PENGUIN REFERENCE

THE PENGUIN TV COMPANION

Jeff Evans was born in South Wales and educated at the University of Reading. A freelance journalist, he specializes in writing not only about television, but also travel and beer, having edited eight editions of the Campaign for Real Ale's best-selling annual *Good Beer Guide*. Among his other works is the award-winning *Good Bottled Beer Guide*. He has also contributed to many TV and radio programmes, newspapers and magazines, including the *Radio Times*. He is married with two sons and lives in Newbury.

THE PENGUIN **TV** COMPANION
Jeff Evans

PENGUIN BOOKS

PENGUIN BOOKS

Published by the Penguin Group
Penguin Books Ltd, 27 Wrights Lane, London w8 5TZ, England
Penguin Putnam Inc., 375 Hudson Street, New York, New York 10014, USA
Penguin Books Australia Ltd, Ringwood, Victoria, Australia
Penguin Books Canada Ltd, 10 Alcorn Avenue, Toronto, Ontario, Canada M4V 3B2
Penguin Books India (P) Ltd, 11, Community Centre, Panchsheel Park, New Delhi – 110 017, India
Penguin Books (NZ) Ltd, Private Bag 102902, NSMC, Auckland, New Zealand
Penguin Books (South Africa) (Pty) Ltd, 5 Watkins Street, Denver Ext 4, Johannesburg 2094, South Africa

Penguin Books Ltd, Registered Offices: Harmondsworth, Middlesex, England

First published 2001
1

Copyright © Jeff Evans, 2001
All rights reserved

The moral right of the author has been asserted

Set in 7.5/9 pt ITC Stone Serif
Typeset by Rowland Phototypesetting Ltd, Bury St Edmunds, Suffolk
Printed in Scotland by Omnia Books Ltd, Glasgow

To Christopher and Andrew,
whose devotion to Doctor Who and Postman Pat saved me hours of research.

CONTENTS

INTRODUCTION

There were times, not so long ago, when producing a book like this would have been unthinkable. Television, it was said, was not something you wrote books about. Film, yes, by all means. The more film guides the better. But television, no. Nobody wants to read about television.

This all sounded a bit bizarre to me. Even taking into account the disdain in which television was held in some quarters during its early years – comedian Ernie Kovacs, for instance, once famously said that television was a medium, because it was neither rare nor well done – I just could not believe that a subject which enthrals hundreds of millions of people each day and which touches all our lives could not be worth a few words in print. Yet, until the first edition of this book surfaced under the title of *The Guinness Television Encyclopedia* in 1995, there were relatively few television books on the market.

What was lacking most until then was a one-volume book of facts and figures about TV programmes and personalities. The books that were on sale either were limited in scope, to comedies, detective series, British programmes, etc., or, if they did have a wider brief, they failed to provide all the information I wanted, whether it be cast-lists, plot synopses or just memory-jogging bits of trivia. So I decided to compile the information myself. Now, six years on, we have arrived in the digital age, tempted by a cornucopia of channels, many of which major on re-runs of classic programmes. The book is therefore more relevant than ever and this new edition is more than overdue.

THE FACTS

The *Penguin TV Companion*'s aim is to provide facts. There are no (deliberate) attempts to rate or criticize programmes or performers. Instead, priority has been given to hard information, both important and trivial. Anyone seeking an answer to some nagging TV query – who played . . . ?; what was the name of . . . ?; when did . . . ? – will, hopefully, find it here. I hope, too, that anyone casually browsing will be drawn nostalgically back into the golden days of television and enjoy some fond memories.

THE ENTRIES

There are nearly 1,300 programmes featured in this book. They are listed with their country of origin, production company, UK channel and transmission dates. Cast-lists highlighting the regular characters follow, then major production credits, centring on creators, writers and producers of programmes. Each programme's description covers the general concept, the main storylines, character details and a good dose of trivia – the sort of facts that you could easily live without, but would prefer not to.

There are also around 1,300 entries for TV stars and behind-the-scenes contributors. Each person's major television work has been highlighted, though film and theatre credits (falling outside the brief) have largely been ignored. Real names and dates of birth have been provided where obtainable, though some performers are famously shy about their ages and others, understandably, prefer to have their privacy respected in such matters.

So what is and isn't included? One thing I learned while compiling the first edition was that any attempt to lay down hard-and-fast ground-rules is sure to end in dissatisfaction. It is possible, for instance, to restrict programme entries to those that have attracted the most viewers, based on audience ratings. Except that this instantly precludes programmes on 'minority' channels like BBC 2, Channel 4 and Channel 5. Would the book be complete without *Father Ted*, *ER* or *This Life*? Based on the ratings charts, it would also rule out children's programmes and other daytime offerings. Other options would have been to consider including only award-winning programmes, peak-hour programming or UK-produced programmes, but these formats would fall down in similar ways. Consequently, I have adopted a loose set of criteria for the programmes featured in this book. These involve general acclaim, historical significance, biggest audiences, cult status and nostalgia value.

The programmes cover nearly all fields: dramas, documentaries, situation comedies, variety shows, current affairs series, children's favourites, quiz shows, panel games, sports programmes, soap operas, mini-series and important one-off plays. TV movies, however, have not been included. As a result, the following pages are a tribute to the good, the bad and the sometimes very ugly moments in TV's past. You will find everything, from the most critically acclaimed to the most cruelly derided, and even some programmes you may just have forgotten.

The entries for people are similarly based on those who have contributed most, or enjoyed most success, in television's first 65 years. They include actors, comedians, presenters, writers, producers, executives and even the brilliant engineers who made television possible in the first place. To complete the picture, there are also entries for television companies and explanations of some of the technical terms that confront the viewer on a day-to-day basis as each programme's credits roll by.

THE RESEARCH
Researching and updating this book has been great fun. It has also proved rather frustrating at times. For instance, while there has been no shortage of information about American programmes, vintage British television is shrouded in obscurity. The main reason for this is the fact that most US programmes (pre-videotape) were captured on film and therefore have been preserved. British programmes in the 1940s and 1950s mainly went out live and any primitive recordings which were made, together with episodes of 1960s classics like *Doctor Who* and *Steptoe and Son*, were famously wiped as an economy and space-saving measure by the BBC in the 1970s. As a result, the detail unearthed about early British programmes is inevitably rather thinner than for American contemporaries.

Programmes are listed with their first and last transmission dates. Where a break of more than one year has occurred during the programme's run, this has been indicated with separate sets of dates. Only the original transmissions (not repeats) have been charted. Programmes shown on BBC Television before the advent of BBC 2 (and therefore BBC 1) in 1964 have the channel listing 'BBC' only. Those beginning before, and continuing after, the BBC was split into two channels have the listing 'BBC 1' or 'BBC 2', depending on which channel they were subsequently allocated.

However, some transmission dates have proved difficult to track down. Often, overseas programmes screened on ITV have not been fully networked, meaning that they have been seen in only some areas. The regions have also transmitted episodes out of sequence, sometimes years apart, and it does not follow that the region offering the first-ever transmission of a programme will also be the first to show the last episode. As a result, the dates listed here for some overseas entries are informed estimates, but any corrections to these dates would be happily received.

All programme details have been updated to the end of 2000, but information concerning people may be even more recent.

THE ACKNOWLEDGEMENTS
To produce a book of this scope and scale, a writer needs more than a little help. I would particularly like to thank Jacqueline Kavanagh, Mike Websell and Neil Somerville at the BBC Written Archives Centre for their assistance, and the numerous other librarians, press officers and agents who have answered my many queries. I am especially indebted to my wife, Jacquie, not only for allowing me to spend most of my waking hours cooped up with a computer, or hidden away in a corner of some library, but also for contributing to much of the research herself.

Always conscious that 'the truth is out there', I have made every effort to ensure the accuracy of the information in these pages. However, without looking for an excuse for errors and omissions, there are so many facts and figures in this book that it would be a miracle if all were totally correct. If you know better, your comments will be more than welcome.

Jeff Evans

A FOR ANDROMEDA/ THE ANDROMEDA BREAKTHROUGH

UK (BBC) Science Fiction. BBC 1961/1962

John Fleming	**Peter Halliday**
Prof. Reinhart	**Esmond Knight**
Dr Geers	**Geoffrey Lewis**
Prof. Madeleine Dawnay	**Mary Morris**
Christine/Andromeda	**Julie Christie** (*A for*)
	Susan Hampshire (*Breakthrough*)
Dennis Bridger	**Frank Windsor**
Dr Hunter	**Peter Ducrow**
Harvey	**John Murray-Scott**
Judy Adamson	**Patricia Kneale**
Major Quadring	**Jack May**
Harries	**John Nettleton**
J. M. Osborne	**Noel Johnson**
Gen. Vandenberg	**Donald Stewart**
Minister of Science	**Ernest Hare**
Prime Minister	**Maurice Hedley**
Minister of Defence Burdett	**David King**
Kaufman	**John Hollis**
Egon	**Peter Henchie**
Prof. Neilson	**Walter Gotell** (*Breakthrough*)
Mlle Gamboule	**Claude Farel** (*Breakthrough*)
Col. Salim	**Barry Linehan** (*Breakthrough*)
Dr Abu Zeki	**David Saire** (*Breakthrough*)
President of Azaran	**Arnold Yarrow** (*Breakthrough*)

Writers: **Fred Hoyle, John Elliot**
Producers: **Michael Hayes, Norman James** (A for
Andromeda), **John Elliot** (*Breakthrough*)

*A beautiful girl is created by a sinister alien
computer.*

In 1970 (nine years into the future), a new giant radio
telescope in the Yorkshire Dales, managed by Professor
Reinhart, picked up a series of signals from the direction
of the constellation Andromeda which had taken 200
years to reach Earth. Working through the messages,
brilliant scientist John Fleming concluded that they
formed plans for a highly sophisticated computer. In a
top-secret project, sponsored by the government and
hidden away at Thorness on a remote Scottish island,
he followed the alien instructions and built the
machine. A battle then began between good and bad
scientists, government agencies and the Swiss business
cartel, Intel, headed by the evil Kaufman, for the use of
its powers.

Through collaboration with amoral biologist Madeleine Dawnay, the computer succeeded in developing
an embryo, based on the biological blueprint of Christine, a lab assistant it had electrocuted. The embryo
rapidly blossomed into a replica of the girl (though
blonde not brunette, as Christine had been) and was
given the name of Andromeda. Unfortunately, the replica girl was mentally linked to the corrupt machine
and became its agent. It wasn't until the conscientious
Fleming drew her warmer, more human emotions to the
fore that she was able to break free from her computer
master.

In a sequel series, *The Andromeda Breakthrough*, shown a year later, Fleming, Dawnay and Andromeda were kidnapped and imprisoned in the Middle Eastern country of Azaran, where Intel had set up its own super-computer. Weather systems had been disrupted, violent storms were raging across the globe and the Earth's atmosphere was being eaten away. In this follow-up, the part of Andromeda was taken over by Susan Hampshire.

Now recognized as classic TV science fiction, *A for Andromeda* and *The Andromeda Breakthrough* were created by BBC producer John Elliot from a storyline by Cambridge astronomer and novelist Fred Hoyle. *A for Andromeda* was the BBC's first attempt at adult science fiction since the QUATERMASS serials and is well remembered for giving young drama school student Julie Christie her first starring role.

A. J. WENTWORTH, BA
UK (Thames) Situation Comedy. ITV 1982

A. J. Wentworth	**Arthur Lowe**
Matron	**Marion Mathie**
Revd R. G. Saunders ('Headmaster')	**Harry Andrews**
Rawlinson	**Ronnie Stevens**
Gilbert	**Michael Bevis**
Miss Coombes	**Debbie Davies**

Writer: **Basil Boothroyd**
Producer: **Michael Mills**

The exploits of an absent-minded schoolteacher.

In his last TV series, recorded just weeks before he died, Arthur Lowe played a maths teacher in a 1940s prep school who was obsessed with old-fashioned school virtues. Fighting internal battles with his arch-enemy, Matron, the disaster-prone teacher (who was weak on discipline but strong on dignity) was constantly pre-occupied by such trivial matters as the high cost of pen nibs. The snobbish cleric, Reverend R. G. Saunders, was the school's headmaster. The series was based on stories by H. F. Ellis, although just six episodes were made.

ABBOT, RUSS
(Russ Roberts; 1947–)

Tall, twinkly-eyed, Chester-born comedian and impressionist who entered showbiz as a member of the Black Abbots cabaret group. His TV breaks came from appearances in WHO DO YOU DO?, *The Comedians* and *Bruce Forsyth's Big Night* and led to a series he shared with its named star, *Freddie Starr's Variety Madhouse*. With Starr's departure, the show became *Russ Abbot's Madhouse* in 1980 (sometimes *Saturday Madhouse*) and allowed Abbot to begin introducing the farcical creations for which he became famous, such as inept superhero Cooperman (an exaggerated impersonation of Tommy Cooper), detective Barratt Holmes, air ace Boggles, Irish crooner Val Hooligan, rock'n'roller Vince Prince, secret agent Basildon Bond, and C. U. Jimmy, the indecipherable, kilted Scotsman. The same format was applied when the show switched to BBC 1 in 1986 and became *The Russ Abbot Show*. Back on ITV in 1994, Abbot pioneered some new creations, including the Noisy Family, Clueless Cleric and the good folk of Pimpletown, such as Percy Pervert and Mrs Verruca. In his sketch work he has been well supported by the likes of Bella Emberg, Les Dennis, Dustin Gee, Michael Barrymore and Jeffrey Holland, but Abbot has also featured in serious and sitcom roles, most notably as retired teacher Ted Fenwick in SEPTEMBER SONG, and as shoe salesman Ted Butler in *Married for Life*.

ABC

Early ITV franchise-holder covering the Midlands and the North of England at weekends only. An offshoot of the ABC (Associated British Cinemas) theatre chain, the company was owned mainly by ABPC (Associated British Picture Corporation), although Warners also held shares in the 1950s. ABC went on air on 18 February 1956 in the Midlands and on 5 May 1956 in the North. Its network programming successes included ARMCHAIR THEATRE, OPPORTUNITY KNOCKS and THE AVENGERS. At the behest of the ITA, during the 1968 franchise re-assessments the company merged with Associated-Rediffusion to create Thames Television. ABC then gave up its Midlands and North of England franchises but, as Thames, took over London's Monday to Friday coverage.

ABC
(American Broadcasting Company)

American television network, for years the least successful of the three national networks. It was founded in 1943 by Edward J. Noble, the maker of Life Savers confectionery, when he purchased a radio network from NBC. In 1953 the company merged with United Paramount Theaters. Despite struggling against its competitors, CBS and NBC, from its earliest days (largely because it owned fewer affiliate stations), ABC has nevertheless made its mark on US television history. It was the first company to bring Hollywood studios into TV production, thereby accelerating the move from live to filmed broadcasts. It notched numerous sports firsts in the USA (its most-watched programme is still *Monday Night Football*), and among its other programming successes have been BATMAN, ROSEANNE, HOME IMPROVEMENT, NYPD BLUE and three of the biggest mini-series ever: ROOTS, THE THORN BIRDS and THE WINDS OF WAR. By the end of the 1970s, ABC had elevated itself into the top bracket of US TV, becoming a very serious competitor to the two big networks. The company was bought by Capital Cities Communications in 1986 and was then acquired by the Walt Disney Corporation in 1995.

ABIGAIL'S PARTY
UK (BBC) Drama. BBC 1 1977

Beverly	**Alison Steadman**
Sue	**Harriet Reynolds**
Laurence	**Tim Stern**

Angela .... **Janine Duvitski**
Tony .... **John Salthouse**

Writer: **Mike Leigh**
Producer: **Margaret Matheson**

A pretentious evening in suburbia turns to disaster as marital frictions take hold.

Abigail, the eponymous entertainer of this exalted PLAY FOR TODAY, was never actually seen. She was in the house next door, throwing a party for her teenage friends. It might, therefore, have been more appropriate to call the drama 'Beverly's Party', for that is where the action took place.

To coincide with the teenage bash, neurotic neighbour Beverly had organized her own little gathering for the grown-ups. Along with Abigail's anxious mother, Sue, local residents Angela and Tony were invited, and making up the select group was Beverly's stressed-out husband, Laurence. As the evening dragged by, the drink flowed freely, the grating Beverly forced everyone to endure the 'fantastic' Demis Roussos on the stereo, and marital tensions reached fever pitch as she obliviously sailed through a series social blunders.

Abigail's Party was the play that confirmed the talents of writer/director Mike Leigh and his then wife, actress Alison Steadman, who had previously collaborated on an earlier *Play for Today*, *Nuts in May* (1976). It had first been performed on stage at the Hampstead Theatre and some of the dialogue, even in the televised version, was improvised. The play has become a cult and, in 1997, BBC 2 presented an *Abigail's Party* night to commemorate the 20th anniversary of its first transmission.

ABOUT THE HOME

UK (BBC) Magazine. BBC 1951–8

Presenter: **Joan Gilbert**
Producer: **S. E. Reynolds**

Practical tips for housewives.

This long-running afternoon programme was designed to help housewives improve their domestic skills such as cookery and needlework, although other items covered included shopping, deportment and even puppy training. Home-improvement tips from Barry Bucknell proved so popular that he gained his own series, *Do It Yourself*, in 1957.

ABSOLUTELY

UK (Absolutely) Comedy. Channel 4 1989–93

Gordon Kennedy, Jack Docherty, Moray Hunter, Morwenna Banks, Peter Baikie, John Sparkes

Producers: **Alan Nixon, David Tyler**

Eccentric comedy sketch show with a Scottish accent.

Absolutely drew together some of Scotland's new breed of comics and gave them a licence for creativity. The result was a collection of surreal and silly sketches.

Morwenna Banks perfected the 'Yes, it's twue', worldly-wise junior schoolgirl, Moray Hunter became the anoraky Calum Gilhooley and the Welsh member of the team, John Sparkes, created accident-prone DIY expert Denzil and the lavatorial Frank Hovis. The parish council of the fictitious village of Stoneybridge was also featured on a regular basis, and Jack Docherty portrayed rabid nationalist McGlashen. Docherty and Hunter (both formerly of *Friday Night Live*) took their creations, Donald McDiarmid and George McDiarmid – 'two friends with but a single surname' – into a spin-off series, *Mr Don and Mr George*, in 1993.

ABSOLUTELY FABULOUS

UK (Saunders & French/BBC) Situation Comedy. BBC 2/BBC 1 1992–6

Edina Monsoon .... **Jennifer Saunders**
Patsy Stone .... **Joanna Lumley**
Saffron Monsoon .... **Julia Sawalha**
Bubble .... **Jane Horrocks**
Mother .... **June Whitfield**

Creators: **Jennifer Saunders, Dawn French**
Writer: **Jennifer Saunders**
Producer: **Jon Plowman**

The drink- and drug-laden world of a neurotic PR agent and her fashion editor friend.

Edina Monsoon, a single mother of two children, by different fathers, was head of her own public relations agency. Her long-time friend, Patsy Stone, was editor of a fashion magazine. Work for both of them, however, was one long lunchbreak at a trendy restaurant, a spell of shopping at Harvey Nicks or an evening's clubbing. Striving to be seen in all the right places, rubbing shoulders with every celebrity they could find, they ladled out the 'darlings' and 'sweeties' as they struggled to reclaim their late-1960s youth.

Edina shared her three-storey, expensively appointed home in Holland Park with her teenage daughter, Saffron (her son was away at university). However, theirs was not the usual mother–teenager relationship, but quite the reverse. Edina was the disruptive influence, staying out late, getting drunk, throwing tantrums and selfishly spoiling all her daughter's fun. Saffy was simply far too sensible to be corrupted by her mother, a plain Jane who preferred science to sex and books to booze. Their incompatibility was highlighted whenever Patsy arrived to drag Edina off to a fashion shoot or some wild party, much to the disapproval of both Saffron and Edina's mother. The archetypal society slag, Patsy lived on a diet of cigarettes, drink, drugs and younger men. She wasn't happy unless she was smoking, slurping, sniffing or sleeping with someone. Also seen was Bubble, Edina's chirpy but brainless northern secretary.

Derived from a sketch in *French and Saunders*, in which Dawn French played the swotty daughter, *Absolutely Fabulous* emerged from its first season clutching a handful of awards, with Joanna Lumley singled out for her successful first stab at comedy and the way in which she gleefully debunked her traditional aristocratic roles. For the second and third seasons, and the final two-parter in 1996, it earned itself a BBC 1 time slot. Edina and Patsy also turned up in one episode of ROSEANNE. A similarly themed, but typically toned-down, US comedy entitled *High Society*, starring Jean Smart and Mary McDonnell, was screened in the States in 1995–6 but was not well received. *Absolutely Fabulous*'s theme song, Bob Dylan's 'This Wheel's on Fire', was sung by Jennifer Saunders's husband, Adrian Edmondson, with Julie Driscoll, vocalist on the original, 1968, hit version by the Brian Auger Trinity. A new series of *Absolutely Fabulous* was planned for 2001, after Saunders, Lumley, Sawalha, Horrocks and Whitfield had all worked together again in 2000 on a one-off comedy penned by Saunders called *Mirrorball*.

ACCESS TELEVISION

Programmes produced by members of the public or by pressure groups, who are given editorial control of the project but are also offered the assistance of a professional crew. It is otherwise known as public access. The BBC's *Open Door*, beginning in 1973, was one of the most famous British examples, while the wacky *Manhattan Cable* compilations revealed just how much further public access is taken in the USA's cable industry.

ACE OF WANDS
UK (Thames) Children's Adventure. ITV 1970–2

Tarot .... **Michael MacKenzie**
Sam Maxsted .... **Tony Selby**
Lillian ('Lulli') Palmer .... **Judy Loe**
Mr Sweet .... **Donald Layne-Smith**
Mikki .... **Petra Markham**
Chas .... **Roy Holder**

Creator: **Trevor Preston**
Producers: **Pamela Lonsdale, John Russell**

A young stage magician tackles crime and evil in his spare time.

Tarot was a magical entertainer, a combination of conjurer and escapologist, whose youthful appearance concealed a mysterious background and a resourceful mind. Billed as 'a 20th-century Robin Hood, with a pinch of Merlin and a dash of Houdini', he was assisted in his adventures by Sam and Lulli. Sam, a reformed ex-convict, shared Tarot's luxury apartment and built many of his stage props, while Lulli, an orphan and fellow telepath, was Tarot's stage partner. Mr Sweet, an eccentric, tweed-suited man who ran an antique bookshop and rode a motorbike, also lent a hand, chipping in with his expert knowledge of the insect world. In the background perched Ozymandias, a Malayan fishing owl.

The so-called 'Ace of Wands' and his companions ran into a host of weird and wonderful, BATMAN-esque supercriminals, with names like Madame Midnight, Mr Stabs and Ceribraun. But perhaps the most sinister was Mama Doc, who turned people into dolls which bled

when broken. In the final season, Sam and Lulli were replaced by Mikki and Chas. Mikki, another telepath, worked as a reporter, and Chas was her photographer brother. Mr Sweet, now based at a university, was also seen again.

ACKLAND, JOSS
CBE (1928–)

London-born actor regularly seen in guest star roles. He supported Alec Guinness in TINKER, TAILOR, SOLDIER, SPY and also appeared in the ITV George Smiley dramatization, *A Murder of Quality*, as well as playing the spymaster Cumming in Somerset Maugham's *Ashenden*. Earlier, he was newspaper editor William Stevens in *Kipling*, D'Artagnan in *The Further Adventures of the Musketeers*, widower Joseph Lockwood in the sitcom *Thicker Than Water*, Charles Bronte in THE CREZZ, and for a while took the part of Inspector Todd in Z CARS. Other credits have included THE GOLD ROBBERS, COUNTRY MATTERS, ENEMY AT THE DOOR, MISS MARPLE, plus numerous single dramas, including *Shadowlands*.

ADAM ADAMANT LIVES!
UK (BBC) Science Fiction. BBC 1 1966–7

Adam Adamant .... **Gerald Harper**
Georgina Jones .... **Juliet Harmer**
William E. Simms .... **Jack May**
The Face .... **Peter Ducrow**

Creators: **Donald Cotton, Richard Harris**
Producer: **Verity Lambert**

An Edwardian adventurer, trapped in ice, thaws out in the Swinging Sixties.

Adam Llewellyn De Vere Adamant was a legend in his own lifetime: a smooth, dashing man of action who countered crooks and defended the weak in turn-of-the-century England. However, in 1902, he was ensnared by his arch-enemy, a megalomaniac in a leather mask known only as 'The Face'. Injected with a preservative drug, Adamant was encased in a block of ice and left to posterity. In 1966 a group of London workmen discovered his body and thawed it out. Adam Adamant, now aged 99, but still with the body of a 36-year-old, was back in action.

However, swinging London, buzzing with loud noise, bright lights and the permissive society, confused the revitalized adventurer. To his rescue rode Georgina Jones, a trendy young nightclub DJ and an Adam Adamant fan (having learned from her grandfather about the great man's exploits). Together with Georgie and William E. Simms, a former music hall artist who became his manservant (still sporting Edwardian clothing) again turned his attentions to the criminal fraternity. They embarked on a series of AVENGERS-style, off-beat adventures in which Adamant's keen intellect (he had an amazing memory and degrees from several universities), athletic abilities (he was a keen boxer) and adroitness with weapons (especially his sword) were put to excellent use. In the second series, his old enemy, The Face, returned to instigate yet more trouble.

Alive with the colour of Carnaby Street (despite being taped in black and white), *Adam Adamant Lives!* was firmly set in the era of mini-skirts, mods and early psychedelia, with much interest derived from the jarring juxtaposition of Edwardian morals with the liberal society of the 1960s. It provided Gerald Harper with a chance to develop his suave toff image which reached its pinnacle in HADLEIGH three years later. It also opened doors for behind-the-scenes crew-members such as Ridley Scott, who went on to direct films like *Alien* and *Blade Runner*. The James Bond-like theme music was sung by Kathy Kirby.

ADAM DALGLIESH
See **P. D. JAMES.**

ADAMS, TOM
(1938–)

London-born actor making his TV debut as a crook in DIXON OF DOCK GREEN and moving on to other supporting, as well as leading, roles, which have generally been of a stern and serious nature. He was Guy Marshall in EMERGENCY – WARD 10, Major Sullivan in *Spy Trap*, Daniel Fogarty in THE ONEDIN LINE, Dr Guy Wallman in GENERAL HOSPITAL, DCI Nick Lewis in *The Enigma Files*, and Malcolm Bates in EMMERDALE FARM. Other credits have included JOURNEY TO THE UNKNOWN, *Villains*, *West Country Tales*, *Strike it Rich* and REMINGTON STEELE.

ADAMSON, PETER
(1930–)

Burly, gruffly spoken, Liverpool-born actor who is remembered by all as Len Fairclough, CORONATION STREET's 1960s/70s he-man. In the 1950s Adamson enjoyed small parts in Granada series like KNIGHT ERRANT and *Skyport*, before joining the *Street* in 1961. He filled the role of heavy-drinking, womanizing builder Fairclough for 22 years, until alleged off-screen indiscretions led to his dismissal by Granada. The writers had the two-timing Fairclough killed in a car crash on the way home from visiting a mistress.

ADDAMS FAMILY, THE
US (Filmways) Situation Comedy. ITV 1965–6

Morticia Addams	**Carolyn Jones**
Gomez Addams	**John Astin**
Uncle Fester Frump	**Jackie Coogan**
Lurch	**Ted Cassidy**
Grandmama Addams	**Blossom Rock**
Pugsley Addams	**Ken Weatherwax**
Wednesday Thursday Addams	**Lisa Loring**
Cousin Itt	**Felix Silla**
Thing	**Ted Cassidy**

Creator: **David Levy**

The misadventures of a macabre family, based on the cartoon strip by Charles Addams.

The weird and wonderful Addams Family was headed by Gomez, a lawyer and man of independent wealth, with his sultry, slinky wife, Morticia. They lived in a musty, spooky Victorian mansion, in a street appropriately called Cemetery Ridge, with Morticia's bald, habit-wearing Uncle Fester, Gomez's mother, Grandmama (a witch), their son Pugsley, daughter Wednesday, and a high-pitched, gobbledegook-speaking mass of hair called Cousin Itt. Their servants were a disembodied hand in a box known as Thing and a 6-foot 9-inch butler named Lurch, who groaned the question 'You rang?' when summoned by a gong which shook the whole house.

In line with their strange but pleasure-filled lifestyle, the family had unusual pets. Gomez took delight in his octopus, Aristotle; Morticia was comforted by her man-eating African Strangler called Cleopatra; and Homer, Wednesday's pet, was a Black Widow spider. For toys, Pugsley had an electric chair and a gallows, while Wednesday played with a headless doll. Gomez, on the other hand, indulged his violent instincts by blowing up toy trains or sword swallowing, if he wasn't fencing his wife or devouring her with kisses at the slightest hint of a French word. Fester lit light bulbs in his mouth, Grandmama practised knife-throwing and Lurch was often called upon to play the harpsichord. Cousin Itt was easily pleased: it hung upside down in the chimney. And yet, for all their eccentricities, the Addams Family believed that they were normal and that it was the world around them that was bizarre. As a result, whenever contact was made with neighbours, or other 'ordinary' folk, misunderstanding was rife. The same premise was used in THE MUNSTERS, which reached TV screens at about the same time. Another memorable feature of the series was its finger-clicking theme song.

The cast had a good pedigree. Carolyn Jones was already a Hollywood name, Astin had previously starred in *I'm Dickens, He's Fenster*, Jackie Coogan at the age of four had appeared with Chaplin in *The Kid*, and Blossom Rock was the sister of singer Jeanette McDonald. A couple of Addams Family movies followed in the early 1990s, with Anjelica Huston as Morticia and Raul Julia as Gomez.

ADIE, KATE
OBE (Kathryn Adie; 1945–)

The BBC's Chief News Correspondent since 1989, Sunderland-born Kate Adie joined the BBC in 1969 as a producer in local radio, having spent three years with the National Youth Theatre. She moved to BBC South as a reporter in 1977 and then joined the BBC national news set-up in 1979. In 1980 she covered the siege of the Iranian Embassy in London and went on to make her name as an on-the-spot reporter in the most hazardous situations, in places as diverse as Libya, Tiananmen Square, the Gulf and Kosovo.

ADMAGS

Short for advertising magazines, admags are programmes that are used to promote commercial products, generally employing less than subtle techniques. The practice was commonplace in Britain following the advent of ITV in 1955 but was outlawed by Parliament in 1963. Probably the best-remembered admag is *Jim's Inn*, a pub-orientated programme set in the fictitious village of Wembleham, hosted by 'landlords' Jimmy and Maggie Hanley. Customers used to wander in and discuss their latest bargains over a pint or two. Other notable admags in the UK were Noele Gordon's *Homes and Gardens* (1956), Peter Butterworth and Janet Brown's *Where Shall We Go?* (also 1956) and John Slater's *Slater's Bazaar* (from 1957).

ADVENTURER, THE
UK (ITC) Secret Agent Drama. ITV 1972–3

Gene Bradley .... **Gene Barry**
Mr Parminter .... **Barry Morse**
Diane Marsh .... **Catherine Schell**
Gavin Jones .... **Garrick Hagon**
Vince .... **Stuart Damon**

Producer: **Monty Berman**

A US secret agent operates under the cover of an international film star.

Gene Bradley was a wealthy, jet-setting movie celebrity who indulged himself in business ventures of all kinds, but whose real job involved secret assignments for US intelligence. Employing his acting skills to the full and taking on various disguises, Bradley was an international knight who came to the rescue of threatened women, defecting scientists and others in need of assistance. His assignments were given to him by his 'manager', Mr Parminter, and he was accompanied by fellow agent, Gavin Jones. Diane was his contact with the agency. John Barry provided the theme music.

ADVENTURES OF BLACK BEAUTY, THE
UK (LWT/Talbot/Freemantle) Children's Adventure. ITV 1972–4

Dr James Gordon .... **William Lucas**
Victoria Gordon .... **Judi Bowker**
Kevin Gordon .... **Roderick Shaw**
Jenny Gordon .... **Stacy Dorning**
Amy Winthrop .... **Charlotte Mitchell**
Albert .... **Tom Maiden**
Squire Armstrong .... **Michael Culver**

Executive Producer: **Paul Knight**
Producer: **Sidney Cole**

A black stallion is the pride and joy of a young Victorian girl.

This series, based on Anna Sewell's classic children's novel, was set in 1877 on a spacious English country estate. Vicky Gordon was the young owner of a thoroughbred, Black Beauty, which had been badly treated by a succession of cruel owners before Vicky and her family took him in and nursed him back to health. Brother Kevin and sister Jenny lent a hand and their dad, a doctor, and Amy, his housekeeper, were also drawn into the horsey goings-on. Most stories had little to do with the original book.

ADVENTURES OF CHAMPION, THE
See CHAMPION THE WONDER HORSE.

ADVENTURES OF LONG JOHN SILVER, THE
Australia (Isola dell'Oro) Adventure. ITV 1957

Long John Silver .... **Robert Newton**
Jim Hawkins .... **Kit Taylor**
Purity Pinker .... **Connie Gilchrist**
Israel Hands .... **Rodney Taylor**
Billy Bowledge .... **Henry Gilbert**
Mendoza .... **Lloyd Berrell**
Patch .... **Grant Taylor**
Governor Strong .... **Harvey Adams**

Producers: **Mark Evans, Joseph Kaufman**

The further adventures of Treasure Island's scurrilous, one-legged ship's cook.

In the 1700s, in this TV follow-up to successful cinema films, Silver and his cabin-boy friend, Jim Hawkins, were based on Portobello, an island in the Spanish Main. Here they worked on behalf of Governor Strong, thwarting the advances of the Spanish fleet and preserving the island for the British Crown, with a dash of treasure-hunting thrown in for good measure. Off-duty, the rolling-eyed, bearded grog-swiller could be found in Purity Pinker's pub. Sadly, Robert Newton died not long after this series was made.

ADVENTURES OF PARSLEY, THE
See THE HERBS.

ADVENTURES OF RIN-TIN-TIN, THE
US (Herbert B. Leonard/Screen Gems) Children's Adventure. ITV 1956–61

Cpl. Rusty 'B' Company .... **Lee Aaker**
Lt. Ripley 'Rip' Masters .... **James L. Brown**
Sgt Aloysius 'Biff' O'Hara .... **Joe Sawyer**
Cpl. Randy Boone .... **Rand Brooks**
Col. Barker .... **John Hoyt**

Producer: **Herbert B. Leonard**

An orphan and his talented Alsatian become members of a US Cavalry troop.

Discovered as the two survivors of a wagon train raid some time in the 1880s, 11-year-old Rusty and his pet German Shepherd dog, Rin-Tin-Tin, were rescued by the US Cavalry. 'B' Company of the 101st unit ('The Fighting Blue Devils') took them back to their camp, somewhere near the fictional town of Mesa Grande in Arizona, where they were adopted by Lt. Rip Masters and Sgt Biff O'Hara and became members of the troop. Hiding themselves away when big-wig Colonel Barker came to inspect the camp, Rusty and 'Rinty' unearthed a plot against the officer's life. They saved the day and Rusty was awarded corporal's stripes and invited to live on the base with 'Private' Rinty (Rin-Tin-Tin) for as long as he wished.

The action dog, a great rival of the collie, Lassie, was quickly at the forefront of Cavalry activity, leading charges against Apache Indians (spurred on by a 'Yo ho, Rinty'), sniffing out danger and wresting weapons from enemy hands. Two of the dogs that played the lead were actually descendants of the former German army dog whose movie debut came in the 1923 film, *Where the North Begins*. He was such a box-office hit in those silent days that he saved Warner Brothers from bankruptcy. In this 1950s series, he generated a new legion of young fans.

ADVENTURES OF ROBIN HOOD, THE
UK (ITC/Sapphire) Adventure. ITV 1955–9

Robin Hood .... **Richard Greene**
Maid Marian .... **Bernadette O'Farrell**
Patricia Driscoll
Friar Tuck .... **Alexander Gauge**
Little John .... **Archie Duncan**
Rufus Cruikshank
Sheriff of Nottingham .... **Alan Wheatley**
Prince John .... **Hubert Gregg**
Brian Haines
Donald Pleasence
Will Scarlett .... **Ronald Howard**
Paul Eddington
Alan-a-Dale .... **Richard Coleman**
Derwent .... **Victor Woolf**
Deputy Sheriff .... **John Arnatt**
Joan .... **Simone Lovell**
Prince Arthur .... **Peter Asher**
Richard O'Sullivan
Jonathan Bailey

Executive Producer: **Hannah Weinstein**
Producer: **Sidney Cole**

Dashing tales of the 12th-century hero.

Robbing the rich and saving the poor in this early costume drama was Richard Greene, a man forever identified thereafter with the man in Lincoln green from Sherwood Forest. The series was broadly based on the Robin Hood legend, with Robin of Locksley, the Earl of Huntingdon, forced to rebel against the cruel Regent, Prince John, and his local henchman, the Sheriff of Nottingham. All the traditional clan were there, from Friar Tuck to Little John, plus Lady Marian Fitzwalter, known to the Merrie Men as Maid Marian.

The Adventures of Robin Hood was one of the pioneers of British television in America. Thoroughly popular with younger viewers, it inspired a host of other rousing costume dramas, such as THE ADVENTURES OF WILLIAM TELL, THE BUCCANEERS and THE ADVENTURES OF SIR LANCELOT. The theme song, sung by Dick James, was a hit single in 1956. Note the famous names in the cast list, especially Paul Eddington, Richard O'Sullivan and PICTURE BOOK presenter, Patricia Driscoll.

ADVENTURES OF ROBINSON CRUSOE, THE
France (Franco London Films) Children's Drama
BBC 1 1965

Robinson Crusoe .... **Robert Hoffman**

A shipwrecked sailor builds a new life on a tropical island.

This adaptation of Daniel Defoe's classic novel was a familiar sight on children's television in the 1960s, being repeated a number of times after its 1965 debut. Made in France and dubbed into English, it told Crusoe's story in full, even exploring his pre-shipwreck life through flashbacks which featured his childhood, his apprenticeship as a lawyer, his running away to sea and his earlier maritime adventures. Now stranded on the island, he set about building himself a new existence. The 12-part series was filmed in the Canary Islands.

ADVENTURES OF SHERLOCK HOLMES, THE/THE RETURN OF SHERLOCK HOLMES/THE CASEBOOK OF SHERLOCK HOLMES/THE MEMOIRS OF SHERLOCK HOLMES
UK (Granada) Detective Drama. ITV 1984–5 (*Adventures*)/
1986–8 (*Return*)/1991 (*Casebook*)/1994 (*Memoirs*)

Sherlock Holmes .... **Jeremy Brett**
Dr John Watson .... **David Burke** (*Adventures*)
Edward Hardwicke
Mrs Hudson .... **Rosalie Williams**
Insp. Lestrade .... **Colin Jeavons**
Mycroft Holmes .... **Charles Gray**

Executive Producer: **Michael Cox**
Producers: **Michael Cox, June Wyndham Davies**

Conan Doyle's celebrated sleuth, depicted in all his original colour.

After 90 years of trying, and with some 70 actors attempting the title role on film and TV, it wasn't until 1984 that fans found the celluloid Sherlock Holmes they really liked. Generally accepted as being the closest in detail, style and mood to the author's original tales (published in the Victorian *Strand Magazine*), Granada's treatment pitched Jeremy Brett into the famous role, a part with which he became indelibly linked. Quite different from the stereotyped Basil Rathbone version, Brett's Holmes was a man of intelligence and courage, but also a reflective, tactful man with a dark side; a man seen wide-eyed and moody under the influence of cocaine; and a man with respect, not just tolerance, for his trusty (and surprisingly spritely) companion, Watson. The settings were realistic, too, and had been well researched, re-creating Sidney Paget's original *Strand* illustrations.

Two series of Holmes tales were initially revived, culminating in *The Final Problem*, in which our hero was seen to meet his end in a confrontation with the evil Moriarty at Reichenbach Falls. But the pipe-smoking, violin-playing detective resurfaced in two further series, entitled *The Return of Sherlock Holmes*, in which Watson was played by Edward Hardwicke. Hardwicke also kept the role for the two-hour versions of *The Sign of Four* and *The Hound of the Baskervilles*, as well as all subsequent adventures, which went out under the titles of *The Casebook of Sherlock Holmes* and *The Memoirs of Sherlock Holmes*.

ADVENTURES OF SIR LANCELOT, THE
UK (ITC/Sapphire) Adventure. ITV 1956–7

Sir Lancelot du Lac	**William Russell**
Queen Guinevere	**Jane Hylton**
King Arthur	**Bruce Seton**
	Ronald Leigh-Hunt
Merlin	**Cyril Smith**
Sir Kay	**David Morrell**
Brian	**Robert Scroggins**

Executive Producer: **Hannah Weinstein**
Producers: **Sidney Cole, Dallas Bower, Bernard Knowles**

Stories of the celebrated Knight of the Round Table, arguably misplaced in the 14th century.

Sir Lancelot du Lac was the Queen's Champion – 'the bravest knight the world has ever seen', according to the theme song – and the man who warded off all threats to her court at Camelot. In the background was King Arthur, his famous sword Excalibur, the revered sorcerer Merlin, plus Lancelot's squire, former kitchen-boy Brian. The authenticity of the settings was researched at Oxford University, but the era was moved from Sir Lancelot's alleged time of the 6th century up to the 1300s. No mention was made of his dalliance with Queen Guinevere or the conception of Sir Galahad behind the King's back.

William Russell became one of TV's first heart-throbs through this role. He later played Ian Chesterton, a DOCTOR WHO assistant, before arousing fond memories in middle-aged female viewers when he returned as Ted Sullivan in CORONATION STREET in the early 1990s.

ADVENTURES OF SUPERMAN, THE
See SUPERMAN.

ADVENTURES OF TUGBOAT ANNIE, THE
Canada (Normandie) Situation Comedy. ITV 1957–8

'Tugboat' Annie Brennan	**Minerva Urecal**
Capt. Horatio Bullwinkle	**Walter Sande**
Whitey	**Don Baker**
Pinto	**Don Orlando**
Jake	**James Barron**

Rivalry and excitement at sea with two tugboat captains.

Widow Annie Brennan was the stocky, booming-voiced skipper of the *Narcissus*, a tug based in a harbour on the north-west coast of America. Her main aim in life was to get the better of fellow skipper, Horatio Bullwinkle, but, though the pair fought keenly for the best jobs and traded generously in insults, they also shared many an ocean adventure. Whitey and Pinto were Annie's deckhands, and Jake was Bullwinkle's crewman. The series was based on a cartoon strip by Norman Reilly Raine, following on from a 1933 film starring Marie Dressler and Wallace Beery.

ADVENTURES OF TWIZZLE, THE
UK (AP Films/Associated-Rediffusion). Children's Entertainment. ITV 1957–8

Twizzle	**Denise Bryer** (*voice*)

Creator/Writer: **Roberta Leigh**

Puppet tales of a toy with elastic arms and legs.

Notable for being Gerry Anderson's first contribution (as director) to British television, *The Adventures of Twizzle* concerned a toy with a Wee Willy Winkie hat and stretchable arms and legs who ran away from a toy shop and ended up in all sorts of scrapes. At Twizzle's side was a large cat named Footso (after his enormous paws). Twizzle and Footso built a haven for stray toys, a sort of refuge from naughty children. They called it Stray Town, and that was where most of the adventures took place. Among the mistreated and neglected toys were Chawky (a white-faced golliwog), Jiffy the Broomstick Man, Polly Moppet, Candy Floss (a 'Mamma doll' which couldn't say 'Mamma') and Bouncy (a ball which had lost its bounce).

The brains behind Twizzle was Roberta Leigh, later noted for TORCHY and SPACE PATROL. However, it is largely for Anderson's direction that the series is remembered today, even though he contributed to only the first 26 episodes.

ADVENTURES OF WILLIAM TELL, THE
UK (ITP/National Telefilm) Adventure. ITV 1958–9

William Tell .... **Conrad Phillips**
Hedda Tell .... **Jennifer Jayne**
Walter Tell .... **Richard Rogers**
Landburgher Gessler .... **Willoughby Goddard**
Fertog ('The Bear') .... **Nigel Greene**

Executive Producer: **Ralph Smart**
Producer: **Leslie Arliss**

A 14th-century freedom fighter helps the poor people of Switzerland.

Loosely based on the original story by Johann von Schiller, this series told the legend of William Tell, an Alpine hero from the settlement of Berglan, who fought at the side of the oppressed people of Altdorf against the occupying Austrians. The first episode saw Tell challenged by Gessler (the hated Austrian leader) to display his crossbow marksmanship by shooting an apple off the head of his own son, Walter. This Tell duly did, but with a second arrow tucked away for Gessler in case his aim had failed. Discovering this subterfuge, the tyrant attempted to arrest Tell, who fled to the mountains with Walter and his wife, Hedda. From here, assisted by a small band of followers, he set about disrupting Austrian activities with clever and cunning forays, taking on the mantle of a Swiss Robin Hood. Gessler never got his man, and as solace ate vast amounts of food. Scene after scene saw him stuffing his face with meat.

The series (filmed partly in Snowdonia) featured a theme song sung by David Whitfield and was punctuated by the appearance of numerous aspiring actors, including Michael Caine and Frazer Hines, and other notable guests such as Christopher Lee, John Le Mesurier, Patrick Troughton and Wilfrid Brambell. Many years later, star Conrad Phillips resurfaced in EMMERDALE FARM, playing Christopher Meadows, MD of NY Estates. Later still (1989), an Anglo-French revamp of *William Tell* was made. This starred Will Lyman and Jeremy Clyde. Conrad Phillips appeared as a guest star.

AFFILIATE STATION

An independent TV station that links up with one of the large networks to take a proportion of the latter's programming in exchange for a fee, but still leaving gaps in its schedule for its own local output. Affiliate stations are commonplace in the USA and are used by the major networks to extend their audiences. The smaller stations gain from being able to offer first-run, highly rated programmes at no expense to themselves.

AFRICAN PATROL
UK (ME/Kenya) Adventure. ITV 1958–9

Insp. Paul Derek .... **John Bentley**

Producer: **Michael Sadler**

Law and order with a jungle policeman.

British Patrol Inspector Paul Derek worked in the African bush, using his expert knowledge of East African safari country to keep the peace. It was his duty to thwart poachers and other criminals who disturbed the natural balance of the environment. The series was filmed entirely on location in Africa. Star John Bentley re-emerged in the 1960s and 1970s as Hugh Mortimer in CROSSROADS.

AFTER HENRY
UK (Thames) Situation Comedy. ITV 1988–92

Sarah France .... **Prunella Scales**
Eleanor Prescott .... **Joan Sanderson**
Clare France .... **Janine Wood**
Russell Bryant .... **Jonathan Newth**
Vera Poling .... **Peggy Ann Wood**

Writer: **Simon Brett**
Producers: **Peter Frazer-Jones, Bill Shepherd**

A widow shares her home with her demanding mother and her obstinate daughter.

This gentle comedy, contrasting the lives of three generations of women, focused chiefly on the one in the middle. Sarah France was the fortysomething widow of the late Dr Henry France, a man who had been much loved and was now greatly missed. She shared her home in Stipton with her young, headstrong daughter, Clare, and suffered intrusions from her domineering mother, Eleanor, who lived in an adjoining granny flat. Much of the humour arose from Sarah's attempts to reconcile the various generations, which were not without pain and anguish. Sarah's confidant was Russell, her boss at the Bygone Books antiquarian bookshop. Vera Poling was Eleanor's geriatric rival.

After Henry transferred to television after three successful years on BBC Radio. Prunella Scales reprised her radio role, as did Joan Sanderson, although Russell was played by Benjamin Whitrow and Clare by Gerry Cowper in the sound version.

AGATHA CHRISTIE HOUR, THE
UK (Thames) Thriller. ITV 1982

Executive Producer: **John Frankau**
Producer: **Pat Sandys**

An anthology of the Mistress of Crime's lesser-known tales.

This series did not feature the mighty Hercule Poirot, nor did Miss Marple steal the limelight. For once, Agatha Christie's earlier characters were introduced to television in these ten 1920s dramas, which were generally lighthearted, unassuming period adventures, with the cast changing each week.

AGATHA CHRISTIE'S POIROT
UK (LWT/Carnival) Detective Drama. ITV 1989–97; 2000

Hercule Poirot .... **David Suchet**
Capt. Arthur Hastings .... **Hugh Fraser**
Insp./Chief Insp. Japp .... **Philip Jackson**
Miss Lemon .... **Pauline Moran**

Executive Producers: **Nick Elliott, Linda Agran**
Producer: **Brian Eastman**

The cases of the famous Belgian detective.

Along with beer, chocolates and Tin Tin, Hercule Poirot is one of Belgium's greatest exports, even if he was only a figment of Agatha Christie's fertile imagination. Having already been characterized by the likes of Albert Finney and Peter Ustinov on film, Poirot came to TV in the capable hands of the British actor, David Suchet, brother of ITN newscaster, John. It pitched him into the art deco London of the 1930s, giving him a small flat in the luxurious Whitehaven Mansions and allowing crime to follow him wherever he went.

Joining the fastidious sleuth with the curly moustache, fancy cane and 'little grey cells' was his loyal companion, Captain Hastings, a sporty, well-heeled ladies' man who drove a green Lagonda. Also on the scene was the inept Inspector Japp, a Scotland Yard officer who never failed to point the finger at the wrong suspect. Putting matters right, Poirot, with his obtuse continental accent and lop-sided, oval head, calmly gathered together all the likely candidates and, after a meticulous explanation of the facts, quietly and efficiently nailed the guilty party.

Two feature-length *Poirot* episodes were shown in 1996 and 1997, after the series as such ended; these were followed after a three-year gap by a two-part dramatization of *The Murder of Roger Ackroyd* in January 2000.

AGE OF KINGS, AN
UK (BBC) Drama Anthology. BBC 1960

Producer: **Peter Dews**

The ambitious dramatization of five Shakespearean plays as an historical project.

In *An Age of Kings*, the kings in question were Richard II, Henry IV, Henry V, Henry VI and Richard III, as portrayed by William Shakespeare in his plays of the same titles. Spread over 15 episodes, a fortnight apart, the plays were dramatized in sequence to give the overall effect of depicting a continuous stretch (86 years) of British history. Always as a backdrop was the lust for the throne and the burdens of wearing the crown. Michael Hayes directed the plays and the theme music was composed by Sir Arthur Bliss. Featured actors included Robert Hardy, Paul Daneman, David William, Sean Connery and Eileen Atkins.

AGONY/AGONY AGAIN
UK (LWT/BBC/Humphrey Barclay) Situation Comedy. ITV 1979–81 (*Agony*); BBC 1 1995 (*Agony Again*)

Jane Lucas .... **Maureen Lipman**
Bea .... **Maria Charles**
Laurence Lucas .... **Simon Williams**
Andy Evol .... **Peter Blake** (*Agony*)
Val .... **Diana Weston** (*Agony*)
Diana .... **Jan Holden** (*Agony*)
Rob .... **Jeremy Bulloch** (*Agony*)
Michael .... **Peter Denyer** (*Agony*)
Mr Mince .... **Robert Gillespie** (*Agony*)
Vincent Fish .... **Bill Nighy** (*Agony*)
Junior Truscombe .... **Robert Austin** (*Agony*)
Richard .... **Niall Buggy** (*Again*)
Michael Lucas .... **Sacha Grunpeter** (*Again*)
Daniel .... **David Harewood** (*Again*)
Debra .... **Doon Mackichan** (*Again*)
Catherine .... **Valerie Edmond** (*Again*)

Creators: **Anna Raeburn, Len Richmond**
Producers: **John Reardon** (*Agony*); **Humphrey Barclay, Christopher Skala** (*Again*)

A successful agony aunt's own life is a mess.

Jane Lucas was the popular problem-page editor for *Person* magazine and also ran her own radio phone-in. However, for all the sound advice she gave to distressed readers and listeners, her personal life was far from straightforward and she was surrounded by people liable to make things worse. There was her psychiatrist husband, Laurence, who didn't understand people (and from whom she eventually parted); her typically Jewish mother, Bea, who dispensed advice and worried over her; and a couple of gay friends (Rob and Michael) who were always quarrelling – all this on top of 'friends' at work who sought her professional advice for their own little worries. These included her dragon-like editor, Diana, her virtuous secretary, Val, and radio DJ, Andy Evol.

The series was created by (and based on the real life of) agony aunt, Anna Raeburn. A sanitized American version, *The Lucy Arnaz Show*, starred Lucille Ball's daughter in the lead role. In 1995 the series was revived by the BBC under the title of *Agony Again*. Now Jane was the host of the TV talk show, *Lucas Live*. However, she was still pestered by her mother and those around her, who included her gay son, her new man, Daniel, and her ex-husband, Laurence, whom she could never quite let go.

AHERNE, CAROLINE
(1963–)

Manchester-born, former BBC secretary and local radio presenter, acclaimed as one of the brightest comic talents of the 1990s, thanks to her creation of geriatric chat show host, Mrs Merton. The character was later spun off into a sitcom, *Mrs Merton and Malcolm*, before being set aside by Aherne as she concentrated more on developing THE ROYLE FAMILY (and playing Denise Royle) with her long-time writing and performing partner, Craig Cash. Aherne has also been a member of THE FAST SHOW team and, again with Cash, compiled the documentary *Back Passage to India*. Initially billed as Caroline Hook for her early TV appearances, she reverted to her maiden name in 1996 after the break-up of her marriage to former New Order bass player, Peter Hook.

AIN'T MISBEHAVIN'
UK (Clapp Trapp) Comedy Drama. ITV 1997

Eric Trapp .... **Robson Green**
Eddie Wallis .... **Jerome Flynn**
Dolly Nightingale .... **Julia Sawalha**
Ray Smiles .... **Warren Mitchell**
Clara Van Trapp .... **Jane Lapotaire**
Maxie Morrell .... **Jim Carter**
Malky Fraser .... **James Cosmo**
Mrs Jilkes .... **June Brown**
Bing Williams .... **George Melly**
Spadger .... **Graham Stark**

Writer: **Bob Larbey**
Producer: **George Gallaccio**

The misadventures of a pair of 1940s big band musicians.

Eddie Wallis would have loved to have had the chance to fight for his country in World War II. Unfortunately, a plane crash left him suffering from the wrong sort of blackouts you need in wartime, and he was retired to civvy street. Falling back on his musical skills, he joined the Ray Smiles Orchestra, a swing band, where he struck up a friendship with wide-boy and ladies' man Eric Trapp who, unlike Eddie, had no intention whatsoever of aiding the war effort. The pair found themselves out of their depth in inter-gang rivalries and other scrapes as the Nazi bombs fell all around and Eddie hankered for the attentions of Berkeley Square beauty Dolly Nightingale, a lady way beyond his social station. Also seen were band singer Bing Williams and band leader Ray Smiles, who fancied his chances with Eric's Jewish mum, Clara.

This three-part comedy drama was produced by Robson Green's and Jerome Flynn's own company, Clapp Trapp Productions. It allowed them to continue their successful screen partnership – echoing their earlier roles in SOLDIER, SOLDIER – as well as advance their singing careers by belting out nostalgic 1940s songs.

AIRD, HOLLY
(1969–)

British actress coming to the fore young in *The History of Mr Polly* in 1980 and *The Flame Trees of Thika* (as Elspeth Grant), before moving on to the sitcoms *Affairs of the Heart* (Rosemary) and *Double First* (Ellen), and the drama MOTHER LOVE. She then secured lead status in the seaside comedy *Hope It Rains* (Jace), SOLDIER, SOLDIER (Nancy

Thorpe), *Dressing for Breakfast* (Carla) and *Have Your Cake and Eat It* (Allie Gray). Other credits include MISS MARPLE, INSPECTOR MORSE, KAVANAGH QC, *Circles of Deceit* (Sarah Ellis) and *Waking the Dead* (Dr Frankie Wharton).

AIRLINE
UK (Yorkshire) Drama. ITV 1982

Jack Ruskin .... **Roy Marsden**
Peter Witney .... **Richard Heffer**
McEvoy .... **Sean Scanlan**
Jennie Shaw .... **Polly Hemingway**
Ernie Cade .... **Terence Rigby**

Creator: **Wilfred Greatorex**
Executive Producer: **David Cunliffe**
Producer: **Michael Ferguson**

An RAF pilot starts his own airline in the immediate post-war years.

In 1946 Jack Ruskin, demobbed after World War II but with flying still in his blood, struggled to find work with civilian airlines and so chanced his arm by founding his own. His partner in the new Ruskin Air Services was forces colleague Peter Witney. Operating with an old Dakota aircraft Ruskin had bought, they aimed to cut themselves a slice of the world cargo market. However, the business had difficulty getting off the ground, in more ways than one.

Ensnared by shady business deals and hampered by bad weather, Ruskin Air Services offered its staff and management an uncomfortable ride, as Jack lurched from one financial crisis to another. But his entrepreneurial spirit was not to be denied. He raised his sights, took on passenger transport and later became involved in the Berlin Airlift. Ernie Cade was the company's dodgy backer, McEvoy was the company engineer and Jennie Shaw was Jack's girlfriend. Tony Hatch provided the music.

Roy Marsden, Polly Hemingway (Marsden's then real-life wife) and the whole *Airline* ethos was borrowed for a British Airports Authority commercial several years later, a move which brought an unsuccessful lawsuit from the show's creator, Wilfred Greatorex.

AIRPORT
UK (BBC) Documentary. BBC 1 1996–

Narrator: **John Nettles**

Executive Producers: **Jeremy Mills, Clare Paterson, Edwina Vardey**

A look at the complicated working lives of staff at Heathrow Airport.

One of the first of the 1990s influx of 'docu-soaps', *Airport* focused on life at the UK's busiest airport, Heathrow. Many facets of the running of the airport were explored, from the inevitable lost luggage and suspect packages to delayed flights and attempted drug smuggling, although attention occasionally wavered from the original focus on the logistics of airport life to more trivial side-issues featuring some of the airport's increasingly famous employees. These included photographer Dennis Stone; British Midland dispatcher Viv Eggins; VIP liaisons Anita Newcourt and Sara Collins; PC Dave Kidd; terminal duty officers Jean Marie Lavillard and Michèle Harris; customs officers Cath Hall and Garth Powell; journalist Steve Meller; photographer Russell Clisby; Air Jamaica co-ordinator Merla Celestine; traffic warden Jean Dibble; animal welfare man Stuart King; Aer Lingus supervisor Siobhan Feeney; immigration officers Rob Scott, Jo Salmon, Eric Day and Caroline Acheson; air traffic controller Phil Hartwick; Canadian Airlines officer Kelvin Ogunjimi; dispatcher Elaine Pringle; and WPC Annabel Davis. However, the undoubted discovery of the series was Aeroflot supervisor Jeremy Spake.

Christmas specials were produced in 1997 and 1998, the latter showing the main characters in a one-off job swap.

AIRWOLF
US (CBS) Adventure. ITV 1984–6

Stringfellow Hawke .... **Jan-Michael Vincent**
Dominic Santini .... **Ernest Borgnine**
Michael Archangel .... **Alex Cord**
Marella .... **Deborah Pratt**
Caitlin O'Shannessy .... **Jean Bruce Scott**

Creator: **Donald Bellisario**
Executive Producers: **Bernard Kowalski, Donald Bellisario**

Thrills and spills with a high-tech helicopter.

When *Airwolf*, a new breed of super helicopter, was spirited away to Libya by its designer, the US Government called on the services of ace pilot Stringfellow Hawke to retrieve it for Uncle Sam. Hawke, a cello-playing mountain recluse, fulfilled his mission but refused to hand the aircraft back until the US found his brother, who was still missing in Vietnam. In the meantime, Hawke flew secret and spectacular assignments with the super chopper for a Government agency known as The Firm. His contact at The Firm was Archangel, who wore a white suit and an eye patch and carried a stick. Hawke's accomplice on his missions was middle-aged co-pilot Dominic Santini, and he was also joined by female pilot Caitlin O'Shannessy in later episodes. Marella, Archangel's attractive assistant, sometimes represented The Firm.

Airwolf itself was a pretty impressive piece of machinery. An attack helicopter, it had a massive array of weapons and was capable of supersonic flight. It was not unique, however. At the same time, another high-tech chopper, *Blue Thunder*, also began its own series.

ALAN, RAY
(1930–)

London-born ventriloquist/comedian ubiquitous in the 1950s and 1960s with his Mikki the Martian, Lord Charles,

Tich and Quackers and Ali Cat dummies. In the 1970s and 1980s, Alan branched out into panel games, compering shows like *Three Little Words* and *Where in the World?* for HTV. He also appeared regularly on THE GOOD OLD DAYS, calling on the experience he gained in variety theatre before TV beckoned (as a teenager, he worked as a call boy at Lewisham Hippodrome). As a writer (often under the pseudonym of Ray Whyberd), Alan contributed scripts for HANCOCK, BOOTSIE AND SNUDGE, THE TWO RONNIES, Dave Allen and the Jimmy Cricket series *And There's More*.

ALAS SMITH AND JONES / SMITH AND JONES
UK (BBC/Talkback) Comedy. BBC 2 1984–7; BBC 1 1989–92; 1995–8

Mel Smith, Griff Rhys-Jones

Producers: **Martin Shardlow, Jimmy Mulville, John Kilby, Jamie Rix, Jon Plowman, Jon Magnusson**

Comedy sketches with two members of the NOT THE NINE O'CLOCK NEWS *team.*

Mimicking the title of the 1970s Western series starring Pete Duel and Ben Murphy, this vehicle for Mel and Griff's talents is best remembered for the 'head-to-head' scenes, where the idiotic Smith attempted to explain something straightforward to the even dimmer Jones. Another notable feature was the spoof home-video slot, years before Jeremy Beadle picked up a camcorder. After several seasons, the first word was dropped and the show, taken into independent production, was retitled simply *Smith and Jones*, with the series switching to BBC 1 at the same time.

ALBERT
See DEAR MOTHER – LOVE ALBERT.

ALBION MARKET
UK (Granada) Drama. ITV 1985–6

Derek Owen .... **David Hargreaves**
Tony Fraser .... **John Michie**
Lynne Harrison .... **Noreen Kershaw**
Roy Harrison .... **Jonathan Barlow**
Lisa O'Shea .... **Sally Baxter**
Morris Ransome .... **Bernard Spear**
Miriam Ransome .... **Carol Kaye**
Duane Rigg .... **Alistair Walker**
Larry Rigg .... **Peter Benson**
Brenda Rigg .... **Valerie Lilley**
Phil Smith .... **Burt Caesar**
Raju Sharma .... **Dev Sagoo**
Jaz Sharma .... **Paul Bhattacharjee**
Lam Quoc Hoa .... **Philip Tan**
Ly Nhu Chan .... **Pik-Sen Lim**
Ted Pilkington .... **Anthony Booth**
Viv Harker .... **Helen Shapiro**
Geoff Travis .... **Geoffrey Leesley**

Keith Naylor .... **Derek Hicks**

Executive Producer: **Bill Podmore**

Day-to-day ups and downs in a Manchester market.

Contrived as a sister programme to CORONATION STREET, with the aim of lifting ITV's weekend schedules (it went out on Fridays and Sundays), *Albion Market* arrived with a bang and left with a whimper. Much was made of the launch of this ambitious new series, but its poor audience ratings (beaten by *Wogan* and OPEN ALL HOURS) resulted in some ITV regions moving it to even less advantageous time-slots and *Albion Market* eventually shut up shop a year after it began, after exactly 100 half-hour episodes.

Set in a covered Manchester market (actually a converted Salford warehouse), the series monitored the complex lives of an ethnically mixed group of stall holders. At the forefront of the action were the likes of hunky, cake-selling wide-boy Tony Fraser, his 19-year-old girlfriend, Lisa O'Shea, her mum, Lynne Harrison, who ran a domestic goods stall, and Lynne's two-timing, no-good husband, Roy. Lam Quoc Hoa and Ly Nhu Chan were Vietnamese refugee cousins, Raju and Jaz Sharma were expelled Ugandan denim merchants, and Morris and Miriam Ransome were the Jewish couple who ran the pottery stall. Derek Owen was the harassed market supervisor, Phil, the West Indian, worked in the café and Duane Rigg was the market's teenage delinquent. Towards the end of its run, two new personalities were introduced in an attempt to give the show a lift. Sixties pop singer Helen Shapiro played Viv, a hairdresser, and former TILL DEATH US DO PART 'Scouse git' Tony Booth was seen as Ted Pilkington, licensee of the market's local, The Waterman's Arms.

ALDA, ALAN
(Alphonso d'Abruzzo; 1936–)

New York City-born actor/comedian/writer/director who shot to fame as Hawkeye Pierce in M*A*S*H. An ever-present in the series' 11-year run (though he did not appear in the original film), he gradually became one of the programme's creative controllers and picked up Emmys for acting, writing and directing on the show. Earlier, Alda had filled a satirist's chair on the US version of THAT WAS THE WEEK THAT WAS and made guest appearances in THE PHIL SILVERS SHOW, and the 1960s American dramas *The Nurses*, *The Trials of O'Brien* and *Coronet Blue*. Thanks to his extensive cinema work, his TV appearances have been thin since M*A*S*H ended, but he did create the sitcom *We'll Get By* and play Jack Burroughs in another sitcom he devised, *The Four Seasons*, based on his film of the same title. In 1999, he returned to the small screen as Dr Gabriel Lawrence in ER. He is the son of actor Robert Alda.

ALDERTON, JOHN
(1940–)

Lincolnshire-born British comedy actor first seen in EMERGENCY – WARD 10 as Dr Richard Moone (alongside his first wife, Jill Browne) but best remembered as the hapless, naïve schoolteacher, Bernard Hedges, in PLEASE SIR! and *The Fenn Street Gang*. It was these series that launched Alderton into a succession of other sitcoms, most notably MY WIFE NEXT DOOR, *The Upchat Line*, WODEHOUSE PLAYHOUSE and *Father's Day*. Straight parts have still been accepted, however. Alderton played chauffeur Thomas Watkins in UPSTAIRS, DOWNSTAIRS (opposite his second wife, Pauline Collins), and this led to a spin-off series, *Thomas and Sarah*. The duo have also starred together in the comedy NO HONESTLY and the rustic drama FOREVER GREEN. Alderton was also the narrator of the animation *Fireman Sam*.

ALDRIDGE, MICHAEL
(1920–94)

Distinguished British actor, a 1960s star as Dimmock in THE MAN IN ROOM 17, who resurfaced in 1985 as Seymour Utterthwaite, Foggy Dewhurst's replacement in LAST OF THE SUMMER WINE, and the inquisitive old buffer Caldicott, in CHARTERS AND CALDICOTT. He was also seen in *Love for Lydia*, *Love in a Cold Climate* and TINKER, TAILOR, SOLDIER, SPY.

ALEXANDER, JEAN
(1926–)

Liverpool-born actress for ever known to viewers as CORONATION STREET's Hilda Ogden. After appearances in DEADLINE MIDNIGHT, *Jacks and Knaves*, TOP SECRET and Z CARS, Jean Alexander joined the regulars on the *Street* in 1964 (having been seen briefly as a landlady in 1962), donning Hilda's curlers and pinny and moving into number 13 with Bernard Youens as her layabout husband, Stan. When she decided to retire, 23 years later, she had made Hilda a national institution. Her finest hour came in 1984 with the death of Youens and the passing of Stan, when she turned in one of the most acclaimed and moving pieces of acting in TV history. Since leaving the *Street*, Alexander has appeared as Granny Trellis in the sitcom *Rich Tea and Sympathy* and Lily in *The Phoenix and the Carpet*, and enjoyed cameo performances in *Adam's Family Tree* and as Auntie Wainwright in LAST OF THE SUMMER WINE.

ALEXANDER, TERENCE
(1923–)

London-born actor who achieved semi-star status as Charlie Hungerford in BERGERAC. His earlier credits ranged from the 1950s aviation adventure series *Garry Halliday*, THE FORSYTE SAGA (as Montague Dartie) and

THE PALLISERS, to the comedies *All Aboard, My Pal Bob*, HANCOCK'S HALF-HOUR, *The Dick Emery Show*, TERRY AND JUNE, THE FALL AND RISE OF REGINALD PERRIN, *Just Liz, Devenish*, and *Ben Travers Farces*. He has also been seen in THE NEW STATESMAN (Sir Greville) and THE DETECTIVES, plus single dramas and as comedy support for the likes of Eric Barker, Les Dawson, Jim Davidson and Allan Stewart.

ALF

US (Lorimar) Situation Comedy. ITV 1987–9

ALF .... **Paul Fusco** (*voice only*)
Willie Tanner .... **Max Wright**
Kate Tanner .... **Anne Schedeen**
Lynn Tanner .... **Andrea Elson**
Brian Tanner .... **Benji Gregory**
Raquel Ochmonek .... **Liz Sheridan**
Trevor Ochmonek .... **John LaMotta**

Creators: **Paul Fusco, Tom Patchett**
Executive Producers: **Bernie Brillstein, Tom Patchett**

An Alien Life Form (ALF) is looked after by a suburban American family.

When ALF crash-landed his spacecraft on the Tanner family's garage roof, they took him into their kitchen and into their care. Just like ET, ALF instantly won over his adoptive family. Unable to return home, as his planet (Melmac) had blown up and his spacecraft was beyond repair, he settled into a domestic lifestyle, to the bemusement of the Tanners' slow-witted neighbours, the Ochmoneks. Although warm-hearted, this furry, wisecracking alien was also somewhat mischievous, with a penchant for watching TV and over-eating. His favourite food was cat, sadly for the Tanners' own pet, Lucky. He was said to be 229 years old and, on his own planet, went by the name of Gordon Shumway. Like Mork in MORK AND MINDY, he presented viewers with a cynical view of the way of life on Earth. ALF's gravelly voice belonged to Paul Fusco, one of the show's creators.

ALFRED HITCHCOCK PRESENTS

US (Universal/Shamley) Suspense Anthology. ITV 1957–66

Host: **Alfred Hitchcock**

Executive Producer: **Joan Harrison**
Producer: **Norman Lloyd**

An anthology of murder mysteries with a sting in the tale, introduced by the 'Master of Suspense'.

Alfred Hitchcock himself directed only about 20 of the 300-plus episodes in this series, but he was very involved in selecting stories and plots (often from the work of authors such as Roald Dahl, Ray Bradbury and H. G. Wells). Other directors who worked on the programmes included Robert Altman, Sydney Pollack and William Friedkin, while famous actors such as Robert Redford, Burt Reynolds, Walter Matthau, Charles Bronson, Steve McQueen and William Shatner occasionally starred.

Each programme was introduced by Hitchcock with a creaky 'Good evening' and wrapped up with his post-script, glibly explaining how the perpetrator of what seemed a perfect crime had been found out. Very often these deadpan intros and tailpieces had nothing at all to do with the actual tale being told, but were just a device allowing Hitchcock to appear in a bizarre and macabre setting – sitting in an electric chair or impaled on a pole like a scarecrow, for instance – highlighting his renowned black humour. No allusion was ever made to these weird props, and he delivered his piece to camera as if all was perfectly normal. The stories themselves were cleverly crafted, centring on crimes such as murder and blackmail, but each had a surprising twist in the tail. The series primarily consisted of 30-minute dramas, but over 90 stories were made in a 60-minute format and went out as *The Alfred Hitchcock Hour*. The doodled caricature used as the show's logo had been drawn by the man himself, while the jaunty but sinister theme music was based on Gounod's *Funeral March of a Marionette*.

The concept was intriguingly revived in the 1980s, using new stories or reworking old tales, but with the original Hitchcock segments repainted in colour by computer technology. The producer of the original series was Norman Lloyd, who also acted and went on to become Dr Daniel Auschlander in ST ELSEWHERE.

ALFRESCO

UK (Granada) Comedy. ITV 1983–4

Stephen Fry, Hugh Laurie, Emma Thompson, Ben Elton, Siobhan Redmond, Robbie Coltrane

Producers: **Sandy Ross, John G. Temple**

Comedy sketch vehicle for future big names.

If asked to name Britain's biggest comedy and drama names at the end of the 20th century, many viewers would have included most of the stars in the above list. Back in 1983, however, Fry, Laurie, Thompson, Elton, Redmond and Coltrane were virtual unknowns, fledgling talents given their wings by Granada, which plucked them from training schools like the Cambridge Footlights and the Edinburgh Fringe in the hope of providing a response to the BBC's NOT THE NINE O'CLOCK NEWS. Here they fooled around in a late-night mélange of skits, most written by Ben Elton and some, experimentally, shot outdoors with hand-held video cameras. Two series were produced.

ALIAS SMITH AND JONES

US (Universal) Western. BBC 2 1971–4

Hannibal Heyes (Joshua Smith) .... **Pete Duel**
Roger Davis
Jed 'Kid' Curry (Thaddeus Jones) .... **Ben Murphy**
Clementine Hale .... **Sally Field**
Harry Briscoe .... **J. D. Cannon**
Narrator .... **Roger Davis**
Ralph Story

Executive Producer: **Roy Huggins**
Creator/Producer: **Glen A. Larson**

Jaunty exploits of a pair of likeable ex-bank robbers on the run in the Wild West.

Hannibal Heyes and Kid Curry were two members of the Devil Hole Gang, wanted for a series of bank robberies. Having given themselves up, they agreed a deal with the Governor of Kansas that if they stayed out of trouble for a year they would be granted a pardon. The only snag was that virtually every lawman thought the pair were still on the run, and plenty of other outlaws still held a grudge against them or were keen to tempt them off the straight and narrow. Under their new identities of Joshua Smith and Thaddeus Jones, they roamed the West, trying desperately to keep their heads down. But by the time the series closed they still hadn't received their pardon. Clementine Hale, a friend of Curry's, was introduced in later episodes.

The series was devised as a TV cash-in on the huge success of the film *Butch Cassidy and the Sundance Kid*, but it was rocked at the end of 1971 by the suicide of Pete Duel. Roger Davis, the narrator of the series, was recast as Hannibal Heyes, and Ralph Story was brought in to do the voice-overs.

ALL CREATURES GREAT AND SMALL
UK (BBC) Drama. BBC 1 1978–80; 1983; 1985; 1988–90

James Herriot	**Christopher Timothy**
Siegfried Farnon	**Robert Hardy**
Tristan Farnon	**Peter Davison**
Helen Alderson/Herriot	**Carol Drinkwater**
	Lynda Bellingham
Mrs Hall	**Mary Hignett**
Mrs Pumphrey	**Margaretta Scott**
Calum Buchanan	**John McGlynn**
Deirdre McEwan	**Andrea Gibb**
Mrs Greenlaw	**Judy Wilson**
Jimmy Herriot	**Oliver Watson**
Rosie Herriot	**Rebecca Smith**
Mrs Alton	**Jean Heywood**

Producer: **Bill Sellars**

Tales from a vet's life in the Yorkshire Dales.

Based on the celebrated autobiographical novels of James Herriot, *All Creatures Great and Small* proved to be an enormous success as a TV series, inspired by a 1974 cinema version featuring Simon Ward, and its 1976 sequel, *It Shouldn't Happen to a Vet*, starring John Alderton. With Christopher Timothy now pulling on the vet's wellies, the TV adaptation (with its echoes of DR FINLAY'S CASEBOOK) took viewers back to the 1930s as Herriot arrived at Skeldale House, home of the veterinary practice in the North Riding town of Darrowby (the real-life Askrigg). There he joined senior partner Siegfried Farnon, his easy-going brother, Tristan, and housekeeper Mrs Hall, helping to build up the practice and dealing with all manner of agricultural and domestic animal ailments. If James was not preventing foot and mouth or groping around up a cow's posterior, he was treating the likes of Tricki-Woo, villager Mrs Pumphrey's pampered Pekinese.

James met and married Helen Alderson (later to bear him a son, Jimmy, and a daughter, Rosie), before the series 'ended' after three years when James and Tristan headed off to join the war effort (Herriot's original novels had run out). A couple of Christmas specials kept the concept alive during the early 1980s, before public clamour was answered with a new series in 1988.

With Peter Davison largely tied up elsewhere and his appearances restricted to a minimum, a new vet was added to the cast. The naïve, badger-keeping idealist, Calum Buchanan, joined the practice. The part of Helen was taken over by 'Oxo mum' Lynda Bellingham, and the time had moved on to the post-war years. The writers invented new stories and situations for the team, but the cosy, slow pace of village life and the warm, gentle humour were maintained. The series ran for three more seasons, plus another Christmas special. The programme's sweeping theme music was composed by Johnny Pearson.

ALL GAS AND GAITERS
UK (BBC) Situation Comedy. BBC 1 1967–71

Revd Mervyn Noote	**Derek Nimmo**
Bishop	**William Mervyn**
Archdeacon	**Robertson Hare**
Dean	**John Barron**
	Ernest Clark

Writers: **Edwin Apps, Pauline Devaney**
Producers: **Stuart Allen, John Howard Davies**

Fun and games in the cloisters of a cathedral.

Gently poking fun at the clergy (one of the first comedies to do so), *All Gas and Gaiters* centred on the farcical team at St Ogg's Cathedral, namely its bishop, archdeacon and, particularly, its bumbling, ultra-sincere, plummy chaplain, Revd Mervyn Noote. Their adversary was the rather sober Dean. Nimmo later took his dithery clerical creation on to OH BROTHER and its sequel, *Oh Father*, playing Brother/Father Dominic. *All Gas and Gaiters* began life as a COMEDY PLAYHOUSE presentation in 1966, with the subsequent five series scripted by husband and wife writers Edwin Apps and Pauline Devaney.

ALL IN THE FAMILY
US (Yorkin-Lear) Situation Comedy. BBC 1/BBC 2 1971–5

Archie Bunker	**Carroll O'Connor**
Edith Bunker	**Jean Stapleton**
Gloria Stivic	**Sally Struthers**
Mike Stivic	**Rob Reiner**
Lionel Jefferson	**Mike Evans**
Louise Jefferson	**Isabel Sanford**
Henry Jefferson	**Mel Stewart**
George Jefferson	**Sherman Hemsley**
Irene Lorenzo	**Betty Garrett**
Frank Lorenzo	**Vincent Gardenia**

Writer/Producer: **Norman Lear**
Creators: **Norman Lear, Bud Yorkin**

Innovative American sitcom centring on an arrogant, bigoted labourer and his loud-mouthed prejudices, unashamedly based on Johnny Speight's TILL DEATH US DO PART.

Archie Bunker was America's Alf Garnett and his family, too, bore a strong resemblance to members of the Garnett household. Archie's wife, Edith, affectionately known as 'Dingbat', was somewhat dim, and his sales assistant daughter, Gloria, had disappointed her father by marrying Mike, an antagonizingly liberal sociology student of Polish extraction, whom Archie called 'Meathead'. They lived with the Bunkers and added to the domestic friction.

Outside characters were more prominent than in the British equivalent. Early victims of Archie's pigheadedness were his mixed-race colleagues at the Prendergast Tool and Die Company, and then there were the Bunkers' ethnic neighbours in Queens, NYC, the Jeffersons (black) and the Lorenzos (Italian). The Jeffersons were eventually given their own series, and another spin-off was *Maude*, based around Edith's cousin, Maude Findlay (played by Bea Arthur).

The series ran until 1983 in the USA, but towards the end of the 1970s the programme format was drastically restructured. Archie bought shares in a bar and Gloria, Mike and their son, Joey, moved to California. A little niece, Stephanie Mills (played by Danielle Brisebois), filled the gap by moving in with Archie and Edith, but actress Jean Stapleton eventually tired of the series and was written out. Edith, it was revealed, died of a stroke. During these changes, the series was renamed *Archie Bunker's Place*.

All in the Family became a landmark in US television comedy and was the top show for five years. This was a programme that dared to raise such issues as race, politics and sex. No one had dared to speak like that on American TV before and, after Archie Bunker, the twee, 'Honey I'm home' domestic sitcom was dead. Like Alf Garnett in the UK, he became part of American society.

ALL OUR YESTERDAYS

UK (Granada) Documentary. ITV 1960–73; 1987–9

Presenters: **James Cameron, Brian Inglis, Bernard Braden**

Producers: **Tim Hewat, Douglas Terry, Jeremy Isaacs, David Plowright, Bill Grundy, Mike Murphy**

Nostalgic documentary series looking back 25 years in time.

Using old cinema newsreels, *All Our Yesterdays* reflected on events taking place in the world in the same week 25 years earlier. Consequently, the first programme looked back to a week in the year 1935. Foreign correspondent James Cameron added footnotes to the film coverage until he was replaced as frontman by Brian Inglis after one year. When the series was resurrected in 1987,

Bernard Braden was the new host and television archives were raided for footage. Over 600 editions were produced.

ALL QUIET ON THE PRESTON FRONT

See **PRESTON FRONT.**

ALL SQUARE

See **IT'S A SQUARE WORLD.**

ALL YOU NEED IS LOVE

UK (LWT/Theatre Projects) Documentary. ITV 1977

Producers: **Richard Pilbrow, Neville C. Thompson**

A history of 20th-century popular music.

Researched in depth, this 13-part documentary traced the development of popular music in all its strands, from jazz and blues to chart pop and progressive rock. Much obscure footage was retrieved and interviews with music legends were wrapped around the narrative. The brains behind the project was Tony Palmer, one of the first heavyweight rock critics and the producer of the controversial 1968 OMNIBUS film, *All My Loving*, which interwove music and musicians with horrifying scenes of war and war crimes.

ALL YOUR OWN

UK (BBC) Children's Entertainment. BBC 1952–61

Presenter: **Huw Wheldon**

Editors: **Cliff Michelmore, Joanne Symons**
Producers: **Michael Westmore, Tony Arnold**

Showcase for young talents and children's hobbies.

Hosted for the most part by future BBC Television Managing Director Huw Wheldon, and edited by a young Cliff Michelmore from 1952, *All Your Own* invited youngsters from all over the UK to show off their skills and talents or discuss their hobbies and pastimes. Guitarist John Williams was featured on one programme and used it as a stepping stone to greater things. Led Zeppelin's Jimmy Page was, reputedly, another youthful guest. Jimmy Logan, Brian Johnston and Cliff Morgan also appeared as hosts.

ALLEN, DAVE

(David Tynan O'Mahony; 1936–)

Suave Irish comedian, a former journalist and Red Coat, famed for monologues casually delivered from a high stool with a drink and cigarette to hand. His favourite hunting grounds are sex and religion (also parodied in short sketches and echoed in his closing catchphrase, 'May your god go with you'). After initially appearing on *The Val Doonican Show* in 1965 and compering SUNDAY

NIGHT AT THE LONDON PALLADIUM, Allen's first solo series was *Tonight With Dave Allen*, for ITV in 1967, which was followed by *The Dave Allen Show* for BBC 2. However, it was through numerous series of *Dave Allen at Large* for the BBC in the 1970s that he became a household name. Later 1970s contributions included *Dave Allen and Friends*, *Dave Allen* and the documentary *Dave Allen in Search of the Great English Eccentric*. He returned to television (and ITV) in the 1990s with a new (and somewhat controversial) series of frank monologues.

ALLEN, GRACIE
(1906–64)

The scatterbrained TV and real-life wife of George Burns. Together they worked their way from vaudeville, through radio to TV, where, in 1950, they created one of America's earliest comedy hits, THE BURNS AND ALLEN SHOW, in which they played themselves in a sitcom environment. Gracie's trademarks were a confused logic and a flair for malapropisms. After eight years, Gracie retired, leaving George to continue alone. She died in 1964 after a long illness.

ALLEN, IRWIN
(1916–91)

American producer/director responsible for some of the most extravagant science-fiction series of the 1960s, all created on the tightest of budgets. Much use was made of stock film footage and cinema cast-offs to add depth to his studio-bound dramas. His first major TV offering was VOYAGE TO THE BOTTOM OF THE SEA in 1964, inspired by his 1962 film release with the same title (and most of the same props). Then came LOST IN SPACE, TIME TUNNEL and LAND OF THE GIANTS, as well as the less memorable *The Swiss Family Robinson*.

ALLEN, JIM
(1926–99)

Manchester-born former miner and socialist-minded playwright, often in collaboration with director Ken Loach, who moved on from scripting for CORONATION STREET to creating some particularly poignant – and controversial – dramas for the BBC, most notably *The Lump* (1967), *The Big Flame* (1969), *The Rank and File* (1971) and the series DAYS OF HOPE. The last enraged pillars of the Establishment, who claimed it crossed the boundary between fiction and propaganda in its story of two young pacifist lovers in the era of the Great War and General Strike. Later works included *The Spongers* (1978), *United Kingdom* (1981) and *The Gathering Seed* (1983).

ALLEN, KEITH
(1952–)

Llanelli-born comedian/actor often associated with 'bad boy' parts, but with a range of roles to his name. These include Rex in MAKING OUT, Thompson in *A Very British Coup*, Jackson Pace in *Jackson Pace: The Great Years*, Jonas Chuzzlewit in *Martin Chuzzlewit*, Byron Flitch in *Born to Run*, Dexter in ROGER ROGER and Jack in *Jack of Hearts*. Previously, he was one of the COMIC STRIP team, featuring in most of their satires, and also appeared in THE YOUNG ONES. He co-wrote the 1990 England World Cup Squad/New Order hit, 'World in Motion'.

ALLEN, PATRICK
(1927–)

Square-jawed, bass-voiced actor and voice-over specialist, perhaps best remembered as the man in the helicopter in the Barratt homes commercial, though also star of several series, including CRANE, *Brett* and *Hard Times*. His other TV credits have included *Glencannon* (as Bosun Hughes), *The Adventures of Aggie*, *The Dick Emery Show*, THE WINDS OF WAR, THE BLACK ADDER, *Body and Soul* and numerous single plays. He is married to actress Sarah Lawson (the third governor in WITHIN THESE WALLS).

ALLEN, RONALD
(1930–91)

Although Ronald Allen is clearly best recalled as the lugubrious David Hunter in CROSSROADS, his career began well before that famous motel opened its doors. His matinee-idol looks could well have seen him in Hollywood in the 1950s, but the several small film roles he gained failed to take him to the top. However, his TV break came in 1962 when he was cast as editor Ian Harman in the woman's magazine drama COMPACT, a part which he followed in 1966 with that of Mark Wilson, one of Brentwich United's managers, in the soccer drama UNITED!. He guested in DOCTOR WHO and joined *Crossroads* in 1969 and remained with the programme for 16 years, until he was surprisingly axed by a new regime in 1985, together with his screen (and future real-life) wife, Sue Lloyd. Later, the suave but rather starchy Allen was seen to 'loosen up', taking a cameo role as the gay Uncle Quentin in the COMIC STRIP's *Five Go Mad In Dorset*.

'ALLO 'ALLO
UK (BBC) Situation Comedy. BBC 1 1984–92

René Artois	Gorden Kaye
Edith Artois	Carmen Silvera
Yvette	Vicki Michelle
Maria	Francesca Gonshaw
Michelle Dubois	Kirsten Cooke
Col. Kurt Von Strohm	Richard Marner
Capt. Hans Geering	Sam Kelly
Lt. Gruber	Guy Siner
Helga Geerhart	Kim Hartman
Herr Otto Flick	Richard Gibson
	David Janson
Von Smallhausen	John Louis Mansi
Officer Crabtree	Arthur Bostrom

Gen. Von Klinkerhoffen	**Hilary Minster**
Mimi La Bonque	**Sue Hodge**
Monsieur Leclerc	**Jack Haig**
	Derek Royle
	Robin Parkinson
Monsieur Alphonse	**Kenneth Connor**
Fanny	**Rose Hill**
Flying Officer Fairfax	**John D. Collins**
Flying Officer Carstairs	**Nicholas Frankau**
Capt. Alberto Bertorelli	**Gavin Richards**
	Roger Kitter

Creators: **Jeremy Lloyd, David Croft**
Producers: **David Croft, John B. Hobbs**

A wartime French café-owner is in demand with both the Germans and the Resistance.

René Artois was the proprietor of a café in the northern French town of Nouvion. He ran the bar with his wife, Edith, and a couple of shapely waitresses, Yvette and Maria. At least, that was until the Germans occupied the town. He then found himself having to pander to the local Nazis, headed by Colonel Von Strohm, the clumsy Captain Geering and the gay Lt. Gruber. At the same time, his bar was taken over as a French Resistance safehouse, primarily to house two gormless British airmen, Fairfax and Carstairs (Adamson in the pilot episode). In this way, this man's war became rather more trying than others'.

Introducing each episode by speaking to camera, René updated viewers on earlier happenings (the show was run as a kind of serial farce). Usually, the highly exaggerated plots centred on René's reluctant attempts to help the airmen escape, or to sabotage the Germans' efforts to steal a priceless painting, the so-called *Fallen Madonna with the Big Boobies* by Van Clomp. Instigator of most of the action was the local Resistance leader, Michelle, comandeerer of René's bar and supplier of the show's prime catchphrase, 'Leesten very carefully. I shall say this only wance.' She was aided by Officer Crabtree, an inept British agent disguised as a gendarme, spouting appalling French which translated into warped English phrases like 'Good moaning'. Indeed, the use of stereotypical accents to convey different languages was one of *'Allo 'Allo*'s success stories. Also influencing affairs was the cruel Herr Flick, the limping local Gestapo chief who demanded kinky affection from his adjutant, Helga, and abused his incompetent sidekick, Von Smallhausen.

Around the central action there were plenty of subplots: René's steamy affairs with both Yvette and Maria (later replaced by Mimi), the marriage of Edith's bedridden mother, Fanny, to ageing Resistance forger Leclerc, and René's alleged death, which allowed Edith to court Monsieur Alphonse, the local undertaker with a 'dicky ticker' and a 'small 'earse with a small 'orse'. But the programme also had some well-rehearsed running jokes: Edith's excruciating singing, for instance, which forced the bar's customers to stuff their ears with cheese, Lt. Gruber's advances to René, and René's (codename Nighthawk) laboured attempts to get the wireless to work from its secret hiding place beneath Fanny's chamber pot (the series took its name from his opening words to London).

Rich in innuendo and slapstick, *'Allo 'Allo* was much criticized for its 'bad taste', though it always claimed to be poking fun at over-the-top wartime dramas and not at the cruelty of war itself. SECRET ARMY was its main target. When it ended, after nearly nine years, the war had finished and Nouvion was liberated. Viewers were treated to a 'flashforward' to the present day and introduced to René's son (again played by Gorden Kaye), who explained what had happened to the locals in the post-war years to a visiting Gruber, who had, surprisingly, married Helga. A West End stage version, with original cast members, was also produced.

ALLY McBEAL
US (20th Century Fox/David E. Kelley) Comedy Drama. Channel 4 1998–

Ally McBeal	**Calista Flockhart**
Georgia Thomas	**Courtney Thorne-Smith**
Billy Thomas	**Gil Bellows**
Richard Fish	**Greg Germann**
Renée Radick	**Lisa Nicole Carson**
Elaine Vassal	**Jane Krakowski**
John 'The Biscuit' Cage	**Peter MacNicol**
Jennifer 'Whipper' Cone	**Dyan Cannon**
Dr Tracey Clark	**Tracey Ullman**
Ling Woo	**Lucy Liu**
Nelle Porter	**Portia de Rossi**

Creator/Executive Producer: **David E. Kelley**
Producers: **Mike Listo, Jonathan Pontell**

An ambitious but neurotic girl works in a quirky law firm.

Described by some critics as a 'love it or loathe it' series, *Ally McBeal* was the US hit of 1997–8, setting a new agenda with its off-beat format, focus on moral dilemmas and exploration of the emotional outpourings of the title character. In the opening episode, the 27-year-old Ms McBeal walked out of her job in a large Boston law practice after being sexually harassed by her boss. She bumped into Richard Fish, an old college friend, and accepted an offer of a job at his law firm instead. Unfortunately, Fish had also taken on Ally's ex-lover, Billy Thomas, the man she had been longing for since their Harvard days. The fact that he was now married to their beautiful and successful colleague, Georgia, made the situation even less comfortable. This emotional triangle featured prominently in the stories to follow.

Fish was an appropriate head of this wacky law firm, which also featured his wily, oddball partner, John Cage – a Barry White fan nicknamed 'The Biscuit' – and gossipy, singing secretary Elaine. Support for the neurotic Ally came from her down-to-earth roommate, district attorney Renée Radick. Also seen at times were Fish's older lover, judge 'Whipper' Cone, and Ally's straight-talking but crazy analyst, Dr Tracey Clark. Icy Nelle Porter and single-minded Ling Woo were later additions to the legal team. Many of the deeper conversations took place in the unisex loo at Cage/Fish and Associates.

To highlight the heroine's mental turmoil, the producers introduced fantasy cartoon elements, like Ally's foot forcing its way into her mouth when she dropped a clanger, or arrows pounding into her heart when she was rejected in love. Her vibrant imagination came to life, too, such as in scenes where she romped naked with her ex-boyfriend in a mug of cappuccino. There was also a computer-generated dancing baby named Mr Huggy that writhed to the song 'Hooked on a Feeling' and personified Ally's subconscious desire to have a child of her own. The baby gained a cult following and a catalogue of successful spin-off merchandise. A CD of *Ally McBeal* music featured tracks by singer Vonda Shepard, who performed in most episodes.

Ally McBeal turned unknown actress Calista Flockhart into a superstar and thrust her into the limelight as a style guru. Her character's comfy pyjamas became the rage at American department stores, her hemlines were attacked by puritans for being much too short, and her ultra-slim figure brought concern for the way it 'promoted' the thin look among impressionable girls. However, plenty of female viewers identified with McBeal's frank expression of a modern woman's mind.

AMBASSADOR
UK (BBC/) Drama. BBC 1 1998–9

Harriet Smith	Pauline Collins
John Stone	Denis Lawson
Stephen Tyler	William Chubb
Kevin Flaherty	Owen Roe
Julian Wadham	Dominic Mafham
Jennifer	Alison McKenna
Becky	Sarah Markland
Nate Smith	Tim Matthews
Sam Smith	Tom Connolly
Catherine Grieve	Eve Matheson
Michael Cochrane	Peter Egan
Eileen	Gina Moxley
Susan	Sinead Clarkin

Producers: **Stephen Smallwood, Louise Berridge**

Problems for a female British ambassador.

Harriet Smith was the new British Ambassador to the Republic of Ireland. The sensitive Anglo-Irish relationship notwithstanding, it was a tricky appointment, made even trickier by Harriet's emotional response to situations, her straight talking and her grammar school upbringing that set her at odds with surrounding Establishment figures. Problems ranged from Irish accusations that the British had sunk one of their trawlers to hostage-taking, drug-smuggling and attempted assassination. It was not the first time that Harriet's life had been placed in threat: previously, in Beirut, her own husband had been killed by a bomb that was intended for her. This left her struggling to manage the upbringing of her two sons, Nate, a hard-to-handle student also living in Dublin, and the young Sam, who still lived with his mother. Supporting Harriet professionally was secret service agent John Stone.

The second series introduced a love interest for Harriet in the form of dodgy construction magnate Michael Cochrane, and Harriet's personal life was placed more under the spotlight than in early episodes. She also gained a new assistant in Catherine Grieve.

AMERICA
UK (BBC) Documentary. BBC 2 1972–3

Presenter: **Alistair Cooke**

Writer: **Alistair Cooke**
Producer: **Michael Gill**

Thoughtful retrospective on the growth of the USA.

'A personal history of the United States' was the subtitle to this well-considered account of the birth and development of a nation, presented from the viewpoint of Alistair Cooke, a top British correspondent and an American citizen. Cooke's dual nationality allowed him to portray the USA from both internal and external viewpoints, fashioning a TV history designed for consumption on both sides of the Atlantic. In 13 weekly episodes he charted the hopes, experiences and achievements of the men who shaped the most powerful country in the world, tracing developments from before Columbus right up to the Nixon era.

His compassionate, gentle narration and poignant anecdotes allowed Cooke to convey the enormity of the problems facing the earliest settlers, and he incisively analysed the political movements and the agricultural and industrial changes that moulded the country over the centuries, winning wide acclaim for his understanding and perception. His conclusion centred on the fact that America at the turn of the 1970s fell a long way short of the dreams of its founding fathers.

Alistair Cooke was for many years the *Guardian*'s Chief America Correspondent. His *Letter from America* is the longest-running single radio programme (since 1946) and can be heard weekly on Radio 4.

AMERICAN BROADCASTING COMPANY
See **ABC**.

AMOS BURKE – SECRET AGENT
See **BURKE'S LAW**.

AMY PRENTISS
US (Universal) Police Drama. ITV 1976

Amy Prentiss	Jessica Walter
Det. Tony Russell	Steve Sandor
Det. Rod Pena	Arthur Metrano
Det. Contreras	Johnny Seven
Jill Prentiss	Helen Hunt
Joan Carter	Gwenn Mitchell

Executive Producer: **Cy Chermak**

A 35-year-old widow becomes San Francisco's first female Chief of Detectives.

When her boss died suddenly, 35-year-old Amy Prentiss was chosen to succeed him. However, there had never been a female Chief of Detectives in the SFPD before and, for her colleagues, that took a bit of getting used to. Fighting prejudice, this was one lady cop who was determined to make the grade. Jill was her young daughter. *Amy Prentiss* aired as part of the MYSTERY MOVIE sequence, but didn't last more than three outings. The pilot had been an episode of A MAN CALLED IRONSIDE.

ANCHOR/ANCHORMAN

The person who presents a news, current affairs, sports or magazine programme, linking contributions from other reporters or cueing in pre-recorded inserts. In some instances, the anchor is instrumental in setting the tone or style of the programme. The term has also been employed for the question master in a game show. It was allegedly first used in 1952 by Sig Mickelson, President of CBS News, when describing the fundamental role played by celebrated news frontman Walter Cronkite in CBS bulletins.

AND MOTHER MAKES THREE/AND MOTHER MAKES FIVE

UK (Thames) Situation Comedy. ITV 1971–3/1974–6

Sally Harrison/Redway	**Wendy Craig**
Simon Harrison	**Robin Davies**
Peter Harrison	**David Parfitt**
Auntie Flo	**Valerie Lush**
Mr Campbell	**George Selway**
David Redway	**Richard Coleman**
Jane Redway	**Miriam Mann** (*Makes Three*)
	Maxine Gordon (*Makes Five*)
Joss Spencer	**Tony Britton** (*Makes Five*)
Monica Spencer	**Charlotte Mitchell** (*Makes Five*)

Creator/Writer: **Richard Waring**
Producer: **Peter Frazer-Jones**

A young widow struggles to cope with her two sons.

Left with her two young boys, Simon and Peter, when her husband died, scatty housewife Sally Harrison took a job at a vet's surgery. Working for Mr Campbell, she struggled along in traditional sitcom fashion with the help of her Auntie Flo, whom she persuaded to join the household. Further assistance came eventually from the new man in her life, David Redway, a widower with a young daughter named Jane. Sally later worked in David's antiquarian bookshop, a marriage ensued and the series turned into *And Mother Makes Five*, in 1974, when they all moved in together. Auntie was rehoused in the flat above the shop and the Spencers became their next-door neighbours.

ANDERSON, CLIVE
(1953–)

Stanmore-born presenter and humorist, coming to the fore as chairman of the improvisation show, WHOSE LINE IS IT ANYWAY? Anderson, a barrister by first profession, was President of the Cambridge Footlights club in the early 1970s and performed stand-up routines at The Comedy Store and other clubs before breaking into television as a writer on programmes such as NOT THE NINE O'CLOCK NEWS and ALAS SMITH AND JONES. After *Whose Line Is It Anyway?*, he graduated to his own Channel 4 chat show, *Clive Anderson Talks Back*, and also stood in on *Wogan* and POINTS OF VIEW. Then came the BBC 2 information programme, *Notes and Queries With Clive Anderson*. From 1995 Anderson appeared in *Our Man In . . .*, a series of light-hearted documentaries from exotic locales around the world. His chat show moved to BBC 1 in 1996 under the title *Clive Anderson All Talk*. Other credits have included hosting *Just for Laughs*, presenting a documentary on the Bayeux Tapestry called *Every Picture Tells a Story*, and taking one of the *Great Railway Journeys of the World*.

ANDERSON, GERRY
(1929–)

British television's puppet-master, Gerry Anderson, actually began his TV career working as director for Roberta Leigh, creator of THE ADVENTURES OF TWIZZLE and TORCHY THE BATTERY BOY. However, Anderson had already set up his own film company with colleague Arthur Provis (Anderson/Provis Films – APF) and, seeing the potential of such animation, launched his own series, FOUR FEATHER FALLS, in 1960. This story of a courageous, crooning Western lawman with magic feathers to protect him was sold to Granada, and Anderson was up and running.

It wasn't until 1962, when he created SUPERCAR, that Anderson embarked on science fiction. These dashing tales of a vehicle that could go anywhere and do anything heralded a new era for TV sci-fi, although it also proved a little too expensive for Granada. Thankfully, Lew Grade stepped in and ITC became Anderson's new backers. *Supercar*'s more adventurous follow-up, FIREBALL XL5, concerning the exploits of Steve Zodiac and his crew, proved very popular, so popular in fact that Anderson decided to go for colour on his next project. This was STINGRAY, the adventures of a supersub and its fearless commander, Troy Tempest. All the while, Anderson's new 'Supermarionation' was reaching maturity, the puppets' strings becoming ever finer and their mouths synchronized with the dialogue for added realism. Working closely with Anderson were Barry Gray (who supplied all the rousing theme tracks), special effects expert Derek Meddings, and co-producer Reg Hill. Involved in the scripting, and supplying some of the female voices, was Gerry's then wife, Sylvia Anderson.

Their next opus proved to be their masterpiece. THUNDERBIRDS, filmed in 50-minute episodes, focused on the agents of International Rescue, an anonymous world-protection force with a fleet of super aircraft. After *Thunderbirds*, Anderson's puppetry was perfected in CAPTAIN SCARLET AND THE MYSTERONS, produced by Century 21 Productions (as APF had now become). Gone were awkward, bulbous-headed puppets, in came perfectly proportioned, beautifully characterized human models, as the indestructible Spectrum agent and his colleagues fought off the vengeful raiders from Mars. Following these last two successes was always going to be difficult, and the Anderson team disappointed fans with two tame offerings, namely JOE 90 and THE SECRET SERVICE. This led Anderson to look more seriously at live action as the way forward, spawning UFO as the next project. Sci-fi was subsequently abandoned when he turned his attention to THE PROTECTORS, starring Robert Vaughn, Nyree Dawn Porter and Tony Anholt as a trio of international crime-fighters; but it was back on the table when SPACE: 1999, with Martin Landau and Barbara Bain, arrived in 1975. The major 1980s offering was TERRAHAWKS, a return to puppetry featuring the grizzly alien Zelda, although there was also a collection of short detective spoofs, *Dick Spanner PI*, shown on Channel 4 in 1985. Ten years later, Anderson was back in orbit, combining live and model action in the expensively produced *Space Precinct*, featuring the exploits of a trans-universal police force.

ANDERSON, GILLIAN
(1968–)

Chicago-born, London-raised actress who became an international star as Dana Scully in THE X-FILES. In 1996 she re-crossed the Atlantic to present the BBC's science series, *Future Fantastic*.

ANDERSON, JEAN
(1907–2001)

Sussex-born actress specializing in crusty, upper-class roles and most familiar as the scheming mother in THE BROTHERS. Her other lead credits included the mother in *The Railway Children* and TENKO (as Joss Holbrook), and there were plenty of supporting roles, from DR FINLAY'S CASEBOOK, THE GOOD GUYS, HEARTBEAT and THE HOUSE OF ELIOTT to INSPECTOR MORSE, GBH, TRAINER and KEEPING UP APPEARANCES.

ANDREWS, ANTHONY
(1948–)

Suave English leading man, coming to the fore as the Earl of Silverbridge in THE PALLISERS and as Lt. Brian Ash in Thames TV's DANGER UXB. BRIDESHEAD REVISITED followed (playing Sebastian Flyte), for which he picked up a BAFTA award as Best Actor on TV. Other notable credits have included UPSTAIRS, DOWNSTAIRS, THE DUCHESS OF DUKE STREET, *Ivanhoe*, *Z for Zachariah*, *Suspicion*, *The Woman He Loved* and the elaborate mini-series *AD (Anno Domini)*, in which he played Nero. Trivia

buffs will recall that Andrews was originally cast as Bodie in THE PROFESSIONALS but lost the part because he looked too much like Martin Shaw in screen tests.

ANDREWS, EAMONN
CBE (1922–87)

Former boxer (the All Ireland Juvenile Champion) and sports commentator who became one of TV's most durable comperes. Having built a successful career in radio, in both Ireland and Britain, Andrews's first TV break came in 1951 when he was selected as host of WHAT'S MY LINE?, the BBC's new panel game. In 1955, he became presenter of THIS IS YOUR LIFE, a light-hearted, biographical tribute show imported from the USA. Ironically, Andrews was surprised in the first show by American compere Ralph Edwards and became the programme's first victim. *What's My Line?* and *This Is Your Life* were to become stalwarts of Andrews's TV career, although he also dabbled in children's television through *Playbox* and, most notably, CRACKERJACK. When his BBC contract elapsed in 1964 (*This Is Your Life* was cancelled), he moved to ITV to host WORLD OF SPORT and his own late-night celebrity series, *The Eamonn Andrews Show* (echoing the title of a 1956 BBC comedy show Eamonn had presented). *This Is Your Life* was revived by Thames in 1969 and *What's My Line?* returned in 1984 (again courtesy of Thames, for whom Andrews presented the nightly news magazine, *Today*, for ten years). His other credits included *Time for Business* and the ambitious satellite quiz *Top of the World* (linking contestants on three continents). Eamonn Andrews died in 1987 from heart disease. In his career, he had been voted Television Personality of the Year four times and had helped to set up RTE, the Irish television corporation.

ANDROMEDA BREAKTHROUGH, THE
See A FOR ANDROMEDA.

ANDY PANDY
UK (BBC) Children's Entertainment. BBC 1950–7; 1970

Creators/Writers: **Freda Lingstrom, Maria Bird**
Narrators: **Maria Bird, Vera McKechnie**
Producers: **Peter Thompson, David Boisseau, Freda Lingstrom**

The tame adventures of a puppet and his toy friends.

Dressed in a blue-and-white-striped suit, with a matching floppy hat, Andy Pandy was one of the pioneers of children's TV in the early 1950s. In fact, he remained a source of fun for infants right through the 1960s, too. Taking up the King of the Kids' Show baton from Muffin the Mule, Andy was a cherub-faced toddler who lived in a picnic basket. He first appeared solo, but then was joined by the moth-eaten Teddy and, later, a rag doll named Looby Loo.

Andy and Teddy's adventures were remarkably uninspiring, stretching no further than a ride on a swing or a turn on the see-saw, accompanied by a rather patronizing commentary from co-creator/writer/narrator Maria Bird and shrill, jingly songs, voiced by Gladys Whitbred and Julia Williams. The greatest excitement came when their backs were turned and Looby Loo sprang to life. With her simple features, yellow plaits and polka-dot dress, Looby played, danced and then skipped to the ditty, 'Here We Go Looby Loo'. At the end of each show, Andy and Teddy popped back in the basket to the strains of the closing song, which declared it was 'Time to go home' (later 'Time to stop play').

Andy Pandy was jointly the brainchild of Maria Bird and Freda Lingstrom, later Head of the BBC's Children's Department, and first aired in 1950, marking an expansion in programmes for younger viewers. Its first slot was Tuesday at 3.45 p.m., and it was soon joined by similar programmes on other days, making up the WATCH WITH MOTHER strand. Only 26 original programmes were made, but they were repeated constantly until 1969. Thirteen new, colour episodes were written and produced by Freda Lingstrom in 1970, to replace the fading black-and-white films, with former PICTURE BOOK presenter Vera McKechnie relating events and Valerie Cardnell providing the songs. The puppets' chunky strings (a world away from the micro-wires used by Gerry Anderson) were initially pulled by Audrey Atterbury and Molly Gibson (Cecil and Madge Stavordale and Christopher Leith in 1970).

ANGELIS, MICHAEL

Liverpudlian actor, often in comic roles like that of Lucien, the rabbit-loving brother of Carol Boswell in THE LIVER BIRDS. He also starred as Chrissie in BOYS FROM THE BLACKSTUFF and Max in *I Woke up One Morning*. More recently, he appeared in GBH and starred as Harold Craven in LUV, as well as playing gay bartender Arnie in SEPTEMBER SONG, DI Kilshaw in *Melissa*, Will Shaker in the comedy *Giving Tongue*, and Chris in PLAYING THE FIELD, and taking over as narrator of THOMAS THE TANK ENGINE AND FRIENDS from Ringo Starr. Other credits have included ROCK FOLLIES, REILLY – ACE OF SPIES, BREAD, BOON, BETWEEN THE LINES, LOVEJOY, CASUALTY and *The Jump*. He married CORONATION STREET actress Helen Worth.

ANGELS

UK (BBC) Drama. BBC 1 1975–83

Patricia Rutherford	**Fiona Fullerton**
Jo Longhurst	**Julie Dawn Cole**
Sita Patel	**Karan David**
Ruth Fullman	**Lesley Dunlop**
Shirley Brent	**Clare Clifford**
Maureen Morahan	**Erin Geraghty**
Miss Heather Windrup	**Faith Brooks**
Stewart Farrar	**Jeremy Wilkin**
Linda Hollis	**Janina Faye**
Elaine Fitzgerald	**Taiwo Ajai**
Sarah Regan	**Debbie Ash**
Jennifer Sorrell	**Marsha Millar**
Sister Easby	**June Watson**
Pauline Smart	**Christine Akehurst**
Anna Newcross	**Joanna Munro**
Jean MacEwen	**Carol Holmes**
Jay Harper	**Shelley King**
Brenda Cotteral	**Kate Saunders**
Sarah Lloyd-Smith	**Claire Walker**
	Kate Lock
Katy Betts/Smart	**Shirley Cheriton**
Sandra Ling	**Angela Bruce**
Fleur Barrett/Frost	**Sharon Rosita**
Adrienne O'Shea	**Fay Howard**
Elizabeth Fitt	**Susan Gilmore**
Rose Butchins	**Kathryn Apanowicz**
Beverley Slater	**Judith Jacob**
Ron Frost	**Martin Barrass**
Den Booth	**Ken Sharrock**
Roger Smart	**Gary Whelan**
Tracey Willoughby/Carr	**Julia Williams**
Valerie Price	**Deborah Manship**
Linda Mo	**Sarah Lam**
Vicky Smith	**Pauline Quirke**
Alison Streeter/Clarke	**Juliet Waley**
Dave Nowell	**Neil West**
Janet Dickens	**Michelle Martin**
Nargis Khan	**Mamta Kash**
Josh Jones	**Tony Armatrading**
Chris Carr	**Martin Rutledge**
Ayo Lapido	**Joy Lemoine**

Creator: **Paula Milne**
Producers: **Ron Craddock, Julia Smith, Ben Rea**

Student nurses struggle to make a success of their lives and careers.

Beginning as a 50-minute drama series, then in 1979 switching to two half-hour episodes a week, *Angels* told the stories of student nurses of St Angela's Hospital, Battersea, and, later, the brand-new Heath Green Hospital in Birmingham. It showed them at work and at play and, shot in semi-documentary style, it exposed their long hours and thankless chores. Although they were angels, these nurses were no saints, which came as a shock to some viewers expecting another dose of EMERGENCY – WARD 10's soppy romance. In many ways, *Angels*, with its grittiness, can be seen as a forerunner of EASTENDERS. Producer Julia Smith went on to create the latter and perhaps used *Angels* as a dress-rehearsal for the East End drama (even though *Angels* was seen only in 13-week blocks and not all year round). Some of the stars, too – Shirley Cheriton, Kathryn Apanowicz and Judith Jacobs – moved to Albert Square, while others, like Pauline Quirke, Fiona Fullerton and Lesley Dunlop, found different avenues to success.

Angels was partly filmed at St James's Hospital, Balham.

ANGLIA TELEVISION

The independent television company serving East Anglia since 27 October 1959 from a headquarters in Norwich and a handful of smaller studios around the region. Inheriting a predominantly agricultural and rural area, the company at first pitched its regional programmes accordingly, although, with gradual expansion into the industrial centres of the East Midlands, its style has become more cosmopolitan. In the early 1970s it relinquished coverage of Lincolnshire and Humberside to Yorkshire Television (thanks to an IBA transmitter swap) and nearly joined Yorkshire and Tyne Tees in a joint holding company, Trident Television. Although the other two companies went ahead, the IBA refused Anglia permission to become Trident's 'third prong'. Nationally, Anglia did very well in the quiz show line in the 1970s, thanks to SALE OF THE CENTURY and *Gambit* in particular. The company has also built up a reputation for talk shows like *Vanessa* and *Trisha* and very competent drama, with the likes of P. D. JAMES's Adam Dalgliesh mysteries, THE CHIEF and *Jilly Cooper's Riders* all contributions to the network. Probably its best-known series, however, was TALES OF THE UNEXPECTED, which notched up huge international sales. Yet Anglia's name for drama has been dwarfed by its worldwide status as a maker of natural history films, thanks to the acclaim showered on SURVIVAL since it began in 1961. Anglia is now part of the Granada Media group.

ANHOLT, TONY
(1941–)

One of TV's smoothies, Singapore-born Tony Anholt's first starring role came as Paul Buchet in THE PROTECTORS, alongside Robert Vaughn and Nyree Dawn Porter. In 1975 he popped up in CORONATION STREET playing David Law, the crooked boss of a model agency, but it was not until the 1980s that his career really revived, when he was cast as tycoon Charles Frere in HOWARDS' WAY. His other TV credits have included THE STRAUSS FAMILY (Eduard), SPACE: 1999 (First Officer Tony Verdeschi), A FAMILY AT WAR, TRIANGLE (Nick Stevens), plus numerous guest spots in the likes of MINDER, BULMAN and ONLY FOOLS AND HORSES. He is the father of actor Christien Anholt.

ANIMAL HOSPITAL
UK (BBC) Factual. BBC 1 1994–

Presenters: **Rolf Harris, Lynda Bryans, Steve Knight, Mairi McHaffie, Shauna Lowry, Rhodri Williams, Christa Hart, Edwina Silver**

Executive Producers: **Lorraine Heggessey, Sarah Hargreaves**

Tears and joy at an RSPCA-run centre for sick animals.

Animal Hospital began as *Animal Hospital Live*, a twice-daily report on events at Harmsworth Memorial Hospital in Holloway, London, in August 1994. The reports ran for five days only, but viewer response to the heart-warming, but also sometimes heart-rending, tales of pet woes was so great that a Christmas Day special followed, then a full series in January 1995. Entitled *Animal Hospital*

Week, it highlighted happenings over seven days at the hospital.

Harmsworth, named after Sir Harold Harmsworth and funded by the RSPCA, takes care of animals whose owners are on benefit and cannot meet veterinary charges, and it also looks after wild animals brought in by caring members of the public. The series proved to be a mixed blessing for the hospital: on the one hand it sent out a clear message about animal welfare, but on the other it caused the hospital to be inundated with injured pets whose owners could and should have paid for treatment elsewhere. Chief vet David Grant was the human star, while celebrity patients included Snowy the poodle and Dolly the bull terrier.

In 1995 the title was simplified to *Animal Hospital* and a 10-minute bulletin for younger viewers was added to the Children's BBC schedules. At Christmas that year a special *Animal Hospital Down Under* saw host Rolf Harris return to his homeland to visit the Currumbin Wildlife Sanctuary in Queensland. (Rolf popped back to Australia in the run-up to the Sydney Olympics for the two-part *Animal Hospital in Oz*.)

Since 1996, the programme has run twice a year, with the autumn series mostly remaining at Harmsworth and the spring series moving to new locations. With the subtitle 'On the Hoof', spring 1996 followed developments at Bedfordshire's Whipsnade Wild Animal Park. In spring 1997, the series headed out to the Hampden Veterinary Hospital in Aylesbury, to reflect on animal stories from the country, while in 1998 the spring programmes focused on Harmsworth's sister RSPCA hospital in Putney, London, featuring vet Tessa Bailey and her team. Putney became the year-round venue in 1999, and in 2000 the team moved north to cover events in Salford and at Stapeley Grange, near Nantwich, before returning to Putney. Highlight packages have been aired under the title *Animal Hospital Revisited*; in summer 1998 the *Animal Hospital Roadshow* toured animal centres around Britain for six weeks; and at Christmas 1998 *Animal Hospital: Fleas and All* offered a behind-the-scenes look at the making of the series.

ANIMAL MAGIC
UK (BBC) Natural History. BBC 1 1962–83

Presenters: **Johnny Morris, Terry Nutkins**

Producers: **Winwood Reade, Jeffrey Boswell, Douglas Thomas, George Inger**

A whimsical look at the world of animals for younger viewers.

Hosted by the inimitable Johnny Morris, the man who talked *for* animals, *Animal Magic* was a stalwart of the BBC's children's output for 21 years. As well as welcoming guest animals into the studio (always a hazardous practice), Morris went out and about (including overseas to places like the Sudan and Japan) to see creatures at work and play. A favourite stamping ground was Bristol Zoo, and 'Keeper Morris' later over-dubbed the films he made, putting humorous words in the animals' mouths. Camels were his favourite beasts because they always looked as if they were talking. Also seen at times were reports from Tony Soper. Terry Nutkins joined Morris in the 1980s.

ANIMAL, VEGETABLE, MINERAL?
UK (BBC) Panel Game. BBC 1952–9

Chairman: **Glyn Daniel**

Producer: **David Attenborough**

Erudite, name-the-item quiz.

Unusually popular, considering its learned tone, *Animal, Vegetable, Mineral?* was one of the BBC's first major panel games. Once a fortnight a team of three experts tried to identify a succession of objects taken from Britain's museums, giving the UK's great 'national inheritance' a plug in the process. The first chairman was Lionel Hale, but, from the second programme, Cambridge University Fellow, Glyn Daniel, hosted proceedings. Among the numerous experts taking part were archaeologist Sir Mortimer Wheeler, Adrian Digby, Norman Cook, Dr W. E. Swinton, Dr Julian Huxley, Jacquetta Hawkes, Professor Thomas Bodkin and other cerebral folk. David Attenborough was the programme's chief producer. A short-lived revival followed in 1971.

ANNIS, FRANCESCA
(1944–)

British actress, best remembered on TV for her acclaimed portrayal of Lillie Langtry in LILLIE, reprising a role she had played in some episodes of EDWARD THE SEVENTH. The earlier MADAME BOVARY for BBC 2, plus the later Agatha Christie dramas, *Why Didn't They Ask Evans?* and *The Secret Adversary*, leading to the series *Partners In Crime* (in which she played Tuppence Beresford), consolidated her appeal in sophisticated roles. In the 1990s she appeared as Kitty O'Shea in *Parnell and the Englishwoman*, Katya Princip in *The Gravy Train Goes East*, Celia Hardcourt in *Deadly Summer* and as Anna Fairley, opposite Robson Green, in *Reckless*. In 2000 she starred as Ellen Richmond in the thriller, *Deceit*. Some of her first TV appearances came in episodes of DANGER MAN and DR FINLAY'S CASEBOOK. Other guest spots have included DALZIEL AND PASCOE.

ANNOUNCER

The person who, either in vision or simply by voice-over, links programmes, reads trails and provides important additional information to viewers. He/she is also known as a continuity announcer. The BBC has long abandoned on-screen announcers, though its early broadcasts were characterized by the presence on camera of personalities such as Jasmine Bligh, Elizabeth Cowell, Leslie Mitchell, Mary Malcolm, McDonald Hobley and Sylvia Peters. ITV stations have held on to in-vision announcers longer, but most now rely on off-screen links.

ANT AND DEC
See McPARTLIN, ANTHONY.

ANTHOLOGY

A collection of dramatic works, generally by various authors, with no continuous characters or plots, even though the stories may share a common theme or style. Examples include OUT OF THE UNKNOWN, THRILLER and COUNTRY MATTERS. Sometimes one character or actor is employed as the host of each programme, to hold the concept together, as exemplified by Alfred Hitchcock in ALFRED HITCHCOCK PRESENTS or Rod Serling in THE TWILIGHT ZONE.

ANTIQUES ROADSHOW
UK (BBC) Antiques. BBC 1 1979–

Presenters: **Angela Rippon, Bruce Parker, Arthur Negus, Hugh Scully, Michael Aspel**

Producers: **Robin Drake, Christopher Lewis, Michele Burgess, Stephen Potter**

A team of experts values the treasured possessions of ordinary citizens.

A Sunday afternoon favourite, *Antiques Roadshow* has travelled the length and breadth of the United Kingdom, inviting viewers to drop in and have their family heirlooms valued. Since the first broadcast in 1979, there has been much raiding of attics and basements across the land, in the hope of discovering something of value. Punters have queued up, cherished items in hand, awaiting the verdict of one of the experts, who have all been drawn from leading auction houses and dealerships.

Participants have explained how the items came into their family's possession, and the specialists have then provided more background information, explaining where, when and by whom it was probably made, and winding up with a financial valuation. One piece a week has usually proved to be a real find – a magnificent specimen of furniture, a long-lost work by a distinguished artist, etc. – much to the delight of both the excited connoisseur and the gasping proprietor. Among the longest-serving experts are David Battie and Hugh Morley-Fletcher (both porcelain), Simon Bull (timepieces), Roy Butler (militaria), and David Collins and Philip Hook (both paintings). Some have become celebrities in their own right – 'potaholic' Henry Sandon, furniture specialist John Bly, and ceramics man Eric Knowles, for instance. Hugh Scully hosted proceedings for many years until his departure in 2000.

A young persons' special, entitled *Antiques Roadshow – the Next Generation*, has been occasionally screened.

AOL-TIME WARNER

The world's largest media and entertainments group was formed in 2000 with the merger of Internet provider America Online and Time Warner, itself a 1989 merger of the Time magazine group – the founder, in 1972, of HBO (the Home Box Office pay-per-view channel) – and Warner Communications, a descendant of Warner Brothers. The group owns the WB Network, launched in 1995 to challenge the big three US TV networks, and the fledgling Fox network, and also part of the corporation is the former Turner Broadcasting System network of stations, which Time Warner absorbed in 1996. TBS, founded by Ted Turner, was the parent company of CNN and CNN International. Part of the group's considerable assets are the film libraries of the MGM and Warner Brothers studios, which have been used to good effect in programming the TNT (Turner Network Television), TCM (Turner Classic Movies) and Cartoon Network channels.

APPLEYARDS, THE
UK (BBC) Children's Drama. BBC 1952–7

Mr Appleyard .... **Frederick Piper**
Douglas Muir
Mrs Appleyard .... **Constance Fraser**
John Appleyard .... **David Edwards**
Janet Appleyard .... **Tessa Clarke**
Tommy Appleyard .... **Derek Rowe**
Margaret Appleyard .... **Pat Fryer**

Writer: **Philip Burton**

Major moments in the life of a suburban, middle-class family.

The Appleyards was an early children's soap opera, transmitted once a fortnight as part of the *Children's Television* slot (around 4.30–5 p.m.). It featured the Appleyard family – mum, dad, teenagers John and Janet, and younger siblings Tommy and Margaret – and picked up a number of awards during its five-year run. A reunion special, entitled *Christmas with the Appleyards*, was shown in 1960.

AQUARIUS
UK (LWT) Arts. ITV 1970–7

Presenters: **Humphrey Burton, Russell Harty, Peter Hall**

Editor: **Humphrey Burton**

Late-night arts magazine.

Produced fortnightly, on Saturday or Sunday nights, *Aquarius* was originally hosted by its editor, Humphrey Burton, though Russell Harty and Peter Hall took over in later years, when the programme was screened weekly. A rival to the BBC's OMNIBUS, *Aquarius* incorporated reports on all aspects of the artistic and cultural world.

During its seven years, the series included items on the likes of Salvador Dali, Artur Rubinstein, Pablo Casals and Stanley Spencer. When it ended in 1977, it was succeeded by THE SOUTH BANK SHOW.

ARCHIE BUNKER'S PLACE
See ALL IN THE FAMILY.

ARE YOU BEING SERVED?
UK (BBC) Situation Comedy. BBC 1 1973–85

Mrs Betty Slocombe .... **Mollie Sugden**
Mr Wilberforce Humphries .... **John Inman**
Capt. Stephen Peacock .... **Frank Thornton**
Mr Cuthbert Rumbold .... **Nicholas Smith**
Miss Shirley Brahms .... **Wendy Richard**
Mr Ernest Grainger .... **Arthur Brough**
Mr Dick Lucas .... **Trevor Bannister**
Mr Mash .... **Larry Martyn**
Mr Harman .... **Arthur English**
Mr Percival Tebbs .... **James Hayter**
Mr Spooner .... **Mike Berry**
Young Mr Grace .... **Harold Bennett**
Mr Harry Goldberg .... **Alfie Bass**

Creators/Writers: **Jeremy Lloyd, David Croft**
Executive Producer: **David Croft**
Producers: **David Croft, Bob Spiers, Michael Shardlow**

Fun and games with the staff of a traditional department store.

Chock-full of nudge-nudge, wink-wink innuendo, this long-running farce centred on the members of staff in the clothing department on the first floor of Grace Brothers. Clearly divided into male and female sections, supervised by department manager Mr Rumbold and floor walker Captain Peacock, the clothing section employed some well-defined comedy stereotypes. On the men's side there was the swishy homosexual, Mr Humphries, declaring 'I'm free' whenever a customer needed attention and always poised to take that inside leg measurement. He worked alongside grouchy old Mr Grainger (in later episodes Mr Tebbs) and the department junior, Mr Lucas, who was later replaced by Mr Spooner. In charge of the ladies' cash desks, amid the intimate apparel, was billowing Mrs Slocombe, a superficially dignified mistress of the unfortunate phrase, who brought howls of laughter from the studio audience with her fluorescent rinses and her constant worries about her pussy. She was ably supported in the battle of the sexes by the buxom, young Miss Brahms. Overseeing the whole operation, and telling everyone that they'd 'all done very well', was the store's owner, doddery Young Mr Grace, a failing geriatric with a dolly bird on each arm. Mr Harman was the cantankerous caretaker who took over from the militant unionist Mr Mash.

Though plots were thin and obvious, the in-jokes kept coming – for 12 years. Even then the characters refused to die, with Messrs Peacock, Humphries and Rumbold, Mrs Slocombe and Miss Brahms resurfacing in a 1992 revival, set at a country hotel. Now under the banner of

Grace and Favour, the team had been made redundant at Grace Brothers, following the death of Young Mr Grace, and discovered that the firm's pension fund had been invested in the run-down Millstone Manor, where Mr Rumbold was the struggling manager. With nothing to lose, the others decided to join him in an attempt to turn the business around, hoping the country air might do them good. Two series were made.

The pilot for *Are You Being Served?* was an episode of COMEDY PLAYHOUSE seen in September 1972, and the series was based on writer Jeremy Lloyd's personal experience of working at Simpson's of Piccadilly. John Inman had a minor hit with a novelty spin-off record, *Are You Being Served Sir*, in 1975, and a feature film version was released in 1977.

ARENA
UK (BBC) Arts. BBC 2 1975–

Editors: **Alan Yentob, Nigel Finch, Anthony Wall**

All-embracing, popular arts series.

The umbrella title of *Arena* has encompassed documentary features on many subjects. Indeed, in its early days each edition was categorized by a subtitle – *Arena: Theatre, Arena: Art and Design, Arena: Cinema, Arena: Television* or *Arena: Rock*. The categories alternated weekly. Some contributions have been seriously arty, others more trivial and populist.

ARISTOCRATS
UK (BBC/Irish Screen/WGBH Boston) Drama. BBC 1 1999

Lady Emily	**Geraldine Somerville**
	Siân Phillips (*older*)
	Hayley Griffiths (*younger*)
Lady Sarah	**Jodhi May**
	Sheila Ruskin (*older*)
Lady Louisa	**Anne-Marie Duff**
	Diana Quick (*older*)
Lady Caroline	**Serena Gordon**
Henry Fox	**Alun Armstrong**
Duke of Richmond	**Julian Fellowes**
Duchess of Richmond	**Diane Fletcher**
Lord Kildare	**Ben Daniels**
King George II	**Clive Swift**
Charles, 3rd Duke of Richmond	**Tom Beard**
	Geoffrey Beevers (*older*)
Mary, 3rd Duchess	**Katherine Wogan**
	Carmen du Sautoy (*older*)
Bunbury	**Andrew Havill**
Lord William Gordon	**Gary Cady**
Prince of Wales	**Luke de Lacey**
Charles James Fox	**Hugh Sachs**
	Trevor Ray (*older*)
Ste Fox	**Toby Jones**
Tom Conolly	**Tom Mullion**
	Paul Ridley (*older*)
Susan Fox-Strangeways	**Pauline McLynn**
William Ogilvie	**George Anton**
	David Grant (*older*)
George Napier	**Martin Glyn Murray**
	Jeremy Bulloch (*older*)
Lord Edward Fitzgerald	**John Light**

Writer: **Harriet O'Carroll**
Producers: **Christopher Hall, David Snodin**

Four great-granddaughters of King Charles II are launched into society from their home in Ireland.

Based on Stella Tillyard's account of the real-life Lennox sisters, this six-part costume drama, set in the 18th century, provided lavish Sunday evening viewing. The sisters were the daughters of the second Duke of Richmond. The eldest, Caroline, was headstrong and eloped with a commoner politician, Henry Fox, more than 20 years her senior. The next daughter, the extravagant Emily, patiently wooed and married Lord Kildare, a less than satisfactory choice for her father, as Kildare was rich but of dubious lineage. The charitable Louisa came next, marrying Ireland's wealthiest man and giving up much of her time to worthwhile causes. Finally there was the unpredictable, flirtatious Sarah, who brought the family name into disrepute through her unbecoming behaviour, especially with the Prince of Wales. Unlike the one-dimensional women often portrayed in this age of powerful men, these sisters showed themselves to be manipulative, liberated and far from submissive.

The serial – reputedly costing over £6 million to create – began in 1742 and continued through to the early 19th century, when the surviving sisters were depicted in their latter years. Although two of the sisters moved to England, the series was shot entirely in Ireland, using some of the houses in which the Lennox sisters once lived. Siân Phillips, who played the older Emily, also acted as narrator.

ARLOTT, JOHN
(1914–91)

Revered cricket commentator and wine expert whose rich Hampshire burr is badly missed in cricketing circles. He joined the BBC in 1945 as a poetry specialist, after 11 years in the police force, and, though he did plenty of TV work in the 1960s, his later contracts were once again with BBC Radio. He pulled stumps on a 33-year commentating career at the Centenary Test in 1980, taking retirement in the Channel Islands.

ARMCHAIR THEATRE
UK (ABC/Thames) Drama Anthology. ITV 1956–74

Producers: **Sydney Newman, Leonard White, Lloyd Shirley**

Influential, long-running series of single dramas.

Although initiated in 1956 (with the play *The Outsider*, starring David Kossoff and Adrienne Corri), *Armchair Theatre* really began to gain authority only in 1958, with the arrival of Canadian producer Sydney Newman. In his five years in charge (before leaving for the BBC, where he created DOCTOR WHO among other offerings),

Newman focused on contemporary themes and 'real' issues, and such grubby realism earned the series the unfortunate nickname of 'Armpit Theatre'.

Newman assembled around him some of the top dramatic talents of the day, including such directors as Philip Saville, George More O'Ferrall and William T. Kotcheff, story editors Irene Shubik and Peter Luke, and young playwrights such as Harold Pinter, Alun Owen, Robert Muller and Ray Rigby. Pinter's first TV play, *A Night Out*, was a 1960 *Armchair Theatre* production and Owen's *Lena, O My Lena* was another of that year's contributions. There were quality performers in front of the camera, too; they included Tyrone Power, Flora Robson, Gracie Fields, Joan Greenwood, Billie Whitelaw, Donald Pleasence, Tom Courtenay and a young Diana Rigg. Some early plays were transmitted live, and the perils of such practice were cruelly highlighted in 1958, when actor Gareth Jones collapsed and died during a rendition of a play entitled *Underground*.

The series produced some notable spin-offs. A 1962 version of John Wyndham's *Dumb Martian* was used as a taster for the new OUT OF THIS WORLD science-fiction anthology which began the following week, while James Mitchell's *A Magnum for Schneider*, in 1967, resulted in the hugely popular CALLAN series. *Armchair Theatre* survived the ITV franchise swap of 1968, with production switching from ABC to the newly formed Thames Television. Thames later tinkered with the format, introducing *Armchair Cinema*, a film-based equivalent, which included *Regan*, the pilot for THE SWEENEY, among its successes.

Armchair Theatre became compulsive Sunday night entertainment for many viewers, particularly during its heyday at the turn of the 1960s. The alternative title of *Armchair Summer Theatre* was occasionally used for seasonal episodes, while *Armchair Mystery Theatre* (1960–5) was a variation on the theme by the same production team.

ARMISTEAD MAUPIN'S TALES OF THE CITY/MORE TALES OF THE CITY

UK (Channel 4/Working Title) Drama. Channel 4 1993; 1998

Anna Madrigal	**Olympia Dukakis**
Mona Ramsey	**Chloe Webb**
	Nina Siemaszko (*More Tales*)
Michael Tolliver	**Marcus D'Amico**
	Paul Hopkins (*More Tales*)
Brian Hawkins	**Paul Gross**
	Whip Hubley (*More Tales*)
Mary Ann Singleton	**Laura Linney**
Edgar Halcyon	**Donald Moffat**
Jon Fielding	**William Campbell**
Beauchamp Day	**Thomas Gibson**
DeDe Halcyon Day	**Barbara Garrick**
Frannie Halcyon	**Nina Foch**
	Diane Leblanc (*More Tales*)
D'orothea Wilson	**Cynda Williams**
	Françoise Robertson (*More Tales*)
Norman Neal Williams	**Stanley Desantis**
Archibald Gidde	**Ian McKellen**
Mother Mucca	**Jackie Burroughs** (*More Tales*)
Burke Andrew	**Colin Ferguson** (*More Tales*)
Betty Ramsey	**Swoosie Kurtz** (*More Tales*)

Writer: **Richard Kramer**
Producers: **Alan Poul, Anthony Root**

Bohemian life in a San Francisco boarding house during the 1970s.

RISING DAMP this wasn't. *Tales of the City* focused on the goings-on at 28 Barbary Place, a San Francisco boarding house run by marijuana-growing transsexual, Anna Madrigal (her name is an anagram of 'a man and a girl'). It opened with the arrival of the naïve, 25-year-old Mary Ann Singleton, fresh from Cleveland, Ohio, and out to enjoy everything San Francisco had to offer. She joined a liberated household that exemplified the *laissez-faire* atmosphere that pervaded the Californian city during the 1970s. Sharing the spotlight were gay Michael 'Mouse' Tolliver; his boyfriend, gynaecologist Jon Fielding; the emotionally strained advertising copywriter, Mona Ramsey; lawyer-turned-waiter Brian Hawkins; and Mrs Madrigal's true love, Edgar Halcyon.

The series was based on the first of six books by local writer Armistead Maupin, which first appeared in serial form in the *San Francisco Chronicle* in 1976. THIRTYSOMETHING writer Richard Kramer was brought in to handle the TV adaptation, which caused a flutter with its gay love scenes, nudity and open treatment of the drugs issue. Rod Steiger made a cameo appearance as a bookstore owner. Five years after Channel 4 screened the five-part series, it broadcast a six-part sequel, entitled *More Tales of the City* (following Maupin's second novel). Still set in Barbary Place, it featured largely the same cast of characters, although there were several actor changes, including the replacement of DUE SOUTH star Paul Gross. New in town was Mother Mucca, a retired madame from Winnemucca, Nevada, who became a guardian figure for the frustrated Mona.

ARMSTRONG, ALUN

(1946–)

Co. Durham-born actor seen in such programmes as *Villains*, *The Stars Look Down*, DAYS OF HOPE, *A Sharp Intake of Breath*, PORRIDGE, INSPECTOR MORSE, BULMAN and *Stanley and the Women*. He was also Squeers in *The Life and Adventures of Nicholas Nickleby* and played Roy Grade in *Goodbye Cruel World*, hated stepfather Gerald in *Goggle Eyes*, Uncle Teddy in *The Life and Times of Henry Pratt*, corrupt politician Austin Donohue in OUR FRIENDS IN THE NORTH, Henry Fox in ARISTOCRATS and gardening gangster Teddy Middlemass in *Underworld*. He has been seen in numerous single dramas, including *Brazen Hussies* and Alan Plater's *Get Lost!*, an early version of THE BEIDERBECKE AFFAIR.

ARMY GAME, THE

UK (Granada) Situation Comedy. ITV 1957–61

Major Upshot-Bagley	**Geoffrey Sumner**
	Jack Allen

CSM Bullimore .... **William Hartnell**
CSM Claude Snudge .... **Bill Fraser**
Cpl. Springer .... **Michael Medwin**
Pte. 'Excused Boots' Bisley .... **Alfie Bass**
Pte. 'Cupcake' Cook .... **Norman Rossington**
                                                        Keith Banks
Pte. 'Popeye' Popplewell .... **Bernard Bresslaw**
Pte. 'Prof' Hatchett .... **Charles Hawtrey**
                                                        Keith Smith
Capt. Pilsworthy .... **Bernard Hunter**
Major Geoffrey Gervaise Duckworth ...... **C. B. Poultney**
Pte. Leonard Bone .... **Ted Lune**
Cpl. 'Flogger' Hoskins .... **Harry Fowler**
Capt. Pocket .... **Frank Williams**
Pte. Dooley .... **Harry Towb**
Lance-Corporal Ernest 'Moosh' Merryweather ....
.... **Mario Fabrizi**
Pte. Billy Baker .... **Robert Desmond**
Pte. 'Chubby' Catchpole .... **Dick Emery**

Creator: **Sid Colin**
Producers: **Milo Lewis, Max Morgan-Witts, Peter Eton,
Eric Fawcett**

*The schemes and scams of a gang of National
Service soldiers.*

This extremely popular early comedy was set in Hut
29 of the Surplus Ordnance Depot at Nether Hopping,
somewhere in remotest Staffordshire, and featured the
exploits of a mixed bag of army conscripts. At the forefront were Pte. 'Bootsie' Bisley, so named because he was
allowed to wear plimsolls instead of boots; Pte. Hatchett,
who knitted to pass the time and was known as 'The
Professor'; Liverpudlian Pte. 'Cupcake' Cook, taking his
name from the many food parcels his mother sent him;
gormless Pte. 'Popeye' Popplewell; and their Cockney
spiv ringleader, Cpl. Springer. Trying to knock them into
shape were the bellowing Sgt-Major Bullimore and then
(when future DOCTOR WHO Bill Hartnell left to star in
the very similar *Carry On Sergeant*) the pompous Sgt
Claude Snudge. Toffee-nosed dimwit Major Upshot-
Bagley was nominal head of the camp.

There were many personnel changes in the series'
four-year run. Upshot-Bagley was replaced by other com-
mandants (Pilsworthy, Duckworth and Pocket) and new
conscripts were brought in. Popeye was succeeded by
the equally dense Pte. Bone, Springer by another chirpy
Londoner, 'Flogger' Hoskins, and other new arrivals
included 'Chubby' Catchpole, Lance-Corporal Ernie
Merryweather and Privates Dooley and Baker. Of the
characters that remained, some changed actors. Barry
Took and Marty Feldman were among the numerous
writers involved.

The Army Game was originally transmitted live once a
fortnight, though when its popularity increased it
switched to once a week. In 1958, the series engendered
a spin-off film, *I Only Arsked* (based on Popeye's
catchphrase). In the same year the signature tune of
the *Army Game* was a top five hit for Michael Medwin,
Bernard Bresslaw, Alfie Bass and Leslie Fyson, and in 1960
a sequel series, BOOTSIE AND SNUDGE, was produced.

ARNAZ, DESI
(Desiderio Alberto Arnaz y de Acha; 1917–86)

Cuban-born musician and band leader who, as Lucille
Ball's real and on-screen husband, became one of TV's
earliest superstars. Arnaz grew up in a wealthy Cuban
family, but in 1933, with the installation of the Batista
regime, he fled, penniless, to Miami with his mother.
His Latin looks and musical abilities secured him work
with bands like Xavier Cugat's and saw him arrive in
Hollywood. There he met the up-and-coming Lucille
Ball and they married in 1940. Ten years later, to save
their turbulent marriage, they agreed to work together
on a new TV comedy, I LOVE LUCY – the mother of all
sitcoms – playing husband and wife duo, Lucy and Ricky
Ricardo. To produce the show, Arnaz founded their own
production company, Desilu (later responsible for shows
such as THE UNTOUCHABLES and MANNIX). However,
their marriage was not to last and they divorced in 1960.
Lucy persevered with her scatterbrained TV characterizations, while Desi turned more to production. In later
years he was seen only rarely on screen.

ARNESS, JAMES
(James Aurness; 1923–)

The brother of MISSION IMPOSSIBLE's Peter Graves, a
strapping giant of an actor who became synonymous
with the Western lawman, thanks to his long-running
portrayal of Marshal Matt Dillon in GUNSMOKE. Arness,
a veteran of the Anzio campaign in World War II,
entered the movie business in the 1940s, winning parts
in assorted B-movies, most memorably *The Thing* and
Them!. In 1955 he was recommended for the *Gunsmoke*
role by his friend, John Wayne, and reluctantly accepted,
fearing that a flopped TV series would jeopardize his
cinema career. To help things along and guarantee a
big audience, Wayne offered to introduce the very first
Gunsmoke episode.

Arness need not have worried. The series ran for 20
years on US TV and during that time he had no cause
to look for other TV work. Indeed, by the close, he
was also part owner of the production. Following the
cancellation of *Gunsmoke* in 1975, Arness returned to the
screen as Zeb Macahan in *How The West Was Won* and
then took on the role of veteran cop Jim McClain in
McCLAIN'S LAW.

ARNOLD, ROSEANNE
See ROSEANNE.

AROUND THE WORLD IN 80 DAYS/
POLE TO POLE/FULL CIRCLE
UK (BBC) Documentary. BBC 1 1989/1992/1997

Presenter: **Michael Palin**
Producer: **Clem Vallence**

Bold but light-hearted expeditions into unlikely quarters of the world.

Michael Palin's hugely successful series of travelogues began with *Around the World in 80 Days* in 1989. Initially earmarked as a vehicle for Alan Whicker, it pitched the ex-*Python* into the role of a modern-day Phileas Fogg. The aim of the venture was to follow closely the path set by Jules Verne's hero, travelling around the world in 80 days and using just land and sea transport (the only methods available 115 years earlier, when Fogg's fictitious journey took place). However, Palin discovered that Fogg's network of passenger liners had long disappeared, and he was forced to rely on unpredictable merchant vessels for large sections of his journey. Delays at customs points, narrowly missed departures and unco-operative locals added to the tension as Palin sought to return to London's Reform Club within the imposed time-limit. His voyage took him on the Orient Express, on numerous ferries and by land across Saudi Arabia and the United Arab Emirates. Most dramatically, he boarded a primitive dhow for the crossing of the Arabian Sea. He then crossed India, China and the USA by train, before steaming into Felixstowe for the last leg into London. The circumnavigation took place in 1988.

Supporting Palin on his travels were his 'Passepartout', an openly acknowledged production team of producer/director Clem Vallence, co-director Roger Mills and a film crew. Half the team followed Palin as far as Hong Kong and the others completed the trip home. They shot film on 77 of the 80 days and their recordings were edited into seven intriguing episodes. An accompanying book, written by Michael Palin, was a massive success, selling over half a million copies.

A second adventure followed in 1991. In *Pole to Pole*, Palin and his team (including several *80 Days* veterans) attempted to travel from the North to the South Pole, using only public transport where available and sticking as closely as possible to the 30° East meridian. The exhausting 141-day voyage took them through the Soviet Union just days before its collapse and then down through civil war-ravaged Africa. Again, a book accompanied the eight-part series, which was screened in 1992.

An even more ambitious venture took place in 1996 (aired in 1997). In the 10-part *Full Circle*, Palin and his pals attempted to follow the line of the Pacific Rim, beginning and ending at Little Diomede Island in the Bering Strait, but taking in stops in Russia, China, Australasia, and South, Central and North America *en route* – a distance of nearly 50,000 miles completed within the set deadline of one calendar year, with just one short stop in the middle, when Palin flew home to visit his wife, who had been receiving treatment for a brain tumour. Another best-selling book followed, as it did for *Michael Palin's Hemingway Adventure* in 1999, a similar but less structured four-part series in which Palin visited the haunts of one of his favourite authors, Ernest Hemingway.

ARREST AND TRIAL
US (Revue/Universal) Detective Drama. BBC 1 1964

DS Nick Anderson .... **Ben Gazzara**
Attorney John Egan .... **Chuck Connors**
Deputy DA Jerry Miller .... **John Larch**
Assistant Deputy DA Barry Pine .... **John Kerr**
DS Dan Kirby .... **Roger Perry**
Det. Lt. Bone .... **Noah Keen**
Jake Shakespeare .... **Joe Higgins**
Mitchell Harris .... **Don Galloway**
Janet Okada .... **Jo Anne Miya**

Producer: **Frank P. Rosenberg**

Innovative drama series, comprising programmes of two separate halves: the first showing a criminal investigation, the second the subsequent trial.

Setting the pattern for a host of crime movies many years later, *Arrest and Trial* depicted the exploits of Detective Sgt Nick Anderson of the LAPD and local defence lawyer John Egan. The first 45-minute segment of each programme concerned itself with the execution of a crime and the efforts of Anderson and his colleagues to find the culprit. The second 45 minutes were then devoted to the trial, giving Egan and his legal eagles the chance to negate Anderson's good work by getting the defendant off the hook.

ARTHUR, BEATRICE
(Bernice Frankel; 1923–)

Tall, deep-voiced, forceful stalwart of American sitcoms, who gained international recognition late in life as Dorothy in THE GOLDEN GIRLS. Earlier, Arthur had played Archie Bunker's cousin, Maude Findlay, in ALL IN THE FAMILY and in her own spin-off, *Maude*. She also starred in *Amanda's*, the US version of FAWLTY TOWERS.

ARTHUR C. CLARKE'S MYSTERIOUS WORLD
UK (Yorkshire) Documentary. ITV 1980

Host: **Arthur C. Clarke**
Narrator: **Gordon Honeycombe**

Executive Producer: **John Fairley**
Producer: **Simon Welfare**

The Earth's strange phenomena investigated by the celebrated science-fiction writer.

Hosting this documentary series from his Sri Lankan home, novelist Arthur C. Clarke turned his attention away from fiction and towards the weird and wonderful, unexplained real-life phenomena to be witnessed around the world. Looking at the strange moving rocks of America's Death Valley, investigating ancient stone circles, and discussing how it can rain frogs were just some of the topics covered as Clarke focused on mysteries of the world that challenge modern-day thinking. Former ITN newscaster Gordon Honeycombe handled the narration of this half-hour series.

ARTHUR OF THE BRITONS
UK (HTV) Adventure. ITV 1972–3

Arthur	**Oliver Tobias**
Llud	**Jack Watson**
Kai	**Michael Gothard**
Mark of Cornwall	**Brian Blessed**
Cerdig	**Rupert Davies**

Executive Producer: **Patrick Dromgoole**
Producer: **Peter Miller**

A dashing young Celtic leader takes on the Saxon invaders.

With no Camelot, no Guinevere and no Merlin, this series dispelled the myth of round tables, chivalrous knights and mystic sorcery, bringing Arthur back down to earth with a bump. Here, young and ruggedly good-looking, the legendary king was depicted as a 6th-century Welsh ruler who fronted a tough, swashbuckling army of Celts against intruders from the East led by Cerdig. Supported by the pagan Llud the Silver Hand and Kai, a Saxon orphan, Arthur's aim was to unite the native tribes of Britain against the invading Saxon forces. Tough battles ensued and there were woodland skirmishes aplenty. The Saxons apart, Arthur's other great rival was the powerful Mark of Cornwall. Many guest artists featured in the series, including Michael Gambon, Tom Baker and Catherine Schell.

AS TIME GOES BY
UK (Theatre of Comedy) Situation Comedy.
BBC 1 1992–

Jean Pargetter	**Judi Dench**
Lionel Hardcastle	**Geoffrey Palmer**
Judith Pargetter	**Moira Brooker**
Alistair Deacon	**Philip Bretherton**
Sandy	**Jenny Funnell**
Rocky Hardcastle	**Frank Middlemass**
Madge Hardcastle	**Joan Sims**
Mrs Bale	**Janet Henfrey**

Creator/Writer: **Bob Larbey**
Producer: **Sydney Lotterby**
Executive Producers: **Philip Jones, John Reynolds**

Two middle-aged former lovers rekindle their romance.

Taking its inspiration from the 1931 song, voiced by Joe Fagin over the credits, *As Time Goes By* was a will-they, won't-they, gentle comedy about two young lovers who had gone their separate ways, only to rediscover each other in middle age. Jean Pargetter and Lionel Hardcastle had each mistakenly believed the other had broken off their youthful romance and both had drifted off to marry someone else. Jean, a nurse, and Lionel, a second lieutenant in the Middlesex Regiment, had met in Hyde Park, but when Lionel was posted to Korea a vital letter from Jean never reached him. After 38 years, fate brought them together again when Lionel, now divorced, employed Jean's secretarial agency (Type For You) to type up his book, *My Life in Kenya*, which described his career as a coffee planter in East Africa. Jean's husband, David, had died and she lived with her daughter, Judith, who one evening brought Lionel home after dinner, with obvious consequences. Jean and Lionel were married in the 1995 series. Also seen were Jean's efficient secretary, Sandy, and Lionel's pushy publisher, Alistair (Judith's boyfriend). The series was created by Bob Larbey from an original idea by Colin Bostock Smith. In 1997, *As Time Goes By* was reworked into a comedy series for Radio 2.

ASCENT OF MAN, THE
UK (BBC/Time-Life) Documentary. BBC 2 1973

Writer/Presenter: **Dr Jacob Bronowski**

Producer: **Adrian Malone**

An inspirational account of man's scientific and philosophical progress.

Through the eyes of Polish-born, California-based historian and philosopher Dr Jacob Bronowski, this 13-part series reflected on the development of man through his technological achievements, considering how the introduction of new inventions and the appreciation of new discoveries changed social and moral patterns. In short, it revealed how man became the shaper of his own environment. From the use of primitive tools to the effects of the Industrial Revolution and beyond, vivid examples and illustrations sugared the pill for less scientifically minded viewers, as did the charisma and enthusiasm of the curious, hunched presenter. Bronowski travelled the world for the series and worked so hard in the four years of production that he collapsed from exhaustion at its completion and died the following year. He was an unlikely TV star, but his series was widely acclaimed.

ASH, LESLIE
(1960–)

British actress, formerly a model and star of a Fairy Liquid advert when aged four. One of her first leading roles was as computer whiz-kid Fred Smith in C.A.T.S. EYES, although there had been plenty of minor parts in series like SECONDS OUT, SHELLEY and THE TWO RONNIES. Ash was also a dancer with the Black and White Minstrels and co-presenter of Channel 4's rock show THE TUBE for a while. More recently, as well as appearances in PERFECT SCOUNDRELS, LOVE HURTS and *Haggard*, she has starred as Nancy Gray in *The Happy Apple*, Deborah in MEN BEHAVING BADLY, Jo in STAY LUCKY and Karen Buckley in WHERE THE HEART IS. Ash was also a panellist in the revival of GOING FOR A SONG. She is married to ex-footballer Lee Chapman, with whom she hosted the series *Dinner Dates*.

ASHCROFT, DAME PEGGY
(Edith Margaret Emily Ashcroft; 1907–91)

Notable British stage and, occasionally, film actress who added television credits to her name in her later years. Most memorably, Dame Peggy appeared as Queen Mary in EDWARD AND MRS SIMPSON and Barbie, the missionary, in Granada's lavish THE JEWEL IN THE CROWN.

ASK ASPEL
UK (BBC) Children's Entertainment. BBC 1 1970–3; 1976–81

Presenter: **Michael Aspel**

Producers: **Iain Johnstone, Will Wyatt, Frances Whitaker, Granville Jenkins**

Long-running children's request show.

Taking over from *Junior Points of View* as the kiddies' feedback series, *Ask Aspel* encouraged youngsters to write in with their views on the BBC's latest offerings. Host Michael Aspel also played requested snippets, and interviews with star guests filled out the programme.

ASK THE FAMILY
UK (BBC) Quiz. BBC 1 1967–84; 1999–

Presenters: **Robert Robinson, Alan Titchmarsh**

Producers: **Cecil Korer, Linda McCarthy, Mark Patterson**

Mind-bending quiz for cerebral families.

Open to families of four (often teachers and their egg-headed offspring), *Ask the Family* was a surprisingly durable early-evening intellectual quiz. Host Robert Robinson fired off a succession of riddles, mental posers and general knowledge questions, some directed to 'children only', 'mother and younger child', 'father and elder child' or other combinations of contestants. The winning family then progressed through the annual knock-out tournament.

Ask the Family was revived on UKGold in spring 1999, with the series screened later in the year on BBC 1. Alan Titchmarsh was the new host.

ASKEY, ARTHUR
CBE (1900–1982)

Indefatigable, Liverpool-born, diminutive music hall veteran who became one of post-war TV's biggest names, appearing in assorted variety spectaculars and, from 1952, his own series, *Before Your Very Eyes* (the title based on one of his catchphrases), with Dickie Henderson, Diana Decker and the busty Sabrina. The series moved to ITV in 1956, a year after the new network had recorded Askey's Blackpool summer show and screened it in five parts under the title *Love and Kisses*. In 1957, Askey appeared with his former partner, Richard Murdoch, in *Living It Up*, a re-creation of their popular 1930s radio show, *Band Waggon*, and then, in 1961, he starred in a sitcom, *The Arthur Askey Show*. The following year, back with the BBC, he shared the limelight with Alan Melville in *Raise Your Glasses*. Always popular, Askey was on our screens till the end. In the 1970s he was one of the regular (and kindest) expert panellists on the talent show, NEW FACES, never failing to shower the contestants with praise, however dire their act.

ASNER, ED
(1929–)

American actor famous as grouchy news editor Lou Grant in THE MARY TYLER MOORE SHOW (a performance which won him three Emmys). When the sitcom ended, he made an unusual move, staying in the same role when Grant was shipped to the West Coast to become editor of the *Los Angeles Tribune* in a straight drama sequel. Another Emmy followed. After several successful seasons, LOU GRANT was cancelled amid rumours of a rift between the producers and the star, revolving around his outspoken political views. Asner's earliest TV credits included guest spots in programmes like THE FBI, THE DEFENDERS, A MAN CALLED IRONSIDE and THE FUGITIVE, as well as a continuous role in a series called *Slattery's People*. He also starred as Axel Jordache in RICH MAN, POOR MAN and the slave ship's Captain Davies in ROOTS (earning two more Emmys), plus the high school drama *The Bronx Zoo*, *Thunder Alley* (about a retired racing driver), and *The Trials of Rosie O'Neill* (Walter Kovatch).

ASPEL, MICHAEL
OBE (1933–)

London-born presenter and chat show host, initially seen on BBC TV news programmes in the 1950s, after working as an actor on BBC Wales radio and as a TV announcer. Since then he has presented CRACKERJACK, COME DANCING, MISS WORLD, the long-running kids' request show ASK ASPEL, *Child's Play*, *Star Games*, GIVE US A CLUE, *The Six O'Clock Show* (London), *Aspel and Company* and the paranormal series *Strange But True*, as well as taking over from Eamonn Andrews as holder of the big red book in THIS IS YOUR LIFE. In 2000 he succeeded Hugh Scully as anchor of ANTIQUES ROADSHOW. He is married to, though separated from, actress Elizabeth Power (Mrs Hewitt in EASTENDERS).

ASSOCIATED-REDIFFUSION

Company formed by Broadcast Relay Services and Associated Newspapers to operate the very first ITV franchise. A-R (as it became known) went on air on 22 September 1955 and covered London on weekdays. The company shortened its name to Rediffusion in the mid-1960s and was forced by the ITA to merge with ABC in 1968. The resulting company, Thames Television, retained the London weekday franchise. Among A-R's successes were TAKE YOUR PICK, DOUBLE YOUR MONEY, DO NOT ADJUST YOUR SET and READY, STEADY, GO!.

ASSOCIATED TELEVISION
See ATV.

ASTIN, JOHN
(1930–)

Tall, moustached American comic actor chiefly remembered as Gomez in THE ADDAMS FAMILY. Previously, he had scored a success as Harry Dickens in the sitcom *I'm Dickens, He's Fenster*, and was later one of the actors to play The Riddler in BATMAN, as well as appearing in *The Pruitts of Southampton*. His attention then switched to directing, working on programmes like CHiPs and *Holmes and Yoyo*, although he continued on screen in series like *Mary, Operation Petticoat, Night Court, Eerie, Indiana* and *The Adventures of Brisco County, Jr.* He was at one time married to former child actress Patty Duke (Astin).

A-TEAM, THE
US (Universal/Stephen J. Cannell) Adventure. ITV 1983–8

Col. John 'Hannibal' Smith	**George Peppard**
Sgt Bosco 'BA' Baracus	**Mr T (Lawrence Tureaud)**
Lt. Templeton Peck ('Faceman')	**Dirk Benedict**
Capt. H. M. 'Howling Mad' Murdock ...	**Dwight Schultz**
Amy Amanda Allen ('Triple A')	**Melinda Culea**
Col. Lynch	**William Lucking**
Col. Roderick Decker	**Lance LeGault**
Tawnia Baker	**Maria Heasley**
Gen. Hunt Stockwell	**Robert Vaughn**
'Dishpan' Frankie Sanchez	**Eddie Velez**
Carla	**Judy Ledford**

Creators/Executive Producers: **Stephen J. Cannell, Frank Lupo**

Four soldiers of fortune, all Vietnam veterans, use their diverse skills to help citizens in trouble.

The A-Team, an unlikely group of heroic renegades, had worked together as commandos in the Vietnam War, only to be captured behind enemy lines and accused of raiding the Bank of Hanoi four days after the war had ended. They maintained they were under orders to do so, but, with no proof, the gang were imprisoned by their own country. Following their escape, the series told how they evaded attempts to recapture them, first by Colonel Lynch, then by Colonel Decker, and their mercenary-style righting of wrongs along the way.

Each member of the Team was a specialist. The cigar-chewing leader, Hannibal Smith, was a master of disguise; Howling Mad Murdock was a brilliant but crazy pilot who had to be sprung from a psychiatric hospital

to join the Team on their missions; the gold-swathed BA ('Bad Attitude') was the inventive mechanic, a Mohican-haired giant of a man who, none the less, dreaded flying with Murdock; while Faceman (played by Tim Dunigan in the pilot episode) was the smooth talker and procurer of their material needs. Together they travelled the world in a heavily armed transit van, initially accompanied by attractive journalist Amy Allen.

Although their escapades were often violent, they were never gory. This was comic-book action, with plenty of crashes and explosions but little blood. A few years into the programme's run, the guys were eventually caught by General Stockwell, but they evaded the firing squad by becoming undercover Government agents. At this time, a new addition, Dishpan, joined the squad.

AT LAST THE 1948 SHOW
UK (Rediffusion) Comedy. ITV 1967

John Cleese, Tim Brooke-Taylor, Graham Chapman, Marty Feldman, Aimi Macdonald

Writers: **John Cleese, Tim Brooke-Taylor, Graham Chapman, Marty Feldman**
Executive Producer: **David Frost**

Manic comedy sketch series.

Emerging from the funny side of THE FROST REPORT and masterminded by David Frost himself, *At Last the 1948 Show* was one of the stepping-stone programmes which led to MONTY PYTHON'S FLYING CIRCUS and a whole new generation of British comedy. Although essentially a sketch show, its skits were unrelated, in the manner perfected later by *Python*. The humour was visual, wacky and verging on the surreal, and there was also a heavy dose of slapstick (foreshadowing Tim Brooke-Taylor's days in THE GOODIES). Aimi Macdonald supported the show's writer-performers, linking events in her trademark whiny voice.

ATKINSON, ROWAN
(1955–)

Newcastle-born, rubber-faced comedian of various talents who began performing while a post-graduate at Oxford. His first TV showcase came in 1979 in a one-off called *Rowan Atkinson Presents . . . Canned Laughter*, but he quickly moved on to NOT THE NINE O'CLOCK NEWS. His major roles since that ground-breaking sketch show have been the weaselly historical blackguard, Edmund BLACKADDER, the gormless mute, MR BEAN, and the pedantic Inspector Raymond Fowler in THE THIN BLUE LINE. Atkinson has his own production company, Tiger Television, for which he devised and narrated the documentary series *Funny Business*.

ATTENBOROUGH, Sir DAVID
CBE (1926–)

Television's leading naturalist, London-born David Attenborough, brother of (Lord) Richard, studied zoology at Cambridge. Joining the BBC as a trainee in 1952, he went on to produce ANIMAL, VEGETABLE, MINERAL? and to host and produce the long-running ZOO QUEST, before being made Controller of BBC 2 in 1965 (overseeing among other things the commissioning of THE WORLD ABOUT US) and the BBC's Director of Programmes in 1969. Although he never totally abandoned wildlife to concentrate on administration, it was not until 1979 that he returned to television in a big way, when he launched his mammoth production, LIFE ON EARTH. This seminal work was followed by THE LIVING PLANET in 1984, TRIALS OF LIFE in 1990, *The Private Life of Plants* in 1995, and *The Life of Birds* in 1998. He has also contributed to *Wildlife on One*, *The Natural World*, *Life in the Freezer* and countless other nature programmes, and presented the documentaries, *Lost Gods of Easter Island* and *State of the Planet*. His whispering, authoritative delivery has been much mimicked by impressionists.

ATV
(Associated Television)

The ITV franchise-holder for London at weekends and the Midlands on weekdays from 1956 to 1968, and then the seven-day contractor for the Midlands from 1968 to 1981. ATV began life as ABC (Associated Broadcasting Company) but was forced to change its name to avoid confusion with Associated British Cinemas, which ran the early franchises for the Midlands and the North at weekends. The company was a merger of interests between Lew Grade and Prince Littler's ITC (which initially owned 50 per cent) and a consortium headed by Norman Collins and Sir Robert Renwick, which had originally been awarded the franchise but which seemed to be having difficulties starting up. ATV went on air on 24 September 1955 in London and on 17 February 1956 in the Midlands. ITC was swallowed up by ATV in 1957, and ATV was itself reconstituted as Central Independent Television to meet the requirements of the IBA's 1981 franchise changes. Central subsequently took over ATV's Midlands area. Among ATV's many programming successes were SUNDAY NIGHT AT THE LONDON PALLADIUM, DANGER MAN, THE SAINT, CROSSROADS and THE MUPPET SHOW, plus the Gerry Anderson futuristic puppet dramas.

AUDIENCE WITH . . ., AN
UK (LWT/Channel 4) Variety. ITV 1980–

One-hour showcase for light entertainment stars.

Beginning on Boxing Day 1980 and continuing, sporadically, ever since, *An Audience with . . .* has featured some of the biggest names in British variety, plus top stars from overseas. The format has been simple: the star has performed highlights from his or her act, sung a few songs, cracked a few gags and taken well-rehearsed 'prompt' questions from the prominent celebrity audience. One 45-minute programme, *An Audience with Sooty*, to celebrate the glove puppet's 40th birthday, was shown during Children's ITV.

The performers featured to date have been: Dame Edna Everage (three times); Dudley Moore; Kenneth Williams; Mel Brooks; Joan Rivers; Billy Connolly; Peter Ustinov; Victoria Wood; Jackie Mason; Bob Monkhouse; Jimmy Tarbuck; Ken Dodd; Shirley Bassey; Freddie Starr (twice); Sooty; Bruce Forsyth; Alf Garnett (Warren Mitchell); Elton John; Ronnie Corbett; The Spice Girls; Rod Stewart; The Bee Gees; Tom Jones; Cliff Richard; and Diana Ross.

AUF WIEDERSEHEN, PET
UK (Witzend/Central) Comedy Drama. ITV 1983–6

Denis Patterson	Tim Healy
'Oz' Osbourne	Jimmy Nail
Neville Hope	Kevin Whately
Wayne	Gary Holton
Bomber	Pat Roach
Barry Taylor	Timothy Spall
Moxey	Christopher Fairbank
Ally Fraser	Bill Paterson

Creators: **Dick Clement, Ian La Frenais, Franc Roddam**
Executive Producer: **Allan McKeown**
Producer: **Martin McKeand**

The misadventures of a gang of building labourers on secondment overseas.

With jobs scarce in the recession-ridden UK of the early 1980s, the Geordie trio of Denis, Neville and Oz decided to leave their wives and girlfriends in search of employment overseas. Denis was the most mature of the three, philosophical and reasonably sensible. Neville was the drippy one, emotionally strained at having to leave his new wife, while Oz was the archetypal slob: big, fat, bigoted and dense. They were taken on as labourers on a Düsseldorf building site, where they shared a hut with four other expatriates – boring Brummie electrician Barry, Cockney carpenter Wayne, level-headed Bristolian wrestler Bomber and Scouse petty crook Moxey. The seven made quite a team. Sharing each other's joys, despairs, hopes and worries, they drank and womanized through their tour of duty, edging from scrape to scrape and from scam to scam.

In the second season, shown two years later, the boys were reunited to renovate the Derbyshire mansion of Newcastle gangster Ally Fraser, for whom Denis had been forced to work after amassing gambling debts. When that ended in the usual chaos, the lads headed off for a few episodes' labour under the Spanish sun. One sad aspect of this last series was the death of actor Gary Holton, who was, nevertheless, still seen in all episodes, thanks to early location filming and the subtle use of a double. Since *Auf Wiedersehen, Pet* most of the cast have progressed to other roles. The closing theme song, 'That's Living Alright' by Joe Fagin, was a top three hit in 1984.

AUNTIE'S BLOOMERS/AUNTIE'S SPORTING BLOOMERS
See IT'LL BE ALRIGHT ON THE NIGHT.

AUTOCUE

Trade name for a means of projecting a script on to a screen in front of a camera lens to allow presenters to read their lines; the words remain unseen by viewers. The system is universally used for news bulletins and other programmes using set scripts. Other trade names include Teleprompt.

AUTRY, GENE
(1907–98)

Texan singing cowboy of the 1930s and 1940s who quickly clambered aboard the TV bandwagon when it began rolling in the 1950s. His *Gene Autry Show*, popular with American kiddies, was a small-screen version of his cinema antics and radio series, with bumbling sidekick Pat Buttram still in tow. 'Back in the Saddle Again' became his theme song. He later developed his own business empire. Apart from owning the Challenge record label, a baseball team, a host of radio and TV stations across the States and assorted hotels, he also founded Flying A Productions. This was the company responsible for such hits as THE RANGE RIDER and CHAMPION THE WONDER HORSE (Champion was Autry's own trusty steed).

AVENGERS, THE
UK (ABC) Secret Agent Drama. ITV 1961–9

John Steed	**Patrick Macnee**
Dr David Keel	**Ian Hendry**
Carol Wilson	**Ingrid Hafner**
Catherine Gale	**Honor Blackman**
Venus Smith	**Julie Stevens**
Dr Martin King	**Jon Rollason**
One-Ten	**Douglas Muir**
One-Twelve	**Arthur Hewlett**
Emma Peel	**Diana Rigg**
Tara King	**Linda Thorson**
'Mother'	**Patrick Newell**
Rhonda	**Rhonda Parker**

Creators: **Sydney Newman, Leonard White**
Executive Producers: **Albert Fennell, Julian Wintle, Gordon L. T. Scott**
Producers: **Leonard White, John Bryce, Julian Wintle, Albert Fennell, Brian Clemens**

Very British crime/science fiction series involving a suave, gentlemanly agent and his athletic female partners.

The Avengers began life as a spin-off from a programme called POLICE SURGEON, which starred Ian Hendry as Dr Geoffrey Brent. In *The Avengers* Hendry played Dr David Keel, who, when his girlfriend was murdered by a drugs gang, went to British Intelligence and an agent called John Steed for help in 'avenging' her death – hence the title. The early episodes, with Steed acting as a foil for the amateur sleuth, were essentially cops-and-robbers fare; also seen at this time were Carol Wilson, Keel's secretary, and Steed's bosses, One-Ten and One-Twelve. Following Hendry's departure during a technicians' strike, Steed was temporarily partnered by Dr Martin King, nightclub singer Venus Smith and then by one Avenger who stayed, Cathy Gale.

Immaculately turned out in a three-piece suit, Steed oozed class. He lived in a select London district, drove a vintage Bentley and, among other idiosyncrasies, insisted on his coffee being stirred anticlockwise. His manners were impeccable at all times. He could defend himself from attack (often with a sword drawn from his umbrella) and still exhibit the utmost courtesy to his adversary. The versatile umbrella (which also performed other remarkable functions), together with Steed's protective bowler hat, became the show's trademark. With Cathy Gale, a widowed anthropologist and judo expert, Steed's career moved from mundane detection and basic counter-intelligence into the world of futuristic international intrigue. Dressed in tight-fitting leather and 'kinky' boots, Gale brought a new raciness to the series. However, after two series, Honor Blackman left to play Pussy Galore in *Goldfinger*. She was replaced by Patrick MacNee's most celebrated colleague, Diana Rigg.

The karate-chopping, kung fu kicking, ultra-fashionable Mrs Peel (widow of test pilot Peter Peel) lived in the fast lane, speeding around in a Lotus Elan. Her name, it is said, was taken from the British film industry expression 'M-Appeal', meaning 'man appeal'. With her arrival *The Avengers* was aimed more at the US market and played up the picture postcard, English village stereotype in its settings. Viewed today, these episodes appear very British and redolent of the Swinging Sixties. It was also during this period that arty programme titles were introduced and Johnny Dankworth's original theme track was replaced by the dramatic Laurie Johnson music.

When Rigg left after three seasons to return to the stage (Peter Peel was, it seemed, found alive), another accomplice was required. Unknown actress Linda Thorson was introduced as farm girl Tara King and, for the first time, a romantic liaison for Steed was suggested. Unlike her predecessors, King was not a martial arts expert, but she was just as aggressive when necessary, laying out opponents with a swipe of her brick-laden handbag or simply with a bunch of fives.

In the 1970s the programme was revived under the title THE NEW AVENGERS, with Steed (now in his 50s) having the benefit of two rather more active assistants, weapons expert Mike Gambit and Purdey, a high-kicking ex-ballet dancer.

The Avengers' plots were always far-fetched but highly inventive, usually focusing on zany attempts to take over the world. They echoed the exploits of James Bond, in a less extravagant way, but still with gadgets and gimmicks galore. Steed and Tara were even given their own version of Bond's boss, 'M', in the form of the wheelchair-bound 'Mother', with his Amazonian secretary, Rhonda. Best remembered among the baddies are the cybernauts (not to be confused with DOCTOR WHO's cybermen).

AWEFUL MR GOODALL, THE
UK (LWT) Spy Drama. ITV 1974

Mr Jack Goodall	**Robert Urquhart**
Millbrook	**Donald Burton**
Alexandra Winfield	**Isabel Dean**

Producer: **Richard Bates**

A retired civil servant still works for the intelligence services.

After more than 15 years as a lieutenant-colonel in MI5 and DI5, 55-year-old widower Jack Goodall had hung up his spy-catching equipment and happily retired to Eastbourne. However, he found the intelligence game hard to give up, especially as he was endowed with a kind of sixth sense, a nose for intrigue which made him invaluable to his former employers. These were fronted by Millbrook, Head of Section at a British security department. Six episodes were produced.

AYCKBOURN, Sir ALAN
(1939–)

London-born playwright responsible for light dramas often concerning the middle classes. His TV credits have included *Bedroom Farce*, the children's single comedy *Ernie's Incredible Illucinations*, episodes of HARK AT BARKER (under the pseudonym of Peter Caulfield), and the trilogy *The Norman Conquests* (consisting of *Table Manners*, *Living Together* and *Round and Round the Garden*), which viewed the relationship between three couples from three individual vantage-points.

AYRES, PAM
(1947–)

British colloquial poet with a yokel accent who came to fame after winning appearances on OPPORTUNITY KNOCKS in 1975. There followed several TV series, such as *What's On Next?* and *The Main Attraction*, and assorted guest appearances on the likes of THE BLACK AND WHITE MINSTREL SHOW.

BACHELOR FATHER

UK (BBC) Situation Comedy. BBC 1 1970–1

Peter Lamb	Ian Carmichael
Harry	Gerald Flood
Mr Gibson	Colin Gordon
Mary	Rona Anderson
Mrs Rathbone	Sonia Graham
Mrs Pugsley	Joan Hickson
Anna	Briony McRoberts
Ben	Ian Johnson
Donald	Roland Pickering
	Andrew Bowen
Jane	Beverley Simons
Freddie	Michael Douglas
Norah	Diana King
Ginny	Jacqueline Cowper
Jo	Geraldine Cowper
Christopher	Kevin Moran

Writer: **Richard Waring**
Producer: **Graeme Muir**

A wealthy bachelor decides he still wants a family, despite not having a wife.

Peter Lamb loved children, but his romantic liaisons had never amounted to much and he still wasn't married. Undaunted, he made himself available as a foster parent, taking in assorted foster children, who caused him plenty of concern. Also in the fray were social workers, teachers, Peter's extended family and next-door neighbour, Harry. The series was based on the real-life story of Peter Lloyd Jeffcock, bachelor foster parent of 12 children.

BAFTA

The British Academy of Film and Television Arts was formed in 1959 as the Society of Film and Television Arts by the amalgamation of the British Film Academy and the Guild of Television Producers and Directors. It was reorganized and given its current name in 1975. Membership is comprised of senior creative workers in the film and television industries, and the aim of the Academy is to raise production standards in both media. The BAFTA Awards, announced annually since 1975, with trophies modelled on classical drama masks, have become a highlight of the TV calendar. These began as The British Film Academy Awards in 1947, developing into The Society of Film and Television Arts Awards in 1969.

BAGPUSS

UK (Smallfilms) Children's Entertainment. BBC 1 1974

Narrator: **Oliver Postgate**

Creators: **Peter Firmin, Oliver Postgate**
Writer: **Oliver Postgate**

A fat, baggy, cloth cat lives on a cushion in a shop window.

Bagpuss was the story of a magic lost-and-found shop, owned by a Victorian girl named Emily. Emily would bring to the shop interesting items she had discovered, with the aim of repairing them and returning them to the owner. To do so, she relied on the help of her fat, pink-and-white-striped cloth cat, Bagpuss, and his industrious little friends. Reciting her magical spell, Emily awoke Bagpuss from sleep (the picture turned from sepia into colour) and he and the other inhabitants of the shop then set about repairing what Emily had found. Down from a shelf came Professor Yaffle, a wooden woodpecker bookend with a German accent. He provided the brains for the task ahead and led the investigation into the identity and usefulness of the object. Up popped Madeleine the rag doll, Gabriel the toad began to strum his banjo and the mice fired up their Marvellous Mechanical Mouse Organ with bellows. Head mouse Charlie kept his crew ahead of the game, and the whole team chanted and sang their way through their chores. Once the item had been mended, it was placed in the window in the hope that its owner would call and, at this point, Bagpuss crawled gratefully back to sleep.

Only 13 episodes of *Bagpuss* were ever produced, but re-runs abounded.

BAILEY, ROBIN
(1919–99)

Nottinghamshire-born actor fond of crusty codger parts, perhaps best remembered as the cynical Uncle Mort in the Brandon saga I DIDN'T KNOW YOU CARED. Previously, however, he had compered *The 64,000 Question* in the 1950s and appeared in a host of major series, including THE PALLISERS, THE NEWCOMERS and UPSTAIRS, DOWNSTAIRS. In 1983 he took over the role of Redvers POTTER from the late Arthur Lowe and, two years later, he was cast as Charters alongside Michael Aldridge's Caldicott in the BBC's revival of the two snoopy old public school duffers, CHARTERS AND CALDI-COTT. Among his other credits were *The Punch Review*, *Sorry I'm A Stranger Here Myself* (as hen-pecked librarian Henry Nunn), JANE (The Colonel), *Tales from a Long Room* (The Brigadier), RUMPOLE OF THE BAILEY (Judge Graves), *Took and Co.*, *A Dance to the Music of Time* (Uncle Alfred) and *Tinniswood Country* (Uncle Mort again).

BAIN, BARBARA
(1931–)

American actress, once the wife and co-star of Martin Landau (in MISSION IMPOSSIBLE and SPACE: 1999). Earlier appearances came in *Richard Diamond, Private Detective* (as Karen Wells, opposite David Janssen) and series such as *Hawaiian Eye*, PERRY MASON, THE DICK VAN DYKE SHOW and WAGON TRAIN.

BAIRD, JOHN LOGIE
(1888–1946)

Scottish inventor, widely acknowledged as the father of television, although not the first to experiment in the field. In 1925 Baird demonstrated a mechanical scanning television system which produced a rudimentary picture. A year later, he had improved its efficiency so that human faces became recognizable. After much badgering, the BBC picked up Baird's invention and placed it central to their television experiments in 1929. However, rival systems, using electronic rather than mechanical scanning, quickly proved more effective and the Corporation switched to EMI-Marconi's cathode-ray tube version a year after regular broadcasts began in 1936. Undaunted, Baird continued to progress his brainchild, experimenting with colour images. Earlier he had also devised a primitive form of video disc, using wax records, and even managed to transmit a TV signal across the Atlantic in 1928, years before satellite relays became a possibility. Just before his death, he had successfully worked on stereoscopic television images.

BAKER, BOB
(1939–)

British scriptwriter, usually in collaboration with Dave Martin, who specializes in children's science fiction. Their biggest successes have been for HTV, with series such as *Sky*, *King of the Castle* and *Into the Labyrinth*. Other credits include the TV movie *Thick As Thieves*, *Murder at the Wedding* and episodes of Z CARS, DOCTOR WHO, BERGERAC and SHOESTRING. Baker has also co-scripted some of the *Wallace & Gromit* films.

BAKER, COLIN
(1943–)

British actor favoured in pompous, confident roles. He first came to light in THE BROTHERS, playing the unscrupulous whiz-kid, Paul Merroney, although his most prominent role was as the sixth DOCTOR WHO. He has also been seen in episodes of THE EDWARDIANS, BLAKE'S 7, *Casualty*, the children's series *Harry's Mad* and the drama *A Dance to the Music of Time* (Canon Fenneau). His first wife was Liza Goddard.

BAKER, DANNY
(1957–)

Garrulous Londoner who specializes in pop culture nostalgia. Formerly a *New Musical Express* journalist, he joined LWT's *Six O'Clock Show* and then moved on to the daytime cartoon quiz, *Win Lose or Draw*. However, greater prominence came after he took over the Radio 5 breakfast show, *Morning Edition*, which led to his hosting assorted panel games, ranging from *Bygones* to *Pets Win Prizes*, as well as his own Saturday night chat show. He is also much seen in TV commercials and presented the series of humorous/nostalgic shorts, *TV Heroes*.

BAKER, GEORGE
(1931–)

Versatile TV actor/writer most closely associated with the rural detective, Inspector Wexford, in THE RUTH RENDELL MYSTERIES (for which he also scripted some episodes). His other major credits have included Tiberius in I, CLAUDIUS, Stanley Bowler in *Bowler* (a spin-off from *The Fenn Street Gang*) and the smarmy Tory, Godfrey Eagan, in NO JOB FOR A LADY. Over the years there have been plenty of other notable appearances, in the likes of *Undermind*, THE PRISONER (as one of the Number 2s), DOCTOR WHO, UP POMPEII (Jamesus Bondus), *Room at the Bottom*, HART TO HART, A WOMAN OF SUBSTANCE, *Dead Head*, and single dramas such as Dennis Potter's *Alice* (playing Lewis Carroll). His third wife is Wexford co-star Louie Ramsay.

BAKER, HYLDA
(1908–86)

Lancashire-born comedienne, for ever identified as Nellie Pledge, one of the squabbling siblings (with Jimmy Jewel) who ran the pickle factory in NEAREST AND DEAREST. However, Hylda Baker's career began in music hall and she toured with many of the big names in the 1940s. In the 1950s, she branched out on her own, hitting the limelight in an episode of THE GOOD OLD DAYS in 1955. In those days it was her act with Cynthia (a man in drag) which brought most laughs. 'She knows you know' became her catchphrase. TV series followed: *Be Soon*, OUR HOUSE (Henrietta), *Best of Friends* and subsequently *Nearest and Dearest* in 1968. Baker also starred as pub landlady Nellie Pickersgill in another sitcom, *Not on Your Nellie*. Although she was equally adept at straight drama (for instance in David Mercer's 1961 play, *Where The Difference Begins*, and in a couple of episodes of Z CARS), her comic timing, jerky mannerisms and flair for the *double entendre* and malapropism made her one of TV's most distinctive comic stars in the 1960s and 1970s.

BAKER, RICHARD
OBE (1925–)

Willesden-born Cambridge Footlights and repertory actor who, in 1954, became BBC Television's first newsreader, having joined the BBC as an announcer on the Third Programme in 1950. Although initially supplying just the voice behind the pictures in BBC TELEVISION NEWSREEL, Baker was later chosen as one of the main three 'in-vision' newsreaders, along with Kenneth Kendall and Robert Dougall. He presented the news until 1982 and has subsequently concentrated on his first love, classical music, appearing on such programmes as OMNIBUS, *The Proms* and FACE THE MUSIC. In contrast, he also provided the narration for the WATCH WITH MOTHER cartoon, *Mary, Mungo and Midge*.

BAKER, ROBERT S.
(1916–)

British producer heavily involved with ITC adventure series of the 1960s, often in collaboration with Monty Berman. Among his efforts were THE SAINT (and, in the 1970s, THE RETURN OF THE SAINT), THE BARON, GIDEON'S WAY and THE PERSUADERS!.

BAKER, TOM
(1934–)

Liverpool-born actor, known for eccentric characters and famous as the fourth DOCTOR WHO. In the 1980s he was the decadent priest in THE LIFE AND LOVES OF A SHE DEVIL, donned the deerstalker of Sherlock Holmes in THE HOUND OF THE BASKERVILLES, played Professor Plum in CLUEDO and guest-starred in BLACKADDER. In recent years, he has filled the role of Professor Geoffrey Hoyt in MEDICS and the ghostly Wyvern in RANDALL AND HOPKIRK (DECEASED). He hosted the kids' literature programme, THE BOOK TOWER, in the 1970s. His second wife was *Doctor Who* co-star Lalla Ward.

BAKEWELL, JOAN
CBE (1933–)

Stockport-born intellectual presenter, one of the early stars of BBC 2 as an interviewer on LATE NIGHT LINE-UP. In subsequent years she struggled to shake off the tag of 'the thinking man's crumpet', bestowed on her by Frank Muir. Other TV credits have included *Reports Action*, *On the Town*, HOLIDAY and 11 years as presenter of the Sunday late-night morality programme, *Heart of the Matter*. More recently, she has fronted the retro series, *My Generation*. Bakewell is married to producer Jack Emery.

BALL, BOBBY
(Robert Harper 1944–) See CANNON, TOMMY.

BALL, JOHNNY
(1938–)

Quirky presenter of intelligent programmes for children. Born in Bristol, he went on to become a Red Coat and clubland comedian, his TV break arriving with PLAY SCHOOL, on which he was a regular for a number of years. He then progressed to the likes of *Star Turn*, *Secret's Out* and *Cabbages and Kings*, before his biggest success, *Think of a Number*, and follow-ups *Think Again* and *Johnny Ball Reveals All*. The father of radio and TV presenter Zoë Ball, he has also written for programmes like DON'T ASK ME and CRACKERJACK.

BALL, LUCILLE
(1911–89)

The doyenne of TV comediennes, Lucille Ball came to television after 20 years' experience on stage and screen. Although considered to be 'the new Harlow' by some, Ball never quite made it to the top in pre-war Hollywood and switched her attention instead to radio in 1948. When she took on the role of a scatterbrained housewife in the series *My Favorite Husband*, her card was marked for the rest of her career. This series was soon translated to television as I LOVE LUCY, co-starring her real-life husband, Desi Arnaz, and produced by their own company, Desilu. The show went on to set standards for other sitcoms to follow. As Lucy Ricardo, Ball became one of TV's earliest superstars and, when her marriage to Arnaz irretrievably broke down, she persevered alone, still as the hapless housewife (albeit in various guises) in the follow-up series, THE LUCY SHOW and HERE'S LUCY. Although a late attempt to return to television in the 1980s with *Life With Lucy* was not a success, viewers have always had plenty of opportunity to enjoy her pioneering comic talents, as re-runs of *I Love Lucy* are never far from the screen.

BALL, NICHOLAS
(1946–)

Actor born in Leamington Spa, who came to light in THE CREZZ and progressed to his own series, HAZELL, playing a cynical London private eye. Among his later credits have been the parts of film director Alan Hunter in COLIN'S SANDWICH and DCI Nick Hall in *Thief Takers*. He was the first husband of Pamela Stephenson.

BALL, ZOË
(1970–)

Lancashire-born, energetic presenter/DJ, the daughter of children's presenter Johnny Ball. Her TV career began as a runner with Granada, from which she progressed to the position of researcher on THE BIG BREAKFAST and then on to fronting Children's BBC and various kids' series, including *Playdays*, *Short Change*, *Fully Booked*, *The O Zone* and the art show, *Smart*. In 1996 she returned to *The Big Breakfast* to replace Gaby Roslin, although she soon moved on to front *Live and Kicking* and editions of TOP OF THE POPS. She has also co-hosted the chat show, *The Priory*, and presented the Radio 1 breakfast show. She is married to DJ Fat Boy Slim.

BALLYKISSANGEL
UK (BBC/Ballykea/World) Drama. BBC 1 1996–

Father Peter Clifford	**Stephen Tompkinson**
Assumpta Fitzgerald	**Dervla Kirwan**
Brian Quigley	**Tony Doyle**
Father MacAnally	**Niall Toibin**
Niamh Quigley/Egan	**Tina Kellegher**
Ambrose Egan	**Peter Hanly**
Brendan Kearney	**Gary Whelan**
Padraig O'Kelly	**Peter Caffrey**
Siobhan Mehigan/Kearney	**Deirdre Donnelly**
Liam	**Joe Savino**
Kathleen	**Áine Ní Mhuiri**
Donal	**Frankie McCafferty**
Eamon	**Birdy Sweeney**
Dr Michael Ryan	**Bosco Hogan**
Timmy Joe Galvin	**Stephen Kennedy**
Enda Sullivan	**Stephen Brennan**
Imelda Egan	**Doreen Keogh**
Kevin	**John Cleere**
Mrs Bella Mooney	**Pauline McLynn**
Sean Dillon	**Lorcan Cranitch**
Orla O'Connell	**Victoria Smurfit**
Father Aidan O'Connell	**Don Wycherley**
Emma Dillon	**Kate McEnery**
Danny Byrne	**Colin Farrell**
Leo	**Jimmy Nesbitt**
Conor Devlin	**Owen Teale**
Kieran Egan	**Sam Farrar**
Uncle Minto	**James Ellis**
Supt./Insp. Foley	**Alan Barry**
Paul Dooley	**Owen Roe**
Oonagh Dooley	**Marion O'Dwyer**
Dermot Dooley	**Ciaran Owens**
Grainne Dooley	**Katie Cullen**
Frankie Sullivan	**Catherine Cusack**

Creator: **Kieran Prendiville**
Producers: **Joy Lale, Chris Griffin, Chris Clough**
Executive Producers: **Tony Garnett, Jeremy Gwilt, Robert Cooper**

A young English priest takes up a challenging new post in a remote Irish town.

Father Peter Clifford, an enthusiastic but naïve Catholic priest, knew that his new posting to St Joseph's church in the town of Ballykissangel would be a trying experience from the moment he set eyes on the community. His superior, Father MacAnally, like the rest of the neighbourhood, was a traditionalist and had simply not moved with the times, and the people were God-fearing, yet loathed the clergy. The archetypal fish out of water, this modern-thinking priest quickly needed to grasp the off-beat logic of the colourful townsfolk and learn all about their different way of life. To do so, he leaned heavily on the town's feisty publican, Assumpta Fitzgerald, landlady of Fitzgerald's bar. Their relationship was stormy but always threatened to break into romance, with all the complications that an affair between a priest and a publican could bring. Even Assumpta's marriage to journalist Leo failed to break the undeclared bond that existed between her and the priest. Clifford also needed to come to terms with the town's Mr Big, the conniving Brian Quigley, the only man (apart from Clifford) with an eye to the future – not to mention a fast punt.

After three hugely successful seasons, stars Stephen Tompkinson and Dervla Kirwan decided to leave the series. After a traumatic finale in which Peter expressed his feelings for Assumpta, only to see her die in his arms after electrocution, the priest decided to seek pastures new. His position at the church was filled by former monk Father Aidan O'Connell, but more attention was given to other new arrivals: unpopular widower Sean Dillon, a self-made man returning home after 20 years; his 17-year-old daughter Emma; and Orla, the new priest's attractive but worldly-wise sister. Fitzgerald's was bought by Quigley.

The series was the brainchild of former TOMORROW'S WORLD presenter Kieran Prendiville, who also scripted many episodes. It drew comparisons with the US series, NORTHERN EXPOSURE, so similar was its premise of a stranded man struggling to cope in a totally alien, and rather kooky, environment. Although loosely based on clerical goings-on in the village of Ballykissanne, County Kerry, where Prendiville spent holidays as a child, *Ballykissangel* was filmed in Avoca, a sleepy County Wicklow town that soon became a major tourist attraction. A new series aired in 2001.

BAMBER, DAVID
(1954–)

English actor, in comic as well as straight parts. His TV highlights have included the roles of Mr Collins in PRIDE AND PREJUDICE and Eric Slatt in *Chalk*. Other credits have included *The Buddha of Suburbia* (Shadwell), *My Night with Reg*, *My Dad's a Boring Nerd*, *Neville's Island* (Angus), MURDER MOST HORRID and *The Railway Children* (Dr Forrest). He is married to actress Julia Swift (daughter of David Swift).

BANACEK
US (Universal) Detective Drama. ITV 1975–7

Thomas Banacek	**George Peppard**
Jay Drury	**Ralph Manza**
Felix Mulholland	**Murray Matheson**
Carlie Kirkland	**Christine Belford**

Creator: **Anthony Wilson**
Executive Producer: **George Eckstein**
Producer: **Howie Horowitz**

Tales of a modern-day bounty hunter.

Cool, calm and sophisticated Thomas Banacek was a wealthy man. He lived in a mansion in Boston's prosperous Beacon Hill area and was driven around by a chauffeur, Jay Drury. The reason for his wealth? He was good at collecting rewards from insurance companies. He specialized in retrieving stolen valuables and, on a 10 per cent rake-off, the greater the prize, the richer he became. The loot may have been gold bullion, or perhaps a prize racehorse. On one occasion it was even a professional footballer. Felix Mulholland, proprietor of Mulholland's Rare Book and Print Shop, was his best friend, and Carlie Kirkland, another insurance agent, became Banacek's rival and romantic interest.

Banacek made George Peppard popular with Polish-Americans. These people had long been the butt of

everyday humour, and at last here was a TV hero to show the world that they really could be clever. Plenty of Polish sayings found their way into the script. The series was shown as part of the MYSTERY MOVIE anthology.

BANANA SPLITS, THE
US (Hanna-Barbera) Children's Comedy. BBC 1 1970

Voices:

Fleegle	**Paul Winchell**
Bingo	**Daws Butler**
Drooper	**Allan Melvin**
Snorky	**Don Messick**

Executive Producers: **William Hanna, Joseph Barbera**

Zany comedy featuring four animal pop stars.

The Banana Splits were an animal pop group, a sort of zoological MONKEES, miming to pre-recorded tracks and dashing around in fast-action sequences. Played by men in outsize costumes, the four were Fleegle, a dog guitarist; Bingo, a bongo-playing gorilla; Drooper, a lion; and Snorky, an elephant. At LAUGH-IN pace, these wacky creatures were used to link various cartoon inserts such as *The Arabian Knights*, *The Micro Ventures*, *The Hillbilly Bears* and *The Three Musketeers*. There was also a live-action adventure entitled *Danger Island* (starring Frank Aletter as Professor Irwin Haydn). Wisecracks and slapstick scenes were the order of the day. Drooper unsuccessfully tried to take out the trash (the bin refused to accept rubbish), Fleegle wrestled with the mailbox for the mail, and the stroppy cuckoo clock made time-telling less than easy. Seldom did an episode pass without someone yelling 'Hold the bus!'. Regular features were Banana Buggie races, song and dance from the rival Sour Grape Girls gang and an 'information' spot called 'Dear Drooper', where the know-all lion attempted to answer viewers' queries. The show is probably best remembered today for its catchy 'One banana, two banana' theme song. Episodes were shown again as part of THE BIG BREAKFAST on Channel 4.

BAND OF GOLD/GOLD
UK (Granada) Drama. ITV 1995–7

Carol Johnson	**Cathy Tyson**
Rose Garrity	**Geraldine James**
Anita Braithwaite	**Barbara Dickson**
Tracy Richards	**Samantha Morton**
George Ferguson	**Tony Doyle**
Curly	**Richard Moore**
Bob	**Anthony Milner**
Steve Dixon	**Ray Stevenson**
Insp./DCI Newall	**David Schofield**
Dez	**Ahsen Bhatti**
Mr Moore	**Philip Martin Brown**
Colette	**Lena Headey**
Joyce Webster	**Rachel Davies**
Smiley	**Darren Tighe**

Vinnie Marshall .... **Adam Kotz**
Brian Roberts .... **Peter Firth**
Rabbit .... **Justin Chadwick**
Brenda Taylor .... **Margo Gunn**
Mrs Minkin .... **Anita Carey**
Emma Johnson .... **Laura Kilgallon**
Alf Black .... **David Bradley**
Paula Graham .... **Janet Dibley** (*Gold*)
DI Cooper .... **Fiona Allen** (*Gold*)
Chubbs .... **David Ross** (*Gold*)
Lloyd .... **Darren Warner** (*Gold*)
Lisa .... **Jayne Ashbourne** (*Gold*)
Insp. Henryson .... **Kern Falconer** (*Gold*)
Mr Smithson .... **Mark Strong** (*Gold*)

Creator: **Kay Mellor**
Writers: **Kay Mellor, Mark Davies Markham** (*Gold*),
Catherine Johnson (*Gold*)
Producers: **Tony Dennis, Elizabeth Bradley, Gillian
McNeill** (*Gold*)

*Gritty, bleak portrayal of the lives of a group of
prostitutes.*

Set in Bradford, *Band of Gold* introduced viewers to the
miserable world of life on the game. It featured four
women who had taken up prostitution for differing
reasons and wrapped their stories around the hunt for
the murderer of young mother Gina Dixon, who had
turned to the game to pay off a loan shark. Carol was
the matter-of-fact, hygiene-obsessed one, happy to be
shocking the neighbours; Rose was the experienced,
matriarchal figure who continually failed to start a new
life; Anita was selfish and scheming; and misguided
teenage blonde Tracy was a drug abuser. George Ferguson was Anita's married boyfriend and the villain who
made the girls' life even more difficult. By the end of the
six-part drama, the foursome had decided to leave the
grime of the streets and set up their own cleaning co-
operative, Scrubbit.

When the series returned for another six episodes a
year later, the girls found it difficult to shake off their
past on the 'Lane'. A new arrival, a sado-masochism
specialist named Colette, joined the throng and more
murders ensued, underlining again the programme's
core message, that prostitution is not a glamorous industry (although, contrarily, Bradford police claimed that
the series had been responsible for an upsurge in activity
in the city's red light area). A third series, of three two-
part stories, arrived in 1997. Re-titled *Gold*, this time only
Rose and Carol remained of the original four girls. Now
both past the age of 40, they once again attempted to go
straight, Rose with a new job as a liaison officer between
the social services and local prostitutes, and Carol with
the help of a generous inheritance from a former punter.
However, they were constantly hindered by their
troubled past and yet more mysterious killings. *Band
of Gold*'s theme song, a version of 'Love Hurts', was
performed by star Barbara Dickson.

BANNISTER, TREVOR
(1936–)

Familiar character and comic actor, starring in the 1967
trilogy *The War of Darkie Pilbeam*, and the sitcoms THE
DUSTBINMEN (Heavy Breathing) and ARE YOU BEING
SERVED? (Mr Lucas). Among other series, Bannister was
also seen in *Wyatt's Watchdogs* (Peter Pitt).

BARBER, GLYNIS
(Glynis van der Reit; 1955–)

South African leading lady who arrived on TV as Soolin,
the blonde gunslinger in BLAKE'S 7, before stripping
down to her underwear in the title role of JANE, BBC 2's
revival of the *Daily Mirror*'s wartime cartoon heroine.
From there, Barber moved on to THE FURTHER ADVEN-
TURES OF LUCKY JIM, then switched to detective work
when cast as the plummy Harriet Makepeace in DEMPSEY
AND MAKEPEACE, opposite her future husband, Michael
Brandon. Her other credits have included THE SAND-
BAGGERS and TALES OF THE UNEXPECTED.

BARCLAY, HUMPHREY

Former Cambridge Footlights graduate and mastermind
of the 1963 revue *Cambridge Circus*, which featured such
up-and-coming performers as John Cleese, Tim Brooke-
Taylor, Bill Oddie, Graham Chapman, Jonathan Lynn
and Graeme Garden. Barclay then moved into tele-
vision, working as a comedy producer with Rediffusion
and then LWT. His many credits have included DO NOT
ADJUST YOUR SET (for which he discovered David Jason),
The Complete and Utter History of Britain, HARK AT BARKER,
DOCTOR IN THE HOUSE (and its sequels), NO – HONESTLY,
THE TOP SECRET LIFE OF EDGAR BRIGGS, *Lucky Feller, Blind
Men*, TWO'S COMPANY, *Nobody's Perfect, End of Part One*,
ME & MY GIRL, A FINE ROMANCE, WHOOPS APOCALYPSE,
HOT METAL and *That's Love*, plus shows starring Cannon
and Ball, Stanley Baxter, Hale and Pace, and Emma
Thompson. In the 1980s Barclay set up his own pro-
duction company, Humphrey Barclay Productions,
which contributed series such as *Dream Stuffing, Relative
Strangers*, DESMOND'S, SURGICAL SPIRIT, *Up the Garden
Path, Brighton Belles, Conjugal Rites* and AGONY AGAIN.

BARKER, RONNIE
OBE (1929–)

Comedian and comic actor born in Bedford, universally
recognized as one of television's finest. From his earliest
appearances in IT'S A SQUARE WORLD (with Michael
Bentine), *The Seven Faces of Jim* (with Jimmy Edwards)
and THE FROST REPORT (alongside John Cleese and
Ronnie Corbett), Barker has enjoyed a reputation second
to none for comic timing and verbal dexterity. He was
given a showcase series in 1968, *The Ronnie Barker
Playhouse*, in one episode of which he introduced the

character of Lord Rustless, who was then spun off into two series of his own, HARK AT BARKER, and *His Lordship Entertains*. In 1971 Barker was paired again with Ronnie Corbett for THE TWO RONNIES, a mixture of monologues, soliloquies and humorous sketches which ran for 15 years, with some material written by Barker himself under the pen-name of Gerald Wiley. *Six Dates with Barker*, aired in 1971, and another anthology series, *Seven of One* in 1973, yielded two major sitcoms and two of TV's brightest creations. The first, PORRIDGE, saw Barker's classic portrayal of the old lag Fletcher (later set free in *Going Straight*). The second, OPEN ALL HOURS, featured the stuttering, penny-pinching grocer Arkwright. Some of his other efforts have been understandably less memorable, namely the short-sighted removal man CLARENCE (written by Barker under the name of Bob Ferris) and the flamboyant, lecherous Welsh photographer THE MAGNIFICENT EVANS. Barker's other credits over the years have included parts in lesser comedies like *The TV Lark*, *Bold as Brass* and *Foreign Affairs*. He retired from showbiz in 1988.

BARKER, SUE
(1956–)

Devon-born former tennis professional (one-time French Open champion) who turned to sports presenting after hanging up her racket in 1985. Following commentating work for Channel 7 in Australia, she joined Sky Sports and then moved to the BBC as presenter of *Sunday Grandstand*, GRANDSTAND and various sporting events, including Wimbledon and the Olympic Games. In 1997 she succeeded David Coleman as chair of A QUESTION OF SPORT.

BARKWORTH, PETER
(1929–)

Kent-born actor, generally in upper-middle-class parts, probably best recalled as the retiring bank manager Mark Telford in TELFORD'S CHANGE. Previously, Barkworth had appeared as Kenneth Bligh in THE POWER GAME, starred as Vincent in the wartime drama MANHUNT, played detective Arthur Hewitt in THE RIVALS OF SHERLOCK HOLMES and added a series of guest appearances in series like OUT OF THE UNKNOWN and COLDITZ. He also took on the role of Eustace Morrow in GOOD GIRL, Stanley Baldwin in WINSTON CHURCHILL – THE WILDERNESS YEARS, and that of computer executive Geoffrey Carr in *The Price*, and was also seen in *Late Starter* and SECRET ARMY. In 1977 Barkworth picked up a BAFTA award for his performance in Tom Stoppard's *Play of the Week, Professional Foul*. More recently, he has been seen in HEARTBEAT.

BARLOW AT LARGE/BARLOW
UK (BBC) Police Drama. BBC 1 1971–3/1974–5

Det. Chief Supt. Charlie Barlow	**Stratford Johns**
DS David Rees	**Norman Corner**
A. G. Fenton	**Neil Stacy**
Det. Insp. Tucker	**Derek Newark** (*Barlow*)

Creator: **Elwyn Jones**
Producers: **Leonard Lewis, Keith Williams**

An aggressive police detective is assigned to the Home Office.

In this, the third part of the Charlie Barlow story, the former Z CARS and SOFTLY, SOFTLY bully boy was somewhat uncomfortably installed in Whitehall, working with a rather smarmy superior, A. G. Fenton, with whom he didn't always see eye to eye. As part of the Police Research Services Branch, his job was to help regional police forces with any difficult cases they encountered. Though he was accompanied by Detective Sgt Rees, he always seemed a little lost without his old mucker, John Watt. The series evolved into another sequel, simply entitled *Barlow*, in which he was joined by Detective Insp. Tucker.

BARNABY JONES
US (Quinn Martin) Detective Drama. ITV 1974–80

Barnaby Jones	**Buddy Ebsen**
Betty Jones	**Lee Meriwether**
Jedediah Romano (J. R.) Jones	**Mark Shera**
Lt. Joe Taylor	**Vince Howard**
Lt. John Biddle	**John Carter**

Executive Producer: **Quinn Martin**
Producers: **Gene Levitt, Philip Salzman, Robert Sherman**

A Los Angeles private eye comes out of retirement to find the killer of his son.

Barnaby Jones, after an impressive career as a private eye, had relaxed into a horse-breeding retirement. But when his son, Hal, the new proprietor of the Jones Detective Agency, was murdered on a case, he set about tracking down the killer. After nailing his man, Barnaby turned his back on retirement and took over control of the firm once more, assisted by his widowed daughter-in-law, Betty (played by Lee Meriwether, Miss America 1955). Barnaby's young cousin, law student J. R. Jones, was recruited to the team in the fifth series, after the murder of his father.

Like most TV private eyes in the 1970s, Barnaby was unconventional. The softly spoken, milk-drinking gumshoe used his vague, totally unassuming appearance to trick criminals into a false sense of security and then pounced when they least expected it. He backed this up by being thoroughly methodical, working on cases in a special crime lab he had constructed at home.

Through this role, star Buddy Ebsen quickly dispelled any fears of typecasting that may have existed following his years as millionaire bumpkin Jed Clampett in THE BEVERLY HILLBILLIES.

BARNETT, LADY ISOBEL
(1918–80)

Elegant, intelligent panellist of WHAT'S MY LINE?. Born in Scotland, Isobel Barnett worked as a GP for a number of years before becoming a Justice of the Peace. It was in 1953 that she joined the new game show *What's My Line?* as a resident panellist, and her graceful manner and shrewd questioning quickly endeared her to viewers. She later appeared in various other panel games, on radio as well as TV, but her life ended on a sad note when she committed suicide in 1980, a week after being found guilty of petty shoplifting. She was the wife of a former Lord Mayor of Leicester, Sir Geoffrey Barnett.

BARNEY MILLER
US (Four D) Situation Comedy. ITV 1979–83

Capt. Barney Miller .... **Hal Linden**
Det. Phil Fish .... **Abe Vigoda**
DS Chano Amenguale .... **Gregory Sierra**
Det. Stanley Wojohowicz ('Wojo') .... **Maxwell Gail**
Det. Nick Yemana .... **Jack Soo**
Det. Ron Harris .... **Ron Glass**
Elizabeth Miller .... **Barbara Barrie**
Rachael Miller .... **Anne Wyndham**
David Miller .... **Michael Tessier**
Bernice Fish .... **Florence Stanley**
Det. Janice Wentworth .... **Linda Lavin**
Insp. Frank Luger .... **James Gregory**
Officer Carl Levitt .... **Ron Carey**
Det. Baptista .... **June Gable**
Det. Arthur Dietrich .... **Steve Landesberg**
Lt. Scanlon .... **George Murdock**

Creators: **Danny Arnold, Theodore J. Flicker**
Executive Producer: **Danny Arnold**
Producers: **Chris Hayward, Arne Sultan**

The ups and downs of life in a Greenwich Village police station under its genial Jewish captain.

Barney Miller was set in New York's 12th Precinct police station. Although Barney's family life featured prominently in the early episodes, it was quickly pushed into the background and all the subsequent action took place in the old precinct house. This soon became home to all kinds of weird and wonderful callers, as well as a motley crew of police officers.

Barney was very much the father figure of the station. He was compassionate and a good listener. His office even had a leather couch for those who needed to pour their hearts out. His colleagues included the decrepit Fish, grumbling his way through his last years on the force and always in need of a bathroom. On retirement, he was given his own spin-off series, *Fish*. There were also the naïve, people-loving Wojo, the philosophical Yemana (who made awful coffee and followed horse racing) and the fast-talking Puerto Rican Amenguale, who was later replaced by Dietrich, a walking encyclopedia. Black jokester Ron Harris eventually had a book

published (*Blood on the Badge*), Levitt was the 5-foot 3-inch officer who longed to be a detective but was 'too short', and Inspector Luger was Barney's boss.

Barney Miller was a police show that relied on talk, not action. There were no car chases, no explosions and none of the fast talk seen in TV's cop dramas. Instead, the humane side of policing was revealed through the inter-personal relationships of the multi-ethnic officers and the social misfits they brought in. As a result, the programme was much appreciated by real-life police officers for its authenticity, and the stars were made honorary members of the New York Police Department. The series ended when the police station was declared a historic site, after the discovery that it had been used by Teddy Roosevelt when he was President of the New York Police Board in the 1890s. Barney and Levitt were promoted, but the gang was dispersed across the city. The pilot for the show was a segment in a comedy anthology *Just For Laughs* called *The Life and Times of Captain Barney Miller*.

BARON, THE
UK (ATV/ITC) Secret Agent Drama. ITV 1966–7

John Mannering ('The Baron') .... **Steve Forrest**
Cordelia Winfield .... **Sue Lloyd**
John Alexander Templeton-Green .... **Colin Gordon**
David Marlowe .... **Paul Ferris**

Producer: **Monty Berman**

An international art dealer works as an undercover agent in his spare time.

In this series, very loosely based on the British Intelligence agent created by John Creasey, Steve Forrest starred as John Mannering, a suave American antiques expert who helped the Secret Service whenever a crime involved the theft of valuable pieces. His nickname, the title of the programme, was taken from his family's ranch in Texas (although in Creasey's stories Mannering was British, not American).

Millionaire Mannering drove a Jensen (registration BAR 1) and owned exclusive antiques shops in London, Washington and Paris, from which he planned his secret missions. In his assignments for John Templeton-Green of British Intelligence, he was joined by attractive Cordelia Winfield of the Special Branch Diplomatic Service. David Marlowe was sometimes seen as Mannering's business associate.

BARR, ROBERT
(1909–99)

Glasgow-born writer and producer with many successes for the BBC, which he joined in 1946, bringing with him a distinguished record as war correspondent. His work included episodes of MAIGRET, Z CARS, SOFTLY, SOFTLY, *Parkin's Patch* and SECRET ARMY, although even earlier credits were the documentary *Germany Under Control* in 1946, *Saturday Night Stories* (as producer) in 1948, a 1949 adaptation of H. G. Wells's *The Time Machine* and the police drama *Pilgrim Street* (again as producer) in 1952. The 1959 series *Spycatcher* and the 1963 series *Moonstrike* were the peaks of his writing career, but he also created *Gazette*, from which HADLEIGH was derived.

BARR, ROSEANNE

See ROSEANNE.

BARRACLOUGH, ROY

(1935–)

Lancashire-born actor and comedian, partner to Les Dawson on numerous occasions (particularly as Cissie and Ada, the two gossipy women), but better known as Alec Gilroy, landlord of the Rovers Return in CORO-NATION STREET, a character he has played on and off since 1972 (in addition to four other *Street* visitors). Earlier appearances included contributions to various dramas and sitcoms from *The War of Darkie Pilbeam*, *Castlehaven* and NEAREST AND DEAREST to NEVER MIND THE QUALITY, FEEL THE WIDTH and LOVE THY NEIGHBOUR. He was also one of the leads in the comedy, *The More We Are Together* (Frank Wilgoose), played major parts in the children's comedies, *Pardon My Genie* (Mr Cobbledick) and *T-Bag Strikes Again*, and starred as Leslie Flitcroft in *Mother's Ruin*. Scores of guest appearances add to his portfolio.

BARRETT, RAY

(1926–)

Australian-born, rugged-looking actor whose first starring role was as Dr Don Nolan in EMERGENCY – WARD 10. As well as making appearances in series like *Educating Archie*, Z CARS and DOCTOR WHO, he starred as Peter Clarke in the GHOST SQUAD sequel, *GS5*, before taking his best-remembered part, that of oil executive Peter Thornton in MOGUL and THE TROUBLESHOOTERS. From then on, Barrett was a regular face in British TV drama, and his voice was familiar, too. Among other voice-overs, he provided the dialogue for STINGRAY's Commander Shore and THUNDERBIRDS' John Tracy in Gerry Anderson's puppet classics. In 1976 he returned to Australia and continued to win plaudits for his performances in film and television Down Under.

BARRIE, AMANDA

(Shirley Ann Broadbent; 1939–)

Although known today as Alma Sedgewick/Baldwin/Halliwell in CORONATION STREET, Lancashire-born Amanda Barrie's TV credits have been numerous and varied, ranging from hostessing on DOUBLE YOUR MONEY and presenting the kids' show, *Hickory House*, to supporting Morecambe and Wise in their first TV outing, *Running Wild* (1954). She was also seen in the likes of THE SEVEN FACES OF JIM, *Bulldog Breed* (Sandra Prentiss), *The Reluctant Romeo* (Geraldine Woods), *Time of My Life* (Jean Archer) and *L for Lester* (Sally Small), plus series such as ARE YOU BEING SERVED? and SPOONER'S PATCH. She

joined the *Street* briefly in 1981 and became a member of the regular cast in 1988.

BARRIE, CHRIS

(1960–)

British comedian, impressionist and comic actor, whose most memorable roles have been as the obnoxious Arnold Rimmer in RED DWARF and the incompetent Gordon Brittas in THE BRITTAS EMPIRE. Barrie has also contributed to shows like *Carrott's Lib*, *Saturday Live*, *Pushing Up Daisies*, *Coming Next . . .* and SPITTING IMAGE, where his impressionist talents were put to good use. Barrie also starred in a third, less successful sitcom, *A Prince Among Men* (ex-footballer Gary Prince). Other credits have included *The Entertainers*, THE YOUNG ONES, FILTHY RICH AND CATFLAP and *Lenny Henry Tonite*.

BARRON, JOHN

(1920–)

Tall, booming, London-born actor generally cast in eccentric roles. He is best known for his C. J. in THE FALL AND RISE OF REGINALD PERRIN ('I didn't get where I am today . . .'), but he first came to viewers' attention in EMERGENCY – WARD 10, *Glencannon* and ALL GAS AND GAITERS (the Dean), before playing the warped scientist Devereaux in the sci-fi serial, TIMESLIP, the Minister in DOOMWATCH, the Vicar in POTTER, US security adviser The Deacon in WHOOPS APOCALYPSE and assorted supporting roles in comedy and drama series.

BARRON, KEITH

(1934–)

Yorkshire-born actor whose TV work has swung between drama and comedy. In the 1960s he made his name as an angry young man in the title role of Dennis Potter's *Vote, Vote, Vote For Nigel Barton* and its prequel, *Stand Up, Nigel Barton*. In the 1980s he starred as David Pearce in DUTY FREE and, in contrast, the love-lorn taxi-driver Tom in the drama *Take Me Home*. He played Guy Lofthouse in THE GOOD GUYS and other credits have included THE ODD MAN and IT'S DARK OUTSIDE (Sgt Swift), THE FURTHER ADVENTURES OF LUCKY JIM (the 1967 version; Jim Dixon), MY GOOD WOMAN (neighbour Philip Broadmore), *No Strings* (Derek), TELFORD'S CHANGE (Tim Hart), *Late Expectations* (Ted Jackson), *Leaving* (Daniel Ford), *Room at the Bottom* (TV boss Kevin Hughes), *Haggard* (title role), *All Night Long* (Bill Chivers), and *Madame Bovary* (L'Heureux). He was also seen in A FAMILY AT WAR, UPSTAIRS, DOWNSTAIRS, *About Face*, HOLDING THE FORT, *Stay With Me 'til Morning*, THE RUTH RENDELL MYSTERIES, *Drovers' Gold*, *Screen One*'s *Gobble* and DALZIEL AND PASCOE. Keith is the father of actor James Barron.

BARRY, GENE
(Eugene Klass; 1921–)

American supporting actor of the 1950s who flourished in the 1960s, winning glamorous title roles in *Bat Masterson*, BURKE'S LAW, *The Name of the Game* and THE ADVENTURER (Steve Bradley). In the 1970s and 1980s he concentrated on more lavish productions, particularly TV movies, but in 1994 he returned to our screens as Amos Burke, the millionaire head of Los Angeles Police's homicide department.

BARRY, MICHAEL
(1910–)

Head of BBC Drama in the pioneering days of the 1950s, responsible for commissioning such classics as QUATERMASS and 1984. Previously, as producer, Barry had introduced the BBC's limited audience to such dramas as Edgar Wallace's *The Case of the Frightened Lady* and *Smoky Cell* (both 1938), *Toad of Toad Hall* (1946) and *Boys in Brown* (1947). In 1965 he produced a Royal Shakespeare Company trilogy of plays under the banner of *The Wars of the Roses*.

BARRYMORE, MICHAEL
(Michael Parker; 1952–)

Tall, energetic, London-born comedian and quiz show host. After appearing on NEW FACES and WHO DO YOU DO? and in support of Russ Abbot, Michael Barrymore found a niche of his own in the 1980s and 1990s in such shows as *Get, Set Go!*, *Michael Barrymore's Saturday Night Out*, *Live from Her Majesty's*, *Barrymore* (a chance for the public to show off their party pieces), the 'strike the screen' quiz, STRIKE IT LUCKY, *Michael Barrymore's My Kind of People*, *Michael Barrymore's My Kind of Music* and the kids' series *Mick and Mac*. His humour is based on physically exhausting, almost acrobatic routines and gentle mimicry of his programme participants, with his catchphrase 'Awight!' well to the fore. In 2000 he accepted his first drama role, playing game show host *Bob Martin* and also presented *Barrymore on Broadway*.

BASEHART, RICHARD
(1914–84)

American actor chiefly remembered by TV viewers as Admiral Harriman Nelson in VOYAGE TO THE BOTTOM OF THE SEA. Other credits (as guest star) included BEN CASEY, THE TWILIGHT ZONE, GUNSMOKE, MARCUS WELBY, MD and THE LOVE BOAT, plus a catalogue of TV movies. Basehart also provided narration for KNIGHT RIDER.

BASS, ALFIE
(1921–87)

Cockney comedian who enjoyed a long film and TV career. One of his earliest small-screen appearances was in the drama *The Bespoke Overcoat* in 1954, although it was as the pessimistic Private 'Excused Boots' Bisley – 'Bootsie' for short – in THE ARMY GAME that he shot to fame in 1957. This led to a sequel, BOOTSIE AND SNUDGE, and then a third sitcom for the character, *Foreign Affairs*. Bass and his co-star Bill Fraser then explored new ground in *Vacant Lot* (with Bass as Alf Grimble). His later TV work included the sitcoms TILL DEATH US DO PART (Bert), ARE YOU BEING SERVED? (Mr Goldberg) and *A Roof Over My Head* (Flamewell), the adventure series DICK TURPIN (Isaac Rag) and a 1974 revival of *Bootsie and Snudge*.

BATES, MICHAEL
(1920–78)

Versatile actor who was part of the original trio of childish old men in LAST OF THE SUMMER WINE (playing Blamire) and starred (blacked up) as the lead wallah, Rangi Ram, in IT AIN'T HALF HOT MUM. His earlier credits included several one-off dramas, such as a 1965 version of *A Passage to India* (again blacked up) and the sitcoms *Mr John Jorrocks* (Duke of Donkeyton), MR DIGBY DARLING (Norman Stanhope) and *Turnbull's Finest Half-Hour* (Major Clifford Turnbull). The Indian connections should not have been surprising: Bates was born in the subcontinent and spoke Urdu.

BATES, RALPH
(1940–91)

Hammer horror actor who showed his versatility in two diverse TV roles, namely the mean, moody George Warleggan in POLDARK and the wimpish lonely heart, John Lacey, in DEAR JOHN. Other TV credits included the 1960s satire series, *Broad and Narrow*, the parts of Caligula in THE CAESARS and Michel Lebrun in *Moonbase 3*, and an appearance in CRIME OF PASSION. Bates, a descendant of French scientist Louis Pasteur, died of cancer in 1991. His two wives were both actresses, Joanna Van Gyseghem and Virginia Wetherall, and he has left two acting children. His daughter Daisy was seen in FOREVER GREEN and his son William appeared as his son in *Dear John*.

BATMAN
US (20th Century-Fox/Greenway) Science Fiction. ITV
1966–8

Bruce Wayne (Batman)	**Adam West**
Dick Grayson (Robin)	**Burt Ward**
Alfred Pennyworth	**Alan Napier**
Aunt Harriet Cooper	**Madge Blake**

Police Commissioner Gordon .... **Neil Hamilton**
Chief O'Hara .... **Stafford Repp**
Barbara Gordon (Batgirl) .... **Yvonne Craig**
The Joker .... **Cesar Romero**
The Riddler .... **Frank Gorshin**
                                                                    John Astin
The Penguin .... **Burgess Meredith**
Catwoman .... **Julie Newmar**
                                                                Eartha Kitt
                                                    Lee Ann Meriwether
Narrator .... **William Dozier**

Executive Producer: **William Dozier**
Producer: **Howie Horowitz**

*Camp TV version of the popular comic strip
created by Bob Kane in 1939.*

Batman was renowned for its purposeful overacting, corny quips and far-fetched storylines. It made a star out of Adam West, albeit a very typecast star, and featured a host of celebrities anxious to grab a piece of what was a very successful series. It played the story very close to the comic book in style and substance, with the addition of Aunt Harriet to detract from the suspicious nature of three men sharing a house. The three were millionaire playboy Bruce Wayne, his 15-year-old ward, Dick Grayson, and their gaunt English butler, Alfred. Only Alfred knew that the other two were really the famous Batman and Robin, crime fighters extraordinaire.

The 'Dynamic Duo' lived 14 miles outside Gotham City, at Wayne Manor, beneath which was concealed Batman's headquarters, the Batcave. A flick of the switch hidden in a bust of Shakespeare revealed firemen's poles (the 'Batpoles') behind a bookcase which allowed them to descend to the cave. Remarkably, on reaching the bottom, they were already clothed in their famous crime-fighting gear and masks. In this high-tech den they puzzled and pondered over the amazing crimes which time and again afflicted the city, before setting out to wreak vengeance on the underworld, a vengeance promised by Wayne when he had been criminally orphaned in his teens.

Their enemies (or 'arch-enemies') were most frequently the Joker, adorned with a sick painted smile, the Riddler, in his question-marked catsuit, the waddling Penguin, with his cigarette holder, and the leather-clad Catwoman, although the series also introduced some baddies not known in the comic strip. These included Egghead (Vincent Price), King Tut (Victor Buono), Mr Freeze (Otto Preminger) and the Bookworm (Roddy McDowall).

Batman and Robin rocketed into action in the Batmobile, a converted 17-foot-long Lincoln Continental, but this was just one of their many gadgets and ingenious devices. Adam West played the lead very drily, while Burt Ward's Robin was dramatically excitable and prone to 'Holy' expressions of farcical topicality, like 'Holy sewer pipe!' as the Riddler emerged from a manhole, and 'Holy fork in the road!'. The villains were ridiculously twisted: the Joker loved to play nasty tricks, while the Riddler always gave the heroes a seemingly unfathomable clue. The action was laughably violent and partially obscured by exclamations like 'Pow!', 'Zap!' and 'Thud'

writ large on the screen. Each episode closed with a cliff-hanger in the style of the old movie serials.

Our heroes were usually summoned into action by the desperate Commissioner Gordon over the Batphone, or by the Batsignal in the sky. However, if Commissioner Gordon was helpless, his librarian daughter certainly was not. She joined the series late in its run as Batgirl, aboard the Batcycle, with her true identity unknown even to her crime-busting colleagues.

BATTLESTAR GALACTICA/ GALACTICA 1980

US (Universal/Glen A. Larson) Science Fiction. ITV 1980–1/ 1984

Commander Adama .... **Lorne Greene**
Capt. Apollo .... **Richard Hatch**
Lt. Starbuck .... **Dirk Benedict**
Lt. Boomer .... **Herb Jefferson, Jr**
Athena .... **Maren Jensen**
Flt Sgt Jolly .... **Tony Swartz**
Boxey .... **Noah Hathaway**
Col. Tigh .... **Terry Carter**
Cassiopeia .... **Laurette Spang**
Count Baltar .... **John Colicos**
Sheba .... **Anne Lockhart** (*Galactica 1980*)
Capt. Troy .... **Kent McCord** (*Galactica 1980*)
Lt. Dillon .... **Barry Van Dyke** (*Galactica 1980*)
Jamie Hamilton .... **Robyn Douglass** (*Galactica 1980*)
Dr Zee .... **Robbie Risk** (*Galactica 1980*)
                                        Patrick Stuart (*Galactica 1980*)
Col. Sydell .... **Allan Miller** (*Galactica 1980*)
Xavier .... **Richard Lynch** (*Galactica 1980*)

Executive Producer: **Glen A. Larson**
Producers: **John Dykstra, Leslie Stevens**

Much-hyped, expensive imitation of Star Wars,
a cross between the BOOK OF EXODUS *and*
WAGON TRAIN.

In the seventh millennium, 12 of the 13 humanoid civilizations had been wiped out by the treacherous Cylons, enemies of humanoids for a thousand years. A motley convoy of 220 small ships joined the battlestar spaceship *Galactica* in making a break for the last remaining refuge, the mythical 'Golden Planet' (Earth). However, as it meandered through the universe, it was stalked by the Cylons and prone to regular attacks.

Adama was the commander of the ship, a Moses figure aided by his son, Apollo, head of the Viper fighter squadron. Starbuck was the impetuous top-gun pilot, roguishly appealing, especially to Adama's daughter, Athena, the communications officer. Other members of the crew included second-in-command Colonel Tigh, Cassiopeia, the medic, and Boomer, another pilot. Villain of the piece was Count Baltar, who had betrayed the humanoids to the Cylons. The players were not clothed in futuristic garments, but in gowns and tunics reminiscent of Earth's early civilizations. The evil, robotic Cylons, on the other hand, had a chrome appearance and peered in sinister fashion through two red light-beam 'eyes'. The malign nature of the enemy was further emphasized by the batlike wings of its spacecraft, whereas Galactica was more of a comfortable city in space, one mile wide.

The special effects, with lasers and colourful explosions aplenty, were spectacular and handled by producer John Dykstra, who had previously worked on *Star Wars*, but the storylines found plenty of critics. As a result the programme was halted and revamped in a new form known as *Galactica 1980*. This moved the time on 30 years and saw the ship arriving on Earth, only to find the Cylons plotting its destruction. Lorne Greene as Adama was the sole survivor of the original cast. He was now assisted by Captain Troy, a grown-up version of Adama's adopted son, Boxey, a star of the original series.

The pilot episode of *Battlestar Galactica* received a cinema release in the UK, in an attempt to recoup money lost after the series flopped in the USA.

BAVERSTOCK, DONALD
(1924–95)

Influential BBC current affairs producer of the 1950s and 1960s, responsible to no small degree for such programmes as *Highlight*, TONIGHT and THAT WAS THE WEEK THAT WAS. He later became head of BBC 1 before moving on to the fledgling Yorkshire Television, where he was programme director from 1968 to 1973.

BAXENDALE, HELEN
(1971–)

Yorkshire-born, Staffordshire-raised actress seen as Dr Claire Maitland in *Cardiac Arrest* before starring as Cordelia Gray in AN UNSUITABLE JOB FOR A WOMAN and Rachel Bradley in COLD FEET. She also appeared in *Screen One*'s *Truth or Dare* (lawyer Lorna Johnston), *Screen Two*'s *Crossing the Floor* (politician's mistress Ruth Clarke) and *The Investigator* (lesbian military policewoman Caroline Meagher), and has also guested in DANGERFIELD and FRIENDS (Ross's girlfriend, Emily).

BAXTER, RAYMOND
(1922–)

Distinguished BBC presenter, born in Ilford. He has been heard to best effect in coverage of air shows (he was a World War II RAF pilot, which led him to join BFBS and then the BBC), royal occasions and motor sports events. He presented the weekly science programme TOMORROW'S WORLD for 12 years and returned for the retrospective *Tomorrow's World Time Machine* in the 1990s. His other credits have included *Eye On Research* and *The Energy File*, and a guest appearance in THE GOODIES.

BAXTER, STANLEY
(1926–)

Scottish comedian and impersonator, fond of mimicking TV's *grandes dames* and Hollywood idols. Following

his breakthrough in 1950s series like CHELSEA AT NINE and *On the Bright Side*, Baxter launched his long-running sketch series, *The Stanley Baxter Show*, in 1963, and appeared in his own fortnightly comedy, *Baxter on . . .*, which included programmes on travel, television, law, and theatre, a year later. He switched channels in 1972 to present *The Stanley Baxter Picture Show*, the first in a series of specials. *The Stanley Baxter Series* in 1981 took him back to weekly productions, but since then he has been seen only in one-offs once more. He did, however, take the lead role in the children's comedy, *Mr Majeika*.

BAYLDON, GEOFFREY
(1924–)

Leeds-born actor fondly remembered as CATWEAZLE, the 11th-century sorcerer trapped in the 20th century. Among his other TV credits have been Z CARS, THE AVENGERS, THE SAINT, *The Victorians*, EDWARD THE SEVENTH, *Devenish* (Neville Liversedge), ALL CREATURES GREAT AND SMALL, BERGERAC, BLOTT ON THE LANDSCAPE (Ganglion), WORZEL GUMMIDGE (The Crowman), *Star Cops* and CASUALTY, plus numerous single dramas and series.

BAYWATCH
US (Tower 12) Drama. ITV 1990–7

Lt. Mitch Buchannon	David Hasselhoff
Jill Riley	Shawn Weatherly
Craig Pomeroy	Parker Stevenson
Eddie Kramer	Billy Warlock
Shauni McLain	Erika Eleniak
Trevor Cole	Peter Phelps
Gina Pomeroy	Holly Gagnier
Hobie Buchannon	Brandon Call
	Jeremy Jackson
Gayle Buchannon	Wendie Malick
John D. Cort	John Allen Nelson
Lt. Garner Ellerbee	Gregory Alan-Williams
Capt. Don Thorpe	Monte Markham
Harvey Miller	Tom McTigue
Lt. Ben Edwards	Richard Jaeckel
Matt Brody	David Charvet
C. J. Parker	Pamela Anderson/Lee
Lt. Stephanie Holden	Alexandra Paul
Summer Quinn	Nicole Eggert
Jimmy Slade	Kelly Slater
Jackie Quinn	Susan Anton
Caroline Holden	Yasmine Bleeth
Logan Fowler	Jaason Simmons
Cody Madison	David Chokachi
Donna	Donna D'Errico
Neely Capshaw	Gina Lee Nolin
Samantha	Nancy Valen

Thrills and spills with scantily clad LA lifeguards.

The Los Angeles County lifeguards were the stars of this all-action seaside romp, known variously as 'Barewatch' and 'Boobwatch' because of its acres of tanned flesh. Chief hunk and programme mastermind was David

Hasselhoff in the guise of Mitch Buchannon, at the outset a newly installed lieutenant in the seaside patrol force. Working alongside Mitch in the early days were his lawyer friend, Parker Stevenson, and Jill Riley, sadly killed by a shark during the first season. Thorpe was Buchannon's officious captain, and assorted rookie lifeguards milled around the team's Malibu Beach headquarters. These included Shauni McLain, Trevor Cole and Eddie Kramer. Part of the fabric was Mitch's son, Hobie, who lived with his dad following Mitch's marriage break-up; and officers from the LAPD beach patrol squad, particularly Garner Ellerbee, were also seen. John D. Cort ran the local beach shop, Sam's Surf and Dive.

Despite success outside the USA, *Baywatch* was cancelled after just one season. Hasselhoff and a consortium of three others pooled resources to finance the production of more episodes, which they sold into syndication and to networks overseas. The almost cult following the series enjoyed in the UK no doubt swayed their decision. With the fresh set-up, new characters appeared, including Ben Edwards, a weather-beaten but good-natured lifeguard, and young joker Harvey Miller. Matt Brody, C. J. Parker and Stephanie Holden were among the later recruits. From 1995, in the UK the series was billed as *New Baywatch*. A spin-off series, *Baywatch Nights*, in which Mitch became a detective, was screened in 1996. *Baywatch* was itself revamped in 2000 with a switch of location to *Baywatch Hawaii*.

BBC
(British Broadcasting Corporation)

Britain's major broadcasting organization was founded as the British Broadcasting Company in 1922, with executives drawn from the ranks of radio receiver manufacturers who had been invited to provide a broadcasting service by the Postmaster General. Then, as today, funding was provided by a licence fee, payable by all users of radio (now TV) sets, at a rate set by Parliament. To this day, neither the BBC's radio nor television service has accepted paid advertising. The company was reconstituted as the British Broadcasting Corporation (a public corporation, working 'as a trustee for the national interest') on 1 January 1927, and since that time has derived its authority from a Royal Charter. The Charter has been considered for renewal on several occasions, each time instigating a heated debate about the role of the BBC and its funding.

Organizationally, the BBC is headed by a board of Governors, all appointed by the Queen on the advice of the Government, for a five-year term. Day-to-day control is assumed by the Director-General and his executives. The BBC's first Director-General, and effectively the father of public service broadcasting in the UK, was John (later Lord) Reith, who instilled in programme-makers his belief in the need to 'Educate, Inform, Entertain'.

The BBC began television experiments in 1932, from a studio in Broadcasting House, Portland Place, London. On 2 November 1936 the Corporation inaugurated the world's first regular high-definition television service, but this was suspended on 1 September 1939 for defence reasons, with war imminent. It resumed on 7 June 1946, with the same Mickey Mouse cartoon that had closed the station down seven years earlier. A major milestone in the development of the television service was the Coronation of Queen Elizabeth II in 1953. The BBC covered the proceedings live, and sales of television sets rocketed. However, its monopoly position as the UK's only television broadcaster was broken with the launch of ITV in 1955.

On 29 June 1960 the BBC opened its new Television Centre in Shepherd's Bush, West London, having previously broadcast from Alexandra Palace and the old film studios at Lime Grove. On 20 April 1964 the Corporation's second channel, BBC 2, was launched (although a power cut curtailed its opening night). Its focus from the beginning has been on minority-interest programmes, innovation and education. Colour broadcasts began on BBC 2 on 1 July 1967 (initially only five hours a week). The colour service was officially inaugurated on 2 December of the same year and spread to BBC 1 (and ITV) on 15 November 1969. Both BBC channels have allowed for regional opt-out programmes, to cover local news, current affairs, sports and entertainments. These are prepared by a network of BBC studios around the country. In 1991, BBC World Service Television was launched. This largely satellite channel beams BBC news and entertainment programmes around much of the world, 24 hours a day. Also in the 1990s, NICAM stereo sound was introduced and, with the arrival of digital broadcasting, the BBC launched a tranche of new channels: BBC News 24, BBC Choice, BBC Knowledge and BBC Parliament.

In technical terms and also programme-wise, the BBC has a reputation second to none in world broadcasting. Its news coverage has been viewed as authoritative, and its drama output – particularly its period classics – is legendary. However, the 1990s witnessed a degree of turmoil within the organization. Under the 1989 Broadcasting Bill, 25 per cent of all programmes now have to be supplied by independent contractors. This inevitably led to an immediate loss of BBC jobs. Another consequence was 'Producer Choice'. This system of allocating cash to BBC programme-makers to buy technical and other services, from either within the BBC or without, was introduced by Director-General John Birt, the man charged with leading the Corporation through its next Royal Charter renewal, in 1996. It did not prove popular with BBC employees. However, the BBC duly gained its seventh Royal Charter and Birt was eventually succeeded as Director-General in January 2000 by Greg Dyke, who immediately aimed to slash bureaucracy and declared his support for programme-makers.

DIRECTORS-GENERAL OF THE BBC

John Reith	1927–38
Frederick Ogilvie	1938–42
Robert Foot	1942–4
Cecil Graves	1942–3
William Haley	1944–52
Ian Jacob	1952–9
Hugh Carleton Greene	1960–9
Charles Curran	1969–77
Ian Trethowan	1977–82

Alasdair Milne 1982–7
Michael Checkland 1987–93
John Birt 1993–2000
Greg Dyke 2000–

BBC CHOICE

Digital, general-interest, free channel launched by the BBC on 23 September 1998, its first programme hosted by Clive Anderson. The channel feeds off BBC 1 and BBC 2, offering selected repeats of the week's programming from these two channels, as well as classic repeats from further back. It also supplements mainstream BBC programmes by offering behind-the-scenes glimpses into production, and comment programmes immediately after the main channels have aired a programme worthy of debate. Extended coverage of sports events terminated by BBCs 1 and 2 has also been a feature. There were also regional opt-outs initially, with separate programming between 10 p.m. and midnight (and occasionally at other times) for BBC Choice, BBC Choice Scotland, BBC Choice Wales and BBC Choice Northern Ireland, these channels being available to the whole of the UK.

BBC KNOWLEDGE

Free-to-view, digital channel launched on 1 June 1999. Immediately embracing all the latest interactive technology, including Internet involvement, the channel set out to revolutionize learning by tapping into viewers' interests rather than pumping out stodgy school fare. Among the major items initially were *The Fix* – variously covering the subjects of languages, history and science – and *The Ology Hour*. More recently, themed days have been introduced, with programmes repeated throughout the day.

BBC NEWS 24

Self-explanatory, all-day and all-night news service provided free by the BBC. The channel was launched on 9 November 1997 and was initially available only via cable networks. It is now broadcast digitally, too. As well as constant news, weather and sports bulletins, the channel features more in-depth programming, like *Hard Talk* (with Tim Sebastian) and *Simpson's World* (John Simpson).

BBC PARLIAMENT

Free BBC digital channel covering events live from the House of Commons and the House of Lords. It was launched in 1999.

BBC TELEVISION NEWSREEL, THE
UK (BBC) News. BBC 1948–54

Editor: **D. A. Smith**
Producer: **Harold Cox**

News events from around the world.

Hardly topical, and consisting largely of fading news items, *The BBC Television Newsreel* was BBC TV's first attempt at presenting news footage. Previously, the news had been conveyed in sound only, radio fashion, and up-to-date, in-vision news bulletins were still six years away (they began in 1954). This programme filled the gap, using the style of cinema newsreels, but running for 15 minutes instead of ten and including fewer stories. International items were incorporated, thanks to an exchange deal with America's NBC network. The same programme was initially transmitted four times a week, on Mondays, Wednesdays and twice on Saturdays.

BBC TELEVISION SHAKESPEARE, THE
UK (BBC) Drama Anthology. BBC 2 1978–85

Producers: **Cedric Messina, Jonathan Miller, Shaun Sutton**

Ambitious staging of all 37 Shakespeare plays.

Creating the definitive television version of Shakespeare's *oeuvre* proved even more difficult than imagined when the BBC launched the project in 1978. Some productions ran into 'technical' troubles and the numerous styles applied by directors resulted in a rather piecemeal effect for the series as a whole. Some plays, for instance, were totally studio-bound, while others were shot on location. Cedric Messina was the brains behind the concept and took charge of production for the first two years. Jonathan Miller was drafted in to continue the project and Shaun Sutton completed affairs.

Among the stars appearing over the seven years were Anthony Hopkins, Helen Mirren, Derek Jacobi, John Gielgud, Wendy Hiller, James Bolam, Virginia McKenna, Timothy West and Anthony Quayle. Perhaps the most unusual casting was of John Cleese as *The Taming of the Shrew*'s Petruchio. Desmond Davis, Herbert Wise, Basil Coleman and David Giles were among the directors employed.

BBC–3
UK (BBC) Comedy. BBC 1 1965–6

John Bird, Robert Robinson, Lynda Baron, David Battley, John Fortune, Bill Oddie, Alan Bennett, Leonard Rossiter, Roy Dotrice

Producer: **Ned Sherrin**

Controversial programme of topical humour and debate.

Son of THAT WAS THE WEEK THAT WAS, by way of NOT

SO MUCH A PROGRAMME, MORE A WAY OF LIFE, this late-night satire show is chiefly remembered today for allowing the first known use of the 'F' word on national television. It came in 1965 during an interview with Kenneth Tynan about theatre censorship. Such frank discussions mingled with sketches, filmed inserts and music in the programme plan, but the show never achieved the heights of *TW3*, despite employing writers like David Frost, Christopher Booker, John Mortimer and Keith Waterhouse. Supporting the principals on screen were the likes of Malcolm Muggeridge, Patrick Campbell, Harvey Orkin, Denis Norden and Norman St John Stevas.

BEACHAM, STEPHANIE
(1947–)

Casablanca-born actress often seen in the determined female role. Her most prominent part has been as Sable Colby in DYNASTY and THE COLBYS, transatlantic success arriving after several notable performances on British television. Among these were the parts of Rose Millar in TENKO and Connie in the series of the same name. Her earlier credits included guest appearances in THE SAINT, ARMCHAIR THEATRE, CALLAN, JASON KING, UFO, THE PROTECTORS, *Marked Personal* and HADLEIGH. More recently, she has been seen in the US sitcom, *Sister Kate*, and as Mrs Peacock in CLUEDO, Molly Carter in *Jilly Cooper's Riders*, Dr Kristin Westphalen in *Seaquest DSV* and Dorothea Grant in *No Bananas*.

BEADLE, JEREMY
MBE (1948–)

Bearded British presenter of audience participation shows, especially those involving pranks, stunts and hidden cameras. Breaking into television as one of the four original presenters of GAME FOR A LAUGH, Beadle has since hosted *Beadle's About*, *Beadle's Box of Tricks*, *People Do the Funniest Things*, YOU'VE BEEN FRAMED and *Win Beadle's Money*. He has also worked as a writer and consultant on other programmes.

BEAN, SEAN
(1958–)

Sheffield-born actor with a Shakespearean stage background. On television he starred as Lovelace in *Clarissa*, Mellors in *Lady Chatterley*, Paul in *A Woman's Guide to Adultery*, Dominic O'Brien in CATHERINE COOKSON's *The Fifteen Streets* and Richard Sharpe in SHARPE. Other credits include INSPECTOR MORSE and Andy McNab in *Bravo Two Zero*. Bean's second wife was actress Melanie Hill and his third wife was his *Sharpe* co-star, Abigail Cruttenden.

BEATON, NORMAN
(1934–94)

Guyanese actor, star of the barber shop series DESMOND'S (Desmond Ambrose). His earlier work took in leading roles in EMPIRE ROAD (Everton Bennett) and THE FOSTERS (Samuel Foster), and he was also seen in *Dead Head*, among other dramas.

BEAUTY AND THE BEAST
US (Republic Pictures) Adventure. ITV 1988–91

Assistant DA Catherine Chandler	**Linda Hamilton**
Vincent	**Ron Perlman**
Father	**Roy Dotrice**
Deputy DA Joe Maxwell	**Jay Acavone**
Edie	**Ren Woods**
Kipper	**Cory Danziger**
Mouse	**David Greenlee**
Diana Bennett	**Jo Anderson**
Gabriel	**Stephen McHattie**
Elliott Burch	**Edward Albert**

Creator: **Ron Koslow**
Executive Producers: **Ron Koslow, Paul Junger Witt, Tony Thomas, Stephen Kurzfeld**

A beautiful girl's life is saved by a deformed man, who then protects her in her fight against crime.

This adventure series had links with both the fairytale world and *The Phantom of the Opera*. When attractive attorney Catherine Chandler was attacked and left for dead in Central Park, New York, her life was saved by the strangely deformed Vincent (his face was marked like a lion), who took her to his underground refuge and nursed her back to health. When she returned to civilization, the love and the strong telepathic bond which had grown between them allowed Vincent to spring to her assistance whenever she fell into danger.

Vincent, for all his grotesque looks, was a compassionate, gentle soul and a lover of poetry. But he lived among the shadows, hitching rides on top of tube trains. Abandoned as a child, he had been taken in by the people who lived in the catacombs beneath Manhattan ('Tunnel World'), where he had been raised by a reclusive genius known as Father. Kipper and Mouse were Father's helpers.

After an initially platonic relationship, Catherine and Vincent fell in love and the fairytale continued until Catherine was kidnapped and murdered by Gabriel, head of a criminal organization, but not before she had given birth to Vincent's son. Diana Bennett was brought in by Catherine's boss to investigate the case, and she became Vincent's new friend. Assisted by businessman Elliott Burch, they tracked down and killed Gabriel, leaving Vincent and his son to retreat to their peaceful underworld home.

BECKINSALE, RICHARD

(1947–79)

Affable comedy actor whose tragic early death cut short a TV career that had already produced some classic roles. He is probably best recalled as Ronnie Barker's cellmate, Godber, in PORRIDGE and *Going Straight*, although he was just as popular as the sex-starved Geoffrey opposite Paula Wilcox in THE LOVERS and Rigsby's medical student tenant, Alan Moore, in RISING DAMP. Among his early work was the kids' sketch show, *Elephant's Eggs in a Rhubarb Tree*. His last series was *Bloomers*, in which he played Stan, a resting actor who became a partner in a florist's. His two daughters, Samantha, from his first marriage, and Kate, from his second marriage to actress Judy Loe, are both also actresses.

BED-SIT GIRL, THE

UK (BBC) Situation Comedy. BBC 1 1965–6

Sheila Ross	Sheila Hancock
Dilys	Dilys Laye
David	Derek Nimmo
Liz	Hy Hazell

Writers: **Ronald Chesney, Ronald Wolfe**
Producers: **Duncan Wood, Graeme Muir**

A single girl dreams of a more glamorous life.

Living in a bed-sit and working as a typist didn't amount to much for dreamy, disorganized Sheila Ross. She envied the exotic lifestyle of her air stewardess neighbour, Dilys, with whom she fought for eligible bachelors with little success. When Dilys moved on after the first season, Sheila gained a boyfriend in the form of David, her next-door neighbour, but her girly chats continued with the worldly-wise Liz, who also lived in the house.

BEENY, CHRISTOPHER

(1941–)

British actor whose first TV outing was as Lenny (aged 12) in THE GROVE FAMILY, the grandmother of all UK soaps, way back in 1954. However, most viewers remember him as Edward, the footman, in UPSTAIRS, DOWNSTAIRS, or as Thora Hird's hapless nephew, Billy, in the funereal sitcom IN LOVING MEMORY. He briefly played Geoffrey, Paula Wilcox's neighbour, in MISS JONES AND SON, and was also seen as Tony in the 1970s revival of THE RAG TRADE, taking on the foreman role vacated by Reg Varney. Other appearances have included DIXON OF DOCK GREEN, EMERGENCY – WARD 10, ARMCHAIR THEATRE, Z CARS, THE PLANE MAKERS and the kids' programme PLAY AWAY.

BEGGAR MY NEIGHBOUR

UK (BBC) Situation Comedy. BBC 1 1967–8

Gerald Garvey	Peter Jones
	Desmond Walter-Ellis
Rose Garvey	June Whitfield
Harry Butt	Reg Varney
Lana Butt	Pat Coombs

Writers: **Ken Hoare, Mike Sharland**
Producers: **David Croft, Eric Fawcett**

Neighbour and family conflict in the London suburbs.

Gerald Garvey lived with his wife, Rose, in Muswell Hill. Rose's sister, Lana Butt, and her husband, Harry, lived next door, but things were far from cosy because of their unequal prosperity. Harry was an overpaid fitter, while Gerald was an underpaid junior executive, which made the flashy Butts the haves and the impoverished Garveys the have-nots. The Garveys' attempts to keep up with the Joneses (or Butts) provided most of the humour. The programme stemmed from a 1966 COMEDY PLAYHOUSE pilot and ran for three series.

BEGGARMAN, THIEF

See RICH MAN, POOR MAN.

BEIDERBECKE AFFAIR, THE/THE BEIDERBECKE TAPES/THE BEIDERBECKE CONNECTION

UK (Yorkshire) Drama. ITV 1985/1987/1988

Trevor Chaplin	James Bolam
Jill Swinburne	Barbara Flynn
DS/DI Hobson	Dominic Jephcott *(Affair/Connection)*
Mr Carter	Dudley Sutton
Mr Wheeler	Keith Smith
Big Al	Terence Rigby *(Affair/Connection)*
Little Norm	Danny Schiller *(Affair/Connection)*
Chief Supt. Forrest	Colin Blakely *(Affair)*
Sylvia	Beryl Reid *(Tapes)*
Peterson	Malcolm Storry *(Tapes)*
John	David Battley *(Tapes)*
Bella Atkinson	Maggie Jones *(Tapes)*
Ivan	Patrick Drury *(Connection)*

Writer: **Alan Plater**
Executive Producers: **David Cunliffe** *(Affair/Tapes)*, **Keith Richardson** *(Connection)*
Producers: **Anne W. Gibbons** *(Affair)*, **Michael Glynn** *(Tapes/Connection)*

Two schoolteachers unravel a web of corruption, against a background of classic jazz.

In *The Beiderbecke Affair*, Leeds comprehensive woodwork master Trevor Chaplin and his English teacher girlfriend Jill Swinburne had really rather modest ambitions. He was looking for a set of Bix Beiderbecke records, following a mix-up in his mail order, and she was seeking election to the local council on a conservation ticket. However, fate took a hand to lead them into a murky world of underhand dealing, bureaucracy and corruption, bringing their relationship into crisis and themselves into conflict with the police.

Such was the success of this quirky, light-hearted six-parter that a sequel, *The Beiderbecke Tapes*, appeared two years later. In this two-part tale, Trevor bought some jazz tapes from the barman of an empty pub, only to find that one contained a recording of plans to dump nuclear waste in the Yorkshire Dales. Having survived that escapade, he and Jill resurfaced for a third and final time in the four-part *The Beiderbecke Connection*, which brought them into contact with a Russian refugee and saw them attract suspicion from the authorities.

Music played a sizeable part in these genial tales of intrigue in which the hero and heroine travelled around in a beat-up old motor, reluctantly playing detective and running into all kinds of odd characters. They were accompanied by the sounds of jazz-great Bix Beiderbecke, re-created for the series by Kenny Baker, with new music by Frank Ricotti. Writer Alan Plater had earlier contributed a similar series under the title of *Get Lost!*. Screened in 1981, this four-parter saw two teachers, played by Alun Armstrong and Bridget Turner, investigating missing persons.

BELL, ANN
(1940–)

Cheshire-born actress, best known as Marion Jefferson, the British group leader, in TENKO and seen later as Gracie Ellis, the finishing school headmistress, in the rock'n'roll retrospective, *Head Over Heels*, with plenty of other credits before and after. These have included the parts of Maria in the 1965 adaptation of FOR WHOM THE BELL TOLLS and Mary Webster in the 1988 sitcom, *Double First*, as well as appearances in THE SAINT, MR ROSE, CALLAN, DANGER MAN, THE BARON, *War and Peace*, *Tumbledown*, *Christabel*, INSPECTOR MORSE, MEDICS, AGATHA CHRISTIE'S POIROT, DOCTOR FINLAY, CASUALTY, *The Ice House* and *The Woman in White*. She is married to actor Robert Lang.

BELL, MARTIN
OBE (1938–)

Experienced BBC reporter, its diplomatic correspondent, chief North American correspondent and foreign affairs correspondent, among other posts, during his 35 years with the Corporation. He is best known, however, for his work as a war reporter, covering 11 major conflicts from Vietnam to Bosnia, in which he was hit by shrapnel and wounded in 1992. After recovery, Bell decided to leave the BBC and stand as independent, 'anti-sleaze' Parliamentary candidate for Neil Hamilton's Tatton constituency in 1997, which he won with the support of the Labour and Liberal Democrat parties. His distinctive attire has earned him the nickname 'the man in the white suit'.

BELL, TOM
(1932–)

Liverpool-born actor, often seen in dry, unsmiling roles. His credits have included ARMCHAIR THEATRE, PLAY FOR TODAY, HOLOCAUST, REILLY – ACE OF SPIES, ANGELS, *The Rainbow*, *Chancer*, SPENDER, *King's Royal*, CATHERINE COOKSON'S *The Cinder Path* and PRIME SUSPECT (DS Bill Otley). His other major parts have varied from menacing hero/villain Frank Ross in OUT and Walter Morel in *Sons and Lovers* to waxworks owner Harry Nash in the sitcom *Hope It Rains* and the patriotic Thomas Slater in *No Bananas*.

BELLAMY, DAVID
OBE (1933–)

Enthusiastic, bearded, London-born naturalist, much mimicked by TV impressionists. After a few early programmes like *Bellamy on Botany* and *Bellamy's Britain* for the BBC, and then prime-time exposure on ITV's DON'T ASK ME, he launched into a run of successful, light-hearted documentary series, which included *Bellamy's Europe*, the award-winning *Botanic Man*, *Up a Gumtree*, *Bellamy's Backyard Safari* (in which he was shrunk by special effects to explore the wilderness of a typical garden), *Bellamy's New World*, *Bellamy's Bugle*, *Bellamy on Top of the World*, *Bellamy's Bird's Eye View* and *Bellamy Rides Again*.

BELLE AND SEBASTIAN
France (Gaumont Television Paris) Children's Drama
BBC 1 1967–8

Sebastian	**Mehdi**
César	**Edmond Beauchamp**
Guillaume	**Jean Michel Audin**
Jean	**Dominique Blondeau**
Angélina	**Paloma Matta**
Céléstine	**Hélène Dieudonné**
Norbert	**Morice Poli**
Pierre Maréchal	**Claude Giraud** (*Horses*)
Sylvia	**Louise Marleau** (*Horses*)

A French gypsy boy befriends a Pyrenean mountain dog and together they enjoy a number of adventures.

Eight-year-old Sebastian, an abandoned gypsy boy, had been found by old César and brought up on his farm, alongside his own grandchildren, Jean and Angélina. One day, tales began to arrive in their French Alpine village, Saint-Martin, close to the Italian border, of a big, wild, white dog which was on the loose in the mountains. Villagers were suspicious of the beast but little Sebastian, using his gypsy know-how, brought the dog under control, named it Belle and proceeded to wander the hills with his new friend, rooting out smugglers and averting avalanches.

Made in France and dubbed into English, the 13-part

serial was a heart-warming element in the BBC's children's output in 1967. A second series of the same length, entitled *Belle, Sebastian and the Horses*, followed a year later. The young star of both series, known simply as Mehdi, was the son of French film star Cécile Aubry, who was also involved in the production.

BELLINGHAM, LYNDA
(1948–)

Canadian-born actress, the mum in the Oxo commercials, but already familiar to TV viewers from series such as GENERAL HOSPITAL (Nurse Hilda Price), Z CARS, *The Pink Medicine Show*, *Tell Tarby* and *The Fuzz* (WPC Purvis). She also guested in DOCTOR WHO, ANGELS, DON'T FORGET TO WRITE, and THE SWEENEY, and replaced Carol Drinkwater as Helen Herriot in ALL CREATURES GREAT AND SMALL, before becoming Faith Grayshot in the comedy SECOND THOUGHTS and its sequel, *Faith in the Future*. She was also Mrs Lupin in *Martin Chuzzlewit* and starred as Penny Martin in *Reach for the Moon*.

BELLISARIO, DONALD P.

The creator and executive producer of MAGNUM PI, *Tales of the Gold Monkey* and AIRWOLF and later founder of his own production company, Bellisarius, responsible for such hits as QUANTUM LEAP. His earlier work took in KOJAK (as writer) and BATTLESTAR GALACTICA (as writer/producer).

BEN CASEY
US (Bing Crosby) Medical Drama. ITV 1961–7

Dr Ben Casey	**Vince Edwards**
Dr David Zorba	**Sam Jaffe**
Dr Maggie Graham	**Bettye Ackerman**
Dr Ted Hoffman	**Harry Landers**
Nick Kanavaras	**Nick Dennis**
Nurse Wills	**Jeanne Bates**
Jane Hancock	**Stella Stevens**
Dr Mike Rogers	**Ben Piazza**
Dr Daniel Niles Freeland	**Franchot Tone**
Dr Terry McDaniel	**Jim McMullan**
Sally Welden	**Marlyn Mason**

Creator: **James Moser**
Producer: **Matthew Rapf**

A gifted but brooding young surgeon works at a large hospital.

Unlike the baby-faced Dr Kildare, his screen rival in the early 1960s, Ben Casey was surly, tough and determined. He worked as a neurosurgeon at the County General Hospital and was very much a rebel who would happily flout the rules if it was in his patient's interest. His stabilizing influence, however, was the venerable Dr Zorba, a white-haired, mad scientist type, whom Casey respected enormously. It was Zorba who spoke the dramatic words which opened each programme and summed up the extremes of hospital life: 'Man; Woman; Birth; Death; Infinity'. When Zorba left, the Chief of Surgery role was assumed by Dr Freeland. Other familiar faces were Nick Kanavaras, the hospital orderly, Dr Ted Hoffman and Nurse Wills.

Ben Casey was a bold series which was never afraid to tackle difficult subjects like abortion. It was also shot in such a way (extreme close-ups, etc.) that the true tension of critical medicine was effectively conveyed. Romance was kept to the sidelines and, for all his macho appeal, Casey was only rarely linked with a woman. His relationship with anaesthetist Maggie Graham was softly alluded to, but his most dramatic entanglement came with beautiful Jane Hancock, a coma victim, for whose attentions he fought with Dr Mike Rogers.

Ben Casey became less convincing and 'soapier' towards the end of its run and finally drew to a close in the USA in 1966, five months before DR KILDARE. During its five years on air it had made a sex symbol out of the profusely hairy Vince Edwards, a handsome young actor discovered by Bing Crosby, whose company produced the series.

BENAUD, RICHIE
(1930–)

Australian former leg-spin bowler, batsman and Test captain who has become one of the most respected commentators on the game of cricket, working for Channel Nine in Australia and for the BBC (1963–99) and, latterly, Channel 4 in the UK. His first career (alongside cricket) was as a crime reporter.

BENEDICT, DIRK
(Dirk Niewoehner; 1944–)

Known in the 1980s as Faceman in THE A-TEAM, Dirk Benedict had earlier appeared on the small screen in the short-lived cop series *Chopper One*, before taking on the mantle of Lt. Starbuck in the sci-fi spectacular, BATTLESTAR GALACTICA. He has also starred in various TV movies.

BENNETT, ALAN
(1934–)

Bespectacled, gently spoken, Leeds-born playwright, actor and narrator, a former *Beyond the Fringe* star, also seen in the satire show BBC-3 and Jonathan Miller's TV version of *Alice in Wonderland* when starting out in television. In the 1990s, he played historian Hugh Trevor-Roper in the drama *Selling Hitler*, provided the voice of Mole in the ITV animation of *The Wind in the Willows*, hosted *The Abbey*, a three-part documentary about Westminster Abbey for BBC 2, and took the role of Sillery in *A Dance to the Music of Time*. However, it has been for his collection of TV dramas that he has won most plaudits. The highlights have included *A Day Out* (1972), *Sunset Across the Bay* (1975), *A Little Outing* (1977),

One Fine Day (1979), *Objects of Affection* (1982), *The Insurance Man* (1986), *A Question of Attribution* (1991) and *An Englishman Abroad* (1983; the tale of a chance meeting between spy Guy Burgess and actress Coral Browne). He has also written a series of comedy sketches, *On the Margin* (1966), an anthology series, *By Alan Bennett – Six Plays* (1978), and received acclaim for TALKING HEADS (1988) and its follow-up, *Talking Heads 2* (1998). These seasons of monologues epitomized Bennett's flair for character observation and realistic dialogue, as well as offering performers like Thora Hird and Bennett himself the chance to shine. More monologues followed in *Telling Tales* in 2000, in which his own early life in Leeds came under the spotlight.

BENNETT, HARVE
(Harve Fischman; 1930–)

US producer of action series like THE SIX MILLION DOLLAR MAN, THE BIONIC WOMAN, GEMINI MAN and THE INVISIBLE MAN, as well as the mini-series, RICH MAN, POOR MAN.

BENNETT, HYWEL
(1944–)

Welsh actor, very popular in British films of the 1960s, whose most durable television role was as the un-employed graduate James SHELLEY. One of his earliest TV appearances was in a 1960s DOCTOR WHO story and he has also played memorable parts in *Malice Afore-thought* (Dr Bickleigh), PENNIES FROM HEAVEN (Tom), TINKER, TAILOR, SOLDIER, SPY (Ricki Tarr), KARAOKE (Arthur 'Pig' Mailion), *Harpur and Iles* (Desmond Iles) and *Neverwhere* (Mr Croup), plus various plays and films, including the sci-fi fantasy, *Artemis 81*. He was formerly married to READY, STEADY, GO! presenter Cathy McGowan and is the brother of actor Alun Lewis.

BENNETT, LENNIE
(Michael Berry; 1938–)

Northern comedian and game show host, formerly one half of Lennie and Jerry (with Jerry Stevens). He first appeared on THE GOOD OLD DAYS in 1966 after working for a while as a journalist, and his later credits have included *Lennie and Jerry*, THE COMEDIANS, *London Night Out*, *Starburst*, *Bennett Bites Back* and *All Star Secrets*. He also hosted *Punchlines* and *Lucky Ladders*.

BENNY, JACK
(Benjamin Kubelsky; 1894–1974)

One of TV's earliest celebrities, Jack Benny's career began in music in the 1920s. As a vaudeville violinist, he billed himself as Ben K. Benny, soon adding humour to his routine and becoming Jack Benny. Although he made a number of films, his greatest success pre-TV came on American radio, where he finely tuned the character

traits that were to become so popular later. Playing him-self in the long-running *Jack Benny Show* (with announcer Don Wilson and Eddie 'Rochester' Anderson, his valet, in support), he quickly gained a reputation for his stinginess, his lied-about age (always 39) and appalling violin playing. He was married to his some-time co-star, Mary Livingstone.

BENTINE, MICHAEL
CBE (1922–96)

Watford-born, part-Peruvian comedian and one-time Goon, the deviser and presenter of some of TV's most bizarre comedy shows. These included *The Bumblies* (a 1954 puppet animation for kids, featuring creatures from the planet Bumble), *Yes, It's The Cathode-Ray Tube Show!* (1957, with Peter Sellers), *After Hours* (1958–9), the influential IT'S A SQUARE WORLD (1960), *All Square* (1966) and *Michael Bentine's Potty Time* (with more puppets in 1973, spun off from *Michael Bentine Time* the previous year). He also hosted the hobbies programme *Madabout* and one of his last credits was providing voices for another puppet series, *The Great Bong*.

BENTLEY, JOHN
(1916–)

British film actor who re-emerged in the 1970s as Hugh Mortimer, Meg Richardson's ill-fated new husband in CROSSROADS. Playing the millionaire businessman, he had attempted to win Meg's hand as far back as 1965, but received the brush-off. Reconciled, their 1975 wedding was one of the TV events of the year. Previously, Bentley had starred as Patrol Inspector Paul Derek in the 1950s jungle adventure series AFRICAN PATROL. His TV port-folio also includes *Strictly Personal* and ARMCHAIR THEATRE.

BERGERAC
UK/Australia (BBC/The Seven Network) Police Drama.
BBC 1 1981–91

DS Jim Bergerac	**John Nettles**
Charlie Hungerford	**Terence Alexander**
Chief Insp. Barney Crozier	**Sean Arnold**
Francine Leland	**Cecile Paoli**
Deborah Bergerac	**Deborah Grant**
Marianne Bellshade	**Celia Imrie**
Susan Young	**Louise Jameson**
Philippa Vale	**Liza Goddard**
DC Terry Wilson	**Geoffrey Leesley**
Danielle Aubry	**Therese Liotard**
Insp. Victor Deffand	**Roger Sloman**
DC Willy Pettit	**John Telfer**
DC Ben Lomas	**David Kershaw**
Diamante Lil	**Mela White**
Charlotte	**Annette Badland**
Peggy Masters	**Nancy Mansfield**
Dr Lejeune	**Jonathan Adams**

Creator: Robert Banks Stewart
Producers: Robert Banks Stewart, Jonathan Alwyn,
George Gallaccio, Juliet Grimm

A single-minded copper roots out smugglers and swindlers in Jersey.

Jim Bergerac did not have the best credentials to be a policeman, physically or mentally – a gammy leg caused him to limp, and he had once been a drunk. His life had been in ruins, with his wife, Deborah, leaving him and his career in the balance. Turning over a new leaf, he became the Channel Islands' most successful detective, displaying genuine determination to get to the bottom of cases.

Working for the Bureau des Etrangers (which dealt with crimes involving non-island folk) and tearing around in a 1947 Triumph sports car, his gaze fell upon visitors and tourists up to no good, and he was never afraid of getting physical in the search for justice. His superiors and colleagues (like Barney Crozier) regularly questioned his methods, but always supportive was his amiable ex-father-in-law, Charlie Hungerford, a businessman constantly on the fringe of dodgy deals.

Despite his new dedication to the job, Bergerac was never far from the temptation of the bottle, especially when there was trouble in his personal life, as the girls came and went. First there was tourist officer Francine Leland, and then lawyer Marianne Bellshade, before estate agent Susan Young provided some stability for a while. Their relationship ended with her murder. There was even more spark in his occasional encounters with Philippa Vale, a glamorous jewel-thief. It was Bergerac's obsession with a woman which eventually brought the series to a close. Jim's relationship with French girl Danielle Aubry resulted in his leaving Jersey to work as a private investigator in Provence. Though the final series saw Jim return to the island on several assignments, it was only a matter of time before the programme finally called it a day.

Bergerac employed a number of semi-regulars who ensured continuity during the programme's 10-year run. These included Diamante Lil, proprietress of the bar, Lil's Place, and pathologist Dr Lejeune. Such longevity was not anticipated when the series began. It was intended as a short filler and was developed only because Trevor Eve had refused to continue with SHOESTRING. *Bergerac* was also good for Jersey. It gave the island's tourist trade an enormous lift. John Nettles, who had become to Jersey what Steve McGarrett had been to Hawaii and Inspector Morse was to become to Oxford, also made it his home.

BERLE, MILTON
(Mendel Berlinger; 1908–)

Although his name means little to younger British viewers, Milton Berle was 'Mr Television' to US audiences in the 1950s. A former silent-movie star as a child and later an established vaudevillian, he broke into television in 1948 as host of the variety show, *The Texaco Star Theatre* (later *The Milton Berle Show*). So popular were his brash comic sketches, buffoonery, outrageous costumes and awful puns that NBC quickly signed him up on a 30-year contract. His best years were in the early 1950s and his humour soon dated, but he continued to appear sporadically until the 1980s. British viewers may have caught 'Uncle Miltie' as guest star in THE DEFENDERS, F TROOP (Wise Owl), BATMAN (Louie the Lilac), in some episodes of THE LOVE BOAT, the comedy compilation *Just for Laughs,* or in one of his TV movies.

BERLUSCONI, SILVIO
(1936–)

Italian media magnate and owner of the AC Milan football club who became his country's Prime Minister for a while in 1994 and was re-elected to the post in 2001. Berlusconi's television interests began almost by chance when he established a small closed-circuit station in the Milan suburb that he was developing as part of his real-estate business. This grew into TeleMilano, which evolved into the national network, Canale 5, following the deregulation of television in Italy. He subsequently added two more commercial channels to his empire, Retequattro and Italia 1 (giving himself three national networks to match the three controlled by the state-owned RAI corporation), as well as pioneering pay TV in Italy via his shareholding in Telepiù. Berlusconi has also had interests in Spanish television, through Tele 5, and France, via La Cinq. His TV and publishing businesses are handled by his company, Fininvest.

BERMAN, MONTY
(1913–)

British TV producer of action series for ITC, working closely with Robert S. Baker in developing programmes like THE SAINT, THE BARON and GIDEON'S WAY, and with Dennis Spooner on RANDALL AND HOPKIRK (DECEASED), DEPARTMENT S and THE CHAMPIONS.

BERNSTEIN, Lord SIDNEY
(1899–1993)

British film and television executive who, after building up his father's cinema chain (and introducing the idea of a Saturday matinee for kids), worked as a consultant for the Ministry of Information in World War II. Later he produced three films for Alfred Hitchcock and went on to found GRANADA TELEVISION (and the whole Granada group) with his brother, Cecil. Granada (the name was inspired by a walking holiday in Spain) introduced commercial television to the North of England in 1956, and Bernstein succeeded in running it almost as a family business for many years. He was made a life peer in 1969.

BERRY, NICK
(1963–)

Former child actor whose best-known television work has been as Simon 'Wicksy' Wicks in EASTENDERS, PC Nick Rowan in HEARTBEAT and harbour master Mike Nicholls in *Harbour Lights*. Other credits have included THE GENTLE TOUCH, *Box of Delights*, CLUEDO, and the single dramas *Paparazzo* (photographer Rick Caulker), *Respect* (ex-boxer Bobby Carr), *Black Velvet Band* (Martin Tusco) and *The Mystery of Men* (Colin Dunbar). He also runs his own production company, Valentine Productions. Berry's wife is actress Rachel Robertson.

BERYL'S LOT
UK (Yorkshire) Comedy Drama. ITV 1973–7

Beryl Humphries	**Carmel McSharry**
Tom Humphries	**Mark Kingston**
	George Selway
Rosie Humphries	**Verna Harvey**
Jack Humphries	**Brian Capron**
Babs Humphries	**Anita Carey**
Trevor Tonks	**Tony Caunter**
Vi Tonks	**Barbara Mitchell**
Horace Harris	**Robert Keegan**
Wully Harris	**Annie Leake**
Charlie Mills	**Norman Mitchell**
Wacky Waters	**Johnny Shannon**
Fred Pickering	**Robin Askwith**
Freda	**Queenie Watts**

Writers: **Kevin Laffan, Bill MacIlwraith, Charles Humphreys**
Executive Producers: **Peter Willes, David Cunliffe**
Producers: **John Frankau, Jacky Stoller, Derek Bennett**

A milkman's wife tries to better herself in middle age.

One morning, at the age of 40, charlady Beryl Humphries woke up and decided she hadn't done enough with her life. Married to Tom, a milkman, she realized she wanted to be more than a cleaner and, to the surprise of her children, Rosie, Jack and Babs, and that of her many friends and neighbours, set about improving her lot, signing up for evening classes.

The series was based on the life of cook Margaret Powell, also a milkman's wife, who passed 'O' and 'A' levels while in her 50s and at the age of 61 had her first book published.

BETAMAX
See VHS.

BETWEEN THE LINES
UK (BBC/Island World) Police Drama. BBC 1 1992–4

Det. Supt. Tony Clark	**Neil Pearson**
DI Harry Naylor	**Tom Georgeson**
DS Maureen Connell	**Siobhan Redmond**
Chief Supt. John Deakin	**Tony Doyle**
Commander Brian Huxtable	**David Lyon**
Sue Clark	**Lynda Steadman**
Jenny Dean	**Lesley Vickerage**
Chief Supt. Graves	**Robin Lermite**
Commander Sullivan	**Hugh Ross**
Angela Berridge	**Francesca Annis**
Joyce Naylor	**Elaine Donnelly**
Kate Roberts	**Barbara Wilshere**
Sarah Teale	**Sylvestra le Touzel**

Creator: **J. C. Wilsher**
Executive Producer: **Tony Garnett**
Producers: **Peter Norris, Joy Lale**

The professional and private lives of a police internal investigator.

Between The Lines revolved around the somewhat complex life of Detective Supt. Tony Clark, an ambitious but headstrong member of the Complaints Investigation Bureau (CIB), a division of the Metropolitan Police. As the head of a team of two detectives, it was Clark's job to root out bent coppers – at all levels in the force. Unfortunately, the hard-drinking, emotionally immature Clark was also a pawn in political games played by his superiors, and his job was further complicated by his own turbulent private life. His biggest problem, it seemed, was keeping his trousers on. Indeed, the series was cruelly nicknamed 'Between the Sheets' and even 'Between the Loins'. His marriage broke up because of an affair with WPC Jenny Dean, and other women, such as Home Office official Angela Berridge and TV producer Sarah Teale, also drifted into his bed during the programme's three-series run.

Clark's sidekicks were Harry Naylor and Mo Connell. Harry, the chain-smoking dependable-copper type, became increasingly more reckless and violent in his work as his wife's terminal illness developed, while Mo's own personal affairs (of the gay variety) began to infiltrate her working world, too. Above Clark initially were Commander Huxtable and Chief Supt. John Deakin. Clark managed to nail the menacing Deakin for corruption at the end of the first series, but Deakin wriggled off the hook and remained a powerful influence in Clark's life, particularly in the third series when Clark, Naylor and Connell found themselves outside the force and Deakin controlled their work as security advisers.

Between The Lines was an unexpected hit, picking up many awards and opening new doors for its star, Neil Pearson, previously seen as randy Dave Charnley in the Channel 4 comedy, DROP THE DEAD DONKEY.

BEVERLY HILLBILLIES, THE
US (Filmways) Situation Comedy. ITV 1963–71

Jed Clampett	**Buddy Ebsen**
Daisy Moses (Granny)	**Irene Ryan**
Elly May Clampett	**Donna Douglas**
Jethro Bodine	**Max Baer, Jr**
Milburn Drysdale	**Raymond Bailey**
Jane Hathaway	**Nancy Kulp**

Cousin Pearl Bodine	**Bea Benaderet**
Mrs Margaret Drysdale	**Harriet MacGibbon**
Jethrene Bodine	**Max Baer, Jr**
John Brewster	**Frank Wilcox**
Ravenswood	**Arthur Gould Porter**
Janet Trego	**Sharon Tate**
Lawrence Chapman	**Milton Frome**
John Cushing	**Roy Roberts**
Dash Riprock	**Larry Pennell**
Homer Cratchit	**Percy Helton**
Shorty Kellems	**George 'Shug' Fisher**
Shifty Shafer	**Phil Silvers**
Flo Shafer	**Kathleen Freeman**
Mark Templeton	**Roger Torrey**

Creator/Producer: **Paul Henning**
Executive Producer: **Al Simon**

A family of country bumpkins strikes oil, becomes rich and moves to Beverly Hills.

When Jed Clampett went out hunting on his land, he found more than he bargained for. Stumbling across a bubbling oil-reservoir meant that life in Bug Tussle in the Ozark Mountains was about to end for Jed and his family. They sold the drilling rights to John Brewster of the OK Oil Company and, with their new-found wealth, packed their bags on to their rickety old boneshaker and headed for the city, taking up residence among the rich and famous of Beverly Hills. And that's where the comedy began, for this family was not designed to live in an urban mansion. They were used to the rough and ready wild outdoors and thought smog was a small hog. It was their inability to adapt to modern conveniences and day-to-day life in a prosperous neighbourhood that provided the laughs.

Although Jed himself was fairly level-headed, the same couldn't be said for the other members of the Clampett family. Granny, his wrinkly, irritable mother-in-law, fought manfully against modern-day comforts and still tried to buy such items as possum innards for her many potions and recipes. Elly May provided the glamour as Jed's animal-loving daughter whom Granny was always trying to marry off, while brawny Cousin Jethro (played by the son of former world boxing champion Max Baer) was a dim, clumsy womanizer.

The Clampetts were chaperoned by Milburn Drysdale, President of the Commerce Bank, which held their money. Assisted by the starchy Jane Hathaway, Drysdale moved the family into the house next to his own, in order to keep an eye on them and to keep out poachers, including his rival, John Cushing, of the Merchant's Bank. Snooty Mrs Drysdale, however, was not so pleased to have the Clampetts as neighbours; they hardly allowed her to keep up appearances, and she hated her husband's grovelling.

Max Baer Jr also took the part of Jethro's sister, Jethrene, in the early days, and another original character was Cousin Pearl Bodine, mother of Jethro and Jethrene. But as the series developed, so the storyline moved along. Jethro finally graduated from school and, in his quest for true playboy status, began investing in flawed business ventures. The Clampetts purchased the majority holding in Mammoth Studios, run by Lawrence

Chapman, which led to Elly May's romance with film star Dash Riprock (né Homer Noodleman). Before the series closed (after nine years on US TV), she at last found her Mr Right, in the shape of navy frogman Mark Templeton. By that time the Clampetts' fortune had risen from a comfortable $25 million to a mighty $95 million.

Occasional visitors to the show throughout its run were musicians Lester Flatt and Earl Scruggs, banjo-picking performers of the memorable theme song, 'The Ballad of Jed Clampett'.

BEVERLY HILLS 90210

US (Twentieth Century-Fox/Torand/Spelling Entertainment) Drama. ITV 1991–2

Brenda Walsh	**Shannen Doherty**
Brandon Walsh	**Jason Priestley**
Jim Walsh	**James Eckhouse**
Cindy Walsh	**Carol Potter**
Kelly Taylor	**Jennie Garth**
Steve Sanders	**Ian Ziering**
Dylan McKay	**Luke Perry**
David Silver	**Brian Austin Green**
Andrea Zuckerman	**Gabrielle Carteris**
Donna Martin	**Tori Spelling**
Scott Scanlon	**Douglas Emerson**
Chris Suiter	**Michael St Gerard**
Nat	**Joe E. Tata**
Henry Thomas	**James Pickens, Jr**
Emily Valentine	**Christine Elise**

Creator: **Darren Star**
Executive Producer: **Charles Rosin**
Producers: **Aaron Spelling, Darren Star, Sigurjon Sighvatsson**

Teenage years in America's most select residential neighbourhood.

Beverly Hills 90210 was a zip code to die for, the zip code of the most fashionable residential area on the West Coast, a place where film stars and hugely successful business folk mingled in an atmosphere of gaudy prosperity. Into this glamorous setting stepped the Walshes, an altogether unassuming new family in town. Arriving from Minnesota, accountant dad Jim, wife Cindy and 16-year-old twins Brenda and Brandon were comfortably well off but strangely content with their lot, unlike their showy, ambitious neighbours. As they settled into their new environment, the kids, with their friends at West Beverly Hills High, provided the real focus of the series.

Dealing with realistic 1990s teen troubles like safe sex and drugs, as well as traditional adolescent woes such as peer pressure and school grades, *Beverly Hills 90210* quickly gathered a cult following among younger viewers. Apart from the Walsh family, the main protagonists were Brenda's snooty friend, Kelly; Steve, Kelly's ex-boyfriend and adopted son of TV star, Samantha Sanders; Brandon's surfing buddy, Dylan (Brenda's boyfriend); Andrea, the editor of the school newspaper; insecure David Silver; David's pal, Scott, and Donna, another of Brenda's friends (played by the daughter of TV executive Aaron Spelling).

So much did the series involve itself in teenage troubles that, in the USA, *Beverly Hills 90210* was followed each week by a list of special help lines, encouraging kids to call if they had experienced the problems highlighted in that particular episode. More recent series have been run on the Sky One satellite channel, as has a spin-off series, *Melrose Place*.

BEWES, RODNEY
(1937–)

Bingley-born comedy actor, one of TV's LIKELY LADS (Bob Ferris) in the 1960s and 1970s. He first appeared as a teenager on children's TV and later starred as Albert Courtnay in DEAR MOTHER . . . LOVE ALBERT (which he co-wrote and co-produced) and its follow-up, *Albert*, as well as playing Reg Last in *Just Liz*, and the straight man to BASIL BRUSH. Numerous guest appearances have included parts in DOCTOR WHO and Z CARS.

BEWITCHED
US (Screen Gems) Situation Comedy. BBC 1 1964–76

Samantha Stephens	**Elizabeth Montgomery**
Darrin Stephens	**Dick York**
	Dick Sargent
Endora	**Agnes Moorehead**
Maurice	**Maurice Evans**
Larry Tate	**David White**
Louise Tate	**Irene Vernon**
	Kasey Rogers
Tabitha Stephens	**Erin and Diane Murphy**
Adam Stephens	**David and Greg Lawrence**
Abner Kravitz	**George Tobias**
Gladys Kravitz	**Alice Pearce**
	Sandra Gould
Aunt Clara	**Marion Lorne**
Uncle Arthur	**Paul Lynde**
Esmerelda	**Alice Ghostley**
Dr Bombay	**Bernard Fox**

Creator: **Sol Saks**
Executive Producer: **Harry Ackerman**
Producer: **William Asher**

An attractive young witch marries a human and tries to settle down. However, she cannot resist using her magical powers, much to her husband's dismay.

Darrin Stephens was given a big surprise on his wedding day: he learned that his beautiful blonde bride, Samantha, was actually a witch who had been around for hundreds if not thousands of years. She was, however, tired of the supernatural life and wanted to become part of normal society. Promising Darrin that she would rein back her magic, the newlyweds set up home deep in Connecticut suburbia.

However, all did not go to plan, largely because of Endora, Samantha's mother, who fiercely opposed this 'mixed' marriage and used every opportunity to cast spells on her unfortunate son-in-law, changing him into chimps and frogs at will. She made no effort to learn his name, calling him variously Darwin, Donald, Durwood or something equally wrong. All of this was rather irritating for the hapless Darrin, an ambitious advertising executive with McMann and Tate. Whenever he managed to worm his way into boss Larry Tate's good books, there was Endora to foul things up. Fortunately, Samantha was always on hand to put things straight.

Samantha herself was very content in her domesticated life. She and Darrin were happy in their marriage, but she could never quite resist the temptation to twiddle her nose and let magic do the housework. Occasional visitors to the bizarre Stephens home were Samantha's confused Aunt Clara, a clumsy witch who forgot how to undo her spells, Maurice, Samantha's father, and practical joker Uncle Arthur. And then there were Abner and Gladys Kravitz, the neighbours. Witnessing the amazing events in the house next door from behind her twitching curtains, Gladys always failed to attract her husband's attention in time. Not surprisingly, he thought she was barmy.

The Stephenses soon began a family, with Tabitha the first born. She inherited her mother's special powers, and the gift was also passed on to her brother, Adam, born a few years later. Later additions to the cast were Esmerelda, a bungling, failing sorceress who was taken on as housekeeper, and the ineffective Dr Bombay.

Bewitched saw many personnel changes in its run and caused much confusion when, unannounced, Dick York was suddenly replaced by Dick Sargent (York suffered continually from back trouble and eventually could not go on). Alice Pearce, who originally played Gladys Kravitz, died in 1966, and the part of Louise Tate, Larry's wife, was also played by two actresses. A convention in American TV production was to use twins to play young children, to circumvent the limited hours minors were allowed to work. As a result, both Tabitha and Adam were played by twins, Tabitha by three sets before one of the last pair, Erin Murphy, took on the role full-time. When Tabitha grew up, she was given her own spin-off series, *Tabitha*, in which, played by Lisa Hartman, she worked for a Los Angeles TV station.

Bewitched was based on the 1942 film, *I Married a Witch*, which, in turn, was taken from Thorne Smith's 1941 novel, *The Passionate Witch*.

BIG BREADWINNER HOG
UK (Granada) Crime Drama. ITV 1969

Hog	**Peter Egan**
Ackerman	**Donald Burton**
Edgeworth	**Rosemary McHale**
Grange	**David Leland**
Lennox	**Timothy West**
Raspery	**Peter Thomas**
Izzard	**Alan Browning**
Singleton	**Tony Steedman**
Ryan	**Godfrey Quigley**

Producer: **Robin Chapman**

A vicious underworld mobster strives to be Mr Big.

Young, handsome Hog was a villain. A nasty villain. The sort of villain you didn't want to cross. He was also ambitious, aiming to be London's gangland king, and he would stop at nothing to achieve that goal. But, with the established city mobsters resisting his rise to power, the scene was set for some particularly violent action. In one episode, acid was thrown in someone's face; in others, beatings were commonplace. Indeed the violence was so heavy that an apology had to be made to viewers. It seems the public were not yet ready for the criminal fraternity to be shown in all their gory colours.

BIG BREAKFAST, THE
UK (Planet 24) Entertainment. Channel 4 1992–

Presenters: **Chris Evans, Gaby Roslin, Paula Yates, Bob Geldof, Mark Lamarr, Keith Chegwin, Mark Little, Paul Ross, Richard Orford, Lily Savage, Zoë Ball, Danni Minogue, Sharron Davies, Rick Adams, Vanessa Feltz, Denise Van Outen, Johnny Vaughan, Melanie Sykes, Kelly Brook, Sara Cox, Liza Tarbuck, Richard Bacon, Gail Porter**

Executive Producers: **Charlie Parsons, Bob Massie, Lisa Clark, Duncan Gray, Ed Forsdick**
Editor: **Sebastian Scott**

Fast-moving, weekday morning (7–9 a.m.) entertainment mix.

Departing from the established news- and magazine-based format of other breakfast TV shows, *The Big Breakfast* placed the emphasis on fun from the start. Its all-action combination of competitions, interviews, film reviews and music videos was designed to appeal to the younger end of the audience spectrum, with news items restrained to brief headlines every 20 minutes (supplied by ITN and read by Peter Smith, Angela Rippon or Phil Gayle). A real house (three converted lock-keepers' cottages) in East London – and not a typical TV studio – was used for production, adding a cramped, chaotic atmosphere.

In the early programmes, Bob Geldof (director of the production company, Planet 24) conducted a series of pre-recorded interviews with major figures on the world stage, although these were soon abandoned in favour of more trivial items. His then wife, Paula Yates, was also involved, welcoming celebrities into her boudoir and discussing fashion and other issues on her bed (her role was later assumed by Lily Savage and Vanessa Feltz, among others). A real family joined the programme each week, and Keith Chegwin or Richard Orford spent many mornings interviewing motorists in traffic jams and knocking up families in 'Down Your Doorstep'. Other features included 'Cupid's Arrow' (real-life tales of romance), American imports like THE BANANA SPLITS, sketches with puppets Zig and Zag (later stars of their own series), and 'Snap, Cackle and Pop' (entertainment news). However, the first real success story of the programme was host Chris Evans, who became TV's hottest property in the mid-1990s.

BIG BROTHER
UK (Bazal) Documentary. Channel 4 2000

Presenter: **Davina McCall**
Executive Producer: **Ruth Wigley**
Editor: **Conrad Green**

Voyeuristic 'reality soap' involving the inhabitants of a TV show-house.

The most talked-about programme of summer 2000 was *Big Brother*. This controversial concept was imported from the Netherlands, where it had taken the country by storm, generating entertainment out of the spectacle of young people living together in a specially adapted house, sealed off from the rest of the world. In the UK, the house was constructed behind barbed-wire fences in Bow, East London, and became home to ten willing participants for seven weeks. Strategically positioned cameras, two-way mirrors and compulsory radio microphones allowed viewers, through edited highlights (and Internet junkies for 24 hours a day), to spy on their every move – even the bathroom was bugged. The overall intention was, as the programme's publicity candidly put it, to provide 'pore-close TV', studying personal interaction and human behaviour. Critics saw it instead as a descent into voyeurism.

The contestants, chosen from an application-list of some 40,000, were vetted for psychological and social strengths and then thrown together for better or for worse. Each week they were assigned a group task and were also responsible for things like compiling their own shopping lists on a tight budget. Also each week, they nominated two of their number to face eviction, with one losing his or her place at the hands of the voting viewing public. In this way their total dwindled down to a final three, the highest-polling of these walking away with a cheque for £70,000. Along the way, one contestant, Nick Bateman, was expelled for breaking the rules and was substituted by Claire Strutton. The other participants were Melanie Hill, Anna Nolan, Darren Ramsey, Andrew Davidson, Thomas McDermott, Nichola Holt, Caroline O'Shea, Sada Walkington and Liverpudlian builder Craig Phillips, who ran out the eventual winner, generously donating his prize to a young friend with Down's syndrome who needed a vital operation in the USA.

From nothing *Big Brother* quickly gained a big following. Contestants enjoyed celebrity status and crowds of fans gathered at the gates of the house's compound to catch sight of the next evictee. Davina McCall summarized proceedings and interviewed the contestants as they left the TV equivalent of a goldfish bowl. The series was re-produced all over the world and led to a plethora of copycat programmes.

BIG DEAL
UK (BBC) Drama. BBC 1 1984–6

Robby Box	**Ray Brooks**
Jan Oliver	**Sharon Duce**
Debby Oliver	**Lisa Geoghan**
Tommy	**James Ottaway**
Henry Diamond	**Tony Caunter**
Joan	**Deirdre Costello**
Geordie	**Andy Mulligan**
Irish	**Alan Mason**
Vi Box	**Pamela Cundell**
Ferret	**Kenneth Waller**
Dick Mayer	**Stephen Tate**
Kipper	**Roger Walker**
Black George	**Alex Tetteh-Lartey**
Alison Diamond	**Marion Bailey**

Creator/Writer: **Geoff McQueen**
Producer: **Terence Williams**

A middle-aged gambler attempts to kick the habit.

At the age of 40 Londoner Robby Box had not done a day's work since leaving school. Instead, he made a living playing poker and betting on horses and dogs. The sudden realization, however, that his life was passing him by and that he had nothing to show for his misspent youth made Box decide to 'go straight', calling on the help of his blonde girlfriend, Jan, and her teenage daughter, Debby. Things didn't always go to plan, though, especially with the taxman on Robby's tail and Jan always likely to walk out on him. Jan, too, had her problems. She wanted Robby to change but she loved him just the way he was. In the second season Robby's efforts to become respectable led to his taking over The Dragon Club, but life didn't get any easier.

BIG TIME, THE
UK (BBC) Documentary. BBC 1 1976–7; 1980

Presenter/Producer: **Esther Rantzen**

Magic wand programme, allowing amateurs to become professionals for a day.

Esther Rantzen was responsible for this series, which enabled ordinary viewers to achieve lifelong ambitions. Among those featured were a housewife who was given the chance to prepare a banquet at a swish hotel, a vicar who wrote a newspaper gossip column and a sales assistant who joined a circus. However, the real success story concerned Scottish teacher Sheena Easton, who, from singing part-time in clubs, not only cut a record but went on to become an international star in her own right. Two series were produced, with a three-year gap in between.

BIG VALLEY, THE
US (Four Star) Western. ITV 1965–70

Victoria Barkley	**Barbara Stanwyck**
Jarrod Barkley	**Richard Long**
Nick Barkley	**Peter Breck**
Heath Barkley	**Lee Majors**
Audra Barkley	**Linda Evans**
Eugene Barkley	**Charles Briles**
Silas	**Napoleon Whiting**

Producers: **Jules Levy, Arthur Gardner, Arnold Laven**

Life with a cattle-ranching family in California's San Joaquin Valley in the 1870s.

The Big Valley told the story of hard-headed widow Victoria Barkley and her ranching family in the Old West. Her sons ranged from the refined lawyer Jarrod, to the brawny Nick, the foreman on the 30,000-acre holding. Heath was the good-looking one, although he was not Victoria's own (being the illegitimate son of her late husband, Tom, and an Indian squaw), and the youngest son was Eugene, a bashful youth seen only in the earliest episodes. Victoria also had a beautiful but impetuous daughter named Audra. Silas was the family's black servant. Storylines followed the usual Western pattern, revolving around constant battles with rustlers, criminals and con men.

Future SIX MILLION DOLLAR MAN Lee Majors made his TV debut in this series, and Linda Evans also went on to bigger and better things (as Krystle in DYNASTY).

BIGGINS, CHRISTOPHER
(1948–)

Cheerful, bespectacled actor/comedian/presenter, initially finding favour as the effeminate Lukewarm in PORRIDGE, the Revd Ossie Whitworth in POLDARK and Nero in I, CLAUDIUS. He was also Adam Painting in RENTAGHOST and co-host of SURPRISE, SURPRISE with Cilla Black. His other TV credits have included *Watch This Space*, THE LIKELY LADS, PAUL TEMPLE, UPSTAIRS, DOWNSTAIRS, SHOESTRING, CLUEDO (Revd Green) and *On Safari*.

BIGGLES
UK (Granada) Children's Adventure. ITV 1960

Insp. 'Biggles' Bigglesworth	**Neville Whiting**
Ginger	**John Leyton**
Bertie	**David Drummond**
Von Stalheim	**Carl Duering**

Producers: **Harry Elton, Kitty Black**

The adventures of a celebrated flying ace.

In this action-packed series, Biggles, Captain W. E. Johns's daredevil pilot, had left the Air Force with his chums Ginger and Bertie and was attached to Scotland Yard. Now a Detective Air Inspector, the intrepid air ace turned his sights away from enemy aircraft and on to airborne villains, ensuring each episode had a thrilling flying sequence and cliff-hanger ending. Among the show's writers was a young man called Tony Warren, who went on to devise CORONATION STREET, while John

Leyton, who played Ginger, became more famous as a pop singer, topping the charts with 'Johnny Remember Me' a year after *Biggles* was screened.

BILL BRAND
UK (Thames) Drama. ITV 1976

Bill Brand .... **Jack Shepherd**

Creator/Writer: **Trevor Griffiths**
Producer: **Stuart Burge**

Problems in the life of a left-wing MP.

Somewhat autobiographical in tone, Trevor Griffiths's *Bill Brand* focused on a young, idealistic lecturer who climbed his way up the socialist ladder to become a Member of Parliament. Courting controversy all the way, he earned himself many enemies. Eleven episodes were made and, although applauded by the critics, viewers remained unimpressed.

BILL, THE
UK (Thames) Police Drama. ITV 1984–

DI Roy Galloway .... **John Salthouse**
Sgt Bob Cryer .... **Eric Richard**
PC Francis 'Taffy' Edwards .... **Colin Blumenau**
PC Dave Litten .... **Gary Olsen**
PC/DC Jim Carver .... **Mark Wingett**
WPC/Sgt June Ackland .... **Trudie Goodwin**
WPC/WDC Viv Martella .... **Nula Conwell**
PC Timothy Able .... **Mark Haddigan**
DS Ted Roach .... **Tony Scannell**
WPC Claire Brind .... **Kelly Lawrence**
PC Reg Hollis .... **Jeff Stewart**
PC Tony 'Yorkie' Smith .... **Robert Hudson**
PC Robin Frank .... **Ashley Gunstock**
Chief Supt. Charles Brownlow .... **Peter Ellis**
PC Abe Lyttleton .... **Ronnie Cush**
PC Richard Turnham .... **Chris Humphreys**
PC Pete Muswell .... **Ralph Brown**
Insp. Brian Kite .... **Simon Slater**
Sgt Tom Penny .... **Roger Leach**
Sgt Alec Peters .... **Larry Dann**
PC Nick Shaw .... **Chris Walker**
PC Ken Melvin .... **Mark Powley**
PC Danesh Patel .... **Sonesh Sira**
Insp. Christine Frazer .... **Barbara Thorn**
PC Pete Ramsey .... **Nick Reding**
DCI Gordon Wray .... **Clive Wood**
PC Malcolm Haynes .... **Eamonn Walker**
PC Phil Young .... **Colin Aldridge**
Chief Insp. Derek Conway .... **Ben Roberts**
Insp. Andrew Monroe .... **Colin Tarrant**
DCI Kim Reid .... **Carolyn Pickles**
DI Frank Burnside .... **Christopher Ellison**
DS Alistair Greig .... **Andrew Mackintosh**
DC Alfred 'Tosh' Lines .... **Kevin Lloyd**
DC Mike Dashwood .... **Jon Iles**
Sgt John Maitland .... **Sam Miller**
PC Tony Stamp .... **Graham Cole**

PC Dave Quinnan .... **Andrew Paul**
WPC Cathy Marshall .... **Lynne Miller**
PC Steven Loxton .... **Tom Butcher**
WPC Norika Datta .... **Seeta Indrani**
WPC Delia French .... **Natasha Williams**
WPC Suzanne Ford .... **Vikki Gee-Dare**
PC George Garfield .... **Huw Higginson**
PC Ron Smollett .... **Nick Stringer**
Sgt Matthew Boyden .... **Tony O'Callaghan**
DI/DCI Jack Meadows .... **Simon Rouse**
PC Barry Stringer .... **Jonathan Dow**
DC Alan Woods .... **Tom Cotcher**
DS/Det. Insp. Harry Haines .... **Gary Whelan**
DS/DI Chris Deakin .... **Shaun Scott**
WPC/WDC Suzi Croft .... **Kerry Peers**
DS Danny Pearce .... **Martin Marquez**
PC Mike Jarvis .... **Stephen Beckett**
Sgt Ray Steele .... **Robert Perkins**
DI Sally Johnson .... **Jaye Griffiths**
WPC Donna Harris .... **Louise Harrison**
DC Rod Skase .... **Iain Fletcher**
PC Gary McCann .... **Clive Wedderburn**
Chief Insp. Philip Cato .... **Philip Whitchurch**
Woman DS Jo Morgan .... **Mary Jo Randle**
WPC Polly Page .... **Lisa Geoghan**
DS Don Beech .... **Billy Murray**
PC Nick Slater .... **Alan Westaway**
WPC Debbie Keane .... **Andrea Mason**
Chief Insp. Paul Stritch .... **Mark Spalding**
DS John Boulton .... **Russell Boulter**
DI Scales .... **Oliver Haden**
WDC Liz Rawton .... **Libby Davison**
WPC Jamilla Blake .... **Lolita Chakrabarti**
DS Geoff Daly .... **Ray Ashcroft**
DS Merrick .... **Tom Mannion**
Sgt Stuart Lamont .... **Steve Morley**
DC Tom Proctor .... **Gregory Donaldson**
PC Luke Ashton .... **Scott Neal**
DC Travis .... **Kevin Doyle**
PC Sam Harker .... **Matthew Crompton**
WPC Vicky Hagen .... **Samantha Robson**
PC Eddie Santini .... **Michael Higgs**
WPC DaSilva .... **Melissa Lloyd**
WDC Kerry Holmes .... **Joy Brook**
DC Duncan Lennox .... **George Rossi**
WPC Di Worrell .... **Jane Wall**
DC Danny Glaze .... **Karl Collins**
DS Acton .... **Clare Swinburne**
PC Dale Smith .... **Alex Walkinshaw**
WPC Cass Rickman .... **Suzanne Maddock**
DS Claire Stanton .... **Clara Salaman**
DC Micky Webb .... **Chris Simmons**
Supt. Tom Chandler .... **Steve Hartley**
DC Paul Riley .... **Gary Grant**
DC Kate Spears .... **Tania Emery**
PC Nick Klein .... **René Zagger**
DI Alex Cullen .... **Ged Simmons**
DS Debbie McAllister .... **Natalie Roles**
DS Vik Singh .... **Raji James**

Creator: **Geoff McQueen**
Executive Producers: **Lloyd Shirley, Peter Cregeen, Michael Chapman**

Producers: **Michael Chapman, Peter Cregeen, Richard Bramall, Brenda Ennis, Michael Ferguson, Geraint Morris, Pat Sandys, Michael Simpson, Tony Virgo, Peter Wolfes, Richard Handford, Mike Dormer, Chris Clough, Jamie Nuttgens, Chris Lovett, Tom Cotter**

The rigours of day-to-day inner-city policing.

The Bill focused on life at the Sun Hill police station, somewhere in London's East End. It showed the local law-enforcers in their everyday work, catching crooks, keeping the peace and dealing with the general public. For once, personal lives were pushed well into the background.

Criticized by some real policemen for its portrayal of policing methods (but loved by other members of the force), *The Bill* was also attacked for suggesting – years ahead of the Stephen Lawrence tragedy and subsequent inquiry – that racism was a facet of today's force. Nevertheless, the series continued to show just how policemen cope with the realities of the modern world, showing officers of the law as people with a job to do, however unpleasant that job may be.

Head of the station was Chief Supt. Charles Brownlow, a man mainly concerned with the image of his force, and beneath him worked an ever-changing squad of inspectors, sergeants, detectives and constables. Most notable were Bob Cryer, the paternal station officer, the hot-headed DCI Galloway (who was never afraid to bend the rules) and his devious successor, DCI Burnside (given his own spin-off series, *Burnside*, in 2000). Young PCs 'Taffy' Edwards and Jim Carver, the hypochondriac Reg Hollis, ambitious Dave Litton, impetuous Ted Roach, well-groomed Mike Dashwood, scruffy 'Tosh' Lines and dependable WPCs Ackland and Martella were also prominent.

The Bill began in 1983 as an episode of Thames TV's STORYBOARD series, entitled *Woodentop* (a CID nickname for uniformed officers). After four years as an hour-long drama, it 'turned tabloid', splitting into two self-contained, half-hour episodes each week. A new rule was added: there had to be a police person in every scene. Hand-held camerawork was introduced to provide a touch of on-the-streets realism and it certainly helped with the pace of the programme, although characterization and plot development were victims of the truncated format. In 1998, the famous 'plodding feet' title-sequence was dropped – to the dismay of some fans – and later that year, with ratings falling, *The Bill* reverted to a one-hour format.

BILLY BUNTER OF GREYFRIARS • SCHOOL
UK (BBC) Situation Comedy. BBC 1952–61

Billy Bunter .... **Gerald Campion**

Creator/Writer: **Frank Richards**
Producers: **Joy Harington, David Goddard, Pharic Maclaren, Shaun Sutton, Clive Parkhurst**

Jolly japes and wizard wheezes with a plump boarding school pupil.

Performed live twice on a Friday night (at 5.25 p.m. for children and at 8 p.m. for grown-ups) in the days before videotape, *Billy Bunter of Greyfriars School* was one of the BBC's earliest long-running comedies. Scripted by Frank Richards and based on his *Magnet* comic stories, it told tales of the ever-hungry William George Bunter, the Fat Owl of the Remove. Twenty-nine-year-old Gerald Campion filled out for the part and let loose a barrage of 'Crikey!'s and 'Yaroo!'s in raiding tuck shops, avoiding canings and waiting for postal orders from Bunter Court. Mocking Bunter was the beastly schoolboy posse of Harry Wharton, Frank Nugent, Bob Cherry, Hurree Jamset Ram Singh and Johnny Bull (played by a host of young performers), all avoiding the clutches of arch-enemy form-master Mr Quelch (played initially by Kynaston Reeves). Guesting among the boys were aspiring actors like Anthony Valentine, Michael Crawford, Melyvn Hayes and David Hemmings.

BIONIC WOMAN, THE
US (Universal/Harve Bennett) Science Fiction. ITV 1976–9

Jaime Sommers .... **Lindsay Wagner**
Oscar Goldman .... **Richard Anderson**
Dr Rudy Wells .... **Martin E. Brooks**
Jim Elgin .... **Ford Rainey**
Helen Elgin .... **Martha Scott**
Peggy Callahan .... **Jennifer Darling**

Creator: **Kenneth Johnson**
Executive Producer: **Harve Bennett**

A girl with superhuman abilities works for a counter-espionage agency.

In this spin-off from THE SIX MILLION DOLLAR MAN, Steve Austin's one-time girlfriend, Jaime Sommers, took centre stage. In the original series, Jaime broke up with Steve when he became an astronaut, but they were temporarily reunited after she was crippled in a sky-diving accident. Jaime was then given the same bionic treatment as her boyfriend, endowing her with special abilities.

She now had bionic legs which allowed her to run fast, a bionic ear for long-distance hearing and the strength of a bionic right arm. With these new skills, and in her own series, she settled down to life as a schoolteacher at the Ventura Air Force base in Ojai, California, although, in repayment for her futuristic medical treatment, she also worked for the anti-espionage agency OSI (Office of Scientific Information). Steve, too, undertook secret missions for OSI and, inevitably, the two were drawn together yet again. Sadly, the damage to Jaime's memory had wiped out her love for him, but this didn't affect their working relationship. Jaime even took up residence in an apartment at the farm owned by Steve's mother and stepfather (Helen and Jim Elgin).

The series also introduced Max, the bionic German Shepherd dog, as a companion for Jaime, and the Bionic Boy (played by Vincent Van Patten). But more often seen were OSI executive Oscar Goldman and Dr Rudy Wells, the pioneer of bionic medicine. These characters, and that of Peggy Callahan, Oscar's secretary, also appeared in *The Six Million Dollar Man*.

BIRD OF PREY

UK (BBC) Drama. BBC 1 1982

Henry Jay	**Richard Griffiths**
Anne Jay	**Carole Nimmons**
Tony Hendersly	**Jeremy Child**
Charles Bridgnorth	**Nigel Davenport**
Harry Tompkins	**Roger Sloman**
Rochelle Halliday	**Ann Pennington**
Mario	**Guido Adorni**
Dino	**Eddie Mineo**
Hugo Jardine	**Christopher Logue**

Writer: **Ron Hutchinson**
Producer: **Michael Wearing**

A Government employee stumbles into
international intrigue.

Henry Jay, a civil servant in his mid-30s, was working on a case of computer fraud when by chance he unearthed a massive financial conspiracy. He decided to investigate further and, despite the close attentions of a shadowy agency known as Le Pouvoir and various bureaucratic attempts to silence him, Jay proved to be a determined detective, discovering clues that pointed to the involvement of a Euro MP by the name of Hugo Jardine.

Following the success of this four-part drama, dubbed 'a thriller for the electronic age', a sequel, entitled *Bird of Prey 2*, was made in 1984. In this, Henry, on the run with his wife, Anne, continued to expose the murky activities of Le Pouvoir.

BIRD, JOHN

(1936–)

Nottingham-born comedian, actor, writer and director, a graduate of the Cambridge Footlights troupe. His earliest TV credits included THAT WAS THE WEEK THAT WAS, NOT SO MUCH A PROGRAMME, MORE A WAY OF LIFE, BBC-3, and Jonathan Miller's *Alice In Wonderland*, although he has more recently enjoyed success as support to Rory Bremner (with long-time partner, John Fortune) and as Douglas Bromley in EL C.I.D. As well as notable appearances in *Blue Remembered Hills*, *Oxbridge Blues*, JANE, *Travelling Man* and A VERY PECULIAR PRACTICE (Ernest Hemmingway), he has starred in a couple of comedies of his own, namely *A Series of Bird's* and *With Bird Will Travel*, plus *Well Anyway*, *The Long Johns* (the last two shared ventures with Fortune), and the sketch shows *The Late Show*, *World in Ferment*, *After That, This*, *Beyond a Joke* and *Grubstreet* (often with Eleanor Bron). Bird has also featured prominently in the sitcoms, THE GROWING PAINS OF ADRIAN MOLE, *If It Moves, File It* (civil servant Quick), *Joint Account* (Ned Race), *Educating Marmalade* (Mr Atkins) and *Chambers* (pompous barrister John Fuller-Carp), plus the game show, CLUEDO (Professor Plum).

BIRDS OF A FEATHER

UK (Alomo) Situation Comedy. BBC 1 1989–94; 1997–8

Sharon Theodopolopoudos	**Pauline Quirke**
Tracey Stubbs	**Linda Robson**
Dorien Green	**Lesley Joseph**
Chris Theodopolopoudos	**David Cardy**
	Peter Polycarpou
Darryl Stubbs	**Alun Lewis**
	Doug McFerran
Garth Stubbs	**Simon Nash**
	Matthew Savage
Marcus Green	**Nickolas Grace**
	Stephen Greif
Melanie Fishman	**Jan Goodman**

Creators: **Laurence Marks, Maurice Gran**
Producers: **Esta Charkham, Nic Phillips, Candida Julian-Jones, Charlie Hanson, Tony Charles**
Executive Producer: **Allan McKeown**

Two sisters live together after their husbands are
sent to jail.

Tracey and Sharon were two adopted sisters from North London. Of the two, Tracey had patently done better for herself. She had a £³/₄-million neo-Georgian home called 'Dalentrace' in Bryan Close in the Essex suburb of Chigwell, whereas Sharon still lived in Camelot House, a seedy council tower block in Edmonton. Furthermore, Tracey's son, Garth, now attended a public school. What she didn't realize was that her childhood-sweetheart husband, Darryl, was paying for all this on the proceeds of crime. All was revealed when he and Sharon's dim Greek husband, Chris, were arrested for armed robbery and earned themselves 12-year prison sentences. At that point Sharon moved in with Tracey and set about finding a new man in her life. Indeed, sex – or at least talk of it – became their main obsession, even though they still visited their partners in Maidstone prison. Money problems formed their other preoccupation as Darryl's ill-gotten cash began to run out, and Sharon opened up a café to earn a living.

The girls' lives were regularly spiced up by Dorien Green, their snooty, man-eating, Jewish next-door neighbour, who enjoyed a succession of toy boys in the absence of her accountant husband, Marcus (who had been impotent since the 1987 stock market crash). Dorien's great rival on the local social scene was Melanie Fishman.

After a two-and-a-half-year hiatus, *Birds of a Feather* returned to the screen in 1997, picking up the story at the point where the two husbands were (temporarily) released from prison. David Cardy returned to take the part of Chris, while Doug McFerran succeeded Alun Lewis as Darryl. The house in Chigwell had to go to make ends meet and the girls were forced to move to humbler accommodation in Hainault. Dorien, too, faced a new future: Marcus (played once more by Nickolas Grace), it seemed, had been sharing his life with another wife and a son, and Dorien, too, had to move downmarket to Hainault. In yet later episodes, the girls founded their own cleaning company, Maids of Ongar.

An American version, made in 1992, called *Stand By Your Man* and featuring characters named Rochelle, Lorraine and Adrienne, was not a great success.

BIRT, Lord JOHN
(1944–)

Director-General of the BBC whose internal reforms caused much unease in the early 1990s. The streamlining of staff and the introduction of the 'Producer Choice' internal market system proved the most inflammatory, as Birt was charged with leading the BBC through a particularly difficult period in a new multi-channel environment and with the BBC's Charter due for renewal in 1996. Birt's career took off at Granada where, as producer, he was responsible in 1968 for NICE TIME, the innovative comedy show starring Jonathan Routh, Kenny Everett and Germaine Greer. He later moved to LWT, where his input into current affairs television proved equally influential (among other projects he was executive producer of WEEKEND WORLD). He eventually took over as head of Features and Current Affairs before rising to Programme Controller in 1981. He joined the BBC as Deputy Director-General in 1987, brought in by the then Director-General, Michael Checkland, to re-appraise the BBC's journalistic operations. He was named, somewhat controversially, as the next Director-General in 1991, while Checkland still had two years of his contract to run. As he bowed out of the BBC hot seat, he was given a life peerage in December 1999.

BIT OF A DO, A
UK (Yorkshire) Comedy Drama. ITV 1989

Ted Simcock	David Jason
Rita Simcock	Gwen Taylor
Elvis Simcock	Wayne Foskett
Paul Simcock	David Thewlis
Laurence Rodenhurst	Paul Chapman
Liz Rodenhurst/Badger	Nicola Pagett
Simon Rodenhurst	Nigel Hastings
Jenny Rodenhurst/Simcock	Sarah-Jane Holm
Neville Badger	Michael Jayston
Rodney Sillitoe	Tim Wylton
Betty Sillitoe	Stephanie Cole
Carol Fordingbridge	Karen Drury
Gerry Lansdown	David Yelland
Corinna Price-Rodgerson	Diana Weston
Geoffrey Ellsworth-Smythe	Malcolm Tierney
Lucinda Snellmarsh	Amanda Wenban
Eric	Malcolm Hebden
Sandra	Tracy Brabin

Creator/Writer: **David Nobbs**
Executive Producer: **Vernon Lawrence**
Producer: **David Reynolds**

Social rivalry between two families who regularly meet at local functions.

Set in a small Yorkshire town, where everyone knew everyone else's business, *A Bit of a Do* focused on the relationships between members of the Rodenhurst and Simcock families. Laurence Rodenhurst was a dentist, while the socially inferior Ted Simcock ran an iron foundry. The first 'do' which brought them together was the marriage of Laurence's daughter, Jenny, to scruffy Paul, Ted's son. During the reception, Ted enjoyed some extra-marital exercise with Laurence's wife, Liz, which resulted in an unplanned offspring and the break-up of Ted's marriage to Rita. That set the tone for the series.

Other 'dos' the families attended included the Angling Club Christmas party, the Dentists' dance and the crowning of Miss Frozen Chicken UK at the Cock-a-Doodle Chickens event. As the series progressed, Laurence died, Liz picked up with widower Neville Badger, Ted's business hit hard times and Jenny married her brother-in-law, Elvis. Rodney and Betty Sillitoe were boozy regulars at every function, and also seen were barman Eric and waitress Sandra. The episodes were dramatized by David Nobbs from his own novels.

BIXBY, BILL
(1934–93)

American actor famous as the mild-mannered Dr David Banner in THE INCREDIBLE HULK, with earlier starring roles as Anthony Blake in THE MAGICIAN (a part for which he learned conjuring tricks) and Tim O'Hara in MY FAVORITE MARTIAN. His other major TV credit was in a comedy series not seen in the UK, *The Courtship of Eddie's Father*. Bixby also turned his hand to directing, calling the shots for TV movies and on some episodes of RICH MAN, POOR MAN, as well as appearing in front of the camera as Willie Abbott in that mini-series.

BLACK AND WHITE MINSTREL SHOW, THE
UK (BBC) Variety. BBC 1 1958–78

Creator: **George Inns**
Producers: **George Inns, Ernest Maxin, Brian Whitehouse**

Sing-along variety show featuring the Mitchell Minstrels and guests.

Stemming from a one-off special entitled *The 1957 Television Minstrels*, this old-fashioned, fast-moving series was a showcase for conductor George Mitchell's Mitchell Minstrels and especially lead vocalists Dai Francis, John Boulter and Tony Mercer. Other long-serving Al Jolson lookalikes were Benny Garcia, Les Rawlings, Andy Cole and Les Want, and female contributions came from Margo Henderson, Margaret Savage, Penny Jewkes, Delia Wicks and others. In the background the Television Toppers dancers (previously stars of *Toppers About Town*) provided the glamour. Adding light relief were comedians like Leslie Crowther, George Chisholm and Stan Stennet.

The Minstrels specialized in schmaltzy medleys in the sing-along vein, some originating from America's deep South (like the 19th-century minstrel concept itself).

Other tunes were of Country and Western origin, or were derived from foreign folk cultures. The programme was a Saturday night favourite, but, by the end of the 1970s, the political incorrectness of men with blacked-up faces and broad white smiles resulted in its cancellation after over 20 years on air.

BLACK BEAUTY
See ADVENTURES OF BLACK BEAUTY, THE.

BLACK, CILLA
OBE (Priscilla White; 1943–)

Liverpudlian singer turned presenter whose career break came while working as a cloakroom attendant and occasional vocalist at The Cavern club, famous for The Beatles' early performances. Spotted by Brian Epstein, Black secured a recording contract and notched up two number ones with 'Anyone Who Had a Heart' and 'You're My World'. She ventured into television in 1968, gaining her own Saturday night series, *Cilla*, on BBC 1, which ran for several years. In these live programmes she sent an outside broadcast team to surprise unsuspecting residents somewhere in the UK. She also gave viewers the chance to choose the Song for Europe. Black later tried her hand at sitcom in *Cilla's Comedy Six* and *Cilla's World of Comedy* and, after a quiet period during the 1970s, she resurfaced as host of SURPRISE, SURPRISE (in 1984) and BLIND DATE (in 1985). In 1998, she launched another Saturday evening show, *The Moment of Truth*.

BLACKADDER
UK (BBC) Situation Comedy. BBC 1 1983–9

The Black Adder (1983)

Edmund, Duke of Edinbugh ('The Black Adder') .... **Rowan Atkinson**
Baldrick .... **Tony Robinson**
Percy .... **Tim McInnerny**
Richard IV .... **Brian Blessed**
Queen .... **Elspet Gray**
Prince Harry .... **Robert East**

Blackadder II (1986)

Lord Edmund Blackadder .... **Rowan Atkinson**
Baldrick .... **Tony Robinson**
Queen Elizabeth I .... **Miranda Richardson**
Lord Melchett .... **Stephen Fry**
Lord Percy .... **Tim McInnerny**
Nursie .... **Patsy Byrne**

Blackadder the Third (1987)

Edmund Blackadder .... **Rowan Atkinson**
Baldrick .... **Tony Robinson**
George, Prince of Wales .... **Hugh Laurie**
Mrs Miggins .... **Helen Atkinson-Wood**

Blackadder Goes Forth (1989)

Capt. Edmund Blackadder .... **Rowan Atkinson**
Pte. S. Baldrick .... **Tony Robinson**
Lt. The Honourable George Colthurst St Barleigh ....
.... **Hugh Laurie**
Gen. Sir Anthony Cecil Hogmanay Melchett ....
.... **Stephen Fry**
Capt. Kevin Darling .... **Tim McInnerny**

Semi-regulars:

Lord Flashheart (*II*/*Goes Forth*) .... **Rik Mayall**
Kate/Bob (*II*)/Driver Parkhurst (*Goes Forth*) ....
.... **Gabrielle Glaister**
Princess Maria (*The Black Adder*)/Lady Whiteadder (*II*) ...
.... **Miriam Margolyes**
Amy Hardwood (*The Third*)/Nurse Mary (*Goes Forth*) ......
.... **Miranda Richardson**

Creators: **Rowan Atkinson, Richard Curtis**
Writers: **Rowan Atkinson, Richard Curtis, Ben Elton**
Producer: **John Lloyd**

Historical double-dealing with various generations of a cowardly family.

Blackadder was a collection of comedies which, although running into four eras, splits neatly into two clear parts: the first series and the rest. Viewers who later came to love the devious, treacherous, selfish rogue of *Blackadder II*, *Blackadder the Third* and *Blackadder Goes Forth* were not over-enamoured of the character portrayed in the first series, which was simply entitled *The Black Adder*. This series was written by Rowan Atkinson and Richard Curtis. By the second generation, Ben Elton had replaced Atkinson as co-writer and the scripts were graced with more rounded plots and filled with choice one-liners.

The Blackadder saga began with Edmund, Duke of Edinburgh. Crudely based on supposedly true historical accounts, the comedy came from the feeble-mindedness of the cringing duke and his sly, cowardly ways. Filmed around Alnwick Castle in Northumberland, at great expense, it was set during the Wars of the Roses, as the houses of Lancaster and York battled for the English throne, with Edmund allegedly the son of Richard IV, one of the Princes in the Tower.

By the second series (the concept having just survived cancellation) Edmund Blackadder, great-great-grandson of the original Black Adder and a courtier of Queen Elizabeth I, had added buoyant confidence to his ancestor's repertoire of deceit and cruelty. He was admirably complemented in his Tudor treachery by an overgrown-schoolgirl version of the Virgin Queen, as well as a pompous rival, Lord Melchett, and a foppish hanger-on, Lord Percy. But the best support came from the rodent-like manservant, Baldrick, like Lord Percy an even stupider descendant of a character first seen in *The Black Adder*.

For *Blackadder the Third*, time had moved on two centuries to the Georgian Age, and the Blackadder in question was butler to the idiotic George, Prince of Wales. In between frequenting Mrs Miggins's coffee shop and cuffing Baldrick about the ear, Blackadder schemed his way in and out of the society groups who surrounded the Prince, meeting the likes of Dr Johnson (Robbie Coltrane) and the Duke of Wellington (Stephen Fry).

The last incarnation came in the World War I trenches of *Blackadder Goes Forth*. Here the weaselly Captain Edmund Blackadder worked every ruse in the book to try to flee the impending carnage, but was inhibited by his imbecile lieutenant, George, and, of course, Private Baldrick. Then there was the arrogant, insensitive General Melchett, booming out orders to his subservient adjutant, Captain Darling, yet another object of contempt for our hero. The tragedy and futility of the Great War were never ridiculed and the series concluded in rich pathos. As all the 'ordinary men' (not the General, of course) were forced 'over the top' to certain death, the slow-motion action faded silently into a field of swaying poppies.

Series two to four were essentially performed by what amounted to a high-class repertory company. Joining Atkinson and Tony Robinson in their roles as Blackadder and Baldrick were Stephen Fry, Hugh Laurie, Miranda Richardson, Tim McInnerny and Rik Mayall, each reprising parts played in earlier series. There was also a Christmas special set in various time zones, including the future, and depicting Blackadder as Ebenezer Scrooge in reverse – he began the story a kind and generous patrician, winding up as the Blackadder we had all grown to know, love and hate. A short insert (*Blackadder: The Cavalier Years*) was produced for COMIC RELIEF in 1988, placing the troupe in the Civil War era, with Stephen Fry as King Charles I, while a special film made for screening at the Millennium Dome, entitled *Blackadder Back and Forth*, was eventually given its TV première by Sky One in October 2000.

BLACKEYES

UK (BBC/Australian Broadcasting Corporation/Television New Zealand) Drama. BBC 2 1989

Maurice James Kingsley	**Michael Gough**
Jessica	**Carol Royle**
Jeff	**Nigel Planer**
Blackeyes	**Gina Bellman**
Jamieson	**Colin Jeavons**
Andrew Stilk	**Nicholas Woodeson**
Det. Blake	**John Shrapnel**
Mark Wilsher	**David Westhead**
Colin	**Gary Love**
Little Jessica	**Hannah Morris**

Writer: **Dennis Potter**
Producer: **Rick McCallum**

A model finds her life story is distorted in a novel.

Controversial, even by Dennis Potter's standards, and predictably slated by the Establishment for its nudity, *Blackeyes* was the story of Jessica, a former model. Angrily discovering that her 77-year-old Uncle Maurice had written a successful sexy novel based on her own real-life modelling experiences, she desperately wanted to rewrite the tale more truthfully, but lacked the required skill. Blackeyes had been her professional name.

Immersed in a typically Potter-esque amalgam of reality and fiction, slimy advertising men like Stilk and the seemingly decent observer Jeff played their parts in showing how young girls can become abused in the glamour industry. Potter also directed the four episodes.

BLACKMAN, HONOR
(1925–)

Blonde British leading lady, a graduate of the Rank charm school who sprang to fame as the athletic Cathy Gale in THE AVENGERS, having already appeared in the series PROBATION OFFICER. After two years as Gale, Blackman headed for Hollywood, winning the part of Pussy Galore in *Goldfinger*. Recently, her most prominent role has been as Laura West in THE UPPER HAND, although she has also been seen in other comedy series like ROBIN'S NEST (Marion Nicholls) and NEVER THE TWAIN (Veronica Barton). Additional credits over the years have ranged from THE FOUR JUST MEN, THE INVISIBLE MAN and GHOST SQUAD to TOP SECRET, the miniseries *Lace* and DOCTOR WHO. Her second husband was actor Maurice Kaufmann.

BLAIR, ISLA
(1946–)

RADA-trained actress born in India, married to actor Julian Glover and mother of actor Jamie Blair. Among her many credits have been roles in *The Liars*, THE CREZZ (Emma Antrobus), *An Englishman's Castle*, *The History Man* (Flora Beniform), WHEN THE BOAT COMES IN (Lady Caroline), THE BOUNDER (Laura), *The Dickie Henderson Show*, TAGGART, *The Advocates* (Katherine Dunbar), THE FINAL CUT (Claire Carlsen), INSPECTOR MORSE, A TOUCH OF FROST, *True Tilda* (Mrs Mortimer) and *Heaven on Earth* (Mary Weston).

BLAIR, LIONEL
(Henry Lionel Ogus; 1932–)

Canadian-born dancer and TV personality, one of the team captains on GIVE US A CLUE and later host of NAME THAT TUNE.

BLAKE'S 7
UK (BBC) Science Fiction. BBC 1 1978–81

Roj Blake	**Gareth Thomas**
Kerr Avon	**Paul Darrow**
Jenna Stannis	**Sally Knyvette**
Vila Restal	**Michael Keating**
Cally	**Jan Chappell**
Zen	**Peter Tuddenham** (*voice only*)
Gan Olag	**David Jackson**
Orac	**Peter Tuddenham** (*voice only*)
Dayna Mellanby	**Josette Simon**
Capt. Del Tarrant	**Steven Pacey**
Soolin	**Glynis Barber**
Supreme Commander Servalan	**Jacqueline Pearce**

Commander Travis .... **Stephen Greif**
Brian Croucher
Slave .... **Peter Tuddenham** (*voice only*)

Creator: **Terry Nation**
Producers: **David Maloney, Vere Lorrimer**

In the distant future, a band of escaped criminals fights back against an oppressive government.

At some time in the 3rd century of the second calendar, the populated worlds of our galaxy found themselves at the mercy of a cruel, remorseless dictatorship known as The Federation. This ruthless regime tolerated no opposition. Petty criminals, by way of pay-offs, were allowed to exist and make life a misery for the population, but no political dissent was tolerated. There were, however, small bands of resistance. One such band was comprised of escaped prisoners, led by the falsely convicted Roj Blake. On their way to exile on the penal colony of Cygnus Alpha, they had made their burst for freedom in an abandoned spacecraft renamed *Liberator*, and now they wandered the galaxy avoiding recapture, hell bent on sabotaging the activities of The Federation.

Blake, a natural-born leader, became a genuine freedom fighter, a hero in a corrupt universe. But even if he was a Robin Hood figure, his followers were far from merry men. His number two, computer genius Kerr Avon, was an ambitious, arrogant man, given only to preserving his own skin, while the safe-cracker, Vila, suffered from a broad yellow streak. There were also smuggler/pilot Jenna Stannis, Cally, a combative, telepathic native of the planet Auron, and the brawny Gan, who had an electronic limiter fitted to his brain to prevent him killing. Although their well-being depended on mutual assistance, this was never a team, rather a collection of squabbling, selfish renegades thrown together by outside pressures.

The seventh member of the group was the *Liberator*'s master computer, Zen, but characters came and went during the course of the programme's run and the composition of the Seven changed. Gone were Gan and Jenna when mercenary Del Tarrant and weapons expert Dayna Mellanby were added to the cast, with the beautiful blonde Soolin, a crack shot, joining later. Not even Blake was a fixture. He disappeared at the end of the second series, to be replaced as leader by the stony-faced Avon. There were also new computers, Orac and, in *Scorpio* (a new spacecraft which replaced the destroyed *Liberator*), Slave. In pursuit of the rebels were Supreme Commander Servalan, icy and calculating, and her vicious henchman, Travis, whom Blake had once blinded in one eye. Blake returned briefly, just long enough to be killed by Avon in the very last episode.

For all their efforts, the Seven only ever succeeded in causing minor problems for The Federation. Their cause was a hopeless one, and a sense of futility pervaded the series. Despite a lacklustre final season, when the budget had clearly been slashed, *Blake's 7* achieved cult status, not just in the UK but in America, too, even though it was never fully networked in the USA. Most of the regulars were reunited for a one-off Radio 4 special in 1998, but with Paula Wilcox providing the voice for Soolin and Angela Bruce playing Dayna.

BLAKELY, COLIN
(1930–87)

Northern Irish classical actor whose TV roles were usually in the quietly determined vein. His most prominent part was Jesus Christ in Dennis Potter's controversial play, *Son of Man*, in 1969, although he also starred as Lew Burnett in *The Hanged Man* and was very nearly cast as the lead in TARGET, the BBC's answer to THE SWEENEY. Other TV credits included the Alun Owen plays *Lena, O My Lena* and *Shelter*, and the dramas *The Breaking of Colonel Keyser, Peer Gynt, The Birthday Party, Drums Along Balmoral Drive, Operation Julie* (DI Richard Lee), *Cousin Bette* (Steinbock), THE BEIDERBECKE AFFAIR (Chief Supt. Forrest) and *Paradise Postponed* (Dr Salter).

BLANC, MEL
(1908–89)

Hollywood's most celebrated cartoon voicer, famous for the likes of Bugs Bunny, Daffy Duck, Sylvester and Tweety Pie, Woody Woodpecker, Porky Pig and Speedy Gonzales. His television voices included Barney Rubble and Dino in THE FLINTSTONES, Cosmo C. Spacely in THE JETSONS and Twiki the robot in BUCK ROGERS IN THE 25TH CENTURY. He actually appeared in vision with Jack Benny in the 1950s, playing Benny's violin teacher, Professor LeBlanc.

BLAND, SIR CHRISTOPHER
(1938–)

Successful businessman, one-time Conservative councillor and TV executive (Deputy Chairman of the IBA, director of ITN and Chairman of LWT), who became the BBC's Chairman in 1996, on a five-year contract. He represented Ireland at fencing in the 1960 Olympics.

BLANKETY BLANK
UK (BBC) Game Show. BBC 1 1979–90; 1997–9/ITV 2001–

Presenters: **Terry Wogan, Les Dawson, Lily Savage**

Producers: **Alan Boyd, Marcus Plantin, Stanley Appel, Dean Jones**

Contrived comic guessing game.

Considering its dire prizes and contrived format, *Blankety Blank* proved remarkably durable. It was undoubtedly established by the appeal of first host Terry Wogan (with his unusual, magic wand-like microphone), but it remained popular when Les Dawson took charge in 1984. What the four contestants (two sets of two) had to do was guess the missing word in a somewhat risqué statement read out by Wogan or Dawson. To edge towards the prizes, their word had to match the guesses made by a panel of six celebrities. The more matches made, the more points (circles or triangles) were accrued. With celebrity help (or hindrance), the winning contestant then had to complete a short, final phrase, hopefully matching it to a word selected in a public survey to win one of the prizes, which were staggeringly modest (Dawson once quipped, 'Some prizes are so bad, they're left in the foyer'). Losing contestants walked away with a *Blankety Blank* cheque book and pen. Of more interest to the viewer were the exchanges between the host and the celebrity panel, which generally overshadowed the main contest.

The show was revived for a Christmas special in 1997, with Lily Savage (Paul O'Grady) at the helm. A series followed in 1998, and a year later the title was changed to *Lily Savage's Blankety Blank*. The programme moved to ITV in 2001.

BLEASDALE, ALAN
(1946–)

Liverpudlian playwright whose work has reflected social injustice through wry humour and sharp characterizations. His first TV play was *Early to Bed* in 1975, but it was his drama *The Black Stuff*, screened in 1980, which attracted more interest. With unemployment poised to soar in Britain, Bleasdale's skilful observation of a band of Scouse tarmac-layers, working away from home and hovering on the brink of the dole, gave more than a hint of his work to come. It ultimately led to a complete series, BOYS FROM THE BLACKSTUFF, a 1982 five-part sequel which explored the stresses life on the dole brought to its main protagonists, including the celebrated Yosser ('Gissa job') Hughes. Earlier, Bleasdale had rewritten the intended first episode of the series as the one-off play, *The Muscle Market*. In 1984 he developed his own *Scully* novels (as first seen in a 1978 PLAY FOR TODAY) for Channel 4, creating a 'real world' teenage drama, before embarking on another controversial series for the BBC. This time it was THE MONOCLED MUTINEER, the four-part story of Percy Toplis, a World War I army rebel who was executed by the Secret Service. The Tory press was outraged. In 1991, back on Channel 4, Bleasdale turned his attention once more to Liverpool and the contrasting lifestyles of rising political star Michael Murray (Robert Lindsay) and gentle schoolteacher Jim Nelson (Michael Palin) in the much-acclaimed GBH. For the same channel he switched to production, offering a helping hand to aspiring writers in the four-part anthology, *Alan Bleasdale Presents*, in 1994, and then wrote and produced *Jake's Progress* in 1995, a drama about family tensions starring Robert Lindsay again and Julie Walters (for whom Bleasdale had contributed material for a one-off showcase in 1991). *Melissa*, a murder-mystery inspired by the writings of Francis Durbridge, followed in 1997.

BLESS THIS HOUSE
UK (Thames) Situation Comedy. ITV 1971–6

Sid Abbott	**Sidney James**
Jean Abbott	**Diana Coupland**
Mike Abbott	**Robin Stewart**
Sally Abbott	**Sally Geeson**
Trevor	**Anthony Jackson**
Betty	**Patsy Rowlands**

Creators: **Vince Powell, Harry Driver**
Producer: **William G. Stewart**

Generation-gap comedy with a suburban family.

Cheery, pipe-chewing Londoner Sid Abbott, a middle-aged stationery salesman, was fond of booze, women and football. He still considered himself one of the lads, but had little chance to prove it, as his long-suffering wife, Jean, was always around to keep him in check. They lived in Birch Avenue, Putney, with their two teenage children, and that was where their real problems began. Mike (trendily garbed in beads and Afghan coat) had just left art college and was far too busy protesting about this and that to find himself a job, and with-it Sally, apple of her dad's eye, was in the final year of grammar school. Sadly their 1970s morals and vices were a touch too daring for their rather staid parents, who were constantly bemused at the permissive society and seldom failed to jump to wrong conclusions. Trevor was Sid's next-door neighbour and drinking pal at the Hare and Hounds, with Betty his nagging wife.

A big ratings success, *Bless This House* numbered among its writers Carla Lane and its creators, Vince Powell and Harry Driver. Produced by future FIFTEEN TO ONE host, William G. Stewart, it was Sid James's last major television series. Geoff Love wrote the theme music. A feature film version was issued in 1972.

BLESSED, BRIAN
(1937–)

Large, Yorkshire-born actor, whose full-blooded performances have earned gentle mimicry. He first came to light in Z CARS, in which, as PC Fancy Smith, he was one of the original stars. Then, in 1966, he played Porthos in the BBC's adaptation of *The Three Musketeers*. In the 1970s and 1980s he was Augustus in I, CLAUDIUS, Mark of Cornwall in ARTHUR OF THE BRITONS and another 'historical' character, King Richard IV, in the first series of BLACKADDER. Blessed then proved to be a well-cast successor to Robert Newton in *John Silver's Return to Treasure Island*. Among his other TV credits have been episodes of JUSTICE, HADLEIGH, PUBLIC EYE, *Churchill's People*, SPACE: 1999, THE SWEENEY, MINDER, *War and Remembrance* and *Tom Jones* (Squire Western). In the footsteps of Hillary and Tensing, he fulfilled a long-held ambition by climbing Mount Everest in the early 1990s. He is married to actress Hildegard Neil.

BLETHYN, BRENDA
(1946–)

Kent-born actress seen in dramatic and comedy roles. She starred as Alison Little and Erica Parsons in the sitcoms *Chance in a Million* and *The Labours of Erica*, respectively; Shirley Frame in the comedy drama *All Good Things*; Margaret Amir in *The Buddah of Suburbia*; and Miriam 'Mim' Dervish in OUTSIDE EDGE. Other credits have included *That Uncertain Feeling* and *Screen One*'s *The Bullion Boys*.

BLIGH, JASMINE
(1913–91)

One of television's first personalities, Jasmine Bligh joined the BBC in 1935, becoming, together with Elizabeth Cowell and Leslie Mitchell, one of the three host-announcers for the Corporation's TV test transmissions. Her earlier experience as an actress stood her in good stead in those days before autocues, as she had to learn all her announcements word for word. Although television was suspended during World War II, Bligh returned to our screens to open up the new post-war service in 1946. After abandoning television work for a while, she returned to the BBC to narrate the *Noddy* series and she resurfaced yet again in the 1970s as presenter of Thames TV's daytime magazine, *Good Afternoon*. Jasmine Bligh was a descendant of Captain Bligh, of *Bounty* fame.

BLIND DATE
UK (LWT) Game Show. ITV 1985–

Presenter: **Cilla Black**

Producers: **Gill Stribling-Wright, Kevin Roast, Michael Longmire, Thelma McGough, Chris O'Dell, Isobel Hatton**

Girls and guys select unseen partners for a prize trip.

In this dating service of the air, young men and women selected a member of the opposite sex to join them on a 'blind date' excursion. Three unseen contestants delivered rehearsed answers to three scripted questions posed by a boy or girl looking for a date. On the strength of their answers, one was chosen to accompany the questioner on a special trip. This may have involved anything from a week on the Mediterranean to a day at a safari park, depending on their luck in drawing envelopes. The following week the blind daters returned to tell all about their experience and to give honest opinions about their unfortunate partners. Cilla Black egged them on.

The first couple to marry as a result of meeting on the programme were Sue Middleton and Alex Tatham. Their 1991 wedding was captured in a special programme entitled *Blind Date Wedding of the Year*.

BLOCKBUSTERS
UK (Central) Quiz. ITV 1983–94

Presenter: **Bob Holness**

Producers: **Graham C. Williams, Tony Wolfe, Terry Steel, Bob Cousins**

Daily general-knowledge quiz for sixth-formers.

In this easy-going contest, Bob Holness asked the questions and three 16–18-year-old students (two played one) provided answers to light up hexagonal blocks on an electronic board. The team of two had to score a line of five blocks across a board to win a game, while the single contestant needed four in a row down the board. Each block selected bore the initial letter of the answer and much fun was had when contestants asked, 'Can I have a P please, Bob?' Money was awarded for every correct answer and matches consisted of three games (the winner won two of the three). The winning pupil (or one of the twosome) was then put on the 'hot spot'. He or she, by answering more questions, had to light up a path across the board in 60 seconds to win a prize. The hot-spot prizes increased in value, the more wins that were achieved, but five wins were the maximum for any contestant(s).

Blockbusters gained a cult following among schoolkids and adults alike, and the studio audience enthusiastically showed their support by hand-jiving to the rousing theme music. *Blockbusters* returned to the screen in 2000, on Sky One, with Liza Tarbuck as host.

BLOCKER, DAN
(1929–72)

Massive American actor, fondly remembered as the gentle giant, Hoss Cartwright, in BONANZA, although he appeared in other earlier TV Westerns, including GUNSMOKE and *Cimarron City*. *Bonanza* lasted only one series after Blocker's untimely death.

BLOTT ON THE LANDSCAPE
UK (BBC) Comedy Drama. BBC 2 1985

Sir Giles Lynchwood, MP	**George Cole**
Lady Maud Lynchwood	**Geraldine James**
Blott	**David Suchet**
Mrs Forthby	**Julia McKenzie**
Dundridge	**Simon Cadell**
Ganglion	**Geoffrey Bayldon**
Hoskins	**Paul Brooke**
Densher	**Jeremy Clyde**

Writer: **Malcolm Bradbury**
Producer: **Evgeny Gridneff**

An unscrupulous MP attempts to build a motorway through his wife's ancestral home.

Sir Giles Lynchwood was the Member of Parliament for South Worfordshire, a man with weird fetishes (which were indulged in extrovert sex sessions down in London) and a greedy desire to make more money. One of his plans was to direct a new motorway through the grounds of his wife's stately home, Handyman Hall, which was picturesquely set in Cleene Gorge. Rallying to its defence, the eccentric Lady Maud (a devotee of country sports) fought tooth and nail to preserve her home, assisted by her surreptitious gardener, Blott. Mrs Forthby was the housekeeper and Dundridge the hapless man from the ministry who found himself immersed in the murky goings-on.

This six-part series was an adaptation by Malcolm Bradbury of Tom Sharpe's black comic novel of the same name. Filming took place at Stanage Park, near Ludlow.

BLUE PETER
UK (BBC) Children's Magazine. BBC 1 1958–

Presenters: **Leila Williams, Christopher Trace, Anita West, Valerie Singleton, John Noakes, Peter Purves, Lesley Judd, Simon Groom, Christopher Wenner, Tina Heath, Sarah Greene, Peter Duncan, Janet Ellis, Michael Sundin, Mark Curry, Caron Keating, Yvette Fielding, John Leslie, Diane-Louise Jordan, Anthea Turner, Tim Vincent, Stuart Miles, Katy Hill, Romana D'Annunzio, Richard Bacon, Konnie Huq, Simon Thomas, Matt Baker, Liz Barker**

Creator: **John Hunter Blair**
Editors: **Biddy Baxter, Lewis Bronze, Oliver MacFarlane, Steve Hocking**

Long-running children's magazine.

Blue Peter is one programme most of Britain's thirty-somethings grew up with. It began as an idea of BBC producer John Hunter Blair in 1958 and was scheduled for a mere seven-week run, with each programme lasting just 15 minutes. Actor Christopher Trace and former Miss Great Britain Leila Williams were the first hosts and helped set the safe, middle-class tone which was to characterize the programme for years to come. However, the golden age of *Blue Peter* was undoubtedly the mid-1960s, when, with the programme extended to a half-hour in length, and well entrenched in its Monday and Thursday tea-time slots, its best-known trio of presenters were Valerie Singleton, John Noakes and Peter Purves.

Over the years, the programme's trademarks have been its unwhistlable hornpipe theme tune (entitled *Barnacle Bill*), and its *Blue Peter* badges (bearing the ship logo devised by Tony Hart) for contributors. (There are five badges to be won: white with a blue ship for correspondents and participants in the programme; blue with a silver ship for contributing recipes or other new creations; green with a white ship for ecologically related letters; competition-winner badges; and the rare, much-coveted gold badge for extraordinary acts and achievements.) The running order has mixed together interviews with guests, chats to precocious kids with unusual hobbies, assorted competitions (design the Christmas stamps was one), the daredevil exploits of the intrepid John Noakes and later Peter Duncan (both went on to star in their own spin-offs, *Go with Noakes* and *Duncan Dares*), and educational and historical inserts. In the early days, the illustrated tales of *Packi* (an elephant drawn, again, by Tony Hart), *Bengo*, a puppy, and space travellers *Bleep and Booster* (the last two sketched by William Timyn) were occasional features and, for years, Percy Thrower looked after the *Blue Peter* garden. Chris Trace diligently cared for the elaborate *Blue Peter* train set, and rides on the programme's namesake steam engine, the 532 *Blue Peter*, have also been scheduled. A new-born baby became a regular visitor to the show in 1968. Daniel Scott became the *Blue Peter* Baby, allowing Noakes and Purves to make a complete hash of changing his nappy.

The programme's animals have shared equal billing with its human hosts. Among the most famous *Blue Peter* pets have been dogs Petra (who actually died after one programme and was replaced by a lookalike for the rest of her days), Patch, Shep, Goldie, Bonnie and Mabel; Jason, the Siamese cat, and fellow felines Jack, Jill and Willow; Joey, the parrot; Honey, the guide dog, and Fred (later discovered to be Freda), the tortoise. Guest animals have proved particularly troublesome (especially as the show has always gone out live), with the chaos caused by Lulu, the defecating elephant, almost matched by a troupe of feuding St Bernards some years later.

Each year the pets have been packed off to the country for the summer while their masters and mistresses have headed for exotic climes in the annual *Blue Peter* expedition. Places visited have included Ceylon (now Sri Lanka) and the USA. Each Christmas has been heralded by the lighting of the advent crown (made from two tinsel-lagged coat-hangers) and a blast from the Chalk Farm Salvation Army Band. Indeed, *Blue Peter*'s Heath Robinson creations like the advent crown have gone into folklore, primarily because of the imaginative use of egg cartons, used toilet-rolls, detergent bottles ('Sqeezy' was never mentioned) and sticky-backed plastic (nor was 'Fablon'). For many years, these were largely the ideas of Margaret Parnell. 'Here's one I made earlier' became a catchphrase.

Another annual feature has been the *Blue Peter* Appeal, raising funds for worthy causes, although not often by asking for money. Instead, used stamps, milk-bottle tops, paperback books, old wool, aluminium cans and other such recyclables have been collected and sold in bulk to bring in cash. Among the best-remembered appeals have been for Guide Dogs for the Blind, inshore lifeboats (seven supplied to date), Biafran war victims, horse-riding centres for handicapped children and equipment for children's hospitals and Romanian orphanages.

As well as the spin-off series mentioned above, another extra was the *Blue Peter Royal Safari to Africa* in 1971, in which Val accompanied HRH Princess Anne (the Princess Royal) into the Kenyan outback. It led to other *Blue Peter Special Assignments* for Val and allowed her to retire from the twice-weekly programme with grace.

Over 40 years after making its debut, *Blue Peter* is still going strong. It survived the retirement of long-serving programme editor, Biddy Baxter, in 1988. Indeed, a third weekly programme was added in 1995, with the schedule changed to Monday, Wednesday and Friday. Even the sacking of presenter Richard Bacon in 1998 for admitting cocaine abuse failed to derail it.

BOCHCO, STEVEN
(1943–)

After a chequered career writing and producing shows like COLUMBO, McMILLAN AND WIFE, THE SIX MILLION DOLLAR MAN, *Griff* and *Delvecchio*, Steven Bochco's career took a sharp upturn when he created HILL STREET BLUES. Although his next series, *Bay City Blues*, was a flop, he then bounced back with LA LAW. Setting a new style for TV drama in these series (ensemble casts, continuing storylines, awkward topics, etc.), he earned himself a prestigious contract with ABC, for whom he went on to develop *Hooperman*, the less successful *Doogie Howser, MD* and *Cop Rock*, which attempted to combine pop songs with police action. Enjoying far greater acclaim was his next offering, NYPD BLUE, topped yet again by the ground-breaking MURDER ONE. His wife, Barbara Bosson, has been seen in many of his productions.

BOHT, JEAN
(1936–)

Although synonymous now with the long-suffering Nellie Boswell in the dole sitcom, BREAD, Jean Boht's television career has stretched over programmes like MR ROSE, THE SWEENEY, JULIET BRAVO, *Spyship* and the Alan Bleasdale dramas BOYS FROM THE BLACKSTUFF and *Scully* (Gran). She also appeared in *I Woke Up One Morning*, *The Cloning of Joanna May* and the unsuccessful *Brighton Belles*, the UK translation of THE GOLDEN GIRLS (Josephine). She is married to composer Carl Davis.

BOLAM, JAMES
(1938–)

Sunderland-born actor/comedian, one of TV's LIKELY LADS (Terry Collier) in the 1960s and 1970s, but enjoying a varied TV career since those days. He gained a new following as Jack Ford in WHEN THE BOAT COMES IN, appeared in the BBC Television Shakespeare production of *As You Like It* and played nosy schoolteacher Trevor Chaplin in THE BEIDERBECKE AFFAIR and its sequels. Not abandoning comedy, he has taken the roles of Roy Figgis in ONLY WHEN I LAUGH, Nesbitt Gunn in *Room at the Bottom*, Father Matthew in *Father Matthew's Daughter*, Bill MacGregor in SECOND THOUGHTS and Ted Whitehead in the one-off *Eleven Men Against Eleven*. He also played the lead in *Andy Capp* and over the years has been seen in programmes like TAKE THREE GIRLS, THE PROTECTORS, *Executive Stress*, *Sticky Wickets*, *Have Your Cake and Eat It* (Nat Oliver), *The Missing Postman* (Clive Peacock), *The Stalker's Apprentice* (serial killer Helmut Kranze), *Dirty Tricks* (Insp. Moss) and *Close and True* (Graham True). He is married to actress Susan Jameson.

BONANZA
US (NBC) Western. ITV 1960–73

Ben Cartwright	**Lorne Greene**
Little Joe Cartwright	**Michael Landon**
Eric 'Hoss' Cartwright	**Dan Blocker**
Adam Cartwright	**Pernell Roberts**
Hop Sing	**Victor Sen Yung**
Sheriff Roy Coffee	**Ray Teal**
Mr Canaday ('Candy')	**David Canary**
Dusty Rhoades	**Lou Frizzel**
Jamie Hunter	**Mitch Vogel**
Griff King	**Tim Matheson**

Creator/Producer: **David Dortort**

The adventures of an all-male ranching family in the 1860s.

This hugely successful Western opened with a pounding theme song and a map which burst into flames. It was the story of the Cartwright family, owners of the 1000-square-mile Ponderosa ranch, set on the edge of Virginia City, Nevada. Head of the family was father Ben, and he was ably supported by his three sons, all from different, deceased mothers. The pensive (and eldest) one was Adam, then came the slow-witted, 21-stone Hoss who, for all his bulk, could be as meek as a kitten. (The name 'Hoss' means 'good luck' in Norwegian and was a tribute to his Scandinavian mother, who had been killed by Indians.) The third son was Little Joe, an impetuous lad with an eye for the girls. The Cartwrights' kitchen was looked after by Chinese cook, Hop Sing.

The series revolved around the family's encounters with the dregs of society, their own self-preservation and the help they gave to others. There were many guest stars throughout its run, but also a few cast changes. Pernell Roberts left the show after six years and was not replaced for a couple of seasons. Then along came Candy, to work as a ranch hand. One of Ben's friends, Dusty Rhoades, was taken on when Candy temporarily moved away, and also seen was orphaned teenager Jamie Hunter. But the series was dealt a mortal blow by the sudden death of actor Dan Blocker in 1972 and, when Lorne Greene suffered a mild heart attack a few months later, the end of the series was in sight. By then *Bonanza* had been a Sunday night favourite in the USA for 14 years.

BOND, JULIAN
(1930–)

British dramatist and producer, contributor to THE SAINT and UPSTAIRS, DOWNSTAIRS, and creator of POLICE SURGEON (the series that led to THE AVENGERS). His later TV successes included *A Man of Our Times*, *The Ferryman* (for the *Haunted* anthology), WINGS, DICK BARTON – SPECIAL AGENT (with Clive Exton), *Love for Lydia*, *Fair Stood the Wind for France*, *Strangers and Brothers* and the Channel 4 adaptation of THE FAR PAVILIONS.

BOND, WARD
(1903–60)

American actor chiefly remembered as the trailmaster, Major Seth Adams, in WAGON TRAIN. He died at the height of the series' success and was replaced by John McIntire as Christopher Hale.

BONEHEAD
UK (BBC) Children's Comedy. BBC 1960–2

Bonehead .... **Colin Douglas**
Boss .... **Paul Whitsun-Jones**
Happy .... **Douglas Blackwell**

Creator/Writer/Producer: **Shaun Sutton**

Three inept crooks prove that crime doesn't pay.

Bonehead introduced kids to three of the most incompetent villains ever seen on television. Head of the trio was the bulky, gangster-like Boss, deviser of great plans which always ended in failure; also in the team was the ironically named Happy. However, it was the dim-witted Bonehead, a lovable imbecile, who was the show's nominal star. Two seasons were made, before actor Colin Douglas moved on to more sensible dramas, like A FAMILY AT WAR.

BONEY
Australia (Norfolk International) Police Drama. ITV 1975

DI Napoleon Bonaparte ('Boney') ..... **James Laurenson**

Executive Producers: **Bob Austin, Lee Robinson**
Producer: **John McCallum**

The cases of an Aborigine detective.

Although a white man 'coloured up', New Zealander James Laurenson took the lead in this popular series about an Aborigine police detective whose beat was the Australian bush. It shouldn't have been the busiest patch for crime, but Boney found plenty to keep him occupied among the farmers, prospectors and drifters of the outback. The series was based on the novels by Arthur Upfield and received only sporadic screenings in the UK.

BOOM

An extendible, manoeuvrable arm holding a microphone which may be positioned, out of shot, over actors' and presenters' heads to pick up voices.

BOON
UK (Central) Comedy Drama. ITV 1986–92

Ken Boon .... **Michael Elphick**
Harry Crawford .... **David Daker**
Doreen Evans .... **Rachel Davies**
Ethel Allard .... **Joan Scott**
Rocky Cassidy .... **Neil Morrissey**
Debbie Yates .... **Lesley-Anne Sharpe**
Laura Marsh .... **Elizabeth Carling**
Alex Wilton .... **Saskia Wickham**

Creators: **Jim Hill, Bill Stair**
Executive Producers: **Ted Childs, William Smethurst**

Producers: **Kenny McBain, Esta Charkham, Michele Buck, Simon Lewis**

A kind-hearted, retired fireman becomes a freelance troubleshooter.

When Ken Boon was forced to leave the fire service on grounds of ill-health (he had damaged his lungs in a heroic rescue), he struggled to make ends meet. After a succession of failed money-making schemes, including a disastrous market-gardening venture, he placed an ad in the local press. It read: 'Ex-fireman seeks interesting work – anything legal considered.' In response he was offered a variety of strange jobs, from child-minding to private detective work, not all of them, as he had hoped, legal. But the stocky, lugubrious Boon, with his heart of gold, was a soft touch, committed to his work and unhappy about letting down employers. His early associates were Doreen Evans and Ethel Allard.

Boon thought of himself as an urban cowboy, cruising the streets of the Midlands on his silver charger, a 650-c.c. BSA Norton motorbike, which he called 'White Lightning'. He soon made his hobby his business by opening a courier agency, The Texas Rangers, and employing a dopey biker by the name of Rocky Cassidy as his sidekick, and teenager Debbie Yates as his secretary. Ken's best friend was fireman-turned-hotelier Harry Crawford, a businessman of little brain who moved from premises to premises, trading up, until he finally went bust as owner of a country house hotel. Ken, who was then working as a private eye with Rocky and a new secretary, Laura Marsh, agreed to join Harry in a new venture, Crawford Boon Security. Laura was later replaced by the resourceful Alex Wilton.

Although the series ended in 1992, one episode remained untransmitted until 1995. The show's theme song, 'Hi Ho Silver', by Jim Diamond, was a UK top five hit in 1986.

BOONE, RICHARD
(1917–81)

American actor, a hit in the roles of hired gun Paladin in HAVE GUN WILL TRAVEL and Wild West detective *Hec Ramsey*. His lesser successes included *Medic* and an anthology, *The Richard Boone Show*, both largely confined to US TV. Like singer Pat Boone, Richard Boone was a descendant of frontiersman Daniel Boone.

BOOTS AND SADDLES
US (California National) Western. BBC 1958–60

Capt. Shank Adams .... **Jack Pickard**
Lt. Col. Hayes .... **Patrick McVey**
Lt. Kelly .... **Gardner McKay**
Lt. Binning .... **David Willock**
Sgt Bullock .... **John Alderson**
Luke Cummings .... **Michael Hinn**

Cavalry patrols in the Wild West.

Subtitled *The Story of the Fifth Cavalry, Boots and Saddles* told of brave uniformed men tackling Indians and other 'baddies' in the American West of the 1870s. Shank Adams was the Captain in charge of the troop, supported by Lt. Colonel Hayes and Lieutenants Kelly and Binning. Luke Cummings was the scout. Thirty-nine half-hour episodes were made, and they appeared to be more popular in the UK than in their native USA.

BOOTSIE AND SNUDGE

UK (Granada) Situation Comedy. ITV 1960–3; 1974

Bootsie Bisley	**Alfie Bass**
Claude Snudge	**Bill Fraser**
Hesketh Pendleton	**Robert Dorning**
Henry Beerbohm 'Old' Johnson	**Clive Dunn**

Producers: **Peter Eton, Milo Lewis, Eric Fawcett, Bill Podmore**

Two National Service veterans find themselves back in Civvy Street.

This spin-off from THE ARMY GAME focused on two of its most popular characters, Pte. 'Excused Boots' Bisley and the bullying Sgt Claude Snudge. It related how the old sparring partners took up positions in a seedy gentlemen's club called The Imperial. Bootsie appropriately became boot boy, while Snudge was the new majordomo. The club was run by its Right Honourable Secretary, Hesketh Pendleton, and Clive Dunn gave one of his first 'old man' performances as the decrepit 83-year-old barman, Old Johnson. Most of the scripts were penned by Marty Feldman and Barry Took.

In 1964 Bootsie and Snudge were seen in diplomatic circles in the series, *Foreign Affairs* (they were given jobs at the British Embassy in the city of Bosnik), and Alfie Bass and Bill Fraser went on to play similar characters (this time known as Alf Grimble and William Bendlove, respectively) in the 1967 series, *Vacant Lot. Bootsie and Snudge* was resurrected in 1974, but the characters' relationship was reversed, with Bootsie now the powerful force, having won the football pools, and Snudge the lowly man from the pools company. The revival was short-lived.

BORDER TELEVISION

Based in Carlisle, Border is the ITV contractor for the extreme north-west of England, the Scottish borders and the Isle of Man, taking to the air on 1 September 1961 (Isle of Man from 26 March 1965). One of the UK's smallest broadcasters, Border has successfully retained its franchise on every occasion but has not contributed significantly to the national ITV network. Perhaps the best-known offering has been the married couples quiz, MR AND MRS, hosted by Derek Batey (who, along with arts critic Melvyn Bragg, has also been a Border director). Having expanded into radio through its Century Radio brand, Border was taken over by the Capital Radio group in 2000.

BORGIAS, THE

UK (BBC) Historical Drama. BBC 2 1981

Rodrigo Borgia	**Adolfo Celi**
Cesare Borgia	**Oliver Cotton**
Giuliano della Rovere	**Alfred Burke**
Lucrezia Borgia	**Anne Louise Lambert**
Juan Borgia	**George Camiller**

Creator/Producer: **Mark Shivas**
Writers: **John Prebble, Ken Taylor**

Much-ridiculed attempt at dramatizing the tyranny of the infamous Borgia family.

Set in the 15th century, *The Borgias* aimed to expose the excesses and vices of late-Renaissance Italy. At the heart of the action was the hideous Rodrigo Borgia, a man who had bribed his way to the title of Pope Alexander VI. A wonderfully impious man, Rodrigo's cruelty and greed were surpassed only by the barbarity of his son, Cesare, and his treacherous daughter, Lucrezia, mistress of poison. They murdered, debased, plundered, raped and violated their way to power, becoming the most hated, but the most potent, family in Italy.

Unhappily, because of star Adolfo Celi's fractured English, the series became rather difficult to follow and collapsed into an unintentional parody of historical drama. Pitched in the same vein as I, CLAUDIUS and other BBC epics, *The Borgias* failed magnificently to reach the same heights. What should have been the most shocking moments were rendered laughable by over-the-top performances and poor scripting. Critics were not impressed, nor was the Vatican, which issued a note of censure.

BOSANQUET, REGINALD

(1932–84)

Popular ITN newsreader of the 1960s and 1970s, whose lively private life became regular tabloid fare. Bosanquet, the son of Middlesex and England cricketer B. J. T. Bosanquet (the man who invented the 'googly', still known as the 'Bosie' Down Under), joined ITN at its inception in 1955 as a trainee. From there he developed into one of its leading reporters, eventually becoming diplomatic correspondent and presenting programmes like ROVING REPORT and *Dateline*. In 1967 he was chosen as one of the newscasters to launch the revolutionary *News at Ten*, and his on-air partnerships with Andrew Gardner and Anna Ford proved particularly popular with viewers, who enjoyed the sense of unpredictability he brought to newsreading. However, his rather stilted delivery and lop-sided smirk were the result of a medical condition and nothing more sinister, like drink, as some columnists had it. Bosanquet resigned from ITN in a blaze of publicity in 1979, during a lengthy technicians' strike and presented a few reports for NATIONWIDE before his death in 1984.

BOSLEY, TOM
(1927–)

American actor, familiar as the sympathetic father, Howard Cunningham, in the nostalgic sitcom, HAPPY DAYS. His 'pop' roles had begun earlier, when he provided the voice for harassed Harry Boyle in *Wait Till Your Father Gets Home*, although later Bosley switched from dad to detective, playing Sheriff Amos Tupper in MURDER, SHE WROTE and the title role in FATHER DOWLING INVESTIGATES. His TV career began in 1964 in the US version of THAT WAS THE WEEK THAT WAS and continued through the likes of *The Debbie Reynolds Show*, in which he played Debbie's brother-in-law, Bob Landers, and *The Dean Martin Show*. He was also narrator for the showbiz restrospective, *That's Hollywood*, and has appeared as guest star in many other series.

BOSS CAT
US (Hanna-Barbera) Cartoon. BBC 1962–3

Voices:

Top Cat ('TC')	**Arnold Stang**
Benny the Ball	**Maurice Gosfield**
Choo Choo	**Marvin Kaplan**
Spook	**Leo De Lyon**
The Brain	**Leo De Lyon**
Fancy-Fancy	**John Stephenson**
Officer Dibble	**Allen Jenkins**
Pierre	**John Stephenson**
Goldie	**Jean Vander Pyl**
Honey Dew	**Sallie Jones**

Creator: **Joseph Barbera**
Executive Producers: **William Hanna, Joseph Barbera**

A scheming tom is leader of a scrounging squad of alley cats.

Boss Cat, or *Top Cat* as it was known outside Britain (the UK already had a cat food of that name), was a feline version of *Sgt Bilko*. Fort Baxter gave way to a Manhattan alleyway and uniforms were swapped for fur coats, but otherwise the guys were all there, from the sweet-talking con cat leader to the dimmest of the dim fall guy. The gang was headed by Top Cat, commonly known as TC, who lived in a luxurious dustbin, ate scraps from the local deli, drank milk from nearby doorsteps and used the local police phone to make his calls, much to the consternation of the neighbourhood copper, Officer Dibble. Like Bilko, TC always had an eye for a fast buck, or the equivalent in cat terms. His dense henchmen, the equivalent of Bilko's platoon, were Brain, Fancy-Fancy, Spook, Choo Choo and Benny the Ball, the last voiced by Maurice Gosfield, Pte. Doberman in THE PHIL SILVERS SHOW. Pierre, Goldie and Honey Dew were other moggies seen.

BOTTOM
UK (BBC) Situation Comedy. BBC 2 1991–2; 1995

Richie Richard	**Rik Mayall**
Eddie Hitler	**Adrian Edmondson**

Creators/Writers: **Rik Mayall, Adrian Edmondson**
Producer: **Ed Bye**

Two no-hopers share a derelict flat.

Bottom – or *Your Bottom*, as its stars had considered calling it (hoping viewers would declare, 'I saw *Your Bottom* on the telly last night') – focused on the directionless lives of a pair of obnoxious flatmates. Richie and Eddie were characters straight out of the Mayall and Edmondson stock repertoire and bore more than a passing resemblance to their roles in THE YOUNG ONES. Richie, cringingly self-centred, dreamed of having sex – with anyone; Eddie, graphically violent and purposefully direct, fouled up his flatmate's best-laid plans. Constantly bickering and endlessly battering each other, they lived in squalor above a Hammersmith shop but virtually destroyed their putrid flat in every episode, amid an avalanche of jokes about smells, vomiting and other disgusting habits. They really were at the *Bottom* of life's pile.

BOUGH, FRANK
(1933–)

Avuncular presenter who, as host of GRANDSTAND from 1968, then NATIONWIDE, HOLIDAY and BREAKFAST TIME, became a household name, although things took a turn for the worse in the late 1980s when indiscretions in his private life hit the headlines. He has since returned to the screen on lower-key programmes for Sky and regional companies, and has occasionally presented sport on ITV (including the 1991 Rugby World Cup).

BOUNDER, THE
UK (Yorkshire) Situation Comedy. ITV 1982–3

Howard	**Peter Bowles**
Trevor Mountjoy	**George Cole**
Mary Mountjoy	**Rosalind Ayres**
Laura	**Isla Blair**

Creator/Writer: **Eric Chappell**
Producer: **Vernon Lawrence**

A conman becomes a cuckoo in his sister and brother-in-law's nest.

Fresh out of jail after serving time for embezzlement, the suave and untrustworthy Howard found a roof over his head, courtesy of his sister, Mary, but much to the dismay of her dependable estate agent husband, Trevor. They hoped he would turn over a new leaf, but then he met Laura, the young, attractive and *rich* widow living next door – just one temptation for him to return to his wicked ways.

BOUQUET OF BARBED WIRE
UK (LWT) Drama. ITV 1976

Peter Manson .... **Frank Finlay**
Prue Manson/Sorenson .... **Susan Penhaligon**
Gavin Sorenson .... **James Aubrey**
Cassie Manson .... **Sheila Allen**
Sarah Francis .... **Deborah Grant**

Writer: **Andrea Newman**
Executive Producer: **Rex Firkin**
Producer: **Tony Wharmby**

A father's incestuous love for his daughter wrecks the family.

Publisher Peter Manson, his wife, Cassie, and daughter, Prue, lived in middle-class harmony in Surrey. Then in stepped American Gavin Sorenson and their lives began to crumble. Gavin married Prue, and a wave of lust, infidelity and incest swept over the family. Peter's obsession with his pouting daughter finally tore the family apart. *Bouquet of Barbed Wire*, written by Andrea Newman from her own novel, graphically revealed the turmoil such steamy, forbidden passions can provoke and fully enjoyed the attentions of the tabloid press. Although Prue died after childbirth at the end of the serial, a sequel, *Another Bouquet*, followed a year later. It saw Cassie resuming a relationship with Gavin, and Peter falling for Gavin's new girlfriend. Clearly, lessons had not been learned.

BOWEN, JIM
(James Whittaker; 1937–)

Cheshire-born comic and game show presenter, a former schoolteacher and nightclub comedian, unearthed by THE COMEDIANS and then part of the *You Must Be Joking!* team. As host of the darts quiz BULLSEYE he gained a reputation for his forthright, down-to-earth treatment of contestants and his fumbling presentation. 'Great', 'smashing' and 'super' became his catchphrases. He also appeared in *Muck and Brass* and EL C.I.D. (playing himself), and in JONATHAN CREEK.

BOWLER, NORMAN
(1932–)

London-born actor who has meandered from one successful series to another. Among his best-known roles are David Martin in *Park Ranger*, DI Harry Hawkins in SOFTLY, SOFTLY, Sam Benson in CROSSROADS and, most recently, Frank Tate in EMMERDALE. His other appearances range from HARPERS WEST ONE and THE RAT-CATCHERS to JESUS OF NAZARETH and DEADLINE MIDNIGHT.

BOWLES, PETER
(1936–)

Suave, London-born actor, star of numerous series, often in a slightly untrustworthy role. His major credits include Toby Meres in the pilot for CALLAN (ARMCHAIR THEATRE's *A Magnum for Schneider*), Guthrie Featherstone in RUMPOLE OF THE BAILEY, Richard DeVere in TO THE MANOR BORN, Archie Glover in ONLY WHEN I LAUGH, Howard in THE BOUNDER, Neville Lytton in LYTTON'S DIARY (which he also created), Major Sinclair Yeates in THE IRISH RM and the conman, Guy Buchanan, in PERFECT SCOUNDRELS. Other appearances have been in *Doctor Knock*, THE SAINT, THE AVENGERS, THE BARON, THE PRISONER, SURVIVORS, *Good Girl* (Colin Peale), *Churchill's People*, SPACE: 1999, I, CLAUDIUS (Caractacus), THE CREZZ (Ken Green) and *Executive Stress* (Donald Fairchild), as well as Ken Russell's 1966 film, *Isadora*, and the mini-series, *A Shadow on the Sun* and *Little White Lies* (Oliver).

BOYD QC
UK (Associated-Rediffusion) Legal Drama. ITV 1956–64

Richard Boyd QC .... **Michael Denison**
Jack .... **Charles Leno**

Writer: **Jack Roffey**
Executive Producer: **Caryl Doncaster**

The ups and downs of a barrister's life.

Suave, elegant Richard Boyd, QC, was the gentle hero of this series of courtroom dramas. Ably supported by his clerk, Jack (who also acted as narrator), he prosecuted at times, but usually defended, generally turning up the right result. Filmed in semi-documentary style, the series was one of the first programmes to explore the world of the British judiciary, becoming a major hit, particularly towards the end of its long run.

BOYD, WILLIAM
(1895–72)

Silver-haired American actor for ever remembered as HOPALONG CASSIDY, a role he literally made his own, buying the TV rights to the character. However, Cassidy had only hopped along when Boyd's career seemed just about over, in 1934, with his days as a leading man in dramatic films of the 1920s fading fast. Boyd, despite his dislike of horses, learned to ride and never looked back. The character made him a millionaire.

BOYLE, KATIE
(Katerina Imperiali di Francabilla; 1926–)

International presenter who graced several EUROVISION SONG CONTESTS and some editions of IT'S A KNOCKOUT, putting her multilingual skills to full use. Born into an aristocratic Italian family, Boyle nevertheless has always seemed eminently English. A former *Vogue* fashion model, she was a familiar face on 1950s and 1960s panel games and variety shows (like *Quite Contrary* and JUKE BOX JURY) and has written an agony aunt column for *TV Times*.

BOYS FROM THE BLACKSTUFF
UK (BBC) Drama. BBC 2 1982

Chrissie Todd	**Michael Angelis**
Yosser Hughes	**Bernard Hill**
Thomas Ralph 'Dixie' Dean	**Tom Georgeson**
George Malone	**Peter Kerrigan**
Loggo Logmond	**Alan Igbon**
Kevin Dean	**Gary Bleasdale**
Angie Todd	**Julie Walters**
Frankie Malloy	**Shay Gorman**
Miss Sutcliffe	**Jean Boht**
Jean	**Gilly Coman**
The Wino	**James Ellis**

Writer: **Alan Bleasdale**
Producer: **Michael Wearing**

A gang of tarmac layers face life on the dole.

In 1980, Alan Bleasdale's single drama, *The Black Stuff*, was shown. It focused on a tarmac gang working away from their home city of Liverpool. It proved so magnetic that the BBC asked Bleasdale to write a series of connected plays, one for each of the main characters. The first of the follow-ups was reworked into a drama called *The Muscle Market*, but the remaining five scripts were put together as a black comedy-drama called *Boys from the Blackstuff*.

In the series the lads were back home. Out of work and signing on in a desolate city riddled with unemployment, their future was bleak and reflected the prospects of millions like them around the country at the time. Undoubtedly the best remembered of the gang was Yosser Hughes, a man so desperate for work to keep his family afloat that he begged people to 'Gissa job', claiming 'I can do dat'.

In these poignant episodes Yosser and his contemporaries became standard-bearers for men who were willing to work but who were having to suffer the indignities of life on the 1980s' scrapheap.

BOYS FROM THE BUSH, THE
UK (Cinema Verity/Entertainment Media/BBC) Comedy Drama. BBC 1 1991–2

Reg Toomer	**Tim Healy**
Dennis Tontine	**Chris Haywood**
Leslie	**Mark Haddigan**
Arlene Toomer	**Nadine Garner**
Doris Toomer	**Pat Thomson**
Delilah	**Kris McQuade**
Corrie	**Kirsty Child**
Stuart Stranks	**Rob Steele**
Stevie Stranks	**Russell Fletcher**

Creator: **Douglas Livingstone**
Producers: **Verity Lambert, David Shanks**

Life with an expat detective and his Australian partner.

Although Reg Toomer had lived in Australia for over 20 years, there was only one Bush for him and that was Shepherd's Bush. However, while pining for his long-lost football team, Queens Park Rangers, he still had a business to look after in Melbourne. Melbourne Confidential was part-marriage consultancy and part-detective agency, but, as long as it paid, any job was considered. Reg's unlikely partner was Aussie Dennis Tontine, a man obsessed with women, but who was on the run from both middle age and his former wife. Also involved were Reg's daydreaming missus, Doris, and their man-hungry, starry-eyed daughter, Arlene. Les was Reg's second cousin and Arlene's on-off lover, who became one of the company's private eyes. Dodgy tycoon Stuart Stranks and his amorous son, Stevie, were added to the cast in the second series.

BRADBURY, Sir MALCOLM
CBE (1932–2000)

Sheffield-born novelist and one-time Professor of American Studies at the University of East Anglia who often reflected his academic background in his writing and became one of TV's most controversial playwrights. Some of his earliest work was for THAT WAS THE WEEK THAT WAS, leading to plays like *The After Dinner Game* in 1975 and *Standing in for Henry* in 1980, although his greatest successes were in adapting Tom Sharpe's BLOTT ON THE LANDSCAPE and PORTERHOUSE BLUE for television in 1985 and 1987. His own novel, *The History Man*, had itself been adapted (by Christopher Hamilton) in 1981 and drew criticism for its raunchy sexual content. Bradbury's later work included *Anything More Would Be Greedy* (1989), *The Gravy Train* (1990) and *The Gravy Train Goes East* (1991), versions of Kingsley Amis's *The Green Man* (also 1991) and *Cold Comfort Farm* (1995), and episodes of DALZIEL AND PASCOE and A TOUCH OF FROST.

BRADEN, BERNARD
(1916–93)

Canadian actor and presenter, one of TV's first consumers' champions. He moved to the UK in 1949 after working in Canadian radio and embarked on a theatre and radio career. On television, he began by presenting schools' programmes, was one of the BBC's team covering the Coronation and was then chairman of THE BRAINS TRUST (1957) and host of the sports magazine, *Let's Go* (1959). Very often he was seen in tandem with his wife, Barbara Kelly, in programmes like *Kaleidoscope* and the sitcom *B and B*, and with other partners in comedies such as *Bath-Night with Braden* and *Early to Braden*. *On the Braden Beat* and BRADEN'S WEEK were other contributions, the last (beginning in 1968) introducing a young researcher by the name of Esther

Rantzen. *Braden's Week*, with its consumer content, proved to be the inspiration for Esther's THAT'S LIFE. Sacked by the BBC for promoting Stork margarine on ITV, Braden returned to Canadian television before resurfacing on programmes such as *After Noon Plus* and a revamped ALL OUR YESTERDAYS in 1987. Among his three children was actress Kim Braden (star of the BBC's version of *Anne of Green Gables*).

BRADEN'S WEEK
UK (BBC) Entertainment. BBC 1 1968–72

Presenter: **Bernard Braden**

Editors: **Desmond Wilcox, Bill Morton**
Producers: **John Lloyd, Adam Clapham, Tom Conway**

Saturday evening slice of light entertainment and consumer affairs.

The clear ancestor of THAT'S LIFE, *Braden's Week* not only humorously reviewed the week's events but was also an early consumers' champion, tackling thorny subjects with a light touch. Bernard Braden fronted affairs, supported by a team of reporter/researchers who included John Pitman, Esther Rantzen and Harold Williamson. Williamson specialized in interviewing children. Rantzen and producer John Lloyd headed off to *That's Life* once *Braden's Week* came to a controversial end in 1972. The BBC were unhappy that Braden had decided to advertise Stork margarine on ITV and dismissed him, claiming it was not viable for the host of a consumer programme to be seen endorsing goods commercially.

BRADY, TERENCE
(1939–)

British writer and actor, the husband of writing partner Charlotte Bingham. Together they have penned a number of successful sitcoms, including NO – HONESTLY, *Yes – Honestly, Father Matthew's Daughter*, TAKE THREE GIRLS and PIG IN THE MIDDLE (in which Brady also starred) and its American clone, *Oh Madeline*, as well as episodes of ROBIN'S NEST and dramas like UPSTAIRS, DOWNSTAIRS, *Thomas and Sarah*, NANNY and *Riders*, plus sketches for MARTI CAINE. On screen, he has been seen in comedies such as *Broad and Narrow, Dig This Rhubarb* and *Cribbins*.

BRAGG, Lord MELVYN
(1939–)

Cumbrian presenter, novelist and playwright, widely acknowledged as TV's Mr Arts after his work as editor and host of THE SOUTH BANK SHOW and the paperback review, *Read All About It*, and appearances on *The Late Show*. Earlier he worked as a producer and writer on the influential MONITOR series, for which he worked closely with Ken Russell. He joined Russell again in 1978 to script *Clouds of Glory*, two films about the Lakeland poets.

Bragg has also edited various other arts programmes, and has been Head of Arts at LWT, as well as chairman of Border Television. His 1992 play, *A Time to Dance*, dramatized from his own novel, drew criticism for its bold sex scenes.

BRAINS TRUST, THE
UK (BBC) Discussion Programme. BBC 1955–61; BBC 2 1996

Chairmen: **Hugh Ross Williamson, Michael Flanders, Mary Ann Sieghart**

Creator: **Howard Thomas**
Producers: **John Furness, Peter Brook, Michael Roberts**

A panel of unprimed intellectuals answer questions from listeners.

This completely unscripted discussion programme began on BBC Radio in 1941, at the height of the Blitz, and became a valuable morale-lifter during the hostilities. Its popularity stemmed as much from the badinage among its three main participants (Professor C. E. M. Joad, Commander A. B. Campbell and Dr Julian Huxley) as from the knowledge it imparted. When this television version began, 14 years later, a more sober tone prevailed, with the intimacy of the cramped radio studio replaced by a TV set filled with armchairs and coffee tables. The first host was Hugh Ross Williamson and the panel changed on a regular basis. Guests included such diverse personalities as Julian Huxley, Egon Ronay and the Archbishop of Cape Town, but one of the stalwarts was Dr Jacob Bronowski (later to compile THE ASCENT OF MAN). Viewers' contributions varied from the sublime to the ridiculous, taking in factual queries, philosophical posers and, at times, almost rhetorical questions, and the panellists (unaware of what was going to be asked) made every effort to provide a coherent and accurate response.

The Brains Trust was exhumed for a six-programme late-night series in 1996, with Assistant Editor of *The Times*, Mary Ann Sieghart, in the chair and panellists including Jonathan Miller, philosopher Edward de Bono and novelist Ben Okri.

BRAKE, PATRICIA
(1942–)

British actress headlining in a number of major series, particularly ELDORADO (Gwen Lockhead). Among her other credits have been PORRIDGE and *Going Straight* (Ingrid Fletcher), *The Glums* (Eth), *Second Time Around* (Vicki), *Troubles and Strife* (Cherry) and 2 POINT 4 CHILDREN (Tina), plus scores of guest appearances. She also played Julie Renfield in the US sitcom, *The Ugliest Girl in Town*.

BRAMBELL, WILFRID
(1912–85)

Diminutive actor for ever cherished by viewers as grubby old Albert Steptoe in STEPTOE AND SON, a role he played, off and on, for 12 years from 1962. Born in Dublin, Brambell's first television appearances were a mixture of comedy parts (in shows that included LIFE WITH THE LYONS) and serious drama. He appeared as a drunk in the science-fiction milestone THE QUATERMASS EXPERIMENT and also popped up in 1984, as an old tortured prisoner, as well as in programmes like *The Adventures of Aggie*. Typecast as old man Steptoe, Brambell's subsequent TV work was thin on the ground, although he did take up a few film roles, playing Paul's grandfather, for instance, in The Beatles' *A Hard Day's Night*, and was also seen in Jonathan Miller's *Alice In Wonderland*, plus a couple of COMEDY PLAYHOUSE pilots. He was another Albert, one of the patients, in Peter Tinniswood's 1970 sitcom, *Never Say Die*, and one of his last television appearances was as a guest in an episode of CITIZEN SMITH.

BRAMWELL
UK (Carlton) Drama. ITV 1995–8

Eleanor Bramwell	**Jemma Redgrave**
Robert Bramwell	**David Calder**
Sir Herbert Hamilton	**Robert Hardy**
Lady Cora Peters	**Michele Dotrice**
Nurse Ethel Carr	**Ruth Sheen**
Kate	**Keeley Gainey**
Daniel Bentley	**Cliff Parisi**
Dr Joe Marsham	**Kevin McMonagle**
Dr Finn O'Neill	**Andrew Connolly**
Sidney Bentley	**Ben Brazier**
Alice Costigan	**Maureen Beattie**

Creator: **Lucy Gannon**
Producers: **Tim Whitby, Harriet Davison**

A female doctor battles against prejudice to care for the urban poor.

Set at the outset in 1895, this Victorian medical drama told the story of ambitious doctor Eleanor Bramwell, who lived in Islington with her physician father, Robert. It told how she launched a crusade to provide medical care for the poor in the East End of London and how she vainly tried to gain the respect of her chauvinistic male peers, such as the blustering Sir Herbert Hamilton. The contrast between the health care available to Eleanor's wealthy private clients in Mayfair and the squalor and degradation endured by her most impoverished patients was the driving force that led her to found the Thrift Infirmary. There she was assisted by the understanding Dr Joe Marsham.

Recalling an age of medical discovery, *Bramwell* reflected on the introduction of such advances as antisepsis and anaesthesia, as well as less successful, often stomach-turning, new treatments. Romantic interest was added for Eleanor by Irish doctor Finn O'Neill (who then jilted her), and later for her father by brewery owner and Thrift benefactor Alice Costigan (whom he married). After three series up to 1997, *Bramwell* returned briefly in 1998 as two feature-length episodes which took the story on to the year 1899 and the Boer War.

BRAND, JO
(1957–)

Dry, self-deprecating, English comedienne, seen in series like *Saturday Live* and eventually her own showcases, *Jo Brand Through the Cakehole* and *Jo Brand: Like It or Lump It*. A former psychiatric nurse, her forthright material has focused on her own appearance (she has referred to herself as the 'Sea Monster') and the inadequacies of the male sex. Other credits have included a comic trawl through the TV archives in *Bad Sports*, the mock debate series, *Head on Comedy with Jo Brand*, and the occasional series *The Horror of . . .*

BRAND, JOSHUA

Writer/producer whose highly successful work with partner John Falsey has included ST ELSEWHERE, NORTHERN EXPOSURE and *I'll Fly Away*. Together they run Falahey-Austin Street Productions.

BRANDED
US (Goodson-Todman) Western. ITV 1965–6

Jason McCord	**Chuck Connors**

The wanderings of an ex-soldier, dismissed from the army on a charge of cowardice.

It was the 1880s and Jason McCord, once a star pupil at West Point, had been dishonourably discharged from the rank of captain in the US Army, accused of cowardice. The only survivor of an Indian massacre at the Battle of Bitter Creek in Wyoming, he had lost consciousness and somehow had been spared. However, the top brass believed he had run away and kicked him out of the force.

In an effort to clear his name, McCord meandered across the Wild West, using his skills as an engineer and a mapmaker in a variety of jobs but predominantly aiming to prove to the world that he was no chicken. He also hoped to gather some clues as to what really happened on that fateful day. But, by the end of the series' short run, despite unearthing occasional evidence in his favour, viewers were no nearer to knowing the truth about poor McCord.

BRANDRETH, GYLES
(1948–)

Professional game show panellist and TV trivialist, wearer of bold sweaters and deviser of various quizzes and puzzles. His work has included CALL MY BLUFF, *Tell* the Truth, Catchword, Babble, The Railway Carriage Game, COUNTDOWN (consulting the dictionary), *Dear Ladies* (as co-writer) and various pieces for breakfast television. A prolific author and Scrabbler, he was Conservative MP for Chester 1992–7.

BRASS

UK (Granada) Situation Comedy. ITV/Channel 4 1983–4/ 1990

Bradley Hardacre	Timothy West
Patience Hardacre	Caroline Blakiston
George Fairchild	Geoffrey Hinsliff
	Geoffrey Hutchings
Agnes Fairchild	Barbara Ewing
Austin Hardacre	Robert Reynolds
	Patrick Pearson
Morris Hardacre	James Saxon
Charlotte Hardacre	Emily Morgan
Isobel Hardacre	Gail Harrison
Dr Macduff	David Ashton
Lord Mountfast	John Nettleton
Jack Fairchild	Shaun Scott
Matthew Fairchild	Gary Cady

Creators/Writers: **John Stevenson, Julian Roach**
Producers: **Bill Podmore, Gareth Jones, Mark Robson**

Social injustice, family rivalries and red-hot passion in a 1930s northern industrial town.

Set in the fictitious town of Utterley, *Brass* exposed the open animosity between two rival families, one rich and powerful, the other poor and subservient, which resulted in much 'trouble at mill'. At the heart of the action was cruel, power-crazed Bradley Hardacre, a self-made man with interests in mining, munitions and especially cotton milling. His loopy, bitter wife, Patience, though confined to a wheelchair, was a chronic alcoholic; and his children, too, all had their quirks: Austin was ambitious and wanted to take over the Empire, Morris was intelligent but immoral, Charlotte was the innocent do-gooder with feminist tendencies, and Isobel was a temptress who later married into nobility. Working for the Hardacres were the Fairchilds, headed by 'Red' Agnes, who, as well as stoking conflict in the workplace, was also Bradley's mistress. Her sons, Jack and Matthew, were openly hostile to their betters, but her husband, George (played by Geoff Hinsliff, later Don Brennan in CORONATION STREET), was just happy to be in their employ.

This tongue-in-cheek parody of TV's gritty, northern industrial dramas was briefly revived by Channel 4 in 1990, with many of the actors resuming their original roles. For the new series the action was set in 1939 at the outset of war.

BRAVO

Launched in 1980 as an American cable station specializing in foreign films and the performing arts, Bravo has since undergone two major conversions. Now available on satellite, cable and digital television in Europe, the channel moved on to focus on cult (mostly American) TV programmes from bygone days (under the umbrella title of *Timewarp Television*), weepy old movies and weird science fiction films. However, it has since changed direction yet again and now targets its appeal on young males with action flicks and laddish programmes revolving around sex. It shares its digital channel with a sister station, Trouble, aimed at the teenage market.

BREAD

UK (BBC) Situation Comedy. BBC 1 1986–91

Nellie Boswell	Jean Boht
Freddie Boswell	Ronald Forfar
Joey Boswell	Peter Howitt
	Graham Bickley
Jack Boswell	Victor McGuire
Aveline Boswell	Gilly Coman
	Melanie Hill
Adrian Boswell	Jonathon Morris
Billy Boswell	Nick Conway
Grandad	Kenneth Waller
Lilo Lil	Eileen Pollock
Shifty	Bryan Murray
Martina	Pamela Power
Julie	Caroline Milmoe
	Hilary Crowson
Oswald	Giles Watling
Derek	Peter Byrne
Celia Higgins	Rita Tushingham
Leonora Campbell	Deborah Grant

Creator/Writer: **Carla Lane**
Producers: **Robin Nash, John B. Hobbs**

The trials of a Liverpool family confidently living life on the dole.

The Boswells were the scourge of the DHSS. Although they attempted to make their own way in the world, like many families in the 1980s they were forced to rely on state handouts. But they did so with pride. They knew their entitlements and exploited all the loopholes. Head of their claustrophobic terraced household at 30 Kelsall Street was Nellie Boswell, a devout Catholic housewife who demanded the presence of her loyal family at mealtimes, which is when most of the squabbling took place. Her husband, Freddie, was a waster who spent most of his time in an allotment shed with the local strumpet, Lilo Lil, so Nellie relied more on her eldest son, the leather-clad Joey, to bring his siblings into line. Squeaky-voiced daughter Aveline was a tasteless dresser who longed to be a model but ended up marrying a vicar named Oswald. Dry, philosophical Jack was the soft-hearted son, Adrian was a poetic, easily hurt, gentle soul, who changed his name from Jimmy to something more appropriate, and the youngest son, Billy, was his antithesis, tactless, big-mouthed and impulsive. Replacing Jack (who had disappeared to America) in some episodes was their cousin Shifty, an appropriately named Irish jailbird. Completing the line-up were the Boswells' impatient and intolerant Grandad, who lived next door and constantly yelled for his dinner, their dog Mongy and the exasperated DHSS counter-clerk, Martina. Also in the action were assorted friends, lovers, wives and neighbours.

BREAKFAST NEWS
See BREAKFAST TIME.

BREAKFAST TIME
UK (BBC) News Magazine. BBC 1 1983–9

Presenters: **Frank Bough, Selina Scott, Nick Ross, Mike Smith, Debbie Greenwood, John Mountford, Sue Cook, Sally Magnusson, Jeremy Paxman**

Editor: **Ron Neil**

Britain's first national breakfast television programme.

Airing at 6.30 a.m. on 17 January 1983, *Breakfast Time* raced past its commercial rival, *Good Morning Britain*, to be the first breakfast television programme seen nationally across the UK. Its bright 'sun' logo and cosy studio set reflected the programme's intention to offer a relaxed and informal introduction to the day. Avuncular Frank Bough and Selina Scott were the main hosts, supported by specialist presenters like Francis Wilson (weather), Diana Moran – the 'Green Goddess' (fitness), Russell Grant (horoscopes), Glynn Christian (cookery) and Chris Wilson (gossip column). The news was read by Debbie Rix and, later, by Fern Britton and Sue Carpenter, while sport was handled by David Icke and then by Bob Wilson. Nick Ross, Mike Smith, Debbie Greenwood, John Mountford, Sue Cook, Sally Magnusson and Jeremy Paxman also took their places on the red leather sofa at various times.

In 1989 the magazine element of the programme was dropped in favour of in-depth news coverage. The programme title was changed to *Breakfast News* and newsreaders such as Nicholas Witchell and Jill Dando replaced the jovial, casual presenters. In 2000, the programme became known simply as *Breakfast*.

BREMNER, RORY
(1961–)

Edinburgh-born impressionist, majoring in topical satire. As well as having his own series for the BBC (*Now – Something Else* and *Rory Bremner*, particularly) and various offerings on Channel 4 (*Rory Bremner . . . Who Else?* and *Bremner, Bird and Fortune*, most notably), Bremner has also contributed to SPITTING IMAGE and *Breakfast with Frost*. In contrast, he took the role of Kevin Beesely in the drama, *You, Me and It*. From beginnings as a cabaret performer while studying at London University, he has become the UK's leading exponent of the impressionist's art. His speciality take-offs include Richie Benaud, Desmond Lynam, Barry Norman and Denis Norden.

BRETT, JEREMY
(Jeremy Huggins; 1935–95)

English Shakespearean and character actor now associated with Conan Doyle's Sherlock Holmes, having given his moody portrayal of the celebrated detective for over ten years. He played D'Artagnan in the BBC's 1966 version of *The Three Musketeers* and Maxim de Winter in its 1979 adaptation of *Rebecca*. He was William Pitt the Younger in *No. 10* and took parts in many series, such as THE CHAMPIONS, COUNTRY MATTERS, *Affairs of the Heart*, *Supernatural*, *Haunted* and MOTHER LOVE. Brett's first wife was actress Anna Massey.

BRIDESHEAD REVISITED
UK (Granada) Drama. ITV 1981

Charles Ryder	**Jeremy Irons**
Lord Sebastian Flyte	**Anthony Andrews**
Lord Alex Marchmain	**Laurence Olivier**
Edward Ryder	**John Gielgud**
Lady Julia Flyte	**Diana Quick**
Lady Marchmain	**Claire Bloom**
Lady Cordelia Flyte	**Phoebe Nicholls**
Lord Brideshead	**Simon Jones**
Anthony Blanche	**Nickolas Grace**
Jasper	**Stephen Moore**
Collins	**Christopher Good**
Lunt	**Bill Owen**
Viscount 'Boy' Mulcaster	**Jeremy Sinden**
Nanny Hawkins	**Mona Washbourne**
Sgt Block	**Kenneth Cranham**
Lt Hooper	**Richard Hope**
Mr Samgrass	**John Grillo**
Rex Mottram	**Charles Keating**
Celia Mulcaster/Ryder	**Jane Asher**
Kurt	**Jonathan Coy**
Cara	**Stephane Audran**

Writer: **John Mortimer**
Producer: **Derek Granger**

Aristocratic decadence in the inter-war years.

Brideshead Revisited told the story of Army Captain Charles Ryder, whose unit found itself stationed in the grounds of Brideshead Castle in Wiltshire in the closing days of World War II (1944). But Ryder himself had been there before, and during this 11-part drama he recounted events in his earlier life, reflecting on the passing of an era.

Charles's connections with Brideshead had begun with Sebastian Flyte, the teddy-bear- ('Aloysius') carrying son of Lord Marchmain, proprietor of the estate. They had met at Oxford in the 1920s and Charles had fallen in with Sebastian's drunkenly decadent troupe of gay young blades. He became a house guest at Brideshead and later fell for Julia, Sebastian's sister. With the family, Charles (a painter) travelled extensively, and life in this aristocratic household opened his eyes to many things. He was fascinated by their behaviour, their mannerisms, their conversations. The beautiful Marchmain estate, with its gardens, fountains and private chapel, held him in awe. Indeed, he was absorbed by their closed, extravagant world and a style of living that belonged to an age rapidly drawing to a close. But it was the overwhelming power that Catholicism held over the family which proved most intriguing.

Brideshead Revisited, closely adapted by John Mortimer from Evelyn Waugh's passionate novel, very nearly became one of television's great disaster stories. Soon after production had begun (using Castle Howard in Yorkshire as the fictitious Brideshead, with other scenes shot at Tatton Park, Cheshire) filming was halted by an ITV technicians' dispute. By the time the strike ended, many of the cast and crew had other commitments, contracts had run out and it seemed that the work would never be finished. But to scrap the project would have been almost as costly as continuing, so the decision was made by Granada to press on. Director Michael Lindsay-Hogg had to be replaced by young Charles Sturridge, and Jeremy Irons was dragged away for three months to make *The French Lieutenant's Woman*. But, at more than twice the original cost, *Brideshead Revisited* did eventually reach the TV screen. For many viewers, it was well worth the wait. The beauty of the photography and easy pace of the rich narrative won many fans. Awards were showered on the production and sales around the world were enormous. The theme music was written by Geoffrey Burgon.

BRIERS, RICHARD
OBE (1934–)

Popular British actor, often in whimsical, slightly eccentric roles. Richard Briers first found TV fame in the early 1960s, as Roger Thursby in BROTHERS IN LAW and George Starling in MARRIAGE LINES. However, it was more than ten years later, after other comedy roles in series like *Ben Travers Farces*, *Tall Stories* and the sitcom, *Birds on the Wing* (Charles Jackson), that he became a household name. His portrayal of Tom Good, with Felicity Kendal as his spirited wife, in THE GOOD LIFE, inspired some viewers to leave the rat race and give self-sufficiency a go. After an appearance in *The Norman Conquests*, and a lead role in the sketch show, *One-Upmanship*, plus lesser success in the sitcoms *The Other One* (Ralph) and GOODBYE MR KENT (Travis Kent), Briers bounced back in EVER DECREASING CIRCLES, as the pedantic Martin Bryce opposite an exasperated Penelope Wilton. In 1985 he took on the role of vicar Philip Lambe in ALL IN GOOD FAITH. After time on the stage, he returned to the small screen in 1993 in *If You See God, Tell Him*, playing Godfrey Spry, a man with an attention span of only 30 seconds, and followed this with the part of George in *Screen Two*'s *Skallagrigg*. In 1995 he starred as ex-diplomat Tony Fairfax in another sitcom, *Down to Earth*, and appeared in the one-off *P. G. Wodehouse's Heavy Weather* (Threepwood). Later he was seen as Sir Charles Fairley in the slave drama, *A Respectable Trade*, and as Hector in *Monarch of the Glen*. Briers is also a voice-over specialist – he narrated the cartoon series ROOBARB and *Noah and Nelly* – and has also won plaudits for his classical roles, which have

included Malvolio in *Twelfth Night*. He is married to actress Ann Davies and is the father of actress Lucy Briers.

BRIGGS, JOHNNY
(1935–)

Short, London-born actor, earlier in his career often seen on the wrong side of the law. His television break came when he switched sides to become DS Russell in NO HIDING PLACE, progressing into soap opera in 1973 with CROSSROADS (Clifford Leyton) and ultimately assuming his present-day *alter ego* , that of devious businessman Mike Baldwin in CORONATION STREET, in 1976. In the 1960s and 1970s Briggs also appeared in programmes as diverse as THE PLANE MAKERS, THE SAINT, Z CARS, MOGUL, THE AVENGERS, LOVE THY NEIGHBOUR, MY WIFE NEXT DOOR, *Bright's Boffins*, NO – HONESTLY, YUS MY DEAR and THICK AS THIEVES.

BRITISH ACADEMY OF FILM AND TELEVISION ARTS
See BAFTA.

BRITISH BROADCASTING CORPORATION
See BBC.

BRITISH COMEDY AWARDS, THE
UK (LWT) Comedy/Awards. ITV 1990–

Presenters: **Michael Parkinson, Jonathan Ross**

Producers: **Michael Hurll, Susie Dark, Alasdair MacMillan**

Annual awards bash dedicated to the art of mirth-making.

The British Comedy Awards has grown from a nervous start in 1990, when Michael Parkinson formally dealt out the honours to the assembled giants of humour at the London Palladium. A year later, the venue was moved to LWT's studios, Jonathan Ross took over as host, a lighter, more risqué tone was adopted and the ceremony was well on its way to establishing itself as one of the focal points of the comedy calendar. Not that everyone has given the proceeds due respect. Chris Evans, having taken his fill of the 'Jester' plaques, promptly announced that he didn't want any more and reputedly gave one of his trophies to a waitress. Among the 'highlights' has been Spike Milligan's uproarious 'grovelling bastard' riposte to the Prince of Wales, who had sent his comedy hero a written tribute to coincide with Spike's receipt of a lifetime achievement award. Equally infamous was Julian Clary's crude remark about Norman Lamont. Such are the risks of broadcasting live.

BRITISH SATELLITE BROADCASTING
See BSKYB.

BRITISH SKY BROADCASTING
See BSKYB.

BRITTAS EMPIRE, THE
UK (BBC) Situation Comedy. BBC 1 1991–7

Gordon Brittas	**Chris Barrie**
Helen Brittas	**Pippa Haywood**
Laura Lancing	**Julia St John**
Carole	**Harriet Thorpe**
Colin Wetherby	**Michael Burns**
Tim Whistler	**Russell Porter**
Gavin Featherly	**Tim Marriott**
Angie	**Andrée Bernard**
Julie	**Judy Flynn**
Linda	**Jill Greenacre**
Penny Bidmead	**Anouschka Menzies**
Councillor Druggett	**Stephen Churchett**

Creators: **Richard Fegen, Andrew Norriss**
Producer: **Mike Stephens**

An over-zealous manager brings daily chaos to a modern sports centre.

Insufferable, pedantic, patronizing, incompetent and accident-prone were all inadequate ways of describing Gordon Brittas, manager of the Whitbury Newtown leisure centre. Whatever he attempted inevitably ended in failure and near loss of life. Brittas ran his little kingdom with a firm hand, planning events meticulously and laying down the law to his unfortunate staff. With disaster always lurking around the corner, it was left to his level-headed number two, Laura, to pick up the pieces and restore calm. Julie, his secretary, simply despaired, and the only member of staff who looked up to Brittas was the loyal Colin, the dim, Geordie maintenance man. Other team members were tearful, often homeless receptionist Carol (who kept her children in a cupboard behind her desk), ambitious coaches Tim and Gavin, and blonde assistant Linda. Gordon's wife, Helen, looked after his children, including twins Matthew and Mark, and popped tranquillizers to keep herself sane.

The series appeared to have ended in 1994, when the sanctimonious menace was appointed a European Commissioner, but the indestructible Brittas survived this, and being flattened by a water tank, only to resurface, to everyone's dismay – especially his wife's – in 1996. A new arrival at the centre was Penny, boss of the privatized sauna/solarium. Even when the end did finally arrive for the series, the grotesque Gordon was not through. He (with wife Helen) resurfaced as a fitness counsellor on BBC 1's short course, *Get Fit with Brittas*, in summer 1997.

Creators Richard Fegen and Andrew Norriss penned all episodes up to the final two series, when various other writers were introduced.

BRITTON, FERN
(1958–)

British presenter of news and lifestyle programmes, the daughter of actor Tony Britton. Among her many credits have been BREAKFAST TIME, *The Brian Conley Show*, GMTV, *Ready Steady Cook*, *This Morning* and regional news magazines like *Coast to Coast*.

BRITTON, TONY
(1924–)

British actor, familiar in snooty, upper-class parts. His most successful TV roles have been as James Nicholls in ROBIN'S NEST, Dr Toby Latimer in DON'T WAIT UP and Vivian Bancroft in *Don't Tell Father*, although other credits have included FATHER, DEAR FATHER, AND MOTHER MAKES FIVE and *Strangers and Brothers*, plus ARMCHAIR THEATRE presentations and plays like *The Nearly Man* (1974) and *The Dame of Sark* (1976). He is the father of presenter Fern Britton.

BROADBENT, JIM
(1949–)

English actor, often in comic roles. His major credits have come in *Gone to the Dogs* (Jim Morley), *Gone to Seed* (Monty Plant) and *The Peter Principle* (Peter Duffley), with other parts in series like *Birth of a Nation*, BIRD OF PREY, THE COMIC STRIP PRESENTS, HAPPY FAMILIES, BLACKADDER, *Victoria Wood*, MURDER MOST HORRID, and a few appearances as the slimy Roy Slater in ONLY FOOLS AND HORSES. (Broadbent, in fact, turned down the role of Del Boy before it was offered to David Jason.) His voice has also been heard in *The Staggering Stories of Ferdinand de Bargos* and in the *Percy the Park Keeper* animations.

BROADCASTING

The transmission of radio or TV signals to be received by the general public, as opposed to narrowcasting, cable or closed-circuit systems that supply signals to only a limited audience.

BRONCO
US (Warner Brothers) Western. BBC 1959–64

Bronco Layne	**Ty Hardin**

A former Confederate Army captain drifts across the Wild West.

Bronco was a series that evolved out of CHEYENNE and a star-versus-studio squabble; the star was Clint Walker, of *Cheyenne*, and the studio was Warner Brothers. Failing to resolve the dispute, Warners recast *Cheyenne* with a new lead character, pitching Ty Hardin into the role of

Bronco Layne. Eventually Walker returned to the fold, but Bronco continued in his own series. To add to the confusion, some *Bronco* episodes were then screened in the USA under the umbrella title of *Cheyenne*, as part of a rotating trilogy which also included *Sugarfoot*, starring Will Hutchins (shown in the UK as *Tenderfoot*).

The character of Bronco was very much a loner. With the end of the Civil War, he headed west, where he met up with the likes of Billy the Kid and Jesse James, but he was never given a regular supporting cast.

BRONOWSKI, JACOB
(1902–74)

Polish-born scientist Jacob Bronowski became an unlikely TV hero in 1973 when his ambitious TV series THE ASCENT OF MAN was screened on BBC 2. His raw enthusiasm, curious hunched poses and evident erudition produced a winning combination for viewers, many of whom would never have watched such an academic series without him. Sadly, he had little time to enjoy his new fame, dying a year later at the age of 72, exhausted by his efforts on the series. Bronowski had been educated at Cambridge and settled with his family in Britain. As well as writing various scientific tomes he had also presented several programmes in the same vein on television and was a member of THE BRAINS TRUST.

BROOKE-TAYLOR, TIM
(1940–)

British comic actor and writer, a product of the Cambridge Footlights. Emerging from innovative 1960s comedy shows like *On the Braden Beat*, THE FROST REPORT (writing with Eric Idle), AT LAST THE 1948 SHOW, *Twice a Fortnight* (largely as writer), *Broaden Your Mind* and *Marty* (straight man to Marty Feldman), Brooke-Taylor hit the big time as one of THE GOODIES. From there he moved into sitcom with less success, appearing in *His and Hers* (Toby Burgess), *The Rough with the Smooth* (Richard Woodville, also as co-writer), ME AND MY GIRL (Derek Yates) and *You Must Be the Husband* (Tom Hammond). He was also seen in the sketch shows, *Hello Cheeky* and *Assaulted Nuts*, and as Victor Meldrew's next-door neighbour in ONE FOOT IN THE GRAVE.

BROOKS, JAMES L.
(1940–)

American writer/producer whose first success came with THE MARY TYLER MOORE SHOW, followed by one of its spin-offs, RHODA (both with his partner, Allen Burns). Brooks moved on to TAXI, *The Associates* and LOU GRANT, before branching out into movies (*Terms of Endearment*, *Broadcast News*, *Big*, etc.), then returning to TV with *The Tracey Ullman Show* and THE SIMPSONS (as executive producer). Other credits include *The Days and Nights of Molly Dodd* and *Eisenhower and Lutz* (as writer).

BROOKS, RAY
(1939–)

Sussex-born actor whose TV break came in the harrowing 1966 play, CATHY COME HOME. After appearances in programmes such as GIDEON'S WAY, CORONATION STREET, RANDALL AND HOPKIRK (DECEASED) and TAXI (the UK version), Brooks narrated the animations MR BENN and *King Rollo*, and then starred as Robbie Box in BIG DEAL in 1984. Subsequently, he has appeared in *Running Wild* (retro teddy boy Max Wild), *The World of Eddie Weary* (title role), and *Growing Pains* (Tom Hollingsworth).

BROOKSIDE
UK (Mersey) Drama. Channel 4 1982–

Roger Huntington	Rob Spendlove
Heather Huntington/Haversham/Black	Amanda Burton
Sheila Grant/Corkhill	Sue Johnston
Bobby Grant	Ricky Tomlinson
Barry Grant	Paul Usher
Damon Grant	Simon O'Brien
Karen Grant	Shelagh O'Hara
Paul Collins	Jim Wiggins
Annabelle Collins	Doreen Sloane
Lucy Collins	Katrin Cartlidge
	Maggie Saunders
Gordon Collins	Nigel Crowley
	Mark Burgess
Gavin Taylor	Daniel Webb
Petra Taylor	Alexandra Pigg
Matty Nolan	Tony Scoggo
Terry Sullivan	Brian Regan
Gizzmo Hawkins	Robert Smith
Ducksie Brown	Mark Birch
George Williams	Doc O'Brien
Alan Partridge	Dicken Ashworth
Samantha Partridge	Dinah May
Harry Cross	Bill Dean
Edna Cross	Betty Alberge
Michelle Jones	Tracey Jay
George Jackson	Cliff Howells
Marie Jackson	Anna Keaveney
Gary Jackson	Allan Patterson
George Jackson, Jr	Steven Patterson
Teresa Nolan	Ann Haydn Edwards
Pat Hancock	David Easter
Kate Moses	Sharon Rosita
Sandra Maghie	Sheila Grier
Tommy McArdle	Malcolm Tierney
Kevin Cross	Stuart Organ
Sally Haynes	Roberta Kerr
Ralph Hardwick	Ray Dunbobbin
Thomas 'Sinbad' Sweeney	Michael Starke
Jack Sullivan	William Maxwell
Vicki Cleary	Cheryl Leigh
Billy Corkhill	John McArdle
Doreen Corkhill	Kate Fitzgerald

Rod Corkhill	Jason Hope
Tracy Corkhill	Justine Kerrigan
Jimmy Corkhill	Dean Sullivan
Nicholas Black	Alan Rothwell
Julia Brogan	Gladys Ambrose
Kirsty Brown	Joanne Black
Madge Richmond	Shirley Stelfox
Christopher Duncan	Stifyn Parri
Debbie McGrath	Gillian Kearney
Sizzler	Renny Krupinski
Mona Harvey/Fallon	Margaret Clifton
Jonathan Gordon-Davies	Steven Pinner
Laura Wright/Gordon-Davies	Jane Cunliffe
Jamie Henderson	Sean McKee
Sue Harper/Sullivan	Annie Miles
Frank Rogers	Peter Christian
Chrissy Rogers	Eithne Browne
Sammy Rogers/Daniels	Rachael Lindsay
Geoff Rogers	Kevin Carson
	Stephen Walters
Katie Rogers	Debbie Reynolds
	Diane Burke
Cheryl Boyanowsky	Jennifer Calvert
Nisha Batra	Sunetra Sarker
Kathy Roach	Noreen Kershaw
'Tommo' Thompson	John O'Gorman
Nikki White	Michelle Byatt
'Bumper' Humphries	James Mawdsley
Michael Choi	David Yip
Caroline Choi	Sarah Lam
Sean Roach	Derek Hicks
Mick Johnson	Louis Emerick
Owen Daniels	Danny McCall
Marcia Barrett	Cheryl Maiker
Josie Johnson	Suzanne Packer
Gemma Johnson	Naomi Kamanga
	Carla Jarrett
Leo Johnson	Leeon Sawyer
	Steven Cole
Diana Spence/Corkhill	Paula Frances
Margaret Clemence	Nicola Stephenson
Derek O'Farrell	Clive Moore
D-D Dixon	Irene Marot
Ron Dixon	Vince Earl
Cyril Dixon	Allan Surtees
Jacqui Dixon	Alexandra Fletcher
Mike Dixon	Paul Byatt
Tony Dixon	Gerard Bostock
	Mark Lennock
Max Farnham	Steven Pinder
Patricia Farnham	Gabrielle Glaister
Jackie Corkhill	Sue Jenkins
Jimmy Corkhill, Jr	George Christopher
Graeme Curtis	David Banks
Fran Pearson	Julie Peasgood
Ellis Johnson	Francis Johnson
John Harrison	Geoffrey Leesley
Barbara Harrison	Angela Morant
Keith Rooney	Kirk Smith
Lindsey Corkhill/Stanlow/Phelan	Claire Sweeney
Susannah Farnham/Morrisey	Karen Drury
Angela Lambert	Hilary Welles
Leanne Powell	Vickie Gates
Peter Harrison	Robert Beck
David 'Bing' Crosbie	John Burgess
Jean Crosbie	Marcia Ashton
Karyn Clark	Joanna Phillips-Lane
Ruth Sweeney	Mary Healey
Anna Wolska	Kazia Pelka
Lyn Matthews/Rogers	Sharon Power
Marianne Dwyer	Jodie Hanson
Joe Halsall	Susie Ann Watkins
Brian Kennedy	Jonathan Caplan
Penny Crosbie	Mary Tamm
Bev McLoughlin	Sarah White
Carol Salter	Angela Walsh
Garry Salter	Stephen Dwyer
Mandy Jordache/Dutton	Sandra Maitland
Trevor Jordache	Brian Murray
Beth Jordache	Anna Friel
Rachel Jordache/Wright	Tiffany Chapman
Brenna Jordache	Gillian Hanna
Simon Howe	Lee Hartney
Mo McGee	Tina Malone
Audrey Manners	Judith Barker
Emma Piper	Paula Bell
Eddie Banks	Paul Broughton
Rosie Banks	Susan Twist
Carl Banks	Stephen Donald
Sarah Banks	Andrea Marshall
Lee Banks	Matthew Lewney
Jenny Swift	Kate Beckett
George Manners	Brian Murphy
Gary Stanlow	Andrew Fillis
Christian Wright	Philip Dowd
Peter Phelan	Samuel Kane
Shane Cochran	Richard Norton
Kenny Maguire	Tommy Boyle
Bel Simpson	Lesley Nightingale
Ollie Simpson	Michael J. Jackson
Georgia Simpson	Helen Grace
Nat Simpson	John Sandford
Danny Simpson	Andrew Butler
Val Walker	Pauline Fleming
Jules Bradley/Simpson	Sarah Withe
J. C. Bradley	Ken Sharrock
Anne Bradley	Faith Brown
Elaine Davies/Johnson	Beverley Hills
Cassie Charlton	Ebony Gray
Gladys Charlton	Eileen O'Brien
Timothy 'Tinhead' O'Leary	Philip Olivier
Tanya Davies	Heather Tomlinson
Carmel O'Leary	Carol Connor
Ben O'Leary	Simon Paul
Melanie O'Leary	Elizabeth Lovelady
Eleanor Kitson	Georgia Reece
Mollie Marchbank	Diane Keen
Lisa Morrisey	Amanda Nolan
Louise Hope	Lisa Faulkner
Greg Shadwick	Mark Moraghan
Margi Shadwick	Bernadette Foley
Nicky Shadwick	Suzanne Collins
Emily Shadwick	Jennifer Ellison
Jason Shadwick	Vincent Price
Jessie Shadwick	Marji Campi
Marcus Seddon	Matthew Brenher

Katrina Evans	**Ann-Marie Davies**
Pauline Robson	**Kim Taylforth**
Andrea Robson	**Juanne Fuller**
Alec O'Brien	**Al T. Kossy**
Niamh Musgrove	**Barbara Drennan**
Joey Musgrove	**Dan Mullane**
Luke Musgrove	**Jason Kavanagh**
Matt Musgrove	**Kristian Ealey**
Kelly Musgrove	**Natalie Earl**
Ryan Musgrove	**Samuel James Hudson**
Franki	**Linda Lusardi**
Anthea Russel/Brindley/Dixon	**Barbara Hatwell**
Megan Brindley	**Cheryl Mackie**
Callum Finnegan	**Gerard Kelly**
Rose Finnegan	**Amanda Noar**
Dr Darren Roebuck	**Timothy Deenihan**
Victoria Seagram/Wilcox/Shadwick	**Patricia Potter**
Nathan Cuddington	**Marcus Hutton**
Jerome Johnson	**Leon Lopez**
Dave Burns	**Simon Chadwick**
Shelley Bowers	**Alexandra Wescourt**
Ray Hilton	**Kenneth Cope**
Diane Murray	**Bernie Nolan**
Marty Murray	**Neil Caple**
Steve Murray	**Steven Fletcher**
Adele Murray	**Katy Lamont**
Anthony Murray	**Raymond Quinn**
Lance Powell	**Mickey Poppins**
Andrew Taylor	**Sean Harrison**
Brigid McKenna	**Meg Johnson**
Clint Moffat	**Greg Pateras**
Robbie Moffat	**Neil Davies**
Kitty Hilton	**Jean Heywood**
Carl Beacham	**David Groves**
Leanne Powell	**Vickie Gates**
Josh McLoughlan	**Adam McCoy**

Creator/Executive Producer: **Phil Redmond**
Producers: **Nicholas Prosser, Mal Young, Ric Mellis, Sue Sutton Mayo, Paul Marquess**

Innovative Channel 4 soap opera.

Brookside was the series that changed the concept of soap opera in Britain. Taking to the air on Channel 4's opening night, it aimed to make realism the key to its success. Creator Phil Redmond (formerly of GRANGE HILL) went out and bought a new housing estate in Liverpool, using the various homes as permanent, 'live-in' sets and shunning the wobbly walls of studio mock-ups. Lightweight, hand-held cameras provided a newsy, ever-moving image of life in Brookside Close. Redmond also went for realism in his characters. They spoke dialectally in heavy, guttural, Merseyside accents, the kids in particular using real swear-words, not transparent euphemisms. Their lives were purposefully down to earth and unromantic, and storylines revolved around the bleakness of life on the dole and the salvation provided by the black economy. Subsequently, other normally 'taboo' subjects such as homosexuality, suicide, AIDS, religious fanaticism, rape and drug abuse have all been given an airing in *Brookside*.

The first residents of the Close included the working-class Grants, the snooty Collinses and young couples Roger and Heather Huntington and Gavin and Petra Taylor. Some characters like Barry Grant have remained with the series for years, but plenty of new faces have moved in and out of the cul-de-sac. Major contributors have included crotchety old Harry Cross, the Corkhills, the Rogers, the Dixons, the Johnsons, the Farnhams, the Crosbies, the Jordaches and window cleaner Sinbad.

Redmond's initial frankness went unrewarded. Audiences dwindled and a change of tack was required. Out went some of the grimmer characters and in came one or two comic creations, to bring some levity. Bad language was toned down and a few more sensationalist elements were introduced. Storylines like the 'Free George Jackson' campaign (revolving around a jailed, innocent fireman) garnered media attention, and a drawn-out siege, ending in a double death, also brought in the viewers. Things have largely settled down again at *Brookside*, although every now and again the hype is turned up for moments like the death of Terry Sullivan's wife and son; the lesbian kiss between Beth Jordache and Margaret Clemence; the discovery of wife-batterer Trevor Jordache's body beneath a patio and the subsequent murder trial; and the incestuous relationship between brother and sister Nat and Georgia Simpson.

Brookside (the working title was *Meadowcroft* until Redmond stumbled across the real Brookside Close) was originally screened twice a week, with a Saturday omnibus, but was expanded to three weekly episodes in 1990. It has also produced some spin-offs. The three-part *Damon and Debbie* (1987) focused on the dispirited son of the Grant family and his school girlfriend as they went on the run from the police in York, while Tracy Corkhill and her boyfriend, Jamie, were seen in a two-part schools programme, *South* (part of Channel 4's *The English Programme* in 1988).

BROSNAN, PIERCE
(1953–)

Irish actor, TV's REMINGTON STEELE but now cast as James Bond, a role earmarked for him for a number of years. Contractual obligations to *Steele* meant that he missed out on the Bond role when Timothy Dalton took over and it seemed his chance had gone. However, when Dalton stepped aside in 1993, Brosnan was once again first choice to play the suave secret agent. His other TV credits have included NANCY ASTOR, *The Manions of America*, THE PROFESSIONALS (guest) and *Noble House*. He was married to actress Cassandra Harris, who died in 1991.

BROTHERS, THE
UK (BBC) Drama. BBC 1 1972–6

Mary Hammond	**Jean Anderson**
Edward Hammond	**Glyn Owen**
	Patrick O'Connell
Brian Hammond	**Richard Easton**
David Hammond	**Robin Chadwick**
Jennifer Kingsley/Hammond	**Jennifer Wilson**
Ann Hammond	**Hilary Tindall**

Carol Hammond	**Nicola Moloney**
	Annabelle Lanyon
	Debbie Farrington
Jill Hammond	**Gabrielle Drake**
Barbara Kingsley/Trent	**Julia Goodman**
Bill Riley	**Derek Benfield**
Harry Carter	**Mark McManus**
Pamela Graham	**Anna Fox**
Nicholas Fox	**Jonathan Newth**
Julie Lane	**Gillian McCutcheon**
Martin Farrell	**Murray Hayne**
Sir Neville Henniswode	**Carleton Hobbs**
Paul Merroney	**Colin Baker**
Clare Miller	**Carole Mowlam**
Gwen Riley	**Margaret Ashcroft**
April Winter/Merroney	**Liza Goddard**
Jane Maxwell	**Kate O'Mara**
Don Stacey	**Mike Pratt**

Creators: **Gerard Glaister, N. J. Crisp**
Producers: **Gerard Glaister, Ken Riddington, Bill Sellars**

Three brothers fight for control of the family haulage business.

When 70-year-old Robert Hammond died, his eldest son, Edward ('Ted'), braced himself to take over the family's long-distance-lorry business, Hammond Transport Services. After all, he had helped to build up the company. However, with the reading of the will, he learned that his two younger brothers had inherited equal shares, and his hard-nosed mother, Mary, who suffered from a heart condition, was just as reluctant to give up her influence. To make matters worse, Robert's mistress, Jennifer Kingsley, had also been handed a slice of the cake.

For over four years *The Brothers* played out the boardroom and bedroom battles of this squabbling family and became a firm Friday, then Sunday, night favourite. Keeping the trucks conveniently in the background, it followed Edward's attempts to assert his authority over his brothers (David, a restless young graduate, and Brian, a boring accountant), and the whole family's concern over the involvement of the prim Jennifer, who eventually married Edward. The truckers were represented by the working-class Bill Riley and his wife, Margaret.

Later additions to the cast were future DOCTOR WHO Colin Baker as obnoxious financial whiz-kid Paul Merroney (an early J. R. Ewing), his disillusioned wife, April, and Kate O'Mara as air-freight baroness Jane Maxwell, and storylines focused on the company's attempts to go public and expand into a global market.

BROTHERS IN LAW

UK (BBC) Situation Comedy. BBC 1962

Roger Thursby	**Richard Briers**
Henry Blagrove	**Richard Waring**
Kendall Grimes	**John Glyn-Jones**
Sally Mannering	**June Barry**

Writers: **Denis Norden, Frank Muir**
Producer: **Graeme Muir**

A trainee barrister fumbles his way through his early cases.

Roger Thursby was an enthusiastic pupil barrister undertaking his first year in chambers. Although he was chaperoned by the more experienced Henry Blagrove and the veteran Kendall Grimes, his courtroom experiences descended into farce as he struggled with the vagaries of legal life. Sally Mannering was his supportive girlfriend.

The series was based on a novel of the same name by Henry Cecil which had been filmed by the Boulting Brothers in 1956. Cecil also contributed to Denis Norden and Frank Muir's TV scripts. *Brothers in Law* gave Richard Briers his first leading role and led to MARRIAGE LINES and greater things. A judge who appeared in the final episode was given his own spin-off series in 1963. Named *Mr Justice Duncannon*, it pitched DR FINLAY'S CASEBOOK star Andrew Cruickshank into the title role.

BROWN, JUNE
(1927–)

Suffolk-born Shakespearean and character actress much seen in films and television before achieving star status as gossipy hypochondriac Dot Cotton in EASTENDERS. Viewers may also recall her as Aunt Sally in the sitcom, *Now and Then*, and in the children's comedy, *Pirates*, as well as in THE DUCHESS OF DUKE STREET (Louisa's mother), THE SWEENEY, *Churchill's People*, SOUTH RIDING, *The Prince and the Pauper*, *Shadows*, THE BILL, *Lace*, MINDER, AIN'T MISBEHAVIN' (Mrs Jilkes) and *Gormenghast* (Nannie Slagg). Her second husband, Robert Arnold, played PC Swain in *Dixon of Dock Green*.

BROWNE, JILL
(1937–91)

One of TV's earliest sweethearts, playing trainee nurse (later Sister) Carole Young in EMERGENCY – WARD 10, Jill Browne found herself inundated with fan mail from male viewers. In 1964, having just been dropped from the hospital soap, she married former co-star John Alderton, although the marriage ended in 1970. Her other major TV role – in the pub variety show, *The New Stars and Garters* – was not a success and she eventually left the business, marrying theatre producer Brian Wolfe in 1971.

BRUCE, FIONA
(1964–)

Singapore-born presenter of such programmes as CRIMEWATCH UK, *The Antiques Show* and *The Search*, as well as BBC news bulletins. She has also reported for programmes like PANORAMA, NEWSNIGHT and *Public Eye*.

BRUNSON, MICHAEL
OBE (1940–)

ITN's Political Editor until his retirement in 2000, Norwich-born Michael Brunson began his broadcasting career with BBC External Services in 1964 as a writer/producer. He moved to BBC Radio South-East the same year, before becoming an assistant producer on 24 HOURS in 1966. He joined ITN in 1968, was its US correspondent, 1972–7, and then European correspondent, 1979–80. Brunson was also seen as a newscaster between 1977 and 1981. In 1980 he took over as Diplomatic Editor, a post he held until becoming Political Editor in 1986.

BRUSH, BASIL

Puppet fox created and voiced by Ivan Owen (formerly the operator of Yoo-Hoo the Cuckoo in the 1950s' *Billy Bean and His Funny Machine* and dog Fred Barker in *Tuesday Rendezvous*, FIVE O'CLOCK CLUB, etc.). Basil's gap-toothed grin, effervescent character and posh voice (more than reminiscent of Terry-Thomas), not to mention his trademark 'Boom boom' and roaring laugh, made him a favourite of both children and adults. The puppet was made for Owen by Peter Firmin, half of the Smallfilms team who devised IVOR THE ENGINE, NOGGIN THE NOG, etc. He first appeared in *The Three Scampis* in 1962 (alongside Howard Williams and a Scottish hedgehog called Spike McPike voiced by Wally Whyton), and then guest-starred with David Nixon, before hiring a succession of straight men to read stories to him on his own Saturday teatime series from 1968 to 1980. Rodney Bewes was first into the role, then came Derek Fowlds, Roy North, Billy Boyle and Howard Williams (again). Basil then resurfaced alongside Doug Ridley in a Border TV series called *Basil's Joke Machine* (ITV 1986), and he was a team captain on *Fantasy Football League* in the 1990s. A new Basil Brush series was planned at the time of writing.

BRUSH STROKES
UK (BBC) Situation Comedy. BBC 1 1986–91

Jacko	**Karl Howman**
Eric	**Mike Walling**
Jean	**Nicky Croydon**
Sandra	**Jackie Lye**
Elmo Putney	**Howard Lew Lewis**
Lionel Bainbridge	**Gary Waldhorn**
Veronica Bainbridge	**Elizabeth Counsell**
Lesley Bainbridge	**Kim Thomson**
	Erika Hoffman

Creators/Writers: **John Esmonde, Bob Larbey**
Producers: **Sydney Lotterby, Mandie Fletcher, Harold Snoad, John B. Hobbs**

A chirpy London decorator has an eye for the ladies, but also a heart of gold.

This gentle comedy focused on the life of Jacko, an appropriately named Cockney Jack the Lad who lived in Motspur Park and worked for Bainbridge's, a small family painting and decorating company. His work colleague (and landlord) was his down-to-earth brother-in-law, Eric (complete with NHS specs), and his boss was the intolerant Lionel. Lionel's wife, Veronica, took over when Lionel died and one of the girls Jacko dated was Lionel's snooty daughter, Lesley. However, Jacko's soft spot was really reserved for Sandra, Bainbridge's Geordie secretary. Also seen was Jean, Eric's wife and Jacko's sensible sister, and bulky Elmo Putney, gormless landlord of the local boozer, The White Hart. Elmo briefly emigrated to Australia, found opals with the aid of his pet dingo and returned in style to London to open a ghastly pink wine-bar (imaginatively dubbed Elmo Putney's Wine Bar), where Lesley took a job waitressing.

The programme's credits showed Jacko working his way along a wall with a paint roller and featured a theme song by Dexy's Midnight Runners. Entitled 'Because of You', it entered the Top Twenty in 1986.

BRYAN, DORA
OBE (Dora Broadbent; 1924–)

Lancashire-born, former child performer who became one of the UK's favourite comediennes in the 1950s–70s, starring in shows like *Our Dora* (Dora), *Happily Ever After* (Dora Morgan), *According to Dora*, *Before the Fringe* and *Both Ends Meet* (Dora Page). In the 1990s she was Mrs Carpenter in ON THE UP and Kitty Flitcroft in *Mother's Ruin*, as well as enjoying a run of high-profile guest appearances.

B SkyB
(British Sky Broadcasting)

The major DBS (Direct Broadcasting by Satellites) station in the UK, formed by a merger of Sky Television and British Satellite Broadcasting (BSB) in 1990. The two companies had previously been rivals.

BSB was the company selected by the IBA to provide satellite television to the UK. In accordance with IBA advice, it opted for a technically advanced system using novel 'squarial' dishes which were designed to receive signals from the specially constructed Marco Polo satellite. However, development problems ensued and BSB was beaten into the marketplace by Sky, an 'unofficial' company, which used larger, round dishes and transmitted from the Astra satellite. Being independently owned, and operating out of Luxembourg, Astra was beyond the control of UK broadcasting regulators. Sky had developed from a primitive satellite channel known as Satellite TV, which broadcast to cable stations (for onward transmission) around Europe from 1982, using existing telecom satellites. Satellite TV was bought by Rupert Murdoch's News International and, with a change of name to Sky, began satellite/cable experiments in the UK, using Swindon as its testing ground. By the time the Astra satellite went into orbit in December 1988, Sky was well established and able to launch four satellite channels direct to homes in February of the following year.

The Marco Polo and Astra systems, however, were incompatible and this meant that viewers had to gamble on which to purchase (in much the same way as the incompatible VHS and Betamax home video systems clashed head to head, with the result that Betamax soon became obsolete). Although Sky continued to lose money, the fact that it was already up and running by the time BSB finally went on air in 1990 proved terminal for BSB, and the latter company was forced into a merger (resembling more of a take-over) with its rival later that year. Only the Astra system is now in use. BSkyB is now the official company name, but just the name Sky is used for the various channels operated by the company.

On 1 October 1998 the company launched Sky Digital and now offers a raft of digital channels, including Sky One (a general entertainments channel); Sky News; various Sky Sports channels; Sky Travel; and countless film and pay-per-view movie channels. The company also markets a wide range of other channels in subscriber packages. These include UK Gold, Style, Play and Drama; Bravo; Living; Disney Channel; Granada Plus, Breeze and Men and Motors; Challenge TV; Paramount Comedy Channel; Sci-Fi; The Discovery Channel and Discovery Home and Leisure; MUTV; British Eurosport; MTV; VH-1; Nickelodeon; Fox Kids; and Cartoon Network. BSkyB also supplies some of its own channels for the terrestrial digital provider, ONdigital, and cable networks.

BSB
See BSKYB.

BUCCANEERS, THE
UK (ITP/Sapphire) Adventure. ITV 1956–7

Dan Tempest	**Robert Shaw**
Lt. Beamish	**Peter Hammond**
Governor Capt. Woodes Rogers	**Alec Clunes**
Blackbeard	**George Margo**
	Terence Cooper
Armando	**Edwin Richfield**
Taffy	**Paul Hansard**
Dickon	**Wilfrid Downing**
Gaff Guernsey	**Brian Rawlinson**
Van Brugh	**Alec Mango**
Bassett	**Neil Hallett**
Pop	**Willoughby Gray**
Costellaux	**Terence Cooper**
Estaban	**Roger Delgado**

Executive Producer: **Hannah Weinstein**
Producer: **Sidney Cole**

A pirate swears loyalty to the king, receives a pardon and defends the colonies from the Spanish.

In 1718 pirate Dan Tempest had been the leader of a band of freebooters in the British Caribbean province of New Providence. However, he was persuaded by Lt. Beamish, the new deputy governor, to switch sides and fight on

behalf of the Crown against the advancing Spanish, and to help counter the disruptive influence of other pirates, such as the famous Blackbeard. Armando, Taffy and Gaff were all loyal members of Tempest's swashbuckling crew on the brig *Sultana*, with Dickon, a stowaway-turned-cabin-boy, and Captain Morgan, Tempest's pet monkey, also seen. Van Brugh was an untrustworthy local businessman in Nassau, where the action mainly took place. Estaban (played by Roger Delgado, the future Master in DOCTOR WHO) was one of the Spanish principals.

With its 'a-roving' theme song, *The Buccaneers* was reputedly TV's first pirate series and was also unusual in that its lead character did not appear until the third episode, the first two being devoted to setting the scene. The sea sequences were filmed off Falmouth and the ship featured was a showbusiness veteran, having already played the part of the *Hispaniola* in Disney's *Treasure Island* and the *Pequod* in John Huston's *Moby Dick*.

BUCHANAN, COLIN

British actor, familiar as detective Peter Pascoe in DALZIEL AND PASCOE and previously as TA man Hodge in PRESTON FRONT. Buchanan has also starred in *Agatha Christie's The Pale Horse* (sculptor Mark Easterbrook) and *Moll Flanders* (Rowland).

BUCK ROGERS IN THE 25TH CENTURY
US (Universal/Glen A. Larson) Science Fiction. ITV 1980–2

Capt. William 'Buck' Rogers	**Gil Gerard**
Col. Wilma Deering	**Erin Gray**
Dr Elias Huer	**Tim O'Connor**
Twiki	**Felix Silla**
	Mel Blanc (*voice*)
	Bob Elyea
Dr Theopolis	**Eric Server** (*voice only*)
Princess Ardala	**Pamela Hensley**
Kane	**Henry Silva**
	Michael Ansara
Hawk	**Thom Christopher**
Dr Goodfellow	**Wilfred Hyde-White**
Admiral Asimov	**Jay Garner**
Crichton	**Jeff David** (*voice only*)
Lt. Devlin	**Paul Carr**
Narrator	**William Conrad**

Executive Producers: **Glen A. Larson, John Mantley**
Producers: **Richard Caffey, John Gaynor, David J. O'Connell, Leslie Stevens, Bruce Lansbury, John G. Stevens, Calvin Clements**

An astronaut is rocketed 500 years into the future.

The comic-strip character Buck Rogers was given a second bite of the TV cherry in this series, following an earlier dramatization seen in the USA in 1950. On this occasion, the space hero found himself in the 25th century, in the year 2491 to be precise. His space capsule (Ranger 3), launched in 1987, had gone missing for 504 years, but, being in suspended animation, Rogers survived the experience, awaking aboard a Draconian spaceship on its way to a peace conference on Earth. The planet, devastated by nuclear war, had forged a new civilization based in a futuristic city (New Chicago) in the Mid West. Outside the city was Anarchia, a wilderness housing the dregs of a mutilated society. The Draconians aimed to take control. Rogers, although initially viewed with suspicion by the Earth Defense Directorate, became the planet's ally in fighting off the aliens, who were led by the glamorous Princess Ardala and her sidekick, Kane. Rogers found romance with attractive defence commander Wilma Deering, and teamed up with top scientist Dr Huer, who supplied a new robot chum, Twiki, and also the computer Dr Theopolis, usually seen as a disc around Twiki's neck.

In its second season the series changed considerably. Buck and Twiki were no longer on Earth but on the spaceship *The Searcher*, seeking out Earthlings who had fled the holocaust. They were now supported by Admiral Asimov (supposedly a descendant of the science-fiction writer, Isaac Asimov), Lt. Devlin and old, inquisitive scientist Dr Goodfellow. Also aboard were Hawk (a half-man, half-bird from the planet Throm) and a pompous robot named Crichton.

While the series was not without its critics, its tongue-in-cheek presentation and elaborate special effects proved to be its saving graces. The pilot, explaining Rogers's arrival in the future, was initially released in cinemas.

BUCKNELL, BARRY

TV 'home improvement' expert whose programmes in the 1950s and early 1960s included *Do It Yourself* and *Bucknell's House*, in which he refitted a derelict Victorian house in Ealing. A former motor engineer, he first appeared in part of the magazine, ABOUT THE HOME.

BUDGIE
UK (LWT) Comedy Drama. ITV 1971–2

Budgie Bird	**Adam Faith**
Charlie Endell	**Iain Cuthbertson**
Hazel	**Lynn Dalby**
Jean	**Georgina Hale**
Mrs Endell	**June Lewis**
Jack Bird	**George Tovey**
Laughing Spam Fritter	**John Rhys-Davies**
Grogan	**Rio Fanning**

Writers: **Keith Waterhouse, Willis Hall**
Executive Producer: **Rex Firkin**
Producer: **Verity Lambert**

A chirpy London spiv keeps hoping things will turn up.

Budgie Bird was a born loser. Always down on his luck, he nevertheless believed that life was about to change. For him Easy Street was just around the corner, but everyone knew that the yellow brick road was leading only to one place – jail. Shunning regular employment, he clung to the fringes of the Soho underworld, filled

with ambitious plans and ideas for his personal betterment, all doomed to instant failure. The best he could manage was a job as a runner for Glaswegian gangster Charlie Endell, proprietor of a dodgy book shop. Endell was a local 'Mr Big' who was always happy to let Budgie take the rap for his illegal activities. But, despite being used and pushed around, the long-haired delinquent remained an eternal optimist, meandering through life, dreaming up worthless ways of making his fortune, ducking and diving and incurring the wrath of the local heavies. Jean was his estranged wife and Hazel his long-suffering girlfriend. Laughing Spam Fritter and Grogan were two other members of the Soho low-life.

The series brought a new direction to the career of 1960s pop star Adam Faith, who returned to TV 20 years later in LOVE HURTS after remarkable interim success as a city wheeler-dealer. A short-lived *Budgie* spin-off, *Charles Endell Esquire*, set in Glasgow and featuring Iain Cuthbertson but not Adam Faith, was seen in 1979.

BUERK, MICHAEL
(1946–)

Solihull-born TV journalist and newsreader whose reports on the Ethiopian famine of 1984 were instrumental in alerting the world to the scale of the human tragedy unfolding in Africa. After starting out in newspapers, Buerk joined BBC Radio Bristol and then moved into television with HTV. He joined BBC TV news in 1973. Among his postings was a four-year stint in South Africa. He has since anchored the BBC's main news bulletins and presented series like *Nature*, *999*, *The Soul of Britain* and a short-lived version of his Radio 4 programme, *The Moral Maze*.

BUFFY THE VAMPIRE SLAYER
US (Mutant Enemy/Kuzui/Sandollar/Twentieth Century-Fox) Comedy Drama. BBC 2 1998–

Buffy Summers	**Sarah Michelle Gellar**
Alexander 'Xander' Harris	**Nicholas Brendon**
Willow Rosenberg	**Alyson Hannigan**
Rupert Giles	**Anthony Stewart Head**
Cordelia Chase	**Charisma Carpenter**
Joyce Summers	**Kristine Sutherland**
The Master	**Mark Metcalf**
Angel	**David Boreanaz**
Oz	**Seth Green**
Spike	**James Marsters**

Creator: **Joss Whedon**

A teenage schoolgirl saves her town from the creatures of Hell.

A 1992 teen movie, starring Kristy Swanson and Donald Sutherland, was responsible for one of TV's biggest cult hits of the turn of the millennium. Adopting the same name, television's *Buffy* pitched Sarah Michelle Gellar into the title role of a high school girl fresh in town but soon to be its saviour.

Buffy Summers had previously been expelled from a

school in LA for starting a fire (actually burning out some demons) and now arrived with her divorcée mother, Joyce, in the town of Sunnydale, California, as sophomore at Sunnydale High School. It turned out that the settlement sat right on top of the gateway to Hell, and it was up to Buffy to don her mantle of vampire-slayer to preserve its residents from the creatures of the deep. Blood-suckers, witches and monsters of all persuasions were seen off by the plucky little blonde. Assigned as Buffy's mentor was school librarian Giles (British actor Anthony Head, late of Nescafé commercials and JONATHAN CREEK). Buffy's friends and some-time rivals in the teen market were Willow, Cordelia and Xander, and outside of school they – and assorted young vampires – frequented The Bronze club. Other notable characters were the menacing Master, punky Spike and Oz, a werewolf who became Willow's boyfriend. One important ally was decent vampire Angel, who became Buffy's beau but whom she was once forced to knife when he turned bad again. He was given his own series, *Angel*, and Buffy moved on to Sunnydale's branch of the University of California.

Camped up to the full, with plenty of butt-kicking, *Buffy*, a veritable death fest wrapped in humorous clothes, was first screened on Sky One in the UK.

BUGS

UK (BBC/Carnival Films) Science Fiction. BBC 1 1995–9

Ed .... **Craig McLachlan**
                                                        Steven Houghton
Ros Henderson .... **Jaye Griffiths**
Nick Beckett .... **Jesse Birdsall**
Jan .... **Jan Harvey**
Alex .... **Paula Hunt**
Channing .... **Michael Grandage**
Adam .... **Joseph May**
Christa .... **Sandra Reinton**

Producer: **Brian Eastman**

A trio of agents armed with high-tech gizmos save the world from subversive forces.

Bugs brought a return to British television of the gadget. What James Bond had been doing in the cinema for decades, and what programmes like THE AVENGERS had once revelled in, was now back in prime time. This Saturday evening escapist fantasy featured three very fit, intelligent, braver-than-brave heroes. Former services man and Government agent Beckett joined forces with the daredevil Ed and the computer/electronics genius Ros to provide answers to the world's many problems. Each week the threesome were tested to the extreme by fiendish villains armed with devices as varied as poisonous electronic mosquitoes, agricultural viruses and voice-activated bombs. To save the day, they were called upon to use their martial arts skills, climb through airducts, dive underwater or even walk in space, usually with a clock counting down in the background. The setting for the series was London, although the location was never officially declared, the producers preferring anonymity with an eye on international sales.

If the futuristic tone of *Bugs* seemed familiar, this was not surprising. The series consultant was Brian Clemens, the man behind most of *The Avengers'* most fondly remembered tales. After three series, *Bugs* gained a more human face. The gadgetry and loud explosions remained, but now personal matters began to intrude on the plot. Romance reared its ugly head, with Beckett chasing Ros and Ros dating businessman Channing. At the same time, the three principals began to work for Jan, head of a secret Government department called the Bureau, and her business-like assistant, Alex. A year later, former NEIGHBOURS star Craig McLachlan left and was replaced in the role of Ed by Steven Houghton. The series concluded with three episodes in August 1999.

BULLSEYE

UK (ATV/Central) Game Show. ITV 1981–95

Presenter: **Jim Bowen**

Creators: **Andrew Wood, Norman Vaughan**
Producers: **Peter Holmans, Bob Cousins**

Quiz based around the game of darts.

A good throwing action and a fair level of general knowledge were what was required in this long-running game show in which comic Jim Bowen welcomed three pairs of contestants to throw darts and answer questions to win cash and prizes. The first segment of the game involved a standard dartboard. One team member aimed three darts and the other collected cash to the value of the score achieved by answering a question correctly. After three rounds of darts the team with the lowest aggregate score was eliminated. The consolation prize was a 'bendy Bully' (a rubber dummy of the show's bull mascot). The two remaining pairs then moved on to the category dartboard, where the thrower aimed for a specialist subject and the partner, again, answered to win cash. Once more the lower scorers were eliminated. The final game saw both partners in the remaining team throwing darts at a prize dartboard (six for the main thrower, three for the non-darter), hoping to hit numbers which corresponded to washing machines, colour TVs, etc. When all the prizes won by the top duo had been totalled up, they were offered the chance to gamble them for a star prize, hidden behind screens. With three darts each, if they scored a total of 101 or more the star prize was theirs. Any less and the prizes were forfeited. Cruelly, Bowen always invited losing contestants to 'Look what you would have won', whipping back the screen to reveal a speedboat, a new car or a foreign holiday for four people. An additional element of the programme involved a guest professional player throwing nine darts for charity. Darts commentator Tony Green kept score throughout.

It is fair to say that *Bullseye* (co-devised by comic Norman Vaughan) was one of the most unlikely TV successes produced by Central Television. Host Jim Bowen became notorious for his insensitive handling of contestants ('What do you do for a living?' 'I'm unemployed, Jim.' 'Super.') and his various gaffes. Some recorded programmes were allegedly binned, being judged too poor to transmit, but the series quickly built up a cult following, particularly among the young.

BULMAN
UK (Granada) Detective Drama. ITV 1985–7

George Bulman .... **Don Henderson**
Lucy McGinty .... **Siobhan Redmond**
William Dugdale .... **Thorley Walters**

Creator: **Kenneth Royce**
Writer: **Murray Smith**
Executive Producer: **Richard Everitt**
Producers: **Steve Hawes, Sita Williams**

An ex-policeman retires to the world of antiques but is coaxed back into private detection.

Sgt George Bulman first appeared in THE XYY MAN, pursuing the aggressive chromosome freak, Spider Scott. The character then re-emerged in the series, STRANGERS, but his personality and character traits had changed dramatically. Although still uncompromising, he had become rather eccentric and less conventional, wearing fingerless grey gloves on duty and sporting gold-rimmed reading spectacles. In this follow-up series of his own, the character became quirkier still.

Bulman had retired from the force to open an antiques shop and repair clocks in the Shanghai Road, southwest London. But his knowledge of the criminal world and his powers of detection were too great to lay to waste and he found himself dragged back into action. Egging him on was Lucy McGinty, the daughter of a former colleague. A Medieval Studies student, she had thrown it all in to work with George and learn his criminology skills. An academic secret serviceman named William Dugdale, a throwback to *Strangers* days, was also seen.

The softly spoken Bulman's trademarks included his 2CV car, a knowledge of the classics and the use of a nasal inhaler. He always carried a plastic bag, too. Several of these gimmicks were introduced by accident. For instance, actor Don Henderson first used an inhaler because he really did have a cold, and the gloves were employed to cover up a stubborn wedding ring which couldn't be removed (Bulman was divorced). A scarf covered Henderson's throat cancer surgery scars, and the fact that he sometimes talked in a whisper was also connected to this ailment.

BURKE, ALFRED
(1918–)

British actor and writer, remembered for his long-running portrayal of the down-at-heel private detective, Frank Marker, in PUBLIC EYE. Among his later roles were Revd Patrick Brontë in *The Brontës of Haworth*, the Nazi Major Richter in ENEMY AT THE DOOR, Long John Silver in *Treasure Island*, Giuliano della Rovere in THE BORGIAS and a guest spot in BERGERAC (as Jim's old headmaster).

BURKE, JAMES
(1936–)

Excitable, bespectacled presenter, particularly adept at explaining complex scientific issues in layman's terms on programmes like TOMORROW'S WORLD and his own series, CONNECTIONS. He was also part of the BBC's team covering the *Apollo* moon missions and was scientific adviser on the drama series, *Moonbase 3*.

BURKE, KATHY
(1964–)

Award-winning English actress seen in both comic and straight drama roles. She first gained attention when providing strong support to Harry Enfield in his various series (playing, among other characters, Waynetta Slob and Perry the teenager). She was Martha in the drama MR WROE'S VIRGINS, Sharon in COMMON AS MUCK, Honour the maid in *Tom Jones* and starred as Linda La Hughes in the comedy, *Gimme Gimme Gimme*. Other credits have included A VERY PECULIAR PRACTICE, ABSOLUTELY FABULOUS (Magda), MURDER MOST HORRID and *Ted and Ralph*.

BURKE'S LAW/AMOS BURKE – SECRET AGENT
US (Four Star) Detective Drama. ITV 1963–6

Capt. Amos Burke .... **Gene Barry**
Det. Tim Tilson .... **Gary Conway**
DS Lester Hart .... **Regis Toomey**
Henry .... **Leon Lontoc**
Sgt Ames .... **Eileen O'Neill**
'The Man' .... **Carl Benton Reid** (*Secret Agent*)

Creators: **Ivan Goff, Ben Roberts**
Producer: **Aaron Spelling**

The cases of the head of the Los Angeles homicide squad, a multi-millionaire.

This glossy series focused on Captain Amos Burke, the obscenely wealthy boss of the LAPD's murder squad, who was dragged away from society functions and expensive wining and dining to head up all manner of homicide investigations. Burke cruised to the scene of crime in the back of a Rolls-Royce, driven by his chauffeur, Henry. There he was assisted by young detective Tim Tilson and wise veteran sergeant Lester Hart. Policewoman Ames was added to Burke's staff later. As unlikely as it seems, the debonair bachelor was evidently the right man for this particular job, as most of the victims appeared to come from the élite end of society. Each programme was subtitled *Who killed . . . ?*, with the name of that week's unfortunate victim filling the gap.

Burke eventually quit the police force to become an undercover agent, and set out on the trail of criminals all over the world. His contact was known only as 'The Man' and was the sole supporting actor in the new-look series. With this change of tack (a response to the success of THE MAN FROM UNCLE), the programme was renamed *Amos Burke – Secret Agent*.

Burke's Law, littered with famous guest stars (sometimes more than half a dozen in one episode), was originally planned as a vehicle for Dick Powell, who had played the character in an American anthology series a year or two earlier. It was revived in 1994, with Gene Barry again in the title role. Taking things somewhat easier, in accordance with his age, he now relied on the help of his son, Peter (played by Peter Barton). The role of Henry was taken over by Danny Kamekona.

BURNET, Sir ALASTAIR
(James Burnet; 1928–)

British news and current affairs presenter who joined ITN as political editor in 1963. Despite taking over as editor of *The Economist*, Burnet preserved his ITN career and became one of the first two newscasters on *News at Ten* in 1967 (with Andrew Gardner). Although he left for the BBC and PANORAMA in 1972, and went on to edit the *Daily Express*, he later returned to ITN to launch *News at 5.45*. Subsequently he anchored *News at Ten* for many years. His other television work included THIS WEEK, as well as numerous election programmes, Budgets, royal interviews and commentaries on State occasions. He was knighted in 1984 and retired in 1990.

BURNS AND ALLEN SHOW, THE
US (CBS) Situation Comedy. BBC 1955–61

George Burns	Himself
Gracie Allen	Herself
Blanche Morton	Bea Benaderet
Harry Morton	Fred Clark
	Larry Keating
Harry Von Zell	Himself
Ronnie Burns	Himself

Producer: **Ralph Levy**

Television vehicle for a vaudeville act that had been running for 30 years.

Real-life husband and wife George Burns and Gracie Allen had long been stage and radio partners. As television began to take off, they moved into this unexplored medium and, in doing so, laid down benchmarks for other comedians to follow. Their series was essentially a sitcom, although extended dialogues between the two stars offered more than an echo of their variety days. In the style of I LOVE LUCY and other contemporary US comedies, this one was domestic-based, with the pair playing a husband and wife living in Beverly Hills. Like Lucy, Gracie's confidante was her next-door neighbour, in this case Blanche Morton. The latter's husband, Harry, had a short fuse which contrasted sharply with the relaxed approach of the philosophical Burns. However, Burns did have an advantage. It was his show and he was able to step out of the action and talk to the audience, pondering what to do next or

how the plot should develop. He even had a TV set to watch scenes involving the others and could drag the show's announcer, Harry Von Zell, into the action. It's easy to see where Garry Shandling's inspiration came from. (See IT'S GARRY SHANDLING'S SHOW.)

Gracie's character was a real scatterbrain, but what drove many guest stars to despair was her alternative logic and strange, convoluted reasoning with which they couldn't argue. Thankfully, tolerant George understood her. Why else would he fall for the same ending each week: 'Say "Goodnight", Gracie'; 'Goodnight Gracie'? (an ending copied by Rowan and Martin in LAUGH-IN). The Burns's son, Ronnie, also appeared, but the show ended in America in 1958, when Gracie announced her retirement from the business. Co-star Bea Benaderet went on to provide the voice for Betty Rubble in THE FLINTSTONES and the irrepressible George soldiered on alone.

BURNS, GEORGE
(Nathan Birnbaum; 1896–1996)

New York-born, cigar-puffing vaudeville comic whose partnership with his scatterbrained wife, Gracie Allen, proved successful on stage, radio and ultimately television. *The Burns and Allen Show* revolutionized TV comedy in the 1950s (with debunking of television conventions) and was a hit on both sides of the Atlantic. With Gracie's retirement and subsequent death, George's career seemed to fade out, but he bounced back in the mid-1970s with a run of cinema successes (such as *The Sunshine Boys* and *Oh God!*) and even began a new US TV series, *The George Burns Comedy Week*, in 1985. He performed right up to his 100th birthday, and a few weeks later he died.

BURNS, GORDON
(1942–)

Presenter, narrator and quiz show host, from 1977 questionmaster on THE KRYPTON FACTOR. Born in Belfast, Burns began his career with Ulster Television (as sports editor and news presenter). From there he moved to Granada, working on WORLD IN ACTION and *Granada Reports*. He has also presented *Password*, SURPRISE, SURPRISE with Cilla Black, various regional programmes, and he devised and hosted the game show, *A Word in Your Ear*.

BURR, RAYMOND
(1917–93)

Canadian actor, star of two of the best-loved series of the 1950s and 1960s, PERRY MASON and A MAN CALLED IRONSIDE. Between them, these series notched up 18 years of continuous success for their star, leaving him little time to play other roles. Burr did take up the offer of a few TV movies and mini-series (including *79 Park Avenue*), but it wasn't until he revived the old legal-eagle Mason in 1986 that he was prominent on our screens again. Earlier in his career Burr had appeared in around 90 movies.

BURTON, AMANDA
(1956–)

Northern Irish actress, best known for her roles as Heather Haversham in BROOKSIDE, Dr Beth Glover in PEAK PRACTICE and Dr Sam Ryan in SILENT WITNESS. Other credits have included the single drama, *The Gift* (dying young mother Lynn Ransom) and *Little Bird* (Rachel, Lewis), BOON (Margaret Daly) and INSPECTOR MORSE, plus a *Born to Be Wild* nature programme about bears.

BURTON, HUMPHREY
CBE (1931–)

British arts presenter and producer, associated with such programmes as MONITOR, OMNIBUS and AQUARIUS.

BUSMAN'S HOLIDAY
UK (Granada/Action Time) Quiz. ITV 1985–93

Presenters: **Julian Pettifer, Sarah Kennedy, Elton Welsby**

Executive Producers: **Stephen Leahy, Dianne Nelmes**
Producers: **Stephen Leahy, Patricia Pearson, Richard Bradley, Jenny Dodd, Kieran Roberts**

Teams compete for a chance to see how their own jobs are done in other corners of the world.

In this occupational quiz, three teams of workers from various professions were cross-examined about each other's jobs and answered questions about their own specialities. A general knowledge element was also thrown in. The three teams were whittled down to one, which then collected a European or worldwide 'Busman's Holiday'. This saw the three members whisked away to an exotic location to see how their jobs were carried out in that part of the world. A film was made of their experience and shown as an insert in the following week's programme. Contestants included the likes of seaside landladies, hovercraft pilots, antiques dealers, osteopaths and wardens of stately homes. Julian Pettifer was the original host, succeeded by Sarah Kennedy and then Elton Welsby.

BUTLER, DAWS
(1916–88)

American cartoon voicer, the voice of Yogi Bear, Huckleberry Hound and scores of Hanna-Barbera characters, including Elroy Jetson, Lambsy in *It's the Wolf* and Peter Perfect and others in WACKY RACES.

BUTTERFLIES
UK (BBC) Situation Comedy. BBC 2 1978–80; 1983

Ria Parkinson	**Wendy Craig**
Ben Parkinson	**Geoffrey Palmer**
Russell Parkinson	**Andrew Hall**
Adam Parkinson	**Nicholas Lyndhurst**
Leonard Dunn	**Bruce Montague**
Ruby	**Joyce Windsor**
Thomas	**Michael Ripper**

Creator/Writer: **Carla Lane**
Producers: **Gareth Gwenlan, Sydney Lotterby**

The frustrations of an overlooked suburban housewife.

It seemed as if Ria Parkinson's role in life was already over, after 19 years of marriage. Her two slightly wayward sons, Russell and Adam, had grown up and now had lives of their own. Her dentist husband, Ben, a manic depressive, was too wrapped up in his work and his hobby (butterfly collecting) and so Ria found herself entering a mini midlife crisis. What was worse, even her housekeeping skills were subject to criticism, particularly her cooking, with anything more complicated than corn flakes becoming a game of chance. To ease the pain, she contemplated an extra-marital affair with the recently divorced Leonard Dunn, a smooth, wealthy businessman she met in a restaurant, although it barely amounted to more than words. Ruby was the Parkinsons' rough-and-ready daily, often bemused at the strange goings-on in the household, and Thomas was Leonard's chauffeur.

The series proved to be a useful stepping-stone for actor Nicholas Lyndhurst, taking him out of the realm of child stars and into adult performances. Before *Butterflies* had ended, ONLY FOOLS AND HORSES had begun. A version of Dolly Parton's 'Love Is Like a Butterfly' was used for the theme tune. The cast was reunited for a special CHILDREN IN NEED sketch in 2000.

BUTTERWORTH, PETER
(1919–79)

Carry On actor whose television work stretched from the 1940s through to his death in 1979. Credits included the children's programmes, *Kept In*, *Those Kids* (Mr Oddy) and *SS Saturday Special*, the early sketch shows, *How Do You View?* and *Two's Company*, plus the sitcoms, *Friends and Neighbours*, *Meet the Champ* (a boxing trainer), *Bulldog Breed* (Henry Broadbent), *Kindly Leave the Kerb* (busker Ernest Tanner), *A Class by Himself* (the valet Clutton) and *Odd Man Out* (Wilf), plus straight drama roles in DOCTOR WHO (the Time Meddler), EMERGENCY – WARD 10, DANGER MAN, THE ODD MAN and PUBLIC EYE. He was married to impressionist Janet Brown and father of actor Tyler Butterworth. He appeared with Janet many times in the 1950s, including on the admag, *Where Shall We Go?*.

BY THE SWORD DIVIDED
UK (BBC) Drama. BBC 1 1983–5

Anne Lacey/Fletcher	**Sharon Mughan**
Sir Thomas Lacey	**Timothy Bentinck**
John Fletcher	**Rob Edwards**
Lucinda Lacey/Ferrar	**Lucy Aston**
Sir Martin Lacey	**Julian Glover**
Major Gen. Horton	**Gareth Thomas**
Susan Protheroe	**Judy Buxton**
Capt. Hannibal Marsh	**Malcolm Stoddard**
King Charles I	**Jeremy Clyde**
Sir Henry Parkin	**Charles Kay**
Nathaniel Cropper	**Andrew Maclauchlan**
Goodwife Margaret	**Rosalie Crutchley**
Will Saltmarsh	**Simon Dutton**
Walter Jackman	**Edward Peel**
Capt. Charles Pike	**Mark Burns**
Rachel	**Debbie Goodman**
Emma Bowen/Skinner	**Janet Lees Price**
Hannah Jackman	**Joanna Myers**
Dick Skinner	**Peter Guinness**
Hugh Brandon	**Simon Butteriss**
Mrs Dumfry	**Claire Davenport**
Sir Ralph Winter	**Robert Stephens**
Sir Austin Fletcher	**Bert Parnaby**
Oliver Cromwell	**Peter Jeffrey**
Frances Neville/Lacey	**Joanna McCallum**
King Charles II/Will Jones	**Simon Treves**
Minty	**Eileen Way**
John Thurloe	**David Collings**

Creator: **John Hawkesworth**
Producers: **Brian Spiby, Jonathan Alwyn**

A family is torn apart by the English Civil War.

Beginning in May 1640, *By the Sword Divided* told the story of a noble English family as Civil War loomed. Head of the family was Sir Martin Lacey, a staunch Royalist who found his relatives siding with his Parliamentarian opponents and his own daughters marrying into 'the other side'. In the course of the first series, Sir Martin fought at Edgehill, the Laceys' home at Arnescote Castle fell under siege from Cromwell's troops and the family silver was smuggled to the King at Oxford, all this taking events up to summer 1647. The second series, which aired in 1985, covered the period 1648–60 and picked up with Arnescote Castle firmly in the hands of Sir Martin's daughter, Anne, and her Parliamentarian husband, John Fletcher. It continued through the execution of Charles I, a visit from Cromwell, assorted witch hunts, the arrival of Charles II, Royalist attempts to regain Arnescote and the eventual restoration of the monarchy, with family turmoil, as always, competing fiercely with the outside hostilities.

BYGRAVES, MAX
(Walter Bygraves; 1922–)

London-born entertainer who earned the nickname 'Max' after an impression he performed of Max Miller while in the RAF. Although training as a carpenter, Bygraves was able to turn professional as a singer and comedian soon after the war, working on stage, radio, records and film, eventually arriving on television with his *Singalongamax* nostalgic music shows, numerous Royal Variety Performances and one-off specials. His hosting of FAMILY FORTUNES proved less successful and the series was cancelled, only to be brought back a few years later with Les Dennis in charge. 'I wanna tell you a story' became his catchphrase.

BYKER GROVE
UK (Zenith North) Children's Drama. BBC 1 1989–

Michael	**Gordon Griffin**
Julie	**Lucy Walsh**
Donna	**Sally McQuillan**
Nicola	**Jill Halfpenny**
Spuggie	**Lyndyann Barrass**
Gill	**Caspar Berry**
Winston	**Craig Reilly**
Mary O'Malley	**Lyn Douglas**
Rajeev	**Daniel Larson**
Clare Warner	**Jenny Twigge**
Cas	**Niall Shearer**
Geoff	**Billy Fane**
Hayley	**Amanda Webster**
Alison	**Victoria Murray**
Jim Bell	**Colin MacLachlan**
Duncan	**Declan Donnelly**
Ian	**Craig Grieveson**
Lisa	**Jayne Mackenzie**
Fraser	**John Jefferson**
Carl	**Peter Eke**
Polly	**Denise Welch**
Brad	**Michael Nicholson**
Jan	**Morten Lind**
Charley	**Michelle Charles**
PJ	**Anthony McPartlin**
Dexter	**Gavin Kitchen**
Robert	**Christopher Hardy**
Jemma	**Nicola Ewart**
Gwen	**Linda Huntley**
Kelly	**Louise Towers**
Beckett	**Roger Lloyd Pack**
Speedy	**Stephen Bradley**
Leah	**Jayni Hoy**
Noddy	**Brett Adams**
Angel	**Vicky Taylor**
Debbie	**Nicola Bell**
Morph	**Tracy Dempster**
Paul	**Joe Caffrey**
Marcus	**David Oliver**
	Oliver Stone
Amanda	**Gemma Graham**

Patsy	Justine McKenzie
Frew	Luke Dale
Kath	Lesley Saint John
Charlie	Donna Air
Lou	Annie Orwin
Barney	Stephen Carr
Lee	Rory Gibson
Greg	Dale Meeks
	Gary Crawford
Gary	George Trotter
Marie	Louise Mostyn
Anna	Claire Graham
Alfie	Andrew Smith
Flora	Kerryann Christiansen
Arran	Neil Blackstone
Dace	Leslie Baines
Ed	Grant Adams
Laura Dobson	Emma Brierley
Karen	Kimberly Dunbar
Brigid	Joanne McIntosh
Ashley	Shaun Mechen
Terry	Chris Woodger
Sita	Gauri Vedhara
Philip	Philip Miller
Leanne	Vikki Spensley
Jake	Nick Figgis
Cher	Jody Baldwin
Rob	Gavin Makel
Teraise	Adele Taylor
Jack	Edward Scott
Sian	Charlie Hardwick
Harry	Leah Jones
Ben	Andrew Smith
Nikki	Siobhan Hanratty
Ollie	Louis Watson
Regina	Jade Turnbull
Laura	Louise Henderson
Barry	Stephen Douglass
Nat	Alexa Gibb
Emma	Holly Wilkinson
Tom	Ronan Patterson
Matt	Adam Scott
Claire	Victoria Hawkins
Liam	Pete Hepple
Stumpy	Paul Meynell
Maggie	Janine Birkett
Tina	Lynne Wilmot
Akili	Patrick Miller
Juliet	Beverley Hills
Peter	Bill Fellows
Joe	Chris Beattie
Bill	Adam John Ironside
Bradley	Nicholas Nancarrow
Paul	Patrice Etienne
Eve	Rory Lewis
Adam	Alex Beebe
Luke	Dominic Beebe

Creator: **Adele Rose**
Producers: **Matthew Robinson, Morag Bain**
Executive Producers: **Andrea Wonfor, Pater Murphy**

Very popular teenage soap, set in a Newcastle youth centre.

When teenager Julie moved with her family to Newcastle, she immediately hated her new home, until she met new friends at Byker Grove youth centre. This was the device used to introduce viewers to a gang of North-Eastern youths who dabbled in all the usual vices but enjoyed lasting friendships along the way. Touchy subjects, including death, homosexuality, racism, teenage marriage, divorce, joy-riding and homelessness, have been tackled during the series' long run.

Byker Grove, predictably, also had its pop successes. Characters PJ and Duncan (launch-pad characters for children's TV presenters Ant and Dec) enjoyed an extended run of hit singles, and 'Love Your Sexy . . . !!' was a minor hit in 1994 for Byker Grooove! (Vicky Taylor, Jayni Hoy and Donna Air).

BYRNE, JOHN

(1940–)

Scottish painter and playwright whose TUTTI FRUTTI was one of the most highly acclaimed drama serials of the late 1980s. He followed it up with *Your Cheatin' Heart*.

BYRNE, PETER

(1928–)

For years Jack Warner's son-in-law, Andy Crawford, in DIXON OF DOCK GREEN, Peter Byrne pleased his female admirers by turning out again in the 1980s, playing the part of Nellie Boswell's fancy man in BREAD. Over the years his other appearances have included parts in *The New Canadians*, BLAKE'S 7 and his earliest programme, *The Pattern of Marriage*, in 1953.

BYRNES, EDD

(Edward Breitenberger; 1933–)

Short-lived cult figure of the late 1950s and early 1960s, otherwise known as Kookie, the jive-talking car-park attendant in 77 SUNSET STRIP. Since that role ended in 1963 the blond-haired Byrnes has found work difficult to come by, meandering in and out of minor series and spaghetti Westerns. He had a hit single (with Connie Stevens) in 1960, entitled 'Kookie, Kookie (Lend Me Your Comb)', based on his excessive grooming in the series.

C.A.T.S. EYES

UK (TVS) Detective Drama. ITV 1985–7

Maggie Forbes .... **Jill Gascoine**
Pru Standfast .... **Rosalyn Landor**
Frederica 'Fred' Smith .... **Leslie Ash**
Nigel Beaumont .... **Don Warrington**
Tessa Robinson .... **Tracy-Louise Ward**

Creator: **Terence Feely**
Executive Producer: **Rex Firkin**
Producers: **Dickie Bamber, Frank Cox, Raymond Menmuir**

A female detective agency is really a front for a Home Office security team.

This was the story of three intrepid girl agents – a sort of British CHARLIE'S ANGELS. Head of the team was Pru Standfast, a tall Oxford graduate once with the War Office, renowned for her organizational abilities. Her colleagues were ex-policewoman Maggie Forbes and young computer buff, Fred Smith. Forbes had 18 years of police experience behind her (see THE GENTLE TOUCH) and brought formal detection skills to the team. Smith, in addition to her computer wizardry, was an ace driver. Together they operated as the Eyes Enquiry Agency, a front for a Home Office investigation team known as Covert Activities Thames Section (C.A.T.S.). Their missions took them into the areas of international espionage, corruption, terrorism and organized crime, and supporting their efforts and keeping an eye on their work was Ministry man Nigel Beaumont. When the show returned for a second season, changes had been made. Most notably, Pru Standfast had gone, Forbes had taken over as leader and a new recruit, Tessa Robinson, had been added.

CABLE

A system involving the relay of television programmes via a network of cables, using one central reception/transmission centre. Initially cable was introduced to provide TV pictures to parts of the country where aerial reception was poor or non-existent. Rediffusion was one such supplier in the UK. However, with the new generation of cabling, and the introduction of optical fibre (allowing many more channels to be carried), a host of new cable companies has sprung up across the UK, the most prominent being NTL and Telewest. These now use digital technology and provide dedicated national cable stations (like Performance), alongside satellite channels and locally made community programmes. The systems are regulated in the UK by the ITC.

CABLE NEWS NETWORK

See CNN.

CADE'S COUNTY

US (Twentieth Century-Fox) Police Drama. ITV 1972

Sam Cade .... **Glenn Ford**
J. J. Jackson .... **Edgar Buchanan**
Arlo Pritchard .... **Taylor Lacher**
Rudy Davillo .... **Victor Campos**
Pete .... **Peter Ford**
Joannie Little Bird .... **Sandra Ego**
Betty Ann Sundown .... **Betty Ann Carr**

Executive Producer: **David Gerber**
Producer: **Charles Larson**

Exciting moments in the life of a chief lawman.

This modern Western focused on Sheriff Sam Cade, leading crimebuster of Madrid County, California. Cade himself was mainly rooted to his Madrid town base, but his deputies out and about, keeping the peace around the large desert county, were J. J. Jackson, an experienced veteran, and younger colleagues Arlo, Rudy and Pete (played by Glenn Ford's son). Two real-life Native American girls, Sandra Ego and Betty Ann Carr, played police dispatchers Joannie Little Bird and Betty Ann Sundown.

CADELL, SIMON

(1950–96)

British dramatic and comedy actor accomplished in strait-laced, nervous roles such as entertainments manager Jeffrey Fairbrother in HI-DE-HI!, the hapless civil servant Dundridge in BLOTT ON THE LANDSCAPE, estate agent Larry Wade in LIFE WITHOUT GEORGE and actor Dennis Duval in SINGLES. His other TV credits included HADLEIGH, HINE, THE GLITTERING PRIZES, WINGS, SPACE: 1999, *About Face*, the 1976 play *The Dame of Sark*, the similar in content *Enemy at the Door* (Hauptmann Reinicke), and EDWARD AND MRS SIMPSON. He was brother of actress Selina Cadell and son-in-law of writer/producer David Croft.

CADFAEL

UK (Central) Detective Drama. ITV 1994–8

Brother Cadfael .... **Derek Jacobi**
Hugh Beringar .... **Sean Pertwee**
                                                                    Eoin McCarthy
                                                                    Anthony Green
Prior Robert .... **Michael Culver**
Abbot Heribert .... **Peter Copley**
Abbot Radulfus .... **Terrence Hardiman**
Brother Jerome .... **Julian Firth**
Brother Oswin .... **Mark Charnock**

Producer: **Stephen Smallwood**

The investigations of a medieval monk detective.

Adapted from, or based on, the novels by Ellis Peters (pseudonym of the late Edith Pargeter), this series of sporadic adventures featured Brother Cadfael, a Benedictine monk living in Shrewsbury's St Peter and St Paul abbey during the reign of King Stephen. His first television outing came in an adaptation of Ms Peters's second novel, *One Corpse Too Many*, and was set during a siege on the Shropshire market town in the year 1138.

The fiftysomething Cadfael had turned to the cloisters late in life, having been a crusader and even fathered a son. However, his inquiring mind would not confine itself to reflections on the Good Book or tending the monastery herb gardens, and the merest sniff of intrigue set the self-effacing sleuth's investigative juices flowing. His success rate was phenomenal, considering he could call on none of today's technology or advances in forensic science. To ensure the correct setting and atmosphere, the producers took filming over to the Fot studios, near Budapest, where they reconstructed medieval Shrewsbury, complete with a mini River Severn. Experts were employed as consultants on historical, religious and musical matters. Each of the 12 episodes ran to 90 minutes and guest stars included soap actors Roy Barraclough, Anna Friel and Peter Baldwin.

CAESARS, THE

UK (Granada) Drama. ITV 1968

Augustus .... **Ronald Culver**
Germanicus .... **Eric Flynn**
Tiberius .... **André Morell**
Sejanus .... **Barrie Ingham**
Caligula .... **Ralph Bates**
Claudius .... **Freddie Jones**
Livia .... **Sonia Dresdel**

Writer/Producer: **Philip Mackie**

Power and corruption in ancient Rome.

Pre-dating the celebrated I, CLAUDIUS by eight years, *The Caesars* tackled the same subject, namely the political dog-fighting of Imperial Rome and the craven pastimes of its foremost citizens. Written and produced by Granada's Head of Drama, Philip Mackie, and directed by Derek Bennett, it was, in critics' eyes, no less successful. The six episodes focused chiefly on the six emperors and generals Augustus, Germanicus, Tiberius, Sejanus, Caligula and Claudius, with the scheming matriarch, Livia, also immersed in the action. Overall, a compact study of Rome's decline and fall was compiled.

CAFE CONTINENTAL

UK (BBC) Variety. BBC 1947–53

Creator/Producer: **Henry Caldwell**

International cabaret presented from a fake nightclub.

This initially 45-minute, later one-hour, variety show took the form of a Saturday night visit to a sophisticated international cabaret and dining club, complete with presiding maître d'hôtel and master/mistress of ceremonies. Claude Frederic and Pier Auguste were two of the artists to take the roles of the former; Al Burnett and Hélène Cordet two to take the latter. Sydney Jerome was the orchestra leader. Probably the biggest name to appear behind the Café's smart swing doors was Folies Bergères star Josephine Baker (in 1948).

CAGNEY AND LACEY
US (Orion) Police Drama. BBC 1 1982–8

Det. Mary Beth Lacey	**Tyne Daly**
Det. Christine Cagney	**Meg Foster**
	Sharon Gless
Lt. Bert Samuels	**Al Waxman**
Det. Mark Petrie	**Carl Lumbly**
Det. Victor Isbecki	**Martin Kove**
Det. Paul La Guardia	**Sidney Clute**
Deputy Insp. Marquette	**Jason Bernard**
Desk Sgt Ronald Coleman	**Harvey Atkin**
Harvey Lacey	**John Karlen**
Harvey Lacey, Jr	**Tony La Torre**
Michael Lacey	**Troy Slaten**
Alice Lacey	**Dana and Paige Bardolph**
	Michelle Sepe
Sgt Dory McKenna	**Barry Primus**
Insp. Knelman	**Michael Fairman**
Det. Jonah Newman	**Dan Shor**
David Keeler	**Stephen Macht**
Det. Manny Esposito	**Robert Hegyes**
Det. Al Corassa	**Paul Mantee**
Josie	**Jo Corday**
Tom Basil	**Barry Laws**
Charlie Cagney	**Dick O'Neill**
Det. Verna Dee Jordan	**Merry Clayton**
Nick Amatucci	**Carl Weintraub**

Creators: **Barney Rosenzweig, Barbara Avedon, Barbara Corday**
Executive Producer: **Barney Rosenzweig**
Producer: **Richard A. Rosenbloom**

Two female cops win through in a man's world, despite the pressures of their personal lives.

Cagney and Lacey was a pioneer among TV cop series. It broke new ground in that it allowed women to be seen in the buddy-buddy context epitomized by series like STARSKY AND HUTCH. It was based on two women, Mary Beth Lacey and Chris Cagney, cops paired together as a team on the New York streets, and it struck a firm feminist stance in rejecting all the established preconceptions of women on television. The two heroines were seen holding their own in a tough, tough world, where the conflict and male prejudice they met within the police force was sometimes as great as the violence outside.

Cagney and Lacey was not the usual cops-and-robbers fare. It showed the grimier side of police work, the ups *and* the downs, and the girls were more than partners. In the sanctuary of the ladies' room at the police station, they poured their hearts out to each other, discussing the strains of work and their personal worries. Mary Beth was married (to construction worker Harvey Lacey) with young sons (Harvey Jr and Michael) and later a daughter

(Alice). She had come from a broken home, had been through an abortion at 19 and had battled her way through a breast cancer scare. Chris was ambitious and single, but, dreading being alone all her life, she was continually drawn into unsuccessful relationships, such as with attorney David Keeler.

The programme never shirked heavy issues, such as Chris's occasional alcohol-dependency and the drug addiction of her one-time boyfriend, fellow cop Dory McKenna. In one episode she was even raped. Her alcoholic father, Charlie, also once on the force, appeared from time to time until he died, ironically just before she won her promotion to sergeant.

The series was not an instant hit in the States. After a pilot starring Loretta Swit of M*A*S*H in the part of Cagney, a short first series was produced, with Meg Foster cast alongside Tyne Daly. However, it was criticized for being too hard and too unfeminine, and so, when the next episodes were made, the producers softened it up, replacing Foster with Sharon Gless. Even then the studio was not impressed with the ratings and they cancelled the show, only for it to be brought back by huge public demand. It seems that the public were right.

CAINE, MARTI
(Lynne Shepherd; 1945–95)

Slim, Sheffield-born comedienne and singer, a former model who came to fame via the NEW FACES talent-spotting show (she won the 1975 series), a programme she hosted for three series on its revival in 1986. In between, she starred in her own comedy/variety shows (*Nobody Does It Like Marti*, *Marti* and *The Marti Caine Show*) and attempted sitcom with *Hilary*, in which she played an accident-prone TV researcher. Her last series was *Joker in the Pack*. Marti's stage name was taken from gardening terminology – 'tomato canes'.

CALL MY BLUFF
UK (BBC) Panel Game. BBC 2/ BBC 1 1965–88; 1996–

Presenters: **Robin Ray, Joe Melia, Peter Wheeler, Robert Robinson; Bob Holness**

Creators: **Mark Goodson, Bill Todman**
Producers: **T. Leslie Jackson, Bryan Sears, Johnny Downes**

Panel game based on the true meaning of obscure words.

Despite lasting just six months in its native USA, *Call My Bluff* was a stalwart of the BBC 2 schedule almost from the channel's inception. In keeping with the more erudite nature of the BBC's second channel, this programme looked at strange words, with two teams of three celebrities attempting to mislead each other as to the true meaning of arcane dictionary entries. Each panellist gave a lengthy, humorous definition of the word offered up by the chairman and the other team had to decide which description was genuine. Success or failure was denoted by the turning over of the description cards to reveal, in big letters, TRUE or BLUFF.

The programme's first chairman was Robin Ray, although the longest serving and best known was Robert Robinson (from 1967). Joe Melia and Peter Wheeler also hosted proceedings in the early days. Frank Muir and Robert Morley were the first team captains, Patrick Campbell later replaced Morley and Arthur Marshall took over from the late Campbell in the 1980s. However, numerous other celebrities also stood in as team captains. They included Kenneth Horne, Alan Melville and Kenneth Williams.

A one-off programme was shown in 1994 with Joanna Lumley opposing Frank Muir and with Robert Robinson in the chair, before the series returned at lunchtimes on BBC 1 in 1996. New chairman was Bob Holness, with Alan Coren and Sandi Toksvig acting as captains.

CALLAN
UK (ABC/Thames) Secret Agent Drama. ITV 1967–72

David Callan .... **Edward Woodward**
Lonely .... **Russell Hunter**
Hunter .... **Ronald Radd**
                                         Michael Goodliffe
                                         Derek Bond
                                         William Squire
Toby Meres .... **Anthony Valentine**
Cross .... **Patrick Mower**
Hunter's secretary .... **Lisa Langdon**

Creator: **James Mitchell**
Executive Producer: **Lloyd Shirley**
Producer: **Reginald Collin**

The assignments of a notoriously tough British Secret Intelligence agent.

Callan was a far cry from the glamorous world of James Bond. The hero was a hard man, edgy and friendless. He worked for the intelligence service, bluntly snuffing out enemies and others who represented a danger to British security. But he was also a rebel and a thinker who brought his own version of justice into play, rather than just killing willy-nilly as instructed. Callan, as a consequence, was constantly in trouble with his superiors.

In his first appearance, in a 1967 episode of ABC's ARMCHAIR THEATRE called *A Magnum for Schneider*, Callan himself was the target. He had been given the chance to retrieve his dodgy reputation within British intelligence by bumping off an enemy agent, but this was merely a ruse to nail him for murder and so dispose of him. Turning the tables, Callan won through and public interest in the character led to a fully fledged series later the same year.

In the series the star was assisted by a dirty, smelly petty crook called Lonely, who supplied him with under-the-counter firearms and useful information. Callan treated Lonely, one of life's perpetual losers, with complete disdain. At the same time, though, he protected his little accomplice, finding him a job as driver of the communications car, a taxi filled with high-tech listening devices. Within the intelligence service, Callan's immediate boss was Hunter, not a specific person but a codename for the various heads of department supervising him. There was also Meres (played by Peter Bowles in the *Armchair Theatre* play), a fellow agent who resented Callan's position and contrived to dislodge him. Another agent seen later, the trigger-happy Cross, shared the same sentiments.

Nine years after the series ended, Callan was brought back in a one-off 90-minute play for ATV entitled *Wet Job*. Now retired and running a militaria shop under the alias of David Tucker, he was re-enlisted by the security services for one last mission. Hunter was played by Hugh Walters and Lonely resurfaced, too, in the unlikely position of a bathroom store proprietor.

Callan, with its distinctive swinging naked light-bulb opening sequences, was created by writer James Mitchell, who was later responsible for WHEN THE BOAT COMES IN. A cinema version was released in 1974.

CAMBERWICK GREEN / TRUMPTON / CHIGLEY
UK (Gordon Murray) Children's Entertainment. BBC 1
1966/1967/1969

Narrator: **Brian Cant**

Creator/Producer: **Gordon Murray**
Writers: **Gordon Murray, Alison Prince** (*Trumpton*)

Rural puppet soap operas for kids.

Animated by Bob Bura and John Hardwick, Gordon Murray's rustic puppet trilogy began in 1966, when *Camberwick Green* took over the Monday WATCH WITH MOTHER slot. It gave children an insight into the lives of the folk of Camberwick Green, a small village deep in the English countryside. Each episode opened and ended with a shot of a musical box, 'wound up and ready to play', from which one of the villagers slowly emerged, allowing viewers to follow them as they went about their typical day. Sadly, a minor tragedy always struck at some point and the gallant lads at Pippin Fort, under the command of Captain Snort and Sgt Major Grout, were usually called in to restore order. The good people of Camberwick Green were: Windy Miller of Colley's Mill; Roger Varley, the chimney sweep; Mr Carraway, the fishmonger; gossipy Mrs Honeyman, the chemist's wife (and her baby boy); Dr Mopp with his boneshaker car; farmer Jonathan Bell; Mr Crockett, the garage owner; Mickey Murphy, the baker (with children Paddy and Mary); salesman Mr Dagenham; Thomas Tripp, the milkman; Peter Hazel, the postman; Mrs Dingle, the postmistress (and Packet, the Post Office puppy), and, of course, PC McGarry (number 452). A pierrot puppet turned over the opening and closing titles.

A few *Camberwick Green* characters appeared in the spin-off series, *Trumpton*, a year later, dropping in on an occasional basis. This time the action had moved to the larger town of Trumpton, where the role played earlier by the soldiers of Pippin Fort was taken over by Capt. Flack's courageous local firemen: Pugh, Pugh, Barney McGrew, Cuthbert, Dibble and Grubb. Mrs Honeyman gave way to the blethering Miss Lovelace and her yapping dogs, and also featured were the Mayor; the Town Clerk, Mr Troop; Mrs Cobbit, and Mr Platt. The start of each episode focused on the Trumpton clock, 'telling the time for Trumpton', and all programmes ended with a fire brigade band concert in the park.

The third instalment of this puppet melodrama came from Chigley, a hamlet described as being 'near Camberwick Green, Trumptonshire'. This was an altogether more modest little settlement, chiefly consisting of a biscuit factory, a canalside wharf, a pottery and a stately home, Wingstead Hall. The last belonged to Lord Belborough, a charitable aristocrat who, with his loyal butler, Mr Brackett, ran a steam train known as *Bessie* for the benefit of the local people. Goods were ferried in and out at Treadles Wharf, where the bargees and dockers were watched over by Mr Swallow. Cresswells Chigley Biscuits, meanwhile, was in the hands of Mr Cresswell, and his employees held a dance to the music of a barrel organ after the six o'clock whistle at the end of each episode. Also seen were Mr Clamp, the greengrocer; Harry Farthing, the potter-cum-sculptor; Mr Clutterbuck, the builder; carpenter Chippy Minton and his son, Nibbs; Mr Bilton, Belborough's gardener, and assorted cross-over characters from both *Camberwick Green* and *Trumpton*.

Despite only 13 episodes being made of each series, repeat showings continued for many years. While the storylines were always very limited and the songs (by Freddie Phillips) crushingly repetitive, Brian Cant's whimsical delivery and the quality of the animation and characterization have made this little trilogy into children's television classics.

CAMCORDER

A video camera and recorder in one smallish unit, much more flexible than separate camera and recording machines.

CAMERON, JAMES
OBE (1911–85)

British current affairs reporter of the 1960s and 1970s. He was the first commentator on the retrospective series, ALL OUR YESTERDAYS, and later turned to drama writing. The 1979 *Screenplay* presentation, *The Sound of the Guns*, was his first offering.

CAMPION
UK (BBC/WGBH Boston) Detective Drama. BBC 1
1989–90

Albert Campion	**Peter Davison**
Magersfontein Lugg	**Brian Glover**
Chief Insp. Stanislaus Oates	**Andrew Burt**

Producers: **Ken Riddington, Jonathan Alwyn**

Murder investigations in the 1930s with an unassuming, bespectacled detective.

Albert Campion, the creation of novelist Margery Allingham and star of 26 books, first reached the TV screen in 1959 in the BBC serial, *Dancers in Mourning*. In this and the follow-up, *Death of a Ghost*, a year later, he was played by Bernard Horsfall. Campion reappeared later in the 1960s in the anthology series, DETECTIVE. On that occasion he was played by Brian Smith. However, it was the 1989–90 series, starring Peter Davison, which really brought him to the attention of the viewing public.

Practising his skills in the 1930s, in the same genteel circles as Lord Peter Wimsey and Hercule Poirot, the aristocratic Campion was a determined and shrewd amateur sleuth, with strong moral principles – even if his mild-mannered appearance conveyed quite the opposite. Sporting large, horn-rimmed glasses and with his amiable and unassuming personality pushed well to the fore, villains thought it easy to shrug off Campion's inquiries. They soon learned better, as our hero doggedly pieced together the relevant clues. Also at hand was Campion's brawny, down-to-earth manservant, a reformed burglar named Lugg, whose duties ranged from taking care of the baggage to obtaining information his master couldn't reach by mixing with the lower classes. The duo rode around the East Anglia countryside in a splendid vintage Lagonda, wrapping up crimes before their Scotland Yard associate, Stanislaus Oates, could move in.

CAMPION, GERALD
(1921–)

British actor, TV's Billy Bunter in the 1950s (even though aged 29 at the time). No other starring roles followed and Campion turned instead (somewhat fittingly) to the restaurant business, although he has still taken small parts in TV comedies and dramas, such as *The World of Beachcomber* and THE RETURN OF SHERLOCK HOLMES.

CANDID CAMERA
UK (ABC) Comedy. ITV 1960–7

Presenters: **Bob Monkhouse, Jonathan Routh**

Creator: **Allen Funt**

Hidden-camera stunts at the expense of the general public.

Candid Camera was imported into the UK from the USA, where it had been devised by arch-prankster Allen Funt. Funt began gauging the public's reaction to unusual, not to say bizarre, situations in his radio show, *Candid Microphone*. It transferred to television in 1949 with the same title, before becoming *Candid Camera* in 1953. ABC produced the UK version, installing Bob Monkhouse as its host and sending Jonathan Routh out and about in search of gullible citizens. Hidden cameras surreptitiously witnessed their reactions to impossible situations – a man selling £5 notes for £4 10s, garage mechanics asked to discover why a car wouldn't start and finding it had no engine, etc. Eventually, the poor punters were put out of their misery with the words

'Smile, you're on *Candid Camera*'. The series was revived by LWT in 1974, when it was produced and presented by Peter Dulay.

CANNELL, STEPHEN J.
(1941–)

American producer and writer of all-action series in the 1970s and 1980s, whose first major success was THE ROCKFORD FILES. His production company was also responsible for THE A-TEAM, *Hardcastle and McCormick*, *Riptide* and *Tenspeed and Brown Shoe*, among other series.

CANNON
US (Quinn Martin) Detective Drama. BBC 1 1972–8

Frank Cannon .... **William Conrad**

Executive Producer: **Quinn Martin**
Producer: **Anthony Spinner**

An overweight, middle-aged private detective puffs and pants after crooks in Los Angeles.

William Conrad was the only star of this successful series, which had been tailor-made for him. After 11 years of providing the voice of Matt Dillon in the American radio version of GUNSMOKE, he was denied the TV role because of his physical appearance (James Arness got the job). *Cannon*, at last, was his overdue reward.

Frank Cannon was an unlikely detective. He loved the good life and his body bore the scars. His hefty frame meant that every case was a real effort, particularly when it came to a sweaty chase after a fleeing murderer, because, having no sidekick, Cannon had to do all the legwork himself. Still, he was well reimbursed for his work, charging enough to keep up his bon viveur lifestyle and to repair the big Lincoln Continental he pranged around the LA streets. Cannon was one of the first gimmicky cops. After him came Kojak, McCloud and Columbo. The series first aired in the UK under the umbrella title of *The Detectives*, in sequence with THE ROCKFORD FILES, HARRY O and A MAN CALLED IRONSIDE.

CANNON, TOMMY
(Thomas Derbyshire; 1938–)

The partner of diminutive northern comic Bobby Ball. After a long apprenticeship as the Shirell Brothers and then the Harper Brothers, former welders Cannon and Ball arrived on television courtesy of a not so promising debut on OPPORTUNITY KNOCKS in 1968 and did not secure their own show until 1979 (following guest appearances with Bruce Forsyth). As well as their own peak-time variety shows (mostly scripted by Sid Green), the duo have also attempted a quiz, *Cannon and Ball's Casino*, and a sitcom, *Plaza Patrol*, playing shopping-centre security men Bernard Cooney (Cannon) and Trevor Purvis (Ball).

CANT, BRIAN
(1933–)

Whimsical children's TV presenter, popular in the 1960s and 1970s in PLAY SCHOOL, PLAY AWAY and as the voice behind CAMBERWICK GREEN, TRUMPTON and CHIGLEY. More recently, he has hosted the series *Bric-a-Brac* and *Dappledown Farm*. As an actor, Cant has guested in various series, including DOCTOR WHO.

CAPITAL CITY
UK (Thames/Euston Films) Drama. ITV 1989–90

Max Lubin	**William Armstrong**
Leonard Ansen	**John Bowe**
James Farrell	**Denys Hawthorne**
Jimmy Destry	**Dorian Healy**
Declan McConnochie	**Douglas Hodge**
Chas Ewell	**Jason Isaacs**
Sirkka Nieminen	**Joanna Kanska**
Lee Wolf	**Richard Le Parmentier**
Michelle Hauptmann	**Trevyn McDowell**
Hannah Burgess	**Anna Nygh**
Wendy Foley	**Joanna Phillips-Lane**
Hudson Talbot	**Rolf Saxon**

Creator: **Andrew MacLear**
Producer: **Irving Teitelbaum**
Executive Producers: **Andrew Brown, John Hambly**

Hectic wheeling and dealing in the offices of a City bank.

Capital City was set in the dealing rooms of the fictitious Shane Longman bank, taking a long look at the perils of currency and Stock Market trading and the pressures these bring to personal lives. Among the prominent characters was eccentric new ideas-man, Max Lubin; outrageous womanizer Declan McConnochie and the German girl he chased after, Michelle Hauptmann; Declan's former live-in lover, Sirkka Nieminen; computer manager Hannah Burgess; Hudson Talbot, an American whose wife had abandoned him with their baby; dealing room manager Wendy Foley, who had worked her way up in the bank; obnoxious junior dealer Jimmy Destry; Jimmy's house sharer, Chas Ewell; and the man who had built the bank's fortune, Head of Banking Activities Leonard Ansen. Flashing computer screens, phones strapped to ears and cries of 'Buy!' and 'Sell!' helped convey the frenetic pace of life in the City. Away from work, the obscene amounts of money being made – and sometimes lost – by the yuppie workers were reflected in their extravagant lifestyles.

CAPTAIN PUGWASH
UK (John Ryan) Children's Entertainment. BBC 1 1957–66; 1974–5; ITV 1998

Narrator: **Peter Hawkins**

Creator/Writer: **John Ryan**

Producers: **Gordon Murray, John Ryan**

The maritime adventures of a blustery pirate and his crew.

Animated by John Ryan in the most basic fashion, with crudely drawn characters making the simplest of movements against a static background, *Captain Pugwash* was a remarkably cheap series to produce. All the same, it became a perennial favourite and a great filler programme for the BBC. First appearing in 1957, and updated in colour in the 1970s, it related tales of the pirate, Captain Horatio Pugwash, podgy skipper of the *Black Pig*. His hapless crew were work-shy and rather dense, and included able seamen Barnabas and Willy, and a loyal cabin boy named Tom. Most of the time they sought to avoid the clutches of the barbarous Cut Throat Jake, a black-bearded pirate of the worst order, and the five-minute episodes ran in serial form, each ending with a cliffhanger finish. The distinctive accordion sea-shanty theme music, 'The Hornblower', was performed by Tommy Edmondson and the many voices belonged to Bill and Ben vocalist, Peter Hawkins.

The jaunty pirate returned to the screen in 13 new stories entitled *The Adventures of Captain Pugwash*, in 1998. Luscious Lill was one of the new characters complementing the old favourites as they plied the seas around the island of Mucho-Buffo.

Such was the success of *Captain Pugwash* that it spawned a *Radio Times* cartoon strip and a successor series in 1972, *The Adventures of Sir Prancelot*, which revolved around a fearless knight in shining armour.

CAPTAIN SCARLET AND THE MYSTERONS

UK (Century 21/ITC) Children's Science Fiction. ITV
1967–8

Voices:

Capt. Scarlet (Paul Metcalfe)	**Francis Matthews**
Col. White (Charles Gray)	**Donald Gray**
Capt. Blue (Adam Svenson)	**Ed Bishop**
Capt. Grey (Bradley Holden)	**Paul Maxwell**
Capt. Magenta (Patrick Donaghue)	**Gary Files**
Capt. Ochre (Richard Frazier)	**Jeremy Wilkin**
Lt. Green (Seymour Griffiths)	**Cy Grant**
Dr Fawn (Edward Wilkie)	**Charles Tingwell**
Melody Angel (Magnolia Jones)	**Sylvia Anderson**
Harmony Angel (Chan Kwan)	**Lian-Shin**
Symphony Angel (Karen Wainwright)	**Janna Hill**
Rhapsody Angel (Diane Sims)	**Liz Morgan**
Destiny Angel (Juliette Pointon)	**Liz Morgan**
Capt. Black (Conrad Turner)	**Donald Gray**
The Voice of the Mysterons	**Donald Gray**
World President	**Paul Maxwell**

Creators: **Gerry Anderson, Sylvia Anderson**
Producer: **Reg Hill**

An indestructible puppet super-agent takes on a vengeful alien force.

In the year 2068, Spectrum, the world's security command, undertook a mission to Mars, a mission which turned to disaster. When the native Mysterons locked their antennae on to the landing party, they were mistaken for guns and the order was given for a Mysteron city to be destroyed. In response, the Mysterons slaughtered the Spectrum envoys, including their leader, Captain Black, vowing to wreak vengeance on the people of Earth.

The Mysterons possessed the remarkable power of retro-metabolism – the re-creation of destroyed matter, which rendered it indestructible at the same time. The first thing they did was to reconstruct their destroyed city and piece together Captain Black, formerly Spectrum's top agent, for use against his former allies. The Mysterons also tried to destroy and re-create another Spectrum officer, Captain Scarlet, but this time their plan failed and, although Scarlet became indestructible, he nevertheless remained loyal to Spectrum and proved time and again crucial in the defence of the Earth.

Spectrum, operating from a floating control-centre called Cloudbase, was run by Colonel White. The other agents and officers were also codenamed after colours, with uniforms to reflect their identities, and they were ably supported by the five female pilots of Angel Interceptor aircraft: Melody, Harmony, Symphony, Destiny and Rhapsody. All operatives raced into action on the command SIG ('Spectrum Is Green').

In each episode the Mysterons threatened the Earth's security by attacking key command centres or personnel, sabotaging world conferences or simply gunning for Spectrum. The aliens themselves were never seen, but the introduction to each programme featured the gravelly 'Voice of the Mysterons', reiterating their avowed intention to gain revenge. As the voice boomed out, two rings of light played over a dead body or wrecked aircraft, indicating that the regeneration process was under way. Spectrum needed to be well equipped to handle the Mysteron threat but, despite its Spectrum Pursuit Vehicles (SPVs), Maximum Security Vehicles (MSVs) and other high-tech wizardry, it still relied heavily on one man – the indestructible (if rather humourless) Captain Scarlet.

The producers' attention to detail in this series was remarkable. For the first time Gerry Anderson puppets were perfect in proportion, with the electronic circuitry that made his earlier marionettes 'big-headed' transferred into the puppets' bodies. The puppets were also made to look like the actors who supplied their voices. Scarlet, for instance, was a model of Francis Matthews. The characterization, too, was more detailed than in previous efforts. The agents were given private lives and real identities (Scarlet was really Paul Metcalfe), and were furnished with other biographical data. It was revealed, for instance, that the Trinidadian communications specialist, Lt. Green, and the American Captain Grey had both previously been assigned to WASP on the STINGRAY project, and that Diane Sims (Rhapsody Angel) had once worked with Lady Penelope of THUNDERBIRDS fame. The closing theme song was performed by 'The Spectrum'.

CAPTION ROLLER

Mechanical system of running continuous captions that can be superimposed over another shot or filmed independently. It has traditionally been used for a programme's closing credits, although computer-generated graphics have now taken over.

CAR 54, WHERE ARE YOU?

US (Euopolis) Situation Comedy. ITV 1964–5

Officer Gunther Toody	**Joe E. Ross**
Officer Francis Muldoon	**Fred Gwynne**
Lucille Toody	**Bea Pons**
Capt. Martin Block	**Paul Reed**
Officer O'Hara	**Albert Henderson**
Officer Anderson	**Nipsey Russell**
Officer Antonnucci	**Jerome Guardino**
Officer Steinmetz	**Joe Warren**
Officer Riley	**Duke Farley**
Officer Murdock	**Shelley Burton**
Officer Leo Schnauser	**Al Lewis**
Sylvia Schnauser	**Charlotte Rae**
Officer Kissel	**Bruce Kirby**
Officer Ed Nicholson	**Hank Garrett**

Creator/Producer: **Nat Hiken**

The slapstick escapades of an inept team of New York City cops.

Hot on the heels of his success with THE PHIL SILVERS SHOW, producer Nat Hiken introduced viewers to *Car 54, Where Are You?* and the ropiest bunch of cops yet seen on TV. At the forefront were Toody and Muldoon, the former short, podgy and amiable, the latter tall and sullen. Not only did they look odd together, they were also pretty hopeless in action. Their beat was in the 53rd Precinct, the troubled Bronx, although you really wouldn't have known it as the series played only on the lighter side of police work. Much of the fun came from within the police station itself.

Hiken brought Joe E. Ross with him from '*Bilko*' (he had played Sgt Rupert Ritzik and Bea Pons played his nagging wife, as here), while Fred Gwynne was to go on to greater fame as Herman in THE MUNSTERS. Al Lewis joined him as Grandpa in that series. *Car 54, Where Are You?* was re-run on Channel 4 in 1983.

CARGILL, PATRICK
(1918–96)

Although gaining a reputation as Britain's leading farceur in the 1970s, thanks to series like FATHER, DEAR FATHER (novelist Patrick Glover), *The Many Wives of Patrick* (antiques dealer Patrick Woodford) and the anthology, *Ooh La La*, London-born Patrick Cargill's earlier television roles had been in quite a different vein. After appearing as a baddie in THE ADVENTURES OF ROBIN HOOD, Cargill was cast as mysterious agent Miguel Garetta (who worked under the identity of an Argentinian businessman) in TOP SECRET, and later played one of the Number 2s in THE PRISONER. He also guest-starred in action series like THE AVENGERS and MAN IN A SUITCASE. However, his flair for comedy was already apparent. He played the doctor in the famous HANCOCK'S HALF HOUR sketch, 'The Blood Donor', for instance, and also appeared in the follow-up series, *Hancock*, and then supported Brian Rix in *Dial RIX*. After his television heyday, Cargill returned to the stage. He died after being knocked down by a hit-and-run driver in Sydney, Australia.

CARLING, LIZ
(1967)

Middlesbrough-born actress, seen in dramas and comedies like BOON (Laura Marsh), *Barbara* (Linda), CROCODILE SHOES (Wendy), GOODNIGHT SWEETHEART (Phoebe) and *Border Café* (Charlotte), as well as guesting in series like MEN BEHAVING BADLY.

CARLTON TELEVISION

The contractor for the London weekday ITV franchise, Carlton is part of Carlton Communications, which also owns Central Television (now renamed Carlton Central), Westcountry (now Carlton Westcountry) and HTV, plus shares in ITN and 50 per cent of ONdigital, the terrestrial digital provider. It also runs the cable/digital channels Carlton Select and Carlton Food Network, and the game show specialists, Action Time. Carlton surprisingly ousted the successful Thames Television from the London area in the 1991 franchise auctions, taking to the air on 1 January 1993. Among the group's best-known contributions to the ITV network have been KAVANAGH QC and PEAK PRACTICE.

CARLYLE, ROBERT
OBE (1961–)

Glasgow-born, noted method actor who made a huge impression with his portrayal of psychotic killer Albie in CRACKER and went on to enjoy a more relaxed encounter with crime as Highland copper HAMISH MACBETH. His other major TV roles have been as Nosty in *Screenplay's Safe*, Graham in *Screen Two's Priest*, petty criminal John Joe 'Jo Jo' McCann in *Looking After Jo Jo* and Ray in *Face*. He has also been seen in series like *The Advocates*, *99–1* and THE BILL.

CARMICHAEL, IAN
(1920–)

RADA-trained, Yorkshire-born actor whose TV high spot was as Lord Peter Wimsey, the toff detective created by Dorothy L. Sayers. In similar style, he had earlier perfected the silly-ass comic character, playing Bertie in THE WORLD OF WOOSTER, before becoming the harassed foster dad, Peter Lamb, in BACHELOR FATHER. His other TV credits have included *All for Love*, *Just A Nimmo*, SURVIVAL (narrator) and the part of Sir James Menzies in *Strathblair*, although he first appeared on television way back in the 1940s and 1950s, in variety and sketch shows.

CARPENTER, HARRY
OBE (1925–)

Durable BBC sports presenter and boxing commentator (over four decades), who retired from GRANDSTAND, SPORTSNIGHT, Wimbledon, the Olympics, the Boat Race and Open Golf coverage in the early 1990s, before finally counting himself out of the boxing game at the 1994 Commonwealth Games. His friendship with heavyweight Frank Bruno marked the latter years of his career – 'Know what I mean, 'Arry?'

CARPENTER, RICHARD

Former actor (Peter Parker in KNIGHT ERRANT and Mr Victor in EMERGENCY – WARD 10) turned writer of juvenile adventures whose major contributions have been CATWEAZLE (allegedly inspired by a word scratched on a gate), *The Ghosts of Motley Hall*, DICK TURPIN, *Smuggler*, ROBIN OF SHERWOOD and *The Borrowers*. He has also contributed to series like THE ADVENTURES OF BLACK BEAUTY and *The Scarlet Pimpernel*.

CARRADINE, DAVID
(John Arthur Carradine; 1936–)

American actor whose TV fame is owed chiefly to the part of Kwai Chang Caine in the 1970s martial arts Western, KUNG FU, a role he revived in the 1990s. If he appeared at home in the character, it was because Caine's philosophical approach to life was not, it has been reported, that far removed from Carradine's own thoughtful disposition. His sad, gaunt features were also put to good use in the 1960s cowboy series, *Shane*, in which he played the title role, and shows like ALFRED HITCHCOCK PRESENTS and A MAN CALLED IRONSIDE. In the 1980s he resurfaced in the mini-series, *North and South*. David is a member of the famous Hollywood acting family, son of John Carradine and half-brother to Keith and Robert.

CARROLL, LEO G.
(1892–1972)

Distinguished British actor, a star in his seventies as the sober Mr Waverly in THE MAN (and *The Girl*) FROM UNCLE. Earlier, playing men of authority, Carroll featured in numerous Hollywood movies, including several Hitchcock classics. He arrived on TV in the ghostly 1950s sitcom, *Topper*, playing the title role, Cosmo Topper, and also starred in a short-lived version of Bing Crosby's film, *Going My Way*, in 1962. Other television credits included A MAN CALLED IRONSIDE. However, it is as the boss of

Napoleon Solo, Illya Kuryakin and April Dancer in the mid-1960s that he is best remembered.

CARROTT, JASPER
(Robert Davis; 1945–)

Broad Brummie comic, a sharp observer of public failings who hosted his own series on BBC 1 throughout most of the 1980s. His earlier work came on BBC regional television, and he gained a cult following which took him into the record charts in 1975 with 'Funky Moped'/'Magic Roundabout'. He contributed material for TISWAS and there followed a series of *The Jasper Carrott Show* for LWT, along with a few one-off shows and spoof documentaries, such as *Carrott Del Sol*. However, it was in *Carrott's Lib*, *Carrott Confidential* and *Canned Carrott* that he established himself in the mainstream of British comedy, combining long, satirical, often ranting monologues (about Reliant Robins, Birmingham City FC, *Sun* readers, etc.) with assorted sketches (assisted at various times by the likes of Emma Thompson, Chris Barrie, Steve Punt and Hugh Dennis). One segment of *Canned Carrott*, THE DETECTIVES, a send-up of ITV cop shows like SPECIAL BRANCH and THE SWEENEY, and co-starring Robert Powell, was spun off into its own half-hour series. *The Jasper Carrott Trial*, in 1997, was a retrospective of his best sketches pieced together as part of a mock court case. He is the father of actress Lucy Davis.

CARSON, FRANK
(1926–)

Irrepressible, Ulster-born, bespectacled stand-up comedian, fond of laughing at his own jokes because 'It's the way I tell 'em'. After coming to light on OPPORTUNITY KNOCKS and as one of THE COMEDIANS, he popped up to spout his juvenile gags on the raucous TISWAS programme. He also contributed to THE GOOD OLD DAYS and, in 1981, starred in his own variety show-cum-sitcom, as Frank O'Grady, manager of *Ballyskillen Opera House*.

CARSON, JOHNNY
(1925–)

An American institution, Johnny Carson hosted *The Tonight Show* for 30 years, garnering huge audiences with his boyish looks, cheeky grin and quick wit. Carson did little else on TV after his run as host of the show began in 1962, save a few guest appearances and the occasional piece of emceeing. In 1981 he attempted to bring his show to Britain but it didn't catch on. On his retirement in 1992, NBC named comedian Jay Leno as Carson's *Tonight* successor.

CARSON, VIOLET
OBE (1898–1983)

In the shape of CORONATION STREET battleaxe, Ena Sharples, Violet Carson brought us one of television's unforgettable characterizations. An original member of the cast in 1960 (at the age of 62), she stayed with the show until 1980, enjoying some glorious spats with the Street's vixen, Elsie Tanner, and some classic moments in the snug of the Rovers with Minnie Caldwell and Martha Longhurst. But beneath Ena's hairnet, Violet Carson's natural talent lay in music. She played piano for Wilfrid Pickles in the radio quiz, *Have A Go*, and in her later years was a regular guest on STARS ON SUNDAY, singing and playing the organ. Once *Coronation Street* had taken off, Carson had few other opportunities to show off her acting skills, however, although some viewers still recalled her as Auntie Vi on radio's *Children's Hour* and as an early contributor to *Woman's Hour*.

CARTER, LYNDA
(1951–)

Statuesque former Miss USA (1973), understandably cast as TV's WONDER WOMAN, given her Amazonian figure. She has since appeared in assorted TV movies, as well as an unsuccessful detective series with Loni Anderson, *Partners in Crime* and *Hawkeye*, a series based on *Last of the Mohicans*.

CARTIER, RUDOLPH
(1904–94)

Viennese director/producer who arrived in the UK in the late 1930s, joining the BBC in 1952. He stayed with the Corporation for 25 years, bringing with him the influences of continental cinema and directing some of its most influential plays and serials. His treatment of Nigel Kneale's THE QUATERMASS EXPERIMENT (and its sequels) shocked the country, his *1984* was a milestone, and both helped to establish him as a seminal figure in TV drama. His work also covered TV opera (*Otello* in 1959 and *Carmen* in 1962, for instance) as he demonstrated his love of the spectacular and his adventurous, extravagant approach to studio drama. Among his other major contributions were *Sunday-Night Theatre* offerings like *The White Falcon* (1956), plus *Arrow to the Heart* (1952), *Wuthering Heights* (1953), *Thunder Rock* (1955), *Captain of Koepenick* (1958), *Mother Courage and Her Children* (1959), *Anna Karenina*, *Rashomon* (both 1961), *Dr Korczak and The Children* (1962), *Stalingrad* (1963, for the *Festival* anthology), *The July Plot* (a 1964 *Wednesday Play*) and *Lee Oswald – Assassin* (a 1966 *Play of the Month*). He also directed more mundane BBC efforts like episodes of MAIGRET, OUT OF THE UNKNOWN and Z CARS.

CARTOON NETWORK

The world's first 24-hour all-cartoon channel was launched by Turner Broadcasting (now owned by AOL-Time Warner) on cable in the USA in 1992. The channel has been available courtesy of the Astra satellite system in Europe since 1993, and also more recently via digital services. It provides a showcase for Hanna-Barbera, Warner Brothers and MGM animations – including classics like SCOOBY DOO, THE FLINTSTONES and TOM AND JERRY – and is available in six languages.

CARTY, TODD
(1963–)

Irish-born actor whose earliest TV appearances came in Z CARS, *Our Mutual Friend* and assorted juvenile parts, although it was as Tucker Jenkins in the school drama, GRANGE HILL, that he gained his first major role. Indeed, out of this came his own spin-off, *Tucker's Luck*, which followed Jenkins as he left school. When actor David Scarboro, who played Mark Fowler in EASTENDERS, died in 1988, Carty was drafted in (two years later) to join numerous other former *Grange Hill* stars in Albert Square. Other credits include Pentecost in the single drama, *Black Velvet Band*.

CASANOVA
UK (BBC) Drama. BBC 2 1971

Giovanni Casanova	Frank Finlay
Lorenzo	Norman Rossington
Cristina	Zienia Merton
Barberina	Christine Noonan
Schalon	Patrick Newell
Senator Bragadin	Geoffrey Wincott
Senior Inquisitor	Ronald Adam
Valenglart	David Swift
Genoveffa	Lyn Yeldham
Anne Roman-Coupier	Ania Merson

Writer: **Dennis Potter**
Producer: **Mark Shivas**

The famed 18th-century Italian poet and lover reflects on his life.

In this six-part, hour-long drama, Giovanni Casanova from his prison cell cast his mind back over the events of his life, evaluating whether his actions had been just and his deeds honourable. He questioned the dogmas of the time and attempted to find escape, physical and mental, from his incarceration at the hands of the Spanish Inquisition. The flashback sequences, taking the romantic writer from the age of 30 to his death at 73, when he was 'imprisoned' as a librarian in the court of a Czech count, majored on bold language, nudity and sexual antics, leading Mrs Whitehouse to accuse the series of gross indecency. Writer Dennis Potter hit back, claiming his work was, on the contrary, very moral.

CASE HISTORIES OF SCOTLAND YARD
UK (Anglo Amalgamated Films) Police Drama Anthology.
ITV 1955

Insp. Duggan	Russell Napier
Insp. Ross	Ken Henry
Sgt Mason	Arthur Mason

Host: **Edgar Lustgarten**

Producer: **Jack Greenwood**

Drama series based on actual Scotland Yard case files.

Introduced by noted journalist and criminologist Edgar Lustgarten, this early half-hour film series was particularly popular in the USA (where it was known simply as *Scotland Yard*). It offered dramatized accounts of real-life crimes which had been investigated by the men of the Metropolitan Police. Although casts changed every week, a few characters like Inspector Duggan appeared on a semi-regular basis.

CASEBOOK OF SHERLOCK HOLMES, THE

See **ADVENTURES OF SHERLOCK HOLMES, THE.**

CASEY JONES

US (Columbia/Briskin) Children's Western. BBC 1958

John Luther 'Casey' Jones	**Alan Hale, Jr**
Casey Jones, Jr	**Bobby Clark**
Alice Jones	**Mary Lawrence**
Wallie Simms	**Dub Taylor**
Red Rock	**Eddy Waller**
Sam Peachpit	**Pat Hogan**

Excitement on a Midwestern railroad in the 1890s.

Based on the mournful ballad in which the hero is tragically killed, this series for youngsters was much more perky. Casey Jones (steamin' and a-rollin') was an engineer for the Illinois Central Railroad, the man behind the throttle of the celebrated *Cannonball Express*. Living with his wife, Alice, his young son, Casey Jr, and dog, Cinders, in Jackson, Tennessee, and loyally supported by his railroad colleagues, Wallie Simms, the fireman, and Red Rock, the conductor, Casey somehow always managed to fulfil his missions, in the face of the greatest adversity. This was one Casey Jones who wouldn't die.

CASSIDY, DAVID
(1950–)

Actor/singer heart-throb of the 1970s, soaring to international fame as Keith Partridge in THE PARTRIDGE FAMILY, in which he starred with his own stepmother, Shirley Jones. On the back of the series he topped the record charts on both sides of the Atlantic with songs like 'How Can I Be Sure' and 'Daydreamer', as well as having Partridge Family hits. Since those heady days TV work has been thin, except for an unusual detective series created specifically for him in 1978, *David Cassidy – Man Undercover*, in which he played Officer Dan Shay. His earliest work consisted of minor roles in series like BONANZA. Cassidy married actress Kay Lenz in 1977. His father was actor Jack Cassidy and his brother, Shaun, has also made showbiz his career.

CASSIDY, TED
(1932–79)

Giant American actor, chiefly remembered in his guise of Lurch, the groaning butler in THE ADDAMS FAMILY. (He also played the hand, Thing, unless Lurch was also in shot.) Later Cassidy appeared as Injun Joe in *The New Adventures of Huck Finn* and provided the voice for numerous Hanna-Barbera characters, including FRANKENSTEIN JR. He died following heart surgery in 1979.

CASTLE, ROY
OBE (1933–94)

Popular, extremely versatile entertainer whose talents stretched from singing and dancing to playing obscure musical instruments. Early in his career he acted as straight man to Jimmy James, coming to the fore as a star in his own right in the 1950s sketch show, *New Look*. He then appeared in numerous films, ranging from *Dr Who and the Daleks* to *Carry On Up the Khyber*. From 1972 he hosted the superlatives show, RECORD BREAKERS (holding some world records himself), and his other TV offerings included *Castle Beats Time*, *The Roy Castle Show* and Ronnie Barker's *Seven of One*. The last years of his life were dedicated to fighting (and raising the profile of) lung cancer, a disease he claimed he had contracted from passive smoking, having spent years playing the trumpet in smoky club rooms.

CASUALTY

UK (BBC) Medical Drama. BBC 1 1986–

Charlie Fairhead	**Derek Thompson**
Lisa 'Duffy' Duffin	**Catherine Shipton**
Megan Roach	**Brenda Fricker**
Dr Ewart Plimmer	**Bernard Gallagher**
Clive King	**George Harris**
Kuba Trzcinski	**Christopher Rozycki**
Susie Mercier	**Debbie Roza**
Dr Barbara 'Baz' Samuels/Hayes/Fairhead	**Julia Watson**
Andrew Ponting	**Robert Pugh**
Sandra Mute	**Lisa Bowerman**
Elizabeth Straker	**Maureen O'Brien**
Karen O'Malley	**Katie Hardie**
Dr Mary Tomlinson	**Helena Little**
Cyril James	**Eddie Nestor**
Dr David Rowe	**Paul Lacoux**
Valerie Sinclair	**Susan Franklyn**
Shirley Franklin	**Ella Wilder**
Kiran Joghill	**Shaheen Khan**
Alison McGrellis	**Julie Graham**
Julie Stevens	**Vivienne McKone**
Keith Cotterill	**Geoffrey Leesley**
Sadie Tomkins	**Carol Leader**
Dr Lucy Perry	**Tam Hoskyns**
Alex Spencer	**Belinda Davison**
Dr Andrew Bower	**William Gaminara**

Dr Beth Ramanee	**Mamta Kaash**
Dr Julian Chapman	**Nigel Le Vaillant**
Jimmy Powell	**Robson Green**
Tony Walker	**Eamon Boland**
Martin Ashford	**Patrick Robinson**
Helen Green	**Maggie McCarthy**
Norma Sullivan	**Anne Kristen**
Josh Griffiths	**Ian Bleasdale**
Jane Scott	**Caroline Webster**
Kelly Liddle	**Adie Allen**
Patricia Baynes	**Maria Friedman**
Dr Rob Khalefa	**Jason Riddington**
Kate Miller	**Joanna Foster**
Sandra Nicholl	**Maureen Beattie**
Maxine Price	**Emma Bird**
Simon Eastman	**Robert Daws**
Dr Mike Barratt	**Clive Mantle**
Brian Crawford	**Brendan O'Hea**
Mark Calder	**Oliver Parker**
Mie Nishi-Kawa	**Naoko Mori**
Frankie Drummer	**Steven O'Donnell**
Dave Masters	**Martin Ball**
Rachel Longworth	**Jane Gurnett**
Dr Karen Goodliffe	**Suzanna Hamilton**
Adele Beckford	**Doña Croll**
Kenneth Hodges	**Christopher Guard**
Helen Chatsworth	**Samantha Edmonds**
Mary Skillett	**Tara Moran**
Lucy Cooper	**Jo Unwin**
Kate Wilson	**Sorcha Cusack**
Eddie Gordon	**Joan Oliver**
Matt Hawley	**Jason Merrells**
Adam Cooke	**Steven Brand**
Jude Kocarnik	**Lisa Coleman**
Liz Harker	**Sue Devaney**
Dr Daniel Perryman	**Craig Kelly**
Laura Milburn/Ashford	**Lizzy McInnerny**
Peter Hayes	**Robert Duncan**
Trevor Wilson	**Michael N. Harbour**
Richard McCabe	**Gray O'Brien**
Gloria Hammond	**Ganiat Kasumu**
Sam Colloby	**Jonathan Kerrigan**
Jack Hathaway	**Peter Birch**
David Sinclair	**Vas Blackwood**
Monica	**Soo Drouet**
Mark Grace	**Paterson Joseph**
Dr Georgina 'George' Woodman	**Rebecca Lacey**
Tina Seabrook	**Claire Goose**
Amy Howard	**Rebecca Wheatley**
Elliot Matthews	**Peter Guinness**
Derek 'Sunny' Sunderland	**Vincenzo Pellegrino**
Penny Hutchens	**Donna Alexander**
Eve Montgomery	**Barbara Marten**
Adam Osman	**Pal Aron**
Chloe Hill	**Jan Anderson**
Max Gallagher	**Robert Gwilym**
Sean Maddox	**Gerald Kyd**
PC Pat Garratt	**Ian Kershaw**
Marius Lupescu	**Patrick Romer**
Holly Miles	**Sandra Huggett**
Finlay Newton	**Kwame Kwei Armah**
Barney Wolfe	**Ronnie McCann**
Mel Dyson	**Michelle Butterly**
Patrick Spiller	**Ian Kelsey**
Spencer	**Ben Keaton**
Dan Robinson	**Grant Masters**
Colette Kierney	**Adjoa Andoh**

Creators: **Jeremy Brock, Paul Unwin**
Producers: **Geraint Morris, Peter Norris, Michael Ferguson, Corinne Hollingworth, Rosalind Anderson, Sally Haynes, Johnathan Young, Alexei de Keyser, Tim Bradley, Rachel Wright**

A hectic night's work in a city's accident and emergency unit.

Set at night-time in the casualty department of Holby (a thinly disguised Bristol) City Hospital, this extremely popular series has echoed American imports like HILL STREET BLUES and ST ELSEWHERE in its construction, with one disturbing lead story merged with one or two more light-hearted sub-plots to ease the tension and add contrast. While the 'stars' of each show have been the various patients, of the regular cast the main man has been Charlie Fairhead, the avuncular charge nurse. In the early years he shared the limelight with maternal Megan Roach and the outspoken, single-mother senior nurse, Lisa 'Duffy' Duffin. Among the other notable cast members have been 'Baz' Hayes, Charlie's ideal woman who left her husband, Peter, to have Charlie's baby (Louis); ex-surgeon Ewart Plimmer; heart-throb Dr Julian Chapman; Geordie porter, Jimmy Powell; and dependable Martin 'Ash' Ashford, who eventually married hospital PR manager, Laura Milburn. There were also nose-stud-wearing union rep, Jude Kocarnik, who was almost stabbed to death; her boyfriend, receptionist Matt Hawley; shopping addict Kate Wilson; and single parent George Woodman. However, new supporting casts have arrived with each season, and only a few characters have lasted any great length of time. This is possibly because the action in *Casualty* has traditionally come more from events in the wards than from the personal lives of its protagonists, although the characters have increasingly come through over the years. Charlie, for example, has suffered from alcohol addiction, a nervous breakdown and numerous romantic upheavals, but life goes on at Holby.

The series has never been afraid to court controversy. The status of the NHS has always been an issue, much to the dismay of some politicians, and touchy medical matters have bravely been covered, including AIDS and anorexia. Other social menaces like terrorism, rioting, rape, arson and plane crashes have been given equal prominence and drawn similar venom from sensitive critics. Production-wise, too, *Casualty* has been daring. The 1994–5 season was initially shot on film to add greater depth and slickness. However, viewers preferred the tamer atmosphere of videotape, and later episodes were electronically recorded as before.

Among the numerous guest stars playing the walking wounded have been Kate Winslet, Robert Carlyle, Alfred Molina, Dorothy Tutin, Norman Wisdom, Minnie Driver and Hywel Bennett.

An episode in November 1998 introduced guest characters as a preamble to a spin-off series, *Holby City*. March 1999 saw the screening of the 250th episode and various celebratory programmes, including a behind-the-scenes look at production and an all-time viewers' favourite repeat.

CATCHPHRASE
UK (TVS/Meridian/Action Time/Carlton) Game Show. ITV 1986–

Presenters: **Roy Walker, Nick Weir**

Executive Producers: **John Kaye Cooper, Stephen Leahy**
Producers: **Graham C. Williams, Frank Hayes, Liddy Oldroyd, Patricia Mordecai, Royston Mayoh, Patricia Pearson**

Spot-the-saying quiz involving complex computer graphics.

'See what you say and say what you see' has become the *Catchphrase* catchphrase. This undemanding game show has asked two contestants to solve a series of computer-generated visual puzzles representing well-known phrases or sayings. Wrong guesses were generously rejected by host Roy Walker with his own trademark quips like 'It's good, but it's not right', until Walker was succeeded by new host Nick Weir in January 2000. Cash and travel prizes have been awarded to successful contestants.

CATHERINE COOKSON
UK (Tyne Tees/Worldwide/Festival Films) Drama. ITV 1989–

The Fifteen Streets (1989)

John O'Brien	**Owen Teale**
Mary Llewellyn	**Clare Holman**
Dominic O'Brien	**Sean Bean**
Peter Bracken	**Ian Bannen**
Christine Bracken	**Jane Horrocks**
Beatrice Llewellyn	**Billie Whitelaw**
James Llewellyn	**Frank Windsor**

Writer: **Gordon Hann**

The Black Candle (1991)

Bridget Mordaunt	**Samantha Bond**
William Filmore	**Denholm Elliott**
Lionel Filmore	**Nathaniel Parker**
Douglas Filmore	**Robert Hines**
Victoria Mordaunt	**Tara Fitzgerald**
Daisy Bennett	**Siân Phillips**

Writer: **Gordon Hann**

The Black Velvet Gown (1991)

Riah Millican	**Janet McTeer**
Percival Miller	**Bob Peck**
Bridget Millican	**Geraldine Somerville**
Madam Gullmington	**Jean Anderson**

Writer: **Gordon Hann**

The Man Who Cried (1993)

Abel Mason	**Ciaran Hinds**
Florrie Donelly	**Kate Buffery**
Hilda Maxwell	**Amanda Root**
Lena Mason	**Angela Walsh**
Dick Mason	**James Tomlinson**
	Ben Walden

Writer: **Stan Barstow**

The Cinder Path (1994)

Victoria Chapman	**Catherine Zeta Jones**
Charlie MacFell	**Lloyd Owen**
Edward MacFell	**Tom Bell**
Nellie Chapman	**Maria Miles**
Mary MacFell	**Rosalind Ayres**
Ginger Slater	**Antony Byrne**

Writer: **Alan Seymour**

The Dwelling Place (1994)

Cissie Brodie	**Tracey Whitwell**
Lord Fischel	**James Fox**
Clive Fischel	**Edward Rawle-Hicks**
Matthew Turnbull	**Ray Stevenson**
Cunningham	**Philip Voss**
Rose Turnbull	**Julie Hesmondhalgh**
Isabelle Fischel	**Lucy Cohu**

Writer: **Gordon Hann**

The Glass Virgin (1995)

Annabella Lagrange	**Emily Mortimer**
Edmund Lagrange	**Nigel Havers**
Manuel Mendoza	**Brendan Coyle**
Rosina	**Christine Kavanagh**
Betty Watford	**Jan Graveson**
Lady Constance	**Sylvia Syms**

Writer: **Alan Seymour**

The Gambling Man (1995)

Rory Connor	**Robson Green**
Charlotte Kean	**Sylvestra Le Touzel**
Frank Nickle	**Bernard Hill**
Janie Waggett	**Stephanie Putson**
Lizzie O'Dowd	**Anne Kent**
Jimmy Connor	**Dave Nellist**

Writer: **T. R. Bowen**

The Tide of Life (1996)

Emily Kennedy	**Gillian Kearney**
Sep McGilby	**John Bowler**
Larry Birch	**Ray Stevenson**
Lucy Kennedy	**Susie Burton**
John Kennedy	**Berwick Kaler**
Con Fulwell	**Justin Chadwick**
Rona Birch	**Diana Hardcastle**
Nick Stuart	**James Purefoy**

Writer: **Gordon Hann**

The Girl (1996)

Hannah Boyle .... **Siobhan Flynn**
Ned Ridley .... **Jonathan Cake**
Anne Thornton .... **Jill Baker**
Matthew Thornton .... **Malcolm Stoddard**
Fred Loam .... **Mark Benton**
Mrs Loam .... **Susan Jameson**

Writer: **Gordon Hann**

The Wingless Bird (1997)

Agnes Conway .... **Claire Skinner**
Charles Farrier .... **Edward Atterton**
Reg Farrier .... **Julian Wadham**
Alice Conway .... **Anne Reid**
Arthur Conway .... **Frank Grimes**
Jessie Conway .... **Michelle Charles**
Robbie Felton .... **Daniel Casey**
Col. Farrier .... **Dinsdale Landen**
Grace Farrier .... **Elspet Gray**

Writer: **Alan Seymour**

The Moth (1997)

Robert Bradley .... **Jack Davenport**
Sarah Thorman .... **Juliet Aubrey**
Dave Waters .... **David Bradley**
Millie Thorman .... **Justine Waddell**
Alice Bradley .... **Janet Dale**
Reginald Thorman .... **Jeremy Clyde**
Kate Thorman .... **Judy Loe**

Writer: **Gordon Hann**

The Rag Nymph (1997)

Aggie Winkowski .... **Val McLane**
Millie Forester .... **Perdita Weeks**
                                                     Honeysuckle Weeks
Ben .... **Alec Newman**
Bernard Thompson .... **Crispin Bonham-Carter**
Raymond Crane-Boulder .... **Patrick Ryecart**

Writer: **T. R. Bowen**

The Round Tower (1998)

Vanessa Ratcliffe .... **Emilia Fox**
Angus Cotton .... **Ben Miles**
Jane Ratcliffe .... **Jan Harvey**
Jonathan Ratcliffe .... **Keith Barron**
Arthur Brett .... **Denis Lawson**

Writer: **T. R. Bowen**

Colour Blind (1998)

Bridget Paterson .... **Niamh Cusack**
Rose Angela Paterson .... **Carmen Ejogo**
Jimmy Paterson .... **Tony Armatrading**
Kathie McQueen .... **Dearbhla Molloy**
Cavan McQueen .... **Walter McMonagle**
Matt McQueen .... **Ian Embleton**

Writer: **Gordon Hann**

Tilly Trotter (1999)

Tilly Trotter .... **Carli Norris**
Mark Sopwith .... **Simon Shepherd**
Simon Bentwood .... **Gavin Abbott**
Ellen Ross .... **Beth Goddard**
Biddy Drew .... **Madelaine Newton**
Katie Drew .... **Sarah Jane Foster**
Mrs Forefoot Meadows .... **Rosemary Leach**

Writer: **Ray Marshall**

The Secret (2000)

Freddie Musgrave .... **Colin Buchanan**
Maggie Hewitt .... **Clare Higgins**
Belle .... **Hannah Yelland**
Marcel Birkstead .... **Stephen Moyer**
Connie .... **Liz Carling**
Mrs Birkstead .... **June Whitfield**
Freeman .... **Terence Hillyer**

Writer: **T. R. Bowen**

A Dinner of Herbs (2000)

Kate Makepeace .... **Billie Whitelaw**
Roddy Greenbank .... **Jonathan Kerrigan**
                                                     Rupert Frazer
Hal Roystan .... **Tom Goodman Hill**
                                                     David Threlfall
Mary Ellen Lee/Roystan .... **Melanie Clark Pullen**
                                                     Jane Arden
Kate Roystan .... **Debra Stephenson**
Mr Mulcaster .... **Tim Healy**

Writers: **Christopher Green, Ray Marshall**
Producer (all series): **Ray Marshall**

Adaptations of the historical novels by one of Britain's best-selling authors.

Worldwide International Television producer Ray Marshall could hardly believe that such a prolific and popular novelist as Dame Catherine Cookson had never seen her works dramatized for television, with the exception of her stories about The Mallens in the 1970s. Consequently, he took the opportunity to bring her book, *The Fifteen Streets*, to the screen in 1989 and hasn't looked back. He followed it up with *The Black Candle* and *The Black Velvet Gown* and then set up his own production company, Festival Films, to work on the rest of Dame Catherine's extensive output (initially in conjunction with Worldwide).

Cookson's tales major on the downtrodden heroine who hopefully wins through. Set in the North-East of England, and usually in the early years of the 20th century (although *The Round Tower* was set in the 1950s and 1960s, and *Tilly Trotter* in the mid-1800s), they have proved as popular on television as in print. Her intricate plots, matter-of-fact social commentaries and three-dimensional characters have provided the TV dramatists with more than enough to work on. Most of the stories (billed as *Catherine Cookson's The Glass Virgin*, etc.) have been dramatized in three parts.

CATHODE RAY TUBE

The electron tube invented by Karl Ferdinand Braun in 1897 which was modified by Philo T. Farnsworth and Vladimir Zworykin in the 1920s to display television pictures. The device includes a gun that fires a stream of electrons at a phosphor-coated screen, causing it to glow and so display the TV image. Familiarly known as the 'tube', early versions were expensive and not known for their longevity. A common gripe with viewers in the 1950s and 1960s was that their 'tube had gone'.

CATHY COME HOME

UK (BBC) Drama. BBC 1 1966

Cathy Ward .... **Carol White**
Reg Ward .... **Ray Brooks**
Mrs Ward .... **Winnifred Dennis**

Writer: **Jeremy Sandford**
Producer: **Tony Garnett**

Documentary-style drama focusing on the plight of a homeless mother and her children.

Cathy Come Home was possibly the most important contribution made by THE WEDNESDAY PLAY. It told of Cathy, a young northern lass who made her way to the bright lights of London, met and married a local van-driver (Reg) and found herself mother of three young children (Sean, Stephen and Marlene). It revealed how the family was torn apart by the fact that they soon had no permanent roof over their heads, following Reg's accident at work and his subsequent struggle for employment. It showed how they lurched steadily downmarket, from a comfortable maisonette to Reg's mum's over-crowded, squalid tenement, to run-down lodgings, to a pokey caravan on an unhealthy site, to a derelict house, and finally to a hostel for the homeless, where the father was separated from his wife and children. Physically torn apart, Cathy and Reg grew increasingly distant emotionally until he stopped paying for the family's keep and they were thrown on to the streets. The despair and helplessness experienced by Cathy as her kids were taken into care touched the hearts of viewers and led to angry calls for action to prevent such tragic circumstances. Shelter, the homeless charity, was able to capitalize on the furore and become an important voice in housing matters.

The play was directed by Ken Loach, who used documentary, news-style camera angles and hand-held cameras in the search for realism. The soundtrack was punctuated with urban noise, and scenes were kept short and snappy to avoid over-dramatization. Housing facts and figures were quoted throughout the play, adding a political commentary to the events in view.

CATWEAZLE

UK (LWT) Children's Science Fiction. ITV 1970–1

Catweazle .... **Geoffrey Bayldon**
Carrot Bennett .... **Robin Davis**
Mr Bennett .... **Charles Tingwell**
Sam .... **Neil McCarthy**
Cedric Collingford .... **Gary Warren**
Lord Collingford .... **Moray Watson**
Lady Collingford .... **Elspet Gray**
Groome .... **Peter Butterworth**

Creator/Writer: **Richard Carpenter**
Executive Producer: **Joy Whitby**
Producers: **Quentin Lawrence, Carl Mannin**

An 11th-century wizard becomes stranded in the 20th century.

Catweazle, an alchemist in Norman times, was attempting to harness the power of flight when his magic failed him and he found himself transported 900 years into the future. In an age when man really could fly, this scrawny rag-bag of a wizard was astounded and absorbed by simple, everyday objects. Items like the light bulb ('electrickery', as he called it) or the telephone ('telling bone') were simply beyond his comprehension. As he strove to find a way back to his own time, Catweazle was befriended by Carrot, a farmer's son, who soon discovered that life wasn't easy with an ancient magician in tow.

Despite at last finding a way home at the end of the first series, Catweazle promptly returned to our time for a second run, on this occasion arriving in the village of King's Farthing and finding a new ally in Cedric, son of Lord and Lady Collingford. Still struggling to master the art of flight, he now also sought the mystic 13th sign of the zodiac, which would enable him to return to his own age. Finally achieving his objective, Catweazle disappeared back into the past for good.

CAZENOVE, CHRISTOPHER

(1945–)

Aristocratic British actor who, after success as Richard Gaunt in THE REGIMENT, George Cornwallis-West in JENNIE, LADY RANDOLPH CHURCHILL and as the Honourable Charles Tyrrell in THE DUCHESS OF DUKE STREET, flew to the USA to star as Ben Carrington in DYNASTY. Among his other credits have been the US comedy *A Fine Romance*, THE RIVALS OF SHERLOCK HOLMES, *Affairs of the Heart, Ladykillers, Jenny's War*, LOU GRANT and *Kane and Abel*. Cazenove was once married to actress Angharad Rees.

CBS

CBS was, for many years, America's number one network. Founded in 1927 as United Independent Broadcasters by Arthur Judson, the company quickly took on a partner, the Columbia Phonograph and Records Company, at the same time renaming itself Columbia Phonograph Broadcasting System. When the phonograph company pulled out because of increasing losses, the name was shortened to Columbia Broadcasting System (CBS). In 1929 William S. Paley bought control of the company and became its most influential executive. He remained on the board until 1983, leading CBS into television, aggressively signing up affiliate stations and making the network America's first choice. In 1974 the company name was changed from Columbia Broadcasting System to CBS Inc., and various internal power struggles in the 1970s and 1980s ensued, reflecting CBS's fall from the top spot. The company temporarily diversified into publishing, toys and other interests and was taken over by the Tisch family, owners of the Loews Corporation. In 1995 CBS was bought by Westinghouse Electric Corporation. In its heyday CBS boasted the biggest stars and the top shows: I LOVE LUCY, *The Honeymooners*, THE DICK VAN DYKE SHOW, ALL IN THE FAMILY and M*A*S*H all aired on CBS, and the station was also home to revered news journalists Ed Murrow and Walter Cronkite. In recent years the biggest hits have been modest in comparison, namely MURDER, SHE WROTE and *Murphy Brown*.

CELEBRITY SQUARES
UK (ATV/Central) Quiz. ITV 1975–9/1993–5

Presenter: **Bob Monkhouse**

Producers: **Paul Stewart Laing, Glyn Edwards, Peter Harris, Gill Stribling-Wright, Danny Greenstone**

Noughts and crosses quiz featuring showbusiness personalities.

In this light-hearted game show nine celebrities inhabited the squares of a giant (18-foot) noughts and crosses board. Two contestants took turns to nominate celebrities to answer general knowledge questions and then tried to work out if the celebrity's answer was right or wrong. If they guessed correctly, they won an X or an O for that space on the board and a line of three noughts or three crosses earned cash and prizes. Quick-fire gags and contrived answers abounded as the quiz element played second fiddle to comedy. Kenny Everett provided the wacky voice-overs. The celebrities taking part in the first show were Diana Dors, Leslie Crowther, Aimi McDonald, Alfred Marks, Vincent Price, Hermione Gingold, Terry Wogan, Arthur Mullard and William Rushton.

One segment of the programme saw the tables turned on host Bob Monkhouse. Each celebrity fired a question at him and his correct answers collected money for charity. *Celebrity Squares*, which was revived in 1993 after a 14-year absence, was a copy of the popular American game show, *Hollywood Squares*.

CENTRAL

The ITV contractor for the Midlands, Central Independent Television came into being as a restructured version of ATV, which previously held the Midlands franchise. It went on air on 1 January 1982 and retained its franchise in 1991 with a bid of just £2,000 (there were no challengers). Central has since been taken over by Carlton Communications, the franchise-holder for London weekdays. The station is now known as Carlton Central. It has two studio bases, in Birmingham and Nottingham, and among the company's many programming successes have been AUF WIEDERSEHEN, PET, CROSSROADS, BLOCKBUSTERS, THE PRICE IS RIGHT and SPITTING IMAGE.

CHALLENGE ANNEKA
UK (Mentorn) BBC 1 1989–95

Presenter: **Anneka Rice**

Creator: **Anneka Rice**
Producer: **Tom Gutteridge**

Anneka Rice works against the clock to complete an ambitious project.

Piloted as part of CHILDREN IN NEED in 1988, when star Anneka Rice battled against the odds to arrange for an orchestra to perform the '1812 Overture' on the Thames, freeze part of the river for a skating ballet and organize a firework display, all within a few days, *Challenge Anneka* was soon launched as a series of 40-minute programmes. Each week, a new challenge was set by a member of the public – seemingly impossible tasks like staging a West End farce, or converting an old church into a circus training school, within 24 hours. Rice – unaware of what was involved until the start of the programme – then donned her bright overalls, boarded her 'Challenger' jeep and set about coercing people into helping her meet the challenge on time. All challenges were aimed at providing lasting benefit and those that gained included charities and other worthy causes. In her *Challenge* role, Rice once guested in 2 POINT 4 CHILDREN.

CHALLENGE TV

Satellite and cable channel that specializes in re-runs of game shows and quizzes. Its daily fare is a diet of CATCHPHRASE, FAMILY FORTUNES, 3-2-1, THE KRYPTON FACTOR and the like, most seen long ago on terrestrial TV. Some new versions of favourites like SALE OF THE CENTURY and one or two first-run series like *Splitsecond* have brought the channel more up to date. Live viewer phone-in competitions, and the inclusion of non-quizzes like CANDID CAMERA from the USA, have broadened its appeal.

Challenge TV is part of the Flextech group but it evolved from a broadcaster called The Family Channel. That had been established in the USA in 1977 as CBN

Satellite Service, providing religious programmes for the non-profit-making Christian Broadcasting Network, later developing into CBN Cable Network and focusing instead on 'wholesome', morally sound entertainment. The channel's Christian roots were further distanced by the change of the name to The Family Channel in 1988, and it was launched in the UK in September 1993, the same year that its then parent company, International Family Entertainment (IFE), bought the disenfranchised TVS and its Maidstone studios for £58 million. The Family Channel's UK broadcasts were based around material suitable for viewing by the entire family, mixing heart-warming drama series like *Road to Avonlea* and THE DARLING BUDS OF MAY with comedy and quiz shows, leading ultimately to the current quiz-show-led format and the change of name to Challenge TV.

CHALMERS, JUDITH
OBE (1935–)

Manchester-born presenter and announcer, for many years host of ITV's travelogue, WISH YOU WERE HERE . . . ?. Chalmers began her career as a child actor at the age of 13, working on BBC Radio's *Children's Hour*, and her later radio credits have included *Family Favourites*, *Woman's Hour* and her own Radio 2 morning show. On TV she has been seen on COME DANCING, *Afternoon Plus* and various beauty contests, including MISS WORLD. Married to former broadcaster Neil Durden-Smith, Chalmers is the mother of sports presenter Mark Durden-Smith.

CHAMBERLAIN, RICHARD
(1935–)

1960s heart-throb actor with boyish looks, gaining international fame as the dedicated young DR KILDARE. Although initially typecast after playing Kildare for five years, Chamberlain has since managed to break into other starring roles in film and on TV, often in mini-series and most notably in *The Count of Monte Cristo* and *The Man in the Iron Mask*, and as Alexander McKeag in *Centennial*, as the English captain John Blackthorne (or Anjin) in SHOGUN and as the troubled Australian priest, Ralph de Bricassart, in THE THORN BIRDS.

CHAMPION THE WONDER HORSE
US (Flying A) Children's Adventure. BBC 1956–7

Ricky North	**Barry Curtis**
Sandy North	**Jim Bannon**
Will Calhoun	**Francis McDonald**
Sheriff Powers	**Ewing Mitchell**

Executive Producer: **Armand Schaefer**
Producer: **Louis Gray**

A 12-year-old boy and his multi-talented horse find adventure in the Wild West.

Ricky North lived on his Uncle Sandy's North Ranch, somewhere in Texas, in the 1880s. His pride and joy was Champion, once leader of a herd of wild horses and now domesticated to the point where Ricky (but no one else) could safely ride him. From the very first episode, when Champion hauled Ricky to safety with a rope looped around his neck, it was clear that this was no ordinary nag. Indeed, the haughty stallion continued to earn his keep, constantly foiling criminals, alerting his owner to freak natural disasters and generally keeping the young boy out of trouble. Rebel, Ricky's German Shepherd dog, also lent a paw from time to time.

The series (known in America, and sometimes billed in the UK, as *The Adventures of Champion*) was created by Gene Autry in celebration of Champion, who was his own horse. Only 26 episodes were ever made.

CHAMPIONS, THE
UK (ITC) Science Fiction. ITV 1968–9

Craig Stirling	**Stuart Damon**
Sharon McCready	**Alexandra Bastedo**
Richard Barrett	**William Gaunt**
Commander W. L. Tremayne	**Anthony Nicholls**

Creators: **Monty Berman, Dennis Spooner**
Producer: **Monty Berman**

Three superhumans help maintain peace in the world.

In this 'SIX MILLION DOLLAR MAN meets *Lost Horizon*' caper, American Craig Stirling and Britons Sharon McCready and Richard Barrett worked for the international peace agency, Nemesis. But these were no ordinary secret agents. Having suffered a plane crash in the Himalayas on a mission to China, they had been saved and healed by an old man from a reclusive Tibetan civilization. Endowed with superhuman powers, they found that their senses had been fine-tuned so that they could hear, see and smell acutely. They also had enhanced strength and stamina, and special mental powers like telepathy.

Promising to preserve the lost city's anonymity, the trio returned to the West and began to use their remarkable talents on behalf of Nemesis. Their boss, Tremayne (who was based in Geneva), issued them with assignments aimed at defusing international flashpoints and potential sources of world tension. The policy was to maintain the existing balance of power between nations. The agents' special attributes, however, always remained a secret, and they were certainly not infallible or invincible, needing to work very much as a team. Although they were as mortal as any other human, they became 'Champions of law, order and justice'.

The series was re-run on BBC 2 in 1995.

CHANDLER AND CO.
UK (Skreba/BBC) Drama BBC 1 1994–5

Elly Chandler	**Catherine Russell**
Dee Tate	**Barbara Flynn**
Larry Blakeston	**Peter Capaldi**
David Tate	**Struan Rodger**

Kate Phillips .... **Susan Fleetwood**
Benji Phillips .... **Graham McGrath**
Simon Wood .... **Bill Britten**
Dr Mark Judd .... **Adrian Lukis**

Creator: **Paula Milne**
Producer: **Anne Skinner**
Executive Producer: **Michael Wearing**

*Two sisters-in-law set up their own private
detection agency.*

Elly Chandler had recently divorced her philandering husband, Max, and needed a new challenge in life. Inspired by Larry Blakeston, the private eye she had hired to expose her husband's infidelity, she decided to set up her own investigation firm, roping in Max's sister, Dee, and turning to the now-retired Blakeston for advice and surveillance equipment. Dee was a reluctant partner and had told her husband, David, that she was going to be involved only until Elly had found her feet. However, it was hard for Dee to detach herself from the business, even though detective work turned out to be a lot less fun than the girls had imagined, bringing danger to themselves and their families.

In the second series, set a couple of years on, Dee had finally left the agency and Larry had also departed. A more confident Elly gained a new partner, Kate Phillips, and new romance with Dr Mark Judd.

CHANGING ROOMS
UK (Bazal/BBC) Lifestyle. BBC 2/BBC 1 1996–

Presenter: **Carol Smillie**

Producers: **Ann Hill, Pauline Doidge, Caspar Peacock,
Ann Booth-Clibborn, Mary Ramsay, Susannah Walker**
Executive Producer: **Linda Clifford**

*Neighbours simultaneously re-decorate each
other's home.*

With a time-limit of two days and a budget of just £500, two sets of neighbour friends attempted to improve a room in each other's home in this surprisingly successful series. Given the help of a professional designer (Graham Wynne, Michael Jewitt, Laura McCree and, more notably, Linda Barker, Laurence Llewelyn-Bowen and Anna Ryder Richardson) and the assistance of crafty carpenter 'Handy Andy' Kane, they set about transforming the look of one of their friends' rooms. The series inspired viewing DIYers, but was also panned for some of its over-the-top designs, quick fixes and cheapo decorations. At the end of each show, the neighbours were taken back to their own home and shown the results – often to delight, but occasionally to heartbreak. Carol Smillie introduced the programme and reported on progress throughout.

Changing Rooms, beginning modestly on BBC 2 but transferring to BBC 1 after two years, was one of the first of a new tranche of lifestyle/DIY programmes – *Home Front, All Mod Cons, Change That*, etc. – that had viewers queuing outside B&Q on a Sunday morning. The series merged with a sister programme for a special in 2000 entitled *When Changing Rooms Met Ground Force*, in which interior decorating and gardening specialists switched jobs.

CHANNEL

The frequency allocated to a TV service.

CHANNEL 3
See ITV.

CHANNEL 4

Britain finally received its fourth channel in 1982, after years of debate. Channel 4 was set up as a wholly owned subsidiary of the IBA, with the brief to serve minority interests and encourage innovation through programming supplied by outside independent producers. Its first chief executive was Jeremy Isaacs and he 'sugared the pill' of minority programming by buying in popular overseas series like CHEERS and *The Paul Hogan Show*. The channel – first airing on 2 November 1982 – proved more successful than doubters had predicted. Some felt that its narrow target audience would not generate sufficient advertising revenue. However, it did so well that the basis of its advertising sales was changed in 1993. Whereas sales were originally the responsibility of the other ITV companies, who then paid for the upkeep of Channel 4 through a levy on their incomes, since 1993 Channel 4 has sold its own advertising. At the same time, its corporate structure was changed so that it became a non-profit-making organization licensed and regulated by the ITC.

Channel 4 has always courted controversy and provided a valuable mouthpiece for minority groups. but it has also excelled at commissioning award-winning films. *Room With a View, The Madness of King George* and *Four Weddings and a Funeral* are just three examples. The first programme seen on Channel 4 was COUNTDOWN, which is still being screened today. Equally durable has been the revolutionary soap, BROOKSIDE, and other Channel 4 successes have included THE TUBE, GBH, THE FAR PAVILIONS and *Channel 4 News*. Michael Grade became chief executive (1989–97), following Jeremy Isaacs's departure. In 2001 Channel 4 launched a sister digital entertainment channel called E4.

Channel 4 does not cover Wales, which is served by a bilingual channel, S4C.

CHANNEL 5

The UK's fifth terrestrial TV channel finally arrived in 1997, after years of uncertainty over the viability of such a service. The channel was first proposed in the late 1980s, when it was suggested that a couple of channels then devoted to non-broadcasting concerns could be freed up for transmissions – although there was a fly in the ointment, in that domestic video recorders in some parts of the country would need retuning to prevent interference from the new signal. This imposed a heavy financial commitment on prospective broadcasters, as they would have had to pay for the retuning exercise.

The ITC advertised the Channel 5 franchise in 1992, but only one application was received and this was declined. After a thorough review of the prospects for the channel, the franchise was re-advertised in 1994, the winning bid announced a year later as coming from C5 Broadcasting, which satisfied the Commission with regard to both programming commitments and commercial viability – including the cost of retuning video recorders. Despite rival bidder Virgin TV gaining a judicial review, C5 Broadcasting took to the air on 30 March 1997, employing the then five Spice Girls to publicize the launch. After a half-hour introductory slot, the first scheduled programme was the new soap, *Family Affairs*. Only about 60 per cent of UK homes were able to receive the channel at first, but its coverage has increased since (helped by the fact it has been carried on both satellite and digital networks).

Initial response to Channel 5's programming from the ITC was good, with the freshness and vitality it brought to children's, religious and news programming being especially welcomed. However, in 2000 there was widespread criticism of the channel's late-night programming, which had come to rely heavily on 'adult' material.

Channel 5 is owned by three major shareholders: United News & Media, Pearson (owners of Thames, Grundy and Alomo) and pan-European media group, CLT/UFA.

CHANNEL TELEVISION

The smallest of the ITV contractors, Channel Television went on air on 1 September 1962 to serve the various Channel Islands (which were represented in the company's first logo of six linked hexagons). Early on there were serious doubts as to whether such a small audience would generate enough advertising income to keep an independent television service alive, but Channel is still afloat after 40 years. (A reflection of the size of the area was the fact that the company retained its franchise in the 1991 auctions with a bid of just £1,000.) To make ends meet, at various times Channel has been forced to link up with Westward, TSW, TVS and Meridian for advertising sales and administration. These companies have also been the suppliers of ITV national output to Channel, beaming programmes over the English Channel for relay by local transmitters.

Another consequence of low advertising turnover has been the almost negligible contribution Channel has been able to make to network programming (the most prominent examples have been editions of *About Britain* and HIGHWAY), although Channel – or CTV, as it has become known – has won many fans for its local news and regional documentary service, including some programmes in French and Portuguese. The station mascot, Oscar Puffin, has enjoyed his own children's series, *Puffin's Pla(i)ce*, for many years.

CHAPMAN, GRAHAM
(1941–89)

Tall, satirical comedian, a qualified doctor and stalwart of the MONTY PYTHON team. Previously Chapman had been seen with John Cleese and others in AT LAST THE 1948 SHOW and he was also a prolific writer for other series (usually in conjunction with Cleese). His script credits included THE FROST REPORT, *Marty*, *Broaden Your Mind*, THE TWO RONNIES and the DOCTOR IN THE HOUSE sequence of sitcoms, as well as the Ronnie Corbett series, NO – THAT'S ME OVER HERE, NOW LOOK HERE . . . and *The Prince of Denmark* (the last two with Barry Cryer).

CHAPPELL, ERIC
(1933–)

British comedy writer, responsible for some of ITV's most popular sitcoms, namely RISING DAMP, THE SQUIRRELS, THE BOUNDER, ONLY WHEN I LAUGH, *Misfits*, *Fiddlers Three*, *Haggard*, HOME TO ROOST, SINGLES and DUTY FREE (the last two in collaboration with Jean Warr).

CHARACTER GENERATOR

A device for superimposing text (captions, names, etc.) on to the TV picture. Also known as a caption generator or by tradenames like Anchor and Aston.

CHARLIE CHAN
See NEW ADVENTURES OF CHARLIE CHAN, THE.

CHARLIE'S ANGELS
US (Spelling-Goldberg) Detective Drama. ITV 1977–82

Sabrina Duncan	**Kate Jackson**
Jill Munroe	**Farrah Fawcett-Majors**
Kelly Garrett	**Jaclyn Smith**
Kris Munroe	**Cheryl Ladd**
Tiffany Welles	**Shelley Hack**
Julie Rogers	**Tanya Roberts**
John Bosley	**David Doyle**
Charlie Townsend	**John Forsythe** (*voice only*)

Executive Producers: **Aaron Spelling, Leonard Goldberg**
Producer: **Rick Husky, David Levinson, Barney Rosenzweig**

Three beautiful ex-policewomen work undercover for a mysterious detective agency boss.

'Once upon a time there were three girls who went to the police academy and they were each assigned very hazardous duties. But I took them away from all that and now they work for me. My name is Charlie.' So stated the opening titles of this glitzy detective series in which Sabrina Duncan, Kelly Garrett and Jill Munroe were the original team of Angels. Sabrina, nominal leader of the trio, was a multilinguist, Kelly was a former showgirl, while Jill was an athletic blonde. Together they had been hired by Charlie Townsend of Townsend Investigations, a Los Angeles detective agency. Charlie himself was never seen, only heard on the telephone (and in the intro), leaving the avuncular John Bosley to act as the girls' personal contact.

The Angels were able to take on missions that were out of bounds for most other investigators. Their stunning looks allowed them to work undercover (often with little cover), as nightclub singers, models, strippers and even army recruits. Although their assignments were rough and dangerous, the girls' appearance was never less than immaculate, and their skimpy outfits (often without bras) led to *Charlie's Angels* being labelled the doyen of 'jiggly' TV.

The first changes in the series came with the departure of Farrah Fawcett-Majors (later just Fawcett after her divorce from Lee Majors) to pursue a film career. She did agree to make occasional guest appearances, but her permanent replacement was Alan Ladd's daughter-in-law, Cheryl, as Jill's younger sister, Kris. Two more Angels were also brought in. Tiffany Welles, daughter of a Connecticut police chief, took over from Sabrina, then she, in turn, was replaced by Julie Rogers. The voice of the enigmatic Charlie was provided by John Forsythe, later Blake Carrington in DYNASTY. A film version starring Drew Barrymore, Cameron Diaz and Lucy Liu was released in 2000.

CHARMER, THE
UK (LWT) Drama. ITV 1987

Ralph Ernest Gorse	**Nigel Havers**
Donald Stimpson	**Bernard Hepton**
Joan Plumleigh-Bruce	**Rosemary Leach**
Clarice Mannors	**Fiona Fullerton**
Alison Warren	**Judy Parfitt**
Pamela Bennett	**Abigail McKern**

Writer: **Allan Prior**
Executive Producer: **Nick Elliott**
Producer: **Philip Hinchcliffe**

A suave young con-merchant wins the hearts of wealthy ladies.

Ralph Gorse was a cad. Exercising his skill at smooth talk, he worked his way around the seaside resorts of 1930s Britain preying on rich, gullible ladies who could not resist his good looks and gentle manner. No sooner had they taken him to their hearts than he was away with the family silver or at least a wallet full of 'borrowed' notes. It all worked very well until he deceived the delightfully tweedy Joan Plumleigh-Bruce, whose estate agent friend, Donald Stimpson, took exception and promised revenge. The series was based on the books by Patrick Hamilton.

CHARTERS AND CALDICOTT
UK (BBC/Network Seven) Detective Drama. BBC 1 1985

Charters	**Robin Bailey**
Caldicott	**Michael Aldridge**

Writer: **Keith Waterhouse**
Producer: **Ron Craddock**

Two retired old buffers immerse themselves in murder.

Appearing initially as bit characters in Hitchcock's *The Lady Vanishes* in 1938, Charters and Caldicott were portrayed by actors Basil Radford and Naunton Wayne as a couple of well-meaning, upper-class twits with no grasp of reality. Their eccentric Englishmen abroad roles simply brought a touch of comic relief to an otherwise spooky and melodramatic tale. Soon afterwards, however, they resurfaced in another cameo role in *Night Train to Munich*, before gaining top billing in their own vehicle, *Crooks' Tour*, in 1940. Over 40 years later they became stars of their own BBC series.

Now in retirement, the two perpetual schoolboys were played by Robin Bailey and Michael Aldridge. They enjoyed regular monthly lunches at their Pall Mall club, where they discussed the inadequacies of women, the wonders of cricket and how things simply weren't as they used to be. Strictly public school, they pitied people who didn't share their backgrounds and interests, and voiced prejudiced concerns about the state of the world. Charters, a widower, lived in a country cottage near Reigate and religiously hailed a Green Line bus on the first Friday of every month to meet his chum, Caldicott, at his residence in Viceroy Court, Kensington. However, when a girl's body was discovered at Caldicott's flats, the old buffers found themselves embarking on the trail of a murderer.

CHAT SHOW
See TALK SHOW.

CHATAWAY, Sir CHRISTOPHER
(1931–)

London-born middle-distance athlete turned broadcaster who read the news for ITN in its early days. He later joined the BBC's PANORAMA, before switching to politics and becoming a Conservative MP and subsequently Postmaster General. He was the BBC's first *Sports Personality of the Year*, in 1954.

CHEATERS, THE
UK (Danziger) Detective Drama. ITV 1960–2

John Hunter	**John Ireland**
Walter Allen	**Robert Ayres**

Producers: **Edward J. Danziger, Harry Lee Danziger**

The investigations of an insurance inspector.

The door-to-door inquiries of claims inspector John Hunter formed the basis of this series. Diligent and honest, Hunter and his assistant, Walter Allen, were relentless in their pursuit of nasty people who were swindling his company, the Eastern Insurance Company, at the ultimate expense of decent policy-holders. Those who attempted crafty frauds and fiddles were quickly sussed out. Star John Ireland went on to play Jed Colby in RAWHIDE.

CHECKLAND, Sir MICHAEL
(1936–)

BBC Director-General from 1987 to 1993, when he was succeeded in rather controversial circumstances by his former deputy, John Birt. Checkland had previously been Deputy Director-General himself (from 1985) and was an expert in the financial affairs of the Corporation, joining the BBC in 1964 as an accountant and working his way up to chief accountant status. In 1977 he became controller of planning and resource management for the television division. The announcement (surprisingly well in advance) of John Birt's promotion to the Director-General position made Checkland's last two years in the position somewhat uncomfortable and led some commentators to label him a lame duck controller.

CHEERS
US (Paramount) Situation Comedy. Channel 4 1982–93

Sam Malone	**Ted Danson**
Diane Chambers	**Shelley Long**
Carla Tortelli/LeBec	**Rhea Perlman**
Ernie Pantusso ('Coach')	**Nicholas Colasanto**
Norm Peterson	**George Wendt**
Cliff Clavin	**John Ratzenberger**
Dr Frasier Crane	**Kelsey Grammer**
Woody Boyd	**Woody Harrelson**
Rebecca Howe	**Kirstie Alley**
Dr Lilith Sternin/Crane	**Bebe Neuwirth**
Janet Eldridge	**Kate Mulgrew**
Evan Drake	**Tom Skerritt**
Eddie LeBec	**Jay Thomas**
Robin Colcord	**Roger Rees**
Kelly Gaines/Boyd	**Jackie Swanson**
John Hill	**Keene Curtis**
Paul	**Paul Willson**

Creators/Producers: **Glen Charles, Les Charles, James Burrows**

Award-winning comedy centring around the staff and regulars at a Boston bar.

Cheers bar (established 1895) was owned by former Boston Red Sox pitcher, Sam 'Mayday' Malone, a reformed alcoholic and a successful womanizer. But he met his match in the first episode of this cult comedy with the arrival of Diane Chambers, an over-educated academic researcher. Ditched by her husband-to-be, she accepted Sam's offer of a job as a waitress, a move which led to years of good-natured sparring and on-off relationships with her boss.

Revolving around Sam and Diane's intermittent romance were the lives of the other staff and bar regulars. Carla Tortelli, a sharp-tongued, streetwise mother of many, was the perfect antidote to the sophisticated Diane, and Ernie Pantusso, the mild-mannered ex-Red Sox coach, was another leading character in the show's early years. His naïvety and absent-mindedness were much missed when actor Nicholas Colasanto died in 1985, but the gap was soon filled with the arrival of Woody Boyd, a young farmboy from the backwaters of Hanover, Indiana. He came to Boston to meet Coach, his pen-pal, took a job behind the bar and eventually married the extremely wealthy but rather dizzy Kelly Gaines.

Woody's innocence and gullibility were genially abused by regulars Norm, Cliff and Frasier. Norm, an accountant, spent most of his waking life in Cheers savouring freedom from his wife, Vera, while know-all Cliff, the mailman, was the butt of all the jokes. The third regular was Frasier Crane, an insecure psychiatrist who was introduced as Diane's new fiancé. However, their relationship broke up and the pompous, emotional shrink joined Cliff and Norm as one of the losers hugging the bar. He eventually found his perfect partner in a severe, intellectual colleague, Dr Lilith Sternin, and they had a son, Frederick.

Four years into its run, *Cheers* was forced into a major recast. Not only had Coach died but Diane, too, said goodbye to the bar – and to Sam – taking herself away for six months to write a book. Sam knew that she would not return, so he sold the bar to a leisure conglomerate, bought a boat and planned to sail around the world. When the next series opened, Sam's boat had sunk and he had returned to Cheers to talk his way into a job. Only this time he was just a member of staff, responsible to sultry new manageress, Rebecca Howe. Another love-hate relationship began.

Frigid and sycophantic, Rebecca was a real career-chaser. For a while she pursued company bigwig Evan Drake, then her attention turned to smarmy English businessman, Robin Colcord. When Colcord used her to gain inside knowledge of her company in order to launch a take-over bid, Sam shopped him and was given his bar back for only $1. Rebecca stayed on as manageress and later as a partner.

In the extended final episode of *Cheers*, Diane walked back into Sammy's life. Her book had been published and had picked up a major award, but she and Sam still could not make their relationship work, and she left once more. This time, it was clearly for good.

Although the inside shots of the bar were studio produced, the exterior of Cheers was a real Boston bar, The Bull and Finch, which now does a roaring tourist trade. After 11 years one element of *Cheers* was allowed to live on as Frasier, now separated from Lilith, was given his own spin-off series, FRASIER.

CHEF!
UK (APC/Crucial) Situation Comedy. BBC 1 1993–6

Gareth Blackstock	**Lenny Henry**
Janice Blackstock	**Caroline Lee Johnson**
Everton	**Roger Griffiths**
Lucinda	**Claire Skinner**
Piers	**Gary Parker**
Otto	**Erkan Mustafa**
Lola	**Elizabeth Bennett**
Gustave	**Ian McNeice**
	Jeff Nuttall
Donald	**Gary Bakewell**
Crispin	**Tim Matthews**
Alice	**Hilary Lyon**
Debra	**Pui Fan Lee**
Alphonse	**Jean Luc Rebaliati**
Cyril Bryson	**Dave Hill**
Savanna	**Lorelei King**
Renee Bryson	**Sophie Walker**
Vincenzo	**Vincent Walsh**

Creator: **Lenny Henry**
Writer: **Peter Tilbury**
Executive Producer: **Polly McDonald**
Producer: **Charlie Hanson**

An ambitious but egocentric chef strives to succeed in his own restaurant.

Gareth Blackstock was the gifted *chef de cuisine* at Le Château Anglais, a stately French restaurant deep in the Oxfordshire Cotswolds. When the Château fell into financial difficulties, he and his wife, Janice, sold Linden Cottage, their picture-postcard home, and bought control themselves. Keen to build on his Michelin two-star status, Blackstock found his ambitions hindered by his inept kitchen hands, especially the accident-prone soul food specialist, Everton. No one escaped the chef's fits of pique, as he lambasted staff and customers alike with pearls of sarcastic abuse. But, although he ruled with a rod of iron, Gareth deep down nursed a fragile ego. This was tested particularly in the third and final series (two years after the second), when his marriage broke down and the restaurant was bought by the rather down-market Cyril Bryson, whose spoilt daughter, Renee, came to work in the kitchen.

Well supported by a team of top chef advisers, particularly John Burton-Race, Lenny Henry and writer Peter Tilbury – who scripted the first two series – gave viewers a revealing insight into the world of a top kitchen, with its exacting standards and finest attention to detail, gently parodying the celebrity status of Britain's leading chefs.

CHEGWIN, KEITH
(1957–)

Liverpudlian actor, presenter and musician (in the band Kenny), whose earliest appearances were in programmes like *Junior Showtime*, THE LIVER BIRDS, THE TOMORROW PEOPLE, *My Old Man*, *The Wackers* (Raymond Clarkson) and OPEN ALL HOURS. In 1976 his big break came with MULTI-COLOURED SWAP SHOP, for which he was roving reporter/entertainer. He stayed with the Saturday morning show when it evolved into *Saturday Superstore*, and was married for some time to one of his co-presenters, Maggie Philbin. His own kids' music show, *Cheggers Plays Pop*, followed, as well as a couple of investigative series, *Cheggers' Action Reports* and *Cheggers Checks It Out*. In the 1990s he appeared regularly on satellite television, hosted THE BIG BREAKFAST, featured on GMTV and presented the revival of IT'S A KNOCKOUT. In 2000 he controversially appeared nude in the Channel 5 naturists' game show, *Naked Jungle*. Chegwin is the brother of radio broadcaster Janice Long.

CHELSEA AT NINE
UK (Granada) Variety. ITV 1957–60

Producer: **Denis Forman**

International cabaret direct from a London theatre.

Chelsea at Nine was Monday night's big variety offering, presented by Granada Television from its Chelsea Palace theatre. It showcased top transatlantic stars (the likes of Billie Holiday, Alan Young and Ferrante and Teicher appeared), with American directors employed to give the show an international sheen. As well as major entertainment names of the day, the programme included regular comedy skits from the team of Mai Zetterling, Dennis Price and Irene Handl, and excerpts from contemporary theatre shows, while The Granadiers were the house song-and-dance troupe, directed by Cliff Adams. With a timing change, the series became *Chelsea at Eight* in 1958 and, in the same year, adopted the title of *Chelsea Summertime* for its seasonal programmes. The first compere was David Hutcheson; Bernard Braden also hosted.

CHESNEY, RONALD

British comedy writer, usually in tandem with Ronald Wolfe. Together they penned THE RAG TRADE, MEET THE WIFE, THE BED-SIT GIRL, *Sorry I'm Single*, *Wild, Wild Women*, ON THE BUSES, *Don't Drink the Water*, ROMANY JONES, *Yus My Dear*, *Watch This Space*, *Take a Letter*, *Mr Jones . . .*, an episode of 'ALLO 'ALLO and sketches for Dora Bryan in *According to Dora*. Chesney also collaborated with Marty Feldman (and Wolfe) on the 1950s series, *Educating Archie*.

CHEYENNE
US (Warner Brothers) Western. ITV 1958–64

Cheyenne Bodie	**Clint Walker**
Bronco Layne	**Ty Hardin**
Smitty	**L. Q. Jones**

A wanderer works his way across the American West.

Based on the 1947 film of the same name starring Dennis Morgan, *Cheyenne* related the adventures of Cheyenne Bodie, a drifter who travelled the Wild West in the years following the Civil War. The hero was a frontier scout, a strapping giant of a man who had learnt Indian skills and who now strayed from town to town, from job to job and from girl to girl. Constantly falling foul of outlaws and villains, Bodie was often on the receiving end of a severe beating. He did, however, enjoy some friendly company during the first series in the shape of Smitty, a mapmaker.

Of as much interest as the programme itself were the behind-the-scenes wrangles. When Clint Walker walked out after a legal dispute with Warner Brothers, he was temporarily replaced in the lead by Ty Hardin as Bronco Layne. When Walker was reinstated, Hardin was not dropped but given his own spin-off series, BRONCO.

CHICAGO HOPE
US (David E. Kelley/Twentieth Century-Fox) Medical Drama. BBC 1 1995–

Dr Jeffrey Geiger	**Mandy Patinkin**
Dr Aaron Shutt	**Adam Arkin**
Nurse Camille Shutt	**Roxanne Hart**
Dr Phillip Watters	**Hector Elizondo**
Dr Arthur Thurmond	**E. G. Marshall**
Alan Birch	**Peter MacNicol**
Angela Giandamenico	**Roma Maffia**
Dr Karen Antonovich	**Margaret Colin**
Dr Daniel Nyland	**Thomas Gibson**
Dr Geri Infante	**Diane Venora**
Dr Billy Kronk	**Peter Berg**
Dr Dennis Hancock	**Vondie Curtis-Hall**
Laurie Geiger	**Kim Greist**
Dr Kate Austin	**Christine Lahti**
Dr Diane Grad	**Jayne Brook**
Maggie Atkisson	**Robyn Lively**
Dr John Sutton	**Jamey Sheridan**
Judge Harold Aldrich	**Stephen Elliott**

Creator: **David E. Kelley**
Executive Producers: **John Tinker, Bill D'Elia**

Earnest medical drama set in a busy city hospital.

Chicago Hope Hospital, in the city of the same name, had more than its fair share of medical and personal crises, but in a more much restrained, soapy way than in its US rival, ER, which was also set in the Windy City and strangely was its cross-channel rival on Thursday evenings in the US. *ER* won that battle, but *Chicago Hope* prospered in another time-slot for several more years.

The state-of-the-art hospital specialized in medical innovation, and chief among the healers were estranged surgeon and wife, Aaron and Camille Shutt, along with level-headed chief surgeon Phillip Watters, fading doctor Arthur Thurmond and the gifted but unnecessarily rude and explosive Dr Jeffrey Geiger. Also prominent was legal adviser Alan 'The Eel' Birch. Viewers of a fragile constitution quailed at the sight of so many organ close-ups and pumping blood, and UK transmission was gradually switched from Saturday peak hours to late

Tuesday nights, as the series began to fade out on this side of the Atlantic.

CHIEF, THE
UK (Anglia Films) Police Drama. ITV 1990–5

Chief Constable John Stafford	**Tim Pigott-Smith**
ACC Anne Stewart	**Karen Archer**
Dr Elizabeth Stafford	**Judy Loe**
Det. Chief Supt. Jim Gray	**Eamon Boland**
Emma Stafford	**Sara Griffiths**
Tim Stafford	**Ross Livingstone**
Martin Stewart	**David Cardy**
ACC/Chief Constable Alan Cade	**Martin Shaw**
Det. Chief Supt. Sean McCloud	**Stuart McGugan**
Nigel Crimmond	**Michael Cochrane**
Colin Fowler	**T. P. McKenna**
Alison Dell	**Ingrid Lacey**
Andrew Blake	**Julian Glover**
DOC Wes Morton	**Bosco Hogan**
Det. Supt. Rose Penfold	**Gillian Bevan**
Sam Lester	**Davyd Harries**
PC Charlie Webb	**Brian Bovell**

Creator: **Jeffrey Caine**
Executive Producer: **Brenda Reid**
Producers: **Ruth Boswell, John Davies**

The problems facing the Chief Constable of a regional police force.

When John Stafford gained promotion to the rank of Chief Constable of Eastland, an East Anglian police force, he quickly made himself a number of enemies. Bringing with him Anne Stewart, his CID supremo from Nottinghamshire, and promoting her to Head of Crime and Operations was not a good start and immediately triggered resentment among Eastland's long-serving officers. But when the outspoken Chief began to lay down the law on police drinking and aggressive police driving, and then refused to ban a student protest against a visiting Government minister, he was made very aware of the disillusionment all around him, including from those who had appointed him. However, *The Chief* was also a personal drama, revealing how Stafford coped with the pressures of office, how he and his doctor wife, Elizabeth, struggled to keep their teenage kids in check, and how Anne's marriage foundered when her husband, Martin, began to resent her devotion to work.

After two seasons a major cast change was enforced. Stafford moved to a job with Europol in Brussels and the race to replace him was won by the smart, ambitious Metropolitan Police officer, Alan Cade, another man set to ruffle feathers in Eastland. First to take umbrage was Anne, who had been overlooked for the job. Some biting home truths from Alison Dell, Cade's PR consultant, helped him sharpen up his act.

This was not a standard cops-and-robbers series. Instead of dwelling on day-to-day routine police work, it focused on the principles and policies of crime prevention, homing in on the crucial decisions that an officer at the top of the ladder has to make. For authenticity,

John Alderson, former Chief Constable of Devon and Cornwall, acted as adviser.

CHIGLEY
See **CAMBERWICK GREEN.**

CHILDREN IN NEED
UK (BBC) Telethon. BBC 1 1980–

Presenters: **Terry Wogan, Esther Rantzen, Sue Cook, Gaby Roslin**

Star-studded annual appeal marathon.

From humble origins on radio on Christmas Day 1927, *Children in Need* has progressed to become one of the highlights of the British TV year, taking over BBC 1's entire evening schedule (apart from the news) on the third Friday in November. The first major TV appeal was held in 1980, when the now established format was launched, involving seven hours of live television. Terry Wogan and Esther Rantzen (later replaced by Sue Cook, herself succeeded by Gaby Roslin) were the first hosts, with the assistance at times of Andi Peters and numerous celebrity guests. Esther Rantzen has also welcomed the year's Children of Courage, and BBC regional presenters have taken charge of the numerous opt-out segments, which have covered fund-raising events locally.

Throughout the evening, appeals for cash donations to help deprived children have been made, with running totals announced on a regular basis. Family-orientated features have filled the early part of the programme – singing chefs, dancing weathermen, soap stars out of character, etc. – with a more mellow atmosphere prevailing towards the closedown at around 2 a.m. After midnight, stars of West End shows have tended to drop in with buckets of cash collected from their own audiences. To generate further interest, novel stunts such as 3-D (a complex DOCTOR WHO meets EASTENDERS story in 1993) and 'scratch and sniff' Smell-o-Vision (1995) experiments have been attempted.

The 1980 appeal raised £1.2 million, but some years have seen in excess of £20 million filling the coffers. Reports on how the money has been spent have been shown in the following year's programme. The appeal's mascot has been Pudsey, a forlorn-looking, bandaged teddy bear.

CHINESE DETECTIVE, THE
UK (BBC) Police Drama. BBC 1 1981–2

DS Johnny Ho .... **David Yip**
DCI Berwick .... **Derek Martin**
DS Donald Chegwyn .... **Arthur Kelly**
Joe Ho .... **Robert Lee**

Creator: **Ian Kennedy Martin**
Producer: **Terence Williams**

Life on the beat for an ethnic copper.

Britain's first Chinese police hero was Detective Sgt Johnny Ho. He had joined the police partly as a means of clearing his father's name, but had been refused entry to the Metropolitan Police on grounds of height. Finding a way in elsewhere, Ho managed to work his way back to London's Limehouse district, where he found the going tough and his colleagues unsupportive. A natural loner, he encountered plenty of harassment, not least from his rigid boss, DCI Berwick, who hated his scruffy appearance and sloppy behaviour. To bring Ho back into line, he paired him with experienced sergeant Donald Chegwyn.

The Chinese Detective came from the pen of THE SWEENEY creator, Ian Kennedy Martin. Not surprisingly, the real police did not appreciate the suggestion that racism existed in the ranks, whether intentional or not.

CHIPS
US (MGM) Police Drama. ITV 1979–87

Officer Francis 'Ponch' Poncherello .... **Erik Estrada**
Officer Jonathan Baker .... **Larry Wilcox**
Sgt Joe Getraer .... **Robert Pine**
Officer Gene Fritz .... **Lew Saunders**
Officer Baricza .... **Brodie Greer**
Officer Sindy Cahill .... **Brianne Leary**
Harlan .... **Lou Wagner**
Officer Grossman .... **Paul Linke**
Officer Bonnie Clark .... **Randi Oakes**
Officer Turner .... **Michael Dorn**
Officer Steve McLeish .... **Bruce Jenner**
Officer Bobby 'Hot Dog' Nelson .... **Tom Reilly**
Officer Kathy Linahan .... **Tina Gayle**
Cadet Bruce Nelson .... **Bruce Penhall**
Officer Webster .... **Clarence Gilyard, Jr**

Creator: **Rick Rosner**
Producers: **Rick Rosner, Cy Chermak, Ric Randall**

The adventures of two hunky police motorcyclists in and around Los Angeles.

Baker and Ponch worked as a team for the California Highway Patrol (CHiPS): the fair-haired Baker was the sensible, serious one, the swarthy Ponch was his devil-may-care partner, often falling foul of their boss, Sgt Getraer. They were both single and their private lives mingled with their crime-fighting in every action-packed episode. The supporting cast included a mechanic, Harlan, and a sequence of female cops, beginning with Sindy Cahill (later replaced by Bonnie Clark and then Kathy Linahan).

At one point Erik Estrada fell into dispute with the programme's makers and was replaced by Olympic decathlon champion, Bruce Jenner, who duly made way for Estrada when the matter was resolved. Larry Wilcox was the first to make a permanent break and Baker was written out before the final season. Ponch then gained a new partner, Bobby Nelson, and Nelson's brother, Bruce, was also seen, played by another sports star, speedway rider Bruce Penhall.

CHROMA KEY

Another term for colour separation overlay, i.e. the electronic technique that allows one colour in the picture (usually blue) to be filled with another image. It has been used over the years for studio backdrops and also for crude special effects. Blue is the most popular choice as it is least common in human skin colourings.

CHRONICLE

UK (BBC) Historical Documentary. BBC 2 1966–91

Presenters: **Glyn Daniel, Magnus Magnusson**

Producers: **Paul Johnstone, Bruce Norman, Roy Davies**

New developments in the world of history and archaeology.

This monthly educational series looked at the latest findings of the world's leading archaeologists and historians. Cambridge archaeologist (and former ANIMAL, VEGETABLE, MINERAL? chairman) Glyn Daniel was the first host, with a pre-MASTERMIND Magnus Magnusson taking over later.

CHRONICLES OF NARNIA, THE

UK (BBC) Children's Drama. BBC 1 1988–90

Peter Pevensie	**Richard Dempsey**
Susan Pevensie	**Sophie Cook**
Edmund Pevensie	**Jonathan R. Scott**
Lucy Pevensie	**Sophie Wilcox**
The White Witch	**Barbara Kellerman**
Prince/King Caspian	**Jean-Marc Perret**
	Samuel West
	Geoffrey Russell
King Miraz	**Robert Lang**
Dr Cornelius	**Henry Woolf**
Reepicheep	**Warwick Davis**
Trumpkin	**Big Mick**
Eustace Scrubb	**David Thwaites**
Jill Pole	**Camilla Power**
Puddleglum	**Tom Baker**
Aslan	**Ronald Pickup** (*voice only*)

Writer: **Alan Seymour**
Producer: **Paul Stone**

Adaptations of the classic children's fantasies by C. S. Lewis.

Employing a plethora of animal costumes and extensive special effects, the BBC set out to dramatize C. S. Lewis's epic stories of the fictitious world of Narnia. In the end, four of his seven books were covered, beginning with the first, *The Lion, the Witch and the Wardrobe. Prince Caspian, Voyage of the Dawn Treader* and *The Silver Chair* followed. A particular feature was the complicated human and mechanical operation of the giant lion which represented Aslan, the awesome Narnia deity.

CHURCHILL, DONALD
(1930–91)

British actor and playwright whose writing credits included *Never a Cross Word, Moody and Pegg* (with Julia Jones), Charlie Drake's comedy, *Who Is Sylvia?* (co-written with Drake), and an adaptation of Dickens's *Our Mutual Friend.* He also wrote for series like ARMCHAIR THEATRE and THE SWEENEY. On screen, he starred in the 1958 sitcom, *Trouble for Two* (a cleaner), *Bulldog Breed* (the hapless Tom Bowler), SPOONER'S PATCH (as Inspector Spooner, succeeding Ronald Fraser), *It's Not Me – It's Them* (the constantly unemployed Albert Curfew), *The Sun Trap* (expat Peter Halliday) and *Good Night and God Bless* (as Ronnie Kemp, a game show host; also as co-writer). Among his other appearances were parts in EL C.I.D. (Metcalf), C.A.T.S. EYES, DON'T WAIT UP, BERGERAC and *Stanley and the Women.* Churchill was married to actress Pauline Yates.

CINEMA

UK (Granada) Film Review. ITV 1964–75

Presenters: **Bamber Gascoigne, Derek Granger, Michael Scott, Mark Shivas, Michael Parkinson, Clive James, Brian Trueman**

Producers: **Derek Granger, John Hamp, Peter Wildeblood, Mark Shivas**

Long-running weekly film magazine.

Eight years before Barry Norman began reviewing films in FILM 72, Granada launched its own half-hour series revolving around the world of the silver screen. *Cinema* ran for 11 years and over 500 episodes, mixing critiques of the latest releases, interviews with film celebrities and some retrospective material. A common theme or a personality linked most items. Its first host, Bamber Gascoigne, occupied the presenter's chair for just three months, and the best-remembered frontmen were later incumbents Mike Scott and Michael Parkinson. The programme's natural 'successor' was the junior film magazine, *Clapperboard* (also from Granada), hosted by Chris Kelly, which began in 1972 and ran for ten years.

CIRCUS BOY

US (Herbert B. Leonard/Screen Gems) Children's Adventure. BBC 1957–8

Corky	**Mickey Braddock**
Joey	**Noah Beery, Jr**
Big Tim Champion	**Robert Lowery**
Hank Miller	**Leo Gordon**
Little Tom	**Billy Barty**
Swifty	**Olin Howlin**
Barker	**Eddie Marr**
Pete	**Guinn Williams**
Col. Jack	**Andy Clyde**
Elmer Purdy	**Sterling Holloway**

Producers: **Herbert B. Leonard, Norman Blackburn**

*The turn-of-the-century adventures of a
12-year-old orphan taken in by a colourful
travelling circus.*

When little Corky's parents had been killed in a wire-walking act, he was adopted by Big Tim Champion, proprietor of the Champion Circus. Earning his keep by caring for Bimbo, the baby elephant, Corky was surrounded by a giant, colourful family, including Little Tom, the midget, Joey, the clown, and animals like Sultan the tiger and Nuba the lion. As the circus moved from town to town, so each story unfolded.

Mickey Braddock later achieved considerably more fame, under his real name of Dolenz, as drummer in The Monkees pop group.

CISCO KID, THE
US (The Cisco Company/Ziv) Children's Western.
BBC 1954

The Cisco Kid .... **Duncan Renaldo**
Pancho .... **Leo Carrillo**

Producer: **Philip N. Krasne**

*The exploits of a Mexican Robin Hood and his fat,
smiling sidekick.*

In the late 19th century, the Cisco Kid and his partner, Pancho, travelled around the south-western United States, helping the oppressed, thwarting bandits and steering clear of sheriffs and deputies who thought that they were outlaws. They kept violence to a minimum, with Cisco confining himself to shooting guns from his opponents' hands, sometimes aided by the totally unathletic Pancho, who was an expert with the whip.

Cisco was a ladies' man, a bit of a dandy, dressed up in finely embroidered shirts and silver spurs. He sported a giant sombrero and was quite a charmer. Pancho's only affair, however, was with his food. Cisco's horse was Diablo (with whom star Duncan Renaldo continued to make personal appearances long after the show had ended), while Pancho rode Loco; but they were two very unlikely cowboys. Their adventures were played largely for laughs and Pancho's abysmal grip of the English language was milked to the full.

The Cisco Kid was created by writer O. Henry and the character appeared in the cinema as early as the 1920s. Duncan Renaldo had already played the part in the movies before the TV series was conceived and was in his 50s by the time it was made. Leo Carrillo was even older, in his 70s. Unusually for TV series of this period, it was filmed in colour.

CITIZEN JAMES
UK (BBC) Situation Comedy. BBC 1960–2

Sidney Balmoral James .... **Sid James**
William 'Bill' Kerr .... **Bill Kerr**
Liz Fraser .... **Liz Fraser**

Charlie .... **Sydney Tafler**

Writers: **Ray Galton, Alan Simpson, Sid Green, Dick
Hills**
Producers: **Duncan Wood, John Street, Ronald Marsh**

*A London sponger takes on society and usually
gets beaten.*

Resuming his role as a Cockney layabout with contempt for authority, Sid James branched out from HANCOCK'S HALF HOUR and into this series of his own. His new sparring partners were Australian Bill Kerr and girlfriend Liz Fraser, the owner of a club. Charlie, a bookie's sidekick, was added later in the series when James set himself up as a champion of the underdog and fighter for lost causes (usually with the wrong result).

CITIZEN SMITH
UK (BBC) Situation Comedy. BBC 1 1977–80

Walter Henry 'Wolfie' Smith .... **Robert Lindsay**
Ken Mills .... **Mike Grady**
Tucker .... **Tony Millan**
Anthony 'Speed' King .... **George Sweeney**
Shirley Johnson .... **Cheryl Hall**
Charlie Johnson .... **Peter Vaughan**
                                                                    Tony Steedman
Florence Johnson .... **Hilda Braid**
Harry Fenning .... **Stephen Greif**
Ronnie Lynch .... **David Garfield**

Creator/Writer: **John Sullivan**
Producers: **Dennis Main Wilson, Ray Butt**

*The farcical exploits of a work-shy Tooting
revolutionary.*

'Power to the People!' Wolfie Smith was the Che Guevara of south-east London – or so he believed. Sporting an Afghan coat and a commando beret, he was the guitar-strumming figurehead of the Tooting Popular Front (TPF), a team of hapless Marxist freedom fighters whose members totalled six in number. His right-hand man was Ken, a weedy, vegetarian pacifist-cum-Buddhist with whom he shared a flat above the home of Charlie and Florence Johnson, the parents of Wolfie's girlfriend, Shirley. (Played by Robert Lindsay's real wife at the time, Cheryl Hall, Shirley appeared in only the first three seasons, when she worked in the Sounds Cool record shop.) Her dad, a security guard at Haydon Electronics, was an irascible social-climbing Yorkshireman who had no time for 'that bloody yeti', as he branded Wolfie. (Peter Vaughan also left the series after three years, handing the role to Tony Steedman.) His dopey wife, on the other hand, was genuinely fond of the lodger she mistakenly knew as 'Foxy'.

The other main characters in the TPF were Tucker and Speed. Tucker, a nervous family man with a formidable wife (June) and nine kids, owned the van the gang used for their 'manoeuvres'. Speed was the team's hard man, a brainless, violent thug who drifted in and out of jail. Lurking in the background was the manor's Mr Big, Harry Fenning, who was owner of Wolfie's local, The

Vigilante. Fenning was replaced in the last series by the just as nasty, but cruelly hen-pecked, Welsh gangster, Ronnie Lynch.

Wolfie's cack-handed attempts at liberating the proletariat, in between shirking jobs and cadging pints, provided the focus for the series. 'Come the glorious day,' he threatened, his enemies would be lined up against the wall for a 'last fag,' then 'bop, bop, bop,' the struggle would be over. But with such inept ideas and such gormless allies, capitalism was never in any danger. After all, who was going to take notice of a revolutionary who rode a scooter?

Citizen Smith was John Sullivan's big break. The writer of ONLY FOOLS AND HORSES, JUST GOOD FRIENDS, DEAR JOHN, etc., was working as a scene shifter at the BBC at the time. Convinced he could produce something better than the humourless sitcoms he was watching, he created the character of an ageing hippie turned working-class hero, whose support for Fulham FC was yet another lost cause. The script was taken up for an episode of COMEDY PLAYHOUSE in 1977 (in which Artro Morris played Shirley's dad) and a full series was commissioned the same year.

CIVILISATION
UK (BBC) Documentary. BBC 2 1969

Presenter: **Kenneth Clark**

Producers: **Michael Gill, Peter Montagnon**

A chronicle of human cultural development and the benefits and comforts it has brought to the world.

This documentary looked at history not from a perspective of dates and battles but through the ideas and values that shaped humankind over the centuries. Charting developments since the Dark Ages, Kenneth Clark's aim was to show viewers, through examples of art and architecture, how man had risen above the common beast, how he had discovered 'Civilisation'. The work was inspired by a fear that man was slipping back into moral chaos and, by profiling men of genius – painters, thinkers, poets and musicians, people who had brought order to our lives – Clark sought to prove that we really were above all the hassles of the modern-day industrial society. Presented in an old-fashioned, simple style, shunning clever TV gimmickry and relying on good prose over well-framed images, the series was a remarkable success, especially considering the contemporary climate in which Andy Warhol, Jackson Pollock, The Beatles and Flower Power had asserted their heavy influence. Clark, a highbrow, learned art historian and former Chairman of the Independent Television Authority, became an unlikely TV hero, a status he did not in the least relish.

CLANGERS
UK (Smallfilms) Children's Entertainment. BBC 1 1969–74

Creators/Writers/Producers: **Oliver Postgate, Peter Firmin**

The moral adventures of the mousey inhabitants of a blue planet.

Strange, pink and woolly, the Clangers were mouse-like creatures with pronounced noses and perky ears who lived inside a small blue planet. They wore personal suits of armour for protection from the many meteorites that broke through the thin atmosphere, and they took their name from the sound made when they battened down their dustbin-lid hatches and retreated underground. The Clangers spoke only in musical whistles – to each other and to the other inhabitants of their planet, the Soup Dragon and the Froglets. The Soup Dragon lived in the soup wells, where the Clangers' staple diet was obtained (they also ate Blue String Pudding), while the Froglets were small orange amphibians who lived in a deep pond and travelled around in a top hat. Also seen was the Iron Chicken (and its chick), a metal bird that nested a little way out in space. The Clangers themselves were Major and Mother Clanger, Grandmother, Small and Tiny.

The Clangers' world was a little haven of peace and happiness. Apart from minor concerns like how to pick notes from music trees to propel Major Clanger's boat, their only worries were occasional disturbances from aliens or stray alien inventions. These instances were used to moral effect, revealing just how happy uncluttered, modest lives could be.

This five-minute, pre-evening news animation came from the Smallfilms duo of Oliver Postgate and Peter Firmin, who were also responsible for NOGGIN THE NOG, POGLES' WOOD, BAGPUSS and IVOR THE ENGINE.

CLAPPERBOARD
See CINEMA.

CLAPPERBOARD

A hinged marker board used during filming to indicate the title of the programme, the scene and the take. The board is hinged to allow its two parts to be 'clapped' together at the start of the take, the noise of the clap then being used to synchronize sound and vision tracks in editing. New electronic systems have gradually undermined the clapperboard's usefulness.

CLARENCE
UK (BBC) Situation Comedy. BBC 1 1988

Clarence Sale .... **Ronnie Barker**
Jane Travers .... **Josephine Tewson**

Writer: **Bob Ferris**
Producer: **Mike Stephens**

A short-sighted removals man sets up home in the country with an out-of-work parlourmaid.

Londoner Clarence Sale, a middle-aged, self-employed removals man with his own company (Get A Move On), was clumsy and short-sighted. Not that this did anything to dampen his confidence. Meeting up with Jane Travers, an unemployed parlourmaid to the rich, on Coronation Day 1937, he took her back to his Peckham flat for some fish and chips. There they began a gentle romance that developed when they moved out to the Oxfordshire countryside, taking up residence in a rundown cottage Travers had inherited from her aunt. The ensuing episodes revolved around Clarence's attempts to bed Travers, their acclimatization in the country and Clarence's abysmal eyesight.

The series was written by Ronnie Barker under the pseudonym of Bob Ferris.

CLARK, LORD KENNETH
(1903–83)

London-born art historian whose 13-part CIVILISATION in 1969 was fêted as a television masterpiece. The spin-off book proved equally profitable for the BBC and was one of the first successful 'TV tie-ins'. Earlier in his life Clark had been Director of the National Gallery, worked for the Ministry of Information in World War II, assumed the chairmanship of the Arts Council and then became first Chairman of the Independent Television Authority (1954–7). In 1964 he presented the series, *Great Temples of the World*, and among his other contributions were talks on Rembrandt and series like *Landscape Into Art*, *Discovering Japanese Art*, *Pioneers of Modern Painting* and *Romantic v. Classic Art*. He was made a life peer in 1969 and one of his sons was the late Conservative MP, Alan Clark.

CLARKE, MARGI
(1954–)

Liverpudlian actress, a former Granada presenter (*What's On*), mostly seen in coarse, down-to-earth roles such as Queenie in MAKING OUT and CORONATION STREET's Jackie Dobbs. Her GOOD SEX GUIDE in 1993 caused quite a stir, and she also appeared in the two-part drama, *Soul Survivors* (Connie). Clarke is the sister of scriptwriter/director Frank Clarke (who wrote the film drama, *Letter to Brezhnev*, that gave Margi her break).

CLARKE, ROY
(1930–)

British comedy writer responsible for such series as THE MISFIT, LAST (and *First*) OF THE SUMMER WINE, OPEN ALL HOURS, ROSIE, THE MAGNIFICENT EVANS, *Mann's Best Friends*, *Flickers*, *Pulaski*, POTTER, *The Clairvoyant*, KEEPING UP APPEARANCES, *Don't Tell Father*, *The Sharp End*, *Ain't Misbehavin'* and *Spark*. His humour is of the gentle nature, relying on shrewd observation of character, and most of his work has been set in his native Yorkshire. Clarke has also contributed to drama series like MR ROSE and THE TROUBLESHOOTERS, and he wrote the *Screen One* drama, *A Foreign Field*.

CLARKE, WARREN
(Alan Clarke; 1947–)

Lancashire-born actor, best known as cop Andy Dalziel in DALZIEL AND PASCOE but seen in a variety of roles (including comic) and most notably in SOFTLY, SOFTLY (DS Stirling), SHELLEY (Paul), *The Home Front*, THE JEWEL IN THE CROWN (Sophie Dixon), THE ONEDIN LINE (Josiah Beaumont), JENNIE, LADY RANDOLPH CHURCHILL (Winston Churchill), *The Manageress*, *Nice Work* (Vic Wilcox), *All Good Things* (Phil Frame), *Gone to the Dogs* (Larry Patterson), *Gone to Seed* (Winston), *All in the Game* (Kenny Dawes), *Conjugal Rites* (voice of Toby the dog), *The House of Windsor* (Max Kelvin), *Moving Story* (Bamber), *A Respectable Trade* (Josiah Cole), *The Locksmith* (Roland Pierce), *Giving Tongue* (Pollin), *In the Red* (George Cragge), *The Mystery of Men* (Vernon) and *Down to Earth* (Brian Addis). His guest appearances have been many (including as Elsie Tanner's nephew, Gary, in CORONATION STREET).

CLARKSON, JEREMY
(1960–)

Forthright, Doncaster-born motoring presenter who made his name in TOP GEAR and has moved on to front his own series, like *Jeremy Clarkson's Motorworld*, *Jeremy Clarkson's Extreme Machines*, *Clarkson's Car Years* and the chat show, *Clarkson*, as well as the mechanical combat contest, *Robot Wars*. He is a cousin of TV doctor Mark Porter.

CLARY, JULIAN
(1959–)

Surbiton-born camp comedian specializing in *double entendres* and innuendo. His TV break came in the game show, *Trick or Treat*, in which he was billed as The Joan Collins Fan Club and was accompanied by his pet, Fanny the Wonderdog. He has since advanced to his own series, such as *Sticky Moments with Julian Clary*, the sitcom *Terry and Julian*, *All Rise for Julian Clary*, *Mr and Mrs with Julian Clary* and *Prickly Heat* (the last for Sky), and has also been a team captain in the comedy quiz, *It's Only TV But I Like It*. Another game show he piloted in both the UK and US, called *In the Dark*, never made it to a series. Clary also appeared in the feature-length comedy, *Brazen Hussies* ('Man in the Moon').

CLEESE, JOHN
(1939–)

Tall, Somerset-born actor/comedian/writer, a Cambridge Footlights graduate who was already a TV legend thanks to MONTY PYTHON'S FLYING CIRCUS when achieving even greater acclaim for his manic FAWLTY TOWERS (star and co-writer with then wife, Connie Booth). Pre-*Python*, Cleese had appeared with Ronnies Barker and Corbett in THE FROST REPORT, and with Graham Chapman *et al.* in AT LAST THE 1948 SHOW. He later supported Les Dawson in SEZ LES. Cleese also wrote (mostly in collaboration with Chapman) for David Frost, THAT WAS THE WEEK THAT WAS, *Broaden Your Mind*, *Marty* and the DOCTOR IN THE HOUSE series. His numerous guest appearances have taken in shows as diverse as WHOOPS APOCALYPSE, CHEERS, THE AVENGERS, THE GOODIES, DOCTOR WHO and THE MUPPET SHOW, although in recent years film work has taken over. He did, however, indulge his fascination with lemurs in a *Born To Be Wild* expedition to Madagascar in 1998.

CLEMENS, BRIAN
(1931–)

British producer and scriptwriter, whose work for ITC in the 1960s earned him a real following among fans of TV adventure. By far his greatest impact was in THE AVENGERS, although he also contributed to THE MAN FROM INTERPOL, THE INVISIBLE MAN, DANGER MAN, ADAM ADAMANT LIVES!, THE CHAMPIONS, THE PERSUADERS!, THE PROTECTORS and BERGERAC, as well as creating THE PROFESSIONALS and the suspense anthology, THRILLER, and co-creating the sitcom, MY WIFE NEXT DOOR (with Richard Waring). Clemens was also series consultant on the high-tech action drama, BUGS.

CLEMENT, DICK
(1937–)

British writer and producer, partner of Ian La Frenais and creator of some of British television's classic comedies. After working as a producer on shows like NOT ONLY ... BUT ALSO ..., Clement teamed up with Geordie insurance salesman La Frenais and scripted a series about two young pals from Newcastle, THE LIKELY LADS, which became one of BBC 2's first hits and was successfully revived in the 1970s as WHATEVER HAPPENED TO THE LIKELY LADS?. The duo went on to create PORRIDGE, and their success continued into the 1980s with AUF WIEDERSEHEN, PET. Among their other offerings over the years have been THE FURTHER ADVENTURES OF LUCKY JIM (two versions), *Mr Aitch*, THICK AS THIEVES, *Mog* and the *Porridge* sequel, *Going Straight*. In the 1990s they penned the limousine-for-hire drama, *Full Stretch*, and the sitcoms *Freddie and Max*, *Old Boy Network* and *Over the Rainbow*, the last inspired by their own screenplay for the film, *The Commitments*. They also contributed episodes to SHINE ON HARVEY MOON and Billy Connolly's US series, *Billy*, as well as material for Tracey Ullman. La Frenais (without Clement) has also adapted Jonathan Gash's LOVEJOY novels for television, co-created SPENDER with Jimmy Nail and contributed to the 1972 sitcom, *The Train Now Standing*. Together and separately, they have worked as script editors on several other programmes.

CLEOPATRAS, THE
UK (BBC) Drama. BBC 2 1983

Cleopatra	Michelle Newell
Pot Belly	Richard Griffiths
Cleopatra II	Elizabeth Shepherd
Cleopatra Thea	Caroline Mortimer
Cleopatra IV	Sue Holderness
Cleopatra Tryphaena	Amanda Boxer
Cleopatra Selene	Prue Clarke
Cleopatra Berenike	Pauline Moran
Chickpea	David Horovitch
Alexander	Ian McNeice
Theodotus	Graham Crowden
Fluter	Adam Bareham
Mark Antony	Christopher Neame
Julius Caesar	Robert Hardy
Charmian	Shirin Taylor
Arsinoe	Francesca Gonshaw
Iras	Carole Harrison

Writer: **Philip Mackie**
Producer: **Guy Slater**

The history of Greek rule in ancient Egypt.

This wry, 'horror-comic' look at the unscrupulous, incestuous dynasty of Greek women who ruled Egypt from 145 BC to 35 BC was played rather deadpan. The aim was to avoid flippancy but also to skip over the more grotesque incidents. In eight parts, the story of the Cleopatras was told by the last Cleo (played by Michelle Newell, who also played her great-grandmother), and flashed back to her six ruthless ancestors of the same name. Also involved in the sordid goings-on was the flabby Pot Belly. Dozens of brave girls with little hair and even less clothing wobbled around in the background. Actress Amanda Boxer even shaved her head for her role. Sadly, the series failed to achieve respect and suffered the ridicule of both critics and viewers.

CLIVE JAMES – FAME IN THE TWENTIETH CENTURY
UK (BBC) Documentary. BBC 1 1993

Writer/Presenter: **Clive James**
Producer: **Beatrice Ballard**

An eight-part, decade-by-decade look at the famous and infamous in the 20th century.

In this nostalgic series, Clive James, with his usual wry observation, looked back over the 20th century, the first century to experience the power of mass media and all its fame-creating potential. He scrutinized the people who had made the news and gained celebrity status in each decade, examining how and why they came to the fore. He then scratched away the veneer to reveal the truth behind the headlines. Archive footage traced the lives of leading politicians, film stars, criminals and pioneers, from Charlie Chaplin and Mahatma Gandhi to Madonna and Norman Schwarzkopf.

CLOCHEMERLE

UK (BBC/Bavaria Atelier) Comedy. BBC 2 1972

Mayor Barthélemy Piechut	**Cyril Cusack**
Curé Ponosse	**Roy Dotrice**
Ernest Tafardel	**Kenneth Griffith**
Justine Putet	**Wendy Hiller**
Adèle Torbayon	**Cyd Hayman**
The Baroness Courtebiche	**Micheline Presle**
Alexandre Bourdillat	**Hugh Griffith**
Nicholas the Beadle	**Bernard Bresslaw**
Hortense Girodot	**Madeline Smith**
Monsieur Girodot	**Wolfe Morris**
Rose Bivaque	**Georgina Moon**
Narrator	**Peter Ustinov**

Writers: **Ray Galton, Alan Simpson**
Producer: **Michael Mills**

*Plans to install a new pissoir in a French village
result in civil unrest.*

Gabriel Chevallier's 1934 comedy was adapted by Ray
Galton and Alan Simpson in nine parts to create this
gentle farce. It concerned the good people of Clochemerle who found themselves divided over plans to open
a new urinal in the centre of the small French village.
Reaction from the snootier members of society, and
especially the prim ladyfolk, reached such a peak that
the army was called in to quell the unrest. Filmed in
France, in the village of Marchampt in Beaujolais, the
series attracted a celebrated cast of both British and
French performers.

CLOONEY, GEORGE

(1961–)

American actor attaining star status thanks largely to his
role as Dr Doug Ross in ER. Previously, Clooney had been
seen as Booker Brooks in ROSEANNE, as well as in several
other US sitcoms (including one called, strangely, *E/R*),
the soap, *Sisters*, and the police dramas *Bodies of Evidence*
and *Sunset Beat*, most of which never aired in the UK.
He is the nephew of 1950s singer Rosemary Clooney and
the son of Nick Clooney, a TV presenter and variety
host. He was once married to actress Talia Balsam.

CLOSE DOWN

In the days before 24-hour television, the final
announcement of the TV day, often involving a look at
the clock, a preview of the next day's fare and a rendition of the national anthem and the station sig-
nature-tune.

CLOSED CIRCUIT

A television system that is not broadcast but transmitted
via a sequence of cables or by microwaves to a restricted
number of receivers. It is generally in use in educational
establishments, but has been used for showing major
sporting or entertainment events to a limited audience
in theatres or stadia.

CLOSE-UP

A detailed shot of an object or, more commonly, a head-
and-shoulders shot of the presenter or actor.

CLOSING TITLES

The roll-call of performers' and technicians' credits seen
at the end of a television programme or film.

CLUEDO

UK (Granada/Action Time) Game Show. ITV 1990–3

Season One:

Host	**James Bellini**
Mrs Peacock	**Stephanie Beacham**
Mrs White	**June Whitfield**
Col. Mustard	**Robin Ellis**
Miss Scarlett	**Tracy-Louise Ward**
Revd Green	**Robin Nedwell**
Prof. Plum	**Kristoffer Tabori**

Season Two:

Host	**Chris Tarrant**
Mrs Peacock	**Rula Lenska**
Mrs White	**Mollie Sugden**
Col. Mustard	**Michael Jayston**
Miss Scarlett	**Koo Stark**
Revd Green	**Richard Wilson**
Prof. Plum	**David McCallum**

Season Three:

Host	**Richard Madeley**
Mrs Peacock	**Susan George**
Mrs White	**Pam Ferris**
Col. Mustard	**Lewis Collins**
Miss Scarlett	**Lysette Anthony**
Revd Green	**Christopher Biggins**
Prof. Plum	**Tom Baker**

Season Four:

Host	**Richard Madeley**
Mrs Peacock	**Joanna Lumley**
Mrs White	**Liz Smith**
Col. Mustard	**Leslie Grantham**
Ms Scarlett	**Jerry Hall**
Revd Green	**Nicholas Parsons**
Prof. Plum	**John Bird**

Executive Producer: **Dianne Nelmes**
Producers: **Stephen Leahy, Brian Park, Kieran Roberts,
Mark Gorton**

Celebrity whodunnit, based on the enormously successful board game invented by Anthony Pratt in 1944.

In this light-hearted, studio-bound mystery, a murder was committed each week at Arlington Grange (not at Tudor Close, as in the board game), a house owned by society widow Mrs Peacock. What the two teams of two celebrities had to do was work out whodunnit, where in the house and with what weapon, having viewed the video evidence and closely questioned the suspects. Apart from Mrs Peacock, there were also the flighty Miss Scarlett, housekeeper Mrs White, retired military man Colonel Mustard, decidedly dodgy vicar Reverend Green and eccentric Professor Plum. The cast changed every season, including for a 1990 Christmas special, which saw Kate O'Mara as Mrs Peacock, Joan Sims as Mrs White, Toyah Wilcox as Miss Scarlett, David Robb as Colonel Mustard, Derek Nimmo as Reverend Green and Ian Lavender in the role of Professor Plum. James Bellini hosted this one-off. The series was not entirely dissimilar to the earlier WHODUNNIT?.

CLUFF

UK (BBC) Police Drama. BBC 1 1964–5

DS Caleb Cluff	**Leslie Sands**
Insp. Mole	**Eric Barker**
	Michael Bates
DC Barker	**John Rolfe**
PC Harry Bullock	**John McKelvey**
Annie Croft	**Olive Milbourne**

Creator: **Gil North**
Producer: **Terence Dudley**

Easy-paced policing with an old-fashioned Yorkshire detective.

Caleb Cluff was a traditional sort of copper. Not for him the exhausting business of tearing around after criminals, largely because there weren't that many where he lived (fictional Gunnershaw) at that time (the early 1960s). No, this detective was painfully slow about his business, much to the annoyance of his superior, Inspector Mole, but he was also good at his job, probably because he was so thorough and took time to get to know everyone. His young sidekick, DC Barker, certainly benefited from his methodical approach.

The tweed-suited Cluff's idea of fun was a good walk, with a pipe in his mouth, chestnut walking stick in his hand and Clive, his loyal black-and-tan dog, at his side. He lived alone, and was looked after by a daily housekeeper, Annie Croft. Created by Gil North, the character had first appeared as part of the DETECTIVE anthology series.

CLUNES, MARTIN

(1962–)

London-born actor-director, the son of the late classical actor, Alec Clunes. His first major TV role came in DOC-TOR WHO and Clunes then moved on to specialize in upper-class roles, although his greatest success has been in quite a different vein, as '90s lad Gary Strang in MEN BEHAVING BADLY. His other major roles have been in *All at Number 20* (lodger Henry), NO PLACE LIKE HOME (son Nigel Crabtree), JEEVES AND WOOSTER (Barmy Fotheringay Phipps), *Demob* (ex-army entertainer Dick Dobson), *An Evening with Gary Lineker* (Dan), *Touch and Go* (wifeswapper Nick Wood), *Over Here* (Group Captain Barker), *Hunting Venus* (New Romantic has-been Simon Delancey, also as director), *Sex 'n' Death* (TV show host Ben Black), *Gormenghast* (Professor Flower), *Dirty Tricks* (Edward), *Lorna Doone* (Jeremy Stickles) and the panto-mime, *Aladdin* (Abanazer), with guest parts in series like *About Face*, HANNAY, BOON, INSPECTOR MORSE, LOVE-JOY, *Gone to the Dogs*, *Rik Mayall Presents*, *Rides*, *Bonjour La Classe* and *Moving Story*. In 2000 he presented the documentary series, *Men Down Under*, with Neil Morrissey.

CNN

(Cable News Network)

CNN was founded in Atlanta by Ted Turner in 1980, against the advice of experts of the day who believed that a dedicated, round-the-clock news channel could not survive in the limited world of cable. Indeed, the first few years in the company's history were unremark-able and it was not until 1985 that it enjoyed its first year in profit. In 1982 a second channel, majoring on continuous 30-minute news summaries and known initially as CNN-2, was launched; it is now called CNN Headline News. In 1985 a third channel, with a global rather than American bias, was opened up. Called CNN International, it is this channel that can be seen all around the planet and that has led the field in inter-national news-gathering and -dissemination. Its unique-ness was underscored by the outbreak of the Gulf War in 1991, when CNN became the channel to watch for 'as it happens' reports on air raids and other unfolding events. CNN International has been supplied to hotels and other broadcasting stations since its earliest days and became available to European homes via the Astra satellite system in 1992 and later via digital services.

COHEN, SACHA BARON

(1970–)

Cambridge history graduate (and Footlights member) Sacha Baron Cohen shot to fame in 1998 in Channel 4's late night comedy offering *The 11 O'Clock Show*, with his wickedly satirical creation, Ali G. Allegedly a black youth (though clearly white) from Staines, Ali G adopted black American slang and teased politicians and other authori-tarian figures with patently stupid questions that they could not afford to dismiss. But the 'hipness' of British youth culture was as much ridiculed as the pomp of celebrity and power. The fact that 'Ali G' was an abbrevi-ation of the name Alistair Graham underlined how tongue-in-cheek the characterisation was. Highlights of Cohen's performances were edited together in *Da Best* of *Ali G* and then in 2000 he gained his own series, *Da Ali G Show*. He has also progressed to other comic creations, including Kazakhstani TV reporter, Borat Karabzhanov, seen exploring English culture in the one-off *The Best of Borat* in 2001. An early TV appearance for Cohen came in *Jack and Jeremy's Police 4* in 1995, a sketch show in which he supported Jack Dee and Jeremy Hardy.

COLBOURNE, MAURICE
(Roger Middleton; 1939–89)

Determined-looking British actor whose big TV break came as John Kline in the violent GANGSTERS series. However, it is as Tom Howard in the maritime soap, HOWARDS' WAY, that he is best remembered, and it was while working on the fifth series of the show that he died of a heart attack. Among his other credits were *The Day of the Triffids*, the part of Charles Marston in THE ONEDIN LINE and guest spots in SHOESTRING, DOCTOR WHO, VAN DER VALK and THE RETURN OF THE SAINT.

COLBYS, THE
US (Aaron Spelling) Drama. BBC 1 1986–7

Jason Colby	**Charlton Heston**
Sable Scott Colby	**Stephanie Beacham**
Francesca Scott Colby/Langdon	**Katherine Ross**
Jeff Colby	**John James**
Fallon Carrington/Colby	**Emma Samms**
Monica Colby	**Tracy Scoggins**
Miles Colby	**Maxwell Caulfield**
Bliss Colby	**Claire Yarlett**
Zachary Powers	**Ricardo Montalban**
Constance Colby	**Barbara Stanwyck**
Lord Roger Langdon	**David Hedison**
Garrett Boydston	**Ken Howard**
Hutch Corrigan	**Joseph Campanella**
Sean McAllister	**Charles Van Eman**
Channing Carter/Colby	**Kim Morgan Greene**
Senator Cash Cassidy	**James Houghton**
Adrienne Cassidy	**Shanna Reed**
Hoyt Parker/Phillip Colby	**Michael Parks**

Creator: **Aaron Spelling**
Writers: **Robert Pollock, Eileen Pollock**
Producers: **Richard Shapiro, Esther Shapiro**

Glamorous spin-off from DYNASTY, *initially entitled* Dynasty II – The Colbys.

This soap was set in Los Angeles, around the wealthy Colby family, who had been introduced in a few episodes of *Dynasty* before being left to their own devices. The central character was Jason Colby, head of Colby Enterprises, a company with a finger in more than one pie. Oil, real estate, aeronautics and shipping all contributed to its success. Similar to *Dynasty*'s Blake Carrington in many respects, Jason was proud, ruthless and exceptionally rich, not that that made him or his family particularly happy. His wife, Sable, was usually in the thick of the action, fighting with her sister, Frankie, and attempting to murder Constance, Jason's sister, who

was the matriarch of Belvedere, the family's estate. The younger generation were represented by Miles (Jason and Sable's son), Monica (their elder daughter), and Bliss (their younger daughter). The link with *Dynasty* came through the character of Jeff Colby, who was Frankie's son and Jason's nephew (though later revealed to be his son, too).

The Colbys ran the gamut of the usual soap stories – illicit affairs, divorce, terminal illness, inheritance disputes, acts of vengeance and commercial wrangles – and introduced a host of temporary characters. But it also took the genre to higher planes (or lower depths, depending on the point of view) when Fallon, Jeff's love from *Dynasty* (who had already been resurrected from a fatal plane crash and had married Miles in a fit of amnesia), witnessed the landing of a UFO and was whisked away to galaxies new. This was meant to be an end-of-season cliffhanger, but *The Colbys* never came back. Despite the enormous sums of money spent on performers, clothes and sets, the ratings were disastrous. It was left to *Dynasty* to bring Fallon back down to Earth.

COLD FEET
UK (Granada) Comedy Drama. ITV 1998–

Adam Williams	**James Nesbitt**
Rachel Bradley	**Helen Baxendale**
Pete Gifford	**John Thomson**
Jenny Gifford	**Fay Ripley**
David Marsden	**Robert Bathurst**
Karen Marsden	**Hermione Norris**

Creator: **Mike Bullen**
Writers: **Mike Bullen, David Nicholls**
Executive Producers: **Andy Harries, Christine Langan, Mike Bullen**
Producers: **Christine Langan, Spencer Campbell**

Ups and downs in the lives of three middle-class thirtysomething couples.

Variously described as 'FRIENDS with children' and 'THIS LIFE with laughs', *Cold Feet* focused on three comfortably-off couples in their 30s, drawing humour from their day-to-day travails and the efforts they made (or didn't) to work at their relationships. Couple number one were Adam, a systems analyst, and Rachel, an advertising executive, who met in the pilot episode, shown at Easter 1997 – 'Cold Feet' referring to his continual fear of commitment. Their friends were insurance clerk Pete and stay-at-home Jenny, trying to conceive in the pilot but giving birth at the start of the first series. Sleepless nights and other baby matters filled their life. Completing the sextet were David and Karen, he a well-heeled, career-dominated management consultant, she a book editor who had given up work to care for their baby son, Joshua, and who now found home life boring. The setting, refreshingly, was Manchester, not London, and there were technical innovations, too, with overlapping scenes and the use of flashbacks providing a novel twist.

Despite winning Montreux's celebrated Golden Rose for the pilot programme, *Cold Feet* almost didn't make it into a series, having performed poorly audience-wise in a late time-slot. However, when it eventually returned, it proved to be one of ITV's major hits of the late 1990s. A second series in 1999 continued to explore the deterioration in each relationship, dealing with adultery, depression and sickness, among other 'difficult' subjects. A more upbeat third series aired in autumn 2000.

COLDITZ

UK (BBC/Universal) Drama. BBC 1 1972–4

Lt. Col. John Preston	**Jack Hedley**
Capt. Pat Grant	**Edward Hardwicke**
Flt Lt./Major Phil Carrington	**Robert Wagner**
Flt Lt. Simon Carter	**David McCallum**
Kommandant	**Bernard Hepton**
Lt. Dick Player	**Christopher Neame**
Capt. George Brent	**Paul Chapman**
Hauptmann Ulmann	**Hans Meyer**
Capt. Tim Downing	**Richard Heffer**
Pilot Officer Muir	**Peter Penry-Jones**
Major Horst Mohn	**Anthony Valentine**
Squadron Leader Tony Shaw	**Jeremy Kemp**
Lt. Col. Max Dodd	**Dan O'Herlihy**

Creators: **Brian Degas, Gerard Glaister**
Producer: **Gerard Glaister**

Prisoners of war attempt to flee an escape-proof German castle.

Based on the book by Major Pat Reid, a genuine survivor of Colditz who acted as technical adviser, this series followed the adventurous bids for freedom of a group of high-level Allied POWs, most of whom had already succeeded in escaping from other prison camps. After an initial three episodes which showed how all the main characters had arrived at Castle Colditz (a supposedly impregnable fortress, known as Oflag IV C, perched high on sheer cliffs in eastern Germany), the series settled down into a portrayal of the rivalry and suspicions that existed among the various Allied nationalities. Their relationship with their German captors was also in focus. Although a mutual respect grew between the POWs, led by the British Lt. Col. Preston, and the camp's tolerant Kommandant, friction increased when the SS threatened to take over the castle and when, in the second series, the sadistic Major Mohn was introduced.

The desperate escape plans included launching homemade gliders off the castle roof, as well as the more conventional guard impersonations and wall scalings. One inmate, Wing Commander Marsh, worked on insanity as a means of getting out. He succeeded but, when finally freed, the stress of acting mad had actually warped his mind. Guest stars came and went, and the progress of the war outside the castle walls was used as a backdrop to events in the closed world of Colditz itself. The series concluded with liberation in 1945.

Colditz revived the flagging career of Robert Wagner, who played Canadian airman Phil Carrington. The series also led to a variety of spin-off ventures, ranging from bizarre holidays at the real castle to a children's board game. The inspiration had been the 1955 film, *The Colditz Story*, starring John Mills and Eric Portman.

COLE, GEORGE
OBE (1925–)

For most viewers, London-born George Cole is, and always will be, Arthur Daley. Though his TV work has been prolific and varied, his portrayal of MINDER's Cockney spiv with a lock-up full of dodgy goods and a fine line in persuasive banter has dwarfed all his other contributions to the small screen. Cole came to television after a successful stage, radio and film career in which he worked closely with Alastair Sim, and his profile as a rather unreliable, Jack-the-lad figure was established by the St Trinian's films, in which he played Flash Harry. In 1960, his radio role of David Bliss, in the comedy A LIFE OF BLISS, moved to television, and Cole never looked back. He went on to star in *A Man of Our Times* (Max Osborne), DON'T FORGET TO WRITE (Gordon Maple), THE BOUNDER (Trevor), BLOTT ON THE LANDSCAPE (Sir Giles Lynchwood), *Comrade Dad* (Reg Dudgeon), *Root Into Europe* (Henry Root), *My Good Friend* (Peter Banks), *Dad* (Brian Hook) and *An Independent Man* (Freddie Patterson), as well as appearing in programmes as diverse as THE GOLD ROBBERS, UFO, *The Voyage of Charles Darwin*, *Natural Causes*, *Heggerty Haggerty* and *The Sleeper* (George Gleeson), plus numerous single dramas.

COLE, JOHN
(1927–)

Northern Ireland-born BBC political editor 1981–92. Cole began his journalistic career with the *Belfast Telegraph*, before joining the *Guardian* in 1956 and moving on to the *Observer* in 1975. In the 1980s he was one of the most familiar faces (and voices) on British television, earning great respect from both viewers and politicians. Cole has also been seen on WHAT THE PAPERS SAY and has compiled some reports for HOLIDAY. His TV memoirs, *A Progress Through Politics*, were shown in 1995.

COLE, STEPHANIE
(1941–)

Warwickshire-born actress, usually seen as a hardheaded female, as exemplified by the roles of Dr Beatrice Mason in TENKO and Diana Trent in WAITING FOR GOD. She was also Mrs Featherstone, a grouchy customer in OPEN ALL HOURS, Sarah Mincing in the children's series, *Return of the Antelope*, Betty Sillitoe in A BIT OF A DO and the senile Peggy in *Keeping Mum*. Cole has also appeared in *Tropic*, *About Face*, AGATHA CHRISTIE'S POIROT and performed one of Alan Bennett's TALKING HEADS monologues.

COLEMAN, CHARLOTTE
(1968–)

British actress, the daughter of actress Ann Beach and sister of actress Lisa Coleman. Charlotte began acting at the age of eight and has moved on to star in WORZEL GUMMIDGE (Sue Peters), *Educating Marmalade* and *Danger – Marmalade at Work* (Marmalade Atkins), ORANGES ARE NOT THE ONLY FRUIT (Jess), *Freddie and Max* (Freddie), *Giving Tongue* (Barb Gale) and *How Do You Want Me?* (Lisa Lyons), with smaller roles in dramas and comedies like *Oliver's Travels* (Cathy) and *Gayle's World*.

COLEMAN, DAVID
OBE (1926–)

Former journalist and Cheshire mile champion who has been one of the BBC's most prominent sports commentators and presenters since the 1950s. Previously editor of the *Cheshire County Express* and a radio presenter, Coleman established himself as a BBC political reporter, then as contributor to *Sports Special*, before becoming main host of GRANDSTAND and one of MATCH OF THE DAY's commentary team. He then took on his own midweek sports magazine, *Sportsnight With Coleman* (later *Sportsnight*). Over the years he has become known for his detailed background research (put to good use when ad-libbing on *Grandstand* during the teleprinter results spot, for instance) and for the rather unfortunate turn of phrase which has given rise to the neologism, 'Colemanballs' (thanks to *Private Eye*). He currently specializes in athletics commentary and was the chairman of A QUESTION OF SPORT 1979–97.

COLIN'S SANDWICH
UK (BBC) Situation Comedy. BBC 2 1988–90

Colin Watkins .... **Mel Smith**
Jenny Anderson .... **Louisa Rix**
Des .... **Mike Grady**
Mr Travers .... **Andrew Robertson**
Trevor Blacklock .... **Tony Haase**
Graham .... **Lee Cornes**
Sarah .... **Jane Booker**
John Langley .... **Michael Medwin**
Alan Hunter .... **Nicholas Ball**

Writers: **Paul Smith, Terry Kyan**
Producer: **John Kilby**

An under-achieving British Rail clerk lacks the conviction to build a new career as a writer.

Described by some as 'Hancock for the 1980s', *Colin's Sandwich* revolved around the efforts of terminal worryguts Colin Watkins to balance his daytime job in the British Rail complaints department with a fledgling career as a writer of thriller stories. The acceptance of one of his tales for the *Langley Book of Horror* did nothing

to ease the pressure as Colin toyed with the idea of becoming a professional scribe. Later episodes saw Colin still holding down his BR position while struggling to pen a screenplay for pig-ignorant, cult film director Alan Hunter. Colin's girlfriend, Jenny, bore the brunt of his neurotic, self-questioning rants, while his anoraky pal, Des, and other yuppie acquaintances, like the love-lorn Sarah, just got in the way. At work, his moronic colleagues, Trevor and Graham, and his delegating boss, Mr Travers, helped drive Watkins further round the bend.

COLLINS, JOAN
OBE (1933–)

London-born movie actress of the 1950s and 1960s who hit the big time through raunchy films and glossy television in the 1970s. Her most prominent role has been as the vicious Alexis Carrington/Colby in DYNASTY, making her queen of the soap bitches. Among her other TV credits (most as a guest) have been THE HUMAN JUNGLE, THE VIRGINIAN, THE MAN FROM UNCLE, BATMAN, STAR TREK, MISSION: IMPOSSIBLE, *Orson Welles Great Mysteries*, SPACE: 1999, THE PERSUADERS!, STARSKY AND HUTCH, FANTASY ISLAND, TALES OF THE UNEXPECTED, *Monte Carlo* and *Sins* (a mini-series produced by her own company). She is the sister of novelist Jackie Collins and was once married to entertainer Anthony Newley (one of four husbands).

COLLINS, LEWIS
(1946–)

British actor whose television break came alongside Diane Keen and David Roper in THE CUCKOO WALTZ, playing unwanted lodger Gavin Rumsey. After this came THE PROFESSIONALS, in which as Bodie he was teamed up with Martin Shaw's Doyle. His other appearances have included parts in WARSHIP, THE NEW AVENGERS, ROBIN OF SHERWOOD, JACK THE RIPPER and CLUEDO (Colonel Mustard).

COLLINS, MICHELLE
(1963–)

London-born actress, once a singer with Mari Wilson and the Wilsations, whose major roles have included Stephanie Wild in the sitcom, *Running Wild*, Cindy Beale in EASTENDERS, Susie in REAL WOMEN, holiday rep Nicki Matthews in *Sunburn* (also singing the theme song), Maxine Gaines in *Up Rising* and Diana Wakeham in *The Sleeper*. In addition, she once hosted THE WORD and in 2000 presented *Michelle in Brazil*, a documentary about the plight of street children.

COLLINS, PAULINE
(1940–)

British actress who shot to fame as Sarah, the parlourmaid in UPSTAIRS, DOWNSTAIRS. So popular was her character that a spin-off, *Thomas and Sarah*, was produced for her and her real-life husband, John Alderton.

Collins's TV break had come with EMERGENCY – WARD 10 and was followed by her first starring role as Dawn in THE LIVER BIRDS, alongside Polly James. However, after a short first series, Nerys Hughes joined as James's new flatmate and Collins left. Post-*Upstairs, Downstairs*, she has starred with hubby Alderton on three further occasions – as Clara Danby in the sitcom NO – HONESTLY, as various characters in WODEHOUSE PLAYHOUSE and as Harriet Boult in FOREVER GREEN. Her most recent starring roles have been as Aileen Matthews in the *Screen Two* drama, *Flowers of the Forest*, and as Harriet Smith in AMBASSADOR.

COLONEL MARCH OF SCOTLAND YARD
UK (Sapphire) Police Drama. ITV 1956–7

Col. Perceval March	**Boris Karloff**
Insp. Ames	**Ewan Roberts**

Producer: **Hannah Weinstein**

The strange cases of a specialist detective.

One-eyed Colonel March worked for D-3, the Department of Queer Complaints at Scotland Yard, a position that led to his involvement in seemingly unsolvable cases. Sometimes it appeared the supernatural had played a hand in murder. On other occasions, supposedly impossible crimes landed on his desk (including a murder in a sealed compression chamber where no one could have reached the victim). March even confronted the Abominable Snowman in one episode. Nevertheless, the dogged detective, who sported a black patch over his left eye, always found the answer. The stories were based on stories by Carter Dickson (John Dickson Carr).

COLOUR TELEVISION

Although initially earmarked for 1956–7, colour television did not officially begin in the UK until 2 December 1967, some 13 years after the USA had begun regular colour broadcasts (although, it is true to say, significant colour viewing figures in the USA were not established until around 1965). The factors that inhibited the development of colour in the UK were varied. They included the need for the Government to approve a suitable system, preferably in conjunction with its European neighbours so that standard technology was achieved. The American NTSC system was initially employed by the BBC for test transmissions, which began in 1962, but was quickly dropped in favour of the French SECAM technology. Eventually it was the German-originated PAL system, a 625-line variant of the 525-line NTSC system, that was adopted in the UK.

COLTRANE, ROBBIE
(Anthony McMillan; 1950–)

Scottish actor whose early television work took in A KICK UP THE EIGHTIES, *Laugh??? I Nearly Paid My Licence Fee*, ALFRESCO and various COMIC STRIP plays. He also appeared in THE YOUNG ONES, GIRLS ON TOP, BLACK-ADDER and *Saturday Live* before starring as Danny McGlone in John Byrne's rock'n'roll comedy drama, TUTTI FRUTTI. He has since had his own show, appeared with Emma Thompson, featured in Dario Fo's *Mistero Buffo*, starred as Captain Chisholm in *The Ebb-Tide* and played Tweedledum in *Alice in Wonderland*, but his best-known role has been that of Fitz in the acclaimed crime drama, CRACKER. In 1993 he made a light-hearted American road film documentary, *Coltrane in a Cadillac*, and in 1995 narrated *The Limit*, a series about structural engineering.

COLUMBO
US (Universal) Detective Drama. ITV 1972–9; 1991–4

Lt. Columbo	**Peter Falk**

Creators: **Richard Levinson, William Link**
Executive Producers: **Roland Kibbee, Dean Hargrove, Richard Alan Simmons**
Producers: **Edward K. Dodds, Everett Chambers, Richard Alan Simmons, Stanley Kallis**

The investigations of a grubby, seemingly ineffective police detective.

Each episode of *Columbo* opened in the thick of the action. A murder was committed and the culprits quickly covered their tracks, pulling off an apparently perfect crime. However, soon on the scene was America's most unlikely policeman, Lt. Columbo, and, by piecing together even the most minute fragments of evidence, the LA-based detective always got his man. Of course, viewers came to expect Columbo to be successful, but the same couldn't be said for the murderers. Lulled into a false sense of security by his tramp's raincoat, battered old car, well-chewed cigar and polite manner, they never believed that this scruffy old cop could nail them. But, by throwing his suspects off guard, Columbo knew he could catch them unawares. From the outset he seemed to know who the murderer was, and viewers were able to watch the battle of wills that developed between the culprit manoeuvring to allay suspicion and the detective homing in on his prey. Much mentioned, but never seen, was his wife, but she did appear in her own spin-off series, *Mrs Columbo*, played by Kate Mulgrew. Columbo's lone companion seemed to be his bassett hound, Fang.

The character of Columbo was allegedly modelled on Petrovich, an inspector in Dostoevsky's *Crime and Punishment*, and first reached the screen in a segment of USA's *Sunday Mystery Hour*, way back in 1961. Then the character was played by Bert Freed. When Columbo was looked at again in the late 1960s, Bing Crosby and Lee J. Cobb were the two names touted for the role. Both were unavailable, so in stepped Peter Falk to appear in two TV movies, *Prescription: Murder* in 1968 (in which we learned Columbo's christian name was Philip) and *Ransom for a Dead Man* in 1971. When in full production, with feature-length episodes, the show aired as part of the MYSTERY MOVIE anthology, although it has also been billed simply under its own title. Guest stars abounded, from Dick Van Dyke and William Shatner to Patrick McGoohan and Donald Pleasence. The detective returned in the 1990s in a new series of two-hour adventures.

COMBAT
US (Selmur) War Drama. ITV 1963–8

Lt. Gil Hanley .... **Rick Jason**
Sgt Chip Saunders .... **Vic Morrow**
PFC Paul 'Caje' Lemay .... **Pierre Jalbert**
Pte. William G. 'Wildman' Kirby .... **Jack Hogan**
Littlejohn .... **Dick Peabody**
Doc Walton .... **Steven Rogers**
Doc .... **Conlan Carter**
Pte. Braddock .... **Shecky Greene**
Pte. Billy Nelson .... **Tom Lowell**

Producer: **Gene Levitt**

A US Army platoon fights its way across Europe in the wake of D-Day.

Filmed for most of its run in black and white, and interspersed with some actual war footage, *Combat* was the most successful of the new breed of 1960s war sagas. It featured K Company, Second Platoon of the US Army, which was headed by Lt. Gil Hanley. With Hanley were Sgt Chip Saunders and a varied company of men, most notably the wisecracking Braddock, a Cajun known simply as 'Caje' and an impressionable young medic, Doc Walton. While the war was hard to avoid, other aspects of platoon life were also handled, and realism was the bedrock of the series. Robert Altman directed many of the episodes, which aired on US TV from 1962 and which were seen sporadically around the ITV network.

COME BACK MRS NOAH
UK (BBC) Situation Comedy. BBC 1 1978

Mrs Noah .... **Mollie Sugden**
Clive Cunliffe .... **Ian Lavender**
Carstairs .... **Donald Hewlett**
Fanshaw .... **Michael Knowles**
Garfield Hawk .... **Tim Barrett**
Scarth Dare .... **Ann Michelle**
TV presenter .... **Gorden Kaye**
Technician .... **Jennifer Lonsdale**

Writers: **Jeremy Lloyd, David Croft**
Producer: **David Croft**

A housewife is lost in space.

When, in the 21st century, housewife Mrs Noah won

herself a trip round *Britannia Seven*, Britain's newest spaceship, little did she know that her voyage would be so adventurous. Accidentally blasted into orbit, she and a hotchpotch crew found themselves floating round the world at 56,325 kmh (35,000 mph), as Mission Control fought desperately to retrieve their craft. Among those alongside Mrs Noah was roving TV reporter Clive Cunliffe.

Despite coming from the pen of the creators of 'ALLO 'ALLO and featuring the usual Croft/Perry/Lloyd repertory company actors, with Mollie Sugden in full sail, this sitcom failed to take off and survived only one short season (plus a pilot at the end of 1977).

COME DANCING
UK (BBC) Entertainment. BBC 1 1950–95

Creator: **Eric Morley**
Producers: **Barrie Edgar, Ray Lakeland, Philip Lewis, Simon Betts**

Enduring ballroom dancing contest.

One of television's longest-running programmes, *Come Dancing* proved remarkably durable. Initially conceived as a showcase for events from regional ballrooms, with professionals Syd Perkins and Edna Duffield offering instruction for viewers at home, it assumed the more familiar dance-contest format in 1953. The competition later took the form of an inter-regional knock-out, pitting teams from areas such as Home Counties North against the South-West, or some other part of the UK. The last series, in 1995, featured contestants from various European countries. Swathed in a sea of sequins, the athletic, mostly amateur, enthusiasts competed in various formal dance categories, from the tango to the paso doble. There was also a section for formation dancing, and newer crazes like rock'n'roll were incorporated over the years. The deviser of the programme, Mecca's Eric Morley, also emceed proceedings, although the programme's presenters and on-the-floor comperes were many. The most notable included McDonald Hobley, Peter Dimmock, Sylvia Peters, Peter West, Brian Johnston, Pete Murray, Don Moss, Keith Fordyce, Michael Aspel, Judith Chalmers, Terry Wogan, Noel Edmonds, Peter Marshall, Angela Rippon, David Jacobs and Rosemarie Ford.

COMEDIANS, THE
UK (Granada) Comedy. ITV 1971–4; 1979; 1984–5; 1992

(1971–4): **Frank Carson, Bernard Manning, Colin Crompton, Ken Goodwin, Mike Reid, Jim Bowen, Charlie Williams, Duggie Brown, Mike Burton, George Roper, Tom O'Connor, Russ Abbot, Lennie Bennett, Jos White, Dave Butler, Steve Faye, Alan Brady, Eddie Flanagan, Pat Mooney, Jimmy Marshall**

(1979): **Stan Boardman, Roy Walker, Johnny Carroll, Vince Earl, Charlie Daze, George King, Harry Scott, Lee Wilson, Mick Miller, Ivor Davis, Hal Nolan, Pat Tansey, Mike Kelly, Bobby Kaye**

Producers: **John Hamp, Ian Hamilton**

Wall-to-wall gags from leading club comics.

With musical interludes from Shep's Banjo Boys, *The Comedians* was a showcase for the top talent from the northern clubs. Producer John Hamp brought the country's fastest wisecrackers into the studio, recorded their (somewhat cleaned-up) routines before a live audience, then inter-cut their gags with those from other contributors to create a non-stop barrage of quick-fire jokes. Snappy editing ensured a lively pace, and a joke a minute, at the very least, was guaranteed.

The Comedians launched the television careers of a number of funny men (and future game show hosts), the best remembered being listed above. These included abrasive Bernard Manning, weedy Colin Crompton (the pair came together again later in WHEELTAPPERS' AND SHUNTERS' SOCIAL CLUB), Ken 'Settle down now' Goodwin, Mike 'Terr-i-fic' Reid, Frank 'It's the way I tell 'em' Carson and Jim 'Smashing, super' Bowen. Lennie Bennett, Tom O'Connor and Russ Abbot were three other performers who carved out new careers after appearances on the show, Duggie Brown (brother of CORONATION STREET's Lynne Perrie) has since turned to acting (with appearances in BROOKSIDE), but Charlie Williams, a black comic with a thick Yorkshire accent, unfortunately failed to make the grade when given charge of THE GOLDEN SHOT and has seldom been seen since.

The Comedians was revived in 1979, with a new intake of stand-up comics that included Roy Walker and Stan Boardman. A third revival in 1984, with yet more new talent (most notably Les Dennis), proved less memorable, as did a fourth in 1992. *The Comedians Christmas Cracker*, a one-off in December 1993, celebrated the programme's 21st birthday in the company of old stalwarts like Manning, Carson, Bowen, Brown, Boardman, Williams and Goodwin.

COMEDY PLAYHOUSE

UK (BBC/Carlton) Situation Comedy Anthology. BBC1
1961–74; ITV 1993

Creator: **Tom Sloan**

Sporadic collections of sitcom pilots.

Comedy Playhouse was an umbrella title given to occasional series of single comedies. Each comedy acted as a pilot and, if successful, stood a fair chance of being extended into a series of its own. Ray Galton and Alan Simpson wrote the first collection, but many other writers (including Johnny Speight, Roy Clarke and Richard Waring) made contributions later. The most famous of *Comedy Playhouse*'s protégés were STEPTOE AND SON (piloted as *The Offer* in 1962), TILL DEATH US DO PART and THE LIVER BIRDS. Others included ALL GAS AND GAITERS, NOT IN FRONT OF THE CHILDREN, ME MAMMY, LAST OF THE SUMMER WINE and HAPPY EVER AFTER.

Similar in concept was *Comedy Special* in 1977, which introduced CITIZEN SMITH, and the 1973 Ronnie Barker showcase, *Seven of One*, which included OPEN ALL HOURS

and *Prisoner and Escort*, the pilot for PORRIDGE. Carlton resurrected *Comedy Playhouse* in 1993, giving birth to two series, *Brighton Belles* (the UK version of THE GOLDEN GIRLS) and *The 10%ers*.

COMIC RELIEF

UK (BBC) Telethon. BBC 1 1988–

Comedy charity marathon.

Exploiting the talents of comedians and comic actors from various generations and backgrounds, *Comic Relief* has been described as CHILDREN IN NEED with gags. It sprang from a 1986 *Omnibus* compilation programme of the highlights of three live Comic Relief concerts staged at the Shaftesbury Theatre, London, in the same year, as an extension to the Live Aid music projects. The first fully fledged *Comic Relief* extravaganza – largely the brainchild of writer Richard Curtis – was hosted by Griff Rhys Jones and Lenny Henry in 1988. Proceeds (over £15 million initially, rising over the years to over £26 million) have gone to help famine victims in Africa, and the needy closer to home. The second *Comic Relief* came a year later, in 1989, but the appeal has since settled into a biennial routine, taking place on a date in February/March which has been dubbed 'Red Nose Day' (clowns' red noses of assorted designs being sold to raise money).

Appeals for cash have been made throughout the evening's live programming, with running totals announced at regular intervals. Reports on how funds have been spent have punctuated each appeal. Viewers have been invited to bid for their favourite clips from old comedy series, and special segments of contemporary comedies have been produced. Among the many comedians giving their time to the show have been Jasper Carrott, Rowan Atkinson, Tony Robinson, Ken Dodd, Jonathan Ross, Stephen Fry, Richard Wilson, Ben Elton, Frank Carson, Jo Brand, Julian Clary, French and Saunders, Harry Enfield, Ernie Wise, Paul Merton, Ian Hislop, Hale and Pace, Rory Bremner, Victoria Wood, Reeves and Mortimer, and the SPITTING IMAGE team, as well as other stars like Hugh Grant, Joanna Lumley, Cilla Black, Chris Tarrant, Bill Wyman, Barry Norman and Tom Jones.

In 1999, *Comic Relief's Great Big Excellent African Adventure*, shown in the weeks leading up to the main broadcast, sent celebrities like Stephen Fry, Geri Halliwell, Ruby Wax, Michael Palin and Paul Bradley to the strife-ridden continent to report on the appalling hardships faced by the local people. *Radio Times* for the week beginning 6 March 1999 was devoted to *Comic Relief* and spoof-edited by Victoria Wood. In June 1999, BBC 1 screened *Comic Relief: the Debt Wish Show*, a recording of two concerts at the Brixton Academy, London, organized to campaign for the cancellation of Third World debt.

COMIC STRIP PRESENTS, THE
UK (Filmworks/Comic Strip) Comedy. Channel 4 1982–8;
BBC 2 1988–93; Channel 4 1998–2000

Peter Richardson, Dawn French, Jennifer Saunders,
Adrian Edmondson, Rik Mayall, Daniel Peacock, Robbie
Coltrane, Nigel Planer, Alexei Sayle, Keith Allen

Producer: Michael White, Ben Swaffer (Channel 4),
Lolli Kimpton (BBC 2)

*Spoof and satire with a new generation of
comedians.*

The Comic Strip, a Soho comedy club opened by writer
Peter Richardson in 1980, was the venue that gave early
opportunities to many of the 1980s' most successful
young comedians. Its compere was Alexei Sayle and
prominent among its performers were French and Saunders, Nigel Planer, Rik Mayall and Adrian Edmondson.
The Comic Strip Presents was its television manifestation,
but, instead of focusing on stand-up routines, it centred
on satire and send-up. The premiere was an Enid Blyton
spoof, *Five Go Mad in Dorset*, which rounded off Channel
4's first night in 1982. A half-hour parody of the snooty,
class themes of Blyton's books, it cast French and Saunders as George and Anne, with Adrian Edmondson as
Dick and Peter Richardson as Julian. Memorably, it also
featured serious-looking CROSSROADS star Ronald Allen
as Uncle Quentin, proudly declaring himself to be a
homosexual.

Five Go Mad in Dorset led to five series of Comic Strip
productions, plus occasional specials, all drawing their
humour more from atmosphere and characterization
than from jokes and one-liners. Titles were as varied as
War, *The Beat Generation*, *A Fistful of Travellers' Cheques*
and *Bad News Tour* (featuring an inept heavy metal
band). One notable episode, entitled *The Strike*, explored
the miners' dispute through the eyes of Hollywood, with
Peter Richardson playing Al Pacino in the role of Arthur
Scargill, and Jennifer Saunders as Meryl Streep, playing
Scargill's wife. The same theme was extended to a later
production, *GLC*, in which Robbie Coltrane was Charles
Bronson playing Ken Livingstone. *The Bullshitters* (a parody of THE PROFESSIONALS) was not officially a Comic
Strip production, but did feature a few members of the
team. With its stars now name performers, *The Comic
Strip Presents* moved to BBC 2 in the 1990s, before resur-
facing on Channel 4 on Easter Sunday 1998 for a one-off
production, *Four Men in a Car*, which was followed by
Four Men in a Plane in January 2000.

COMMENTATOR

A person who expresses a view on news and current
affairs or reports direct from sporting events, usually
describing the action as it happens.

COMMERCIAL

A television advertisement that may vary in length from
a few seconds to a few minutes. In the UK these are
grouped together in commercial breaks lasting several
minutes, which are screened between and also during
programmes. In other countries and on some satellite
networks commercials are seen between programmes
only. In the USA, breaks are more frequent and have
traditionally been more rigidly enforced, causing much
concern when programmes have been halted to accommodate a break. Commercial television (aka ITV) arrived
in the UK on 22 September 1955 and the first advert in
the first 'natural break' (as it was then termed) was for
Gibbs SR toothpaste. Then, as now, there were strict
rules regarding advertising. Today the ITC monitors
commercials, with the main concerns being that they
do not mislead, do not encourage or condone harmful
behaviour and do not cause widespread or exceptional
offence. Certain products, in line with Government
legislation, are prohibited (tobacco, etc.), and controversial subjects like alcohol, financial services, children's
goods, medical products and religious and charitable
concerns are subject to more detailed regulation. An
average of seven minutes per hour of advertising are
now allowed on ITV, Channel 4 and Channel 5, with
an average of eight minutes per hour during peak hours
(7–9 a.m. and 6–11 p.m.) and a maximum of 12 minutes
in any hour. Satellite stations can offer an average of
nine minutes' worth per hour (maximum 12 minutes per
hour), although shopping channels are not restricted
in the same way. The timing of commercials is also
controlled. No advertising is allowed during religious
services, for example.

COMMON AS MUCK
UK (BBC) Drama. BBC 1 1994; 1997

Nev	Edward Woodward
Foxy	Tim Healy
Ken	Neil Dudgeon
Bernard	Richard Ridings
Sunil	Anthony Barclay
Jonno	Stephen Lord
John Parry	Roy Hudd
Dulcie	Freda Dowie
George Ward	Paul Kember
Denice	Nimmy March
Guy Simmons	Ian Mercer
Mr Arnold	George Raistrick
Jean	Shirley Stelfox
Philip Edwards	Thomas Craig
Moira	Tina Malone
Sandra	Candida Rundle
Marie	Michelle Holmes
Ted	Mike Kelly
Brian Forget	Douglas Henshall
Sharon	Kathy Burke
Diane Parry	June Watson
Derek	Frank Finlay

Irene	**June Whitfield**
Mike Roberts	**Paul Shane**
Christine Stranks	**Lesley Sharp**
Nat Prabhaker	**Saeed Jaffrey**
Dougie Hodd	**Terence Rigby**
Reg Vickers	**Alexei Sayle**
Vinny	**William Ivory**

Writer: **William Ivory**
Producers: **John Chapman, Catherine Wearing**

*A team of refuse collectors fight to save their jobs
from being privatized.*

Set in the fictional northern town of Hepworth, this
comedy drama explored the lives of a team of unruly
dustbinmen – the so-called 'Supercrew' – who discovered
that the local council was planning to put out their work
to private tender because of their lousy attitude and poor
performance. In a panic over likely job-losses, the lads
pulled out the stops to try to keep the contract for their
DOG (Direct Operations Group) council subsidiary, in
the face of glossy promises from Belgian outsiders,
Propre UK. Among the numerous colourful characters
were gloomy veteran Nev; mad driver Foxy; Foxy's son,
Jonno; punchy Ken; simple-minded Bernard; student
Sunil; and cleansing manager John Parry. Their families
also played a part. Stripper/Miss Parks and Gardens
Marie was played by Michelle Holmes, who (as Tina
Fowler to his Eddie Ramsden) had once played writer
William Ivory's girlfriend in CORONATION STREET.

When the lads returned for a second series, a new
threat hung over their workplace: property tycoons
wanted to redevelop their yard. Nev had retired after 45
years and was planning to marry gold-digging new flame
Irene, while the other guys found themselves involved
in new ventures like interior decorating and owning a
hairdressing salon. Corruption hung heavy in the air
and the crew did their best to expose it.

At times dark and moody, but always capable of breaking into mirth, *Common as Muck* was well received by
viewers and critics.

COMO, PERRY

(Pierino Como; 1913–2001)

Laid-back Italian-American crooner whose variety
shows in the 1950s (and extravagant Christmas specials
later) were hits on both sides of the Atlantic.

COMPACT

UK (BBC) Drama. BBC 1 1962–5

Joanne Minster	**Jean Harvey**
Jimmy Saunders	**Nicholas Selby**
Richard Lowe	**Moray Watson**
Mark Viccars	**Gareth Davies**
Alison Gray/Morley	**Betty Cooper**
Alec Gordon	**Leo Maguire**
Sally Henderson/Harmon	**Monica Evans**
Lily Todd/Kipling	**Marcia Ashton**
Maggie Clifford/Brent	**Sonia Graham**

Ruth Munday	**Anna Castaldini**
Sir Charles Harmon	**Newton Blick**
Arnold Babbage	**Donald Morley**
Mary/Augusta 'Gussie' Brown/Beatty ..	**Frances Bennett**
Kay Livingstone/Babbage	**Justine Lord**
Iris Alcott/Millet	**Louise Dunn**
Ian Hart/Harmon	**Ronald Allen**
Gillian Nesbitt	**Dilys Watling**
Sylvia Grant	**Vicky Harrington**
Eddie Goldsmith	**Patrick Troughton**
Paul Constantine	**Tony Wright**
Clancey	**Ann Morrish**
Mr Kipling	**Blake Butler**
Lois James/McClusky	**Dawn Beret**
Mike McClusky	**Clinton Greyn**
Lynn Bolton	**Bridget McConnel**
Tim Gray	**Scot Finch**
Kathy Sherwood	**Penny Morrell**
Adrian Coombs	**Robert Desmond**
Carol 'Copper' Beach	**Mandy Miller**
Bryan Marchant	**Keith Buckley**
Clare Farrell/Viccars	**Janet Hargreaves**
Stan Millet	**Johnny Wade**
Susan Caley	**Sonia Fox**
Edmund Bruce	**Robert Flemyng**
Tony Marchesi	**Norman Florence**
Mrs Chater	**Beryl Cooke**
Alan Drew	**Basil Moss**
Anthea Keane	**Julia Lockwood**
Camilla Hope	**Carmen Silvera**
Celia Randall	**Rachel Gurney**
David Rome	**Vincent Ball**
Lorna Wills-Ede	**Brenda Kaye**
Ken Hawkins/Geoffrey Gray	**Edward Evans**
Doug Beatty	**Lawrence James**
Michele 'Mitch' Donnelly	**Diana Beevers**
Ben Bishop	**Bill Kerr**
Cheryl Fine	**Jan Miller**
Rosalind Garner	**Jennifer Wood**
Tessa March	**Bridget Armstrong**
Harry Cornell	**Lionel Murton**
Elliot Morrow	**Maurice Browning**
Anne Appleby	**Jennifer Wilson**

Creators: **Hazel Adair, Peter Ling**
Producers: **Alan Bromly, Douglas Allen, Morris Barry,
Bernard Hepton, Joan Craft, Harold Clayton, William
Sterling**

*The lives and loves of the staff at a women's
magazine.*

Compact was the BBC's first soap opera since the demise
of THE GROVE FAMILY in 1957. It took place in the high-
rise, Victoria offices (Enterprise House) of *Compact*, a
glossy magazine that majored in schmaltzy fiction and
other matters of female interest, and, as the programme
blurb declared, focused on 'the talented and temperamental people who worked on a topical magazine for
the busy woman'.

The magazine's first editor was Joanne Minster. Also
part of the team were fiction editor Mark Viccars, photographer Alec Gordon, features editor Jimmy Saunders,
art director Richard Lowe, accountant Mr Babbage and

assorted writers and secretaries. The problem page editor was Alison Morley. Her name was originally given as Alison Gray, until the producers realized there was already a contributor to *Reader's Digest* with that name.

Action centred around the hassle of getting the magazine on to the presses each week, with staff squabbles promoted to the realms of high drama. Personal relationships bloomed and died, and there was much sparring for position in the office. Ian Harmon, son of Sir Charles Harmon (the chairman of Harmon Enterprises Incorporated, the magazine's proprietor), arrived from America, using the undercover name of Ian Hart and bringing with him suave looks and gentlemanly behaviour. Before long he married Sally, his secretary. Other major figures to work on the magazine included features editor Gussie Brown (who, embarrassed by her Christian name, at first pretended her name was Mary), American fashion editor Lois James, managing editor Edmund Bruce (brought in from rival magazine, *Lady Fair*), novelist-turned-fiction editor Camilla Hope, librarian Alan Drew and showbusiness editor David Rome.

Compact was screened twice a week. It was criticized for being too wholesome and goody-goody (despite touching on one or two controversial items, like unmarried mothers and drug abuse), but it was very successful in the ratings. All the same, the BBC bosses were less than satisfied. They pulled the plug on the series in July 1965, after just three years on air – ironically assigning *Compact* the same fate that had befallen *The Grove Family*.

CONLEY, BRIAN
(1961–)

London-born entertainer, hosting his own comedy-variety shows – including *Brian Conley – This Way Up* and *The Brian Conley Show* – plus *The National Lottery – We've Got Your Number*, and also starring as petty crook Kenny Conway in *Time After Time* and sadistic gym teacher Doug Digby in THE GRIMLEYS. *Five Alive* and *Summertime Special* featured among his earlier credits.

CONNECTIONS
UK (BBC/Time-Life) Documentary. BBC 1 1978

Presenter: **James Burke**

How scientific progress has changed the world.

This ambitious series attempted to explain the relationship between technological achievement and the course of world history. The case was argued in a lively but highly informative manner by ex-TOMORROW'S WORLD presenter, James Burke.

CONNOLLY, BILLY
(1942–)

Partick-born comedian and actor, familiarly known as 'The Big Yin'. Connolly, a former shipyard welder, was once a member of the Humblebums folk duo with Gerry Rafferty, before turning to stand-up comedy. His TV successes have come on both sides of the Atlantic. He starred in the US series, *Head of the Class* and *Billy* (in both as teacher Billy MacGregor), and in the UK has made appearances on NOT THE NINE O'CLOCK NEWS, THE COMIC STRIP PRESENTS, *The Kenny Everett Video Show* and MINDER. He has starred in his own comedy specials and in 1994 went on *Billy Connolly's World Tour of Scotland*, followed two years later by *Billy Connolly's World Tour of Australia*. In between, the BBC packed him off to the North Pole for a survival course in *Billy Connolly: a Scot in the Arctic*, and then rewarded him with *An Evening in with Billy Connolly* (four hours on BBC 2) in 1996. A year later, he took the lead in the *Screen One* drama, *Deacon Brodie*. This followed the 1993 *Screen One* offering, *Down Among the Big Boys*, in which Connolly starred as criminal JoJo Donnelly. He is married to former comic actress Pamela Stephenson.

CONNORS, CHUCK
(Kevin Connors; 1921–92)

Athletic American actor, a former professional baseball player who turned to film and television and starred in various action series, particularly as Lucas McCain in THE RIFLEMAN, Jason McCord in BRANDED and Jim Sinclair in *Cowboy in Africa*. He also played defence attorney John Egan in ARREST AND TRIAL and, in the 1970s, resurfaced in ROOTS, taking the part of Tom Moore. Other TV credits included episodes of FANTASY ISLAND, THE SIX MILLION DOLLAR MAN and MURDER, SHE WROTE.

CONRAD, WILLIAM
(1920–94)

Gravel-voiced American actor, a fighter pilot in World War II but for ever remembered by viewers as the huffing and puffing, overweight private eye, Frank CANNON. It was a starring role at last for Conrad, who had missed out on several previous occasions. His resonant voice had made him a prolific radio actor and announcer, and he had been seen in numerous films in the 1940s and 1950s, but his portly frame always spoiled his chances of on-screen TV success. GUNSMOKE was a point in question. Although he had voiced the part of Matt Dillon for years on US radio, there was no way the producers could cast Conrad as the strapping marshal of Dodge City, and the role went instead to James Arness. Conrad, consequently, concentrated on work behind the camera. He produced/directed series like NAKED CITY, 77 SUNSET STRIP and, ironically, *Gunsmoke*. He also provided narration for such programmes as THE FUGITIVE, THE INVADERS and BUCK ROGERS IN THE 25TH CENTURY, but it wasn't until Frank Cannon was born that his screen success was assured. He followed it with two more detective romps, *Nero Wolfe* and *Jake and the Fatman*, but he still continued to dabble in voice-overs, speaking the lines of the Lone Ranger in the 1980s cartoon revival, for instance.

CONTI, TOM
(1941–)

Latin-looking Scottish actor, popular on stage and film but also prominent on TV thanks to dramas like *Madame Bovary*, THE GLITTERING PRIZES (Adam Morris), *The Norman Conquests*, *Voices Within* and Dennis Potter's *Blade on the Feather*, as well as comedies like *Old Boy Network* (Lucas Frye). He has also narrated series such as the music documentary, *Sound Stories*.

CONTINUITY ANNOUNCER
See ANNOUNCER.

CONTRAST

The relationship between the lightest and darkest elements of a TV picture.

CONTROL DESK

Found in the control room or gallery, the control desk houses the vision mixer and other technical apparatus used by the director, his production assistant and other technicians as they monitor recordings or live transmissions.

CONWAY, RUSS
(Trevor Stanford, DSM; 1925–2000)

British piano-playing celebrity of the late 1950s and early 1960s, a stalwart of variety spectaculars and series like *The Billy Cotton Band Show*. Self-taught, he sold millions of copies of records like 'Sidesaddle' and 'Roulette' before he faded off UK TV screens.

COOGAN, STEVE
(1965–)

Manchester-born comedian and actor, acclaimed for a series of character creations, most notably self-important sports presenter-turned-chat-show host, Alan Partridge. Partridge was first seen in THE DAY TODAY (based on earlier success in Radio 4's *On The Hour*) and later in his own series, *Knowing Me, Knowing You with Alan Partridge* (another follow-up from radio) and *I'm Alan Partridge*. Almost as popular has been the foul-mouthed brother-and-sister combination of boozy Paul and slutty Pauline Calf, who first appeared in comedy revues like *Saturday Zoo* and went on to feature in their own one-off programmes, *The Paul Calf Video Diary* and *Three Fights, Two Weddings and a Funeral*. The squabbling siblings also appeared in a series of comedy playlets called *Coogan's Run*, along with new characters such as obnoxious salesman Gareth Cheeseman, quiz machine freaks Guy and Stuart Crump, museum creator Tim Fleck, club singer Mike Crystal and handyman Ernest Moss. Another Coogan creation was Portuguese crooner Tony Ferrino. Previously, Coogan had supplied voices for SPITTING IMAGE and had featured regularly in THE KRYPTON FACTOR inserts. In 1997 he made his straight acting debut as journalist Mike Gabbart in soccer scandal drama, *The Fix*.

COOK, PETER
(1937–95)

Dry, satirical, Torquay-born comedian, a Cambridge Footlights graduate whose celebrated two-year partnership with Dudley Moore in NOT ONLY . . . BUT ALSO . . . in the mid-1960s followed a couple of years of success with the *Beyond the Fringe* revue. Cook's collaborators in those early days included Moore, Jonathan Miller and Alan Bennett, and it was during that time that he developed his philosophical E. L. Wisty character, complete with grubby mac and flat cap, which he brought to TV in *On the Braden Beat* in 1964. In 1966 he played the Mad Hatter in Miller's adaptation of *Alice In Wonderland*. After moving into film, Cook returned to television in the late 1970s, appearing as a seedy dance-hall manager in the late-night rock show, *Revolver*, and in 1981 he switched to sitcom, starring with Mimi Kennedy in *The Two of Us*, the American version of TWO'S COMPANY (as butler Robert Brentwood). Among his other credits were *Gone to Seed* (unscrupulous property developer Wesley Willis), THE BLACK ADDER (King Richard III), the series of spoof shorts, *A Life in Pieces* (his long-established creation Sir Arthur Streeb-Greebling being interviewed by Ludovic Kennedy), the voice of the *Viz* cartoon character, Roger Mellie, and assorted cameo performances. Cook was co-founder of London's Establishment Club in 1960 and became a major shareholder in the fledgling *Private Eye* magazine in the same year.

COOK, ROGER
(1943–)

New Zealand-born, Australia-raised investigative reporter, first on radio in the UK (*The World At One* and *Checkpoint*), after working for Australian TV. Through his ITV series, *The Cook Report*, Cook has exposed any number of fraudsters and con men, as well as upbraiding the authorities on behalf of the consumer. Cook has bravely tackled the most risqué of subjects and the most violent of characters, from child pornographers and badger-baiters to terrorists and racketeers. His camera-in-the-face method of confronting his targets has been much mimicked.

COOK, SUE
(1949–)

Middlesex-born, former radio broadcaster and TV news and current affairs presenter (NATIONWIDE) who for many years was co-host of the annual CHILDREN IN NEED appeals. She has also presented BREAKFAST TIME and *Out of Court*, worked on various magazine programmes and fronted CRIMEWATCH UK for 11 years. She was once married to classical guitarist John Williams.

COOKE, ALISTAIR
KBE (Hon.) (1908–)

Manchester-born journalist, now an American citizen, who has presented Radio 4's *Letter from America* since 1946. A one-time BBC film critic, for many years Cooke was the *Guardian*'s chief US correspondent and he also worked for American radio stations as a specialist in British affairs. He first appeared on British television in the 1930s, presenting a short programme, *Accent in America*, although his TV masterpiece was undoubtedly AMERICA, a 13-week personal analysis of the birth and development of a nation, delivered in his customarily modest but incisively knowledgeable style and filled with feeling and affection for his adopted homeland. In the USA he has been the host of *Masterpiece Theater*, an anthology series of top British drama programmes like UPSTAIRS, DOWNSTAIRS, THE SIX WIVES OF HENRY VIII and POLDARK.

COOKE, BRIAN

British comedy scriptwriter, often in collaboration with Johnnie Mortimer (see Mortimer's entry for joint credits). Individually, Cooke has also contributed TRIPPER'S/SLINGER'S DAY plus *Close to Home* and KEEP IT IN THE FAMILY, both of which went on to have US versions scripted by Cooke himself (*Starting from Scratch* and *Too Close for Comfort*, respectively).

COOL FOR CATS
UK (Associated-Rediffusion) Pop Music. ITV 1956–61

Hosts: **Ker Robertson, Kent Walton**

Creator: **Joan Kemp-Welch**

Britain's first pop music show.

Billed variously as 'A disc programme for Squares', and 'A square disc programme', *Cool for Cats* was British TV's first pop music showcase, airing the latest single releases. Given its minuscule budget, the programme was forced to rely on artists miming and the talents of a resident dance group (led by Douglas Squires) which, to ring the changes, used the stairs and passageways of Associated-Rediffusion's offices as well as its studios. All the same, the 15-minute programme proved particularly popular and was screened more than once a week. Journalist Ker Robertson, the first host, was succeeded after a few weeks by Kent Walton, later better known for his ITV wrestling commentaries. Robertson went on to become the show's record arranger.

COOMBS, PAT
(1930–)

Wiry Cockney comedy actress, typically in dithery or distressed parts, or as a timid soul dominated by a female dragon. She appeared in just such a role with Peggy Mount in the retirement home comedy, *You're Only Young Twice*, playing Cissie Lupin, having previously played Violet, Mount's sister-in-law, in LOLLIPOP LOVES MR MOLE. Her comedy career began with Arthur Askey (she was Nola in the radio show, *Hello Playmates*) and some of her earliest TV appearances were with Bill Maynard, Terry Scott, Tony Hancock, Cyril Fletcher and Jimmy Edwards. Coombs then appeared in *Barney Is My Darling* (Miss Hobbitt) and starred in the sitcom, BEGGAR MY NEIGHBOUR, as Reg Varney's wife, Lana Butt. She later joined Stephen Lewis (playing his sister, Dorothy) in the ON THE BUSES spin-off, *Don't Drink the Water*, and over the years has also been seen in programmes like *Marty*, *The Dick Emery Show*, TILL DEATH US DO PART, *Wild, Wild Women* (Daisy), *The Lady is A Tramp* (Lanky Pat) and the kids' series, *Hogg's Back* (Mrs Mac), *Roy's Raiders*, *Ragdolly Anna* and *Mr Majeika*. Coombs also spent some time in EASTENDERS, as Girl Guide leader Marge Green.

COOPER, TOMMY
(1922–84)

Tall, Caerphilly-born comedian, notorious as the fez-wearing magician with the bad gags and bemused look whose tricks always failed. Tommy Cooper's hugely successful career began in the army and continued after the war on the London variety circuit. In the 1950s he branched out into television, appearing in series like *It's Magic* and winning a run of his own series, including *Cooper – Life with Tommy*, *Cooper's Capers*, *Cooperama*, *Life With Cooper*, *Cooper at Large*, *The Tommy Cooper Hour*, *Cooper King-Size* and *Cooper – Just Like That!* (after his catchphrase). He became a cult comedian and enjoyed great respect among his fellow artistes. It was actually on television that he died, suffering a heart attack while appearing on *Live from Her Majesty's*.

COPE, KENNETH
(1931–)

British actor/scriptwriter who came to the fore as one of the presenters of THAT WAS THE WEEK THAT WAS before joining CORONATION STREET as a semi-regular in the mid-1960s, turning up from time to time as Scouser Jed Stone, the petty crook Minnie Caldwell adored and knew as Sonny Jim. However, it was as the deceased part of RANDALL AND HOPKIRK (DECEASED) that he is best remembered, playing the ghost detective, Marty Hopkirk. Other credits have included WHACK-O! (schoolmaster Price Whittaker), DIXON OF DOCK GREEN, Z CARS, THE AVENGERS, *We Have Ways of Making You Laugh*, BERGERAC, SHELLEY (DHSS clerk Forsyth), MINDER, STRANGERS, *Bootle Saddles*, DOCTOR WHO, BROOKSIDE (Ray Hilton) and CASUALTY. Among his writing successes have been the kids' soccer series, *Striker*, the sitcom *Thingumybob* and episodes of THE DUSTBINMEN, THE SQUIRRELS and *A Sharp Intake of Breath*.

CO-PRODUCTION

A programme made jointly by two or more companies, sometimes from more than one country, in an effort to spread the financial risk.

COPS, THE
UK (World/BBC) Police Drama. BBC 2 1998–

WPC Mel Draper .... **Katy Cavanagh**
Sgt Edward Giffen .... **Rob Dixon**
PC Roy Bramell .... **John Henshaw**
PC Mike Thompson .... **Steve Jackson**
PC Danny Rylands .... **Jack Marsden**
WPC/Sgt Natalie Metcalf .... **Clare McGlinn**
PC Jaz Shundara .... **Parvez Qadir**
DS Alan Wakefield .... **David Crellin**
PC Colin Jellicoe .... **Steve Garti**
PC Dean Wishaw .... **Danny Seward**
Cindy .... **Margaret Blakemore**
Standish .... **Sue Cleaver**
Chief Insp. Newland .... **Mark Chatterton**
Stowe .... **Ken Kitson**
Maggie Hayes .... **Jan Pearson**
WPC Amanda Kennett .... **Paulette Williams**
Darril Stone .... **Stuart Goodwin**
Ellen .... **Deirdre Costello**

Producers: **Eric Coulter, Ann Harrison-Baxter**
Executive Producer: **Tony Garnett**

Innovative police drama with the feel of a documentary.

Set in the northern town of Stanton (in real life Bury), and particularly on the streets of the troublesome Skeetsmore estate, *The Cops* left viewers wondering whether this police work was real or fictitious, thanks to the employment of documentary-style camerawork and a largely unknown cast of actors. Stories majored on the stresses of being a part of the force, rather than the traditional cops-and-robbers fare; violence featured prominently and strong language ensured the series was light years away from the days of DIXON OF DOCK GREEN.

These boys and girls in blue were hardly a perfect bunch. The leading characters included probationary WPC Mel Draper, whose drug use helped her through the shifts; modernizing new sergeant Edward Giffen; Asian probationer PC Jaz; his wily partner, Colin Jellicoe; old-fashioned, non-PC PC Roy Bramell; level-headed Danny Rylance; socially aware, ambitious WPC Natalie Metcalf; and the mostly sensible but always volatile Dean Wishaw. Experienced producer Tony Garnett worked on getting the right balance, with the odd flash of humour lightening the load and occasional heart-rending moments adding sentiment.

Though quite different in tone, *The Cops* was not unlike Z CARS in that it moved police drama on to a new level and drew immediate criticism from the police force itself – which had co-operated in the filming – for the unfavourable image it portrayed of today's law-enforcers. Unsurprisingly, assistance was not forthcoming for series two.

CORBETT, HARRY
OBE (1918–89)

'Bye bye, everybody, bye, bye.' These weary, resigned closing words of each show became the catchphrase of Harry Corbett, a genial northern entertainer, the man who gave the world Sooty and Sweep. Beginning his working life as an electrical engineer, Corbett, an amateur pianist and magician, transformed his life in 1948 when he purchased a bear glove-puppet on Blackpool's North Pier for 7/6d (38p). He built the bear into his magic act, which led to an appearance on the BBC's *Talent Night* in 1952. The bear was simply known as Teddy at the time, but after applying some chimney soot to his ears and nose, in order to add more character, he was re-christened Sooty. Five years later, Sweep, a squeaky, rather dim dog with a lust for sausages, joined Sooty, making Corbett's life a misery as they spoiled his magic tricks, sprayed him with water and hit him around the head with a balsa-wood hammer. Corbett then introduced other characters to the show, including Kipper the cat, Butch the dog and Ramsbottom the snake, but most controversial was its first female star, Soo, a cute panda who did all the housework. In 1968 Corbett switched channels, taking his puppets to ITV, where he stayed until he suffered a heart attack in 1975. His son, Matthew, then took over as Sooty and Sweep's harassed straight man, eventually selling the rights to the puppets for £1.4 million in 1996, but keeping a hand in the business, so to speak, for another two years.

CORBETT, HARRY H.
OBE (1925–82)

Although he subsequently appeared in a range of TV shows, Harry H. Corbett will for ever be remembered as Harold Steptoe, the seedy rag-and-bone man with artistic pretensions whose dreams were constantly shattered by his vulgar old dad. Corbett came to television via film and the Shakespearean and classical stage, having served in the Marines in the war and then training as a radiographer. STEPTOE AND SON arrived in 1962 and ran – off and on – for 12 years, leaving Corbett heavily typecast, despite numerous appearances in programmes like THE GOODIES, TALES OF THE UNEXPECTED and SHOESTRING, his own three sitcoms – as the status-seeking *Mr Aitch* in 1967, the determined bachelor Alfred Wilcox in *The Best*

Things in Life in 1969, and newsagent *Grundy* in 1980 – and a prominent role in the comedy, POTTER, as local gangster Harry Tooms. Corbett, whose first wife had been comedienne Sheila Steafel, died of a heart attack in 1982, ironically three years before his TV father, Wilfrid Brambell. The 'H' in his name stood, allegedly, for 'Hanything' and was included to avoid confusion with Harry Corbett of Sooty fame. His daughter is actress Susannah Corbett.

CORBETT, RONNIE
(1930–)

Tiny, bespectacled, Edinburgh-born comedian and comic actor, one half of the celebrated TWO RONNIES partnership. Ronnie Corbett's TV career actually began on CRACKERJACK in the 1950s and progressed via series like *The Dickie Henderson Show* and *It's Tarbuck* to THE FROST REPORT (on which he worked for the first time with Barker). His own sitcom, NO – THAT'S ME OVER HERE, and a comedy/variety series, *The Corbett Follies*, followed. Then, in 1971, he was teamed once again with Barker for *The Two Ronnies*. One of the show's highlights was Corbett's drawn-out monologue, delivered from an outsize armchair. During the programme's lengthy run, Corbett moved back into situation comedy with the series, NOW LOOK HERE . . ., *The Prince of Denmark* and SORRY!, the last providing the final outing for his various 'mummy's boy' comedy roles. His own sit-down/sketch series, *The Ronnie Corbett Show*, was shown in 1987. In the 1990s he hosted *Small Talk*, a humorous quiz game based on children's views of the world, and was a regular on *The Ben Elton Show*. Corbett also has plenty of guest appearances to his name.

CORONATION STREET
UK (Granada) Drama. ITV 1960–

Ena Sharples	Violet Carson
Annie Walker	Doris Speed
Jack Walker	Arthur Leslie
Elsie Tanner/Howard	Pat Phoenix
Dennis Tanner	Philip Lowrie
Frank Barlow	Frank Pemberton
Ida Barlow	Noel Dyson
Ken Barlow	William Roache
David Barlow	Alan Rothwell
Martha Longhurst	Lynne Carol
Minnie Caldwell	Margot Bryant
Elsie Lappin	Maudie Edwards
Ivan Cheveski	Ernst Walder
Linda Cheveski	Anne Cunningham
Harry Hewitt	Ivan Beavis
Christine Hardman/Appleby	Christine Hargreaves
May Hardman	Joan Heath
Susan Cunningham	Patricia Shakesby
Albert Tatlock	Jack Howarth
Florrie Lindley	Betty Alberge
Esther Hayes	Daphne Oxenford
Leonard Swindley	Arthur Lowe
Concepta Riley/Hewitt/Regan	Doreen Keogh
Lucille Hewitt	Jennifer Moss
Valerie Tatlock/Barlow	Anne Reid
Emily Nugent/Bishop	Eileen Derbyshire
Billy Walker	Kenneth Farrington
Joan Walker/Davies	June Barry
	Dorothy White
Len Fairclough	Peter Adamson
Alf Roberts OBE	Bryan Mosley
Bill Gregory	Jack Watson
Jed Stone	Kenneth Cope
Sheila Birtles/Crossley	Eileen Mayers
Doreen Lostock	Angela Crow
Dot Greenhalgh	Joan Francis
Nancy Leathers	Norah Hammond
Joe Makinson	Brian Rawlinson
Arnold Tanner	Frank Crawshaw
Jerry Booth	Graham Haberfield
Dave Smith	Reginald Marsh
Myra Dickenson/Booth	Susan Jameson
Neil Crossley	Geoffrey Matthews
David Robbins	Jon Rollason
Charlie Moffitt	Gordon Rollings
Hilda Ogden	Jean Alexander
Stan Ogden	Bernard Youens
Irma Ogden/Barlow	Sandra Gough
Trevor Ogden	Jonathan Collins
	Don Hawkins
Rita Bates/Littlewood/Fairclough/Sullivan	Barbara Mullaney/Knox
William Piggott	George A. Cooper
Sandra Petty	Heather Moore
Lionel Petty	Edward Evans
Susan Barlow/Baldwin	Katie Heanneau (*Barlow* only)
	Susi Patterson (*Barlow* only)
	Wendy Jane Walker
	Joanna Foster
Peter Barlow	John Heanneau
	Mark Duncan
	Christopher Dormerr
	Linus Roache
	Joseph McKenna
	David Lonsdale
	Chris Gascoyne
Nellie Harvey	Mollie Sugden
Ray Langton	Neville Buswell
Bet Lynch/Gilroy	Julie Goodyear
Ernest Bishop	Stephen Hancock
Steve Tanner	Paul Maxwell
Joe Donnelli	Shane Rimmer
Audrey Bright/Fleming	Gillian McCann
Dickie Fleming	Nigel Humphreys
Maggie Clegg/Cooke	Irene Sutcliffe
Les Clegg	John Sharp
Gordon Clegg	Bill Kenwright
George Greenwood	Arthur Pentelow
Tommy Deakin	Paddy Joyce
Betty Turpin/Williams	Betty Driver
Cyril Turpin	William Moore
Alice Pickens	Doris Hare
Janet Reid/Barlow	Judith Barker
Bernard Butler	Gorden Kaye
Ted Loftus	Ted Morris
Alan Howard	Alan Browning

Mavis Riley/Wilton	**Thelma Barlow**
Frank Bradley	**Tommy Boyle**
Ivy Tilsley/Brennan	**Lynne Perrie**
Edna Gee	**Mavis Rogerson**
Norma Ford	**Diana Davies**
Jacko Ford	**Robert Keegan**
Ron Cooke	**Eric Lander**
Alec Gilroy	**Roy Barraclough**
Deirdre Hunt/Langton/Barlow/Rachid	**Anne Kirkbride**
Vera Hopkins	**Kathy Staff**
Tricia Hopkins	**Kathy Jones**
Idris Hopkins	**Richard Davies**
Granny Megan Hopkins	**Jesse Evans**
Blanche Hunt	**Maggie Jones**
Eddie Yeats	**Geoffrey Hughes**
Vera Duckworth	**Elizabeth Dawn**
Gail Potter/Tilsley/Platt	**Helen Worth**
Ralph Lancaster	**Kenneth Watson**
Fred Gee	**Fred Feast**
Derek Wilton	**Peter Baldwin**
Mike Baldwin	**Johnny Briggs**
Suzie Birchall	**Cheryl Murray**
Renee Bradshaw/Roberts	**Madge Hindle**
Tracy Langton/Barlow	**Christabel Finch**
	Holly Chamarette
	Dawn Acton
Steve Fisher	**Lawrence Mullin**
Ida Clough	**Helene Palmer**
Brian Tilsley	**Christopher Quinten**
Bert Tilsley	**Peter Dudley**
Audrey Potter/Roberts	**Sue Nicholls**
Arnold Swain	**George Waring**
Martin Cheveski	**Jonathon Caplan**
Ron Sykes	**Bobby Knutt**
Johnny Webb	**Jack Smethurst**
Nicky/Nick Tilsley/Platt	**Warren Jackson**
	Adam Rickitt
Alma Sedgewick/Baldwin/Halliwell	**Amanda Barrie**
Eunice Nuttall/Gee	**Meg Johnson**
Gordon Lewis	**David Daker**
Marion Willis/Yeats	**Veronica Doran**
Sharon Gaskell	**Tracie Bennett**
Maggie Dunlop/Redman	**Jill Kerman**
Tom 'Chalkie' Whitely	**Teddy Turner**
Craig Whitely	**Mark Price**
Phyllis Pearce	**Jill Summers**
Victor Pendlebury	**Christopher Coll**
Dr Lowther	**Robert Scase**
Percy Sugden	**Bill Waddington**
Jack Duckworth	**William Tarmey**
Terry Duckworth	**Nigel Pivaro**
Norman 'Curly' Watts	**Kevin Kennedy**
Shirley Armitage	**Lisa Lewis**
Kevin Webster	**Michael Le Vell**
Sally Waterman	**Vicki Chambers**
Mark Redman	**Thomas Hawkeswood**
	Christopher Oakes
	Chris Cook
	Paul Fox
Bill Webster	**Peter Armitage**
Debbie Webster	**Sue Devaney**
George Wardle	**Ron Davies**
Gloria Todd	**Sue Jenkins**
Martin Platt	**Sean Wilson**
Harry Clayton	**Johnny Leeze**
Connie Clayton	**Susan Brown**
Andrea Clayton	**Caroline O'Neill**
Sue Clayton	**Jane Hazelgrove**
Sam Tindall	**Tom Mennard**
Frank Mills	**Nigel Gregory**
Stella Rigby	**Vivienne Ross**
Jenny Bradley	**Sally Ann Matthews**
Alan Bradley	**Mark Eden**
Sally Seddon/Webster	**Sally Whittaker**
Ian Latimer	**Michael Looney**
Sarah Louise Tilsley/Platt	**Lynsay King**
	Tina O'Brien
Don Brennan	**Geoff Hinsliff**
Sandra Stubbs	**Sally Watts**
Tina Fowler	**Michelle Holmes**
Dawn Prescott	**Louise Harrison**
Liz McDonald	**Beverley Callard**
Jim McDonald	**Charles Lawson**
Andy McDonald	**Nicholas Cochrane**
Steve McDonald	**Simon Gregory**
Wendy Crozier	**Roberta Kerr**
Mark Casey	**Stuart Wolfenden**
Reg Holdsworth	**Ken Morley**
Kimberley Taylor	**Suzanne Hall**
Eddie Ramsden	**William Ivory**
Nigel Ridley	**John Basham**
Maurice Jones	**Alan Moore**
Des Barnes	**Philip Middlemiss**
Steph Barnes	**Amelia Bullmore**
Vicky Arden	**Helen Warburton**
	Chloë Newsome
Felicity 'Flick' Khan	**Rita Wolf**
Angie Freeman	**Deborah McAndrew**
Phil Jennings	**Tommy Boyle**
Rosie Webster	**Emma Collinge**
	Helen Flanagan
Marie Lancaster/Ramsden	**Joy Blakeman**
Peter Ingram	**Tony Osoba**
Jackie Ingram/Baldwin	**Shirin Taylor**
Raquel Wolstenhulme/Watts	**Sarah Lancashire**
Brendan Scott	**Milton Johns**
Lisa Horten/Duckworth	**Caroline Milmoe**
Ted Sullivan	**William Russell**
Denise Osbourne	**Denise Black**
Neil Mitchell	**John Lloyd Fillingham**
Carmel Finnan	**Catherine Cusack**
Doug Murray	**Brian Hibbard**
Paula Maxwell	**Judy Brooke**
Maureen Naylor/Holdsworth/Elliott	**Sherrie Hewson**
Maud Grimes	**Elizabeth Bradley**
Fiona Middleton	**Angela Griffin**
Tanya Pooley	**Eva Pope**
Charlie Whelan	**John St Ryan**
Norris Cole	**Malcolm Hebden**
Tricia Armstrong	**Tracy Brabin**
Jamie Armstrong	**Joseph Gilgun**
Revd Bernard Morten	**Roland MacLeod**
Samir Rachid	**Al Nedjari**
Maxine Heavey/Peacock	**Tracy Shaw**
Rodney Bostock	**Colin Proctor**
Billy Williams	**Frank Mills**

Josie Clarke	**Ellie Haddington**
Anne Malone	**Eve Steele**
Daniel Osbourne	**Lewis Harney**
Eric Firman	**Malcolm Terris**
Tony Horrocks	**Lee Warburton**
Judy Mallett	**Gaynor Faye**
Gary Mallett	**Ian Mercer**
Stephen Reid	**Todd Boyce**
Fred Elliott	**John Savident**
Ashley Peacock	**Stephen Arnold**
Joyce Smedley	**Anita Carey**
Kelly Thomson	**Sarah Moffett**
Sophie Webster	**Ashleigh Middleton**
	Emma Woodward
Claire Palmer	**Maggie Norris**
Becky Palmer	**Emily Aston**
Sean Skinner	**Terence Hillyer**
Samantha Failsworth	**Tina Hobley**
Roy Cropper	**David Neilson**
Alan McKenna	**Glenn Hugill**
Chris Collins	**Matthew Marsden**
Natalie Horrocks/Barnes	**Denise Welch**
Zoe Tattersall	**Joanne Froggatt**
Les Battersby	**Bruce Jones**
Janice Battersby	**Vicky Entwistle**
Leanne Battersby/Tilsley	**Jane Danson**
Toyah Battersby	**Georgia Taylor**
Jon Lindsay	**Owen Aaronovitch**
Pam Middleton	**Elizabeth Estensen**
Geoffrey 'Spider' Nugent	**Martin Hancock**
Hayley Patterson/Cropper	**Julie Hesmondalgh**
David Platt	**Thomas Ormson**
	Jack P. Shepherd
Greg Kelly	**Stephen Billington**
Jackie Dobbs	**Margi Clarke**
Charlie West	**Keith Clifford**
Michael Wall	**Dominic Rickhards**
Lorraine Brownlow	**Holly Newman**
Linda Sykes/Baldwin	**Jacqueline Pirie**
Alison Wakefield/Webster	**Naomi Radcliffe**
Aiden O'Donnall	**Kieran Flynn**
Ian Bentley	**Jonathan Guy Lewis**
Ravi Desai	**Saeed Jaffrey**
Nita Desai	**Rebecca Sarker**
Vikram Desai	**Chris Bisson**
Julia Stone	**Fiona Allen**
Ted Cooper	**David Peart**
Tyrone Dobbs	**Alan Halsall**
Danny Hargreaves	**Richard Standing**
Vinny Sorrell	**James Gaddas**
Melanie Tindell	**Nichola Wheeler**
Tom Ferguson	**Tom Wisdom**
Doreen Heavey	**Prunella Gee**
Beryl Peacock	**Anny Tobin**
Rebecca Hopkins	**Jill Halfpenny**
Gwen Loveday/Davies	**Annie Hulley**
Debs Brownlow	**Gabrielle Glaister**
Duggie Ferguson	**John Bowe**
Dev Alahan	**Jimmi Harkishin**
Maria Sutherland	**Samia Ghadie**
Jez Quigley	**Lee Boardman**
Dennis Stringer	**Charles Dale**
Eileen Grimshaw	**Sue Cleaver**

Geena Gregory	**Jennifer James**
Anthony Stephens	**John Quayle**
Edna Miller	**Joan Kempson**
Emma Taylor	**Angela Lonsdale**
Charlie Ramsden	**Clare McGlinn**
Dr Matt Ramsden	**Stephen Beckett**
Candice Stowe	**Nikki Sanderson**
Karen Phillips	**Suzanne Jones**
Bobbi Lewis	**Naomi Russell**
Sam Kingston	**Scott Wright**

Creator: **Tony Warren**
Producers: **Stuart Latham, Derek Granger, H. V. Kershaw, Margaret Morris, Tim Aspinall, Howard Baker, Peter Eckersley, Jack Rosenthal, Michael Cox, Richard Everitt, Richard Doubleday, John Finch, June Howson, Brian Armstrong, Eric Prytherch, Susie Hush, Bill Podmore, Leslie Duxbury, Pauline Shaw, Mervyn Watson, John G. Temple, David Liddiment, Carolyn Reynolds, Tony Wood, Sue Pritchard, Brian Park, David Hanson, Jane Macnaught**

Working-class life in a northern back-street.

Coronation Street is a British institution. However, after the first episode went out at 7 p.m. on 9 December 1960 one critic famously declared that it had no future, being all doom and gloom. Like the Decca records executive who turned down The Beatles, he couldn't have been more wrong. The *'Street'* is now over 40 years old and still at the top of the ratings. That said, anyone viewing early recordings will immediately recognize how the series has changed over the years. It began in an age of industrial grime and sweat but has progressed to reflect the many changes that have taken place in British life. The smoking chimney pots and leaden skies of the early programme credits echoed a dour but vibrant society, and creator Tony Warren (a 23-year-old Granada staff-writer, tired of adapting BIGGLES stories) initially produced scripts similar to the kitchen-sink dramas seen on ARMCHAIR THEATRE. But the programme quickly mellowed, introducing more humour and occasional farcical elements. Indeed, the programme wandered so far from Warren's original goals that at one time he disowned it. These days, *Coronation Street* plays almost like a situation comedy, although shocks, tragedy and moments of high drama are liberally dispersed throughout its episodes. Warren himself has now conceded that with society growing 'softer', *Coronation Street* has had to follow suit.

The programme is set in the fictional Manchester suburb of Weatherfield, Coronation Street (the working name was *Florizel Street* but, allegedly, sounded too much like a lavatory cleaner) being a typical northern back-street terrace with a pub on one corner and a shop on the other. The first ever scene took place in the shop on the day that Florrie Lindley arrived to take over the business from the retiring Elsie Lappin. Also in that historic original cast were Annie and Jack Walker, landlords of the pub, the Rovers Return. The genial Jack (and actor Arthur Leslie) died in 1970, but Annie, the *Street's* duchess and mistress of the withering look, held the licence until 1983, when she retired and left the series. Ena Sharples was the local hair-netted battleaxe, caretaker of the Glad Tidings Mission. Her OAP friends in the pub's snug were meek-and-mild Minnie Caldwell and Martha Longhurst, who was sensationally killed off in 1964, slumping dead over her milk stout. Another veteran was pensioner Albert Tatlock, proud of his war medals but never too proud to cadge a free rum if one was offered. Elsie Tanner was the fiery brunette whose promiscuity nettled the local puritans (especially Ena), and Dennis was her layabout son. And then there were the Barlows, hard-working, salt of the earth dad, Frank, his loyal wife, Ida (soon to be crushed by a bus), and two sons, Ken and David. David, a one-time professional footballer, was subsequently killed in a car accident in Australia, while Ken, always the *Street*'s intellectual (thrice-married: to Albert Tatlock's niece Valerie, to suicide victim Janet Reid and to Deirdre Langton), is today the only remaining original cast member.

Over the years the series has introduced plenty of other memorable characters. Leonard Swindley, the teetotal, lay-preaching draper at Gamma Garments, was jilted at the altar by the mousey Emily Nugent. Swindley later starred in the spin-off series, PARDON THE EXPRESSION. Nugent, another long-serving member of the cast, went on to marry photographer Ernie Bishop and, after he was shot dead in a wages snatch, wed bigamist Arnold Swain. Lucille Hewitt was the troublesome teenager who lived with the Walkers after her father, Harry, and barmaid step-mother, Concepta, left for Ireland, while Len Fairclough was the *Street*'s he-man, a hard-drinking, roughly hewn builder who eventually signed away his bachelorhood (after years of flirtation with Elsie Tanner) in a marriage to red-headed singer Rita Littlewood. After 23 years in the series, he was killed off in a car crash in 1983, following a visit to his mistress. Lovable Jerry Booth was Len's stuttering assistant at the builder's yard. His place was taken later by the untrustworthy Ray Langton.

Stan and Hilda Ogden moved into number 13 in 1964 and forged one of TV's great double acts, a partnership that was broken only by actor Bernard Youens's illness and subsequent death in 1984. A combination of a workshy boozer and a tittle-tattling skivvy, the Ogdens were the unluckiest couple on television, although their misfortune was usually self-inflicted. For many, Hilda's grief when Stan died provided moments of unsurpassable drama, and actress Jean Alexander's performance won universal acclaim. The Ogdens' wayward daughter, Irma (she of the rasping voice), became David Barlow's wife, while their lodger, chortling jailbird dustman Eddie Yeats, was one of the show's most popular stars of the 1970s.

With the retirement of Annie Walker, the Rovers Return eventually passed into the hands of brassy, buxom Bet Lynch, the tarty, blonde barmaid who first arrived in the series in 1966 and became a fixture in 1970. Bet took over as the *Street*'s mother confessor, although her own problems (notably with men – including her failed marriage to entertainments agent Alec Gilroy) were far from trivial. One of her liaisons was with ragtrade wide boy, Mike Baldwin, arch-enemy of Ken Barlow (having tried to steal Ken's wife, Deirdre, and then marrying his daughter, Susan). Rita Fairclough's harrowing ordeal at the hands of vicious Alan Bradley

was another *Coronation Street* highlight, ending with Bradley's death beneath the wheels of a Blackpool tram. Twittering away behind Rita was Mavis, her dithery colleague in The Kabin newsagent's shop, and regular interruptions came from Mavis's wimpy suitors, Derek Wilton and Victor Pendlebury.

The younger element has also been well represented. In the 1970s action focused around flighty shop assistant Suzie Birchall, corner shop girl Tricia Hopkins and insecure Gail Potter. Gail has since matured into a mother of three – and wife of two. Her first husband was the brawny Brian Tilsley (son of Ivy, arch-nagger, devout Catholic and one-time factory shop steward), while her second husband was trainee nurse Martin Platt, one of the 1980s' intake of teenagers. Along with Martin, the 1980s brought in star-gazing binman (later supermarket manager) Curly Watts, bookie Des Barnes and mechanic Kevin Webster and his blonde wife, Sally. Occasionally on the scene was sneering Terry Duckworth, the ne'er-do-well son of shiftless Jack and loud-mouthed Vera, who have assumed the Ogdens' crown as the *Street*'s perpetual losers.

Shopkeeper Alf Roberts was one of the series' senior figures after becoming a permanent cast member in 1968, no doubt helped by the fact that he was Weatherfield's mayor on two occasions. His second wife, Renee, was killed in a car accident, and Alf later suffered at the hands of his spendthrift third wife, Audrey, Gail's unreliable mother. Among the other senior characters have been policeman's widow Betty Turpin (the pub's homely barmaid and ace hot-pot cook); gravel-voiced blue-rinsed Phyllis Pearce and the apple of her eye, war cook Percy Sugden, Emily's interfering, insensitive lodger; and the endlessly bickering McDonald family. Another cult character was Reg Holdsworth, the pompous, vain retail executive.

In recent years, the most notable newcomers have included the 'neighbours from hell', the Battersbys; black-pudding-maker-turned-corner-shop-keeper Fred Elliott, and transsexual Hayley Patterson. Dramatic high spots have continued to keep the series at the top of the ratings. The exits (in various styles) of Bet, Derek and Mavis brought a tear to many a viewer's eye, as did the short-lived marriage of Curly and Raquel. The wrongful conviction of Deirdre for financial fraud ignited the nation and campaigns were organized to 'free the Weatherfield one'.

Coronation Street's writers have been many, with the most notable including John Finch, Jack Rosenthal, Harry Driver, Harry (H. V.) Kershaw, Adele Rose, Jim Allen and John Stevenson. The series' melancholic solo-cornet theme tune was written by Eric Spear. In addition to the cast list above, the roll-call of 'guesting' actors and actresses is impressive to say the least. Among those cutting their teeth in the series have been singers Peter Noone of Herman's Hermits (Len Fairclough's son, Stanley), Monkee Davy Jones (Ena Sharples's grandson, Colin Lomax) and Michael Ball (Malcolm Nuttall, Kevin Webster's one-time rival in love), as well as the likes of Joanna Lumley (Ken Barlow's girlfriend, Elaine Perkins), Prunella Scales (bus conductress Eileen Hughes), Martin Shaw (hippie Robert Croft), Ray Brooks (Norman Phillips), Michael Elphick (Douglas Wormald, who wanted to buy The Kabin), Paula Wilcox (Ray Langton's sister, Janice), Peter Dean (lorry driver Fangio Bateman), Stan Stennett (Norman Crabtree, Hilda Ogden's chip-shop-owning brother), Richard Beckinsale (a policeman), THE GOOD OLD DAYS compere Leonard Sachs (Sir Julius Berlin), Paul Shane (Post Office worker Frank Draper), Bill Maynard (music agent Mickey Malone), Ben Kingsley (a Jack-the-lad who chatted up Irma Ogden and Valerie Barlow), Max Wall (Elsie Tanner's friend, Harry Payne) and a very young Joanne Whalley-Kilmer (Pamela Graham). Singer Chris Sandford appeared as binman Walter Potts, aka pop hopeful Brett Falcon, who recorded the song, 'Not Too Little Not Too Much', a real-life Top Twenty hit in 1963.

Originally screened live on Fridays, *Coronation Street* switched to Monday and Wednesday evenings in 1961 and was, for the first time, fully networked (the earliest episodes were not seen in the Midlands or in the Tyne-Tees area). From 1989, a third helping was served up on Fridays in a bid to win the soap war with BBC rival, EASTENDERS, and a fourth weekly episode – on Sunday – was added in 1996. *Coronation Street* has also been viewed with much pleasure all around the world, although one of the few places it has yet to catch on is the USA. America did produce its own copycat soap, however, in the shape of PEYTON PLACE. Outliving its glamorous American clone by many years, *Coronation Street* is now the world's longest-running fictitious television series.

COSBY, BILL
(1937–)

Hugely successful American comedian/actor/producer, a former nightclub comic whose TV career began with *I Spy* in 1965. In playing the part of Alexander Scott, Cosby became the first black actor to co-star in a US prime-time drama series. He followed *I Spy* with a succession of comedy, variety and children's programmes, most of which were not aired in the UK. After spending eight years out of television, during which he gained a doctorate in education, he was tempted back by the offer of a sitcom over which he had complete creative control. The result was THE COSBY SHOW, and his portrayal of caring dad Cliff Huxtable enabled Cosby to give vent to his own philosophies of how to raise and educate children. The show picked up numerous awards and was a massive ratings success. More recently Cosby has filled Groucho Marx's shoes in the revival of the 1950s US quiz show, *You Bet Your Life*, played criminologist Guy Hanks in *The Cosby Mysteries*, and starred in the US version of ONE FOOT IN THE GRAVE, known simply as *Cosby*.

COSBY SHOW, THE
US (Carsey-Werner) Situation Comedy. Channel 4
1985–94

Dr Heathcliff (Cliff) Huxtable	**Bill Cosby**
Clair Huxtable	**Phylicia Ayres-Allen/Rashad**
Denise Huxtable Kendall	**Lisa Bonet**
Theodore Huxtable	**Malcolm-Jamal Warner**
Vanessa Huxtable	**Tempestt Bledsoe**
Rudy Huxtable	**Keshia Knight Pulliam**
Sondra Huxtable/Tibideaux	**Sabrina Le Beauf**
Peter Chiara	**Peter Costa**
Anna Huxtable	**Clarice Taylor**
Russell Huxtable	**Earle Hyman**
Elvin Tibideaux	**Geoffrey Owens**
Kenny ('Bud')	**Deon Richmond**
Cockroach	**Carl Anthony Payne**
Denny	**Troy Winbush**
Lt. Martin Kendall	**Joseph C. Phillips**
Olivia Kendall	**Raven Symone**
Pam Turner	**Erika Alexander**

Creators: **Bill Cosby, Ed Weinberger, Michael Leeson**
Producer: **Bill Cosby**

Family life in a caring New York household.

After a chequered TV past, Bill Cosby created this gentle sitcom and turned it into one of US TV's biggest ever moneyspinners. *The Cosby Show* followed developments in the life of a black middle-class family, showing the children growing up, leaving school and college, eventually getting married and having children of their own. The parents were the charming Cliff Huxtable, an obstetrician, and his confident lawyer wife, Clair. Their children ranged in age from Sondra, a Princeton student, to five-year-old Rudy with, in between, teenagers Denise and Theo and eight-year-old Vanessa. The children's friends were also included. Cockroach was a pal of Theo's, while Peter and Bud were two of Rudy's classmates. Anna and Russell, Cliff's parents, made occasional appearances and, later, the Huxtables took in Pam Turner, the teenage daughter of a distant cousin from the Brooklyn slums. The family lived in a New York terraced house, from where Cliff also practised his medicine.

Bill Cosby wasn't just the show's creator, his control was evident throughout. He was involved in many aspects of the production and the series became a personal statement about how he felt children should be brought up, i.e. with firmness and love, a philosophy he had developed while taking an education degree in the 1970s.

COTTON, BILL
CBE (1928–)

The son of bandleader Billy Cotton, Bill Cotton's showbusiness career began in Tin Pan Alley as a record plugger. He was joint MD of Michael Reine Music Co., 1952–6, before joining the BBC as a light entertainment producer. He became Assistant Head of Light Entertainment in 1962, moving up to Head of Variety in 1967. From 1970 he was Head of Light Entertainment and progressed to Controller of BBC 1 in 1977, and then Deputy Managing Director of BBC Television in 1981. After time spent chairing BBC Enterprises, Cotton was installed as Managing Director of BBC Television in 1984. In 1988 he left to join the Noel Gay Organization. He became deputy chairman of Meridian in 1991, and chairman from 1996.

COTTON, BILLY
(1899–1969)

'Wakey, wakey!' With a yell like this, and a rousing rendition of his theme tune, 'Somebody Stole My Girl', jovial bandleader Billy Cotton ensured viewers never missed the start of his weekly variety revue. With its emphasis on comedy and music, *The Billy Cotton Band Show* was a stalwart of the BBC's programming for 12 years from 1956, and Cotton also had success with *Wakey Wakey Tavern* and *Billy Cotton's Music Hall*, as well as being seen in variety programmes like *Saturday Showtime* and *The Tin Pan Alley Show*. Cotton arrived on television via BBC radio. He first broadcast in 1924, and his Band Show was a Sunday lunchtime favourite for 19 years from 1949. He was also a keen sportsman, despite his 17-stone frame. His son, Bill Cotton Jr (who also produced some of his dad's programmes), later became Managing Director of BBC Television.

COUNT OF MONTE CRISTO, THE
UK (ITP) Adventure. ITV 1956

Edmund Dantès	**George Dolenz**
Jacopo	**Nick Cravat**
Rico	**Robert Cawdron**

Producers: **Sidney Marshall, Dennis Vance**

A falsely imprisoned man learns of lost treasure from a fellow prisoner and escapes to claim it.

In 18th-century France, Edmund Dantès had been wrongly convicted of crimes against the state and incarcerated in the infamous Château d'If. There, a dying prisoner told of the treasure to be found on the island of Monte Cristo and Dantès broke free to take it for his own, setting himself up as a nobleman on the proceeds. The original story came from the novel of the same name by Alexandre Dumas, although the TV series expanded on Dantès's swashbuckling adventures, making the Frenchman a kind of Robin Hood battling for fairness and justice for all, and travelling all around Europe. Star George Dolenz was the father of future Monkee, Mickey.

COUNTDOWN
UK (Yorkshire) Game Show. Channel 4 1982–

Presenters: **Richard Whiteley, Carol Vorderman**
Creator: **Armand Jammot**
Executive Producers: **Frank Smith, John Meade**

Daily afternoon words-and-numbers game.

The aim for the two *Countdown* contestants has been to construct, in 30 seconds, the longest word they can from nine letters chosen at random. Whoever has used up the most letters in forming a word has earned the same number of points as letters used. Between word rounds a couple of numbers games have been introduced. For these, the contestants have needed to add, subtract, multiply and divide randomly selected numbers to arrive at a given total (or as close to it as possible). The contestant with the sum nearest the total has gained up to ten more points. The final round has been the *Countdown* conundrum, an anagram worth ten points for first correct solution. The higher-scoring contestant has then met a new challenger on the following day, and the series' best participants have taken part in an end-of-term knockout to find the overall champion.

Richard Whiteley – master of the excruciating pun – has hosted proceedings from day one, Carol Vorderman has been the numbers and letters girl and Beverley Isherwood and Kathy Hytner acted as hostesses in the early programmes. A guest celebrity has helped verify the words, and those gleefully undertaking this chore have included Ted Moult, Kenneth Williams, Sylvia Syms, Richard Stilgoe and Gyles Brandreth. *Countdown* was the first programme to be seen on Channel 4 and was based on a French concept.

COUNTRY MATTERS
UK (Granada) Drama Anthology. ITV 1972–3

Producer: **Derek Granger**

Dramatization of assorted rustic stories.

This anthology of 13 attractively framed rustic tales was adapted from the works of H. E. Bates and A. E. Coppard. It featured stars like Ian McKellen, Joss Ackland, Pauline Collins, Jane Lapotaire, Michael Elphick, Jeremy Brett and Gareth Thomas, and the plays revolved around love, rivalry and times of adversity in beautiful country locations.

COURT MARTIAL
UK/US (Roncom/ITC) Legal Drama. ITV 1965–7

Capt. David Young	**Bradford Dillman**
Major Frank Whittaker	**Peter Graves**
Master Sgt John MacCaskey	**Kenneth J. Warren**
Sgt Wendy	**Diane Clare**

Producers: **Robert Douglas, Bill Hill**

A team of military lawyers investigates crimes committed during the war.

Based in England during World War II, the industrious legal eagles of the US Army Judge Advocate General's Office were assigned to the continent of Europe. Their mission: to track down perpetrators of war crimes and bring them to justice. Each episode devoted much time to their excursions into war-torn Europe, winding up with the court martial proceedings themselves. Major Frank Whittaker was senior officer and chief prosecutor, Captain David Young the defending barrister. Sgt John MacCaskey was their aide and Sgt Wendy their secretary. The series was spun off a two-part story entitled *The Case Against Paul Ryker*, which aired as part of the *Kraft Suspense Theater* anthology in the USA.

COUSTEAU, JACQUES
(1910–97)

French marine expert and former Navy officer who was largely responsible for the development of the aqualung (and the new freedom it gave divers) during World War II. He also won his country's prestigious *Légion d'honneur* medal. In the post-war years he branched out into cinematic documentaries that charted his scientific explorations beneath the waves. Working from his converted minesweeper, *Calypso*, Cousteau later revealed the mysteries of the deep to TV viewers, in series like *Under the Sea*, THE WORLD ABOUT US, the internationally successful *Undersea World of Jacques Cousteau* (which ran for eight years) and *The Cousteau Odyssey*. His entertaining, authoritative, rather nasal delivery opened up the complexities of marine biology to an enthralled general public and earned him numerous awards. In his later years he was a vociferous environmental campaigner.

CRACKER
UK (Granada) Drama. ITV 1993–6

Eddie 'Fitz' Fitzgerald	**Robbie Coltrane**
Judith Fitzgerald	**Barbara Flynn**
DS Jane Penhaligon	**Geraldine Somerville**
DCI David Bilborough	**Christopher Eccleston**
DS Jimmy Beck	**Lorcan Cranitch**
Mark Fitzgerald	**Kieran O'Brien**
DCI Wise	**Ricky Tomlinson**
DC Harriman	**Colin Tierney**
Temple	**Robert Cavanah**
Skelton	**Wilbert Johnson**

Creator: **Jimmy McGovern**
Producers: **Gub Neal, Paul Abbott, Hilary Bevan Jones**

A larger-than-life police psychologist cracks complicated crimes but fails to keep his own life in order.

'Fitz' Fitzgerald was an outstanding but totally unconventional criminal psychologist, working freelance for the Greater Manchester Police. His speciality was reading a criminal's mind, drawing up character profiles and helping the police break down a suspect's outer shell, although his approach was often crude, insensitive and far from gentle. Bilborough (and later Wise) was the DCI at the Anson Road station who called on Fitz's services, and 'Panhandle' Penhaligon was the sergeant usually dispatched to chaperone him. As brilliant as Fitz was at his job, his own personal life was in a mess. Grossly overweight, a heavy drinker, a compulsive gambler and a chain-smoker, Fitz could 'spot a guilty cough in a football crowd but not know if World War III was breaking out in his living room', according to Panhandle. And when Fitz's long-suffering wife, Judith, walked out on him, he only made matters worse by embarking on a stormy affair with his attractive police associate.

Intense, shocking and riddled with unexpected twists and turns, *Cracker* won universal acclaim, with Robbie Coltrane collecting the BAFTA Best Actor award for his efforts. It was also graphically and realistically violent, although such excesses were presented in a defiantly unglorified manner. The programme ended after three series in 1995, but a two-hour special, set in Hong Kong, followed in October 1996. An American version, entitled *Fitz* and starring Robert Pastorelli, was shown on ITV in 1998.

CRACKERJACK
UK (BBC) Children's Entertainment. BBC 1955–84

Presenters: **Eamonn Andrews, Leslie Crowther, Michael Aspel, Ed Stewart, Stu Francis**

Other regulars: **Joe Baker, Jack Douglas, Ronnie Corbett, Michael Derbyshire, Eddie Leslie, Pearl Carr, Teddy Johnson, Raymond Rollett, Vivienne Martin, Peter Glaze, Jillian Comber, Pip Hinton, Valerie Walsh, Christine Holmes, Rod McLennan, Frances Barlow, Don Maclean, Little and Large, Stuart Sherwin, Heather Barbour, Elaine Paige, Jacqueline Clarke, Jan Hunt, Bernie Clifton, Val Mitchell, The Krankies, Jan Michelle, Leigh Miles, Sally Ann Triplett, Julie Dorne Brown, Sara Hollamby, Ling Tai**

Producers: **Johnny Downes, Peter Whitmore, Brian S. Jones, Robin Nash, Brian Whitehouse, Paul Ciani**

Live music and comedy show for kids.

In the USA, *Crackerjack* is a brand of popcorn – an appropriate name for this variety show, which leaned heavily on top pop stars and corny jokes to carry the day. But carry the day it did – mostly on Thursdays or Fridays, at five to five (or thereabouts), for no less than 29 years. With its trademark 'Crackerjack' echo from the studio audience every time the programme's name was mentioned, it offered speeded-up slapstick sketches (most memorably featuring a young Leslie Crowther and former Crazy Gang extra, Peter Glaze), the latest pop hits (big names appearing included Roy Orbison, Tom Jones and Cliff Richard) and a sing-along, grand finale, usually comprising a medley of chart records with 'funny' new words added. Music was provided for many years by the Bert Hayes Octet. In between, competitions held sway. These were strictly divided into boys' and girls' games in the show's formative years, and best remembered is *Double or Drop* (which was devised by the programme's first host, Eamonn Andrews, and ran until 1964). In *Double or Drop*, kids answered questions and were then loaded up with prizes which, if dropped, were confiscated. Wrong answers led to armfuls of boobyprize cabbages. Another popular game was *Jig-Jak*, introduced in 1964. This involved answering questions to gain a piece of a jigsaw featuring a famous person's face. The first competitor to spot the celebrity gained the prize, but all contestants, win or lose, walked away with a coveted *Crackerjack* pencil. *Take a Letter* featured prominently in later series.

Ronnie Corbett and Jack Douglas cut their TV teeth on *Crackerjack* and Leslie Crowther's career was done no harm by an eight-year stretch as comic and then compere. Richard Hearne's Mr Pastry was also a regular guest in the 1950s. Eamonn Andrews and Michael Aspel moved on to bigger and better things, while later hosts Ed 'Stewpot' Stewart and Stu 'I could crush a grape' Francis were established children's entertainers who found their niche with the programme. Reassuring female hostesses like Jillian Comber, Pip Hinton and Christine Holmes became almost as popular as the male stars.

CRADOCK, FANNY
(Phyllis Cradock; 1909–94)

Fanny Cradock was one of the small screen's first cooks and an unlikely star of TV's golden age. Shunning the apron in favour of impractical evening gowns and pearls, she epitomized the rather starchy attitude prevalent in the BBC in the 1950s. She and her third husband, Major John Cradock, were published gourmets, writing the *Bon Viveur* column in the *Daily Telegraph*, for instance. They joined the BBC in 1955 to present *Kitchen Magic* but were soon snapped up by the new, less pompous ITV, where, instead of being Phyllis and John, they became Fanny and Johnny and hosted *Fanny's Kitchen, Chez Bon Viveur* and *The Cradocks*. They also chipped in with the *Happy Cooking* sequence in the kids' series, *Lucky Dip*. Although they were generally billed as a twosome, it was Fanny who was clearly in charge, leaving the monocled Johnny hovering in the background as she thrashed a few eggs around or whipped up a pudding. Her rather brusque, demanding style made her and Johnny (often jokingly portrayed as a kitchen boozer) easy targets for comedians like Benny Hill. They rejoined the BBC in the 1960s, presenting programmes like *Giving A Dinner Party, Fanny Cradock Invites* and *Fanny Cradock Cooks for Christmas*, carrying on until retirement in the 1970s. Johnny died in 1987.

CRAIG, MICHAEL
(Michael Gregson; 1929–)

Silver-haired British actor, born in India. A Rank movie star of the 1950s and 1960s, his starring TV roles have included Johann in the steamy *Husbands and Lovers*; 50-year-old Harry who fell in love with a girl half his age in the sitcom, *Second Time Around*; William Parker, the dad of the Australia-bound family in *The Emigrants*; and ship's officer John Anderson in TRIANGLE. Other credits have included EMERGENCY – WARD 10 and DOCTOR WHO.

CRAIG, WENDY
(1934–)

Durham-born actress strongly associated with daffy, harassed-mother roles, evidenced in such series as NOT IN FRONT OF THE CHILDREN (Jennifer Corner), AND MOTHER MAKES THREE/FIVE (Sally Harrison/Redway) and BUTTERFLIES (Ria Parkinson). She branched out into serious drama in her own creation, NANNY (playing 1930s

nanny, Barbara Gray), but returned to sitcom with the short-lived *Laura and Disorder*, a series that she co-wrote (under her pen-name of Jonathan Marr) and in which she played accident-prone divorcée Laura Kingsley arriving back in the UK after ten years in America. In the 1990s, Craig was seen in THE GOLDEN GIRLS clone, *Brighton Belles* (Annie), while her earliest credits included the 1964 comedy, *Room at the Bottom*, and various single dramas.

CRANE
UK (Associated-Rediffusion) Adventure. ITV 1963–5

Richard Crane	**Patrick Allen**
Orlando O'Connor	**Sam Kydd**
Col. Mahmoud	**Gerald Flood**
Halima	**Laya Raki**

Creators: **Patrick Alexander, Jordan Lawrence**
Producer: **Jordan Lawrence**

The adventures of a city businessman turned contrabrand dealer in North Africa.

Bored by the routine of city life, Richard Crane took himself off to sunny Morocco, bought a boat and opened a beachfront bar near Casablanca. To pass the time, he indulged himself in petty smuggling: minor items like tobacco and booze. Keeping an eye on his activities was elegant local police chief Colonel Mahmoud, although he and Crane sometimes worked together against 'serious' criminals. Crane's well-worn friend and accomplice was Orlando O'Connor, a former member of the French Foreign Legion. He later appeared in his own spin-off series for children, ORLANDO. Halima was the café's sultry young bartender. Star Patrick Allen, an actor with a booming, authoritative voice, went on to further success off-camera, cornering the market in advert voice-overs.

CRANHAM, KENNETH
(1944–)

Dunfermline-born actor, well versed in rough-diamond roles and with a host of one-off dramas and guest appearances to his name. Among his starring roles have been Harvey Moon, the demobbed RAF corporal in SHINE ON HARVEY MOON, the over-zealous Pastor Finch in ORANGES ARE NOT THE ONLY FRUIT and villain Gus Mercer in EL C.I.D. Other credits have included *A Sort of Innocence*, CORONATION STREET, DANGER UXB (Jack Salt), *Thérèse Raquin*, REILLY – ACE OF SPIES (Lenin), *Chimera* (Hennessey), INSPECTOR MORSE, BOON, *Rules of Engagement*, VAN DER VALK, BERGERAC, MURDER MOST HORRID, *The Tenant of Wildfell Hall* (Revd Millward), *Our Mutual Friend* (Silas Wegg) and *Without Motive* (DC Supt. Derek Henderson). His first wife was actress Diana Quick and second wife actress Fiona Victory.

CRANITCH, LORCAN
(1959–)

Dublin-born actor coming to light as the devious DS Jimmy Beck in CRACKER and moving on to star as George Smith in *Screen One*'s *Deacon Brodie*, Larry Duggan in *The Heart Surgeon*, Stephen in *Close Relations*, Sean Dillon in BALLYKISSANGEL, Michael McCready in *McCready and Daughter* and Bernard Cleve in *My Fragile Heart*.

CRAVEN, JOHN
CBE (1940–)

Leeds-born presenter whose first TV appearances came at the age of 16 on *Sunday Break*. Later he was seen on regional news magazines, including *Look North* and *Points West*, and the kids' show, *Search*, before he secured the job of children's news presenter on his own JOHN CRAVEN'S NEWSROUND. From this came MULTI-COLOURED SWAP SHOP (encouraging a 'News Swap'), its successor, *Saturday Superstore*, and programmes like *Brainchild* and *The Show Me Show*. Most recently he has been host of *Country File* and programmes such as *Animal Sanctuary*.

CRAWFORD, BRODERICK
(William Broderick Crawford; 1911–86)

The man who gave the world the catchphrase 'Ten-Four', brawny Broderick Crawford's career began in 1930s gangster movies, in the sort of shady role he was initially to take into television. However, it was on the other side of the law that he made his name, playing Chief Dan Matthews in the hugely successful HIGHWAY PATROL. His bulky frame leaning against a car window, hollering 'Ten-Four' down the radio, is fondly remembered by viewers. Although he did secure lead roles in a couple of other American series (*King of Diamonds* and *The Interns*) after *Highway Patrol* ended in 1959, he was mostly seen by British viewers in guest appearances in TV movies and shows such as GET SMART, BURKE'S LAW and FANTASY ISLAND. The son of comedienne Helen Broderick, he won the Oscar for Best Actor in 1949 for his performance in *All the King's Men*.

CRAWFORD, MICHAEL
OBE (Michael Dumble Smith; 1942–)

Salisbury-born actor whose starring role in SOME MOTHERS DO 'AVE 'EM came after years of supporting parts in early ITC adventures like SIR FRANCIS DRAKE (playing Drake's nephew, John), comedies such as BILLY BUNTER OF GREYFRIARS SCHOOL and NOT SO MUCH A PROGRAMME, MORE A WAY OF LIFE, and such dramas as POLICE SURGEON, PROBATION OFFICER and EMERGENCY – WARD 10. However, it was as the accident-prone Frank Spencer that he made his name, winning huge acclaim for his comic performances and exhausting stunt routines. From this base, Crawford moved on to the less successful *Chalk and Cheese* (Dave Finn, a Cockney among posher neighbours), and then more into theatre, although still finding time to pop up as a guest star and singer on variety shows.

CREDITS

The roll-call of programme participants (both in front of and behind the cameras), usually seen at the end of the programme. Occasionally credits are given during the opening titles, but usually these are confined to the major stars and the writers.

CREW

The technical team working on a programme, essentially the operators of sound, lighting and camera equipment, but, in wider terms, associated staff involved in make-up, wardrobe, set construction, etc.

CREZZ, THE
UK (Thames) Drama. ITV 1976

Charles Bronte	**Joss Ackland**
Emma Antrobus	**Isla Blair**
Ken Green	**Peter Bowles**
Dr Balfour-Harvey	**Hugh Burden**
Brenda Pitman	**Janet Key**
Jackie Bronte	**Elspet Gray**

Creator: **Clive Exton**
Producer: **Paul Knight**

Tales of the residents of a London crescent.

Set in fictitious Carlisle Crescent, a middle-class London residential street, this series delivered 12 soapy, hour-long plays about the people who lived in *The Crezz*. It analysed their personal lives and monitored their inter-relationships, with one household assuming centre stage in each episode.

CRIBB
UK (Granada) Police Drama. ITV 1980–1

DS Cribb	**Alan Dobie**
Constable Thackeray	**William Simons**
Chief Insp. Jowett	**David Waller**

Executive Producer: **Peter Eckersley**
Producer: **June Wyndham Davies**

Victorian crime detection with a persistent CID officer.

Sgt Cribb, a dry, stubborn detective, worked for the newly formed Criminal Investigation Department, inaugurated to clean up the grimy streets of London in the time of Jack the Ripper. Cribb, a tough and determined officer with an eye for the ladies, outwitted the city's cleverest crooks (and his smartest colleagues) to bring to book all who crossed his path. He was assisted in his investigations by loyal Constable Thackeray, with Chief Inspector Jowett, the commanding officer, often getting in the way.

The series, based on the novels of Peter Lovesey, involved its hero in all manner of crimes, from blackmail to murder, usually set against the backdrop of the Victorians at leisure, with prize-fighting, the music hall and a six-day walking marathon among the featured activities. The detail was well researched and genuine events like the publication of Jerome K. Jerome's *Three Men in a Boat* and the purchase of London Zoo's elephant, Jumbo, by Barnum & Bailey's Circus, were woven into the plots. The series was spun off a 90-minute pilot episode, seen as part of Granada's *Screenplay* anthology in 1979.

CRIBBINS, BERNARD
(1928–)

Whimsical British actor/comedian, a familiar voice as well as face on television. The milestones of his long TV career have been his own show, *Cribbins*, the sketch show, *Get the Drift*, THE WOMBLES (for which he provided the narration), *Cuffy* (as the eponymous tinker, spun off from SHILLINGBURY TALES), *High and Dry* (Ron Archer, owner of a seaside pier) and *Langley Bottom* (Seth Raven). These accompany numerous contributions to THE GOOD OLD DAYS and JACKANORY, guest spots (in series as varied as THE AVENGERS and FAWLTY TOWERS) and assorted panel-game appearances, including as host of *Star Turn*. Cribbins was also the voice of Buzby, the chatty bird in the BT commercials.

CRIME OF PASSION
UK (ATV) Legal Drama Anthology. ITV 1970–3

President of the Court .... **Anthony Newlands**
Maître Savel .... **Daniel Moynihan**
Maître Lacan .... **John Phillips**
Maître Dubois .... **Bernard Archer**

Creator: **Ted Willis**
Producers: **Cecil Clarke, Robert D. Cardona, Ian Fordyce**

French barristers do battle over crimes of the heart.

Created by Ted Willis, using authentic French court cases ('Crime of Passion' is a legitimate defence in France), this series featured Maître Lacan for the prosecution and Maître Savel for the defence. Another lawyer, Maître Dubois, was seen in the last series. Each episode, poignantly given the name of its lead character – 'Catherine', 'Danielle', 'Gerard', etc. – opened showing the crime in question, before moving on to the trial and finally the verdict of the Judge, the President of the Court. Among the guest stars were Felicity Kendal, Johnny Briggs, Ralph Bates and Tessa Wyatt.

CRIME SHEET
UK (Associated-Rediffusion) Police Drama. ITV 1959

Det. Chief Supt. Tom Lockhart .... **Raymond Francis**

Creator: **Glyn Davies**
Producer: **Barry Baker**

The second part of the Supt. Lockhart trilogy.

In this series, the sharp-witted, snuff-taking Supt. Lockhart of MURDER BAG had been promoted to detective chief superintendent and now cast his net farther afield than mere murder investigations. His talents were employed on crime of all sorts, but he remained so diligent and infallible in his pursuit of villains that he was quickly transferred to Scotland Yard and NO HIDING PLACE. Two years later, Associated-Rediffusion revived the title *Crime Sheet* for a play starring Gerald Case as Chief Supt. Carr.

CRIME TRAVELLER
UK (Carnival Films) Science Fiction. BBC1 1997

Jeff Slade .... **Michael French**
Holly Turner .... **Chloë Annett**
Chief Insp. Kate Grisham .... **Sue Johnston**
Morris .... **Paul Trussell**
Nicky Robson .... **Richard Dempsey**
Danny .... **Bob Goodey**

Creator/Writer: **Anthony Horowitz**
Producer: **Brian Eastman**
Executive Producer: **Caroline Oulton**

A policeman discovers he can crack crime by nipping back in time to observe events.

Unconventional copper Jeff Slade had just made one mistake too many. Blowing an undercover operation by chasing the main suspect, against the orders of his no-nonsense boss, Grisham, he had put his job on the line. He was saved, however, by police science officer Holly Turner, who decided to use the time machine developed by her late dad to unearth vital evidence that would help out Slade. Realizing something funny had occurred, Slade confronted Holly, who revealed the time machine which was built into her flat. The temptation proving too great, Slade used the machine for his own ends to trap a killer, and, much against Holly's wishes, the duo continued to dart back in time to solve some baffling crimes. The usual time-travelling caveats – making sure you don't bump into yourself, getting back within a set time-limit, etc. – added to the tension. Also seen were new-graduate policeman Nicky Robson, the somewhat dim copper, Morris, and Danny, the constantly bemused janitor at Holly's apartment block.

Despite good pre-publicity and the fact that this was Michael French's first starring role after EASTENDERS, *Crime Traveller* failed to hit the spot with the viewing public and only one series of eight 50-minute episodes was made.

CRIMEWATCH UK
UK (BBC) Factual. BBC 1 1984–

Presenters: **Nick Ross, Sue Cook, Jill Dando, Fiona Bruce**

Editors/Producers: **Peter Chafer, Nikki Cheetham, Gerry McClellend, Liz Mills, Seetha Kumar, Kate Thomson, Gaby Koppel**

Crime reconstruction series inviting viewer assistance in catching villains.

Based on the German series, *File XY Unsolved*, and originally scheduled for just three editions, *Crimewatch UK* has combined dramatic re-enactments of unsolved crimes with a plea to the general public to ring in with further information. Tips on crime prevention have also been included and 'treasure trove' spots have allowed burgled viewers to reclaim stolen property. Two resident police officers, David Hatcher and Helen Phelps, plus visiting detectives, initially helped give the police side of each story. Phelps later left the force and joined the programme's production team. Her place alongside Hatcher has since been taken by Jacqui Hames. Original co-presenter Sue Cook left in 1995 and was succeeded by Jill Dando, who fronted the programme with Nick Ross until her tragic death in 1999, when she was replaced by Fiona Bruce. The programme has been aired monthly, and occasional review programmes (entitled *Crimewatch File*) have also been made, bringing viewers up to date with past stories. The series' clear-up rate has been impressive, with nearly 400 arrests made as a result of new information given by viewers. To allay viewers' fears, Ross has nearly always signed off with the words: 'Don't have nightmares. Do sleep well.'

CRISS CROSS QUIZ
UK (Granada) Quiz. ITV 1957–67

Presenter: **Jeremy Hawk**

Long-running noughts and crosses quiz.

This popular game show took the form of noughts and crosses with questions. One contestant scored crosses, the other scored noughts and, by giving correct answers, both sought to make a line of three, either vertically, diagonally or horizontally. For each correct answer cash was forthcoming, and large totals were possible. Jeremy Hawk (father of actress Belinda Lang) was the original questionmaster of this thrice-weekly show, and he also hosted a children's version, *Junior Criss Cross Quiz*, which ran for the same number of years. Chris Kelly was another presenter of the youth version, as were (at various times) Bob Holness, Mike Sarne, Chris Howland, Gordon Luck, Peter Wheeler, Mark Kelly, Bill Grundy and soccer star Danny Blanchflower. *Criss Cross Quiz* was derived from the American game show, *Tic Tac Dough*.

CROCODILE SHOES
UK (Big Boy) Drama. BBC 1 1994–6

Jed Shepperd	Jimmy Nail
Ade Lynn	James Wilby
Emma Shepperd	Melanie Hill
Pep	John Bowler
Caroline Carrlson	Alex Kingston
Alan Clarke	Christopher Fairbank
Snotter	Vince Pellegrino
Ox	Oliver Haden
Carmel Cantrell	Amy Madigan
Lou Benedetti	Burt Young
Archie Tate	Sammy Johnson
Wendy	Ellzabeth Carling
Lucy	Sara Stewart
Roxanne Pallenberg	Nadeshda Richter Brennicke
Omo	Jeffrey Knox
Big Chrissie	Paul Palance
Warren Bowles	Robert Morgan

Creator/Writer: **Jimmy Nail**
Producer: **Peter Richardson**
Executive Producers: **Linda James, Jimmy Nail, Jen Samson**

A Geordie manual worker becomes an international Country and Western star.

Jed Shepperd worked as a lathe-operator in a Newcastle factory but harboured hopes of becoming a country singer. His dreams came to reality when his sister, Emma, secretly sent a tape of Jed's songs off to Ade Lynn, a struggling A&R man for a London-based record company. Lynn recognized the talent and signed up Shepperd for himself, re-fashioning his image, propelling him to fame and using his cut of the proceedings to fuel his drugs habit. The ingenuous Shepperd was whisked to Nashville, where he attracted the romantic attentions of top country star Carmel Cantrell. In the second series, shown two years later, the drugs dealers had caught up with Lynn, and Shepperd was suspected of his murder. His record company was keen to recover a £500,000 advance on his second album (not yet recorded), a tabloid journalist was on his tail, and he found himself framed for drug peddling. Right back on his uppers, the former star set about clearing his name and finding the real killers.

Allowing creator Jimmy Nail to indulge his own passion for singing, *Crocodile Shoes* spawned a handful of hit singles.

CROFT, DAVID
OBE (David Sharland; 1922–)

British child actor turned comedy writer and producer, particularly in collaboration with Jimmy Perry and Jeremy Lloyd. With Perry, Croft created the doyen of British sitcoms, DAD'S ARMY, and went on to script (and produce) comedy favourites, IT AIN'T HALF HOT, MUM and HI-DE-HI!. These reflected Croft's experiences as an

ARP warden, a military entertainments officer in India and a producer of stage shows at Butlins. Croft and Perry also contributed YOU RANG, M'LORD?. With Lloyd, Croft wrote *Oh Happy Band!*, ARE YOU BEING SERVED?, COME BACK MRS NOAH, 'ALLO 'ALLO and *Grace and Favour*. With Richard Spendlove, he created OH DOCTOR BEECHING!. Croft's production credits have also included the sitcoms, *The Eggheads* (also as co-writer with Richard Waring), *A World of His Own*, HUGH AND I, BEGGAR MY NEIGHBOUR and UP POMPEII!, *as well as The Benny Hill Show* and *The Dick Emery Show*. His daughter, Penny, co-wrote the sitcom, LIFE WITHOUT GEORGE, which starred his son-in-law, the late Simon Cadell.

CRONKITE, WALTER
(1916–)

An American institution, Walter Cronkite was the USA's foremost newsreader and commentator for some 20 years. Joining CBS as a reporter in 1950, he moved up to newsreader and news editor on the network's *Evening News* in 1962, quickly establishing himself as the country's most trusted anchorman. His avuncular, cosy, sometimes emotional style and his 'That's the way it is' sign-off became his trademarks.

CROSBIE, ANNETTE
(1934–)

Scottish actress best known as Margaret, the long-suffering wife of Victor Meldrew, in ONE FOOT IN THE GRAVE. Her television career, however, has spanned over three decades and has included the role of Catherine of Aragon in the acclaimed drama, THE SIX WIVES OF HENRY VIII, and a BAFTA award-winning portrayal of Queen Victoria in EDWARD THE SEVENTH. In addition to assorted one-off plays, Crosbie's other notable performances have included a Resistance worker in *The White Rabbit*, Henrietta Labouchere in *Lillie*, Liz, Keith Barron's frumpy wife, in *Take Me Home*, and Joyce, Mel Smith's mother, in COLIN'S SANDWICH. She was also seen in John Mortimer's *Paradise Postponed* and played Janet in the 1993 revival of DOCTOR FINLAY, Edith Sparshott in AN UNSUITABLE JOB FOR A WOMAN, Aunt Doreen in *Underworld* and Hattie in *Anchor Me*, as well as supporting Rory Bremner.

CROSBY, BING
(Harry Lillis Crosby; 1903–77)

Internationally renowned crooner and light actor whose television work was largely confined to guest appearances and variety shows, with an attempt at sitcom in *The Bing Crosby Show* (as structural designer Bing Collins) proving less rewarding. However, his behind-the-scenes credits were important and his film company, Bing Crosby Productions, was responsible for several US hit series, including BEN CASEY. Trivia buffs will note that Crosby was the first choice for the role of COLUMBO

but turned it down, allegedly because it would have interfered with his golf.

CROSSROADS
UK (ATV/Central) Drama. ITV 1964–88

Meg Richardson/Ryder/Mortimer	Noele Gordon
Jill Richardson/Crane/Harvey/Chance	Jane Rossington
Sandy Richardson	Roger Tonge
Kitty Jarvis	Beryl Johnstone
Dick Jarvis	Brian Kent
Brian Jarvis	David Fennell
Janice Gifford/Jarvis	Carolyn Lyster
Carlos Rafael	Anthony Morton
Marilyn Gates/Hope	Sue Nicholls
	Nadine Hanwell
Christine Fuller/Palmer	Alex Marshall
Mrs Blundell	Peggy Aitchison
Owen Webb	George Skillan
Benny Willmot	Deke Arlon
Amy Turtle	Ann George
Hugh Mortimer	John Bentley
Philip Carroll	Malcolm Young
Josefina Rafael	Gillian Betts
Ralph Palmer	Norman Jones
Ruth Bailey/Fraser	Pamela Greenall
Sam Redway	John Porter Davison
Stephanie 'Stevie' Harris	Wendy Padbury
Penny Richardson	Diane Grayson
Diane Lawton/Parker/Hunter	Susan Hanson
Andy Fraser	Ian Paterson
Derek Maynard	Brian Hankins
Dave Cartwright	John Hamill
Barry Hughes	Patrick Marley
Kevin McArthur	Vincent Ball
Geoffrey Steele	Lew Luton
Shirley Perkins	Jacqueline Holborough
Enoch Jarvis	Jack Hayes
Eleanor Chase	Gillian Wray
Marie Massinet	Colette Gleeson
Pepe Costa	Stephen Rea
Miss Edith Tatum	Elisabeth Croft
Vince Parker	Peter Brookes
Malcolm Ryder	David Davenport
Ted Hope	Charles Stapley
Tish Hope	Joy Andrews
Peter Hope	Neville Hughes
Lynn Hope	Patsy Blower
Mrs Witten	Jo Richardson
Joyce Wood	Penelope Goddard
Myrtle Cavendish	Gretchen Franklin
Nick Van Doren	Peter Boyes
David Hunter	Ronald Allen
Rosemary Hunter	Janet Hargreaves
Chris Hunter	Freddie Foot
	Stephen Hoye
Tessa Wyvern	Eva Wishaw
John Crayne	Mark Rives
Sandra Gould	Diane Keen
Paul Stevens	Paul Greenwood
Don Rogers	Albert Shepherd
Melanie Harper	Cleo Sylvestre

Mrs Ash	**Kathleen St John**
Archie Gibbs	**Jack Haig**
Mr Lovejoy	**William Avenell**
Wilf Harvey	**Morris Parsons**
Stan Harvey	**Edward Clayton**
Sheila Harvey/Mollison	**Sonia Fox**
Vera Downend	**Zeph Gladstone**
Jane Smith	**Sally Adcock**
Clifford Leyton	**Johnny Briggs**
Sharon Metcalfe	**Carolyn Jones**
Mr Booth	**David Lawton**
Shughie McFee	**Angus Lennie**
Dr Butterworth	**Tony Steedman**
Kate Hamilton	**Frances White**
Anthony Mortimer	**Jeremy Sinden**
Paul Ross	**Sandor Elès**
Carney	**Jack Woolgar**
Jim Baines	**John Forgeham**
Benny Hawkins	**Paul Henry**
Ed Lawton	**Thomas Heathcote**
Doris Luke	**Kathy Staff**
Marian Owen	**Margaret John**
Iris Scott	**Angela Webb**
Kath Brownlow/Fellowes	**Pamela Vezey**
Arthur Brownlow	**Peter Hill**
Glenda Brownlow/Banks	**Lynette McMorrough**
Ron Brownlow	**Ian Liston**
Dr Farnham	**Allan Lander**
Kevin Banks	**David Moran**
Joe MacDonald	**Carl Andrews**
Adam Chance	**Tony Adams**
Lloyd Munro	**Alan Gifford**
Barbara Brady/Hunter	**Sue Lloyd**
Reg Cotterill	**Ivor Salter**
Alison Cotterill	**Carina Wyeth**
J. Henry Pollard	**Michael Turner**
Miranda Pollard	**Claire Faulconbridge**
Valerie Pollard	**Heather Chasen**
Oliver Banks	**Kenneth Gilbert**
Sally Banks	**Wendy Williams**
Eddie Lee	**Roy Boyd**
Victor Lee	**Victor Winding**
Tom Peterson	**Graham Rees**
Rita Hughes	**Lynn Dalby**
Becky Foster	**Maxine Gordon**
Gilbert Latham	**Royce Mills**
Carole Sands	**Jo-Anne Good**
Sid Hooper	**Stan Stennett**
Mavis Hooper	**Charmian Eyre**
Roy Lambert	**Steven Pinder**
Anne-Marie Wade	**Dee Hepburn**
Reg Lamont	**Reginald Marsh**
Jennifer Lamont	**Jean Kent**
Ashley Lamont	**Martyn Whitby**
Rose Scott	**Val Boothman**
Richard Lord	**Jeremy Mason**
Walter Soper	**Max Wall**
Colin Sands	**Paul Blake**
Ken Sands	**John Malcolm**
Lisa Walters	**Francesca Gonshaw**
John Latchford	**Arthur White**
Dr James Wilcox	**Robert Grange**
Douglas Brady	**Nigel Williams**
Larry Wilcox	**Paul Ashe**
Stephen Fellowes	**John Line**
Pat Reddington	**Rosemary Smith**
Nicola Freeman	**Gabrielle Drake**
Daniel Freeman	**Philip Goodhew**
Barry Hart	**Harry Nurmi**
Clifford Wayne	**Michael Drew**
Sam Benson	**Norman Bowler**
Mickey Doyle	**Martin Smith**
Mr Darby	**Patrick Jordan**
Lorraine Baker	**Dorothy Brown**
Mrs Meacher	**Stella Moray**
Georges-André Arnaud	**Jean Badin**
Tracey Hobbs	**Colette Barker**
Mrs Tardebigge	**Elsie Kelly**
Charlie Mycroft	**Graham Seed**
Tommy Lancaster	**Terence Rigby**
Mary Lancaster	**Francis Cuka**
Debbie Lancaster	**Kathryn Hurlbutt**
Lisa Lancaster	**Alison Dowling**
Mrs Babbitt	**Margaret Stallard**
Beverley Grice	**Karen Murden**
Margaret Grice	**Meryl Hampton**
Ray Grice	**Al Ashton**
Ranjit Rampul	**Ashok Kumar**
John Maddingham	**Jeremy Nicholas**
Jamie Maddingham	**Christopher Duffy**

Creators: **Hazel Adair, Peter Ling**
Producers: **Reg Watson, Pieter Rogers, Jack Barton, Phillip Bowman, Marian Nelson, William Smethurst, Michele Buck**

The day-to-day events at a Midlands motel.

Few programmes have endured as much ridicule as *Crossroads*. At the same time, few programmes have won the hearts of so many viewers. From its earliest days, *Crossroads* was taunted with criticisms of its wobbly sets and often wobblier performers. Lines were fluffed or simply forgotten, scripts were wooden and plots transparent, but much of this could be put down to the demands of a hectic recording schedule, given that *Crossroads* began as a five-times-a-week early-evening serial. Despite this and the constraints of a small budget, its popularity was such that it ran and ran – for 24 years in all.

The programme's queen bee was Meg Richardson, widowed owner of the Crossroads Motel, set in the fictitious village of King's Oak, somewhere in the West Midlands. Around her buzzed her next-of-kin: daughter Jill, son Sandy and sister Kitty, with Kitty's husband, Dick, and architect son, Brian. Meg's extended family were the motel staff, most of them dyed-in-the-wool Brummies, with the notable exception of Spanish chef Carlos Rafael. The most popular employees over the years included Diane Lawton, the blonde waitress who steadily worked her way up the motel ladder, singing waitress Marilyn Gates, gossipy little Amy Turtle, pompous chef Mr Lovejoy, hairstylist Vera Downend (who lived on a houseboat), coffee bar worker Benny Willmot, gardener Archie Gibbs, gruff nightwatchman Carney, spinster Doris Luke, oily restaurant manager Paul Ross, Scots chef Shughie McFee and receptionist Anne-Marie Wade. At the Crossroads garage worked Jim Baines, Sid Hooper and Joe McDonald, and the good folk of King's Oak also had a look-in, especially miserable old Wilf Harvey (whose electrician son, Stan, married Jill), postmistress Miss Tatum, antiques dealers Tish and Ted Hope and shopkeeper Roy Lambert. Probably the best loved of all *Crossroads* characters, however, was the slow-witted, woolly-hatted Benny Hawkins, first seen as a labourer at Diane's uncle's farm. He followed 'Miss Diane' back to King's Oak, but continued to suffer more than his fair share of misfortune, including the death of his gypsy girlfriend, Maureen Flynn, on their wedding day.

But tragedy and romance were the name of the game at Crossroads. Young Sandy was crippled in a car accident and spent most of his time afterwards in a wheelchair (actor Roger Tonge was later confined to a wheelchair himself, before dying prematurely in 1981). Jill married three times (once bigamously) and Meg herself married twice. Her first new husband, Malcolm Ryder, tried to poison her, and she later fell for old flame Hugh Mortimer, a millionaire businessman who then died of a heart attack while being held as a terrorists' hostage. This may sound rather far-fetched, but such extravagant storylines were always possible. In 1967, a rediscovered wartime bomb blew up the motel. In 1981 it was destroyed by fire but rose again, phoenix-like, from the ashes. However, *Crossroads* was also a brave serial and could be stonily earnest at times. It tackled issues other soaps happily shirked, these ranging from teenage runaways, abortion and test-tube babies to racism, rape and physical handicaps.

Power struggles contributed to much of the action, too. Suave David Hunter was brought in as partner in 1969 and he shared Meg's limelight until she was written out in 1981 (she sailed away on the *QE II* to a new life). Four years later, David and his novelist wife Barbara were also dispatched to pastures new. In their place, fighting for control of the motel, were Jill, Adam Chance (her smoothie husband), tycoon J. Henry Pollard, new leading lady Nicola Freeman and businessman Tommy Lancaster. It was when Daniel Freeman, Nicola's stepson, assumed control in 1988 that the series finally ended. By this time, the motel had changed its name to King's Oak Country Hotel. Jill, who had spoken the first ever words on the series – 'Crossroads Motel. Can I help you?' – also spoke the last, as she drove away with the new man in her life, John Maddingham, to open up a small hotel in the west.

Crossroads also focused on the motel guests, some of whom were celebrities indulging a fancy to appear in the show. These included Bob Monkhouse, Ken Dodd and Larry Grayson, who in one of his appearances acted as chauffeur to Meg and Hugh Mortimer on their wedding day. Some big names were given their break on the series. Malcolm McDowell played PR man Crispin Ryder, Diane Keen was waitress Sandra Gould and Elaine Paige was seen in the guise of Caroline Winthrop. Another guest was singer Harriet Blair, played by Stephanie de Sykes, who then took her song in the programme, 'Born With A Smile On My Face', to number two in the 1974 charts. It wasn't the first *Crossroads* hit: Sue Nicholls (later Audrey Roberts in CORONATION STREET) made the Top Twenty with 'Where Will You Be' in 1968. Nor was it the last: Simon May recorded a vocal version of his 'Summer Of My Life' tune in 1976, Paul Henry spoke the words of 'Benny's Theme' (played by the Mason Glen Orchestra) in 1978 and Kate Robbins (in the series as Kate Loring) succeeded with 'More Than In Love' in 1982. Paul McCartney and Wings' reworking of Tony Hatch's thumpingly catchy theme tune was used on some episodes (particularly those with sad or soppy endings) but, under producer William Smethurst in 1987, a new theme tune by Max Early and Raf Ravenscroft was introduced.

Devised by former COMPACT writers Hazel Adair and Peter Ling, from an idea by producer Reg Watson (later of PRISONER: CELL BLOCK H and NEIGHBOURS fame), *Crossroads'* working title was *The Midland Road*. Adopting the snappier name, the series began in 1964 but, despite gaining a cult following, was not fully networked by ITV until 1972. Its heavy workload was cut to four episodes a week in 1967, and then, on the instructions of the IBA, which was concerned about its quality, to three episodes a week in 1980. When the plug was pulled altogether in 1988, after over 4,500 programmes, there was a huge outcry, but the bosses at Central Television were adamant that *Crossroads'* day was done and refused to reconsider. In its place, fans had to make do with Victoria Wood's cheeky send-up, *Acorn Antiques*. *Crossroads* was revived as a daily serial by ITV in 2001.

CROW ROAD, THE
UK (Union Pictures/BBC) Drama. BBC 2 1996

Prentice McHoan	**Joseph McFadden**
Kenneth McHoan	**Bill Paterson**
Rory McHoan	**Peter Capaldi**
Ashley Watt	**Valerie Edmond**
Fiona Urvill	**Stella Gonet**
Fergus Urvill	**David Robb**
Lewis McHoan	**Dougray Scott**
Janice	**Patricia Kerrigan**
Hamish McHoan	**Paul Young**
Lachlan Watt	**Alex Norton**
Mary McHoan	**Elizabeth Sinclair**
Verity	**Simone Bendix**
Aunt Antonia	**Claire Nielsen**
Margot McHoan	**Gudrun Ure**

Writer: **Bryan Elsley**
Producer: **Bradley Adams**
Executive Producers: **Andrea Calderwood, Kevin Loader, Franc Roddam**

A Scottish lad tries to unearth the truth about his uncle's disappearance.

Student Prentice McHoan had always been puzzled by the fact that his Uncle Rory had disappeared in strange circumstances several years before, after setting out to visit the family home. He finally decided to find out more and, armed with extracts from Rory's written work, followed his trail back to the Highlands. Several other family mysteries and personal animosities within the clan contrived to make the discovery of the truth only more difficult. Verity was the cousin Prentice set his heart on, but she was stolen by his brother, Lewis, a stand-up comedian; but at least he was comforted by Rory's former girlfriend, Janice, and his own life-long friend, Ashley Watt, as he gradually learned the truth about his family and himself.

This intriguing serial, based on the novel by Iain Banks, was made in four one-hour episodes, with flash-backs revealing important evidence from years gone by and the lost Uncle Rory reappearing as a figment of Prentice's imagination. Plenty of sharp humour provided balance, and *The Crow Road* earned itself a host of commendations.

CROWN COURT
UK (Granada) Drama. ITV 1972–84

Long-running afternoon courtroom drama.

Presenting a different case each week, over three half-hour episodes, *Crown Court* was a stalwart of ITV's first afternoon schedules. Viewers were treated to hearings on a variety of subjects, from drug-pushing to murder, and then awaited the deliberations of the jury (a panel of viewers), which were revealed at the close of the last episode. Many distinguished actors graced this popular series, including the likes of John Le Mesurier, Bob Hoskins, Ben Kingsley, Juliet Stevenson, Pauline Quirke, Michael Elphick, Liz Fraser, Michael Gough, Jack Shepherd and Connie Booth. Richard Wilson was a regular, playing barrister Jeremy Parsons QC. The setting was the fictitious Fulchester Crown Court. A similarly styled series, *Verdict*, was screened on ITV in 1998.

CROWTHER, LESLIE
CBE (1933–96)

Nottingham-born funny man – the son of stage actor Leslie Crowther Sr – who sprang to fame as resident clown on the kids' show CRACKERJACK in 1960 and stayed with the series for eight years, finally acting as compere. As well as regular appearances in variety programmes like THE BLACK AND WHITE MINSTREL SHOW, *Hi Summer*, *The Saturday Crowd* and *Starburst*, Crowther also dabbled in sitcom. He starred as bachelor Thomas Jones in *The Reluctant Romeo*, Clive Gibbons, a husband beholden to a charity-obsessed wife, in MY GOOD WOMAN, and mummy's boy Tony Marchant in *Big Boy Now*. He also ventured into game shows, hosting the 'Come on down' shopping quiz, THE PRICE IS RIGHT, and also presented *Whose Baby?* and the look-alike talent show, STARS IN THEIR EYES. Over the years he had various showcases of his own, including *Crowther's In Town*, *The Crowther Collection* and *Leslie Crowther's Scrapbook*, but his career was abruptly halted by a serious car accident in 1992. Leslie was the father of actress Liz Crowther.

CRUICKSHANK, ANDREW
MBE (1907–88)

Distinguished Scottish stage and screen actor who arrived on television in the 1930s in early productions like *Bleak House*. In 1962 he was cast as the grouchy Dr Cameron in DR FINLAY'S CASEBOOK, a role he filled until the series ended in 1971. His other TV work included *Mr Justice Duncannon*, the satire *The Old Men at the Zoo* (Mr Sanderson) and the part of eccentric old Mr Hodinett in *King and Castle*.

CRYER, BARRY
(1935–)

Leeds-born comedian and sketch-writer, at times providing scripts for some of the world's finest, including Bob Hope and George Burns. As well as behind-the-scenes work on the comedies NO – THAT'S ME OVER HERE!, DOCTOR IN THE HOUSE, NOW LOOK HERE . . ., *The Prince of Denmark* and *Langley Bottom* (in collaboration with such writers as Graham Chapman and John Junkin), Cryer has also been a familiar face in front of the camera, particularly on panel games and sketch shows like AT LAST THE 1948 SHOW and *Hello Cheeky*. He hosted the quick-fire gag show, *Jokers Wild*, in the 1970s and *The Stand Up Show* in the 1990s, and was one of the team on *What's On Next?*, a regular in *The Steam Video Company*, and part of the *Assaulted Nuts* sketch show gang. The roll-call of artists he has supplied gags for reads like a Who's Who of TV comedy: The Two Ronnies, Morecambe and Wise, Bruce Forsyth, Max Bygraves, Bob Monkhouse, Marty Feldman, Dick Emery, Frankie Howerd, Mike Yarwood, Bernie Winters, Stanley Baxter, Des O'Connor, Kenny Everett, Jasper Carrott, Tommy Cooper, Leslie Crowther, Bobby Davro, Jim Davidson, Les Dennis, Little and Large, Les Dawson, Russ Abbot and Rory Bremner.

CRYSTAL MAZE, THE
UK (Chatsworth) Game Show. Channel 4 1990–5

Presenters: **Richard O'Brien, Edward Tudor-Pole**

Producers: **Malcolm Heyworth, David G. Croft**

Prizes await contestants skilled at physical and mental puzzles.

In this cross between THE KRYPTON FACTOR and Indiana Jones, impish Mazemaster Richard O'Brien invited a team of contestants (all aged strictly under 40) to tackle a series of mental and physical games with the aim of winning time-crystals. The more crystals collected, the longer the team were given in the finale to gather floating strips of gold foil which then translated into prizes. If a contestant ran out of time in any of the games, he or she was sealed into the room housing the game and a crystal was forfeited to extricate him or her if necessary. All the games were thematically linked to four fantasy zones (Aztec, Futuristic, Medieval and Industrial, the last giving way to Ocean later) similar to those seen in computer games, and the quality of the imaginative sets ensured a good 'Dungeons and Dragons' atmosphere. The programme quickly earned itself a cult following, and a children's edition was shown at Christmas 1991. In 1994 O'Brien left and was replaced by Ed Tudor-Pole.

CRYSTAL TIPPS AND ALISTAIR
UK (BBC) Animation. BBC 1 1971–4

Creator: **Hilary Hayton**
Writers: **Hilary Hayton, Graham McCallum**
Producer: **Michael Grafton-Robinson**

Quirky, psychedelic animation about a girl and her dog.

Crystal Tipps and Alistair was a product of the BBC's animation department, a unit that barely got off the ground in the early 1970s. Employing just one illustra-Tor and one animator, it was soon disbanded and this series was subsequently made by outside contractors. It featured the adventures of a girl with a very bushy, violet-coloured hair-do (Crystal Tipps) and her large, square-headed dog (Alistair). The five-minute programmes were screened in the 'MAGIC ROUNDABOUT slot' just before the early evening news.

CTV
See **CHANNEL TELEVISION.**

CUCKOO WALTZ, THE
UK (Granada) Situation Comedy. ITV 1975–7; 1980

Chris Hawthorne .... **David Roper**
Felicity 'Fliss' Hawthorne .... **Diane Keen**
Gavin Rumsey .... **Lewis Collins**
Connie Wagstaffe .... **Clare Kelly**
Austen Tweedale .... **John McKelvey**
Adrian Lockett .... **Ian Saynor**

Writers: **Geoffrey Lancashire, John G. Temple**
Producers: **Bill Gilmour, Brian Armstrong, John G. Temple**

Two hard-up newlyweds take in a lodger and live to regret it.

Chris and Fliss Hawthorne were young, recently married and in love. However, their cash flow was virtually non-existent and they were as poor as the proverbial church mice. Their living-room furniture consisted of a deck-chair marked 'Property of Prestatyn UDC' and they had no room for the luxuries of life, a fact which made Chris rather doleful. Fliss generally cheered him up with a murmur of 'Chris-Fliss-Kiss', followed by a quick snog. To ease their financial problems, the Hawthornes took in Chris's friend, Gavin Rumsey, a refugee from a broken marriage, as their lodger. Unlike his hosts, sporty Gavin always had cash to burn. He brought with him a van-load of expensive furniture and a flashy car. He also tended to flirt with his pretty landlady, who always remainded loyal to her lacklustre journalist husband. When Fliss gave birth to twins, further demands were placed on the Hawthornes' meagre resources and, as a result, Gavin remained the 'cuckoo' for three seasons. However, when the series returned after a three-year hiatus, he had given way to another lodger, Adrian

Lockett, who, to complicate matters, quickly became besotted with Fliss.

CUE
The signal (usually visual) given to a presenter or actor to start speaking or moving. Camera operators and other technicians also have to be 'cued', although their cues are usually vocal and given via their headphones.

CUE CARD
See **IDIOT BOARD.**

CUNLIFFE, DAVID
(1935–)

British TV executive, for a number of years Controller of Drama at Yorkshire Television, although previously working as producer/director for Granada, LWT and the BBC. Among his credits have been *Saturday Night Theatre*, THE ONEDIN LINE, BERYL'S LOT, HARRY'S GAME, HADLEIGH, THE MAIN CHANCE and EMMERDALE FARM.

CURRAN, Sir CHARLES
(1921–80)

BBC Director-General, 1969–77, Dublin-born Charles Curran joined the BBC as a radio producer in 1947, before leaving for a career in newspapers. He rejoined the Corporation in 1951 and worked his way up the administrative ladder, eventually succeeding Hugh Greene as Director-General. Curran was also President of the European Broadcasting Union and chief executive of the Visnews news agency.

CURRY AND CHIPS
UK (LWT) Situation Comedy. ITV 1969

The Foreman .... **Eric Sykes**
Kevin O'Grady ('Paki-Paddy') .... **Spike Milligan**

Creator/Writer: **Johnny Speight**
Producer: **Keith Beckett**

A Pakistani immigrant starts work at a factory and suffers the expected racial abuse.

There have been few comedy series more controversial than *Curry and Chips*. Penned by TILL DEATH US DO PART creator Johnny Speight, it looked at life in the factory of Lillicrap Ltd, a factory making cheap souvenirs. Newly arrived was Kevin O'Grady, an Asian with an Irish father, a genetic combination that resulted in his nickname of Paki-Paddy. Played by a blacked-up Spike Milligan, Paki-Paddy suffered the racist taunts of his workmates, even though Eric Sykes's foreman was rather more liberal in his outlook. Speight's intention was to turn such bigotry and narrow-mindedness into ridiculous carica-tures, but viewers and critics found the crude 'factory' language too much to swallow, and only one series was made. Actors like Kenny Lynch, Sam Kydd, Geoffrey Hughes and Norman Rossington provided support for the principals.

CURTIS, RICHARD
CBE (1956–)

British comedy writer, best known for his screenplays for the award-winning films, *Four Weddings and a Funeral* and *Notting Hill*. His earlier writing was in collaboration with former Oxford colleague Rowan Atkinson and then with Ben Elton, and his major credits are NOT THE NINE O'CLOCK NEWS, SPITTING IMAGE, BLACKADDER, MR BEAN and THE VICAR OF DIBLEY. Curtis has also been the brains behind COMIC RELIEF.

CURTIS, TONY
(Bernard Schwarz; 1925–)

Hollywood film name whose television experience has been confined to action adventures such as THE PERSUADERS! (playing millionaire Danny Wilde), *McCoy* (a confidence trickster) and *Vega$* (casino boss Phil Roth).

CUSACK, SINÉAD
(1948–), SORCHA (1949–), NIAMH (1961–), CATHERINE (1969–)

Four Irish actress sisters, the daughters of actor Cyril Cusack (1910–93). Sinead is married to Jeremy Irons and has been seen in programmes like *Scoop, Quiller, Have Your Cake and Eat It* (Charlotte Dawson) and *Oliver's Travels* (WPC Diane Priest); Sorcha is probably best known as Kate Wilson in CASUALTY but also starred in *Plastic Man* (Erin MacConnell) and *Eureka Street* (Caroline), and has featured in BROOKSIDE, INSPECTOR MORSE, MAIGRET, AGATHA CHRISTIE'S POIROT and the kids' series, *The Square Leopard*; Niamh's biggest roles have been as Kate Rowan in HEARTBEAT and Christine Fletcher in *Always and Everyone*, and she has also

appeared in JEEVES AND WOOSTER, CATHERINE COOKSON's *Colour Blind* (Bridget Paterson), QED's dramatization, *Cause of Death* (solicitor Mary McGuire), and the single dramas, *Rhinoceros* (Julie Flynn) and *Little Bird* (Ellen Hall); while half-sister Catherine's most prominent appearances have been as psychotic student nurse Carmel Finnan in CORONATION STREET and as Frankie Sullivan in BALLYKISSANGEL, with other parts in DOCTOR WHO, THE CHIEF, THE BILL and CADFAEL.

CUSHING, PETER
OBE (1913–94)

Hammer horror master Peter Cushing was also a prolific TV performer, even if you just take into account the number of times he appeared on *The Morecambe and Wise Show* requesting a cheque. He played Winston Smith in the controversial 1954 adaptation of George Orwell's *1984*, Sherlock Holmes for the BBC in 1968 and cropped up in many other single dramas and series as a guest performer, from THE AVENGERS to SPACE: 1999 and, of course, HAMMER HOUSE OF HORROR.

CUTHBERTSON, IAIN
(1930–)

Glaswegian actor, chiefly remembered as seedy spiv Charlie Endell in BUDGIE and its sequel, *Charles Endell Esquire*, and the Scottish lawyer, John Sutherland, in SUTHERLAND'S LAW. His other starring performances have included roles in *The Borderers, Diamond Crack Diamond* (lawyer Mark Terson), *Scotch on the Rocks, Tom Brown's Schooldays* (Dr Arnold), *Children of the Stones* (psychic megalomaniac Hendrick), *The Voyage of Charles Darwin, Rep* (theatre troupe manager J. C. Benton), SUPERGRAN (the nasty Scunner Campbell) and *Headhunters* (Malcolm Standish). Cuthbertson has also enjoyed many guest appearances in series as varied as Z CARS, THE DUCHESS OF DUKE STREET, SURVIVORS, RIPPING YARNS, DANGER UXB, DOCTOR WHO, *Return of the Antelope*, RAB C. NESBITT, MINDER and INSPECTOR MORSE. He is married to actress Anne Kirsten.

DAD'S ARMY
UK (BBC) Situation Comedy. BBC 1 1968–77

Capt. George Mainwaring	**Arthur Lowe**
Sgt Arthur Wilson	**John Le Mesurier**
L/Cpl. Jack Jones	**Clive Dunn**
Pte. James Fraser	**John Laurie**
Pte. Joe Walker	**James Beck**
Pte. Frank Pike	**Ian Lavender**
Pte. Charles Godfrey	**Arnold Ridley**
Chief ARP Warden William Hodges	**Bill Pertwee**
The Vicar (Revd Timothy Farthing)	**Frank Williams**
The Verger (Mr Henry Yeatman)	**Edward Sinclair**
Mrs Mavis Pike	**Janet Davies**
Mr/Pte. Cheeseman	**Talfryn Thomas**
Mrs Mildred Fox	**Pamela Cundell**
Mrs Anthea Yeatman	**Olive Mercer**
Pte. Sponge	**Colin Bean**

Creators/Writers: **Jimmy Perry, David Croft**
Producer: **David Croft**

The bumbling exploits of a World War II Home Guard platoon in an English coastal town.

Drawing nostalgically on 1940s Britain, this long-running farce has been described as *the* classic British sitcom. It focused on the misadventures of the Local Defence Volunteers of fictional Walmington-on-Sea (supposedly Bexhill). In true Home Guard tradition, the platoon was comprised of men too old, too young or too weak to take their place on the front line (hence, 'Dad's Army').

Self-appointed head of the unit was Captain George Mainwaring, the town's pompous, incompetent bank manager with a tragically misplaced sense of his own importance. His much-maligned second in command, in the bank as well as in uniform, was Arthur Wilson. Public-school educated and polite to the point of asking the platoon if they 'would mind awfully falling in', he was far more level-headed than Mainwaring and never failed unwittingly to undermine his CO. Next in line was the town's butcher, fading Boer War veteran Jack Jones, master of the long-winded, far from pertinent tale, but a man with the heart of a lion and always the first to volunteer for the most dangerous tasks.

The other key members of the platoon were just as distinctive. Private Fraser was a rolling-eyed, penny-pinching Scottish undertaker, and Godfrey was the company's doddery, weak-bladdered first-aider, who lived in a picture-postcard cottage with his sisters, Dolly and Cissy. Private Walker and movie-mad teenager Frank Pike were the other two principals, Walker a black market spiv (a role originally earmarked for writer Jimmy Perry himself) and Pike a bank clerk and mummy's boy whose mother conducted a semi-covert affair with Sgt Wilson – his 'Uncle Arthur'.

Valiantly failing to patrol the resort or to fulfil demanding military exercises, the platoon were constantly nettled by the local ARP warden, Mr Hodges, the greengrocer. He and 'Napoleon' (as he labelled Mainwaring) jostled for military command in the town, and disputes over the use of the church hall for parade nights led to the interference of the whingeing Vicar and his loyal verger, Mr Yeatman. Other characters who popped up from time to time included toothy Welsh reporter Mr Cheeseman and Jones's rotund lady friend, Mrs Fox.

Bound together with 1940s tunes vocalized by Bud Flanagan, the series threw up some of the most memorable lines in TV comedy. Mainwaring's 'Stupid boy' (to Pike), Wilson's ominous 'Do you think that's wise, Sir', Jones's 'Permission to speak, Sir' and 'Don't panic', and Fraser's 'We're doomed' all became catchphrases. With the exception of young Ian Lavender, the cast had all done their time on stage and screen, and Arnold Ridley was also the author of *The Ghost Train*, a much-adapted stage play. The death of James Beck in 1973 (ironically one of the youngest cast members) was not allowed to stop the series. The cast was full and talented enough to continue, and lesser characters like Private Sponge were given more prominence in support. A film version of *Dad's Army* was released in 1971.

DAKTARI
US (MGM/Ivan Tors) Adventure. BBC 1 1966–9

Dr Marsh Tracy	**Marshall Thompson**
Paula Tracy	**Cheryl Miller**
Jack Dane	**Yale Summers**
District Officer Hedley	**Hedley Mattingly**
Mike	**Hari Rhodes**
Bart Jason	**Ross Hagen**
Jenny Jones	**Erin Moran**

Creators: **Ivan Tors, Art Arthur**
Executive Producer: **Ivan Tors**
Producer: **Leonard Kaufman**

The adventures of an American vet based at an African wildlife compound.

'Daktari' means 'doctor' in an African language, and this series revolved around Marsh Tracy, respected animal doctor and head of the Wameru Study Centre for Animal Behaviour. He was assisted by his daughter, Paula, American conservationist Jack Dane, and Mike, a native African. Hedley, a British game-warden, called upon Tracy for advice and help from time to time. Later arrivals were hunter-turned-guide Bart Jason and a seven-year-old orphan, Jenny Jones, whom the Tracys adopted. Together they found themselves dealing with conservation issues, tackling the iniquitous hunting trade and riding to the rescue of stranded cubs and badly injured beasts.

The animals were the real stars of *Daktari*, especially Judy, the mischievous chimpanzee, and Clarence, who had already appeared in his own film, *Clarence the Cross-Eyed Lion* (also featuring Marshall Thompson and Cheryl Miller). It was this cinema release that inspired the TV series, which was filmed at producer Ivan Tors's Africa, USA wildlife park near Los Angeles. Child actress Erin Moran went on to greater success as Joanie in HAPPY DAYS.

DALLAS
US (Lorimar) Drama. BBC 1 1978–91

John Ross (JR) Ewing, Jr	**Larry Hagman**
Eleanor Southworth (Miss Ellie) Ewing/Farlow	**Barbara Bel Geddes**
	Donna Reed
John Ross (Jock) Ewing	**Jim Davis**
Bobby Ewing	**Patrick Duffy**
Pamela Barnes/Ewing	**Victoria Principal**
Lucy Ewing/Cooper	**Charlene Tilton**
Sue Ellen Ewing	**Linda Gray**
Ray Krebbs	**Steve Kanaly**
Cliff Barnes	**Ken Kercheval**
Willard 'Digger' Barnes	**David Wayne**
	Keenan Wynn
Gary Ewing	**David Ackroyd**
	Ted Shackelford
Valene Ewing	**Joan Van Ark**
Liz Craig	**Barbara Babcock**
Jenna Wade	**Morgan Fairchild**
	Francine Tacker
	Priscilla Presley
Kristin Shepard	**Colleen Camp**
	Mary Crosby
'Dusty Farlow'	**Jared Martin**
Dr Ellby	**Jeff Cooper**
Donna Culver/Krebbs	**Susan Howard**
Dave Culver	**Tom Fuccello**
Harve Smithfield	**George O. Petrie**
Vaughn Leland	**Dennis Patrick**
Connie	**Jeanna Michaels**
Louella	**Meg Gallagher**
Jordan Lee	**Don Starr**
Mitch Cooper	**Leigh McCloskey**
John Ross Ewing III	**Tyler Banks**
	Omri Katz
Punk Anderson	**Morgan Woodward**
Mavis Anderson	**Alice Hirson**
Marilee Stone	**Fern Fitzgerald**
Afton Cooper	**Audrey Landers**
Rebecca Wentworth	**Priscilla Pointer**
Jeremy Wendell	**William Smithers**
Clayton Farlow	**Howard Keel**
Katherine Wentworth	**Morgan Brittany**
Mickey Trotter	**Timothy Patrick Murphy**
Holly Harwood	**Lois Chiles**
Mark Graison	**John Beck**
Peter Richards	**Christopher Atkins**
Serena Wald	**Stephanie Blackmore**
Paul Morgan	**Glenn Corbett**
Charlie Wade	**Shalane McCall**
Sly	**Deborah Rennard**
Phyllis	**Deborah Tranelli**
Jessica Montford	**Alexis Smith**
Mandy Winger	**Deborah Shelton**
Jamie Ewing/Barnes	**Jenilee Harrison**
Christopher Ewing	**Joshua Harris**
Jack Ewing	**Dack Rambo**
Angelica Nero	**Barbara Carrera**
April Stevens	**Sheree J. Wilson**

Ben Stivers/Wes Parmalee	**Steve Forrest**
Bruce Harvey	**Jonathan Goldsmith**
Casey Denault	**Andrew Stevens**
Carter McKay	**George Kennedy**
Rose McKay	**Jeri Gaile**
Don Lockwood	**Ian McShane**
Cally Harper/Ewing	**Cathy Podewell**
Tracy Lawton	**Beth Toussaint**
James Richard Beaumont	**Sasha Mitchell**
Michelle Stevens	**Kimberly Foster**
Jackie Dugan	**Sherril Lynn Rettino**
Kendall	**Danone Simpson**
Vanessa Beaumont	**Gayle Hunnicutt**
Stephanie Rogers	**Lesley-Anne Down**
Liz Adams	**Barbara Stock**
Sheila Foley/Hillary Taylor	**Susan Lucci**
Breslin	**Peter White**
LeeAnn De La Vega	**Barbara Eden**

Creator: **David Jacobs**
Producer: **Leonard Katzman**

A wealthy Texan oil family indulge in sexual and commercial intrigue, in a bid to unsettle their rivals and each other.

This prime-time American soap was based around the life and affairs (business and personal) of the Texan Ewing family and their associates and introduced one of television's all-time great bad guys, the legendary JR Ewing. The Ewings' wealth flowed from the oil industry, thanks to the manoeuvring of John Ross ('Jock') Ewing, the head of the clan, who had cheated his great rival, Digger Barnes, out of the proceeds of a giant oil-strike some 40 years earlier. Jock also stole Digger's girl, Eleanor Southworth ('Miss Ellie'), leaving the two families the bitterest enemies since the Capulets and Montagues.

Jock and Ellie's three sons were John Ross Jr ('JR'), the rarely seen Gary, and Bobby. They lived on the Southfork ranch in Braddock County, just outside Dallas. Gary moved away and into his own spin-off series, KNOTS LANDING, leaving JR and Bobby prime heirs to the Ewing fortune. Whereas JR was ruthless and bad and never happy unless he was hurting someone, Bobby was honest and good, almost his brother's missing conscience. Their relationship was always uneasy, and JR resented Bobby's involvement in Ewing Oil. Another leading character was ranch foreman Ray Krebbs, who turned out to be Jock's illegitimate son, and therefore a Ewing.

The Ewing–Barnes rivalry passed down a generation from Jock and Digger to JR and Cliff Barnes, who, as an Assistant District Attorney, explored every avenue for exposing Ewing corruption, in the hope of gaining revenge for his father's humiliation. Cliff eventually became head of his own family's oil enterprise, Barnes-Wentworth. The Ewings and the Barneses were forced together in the first episode of *Dallas* when Bobby controversially married Cliff's sister, Pam. It was a sign of things to come, with marriage and divorce commonplace among these excessively wealthy, beautiful people. JR was married (twice) to Sue Ellen, a former Miss Texas but a helpless drunk, whom he cheated on unmercifully. Bobby had his girlfriends, too. Jenna was one, April

another. And when Jock was killed in a helicopter accident in South America, Miss Ellie was remarried, to Clayton Farlow.

Amid all the marriages, extra-marital alliances and underhand wheeling and dealing, the series was punctuated by two key storylines. In the first, JR received his come-uppance when he was victim of an attempted assassination. The whole world spent months between series agonizing over 'Who shot JR?', and it wasn't an easy question to answer, so many were his enemies. In order to hold the suspense, the studio filmed several possible conclusions, so that not even the cast knew who had pulled the trigger. It turned out to be Kristin, Sue Ellen's pregnant (by JR) sister. JR recovered, Kristin left town and the baby, Christopher, was adopted by Bobby and Pam.

The other storyline on which the series turned was the death and resurrection of Bobby. In one of TV's greatest comebacks, he was first murdered in a hit-and-run accident after saving Pam's life, and then, when the series began slipping in the ratings, he was miraculously reintroduced. This was achieved, quite unashamedly, by waking Pam from a dream to find Bobby lathering himself in the shower, turning all that had happened in the previous series into just a nightmare. During the 'dream sequence' Pam had married Mark Graison.

Other highlights in the series' long run were JR's loss of control of Ewing Oil to Bobby when his criminal dealings were discovered; his fight to regain power; his attempts to get Sue Ellen institutionalized for her alcoholism; Bobby being shot by his wife's half-sister, Katherine Wentworth, and the arrival of the suspicious Wes Parmalee, who claimed to be Jock back from the dead and who very nearly convinced Miss Ellie in the process. JR floated in and out of prisons and mental asylums, as his manoeuvring was matched by those around him. The marriages, divorces, illicit affairs, sneaky business-deals and overwhelming duplicity continued throughout the show's run.

By the series' close, JR's world had collapsed around him. His various ex-wives and children had all left home, Bobby had been given Southfork by Miss Ellie, who had gone to Europe with Clayton, and, worst of all, Cliff Barnes now owned Ewing Oil. In the final episode, inspired by the film, *It's A Wonderful Life*, JR sat, drank and reflected on his life. An angel/devil popped up to show him just how others might have lived had JR never been born. Some had a much happier life, others were less fortunate; but it all seemed a bit much for JR to take. As he pulled out a revolver, viewers heard a shot. Only Bobby, who dashed into the room, saw exactly what had occurred.

As evidenced by its cast list, *Dallas* was never afraid to introduce new characters and situations. Nor did it ever shy from switching actors and actresses when pressed into it. When Barbara Bel Geddes became ill, a far from convincing replacement was found in Donna Reed. There were two Garys, two John Rosses (JR and Sue Ellen's son), two Diggers and two Kristins, including Mary Crosby (Bing's daughter). There were actually three Jennas, with Morgan Fairchild and Francine Tacker both making the odd appearance before Priscilla Presley (wife of Elvis) made the part her own.

DALY, TYNE
(1946–)

Born to an acting family, Tyne Daly's first TV appearance came in an episode of THE VIRGINIAN, which she followed up with a stint in the US daytime soap, *General Hospital*. After numerous TV and cinema movies, she finally gained stardom as Mary Beth Lacey in the detective series, CAGNEY AND LACEY. She followed this in the 1990s with a part in the US drama series, *Christy*.

DALZIEL AND PASCOE
UK (BBC) Police Drama. BBC 1 1996–

Det. Supt. Andy Dalziel	Warren Clarke
DS/DI Peter Pascoe	Colin Buchanan
Ellie Soper/Pascoe	Susannah Corbett
DS Edgar Wield	David Royle
Cadet Sanjay Singh	Navin Chowdhry
Edward Soper	Peter Halliday
Mary Soper	Sylvia Kay
Dr Vickery	Fred Pearson
Deputy Chief Constable Raymond	Malcolm Tierney
WDC Shirley Novello	Jo-Anne Stockham
ACC Rebecca Fenning	Pippa Haywood

Producers: **Eric Abraham, Chris Parr, Paddy Higson, Lars MacFarlane, Nick Pitt, Andrew Rowley**

Two seemingly incompatible coppers crack crime in the North.

Detective Superintendent Andy Dalziel (pronounced 'De-yell') was a traditional Yorkshire copper, an abrasive, not surprisingly divorced, man with plenty of bark and the social deportment of a monkey. His new partner, sociology graduate DS (later DI) Peter Pascoe, was not only much younger, but gently spoken, more sensitive to civil liberties and considerably better mannered. Together, they made an unlikely but effective team, rooting out plenty of villains – mostly in Yorkshire's more industrial centres (in and around the fictional town of Wetherton). In the background (and sometimes more prominent) was Ellie, Pascoe's liberal-minded girlfriend/wife, a teacher of creative writing.

The characters were created by novelist Reginald Hill and were first seen on television in the three-part ITV drama, *A Pinch of Snuff*, which starred comedians Hale and Pace in straight dramatic roles. Writers on the BBC series included Alan Plater and Malcolm Bradbury.

DAN AUGUST
US (Quinn Martin) Police Drama. ITV 1976–8

Det. Lt. Dan August	Burt Reynolds
Sgt Charles Wilentz	Norman Fell
Sgt Joe Rivera	Ned Romero
Chief George Untermeyer	Richard Anderson
Katy Grant	Ena Hartmann

Executive Producer: **Quinn Martin**

Producer: **Adrian Samish**

A home-town cop uses his local knowledge to track down criminals.

In this short-lived series, Detective Lt. Dan August patrolled his home-town beat in Santa Luisa, California. Having grown up with many of the area's offenders and their victims, the tough young cop took a deep personal interest in his investigations, an interest which earned him respect and brought him results. Made before Burt Reynolds hit the box office big time, the series lasted only one year but, capitalizing on the star's success, it fared much better on its re-runs.

DANCE, CHARLES
(1946–)

Worcestershire-born heart-throb actor seen to best light in dramas like THE JEWEL IN THE CROWN, in which he played Guy Perron, the thriller series, *The Secret Servant*, and the sci-fi drama, FIRST BORN (Edward Forester). He also played the title role in the mini-series version of *Phantom of the Opera*, with other credits including EDWARD THE SEVENTH, NANCY ASTOR and the *Screen Two* presentation, *Century*.

DANDO, JILL
(1961–99)

Weston-super-Mare-born news and travel presenter whose brutal murder in 1999 shocked the nation. Jill had become a favourite with viewers, thanks to her homely, genuine presentation style. Her career began in local newspapers and BBC local radio before she joined ITV in the South West and then the BBC in the same region. In 1998 she moved to BREAKFAST TIME, and her national TV credits went on to include *Safari UK*, SONGS OF PRAISE, HOLIDAY (host from 1993, plus its spin-offs), CRIMEWATCH UK (from 1995) and the *Six O'Clock News*. Her last series, *Antiques Inspectors*, was first aired the day before she died.

DANGER MAN
UK (ATV/Pimlico Films) Secret Agent Drama. ITV 1960–8

John Drake	Patrick McGoohan
Hobbs	Peter Madden

Creator: **Ralph Smart**
Executive Producer: **Ralph Smart**
Producers: **Sidney Cole, Aida Young**

The adventures of a sophisticated, globe-trotting intelligence agent.

John Drake worked for NATO, covertly assisting governments wherever security breaches were suspected. His aim was to preserve world peace and he risked life and limb to achieve it. He was highly competent, athletic, cool and sharp-witted. He was a man of few words who intensely disliked violence but often needed to tackle his enemies head on. He drank only little, and womanized to the same modest extent. His missions took him to all parts of the world.

Two years after the initial half-hour episodes had ended in 1962, the producers were spurred back into action by the success of the first James Bond movies. Drake was recast in a new, hour-long series, as a member of the British Secret Service, a Special Security Agent working for MI9. This time he also had an immediate boss, Hobbs, and, inspired by Bond, his array of electronic gadgetry had increased. This series was screened under the title of *Secret Agent* in the USA. Patrick McGoohan directed some episodes himself.

DANGER UXB
UK (Thames/Euston Films) Drama. ITV 1979

Lt. Brian Ash	**Anthony Andrews**
Sgt James	**Maurice Roëves**
Susan Mount	**Judy Geeson**
Cpl. Mould	**Norman Chappell**
Sapper Jim Wilkins	**George Innes**
Norma Baker	**Deborah Watling**
Mrs Baker	**Marjie Lawrence**
Cpl. Samuel Horrocks	**Ken Kitson**
Sapper/L/Cpl. Jack Salt	**Kenneth Cranham**
Dr David Gillespie	**Iain Cuthbertson**
Capt./Major Francis	**Ken Farrington**
Lt. Ivor Rogers	**Jeremy Sinden**

Creators: **John Hawkesworth, John Whitney**
Producer: **John Hawkesworth**
Executive Producer: **Johnny Goodman**

High-drama series charting the bravery of a World War II bomb disposal squad.

These stories were drawn from the memoirs of real-life sapper Major A. P. Hartley and followed the progress of a bomb disposal company (UXB standing for unexploded bomb) from the Blitz to D-Day. Hero of the piece was young Lt. Brian Ash, like many of his colleagues learning the ropes as he went along. Newly commissioned, he had joined the 97 Tunnelling Company of the Royal Engineers, only to discover, to his horror, that the regiment was now involved in bomb disposal. The bare minimum of training was provided and the life-expectancy of a sapper was a mere seven weeks. Ash was thrown immediately in at the deep end as commander of 347 Section, taking the position (and the lodgings) of a recently killed officer. Susan Mount, married daughter of explosives boffin Dr Gillespie, provided Ash's romantic interest, although he also needed to fend off the attentions of Norma, the flighty daughter of his landlady, Mrs Baker.

In his work, there was no room for trial and error, and Ash relied heavily on the knowledgeable Sgt James. Each mission placed the sappers in impossible positions, a hair's breadth away from oblivion. Some did not make it, dragging emotion into the plots; others, like Brian Ash, survived to dispose of other bombs.

DANGERFIELD
UK (BBC) Drama. BBC 1 1995–

Dr Paul Dangerfield	**Nigel Le Vaillant**
Dr Joanna Stevens	**Amanda Redman**
DI Ken Jackson	**George Irving**
Marty Dangerfield	**Sean Maguire**
	Tim Vincent
Al Dangerfield	**Lisa Faulkner**
	Tamzin Malleson
Terri Morgan	**Katy Murphy**
Dr Nick McKenzie	**Bill Wallis**
Dr Shaaban Hamada	**Nadim Sawalha**
Kate Durrani	**Kim Vithana**
DC Nicky Green	**Tracy Gillman**
Julia Caxton	**Catherine Terris**
PC Nigel Spenser	**Mo Sesay**
PC Georgie Cudworth	**Eleanor Martin**
Sgt Keith Lardner	**Roderick Smith**
Liz Moss	**Jacquetta May**
Dr Annie Robbins	**Fiona Victory**
DS Helen Diamond	**Nicola Cowper**
DI Frank Dagley	**Michael Melia**
Angela Wakefield	**Marcia Warren**
Dr Jonathan Paige	**Nigel Havers**
PC Liam Walsh	**Linford Brown**
Jojo	**Sam Loggin**
Dr Ross Freeman	**Adrian Bower**
DI Gillian Cramer	**Jane Gurnett**
DC Gary Monk	**Ian Gain**
PC Tom Allen	**Julian Kay**
Beth Saunders	**Lynsey Baxter**
Matt Gregory	**Idris Elba**
Molly Cramer	**Frances White**

Creator: **Don Shaw**
Producers: **Adrian Bate, Peter Wolfes, Beverley Dartnall**
Executive Producer: **Chris Parr**

A GP solves murder cases in rural Warwickshire.

Doctor Paul Dangerfield had been through an emotional time. Scarred by the car-crash death of his wife, he had been left with the care of their two teenage children, Alison and Marty. He threw himself into his work, charging around in a Land Rover Discovery with a mobile phone pressed to his ear (much to the concern of viewers, who complained so much that a hands-free version was fitted for later series). His day job was that of a country GP, but Dangerfield also helped out the local constabulary as a police surgeon – a mix of roles that ensured he had feet in both medicine and crime camps, but often to the satisfaction of neither. Family troubles added yet another dimension.

Dangerfield's colleagues included fellow doctor Joanna Stevens and solicitor Kate Durrani, both of whom had designs on the handsome hero. DI Ken Jackson was his accomplice on the force. In the second series, a new arrival, forensics expert – and falconry addict – Terri Morgan had been introduced to allow Dangerfield to delve that much more deeply into his criminal investigations. A series later, this had been toned down with the departure of Terri. Dangerfield had moved out of his country home into a more modest house in Warwick, and his children were now played by different actors. There were new colleagues in the surgery (Dr Annie Robbins) and at the station (DI Frank Dagley and DS Helen Diamond) and, as his tragic past finally caught up with him, Dangerfield sought help from bereavement counsellor Liz Moss. In the next series, Dr Jonathan Paige, an old friend of Dangerfield's played by Nigel Havers, was introduced in preparation for the exit of star Nigel Le Vaillant. Havers took over the lead from the next season, the series keeping the same title as Paige was installed in the Dangerfield Health Centre. He was joined on the police side by DI Gillian Cramer, with added romantic interest coming from art critic Beth Saunders. Soon Paige had succumbed to the inevitable and abandoned his general practice in favour of full-time police work.

DANGERMOUSE

UK (Cosgrove Hall/Thames) Cartoon. ITV 1981–7; 1991–2

Voices:

Dangermouse .... **David Jason**
Penfold .... **Terry Scott**
Baron Greenback .... **Edward Kelsey**
Nero .... **David Jason**
Col. K .... **David Jason**
Stiletto Mafioso .... **Brian Trueman**
Narrator .... **David Jason**

Creators: **Mike Harding, Brian Trueman**
Writers: **Brian Trueman, Angus Allen**
Executive Producer: **John Hambley**
Producers: **Brian Cosgrove, Mark Hall**

The all-action adventures of a mouse secret agent and his nervous sidekick.

Working for the British Secret Service from a base in a Baker Street postbox, Dangermouse – 'the greatest secret agent in the world' – was the saviour of civilization on more than one occasion. This eye-patch-wearing, white-suited, daring hero was usually called into action by his whiskery boss, Colonel K, to deal with the fiendishly inventive plans of megalomaniac toad, Baron Greenback. At the cool-headed Dangermouse's side was the timid, bespectacled Penfold (prone to fretful exclamations like 'Crikey'), while Greenback's chief henchman was the caterpillar, Nero, supported by a group of gangster crows headed by Stiletto Mafioso. Another adversary, Count Duckula, a vegetarian vampire (also voiced by David Jason), was later spun off into his own series.

Pacily narrated, with parodies on James Bond and other dashing heroes (not to mention plays on adult literature), the *Dangermouse* stories were often episodic (five parts to each tale) and proved a hit with all ages. Co-creator Mike Harding supplied the musical content.

DANIEL BOONE

US (Arcola-Fesspar/Twentieth Century-Fox) Western. ITV 1965–71

Daniel Boone .... **Fess Parker**
Yadkin .... **Albert Salmi**
Mingo .... **Ed Ames**
Rebecca Boone .... **Patricia Blair**
Jemima Boone .... **Veronica Cartwright**
Israel Boone .... **Darby Hinton**
Cincinnatus .... **Dal McKennon**
Jericho Jones .... **Robert Logan**
Gideon .... **Don Pedro Colley**
Gabe Cooper .... **Roosevelt Grier**
Josh Clements .... **Jimmy Dean**

Executive Producers: **Aaron Rosenberg, Aaron Spelling**
Producers: **George Sherman, Barney Rosenzweig, Joseph Silver**

Tales of one of America's great folk heroes.

In this series, created to capitalize on Fess Parker's earlier success as Davy Crockett, the actor played the lead in much the same way, even to the point of wearing the same racoon-skin cap. It was, of course, something of an exaggeration of the life of the real Daniel Boone, who was one of America's great frontiersmen.

Boone lived during the American Wars of Independence, in the area bordering North Carolina, Kentucky and Tennessee. As played by Parker, he was one of the pioneers: a calm, peaceful, strong hero who carved new paths into the vast unknown continent, surveying and mapping the landscape, hunting wild animals, and befriending or fighting off Indians. Larger than life, he was seen in the title sequence splitting a tree with a single throw of an axe.

With his wife, Rebecca, and children, Jemima and Israel, Boone was based in the town of Boonesborough, where among his associates were the town barkeeper, Cincinnatus, and an Oxford-educated Cherokee Indian named Mingo. Yadkin, a friend from the backwoods, travelled with him on his early forays, and another pioneer, Jericho Jones, joined Boone later in the series. Also seen were Josh Clements, a trapper, Gideon, an Indian, and the escaped slave, Gabe Cooper.

The series was first screened in its native USA in 1964 and received sporadic showings around the ITV network.

DANIEL, GLYN

(1914–86)

British archaeologist who became a prominent TV personality in the 1950s and 1960s, thanks to his appearances as host of ANIMAL, VEGETABLE, MINERAL? and CHRONICLE. He was a don at Cambridge.

DANIELS, PAUL
(Newton Edward Daniels; 1938–)

Middlesbrough-born comedian and illusionist, also a host of quiz shows and panel games. Before gaining his own BBC magic show, Daniels took his nightclub act in and out of TV variety programmes, appearing on OPPORTUNITY KNOCKS and WHEELTAPPERS' AND SHUNTERS' SOCIAL CLUB among other series, and briefly presenting his own variety showcase for Granada, *Paul Daniels' Blackpool Bonanza*. In the 1980s he became TV's most popular magician and used his success to branch out into kids' television with *Wizbit* and game shows, hosting *Odd One Out*, EVERY SECOND COUNTS and *Wipeout*, before continuing with stage trickery in *Paul Daniels' Secrets*. He is married to his glamorous assistant, Debbie McGee, and his son (and former assistant) Martin is now an entertainer in his own right, a one-time presenter of GAME FOR A LAUGH.

DANSON, TED
(1947–)

Square-jawed American actor whose huge success as romeo bartender Sam Malone in the sitcom, CHEERS, won him a run of Hollywood starring parts and the title role in the TV adaptation of *Gulliver's Travels*. His earlier work included a couple of years in the US daytime soap, *Somerset*, and minor appearances in MAGNUM, PI and *Benson*, with his most recent credits coming in the US series, *Ink* and *Becker*. He is married to actress Mary Steenburgen.

DARLING BUDS OF MAY, THE
UK (Yorkshire/Excelsior Group) Comedy Drama. ITV
1991–3

Sidney Charles 'Pop' Larkin	**David Jason**
Ma Larkin	**Pam Ferris**
Mariette Larkin/Charlton	**Catherine Zeta Jones**
Cedric 'Charley' Charlton	**Philip Franks**
Primrose Larkin	**Julie Davies**
	Abigail Romison
Montgomery Larkin	**Ian Tucker**
Petunia Larkin	**Christina Giles**
Zinnia Larkin	**Katherine Giles**
Victoria Larkin	**Stephanie Ralph**
Edith Pilchester	**Rachel Bell**
Ernest Bristow	**Michael Jayston**
The Brigadier	**Moray Watson**

Writers: **Bob Larbey, Richard Harris, Paul Wheeler**
Executive Producers: **Richard Bates, Vernon Lawrence**
Producers: **Robert Banks Stewart, Peter Norris, Simon Lewis**

Tales of a happy-go-lucky rural Kent family in the 1950s.

Based on H. E. Bates's five Larkin books (which began with a novel entitled *The Darling Buds of May*), this hugely popular, wholesome series engendered a 'feel good' factor in viewers. Here was a family that chortled its way through life, enjoying the simple pleasures of the countryside and having little time for the stresses of the real world. Head of the clan was the boisterous Pop Larkin, a man of independent means who ran a 22-acre smallholding and earned a bob or two wherever he could. Larkin by name and larking by nature, Pop was seldom flustered and usually had an answer for every problem. His irrepressible common-law wife (they had skipped the formality of marriage), known to all as Ma, was a roly-poly, laugh-a-minute character, always at work in the kitchen preparing gigantic feasts for breakfast, lunch and dinner (which Pop liberally doused with ketchup) and snacks for moments in between. Their six children began with their beautiful eldest daughter, Mariette, and were generally named after assorted flowers. In the first episode, Cedric Charlton, a naïve, young, poetry-loving Inland Revenue official, called to investigate Pop's affairs. Befuddled by Pop's anti-tax logic, 'Charley' stayed for lunch, fell in love with Mariette and never left. They married and Mariette gave birth to a son, John Blenheim. 'Perfick', as Pop would have put it.

Working as executive producer on the series was Richard Bates, son of the Larkins' creator, who had originally sold the rights of the novels to an American company, but bought them back when their adaptation was slow to get off the ground. He took the idea to Yorkshire Television and gave the company one of its greatest hits. Bob Larbey wrote the first series, with other writers employed for later episodes. A less subtle American film version of *Darling Buds*, entitled *The Mating Game*, starring Debbie Reynolds and Tony Randall, was released in 1959.

DARREN, JAMES
(James Ercolani; 1936–)

American leading man whose TV high spots have included THE TIME TUNNEL (lost scientist Dr Tony Newman) and T. J. HOOKER (Officer Jim Corrigan). He has also appeared as a guest star on FANTASY ISLAND and *Vega$*, among many other series. Small-screen success came after movie fame in the 1950s, when he was cast as a teenage heart-throb figure. He even branched out into singing, hitting the UK charts in the early 1960s with 'Goodbye Cruel World' and three other discs.

DAVENPORT, JACK
(1973–)

English actor, the son of Maria Aitken and Nigel Davenport. His TV break came with the series, THIS LIFE, in which he played Miles. This led to the lead roles of Robert Bradley in CATHERINE COOKSON'S *The Moth*, DS Michael Colefield in *Ultraviolet*, Harry Fairfield in *The Wyvern Mystery* and Steve in the comedy, *Coupling*. His brother and sister, Hugo and Laura, are also both actors.

DAVENPORT, NIGEL
(1928–)

Cambridgeshire-born actor, much seen on television. He is particularly associated today with tetchy businessman roles, thanks to appearances as Sir Edward Frere in HOWARDS' WAY and James Brant in TRAINER. Among his career high spots have been the parts of Councillor Robert Carne in SOUTH RIDING, Jack Hoxton in the sitcom, *Don't Rock the Boat*, King George III in *Prince Regent*, the South African police chief in *The Biko Inquest* and Sir Charles Pelham in *Longitude*. He also starred in OIL STRIKE NORTH (Jim Fraser) and has had credits in such series as *Travelling Man*, *Madame Bovary*, BIRD OF PREY and MIDSOMER MURDERS. His second wife was actress Maria Aitken and he is the father of actors Jack, Hugo and Laura Davenport.

DAVIDSON, JIM
OBE (1953–)

Chirpy, Cockney comedian, fond of dirty jokes but somewhat toned down for television appeal. He came to light on the talent show, NEW FACES, and has subsequently appeared in assorted variety specials, the gag show, *What's On Next?*, his own sitcoms, *Up the Elephant and Round the Castle* and *Home James* (Jim London in both), and his own game shows, *Big Break* and JIM DAVIDSON'S GENERATION GAME. His third wife was presenter Alison Holloway.

DAVIES, ALAN
(1966–)

Mop-haired comedian and actor, most familiar as sleuth JONATHAN CREEK, but also starring as travelling time-share salesman Simon Treat in the series, *One for the Road*, and as Russel Boyd in *A Many Splintered Thing*. He was a team captain in the advert quiz, *The Best Show in the World . . . Probably* and has also featured in *Urban Trauma* and *Stand Up with Alan Davies* – profiles and recordings of his stage work.

DAVIES, ANDREW
(1936–)

Former university lecturer and one of British TV's foremost screenwriters. Davies began his scripting career with one-off adaptations and plays like *The Signalman* (starring Denholm Elliott) in 1976 and *Fearless Frank* (starring Leonard Rossiter) in 1978, although his first series successes were *The Legend of King Arthur* and the kids' comedy, *Educating Marmalade*, and its sequel, *Danger – Marmalade At Work*. He adapted R. F. Delderfield's *To Serve Them All My Days* and *Diana* for the BBC and went on to deliver the surreal A VERY PECULIAR PRACTICE, set in the quirky world of Lowlands University. Davies then scripted MOTHER LOVE and reworked

Michael Dobbs's HOUSE OF CARDS, TO PLAY THE KING, and THE FINAL CUT, with great success. The most recent acclaim has come from his adaptations of MIDDLE-MARCH, PRIDE AND PREJUDICE, *Moll Flanders*, *Jane Austen's Emma*, *Vanity Fair* and *Take a Girl Like You*. In quite a different vein, he co-wrote the flat-share sitcom, GAME ON, with Bernadette Davis and the kids' comedy, *The Boot Street Band*, with Steve Attridge. Over the years, there have also been other notable pieces, such as *The Old Devils* and *Anglo-Saxon Attitudes*, as well as numerous one-off dramas like *Harnessing Peacocks*, *Getting Hurt* (part of the *Obsessions* season) and *Screen One/Two* productions like *Bavarian Night*, *Ball Trap on the Côte d'Azur* and *A Very Polish Practice* (picking up where the earlier series left off).

DAVIES, BARRY
(1940–)

Sports commentator, with the BBC since 1969, and previously with ITV. Davies has commentated on most events, from soccer, tennis and ice skating to various Olympic sports. He also hosted QUIZ BALL.

DAVIES, DIANA
(1936–)

Manchester-born actress, first coming to light as Freda Ashton's friend, Doris, in A FAMILY AT WAR but familiar to soap fans as Norma Ford in CORONATION STREET in the 1970s and, more recently, Caroline Bates in EMMER-DALE. She has also enjoyed many other smaller roles over the years.

DAVIES, DICKIE
(1933–)

Sports presenter, initially with Southern Television but host of WORLD OF SPORT from 1968. Davies, with his trademark 'badger' streak in his hair, has also hosted other sporting events, including boxing, snooker and the Olympic Games, as well as the quiz show, *Sportsmasters* (which he produced for HTV). He suffered a stroke in 1995 but has recuperated well and returned to presentation with Sky Sports.

DAVIES, FREDDIE
(1937–)

British comedian known for his 'Parrotface' routine and his spluttering pronunciation. He found his way into television via OPPORTUNITY KNOCKS and was a variety show regular in the 1960s and 1970s, becoming particularly popular with younger viewers. He went on to star in his own kids' sitcom, *The Small World of Samuel Tweet* (as Tweet) but, more recently, Davies has been seen in straight roles in series like ALL QUIET ON THE PRESTON FRONT (Heron Man), BAND OF GOLD and HEARTBEAT.

DAVIES, JOHN HOWARD
(1939–)

Former child actor, star of such film classics as *Oliver Twist* and *Tom Brown's Schooldays*, who became a BBC producer/director (later with Thames), working largely on comedy shows. Among his contributions have been STEPTOE AND SON, ALL GAS AND GAITERS, *The Very Merry Widow*, *The World of Beachcomber*, MONTY PYTHON'S FLYING CIRCUS, *Misleading Cases*, THE GOODIES, *As Good Cooks Go*, *No Strings*, WHOOPS BAGHDAD!, THE FALL AND RISE OF REGINALD PERRIN, THE GOOD LIFE, FAWLTY TOWERS, *The Other One*, *Andy Capp*, *We'll Think of Something*, *Executive Stress*, *All in Good Faith*, AFTER HENRY, NO JOB FOR A LADY, *Hope It Rains*, MR BEAN and *Law and Disorder*.

DAVIES, RICHARD

Overtly Welsh character and comic actor, usually sporting National Health glasses. Although remembered by many as the couldn't-give-a-damn sports teacher, Pricey, in PLEASE SIR!, Davies has popped up in all manner of programmes, especially those needing a strong Welsh presence, including the drama *The Citadel* (Mr Watkins), the sitcom *Rule Britannia* (Taffy Evans) and the short-lived HTV soap *Taff Acre* (Max Johnson). For a while in the mid-1970s, as Idris Hopkins (married to Kathy Staff's Vera), he ran the corner shop in CORONATION STREET. Davies has also been seen in the comedies OH NO! IT'S SELWYN FROGGITT (Clive), BOTTLE BOYS (Stan Evans) and WHOOPS APOCALYPSE (Chancellor of the Exchequer), plus the children's series, *Robert's Robots* and *The Boot Street Band* (caretaker Dai Cramp).

DAVIES, RUPERT
(1916–76)

With the strike of a match and a puff on his pipe at the start of each episode, Rupert Davies instantly became the French detective MAIGRET, a character he played for three years from 1960 and which he remained heavily associated with for the rest of his life. As Maigret, Davies also introduced the BBC's DETECTIVE anthology series, although it wasn't his first TV detective role; that was as Inspector Duff in the late-1950s production of THE NEW ADVENTURES OF CHARLIE CHAN. Earlier, Davies had taken the part of Vincent Broadhead in QUATERMASS II and played Seamus in SAILOR OF FORTUNE (alongside Lorne Greene), after moving into TV and films from the stage and radio. He also made guest appearances in programmes like THE INVISIBLE MAN and *The Adventures of Aggie*. In 1968 he provided the voice for Professor McClaine in JOE 90, and a few years later was Cerdig in ARTHUR OF THE BRITONS and Count Rostov in *War and Peace*, but his subsequent work was thin on the ground, as the millstone of *Maigret* hung ever heavier.

DAVIES, WINDSOR
(1930–)

London-born but predominantly Welsh comic actor, the bawling Sgt Major Williams in IT AIN'T HALF HOT MUM. Davies's other major TV role has been as Oliver Smallbridge in the antique trade sitcom, NEVER THE TWAIN, although his TV appearances have been plentiful, regular and have also included the parts of George Vance in a 1985 sitcom called *The New Statesman*, Lloyd George in *Mosley*, Pugh in *Mortimer's Law*, General Tufto in *Vanity Fair* and Rottcodd in *Gormenghast*. Where his face hasn't appeared, his voice has been heard, as in the Gerry Anderson puppet series, TERRAHAWKS (speaking the lines of Sgt Major Zero). 'Whispering Grass', his recording with *It Ain't Half Hot Mum* co-star Don Estelle, topped the charts in 1975.

DAVISON, PETER
(Peter Moffet; 1951–)

London-born actor, Tristan Farnon in ALL CREATURES GREAT AND SMALL, Dr Stephen Daker in A VERY PECULIAR PRACTICE, the 1930s detective Albert CAMPION and TV's fifth DOCTOR WHO. Added to this notable list of starring roles are a handful of sitcoms, of varying success: *Sink or Swim* (Brian Webber), HOLDING THE FORT (Russell Milburn), *Fiddlers Three* (Ralph) and *Ain't Misbehavin'* (Clive Quigley), plus dramas like *Love for Lydia* (Tom Holland), *Harnessing Peacocks* (Jim), *The Stalker's Apprentice* (DI Maurice Birt), *Cuts* (Henry Babbacombe), *At Home with the Braithwaites* (David Braithwaite) and *The Mrs Bradley Mysteries* (Inspector Christmas). Guest appearances in programmes such as THE TOMORROW PEOPLE, *Kinsey*, MISS MARPLE and THE HITCH-HIKER'S GUIDE TO THE GALAXY, and a theme-music credit for the sitcom, MIXED BLESSINGS, add yet more to his portfolio. He was once married to actress Sandra Dickinson.

DAVRO, BOBBY
(Robert Nankeville; 1959–)

Middlesex-born comedian and impressionist, coming to the fore via *Copy Cats* and much seen on variety and game shows, from *Go For It* to *Punchlines*. He has hosted several series of his own, including *Bobby Davro on the Box*, *Bobby Davro's TV Weekly*, *Davro's Sketch Pad*, *Davro* and *Bobby Davro: Rock with Laughter*. He has also taken charge of the *Run the Risk* game segment of *Live and Kicking*. and presented a revival of WINNER TAKES ALL for Challenge TV. His stage name was taken from the name of his dad's shop – Davro's, which was itself derived from the names of Bobby and his brother (David and Robert).

DAVY CROCKETT
US (Disney) Adventure. ITV 1956

Davy Crockett .... **Fess Parker**
Georgie Russell .... **Buddy Ebsen**

Executive Producer: **Walt Disney**
Producer: **Bill Walsh**

Tales of the great American frontiersman.

'Born on a mountain top in Tennessee', according to the enormously successful theme song, Davy Crockett in reality was a one-time militia scout and a US Congressman who died in the legendary siege of the Alamo. For this action series, Crockett became an all-American hero, helping to tame the Wild West and thwarting the advances of the Mexicans with the aid of his trusty rifle, Old Betsy, and his loyal sidekick, Georgie Russell. His racoon-skin cap became his trademark and was adopted by addicted children on both sides of the Atlantic as the merchandising spin-offs took hold. The series originally aired in the USA as part of the anthology series, *Disneyland*.

Fess Parker took on a similar part in the 1960s, when he again donned a furry hat for the role of another American hero, DANIEL BOONE. Buddy Ebsen, meanwhile, went on to play a different sort of backwoodsman, Jed Clampett, in THE BEVERLY HILLBILLIES.

DAWN, ELIZABETH
MBE (Sylvia Butterfield; 1939–)

CORONATION STREET's formidable Vera Duckworth, who arrived in Weatherfield in 1976 as one of the girls in Mike Baldwin's sweat-shop. Leeds-born Elizabeth Dawn's working life had begun in a real factory, before progressing via a stint in Woolworth's to singing in nightclubs. *Street* stardom eventually came after TV commercials, waitressing on WHEELTAPPERS' AND SHUNTERS' SOCIAL CLUB, playing a warden in *Crown Court*, guesting with Larry Grayson, minor roles in series like Z CARS and COUNTRY MATTERS, and notable one-off plays like *Kisses at Fifty*, *Leeds United* and *The Greenhill Pals*. Other credits include *One Foot in the Past*.

DAWS, ROBERT
(1959–)

English actor often seen in lighter roles, such as Peter James in *There Comes a Time . . .*, Roger Dervish in OUT-SIDE EDGE, Tuppy Glossop in JEEVES AND WOOSTER, Sam in ROGER ROGER and Oscar in the single comedy, *The Mystery of Men*. Daws was also Simon Eastman in CASUALTY and Piggy Garstone in THE HOUSE OF ELIOTT. Other credits have included ROBIN OF SHERWOOD (Giscard), *The Missing Postman* (Peter Robson) and *Take a Girl Like You* (Dick Thompson). He is married to actress Amanda Waring.

DAWSON, LES
(1933–93)

Manchester-born comedian, a former jazz pianist who used his keyboard skills to great effect in his useless-pianist routine. Otherwise, Dawson was noted for his dry, pessimistic delivery and his catalogue of mother-in-law and wife jokes. Discovered on OPPORTUNITY KNOCKS, he quickly moved on to star in his own YTV series, *Sez Les*, in which he developed characters like the seedy Cosmo Smallpiece, and perfected a gossipy housewife double act (Cissie and Ada) with Roy Barraclough. Taking over BLANKETY BLANK from Terry Wogan, he maintained the show's high ratings and, still with the BBC, he also hosted *The Les Dawson Show*. His career came full circle in 1990, when he became compere of *Opportunity Knocks*, succeeding Bob Monkhouse. One of his most unusual roles was that of a 100-year-old woman in the straight drama, *Nona*, but his last appearance came in the comedy-drama, *Demob*, in which he took the role of comic Morton Stanley.

DAWSON'S CREEK
US (Columbia TriStar) Drama Channel 4 1998–

Dawson Leery .... **James Van Der Beek**
Josephine 'Joey' Potter .... **Katie Holmes**
Jennifer Lindley .... **Michelle Williams**
Pacey Witter .... **Joshua Jackson**
Mr Mitchell Leery .... **John Wesley Shipp**
Mrs Gail Leery .... **Mary-Margaret Humes**
Miss Tamara Jacobs .... **Leann Hunley**
Grams .... **Mary Beth Peil**
Bessie Potter .... **Nina Repeta**
Abby Morgan .... **Monica Keena**
Andie McPhee .... **Meredith Monroe**
Jack McPhee .... **Kerr Smith**
Gretchen .... **Sasha Alexander**

Creator: **Kevin Williamson**
Executive Producers: **Paul Stupin, Greg Berlanti, Greg Prange**

The pains of adolescent life in a quiet Massachusetts town.

Set in the picturesque coastal settlement of Capeside, *Dawson's Creek* was a story of boys becoming men and girls becoming women during the traumatic high school years. Nominal star was Dawson Leery, an intense, 15-year-old would-be film-maker obsessed with Steven Spielberg and the only child of immature, squabbling parents (his mum was a TV newsreader, his dad ran a restaurant). Dawson's best friend was the tomboyish girl next door, Joey Potter, daughter of a jailbird dad and a mother who had died of cancer. She had been raised by her sister, Bessie. Third buddy was Pacey Witter, the lusty son of a police family who had a relationship with his English teacher, Miss Jacobs, and whose eventual affair with Joey led to friction between Joey and Dawson. Then there was Jen, a blonde, promiscuous New York escapee who, like all the principals, learned maturity at Capeside High as the series developed. New in town later were Andie McPhee, Pacey's one-time girlfriend who fell into drug dependency, and her brother, Jack, who struggled with his homosexuality. Another arrival was the troublesome Abby Morgan, who drowned after falling off a bridge.

Dawson's Creek was created by film-maker Kevin Williamson (*Scream* and *I Know What You Did Last Summer*). Outdoor action was shot in Wilmington, North Carolina, with the University of North Carolina doubling up as Capeside High.

DAY, Sir ROBIN
(1923–2000)

The doyen of British political interviewers, London-born Robin Day was a barrister who joined the BBC as a radio producer in 1955. With the start of ITV, he moved to ITN to become one of its first two newscasters (along with Chris Chataway), also presenting the company's ROVING REPORT and *Tell the People*. In 1959 he left in order to stand as Liberal parliamentary candidate for Hereford, but, failing to win the seat, he returned to television as a reporter/presenter on PANORAMA, staying with the programme until 1972. In later years he hosted *Newsday*, all the BBC's main political events (as well as Radio 4's *The World at One*) and initiated QUESTION TIME in 1979. One famous interview for NATIONWIDE during the Falklands conflict was rudely interrupted when his interviewee, Defence Secretary John Nott, stormed out after being dubbed a 'here today, gone tomorrow politician'. Retiring in 1989, Day later took his brusque, breathy, yet dogged interviewing style – and his famous spotted bow-tie – to satellite and regional television.

DAY TODAY, THE
UK (Talkback) Comedy. BBC 2 1994

Christopher Morris, Steve Coogan, Rebecca Front, Doon MacKichan, Patrick Marber, David Schneider

Creators/Writers: **Christopher Morris, Armando Iannucci**
Executive Producer: **Peter Fincham**
Producer: **Armando Iannucci**

Award-winning spoof news and current affairs programme.

A sort of MONTY PYTHON meets NEWSNIGHT, *The Day Today* was the television manifestation of Radio 4's *On the Hour*. It took the form of a TV news magazine, anchored by Christopher Morris, an argumentative, disdainful, Jeremy Paxman-like interviewer and reader of sensational but obscure headlines. Doon MacKichan presented business news in the guise of Collaterlie Sisters and Steve Coogan's cringingly awful sports correspondent, Alan Partridge, was later given his own chat show, *Knowing Me, Knowing You with Alan Partridge*. Typically quirky reports from the USA were provided by CBN's Barbara Wintergreen; Sylvester Stuart was the decapi-

tated weatherman with the innovative graphics; Peter O'Hanraha'hanrahan dealt with economic issues; Valerie Sinatra warned of traffic chaos from her mile-high travel tower, and Speak Your Brains was the weekly *vox pop* spot. The voice of Michael Alexander St John was also heard.

DAYS OF HOPE
UK (BBC) Drama. BBC 1 1975

Ben Matthews .... **Paul Copley**
Sarah Hargreaves .... **Pamela Brighton**
Philip Hargreaves .... **Nikolas Simmonds**

Writer: **Jim Allen**
Producer: **Tony Garnett**

Young idealism during the turbulent days of World War I and the General Strike.

Much acclaimed but highly controversial, *Days of Hope*, set in the years 1916 to 1926, was the four-part story of three young northern Christians: farmer Ben Matthews, his sister, Sarah, and her husband, Philip. As well as being pacifists they were also socialists, working towards the election of a Labour Government, their lives touched by the dramatic events of the time and the poverty and injustice which surrounded them. Applauded for its courageous stance and undeniably impressive production, the mini-series was viciously slated by Conservative-minded critics for its subversive tone, historical inaccuracy and socialist sentiments. Ken Loach directed all four parts: *1916: Joining Up*, *1921: Black Friday*, *1924: The First Labour Government* and *1926: The General Strike*.

DBS
(Direct Broadcasting by Satellites)

Direct Broadcasting by Satellites was first conceived in the 1970s as a means of relaying TV signals to homes without the need for terrestrial transmitters or masts. At an international conference in 1977, Britain was allocated five channels, and the BBC was charged with setting up the first two, with a proposed air date of 1986. Unfortunately, numerous difficulties (not least lack of Government financial support) resulted in the concept, as it stood, being scrapped. The IBA took over the idea instead, eventually issuing a licence to a consortium known as British Satellite Broadcasting (BSB). BSB, in turn, ran into problems of its own. Although its Marco Polo satellite was soon in position, delays resulted from technical difficulties (particularly with the revolutionary smaller reception dish, the 'squarial'). BSB eventually went on air in spring 1990, but Rupert Murdoch's company, Sky, had stolen a march and was already broadcasting from the Luxembourg-owned Astra satellite, enjoying over a million viewers. In November of the same year, with both companies operating at a loss, BSB was forced to merge with Sky, creating British Sky Broadcasting (BSKYB).

DE LA TOUR, FRANCES
(1944–)

British Shakespearean actress finding a comedy niche as the plain Jane, Miss Jones, in RISING DAMP. Among her other credits have been the anthologies, CRIME OF PASSION and *Cottage To Let*, *Flickers*, *Tom Jones* (Aunt Western), the *Screen Two* drama, *Genghis Cohen* (Dr Helga Feuchtwanger), COLD LAZARUS (Emma Porlock) and the sitcoms *A Kind of Living* (Carol Beasley), *Every Silver Lining* (Shirley Silver) and *Downwardly Mobile* (Rosemary).

DEADLINE MIDNIGHT
UK (ATV) Drama. ITV 1960–1

Joe Dunn	**Peter Vaughan**
Neville Crane	**Jeremy Young**
Matt Stewart	**Bruce Beeby**
Tom Douglas	**James Culliford**
Peggy Simpson	**Mary Law**
Mike Grieves	**Glyn Houston**
Mark Byron	**Olaf Pooley**

Producers: **Hugh Rennie, Rex Firkin**

Action and adventure with the reporters of a fictitious daily newspaper.

Focusing on the investigations of the journalists of the *Daily Globe*, *Deadline Midnight* took its inspiration from the intrepid reporters of Fleet Street. Former *Daily Express* editor Arthur Christiansen acted as programme consultant to ensure authenticity, although many Fleet Street hacks were not impressed with proceedings. Peter Vaughan starred as the *Globe*'s news editor, Joe Dunn (replaced later by Glyn Houston as Mike Grieves), and the ever-changing cast was filled with relatively unknown actors in a quest for a realistic atmosphere.

DEAN, LETITIA
(1968–)

English actress whose early TV work included the parts of Lucinda in GRANGE HILL and Dawn in BROOKSIDE. However, it was as Sharon in EASTENDERS that she made her mark, following this up by playing Barbara, one of Charles II's 39 mistresses, in the musical drama, *England, My England*, and then with the parts of Chris Cross in THE HELLO GIRLS and Charlotte in *Lucy Sullivan Is Getting Married*. Other credits have included THE BILL, CASUALTY and DROP THE DEAD DONKEY.

DEAR JOHN
UK (BBC) Situation Comedy. BBC 1 1986–7

John Lacey	**Ralph Bates**
Kate	**Belinda Lang**
Kirk St Moritz	**Peter Blake**
Ralph Dring	**Peter Denyer**

Louise Williams	**Rachel Bell**
Mrs Arnott	**Jean Challis**
Mrs Lemenski	**Irène Prador**
Sylvia Watkins	**Lucinda Curtis**
Ricky Fortune	**Kevin Lloyd**
Wendy	**Wendy Allnutt**

Creator/Writer: **John Sullivan**
Producer: **Ray Butt**

A wimpy divorcé finds solace in an encounter group.

Language teacher John Lacey had a shock on returning home from work one day. He found a note from his wife, Wendy, revealing that she had left him for his best friend, taking Toby, their eight-year-old son, with her. In the subsequent divorce proceedings, John lost his house and was forced to move into a crummy bedsit. Among his new neighbours was the elderly Mrs Lemenski, a foreign immigrant who was sure John was crazy.

His social life in tatters, John spotted an advert in a newspaper for The 1-2-1 Club, a divorced persons' encounter group, and decided to give it a go. The class was run by officious beauty consultant Louise Williams, whose chief interest was in her members' sexual problems and fetishes. Joining John in the group was Ralph Dring, one of life's great bores and the proud driver of a motorcycle combination. His Polish wife had married him to avoid extradition and had left him during their wedding reception. Also seen was Kate, an attractive but uptight girl whose three marriages had broken down because of her frigidity. This also seemed to prevent her warming to John. While other minor characters hovered in the background (including the virtually silent Mrs Arnott, Sylvia with the silly laugh and faded rock star Ricky Fortune – of Ricky Fortune and the Fortunates), the other main protagonist was Kirk St Moritz, a John Travolta lookalike, who had not even been married, let alone divorced, and attended simply to pick up 'frustrated chicks'. This spinner of exotic yarns, who claimed to be a spy, turned out to be a dowdy mummy's boy whose real name was Eric Morris.

Writer John Sullivan sold the idea to an American company and spent some time as a consultant and writer on their version of the series. This aired in the UK as *Dear John: USA* and starred Judd Hirsch.

DEAR MOTHER – LOVE ALBERT
UK (Thames/Yorkshire) Situation Comedy. ITV 1969–72

Albert Courtnay	**Rodney Bewes**
Mr A. C. Strain	**Garfield Morgan**
Vivian McKewan	**Sheila White**
Mrs McKewan	**Geraldine Newman**
Frances Ross	**Mary Land**
Leslie Willis	**Luan Peters**
Doreen Bissel	**Liz Gebhardt**
	Cheryl Hall (*Albert*)
Mrs Ada Bissel	**Amelia Bayntun**

Creators/Writers/Producers: **Rodney Bewes, Derrick Goodwin**

A young man's letters home to his mother exaggerate his success in the big city.

When naïve North Country lad Albert Courtnay moved to the bright lights of London he had high hopes. Unfortunately, life turned out to be rather more mundane than anticipated, not that he told his mother this in his weekly letters home. Albert worked for Mr A. C. Strain as a sales and marketing consultant in a confectionery factory. Vivian McKewan was the girl in his life, and her mother was also seen. Later Albert moved into a flat with two girls, Frances and Leslie, to the disapproval of his new fiancée, Doreen Bissel, and his prospective mother-in-law. After three seasons, the title was shortened to *Albert*.

DEATH OF A PRINCESS
UK (ATV) Drama Documentary. ITV 1980

Princess Misha'al .... **Suzanne Abou Taleb**
Ryder .... **Paul Freeman**

Writer: **Antony Thomas**
Producers: **Antony Thomas, Martin McKeand**

Highly controversial simulated documentary about the execution of an Islamic princess.

Death of a Princess, a two-hour special, sparked off one of the mightiest rows ever caused by a television programme. It reconstructed the investigations made by writer/co-producer Antony Thomas into the case of a 19-year-old Arab princess who had wavered from strict adherence to the Islamic religion and committed adultery. The price she paid for this capital crime was public execution. No country was named in evidence, but Saudi Arabia was so offended with the programme and its open criticism of Islamic culture that it cut diplomatic ties with the United Kingdom. Arguments raged over the accuracy of the information, although Thomas claimed to have travelled widely and talked to various witnesses in the course of his research. Normality was restored only once Foreign Secretary Lord Carrington had openly condemned the film.

DEATH OF AN EXPERT WITNESS
See P. D. JAMES.

DEAYTON, ANGUS
(1956–)

British writer, comedian and comic actor, an Oxford graduate and one-time collaborator with Rowan Atkinson. However, Deayton is best known as Patrick, Victor Meldrew's frustrated neighbour, in ONE FOOT IN THE GRAVE and as the chairman of the topical satire show, HAVE I GOT NEWS FOR YOU. His other major credits have included KYTV (Mike Channel), MR BEAN, *Chelmsford*

123, *Alexei Sayle's Stuff*, TISWAS, *Doctor at the Top*, *Bad Company* (Paul Foot) and the *Screen One* presentation, *Lord of Misrule* (MI5 man), plus quirky documentary and feature programmes such as *In Search of Happiness*, *The Temptation Game*, *The Lying Game*, *A History of Alternative Comedy* and *Before They Were Famous*. He has also written for Rory Bremner and *Aspel & Co.*, and is a popular choice for commercial voice-overs.

DEE, JACK
(1961–)

Kent-born comedian and actor, known for his dry, unsmiling delivery. He was launched on television in *The Jack Dee Show* for Channel 4, following this with a sketch show, *Jack and Jeremy's Real Lives*, which he shared with Jeremy Hardy, before moving over to ITV with the cabaret show, *Jack Dee's Saturday Night*, and then *Jack Dee's Sunday Service*. In 2000 he presented an eight-part feature on Canada's *Just for Laughs* festival in *Jack Dee's Full Mountie* for the BBC and then fronted the topical *Jack Dee's Happy Hour*. He was team captain for the first series of *It's Only TV But I Like It* (developed, like his other shows, by his own production company, Open Mike) and has also presented TOP OF THE POPS and, as an actor, has appeared in SILENT WITNESS and AMBASSADOR.

DEE, SIMON
(Nicholas Henty Dodd; 1935–)

Controversial DJ and talk show presenter, at one time all the rage but quickly fading out of view. His heyday came with the trendy tea-time pop and chat show, *Dee Time*, in 1967, the year in which he also compered MISS WORLD. Previously, he had been the first voice on the pirate radio station, Radio Caroline, when it opened in 1964 and remained on the high seas until the following year. He then joined the BBC, presenting programmes like *Housewives' Choice* and *Midday Spin*, as well as contributing to Radio Luxembourg. Although he made a small comeback with LWT in the early 1970s, hosting *The Simon Dee Show*, little has been seen of him in recent years.

DEF II
UK (BBC) Youth Magazine. BBC 2 1988–94

Executive Producer: **Janet Street-Porter**

Early-evening youth programming strand.

The *DEF II* slot (roughly between 6 and 7.30 p.m. on Mondays and Wednesdays) was aimed at the 16–25-year-old market and emulated Channel 4's *Network 7* (also once in the care of Janet Street-Porter). Among the programmes airing under the *DEF II* umbrella were the *Rough Guides* series with Magenta De Vine and Sankha Guha, *Rapido* with Antoine de Caunes, the US comedies *Wayne's World* and *The Fresh Prince of Bel-Air*, *Dance Energy* (later *D Energy*) with Normski, *Job Bank* (career profiles), *Liquid Television* (animations), the football magazine *Standing Room Only*, *Cyberzone* (a virtual-reality game show), *Behind the Beat* (a black music show), *Reportage* (news and views from around the world) and *Open to Question*, in which youngsters interviewed celebrities.

DEFENDERS, THE
US (Plautus) Legal Drama. BBC 1962–7

Lawrence Preston .... **E. G. Marshall**
Kenneth Preston .... **Robert Reed**
Helen Donaldson .... **Polly Rowles**
Joan Miller .... **Joan Hackett**

Creator: **Reginald Rose**
Producers: **Herbert Brodkin, Robert Markell**

Father and son lawyers defend clients accused of socially 'difficult' crimes.

In this very well-respected courtroom series, two generations of a legally minded family were brought together in the conscientious partnership of Preston and Preston. Lawrence Preston was the father and the old hand, educating his rookie son, Kenneth, who was fresh from law school and full of worthy ideas. Together they undertook a variety of cases, often dealing with subjects that pricked the public's conscience, such as civil rights, abortion and mercy killing; but, unusually for TV advocates, they didn't always win. In early episodes the pair were supported by secretary Helen Donaldson, and Kenneth's girlfriend, Joan Miller, a social worker, was also seen.

Ralph Bellamy and William Shatner were the stars of the pilot episode, which was shown in 1957, four years before *The Defenders* became a series in the USA. In that pilot, the pair acted on behalf of a client played by Steve McQueen. Many famous guest stars embellished the show over the years, from the likes of Gene Hackman and Jon Voight to Robert Redford and Dustin Hoffman.

DEFINITION

The clarity and sharpness of the TV screen picture.

DEMPSEY AND MAKEPEACE
UK (LWT/Golden Eagle) Police Drama. ITV 1985–6

Lt. James Dempsey .... **Michael Brandon**
DS Harriet Makepeace (Harry) .... **Glynis Barber**
Chief Supt. Gordon Spikings .... **Ray Smith**
DS Charles Jarvis (Chas) .... **Tony Osoba**

Creator/Producer: **Tony Wharmby**
Executive Producer: **Nick Elliott**

A streetwise Yank and a plummy member of the British aristocracy form an unlikely police partnership.

James Dempsey was a New York cop from Manhattan's Ninth Precinct who, having uncovered corruption in his own force and shot dead his own partner, was transferred to Britain for safety. There he was teamed with Lady Harriet Makepeace, a stunning blonde Cambridge science graduate with distant claims to the throne who, for some reason, had decided to pursue a police career. The two formed an uneasy partnership, working for SI 10, a covert division of Scotland Yard.

Dempsey was the typical brash American, a Vietnam veteran, hasty in his actions and fast on the trigger. Makepeace was a crack shot, a former archery champion, who, rather more subtly, achieved results by using her contacts in high places. In charge of the pair was vociferous Liverpudlian Gordon Spikings, with Chas, another detective, occasionally joining them in their investigations.

In all, *Dempsey and Makepeace* was a rather violent series, offering car chases aplenty and dragging in all sorts of criminals, from terrorists to drug-pushers. Stars Michael Brandon and Glynis Barber took their partnership on to a new footing when they were later married in real life.

DENCH, Dame JUDI
OBE (Judith Dench; 1934–)

Award-winning York-born actress, in straight drama and classical roles as well as comedy. While the 1980s and 1990s saw her star in two cosy domestic sitcoms – as Laura in A FINE ROMANCE (opposite her real-life husband, Michael Williams) and Jean in AS TIME GOES BY – Dench's TV career began in the mid-1960s, with appearances in Z CARS, MOGUL and assorted Shakespearean adaptations. Other notable performances have come in *Love in a Cold Climate* (again with Williams), *Saigon, Year of the Cat*, *Going Gently*, *Behaving Badly*, *Langrishe, Go Down*, *Absolute Hell* (part of BBC 2's *Performance* season), *Last of the Blonde Bombshells* (Elizabeth) and John Hopkins's *Theatre 625* quartet, *Talking to a Stranger*. She is the mother of actress Finty Williams.

DENIS, ARMAND
(1897–1971) and **MICHAELA** (1914–)

A cross between David Attenborough and Fanny and Johnny Cradock, Armand and Michaela Denis were UK TV's first wildlife specialists. Through his interest in photography, Armand, a Belgian-born but Oxford-educated chemist, branched out into filming wildlife and met London-born Michaela in New York and again while filming in South America. They married and also teamed up professionally to bring the great outdoors to BBC viewers. Their distinctive presentation – he with his Belgian accent and she with her blonde, pin-up looks – brought them instant fame. Their series *Filming Wild Animals* and *Filming in Africa* in 1954 and 1955 were followed by *Michaela and Armand Denis* for ITV, before they returned to the BBC in 1957 to present *On Safari*, a series that ran for many years. On leaving television they retired to their home in Kenya, where Armand died in 1971. After a tragically short second marriage to Sir William O'Brien Lindsay, the last English Chief Justice of Sudan (he died weeks after the ceremony), Michaela turned to spritual healing, setting up a centre in Nairobi.

DENISON, MICHAEL
CBE (1915–98)

Distinguished, Doncaster-born, Harrow- and Oxford-educated actor, first seen on TV in the 1930s in plays like Eugene O'Neill's *Marco Millions*. For eight years Denison was the suave Richard Boyd in ITV's BOYD QC, Britain's answer to PERRY MASON, although his later television appearances were less prominent, but included CROWN COURT, PRIVATE SCHULTZ, THE AGATHA CHRISTIE HOUR, RUMPOLE OF THE BAILEY, *Cold Warrior*, *Blood Money*, HOWARDS' WAY (Admiral Redfern) and one-off plays, including Joe Orton's *Funeral Games*. He was married to actress Dulcie Gray.

DENNIS, LES
(Leslie Heseltine; 1954–)

Liverpudlian light comedian, impressionist and actor, for a few years partner of the late Dustin Gee. His TV break came when winning NEW FACES, from which he progressed to WHO DO YOU DO?, THE COMEDIANS, *Russ Abbot's Madhouse*, *Go For It*, assorted variety shows and his own vehicle (originally with Gee), *The Laughter Show*. In 1987 he took over as host of the quiz game, FAMILY FORTUNES, and he has also hosted the talent show, *Give Your Mate a Break*. Dennis has been increasingly seen in acting cameos, too. His second wife is actress Amanda Holden.

DEPARTMENT S
UK (ITC) Detective Drama. ITV 1969–70

Jason King	Peter Wyngarde
Stewart Sullivan	Joel Fabiani
Annabelle Hurst	Rosemary Nicols
Sir Curtis Seretse	Dennis Alaba Peters

Creators: **Monty Berman, Dennis Spooner**
Producer: **Monty Berman**

A trio of special agents solve impossible cases for a division of Interpol.

Department S was the Paris-based secret wing of Interpol, the international police force, undertaking assignments that baffled regular detectives and government agents alike. The team's figurehead was the rakish Jason King, a thriller novelist who grappled with the facts of each case by putting himself in the shoes of his detective creation, Mark Caine. He was joined by the equally perceptive American action man, Stewart Sullivan (who loved to shoot down King's extravagant theories), and Annabelle Hurst, an attractive computer buff with an eye for detail. Their head of section was Oxbridge-educated black African Sir Curtis Seretse.

The trio's cases ranged from investigating what had happened to an airliner strangely lost for six days to discovering how a tailor's dummy managed to crash a car. The inquiries called more for lateral thinking than for pure detection, but the unorthodox team always achieved results, despite striving to outdo each other along the way. The undoubted star, the flamboyant, womanizing King – wearer of the magnificently psychedelic shirts and kipper ties – was soon given his own spin-off series, JASON KING.

DEPUTY DAWG
US (Terrytoons) Cartoon. BBC 1 1963–4

Voices: **Dayton Allen**

Creator: **Larz Bourne**
Executive Producer: **Bill Weiss**

The misadventures of an inept and accident-prone lawkeeper.

Hounded by pesky varmints like the short-sighted Vince (Vincent Van Gopher), the dicky-bowed racoon Ty Coon, Muskie the muskrat and Pig Newton, Deputy Dawg strove in vain to maintain law and order in sleepy Mississippi. With frustrated yells of 'Just a cotton-picking moment' and 'Dagnabit Muskie', the drawling canine in the wide black hat tried desperately to defend a hen-house from would-be invaders. He answered to the show's only human, The Sheriff, for the succession of disasters and mishaps that befell him and from which he was rescued only by a stroke of good luck. Dayton Allen voiced Deputy Dawg, plus most of his adversaries. Ralph Bakshi, one of the show's directors, later enjoyed success with the controversial adult cartoon film, *Fritz the Cat*.

DESMOND'S
UK (Humphrey Barclay) Situation Comedy. Channel 4
1989–94

Desmond Ambrose	Norman Beaton
Shirley Ambrose	Carmen Munroe
Matthew	Gyearbuor Asante
Porkpie Grant	Ram John Holder
Lee	Robbie Gee
Tony	Dominic Keating
Sean Ambrose	Justin Pickett
Michael Ambrose	Geff Francis
Gloria Ambrose	Kim Walker
Louise	Lisa Geoghan
Beverley	Joan Ann Maynard
Mandy	Matilda Thorpe

Creator: **Trix Worrell**
Producers: **Humphrey Barclay, Charlie Hanson, Paulette Randall**

A Peckham barber's shop is the hub of the local West Indian community.

Grumpy Desmond Ambrose was the proprietor of Desmond's barber's shop in south-east London. He ran it with his wife, Shirley, with whom he had three children,

Michael, Sean and Gloria. He also had many friends and acquaintances who used the shop as a meeting place. There they chewed the fat, enjoyed Shirley's refreshments, indulged in various social events and occasionally had their hair cut as well. Mixing various generations of black Londoners, *Desmond's* drew its humour from London street life and West Indian generation-gap conflicts, contrasting the ways and attitudes of the older, immigrant members with those of the youngsters, who had been born and bred locally. Creator Trix Worrell wrote the majority of the episodes, and then all the scripts for the spin-off, *Porkpie* (1995–6), focusing on lollipop man Porkpie Grant, one of Desmond's friends from the old country, who went on to win the Lottery.

DESTINATION DOWNING STREET

UK (TV Scripts/Associated-Rediffusion) Spy Drama.
ITV 1957

Mike Anson	**John Stone**
Jacques	**Donald Morley**
Sylva	**Sylva Langova**
Colin	**Graham Crowden**
Phoebe	**Diana Lambert**

Creator/Writer: **St John Curzon**
Producer: **Eric Maschwitz**

The adventures of a select team of secret agents, responsible directly to the Prime Minister.

When Britain was threatened by ruthless foreign saboteurs, there was only one person to call: Major Mike Anson. Anson, a former commando, was one of TV's first secret agents, ably assisted in his counter-espionage by two former resistance fighters, the Frenchman Jacques and Sylva, a Czech girl. Colin, a university don-cum-explosives expert, and Phoebe, a WAAF officer who worked as the team's organizer, completed the line-up.

The quintet were brought together after a trio of disasters had all struck uncannily at one time – an atomic scientist went missing, a ship sank and an African village disappeared – the work, it seemed, of the evil spy syndicate, ARKAB. Other similarly bizarre encounters followed. Such was the prestige of this hand-picked squad that they were answerable only to the PM himself (hence the title).

DETECTIVE

UK (BBC) Detective Drama Anthology. BBC 1 1964;
1968–9

Chief Insp. Maigret	**Rupert Davies**

Producers: **David Goddard, Verity Lambert, Jordan Lawrence**

Anthology series giving air time to some of literature's finest detectives, as well as some novel TV sleuths.

This intriguing collection of detective tales appears just as interesting in retrospect as when it first reached the screens, for among the selected sleuths were characters who would soon gain their own series, albeit sometimes in the hands of other actors. *Detective* introduced viewers to Margery Allingham's Albert Campion, for instance, played here by Brian Smith, as well as G. K. Chesterton's Father Brown, as portrayed by Mervyn Johns, and Ngaio Marsh's Inspector Roderick Alleyne, depicted by Geoffrey Keen and Michael Allinson. Cluff and Sherlock Holmes, with their stars Leslie Sands and Douglas Wilmer, were launched into full series virtually straight away.

The other characters (some of whom appeared more than once) were Carter Dickson's Sir Henry Merrivale (David Horne and Martin Wyldeck), E. C. Bentley's Philip Trent (Michael Gwynn), Edmund Crispin's Professor Gervase Fen (Richard Wordsworth), Nicholas Blake's Nigel Strangeways (Glyn Houston and Bernard Horsfall), John Trench's Martin Cotterell (Alan Dobie) and Roy Vickers's Inspector Rason (Michael Hordern and John Welsh). Jeffery Farnol's Jasper Shrig (Patrick Troughton and Colin Blakely) was another featured investigator, as were Douglas Sanderson's Bob Race (Frank Lieberman), Selwyn Jepson's Eve Gill (Jane Merrow and Penelope Horner), Austin Freeman's Dr Thorndyke (Peter Copley), Delano Ames's Jane and Dagobert Brown (Joan Reynolds and Leslie Randall), H. C. Bailey's Reggie Fortune (Denholm Elliott), Joyce Porter's Detective Chief Inspector Dover (Paul Dawkins), and Colin Morris's Detective Chief Inspector Dew (Glynn Edwards). Also featured were Ethel Lina White's Miss Pye (Angela Baddeley), Clifford Witting's DC Peter Bradfield (Mark Eden), Clark Smith's Nicky Mahoun (Frederick Jaeger), Michael Innes's Sir John Appleby (Dennis Price and Ian Ogilvy), Ursula Curtiss's Robert Carmichael (Dudley Sutton), Anthony Berkeley's Roger Sheringham (John Carson), Hillary Waugh's Police Chief Fellows (Lee Montague), William Haggard's Charles Russell (Roland Culver), MacDonald Hastings's Montague Cork (Colin Douglas), Josephine Tey's Alan Grant (John Carson), R. C. Woodthorpe's Sir Luke Frinsby (Cyril Luckham), Edgar Jepson and Robert Eustace's Ruth Kelstern (Hannah Gordon), H. R. F. Keating's Inspector Ghote (Zia Mohyeddin), Ludovic Peters's Ian Firth (David Buck) and John Smith (Meredith Edwards), Francis Didelot's Commissaire Bignon (Derek Godfrey and Edward Woodward), Edgar Allan Poe's Auguste Dupin (Edward Woodward, again) and Bill Fraser as William Guppy (based on Dickens's *Bleak House*).

The series was introduced for the first season by Rupert Davies in his famous guise of MAIGRET, although no Maigret tales were actually included. A gap of four years lapsed before the series resumed in 1968, continuing through to 1969.

DETECTIVES, THE

UK (Celador) Situation Comedy. BBC 1 1993–7

DC Bob Louis	**Jasper Carrott**
DC Dave Briggs	**Robert Powell**
Supt. Frank Cottam	**George Sewell**

Writers: **Steve Knight, Mike Whitehill**

Producers: **Ed Bye, Nic Phillips**

Spin-off series from Canned Carrott, *featuring the two incompetent detectives.*

Bob Louis and Dave Briggs were two gormless plain-clothes detectives who achieved results despite their best efforts. Paired on undercover investigations by their no-nonsense boss, Supt. Cottam, their bumbling and bickering, petty rivalry and hare-brained schemes usually spelt disaster for themselves but, somehow, success for the force. Star names from other BBC series cropped up from time to time: Jim Bergerac and Charlie Hungerford in an episode set on Jersey, and Danny Kane from THE PARADISE CLUB in an East London gang story. Jerry Hall, Jimmy Tarbuck, Tony Jacklin, Frank Windsor, Noel Edmonds, John Ratzenberger and Tony Head all made cameo appearances.

The characters were named after television executives known to creators Steve Knight and Mike Whitehill (who went on to co-devise WHO WANTS TO BE A MILLIONAIRE? with the real-life Dave Briggs).

DIAL 999

UK (Towers of London/ZIV) Police Drama. ITV 1958–9

DI Mike Maguire	**Robert Beatty**
DI Winter	**Duncan Lamont**
DS West	**John Witty**

Producer: **Harry Alan Towers**

A Canadian Mountie is seconded to the Metropolitan Police.

Inspector Mike Maguire was sent to London by the Royal Canadian Mounted Police to study advanced crime-detection techniques. Operating on a sort of 'work experience' basis, he was given an acting rank of detective inspector and assisted in his investigations by Detective Inspector Winter and Detective Sgt West. Like other mounties, the tough but fair Maguire always got his man. The series was made in conjunction with Scotland Yard and involved much location filming.

DIAMOND, ANNE

(1954–)

Birmingham-born journalist and presenter, whose work on ATV and Central's regional news programmes and then NATIONWIDE eventually led to her appointment as co-host of the TV-am breakfast show, *Good Morning Britain,* as the company sought to brighten up its act. Alongside Nick Owen, she helped reconstruct the ailing station's viewing figures. After leaving the breakfast sofa she moved into quiz shows (*The Birthday Show*, with Benny Green) and daytime TV, hosting *The Time, The Place, This Morning* and *TV Weekly*, before teaming up with Nick Owen again for the BBC's *Good Morning With Anne and Nick.*

DICK BARTON – SPECIAL AGENT

UK (Southern) Secret Agent Drama. ITV 1979

Dick Barton	**Tony Vogel**
Snowey White	**Anthony Heaton**
Jock Anderson	**James Cosmo**
Sir Richard Marley	**John Gantrel**
Melganik	**John G. Heller**

Writers: **Clive Exton, Julian Bond**
Executive Producers: **Terence Baker, Lewis Rudd**
Producer: **Jon Scoffield**

Light-hearted television revival of a legendary radio hero.

Fearless, dependable Dick Barton, demobbed after six years in the Army, found civilian life a touch too mundane for his liking. So, when he received a call from an old friend, Sir Richard Marley, asking him to find his missing son and daughter, he willingly dashed once more into the fray, in the company of his former colleagues, Snowey and Jock. The trio then stumbled into other inquiries, and more than once confronted their evil adversary, Melganik.

Unfortunately, this twice-weekly, 15-minute serial failed to capture the public's imagination in the same way as the original radio series, which went out between 1946 and 1951 and drew audiences of 15 million. Radio's Barton, Noel Johnson, reputedly received 2,000 letters a week. Perhaps it was his very clean-cut, wholesome portrayal of the dashing former commando who shunned hard drink and loose women which endeared him to listeners. On TV, Tony Vogel's Barton was considerably more earthy.

DICK TURPIN

UK (Gatetarn/Seacastle/LWT) Adventure. ITV 1979–82

Dick Turpin	**Richard O'Sullivan**
Nick Smith ('Swiftnick')	**Michael Deeks**
Sir John Glutton	**Christopher Benjamin**
Capt. Nathan Spiker	**David Daker**

Creator/Writer: **Richard Carpenter**
Producers: **Paul Knight, Sidney Cole**

Tales of the famous 18th-century highwayman.

Dick Turpin, cheated out of his wealth while on war duty in Flanders, decided to flout the law to regain his prosperity. His chief adversaries were the corrupt (and appropriately named) Sir John Glutton and Glutton's sneering, ambitious steward, Spiker. Assisted by Swiftnick, a young tearaway who became his closest companion, Turpin soon became a folk hero and rode to the aid of many a troubled countryman. These swash-buckling adventures saw the pair in and out of prison before Turpin's final capture and sentencing to death by hanging.

DICK VAN DYKE SHOW, THE
US (Calvada/T&L) Situation Comedy. BBC 1963–7

Rob Petrie .... **Dick Van Dyke**
Laura Petrie .... **Mary Tyler Moore**
Sally Rogers .... **Rose Marie**
Maurice 'Buddy' Sorrell .... **Morey Amsterdam**
Ritchie Petrie .... **Larry Mathews**
Melvin Cooley .... **Richard Deacon**
Dr Jerry Helper .... **Jerry Paris**
Millie Helper .... **Ann Morgan Guilbert**
Alan Brady .... **Carl Reiner**

Creator: **Carl Reiner**
Executive Producer: **Sheldon Leonard**
Producers: **Carl Reiner, Sam Denoff**

Gentle mishaps in the life of a TV scriptwriter.

Rob Petrie was head writer for *The Alan Brady Show*, a TV comedy programme. With his wife, Laura (a former dancer), and son, Ritchie, he lived in the suburbia of New Rochelle, where dentist Jerry Helper and his wife, Millie, were their next-door neighbours. Rob's life also extended to the TV studio in New York where he worked. His 'family' there included the man-hungry Sally Rogers and the wisecracking, loud-mouthed Buddy Sorrell. As a trio, they were constantly harassed by the arrogant Mel Cooley, the show's bald producer who was also the brother-in-law of the star, Alan Brady. Carl Reiner, who played the neurotic Brady, was, in fact, the show's creator and was not seen, only heard, for the first few seasons, before eventually making a visual appearance. Reiner had developed the series with himself in mind for the Dick Van Dyke role, but the networks were not impressed.

Many of the stars went on to further success: Jerry Paris became a successful producer and director, working on HAPPY DAYS among other programmes, while Mary Tyler Moore became a TV superstar, having her own series, THE MARY TYLER MOORE SHOW, and setting up the MTM production company.

DICKENS OF LONDON
UK (YTV) Drama. ITV 1976

Charles Dickens .... **Simon Bell** (*child*)
Roy Dotrice (*old man*)
Gene Foad (*young man*)
John Dickens .... **Roy Dotrice**
Catherine Dickens .... **Diana Coupland**
Catherine Hogarth/Dickens .... **Patsy Kensit** (*child*)
Adrienne Burgess (*woman*)
Georgiana Hogarth .... **Christine McKenna**
Fanny Dickens .... **Pheona McLellan** (*child*)
Henrietta Baynes (*woman*)
Maria Beadnell .... **Karen Dotrice**
Mr Hogarth .... **Richard Leech**

Executive Producer: **David Cunliffe**
Producer: **Marc Miller**

The great writer looks back on his formative years.

This biopic focused on an ageing, failing Charles Dickens as he recalled scenes from his early life. It followed his development up to the age of 32 and offered ample opportunity for viewers to identify people and events that were to shape his writings. Roy Dotrice played Dickens as an old man and also the young Dickens's father.

DICKINSON, ANGIE
(Angeline Brown; 1931–)

TV fame came quite late to former beauty queen Angie Dickinson, who had appeared with John Wayne in the film, *Rio Bravo* (among other movies), way back in the 1950s. Although she won herself a selection of interesting guest-spots in programmes like PERRY MASON, THE FUGITIVE, ALFRED HITCHCOCK PRESENTS and DR KILDARE, it wasn't until 1974 that she was cast in a lead role, that of Sgt Pepper Anderson in POLICE WOMAN. The programme ran for four years, and she followed it up with the mini-series, *Hollywood Wives*, and then a couple of other drama series in the USA, neither of which made inroads on the other side of the Atlantic. Dickinson does, however, have plenty of TV movies to her name. She was once married to composer Burt Bacharach.

DICKINSON, SANDRA
(Sandra Searles; 1940–)

Squeaky-voiced, blonde-haired, mainly comedy actress, the former wife of actor Peter Davison. Although born in Washington, DC, Dickinson's television work has been concentrated in the UK, taking in series as varied as THE TOMORROW PEOPLE, *What's On Next?*, TRIANGLE and THE TWO RONNIES. She also appeared with Roy Kinnear in *The Clairvoyant* (Lily), THE HITCH-HIKER'S GUIDE TO THE GALAXY (Trillian) and 2 POINT 4 CHILDREN (Tina).

DID YOU SEE . . . ?
UK (BBC) TV Review. BBC 2 1980–7; 1991–3

Presenters: **Ludovic Kennedy, Jeremy Paxman**

Producers/Editors: **John Archer, Sue Mallinson, Chris Mohr, Anne Tyerman**

Intellectual reviews of the week's television programming.

Chaired initially by Ludovic Kennedy, but from 1991 by Jeremy Paxman, *Did You See . . . ?* invited guests (usually writers, producers and politicians, rather than professional critics) to examine three of the previous week's TV offerings. Each guest was assigned one programme for close study and gave a full appraisal, with the others chipping in with their views in due course. Before the debate began, a brief overview of the week's TV happenings was provided by the host.

DIGITAL

Digital television was launched in the UK in October 1998. The new technology squeezes more channels into the space normally used to carry old-fashioned analogue TV channels, not only allowing more programming choice but also freeing up frequencies for uses such as mobile communications. It works by transmitting signals as a stream of binary digits, which helps eliminate interference. The signals are also compressed to discard unnecessary information, hence taking up less space.

There are three ways of receiving digital television. The first is by Digital Terrestrial Television, which uses existing transmitters and existing domestic aerials. Because digital signals require less space, six channels can be crammed into the same frequency as the old broadcasting system. These collections of channels are known as multiplexes, and initially six multiplexes were set up. One was operated by the BBC, another by ITV, Channel 4 and Teletext. A third was awarded to S4C Digital Networks to supply Channel 5, S4C and Scottish Gaelic programming, with the last three given to ONdigital for its 'satellite'-style content of films, sport and minority channels.

The second means of receiving digital (and the first on air) is by Digital Satellite Television. Operated by BSkyB, this system uses satellite technology to beam down signals to a domestic digital dish (smaller than the former analogue dishes). Just as for its terrestrial equivalent, the fact that digital signals use less space means that there is room for more channels. The third method of digital broadcasting is Digital Cable Television, where channels are piped through cable networks to the home. All three systems require the use of a decoder box that reconstitutes digital signals for television sets, although increasingly new televisions include built-in decoders. Programmes broadcast digitally by the BBC, ITV, Channel 4, Channel 5 and S4C are free to view, as are some satellite/cable services; other channels are sold as part of a subscriber package.

Additional benefits of digital include CD-quality sound, widescreen pictures, on-screen programme listings, limited 'ghosting' and other interference, the opportunity to order pay-per-view films and sporting events, the chance to 'interact' with broadcasts (casting votes, selecting news items, choosing camera angles, etc.), and scope for the development of commercial activities, such as home shopping and banking. On the negative side, if for some reason the signal becomes poor, reception will not simply deteriorate but will disappear altogether. It is planned that analogue services will continue to run simultaneously for a number of years, until digital coverage is comprehensive and decoder ownership is widespread and cheap.

DIMBLEBY, DAVID
(1938–)

Son of Richard and brother of Jonathan, David Dimbleby joined the BBC as a reporter in 1960 and has long been one of the Corporation's foremost political commentators and interviewers, working on programmes like PANORAMA, NATIONWIDE, *This Week, Next Week, The Dimbleby Talk-in* and most election coverages. In 1971 he ran into controversy when his 24 HOURS programme, *Yesterday's Men*, provoked anger among Labour politicians for an unfair and biased (they claimed) interview with deposed premier Harold Wilson. Dimbleby has also presented TOP OF THE FORM and, more notably, such documentaries as the award-winning *The White Tribe Of Africa*, the analytical series, *An Ocean Apart*, which looked at how the UK and the USA had developed in different cultural directions, and *Rebellion!*, which told the story of Rhodesia's transition into Zimbabwe. He is the current chairman of QUESTION TIME and was once married to cookery writer Josceline Dimbleby.

DIMBLEBY, JONATHAN
(1944–)

Following his father, Richard, and elder brother, David, into the current affairs side of television (and radio), Jonathan Dimbleby's progress came largely thanks to the independent sector. Beginning as a reporter with the BBC in Bristol, Dimbleby switched to ITV to present THIS WEEK, *TV Eye* and some prominent individual documentaries. Then came FIRST TUESDAY (also as associate editor), before he joined the BBC to host the lunchtime political analysis show, *On the Record*. In 1994 his interview with the Prince of Wales hit the headlines, Prince Charles conceding, at Dimbleby's prompting, that he had been unfaithful to Princess Diana. In 1997 his series, *The Last Governor*, chronicled the closing months of British rule in Hong Kong. Dimbleby is married to writer Bel Mooney. More recently, he has hosted *Jonathan Dimbleby*, a Sunday lunchtime political debate for ITV.

DIMBLEBY, RICHARD
CBE (1913–65)

Celebrated as one of Britain's finest broadcasters, Richard Dimbleby's radio work veered between light-hearted items like *Down Your Way* and *Twenty Questions* and sombre, graphic reporting. Joining the Corporation's news department in 1936, he became its first war correspondent and was the reporter who brought British listeners on-the-spot coverage of events like El Alamein and D-Day, even commentating from an RAF bomber over Germany. In doing so, he revealed a remarkable flair for conveying the awesome nature and true horror of such campaigns. Moving into television, he became synonymous with State occasions (the 1953 Coronation was one of the high spots of his career), technical innovations (such as presenting new Eurovision and satellite links) and political debates. Once he was installed as anchorman of PANORAMA in 1955, the programme quickly took off and Dimbleby earned himself a unique position of trust in the country, at the same time becoming recognized internationally as the voice of the BBC.

He died in 1965, not long after presenting the BBC's coverage of the state funeral of Sir Winston Churchill. His two sons, David and Jonathan, have both followed him into current affairs broadcasting.

DIMMOCK, CHARLIE
(Charlotte Dimmock; 1966–)

Red-haired, Southampton-born gardening presenter whose job as manager of a Romsey garden centre proved to be the launch-pad for a new TV career. Through series such as *Grass Roots*, GROUND FORCE, *Charlie's Garden Army* and *Charlie's Wildlife Gardens*, she put glamour into gardening at the turn of the millennium, drawing new viewers into the garden not just with her horticultural skills but also with her famously relaxed approach to upper-body support.

DIMMOCK, PETER
CVO, OBE (1920–)

Former RAF pilot who became one of BBC Television's first outside broadcast producers and sports commentators, joining the Corporation in 1946. He hosted COME DANCING and SPORTSVIEW, and was in the chair for the first edition of GRANDSTAND in 1958. Dimmock was sports adviser to the European Broadcasting Union 1959–72, as well as being the liaison executive between the BBC and the royal family, 1963–77. In the 1970s he was General Manager of BBC Enterprises and then became an executive with America's ABC network.

DINNERLADIES
UK (Good Fun/Pozzitive/BBC) Situation Comedy. BBC 1
1998–2000

Bren	**Victoria Wood**
Dolly Bellfield	**Thelma Barlow**
Tony Martin	**Andrew Gunn**
Anita	**Shobna Gulati**
Philippa Moorcroft	**Celia Imrie**
Twinkle	**Maxine Peake**
Stan Meadowcroft	**Duncan Preston**
Jean	**Anne Reid**
Petula Gardeno	**Julie Walters**
Mr Michael	**Christopher Greet**
Jane	**Sue Devaney**

Producers: **Geoff Posner, Victoria Wood**

Day-to-day laughs with the staff of a factory canteen in Manchester.

Victoria Wood's first sitcom was a character-led affair in which events played second fiddle to the personalities and the sort of socially observant banter that fills her stage shows. The ensemble was headed by the down-to-earth Bren, the sort of person who keeps her head when all about her are losing theirs and who can butter rolls and wash lettuce with the best, even if she does have trouble remembering words. She coped admirably with boss Tony (a chemotherapy survivor, later her boyfriend); daffy *Daily Mail*-reader Dolly; laid-back, oversexed Jean; punctilious handyman Stan (his dander permanently up); and drippy young helpers Twinkle and Anita. Highly-strung personnel manager Philippa flitted in and out with news of happenings in the Manchester factory (HWD Components), and Bren's wacky mum, Petula, occasionally left her grubby caravan home to reveal her latest sexual conquests. Although stories nominally revolved around the visit of royalty or a Japanese take-over of the company, of greater importance to Bren and her colleagues was whether the bread man had delivered the right order or if the toaster would actually work. But even these played second fiddle to the human dramas that unfolded. With its heavy word-count and complex and witty dialogue, each *dinnerladies* (deliberately billed with a small initial 'd') episode was actually recorded twice, to allow the cast to guarantee spot-on performances. Just two series were made.

DIRECT BROADCASTING BY SATELLITES
See DBS.

DIRECTOR

The creative/artistic executive in a production team. The director is the one who takes charge of the performances of the actors and camera crew, and who also supervises the post-production stages.

DIRECTOR-GENERAL

The title given to the chief executive of the BBC.

DISAPPEARING WORLD
UK (Granada) Natural History. ITV 1970–93

Creator/Editor: **Brian Moser**

Long-running, intermittently screened documentary series looking at civilizations in the far corners of the world.

Former WORLD IN ACTION producer Brian Moser was the brains behind this award-winning collection of films on 'lost' tribes hidden away in the remotest parts of the planet. His reports on the customs and ways of life of such peoples as the Cuiva in Colombia, the Meo in Laos, the Mursi in Ethiopia and the Mehinacu in Brazil brought anthropology into the living room and revealed how ancient lifestyles were being threatened by the advance of the modern world. No commentators were used. The subjects spoke for themselves, in their own languages, and subtitles provided an English translation.

DISCOVERY CHANNEL, THE

Founded in 1985 by John S. Hendricks, The Discovery Channel has broadcast in Europe via the Astra satellite system since 1993 and on digital networks since 1998, but has been available on cable in the UK since 1989. The service is provided by The Discovery Channel Europe, which is programmed separately from the original American channel to take account of European interests. Through documentaries and other factual programmes, Discovery covers a very wide range of subjects in five programme genres: adventure, travel, nature, history and technology. It does not feature current affairs or the arts. The channel commissions many programmes of its own, some in conjunction with other broadcasters, but also carries suitable material first seen on terrestrial channels. Its sister (spin-off) channels include Discovery Home and Leisure, Discovery Civilisation, Discovery Travel and Adventure, Discovery Sci-Trek and Animal Planet.

DISH

A round aerial for receiving satellite transmissions. Attempts by the ill-fated British Satellite Broadcasting (BSB) to introduce a smaller, more angular 'squarial' for domestic use met with initial technical difficulties, although some versions were made available.

DISNEY, WALT
(Walter Elias Disney; 1901–66)

Although Walt Disney's contributions to television are small beer when compared to his influence in the cinema, nevertheless the man and his organization have been responsible for some notable achievements on the box. His *Disneyland* anthology, first shown to US audiences in 1954, was instrumental in bringing Hollywood studios into the mainstream of television production. The series continued right into the 1990s, under various names, including *Walt Disney's Wonderful World of Color* and *The Wonderful World of Disney*, and has been given credit for raising the standards of children's TV entertainment and education. Out of *Disneyland* came DAVY CROCKETT, an adventure series based loosely around the legendary frontiersman, and, a year after *Disneyland* started, *The Mickey Mouse Club* was launched, proving a huge hit with young mousketeers (ears and all) all across the States. Also popular in the 1950s was another Disney series, ZORRO. Although Disney himself refused to release his movie classics for TV consumption, believing that there would always be a new market for his theatrical cartoons, his company did instigate The Disney Channel in 1983, allowing this cable station to benefit from the organization's treasure trove of films and past programmes.

DISSOLVE

The merging of one shot into another, by fading one out at the same time as fading another in. It is also known as a mix.

DISTRICT NURSE, THE
UK (BBC) Drama. BBC 1 1984; 1987

Megan Roberts	Nerys Hughes
David Price	John Ogwen
Gwen Harries	Margaret John
Hugh Morris	Philip Raymond
Dr O'Casey	Rio Fanning
Nesta Mogg	Deborah Manship
Teg	Ken Morgan
Bryn Morris	Gareth Potter
Dylan Roderick	Ian Saynor
Sarah Hopkin	Elen Roger Jones
Wil Hopkin	Ernest Evans
Evelina Williams	Beth Morris
Mrs Prosser-Davies	Elizabeth Morgan
Nora	Nathalie Price
Dr Charles Barclay	Philip Hurdwood
Revd Geraint Rhys	Ifan Huw Dafydd
Dr Emlyn Isaacs	Freddie Jones
Dr James Isaacs	Nicholas Jones
'Captain' Mansel	Jack Walters
Dilys Humphries	Christine Pollon
Ruth Jones	Janet Aethwy
R. T. Williams	Owen Garmon
Marie Anderson	Carol Holmes

Creators: **Julia Smith, Tony Holland**
Producers: **Julia Smith, Peter Edwards**

A nurse fights for respect in the poverty-ridden South Wales valleys of the 1920s.

Megan Roberts was the new 'Queen's Nurse' in the mining village of Pencwm. Typically conservative (with a small 'c'), the local residents treated their new arrival with suspicion. Perhaps it was her sit-up-and-beg pushbike and hideous hat that frightened the miners. More probably it was because she came from *North* Wales and, what's more, was a walking symbol of uniformed authority. The fact that she was a woman, taking control in a man's world, only made matters worse. Battling prejudice and ignorance at every turn, the determined and bossy Megan finally won acceptance and was able to improve medical practice in the village. For the third series, shown three years later and set in 1932, Megan had moved to the seaside town of Glanmôr, where she lived in the busy household of Dr Emlyn Isaacs.

DIVING TO ADVENTURE
See HASS, HANS AND LOTTE.

DIXON OF DOCK GREEN
UK (BBC) Police Drama. BBC 1 1955–76

PC/Sgt George Dixon	Jack Warner
PC/DS/DI Andy Crawford	Peter Byrne
Mary Crawford	Billie Whitelaw
	Jeanette Hutchinson
	Anna Dawson
Insp./DI Cherry	Robert Cawdron
PC/DC 'Laudy' Lauderdale	Geoffrey Adams
Sgt Flint	Arthur Rigby
PC/Sgt Johnny Wills	Nicholas Donnelly
PC 'Tubb' Barrell	Neil Wilson
Sgt Grace Millard	Moira Mannion
Cadet/PC Jamie MacPherson	David Webster
PC Bob Penney	Anthony Parker
WPC Kay Shaw/Lauderdale	Jocelyne Rhodes
Jenny Wren	Hilda Fenemore
Duffy Clayton	Harold Scott
PC/DC Tommy Hughes	Graham Ashley
DC Jack Cotton	Michael Nightingale
WP Sgt 'Scotty' Scott	Ruth Lodge
PC Bush	Max Latimer
WP Sgt Christine Freeman	Anne Ridler
WPC 'Barney' Barnes	Janet Morris
PC Clyde	Christopher Gilmore
PC Jones	John Hughes
WPC Alex Johns	Jan Miller
Cadet Michael Bonnet	Paul Elliott
PC/Sgt Wills	Nicholas Donnelly
PC/DC Swain	Robert Arnold
WPC Liz Harris/Swain	Zeph Gladstone
WP Sgt Jean Bell	Patricia Forde
PC Roberts	Geoffrey Kenion
WPC Shirley Palmer	Anne Carroll
PC Burton	Peter Thornton
Sgt Cooper	Duncan Lamont
WPC Betty Williams	Jean Dallas
PC Ted Bryant	Ronald Bridges
Det. Supt. Harvey	Geoffrey Keen
DC Pearson	Joe Dunlop
WDC Ann Foster	Pamela Buchner
PC Brian Turner	Andrew Bradford
WPC Sally Reed	Jenny Logan
PC Newton	Michael Osborne
PC Forbes	Scott Fredericks
DC Webb	Derek Anders
DI/DCI Scott	Kenneth Watson
DS Brewer	Gregory De Polnay
PC Harry Dunne	Stephen Marsh
DC Len Clayton	Ben Howard
DS Alan Bruton	Richard Heffer

Creator: **Ted Willis**
Producers: **Douglas Moodie, Ronald Marsh, Eric Fawcett, Joe Waters**

The cases of a traditional London bobby.

George Dixon was a policeman of the old school, the sort of dependable copper who helped old ladies across the road and whose idea of justice for young tearaways was a clip around the ear. Perhaps that was not surprising, given that the series began in the mid-1950s. But when you consider that it was still on our screens 21 years later, at a time when Jack Regan (THE SWEENEY) was dishing out knuckle sandwiches on the same London streets, it is easy to see just how dated this series had become. Indeed, even by 1962, the series was beginning to show its age, with the all-action men of Z CARS vying for viewers' attentions. But *Dixon of Dock Green* soldiered on, plodding its own beat, unashamedly unspectacular in style and content, and almost turning a blind eye to the rapidly rising crime rate.

George Dixon first saw the light of day in the 1949 Rank film, *The Blue Lamp*, in which the genial veteran was gunned down by armed robber Dirk Bogarde. His creator, Ted Willis, exhumed the character six years later when the BBC were looking for a replacement for FABIAN OF THE YARD. He placed PC Dixon at London's Dock Green police station, where he became a source of inspiration and comfort not only to the community but also to his younger colleagues. One such colleague was PC Andy Crawford, who went on to marry George's daughter, Mary (played by Billie Whitelaw in the first year), and provide him with twin grandchildren.

It was Crawford and his more sprightly pals who took over the running around as Dixon grew older and was promoted in 1964 to the rank of desk sergeant, replacing Sgt Flint. Other familiar faces at the Dock Green nick in the early days were PCs 'Laudy' Lauderdale and 'Tubb' Barrell, and Sgt Grace Millard; but many other officers came and went over the years, including the ill-fated Bob Penney, shot on duty. With his promotion, Dixon rarely strayed beyond the station counter, as Warner's advancing years began to take their toll. By the time the series ended in 1976, he was aged 80, and the last two seasons had shown him coming to terms with retirement.

Although it became atypical of a London policeman's lot (despite Ted Willis's thorough initial research at Paddington Green nick and regular story feeds from active force members), cosy *Dixon of Dock Green* remains one of British TV's most fondly remembered series. George's opening and closing monologues beneath the famous blue lamp, whistling 'Maybe It's Because I'm a Londoner' as he drifted into shot from the murky night, are classic TV memories, as is the lilting theme music, 'An Ordinary Copper', that wafted into living rooms every Saturday teatime.

Jack Warner, brother of music-hall stars Elsie and Doris Waters, died five years after the series ended and his funeral turned into a tribute from fans and policemen alike. At the ripe old age of 85, George had bidden viewers his final 'Evening All'.

DO NOT ADJUST YOUR SET
UK (Rediffusion/Thames) Children's Comedy. ITV 1967–8/1968–9

Eric Idle, Michael Palin, Terry Jones, David Jason, Denise Coffey, Terry Gilliam, The Bonzo Dog Doo-Dah Band

Writers: **Eric Idle, Michael Palin, Terry Jones**
Producers: **Humphrey Barclay, Ian Davidson**

Silly sketches and goofy gags for younger viewers.

Although aimed at the children's hour audience, this wacky series was a direct predecessor of MONTY PYTHON'S FLYING CIRCUS and all that programme was to achieve. Corralling together for the first time the talents of Eric Idle, Michael Palin, Terry Jones and animator Terry Gilliam, plus comic actress Denise Coffey and promising newcomer David Jason, producer Humphrey Barclay offered a madcap, 25-minute show of sketches and sight gags. One element featured the zany adventures of superhero Captain Fantastic (Jason), who was hounded by his nemesis, Mrs Black (Coffey). Fantastic was also seen in MAGPIE. The Bonzo Dog Doo-Dah Band provided musical relief.

DOBIE, ALAN
(1932–)

Yorkshire-born actor, most highly acclaimed for his performance as the Victorian Detective Sgt CRIBB in the 1980 series of the same name. He played David Corbett in THE PLANE MAKERS in the mid-1960s, John Diamond in *Diamond Crack Diamond* in 1970, Prince Dmitri in Tolstoy's *Resurrection* in 1971 and Prince Andrei Bolkonsky in his *War and Peace* in 1973. Other credits have included THE TROUBLESHOOTERS, *Hard Times*, *Kessler, Master of the Game* and numerous single dramas. His first wife was actress Rachel Roberts.

DOBSON, ANITA
(1949–)

London-born actress still best known as boozy pub landlady Angie Watts in EASTENDERS. She arrived in Albert Square at the programme's inception, taking advantage of the show's popularity to have a Top Five hit with a vocal version of its theme song, 'Anyone Can Fall In Love', in 1986. Her other TV has ranged from appearances in programmes as diverse as PLAY AWAY, NANNY, *Partners in Crime*, *Up the Elephant and Round the Castle*, the single drama *The World of Eddie Weary* and DANGERFIELD. She also played Cath in the short-lived hairdressers' sitcom, *Split Ends*, Ivy Osborne in the comedy, *Get Well Soon*, Donna Slaney in the drama series, *Hearts and Bones*, and Sam Greene in Sky One's *The Stretch*.

DOCTOR AT LARGE/IN CHARGE/AT SEA/ON THE GO/DOWN UNDER/AT THE TOP
See DOCTOR IN THE HOUSE.

DOCTOR FINLAY
UK (Scottish) Medical Drama. ITV 1993–6

Dr John Finlay	**David Rintoul**
Dr Cameron	**Ian Bannen**
Dr Neil	**Jason Flemyng**
Janet MacPherson/Livingstone	**Annette Crosbie**
Brenda Maitland	**Margo Gunn**
Dr Gilmore	**Ralph Riach**
Angus Livingstone	**Gordon Reid**
Rhona Swanson	**Jackie Morrison**
Dr Napier	**Jessica Turner**

Producers: **Peter Wolfes, Bernard Krichefski**

In 1946 John Finlay returns to Tannochbrae after wartime service and finds things have changed.

Moving on two decades from the classic 1960s series (DR FINLAY'S CASEBOOK), this *Doctor Finlay* was set amid the struggles of post-war revival. The old Arden House practice was now run down. Dr Cameron had grown tired and was troubled by the changes being enforced by the new National Health Service. Janet was no longer the gentle, inconspicuous housekeeper of the 1920s but a woman of the 1940s, hardened to the stresses, crises and inadequacies of wartime life. Into this background ambled Dr John Finlay, fresh from service as a major in the Royal Army Medical Corps, and, with some uncertainty, now reaching a crossroads in his career. He was not overpleased to be joined as partner by the young, impulsive Dr Neil, who was taken on to help with Dr Cameron's workload.

With the arrival of the third series, in 1995, the year had progressed to 1949. Janet had married Angus Livingstone, abdicating her place as housekeeper to young Rhona Swanson, but still keeping an eye on Arden House in her new role of practice receptionist. Dr Neil had moved on to pastures new and his replacement was, somewhat provocatively, a woman, Dr Napier.

Although the village of Callander had served admirably as a setting for the original series, a new location had to be sought for the Tannochbrae of the 1940s. It was discovered in the Fife town of Auchtermuchty.

DR FINLAY'S CASEBOOK
UK (BBC) Medical Drama. BBC 1962–71

Dr Alan Finlay	**Bill Simpson**
Dr Angus Cameron	**Andrew Cruickshank**
Janet	**Barbara Mullen**
Dr Snoddie	**Eric Woodburn**
Mistress Niven	**Effie Morrison**

Producers: **Campbell Logan, Andrew Osborn, Gerard Glaister, Douglas Allen, Royston Morley, John Henderson**

Young and old doctors share a Scottish village practice.

Set in and around the settlement of Tannochbrae (real-life Callander) and starting in 1928, *Dr Finlay's Casebook* related the ups and downs in the life of young, ambitious Dr Alan Finlay and his crusty ex-surgeon partner, Dr Angus Cameron (who was only 65 when the series ended, despite seeming much older). In the best tradition of medical dramas, the whippersnapper with the newfangled ideas did not always see eye to eye with the stick-in-the-mud old hand; but all the same Tannoch-brae was well served by its two dedicated GPs, who mutually benefited from their working arrangement. Watching over proceedings at their base, Arden House, was their trusty housekeeper, Janet, and also seen from time to time were the odious Dr Snoddie and the gossipy midwife, Mistress Niven.

The series, which ran for nine years, despite keen competition from the likes of DR KILDARE and BEN CASEY, was based on stories published as *The Adventures of a Black Bag* by doctor-novelist A. J. Cronin. The series was revived by ITV in 1993 (see DOCTOR FINLAY).

DOCTOR IN THE HOUSE
UK (LWT) Situation Comedy. ITV 1969–70

Michael Upton	Barry Evans
Duncan Waring	Robin Nedwell
Dick Stuart-Clark	Geoffrey Davies
Paul Collier	George Layton
Huw Evans	Martin Shaw
Dave Briddock	Simon Cuff
Prof. Geoffrey Loftus	Ernest Clark
The Dean	Ralph Michael
Danny Hooley	Jonathan Lynn

Producer: **Humphrey Barclay**

Medical students at London's St Swithin's Teaching Hospital run riot.

Loosely based on the *Doctor* books by Richard Gordon, which had been filmed in the 1950s with Dirk Bogarde in the lead role, this TV comedy led to a run of spin-off series: *Doctor at Large* (1971), *Doctor in Charge* (1972–3), *Doctor at Sea* (1974) and *Doctor on the Go* (1975–7). There was also an Australian version, *Doctor Down Under* (1981). The central character was initially naïve young student Michael Upton, but when Barry Evans left the show in 1972, Robin Nedwell as Duncan Waring, one of Upton's friends in the first series, returned to take over centre stage. Among the other hell-raisers were the upper-crust, work-shy Dick Stuart-Clark, Welshman Huw Evans, genial Paul Collier and crazy Irishman Danny Hooley. Prim spoilsport Laurence Bingham (Richard O'Sullivan) was seen in the *Doctor at Large* and *Doctor in Charge* series. Haughty Professor Loftus cast a disapproving eye on the goings-on as the red-blooded students chased nurses, played childish pranks and generally caused chaos. The characters were revived in 1991 in a new BBC series, *Doctor at the Top*, which viewed the lads 20 years on in their respective practices.

Doctor in the House was a decisive step forward in the careers of several actors who played a major part in British sitcoms of the 1970s and 1980s. Richard O'Sullivan went on to his own series, MAN ABOUT THE HOUSE, Barry Evans to MIND YOUR LANGUAGE, George Layton to IT AIN'T HALF HOT MUM and behind-the-scenes scriptwriting on a host of comedy shows, and Jonathan Lynn teamed up with Anthony Jay to create the hugely successful YES, MINISTER. Writers on the *Doctor* series themselves included THE GOODIES duo of Bill Oddie and Graeme Garden, as well as *Python*s Graham Chapman and John Cleese. Cleese allegedly based his FAWLTY TOWERS on a hotelkeeper he had created for one of the *Doctor* episodes.

DR KILDARE
US (Arena/MGM) Medical Drama. BBC 1 1962–6

Dr James Kildare	Richard Chamberlain
Dr Leonard Gillespie	Raymond Massey
Dr Simon Agurski	Eddie Ryder
Dr Thomas Gerson	Jud Taylor
Susan Deigh	Joan Patrick
Nurse Zoe Lawton	Lee Kurty
Dr Lowry	Steven Bell
Nurse Fain	Jean Inness

Executive Producer: **Norman Felton**

A sensitive young doctor learns the ropes from an experienced senior physician.

Baby-faced James Kildare worked at the Blair General Hospital under the watchful eye of wise old Leonard Gillespie. The series began with Kildare and two other doctors, Agurski and Gerson, taking up new posts at the hospital. The others left after one season but the dedicated Kildare stayed on, battling with medical matters, furthering his knowledge and education, and striving to meet the standards set by his mentor, Gillespie.

The programme kept fairly true to life, exposing the moral and ethical dilemmas experienced by the medical fraternity and the suffering endured by patients and their families, although the initial hour-long dramas later gave way to a half-hour serial format. Its big TV rival was always BEN CASEY, which ran for about the same length of time.

Dr Kildare made Richard Chamberlain into a household name. He even hit the charts with a vocal version of the theme song, 'Three Stars Will Shine Tonight', in 1962, and found it difficult to shake off the persona of the heart-throb doctor he portrayed so effectively. The character, which was created by Max Brand, had already appeared in several films in the 1930s and 1940s, played mainly by Lew Ayres, with Lionel Barrymore in the role of Gillespie.

DR QUINN: MEDICINE WOMAN
US (The Sullivan Company/CBS) Drama. ITV 1993–

Dr Michaela 'Mike' Quinn	Jane Seymour
Byron Sully	Joe Lando
Loren Brey	Orson Bean
Matthew Cooper	Chad Allen
Colleen Cooper	Erika Flores
	Jessica Bowman
Brian Cooper	Shawn Toovey
Jake Slicker	Jim Knobeloch
Revd Timothy Johnson	Geoffrey Lower
Horace Bing	Frank Collison
Robert E	Henry Sanders
Grace	Jonelle Allen

Emily .... **Heidi Kozak**
Cloud Dancing .... **Larry Sellers**
Hank Claggerty/Lawson .... **William Shockley**
Myra .... **Helene Udy**
Ingrid .... **Jennifer Youngs**
Dorothy Jennings .... **Barbara Babcock**
Olive Davis .... **Gail Strickland**
Preston A. Lodge III .... **Jason Leland Adams**
Dr Andrew Cook .... **Brandon Douglas**
Teresa Morales .... **Alex Meneses**
Daniel Simon .... **John Schneider**

Creator: **Beth Sullivan**
Executive Producers: **Beth Sullivan, Carl Binder, Philip Gerson, Chris Abbott**

A female doctor challenges tradition in the Wild West.

Michaela 'Mike' Quinn was a revolutionary. She had defied the prevailing logic and convention by qualifying as a surgeon in Boston (it was 1860) and working at her father's practice. When he died, she decided to take a job in the frontier town of Colorado Springs, much against her mother's wishes. The townsfolk were equally aghast when they realized their new medical person was a woman. But Mike quickly gained their confidence, aided by support from the rugged, mysterious Byron Sully (a future husband) and his pet wolf. She also became a surrogate mother, being handed the care of three orphans (Matthew, Colleen and Brian) when their mother, boarding-house keeper Charlotte Cooper, an early friend in the town, died from a snake bite. Among the initially sceptical townsfolk were storekeeper Loren Brey, barber Jake Slicker, saloon-keeper Hank Claggerty, saloon girl Myra and newspaper editor Dorothy Jennings. Cloud Dancing was the local friendly Indian.

DOCTOR WHO

UK (BBC) Science Fiction. BBC 1 1963–89; (Universal/BBC Worldwide/MCA) 1996

Doctor Who .... **William Hartnell**
Patrick Troughton
Jon Pertwee
Tom Baker
Peter Davison
Colin Baker
Sylvester McCoy
Paul McGann

The Doctor's Assistants:

Susan Foreman (*Hartnell*) .... **Carole Ann Ford**
Ian Chesterton (*Hartnell*) .... **William Russell**
Barbara Wright (*Hartnell*) .... **Jacqueline Hill**
Vicki (*Hartnell*) .... **Maureen O'Brien**
Steven Taylor (*Hartnell*) .... **Peter Purves**
Katarina (*Hartnell*) .... **Adrienne Hill**
Dorothea 'Dodo' Chaplet (*Hartnell*) .... **Jackie Lane**
Polly (*Hartnell/Troughton*) .... **Anneke Wills**
Ben Jackson (*Hartnell/Troughton*) .... **Michael Craze**
Jamie McCrimmon (*Troughton*) .... **Frazer Hines**
Victoria Waterfield (*Troughton*) .... **Deborah Watling**

Zoe Herriot (*Troughton*) .... **Wendy Padbury**
Liz Shaw (*Pertwee*) .... **Caroline John**
Jo Grant (*Pertwee*) .... **Katy Manning**
Sarah Jane Smith (*Pertwee/ Tom Baker*) **Elisabeth Sladen**
Lt. Harry Sullivan (*Tom Baker*) .... **Ian Marter**
Leela (*Tom Baker*) .... **Louise Jameson**
K9 (*Tom Baker*) .... **John Leeson** (*voice only*)
David Brierley (*voice only*)
Romana (*Tom Baker*) .... **Mary Tamm**
Lalla Ward
Adric (*Tom Baker/Davison*) .... **Matthew Waterhouse**
Nyssa (*Tom Baker/Davison*) .... **Sarah Sutton**
Tegan Jovanka (*Tom Baker/Davison*) .... **Janet Fielding**
Vizlor Turlough (*Davison*) .... **Mark Strickson**
Perpugillian ('Peri') Brown (*Davison/Colin Baker*) ....
.... **Nicola Bryant**
Melanie Bush (*Colin Baker/McCoy*) .... **Bonnie Langford**
Dorothy 'Ace' (*McCoy*) .... **Sophie Aldred**
Dr Grace Holloway (*McGann*) .... **Daphne Ashbrook**
Chang Lee (*McGann*) .... **Yee Jee Tso**

Others:

Col./Brigadier Alastair Gordon Lethbridge Stewart
(*Troughton/Pertwee/Tom Baker/Davison/McCoy*) ....
.... **Nicholas Courtney**
Sgt/RSM Benton (*Pertwee/Tom Baker*) .... **John Levene**
Capt. Mike Yates (*Pertwee*) .... **Richard Franklin**
The Master (*Pertwee/Tom Baker/Davison/Colin Baker/ McCoy/McGann*) .... **Roger Delgado**
Anthony Ainley
Eric Roberts
Davros (*Tom Baker/Davison/Colin Baker/McCoy*) ....
.... **Michael Wisher**
David Gooderson
Terry Molloy
The Black Guardian (*Tom Baker/Davison*) ....
.... **Valentine Dyall**
The White Guardian (*Tom Baker/Davison*) ....
.... **Cyril Luckham**
The Valeyard (*Colin Baker*) .... **Michael Jayston**
The Inquisitor (*Colin Baker*) .... **Lynda Bellingham**
The Rani (*Colin Baker/McCoy*) .... **Kate O'Mara**

Creator: **Sydney Newman**
Producers: **Verity Lambert, Innes Lloyd, Peter Bryant, Barry Letts, Philip Hinchcliffe, Graham Williams, John Nathan-Turner**
Executive Producers (*1996 film*): **Alex Beaton, Philip Segal, Jo Wright**

Classic BBC science-fiction series concerning an eccentric time traveller.

Doctor Who first reached the TV screens on the day after President Kennedy was assassinated. It quickly lodged itself into the Saturday teatime slot and gained a wonderful reputation for frightening children and entertaining adults. From behind the sofa, kids of all ages wallowed in the concept of a galactic do-gooder with unusual habits working his way around the dimensions of time and space, protecting the innocent and thwarting the oppressive.

Initially, *Doctor Who* had an educational thrust, with

creator Sydney Newman intending to involve The Doctor in real historical events, showing viewers just how things had actually happened. But, although there were instances when our hero found himself at the Gunfight at the OK Corral, among the Aztecs, alongside Marco Polo or at the start of the Great Fire of Rome, for example, the idea was quickly dropped in favour of more popular scary monsters and superbeasts.

The Doctor was first encountered in the then today of 1963 in the episode, *An Unearthly Child*. The child in question was his alleged granddaughter, Susan, a hyperintelligent pupil at a London school. Her snooping teachers, Ian Chesterton and Barbara Wright, discovered her home was an old police box, parked in a junk yard, where she lived with her grandfather, a mysterious, white-haired, tetchy old man dressed in Edwardian clothing. They sneaked into the police box, only to find it was larger inside than out and was, in fact, a kind of spaceship. Fearing his secret would be made public, The Doctor activated the ship, took off (dematerialized) and landed (materialized) on a prehistoric Earth inhabited by primitive tribesmen. The first *Doctor Who* adventure had begun.

It was at this point that we learned more about The Doctor's spaceship. It was known as the TARDIS, standing for Time And Relative Dimensions In Space, and, as implied, it could travel through time as well as space. Sadly, The Doctor had little control over it, and, as one adventure ended, so another began, with the TARDIS depositing its reluctant crew in yet another perilous situation. The cliffhangers at the end of the programme were always worth waiting for.

As the series progressed, The Doctor's companions changed frequently. Susan left her grandfather to stay on Earth in the year 2167, and Ian and Barbara eventually returned to their own time. In their places, The Doctor picked up Vicki (a stranded Earth girl), Steven Taylor (a space pilot, played by future BLUE PETER presenter Peter Purves) and Dodo, from Wimbledon. Then came Polly, a scientist's secretary, and Ben, a Cockney merchant seaman, before The Doctor himself changed. In an episode called *The Tenth Planet*, something happened that was to prove vital to the longevity of the series: The Doctor regenerated. Viewers learned that he had the power to revitalize himself when close to death and, by the time the series ended, there had, in fact, been six regenerations. On this occasion, the grey locks and craggy features of William Hartnell gave way to the pudding-basin haircut and elfish grin of Patrick Troughton. Along with his appearance, The Doctor's character also changed. His dour snappiness was replaced by sprightly *joie de vivre*, as Troughton turned The Doctor into a kind of scientific clown, a cosmic hobo in baggy checked trousers who passed the time piping up tunes on a recorder. With Doctor No. 2 travelled Polly, Ben and then some of his best-remembered assistants, the Scots Highlander Jamie (a pre-EMMERDALE Frazer Hines), Victoria, the orphaned daughter of an antiques shop owner, and a superintelligent alien, Zoe.

When Troughton decided to bow out, it was easy to drop in a replacement, given that the regeneration idea had been comfortably established, and, with his departure, another of The Doctor's many secrets was revealed.

Viewers learned that The Doctor was actually one of the Time Lords, a race which lived on the planet Gallifrey and acted as guardians of the time concept. In fact, he had been a bit of a rebel, a runaway who had stolen a TARDIS, albeit not a very good one. Not only was its navigation control hopelessly flawed, but its chameleon circuits were also defunct. Consequently, instead of being able to change appearance to blend in with the background (as it had done in 1963), it was now stuck in its police box guise. All the same, the Time Lords were not forgiving. Finally catching up with The Doctor, they put him on trial and exiled him to Earth.

Troughton's successor, Jon Pertwee, played the role as a brilliant scientist with martial arts skills, a dandy in a frilly shirt and a velvet jacket who drove a yellow vintage car named Bessie (registration WHO 1). He worked as a consultant at UNIT (United Nations Intelligence Taskforce), commanded by Brigadier Lethbridge Stewart, a by-the-book, traditional army man who had first appeared as a Colonel in the Troughton days and who appeared with all The Doctors except William Hartnell and Colin Baker. Earth was suddenly under threat from all quarters, as malevolent aliens cast their eyes on the planet, and it was during this period that The Doctor's arch-rival, The Master, a scheming, mesmeric, renegade Time Lord with a goatee beard and a sinister smirk, made his debut. Working with The Doctor at UNIT to counter such adversaries were scientist Liz Shaw, headstrong agent Jo Grant and the tomboyish journalist Sarah Jane Smith.

Sarah Jane continued with the next Doctor, a madcap, mop-haired adventurer played by Tom Baker. Sporting a floppy hat, a flowing scarf and an inane grin, chewing jelly babies in times of danger, Baker's Doctor was once again airborne, the Pertwee version having regained his freedom late in the day. Baker's reign as The Doctor proved to be the longest (seven years) and spanned no fewer than eight assistants, most notably alien warrior girl Leela, Time Lady Romana (or Romanadvoratrelundar, who regenerated, like The Doctor, into a new body), the artful Adric, the aristocratic Nyssa and, briefly, the Australian air stewardess, Tegan. There was also a robot dog, K9.

Baker was succeeded by the gentler, conscientious, cricket-loving Peter Davison depiction, who was admirably supported by Nyssa, Tegan and the schoolboy/alien, Turlough. On Davison's departure, a Baker returned, but this time Colin, not Tom. Adding a touch more whimsy and a hefty dose of arrogance to the part, this plumper, curly-headed Doctor's time was short-lived, and he was not generally liked (he even squabbled with his American companion, Peri). He was briefly joined by the red-haired Mel before Sylvester McCoy was drafted in for the seventh portrayal of The Doctor. On this occasion, our hero was a dashing but dotty man of action, carrying a question-mark-shaped umbrella that mirrored his studious but quirky temperament. His best-remembered travelling chum was the aggressive Ace. The most recent incarnation of the Doctor was provided by Paul McGann in a one-off TV movie shown in 1996. Sylvester McCoy was briefly involved at the start but his Doctor 'died' and was regenerated into a dashing new body. Set in San Francisco on New Year's Eve 1999, it saw the Doctor fighting once again to save the Earth from destruction at the hands of The Master (played by Eric Roberts, brother of Julia), assisted only by Dr Grace Holloway and Chinese youth Chang Lee.

Over the years, the Doctor's enemies were easily as important as his assistants. Among the most menacing were the Cybermen, inhabitants of Earth's twin planet, Mondas, who had replaced their decaying organs with artificial ones and had gradually turned into aggressive silver robot men. The Yeti were furry little robots sent to conquer the Earth; and other memorable invaders included the Ice Warriors (from Mars), the Sea Devils (prehistoric creatures reclaiming their planet from beneath the waves), the Silurians (the Sea Devils' reptile cousins) and The Rani, another rebel Time Lord. The giant ants called Zarbi were some viewers' favourite aliens, but top of the list for most had to be the Daleks, a ruthless race of metal megalomaniacs.

The Daleks were first encountered in the second *Doctor Who* story, *The Dead Planet*. Set on the planet Skaro, it revealed how the Daleks, a dying race, had developed special transporter machines, armed with deadly ray guns, and were seeking to overcome the Thals, their peace-loving rivals. These transporters (with the seldom-seen squidgy Dalek mutants inside), skated around on castors, operating controls with a long suction arm (or occasionally a claw), and viewing the world out of one Cyclops-style eye stick. Their grating electronic voices provided one of the show's most frightening catch-phrases: 'Ex-ter-min-ate!' In later, retrospective episodes, it was revealed that the Daleks had been the mutated remains of the Kaled race, saved by a power-crazed scientist, Davros. Sadly, he had refused to program the Daleks with compassion and they had turned on him, too, in their relentless quest for domination.

Although often mocked for its primitive special effects and ridiculous soundtracks, few programmes have earned more respect than *Doctor Who*. Two feature film copies were made in the early days – *Doctor Who and the Daleks* and *Daleks: Invasion Earth 2150 AD*, both starring Peter Cushing in the title role. The various incarnations of The Doctor have actually appeared together on more than one occasion. The first was in 1972 in a story entitled *The Three Doctors*, in which the incumbent, Pertwee, was given the help of his two predecessors to combat a threat to the Time Lords. By the time of the next reunion, *The Five Doctors*, in 1983, William Hartnell had died and his portrayal was given by Richard Hurndall. Tom Baker declined to appear, and footage from a never-finished production, *Shada*, was used to bring him into the action. Troughton and Colin Baker met up in *The Two Doctors* in 1985, and all except Hartnell/Hurndall and the late Troughton resurfaced for a short and extremely confusing 3-D TV experiment for 1993's CHILDREN IN NEED, in which they fought a collection of old enemies (particularly The Rani) in and around EASTENDERS' Albert Square. In 1999, a spoof *Doctor Who* was produced for COMIC RELIEF, beginning with Rowan Atkinson as the Doctor and Julia Sawalha as his assistant. The Doctor then progressed through various regenerations and ended up as Joanna Lumley. Jonathan Pryce played The Master. A new radio version, starring Jon Pertwee, Elisabeth Sladen and Nicholas Courtney, was aired on Radio

2 in 1996. There are currently no plans for new television programmes, but *Doctor Who*'s fans will never give up the fight to see their hero restored to the small screen – a fact confirmed by the large audience for BBC 2's *Doctor Who Night* in November 1999.

Doctor Who trivia is available in abundance. Allegedly he was around 750 years old and, being a Time Lord, had two hearts and was allowed 13 regenerations. Among his favourite gadgets was the sonic screwdriver, used for anything from opening electronic doors to detonating unexploded bombs. He was seldom called 'Doctor Who', but simply 'The Doctor' (or, somewhat confusingly, 'The Professor' by Ace). The atmospheric original theme music (modernized by later producers) was composed by Ron Grainer of the BBC's Radiophonic Workshop.

DOCTORS, THE
UK (BBC) Drama. BBC 1 1969–71

Dr John Somers	**John Barrie**
Dr Roger Hayman	**Richard Leech**
Dr Elizabeth McNeal	**Justine Lord**
Mrs Hayman	**Irene Hamilton**
Dr Bill Conrad	**Barry Justice**
Tom Durham	**Paul Massie**
Nella Somers	**Alexandra Dane**
Molly Dolan	**Lynda Marchal**
Louise Hayman	**Irene Hamilton**
Mrs Baynes	**Maureen O'Reilly**
Mrs Groom	**Pamela Duncan**
Mrs Parsons	**Elsie Wagstaff**
Dr Linda Carpenter	**Isla Blair**
Dr Thomas Owens/Owen	**Nigel Stock**
Meg Owens/Owen	**Joan Newell**
Dr David Owens/Owen	**Drewe Henley**
Jo Hayman	**Elaine Mileham**
Dr Cheryl Barnes	**Janet Hargreaves**

Creator: **Donald Bull**
Producers: **Colin Morris, Bill Sellars**

Visits to a fictitious NHS practice.

The first twice-weekly BBC serial to be recorded in colour, *The Doctors* was another attempt by the Corporation to crack the soap-opera market, having had only limited success with COMPACT, UNITED! and THE NEWCOMERS. This time the setting was a general practice in North London which was headed by serious, pipe-smoking Dr John Somers. He was ably supported by the likes of Drs Roger Hayman, Liz McNeal and Bill Conrad, as well as, towards the close, Linda Carpenter and Welsh veteran Dr Thomas Owens – his surname eventually simplified to Owen in readiness for the spin-off, *Owen, MD* (1971–3). With limited resources, they aimed to care for 9,000 patients.

The idea was to portray events with due realism, avoiding the schmaltz of American doctors series and skipping the romantic liaisons that characterized EMERGENCY – WARD 10 and similar UK offerings. However, despite the efforts of writers like Elaine Morgan and Fay Weldon, the net result was considered to be a worthy BBC drama without the hoped-for grittiness seen in EASTENDERS, which was still 14 years away.

DOCUMENTARY

A programme focusing on facts – factual people, objects, instances or circumstances – for the purpose of reporting truth or educating the viewer. Inevitably, the maker's viewpoint is incorporated into the programme (whether directly in the narration or through the camera techniques and editing) and comment is made (sometimes purposefully, at other times unintentionally) on the matter in hand. This led 1930s documentary supremo John Grierson to describe the medium as 'the creative treatment of reality'. Documentary techniques have sometimes been borrowed by drama producers to bring an extra degree of realism or objectivity to their work.

DOCU-SOAP

Documentaries that follow events in the everyday lives of ordinary citizens are not new. Paul Watson captured the viewers' attention with THE FAMILY in 1974, for instance. However, in the late 1990s, the docu-soap, as it became known, gained a new lease of life. The major catalysts were AIRPORT, *Vets' School* and *Driving School*, all in theory showing the general public going about their daily business, but of course really focusing only on moments of high drama or comedy. Selective editing ensured that there were no mundane moments to bore the audience, and only the most charismatic of personalities found their way on to the screen. These series inspired a whole raft of look-alikes as producers desperately sought new locations and professions that might just be good for a series or two. Traffic wardens, hotel workers, shop assistants, doctors, zoo keepers, policemen, holiday reps and rat-catchers all found their 15 minutes of fame before the craze – which had started to dominate peak-time schedules – began to subside.

DODD, KEN
OBE (1927–)

Merseyside comic, a stalwart of variety shows and his own comedy programmes during the 1960s and 1970s. As well as stand-up routines in the classic music hall style (complete with tickling stick), Dodd has been known to burst into sentimental song (he had a string of hits in the 1960s, including the chart-topping 'Tears'). He also introduced us to the Diddymen – Dicky Mint, Mick the Marmalizer, Evan, Hamish McDiddy, Nigel Ponsonby-Smallpiece, *et al.* – who worked the jam-butty mines of Knotty Ash. They were presented either as kids in costume or in animated puppet sketches, with Dodd providing the voices. His programme titles have included *The Ken Dodd Show, Doddy's Music Box, Funny You Should Say That, Ken Dodd's World of Laughter, The Ken Dodd Laughter Show* and *Ken Dodd's Showbiz*, and other appearances have come in THE GOOD OLD DAYS, STARS ON SUNDAY, *A Question of Entertainment* (team captain)

and *Alice in Wonderland* (Mr Mouse), with more intriguing 'straight' guest spots in CROSSROADS and DOCTOR WHO.

DOLLY

A mounting for a camera, usually on wheels or rails to allow camera movement.

DON'T ASK ME
UK (Yorkshire) Science. ITV 1974–8

Presenters: **Derek Griffiths, Miriam Stoppard, Magnus Pyke, David Bellamy, Robert Buckman, Austin Mitchell, Brian Glover**

Producer: **Duncan Dallas**

The hows, whys and wherefores of science explained in everyday terms.

Prompted by questions from a studio audience, Dr Magnus Pyke, Dr Miriam Stoppard and David Bellamy took the wonders of science, medicine and technology into Britain's living rooms. 'Why do golf balls have dimples?' and 'Do crocodiles shed tears?' were two typical queries, with one question always coming from a celebrity guest. Derek Griffiths hosted proceedings in the early days, before he was succeeded (briefly) by Adrienne Posta and then by Brian Glover. Dr Rob Buckman and future Labour MP Austin Mitchell also became part of the team. A follow-up series, *Don't Just Sit There*, featured the same pundits.

DON'T FORGET TO WRITE!
UK (BBC) Situation Comedy. BBC 1 1977–9

Gordon Maple .... **George Cole**
Mabel Maple .... **Gwen Watford**
Tom Lawrence .... **Francis Matthews**

Creator/Writer: **Charles Wood**
Producer: **Joe Waters**

A dramatist encounters problems in his personal and professional life.

Gordon Maple was a moody, struggling screenwriter, supplying scripts for feature films that were never actually made, dealing with awkward movie producers who made his life difficult with their niggling demands. Maple was also prone to bouts of writers' block and, to compound the agony, his writer friend Tom Lawrence was altogether more successful. Mabel was Gordon's long-suffering wife.

Don't Forget To Write! had its origins in two plays which, like this series, were written by Charles Wood and starred George Cole and Gwen Watford. The first, entitled *A Bit of a Holiday*, was screened by Yorkshire Television as part of its 1968 anthology, *The Root of All Evil*. The second, *A Bit of a Family Feeling*, aired in 1971 as part of Yorkshire's *The Ten Commandments* season.

DON'T FORGET YOUR TOOTHBRUSH

UK (Ginger) Game Show. Channel 4 1994–5

Presenters: **Chris Evans, Jadene Doran**

Producer: **Lisa Clarke**

Innovative comedy game show offering a chance of a dream holiday to anyone in the studio audience.

Musically supported by Jools Holland and guest bands, Chris Evans broke new ground with this live Saturday night game show. The entire studio audience was told to bring their passports and toothbrushes along, with the possibility that any of them could be leaving immediately at the end of the show on the holiday of a lifetime.

By 'exploding seats' to choose contestants and putting them through a sequence of wacky games and quizzes, winners were chosen and ultimately given the chance to answer enough questions to ensure their holiday was in Rio, not Rhyl, or Barbados, not Bognor. One week the whole audience was packed on to buses and taken away to EuroDisney. Among the games featured were a quiz involving a pop star who had to answer more questions about him or herself than an ardent fan, and an outside broadcast which called on an unsuspecting household and demanded that its residents throw a number of domestic items out of a bedroom window within a given time. Despite immense popularity, only two series were made, Evans preferring to move on to new projects.

DON'T WAIT UP

UK (BBC) Situation Comedy. BBC 1 1983–90

Dr Tom Latimer	**Nigel Havers**
Dr Toby Latimer	**Tony Britton**
Helen Latimer	**Jane How**
Angela Latimer	**Dinah Sheridan**
Madeleine Forbes/Latimer	**Susan Skipper**
Dr Charles Cartwright	**Richard Heffer**
	Simon Williams
Susan Cartwright	**Tricia George**
Felicity Spicer-Gibbs	**Jane Booker**

Creator/Writer: **George Layton**
Producer: **Harold Snoad**

Father and son doctors are brought together by divorce.

Hard-working GP Tom Latimer, newly divorced from Helen, lost his home and his surgery in the ensuing settlement. He managed to rent back the surgery but was forced to share a flat with his pompous dad, Toby, a Harley Street dermatologist who had just seen the break-up of his own marriage to Tom's mother, Angela. Playing on the generation gap, and also on the conflict between NHS and private medicine, the series saw the two men at each other's throats as they tried to rebuild their lives, with Tom working for a reconciliation between his parents. Madeleine was Toby's secretary and Tom's new girlfriend (later wife). Charles Cartwright was Tom's practice partner.

DONAHUE, PHIL

(1935–)

Silver-haired American talk show host, the presenter of a long-running national daytime programme (*Donahue*) in which the audience reveal their views on political and social topics, not to mention sexual matters. His programmes have been aired late at night in the UK. He is married to actress Marlo Thomas.

DONNELLY, DECLAN

(1975–) See McPARTLIN, ANTHONY.

DONOVAN, JASON

(1968–)

Blond Australian actor who shot to fame as Scott Robinson in NEIGHBOURS, using the series to launch a successful singing career. He was the second actor to take the part (following Darius Perkins) and came to Erinsborough via shows like *The Henderson Kids*. Outside Ramsay Street, Donovan also starred in the dramas, *The Heroes*, playing a nervous young sailor, and *I Can Jump Puddles* (Freddy). His father, Terence Donovan, a veteran of Australian TV, also joined the *Neighbours* cast as Doug Willis.

DOOMWATCH

UK (BBC) Science Fiction. BBC 1 1970–2

Dr Spencer Quist	**John Paul**
Dr John Ridge	**Simon Oates**
Tobias 'Toby' Wren	**Robert Powell**
Colin Bradley	**Joby Blanshard**
Pat Hunisett	**Wendy Hall**
Minister	**John Barron**
Barbara Mason	**Vivien Sherrard**
Geoff Hardcastle	**John Nolan**
Dr Fay Chantry	**Jean Trend**
Dr Anne Tarrant	**Elizabeth Weaver**
Commander Neil Stafford	**John Brown**

Creators: **Gerry Davis, Kit Pedler**
Producer: **Terence Dudley**

A special government department monitors dangers to society from scientific 'progress'.

Standing for the Department for the Observation and Measurement of Science, Doomwatch was a governmental agency dedicated to preserving the world from the dangers of unprincipled scientific research. The Government's intention in setting up the agency had been to stifle protest and secure votes, and it believed it was establishing a quango with little power. However, its principal activists, the incorruptible Dr Spencer Quist and the heroic pairing of Dr John Ridge and Toby Wren, soon gave *Doomwatch* some real bite.

Quist had worked on the creation of the atomic bomb but had then seen his wife die of radiation poisoning. Ridge was an all-action, woman-chasing, secret agent type, and Wren was a conscientious researcher. Together they took ecology into viewers' living rooms, questioning the real value of certain scientific discoveries in a series of dramas which, in many respects, were years ahead of their time. Among the problems they tackled were embryo research, subliminal messages, so-called 'wonder drugs', the dumping of toxic waste, noise pollution, nuclear weaponry, man-made viruses, genetic manipulation and animal exploitation. Consequently, *Doomwatch* has been described as the first 'green' TV drama series. It was novel in another TV sense, too, taking the drastic and risky step of killing off one of its lead characters at the end of the first season: Wren was blown up while defusing a bomb on a seaside pier. Among his replacements was Dr Fay Chantry, who was introduced to strengthen the female content.

Radical, unusual and controversial, *Doomwatch* was the brainchild of former DOCTOR WHO collaborators, Gerry Davis and Kit Pedler. However, they became increasingly disillusioned with the series as mundane drama elements took hold. By the third and final season, they had severed their link completely and were openly voicing criticisms of storylines. A feature film of the same title was released in 1972, starring Ian Bannen, but Ridge, Quist and their Yorkshireman lab assistant, Colin Bradley, made only fleeting appearances in it.

DOONICAN, VAL
(1929–)

Relaxed Irish singer whose Saturday night variety shows became a staple of the BBC (and, briefly, ITV) diet in the late 1960s and 1970s. Mixing sentimental ballads with novelty songs like 'O'Rafferty's Motor Car', 'Delaney's Donkey' and 'Paddy McGinty's Goat', Doonican was a firm favourite with both old and young viewers, and his distinctive sweaters and cosy rocking-chair established themselves as his trademarks. Comedian Dave Allen was 'discovered' thanks to the weekly slot Doonican gave him.

DORS, DIANA
(Diana Fluck; 1931–84)

Bold, blonde Swindon-born leading lady, a product of the Rank Charm School whose film career never quite reached the heights it promised. Later in life she found herself in more demand on television. She starred as Queenie Shepherd in the 1970 sitcom, QUEENIE'S CASTLE, as rugby league manageress Di Dorkins in the 1973 comedy, *All Our Saturdays*, played the commandant in THE TWO RONNIES saga, *The Worm That Turned*, and also appeared as Mrs Bott in JUST WILLIAM. Her numerous guest spots included HAMMER HOUSE OF HORROR, THRILLER and villainous roles in both SHOESTRING and THE SWEENEY. She also briefly presented an afternoon

chat show for Southern TV. Never short of personal problems, Diana Dors died in 1984 after major surgery. One of her last TV roles was as slimming presenter on TV-am's *Good Morning Britain*. In 1999 ITV dramatized her life story in *The Blonde Bombshell*, starring Keeley Hawes and Amanda Redman as Dors.

DOTTO
UK (ATV) Quiz. ITV 1958–60

Presenters: **Robert Gladwell, Jimmy Hanley, Shaw Taylor**

Producer: **John Irwin**

Join-the-dots-based game show.

In *Dotto*, a quiz show brought over to the UK from the USA, two contestants, by answering questions, joined dots to reveal a celebrity's face. The first contestant to guess the mystery person received a cash sum for every unjoined dot left on the board. There were 50 dots at the start of each round. Robert Gladwell was the show's original host, and he was succeeded by Jimmy Hanley and then future POLICE FIVE presenter, Shaw Taylor, during the programme's two-year run.

The original American version was forced off the screen after being implicated in the so-called 'Quiz Show Scandal' which rocked US game shows in the late 1950s. It was alleged that certain 'interesting' contestants (those whom viewers liked and who generated good audiences) were favoured by programme sponsors and were given the answers to questions in advance so they could continue as reigning champions from programme to programme.

DOUBLE DECKERS, THE
See HERE COME THE DOUBLE DECKERS.

DOUBLE YOUR MONEY
UK (Associated-Rediffusion/Arlington) Quiz. ITV 1955–68

Host: **Hughie Green**

Creator: **John Beard**

Extremely popular double-or-quit quiz show.

Airing first on Radio Luxembourg, *Double Your Money* was brought to television by Associated-Rediffusion, with its Canadian compere, Hughie Green, once again in charge of events. Participants had the chance to win up to £1,000 by answering questions on specialized subjects. Beginning with a lowly £1 question, the contestants selected from 42 available topics and then 'doubled or quit' with each answer to a total of £32. They were then eligible to enter the Treasure Trail, which led to the jackpot prize. For the nail-biting £1,000 question, contestants were isolated in a sound-proofed booth.

As much a part of the programme as the quiz itself was Hughie Green's over-the-top showmanship, as he clowned around, telling corny jokes and poking fun at his contestants. The show's hostesses were also part of the act. The most prominent were Valerie Drew, Jean Clarke, Alice Earrey (a 77-year-old former charlady who had appeared as a contestant), Nancy Roberts, Barbara Roscoe, Julie de Marco and chirpy Cockney teenager Monica Rose, who became Hughie's sidekick for most of the 1960s. Robin Richmond was the programme's resident organist.

Along with TAKE YOUR PICK, *Double Your Money* was a stalwart of ITV's earliest programme schedules and ran until Associated-Rediffusion lost its franchise in 1968. One edition, in 1966, was recorded in Moscow and, because the Communist Party banned cash prizes, the winner picked up a television set instead. In 1971 the concept was revived by Yorkshire Television as *The Sky's the Limit*, in which air miles (up to 21,000) and spending money (£600) replaced pure cash as prizes. Monica Rose was again seen at Hughie Green's side.

Double Your Money was based on the American show, *The $64,000 Question*, which, somewhat confusingly, also aired in the UK in 1956–8 as *The 64,000 Question*, hosted by Jerry Desmonde and, for a while, Robin Bailey. Impoverished Britain offered only multiples of sixpence a question instead of dollars, with the top prize fixed at £1,600 (later doubled). Nevertheless, matters were taken extremely seriously and retired copper, Detective Supt. Robert Fabian, was employed as custodian of the questions. With its original title of *The $64,000 Question*, it was revived in 1990 with Bob Monkhouse asking the questions.

DOUGALL, ROBERT
MBE (1913–99)

Distinguished and genial BBC newsreader, one of the Corporation's first TV news presenters. Croydon-born Dougall joined the BBC via its accounts department, before moving to the Empire Service as an announcer in the early 1930s. After spending the war with the Royal Naval Volunteer Reserve, he returned to the BBC in 1946, working as a reporter for its European and Far Eastern services, before switching to the Light Programme, again as announcer. When TV news began in 1954, he (like his early colleagues, Richard Baker and Kenneth Kendall) was kept out of sight, reaching the limelight only when ITN pushed their newscasters into the picture. Dougall read the news until 1973 and subsequently made programmes about bird-watching (he was at one time President of the RSPB). He also hosted STARS ON SUNDAY and Channel 4's senior citizens' magazine, *Years Ahead*, and was seen in programmes like NATIONWIDE, GOING FOR A SONG and, famously, dancing on *The Morecambe and Wise Show*.

DOUGLAS, COLIN
(1912–91)

Northern actor whose most prominent roles were as dim-witted crook BONEHEAD in the children's series of the same name and as Edwin Ashton, the father of A FAMILY AT WAR. Among his other credits were parts in the 1955 version of *The Children of the New Forest*, *Dial RIX*, FIRE CRACKERS (George), *Love Story*, FOLLYFOOT, TELFORD'S CHANGE, THE SWEENEY, DICK BARTON – SPECIAL AGENT and NANNY, with his last performance coming in Alan Bleasdale's GBH, as troubled Labour Party veteran Frank Twist.

DOUGLAS FAIRBANKS PRESENTS
UK (Douglas Fairbanks) Drama Anthology. ITV 1955–9

Host/Executive Producer: **Douglas Fairbanks Jr**

Popular, filmed collection of single stories.

Hollywood leading man Douglas Fairbanks Jr introduced, produced and occasionally starred in this anthology of dramas, which ranged from murders to farces. Guest stars included Buster Keaton and Christopher Lee. Production took place at the British National Studios in Elstree and around 120 half-hour episodes were made.

DOUGLAS, JACK
(1927–)

British comedian and stooge whose Alf Ippititimus act (complete with nervous tics) was much played to TV audiences in the 1960s, especially on *The Des O'Connor Show*. He was also at one time the resident comic on CRACKERJACK and was seen in *Not on Your Nellie* (as Stanley Pickersgill), THE SHILLINGBURY TALES and its sequel, *Cuffy* (Jake), and *Carry On Laughing*.

DOUGLAS, MICHAEL
(1944–)

The son of Kirk Douglas and now a Hollywood giant in his own right, Michael Douglas came to the fore as Inspector Steve Keller, Mike Stone's (Karl Malden) partner in THE STREETS OF SAN FRANCISCO. While working on the series, he was busy furthering his film executive career, producing *One Flew Over the Cuckoo's Nest*, and television has since played a poor second fiddle.

DOYLE, TONY
(1942–2000)

Irish actor known for a number of prominent roles, including bent policeman John Deakin in BETWEEN THE LINES, villainous George Ferguson in BAND OF GOLD and roguish Brian Quigley in BALLYKISSANGEL. Among his other credits were 1990 (Dave Brett) and *Circle of Deceit* (Graham). He was the father of actress Susannah Doyle.

DRAGNET
US (MCA/Mark VII) Police Drama. ITV 1955–68

Sgt Joe Friday	**Jack Webb**
Sgt Ben Romero	**Barton Yarborough**
Sgt Ed Jacobs	**Barney Phillips**

Officer Frank Smith .... **Herb Ellis**
Ben Alexander
Officer Bill Gannon .... **Harry Morgan**
Announcer .... **George Fenneman**
Hal Gibney

Creator/Producer: **Jack Webb**

Documentary-style police series relating the cases
of a no-nonsense, strait-laced cop.

'Ladies and gentlemen, the story you are about to see is
true. Only the names have been changed to protect
the innocent.' So began every episode of this highly
successful police drama which was the first to portray a
policeman's lot realistically, including the pressures of
his private life. It centred on plodding bachelor cop, Sgt
Joe Friday, badge number 714 in the Los Angeles Police
Department. His earliest colleague was Ben Romero, but
when actor Barton Yarborough died after only three
episodes, Friday was briefly accompanied by Ed Jacobs
and then through the show's glory years by Officer Frank
Smith (usually played by the chubby Ben Alexander).
When the programme was relaunched in 1967, after
seven years off the air, Harry Morgan (later Colonel
Potter in M*A*S*H) joined Friday on the beat as the
hypochondriac Bill Gannon. This series was entitled
Dragnet '67 and brought the 1950s series bang up to
date, dealing with topical issues like drug-pushing and
student protest.

Dragnet had previously been a hit on US radio and was
the brainchild of actor Jack Webb, who also directed the
series and researched the concept tirelessly. His contacts
in the real-life police department allowed him access to
genuine case files, from which the programme's storylines were adapted. Right from the show's characteristic
'dum-de-dum-dum' opening bars, music was skilfully
used to heighten the tension. Documentary-style
camera angles were often employed, and Webb himself
provided a clinical, ultra-serious narration throughout
each episode, incorporating dates and times as a policeman would when relating the facts to a courtroom. An
announcer wound up the show, explaining the fate of
the captured criminals.

Friday became known for his frank dialogues. He
demanded 'just the facts, ma'am', and matter-of-factly
explained, 'My name's Friday, I'm a cop.' Towards the
end of the first run of the series, he was promoted to
lieutenant, although, strangely, when the show was
revived in 1967 he was a sergeant again. Harry Morgan
paid tribute to his time in *Dragnet* (which was the first
American police drama to be seen on British television)
by appearing in a 1987 film parody which starred Dan
Aykroyd and Tom Hanks.

DRAKE, CHARLIE

(Charles Springall; 1925–)

Short, ginger, cherubic comedian, fond of slapstick routines and mispronunciations. It was as THE WORKER that
he became a 1960s TV favourite, turning up at the Labour
Exchange to make Henry McGee's life (as Mr Pugh – or,
rather, 'Mr Pee-yew') a misery. Drake's TV break came

in the 1950s, when he appeared with Bob Monkhouse
and Dennis Goodwin in *Fast and Loose* (in which Monkhouse blew off his left ear with a blank bullet). He also
starred in children's shows, often as part of an unlikely
double act, *Mick and Montmorency*, with lanky comedian
Jack Edwardes. His own series, *Drake's Progress, Charlie*
Drake in . . . and *The Charlie Drake Show*, followed. In one
episode of the last (entitled *Bingo Madness*), Drake was
knocked unconscious when a stunt went wrong during
a live transmission. After a period of 'retirement', the
jaunty Londoner bounced back and *The Worker* arrived
in 1965. Drake also appeared in the marriage-agency sitcom, *Who Is Sylvia?* (which he co-wrote with Donald
Churchill) and the vaudeville series, *Slapstick and Old*
Lace, before switching to straight roles in dramas like
Crime and Punishment, Endgame, Bleak House and *Filipina*
Dreamgirls. However, he did revive *The Worker* in 1978 as
a segment of *Bruce Forsyth's Big Night*. At the peak of his
comedy career, Drake ventured into films, with limited
success, and even into the pop charts, notching up a
run of novelty hits. 'Hallo my dahlings' became his
catchphrase.

DRAKE, GABRIELLE

(1944–)

British actress, born in Pakistan and much seen on television from the late 1960s onwards. Having appeared in
series like THE SAINT and THE CHAMPIONS, Drake was
cast as Lt. Gay Ellis in another ITC romp, UFO, and then
appeared as Jill Hammond in the road-haulage saga, THE
BROTHERS. However, it was as motel supremo Nicola
Freeman in CROSSROADS that she made a name for herself in the world of soap, staying with the series for a
couple of years and rejoining it again very briefly just
before the programme was cancelled. Among her other
credits have been the sitcom, *Ffizz, Kelly Monteith* (playing his wife), *No. 10, The Importance of Being Earnest* and
MEDICS (Diana Hardy).

DRAMA-DOC

Short for dramatized documentary, the style of programming that reconstructs historical events using actors
working from a script built around a number of known
facts. It is a style of programming that has brought much
confusion in the past, with facts sometimes embroidered
or assumptions introduced. Consequently, some
viewers have been unsure of the real or fictional nature
of the programme. Genuinely fictional dramas, made
using documentary camera techniques and editing in a
search for extra realism, have clouded the issue even
further, although this convention is now widely
accepted and acknowledged.

DREAM ON

US (HBO) Situation Comedy. Channel 4 1991–2

Martin Tupper .... **Brian Benben**
Judith Tupper/Stone .... **Wendie Malick**

Toby Pedalbee .... **Denny Dillon**
Jeremy Tupper .... **Chris Demetral**
Eddie Charles .... **Jeffrey Joseph**

Creators/Writers: **David Crane, Marta Kauffman**
Executive Producers: **John Landis, Kevin Bright**
Producers: **Ribb Idels, David Crane, Marta Kauffman**

A hapless American's life is dominated by old TV programmes.

Martin Tupper was a 36-year-old New York publishing executive recently divorced from Judith, the psychiatrist mother of his 11-year-old son, Jeremy. Martin, however, found it difficult to adapt to his re-found bachelorhood. Stumbling from one-night stand to one-night stand, and always keeping an eye on Judith's new relationship with 'Mr Perfect', Dr Richard Stone, Martin sought guidance in the ways of the single man from his friend, Eddie Charles, a local talk show host. There was little comfort at work, however, from his bulldog secretary, Toby.

Martin, a neurotic type, rode an emotional rollercoaster, and for every emotion there was a TV clip from his youth. Having been sat in front of the television as a child in the 1950s, Martin's mind now worked overtime, dredging up moments from classic black-and-white series that encapsulated his prevailing moods and feelings. For viewers, the clips (usually just one-liners) acted as Martin's thought-bubbles.

Dream On was created to make use of a library of old material that could no longer find a market in syndication. The writers viewed hundreds of classic programmes in the search for snappy lines around which they could build a story. Sometimes the story came first and the lines followed. Among the vintage cuttings were pieces by Ronald Reagan, Lee Marvin, Jack Benny, Groucho Marx, Bette Davis, George Burns and Vincent Price. The series was not networked in the USA but aired on the HBO cable channel, giving the producers greater freedom with sexual content. In the UK, later series were shown on Sky One. Its executive producer, John Landis, is better known for feature films like *The Blues Brothers*, *Trading Places* and *An American Werewolf in London*.

DRISCOLL, PATRICIA
(1930–)

A familiar face with younger viewers in the 1950s, it was Cork-born Patricia Driscoll who originally related the contents of PICTURE BOOK for Monday's WATCH WITH MOTHER. However, in 1957, she left to replace Bernadette O'Farrell as Maid Marian in THE ADVENTURES OF ROBIN HOOD, allowing Vera McKechnie to take over as page-turner for the toddlers. Despite continuing with her acting career, Driscoll never gained another major TV role after she left Sherwood Forest.

DRIVER, BETTY
MBE (1920–)

Although universally known today as Betty Turpin/Williams, homely barmaid and queen of the hotpot, Leicester-born Betty Driver's TV career predates even CORONATION STREET by a number of years. As a child star she took over from Gracie Fields on a stage tour and later spent seven years as singer with Henry Hall's band, entertaining the troops in World War II. After appearing in a number of stage plays and Ealing comedies, Driver was given her own variety programme, *The Betty Driver Show*, by the BBC in 1952. She later turned to drama and appeared as the bossy canteen manageress, Mrs Edgeley, in the *Coronation Street* spin-off, PARDON THE EXPRESSION (with Arthur Lowe), and then in Granada's *Love on the Dole*, before being signed by the company in 1969 to appear in the *Street* proper as policeman Cyril Turpin's wife.

DRIVER, HARRY
(?–1973)

British scriptwriter and producer, one-time partner of Jack Rosenthal and later in collaboration with Vince Powell on sitcoms. As well as contributing to CORONATION STREET, Driver also penned (with Rosenthal) a few episodes of the crime drama, THE ODD MAN, and some scripts for TAXI. He worked with Powell on the comedies, *Bulldog Breed*, BOOTSIE AND SNUDGE, HERE'S HARRY and PARDON THE EXPRESSION, although his straight-drama work continued through series like ADAM ADAMANT LIVES!. Driver and Powell's best-remembered contributions were still to come, however. Among their later creations were GEORGE AND THE DRAGON, TWO IN CLOVER, NEVER MIND THE QUALITY, FEEL THE WIDTH, *The Best of Enemies*, BLESS THIS HOUSE, FOR THE LOVE OF ADA, NEAREST AND DEAREST, SPRING AND AUTUMN and *Mike and Bernie*, with certainly the most controversial of all being the racist comedy, LOVE THY NEIGHBOUR.

DROP THE DEAD DONKEY
UK (Hat Trick) Situation Comedy. Channel 4 1990–8

Gus Hedges .... **Robert Duncan**
George Dent .... **Jeff Rawle**
Alex Pates .... **Haydn Gwynne**
Henry Davenport .... **David Swift**
Sally Smedley .... **Victoria Wicks**
Damien Day .... **Stephen Tompkinson**
Dave Charnley .... **Neil Pearson**
Joy Merryweather .... **Susannah Doyle**
Helen Cooper .... **Ingrid Lacey**

Creators/Producers: **Guy Jenkin, Andy Hamilton**
Executive Producer: **Denise O'Donoghue**

Topical satire based around the staff of a TV newsroom.

It would be difficult to make comedy more up to date than *Drop the Dead Donkey*. By recording each episode the night before transmission and editing it on the day, with voice-overs on the closing credits for up-to-the-minute comment on breaking news, this was a situation comedy with a difference. However, considering the 'situation' was a TV newsroom, it needed to be hyper-topical to succeed.

The newsroom in question was that of Globelink News, owned by the unseen Sir Roysten Merchant but run by his responsibility-shirking, yuppie yes-man, Gus Hedges. Editor of the news team was George Dent, a hypochondriac divorcé and father of a rebellious teenager. His assistant in the first two series was the wily Alex Pates, whose mum was seldom off the phone. The rest of the team consisted of a cynical production secretary (the inappropriately named Joy Merryweather), an alcoholic, toupee-wearing news anchor, Henry Davenport, and his sanctimonious on-air colleague, Sally Smedley, plus reporters Dave Charnley (the office Romeo and compulsive gambler) and unscrupulous Damien Day (known to fabricate tragedy to enliven a story). Helen Cooper, a lesbian single mother, later joined the news team as Alex's replacement.

Drop the Dead Donkey was an instant hit and quickly picked up a cult following, with the result that celebrities and politicians queued up for cameo roles. However, as the characterizations became more defined, reliance on real-life news for humour decreased, and the programme focused more on its protagonists, using topical stories more as fillers. There were no series in 1995 or 1997, but *Drop the Dead Donkey* returned for a final fling at the end of 1998. In a world grappling with the arrival of digital TV, the future for Globelink and its news team appeared bleak; the series showed the characters scrabbling for new careers as the station headed for closure.

Creators Andy Hamilton and Guy Jenkin wrote the vast majority of episodes.

DRURY, JAMES
(1934–)

As the classic strong, silent cowboy, James Drury was TV's THE VIRGINIAN, the eastern ranch foreman who travelled west to bring new ideas to the Shiloh estate in Wyoming. Drury first played the role in 1958, when he starred in the pilot. But, in that seldom-seen episode, *The Virginian* was a dandy, dressed in fancy clothes and sporting short pistols, and it took four years before the series was revamped and accepted by the network. Drury's TV fame arrived after some teenage theatre work and films like *Forbidden Planet*, *Love Me Tender* and *Pollyanna*. His other television performances included episodes of GUNSMOKE and THE RIFLEMAN, but little was seen of him after *The Virginian* ended its nine-year run. He did star in *Firehouse*, a short-lived adventure series, and he has also been seen in TV movies (including the pilot for ALIAS SMITH AND JONES) and guest spots.

DRY RUN

A rehearsal in which the crew merely observe the script and the movement of the performers, without the equipment running.

DUBBING MIXER

The technician responsible for mixing the soundtracks on a programme.

DUCE, SHARON
(1950–)

Sheffield-born actress much seen on TV as the star of series like BIG DEAL (Jan Oliver), *Growing Pains* (Pat Hollingsworth, both opposite Ray Brooks) and *Coming Home* (Sheila Maddocks). She also appeared as Carole, the other woman, in HELEN – A WOMAN OF TODAY, was WPC Cameron in Z CARS, and played Emily Jessop in FIRST BORN, Maggie Fell in the three-part thriller, *Natural Lies*, and Anita in another drama, *Into the Fire*. Among her other credits has been MINDER.

DUCHESS OF DUKE STREET, THE
UK (BBC/Time-Life) Drama. BBC 1 1976–7

Louisa Leyton/Trotter	**Gemma Jones**
Charlie Tyrrell	**Christopher Cazenove**
Mary Phillips	**Victoria Plucknett**
Merriman	**John Welsh**
Joseph Starr	**John Cater**
Major Toby Smith-Barton	**Richard Vernon**
Lizzie	**Maureen O'Brien**
Irene Baker	**Jan Francis**
Augustus Trotter	**Donald Burton**
Mrs Violet Leyton	**June Brown**
Mr Ernest Leyton	**John Rapley**
Lord Henry Norton	**Bryan Coleman**
Mrs Catchpole	**Doreen Mantle**
Monsieur Alex	**George Pravda**
Major Johnny Farjeon	**Michael Culver**
Prince of Wales	**Roger Hammond**
Mrs Wellkin	**Kate Lansbury**
Mrs Cochran	**Mary Healey**
Violet	**Holly De Jong**
Lottie	**Lalla Ward**

Creator/Producer: **John Hawkesworth**
Executive Producer: **Richard Beynon**

A cook in Edwardian London works her way out of the kitchen to become the owner of a select hotel.

Loosely based on the life-story of Rosa Lewis, a kitchen maid who became manageress of the fashionable Cavendish Hotel in Jermyn Street, this series introduced viewers to Louisa Leyton, a gruff, hard-working, Cockney girl determined to better herself. The series began in the year 1900 with Louisa's arrival as assistant chef to Monsieur Alex in the household of Lord Henry Norton. There she met sommelier Augustus Trotter and the Honourable Charles Tyrrell, who admired her cooking and her ambition. Deputizing for the chef when the Prince of Wales called for dinner, Louisa found herself courted by royalty. Pressurized by the Prince's supporters, Louisa was badgered into marrying Gus Trotter (the Prince would not consider compromising a single woman, and her career faced ruin if she rejected him). The Trotters were financially supported and bought the Bentinck Hotel at 20 Duke Street, but the marriage fell apart amid soaring bills and Gus's heavy drinking. Louisa worked herself sick to save the hotel but was rescued by Charlie Tyrrell – soon to inherit the title of Lord Haslemere – who bought up the premises and employed Louisa to run it. Without her husband's hindrance, she bustled around, barking out orders, and turned the Bentinck into one of the best hotels in London, with the help of her loyal staff, principally Mary, the Welsh maid; Starr, the hall porter (and his fox-terrier, Fred); doddery butler Merriman; and Major Smith-Barton, a penniless military man who worked for his keep by smooth-talking the aristocratic guests.

As the series progressed, personal and commercial calamities befell the staff, most notably Louisa's pregnancy by Charlie (resulting in baby Lottie, who was brought up secretly in the country), and reminders of her working-class background that never failed to dog our heroine. The mouth-watering displays of traditional English food were created by chef Michael Smith.

If the programme had more than an echo of UPSTAIRS, DOWNSTAIRS about it, that wasn't coincidental. It was also created by John Hawkesworth and featured theme music by the same composer, Alexander Faris.

DUCHOVNY, DAVID
(1960–)

American actor – a Masters graduate in English Literature from Yale – who gained international stardom in his role of FBI agent Fox Mulder in THE X-FILES. His TV break came in TWIN PEAKS, playing transvestite FBI agent Denis/Denise. He has also narrated the erotic series, *Red Shoe Diaries*. He is married to actress Téa Leoni.

DUE SOUTH
Canada (Alliance) Comedy Drama. BBC 1/BBC 2 1995–9

Constable Benton Fraser .... **Paul Gross**
Det. Ray Vecchio .... **David Marciano**
Capt./Lt. Harding Welsh .... **Beau Starr**
Det. Louis Guardino .... **Daniel Kash**
Det. Jack Huey .... **Tony Craig**
Elaine .... **Catherine Bruhier**
Fraser Sr .... **Gordon Pinsent**
Francesca Vecchio .... **Ramona Milano**
Insp. Meg Thatcher .... **Camilla Scott**
Det. Stanley Raymond Kowalski .. **Callum Keith Rennie**
Det. Thomas E. Dewey .... **Tom Melissis**

Creator: **Paul Haggis**
Executive Producer: **Paul Gross**

A Canadian mountie always gets his man in Chicago.

Mountie Benton Fraser abandoned his Rockies patch when he set out to find the killer of his father. He ended up in Chicago, where he stayed as an attachment at the Canadian consulate, somehow always getting involved in local law-enforcement. Here he applied his own moral code – not to mention heightened animal instincts – and cut through the corruption and cynicism that dogged the city justice scene. Joining the ultra-polite, and often naïve, Fraser – still in his scarlet Mountie uniform – on his adventures in the Windy City were his deaf (but lip-reading) white husky-wolf cross, Diefenbaker, and his street-wise, local cop pal, Ray Vecchio. Three seasons along, Fraser gained a new police partner when Stanley Raymond Kowalski replaced Ray Vecchio, assuming the latter's identity while Vecchio went undercover. Leslie Nielsen guested early on as Mountie Sgt Buck Frobisher.

With its dry humour and quirky feel (reminiscent of NORTHERN EXPOSURE), *Due South* poked gentle fun at both American and Canadian stereotypes. It was produced in Canada, with a grimed-up and newly graffiti-ridden Toronto doubling for the real Chicago. In the UK, the series was initially shown on Sky One but suffered badly at the hands of terrestrial TV schedulers, despite its considerable popularity, jumping days, skipping weeks and even switching channels during its sporadic four-year run.

DUEL, PETE
(Peter Deuel; 1940–71)

Popular and handsome leading American actor of the 1960s, whose TV high spot (and, sadly, last role) was as Hannibal Heyes in ALIAS SMITH AND JONES. Originally using his real name, Deuel, he appeared in shows like COMBAT, THE BIG VALLEY and THE FUGITIVE, and then gained more fame as a regular in the popular US sitcom, *Gidget*. His own comedy, *Love on a Rooftop*, followed, as well as a handful of movie roles. During the first season of *Alias Smith and Jones*, Duel, always highly ambitious and politically sensitive, was found dead of a bullet wound to his head. That was on New Year's Eve 1971 and, although some contend that it was an accident, or even murder, it was judged that he was a suicide victim. His role as Heyes was taken over by the show's narrator, Roger Davis.

DUFFY, PATRICK
(1949–)

A 1970s and 1980s heart-throb, Patrick Duffy's most celebrated role was as Bobby Ewing, JR's brother, in DALLAS. Such was his importance to the series that, after leaving the show in 1985 (and being killed off in a car accident), he was coaxed back to boost the viewing figures, his death (and the whole of one season) being bizarrely explained away as just a dream experienced by his screen wife, Pam. Previously, Duffy had starred as the amphibious hero (Mark Harris) of THE MAN FROM ATLANTIS, and since *Dallas* he has appeared in the sitcom, *Step by Step* (Frank Lambert).

DUKES OF HAZZARD, THE

US (Warner Brothers/Piggy) Adventure. BBC 1 1979–85

Luke Duke	**Tom Wopat**
Bo Duke	**John Schneider**
Daisy Duke	**Catherine Bach**
Uncle Jesse Duke	**Denver Pyle**
Sheriff Roscoe P. Coltrane	**James Best**
Jefferson Davis 'Boss' Hogg	**Sorrell Booke**
Deputy Enos Strate	**Sonny Shroyer**
Cooter	**Ben Jones**
Deputy Cletus	**Rick Hurst**
Lulu Hogg	**Peggy Rea**
Miz Emma Tisdale	**Nedra Volz**
Sheriff Little	**Don Pedro Colley**
Laverne	**Lila Kent**
Emery Potter	**Charlie Dell**
Coy Duke	**Byron Cherry**
Vance Duke	**Christopher Mayer**
The Balladeer	**Waylon Jennings** (*voice only*)

Creator: **Guy Waldron**
Producers: **Joseph Gantman, Paul Picard**

High-speed, slapstick action with two modern-day Robin Hoods.

The Dukes of Hazzard were cousins Luke and Bo Duke, who lived with third cousin, the stunning Daisy, and their wise old Uncle Jesse somewhere east of the Mississippi and south of the Ohio. Avoiding traps set by their corrupt adversaries – the fat, white-suited Boss Hogg (a local politician) and his incompetent brother-in-law, Sheriff Coltrane – the Dukes rode to the rescue of the good folk of Hazzard County. They raced around in a beefed-up, red-and-white, 1969 Dodge Charger, known as 'General Lee', often getting involved in spectacular chases and crashes, and becoming extremely popular with younger viewers.

After a year or so, Sonny Shroyer, who played Coltrane's grinning deputy, Enos Strate, was given his own spin-off series on US TV, temporarily making way for Rick Hurst in the new role of Deputy Cletus. However, more substantial cast changes were required when stars Tom Wopat and John Schneider fell out with producers over merchandising royalties. For a while they were replaced by Byron Cherry and Christopher Mayer as two other Duke cousins (the storyline had it that Luke and Bo had gone to try their luck in a motor-racing circuit), but they were brought back when ratings fell, the two new boys leaving at the same time. Banjo-picking country music accompanied all the action and Waylon Jennings, who acted as narrator, also performed the show's theme song.

DUMONT, ALLEN B.
(1901–65)

American TV pioneer, largely responsible for the development of the cathode ray tube. He founded the DuMont TV network in 1946 but the channel struggled to survive and, when comprehensively beaten by CBS for status as America's third network, DuMont closed in 1955. In its short time it had specialized in sports events, political coverage and quiz and variety shows.

DUNCAN, LINDSAY
(1950–)

Edinburgh-born actress best remembered for her roles in *Traffik* (Helen), GBH (Barbara Douglas), A YEAR IN PROVENCE (Annie Mayle), *The Rector's Wife* (Anna), *Jake's Progress* (Monica), *Just William* (Lady Walton), *Tom Jones* (Lady Bellaston), *Shooting the Past* (Marilyn Truman), *Oliver Twist* (Elizabeth Leeford) and *Dirty Tricks* (Alison). Other credits include *The Kit Curran Radio Show*, *TECX*, *Travelling Man*, REILLY – ACE OF SPIES and numerous single dramas. She is married to actor Hilton McRae.

DUNLOP, LESLEY
(1956–)

Newcastle-born actress with an extensive television portfolio. Although probably best known as Zoe Callender in MAY TO DECEMBER (replacing Eve Matheson), Dunlop has also appeared as Ruth Fullman in ANGELS and Sara in *Capstick's Law*, as well as in the dramas *Rich Deceiver* (Ellie Freeman), *The Phoenix and the Carpet* (Eliza), *Wokenwell* (Lucky Whiteside), *Tess of the D'Urbervilles* (Joan Durbeyfield), *Pure Wickedness* (Mo Healy) and WHERE THE HEART IS (Anna Kirkwall). Among her other credits have been SOUTH RIDING, *Penmarric*, THE ADVENTURES OF BLACK BEAUTY, *Our Mutual Friend*, *Smuggler*, DOCTOR WHO and SILENT WITNESS.

DUNN, CLIVE
OBE (1922–)

Clive Dunn has been playing old men for five decades. He will always be remembered principally as the senile butcher, Jack Jones, panicky veteran of Boer War conflicts, in DAD'S ARMY, but he also brought his doddery charms to kids' TV as Charlie Quick, aka Grandad, in the series of the same name in the late 1970s. Dunn had come to light on children's TV in the 1950s, before appearing on *The Tony Hancock Show*, *The Dickie Henderson Half-Hour*, IT'S A SQUARE WORLD and *The World of Beachcomber*. In 1960 he took the part of Old Johnson in BOOTSIE AND SNUDGE, and 14 years later starred as Sam Cobbett in the YTV sitcom, *My Old Man*, with his real-life wife Priscilla Morgan taking the role of his daughter, Doris.

DURBRIDGE, FRANCIS
(1912–98)

British writer of suspense serials, working for the BBC from the early 1950s. Among his most prominent contributions were *The Broken Horseshoe*, *Operation Diplomat* (both 1952), *Portrait of Alison* (1955), *The Scarf* (1959), *The*

World of Tim Frazer (1960–1, starring Jack Hedley), *The Desperate People* (1963), *Melissa* (1964, remade in 1974 and reworked by Alan Bleasdale in 1997), *A Man Called Harry Brent* (1965), *A Game of Murder* and *Bat out of Hell* (both 1966), *The Passenger* and *Stupid Like a Fox* (both 1971), *The Doll* (1975) and *Breakaway* (1980) – many packaged under the umbrella title, *Francis Durbridge Presents*. Durbridge was also the creator of wealthy sleuth PAUL TEMPLE.

DUSTBINMEN, THE
UK (Granada) Situation Comedy. ITV 1969–70

Bloody Delilah	**John Woodvine**
	Brian Wilde
Cheese and Egg	**Bryan Pringle**
Winston Platt	**Graham Haberfield**
'Smellie' Ibbotson	**John Barrett**
Heavy Breathing	**Trevor Bannister**
Eric	**Tim Wylton**

Creator: **Jack Rosenthal**
Producers: **Jack Rosenthal, Richard Everitt**

The misadventures of a team of refuse collectors.

Based on a 1968 play by Jack Rosenthal, entitled *There's a Hole in Your Dustbin, Delilah*, *The Dustbinmen* was Rosenthal's series about a gang of northern binmen, viewing their progress as they set about their rounds, shirking work and lusting after housewives. Leader of the team was Cheese and Egg (his initials were C. E.) and riding with him on their bin lorry (affectionately dubbed *Thunderbird Three*) were Manchester City fanatic Winston, slow-witted Eric, ladies' man Heavy Breathing and the unfortunately nicknamed Smellie. Their boss at the corporation depot was the so-called Bloody Delilah.

Despite its vulgarity and coarse language, *The Dustbinmen* was a big hit with viewers, and all six first series episodes topped the ratings. Rosenthal opted out after the first two seasons, leaving the scriptwriting to others, having already passed the producer's chair over to Richard Everitt. The original one-off play had three cast differences: Frank Windsor played Bloody Delilah, Jack MacGowran played Cheese and Egg and Harold Innocent was Heavy Breathing.

DUTY FREE
UK (Yorkshire) Situation Comedy. ITV 1984–6

David Pearce	**Keith Barron**
Amy Pearce	**Gwen Taylor**
Robert Cochran	**Neil Stacy**
Linda Cochran	**Joanna Van Gyseghem**
Carlos	**Carlos Douglas**

Writers: **Eric Chappell, Jean Warr**
Producer: **Vernon Lawrence**

Two couples toy with adultery in the Spanish sun.

When David Pearce was made redundant, he and his wife, Amy, used some of the pay-off for a holiday in Spain, where they palled up with Robert and Linda Cochran. Through various compromising and farcical situations, including much hiding in wardrobes and under beds, the series focused on David and Linda's attempts at adultery, with Robert and Amy remaining rather strait-laced throughout. Carlos was the bemused waiter who witnessed the bizarre goings-on. Their package holiday lasted seven weeks on screen and indeed was not completed until a second series ended, a year later. A third season saw the foursome reunited on a winter holiday in the same hotel, and there was also a Christmas special in the same location.

DYKE, GREG
(1947–)

English TV executive, the BBC's Director-General since January 2000. Previously, Dyke had been credited with saving TV-am (by introducing Roland Rat, among other moves) and had been Chief Executive of LWT, programme controller of TVS, Chairman of GMTV and Chief Executive of Pearson Television.

DYKSTRA, JOHN
(1947–)

American special-effects producer, the man behind the *Star Wars* stunts who has also been in demand for television sci-fi offerings like BATTLESTAR GALACTICA.

DYNASTY
US (Aaron Spelling/Fox-Cat) Drama. BBC 1 1982–9

Blake Carrington	**John Forsythe**
Krystle Jennings/Carrington	**Linda Evans**
Alexis Carrington/Colby/Dexter	**Joan Collins**
Fallon Carrington/Colby	**Pamela Sue Martin**
	Emma Samms
Steven Carrington	**Al Corley**
	Jack Coleman
Adam Carrington/Michael Torrance	
....	**Gordon Thomson**
Cecil Colby	**Lloyd Bochner**
Jeff Colby	**John James**
Claudia Blaisdel	**Pamela Bellwood**
Matthew Blaisdel	**Bo Hopkins**
Lindsay Blaisdel	**Katy Kurtzman**
Walter Lankersheim	**Dale Robertson**
Joseph Anders	**Lee Bergere**
Kirby Anders/Colby	**Kathleen Beller**
Andrew Laird	**Peter Mark Richman**
Sammy Jo Dean/Carrington/Fallmont	
....	**Heather Locklear**
Michael Culhane	**Wayne Northrop**
Dr Nick Toscanni	**James Farentino**
Mark Jennings	**Geoffrey Scott**
Congressman Neal McVane	**Paul Burke**
Farnsworth 'Dex' Dexter	**Michael Nader**
Amanda Carrington	**Catherine Oxenberg**
	Karen Cellini
Dominique Deveraux	**Diahann Carroll**

Gerard .... **William Beckley**
Gordon Wales .... **James Sutorius**
Daniel Reece .... **Rock Hudson**
Lady Ashley Mitchell .... **Ali MacGraw**
Danny Carrington .... **Jameson Sampley**
Joel Abrigore .... **George Hamilton**
King Galen .... **Joel Fabiani**
Prince Michael .... **Michael Praed**
Clay Fallmont .... **Ted McGinley**
Ben Carrington .... **Christopher Cazenove**
Caress Morell .... **Kate O'Mara**
Dana Waring/Carrington .... **Leann Hunley**
Krystina Carrington .... **Jessica Player**
Sable Colby .... **Stephanie Beacham**
Sgt Johnny Zorelli .... **Ray Abruzzo**
Virginia Metheny .... **Liza Morrow**
Capt. William Handler .... **John Brandon**
Rudy Richards .... **Lou Beatty, Jr**
Joanna Clauss/Sills .... **Kim Terry-Costin**
Monica Colby .... **Tracy Scoggins**

Creators: **Richard Shapiro, Esther Shapiro**
Executive Producer: **Aaron Spelling**
Producer: **Douglas Cramer**

Oil, money and family rivalries in a Denver setting.

Closely modelled on DALLAS, *Dynasty* almost bettered it in the ratings. As with the saga of the Ewings, the wealth came from oil (indeed, the programme's working-title was *Oil*), with the beneficiaries this time the Carrington family and the setting Denver, Colorado. Head of the family was Blake Carrington, who married his blonde secretary, Krystle Jennings, in the first episode. His children by previous marriages were a man-hungry, precocious daughter named Fallon and a bisexual son, Steve. Other original cast members included geologist Matthew Blaisdel, once a lover of Krystle, Claudia, his disturbed wife, and their attractive young daughter, Lindsay.

From the start Krystle's unhappiness in her marriage was clear, as Blake devoted most of his time to keeping his empire intact. Her problems were only beginning, however, for at the end of the first season Blake's vindictive ex-wife, Alexis, arrived, seeking to regain her share of the family fortune. From this point on, the programme hinged around this female JR's attempts to remove Krystle or unseat Blake himself. Alexis married Blake's great rival, Cecil Colby, and, though he died of a heart-attack soon after, she inherited the power of his oil company, Colbyco, and became even more formidable. Meanwhile, daughter Fallon continued her promiscuous ways, having affairs with all and sundry, including Jeff Colby, whom she married, producing LB ('Little Blake'). Steve married Sammy Jo Dean and conceived a son, Danny. He also became involved with Claudia, endured a period of exile in Indonesia and underwent plastic surgery following an explosion (actor Al Corley left the series). This clumsy switch of actors was later repeated with Fallon, who strangely lost three inches in height, became 14 years younger and began to speak with an English accent.

As in *Dallas*, new characters were constantly being introduced, some of them members of the Carrington clan, keen to get their hands on the family silver. These included Adam Carrington, Blake's illegitimate son (it was later proven that this was not so), who arrived using the name Mark Torrance; black singer Dominique Deveraux, one of Tom's (Blake's dad) unplanned offspring; and Blake's younger brother, Ben. Alexis was far from pleased to see the arrival of her sister, Caress, who tried to publish a damaging book about her called *Sister Dearest*. Alexis bought the publishers to prevent her doing so.

Always keen to better its mentor, *Dynasty* took the high road, introducing world statesmen and royalty into its plots. Ex-President Gerald Ford and his wife, Betty, were joined in one episode by former Secretary of State Henry Kissinger. The royalty came in the form of the fictitious Prince Michael of Moldavia, who planned to wed Alexis's daughter, Amanda. But, in a sensational cliffhanger, the Carringtons were 'massacred' at the European wedding reception by gun-toting revolutionaries. However, it turned out that only two guests had died and the action returned once more to Denver.

Other highlights of the show's run were the conviction of Alexis for murdering Mark Jennings (Krystle's former husband), although the deed was actually done by Congressman Neal McVane in an Alexis disguise; the birth of Blake and Krystle's daughter, Krystina; Krystle's affair with Daniel Reece (Rock Hudson's last role); the abduction of Krystle and her replacement by a lookalike actress, so good she even fooled Blake; Alexis finally wresting power from Blake, before kicking him and Krystle out of the 48-room Carrington mansion; and the destruction in a fire of Blake's hotel, La Mirage, in which Claudia, who had started it, was killed. Marriages came and went, Blake lost his memory and thought he was still married to Alexis, little Krystina needed a heart transplant and was then abducted, and Blake finally regained his company.

Sensational to the end, the last season saw a mummified body dragged from the Carringtons' lake (it turned out to be one of Alexis's old flames, but who had killed him?). Cousin Sable arrived from Los Angeles to sort out Alexis, Krystle fell into a coma in a Swiss hospital, Blake and a bent policeman shot each other, Alexis and her husband, Dex, were pushed off a balcony by Adam, and Fallon and little Krystina found themselves trapped down an old mineshaft with a Nazi art collection! A two-hour special, *Dynasty: The Reunion*, seen in 1992, aimed to conclude matters. This revealed that Alexis had survived, somehow, and explained how Fallon and Krystina were pulled free, how Krystle returned from her sanitarium, and how Blake both lost and won back his business empire, going to prison for murder in between.

In the pilot for *Dynasty*, the role of Blake was filled by George Peppard but, for the series proper, he was replaced by John Forsythe, the man who had earlier provided the voice for Charlie in CHARLIE'S ANGELS. *Dynasty* was also responsible for the spin-off, THE COLBYS, which temporarily took Jeff and Fallon away from the original series.

EASTENDERS
UK (BBC) Drama. BBC 1 1985–

Arthur Fowler	Bill Treacher
Pauline Fowler	Wendy Richard
Michelle Fowler/Holloway	Susan Tully
Mark Fowler	David Scarboro
	Todd Carty
Lou Beale	Anna Wing
Pete Beale	Peter Dean
Kathy Beale/Mitchell	Gillian Taylforth
Ian Beale	Adam Woodyatt
Dennis Watts	Leslie Grantham
Angie Watts	Anita Dobson
Sharon Watts/Mitchell	Letitia Dean
Dot Cotton	June Brown
Nick Cotton	John Altman
Charlie Cotton	Christopher Hancock
Ethel Skinner	Gretchen Franklin
Simon Wicks	Nick Berry
Pat Wicks/Butcher/Evans	Pam St Clement
George 'Lofty' Holloway	Tom Watt
Mary Smith	Linda Davidson
Dr Harold Legg	Leonard Fenton
Ali Osman	Nejdet Salih
Sue Osman	Sandy Ratcliff
Mehmet Osman	Haluk Bilginer
Guizin Osman	Ishia Bennison
Tony Carpenter	Oscar James
Cassie Carpenter	Delanie Forbes
Hannah Carpenter	Sally Sagoe
Kelvin Carpenter	Paul J. Medford
Andy O'Brien	Ross Davidson
Debbie Wilkins	Shirley Cheriton
Naima Jeffery	Shreela Ghosh
Saeed Jeffery	Andrew Johnson
Martin Fowler	Jon Peyton Price
	James Alexandrou
Vicki Fowler	Samantha Leigh Martin
James Willmott-Brown	William Boyde
Cindy Williams/Beale	Michelle Collins
Tom Clements	Donald Tandy
Donna Ludlow	Matilda Ziegler
Colin Russell	Michael Cashman
Barry Clark	Gary Hailes
Duncan Boyd	David Gillespie
Jan Hammond	Jane How
Danny Whiting	Saul Jephcott
Rod Norman	Christopher McHallem
Carmel Roberts/Jackson	Judith Jacob
Matthew Jackson	Steven Hartley
Darren Roberts	Gary MacDonald
Junior Roberts	Aaron Carrington
Aisha Roberts	Aisha Jacob
Ashraf Karim	Aftab Sachak
Sufia Karim	Rani Singh
Shireen Karim	Nisha Kapur
Sohail Karim	Ronnie Jhutti
Dr David Samuels	Christopher Reich
Magda 'Mags' Czajkowski	Kathryn Apanowicz
Frank Butcher	Mike Reid

Mo Butcher	Edna Doré
Diane Butcher	Sophie Lawrence
Ricky Butcher	Sid Owen
Sam Mitchell/Butcher	Danniella Westbrook/Morgan
Janine Butcher	Rebecca Michael
	Alexia Demetriou
	Charlene/Charlie Brooks
Paul Priestley	Mark Thrippleton
Trevor Short	Phil McDermott
Disa O'Brian	Jan Graveson
Marge Green	Pat Coombs
Julie Cooper	Louise Plowright
Eddie Royle	Michael Melia
Grant Mitchell	Ross Kemp
Phil Mitchell	Steve McFadden
Peggy Mitchell/Butcher	Jo Warne
	Barbara Windsor
Rachel Kominsky	Jacquetta May
Jules Tavernier	Tommy Eytle
Celestine Tavernier	Leroy Golding
Etta Tavernier	Jacqui Gordon-Lawrence
Clyde Tavernier	Steven Woodcock
Hattie Tavernier	Michelle Gayle
Lloyd Tavernier	Garey Bridges
Kofi Tavernier	Marcel Smith
Christine Hewitt	Elizabeth Power
Mandy Salter	Nicola Stapleton
Aidan Brosnan	Sean Maguire
Steve Elliot	Mark Monero
Richard 'Tricky Dicky' Cole	Ian Reddington
Nigel Bates	Paul Bradley
Debbie Tyler/Bates	Nicola Duffett
Clare Tyler	Gemma Bissix
Gill Fowler	Susannah Dawson
Shelley	Nicole Arumugam
Sanjay Kapoor	Deepak Verma
Gita Kapoor	Shobu Kapoor
Carol Jackson	Lindsey Coulson
Alan Jackson	Howard Antony
Bianca Jackson/Butcher	Patsy Palmer
Robbie Jackson	Dean Gaffney
Sonia Jackson	Natalie Cassidy
Blossom Jackson	Mona Hammond
Billy Jackson	Devon Anderson
Natalie Price/Evans	Lucy Speed
Nellie Ellis	Elizabeth Kelly
David Wicks	Michael French
Geoff Barnes	David Roper
Ruth Aitken/Fowler	Caroline Paterson
Della Alexander	Michelle Joseph
Binnie Roberts	Sophie Langham
Big Ron	Ron Tarr
Roy Evans	Tony Caunter
Tiffany Raymond/Mitchell	Martine McCutcheon
Vicki Fowler	Samantha Leigh Martin
Stan Dougan	Jack Chissick
Barry Evans	Shaun Williamson
Liam Tyler	Francis Magee
Willy Roper	Michael Tudor Barnes
Lydia	Marlaine Gordon
Ted Hills	Brian Croucher
Tony Hills	Mark Homer
Sarah Hills	Daniela Denby-Ashe
Felix Kawalski	Harry Landis
Guppy Sharma	Lyndam Gregory
Meena McKenzie	Sudha Bhuchar
Joe Wicks	Paul Nicholls
Lorraine Wicks	Jacqueline Leonard
Michael Rose	Russell Floyd
Dan Zappieri	Carl Pizzie
Alistair Matthews	Neil Clark
Sue Taylor	Charlotte Bellamy
Simon Raymond	Andrew Lynford
Lenny Wallace	Desune Coleman
Huw Edwards	Richard Elis
April Branning	Debbie Arnold
Frankie	Syan Blake
Mick McFarlane	Sylvester Williams
Stephen Beale	Stuart Stevens
	Edward Savage
DCI Mason	Campbell Morrison
Neelam Kapoor	Jamila Massey
George Palmer	Paul Moriarty
Alex Healy	Richard Driscoll
Polly Becker	Victoria Gould
Annie Palmer	Nadia Sawalha
Lorna Cartwright	Janet Dibley
Irene Hills/Raymond	Roberta Taylor
Vanessa Carlton	Adele Salem
Mary Flaherty	Melanie Clark Pullen
Conor Flaherty	Sean Gleeson
Matthew Rose	Joe Absolom
Susan Rose	Tilly Vosburgh
Jessie Moore	Chelsey Paden
Jeff Healy	Leslie Schofield
Julie Haye	Karen Henthorn
Nick Holland	Dominic Taylor
Terry Raymond	Gavin Richards
Chris Clark	Matthew Jay Lewis
Louise Raymond/Simmonds	Carol Harrison
Rosa di Marco	Louise Jameson
Gianni di Marco	Marc Bannerman
Beppe di Marco	Michael Greco
Teresa di Marco	Leila Birch
Nicky di Marco	Carly Hillman
Lilly Mattock	Barbara Keogh
Melanie Healy	Tamzin Outhwaite
Josie McFarlane	Joan Hooley
Billy Mitchell	Perry Fenwick
Jamie Mitchell	Jack Ryder
Lisa Shaw	Lucy Benjamin
Steve Owen	Martin Kemp
Saskia Duncan	Deborah Sheridan-Taylor
Nina Harris	Troy Titus-Adams
Dr Fonseca	Jimi Mistry
Dan Sullivan	Craig Fairbrass
Andrea Price	Cindy O'Callaghan
Jackie Owen	Race Davies
Troy Harvey	Jamie Jarvis
Jim Branning	John Bardon
Sandra di Marco	Clare Wilkie
Laura Dunn	Hannah Waterman
Joe di Marco	Jake Kyprianou
Mo Harris	Laila Morse
Charlie Slater	Derek Martin
Zoe Slater	Michelle Ryan

Lynne Slater .... **Elaine Lordan**
Kat Slater .... **Jessie Wallace**
Little Mo Morgan .... **Kacey Ainsworth**
Kim McFarlane .... **Krystle Williams**
Ashley Cotton .... **Frankie Fitzgerald**
Kerry Skinner .... **Gemma McCluskie**
Garry Hobbs .... **Ricky Groves**
Audrey Trueman .... **Corinne Skinner Carter**
Dr Trueman .... **Nicholas R. Bailey**

Creators: **Julia Smith, Tony Holland**
Producers: **Julia Smith, Mike Gibbon, Corinne
Hollingworth, Richard Bramall, Michael Ferguson, Pat
Sandys, Helen Greaves, Leonard Lewis, Barbara Emile,
Mike Hudson, Jane Fallon, Diana Kyle, Nicholas
Hicks-Beach, Alison Davis, Jane Harris, Josephine Ward,
Johnathan Young, Miriam Segal, Lis Steele, Stephen
Garwood, Matthew Robinson, David Boulter, Paul
Annett, Jon East, Emma Turner, Gordon Ronald,
Helena Pope, Anne Edyvean, Diana Barton**

The continuing story of working-class East End folk.

EastEnders has succeeded where COMPACT, UNITED! and
THE NEWCOMERS all failed, namely in providing a serious, lasting, 52-weeks-a-year challenger to CORONATION
STREET in the great soap opera war. Set in the fictitious
London borough of Walford E20, the series has focused
on life in and around grimy Albert Square, a decaying
Victorian residential area with a market tagged on the
side. A greasy-spoon café and a downbeat pub, The
Queen Victoria, have seen as much of the action as any
of the houses. The major characters at the start were the
related Beale and Fowler families. Head of the clan was
crotchety Lou Beale, who lived with her daughter, Pauline Fowler, Pauline's husband, Arthur, and children,
Michelle and Mark. New baby, Martin, arrived soon
after. Pauline's twin brother, Pete Beale, ran the market
fruit-and-veg stall, occasionally assisted by his blonde
wife, Kathy, and schoolboy son, Ian. Den and Angie
Watts were the squabbling pub landlords, fighting for
the attentions of their adopted daughter, Sharon. Café
Osman was run by Turk Ali Osman and his English
wife, Sue; and other major characters in the early days
included gossipy hypochondriac Dot Cotton, her villainous son, Nick, daffy old Ethel Skinner, barman
Simon 'Wicksy' Wicks, dopey Lofty Holloway, yuppie
boy- and girlfriend Andy O'Brien and Debbie Wilkins,
Naima and Saeed Jeffery, two Asian grocers, and the
Carpenters, a West Indian family. As the cast list above
shows, many other characters have taken up residence
in Albert Square over the years.

EastEnders has always kept up a good pace, bustling
along twice a week, with an omnibus edition on Sundays. A third weekly episode was added in April 1994.
The best-remembered storylines have generally revolved
around love triangles, infidelity and deceit, with more
than a pinch of medical crisis and gangsterish crime for
good measure. They have included Michelle's pregnancy
by 'Dirty' Den and her subsequent jilting of Lofty.
Arthur's endless unemployment and eventual nervous
breakdown was a long-running saga, and Kathy's rape
at the hands of smoothie Willmott-Brown was another
pot-boiler. The break-up of Den and Angie's marriage;

Den's disappearance (murder?); Nick's attempts to
poison his mother; the break-up of hardman Grant Mitchell's marriage to Sharon, following his cuckoldry by
his own brother, Phil; the break-up of Grant's next marriage, to Tiffany, involving his sleeping with her mother,
Louise; and Ian and Cindy Beale's child-custody battle
(after she had arranged to have him shot) were further
high spots. To boost viewing figures, the series has
occasionally ventured abroad – to Spain, Paris, Italy and
Ireland, for example, with episodes sometimes extended
to five nights a week to cover the foreign action.

Never afraid to court controversy, *EastEnders* has
bravely tackled touchy issues such as prostitution
(through unmarried mum Mary); homosexuality (with
lovers Colin and Barry); homelessness (of teenagers
Mandy and Aidan); abortion (Michelle's unborn child
by Lofty); Alzheimer's Disease (the mental deterioration
of Mo Butcher); alcoholism (Phil Mitchell); and AIDS
(the HIV infection of Mark Fowler). Murder was the first
subject on the programme's lips, and the series raced to
a flying start with the death of resident Reg Cox in
episode one (killed, it was revealed later, by Nick
Cotton). But through all the doom and gloom that has
dominated *EastEnders*, there have also been many lighter
and funnier moments.

The series was the brainchild of producer Julia Smith
and script editor Tony Holland, who had worked
together on dramas like ANGELS and DISTRICT NURSE.
Legend has it that the idea was concocted in 45 minutes
in a Shepherd's Bush wine bar. The execution of the
idea was far more thorough, however, and saw the
flimsy working titles of *East 8* and *London Pride* quickly
dropped. With its enormous initial publicity push, *East-
Enders* was a hit from day one. It has gained more than
its share of moral critics, but the audience figures have
spoken for themselves. Not only matching *Coronation
Street*, *EastEnders* has regularly knocked its northern rival
off the top of the ratings.

EastEnders trivia is boundless. Fans can reveal that the
beer served at The Vic has been brewed by Luxford &
Copley, that the pub poodle was Roly, and Ethel's dog
was named Willy. They'll tell you the name of Willmott-
Brown's pub (The Dagmar) and the man who owns the
grotty launderette (Mr Opidopoulous), as well as the
numbers of the houses where the characters have lived:
the Fowlers at number 45 and Dr Legg at number 1,
for instance. And they'll recall the spin-off records that
made the UK charts: 'Anyone Can Fall in Love' (a vocal
version of the theme music) by Anita Dobson, 'Every
Loser Wins' by Nick Berry and 'Something Outa Nothing' by Letitia Dean and Paul Medford (known as The
Banned in the series). All were hits in 1986. There was
also an *EastEnders* spin-off programme: *Civvy Street*, a
one-hour special screened in 1988, looked back to the
Albert Square of 1942, and featured a young Lou Beale
played by Karen Meagher and her friend, Ethel, played
by Alison Bettles.

EASTWOOD, CLINT
(1930–)

Legendary movie cowboy-turned-award-winning director, whose rise to fame was greatly assisted by his seven-
year portrayal of trail rider Rowdy Yates in RAWHIDE.
Previously, Eastwood had gained parts only in B-movies
and guest spots in minor TV series.

EBSEN, BUDDY
(Christian Rudolf Ebsen; 1908–)

Versatile American actor who appeared to be typecast
when his marathon stint as country bumpkin Jed Clampett in THE BEVERLY HILLBILLIES came to an end, but
who branched out effectively into detective work as the
ageing private eye, BARNABY JONES, and returned yet
again in the 1980s as retired investigator Roy Houston in
MATT HOUSTON. In his pre-TV days (which effectively
comprised most of his career), Ebsen had been a Hollywood song-and-dance man, appearing in lavish stage
and movie musicals in the 1930s and 1940s. His first
foray on to the small screen came in Walt Disney's DAVY
CROCKETT, playing Crockett's sidekick, Georgie Russell,
and this led to parts in western series such as MAVERICK,
HAVE GUN, WILL TRAVEL, BONANZA, RAWHIDE and
GUNSMOKE, as well as the adventure series, *Northwest
Passage*. When *The Beverly Hillbillies* beckoned, Ebsen
was already in his mid-fifties. Among his other TV
appearances have been guest spots in HAWAII FIVE-O,
Hardcastle and McCormick and ALIAS SMITH AND JONES.
He is also a published song writer.

ECCLESTON, CHRISTOPHER
(1964–)

Salford-born actor, favouring gritty roles, whose most
notable work has been as welfare officer Sean Maddox
in *Friday on My Mind*, DCI David Bilborough in CRACKER,
teacher Drew McKenzie in *Hearts and Minds*, Nicky Hutchinson in OUR FRIENDS IN THE NORTH, Trevor Hicks in
Hillsborough, and Jim Calvert in *Clocking Off*. CASUALTY,
BOON and AGATHA CHRISTIE'S POIROT feature among
his other credits.

ECHO FOUR-TWO
UK (Associated-Rediffusion) Police Drama. ITV 1961

DI Harry Baxter .... **Eric Lander**
DS Joe York .... **Geoffrey Russell**
Acting Supt. Dean .... **Geoffrey Chater**

Producer: **Richard Matthews**

NO HIDING PLACE *spin-off, which gave bright
young detective Harry Baxter more of the
limelight.*

Promoted from sergeant to inspector, Harry Baxter,

Chief Detective Supt. Lockhart's sidekick in *No Hiding
Place*, became the star of this short-lived series. He was
now placed in charge of E Division's Q-cars, a squad of
unmarked vehicles used for surveillance, and, with his
assistant, Joe York, tackled various assignments from an
office in Bow Street. A strong female following for Eric
Lander instigated this series, but an actors' strike
hastened its downfall before all 13 planned episodes were
produced. Lander then returned to the mother series.

EDDINGTON, PAUL
CBE (1927–95)

British actor whose TV work began in the 1950s when
he played Will Scarlett in THE ADVENTURES OF ROBIN
HOOD. A plethora of other ITC adventures followed,
and Eddington was easily spotted in the likes of THE
AVENGERS, THE PRISONER and THE CHAMPIONS. He also
popped up as a bent copper in DIXON OF DOCK GREEN,
played Brutus in *The Spread of the Eagle* presentation of
Julius Caesar, was a reporter in the Raj series, *Frontier*,
and played the civil servant Strand in SPECIAL BRANCH.
However, it was as Jerry Leadbeatter, wife of Margo and
neighbour of the Goods, in THE GOOD LIFE that he at
last achieved top billing. This was followed by the enormously successful YES, MINISTER and *Yes, Prime Minister*
(in which he starred as the bamboozled MP and PM, Jim
Hacker), the sitcom *Let There Be Love* (bachelor Timothy
Love) and numerous other high-profile performances.
These included the play, OUTSIDE EDGE, MISS MARPLE
and *The Camomile Lawn* (Uncle Richard). His last appearance was as Justice Shallow in BBC 2's *Henry IV*. He was
the father of actress Gemma Eddington.

EDEN, MARK
(1928–)

Shakespearean stage and film actor whose most dramatic
television role has been as Alan Bradley in CORONATION
STREET. Moving in with Rita Fairclough, Bradley's persona gradually changed from gentle man-friend to psychotic misogynist, making him one of the *Street*'s most
evil creations. Eden's earlier TV appearances had been
as crusading sports writer Ray Saxon in the 1968 series,
Crimebuster, Detective Inspector Parker in LORD PETER
WIMSEY, Spencer in *The Top Secret Life of Edgar Briggs*,
plus parts in CRIBB, POLDARK and JESUS OF NAZARETH,
as well as a pre-Bradley incarnation in *Coronation Street*
as one of Elsie Tanner's boyfriends, Wally Randle. He is
married to *Street* star Sue Nicholls.

EDGE OF DARKNESS
UK (BBC) Drama. BBC 2 1985

Ronald Craven .... **Bob Peck**
Emma Craven .... **Joanne Whalley**
Darius Jedburgh .... **Joe Don Baker**
James Godbolt .... **Jack Watson**
Grogan .... **Kenneth Nelson**
Bennett .... **Hugh Fraser**

Pendleton	**Charles Kay**
Det. Chief Supt. Ross	**John Woodvine**
Harcourt	**Ian McNeice**
Terry Shields	**Tim McInnerny**
Clemmy	**Zoe Wanamaker**
Chilwell	**Alan Cuthbertson**
Childs	**Trevor Bowen**

Writer: **Troy Kennedy Martin**
Producer: **Michael Wearing**

A Yorkshire policeman, following up the murder of his daughter, is drawn into nuclear subterfuge.

When Detective Inspector Ronald Craven's scientist daughter, Emma, was gunned down at his side by a shotgun-wielding Irishman, he initially believed the murder was a botched attempt to kill him. After all, he had been involved with terrorist informers in Northern Ireland. However, the more he considered the case, and the more he discovered about his daughter's links with an environmental action group called Gaia, the less certain he became. Branching out into some lone detective work, Craven found himself immersed in political intrigue, egged on by two devious civil servants, Pendleton and Harcourt, and drawing in interested parties from around the globe. The trail led to Northmoor, a disused coal mine, which was revealed to be a secret nuclear waste dump that had been infiltrated by Gaia activists, including Emma, shortly before her death. With the assistance of Darius Jedburgh, an abrasive Texan CIA agent, Craven penetrated the site. Both were fatally contaminated and the whole affair was eventually swept under the carpet by the authorities. The only hope of exposing the scandal then rested with Gaia, with whom Craven filed a report.

Edge of Darkness was one of the BBC's most successful drama series of all time. Screened initially to great acclaim on BBC 2, it earned itself a repeat showing on BBC 1 just a few weeks later, before picking up various awards the following year. Its dark, gloomy imagery enhanced the gravity of its subject matter; the ghostly appearances of Craven's dead daughter, supplying him with snippets of information, added to the 'out of our hands' atmosphere, and Eric Clapton's bluesy electric guitar provided powerful incidental music.

EDITOR

The creative technician who cuts and arranges the recorded material into the finished form. The term is also applied to the ultimate decision-maker or chief producer of a current affairs, news, sport or magazine programme.

EDMONDS, NOEL
(1948–)

Bearded disc jockey turned TV presenter, fond of gentle pranks and hidden camera routines. A Radio Luxembourg DJ as a teenager, Edmonds quickly moved to Radio 1, where his breakfast show was a huge success, 1972–7.

His TV breaks came with TOP OF THE POPS, *Z-Shed* and then a new-style Saturday morning programme for kids, MULTI-COLOURED SWAP SHOP. Moving on from *Swap Shop*, Edmonds dominated Saturday teatimes for many years, with (mostly live) programmes like *Lucky Numbers*, THE LATE, LATE BREAKFAST SHOW, *The Saturday Roadshow* and NOEL'S HOUSE PARTY. He has also presented TOP GEAR (reflecting his interest in motor sports), a revival of JUKE BOX JURY, COME DANCING, the junior MASTERMIND series, *Hobby Horse*, the nostalgic *Time of Your Life* and *Noel's Telly Years*, the guessing game, *Whatever Next?*, the TV quiz, TELLY ADDICTS, and the annual *Noel's Christmas Presents*. His dazzling shirts and sweaters have become a trademark. Despite his success in the UK, an attempt at a talk show in the USA in 1986 failed to work out.

EDMONDSON, ADRIAN
(1957–)

English comedian and comic actor, once part of an act known as 20th Century Coyote with Rik Mayall. As Vyvyan in THE YOUNG ONES he perfected his violent moron character, which he carried through into FILTHY, RICH AND CATFLAP (Eddie Catflap) and BOTTOM (Eddie Hitler). He is married to Jennifer Saunders, with whom he appeared in HAPPY FAMILIES (idiot Guy Fuddle), GIRLS ON TOP, *French and Saunders* and assorted COMIC STRIP satires. He has also appeared in BLACKADDER (Baron Von Richthoven), *Saturday Live* (with Rik Mayall, as the Dangerous Brothers), the futuristic comedy *Snakes and Ladders* (Giles) and the Richard Briers comedy-drama, *If You See God, Tell Him* (Gordon Spry). In addition, Edmondson sang the theme song, 'This Wheel's on Fire', for ABSOLUTELY FABULOUS.

EDWARD AND MRS SIMPSON
UK (Thames) Historical Drama. ITV 1978

Edward	**Edward Fox**
Mrs Wallis Warfield Simpson	**Cynthia Harris**
Queen Mary	**Peggy Ashcroft**
Stanley Baldwin	**David Waller**
George, Duke of York	**Andrew Ray**
King George V	**Marius Goring**
Walter Monckton	**Nigel Hawthorne**
Aunt Bessie	**Jessie Matthews**

Writer: **Simon Raven**
Producer: **Allan Cameron**

The story of King Edward VIII's abdication.

This expensive seven-part drama related events leading up to the abdication crisis of 1936, with particular focus on the controversial affair between Prince Edward (later King Edward VIII) and American divorcée Wallis Simpson. Based on the biography by Frances Donaldson, the series portrayed Mrs Simpson as a calculating schemer, something which distressed the real Duchess of Windsor, who was still alive and residing in France. Edward

Fox won much acclaim for his performance as the emotionally torn king.

EDWARD THE SEVENTH
UK (ATV) Historical Drama. ITV 1975

Edward .... Timothy West (*adult*)
Charles Sturridge (*teenager*)
Queen Victoria .... Annette Crosbie
Prince Albert .... Robert Hardy
Princess Alexandra .... Deborah Grant
Helen Ryan
Princess Vicky .... Felicity Kendal
Duchess of Kent .... Alison Leggatt
Col. Bruce .... Harry Andrews
Lord Palmerston .... André Morell
Benjamin Disraeli .... John Gielgud
William Gladstone .... Michael Hordern
Princess Dagmar .... Jane Lapotaire
Lillie Langtry .... Francesca Annis
Lord Salisbury .... Richard Vernon
Lord Coventry .... Robert Flemyng
Lady Brooke .... Carolyn Seymour
Kaiser Wilhelm .... Christopher Neame
Prince Eddy .... Charles Dance
Herbert Asquith .... Basil Dignam
Sir Henry Campbell-Bannerman ...... Geoffrey Bayldon

Writer: **David Butler**
Producer: **Cecil Clarke**

A detailed dramatization of the life of King Edward VII.

Edward was 60 years of age when he succeeded his long-reigning mother, Queen Victoria, to the throne, which meant that his better years were behind him. This 13-part biopic looked closely at the life and loves of the Prince and also focused on the personality of the great Queen herself and other members of the royal family. With scenes filmed within Osborne House, Sandringham and other royal properties, by permission of the present Queen, the series was much applauded for its attention to detail, production techniques and the performances of the lead actors. Based on a biography by Philip Magnus, it was written mainly by David Butler, formerly Dr Nick Williams in EMERGENCY – WARD 10. Butler went on to co-write LILLIE for LWT in 1978, in which Francesca Annis reprised her Lillie Langtry role. *Edward the Seventh* was retitled *Edward the King* when shown in the USA.

EDWARDIANS, THE
UK (BBC) Drama. BBC 2 1972–3

Producer: **Mark Shivas**

Eight dramatizations of the lives of turn-of-the-century British pioneers.

This series of drama-documentaries looked closely at nine early 20th-century figures of note: Messrs Charles Rolls and Frederick Royce (played by Michael Jayston and Robert Powell); writers E. Nesbit (Judy Parfitt) and Arthur Conan Doyle (Nigel Davenport); Daisy, mistress of Edward VII (Virginia McKenna); scout-founder Robert Baden-Powell (Ron Moody); music-hall star Marie Lloyd (Georgia Brown); journalist and MP Horatio Bottomley (Timothy West); and Prime Minister David Lloyd-George (Anthony Hopkins).

EDWARDS, ANTHONY
(1962–)

California-born actor best known as Dr Mark Greene in ER, but also seen as murderer Dick Hickock in the dramatization of Truman Capote's *In Cold Blood*. His early credits included a sitcom, *It Takes Two*, and NORTHERN EXPOSURE (boy in the bubble Mike Monroe).

EDWARDS, JIMMY
DFC (1920–88)

English comedian whose handlebar moustache became a trademark. Awarded the DFC for his wartime RAF efforts, Edwards broke into radio in the late 1940s, when, as Pa Glum, he appeared in *Take It from Here*. This ran for 12 years and The Glums were revived on TV as part of *Bruce Forsyth's Big Night* in 1978. However, it is as Professor Jimmy Edwards, the corrupt principal of Chiselbury School in WHACK-O!, that he will always be remembered by viewers and, after playing the role for four years, 1956–60, he donned his gown and picked up his cane once more for a revival in 1971. His other TV starring roles were in SEVEN FACES OF JIM, *Six More Faces of Jim, More Faces of Jim, Bold as Brass* (musician Ernie Briggs), *Mr John Jorrocks* (Jorrocks, Master of Foxhounds), *The Fossett Saga* (Victorian writer James Fossett) and as the cowardly knight, *Sir Yellow*. The famous moustache was apparently grown to obscure facial injuries received when one of his aircraft crashed in the war.

EDWARDS, VINCE
(Vincento Eduardo Zoine; 1928–96)

American leading man of the 1960s, an international heart-throb thanks to his star status in BEN CASEY. He was generally seen in the UK only in guest spots and in TV movies (including the pilot for KNIGHT RIDER) after the series ended in 1966, moving more into directing, although he did pop up in a couple of lesser dramas in the USA (notably *Matt Lincoln*). His earliest TV performances came in shows such as ALFRED HITCHCOCK PRESENTS and THE UNTOUCHABLES.

EGAN, PETER
(1946–)

Suave English actor whose many roles have encompassed both drama and comedy. Following his performance as a violent gangster in 1969's BIG BREADWINNER HOG and the somewhat different part of the Earl of Southampton in ELIZABETH R in 1971, Egan remained in period costume for PRINCE REGENT in 1979. In the 1980s he charmed sitcom viewers as the super-smooth Paul Ryman in EVER DECREASING CIRCLES, before becoming Hannah Gordon's house husband, David Braithwaite, in the banking comedy, *Joint Account*. He still found time to win acclaim as Magnus Pym in the BBC's adaptation of Le Carré's *A Perfect Spy* and as a war cripple in the one-off play, *A Day in Summer*, for YTV. Among his other credits have been Oscar Wilde in LILLIE, MOTHER LOVE, REILLY – ACE OF SPIES, *The Dark Side of the Sun*, *The Organisation*, TALES OF THE UNEXPECTED, THRILLER, *Paradise Postponed*, THE RUTH RENDELL MYSTERIES and A WOMAN OF SUBSTANCE. In recent years, Egan has been seen in *The Peacock Spring* (Sir Gwithiam), the film comedy *Gobble* (Peter Villiers), *Chiller* (Richard Cramer), AMBASSADOR (Michael Cochrane) and *Cry Wolf* (Dr Hook).

EHLE, JENNIFER
(1970–)

British actress, the daughter of actress Rosemary Harris. Undoubtedly her biggest role to date has been as Elizabeth Bennet in PRIDE AND PREJUDICE, although she also made the headlines with her portrayal of Calypso in *The Camomile Lawn*. Later work has included *Melissa* (title role), and other credits take in *Rik Mayall Presents*.

EL C.I.D.
UK (Granada) Comedy Drama. ITV 1990–2

Douglas Bromley	John Bird
Bernard Blake	Alfred Molina
Frank	Tony Haygarth
Metcalf	Donald Churchill
Delgado	Simon Andreu
Mercedes	Viviane Vives
Stevie Blake	Robert Reynolds
Rosie Bromley	Amanda Redman
Gus Mercer	Kenneth Cranham
Graham	Niven Boyd
Señora Sanchez	Maria Isbert

Creators: **Chris Kelly, Iain Roy**
Executive Producer: **Sally Head**
Producer: **Matthew Bird**

Two former Scotland Yard officers take up residence on the Costa del Crime.

When police clerk Douglas Bromley was told he was being relocated to Derbyshire, the idea didn't greatly appeal, so he encouraged his beefy CID colleague, Bernard Blake, to join him in early retirement and a voyage of adventure to Spain. Setting out in a motorized yacht, aptly named *El C.I.D.*, they moored up on the Costa del Sol, near Marbella, where they quickly immersed themselves in the area's dodgy goings-on. The bar they intended to open was criminally destroyed and the hapless duo joined forces with Delgado and Mercedes, father and daughter detectives, in a long-running battle with the local underworld (and, in particular, nasty Gus Mer-

cer and his henchman, Graham). Metcalf was the bombastic owner of the marina where their boat was berthed and Frank was the expat proprietor of the snappily named Chez Frank restaurant. Blake's troublesome brother, Stevie, turned up in the second season, before Blake himself left in the third series, to be replaced by Rosie, Bromley's long-lost daughter. She arrived in Marbella after being dumped by her boyfriend, and she joined her dad as an accomplice in Delgado and Partners.

ELDORADO
UK (Cinema Verity/J Dy T) Drama. BBC 1 1992–3

Gwen Lockhead	Patricia Brake
Drew Lockhead	Campbell Morrison
Blair Lockhead	Josh Nathan
Nessa Lockhead	Julie Fernandez
Trish Valentine	Polly Perkins
Dieter Schultz	Kai Maurer
Joy Slater	Leslee Udwin
Snowy White	Patch Connolly
Roberto Fernandez	Franco Rey
Rosario Fernandez	Stella Maris
Maria Fernandez	Maria Sanchez
Abuela Fernandez	Maria Vega
Javier Fernandez	Iker Ibanez
Ingrid Olsson	Bo Corre
Marcus Tandy	Jesse Birdsall
Pilar Moreno	Sandra Sandri
Olive King	Faith Kent
Isabelle Leduc	Framboise Gommendy
Philippe Leduc	Daniel Lombart
Arnaud Leduc	Mikael Philippe
Lene Svendsen	Nanna Moller
Per Svendsen	Kim Romer
Trine Svendsen	Marchell Betak
	Clare Wilkie
Gavin Hindle	Darren Newton
Allan Hindle	Jon Morrey
Gerry Peters-Smith	Buki Armstrong
Bunny Charlson	Roger Walker
Freddie Martin	Roland Curram
Fizz Charlson	Kathy Pitkin
Stanley Webb	William Lucas
Rosemary Webb	Hilary Crane
Tracy	Hayley Bromley
Antonio	Jose Antonio Navarro
'Razor' Sharpe	Kevin Hay
Sergio Munoz D'Avila	Alexander Torriglia
Alex Morris	Derek Martin

Creators: **Julia Smith, Tony Holland**
Executive Producers: **Verity Lambert, John Dark**
Producers: **Julia Smith, Corinne Hollingworth**

Drama with an expatriate community in Spain.

In 1992, the year of falling European barriers, the BBC did its bit for the cause by launching a thrice-weekly 'soap for Europe'. Trailed in the tabloids as 'sex, sun and sangria', *Eldorado* was set in the Spanish fishing village of Los Barcos and focused on its community of expatriate Brits, Frenchmen and Danes, all 'living their dream' of a home in the sun but discovering that their new life was not one long holiday after all.

The community's mother figure was Gwen Lockhead, a teacher who ran the English-language newspaper. Gwen's husband, Drew, was a lazy, hard-drinking Glaswegian, her son, Blair, was a typically troublesome teenager and her daughter, Nessa, although wheelchair bound, was determinedly independent. The Lockheads' neighbours were retired military man Stanley Webb, who lived with his young-at-heart wife, Rosemary, Olive King, the local nosy parker, and another ex-army man, Bunny Charlson, who was shacked up with Fizz, a 17-year-old runaway. Charmer Marcus Tandy was the 'Costa del Crime' villain in hiding, gay Freddie Martin knocked about with the rebellious Gerry (a girl), and Snowy White was the Los Barcos handyman. Brothers Gavin and Allan Hindle ran the beach bar, Joy Slater owned the wine bar and Trish Valentine was the ageing nightclub singer who enjoyed a stormy relationship with Dieter Schultz, a 19-year-old German windsurfing teacher. The French were represented by tennis coach Philippe Leduc, his flirty wife, Isabelle, and their 16-year-old romantic son, Arnaud. The Svendsen family offered the Danish input. Dad Per ran a chandlery business, mum Lene was a beautician and their 14-year-old daughter was called Trine. Completing the line-up of Los Barcos principals were Swedish tour guide Ingrid Olssen and a handful of local Spaniards, mostly from the Fernandez family: Roberto, the town doctor, his wife, Rosario, and two teenage children, Maria and Javier. Abuella was Roberto's traditionally minded mother. Pilar Moreno was the other native and she worked at Marcus Tandy's stables, eventually becoming his girlfriend. The interaction of this motley band of retirees, escapees from the rat race, old bigots and young new Europeans was the source of the series' drama.

Eldorado was the biggest and most ambitious series yet awarded to an independent production company (Cinema Verity) by the BBC. A whole village was specially constructed in Spanish woodland for filming and the cast and crew took up residence locally. Sadly, *Eldorado* did not capture the public's imagination in the way Julia Smith and Tony Holland's earlier creation, EASTENDERS, had, and critics piled on the agony. Although viewing figures were on the mend, it was cancelled by new BBC 1 boss, Alan Yentob, just a year after it had begun.

ELECTRONIC NEWS GATHERING
See ENG.

ELIZABETH R
UK (BBC) Historical Drama. BBC 2 1971

Elizabeth I	Glenda Jackson
Robert Dudley	Robert Hardy
William Cecil	Ronald Hines
Mary Tudor	Daphne Slater
Thomas Cranmer	Bernard Hepton
Kat Ashley	Rachel Kempson
Edward VI	Jason Kemp
Catherine Parr	Rosalie Crutchley
Count de Feria	Leonard Sachs
Bishop de Quadra	Esmond Knight
Sir James Melville	John Cairney
Mary, Queen of Scots	Vivian Pickles
Sir Francis Walsingham	Stephen Murray
Duke of Alençon	Michael Williams
Catherine de Medici	Margareta Scott
Earl of Essex	Robin Ellis
Sir Anthony Babington	David Collings
Phillip II, King of Spain	Peter Jeffrey
Sir Francis Drake	John Woodvine
Sir Walter Raleigh	Nicholas Selby
Francis Bacon	John Nettleton
Father Robert Parsons	Paul Hardwick
Lettice Knollys	Angela Thorne
O'Neill, Earl of Tyrone	Patrick O'Connell
Sir Robert Cecil	Hugh Dickson
Earl of Southampton	Peter Egan

Producer: **Roderick Graham**

The troubled life of England's Virgin Queen.

In six self-contained episodes, each of 90 minutes' length, *Elizabeth R* dramatized the tortuous life of the famous 16th-century monarch, beginning with her difficult road to the throne and ending with her lonely death. In doing so, it also afforded viewers an insight into court life in Tudor times.

Following hot on the heels of the enormously successful THE SIX WIVES OF HENRY VIII, *Elizabeth R* had much to achieve but, thanks to its large (for the time) budget of £237,000, close attention to detail and an excellent cast (some reprising the roles they had taken in *Six Wives*), it enjoyed similar acclaim. For her role as Elizabeth, Glenda Jackson shaved her forehead, donned eccentric hairpieces and wore a false nose. Courtesy of hours in the make-up room, she was seen to age from a youthful, determined 15 to a grotesque, pallid 70-year-old over the course of the series.

ELLIOT, JOHN
(1918–)

Early BBC documentary maker, writer, producer and director (1954's WAR IN THE AIR was his greatest achievement) who went on to script some influential dramas, including A FOR ANDROMEDA and *The Andromeda Breakthrough* (both with Fred Hoyle, the latter also as producer). Elliot also created MOGUL and penned some episodes of *Z Cars*, as well as producing the drama anthology, *The Sunday Play*, in 1963. He later became a BBC executive.

ELLIOTT, DENHOLM
CBE (1922–92)

Actor readily cast as a distinguished, but slightly dodgy or sinister Englishman in many films and TV dramas. His major television performances were in THE MAN IN ROOM 17 (Imlac Defraits), MYSTERY AND IMAGINATION

(Count Dracula), *Clayhanger, The Signalman, Blade on the Feather, Hôtel du Lac, Bleak House, Scoop,* RIPPING YARNS, *Codename Kyril* and the mini-series, *Marco Polo* (Niccolò Polo). He also played George Smiley in *A Murder of Quality*. His first wife was Virginia McKenna.

ELPHICK, MICHAEL
(1946–)

Chichester-born actor, headlining in a range of comedies and dramas, especially as German petty crook PRI-VATE SCHULZ, fireman turned adventurer Ken Boon, working-class taxidermist Sam Tyler in THREE UP, TWO DOWN, and news agency boss Harry Salter in *Harry*. Among his many other credits have been the comedy, *Pull the Other One* (Sidney Mundy), AUF WIEDERSEHEN, PET (Irish labourer Magowan), CORONATION STREET, CROWN COURT, *Blue Remembered Hills, This Year, Next Year,* THE SWEENEY, SHOESTRING, *Roger Doesn't Live Here Anymore* (wrestler Stanley), *Masada,* SUPERGRAN, *Jenny's War, Stanley and the Women, The One and Only Phyllis Dixey, The Fix* (Peter Campling) and *David Copperfield* (Barkiss).

ELTON, BEN
(1959–)

British stand-up comic and comedy scriptwriter. Among his writing credits have been THE YOUNG ONES (with Rik Mayall and Lise Mayer), GIRLS ON TOP (script editor), HAPPY FAMILIES, FILTHY RICH AND CATFLAP, *Lenny Henry Tonite,* THE THIN BLUE LINE and, with Richard Curtis, BLACKADDER (apart from the first series). In front of the camera (often complete with sparkling jacket), he has hosted *South of Watford* and *Saturday Live*, appeared in Granada's ALFRESCO and once stood in for *Wogan*. Elton has also been *The Man from Auntie* in a monologue and sketch show (later revamped as *The Ben Elton Show*) that has given a thorough airing to his sharp social and political observations. Outside of television, he has had several novels published (including *Stark*, in which he appeared on its adaptation for BBC 2) and has scripted West End plays.

EMERGENCY – WARD 10
UK (ATV) Drama. ITV 1957–67

Nurse Pat Roberts	**Rosemary Miller**
Nurse/Sister Carole Young	**Jill Browne**
Sister Cowley	**Elizabeth Kentish**
Nurse/Sister/Matron Mary Stevenson	**Iris Russell**
Dr Alan Dawson	**Charles Tingwell**
Dr Patrick 'Paddy' O'Meara	**Glyn Owen**
Potter	**Douglas Ives**
Dr Chris Anderson	**Desmond Carrington**
Dr Simon Forrester	**Frederick Bartman**
Mr Stephen Brooks	**John Brooking**
Dr Peter Harrison	**Peter Howell**
RSO Hughes	**John Paul**
Nurse Ann Guthridge	**Norah Gorsen**
Staff Nurse Jane Morley	**Ann Sears**
Dr John Rennie	**Richard Thorp**
Nurse Jo Buckley/Anderson	**Barbara Clegg**
Nurse Julie Wayne	**Jean Aubrey**
Sister Shelley	**Gene Anderson**
Nurse O'Keefe	**Kerry Marsh**
Donald Latimer	**John Carson**
Jake O'Dowd	**Shaun O'Riordan**
Staff Nurse Craigie	**Shirley Thieman**
Mr Harold de la Roux	**John Barron**
Margaret de la Roux	**Kathleen Byron**
Dr Whittaker	**Robert Macleod**
Sister Crawford	**Cicely Hullett**
Audrey Blake/Dawson	**Jane Downs**
RSO Miller	**John Barrie**
Dr Don Nolan	**Ray Barrett**
Dr Nick Williams	**David Butler**
Miss Nesbitt	**Ann Firbank**
Nurse Gregg	**Felicity Young**
Derek Bailey	**Brian Nissen**
Sister Rhys	**Joan Matheson**
Mr Lester Large	**John Carlisle**
Dr Frances Whitney	**Paula Byrne**
Dr Richard Moone	**John Alderton**
Sister MacNab	**Dorothy Smith**
Rupert Marsden	**Ian Colin**
Andrew Shaw	**John Line**
Dr Ted Bryan	**Richard Bidlake**
Dr Bob Coughlin	**Desmond Jordan**
Dr Griffiths	**Robert Lang**
Nurse Ann Webb	**Jean Trend**
Sally Bowen	**Carol Davies**
Linda Stanley	**Jennifer Wright**
Dr Beckett	**Geoffrey Colvile**
Dr James Gordon	**Michael McKevitt**
Elizabeth Benskin	**Sheila Fearn**
Sister Doughty	**Pamela Duncan**
Staff Nurse Jill Craig	**Anne Brooks**
Mr Fitzgerald	**John Arnatt**
Nurse Kate Ford	**Jane Rossington**
Nurse Michaela Davies/Large	**Tricia Money**
Mr Giles Farmer	**John White**
Nurse Kwe Kim-Yen/Kwei	**Pik-Sen Lim**
Estelle Waterman	**Pauline Yates**
Mr Victor	**Richard Carpenter**
Jean Twillow	**Elisabeth Murray**
Tim Birch	**Frazer Hines**
Mr Guy Marshall	**Tom Adams**
Mr Barrett	**Geoffrey Russell**
Dr Rex Lane Russell	**Basil Hoskins**
Lena Hyde	**Caroline Blakiston**
Staff Nurse/Sister Jane Beattie	**Anne Lloyd**
Amanda Brown	**Hilary Tindall**
Dr Alex Grant	**Michael Baxter**
Sister Ransome	**Stella Tanner**
Mr Booth	**Jonathan Newth**
Mr Bacon	**David Pinner**
Mr Dorsey	**David Garth**
Dr Brook	**William Wilde**
Dr Louise Mahler	**Joan Hooley**
Dr Murad	**Salmaan Peer**
Prof. Jenkins	**John Welsh**
Staff Nurse Lyle	**Colette Dunne**

Helen Booth	**Rosemary Frankau**
Nurse Parkin	**Therese McMurray**
Dr Fairfax	**Victor Winding**
Elizabeth Fairfax	**Honor Shepherd**
Sister Wright	**Zulema Dene**
Nurse Jones	**Janet Lees Price**
Mr Bailey	**David King**
Mr Verity	**Paul Darrow**
Dr Richmond	**Noel Coleman**
Mr Kent	**Ian Cullen**
Staff Nurse Amy Williams	**Sonia Fox**
Dr Green	**Langton Jones**

Creator: **Tessa Diamond**
Producers: **Antony Kearey, Rex Firkin, Hugh Rennie, John Cooper, Cecil Petty, Josephine Douglas, Pieter Rogers**

Britain's first twice-weekly, long-running drama series, focusing on the staff and patients in a large general hospital.

Emergency – Ward 10, the brainchild of ATV staff writer Tessa Diamond, ran for ten years and drew huge audiences. Its cancellation in 1967 was, according to Lew Grade, boss of ATV, one of his biggest mistakes. The series initially focused on trainee nurse Pat Roberts, a farm girl getting to grips with life in a city hospital. She was quickly joined in the limelight by a host of budding stars. Jill Browne as her roommate, Nurse (later Sister) Carole Young, won most male admirers, although some of her male colleagues also became heart-throbs for female viewers. These included Charles Tingwell as surgeon Alan Dawson, Desmond Carrington as Dr Chris Anderson, Ray Barrett as Dr Don Nolan, and Dr John Rennie who was played by a youngster by the name of Richard Thorp, now better known as EMMERDALE's Alan Turner. John Alderton joined the cast in 1963 as youthful Dr Richard Moone (he was later to marry his co-star, Jill Browne).

The action took place at Oxbridge General Hospital and, although drama was high, tragedy was scarce; of more concern were the lives and loves of the hospital staff. Patient deaths were strictly limited to five per year, and this was later reduced to just two. That was good news for emerging names like Ian Hendry, Albert Finney and Joanna Lumley, who all signed up for treatment. *Emergency – Ward 10*'s success spawned a feature film, *Life in Emergency Ward 10*, in 1958, and also one spin-off series, *Call Oxbridge 2000*. This saw Dr Rennie heading off into private practice and itself led to another series, entitled *24-Hour Call*. *Emergency – Ward 10*, for all intents and purposes, was resurrected by ATV in the 1970s in the guise of GENERAL HOSPITAL.

EMERY, DICK
(1917–83)

British comedian, fond of outrageous characterizations and drag sketches. His *Dick Emery Show*, which began in 1963 and ran for nearly two decades, saw him adopting the guises of a sex-starved spinster (always 'Miss' not 'Madam'); an effeminate swinger ('Hello, Honky Tonk');

a toothy vicar; a dim bovver-boy; Farmer Finch; a classy tramp; the conniving, chortling old codger, Lampwick; and Mandy, the brassy blonde who always misunderstood the interviewer, so providing Emery with his catchphrase, 'Ooh, you are awful, but I like you!' After radio (and, later, TV success) in *Educating Archie*, Emery had arrived on the small screen in the 1950s, in *The Tony Hancock Show* and with Libby Morris in *Two's Company*. He also supported Michael Bentine in IT'S A SQUARE WORLD and played Chubby Catchpole in the last series of THE ARMY GAME. In 1964 he took the role of Mr Hughes in the early version of the TV station comedy, *Room at the Bottom*. Emery hosted *The Dick Emery Hour* for Thames in 1979, but returned to the BBC in 1982 to star in a comedy-thriller series entitled simply *Emery*, playing the part of investigator Bernie Weinstock (and several of his suspects) in cases entitled *Legacy of Murder* and *Jack of Diamonds*.

EMMERDALE FARM/EMMERDALE
UK (Yorkshire) Drama. ITV 1972–

Annie Sugden/Kempinski	**Sheila Mercier**
Jack Sugden	**Andrew Burt**
	Clive Hornby
Joe Sugden	**Frazer Hines**
Sam Pearson	**Toke Townley**
Peggy Skilbeck	**Jo Kendall**
Matt Skilbeck	**Frederick Pyne**
Amos Brearly	**Ronald Magill**
Henry Wilks	**Arthur Pentelow**
Marian Wilks	**Gail Harrison**
Rosemary Kendall	**Lesley Manville**
Dolly Acaster/Skilbeck	**Katherine Barker**
	Jean Rogers
Ruth Merrick	**Lynn Dalby**
Tom Merrick	**David Hill**
	Edward Peel
	Jack Carr
Pat Merrick/Sugden	**Helen Weir**
Jackie Merrick	**Ian Sharrock**
Sandie Merrick	**Jane Hutcheson**
Revd Donald Hinton	**Hugh Manning**
Seth Armstrong	**Stan Richards**
Alan Turner	**Richard Thorp**
Caroline Bates	**Diana Davies**
Kathy Bates/Merrick/Tate/Glover	**Malandra Burrows**
Phil Pearce	**Peter Alexander**
Nick Bates	**Cy Chadwick**
Archie Brooks	**Tony Pitts**
Bill Middleton	**Johnny Caesar**
Eric Pollard	**Christopher Chittell**
Mark Hughes	**Craig McKay**
Rachel Hughes	**Glenda McKay**
Sarah Connolly/Sugden	**Madeleine Howard**
	Alyson Spiro
Stephen Fuller	**Gregory Floy**
Karen Moore	**Annie Hulley**
Elsa Feldmann	**Naomi Lewis**
Michael Feldmann	**Matthew Vaughan**
Elizabeth Feldmann/Pollard	**Kate Dove**
Frank Tate	**Norman Bowler**

Christopher Tate .... **Peter Amory**
Kim Tate/Barker/Marchant .... **Claire King**
Zoe Tate .... **Leah Bracknell**
Revd Tony Charlton .... **Stephen Rashbrook**
Richard Anstey .... **Carl Rigg**
Sita Sharma .... **Mamta Kash**
Kate Hughes/Sugden .... **Sally Knyvette**
Lynn Whiteley .... **Fionnuala Ellwood**
Carol Nelson .... **Philomena McDonagh**
Leonard Kempinski .... **Bernard Archard**
Vic Windsor .... **Alun Lewis**
Viv Windsor .... **Deena Payne**
Scott Windsor .... **Toby Cockerell**
Ben Freeman
Kelly Windsor/Glover .... **Adele Silva**
Donna Windsor .... **Sophie Jeffrey**
Verity Rushworth
Shirley Foster/Turner .... **Rachel Davies**
Bernard McAllister .... **Brendan Price**
Angharad McAllister .... **Amanda Wenban**
Jessica McAllister .... **Camilla Power**
Luke McAllister .... **Noah Huntley**
Betty Eagleton .... **Paula Tilbrook**
Britt Woods .... **Michelle Holmes**
Terry Woods .... **Billy Hartman**
Robert Sugden .... **Christopher Smith**
Nellie Dingle .... **Sandra Gough**
Maggie Tagney
Butch Dingle .... **Paul Loughran**
Sam Dingle .... **James Hooton**
Tina Dingle .... **Jacqueline Pirie**
Zak Dingle .... **Steve Halliwell**
Ned Glover .... **Johnny Leeze**
Jan Glover .... **Roberta Kerr**
Roy Glover .... **Nicky Evans**
David Glover .... **Ian Kelsey**
Linda Glover/Fowler .... **Tonicha Jeronimo**
Biff Fowler .... **Stuart Wade**
Emma Nightingale .... **Rachel Ambler**
Mandy Dingle .... **Lisa Riley**
Sean Rossi .... **Mark Cameron**
Susan Wilde .... **Louise Heaney**
Marcus Ellis .... **Richard Burke**
Andy Hopwood/Sugden .... **Kelvin Fletcher**
Steve Marchant .... **Paul Opacic**
Lisa Clegg/Dingle .... **Jane Cox**
Albert Dingle .... **Bobby Knutt**
Marlon Dingle .... **Mark Charnock**
Sophie Wright .... **Jane Cameron**
Will Cairns .... **Paul Fox**
Emma Cairns .... **Rebecca Loudonsack**
Anthony Cairns .... **Edward Peel**
Rebecca Cairns .... **Sarah Neville**
Lord Alex Oakwell .... **Rupam Maxwell**
Lady Tara Oakwell/Thornfield .... **Anna Brecon**
Billy Hopwood .... **David Crellin**
Dee Pollard .... **Claudia Malkovich**
Patrick 'Paddy' Kirk .... **Dominic Brunt**
Graham Clark .... **Kevin Pallister**
Heather Hutchinson .... **Siobhan Finneran**
Lyn Hutchinson .... **Sally Walsh**
Laura Johnstone .... **Louise Beattie**
Tricia Stokes .... **Sheree Murphy**

Revd Ashley Thomas .... **John Middleton**
DI Spalding .... **Davyd Harries**
Stella Jones .... **Stephanie Schonfield**
Bernice Blackstock/Thomas .... **Samantha Giles**
Gavin Ferris .... **Robert Beck**
Sean Reynolds .... **Stephen McGann**
Emily Wylie/Dingle .... **Kate McGregor**
John Wylie .... **Seamus O'Neill**
Frankie Smith .... **Gina Aris**
Pete Collins .... **Kirk Smith**
Alice Bates .... **Rachel Tolboys**
Claudia Nash .... **Susan Duerden**
Elsa Chappell .... **Natasha Gray**
Richie Carter .... **Glenn Lamont**
Angie Reynolds .... **Freya Copeland**
Diane Blackstock .... **Elizabeth Estensen**
Adam Forrester .... **Tim Vincent**
Cain Dingle .... **Jeff Hordley**
Ollie Reynolds .... **Vicky Binns**
Jason Kirk .... **James Carlton**
Paddy Kirk .... **Dominic Brunt**
Edna Birch .... **Shirley Stelfox**
Carlos Diaz .... **Gary Turner**
Marc Reynolds .... **Anthony Lewis**
Gloria Weaver .... **Janice McKenzie**
Rodney Blackstock .... **Patrick Mower**
Joe Fisher .... **Edward Baker-Duly**
Virginia West .... **Bridget Fry**

Creator: **Kevin Laffan**
Executive Producers: **Peter Holmans, David Cunliffe,
Michael Glynn, Keith Richardson**
Producers: **David Goddard, Robert D. Cardona,
Michael Glynn, Anne W. Gibbons, Richard Handford,
Michael Russell, Stuart Doughty, Morag Bain, Nicholas
Prosser, Mervyn Watson, Kieran Roberts**

Long-running saga of Yorkshire farming folk.

Airing twice a week, *Emmerdale Farm* began life as one
of the dramas commissioned by ITV to fill its afternoon
schedules. It quickly attracted sizeable audiences and
was moved to an early evening slot in 1977, eventually
becoming fully networked in 1988 and so developing
into one of the UK's major soaps.

The focus of the series was, for many years, the Sugden
family, inhabitants of Emmerdale Farm itself, set on the
fringes of the fictitious rural village of Beckindale. The
first ever episode saw the funeral of Jacob Sugden, the
family's wastrel father, leaving his wife Annie to take
charge of farm affairs. Annie, a wholesome farmer's wife
in the old tradition, was supported by her sons, Jack and
Joe, daughter Peggy, and crusty old Sam Pearson, Annie's
dad, who was known to all as Grandad. Also on hand
was Peggy's husband, shepherd Matt Skilbeck. Down in
the village, the local hostelry (purveyor of Ephraim
Monk ales) was The Woolpack, jointly owned and managed by stroppy Amos Brearly (a part-time columnist
for the *Hotten Courier*) and kindly, pipe-smoking Henry
Wilks, whose daughter Marian was also seen. The parish
vicar was Mr Hinton. Storylines generally followed the
farming calendar, with worries over crop yield, river
pollution or lamb sickness merging with the usual
stresses and strains of family life.

Unavoidable in such soap marathons, cast changes followed aplenty. Peggy was killed off, leaving Matt to marry Dolly Acaster. Jack disappeared to Rome and resumed his career as a writer, only to return (played by a different actor) several years later. And Joe spent some time in France. New characters came and went. Among the most durable have been poacher-turned-gamekeeper Seth Armstrong and Alan Turner, once-hated manager of NY Estates, who displayed more geniality as The Woolpack's landlord, on the retirement of Amos Brierly. The Emmerdale farmhouse resounded to the bickering of several new families as the Sugden boys brought home their latest wives and step-offspring. But, through it all, until her death, Annie remained the matriarchal figure, barking words of advice to her wayward children between cooking meals and doing the ironing. However, major changes were afoot.

In the mid-1980s the programme was taken by the neck and given a good shake. In came grittier plots and meaner characters. Now the lads not only baled the hay but rolled in it, too. Extra-marital liaisons became a speciality, much to the dismay of the programme's creator, Kevin Laffan. Finally, in recognition of the changes that had swept through the series, the name was shortened to the snappier *Emmerdale* in November 1989. Even since then, there have been new brooms at work and, in an effort to boost viewing figures, increasingly sensational storylines – from murders to a siege at the post office – have been introduced. The Christmas 1993 plot, involving a plane crashing on the village, provoked much controversy but enabled the producers to clear out the dead wood and bring in some fresh faces. This 'coming of age' of *Emmerdale* has been much lamented by those viewers who enjoyed the slow-paced, pastoral pleasures of the early years. A third weekly episode was introduced in January 1997 and the series settled into a Tuesday–Thursday schedule, before the series went five nights a week in 2000.

For many years, the screen Beckindale was actually the Yorkshire village of Esholt, near Bradford (although initially another village, Arncliffe, was used), and The Woolpack's exterior was really that of Esholt's Commercial Inn. However, in order to relieve the real-life village of tourist congestion, a lookalike film set was constructed in the 1990s.

EMPIRE ROAD
UK (BBC) Drama. BBC 2 1978–9

Everton Bennett	**Norman Beaton**
Walter Issacs	**Joe Marcell**
Hortense Bennett	**Corinne Skinner-Carter**
Marcus Bennett	**Wayne Laryea**
Ranjanaa Kapoor	**Nalini Moonasar**
Miss May	**Rosa Roberts**
Desmond	**Trevor Butler**
Royston	**Vincent Taylor**
Mr Kapoor	**Melan Mitchell**
Sebastian Moses	**Rudolph Walker**

Writer: **Michael Abbensetts**
Producer: **Peter Ansorge**

Life in a racially mixed Midlands street.

Filmed in the Handsworth area of Birmingham, *Empire Road* focused on the relationship between the West Indian and Asian inhabitants of a residential street. At the centre of the action were Guyanan grocer Everton Bennett, owner of four of the houses, and his stuttering brother-in-law, Walter Issacs. Through the romance of Everton's son, Marcus, and their Asian neighbour, Ranjanaa, the series exposed inter-racial friction. It also revealed the different outlooks and mentalities of the various generations.

Empire Road broke new ground in being the first drama to be written, performed and directed entirely by black artists. Its writer was Guyanan Michael Abbensetts. The 1978 first season consisted of only five episodes, but ten more episodes followed a year later. In that second series, two white women were added to provide balance, and former LOVE THY NEIGHBOUR star Rudolph Walker was introduced as Sebastian Moses, a new and menacing landlord. The final episode focused on Marcus and Ranjanaa's wedding and the hopes it brought for racial harmony in Empire Road.

ENCRYPTION

The scrambling of a TV signal, allowing it to be decoded only by those who have paid the relevant subscription and have the appropriate equipment or viewing card. It is the everyday working basis for most satellite and cable channels.

ENEMY AT THE DOOR
UK (LWT) Drama. ITV 1978–80

Major Richter	**Alfred Burke**
Clare Martel	**Emily Richard**
Olive Martel	**Antonia Pemberton**
Dr Philip Martel	**Bernard Horsfall**
Oberleutnant Kluge	**John Malcolm**
Hauptmann Reinicke	**Simon Cadell**
Major Freidel	**Simon Lack**
Peter Porteous	**Richard Heffer**

Creator/Writer: **Michael Chapman**
Producers: **Michael Chapman, Jonathan Alwyn**
Executive Producer: **Tony Wharmby**

Life in the Channel Islands during the German occupation.

The Channel Islands were the only part of the United Kingdom to be occupied by the Germans during World War II. This 13-part drama analysed the effect the occupation had on the day-to-day life of the local residents, looking particularly at the Guernsey-based Martel family and especially their 20-year-old daughter, Clare. The action began in June 1940, with the islanders awaiting with trepidation the impending invasion, and continued through the darkest days of the war itself.

ENFIELD, HARRY
(1961–)

Sussex-born comedian coming to the fore on *Saturday Live* with his characterization of Stavros, the Greek kebab-shop owner. On the back of Stavros he created the brash plasterer, Loadsamoney, and his antithesis, hard-up Geordie Buggerallmoney. Enfield then gained his own BBC series, *Harry Enfield's Television Programme*, in which a host of new characters were introduced (some in collaboration with Paul Whitehouse and Kathy Burke), most notably the sadistic Old Gits, Tim Nice-but-Dim, Wayne and Waynetta Slob, the constantly surprised Double-Take Brothers, mechanics Lee and Lance, and Miles Cholmondely-Warner, whose cracked and jumpy bits of old documentary inspired Enfield's commercials for Mercury. There were also The Scousers (a send-up of BROOKSIDE), sensational DJs Mike Smash and Dave Nice from Radio Fab FM and the constantly interfering father-in-law ('Only me . . . You don't want to do that'). Once bored with his creations, Enfield has tended to drop them and introduce new characters. For instance, his later series, *Harry Enfield and Chums*, gave birth to, among others, the Lovely Wobbly Randy Old Ladies, the Self-Righteous Brothers, a war-contrite young German tourist, a pair of gay Dutch policemen, Harry the naughty toddler and Kevin the sulky teenager (who eventually gained his own special, *Kevin's Guide to Being a Teenager*, in 1999). Enfield also provided voices for SPITTING IMAGE (Jimmy Greaves, Douglas Hurd, etc.) and starred as Little Jim Morley in *Gone to the Dogs* and as Dermot in the first series of MEN BEHAVING BADLY. In 1989 he presented the old thespian send-up, *Norbert Smith – A Life*, and in 1993 hosted the mostly serious *Harry Enfield's Guide to Opera*. In yet further contrast, in the 1980s Enfield was seen in the fashion show, *Frocks on the Box*, played Revd Tony Blair in *Sermon from St Albion's* and *Norman Ormal: a Very Political Turtle* in 1998, and in 2000 presented a documentary on teenagers, *Harry Enfield's Real Kevins*, before moving to Sky One for a new series entitled *Harry Enfield's Brand Spanking New Show*.

ENG
(Electronic News Gathering)

Traditionally, news departments have relied on filmed reports from correspondents, which are slow to process and require a large crew to produce. With the development of videotape technology, including smaller, lighter cameras and camcorders, and the use of microwave or satellite links back to the studio (collectively known as ENG), news coverage has become more immediate and much more flexible.

ENGLISH, ARTHUR
(1919–95)

Veteran British entertainer who arrived in television after years on the music-hall boards, playing wide-boy characters. In the early 1970s he took the part of Slugger in the horsey series, FOLLYFOOT, which led to roles in series like *Copper's End* and CROWN COURT. He played Ted Cropper in *How's Your Father*, Bodkin in *The Ghosts of Motley Hall*, caretaker Mr Harman in ARE YOU BEING SERVED? and became Arthur, one of Alf Garnett's new sparring partners, in IN SICKNESS AND IN HEALTH. English was also seen in the drama, *Funny Man*, and played Sid in Channel 4's 1987 retirement home sitcom, *Never Say Die*.

EPILOGUE

A tailpiece to the day's viewing (now seldom seen, thanks to 24-hour TV), in which usually some religious or moral reflection was delivered by a guest speaker.

EQUALIZER, THE
US (Universal) Detective Drama. ITV 1986–90

Robert McCall .... **Edward Woodward**
Control .... **Robert Lansing**
Lt. Burnett .... **Steven Williams**
Lt. Isadore Smalls .... **Ron O'Neal**
Scott McCall .... **William Zabka**
Mickey Kostmayer .... **Keith Szarabajka**
Sgt Alice Shepherd .... **Maureen Anderman**
Pete O'Phelan .... **Chad Redding**
Harley Gage .... **Richard Jordan**

Creators: **Michael Sloan, Richard Lindheim**
Executive Producers: **Michael Sloan, James McAdams**
Producer: **Alan Barnette**

A former secret agent hires himself out to those seeking justice.

Robert McCall had retired from the world of US Government espionage in which he had been given the name, 'The Equalizer'. Now, somewhat ashamed of his duplicitous past, he sought to make amends with his son and ex-wife for the neglect he had shown them over the years, and also hired himself out, via newspaper classified ads, to clients in big trouble. The ads read: 'Got a problem? Odds against you? Call The Equalizer. Tel: 212 555 4200.' Weeding out the callers on his answerphone, he then set out to adjust the balance of good and evil on their behalf, acting as a private eye, or simply as a bodyguard, but often bringing his gun into play. His fee was small, if he ever charged one.

Despite his tough, streetwise exterior, McCall was really compassionate, intelligent and articulate. Always immaculately turned-out, he lived in a stylish Manhattan apartment, loved music and drove a swish black Jaguar. In his work he was supported by Mickey Kostmayer (who did much of the running around) and from time to time he linked up with Control, his former agency boss. His son, Scott, a music student, also appeared, as did Pete O'Phelan, an old friend from his spying days, who ran the bistro where McCall went to relax. Stewart Copeland of The Police rock group composed the theme music.

ER

US (Constant c/Amblin/Warner Brothers) Medical Drama.
Channel 4 1995–

Dr Mark Greene	Anthony Edwards
Dr Douglas Ross	George Clooney
Dr Susan Lewis	Sherry Stringfield
Dr Peter Benton	Eriq La Salle
Dr John Carter	Noah Wyle
Dr David Morgenstern	William H. Macy
Dr William Swift	Michael Ironside
Head Nurse Carol Hathaway	Julianna Margulies
Jerry	Abraham Benrubi
Jennifer Greene	Christine Harnos
Dr John Taglieri	Rick Rossovich
Dr Angela Hicks	C. C. H. Pounder
Dr Deb/Jing-Mei Chen	Ming-Na
Jeanie Boulet	Gloria Reuben
Harper Tracy	Christine Elise
Dr Kerry Weaver	Laura Innes
Chloe Lewis	Kathleen Wilhoite
Shepherd	Ron Eldard
Dr Carl Vucelich	Ron Rifkin
Dr Abby Keaton	Glenne Headly
Dr Donald Anspaugh	John Aylward
Carla Harris	Lisa Nicole Carson
Al Grabarsky	Mark Genovese
Nurse Lydia Wright	Ellen Crawford
Nurse Rhonda Sterling	Jenny O'Hara
Dennis Gant	Omar Epps
Dr Anna Del Amico	Maria Bello
Dr Elizabeth Corday	Alex Kingston
Lucy Knight	Kellie Martin
Dr Maggie Doyle	Jorja Fox
Dr Robert Romano	Paul McCrane
Dr Luka Kovac	Goran Visnjic
Dr Gabriel Lawrence	Alan Alda
Nurse Haleh Adams	Yvette Freeman
Dr Cleo Finch	Michael Michele
Abby Lockhart	Maura Tierney
Dr Dave Malucci	Erik Palladino

Creator: **Michael Crichton**
Executive Producers: **John Wells, Michael Crichton,
Lydia Woodward**

*Breathless action in the casualty unit of a Chicago
hospital.*

'ER' stands for Emergency Room, and this ground-
breaking medical drama was set in that vital section of
Chicago's Cook County General Hospital. What was so
innovative was the sheer relentlessness of the action,
with new characters arriving every minute and countless
storylines woven into each episode, defying the received
wisdom that American audiences would not be able to
follow such complexity. (The series went on to top the
annual ratings, with an audience reach of some 33 million.) Unlike earlier, heart-warming doctors-and-nurses
series, *ER* was not afraid to show the staff failing in their
efforts to preserve life, hand-held cameras racing around
after them as they exhaustingly dashed from patient to
patient. Complex technical language was not forsaken,
and there was no shortage of spurting blood and organ
close-ups.

The series' heart-throb was womanizing paediatrician
Doug Ross, sometimes a victim of his own attitude but
at other times a genuine hero. His romantic past with
Nurse Carol Hathaway was a running theme. Attracting
equal attention was level-headed chief resident Dr Mark
Greene, with other key figures over the years including
Greene's lawyer wife, Jennifer, and his potential lover,
Dr Susan Lewis; shaky intern John Carter; fearsome black
surgeon Peter Benton; English doctor Elizabeth Corday;
and an older version of M*A*S*H's Hawkeye Pierce in Dr
Gabriel Lawrence (Alan Alda returning to the operating
theatre).

The series was created by *Jurassic Park* writer Michael
Crichton, himself a junior doctor in his youth. One
episode was 'guest' directed by Quentin Tarantino;
another episode was transmitted live – another brave
departure from the US television norm.

ESMONDE, JOHN

British comedy writer, usually in collaboration with Bob
Larbey. Their joint successes have included *Room at the
Bottom*, PLEASE SIR!, *The Fenn Street Gang*, *Bowler*, GET
SOME IN!, THE GOOD LIFE, *Don't Rock the Boat*, *Feet First*,
The Other One, *Double First*, *Just Liz*, *Now and Then*, EVER
DECREASING CIRCLES, BRUSH STROKES, MULBERRY, *Hope
It Rains* and *Down to Earth*.

ESPIONAGE

UK (ATV/Plautus) Spy Drama Anthology. ITV 1963–4

Executive Producer: **Herbert Hirschman**
Producer: **George Justin**

Collection of spy dramas based on true stories.

This series, filmed throughout Europe, treated the subject of espionage much more sombrely than its spoofy
successors like THE MAN FROM UNCLE, especially as it
gleaned its facts from real events (some newsreel footage
was used in production). The gloom was lightened somewhat by the appearances of talented guest-stars like Patrick Troughton, Jim Backus and Bernard Lee ('M' from
the James Bond films).

EUROSPORT

Trans-continental sports channel operated by the
French network, TF1. It broadcasts, unscrambled and
free of charge, from the Astra satellites, offering a variety
of sports from soccer to basketball. Viewers can select
the language of the commentaries. Its digital descendant
in the UK is British Eurosport.

EUROTRASH

UK (Rapido) Magazine Channel 4 1993–

Presenters: **Antoine de Caunes, John-Paul Gaultier, Lolo Ferrari**

Producers: **Peter Stuart, John Godfrey, Ian Dunkley**

Irreverent look at eccentric activity across the English Channel.

The title says it all: this late-night selection of lewd and off-beat continental goings-on was not to everyone's taste. French hosts Antoine de Caunes and (initially) fashion designer John-Paul Gaultier smirked their way through a series of smutty reports, overlaid with a cheeky commentary, that investigated the most bizarre pastimes enjoyed by our European neighbours. The first programme featured a Belgian rat restaurant and an amateur pornographer, which nicely set the tone for the weeks to come. Later features involved a nude cleaning service, an Italian ugly club and rabbit showjumping. A big, brash, cartoon-like set underlined the ridiculousness of the whole affair, complemented by the equally cartoon-like, mammoth figure of later co-presenter Lolo Ferrari (who tragically died in 2000). Other regulars included toy giraffes Pee Pee & Po Po, Mr Penguin, the Romeo Cleaners, Eddy Wally and Eva and Adele. Katie Boyle joined de Caunes in 1998 for a one-off review of Eurovision's most memorable moments entitled *A Song for Eurotrash*.

EUROVISION

The international network of cable and satellite links established by the European Broadcasting Union in 1954 to facilitate the transfer of programmes, news items and sports events between countries and to allow simultaneous broadcasts across the Continent.

EUROVISION SONG CONTEST

Europe (including BBC) Entertainment. BBC 1 1956–

Annual Europe-wide song competition.

Much ridiculed but nevertheless a big crowd-puller (if only for the voting at the end), the *Eurovision Song Contest* has been a fixture of the television calendar for over 40 years. Originally devised as a showcase for the new Eurovision network, which linked broadcasters across the Continent, its popularity has now increased to the point where over 40 nations wish to compete, and countries such as Israel, Turkey and members of the former Eastern Bloc have joined the fray. To accommodate allcomers, the lowest-scoring countries now have to sit out the following year's event.

The format involves each country presenting an original song in turn and then voting (via the Eurovision link) on each other's contributions to find the winner, allocating marks from 12 points down to one. The winning country stages the next year's *Contest*. Scores are conveyed multilingually by the show's compere (Katie Boyle is one of the best-remembered hostesses), with individual, voice-only commentaries provided for each country (the drily sarcastic Terry Wogan has become associated with this role for the UK, although the likes of David Jacobs, Rolf Harris, David Gell, Dave Lee Travis, Pete Murray, Michael Aspel and John Dunn have also performed this task). Technical hiccups, unavoidable in a live, pan-European link-up of this magnitude, have become part of the attraction for viewers.

The United Kingdom did not participate in the inaugural *Contest* in 1956, but soon initiated its own monthly competition, known as the *Festival of Popular Songs*. The 1956 *Festival* winner, 'All', sung by Patricia Bredin, went on to represent the UK (and finish seventh) in the 1957 *Contest*. In recent years, the British entry has been selected through an annual *Song for Europe* showdown.

Ireland has become the king of the contest, with four wins in the 1990s and seven in all; the UK has won the competition on five occasions, and the *Contest*'s whipping boys traditionally have been the Norwegians, thanks to their glorious nil scores. *Eurovision* music has been roundly condemned for not moving with the times and for rewarding countries who regurgitate the established 'Boom-bang-a-puppet-in-a-box' catchy-song formula. Only on rare occasions has the real music world peeped through – Abba's 1974 victory with 'Waterloo', for instance, and Love City Groove's rap contribution for the UK in 1995.

EVANS, BARRY
(1945–97)

Fresh-faced British actor whose major roles were in situation comedy. He starred in DOCTOR IN THE HOUSE and *Doctor at Large* as naïve young Michael Upton, although he didn't stay with the series' sequels, relinquishing the lead to Robin Nedwell. He also played Jeremy Brown, the hapless night-school teacher in the controversial MIND YOUR LANGUAGE, and was seen in the Emery comedy-thriller, *Legacy of Murder*, among other programmes.

EVANS, CHRIS
(1966–)

Bespectacled, ginger, controversial DJ, media entrepreneur and presenter of light entertainment shows such as DON'T FORGET YOUR TOOTHBRUSH and TFI FRIDAY, and also the golf travelogue, *Tee Time*. Evans began in radio with Piccadilly in Manchester, before moving to GLR in London and then Radio 1. His television work commenced with the satellite channel, The Power Station, before he switched to Channel 4's THE BIG BREAKFAST, where he quickly established himself as one of TV's most adaptable live-programme presenters. He now presents Virgin Radio's breakfast show (having bought and sold the company) and was the founder of the Ginger Media Group.

EUROVISION SONG CONTEST WINNERS

Year	Winning Country	Winning Song	Winning Singer	UK Song	UK Singer
1956	Switzerland	*Refrain*	Lys Assia	—	—
1957	Netherlands	*Net Als Toen*	Corry Brokken	*All* (7th)	Patricia Bredin
1958	France	*Dors, Mon Amour*	André Claveau	—	—
1959	Netherlands	*Een Beetje*	Teddy Scholten	*Sing Little Birdie* (2nd)	Teddy Johnson and Pearl Carr
1960	France	*Tom Pillibi*	Jacqueline Boyer	*Looking High High High* (2nd)	Bryan Johnson
1961	Luxembourg	*Nous, Les Amoureux*	Jean-Claude Pascal	*Are You Sure?* (2nd)	The Allisons
1962	France	*Un Premier Amour*	Isabelle Aubret	*Ring A Ding Girl* (4th)	Ronnie Carroll
1963	Denmark	*Dansevise*	Grethe and Jørgen Ingmann	*Say Wonderful Things* (4th)	Ronnie Carroll
1964	Italy	*Non Ho l'Età Per Amarti*	Gigliola Cinquetti	*I Love The Little Things* (2nd)	Matt Monro
1965	Luxembourg	*Poupée de Cire, Poupée de Son*	France Gall	*I Belong* (2nd)	Kathy Kirby
1966	Austria	*Merci Chérie*	Udo Jurgens	*A Man Without Love* (9th)	Kenneth McKellar
1967	UK	*Puppet On A String*	Sandie Shaw	*Puppet On A String* (1st)	Sandie Shaw
1968	Spain	*La, la, la*	Massiel	*Congratulations* (2nd)	Cliff Richard
1969	4 countries tied:				
	Spain	*Viva Cantando*	Salome	*Boom Bang-A-Bang* (joint 1st)	Lulu
	UK	*Boom Bang-A-Bang*	Lulu		
	Holland	*De Troubadour*	Lennie Kuhr		
	France	*Un Jour, Un Enfant*	Frida Boccara		
1970	Ireland	*All Kinds Of Everything*	Dana	*Knock Knock Who's There* (2nd)	Mary Hopkin
1971	Monaco	*Un Banc, Un Arbre, Une Rue*	Severine	*Jack In The Box* (4th)	Clodagh Rodgers
1972	Luxembourg	*Après Toi (Come What May)*	Vicky Leandros	*Beg, Steal Or Borrow* (2nd)	New Seekers
1973	Luxembourg	*Tu Te Reconnaîtras (Wonderful Dream)*	Anne-Marie David	*Power To All Our Friends* (3rd)	Cliff Richard
1974	Sweden	*Waterloo*	Abba	*Long Live Love* (joint 4th)	Olivia Newton-John
1975	Netherlands	*Ding-Dinge-Dong (Ding-a-Dong)*	Teach-In	*Let Me Be The One* (2nd)	The Shadows
1976	UK	*Save Your Kisses For Me*	Brotherhood of Man	*Save Your Kisses For Me* (1st)	Brotherhood of Man
1977	France	*L'Oiseau Et L'Enfant*	Marie Myriam	*Rock Bottom* (2nd)	Lynsey De Paul and Mike Moran
1978	Israel	*A Ba Ni Bi*	Izhar Cohen and Alphabeta	*Bad Old Days* (11th)	Co-Co
1979	Israel	*Hallelujah*	Milk and Honey	*Mary Ann* (7th)	Black Lace
1980	Ireland	*What's Another Year?*	Johnny Logan	*Love Enough For Two* (3rd)	Prima Donna
1981	UK	*Making Your Mind Up*	Bucks Fizz	*Making Your Mind Up* (1st)	Bucks Fizz
1982	West Germany	*Ein bisschen Frieden (A Little Peace)*	Nicole	*One Step Further* (7th)	Bardo
1983	Luxembourg	*Si La Vie Est Cadeau*	Corinne Hermès	*I'm Never Giving Up* (6th)	Sweet Dreams
1984	Sweden	*Diggy Loo-Diggy Ley*	The Herreys	*Love Games* (7th)	Belle and the Devotions
1985	Norway	*La det Swinge (Let It Swing)*	The Bobbysocks	*Love Is . . .* (4th)	Vikki
1986	Belgium	*J'aime La Vie*	Sandra Kim	*Runner In The Night* (7th)	Ryder
1987	Ireland	*Hold Me Now*	Johnny Logan	*Only The Light* (13th)	Rikki
1988	Switzerland	*Ne Partez Pas Sans Moi*	Céline Dion	*Go* (2nd)	Scott Fitzgerald
1989	Yugoslavia	*Rock Me*	Riva	*Why Do I Always Get It Wrong?* (2nd)	Live Report
1990	Italy	*Insieme: 1992 (Altogether: 1992)*	Toto Cotugno	*Give A Little Love Back To The World* (6th)	Emma
1991	Sweden	*Fangad av en Stormvind (Captured By A Love Storm)*	Carola	*A Message To Your Heart* (10th)	Samantha Janus
1992	Ireland	*Why Me?*	Linda Martin	*One Step Out Of Time* (2nd)	Michael Ball
1993	Ireland	*In Your Eyes*	Niamh Kavanagh	*Better The Devil You Know* (2nd)	Sonia
1994	Ireland	*Rock 'n' Roll Kids*	Paul Harrington and Charlie McGettigan	*We Will Be Free (Lonely Symphony)* (10th)	Frances Ruffelle
1995	Norway	*Nocturne*	Secret Garden	*Love City Groove* (joint 10th)	Love City Groove
1996	Ireland	*The Voice*	Eimear Quinn	*Ooh Aah . . . Just a Little Bit* (8th)	Gina G
1997	UK	*Love Shine A Light*	Katrina and the Waves	*Love Shine A Light* (1st)	Katrina and the Waves
1998	Israel	*Diva*	Dana International	*Where Are You?* (2nd)	Imaani
1999	Sweden	*Take Me To Your Heaven*	Charlotte Nilsson	*Say It Again* (equal 12th)	Precious
2000	Denmark	*Fly On The Wings Of Love*	Olsen Brothers	*Don't Play That Song Again* (16th)	Nicki French
2001	Estonia	*Everybody*	Tanel Padar and Dave Benton	*No Dream Impossible* (15th)	Lindsey Dracass

EVANS, LINDA
(1942–)

Blonde American actress who endured a 12-year wait between starring roles. Her TV career began with bit parts in popular US series like *Bachelor Father* and MY FAVORITE MARTIAN, but her major break arrived with THE BIG VALLEY, in which she was cast as Audra Barkley. *The Big Valley* ended in 1969, and the 1970s proved more difficult for Evans. She appeared for a while in a spy series called *Hunter* and made a few TV movies, but it wasn't until DYNASTY arrived in 1981 that she regained a high profile, starring as Krystle Jennings/Carrington. Ironically, she had been earmarked for an undefined role which turned out to be that of Pam in DALLAS, but the concept took too long to reach the studio and Evans was released from her contract. Her first husband was film director John Derek.

EVE, TREVOR
(1951–)

Birmingham-born actor, largely seen in the theatre but coming to television prominence in the role of the radio detective, SHOESTRING. Eve's subsequent TV work (often seeing him cast as unpleasant, untrustworthy characters) has included *Jamaica Inn, Lace, The Corsican Brothers, Shadow Chasers* (Professor Jonathan MacKensie), the steamy drama, A SENSE OF GUILT (irresponsible writer Felix Cramer), *Parnell and the Englishwoman* (Charles Stewart Parnell), *A Doll's House, Screen One*'s *Murder in Mind* (policeman Malcolm Iverson), *Screen Two*'s *Black Easter* (detective Alex Fischer), *The Politician's Wife* (MP Duncan Matlock), *Heat of the Sun* (Supt. Albert Tynan), *An Evil Streak* (scheming uncle Alex Kyle) and *Waking the Dead* (DCI Peter Boyd). He is married to actress Sharon Maughan.

EVER DECREASING CIRCLES
UK (BBC) Situation Comedy. BBC 1 1984–9

Martin Bryce	**Richard Briers**
Ann Bryce	**Penelope Wilton**
Paul Ryman	**Peter Egan**
Howard Hughes	**Stanley Lebor**
Hilda Hughes	**Geraldine Newman**

Creators/Writers: **John Esmonde, Bob Larbey**
Producers: **Sydney Lotterby, Harold Snoad**

A pedantic neighbourhood do-gooder is continually upstaged by the smoothie next door.

Martin Bryce, employee of Mole Valley Valves, former REME regiment member, and driver of a light blue Dormobile, liked things done properly. And because no one else could be trusted, he liked to do them himself. By immersing himself in the well-being of his local suburban community, endlessly chairing meetings, organizing functions, tackling bureaucracy and gener-

ally leading from the front, Martin would have severely tested the patience of Job, let alone his long-suffering wife, Ann. For Martin, bedtime meant only one thing – drawing up rotas. Next door to the Bryces (who lived at 'Brooksmead', in The Close) moved Paul Ryman, the suave proprietor of a beauty salon, for whom things seemed to fall very nicely. Without the slightest effort, he always managed unintentionally to steal the limelight and rob Martin of all the credit. From the way he flirted with Ann, it was clear that he could also have stolen Martin's wife, but Paul was too nice for that, and Ann too loyal. Friends to all were their childlike neighbours, Howard and Hilda Hughes, who usually dressed in matching sweaters.

EVERETT, KENNY
(Maurice Cole; 1944–95)

Zany, controversial DJ turned TV comedian. After working for the pirate radio station, Radio London, and for Radio Luxembourg, Kenny Everett became one of Radio 1's first presenters and quickly moved into television. In 1968 he was one of the presenters of NICE TIME (with Germaine Greer and Jonathan Routh), was given his own series, *The Kenny Everett Explosion*, in 1970 and subsequently became a familiar face on panel games, also announcing the prizes on CELEBRITY SQUARES. He appeared in the satire show, *Up Sunday*, and then, in 1978, along came the comedy series, *The Kenny Everett Video Show*, which he hosted in front of a bank of TV monitors. Sketches involved his own characterizations like Cupid Stunt (the buxom movie star who did everything 'in the best possible taste'), Sid Snot (the greaser), hairdresser Marcel Wave and the space animation, Captain Kremmen. Arlene Phillips's Hot Gossip writhed around between sketches, and Everett was also supported by Miss Whiplash, Cleo Rocos. In 1982, after numerous guest appearances on BLANKETY BLANK, Everett returned to the BBC, where his show was renamed *The Kenny Everett Television Show* but his larger-than-life characters remained to the fore (including some new faces like punk Gizzard Puke). Among his other series were *Making Whoopee, Ev* and the game shows, *Gibberish* and *Brainstorm*. Everett died of an AIDS-related illness in 1995.

EVERY SECOND COUNTS
UK (BBC) Quiz. BBC 1 1986–9

Presenter: **Paul Daniels**

Producers: **David Taylor, Stanley Appel**

Light-hearted quiz for married couples.

Hosted by Paul Daniels, *Every Second Counts* invited three married couples to answer questions which earned them vital seconds on a clock. The highest-scoring couple then progressed to the final, in which they used the seconds they had accrued to answer yet more questions and win progressively better prizes. Each set of questions related to a subject and, in the 'true or false' fashion, contestants had to state whether Daniels was reading a correct answer. Red herrings and contrived gags abounded. For the final stage, the couple needed to extinguish a series of triangular lamps with quick and accurate responses to tricky little posers.

EXECUTIVE PRODUCER

The chief overseer of a programme or a series of programmes, usually responsible for the control of budgets. Sometimes the executive producer is the head of the department in a television company. In other cases, it is the programme creator or the star performer, who have vested interests in the direction which the series takes.

EXPERT, THE

UK (BBC) Detective Drama. BBC 2 1968–71; 1976

Prof. John Hardy	**Marius Goring**
Dr Jo Hardy	**Ann Morrish**
DCI Fleming	**Victor Winding**
Jane Carter	**Sally Nesbitt**
DS Ashe	**Michael Farnsworth**
Sandra Hughes	**Valerie Murray**
Susan Bartlett	**Virginia Stride**

Creators: **Gerard Glaister, N. J. Crisp**
Producers: **Gerard Glaister, Andrew Osborn**

A pathologist digs deep to help police with their investigations.

John Hardy was a Warwickshire pathologist who, with the help of his somewhat younger wife, Jo (a GP), and his receptionist, Jane Carter, turned up the vital evidence needed by police to secure tricky convictions. Detective Chief Inspector Fleming was his police ally, and the two men enjoyed a strong mutual respect and a close friendship.

Meticulously researched by actor Marius Goring (formerly TV's SCARLET PIMPERNEL), the character was the invention of producer Gerard Glaister, whose own uncle had been Professor of Forensic Science at Glasgow University. *The Expert* ran from 1968 to 1971, before returning for one more run in 1976. With its modest, thoughtful tone, it contrasted sharply with TV's other major pathologist series, QUINCY.

f

F TROOP
US (Warner Brothers) Situation Comedy. ITV 1968–74

Capt. Wilton Parmenter .... **Ken Berry**
Sgt Morgan O'Rourke .... **Forrest Tucker**
Cpl. Randolph Agarn .... **Larry Storch**
Wrangler Jane .... **Melody Patterson**
Chief Wild Eagle .... **Frank DeKova**
Crazy Cat .... **Don Diamond**
Bugler Hannibal Dobbs .... **James Hampton**
Trooper Duffy .... **Bob Steele**
Trooper Vanderbilt .... **Joe Brooks**
Trooper Hoffenmuller .... **John Mitchum**
Roaring Chicken .... **Edward Everett Horton**

Creator: **Richard M. Bluel**
Producers: **Richard M. Bluel, Hy Averback**

The farcical exploits of a cavalry troop on the Indian front line.

Fort Courage, a cavalry outpost somewhere in deepest Kansas, was commanded by Captain Wilton Parmenter. Well, that's what he thought. Parmenter had been a laundry orderly in the Union army at the end of the Civil War, but one day a simple sneeze changed his life. The loud snort apparently sounded just like 'Charge!' to his own side's cavalry, which sped into action just in time to thwart an attack by the Confederacy. Parmenter was commended for his initiative, promoted to captain and given the posting at Fort Courage. Unfortunately, he was not the real boss of the outfit. That honour was usurped by his sergeant, Morgan O'Rourke, a kind of Wild West Bilko figure who ran the show with his side-kick, Corporal Agarn, but always gave the credit to his nominal camp commander. O'Rourke had even agreed a secret pact with the supposedly hostile Hekawi Indians, headed by the canny Chief Wild Eagle. Between them, O'Rourke and Wild Eagle ran an Indian souvenir racket and protected their business interests by staging fake attacks on the fort whenever the top brass came for an inspection.

O'Rourke's work-shy soldiers were as incompetent as the fort's captain. The bugler, Dobbs, always played a bum note, one private, Hoffenmuller, was a German who spoke no English and Vanderbilt, the look-out, was officially blind. Little wonder the Indians couldn't be bothered to fight them. Also on the scene was Wrangler Jane, a sharp-shooting cowgirl who ran the post office and chased after the boyish Parmenter.

FABIAN OF THE YARD
UK (BBC) Police Drama. BBC 1954–6

DI Robert Fabian .... **Bruce Seton**

Producers: **John Larkin, Anthony Beauchamp**

The cases of a po-faced London detective.

Screaming around the streets of the capital in a heavy, black Humber Hawk squad car, pipe-smoking Detective

Inspector Robert Fabian was one of TV's first police heroes. Based on the life of a real Detective Inspector Fabian (a Flying Squad officer who, on retirement from the force, went on to be 'Guardian of the Questions' on ITV's big-money quiz show, *The 64,000 Question*), this was strait-laced, by-the-book, 1950s detective work, dramatizing cases from the files of Scotland Yard.

Fabian's success was largely down to his innovative detection methods, as he dragged the police force into the 1950s with all its forensic advances. The series, made on film and heavily laden with plummy accents, was screened in the USA as *Fabian of Scotland Yard* or *Patrol Car*, and included brief tourism guides for American viewers, explaining where and what were Hampton Court or Somerset House, for instance, if the plot required Fabian to visit them. The real Inspector Fabian popped up at the end of each programme to deliver some personal homilies on the events taking place. Some episodes were re-edited into feature films for cinema release. These went out as *Fabian of the Yard* (1954) and *Handcuffs, London* (1955).

FACE THE MUSIC
UK (BBC) Quiz. BBC 2/BBC 1 1967–84

Presenter: **Joseph Cooper**

Producer: **Walter Todds**

High-brow music quiz.

Hosted at the piano by the jovial Joseph Cooper, *Face the Music* was the BBC's long-running music quiz for celebrities, focusing mainly on the classical world but also drawing on other musical styles. Regular panel members who attempted to identify snippets of tunes included Joyce Grenfell, Richard Baker and Robin Ray.

FACE TO FACE
UK (BBC) Interview Programme. BBC 1959–62; BBC 2 1995–7

Presenters: **John Freeman, Jeremy Isaacs**

Producers/Editors: **Hugh Burnett, Michael Poole, David Herman, Julian Birkett**

Series of incisive interviews with famous people, probing their personalities and lifestyles.

Face to Face broke new ground in TV interviewing. Although celebrities had faced the camera before, the public had never seen them so exposed by what was essentially a cross-examination. The interrogator was PANORAMA presenter John Freeman. As he probed he never wavered from the courteous and polite, but his assault on the interviewee was relentless and seldom failed to open up the real person behind the famous front. Strangely, the victims seemed quite happy to bare their souls.

Each programme began with caricature sketches of the week's guest by Felix Topolski, which faded into the real image to the lilting strains of a Berlioz overture. The set was stark – simply two uncomfortable chairs a yard apart – and the whole atmosphere one of interrogation. Seldom was Freeman himself seen, and then usually only from the back of his head. The focus was always on the interviewee as he or she was gradually dissected. Over 30 guests in all appeared, although only a couple of them were women. Guests included Martin Luther King, Adam Faith, Stirling Moss, Bertrand Russell, Dame Edith Sitwell, King Hussein of Jordan, Tony Hancock, John Osborne, Evelyn Waugh, Carl Jung and Henry Moore, but by far the most controversial appearance was by Gilbert Harding. The WHAT'S MY LINE? panellist was notorious for being gruff, rude and intolerant, but Freeman exposed a gentler, more humane side. During the interview, Harding was even reduced to tears when questioned about his mother who, unknown to Freeman, had just died.

The highlights of the series were repeated in 1988 with introductions by Joan Bakewell and, in a special episode, Freeman himself was quizzed by Dr Anthony Clare. In the interim years he had been editor of the *New Statesman*, Ambassador to the USA and head of London Weekend Television. *Face to Face* resurfaced in the 1990s as an occasional segment of *The Late Show*, with Jeremy Isaacs as interrogator, and then as a series in its own right. Among Isaacs's interviewees were Arthur Miller, Lauren Bacall, Ken Dodd, Anthony Hopkins, Norman Mailer, Germaine Greer, Stephen Sondheim, Harold Pinter, Kate Adie, Roddy Doyle, Diana Rigg, Bob Monkhouse and, shortly before his death, Paul Eddington.

FAIRBANKS, DOUGLAS, JR
KBE (Hon.) (1909–2000)

American actor, the son of silent film star Douglas Fairbanks. After a career in films and distinguished service during World War II, he turned to television in the 1950s, hosting and sometimes acting in an anthology series of half-hour dramas entitled DOUGLAS FAIRBANKS PRESENTS, which was made in the UK (where he lived for a number of years) but seen around the world. The stories generally had the theme of people caught up in unusual circumstances. His later TV performances included a guest spot on THE LOVE BOAT. Fairbanks's first wife was Joan Crawford.

FAIRLY SECRET ARMY
UK (Video Arts) Situation Comedy. Channel 4 1984–6

Major Harry Kitchener Wellington Truscott	**Geoffrey Palmer**
Nancy	**Diane Fletcher**
Beamish	**Jeremy Child**
Sgt Major Throttle	**Michael Robbins**
Doris Entwistle	**Liz Fraser**
Stubby Collins	**Ray Winstone**
Crazy Colin Carstairs	**James Cosmo**
Jill	**Diana Weston**
Peg Leg Pogson	**Paul Chapman**
Ron Boat	**Richard Ridings**

Writer: **David Nobbs**
Producer: **Peter Robinson**

*An inept retired military man sets up his own
right-wing army to keep moral standards high.*

With the influence of left-wing sympathizers, anarchists
and feminists increasing in Britain – or so he perceived
– Major Harry Kitchener Wellington Truscott, a quite
unemployable old army bigot, once of the Queen's Own
West Mercian Lowlanders, decided to combat growing
subversion by forming a private army of sympathizers.
Rallying to his cause was a motley crew of half-wits,
National Front supporters, ex-military colleagues and
people with nothing better to do. To take on the loony
left, Truscott assembled the raving right and, as he tried
to whip them into shape, sounded not unlike a latter-day
Alf Garnett.

FAITH, ADAM
(Terence Nelhams; 1940–)

Cockney teen singer of the late 1950s/early 1960s, much
seen on pop shows of the day, including OH BOY! and
Boy Meets Girls. He later branched out into acting,
appearing in the anthology series, *Seven Deadly Sins*, in
1966 and earning his own series, BUDGIE, in 1971. After a
couple of years as Soho's perennial loser, Budgie Bird,
Faith didn't return to the small screen, apart from the
odd guest appearance, until LOVE HURTS arrived in 1991.
As Frank Carver opposite Zoe Wanamaker's Tessa Piggott, he found himself with yet another hit on his hands.

FALCON CREST
US (Lorimar) Drama. ITV 1982–91

Angela Channing/Stavros	**Jane Wyman**
Chase Gioberti	**Robert Foxworth**
Maggie Gioberti/Channing	**Susan Sullivan**
Lance Cumson	**Lorenzo Lamas**
Tony Cumson	**John Saxon**
Cole Gioberti	**William R. Moses**
Victoria Gioberti/Hogan/Stavros	**Jamie Rose**
	Dana Sparks
Julia Cumson	**Abby Dalton**
Gus Nunouz	**Nick Ramus**
Phillip Erikson	**Mel Ferrer**
Emma Channing	**Margaret Ladd**
Douglas Channing	**Stephen Elliott**
Sheriff Turk Tobias	**Robert Sampson**
Mario Nunouz	**Mario Marcelino**
Chau-Li	**Chau-Li Chi**
Melissa Agretti/Cumson/Gioberti	**Ana Alicia**
Carlo Agretti	**Carlos Romero**
Richard Channing	**David Selby**
John Costello	**Roger Perry**
Diana Hunter	**Shannon Tweed**
Jacqueline Perrault	**Lana Turner**
Nick Hogan	**Roy Thinnes**
Darryl Clayton	**Bradford Dillman**
Lori Stevens	**Maggie Cooper**
Sheriff Robbins	**Joe Lambie**
Linda Caproni/Gioberti	**Mary Kate McGeehan**
Vince Caproni	**Harry Basch**
Dr Michael Ranson	**Cliff Robertson**
Pamela Lynch	**Sarah Douglas**
Terry Hartford/Ranson	**Laura Johnson**
Joseph Gioberti	**Jason Goldberg**
Norton Crane	**Jordan Charney**
Francesca Gioberti	**Gina Lollobrigida**
Greg Reardon	**Simon MacCorkindale**
Lorraine Prescott	**Kate Vernon**
Joel McCarthy	**Parker Stevenson**
Gustav Riebmann	**J. Paul Freeman**
Father Bob	**Bob Curtis**
Jordan Roberts	**Morgan Fairchild**
Father Christopher	**Ken Olin**
Cassandra Wilder	**Anne Archer**
Robin Agretti	**Barbara Howard**
Apollonia	**Patricia 'Apollonia' Kotero**
Peter Stavros	**Cesar Romero**
Eric Stavros	**John Callahan**
Erin Jones	**Jill Jacobson**
Kit Marlowe	**Kim Novak**
Dan Fixx	**Brett Cullen**
Meredith Braxton	**Jane Badler**
Dina Wells	**Robin Greer**
Guy Stafford	**Jeff Kober**
Mrs Whitaker	**Laurel Schaefer**
Carly Fixx	**Mariska Hartigay**
Garth	**Carl Heid**
Frank Agretti	**Rod Taylor**
Pilar Ortega/Cumson	**Kristian Alfonso**
Nick Agretti	**David Beecroft**
Ben Agretti	**Brandon Douglas**
Tommy Ortega	**Dan Ferro**
Cesar Ortega	**Castulo Guerra**
Gabriel Ortega	**Danny Nucci**
R. D. Young	**Allan Royal**
Michael Channing	**Robert Gorman**
Michael Sharpe	**Gregory Harrison**
Julius Karnow	**Norman Parker**
Ed Meyers	**Philip Baker Hall**
Brian	**Thom Adcox**
Lauren Daniels	**Wendy Phillips**
Walker Daniels	**Robert Ginty**
Jace Sampson	**Stuart Pankin**
Genele Ericson	**Andrea Thompson**

Creator: **Earl Hamner**
Executive Producers: **Earl Hamner, Michael Filerman**

*Family and business rivalries in Californian wine
country.*

Hot on the heels of DALLAS and DYNASTY came *Falcon
Crest*, an American soap born of the same stock as its
predecessors. The setting this time was California's Napa
Valley ('Tuscany Valley' in the series), the industry providing the opulence was wine production and the central character was ruthless Angela Channing. Angela's
rival was Chase Gioberti, who had moved from New
York to take up his share of the Falcon Crest vineyard
fortune. He was the son of her late brother, Jason, and
the two sparred, fought and tussled over power and

prestige. The difference between them was that where Angela was hard and cruel, Chase was essentially good, caring for his employees and the people of the valley. Other principals included Chase's wife, Maggie, his son, Cole, and daughter, Victoria, as well as Angela's family, consisting of daughters Julia and Emma (the former mentally deranged, the latter a man-eater), Julia's son, Lance Cumson, and his wife, Melissa Agretti, daughter of another big wine family. As the series progressed, Angela's tyranny was challenged by a new rival, newspaper magnate Richard Channing, the son of her former husband, Douglas. Richard had inherited half of *The Globe* newspaper in San Francisco (Julia and Emma each had 25 per cent) and fought unscrupulously for yet more power, including control of the vineyards (which he eventually achieved).

The series became more and more violent as the years went by, stretching credulity as it did so. First a sinister business co-operative called 'The Cartel', led by Gustav Riebmann, was introduced. Then another treacherous institution, an underworld gang described as 'The Thirteen', made its bow. Like *Dallas* and *Dynasty*, *Falcon Crest* was well endowed with shootings, framings, trials, stormy marriages, unknown heirs, disputed fathers, amnesiacs, schizophrenics, bombings, plane crashes, white slave rings and numerous skeletons which popped out of cupboards. It did, however, allow its cast a happy ending.

In the final episode, after years of wrangling, attempted murders and the like, the family were reunited and reconciled. Richard (who had turned out to be Angela's son after all) married newcomer Lauren Daniels and sold the vineyard back to Angela, whom he recognized at last as its 'rightful owner'. Plans were made for Falcon Crest to be handed down after her death, hopefully without recrimination.

Falcon Crest was the brainchild of THE WALTONS creator, Earl Hamner. Interestingly, it made a point of casting famous film stars who seldom appeared on television, and the likes of Rod Taylor, Gina Lollobrigida, Kim Novak and Lana Turner all made appearances.

FALK, PETER

(1927–)

New York-born actor who arrived on US television in the late 1950s, moving on to play gangster roles in series like THE UNTOUCHABLES and NAKED CITY. He picked up an Emmy for a performance on *The Dick Powell Show* and was given his first star billing in the legal drama series, *The Trials of O'Brien*. However, in 1968, Falk won the part of a character that was to change his life. In the TV movie, *Prescription: Murder*, he donned the grubby mac and picked up the stubby cigar of offbeat detective Lt. Columbo, after Bing Crosby had turned down the part. COLUMBO proved popular and returned in another movie in 1971, before steady production began and the series became part of the MYSTERY MOVIE anthology. With his grouchy voice, scruffy appearance and sad squint (Falk had lost an eye as a child), Columbo became one of TV's classic creations, resurfacing again in the 1980s.

FALL AND RISE OF REGINALD PERRIN, THE/THE LEGACY OF REGINALD PERRIN

UK (BBC) Situation Comedy. BBC 1 1976–9/BBC 1 1996

Reginald Perrin	**Leonard Rossiter** (*Fall*)
Elizabeth Perrin	**Pauline Yates**
CJ	**John Barron**
Joan Greengross	**Sue Nicholls**
David Harris-Jones	**Bruce Bould**
Tony Webster	**Trevor Adams** (*Fall*)
Jimmy	**Geoffrey Palmer**
Linda	**Sally-Jane Spencer**
Tom	**Tim Preece**
	Leslie Schofield (*Fall*)
Doc Morrissey	**John Horsley**
Prue Harris-Jones	**Theresa Watson**
McBlane	**Joseph Brady** (*Fall*)
Geraldine Hackstraw	**Patricia Hodge** (*Legacy*)
Hank	**Michael Fenton-Stevens** (*Legacy*)
Welton Ormsby	**David Ryall** (*Legacy*)

Creator/Writer: **David Nobbs**
Producers: **Gareth Gwenlan, John Howard Davies**

When a mid-life crisis strikes, a suburban commuter decides to fake his death and seek new horizons under another identity.

Reginald Iolanthe Perrin worked for Sunshine Desserts in a boring office job. He travelled to work each morning from his Norbiton home on the same crowded commuter train, always arriving eleven minutes late for a variety of wacky British Rail reasons (including dead dog on the line). There, despite the attentions of his loyal secretary, Joan Greengross, his career was going nowhere (perhaps symbolized by the crumbling letters on the company sign) and he was constantly browbeaten by his bumptious boss, CJ, who regaled him with advice beginning 'I didn't get where I am today . . .' Home life had become rather mundane, too, with his wife's day revolving around waving him off in the morning and greeting him in the evening, and the thought of visiting his mother-in-law inexplicably filled him with images of a waddling hippopotamus.

It all became too much and Reggie planned a way out. He took himself off to the seaside, abandoned his clothes on the beach to fake drowning and branched out into a new life. After a period wandering Britain's country lanes, he resurfaced back in suburbia, courting his wife, Elizabeth, under the new identity of Martin Wellbourne. He soon reassumed his true name, although by now he had developed an anarchic streak.

Perrin set up his own chain of shops, Grot, which specialized in selling useless objects – cruet sets without holes, square footballs, etc. – and employed his former colleagues from the defunct Sunshine Desserts. Joan once again became his secretary, tempting him with her womanly wiles, and he took delight in taking on CJ as a minor executive. There was also room for his two sycophantic juniors from the old company, Tony 'Great' Webster and David 'Super' Harris-Jones, as well as

Elizabeth. But things went too well for Grot and, resenting the success, Reggie set out to bring the company to its knees before, once again, embarking on a new existence. This time the whole cast joined him in the mock seaside suicide. When they resurfaced in a third season, Reggie had opened Perrins, a rehabilitation commune for stressed executives, finding room for all the usual cronies, including his military-minded brother-in-law, Jimmy (who was always apologizing for something, claiming there had been a 'bit of a cock-up'), and an indecipherable Scottish cook, McBlane.

The role was a marvellous vehicle for Leonard Rossiter, who won acclaim for his portrayal of the highly agitated, stuttering eccentric. Filled with memorable catchphrases, it was scripted by David Nobbs from his original novel, *The Death of Reginald Perrin*, which, some claim, inspired MP John Stonehouse to fake his death in the same way.

In 1996, the BBC bravely decided to resurrect the concept. Considered by some at the time as an attempt to perform *Hamlet* without the prince, *The Legacy of Reginald Perrin* brought together most of the original cast members, but failed to excite the critics. In the new series, Reggie had died once and for all – in the series a billboard advertising the insurance company to which he subscribed had fallen on him in real life actor Leonard Rossiter had died in 1984 – to be commemorated in the opening titles which showed his RIP headstone marked with the tribute 'Forever Revolting'. Reggie may have gone, but his spirit lived in his will, which bequeathed £1 million to each of his associates if they could prove they had done something totally absurd. To achieve their goal, the team formed a new company named Broscor – the Bloodless Revolution of Senior Citizens and the Occupationally Rejected – with the intention of reclaiming the world for those cast aside by thrusting society. Actor Trevor Adams, who had played Tony Webster, could not be traced, so a new, but similar, character named Hank (catchphrase 'wicked') filled his shoes. Another key addition to the cast was solicitor Geraldine Hackstraw. Writer David Nobbs released a novel of the same name to coincide with the new series.

FALL GUY, THE
US (Twentieth Century-Fox) Adventure. ITV 1982–7

Colt Seavers	**Lee Majors**
Howie Munson	**Douglas Barr**
Jody Banks	**Heather Thomas**
Samantha 'Big Jack' Jack	**Jo Ann Pflug**
Terri Shannon/Michaels	**Markie Post**
Pearl Sperling	**Nedra Volz**

Creator/Producer: **Glen A. Larson**

A movie stuntman doubles up as a modern-day bounty hunter.

Colt Seavers was the Fall Guy, a courageous, daring movie stunt double who topped up his income by acting as a bounty hunter, tracking down bail jumpers and other fugitives who had a price on their heads. The spectacular stunts he had perfected in films often came

in handy when apprehending the runaways. Seavers was assisted by beautiful stuntwoman Jody Banks, as well as by his cousin, Howie Munson, who acted as his business manager. Big Jack, the bail bondswoman, handed out the orders, until she was replaced by Terri Shannon (her surname was later changed to Michaels), who then gave way to a grumpy old lady named Pearl Sperling. Star Lee Majors also sang the theme song.

FALSEY, JOHN
(1951–) See **BRAND, JOSHUA**.

FAME
US (MGM/United Artists) Drama. BBC 1 1982–5

Lydia Grant	**Debbie Allen**
Coco Hernandez	**Erica Gimpel**
Danny Amatullo	**Carlo Imperato**
Leroy Johnson	**Gene Anthony Ray**
Bruno Martelli	**Lee Curreri**
Doris Schwartz	**Valerie Landsburg**
Julie Miller	**Lori Singer**
Montgomery MacNeil	**P. R. Paul**
Mr Benjamin Shorofsky	**Albert Hague**
Elizabeth Sherwood	**Carol Mayo Jenkins**
Mr Greg Crandall	**Michael Thoma**
Mrs Charlotte Miller	**Judy Farrell**
Angelo Martelli	**Carmine Caridi**
Dwight	**David Greenlee**
David Reardon	**Morgan Stevens**
Mrs Gertrude Berg	**Ann Nelson**
Holly Laird	**Cynthia Gibb**
Christopher Donlon	**Billy Hufsey**
Quentin Morloch	**Ken Swofford**
Cleo Hewitt	**Janet Jackson**
Jesse Valesquez	**Jesse Borrego**
Nicole Chapman	**Nia Peeples**

Producer: **Stanley C. Rogow**

Energetic musical drama following the lives of students and staff at a performing arts college.

Based on Alan Parker's film of the same name, *Fame* was set in the New York High School for the Performing Arts and focused on a group of talented youngsters learning how to take their place in the world of show business. The emphasis was on sweat, the only way to the top being through dedication and hard work, and the series traced the students' ambitions, their progress, their personal crises and their hard-earned successes, beginning with their arrival as freshers and running through to graduation.

The teachers and instructors were led by sultry Lydia Grant, the demanding dance teacher. She was supported by the much-revered, white-bearded Mr Shorofsky, the music teacher, no-nonsense English tutor Elizabeth Sherwood and drama teacher Mr Crandall, who was later replaced by David Reardon. Quentin Morloch was the stuffy Principal and the dippy school secretary was Mrs Berg.

The real stars, however, were the kids themselves:

Leroy, an agile, creative dancer from Harlem; Coco, an over-ambitious, impetuous singer and dancer; Bruno, a keyboard genius; Doris, a talented comedienne and actress, and Danny, another comic. Julie was a brilliant cellist from the backwoods of Grand Rapids, Michigan, who struggled to come to terms with life in the city, while Montgomery was the son of a successful actress. Characters introduced later included a second influx of students. These included dancers Jesse and Christopher, Holly, who concentrated on drama, Dwight, a chubby tuba player, and singer/dancer Nicole.

Four of the original film's stars reprised their roles in this TV version, namely Gene Anthony Ray, Lee Curreri, Albert Hague and Debbie Allen (who also took charge of the show's choreography). The theme song from the film had been a number one hit for Irene Cara in 1982, but Erica Gimpel, her successor as Coco, provided the vocals on the TV version. The programme also spun off several British chart hits, performed by The Kids from Fame, with 'Hi-Fidelity' and 'Starmaker' being the most successful. There were no hits in the States, but *Fame* was always more successful in the UK than in its native USA.

FAMILY, THE

UK (BBC) Documentary. BBC 1 1974

Producer: **Paul Watson**

Fly-on-the-wall documentary series about a working-class Reading family.

The Wilkins family enjoyed temporary stardom through this warts-and-all, 12-part look at their turbulent domestic life. Terry Wilkins was a bus conductor living with his outspoken wife, Margaret. Sons Gary and Christopher, daughters Marion and Heather, plus Gary's wife, Karen, and two-year-old son, Scott, and Marion's live-in boyfriend, Tom Bernes, completed the crowded family group housed in a maisonette above a greengrocer's shop in Whitley Street, Reading. Also seen was Heather's teenage boyfriend, Melvin Applethwaite. A camera crew virtually lived with the family for three months and recorded their high spots and their lowest ebbs. Blazing rows made colourful viewing and the Wilkinses' flair for letting family skeletons out of the cupboard added to the drama. Later, one-off retrospectives revealed how the family had gradually drifted apart once the series had ended.

Producer Paul Watson repeated the experiment nearly 20 years later, although in rather sunnier climes, in his Australian documentary series, SYLVANIA WATERS.

FAMILY AT WAR, A

UK (Granada) Drama. ITV 1970–2

Edwin Ashton	**Colin Douglas**
Jean Ashton	**Shelagh Fraser**
Margaret Ashton/Porter	**Lesley Nunnerley**
Philip Ashton	**Keith Drinkel**
Sheila Ashton	**Coral Atkins**
David Ashton	**Colin Campbell**
Freda Ashton	**Barbara Flynn**
Robert Ashton	**David Dixon**
Sefton Briggs	**John McKelvey**
Tony Briggs	**Trevor Bowen**
John Porter	**Ian Thompson**
Celia Porter	**Margery Mason**
Harry Porter	**Patrick Troughton**
Ian McKenzie	**John Nettles**

Creator: **John Finch**
Producers: **Richard Doubleday, James Brabazon, Michael Cox**

Glum portrayal of 1930s and 1940s hardships, seen through the lives of a Liverpool family.

Granada's most expensive-ever serial at the time, *A Family at War* focused on the middle-class Ashton family as they struggled through the lean war years. Starting in May 1938 and running on to 1945, it saw them emerge from the decay of the Depression to face the even more bitter realities of World War II, and witnessed family and romantic relationships disintegrate along the way. Never a day passed without a new worry for the Ashtons, headed by morose Yorkshire dad Edwin, who was beholden at work to his pompous brother-in-law, Sefton Briggs. Sefton and his sister, Edwin's wife Jean, had inherited the family printing works. Eldest child was David, a docks worker who had married too young to Sheila, produced two children, Peter and Janet, and was constantly in debt until he joined the RAF. Next came schoolteacher Margaret, who married John Porter, who went missing in action. Philip was the 21-year-old Oxford student who fought in the Spanish Civil War, while Freda, the youngest daughter, was just starting work and Robert, the youngest son, was away at nautical school.

The programme's symbolic titles-sequence, showing a demolished sandcastle, is as well remembered as the series itself.

FAMILY FORTUNES

UK (Central) Game Show. ITV 1980–5; 1987–

Presenters: **Bob Monkhouse, Max Bygraves, Les Dennis**

Producers: **William G. Stewart, Graham C. Williams, Tony Wolfe, Dennis Liddington, Andrew Wightman**

Game show in which families guess what the public thinks.

Based on the American quiz, *Family Feud*, *Family Fortunes* has used a giant computer (initially known as Mr Babbage – after the inventor of the first computer) to display the findings of a public survey. One hundred members of the public have been asked to name various items – a song you sing at parties, things you find at the seaside, etc. – and the two competing families (each consisting of five contestants) have tried to work out which answers have been given. The most popular answers have provided the most points. There have been cash prizes and other valuables to be won. Bob Monkhouse was the first host, succeeded in 1983 by Max Bygraves. After a two-year gap in production, the series returned with Les Dennis as host. *Family Fortunes* has become famous for the off-beam answers given by some contestants. Among the best remembered have been: 'Name something you do in the bathroom' *Answer*: 'Decorate'; 'Name a famous Royal' *Answer*: 'Mail'; 'Name something that flies without an engine' *Answer*: 'A bicycle with wings'.

FANTASY ISLAND
US (Spelling-Goldberg) Drama. ITV 1978–85

Mr Roarke	**Ricardo Montalban**
Tattoo	**Herve Villechaize**
Julie	**Wendy Schaal**
Lawrence	**Christopher Hewett**

Executive Producers: **Aaron Spelling, Leonard Goldberg**

Dreams come true for visitors to a mysterious tropical island.

Fantasy Island, owned and run by the enigmatic Mr Roarke, was the place where, temporarily at least, dreams really could come true. By paying a mere $10,000 for their trip, each visitor could have one wish fulfilled, provided it wasn't *too* fanciful. Whether it was to date attractive women or to make lots of money, this was the chance of a lifetime, and the customers were not short-changed. Things always worked out and endings tended to be happy, even if a few problems or hiccups had been encountered along the way. What's more, all the guests went away having learned some valuable lessons about themselves.

Helping Mr Roarke to keep the customer satisfied were his assistants, initially the midget, Tattoo, and then Lawrence. Roarke's goddaughter, Julie, was also featured for a while. Roarke himself became more and more obscure as the series progressed. It was ultimately revealed that it was his sorcery which lay behind the fantasy factory and in one episode he was seen to face up to the Devil. Each hour-long programme was built around two or three separate fantasies, and the series was modelled on THE LOVE BOAT, also a hit for the Aaron Spelling production team.

Fantasy Island was remade in 1998 with Malcolm McDowell as Mr Roarke. This time there was a more sinister air about proceedings and greater use of special effects to convey the supernatural. It was screened on satellite TV in the UK.

FAR PAVILIONS, THE
UK (Geoff Reeve and Associates/Goldcrest) Drama. Channel 4 1984

Ashton Pelham-Martyn	**Ben Cross**
Princess Anjuli	**Amy Irving**
Kaka Ji Rao	**Christopher Lee**
Koda Dad	**Omar Sharif**
Major Sir Louis Cavagnari	**John Gielgud**
Lt. Wally Hamilton	**Benedict Taylor**
The Rana of Bhithor	**Rossano Brazzi**

Biju Ram	**Saeed Jaffrey**
Major Jenkins	**Robert Hardy**
Princess Shushila	**Sneh Gupta**
Belinda Harlowe	**Felicity Dean**
George Garforth	**Rupert Everett**
Mrs Viccary	**Jennifer Kendal**

Writer: **Julian Bond**
Producer: **Geoffrey Reeve**

Sumptuous story from the days of the Raj.

Costing some £8 million to make, *The Far Pavilions*, like THE JEWEL IN THE CROWN, capitalized on the interest in Raj India generated by Richard Attenborough's film, *Gandhi*. In three two-hour episodes, it told of a young British army officer, Ash Pelham-Martyn, in service with the élite Corps of Guards. Because of his Indian upbringing, Ash found himself torn between the British and Indian cultures, and his forbidden love for former childhood playmate Princess Anjuli added to the torment. On a wider stage, political intrigue and civil unrest led to battles galore. The series was adapted by Julian Bond from the novel by M. M. Kaye. Music was provided by Carl Davis.

FARROW, MIA
(Maria Farrow; 1945–)

The daughter of actress Maureen O'Sullivan, Mia Farrow owes much of her movie fame to her single prime-time TV role, that of Allison McKenzie in PEYTON PLACE. Even though she stayed only two years with the series, it allowed her to gain important exposure and led to a succession of film roles. However, once she had left the series, her character was not forgotten, and the mysterious whereabouts of Allison continued to pervade the storylines of *Peyton Place* right through to its end. Her two husbands were Frank Sinatra and André Previn, and she has also lived with Woody Allen.

FARSON, DANIEL
(1927–97)

Effective Anglo-American TV journalist of the 1950s and early 1960s, when, for ITV, he presented some of the channel's more revealing documentaries. A ground-breaking live TV interviewer who went for the jugular, his credits included THIS WEEK, *People in Trouble, Dan Farson Meets, Now What Do I Do?* and *Pursuit of Happiness*, plus a film on pub entertainers entitled *Time, Gentlemen, Please!*. He also introduced *SMS*, a series of adaptations of stories by Somerset Maugham, in 1960.

FAST SHOW, THE
UK (BBC) Comedy. BBC 2 1994–7; 2000

Paul Whitehouse, Charlie Higson, Caroline Aherne, John Thomson, Arabella Weir, Mark Williams, Simon Day

Producers: **Paul Whitehouse, Charlie Higson**
Executive Producer: **Geoffrey Perkins**

*Inventive, pacy, character- and punchline-driven
sketch show.*

The Fast Show was born out of Harry Enfield's TV programmes. Enfield's close associates, Paul Whitehouse
and Charlie Higson, were watching a package of Enfield's
sketches which had been edited down for a press preview. They realized that these quick, straight-to-the-
punchline highlights were all that was needed to get a
laugh. They picked up the idea and, supported by Caroline Aherne, John Thomson, Arabella Weir, Mark Williams and Simon Day, created *The Fast Show*: as its name
suggests, a swiftly moving barrage of short skits in which
recurring characters never failed to delight viewers by
churning out their favourite catchphrases.

The major players over the show's three-year run were:
music hall comedian Arthur Atkinson ('How queer!'),
often introduced by fellow veteran Tommy Cockles;
Lord of the Manor Ralph, who had a crush on his Irish
estate worker, Ted; romantic car salesman Swiss Toni
(his smoothie lines written by Bob Mortimer); rambling
toff Rowley Birkin QC ('I was very, very drunk'); Unlucky
Alf ('Oh bugger!'); diet- and fashion-conscious Jesse
('This week I shall be mostly eating . . .'); Kenneth and
Kenneth, the provocative menswear assistants ('Suits
you, sir!'); Colin Hunt, the office nerd; TV pundit Ron
Manager (allegedly based on former Luton boss Alec
Stock); the Oz-TV presenters of 'That's Amazing'; the
consumptive country TV host, Bob Fleming; Andy, the
paranoid shirker of office romances; Sir Geoffrey Nor-
man, a deny-everything Tory MP; Louis Balfour, host of
'Jazz Club' ('Nice'); hen-pecked Roy and his wife, Renee
('What did I say, Roy?'); the Fat Sweaty Coppers; US
TV reporter Ed Winchester; the caddish 13th Duke of
Wymborne, usually to be found in a schoolgirl dormi-
tory; cop/doctor Monkfish; US mobsters 'The Unpro-
nouncables'; the crew of Chanel 9, a Mediterranean TV
station ('Chrissie Waddle' and 'Scorchio'); Dave Angel,
Eco-Warrior; deaf stuntsman Chip Cobb; Cockney
Chris, the would-be thief ('I'm a geezer, a little bit whoor,
a little bit waay'); the squeamish zoo-keeper; manic-
depressive painter Johnny ('Black!'); middle-class liar
Patrick Nice ('Which was nice'); incompetent Californian Professor Denzil Dexter; the competitive dad; a
band of itinerant pan-pipers; the equally restless family
with luggage; a vampire-cum-racing-tipster; and Archie,
the intrusive pub codger who's done everything ('Hardest game in the world'). There were also other assorted
unnamed characters such as Weir's insecure girl ('Does
my bum look big in this'), rude South African cosmetics
assistant ('No offence!'), and the woman with the good
idea that men always ignored; Day's 'Someone's sitting
there, mate' man and his pub know-all; Aherne's tactless
supermarket checkout girl and easily impressed, gum-
chewing teenager; Williams's man on the run ('You ain't
seen me, right?'); and Whitehouse's excited Northern
youth ('brilliant'). Funny as they were, there was always
something sad and pathetic about these novel creations.

The show's theme music was 'Release Me'. A spin-off
comedy, *Ted and Ralph*, was screened in December 1998

and three instalments comprising *The Last Fast Show
Ever* were screened at Christmas 2000.

FATHER BROWN
UK (ATV) Detective Drama. ITV 1974

Father Brown .... **Kenneth More**
Flambeau .... **Dennis Burgess**

Writer: **Hugh Leonard**
Producer: **Ian Fordyce**

The cases of a clerical detective in the 1920s.

Fifteen years before Father Dowling began investigating,
this quaint, period series featured Father Brown, TV's
first detective in holy orders. Wily and perceptive, Brown
was a mild-mannered, easy-going criminologist who
solved cases using a mixture of human understanding
and conventional detection. Whether it was identifying
a decapitated corpse at a garden party or helping a young
girl to avoid blackmail, the saintly sleuth came through.
His motto was 'Have Bible, will travel'. Flambeau was his
close friend. The series was based on the short stories of
G. K. Chesterton.

FATHER, DEAR FATHER
UK (Thames) Situation Comedy. ITV 1968–73

Patrick Glover .... **Patrick Cargill**
Anna Glover .... **Natasha Pyne**
Karen Glover .... **Ann Holloway**
Matilda 'Nanny' Harris .... **Noël Dyson**
Barbara Mossman .... **Ursula Howells**
Mrs Glover .... **Joyce Carey**
Georgie .... **Sally Bazely**
                                                 Dawn Addams
Bill Mossman .... **Patrick Holt**
                                                 Tony Britton

Creators/Writers: **Johnny Mortimer, Brian Cooke**
Producer: **William G. Stewart**

*A womanizing novelist struggles to keep his family
and friends in check.*

Patrick Glover, writer of spy novels, was divorced and a
free spirit – in principle. However, plagued by his dotty
mother, his agent (Georgie), his ex-wife (Barbara), her
new, scrap-metal-merchant husband (Bill), a fussy
nanny and two trendy daughters (Anna and Karen), his
life was never his own. Although he drove a swish sports
car and lived in a spacious, well-appointed house in
Hillsdown Avenue, Hampstead, complete with a cuddly
St Bernard named H. G. Wells, his peace and privacy
were constantly being shattered by the household
entourage. This archetypal TV farce was produced by
future FIFTEEN-TO-ONE host William G. Stewart. An Australian version (with only Patrick Cargill and Noël Dyson
from the original cast) was shown in the UK in 1978–80.
A spin-off feature film was released in 1973.

FATHER DOWLING INVESTIGATES
US (Viacom) Detective Drama. ITV 1990–94

Father Frank Dowling .... **Tom Bosley**
Sister Stephanie ('Sister Steve') .... **Tracy Nelson**
Marie Brody .... **Mary Wickes**
Father Philip Prestwick .... **James Stephens**
Sgt Clancy .... **Regina Krueger**

Creators: **Ralph McInerny, Dean Hargrove, Joel Steiger**
Executive Producers: **Fred Silverman, Dean Hargrove**
Producer: **Barry Steinberg**

A Catholic priest has a nose for crime.

Amiable Father Frank Dowling was the parish priest of St Michael's in Chicago, but he found his true vocation in amateur detective work. Joined in his investigations by a nun, Sister Stephanie (or Sister Steve as she preferred to be known), the detective in the dog collar found himself drawn into the most complicated murder mysteries, which he unravelled with great aplomb. Steve, a street-kid-turned-nun, was a more than useful ally. She still knew all the tricks of the trade, from picking locks to gathering information. She even dropped her nun's habit, on occasions, to go incognito. The unlikely duo drove around in Dowling's run-down old station wagon and, using their clerical appearances, were able to go where normal detectives feared to tread. In the background were the bumbling Father Prestwick, a junior priest dispatched by the Bishop to keep an eye on the wayward Dowling, and Marie, the loyal housekeeper at the St Michael's vicarage. Sgt Clancy acted as Dowling's police contact.

The character was created by novelist Ralph McInerny and the series – known as *The Father Dowling Mysteries* in the USA – gave Tom Bosley his first starring role after HAPPY DAYS.

FATHER TED
UK (Hat Trick/Channel 4) Situation Comedy. Channel 4
1995–8

Father Ted Crilly .... **Dermot Morgan**
Father Dougal McGuire .... **Ardal O'Hanlon**
Father Jack Hackett .... **Frank Kelly**
Mrs Doyle .... **Pauline McLynn**
Father Noel Furlong .... **Graham Norton**

Writers: **Graham Linehan, Arthur Mathews**
Producers: **Geoffrey Perkins, Lissa Evans**

*The surreal adventures of three delinquent
Irish priests.*

Bleakly set on fictitious Craggy Island, somewhere off the coast of Galway, this cult comedy focused on the stressed life of Father Ted Crilly, a heavy smoking, bad-mouthed ('Feck!') Catholic priest with more of a lust for the temporal world than for the spiritual. Fast cars and fast women were more his cup of tea than faith and funerals, but they remained but distant dreams to the generally good-natured, slightly wayward cleric. However, Ted's patience was sorely tried by his young assistant, the enthusiastic but ultra-thick (actually profoundly unworldly) Father Dougal McGuire, the sort of man who takes instructions literally, with disastrous consequences. The senior priest in the house was the blasphemous Father Jack Hackett, an angry, often wheelchair-bound psychopath who was perhaps a future version of Ted himself, having finally descended without hope into the mire of 'Drink!' (literally anything, from toilet cleaner to engine oil) and 'Girls!'. It seems that the Church was already well aware of this dubious trio, for they had all been 'exiled' to the island for various reasons: Ted for the embezzlement of a charity fund (the sick child hoping for a visit to Lourdes was deprived and Ted went to Las Vegas on the proceeds); Dougal for some incident involving nuns; and Jack for an unspecified wedding ceremony outrage. The three lived in a particularly grim-looking parochial house (actually a building near Ennistymon, County Clare), where they were dutifully looked after by the equally bizarre Mrs Doyle, forever insisting that they have a cup of tea ('Oh go on!').

Adding to this explosive mix were the inbred islanders, who never failed to cause Ted grief, and occasional religious visitors like the phlegmatic, unentertainable Father Stone and incessantly irritating Father Noel Furlong. The thought of nuns coming to the house was just too much to bear.

The Catholic church did not escape lightly in *Father Ted* – its conventions, sacred places and even its very creed were held up to ridicule, but always in a fashion that was so over the top that it had no grounding in reality. The action was always farcical, with moments of violent slapstick. Nor were the stars ever shown conducting major ceremonies or taking confession.

Three seasons of wild acclaim were brought suddenly to an end with the premature death of star Dermot Morgan from a heart attack in March 1998 (just days before the third series was due to be screened). The only consolation was that at least the series ended while still in its prime. The Father Ted character had previously been performed in stand-up by co-writer Arthur Mathews.

FAWCETT, FARRAH
(1946–)

Shaggy-haired American actress, the face of 1977 after starring as one of CHARLIE'S ANGELS (sporty Jill Munroe). On a wave of lookalike dolls and merchandising, Fawcett left the series after just one season but was forced to make occasional return appearances (to avoid contractual difficulties). Previously, she had gained bit parts in series like *The Flying Nun*, MARCUS WELBY, MD and THE SIX MILLION DOLLAR MAN, and had also appeared as David Janssen's neighbour in HARRY-O. Little television has come her way after leaving *Charlie's Angels*, apart from a short-lived sitcom, *Good Sports*, in 1991, but she has won a fair amount of film work. She was at one time married to actor Lee Majors and was known as Farrah Fawcett-Majors when *Charlie's Angels* began.

FAWLTY TOWERS
UK (BBC) Situation Comedy. BBC 2 1975; 1979

Basil Fawlty	**John Cleese**
Sybil Fawlty	**Prunella Scales**
Manuel	**Andrew Sachs**
Polly Sherman	**Connie Booth**
Major Gowen	**Ballard Berkeley**
Miss Tibbs	**Gilly Flower**
Miss Gatsby	**Renee Roberts**
Terry	**Brian Hall**

Writers: **John Cleese and Connie Booth**
Producers: **John Howard Davies, Douglas Argent**

Chaos in a seaside hotel, courtesy of its manic owner.

Fawlty Towers, a modest little Torquay hotel, was run by husband and wife Basil and Sybil Fawlty. Modest the hotel may have been, but Basil had ambitious plans for his small empire and ran it with great enthusiasm. Sadly, the guests tended to get in the way. Inhibited also by his nagging, droning, gossiping wife and by Manuel, a useless Spanish waiter from Barcelona who understood little English ('I know nathing'), Fawlty's best-laid plans always ended in disaster.

Fawlty was a master at turning the simplest procedures – like serving dinner to late guests – into complete chaos, and his patronizing air, biting sarcasm and bouts of rage all contrived to make matters worse. When practising a fire drill, he refused to allow a real kitchen fire to interrupt the flow of proceedings; when entertaining German guests, a blow on the head encouraged the already unbalanced hotelier to goosestep around the dining room, magnificently failing not to 'mention the war'. When an undercover hotel inspector came to town, Fawlty unctuously fawned over every guest except the right one, and on a planned gourmet evening, Terry, his chef, got blind drunk.

Hovering on the fringe at all times were the hotel's permanent guests, two doddery old ladies (Miss Tibbs and Miss Gatsby) and the senile and deaf Major Gowen. But, thankfully, there was also Polly, the chambermaid, who attempted to bring some order back to the hotel. Hers was generally only a limited success, with her lanky, hot-headed boss screwing things up time and again. He couldn't even keep control of the hotel's name plate, which was constantly tampered with by meddling hands to offer Fatty Owls, Farty Towels, Watery Fowls or other anagrammatic names.

The series combined the best aspect of farce – misconstrued conversations, well-timed exits and entrances, etc. – with some classic one-liners and insults. Very few series have managed to imbue the viewers with so much tension, frustration and exasperation, but *Fawlty Towers* has been generally accepted as one of the gems of British TV comedy. It was allegedly inspired by a visit by the MONTY PYTHON team to a Torquay hotel and their discovery of a rude hotelier who threw Eric Idle's briefcase into the street, thinking it was a bomb. The character was written into one of John Cleese and Graham Chapman's

DOCTOR AT LARGE scripts, before finally achieving greatness in his own right in this sitcom, several years later. After the acclaim of the first six *Fawlty Towers* episodes, the second series took four years to arrive (partly because Cleese and his co-writer wife, Connie Booth, had split up), but most people thought it well worth the wait.

FBI, THE
US (Warner Brothers/Quinn Martin) Police Drama. ITV 1965–75

Insp. Lewis Erskine	**Efrem Zimbalist, Jr**
Agent Arthur Ward	**Philip Abbott**
Barbara Erskine	**Lynn Loring**
Special Agent Jim Rhodes	**Stephen Brooks**
Special Agent Tom Colby	**William Reynolds**
Agent Chris Daniels	**Shelly Novack**
Narrator	**Marvin Miller**

Executive Producer: **Quinn Martin**
Producer: **Charles Lawton**

Successful series highlighting the cases of a fictitious FBI agent.

Inspector Lew Erskine worked for the Federal Bureau of Investigation and travelled the length and breadth of the USA, seeking out criminals and fraudsters and unearthing political subversives and other enemies of the state. During the course of the programme's run he was assisted by a number of different colleagues. One of these, Jim Rhodes, was romantically entwined with Barbara, Erskine's daughter, in the first series, but she was then dropped from the cast. This was a deliberate ploy by the producers, who wanted to isolate the cold, methodical Erskine even further (his wife had already been killed in a shoot-out). Not that Erskine, a dedicated, businesslike operator, appeared to mind. He insisted his work *always* took precedence over his private life. A career detective, he had been with the Bureau for 30 years, right from the turbulent days of the 1930s, when he had helped round up gangsters. Now he reported to Arthur Ward, assistant to the Bureau's Director.

The series won the approval of the real FBI chief, J. Edgar Hoover, who permitted filming at their Washington headquarters. Many of the stories were allegedly based on true cases and, in America, appeals for assistance in tracking down real villains were sometimes made at the end of the show.

FELDMAN, MARTY
(1933–82)

Mop-haired, wide-eyed English comedian, a companion of Mel Brooks and Gene Wilder in the cinema but, before his movie days, a success on the small screen. Feldman's career began in writing. His collaborator was Barry Took and between them they penned scores of scripts for radio series like *Round the Horne* and *Educating Archie*, and TV comedies such as THE ARMY GAME, BOOTSIE AND SNUDGE, *Scott On . . .*, *The Walrus and the Carpenter*, *Barney Is My Darling*, *Broaden Your Mind* and *On The*

Braden Beat. They also wrote for comics like Dick Emery, Harry Secombe and Frankie Howerd, and Feldman (with John Law) provided the famous 'class' sketch, featuring Barker, Corbett and Cleese, for THE FROST REPORT. He also co-produced Corbett's comedy, NO – THAT'S ME OVER HERE!. Moving in front of the camera, he starred in the manic AT LAST THE 1948 SHOW and out of this gained his own BBC 2 series, *Marty*, which developed the zany visual humour that was to characterize his later movie work. Other series followed, such as *The Marty Feldman Comedy Machine* and *Marty Back Together Again.* Feldman died of a heart attack while filming in Mexico in December 1982.

FELLOWS, THE

UK (Granada) Detective Drama. ITV 1967

Oldenshaw	**Richard Vernon**
Dimmock	**Michael Aldridge**
Mrs Hollinsczech	**Jill Booty**
Thomas Anthem	**James Ottaway**
Alec Spindoe	**Ray McAnally**

Creator: **Robin Chapman**
Producers: **Robin Chapman, Peter Plummer**

Two academic criminologists solve crimes from a Cambridge college.

A follow-up series to THE MAN IN ROOM 17 (and indeed subtitled *Late of Room 17*), *The Fellows* focused on two Government-financed crime-crackers, Oldenshaw and Dimmock, who had, at last, left the famous Room 17 to take up residence at All Saints' College, Cambridge. Appointed by the Home Office to the Peel Research Fellowship, their role now was to study how the nature of crime changed as society evolved. However, they soon re-established themselves as formidable detectives, calling on the assistance of number-cruncher Mrs Hollinsczech and servant Thomas Anthem. Alec Spindoe, a gangster convicted during the series, was later given his own TV spin-off series, *Spindoe.*

FELTON, NORMAN

(1922–)

American producer responsible for such hits as DR KILDARE and THE MAN FROM UNCLE (also as co-creator).

FELTZ, VANESSA

(1962–)

London-born, Cambridge graduate presenter, hosting her own talk shows, *Vanessa* and *The Vanessa Show*, until the latter was axed amid a scandal over planted studio guests. Feltz has also fronted *Watchdog: Value for Money* and the quiz, *Quotation Marks*, appeared on programmes like *Good Morning* and, in 1996, was 'on the bed' in THE BIG BREAKFAST.

FENN STREET GANG, THE

See PLEASE SIR!.

FENNELL, ALBERT

(1920–88)

British producer, closely associated with THE AVENGERS and, later, THE PROFESSIONALS, both in collaboration with Brian Clemens.

FERRIS, PAM

(1948–)

British actress, famous as Ma Larkin in THE DARLING BUDS OF MAY and also starring as district nurse Peggy Snow in WHERE THE HEART IS. Other credits have included *Connie* (Nesta), *All Change* (Maggie Oldfield), *Hardwicke House* (Cynthia, the French mistress), ORANGES ARE NOT THE ONLY FRUIT (Mrs Arkwright), *Mr Wakefield's Crusade* (Mad Marion), *Performance's Roots* (Mrs Bryant), MIDDLEMARCH (Mrs Dollop), *The Rector's Wife* (Eleanor Ramsay), *Death of a Salesman* (The Woman), *Screen Two's Mrs Hartley and the Growth Centre* (Alice Hartley), *Our Mutual Friend* (Mrs Boffin), *The Tenant of Wildfell Hall* (Mrs Markham) and *The Turn of the Screw* (Mrs Grose). She is married to actor Roger Frost.

FIFTEEN TO ONE

UK (Regent) Quiz. Channel 4 1988–

Presenter: **William G. Stewart**

Creator: **John M. Lewis**
Producers: **William G. Stewart, Mark Noades**

Fast-moving daily general knowledge quiz involving 15 contestants.

Drily compered by experienced producer William G. Stewart (formerly of FATHER, DEAR FATHER, BLESS THIS HOUSE and THE PRICE IS RIGHT, among other popular series), *Fifteen to One*'s aim has been to whittle down 15 hopefuls into one daily winner. Arranged in an arc around Stewart, the contestants have been asked two questions in turn. Those failing to get at least one right have been eliminated. For the next stage, the contestants have defended what has remained of their initial three lives by nominating one another to answer questions. The last three contestants, with a life intact, have progressed to the last round. In this, they have battled head to head, trying to eliminate each other through nomination and also looking to notch a high score for themselves. The 15 highest-scoring daily winners have competed in the grand final at the end of the series. As on MASTERMIND, no flashy prizes have been on offer, just a simple but tasteful commemorative trophy and the prestige of being a *Fifteen to One* champion.

FILM

UK (BBC) Film Review. BBC 1 1971–

Presenters: **Jacky Gillott, Joan Bakewell, Barry Norman, Frederic Raphael, Jonathan Ross**

Producers: **Iain Johnstone, Patricia Ingram, Don Bennetts, Barry Brown, Jane Lush, Bruce Thompson, Allan Campbell**

Topical review of the cinema world.

Beginning in 1971 as a programme for the South-East only, the *Film* series has since established itself as the most valuable cinema review on television, incorporating appraisals of the latest releases, interviews with major stars about their forthcoming films and details of the current box-office hits. In its early days, as *Film 71*, the presenter was Jacky Gillott. However, Barry Norman took over the hot seat in 1972, alternating with Joan Bakewell and Frederic Raphael, then claimed the series as his own the following year. When he stood down briefly in 1982 to front OMNIBUS, a succession of temporary stand-ins (including producer Iain Johnstone) held the fort, pending his return. When Norman moved to Sky, he was succeeded by Jonathan Ross (from 1999). The programme's title has changed with each year, becoming *Film 72*, etc.

FILTHY RICH AND CATFLAP

UK (BBC) Situation Comedy. BBC 2 1987

Ralph Filthy .... **Nigel Planer**
Richard Rich .... **Rik Mayall**
Eddie Catflap .... **Adrian Edmondson**

Writer: **Ben Elton**
Producer: **Paul Jackson**

Aggression and anarchy dominate the lives of a TV performer, his minder and his agent.

This send-up of television celebrity saw comedian and 'TV star' Richie Rich striving to keep in with his peers (the likes of 'Brucie' and 'Tarby'), but continually hampered by his useless hypochondriac agent, Ralph Filthy, who could never get him any work, and his mindless minder, Eddie Catflap. The sketches were punctuated by various asides to the camera. Penned by Ben Elton, the series offered more than an echo of the team's earlier success with THE YOUNG ONES.

THE FINAL CUT

See HOUSE OF CARDS.

FINCH, JOHN

Scriptwriter whose work has generally focused on Northern working-class situations. Among his credits have been A FAMILY AT WAR, SAM, *This Year, Next Year, Flesh*

and *Blood, Nightingale's Boys, Spoils of War* and numerous episodes of CORONATION STREET.

FINE ROMANCE, A

UK (LWT) Situation Comedy. ITV 1981–4

Laura Dalton .... **Judi Dench**
Mike Selway .... **Michael Williams**
Helen Barker .... **Susan Penhaligon**
Phil Barker .... **Richard Warwick**
Harry .... **Geoffrey Rose**

Creator/Writer: **Bob Larbey**
Producers: **James Cellan Jones, Don Leaver**

A middle-aged couple fumble their way through a relationship.

Laura Dalton, a linguist from Fulham, and Mike Selway, a landscape gardener, were perfect for each other, or so it seemed to their friends and relations. They themselves were unsure, though, which led to much humming and ha-ing and an on-off romance. In their early 40s and each set in their ways, they were incapable of grasping the nettle and, despite much prompting from Laura's sister, Helen, and her husband, Phil (who instigated their meeting by arranging a party), it took them three years to make the right decision.

Things proved simpler in real life, where stars Judi Dench and Michael Williams were husband and wife. Judi Dench also sang the theme song.

FINLAY, FRANK

CBE (1926–)

Lancashire-born actor, often in controversial roles. His portrayal of CASANOVA in Dennis Potter's 1971 series enraged Mrs Whitehouse, and he followed it up with performances as publisher Peter Manson in the equally sensational BOUQUET OF BARBED WIRE and *Another Bouquet*. He was the Führer in the drama, *The Death of Adolf Hitler*, and among his many other appearances have been parts in plays and series like *Target Luna, Doctor Knock, This Happy Breed, Candide, The Adventures of Don Quixote* (Sancho Panza), *84 Charing Cross Road, Count Dracula* (Van Helsing), *Saturday, Sunday, Monday, The Last Campaign*, TALES OF THE UNEXPECTED, BLACKADDER, *Aspects of Love, The Other Side*, LOVEJOY, HEARTBEAT, COMMON AS MUCK (Derek), *How Do You Want Me?* (Astley Yardley), *Longitude* (Admiral Wager) and *The Sins* (Uncle Irwin Green), as well as assorted Shakespearean roles. He also starred in the ARMCHAIR THEATRE pilot for the comedy, NEVER MIND THE QUALITY, FEEL THE WIDTH (Patrick Kelly).

FINNIGAN, JUDY

(1948–)

Daytime TV presenter, co-host of ITV's *This Morning* with her second husband, Richard Madeley, and for a while a live evening chat show, *Tonight with Richard*

Madeley and Judy Finnigan. Finnigan's career began as a researcher with Granada and progressed via the company's regional news magazines. She also reported for Anglia TV. *Classic Coronation Street* saw her introduce epic moments from the long-running soap, while, as first presenter of *We Can Work It Out*, she fronted ITV's answer to WATCHDOG.

FIRE CRACKERS
UK (ATV) Situation Comedy. ITV 1964–5

Charlie	**Alfred Marks**
Jumbo	**Joe Baker**
Weary Willie	**Sidney Bromley**
Loverboy	**Ronnie Brody**
Hairpin	**Cardew Robinson**
Tadpole	**Clive Elliott**
George	**Colin Douglas**
Station Officer Blazer	**John Arnatt**
Leading Fireman Piggott	**Norman Chappell**

Producer: **Alan Tarrant**

The slapstick adventures of an incompetent village fire brigade.

Set in the fictitious settlement of Cropper's End (population 70), *Fire Crackers* concerned the inept local firemen and their decrepit 1907 engine, which was known as Bessie. Somehow this particular band of fire-fighters had been forgotten by the powers that be, so, even though they happily drew their salary, they didn't need to man the pumps. Instead, in times of trouble they called out Station Officer Blazer and his crew from the neighbouring town, which meant that Charlie, the fire chief, and his work-shy team could spend more time cadging pints in The Cropper's Arms. It was just as well, as their token attempts at fire drills usually ended in disaster anyway.

FIREBALL XL5
UK (AP Films/ATV/ITC) Children's Science Fiction.
ITV 1962–3

Voices:

Col. Steve Zodiac	**Paul Maxwell**
Prof. Matthew Matic	**David Graham**
Venus	**Sylvia Anderson**
Commander Zero	**John Bluthal**
Lt. 90	**David Graham**
Zoonie	**David Graham**
Robert the Robot	**Gerry Anderson**

Creators: **Gerry Anderson, Sylvia Anderson**
Producer: **Gerry Anderson**

The crew of a state-of-the-art spacecraft protects Earth from invaders.

This was Gerry Anderson's second venture into Supermarionation (high-tech puppetry) and centred on the exploits of dashing Steve Zodiac, the handsome, blond, dare-devil commander of the spacecraft, *Fireball XL5,*

one of the XL series of faster-than-light rockets. Working for World Space Patrol in the year 2063, the ship was assigned to Sector 25 of the Solar System to counter the aggressive advances and cunning subterfuge of extra-terrestrials like Mr and Mrs Spacespy. Zodiac was ably supported by Venus, his French girlfriend, who was also a Doctor of Space Medicine, and Professor Matt Matic, the navigator, technical genius and designer of *XL5*. Robert, a transparent robot, was the co-pilot and a 'Lazoon' named Zoonie was also aboard. Missions were co-ordinated by Commander Zero and his junior, Lt. 90, from Space City.

The adventures took Zodiac and his crew all across the galaxy. If a planetary landing was in order, the rocket's nose-cone (*Fireball Junior*) detached itself and took the team to the surface. On the planet, they travelled on souped-up scooters known as jet-mobiles. *Fireball XL5* was the only Gerry Anderson series to be fully networked in the USA. Its theme song, 'Fireball', by Don Spencer, narrowly missed the UK Top 30 in 1963.

FIRST BORN
UK (BBC/Australian Broadcasting Corporation/Television New Zealand) Science Fiction. BBC 1 1988

Edward Forester	**Charles Dance**
Ann Forester	**Julie Peasgood**
Lancing	**Philip Madoc**
Chris Knott	**Peter Tilbury**
Nancy Knott	**Rosemary McHale**
Dr Graham	**Roshan Seth**
Marais	**Marc de Jonge**
Jessop	**Niven Boyd**
Emily Jessop	**Sharon Duce**
Gor	**Jamie Foster**
Young Gor	**Peter Wiggins**
Gerry	**Nina Zuckerman**
Nell Forester	**Gabrielle Anwar**
Young Nell	**Beth Pearce**

Writer: **Ted Whitehead**
Producer: **Sally Head**

A scientist creates a man/gorilla hybrid, with dangerous consequences.

It was genetics specialist Edward Forester's God-like desire to create a new breed of creature, one endowed with all man's intelligence but without the aggressive instincts associated with humankind. To this end, he began experimenting with female gorilla cells and his own sperm. The result was the birth of a man-gorilla, which he named Gordon, or Gor. After losing his infantile ape hair, Gor matured into a model son but, eventually confronted with facts about his birth, demanded to see his mother, a gorilla named Mary, who beat him to death in a violent rage. The consequences of Forester's genetic tamperings were not at an end, however, as his daughter, Nell, then gave birth to Gor's child, a baby clearly of mixed species.

This three-part series was an adaptation of the novel, *Gorsaga,* by Maureen Duffy.

FIRST CHURCHILLS, THE
UK (BBC) Historical Drama. BBC 2 1969

John Churchill	John Neville
Sarah Churchill	Susan Hampshire
Sidney Godolphin	John Standing
Charles II	James Villiers
York	John Westbrook
Princess Mary	Lisa Daniely
Princess Anne	Margaret Tyzack
Shaftesbury	Frederick Peisley

Writer/Producer: **Donald Wilson**

Period drama charting the distant ancestry of the famous 20th-century prime minister.

Long before Sir Winston was even a twinkle in his father's eye, his family was heavily entwined with British politics – as far back as Stuart times, when John Churchill wrestled for power in the court of King Charles II. Putting his military skills to good use in assorted European battles, Churchill won from the sovereign the title of the first Duke of Marlborough and, with his wife, Sarah (a lady-in-waiting to the future Queen Anne), instigated the famous line of statesmen bearing his name. Written, directed and produced by Donald Wilson, the series ran to 12 episodes.

FIRST OF THE SUMMER WINE
See **LAST OF THE SUMMER WINE**.

FIRST TUESDAY
UK (Yorkshire) Documentary. ITV 1983–93

Presenters: **Jonathan Dimbleby, Olivia O'Leary**

Powerful series of documentaries on wide-ranging subjects of contemporary significance.

Shown in a post-*News at Ten* slot, *First Tuesday* offered a collection of influential documentaries on subjects as diverse as housewife strippers, joy riders, radioactive pollution and Siamese twins. One notable programme followed a Geordie living and working in China and another investigated the man who shot John Lennon. Using pictures to tell their own story, the series also exposed the abuse dished out in old people's homes, went behind the scenes of the Hillsborough disaster and looked again at the case of the Guildford Four. Jonathan Dimbleby was the first presenter, succeeded by Olivia O'Leary in later years. The name was derived from the fact that the programme was screened on the first Tuesday of the month.

FIRTH, COLIN
(1960–)

Hampshire-born actor whose most celebrated role has been as Mr Darcy in PRIDE AND PREJUDICE. His other credits have included *Camille*, *Dutch Girls*, *Lost Empires* (Richard Herncastle), *Tumbledown* (Robert Lawrence), *Hostages*, THE RUTH RENDELL MYSTERIES' *Master of the Moor* (Stephen Whalby), *Performance*'s *The Deep Blue Sea* (Freddie Page) and *The Widowing of Mrs Holroyd* (Charles Holroyd), *Screen Two*'s *The Hour of the Pig* (Richard Courtois), plus *Nostromo* (Charles Gould), *The Turn of the Screw* (Master) and *Donovan Quick* (title role). He is the brother of actor Jonathan Firth.

FISH, MICHAEL
(1944–)

Long-serving BBC weatherman (since 1974), the presenter who unfortunately assured viewers that there were no hurricanes on the way in 1987. He has also made guest appearances on other shows.

FISHER, GREGOR

Scottish comic actor, best known as the string-vested philosopher, RAB C. NESBITT, a spin-off character from NAKED VIDEO. Another *Naked Video* product which Fisher took into its own off-shoot was *The Baldy Man*. Fisher also starred as Para Handy in *The Tales of Para Handy*, The Fly in *Gormenghast*, and Perks in *The Railway Children*, and earlier appearances came in such series as FOXY LADY (Hector Ross), *City Lights*, THE BILL and BOON.

FIVE O'CLOCK CLUB
UK (Associated-Rediffusion) Children's Entertainment. ITV 1963–6

Presenters: **Muriel Young, Howard Williams, Wally Whyton**

Twice-weekly light magazine for younger viewers.

Taking its cue from the earlier series, *Lucky Dip* and *Tuesday Rendezvous*, very much in the same vein, *Five O'Clock Club* was a popular Tuesday and Friday offering for the under-12s. Its hosts, Muriel Young, Howard Williams and, later, Wally Whyton, presented a mixed bag of pop singers and other guests, and gently sparred with their puppet co-stars, Fred Barker (a dog voiced by Basil Brush man Ivan Owen) and Ollie Beak (an opinionated Liverpudlian owl in a school cap, voiced by Whyton, who resurfaced in the 1970s pop show, *Get It Together*). Additional items included guitar tips from Bert Weedon, hobbies with Jimmy Hanley and animals with Grahame Dangerfield. The programme became *Ollie and Fred's Five O'Clock Club* in 1965. The same year, the cheeky puppets popped up alongside presenter Marjorie Sigley in *Five O'Clock Funfair*.

FLAMBARDS
UK (YTV) Drama. ITV 1979

Christina Parsons/Russell	Christine McKenna

Mr Russell	**Edward Judd**
Mark Russell	**Steven Grives**
William Russell	**Alan Parnaby**
Dick	**Sebastian Abineri**
Dorothy	**Carol Leader**
Sandy	**Peter Settelen**

Executive Producer: **David Cunliffe**
Producer: **Leonard Lewis**

A teenage orphan is terrorized by her uncle and cousin.

In 1909 Christina Parsons, a young orphan girl, was taken under the wing of her boozy, tyrannical uncle, Mr Russell, at Flambards, his decaying estate in the Essex countryside. There her life was made a misery by her cousin, Mark, a sadistic bully who wanted her for his wife. His gentler brother, William, sympathized with Christina but found a more important interest in the new craze of aviation, a passion Christina grew to love, too. The series followed her life, through her marriage to William and the difficulties of the World War I years.

Based on a trilogy of romantic novels by Kathleen Peyton, the 12-part series was adapted by various writers, including Alan Plater. David Fanshawe provided the music.

FLAMINGO ROAD

US (Lorimar/MF) Drama. BBC 1 1981–3

Sheriff Titus Semple	**Howard Duff**
Sam Curtis	**John Beck**
Claude Weldon	**Kevin McCarthy**
Eudora Weldon	**Barbara Rush**
Skipper Weldon	**Woody Brown**
Constance Weldon/Carlyle	**Morgan Fairchild**
Fielding Carlyle	**Mark Harmon**
Lane Ballou	**Cristina Raines**
Lute-Mae Sanders	**Stella Stevens**
Sande Swanson	**Cynthia Sikes**
Elmo Tyson	**Peter Donat**
Michael Tyrone	**David Selby**

Greed, corruption and scandal in a sleepy Southern town.

Based on the 1949 film starring Joan Crawford, *Flamingo Road* was another of the DALLAS/DYNASTY clones that attempted to secure a permanent prime-time slot. In the event, the series was short-lived, lasting only two seasons.

It was set in the small town of Truro, Florida, where the wealthiest street was Flamingo Road. On Flamingo Road lived Claude Weldon, proprietor of the local paper mill, together with his wife Eudora, son Skipper (who ran the mill) and spoiled adopted daughter, Constance. Constance married Fielding Carlyle, a local politician, whose advancement was owed in no small measure to the manipulative sheriff of Truro, Titus Semple. Semple knew the ins and outs of the whole neighbourhood, including the sort of secrets that made him all-powerful. Fielding had really loved Lane Ballou, singer at Lute-

Mae's casino-cum-brothel, but was badgered into the marriage that would best suit his – or, rather, Semple's – plans. Lane was now romantically entwined with construction developer Sam Curtis.

Also featured was Elmo Tyson, the owner of the town's newspaper, *The Clarion*, and another major character arrived in the shape of Michael Tyrone, an angry tycoon out to avenge the execution of his innocent father. His schemes introduced murder and voodoo to the dozy old town, spicing up the family jealousies, business rivalries and political intrigue that dominated the sleazy storylines.

FLETCHER, CYRIL

(1913–)

THAT'S LIFE's 'odd ode' performer, Cyril Fletcher's TV career stretches way back to the medium's earliest days. It was in 1936 that he appeared on the fledgling BBC service, reciting his novel poems and participating in the Corporation's first pantomime, *Dick Whittington*. He also appeared in revues like *Tele-Ho!*. After the war, he was often seen on TV in the company of his wife, Betty Astell. His seaside pier show, *Saturday Night Attraction*, was screened in 1949, and he went on to join the panel of WHAT'S MY LINE?, take part in the religious series, *Sunday Story*, and star in his own ITV show. He joined *That's Life* in the 1970s, composing his odd odes and selecting bizarre newspaper clippings. He has also presented gardening programmes.

FLEXTECH

International media company which has notable television holdings in the UK, including the satellite/cable/digital channels Bravo, Living, Trouble and Challenge TV. In addition, Flextech owns 50 per cent of UKTV, provider of UK Gold, UK Style, UK Drama, UK Horizons and Play UK. It also has a stake in Scottish Media Group, which covers Scottish Television and Grampian Television and itself has a share in GMTV. Another Flextech business is the Maidstone TV studios once owned by TVS.

FLINTSTONES, THE

US (Hanna-Barbera) Cartoon. ITV 1961–6

Voices:

Fred Flintstone	**Alan Reed**
Wilma Flintstone	**Jean Vander Pyl**
Barney Rubble	**Mel Blanc**
Betty Rubble	**Bea Benaderet**
	Gerry Johnson
Dino	**Mel Blanc**
Pebbles Flintstone	**Jean Vander Pyl**
Bamm Bamm Rubble	**Don Messick**

Creators/Executive Producers: **William Hanna, Joseph Barbera**

Comic animation imaginatively placing 1960s lifestyles in a Stone Age setting.

The Flintstones were Fred and Wilma, with little daughter Pebbles an addition to the family in later years. They lived (with their pet dinosaur, Dino) in the city of Bedrock some time around one million years BC. Loudmouthed, hapless Fred worked as a crane operator at the Bedrock Construction Co., alongside his next-door neighbour and best buddy, Barney Rubble. Barney's wife, Betty, was a close friend of Wilma's and the Rubbles soon extended their family, too, when they adopted a baby boy, Bamm Bamm.

The cartoon's humour was largely due to the fanciful idea of presenting prehistoric man with 20th-century mod. cons. The primitive inhabitants of Bedrock had the lot, if in a very basic form. Fred's hi-fi system, for example, consisted of a bird with a large beak scratching out sounds from a stone disc, and the Flintstones' car, complete with tail fins, ran only when they ran (it was feet-powered). The household waste-disposal system was a gluttonous buzzard hidden under the sink; a baby elephant on roller skates acted as Wilma's vacuum cleaner, while Fred's crane at work was a dinosaur. Their newspaper, *The Daily Slate*, arrived on heavy stone slabs and, of course, they owned a Stoneway piano. Several famous 'guest stars' made appearances, including Perry Masonry, the crack barrister, actor Stony Curtis and TV host Ed Sullystone. Meanwhile Fred's yell of 'Yabba Dabba Do!' became one of TV's best-remembered catchphrases.

The Flintstones (originally planned as *The Flagstones*) had the honour of being the first animation to be made specifically for US TV's prime time, and is still being run on TV stations across the world. The Stone Age setting apart, it borrowed much from the hit American series, *The Honeymooners* (seldom seen in the UK), which starred Jackie Gleason and revolved around pal-neighbours who were constantly in hot water. A feature film, *A Man Called Flintstone*, reached the cinema in 1966 and a spin-off series, *Pebbles and Bamm Bamm*, premiered in 1971. In 1994 John Goodman starred in a live-action film version. *The Flintstones* concept was reworked in another Hanna-Barbera production, THE JETSONS. This time the 20th-century way of life was applied to the space age.

FLIP SIDE OF DOMINICK HIDE, THE / ANOTHER FLIP FOR DOMINICK

UK (BBC) Science Fiction. BBC 1 1980/1982

Dominick Hide	**Peter Firth**
Jane	**Caroline Langrishe**
Ava	**Pippa Guard**
Caleb Line	**Patrick Magee**
Great Aunt Mavis	**Sylvia Coleridge**
Helda	**Jean Trend**

Writers: **Alan Gibson, Jeremy Paul**
Producer: **Chris Cherry**

A time traveller from the future is bewildered by 1980s London.

This PLAY FOR TODAY achieved almost cult status with its tale of a friendly but naïve lad from 150 years in the future who visited Britain in the 1980s. By sending his flying saucer through a time warp, Dominick Hide left the year 2130 and returned to London in 1980 to do some historical research. He discovered a city far removed from the one he had just left. In his time, the world was a hygienic place of order and calm, and Hide was bemused and confused by the hustle and bustle he now encountered. Happily, he was befriended by a girl named Jane who became his lover and, in a quirk of fate, gave birth to Dominick's own great-great-grandfather.

Hide resurfaced in a second *Play for Today* two years later entitled *Another Flip for Dominick*, in which his boss, Caleb Line, sent him back to 1982 to find a missing researcher. Once again Dominick met up with Jane (and his two-year-old son/great-great-grandfather), before returning to his wife, Ava, in his own time.

FLIPPER

US (MGM/Ivan Tors) Adventure. ITV 1966–9

Porter 'Po' Ricks	**Brian Kelly**
Sandy Ricks	**Luke Halpin**
Bud Ricks	**Tommy Norden**
Hap Gorman	**Andy Devine**
Ulla Norstrand	**Ulla Stromstedt**

Creator/Executive Producer: **Ivan Tors**
Producer: **Stanley Colbert**

The adventures of two young boys and their pet dolphin at a Florida marine park – a kind of underwater Lassie.

Fifteen-year-old Sandy Ricks and his ten-year-old brother, Bud, lived at the Coral Key Park in Florida, where their widower father, Po Ricks, was Chief Ranger. In the early episodes, carpenter Hap Gorman, an old sea-dog, also hung around, regaling the boys with tall stories, but he was replaced by glamorous Scandinavian biochemist Ulla Norstrand. The family had a pet labrador, Spray, and even a pet pelican, Pete, but it was with Flipper, their tame dolphin, that they had the most fun. This incredibly intelligent sea mammal led Bud and Sandy into a host of maritime adventures and was often at hand to help them out of awkward or dangerous situations. Together they flushed out crooks, averted disasters and swam to the rescue of struggling sailors.

The bottle-nosed dolphin was played most often by an animal named Suzy, and the series was based on the 1963 film of the same name, which starred Chuck Connors as dad alongside son Luke Halpin.

FLOCKHART, CALISTA

(1964–)

American theatre actress who shot to fame as neurotic lawyer ALLY McBEAL, after previously taking only minor roles in a couple of low-key US programmes.

FLOOR MANAGER

The person who takes charge on the studio floor during production, passing on instructions given through headphones by the director in the control room. It is the floor manager who cues the presenters, etc. The term is often abbreviated to FM.

FLOWER POT MEN

UK (BBC) Children's Entertainment. BBC 1952–4

Voices: **Peter Hawkins**

Creators: **Freda Lingstrom, Maria Bird**
Writer: **Maria Bird**

The secret adventures of two flowerpot dwellers who live at the bottom of a garden.

Airing in Wednesday's WATCH WITH MOTHER slot, *Flower Pot Men* exposed the covert activities of identical puppets Bill and Ben. Made out of pots themselves, their hands covered in big gardening gloves and their feet in hobnail boots, Bill and Ben lived in two giant (normal size to humans) flowerpots down by a potting shed. Whenever the gardener popped home for a spot of lunch, the two rascals would slowly raise their heads out of the pots to see if the coast was clear, before leaping out to play. Adventures generally centred around whatever object they could find, but a constant guessing game for viewers was which of the twin puppets had done this or that in the programme. 'Was it Bill or was it Ben?' toddlers were asked, and the truth came out when the culprit turned around to reveal his name on his back. (Older viewers knew instantly, as Bill's voice was a few octaves higher than his pal's.) When the man who worked in the garden had finished his lunch and was on his way down the garden path, the Flower Pot Men scrambled back into their pots in the nick of time. Keeping counsel was their neighbour, Weed, who kindly alerted them to signs of danger. Also in on the boys' secret was the little house, which probably 'knew something about it, too', if its smile was anything to go by.

Flower Pot Men was *Watch with Mother*'s second offering, hot on the heels of ANDY PANDY. Behind the project were *Andy Pandy*'s creators, Freda Lingstrom and Maria Bird, with Audrey Atterbury and Molly Gibson once again pulling the strings and Gladys Whitred and Julia Williams adding the songs. Bill and Ben's 'flobbalot' gibberish was provided by master voicer Peter Hawkins, later to add his talents to THE WOODENTOPS and CAPTAIN PUGWASH, among other animations. A new, 'string-free' version, entitled *Bill and Ben*, was launched in January 2001, with John Thomson voicing Bill and Jimmy Hibbert speaking for Ben.

FLOYD, KEITH
(1943–)

Restaurateur turned TV celebrity, Keith Floyd made his name in a series of programmes for the BBC which dissected the culinary traditions of various corners of the world. These included *Floyd on France, Floyd on Spain, Floyd on Italy, Floyd on Britain and Ireland, Floyd's American Pie, Floyd on Oz* and *Far Flung Floyd*. Other series were *Floyd on Food* and *Floyd on Fish*. He later moved into independent production for series like *Floyd on Africa* and *Capital Floyd*. Establishing himself as a popular, if garrulous frontman, he barked out orders to his camera crew while clutching his trademark glass of wine. Floyd was also chosen to succeed Clive James in what became *Floyd on TV*, before himself making way for Chris Tarrant.

FLYING DOCTOR, THE
UK (ABC) Adventure. ITV 1959–61

Dr Greg Graham	**Richard Denning**
Mary Meredith	**Jill Adams**
Dr Jim Harrison	**Peter Madden**
Charley Wood	**Alan White**

Producer: **David Macdonald**

Adventures in the bush with an American doctor.

Nearly 30 years before *The Flying Doctors* took off from Cooper's Crossing, tall, handsome American doctor Greg Graham, his blind assistant, Dr Harrison, and his trusty nurse, Mary, were life-savers in the Australian outback. Responding to urgent radio messages, they winged their way (always in the nick of time) to remote patients in a small plane piloted by their friend, Charley. Graham had arrived in Australia on leave from a research institute in San Francisco. The series was filmed partly at Elstree and partly on location in Australia.

FLYNN, BARBARA
(Barbara McMurray; 1948–)

Sussex-born actress whose most memorable performances have been as Freda Ashton in Granada's A FAMILY AT WAR, schoolteacher Jill Swinburne in the BEIDERBECKE trilogy and the feminist Dr Rose Marie in A VERY PECULIAR PRACTICE, although she has many other programme credits to her name. These include KEEP IT IN THE FAMILY, OPEN ALL HOURS, *The Last Song, Second Chance, Maybury, Barchester Towers, Day To Remember* and INSPECTOR MORSE. She also played Mme Maigret in the 1990s revival of MAIGRET and was seen as Judith, Fitz's wife, in CRACKER, as private investigator Dee Tate in CHANDLER AND CO., and as Sarah Ridd in *Lorna Doone*.

FLYNN, JEROME
(1963–)

British actor, best known for his work alongside Robson Green in SOLDIER, SOLDIER (Paddy Garvey) and AIN'T MISBEHAVIN' (Eddie Wallis). The pair also enjoyed a run of hugely successful pop records. A keen environmentalist, Flynn was well suited to the later role of wildlife policeman Tom McCabe in *Badger*. Other credits have included *The Fear*, BETWEEN THE LINES (DS Eddie Hargreaves) and *Ruth Rendell's The Lake of Darkness* (Martin Urban). He is the son of actor Eric Flynn and the brother of actor Daniel Flynn.

FOLLYFOOT
UK (Yorkshire) Children's Drama. ITV 1971–3

Dora .... **Gillian Blake**
Steve .... **Steve Hodson**
Slugger .... **Arthur English**
The Colonel .... **Desmond Llewellyn**
Ron Stryker .... **Christian Rodska**
Lewis Hammond .... **Paul Guess**

Executive Producer: **Tony Essex**
Producer: **Audley Southcott**

Eventful days at a home for neglected horses in Yorkshire.

Follyfoot Farm was a retirement home for old and unwanted horses. It was owned by a patrician former army man known as The Colonel and run by his niece, Dora, and Steve, a formerly wayward youth turned reliable stable hand. The farm kitchen was run by a rough-and-ready old boxer named Slugger (once The Colonel's batman), and also in the action was daily hand Ron Stryker, a layabout biker with a heart of gold beneath an abrasive exterior.

Adventures at Follyfoot revolved around the rehabilitation of distressed and neglected horses and were broadly based on the novels by Monica Dickens (particularly the first one, *Cobbler's Dream*, published in 1963). In the farmyard stood a burnt-out tree, victim of a lightning bolt. The Colonel reckoned it would bloom again if given enough attention, so everyone who passed by was required to throw a bucket of water on to its roots. The tree became a good luck charm to the farm folk (and a symbol of hope for worn-out horses) and was featured in the programme's theme song, 'The Lightning Tree', performed by The Settlers, which was a minor chart hit in 1971.

FOOD AND DRINK
UK (BBC/Bazal) Food Magazine. BBC 2 1982–

Presenters: **Simon Bates, Gillian Miles, Henry Kelly, Susan Grossman, Jilly Goolden, Chris Kelly, Michael Barry, Oz Clarke, Paul Heiney, Antony Worrall Thompson, Emma Crowhurst**

Producers: **Henry Murray, Peter Bazalgette, Alison Field, Tim Hincks, Elaine Bancroft, Geraldine McClelland, Gloria Wood**

Eating and drinking magazine.

Crafty recipes, drink reviews and the latest news from the catering world have formed the basis of this popular BBC 2 programme. Simon Bates and Gillian Miles were the original hosts, succeeded by Henry Kelly and Susan Grossman, but the main line-up for several years was Chris Kelly as anchor, Michael Barry in charge of cooking and Jilly Goolden judging various drinks from wines to teas, conveying her findings in an avalanche of over-the-top adjectives. Goolden was later joined by Oz Clarke. In 1997, Barry was succeeded as resident chef by Antony Worrall Thompson. Paul Heiney hosted one series (1991–2) while Chris Kelly was working on another project, and when Kelly finally left the programme in 1999 Goolden took over as host, assisted by Leith's cookery school headteacher Emma Crowhurst. Goolden herself left in 2000, when topical features were abandoned in favour of pre-recordings.

FOOTPRINT

The area of the Earth that a satellite's transmissions reach. If you live outside the footprint area, you can't pick up the signals.

FOR THE CHILDREN
UK (BBC) Children's Entertainment. BBC 1946–51

Producers: **Mary Adams, Andrew Miller Jones**

Early entertainment for school-age children.

Among the items offered under this umbrella title were features on stamp collecting and other wholesome pursuits, classic stories and tales and, from August 1946, music and fun with MUFFIN THE MULE and his piano-playing escort, Annette Mills. Muffin was originally just one of the puppets Annette (and her puppeteer, Ann Hogarth) worked with, but he quickly outshone the likes of Peregrine the Penguin, Sally the Sea Lion, Oswald the Ostrich and Louise the Lamb, to the point where he was given his own series. Only Prudence and Primrose Kitten came close to equalling his popularity, also appearing in their own series in the 1950s. *For the Children*, meanwhile, gave way to ANDY PANDY and the WATCH WITH MOTHER crew.

FOR THE LOVE OF ADA
UK (Thames) Situation Comedy. ITV 1970–1

Ada Cresswell/Bingley .... **Irene Handl**
Walter Bingley .... **Wilfred Pickles**
Leslie Pollitt .... **Jack Smethurst**
Ruth Pollitt .... **Barbara Mitchell**

Creators/Writers: **Vince Powell, Harry Driver**
Producer: **Ronnie Baxter**

Romance in the twilight years with two game pensioners.

When Ada Cresswell buried her late husband, little did she know that the man who had dug the grave would be her next spouse. Beginning a gentle love affair with fellow senior citizen Walter Bingley, Ada moved into his home at Cemetery Lodge, much to the surprise of her daughter, Ruth, and Manchester Utd fanatic son-in-law, Leslie. The sprightly 70-year-olds were eventually married. A feature-film version was released in 1972 and a US copy, *A Touch of Grace*, starring J. Pat O'Malley and Shirley Booth, followed in 1973.

FORBES, EMMA
(1965–)

London-born presenter, first seen in a cookery slot on GOING LIVE!, which led to her co-presenting the Saturday morning programme's successor, *Live and Kicking*, with Andi Peters. She then co-hosted the game show, *Talking Telephone Numbers*, with Phillip Schofield and a regional version of WHAT'S MY LINE?. Her other credits have included *Speakeasy*, LWT's *The Weekend Show*, *Esther* (standing in for Esther Rantzen), *Tip Top Challenge* and *The Club*. She is the daughter of film director Bryan Forbes and actress Nanette Newman.

FORD, ANNA
(1943–)

Gloucestershire-born newsreader and presenter, one of TV-am's 'Famous Five'. Prior to her short stint on breakfast television, Ford had been an ITN newscaster (on *News at Ten*), TOMORROW'S WORLD presenter and a reporter on MAN ALIVE and *Reports Action*, arriving on TV after a time as an Open University tutor. She is now one of the BBC's senior newsreaders and has presented an arts programme for the Performance cable channel.

FORDYCE, KEITH
(1928–)

Former Radio Luxembourg and Light Programme disc jockey, a Cambridge law graduate who presented some of the early 1960s pop shows, especially *Wham!!*, THANK YOUR LUCKY STARS and READY, STEADY, GO!. He also hosted COME DANCING, a few gardening programmes and Westward's regional quiz, *Treasure Hunt*.

FOREVER GREEN
UK (LWT/Picture Partnership) Drama. ITV 1989; 1992

Jack Boult	John Alderton
Harriet Boult	Pauline Collins
Freddy Boult	Daisy Bates
Tom Boult	Nimer Rashed
Lady Patricia Broughall	Paola Dionisotti
Hilly	Wendy Van Der Plank

Executive Producer: **Nick Elliott**
Producer: **Brian Eastman**

A town family moves to the country and discovers rural life is tougher than it looks.

Jack and Harriet Boult, concerned for the health of their asthmatic daughter, Freddy, decided to up-sticks from London and head for the country. Taking up residence at the run-down Meadows Green Farm, somewhere in deepest Gloucestershire, the townies soon discovered that country life had its downs as well as its ups. They found themselves immersed in protests against toxic waste, battling against horse rustlers and protecting barn owls in danger. Tom was their son, and also seen were cranky aristocrat Lady Pat and animal-loving local girl Hilly. Two series of this slow-moving, sentimental drama were made, three years apart.

FORREST, STEVE
(William Forrest Andrews; 1924–)

The brother of actor Dana Andrews, Steve Forrest was one of TV's action men in the 1960s, taking the part of Texas antiques-dealer-cum-investigator John Mannering, aka THE BARON. He followed this up with the role of Lt. Hondo Harrelson in *SWAT* in the mid-1970s and resurfaced in the 1980s as Ben Stivers in DALLAS. He also has plenty of TV movies to his name.

FORSYTE SAGA, THE
UK (BBC/MGM) Drama. BBC 2 1967

Jolyon 'Jo' Forsyte	Kenneth More
Soames Forsyte	Eric Porter
Irene Heron/Forsyte	Nyree Dawn Porter
Jolyon 'Old Jolyon' Forsyte	Joseph O'Conor
James Forsyte	John Welsh
Winifred Forsyte/Dartie	Margaret Tyzack
Ann Forsyte	Fay Compton
Montague Dartie	Terence Alexander
Hélène Hilmer/Forsyte	Lana Morris
Philip Bosinney	John Bennett
Michael Mont	Nicholas Pennell
Frances Crisson/Forsyte	Ursula Howells
Swithin Forsyte	George Woodbridge
Mrs Heron	Jenny Laird
Fleur Forsyte	Susan Hampshire
Annette Lamotte/Forsyte	Dallia Penn
Jolyon 'Jolly' Forsyte	Michael York
Jolyon 'Jon' Forsyte	Martin Jarvis
June Forsyte	Susan Pennick
	June Barry

Producer: **Donald Wilson**

Family squabbles and scandals in the Victorian and Edwardian ages.

The Forsyte Saga was the BBC's last major drama to be produced in black and white, which probably explains why it has not been repeated in recent years, despite its enormous worldwide success. It was the serial which put BBC 2 on the map, attracting six million viewers on Sunday evenings, disrupting church services and emptying pubs. A year later, it was repeated on BBC 1, gaining an audience of 18 million. It was the first serial the BBC ever sold to the Soviet Union and was purchased by stations all over America. And yet *The Forsyte Saga* almost never happened. Producer Donald Wilson had longed to televise John Galsworthy's novels for years, but a combination of problems over rights and stubbornness at the BBC had thwarted him. However, putting together a star cast, Wilson got his way and the series was produced in 26 episodes, each presented as a separate act but with a cliffhanger ending to draw viewers back the following week.

The television script extended the time-scale of Galsworthy's novels, running from 1879 to 1926 and charting the feuding and fighting of the Forsytes, a London merchant family headed by Jolyon (Jo) and his cousin, Soames. Other notable family members included Old Jolyon, the ageing patriarch, and Irene, Soames's wife in a loveless marriage, who was cruelly raped by her husband in one memorably shocking scene. Irene later married Jo and gave birth to Jon, who became illicitly entwined with Fleur, Soames's daughter by a second marriage.

The series confirmed the BBC's reputation for costume dramas and spawned a host of lookalikes, such as THE FIRST CHURCHILLS and THE PALLISERS. Its influence was also seen in the glossy American soaps of the next decade (like DALLAS). More immediately, it revived the flagging career of Kenneth More and made a star out of Susan Hampshire. Eric Porter reaped the accolades, too.

FORSYTH, BRIGIT

(1940–)

Edinburgh-born actress, much seen in supporting roles, such as Bob's bossy wife, Thelma, in WHATEVER HAPPENED TO THE LIKELY LADS?. However, she has enjoyed lead roles of her own, particularly in the sitcoms, *Tom, Dick and Harriet* (Harriet Maddison) and SHARON AND ELSIE (Elsie Beecroft), and the drama, *Holly*. She also played Veronica Haslett in *The Glamour Girls*, Dr Judith Vincent in *The Practice*, Rosemary Dobson in *Nice Town*, Mrs Wells in *Spark* and Francine Pratt in PLAYING THE FIELD, and among her other appearances have been parts in *Adam Smith*, HOLDING THE FORT, *The Master of Ballantrae*, BOON, *Running Wild*, AGATHA CHRISTIE'S POIROT and assorted plays.

FORSYTH, BRUCE

OBE (Bruce Forsyth-Johnson; 1928–)

Highly popular British entertainer whose career stretches back to stage variety performances as Boy Bruce, The Mighty Atom (aged 14). He broke into television in the 1950s and became the main compere of SUNDAY NIGHT AT THE LONDON PALLADIUM in 1958, where he demonstrated his unique and gently aggressive style of handling live audiences and nervous amateur contestants, gaining one of his many catchphrases, 'I'm in charge.' (Forsyth revived the show as *Tonight at the London Palladium* in 2000.) Becoming one of TV's top entertainers, he was given his own variety series, *The Bruce Forsyth Show*, by ATV and proceeded to develop a one-man cabaret routine, singing, dancing, playing the piano and cracking jokes along the way. 'Nice to see you, to see you nice' became another of his catchphrases. In the 1970s he hosted THE GENERATION GAME (picking up yet more gimmicks: 'Didn't he do well!', 'Good game. Good game', etc.) and then, moving to ITV, presented *Bruce Forsyth's Big Night*, PLAY YOUR CARDS RIGHT, *Hollywood or Bust* and YOU BET!. Back with the BBC, he hosted the game show, *Takeover Bid*, and a relaunched *Generation Game*, before switching again to ITV to revamp *Play Your Cards Right* and Leslie Crowther's THE PRICE IS RIGHT. He has also tried his hand at situation comedy, replacing the late Leonard Rossiter in the supermarket farce, TRIPPER'S DAY (as Cecil Slinger in the renamed *Slinger's Day*), and drama, in a 1960s version of Oscar Wilde's *The Canterville Ghost*. His first wife was actress Penny Calvert and his second wife was *Generation Game* hostess Anthea Redfern. His third wife is Miss World 1975, Wilnelia Merced. His daughter Julie is a singer with the Guys and Dolls vocal group.

FORSYTHE, JOHN

(John Freund; 1918–)

American actor well versed in father-figure roles. A one-time baseball commentator, Forsythe switched to acting, appearing on stage, radio and film, before – on Alfred Hitchcock's advice – concentrating on television. He appeared as a guest in ALFRED HITCHCOCK PRESENTS and other anthology series, before headlining in *Bachelor Father* from 1957 to 1962. *The John Forsythe Show* followed and then another comedy, *To Rome with Love*. Neither of these made it on to British screens. A quiet spell as narrator and voice-over actor resulted in the role of Charlie in CHARLIE'S ANGELS, a part in which he was never seen, only heard. In 1981 he was enticed back in front of the camera as tycoon Blake Carrington in DYNASTY and became an international celebrity. His most recent starring role was as Senator William Powers in the sitcom, *The Powers That Be*.

FORTUNES OF WAR

UK (BBC) Drama. BBC 1 1987

Guy Pringle	Kenneth Branagh
Harriet Pringle	Emma Thompson
Prince Yakimov	Ronald Pickup
Dobson	Charles Kay
Inchcape	James Villiers
Sasha Drucker	Harry Burton
Bella Niculesco	Caroline Langrishe
Lord Pinkrose	Alan Bennett
Simon Boulderstone	Robert Graves
Edwina Little	Diana Hardcastle
Toby Lush	Christopher Strauli
Castlebar	Robert Stephens

Writer: **Alan Plater**
Producer: **Betty Willingale**

A young couple's life and relationship are thrown into turmoil by global conflict.

Opening in Bucharest in 1939, at the outset of World War II, and running through to 1943, *Fortunes of War* was the story of newlyweds Guy and Harriet Pringle. Naïve, outgoing Guy worked as a lecturer for the British Council and with his sensible, more reserved wife lived in a cosy little academic community, seemingly oblivious to the events unfolding outside. However, as the conflict deepened and the Pringles were separated from home (in Romania, in Greece and in Egypt, behind the German front), they found themselves inconvenienced by friends like Prince Yakimov. More importantly, parted from each other, their love was put to the test and their characters and personalities forced to change.

Costing £6 million, *Fortunes of War* was the BBC's response to Granada's success with lavish dramas like BRIDESHEAD REVISITED and THE JEWEL IN THE CROWN. It was adapted in seven parts by Alan Plater from Olivia Manning's two trilogies, comprising the novels *The Great Fortune*, *The Spoilt City*, *Friends and Heroes* (*The Balkan Trilogy*), *The Danger Tree*, *The Battle Lost* and *The Sum of Things* (*The Levant Trilogy*).

FORTY MINUTES
UK (BBC) Documentary. BBC 2 1981–94

Editors: **Roger Mills, Edward Mirzoeff, Caroline Pick, Paul Watson**

Acclaimed documentary series tackling a variety of offbeat subjects.

With each programme lasting, as expected, 40 minutes, this collection of documentaries looked at subjects as varied as child prostitution, lavatories, gifted children, homing pigeons, battered husbands, amateur dramatics and prize-winning leeks. A well-remembered 1986 contribution was entitled *The Fishing Party* and focused on four well-bred men having a laugh on an angling trip, while another, *Away the Lads* in 1994, followed boisterous English youths on holiday in Benidorm.

FOSTER, BARRY
(1931–)

Fair, curly-haired, Nottinghamshire-born actor whose TV high spot was the VAN DER VALK series of the early 1970s, in which he played the lead character, a Dutch police detective. The series was briefly revived in 1991. Among his other credits have been parts in *Skyport*, MOGUL (Robert Driscoll), *Divorce His, Divorce Hers*, *The Fall of Eagles* (Kaiser Wilhelm), *The Three Hostages* (Richard Hannay), *Smiley's People*, *A Woman Called Golda*, *Death of an Expert Witness*, *Hôtel Du Lac*, BERGERAC, INSPECTOR MORSE and ROGER ROGER (Pieter Eugene).

FOSTER, JULIA
(1941–)

Fair-haired British actress. She appeared in EMERGENCY – WARD 10, starred as Angie Botley in *Good Girl*, played Amy Wilde in WILDE ALLIANCE and took the title role in a version of *Moll Flanders*. She was also Janet in the domestic sitcom, *The Cabbage Patch*, Carol Bolitho in *Virtual Murder*, and Doris Doyle, the mum, in the kids' fantasy, *News at Twelve*. Among her other credits have been numerous single dramas, some in anthologies like LOVE STORY and *Play for Tomorrow*.

FOSTERS, THE
UK (LWT) Situation Comedy. ITV 1976–7

Samuel Foster	**Norman Beaton**
Pearl Foster	**Isabelle Lucas**
Vilma	**Carmen Munro**
Sonny Foster	**Lenny Henry**
Shirley Foster	**Sharon Rosita**
Benjamin Foster	**Lawrie Mark**

Producer: **Stuart Allen**

Fun and games with a black family in south London.

Breaking new ground as the first British series to feature an all-black cast, *The Fosters* was based on an American sitcom entitled *Good Times* (a spin-off from *Maude*, itself a spin-off from ALL IN THE FAMILY). Using anglicized original scripts, it featured an immigrant family living in a south London tower block. The Fosters were harassed dad Samuel, coping mum Pearl, artistic eldest son Sonny, 16-year-old Shirley and young Benjamin. In the same block lived Vilma, Pearl's friend and confidante. The programme was also notable for giving Lenny Henry (then aged 17) his first series role, but was attacked by some critics for reinforcing racial stereotypes.

FOUR FEATHER FALLS
UK (AP Films/Granada) Children's Western. ITV 1960

Voices:

Tex Tucker	**Nicholas Parsons**
Rocky	**Kenneth Connor**
Dusty	**Kenneth Connor**
Pedro	**Kenneth Connor**
Grandpa Twink	**David Graham**
Fernando	**David Graham**
Ma Jones	**Denise Bryer**
Little Jake	**Denise Bryer**

Producer: **Gerry Anderson**

Cowboy puppetry featuring a fair but tough sheriff who keeps order with the help of a little magic.

Tex Tucker was the sheriff of the Western town of Four

Feather Falls, but he was no ordinary lawman. His job was made considerably more comfortable by four magical feathers that he wore in his stetson. The feathers, given to Tex by Indian Chief Kalamakooya for rescuing his injured son, each had a function: one feather enabled Tex's dog, Dusty, to speak; another gave the power of speech to his horse, Rocky. The last two feathers controlled his two pistols, which swivelled and fired accurately whenever the sheriff was in danger.

Ably supported by Rocky and Dusty, his unofficial deputies, Tex was a true Western hero, standing for no nonsense in a typical cowboy town. Among the villains were Fernando, Big Bad Ben and Pedro the Bandit, and the townsfolk who relied on their hero included Doc Haggerty, Ma Jones the storekeeper, Grandpa Twink and his grandson, Little Jake. Short on killing and big on songs (Michael Holliday provided Tex's singing voice), the 15-minute series ran to 39 episodes.

FOUR JUST MEN, THE

UK (Sapphire/ATV) Adventure. ITV 1959–60

Ben Manfred MP	**Jack Hawkins**
Tim Collier	**Dan Dailey**
Jeff Ryder	**Richard Conte**
Ricco Poccari	**Vittorio De Sica**
Nicole	**Honor Blackman**
Vicky	**June Thorburn**
Giulia	**Lisa Gastoni**

Executive Producer: **Hannah Weinstein**
Producers: **Sidney Cole, Jud Kinberg**

Four wartime colleagues reunite to combat crime.

The Four Just Men, as they styled themselves, were MP and amateur detective Ben Manfred, American reporter Tim Collier, who was based in Paris, New York lawyer Jeff Ryder and wealthy Roman hotelier Ricco Poccari. They had all been members of the same Allied unit during the war and were brought together again by Manfred at the dying request of their wartime leader, Colonel Bacon, to tackle injustice around the world. The men generally worked alone (with each episode featuring only one star), although Manfred's men were also supported by their personal assistants: Nicole for Collier, Vicky for Ryder and Giulia for Poccari. The series was based on the 1906 novel by Edgar Wallace and the 1939 film, which cast the men in a more sinister light.

FOWLDS, DEREK

(1937–)

British actor whose career has veered between reading stories to an animal puppet, manoeuvring a confused politician and supervising young policemen. It was as Basil Brush's straight man that Fowlds first became known, a role he followed up with appearances in dramas such as EDWARD THE SEVENTH, *Clayhanger*, STRANGERS, CRIBB, TRIANGLE, *Affairs of the Heart* (heart-attack victim Peter Bonamy), *My Son, My Son, Rules of Engagement*, BOON, *Chancer* and *Firm Friends* (John

Gutteridge), as well as comedies such as *After This, That*, MISS JONES AND SON, ROBIN'S NEST and RINGS ON THEIR FINGERS. As private secretary Bernard Wooley in YES, MINISTER and its sequel, *Yes, Prime Minister*, he helped keep Paul Eddington's Jim Hacker on the straight and narrow, and in HEARTBEAT, as the fatherly if set-in-his-ways Sgt Blaketon, he kept an eye on young coppers like Nick Berry's PC Rowan. His second wife was BLUE PETER presenter Lesley Judd. His son, Jeremy, is also an actor.

FOWLER, HARRY

MBE (Henry Fowler; 1926–)

Chirpy Cockney actor and presenter, a star of THE ARMY GAME (Corporal Flogger Hoskins) and OUR MAN AT ST MARK'S (Harry the Yo Yo), before branching out into children's programmes, hosting *Going a Bundle* with Kenny Lynch and *Get This* with James Villiers. He has also appeared in series like SPOONER'S PATCH (Jimmy the Con), *Dead Ernest* (Cherub Fred), *Dramarama, Scarecrow and Mrs King*, SUPERGRAN, *Davro's Sketch Pad*, THE BILL, CASUALTY, IN SICKNESS AND IN HEALTH, *World's End* and LOVE HURTS, as well as around 80 films.

FOX

UK (Thames/Euston Films) Drama. ITV 1980

Billy Fox	**Peter Vaughan**
Connie Fox	**Elizabeth Spriggs**
Kenny Fox	**Ray Winstone**
Joey Fox	**Larry Lamb**
Vin Fox	**Bernard Hill**
Ray Fox	**Derrick O'Connor**
Phil Fox	**Eamon Boland**
Renie Fox	**Rosemary Martin**
Andy Fox	**Richard Weinbaum**
Nan	**Cindy O'Callaghan**

Writer: **Trevor Preston**
Executive Producer: **Verity Lambert**
Producer: **Graham Benson**

The singular and collective lives of a south London family with shady connections.

This 13-part filmed drama revolved around the Fox family, headed by local Mr Big, Billy Fox, who celebrated his 70th birthday in the opening episode. The same episode introduced his clan, made up of his second wife, Connie, his five sons and their respective wives, mistresses and offspring. The boys were Vin, working in the construction industry, Kenny, an aspiring welterweight boxer, Joey, a womanizing taxi-driver, Phil, a student, and finally Ray. Also prominent were Vin's wife, Renie, and their deaf son, Andy (Billy's pride and joy). The drama unfolded in two phases: before and after 'King' Billy's death, showing how the family struggled to deal with the loss of this larger-than-life figure who terrified other villains but was kind to the ordinary folk on his manor.

FOX BROADCASTING COMPANY

America's fourth network, making inroads where others (particularly DuMont in the 1940s and 1950s) failed. The company is headed by Rupert Murdoch and former Paramount executive Barry Diller, and takes its name from the old Twentieth Century-Fox studios, which are now part of the company. Fox went on air in November 1986 and soon began to eat into the market share of America's big three networks (CBS, NBC and ABC), adopting a trendier attitude and cleverly launching new programmes in August when the other stations have traditionally scheduled re-runs. While Fox is still not in the same league as the established networks, it is having its successes (including poaching the Superbowl) and among its innovative programmes have been THE SIMPSONS, *The Joan Rivers Show* and *Married . . . with Children*.

FOX, EDWARD
(1937–)

Upright British actor, star of EDWARD AND MRS SIMPSON. Among his other credits have been parts in THE AVENGERS, MAN IN A SUITCASE, JOURNEY TO THE UNKNOWN, *Hard Times, Shaka Zulu, Gulliver's Travels* (General Limtoc) and *A Dance to the Music of Time* (Uncle Giles), although he has been more prolific in the cinema. He is the brother of actor James Fox and father of actress Emilia Fox.

FOX, Sir PAUL
CBE (1925–)

Former paratrooper and journalist Paul Fox joined the BBC in 1950 as holiday relief writer on BBC TELEVISION NEWSREEL, but he quickly put down roots. He was influential in the setting-up of the SPORTSVIEW unit and was the programme's editor from 1953. Fox went on to edit PANORAMA and then progressed up the ladder to the position of Controller of BBC 1 in 1967. He was lured away to Yorkshire Television in 1973, to succeed Donald Baverstock as programme controller, becoming the company's managing director in 1977. He also chaired ITN for two years. In 1988 Fox returned to the BBC on a three-year contract as Managing Director of BBC Television. He has since left broadcasting to work with the Race Courses Association.

FOXY LADY
UK (Granada) Situation Comedy. ITV 1982–4

Daisy Jackson	**Diane Keen**
Joe Prince	**Geoffrey Burridge**
J. P. Schofield	**Patrick Troughton**
Ben Marsh	**Milton Johns**
Tancred Taylour	**Alan David**
Hector Ross	**Gregor Fisher**
Owen Buckley	**Steven Pinder**
Acorn Henshaw	**Tom Mennard**

Writer: **Geoffrey Lancashire**
Producer: **John G. Temple**

A new female editor rides to the rescue of an ailing northern newspaper.

Set in 1959, *Foxy Lady* related how Daisy Jackson gamely took on the editorship of the *Ramsden Reminder*, a weekly local rag tottering on the brink of bankruptcy following the death of the previous incumbent. Her all-male team consisted of accountant Joe Prince, feature writer J. P. Schofield, gambling sports writer Ben Marsh, women's page editor Hector Ross, arts editor Tancred Taylour, print trainee Owen Buckley and odd-job man Acorn Henshaw. Circulation initially picked up, but life was never easy for Daisy.

The cast list makes interesting reading today. Not only did it feature veterans like former DOCTOR WHO Patrick Troughton and Tom Mennard (CORONATION STREET'S Sam Tindall), but also a pre-CROSSROADS and BROOKSIDE Steven Pinder, and Gregor Fisher before he donned the string vest of RAB C. NESBITT.

FRANCIS, CLIVE
(1946–)

The son of NO HIDING PLACE star Raymond Francis, Clive Francis has enjoyed a successful (and more varied) TV career of his own. Among his major roles have been Francis Poldark in POLDARK, DS Dexter in NEW SCOTLAND YARD, Miles Henty in MAY TO DECEMBER, Major Maurice Drummond in *The Piglet Files* and Dominic Eden in *The 10%ers*. He has also been seen in BULMAN, THE FAR PAVILIONS, *David Copperfield*, YES, PRIME MINISTER, *Old Flames*, LIPSTICK ON YOUR COLLAR (Major Hedges), SHARPE and *Longitude* (Captain Digges).

FRANCIS, JAN
(1951–)

Dark-haired English actress, seen in both dramatic and comedy roles. Her most prominent performance was as Penny Warrender in the sitcom, JUST GOOD FRIENDS. However, she has enjoyed several other starring roles, as resistance worker Lisa Colbert in SECRET ARMY, newly widowed Sally Hardcastle in STAY LUCKY, and Maggie Perowne in *Under the Hammer*, for instance. Her ballet training came in useful for her part in *A Chance to Sit Down*, and among the many other programmes she has contributed to have been JACKANORY, SUTHERLAND'S LAW, *Looking for Clancy, Rooms*, THE DUCHESS OF DUKE STREET, RAFFLES, *A Play for Love*, THE RACING GAME, TARGET, RIPPING YARNS, *The Good Companions*, TALES OF THE UNEXPECTED, Alan Plater's *Premiere* offering, *Give Us a Kiss, Christabel, The Ghostbusters of East Finchley* (Grace Pullen) and *Spark* (Colette).

FRANCIS, RAYMOND
(1911–87)

One of British television's earliest coppers, London-born Raymond Francis played the snuff-taking Tom Lockhart in three different series: MURDER BAG in 1957, CRIME SHEET in 1959, and finally NO HIDING PLACE, which ran for eight years up to 1967. Francis had previously appeared in a handful of TV plays and starred as Dr Watson in a 1951 BBC version of *Sherlock Holmes*. Not long before he died he returned to make a cameo appearance as Lockhart in the COMIC STRIP's *Five Go Mad in Dorset* (one of several such appearances for Lockhart over the years). Francis was also seen in series like *Thomas and Sarah*, EDWARD AND MRS SIMPSON, MISS MARPLE and ME AND MY GIRL. He was the father of actor Clive Francis.

FRANCISCUS, JAMES
(1934–91)

American leading man who guested in various 1950s series like HAVE GUN, WILL TRAVEL and THE TWILIGHT ZONE, before winning a lead role in NAKED CITY. As Detective Jim Halloran, he stayed with the series for just one year. Throughout the 1960s and 1970s, he was never short of work. US dramas, including *The Investigators* and *Mr Novak*, plus smaller parts in programmes like THE FBI, kept him busy for most of the time. In 1971 he played the blind private detective, *Longstreet*, and later starred in a couple of other series, *Doc Elliott* and *Hunter*. He had several TV movies to his name, too.

FRANK STUBBS PROMOTES/FRANK STUBBS
UK (Carlton/Noel Gay) Comedy Drama. ITV 1993–4

Frank Stubbs	Timothy Spall
Petra Dillon	Lesley Sharp
Dawn Dillon	Danniella Westbrook
Archie Nash	Trevor Cooper
Dave Giddings	Nick Reding
Karen Lai	Choy-Ling Man
Diane Stubbs	Hazel Ellerby
Blick	Roy Marsden

Creator: **Simon Nye**
Producer: **Hilary Bevan Jones**

An aspiring showbiz promoter never quite makes it big.

Ticket-tout Frank Stubbs was tired of pacing the West End streets hawking overpriced tickets for the top shows. He was even more tired of being nicked and having to spend the night in the cells. Inspired by the success of smooth, young Dave Giddings, he decided that promotion was to be the name of the game from then on. His first break came with an Australian Country and Western singer, whom he staged despite the best efforts of his more established rivals. Predictably, she then left him for a real professional. After that, the ever-optimistic Frank and his colleague, Archie, found themselves ducking and diving in and out of schemes to promote kit cars, Russian skaters, graffiti artists, hopeful actresses, ambitious film directors, a low-profile politician and an American evangelist. Frank had just as many troubles in his personal life, too. He lived with his recently widowed (and virtually bankrupted) sister, Petra, and her daughter, Dawn, in a flat above a betting shop. His own wife, Diane, had kicked him out after his much-regretted fling with a teenager. In the second series, shown in 1994, Stubbs had moved to a swish new office-block, owned by a character named Blick.

Borrowing heavily from the Arthur Daley school of wheeling and dealing, the series was based on Simon Nye's novel, *Wideboy*. Nye also wrote some of the episodes.

FRANKENSTEIN JR AND THE IMPOSSIBLES
US (Hanna-Barbera) Cartoon. BBC 1 1967

Voices:

Frankenstein Jr	Ted Cassidy
Buzz Conroy	Dick Beals
Prof. Conroy	John Stephenson
Multi Man	Don Messick
Fluid Man	Paul Frees
Coil Man	Hal Smith

Executive Producers: **William Hanna, Joseph Barbera**

Cartoon package featuring two helpings of superheroes – a giant Frankenstein robot and a vigilante pop group.

Frankenstein Jr was the invention of red-headed boy scientist Buzz Conroy, son of the eminent Professor Conroy. A huge, talking, thinking, rocket-powered robot, Frankenstein Jr looked just like his horror movie namesake but was used entirely for good causes, defeating supervillains like Dr Shock and Birdman. Buzz controlled Jr with a special radar ring and also joined the robot on his missions. Clambering up on his back, Buzz uttered the magic command 'Allakazoom!', which blasted them off from the Professor's mountain lab. Once in action, Buzz donned his rocket-belt, which enabled him to fly, and Jr employed an armoury of ingenious weapons.

The Impossibles were a three-man, touring pop-group whose performances were constantly interrupted by their boss, Big D, who spoke to them from a video screen hidden in a guitar. With the cry of 'Rally-Ho!', the trio bounded into action against crooks, making full use of their incredible abilities. Coil Man had spring-loaded, extending limbs, Fluid Man had the power to become any kind of liquid (allowing him to trickle under doors, for example) and Multi Man could make instant and unlimited copies of himself. The 'Impossicar' took them from gig to gig.

Any actors worried about typecasting ought to

consider Ted Cassidy's role in this series. Fresh from playing Lurch in THE ADDAMS FAMILY, he now found himself voicing a Frankenstein robot. The giant robot idea was derived from a Japanese series called *Gigantor*.

FRANKLIN, GRETCHEN
(1911–)

London-born actress familiar in down-to-earth, dithery female roles, most notably as Ethel Skinner in EAST-ENDERS. She played Alf Garnett's wife (then Alf *Ramsey*) in the COMEDY PLAYHOUSE pilot of TILL DEATH US DO PART, but didn't continue into the series. Programmes she has appeared in, in a varied career, have included QUATERMASS, *The Artful Dodger*, COMPACT, *The Dick Emery Show*, GEORGE AND MILDRED, *Bowler*, *Churchill's People*, plus various dramas. She was also Myrtle Cavendish in CROSSROADS, Auntie Lil in I DIDN'T KNOW YOU CARED and Alice in *Dead Ernest*.

FRANKLYN, WILLIAM
(1926–)

For all his TV work, smoothie William Franklyn may be best remembered as the 'Schh! You know who' man, after his commercials for Schweppes soft drinks. However, he entered television in the mid-1950s, taking roles in series like DOUGLAS FAIRBANKS PRESENTS, THE COUNT OF MONTE CRISTO and INTERNATIONAL DETECTIVE, before securing star billing in the 1961 adventure series, TOP SECRET, in which he played undercover agent Peter Dallas. He was a familiar face in the 1960s and 1970s, cropping up in action series like THE AVENGERS and THE BARON, and detective stories like MAIGRET and PUBLIC EYE, fronting the sketch show, *What's On Next?*, and taking parts in the comedies, *Paradise Island* (shipwrecked entertainments officer Cuthbert Fullworthy) and *The Steam Video Company*. He hosted the panel game, *Masterspy*, and was also seen in *Moon and Son*, THE UPPER HAND, LOVEJOY and GBH. He is the father of actress Sabina Franklyn.

FRASER, BILL
(1908–87)

Busy British character actor, best remembered as Sgt Claude Snudge in THE ARMY GAME and its sequels, BOOTSIE AND SNUDGE and *Foreign Affairs*, as well as the slightly different *Vacant Lot* (builder William Bendlove). His other performances included Barney Pank in *Barney Is My Darling*, a defrocked priest in Joe Orton's play, *Funeral Games*, undertaker Basil Bulstrode in *That's Your Funeral* and station-master Hedley Green in *The Train Now Standing*. Fraser was also seen as one of Alf Garnett's buddies in TILL DEATH US DO PART, and played Mr Micawber in a BBC version of *David Copperfield*, Henry Brassington in *Flesh and Blood*, Bert Baxter in THE SECRET DIARY OF ADRIAN MOLE, Dr Fellows-Smith in *Doctors' Daughters* and Mr Justice Bullingham in RUMPOLE OF

THE BAILEY, although his TV credits dated way back to the 1940s. His wife was actress Pamela Cundell.

FRASER, RONALD
(1930–97)

Lancashire-born actor, star of the 1970 sitcom, THE MISFIT, in which he played Basil 'Badger' Allenby-Johnson. Fraser also took the role of Inspector Spooner in the first series of SPOONER'S PATCH and enjoyed plenty of other TV credits, popping up in drama anthologies like *Rogues' Gallery* and *Conceptions of Murder*, comedies such as LIFE WITHOUT GEORGE (senile pianist Mr Chambers), and taking parts like Sir Richard Gregory in *Moll Flanders*.

FRASIER
US (Grub Street/Paramount) Situation Comedy.
Channel 4 1994–

Dr Frasier Crane	**Kelsey Grammer**
Dr Niles Crane	**David Hyde Pierce**
Daphne Moon	**Jane Leeves**
Martin Crane	**John Mahoney**
Roz Doyle	**Peri Gilpin**
Bob 'Bulldog' Briscoe	**Dan Butler**

Creators: **David Angell, Peter Casey, David Lee**
Executive Producers: **David Angell, Peter Casey, David Lee, Kelsey Grammer, Christopher Lloyd, Joe Keenan**

The turbulent life of a pompous radio psychiatrist.

Frasier Crane, formerly the intellectual at the bar of CHEERS, had divorced wife Lilith, left Boston and returned to his home town of Seattle. Settling into a new job as resident shrink on the radio station, KACL, he was just beginning to enjoy life in his luxurious new apartment in Elliott Bay Towers when his independence was shattered by the arrival of his invalid father. Martin was an ex-cop who had taken a bullet on duty, and moving in with him were his physical therapist, the semi-psychic Mancunian, Daphne Moon, and an irritatingly intelligent terrier named Eddie (played by a dog called Moose). Not that this was the limit of Frasier's extended family, as his even-more-effete brother, Niles (also an analyst), was seldom away from his doorstep, bemoaning his life with his never-seen, extremely wealthy, hypochondriac wife, Maris. At work, too, Frasier's sanity was tested during his daily phone-in, this time by wacky callers (played by celebrities like Art Garfunkel and Mel Brooks), nymphomaniac producer Roz and vulgar, practical-joking sports presenter Bulldog. The strain also spilled over to the aptly named local coffee shop, Café Nervosa.

Although exhibiting all the best traits of the US sitcom – precise characterization, sharp dialogue and rich farce among them – *Frasier* was also a comedy of manners. The upper-class pretensions of Frasier (who was considerably more refined here than in his latter days at *Cheers*) and Niles were sharply contrasted with the working-class ethics of their good-hearted dad – designer furniture opposite a tatty old armchair, expensive wines against cans of Ballantine's beer, snooty restaurant dinners before the opera versus a hot dog at the ball game, etc. Recurring strands included Frasier's struggle to find a new woman, Roz's similar unhappiness in her single life and Niles's crush on the oblivious Daphne.

As the series developed, the storylines moved on. Maris divorced Niles, Martin dated a barmaid named Sherry, Roz became a single mum and Niles married a demandingly fussy plastic surgeon named Mel. In one memorable season-closer, Daphne's wedding to attorney Donny Douglas was wrecked when she and Niles finally got it together and headed off in Martin's Winnebago.

Cheers had been lauded by both viewers and critics, but its spin-off proved even more successful, being showered with Emmys and almost topping the Nielsen audience ratings.

FRAUD SQUAD
UK (ATV) Police Drama. ITV 1969–70

DI Gamble .... **Patrick O'Connell**
DS Vicky Hicks .... **Joanna Van Gyseghem**
Helen Gamble .... **Elizabeth Weaver**
Lucy Gamble .... **Katherine O'Connell**
Supt. Proud .... **Ralph Nossek**

Creator: **Ivor Jay**
Producer: **Nicholas Palmer**

The inquiries of Scotland Yard's Fraudulent Crimes Squad.

The featured members of the Fraud Squad were Detective Inspector Gamble and his assistant, DS Hicks (one of TV's first prominent female detectives). Together they tackled fraud in all areas, from the activities of con-men to the dubious financial status of a religious sect. Problems within Gamble's own family also came to the fore. The series was created by Ivor Jay, a former DIXON OF DOCK GREEN and CROSSROADS scriptwriter.

FREEMAN, RIGHT HON. JOHN
MBE (1915–)

Serious, determined British interviewer (almost interrogator) of the late 1950s/early 1960s, mostly on FACE TO FACE. A former PANORAMA contributor and Labour MP for Watford, he went on to edit *New Statesman*, become British High Commissioner in India, Ambassador to the USA and chairman of both London Weekend Television and ITN.

FREETIME
See MAGPIE.

FRENCH, DAWN
(1957–)

British comic actress, long-time partner of Jennifer Saunders and wife of Lenny Henry. After a spell as a teacher and some club work with Saunders, she broke into television as part of the *Comic Strip* team, appearing in all their films. With Saunders, Ruby Wax and Tracey Ullman, she starred as Amanda in GIRLS ON TOP (also as co-writer) and then appeared in the comic mystery plays, MURDER MOST HORRID. She has starred as Geraldine Granger, THE VICAR OF DIBLEY, Lisette in *Let Them Eat Cake*, murdering nurse Elaine Dobbs in the *Screen One* presentation, *Tender Loving Care*, and Bev Bodger in the drama, *Sex and Chocolate*, as well as hosting the food and fashion programmes, *Scoff* and *Swank*, and being seen in THE YOUNG ONES, THE STORYTELLER, HAPPY FAMILIES (the cook), *David Copperfield* (Mrs Crupp) and, of course, *French and Saunders*.

FRENCH FIELDS
See FRESH FIELDS.

FRESH FIELDS/FRENCH FIELDS
UK (Thames) Situation Comedy. ITV 1984–6/1989–91

Hester Fields .... **Julia McKenzie**
William Fields .... **Anton Rodgers**
Sonia Barratt .... **Ann Beach**
Nancy Penrose .... **Fanny Rowe**
Guy Penrose .... **Ballard Berkeley**
Peter Richardson .... **Philip Bird**
Emma Richardson .... **Debbie Cumming**
Sally Baxter (*Fresh Fields*)
Karen Ascoe (*French Fields*)
Monsieur Dax .... **Olivier Pierre** (*French Fields*)
Marie-Christine .... **Victoria Baker** (*French Fields*)
Madame Remoleux .... **Valerie Lush** (*French Fields*)
Chantal Moriac .... **Pamela Salem** (*French Fields*)
Jill Trendle .... **Liz Crowther** (*French Fields*)
Hugh Trendle .... **Robin Kermode** (*French Fields*)

Creators/Writers: **John Chapman** (*Fresh Fields/French Fields*), **Ian Davidson** (*French Fields*)
Producers: **Peter Frazer-Jones** (*Fresh Fields*), **James Gilbert** (*French Fields*)

A middle-aged couple spice up their life after the kids leave home.

With the children, Tom and Emma, having flown the nest, Hester and William Fields needed new challenges and new zest in their life. They embarked on a rejuvenated relationship, enjoying each other's company and bouncing along in their new-found freedom, trying out new hobbies and pastimes. They lived in Barnes, west London. The slightly scatty Hester (a cordon bleu cook) worked one day a week at Lucy's Kitchen, and William was an accountant in the City, but their lives were playfully entwined, even if interrupted (especially at mealtimes) by nosy, scrounging neighbour Sonia and by Nancy, Hester's mum, who lived in the granny flat in the garden. Nancy's former husband (and Hester's father), Guy, was also seen from time to time. In 1989, the programme was revived after a three-year hiatus, but with its format and title changed. William was headhunted for a job in France, so the Fields jumped on the foreign property bandwagon and grappled with the language across the Channel. Their tactless, yuppie neighbours there were the Trendles, with Mme Remoleux the Fields' interfering housekeeper.

FREUD, Sir CLEMENT
(1924–)

TV personality, writer, humorist and gourmet, much seen on dog food adverts. For many years Freud was a Liberal MP. He is the father of radio and TV presenter Emma Freud.

FRIEL, ANNA
(1975–)

Actress born in Belfast and raised in Rochdale, achieving star status as Beth Jordache in BROOKSIDE. Earlier, she had appeared in small roles in a variety of series, including *8:15 From Manchester*, EMMERDALE, CORONATION STREET, MEDICS, *In Suspicious Circumstances* and GBH (Michael Palin's daughter). Since leaving *Brookside*, she has been seen in *Shakespeare Shorts: A Midsummer Night's Dream* (Hermia), *Our Mutual Friend* (Bella Wilfer), CAD-FAEL, *Tales from the Crypt* and the single drama, *All For Love* (Flora).

FRIENDS
US (Bright/Kauffman/Crane/Warner Brothers) Situation Comedy. Channel 4 1995–

Rachel Green .... **Jennifer Aniston**
Monica Geller .... **Courteney Cox Arquette**
Phoebe Buffay .... **Lisa Kudrow**
Joey Tribbiani .... **Matt LeBlanc**
Chandler Bing .... **Matthew Perry**
Ross Geller .... **David Schwimmer**

Creators: **Marta Kauffman, David Crane**
Executive Producers: **Kevin S. Bright, Marta Kauffman, David Crane, Adam Chase, Greg Malins**

Six twentysomethings share life in New York City.

This hugely successful sitcom, noted for its sharp one-liners, focused on a group of six mates who lived in the Big Apple and hung out at Central Perk, a Greenwich Village coffee-shop. The three girls were the rather spoilt Rachel Green, now – having walked out of her wedding and alienating her father – struggling to make her own way in the world as a waitress (and, later, as a fashion buyer); assistant-chef Monica Geller, in whose apartment Rachel sought refuge; and their off-beat, New Age, masseuse pal, Phoebe Buffay. The three boys were

museum worker Ross Geller, Monica's brother, who had just divorced his wife, Carol; dim, would-be actor Joey Tribbiani; and Joey's clownish, office worker roommate, Chandler Bing. The last two lived across the hall from Rachel and Monica. The friends' lives revolved around career ambitions, romantic tie-ups and memories of their past (complete with flashbacks).

The biggest traumas seemed to involve Ross, who discovered his wife was having his baby while living with her lesbian lover. He then began an affair with Rachel, whom he'd had a crush on at school. He later married English girl Emily, but the marriage was not a success. Of the others, Chandler and Monica became more than 'friends' and tried desperately to keep their relationship from the rest of the gang. This was after Monica had had a fling with Dr Richard Burke, a friend of her parents. Actress Lisa Kudrow also occasionally appeared as Phoebe's twin sister, Ursula, who was a cross-over character from another sitcom, *Mad About You*. One other (thankfully unseen) regular was the Ugly Naked Guy, spied on by the gang from Monica's apartment.

All episodes were titled 'The One with . . .' (fill in the gap), and the show's theme song, 'I'll Be There for You', was a UK hit for The Rembrandts in 1995.

FRONT MAN

The main presenter of a news, sports or magazine programme, the link between the various items that make up the programme. Also known as anchor.

FROST REPORT, THE
UK (BBC) Comedy. BBC 1 1966–7

David Frost, Ronnie Barker, Ronnie Corbett, John Cleese, Julie Felix, Tom Lehrer, Nicky Henson, Sheila Steafel

Producer: **James Gilbert**

Topical satire show, debunking a different subject every week.

Whereas David Frost's 1968 offering, *The Frost Programme*, focused on in-depth interviews and exposés, the earlier *Frost Report* was a light-hearted affair. It took a different topic each week – holidays, Parliament, sin, etc. – and reviewed it satirically through sketches performed by the likes of John Cleese and Ronnies Barker and Corbett, complemented by a suitable song from Julie Felix. Offerings included the famous 'class' sketch in which the tall, upper-class Cleese looked down on the shorter, middle-class Barker who in turn looked down on the diminutive, working-class Corbett. The programme's writers included the MONTY PYTHON team of Eric Idle, John Cleese, Graham Chapman, Michael Palin and Terry Jones (in tandem for the first time), as well as Tim Brooke-Taylor, John Law and Marty Feldman. A compilation of the best moments, *Frost Over England*, won the Golden Rose at the Montreux Festival in 1967.

FROST, Sir DAVID
OBE (1939–)

Kent-born broadcaster who became an overnight success (or who 'rose without trace', as Malcolm Muggeridge's wife is alleged to have put it) on the revolutionary satire show, THAT WAS THE WEEK THAT WAS, in 1962. Having presented a few low-key programmes for ITV, Frost, the Cambridge graduate son of a Beccles minister, was thrust into the *TW3* host's chair when Brian Redhead pulled out. His unflappability shone through and he also took the show to the USA, where it established itself but failed to win the same acclaim. Back in the UK, Frost compered *TW3*'s less successful offspring, NOT SO MUCH A PRO-GRAMME, MORE A WAY OF LIFE, and then married comedy with hard-hitting interviews, hosting THE FROST REPORT (complete with sketches from Messrs Barker, Corbett and Cleese) on the BBC and *The Frost Programme* (instigating 'trials by television') on ITV. He was executive producer of AT LAST THE 1948 SHOW, NO – THAT'S ME OVER HERE! and *The Ronnie Barker Playhouse*, and starred in his own *Frost On Saturday* and *Frost On Sunday* (while commuting across to the USA), plus various *Frost Over . . .* programmes on countries like New Zealand and Australia. In 1974 he presented *Frost's Weekly* for the BBC and two years later secured a series of exclusive interviews with disgraced President Nixon which were screened on both sides of the Atlantic and offered some important revelations and disclosures. In 1982 he formed part of TV-am's 'Famous Five' as they launched commercial breakfast television in the UK. With the company's problems spilling over into the public domain, he soon found himself the last of the five still at the station. His TV-am Sunday morning show established itself as an important weekly focal point for the political world and he was enticed to take it across to the BBC as *Breakfast with Frost*. However, he did return to ITV in a regional late-night discussion show, again called *The Frost Programme*, in 1993. To underline his versatility, Frost has also produced a couple of TV movies, hosted the panel game, THROUGH THE KEYHOLE, and presented superlative facts and feats in special editions of *The Guinness Book of Records*. As an executive, Frost has been a member of the LWT and TV-am boards and owns his own company, David Paradine Productions (using his middle name). 'Hello, good evening and welcome' has been his much-mimicked catchphrase. His first wife was actress Lynne Frederick.

FRY, STEPHEN
(1957–)

Hampstead-born comedian and actor, the partner of Hugh Laurie in *Saturday Live*, *A Bit of Fry and Laurie*, and JEEVES AND WOOSTER (Jeeves). He played the conniving Lord Melchett in BLACKADDER II and his descendant, the booming General Melchett, in BLACKADDER GOES FORTH; and his other contributions have come in ALFRESCO, THE YOUNG ONES, FILTHY RICH AND CATFLAP, HAPPY FAMILIES (Dr De Quincy), ALAS SMITH AND JONES,

Old Flames, *In the Red* (Radio 2 Controller), *The Magician's House* (voice of Jasper the Owl), *Gormenghast* (Professor Bellgrove) and the investigative reporter spoof, *This Is David Lander*. Fry also appeared in *Stalag Luft* and as Mybug in *Cold Comfort Farm*. While a student at Cambridge, Fry reworked the musical, *Me and My Girl*, which was taken to the West End with great success. He has also written some best-selling novels.

FUGITIVE, THE
US (QM) Drama. ITV 1964–7

Dr Richard Kimble	David Janssen
Lt. Philip Gerard	Barry Morse
Donna Taft	Jacqueline Scott
Fred Johnson ('The One-Armed Man')	Bill Raisch
Helen Kimble	Diane Brewster
Narrator	William Conrad

Executive Producer: **Quinn Martin**

A doctor wrongly convicted of the murder of his wife goes on the run, trying to find her killer before he himself is apprehended.

Dr Richard Kimble had returned home one evening to find his wife dead and a mysterious one-armed man running from the direction of the house. Kimble was arrested for murder and convicted on circumstantial evidence – no one else had seen the one-armed man, but the neighbours had heard the Kimbles quarrelling. Fortunately for Kimble, the train taking him to prison for execution was derailed and he took the chance to slip his unconscious guard, Lt. Gerard, and make a break. Realizing his only chance of redemption lay in finding the real culprit, he began to comb the entire United States for the one-armed man, all the while knowing that Gerard was always only one step behind him.

Plagued by Gerard's relentless pursuit, Kimble was forced to shift from town to town, from low-paid job to low-paid job and from identity to identity, only occasionally making contact with his sister, Donna Taft. His tense life on the run even took him to Mexico and Canada, and the different setting for each episode kept the show fresh, giving producers the scope to try out new ideas and to bring in guest stars.

Unlike most suspense series, *The Fugitive* was allowed a proper conclusion in its final episode, which drew massive audiences all round the world. Kimble at last quarried the one-armed man in a deserted amusement park. As the two men struggled, Gerard arrived to shoot the man he now realized was the real murderer. This day, 29 August 1967, was, as narrator William Conrad affirmed, 'the day the running stopped'. (The episode was shown a day later in the UK.)

The Fugitive was inspired by Victor Hugo's 19th-century French classic, *Les Misérables*, and the real-life case of Dr Sam Sheppard, who was convicted of killing his wife in 1954. The concept was revived in 1993, when Harrison Ford starred in a new cinema version of the Kimble story.

FULL CIRCLE
See **AROUND THE WORLD IN 80 DAYS**.

FULLERTON, FIONA
(1956–)

Fair-haired actress, born in Nigeria, progressing from youthful roles in the 1970s to star in series like ANGELS (Patricia Rutherford), THE CHARMER (Clarice Mannors) and various other dramas. Her first husband was actor Simon MacCorkindale.

FUNT, ALLEN
(1914–99)

The grandfather of today's TV pranksters like Jeremy Beadle and Noel Edmonds, Funt was the man who devised CANDID CAMERA, a series which evolved from his forces radio series, *Candid Microphone*, which captured people unawares, with humorous results.

FURTHER ADVENTURES OF LUCKY JIM, THE
UK (BBC) Situation Comedy. BBC 2 1967; 1982

Jim Dixon	**Keith Barron** (*1967*)
	Enn Reitel (*1982*)
Lucy	**Glynis Barber** (*1982*)
Philip	**David Simeon** (*1982*)
Joanna	**Barbara Flynn** (*1982*)

Writers: **Dick Clement, Ian La Frenais**
Producers: **Duncan Wood** (*1967*), **Harold Snoad** (*1982*)

A North Country lad finds it hard to settle in Swinging London.

Based on, and updated from, Kingsley Amis's 1954 novel, *Lucky Jim*, this series related happenings in the life of Jim Dixon, a cautious lad from Eckersley, Yorkshire, new in London in the permissive 1960s. Not liking what he saw, and finding it hard to fit in, Jim indulged himself in Walter Mitty-like fantasies and private rants about the state of society around him. In 1982 the series was revived with Enn Reitel as Dixon, returning to London in 1967 after a year in Holland, and resuming his position as a teacher of Medieval History at a red-brick university.

GAFFER

The chief electrician in a team.

GALL, SANDY
CBE (1927–)

Former ITN newscaster and foreign correspondent, joining the organization from Reuters in 1963. In his 29 years with ITN, he gained a reputation for venturing behind the front lines and into trouble spots like Uganda, Vietnam and Afghanistan, presenting his findings in a series of important documentaries. He is also a well-published author.

GALLERY

The control room: home of the director, production assistant, vision mixer and other technicians during recording or live transmission.

GALTON, RAY
OBE (1930–)

British comedy scriptwriter, usually in collaboration with Alan Simpson. After meeting while both were convalescing from TB, Galton and Simpson were jointly responsible for Tony Hancock's scripts on HANCOCK'S HALF HOUR on radio and television, later moving on to pen CITIZEN JAMES for Sid James and then, in 1962, an episode of COMEDY PLAYHOUSE entitled *The Offer*. This proved to be the pilot for STEPTOE AND SON, a series they wrote for 12 years (with a five-year hiatus in the middle). Their later work (scripts for Frankie Howerd and Spike Milligan, scores of individual comedies – some billed under the *The Galton & Simpson Comedy* umbrella – and efforts like *Casanova '73*, *Dawson's Weekly* and episodes of *Mr Aitch*) by common consent was not, understandably, in the same league, although they did win fans with their 1972 adaptation of Gabriel Chevalier's CLOCHEMERLE and there was plenty of interest in 1996–7 when Paul Merton resurrected a number of their scripts in *Paul Merton in Galton & Simpson's* . . . Galton, without Simpson, joined forces with Johnny Speight to write the police comedy, SPOONER'S PATCH, in 1979, and with 78John Antrobus to script *Room at the Bottom* in 1986 and *Get Well Soon* – which recalled his meeting with Simpson in hospital – in 1997.

GAMBON, Sir MICHAEL
CBE (1940–)

Dublin-born actor best known for his award-winning portrayal of Philip Marlow in Dennis Potter's THE SINGING DETECTIVE. Subsequently, he starred in the revival of MAIGRET. Gambon's other television work has included the 1968 adventure series, *The Borderers*, and dramas like

The Seagull, Eyeless In Gaza, Oscar Wilde (Wilde), *The Heat of the Day, The Entertainer* (Archie Rice), the thriller, *Faith* (Peter John Moreton), and *Screen Two*'s *A Man of No Importance* (bigoted butcher Carney), although he also starred as Brian in the sitcom, *The Other One*, and appeared in series like *About Face*, MINDER, BERGERAC and THE STORYTELLER. More recently, he was Squire Hamley in *Wives and Daughters* and clockmaker John Harrison in *Longitude*.

GAME FOR A LAUGH
UK (LWT) Comedy. ITV 1981–5

Presenters: **Jeremy Beadle, Henry Kelly, Matthew Kelly, Sarah Kennedy, Rustie Lee, Martin Daniels, Lee Peck, Debbie Rix**

Executive Producer: **Alan Boyd**
Producers: **Phil Bishop, Keith Stewart, Brian Wesley, Bob Merrilees**

Practical jokes and silly stunts designed to make a fool out of the public.

In the vein of CANDID CAMERA, *Game for a Laugh* was a combination of pre-filmed hidden-camera pranks and studio-based stunts, all aimed at catching out Joe Public. Victims' embarrassment was glossed over by shrieks of laughter from the studio audience. Each week the hosts – perched on four high stools – signed off with a contrived 'Watching us, watching you' farewell. Rustie Lee, Lee Peck, Debbie Rix and Martin Daniels later joined the team, and Jeremy Beadle moved on to even greater practical joking in *Beadle's About*. *Game for a Laugh* was based on the 1950s US game show, *People Are Funny*.

GAME ON
UK (Hat Trick) Situation Comedy. BBC 2 1995–8

Matthew Malone	**Ben Chaplin**
	Neil Stuke
Martin Henson	**Matthew Cottle**
Mandy Wilkins	**Samantha Janus**
Clare Monohan	**Tracy Keating**
Jason	**Mark Powley**
Archie	**Crispin Bonham-Carter**

Writers: **Andrew Davies, Bernadette Davis**
Producers: **Geoffrey Perkins, Sioned Wiliam**

Three London flatmates battle their way through life.

Game On was like a dysfunctional, cruder version of *Friends*. It focused on three young flatsharers, each with his or her own personal problems. Most screwed-up was 'double hard' Matthew, whose parents had died, leaving him the money to buy his Battersea flat, but who now suffered from agoraphobia and never ventured outside its door. He whiled away his days watching TV, dressing up as macho film characters or polishing his surfboard, if not exploring the secret contents of the drawers in the room he let to Mandy. Blonde but not dumb, Mandy

worked as a temp and struggled to combat her bimbo image and build a real career, always finding herself taken advantage of, and never being able to say no to a man's advances. Dating losers was her way of life. The third member of this Sartre-esque trio was ingenuous Martin, a ginger-haired, freckly bank worker, a 'sad bastard' whose mother still sent him frozen meals and who was desperate to find a girlfriend and savour his first sexual experience. He was constantly bullied by his life-long 'mate', Matthew. Martin did eventually find a girl, in the shape of Irish nurse Clare, and was heart-broken when she dumped him and then gave birth to his child. Mandy almost married into the aristocracy through Archie, and Matthew inadvertently hooked up with the gay Jason.

Game On was a return to comedy for co-writer Andrew 'PRIDE AND PREJUDICE' Davies and helped make a star out of Ben Chaplin, who left for Hollywood after one series and was replaced as Matthew by Neil Stuke. The theme song, 'Where I Find My Heaven', was performed by the Gigolo Aunts and was a UK hit in 1995.

GAME, SET AND MATCH
UK (Granada) Spy Drama. ITV 1988

Bernard Samson	**Ian Holm**
Fiona Samson	**Mel Martin**
Erich Stinnes	**Gottfried John**
Werner Volkmann	**Michael Degen**
Dicky Cruyer	**Michael Culver**
Gloria Kent	**Amanda Donohoe**
Bret Rensselaer	**Anthony Bate**
Frank Harrington	**Frederick Treves**
Silas Gaunt	**Michael Aldridge**
Julian MacKenzie	**John Wheatley**
Morgan	**Struan Rodger**
Zena Volkmann	**Brigitte Karner**
David Kimber-Hutchinson	**Peter Vaughan**
Henry Tiptree	**Jeremy Child**

Writer: **John Howlett**
Producer: **Brian Armstrong**

A desk-bound intelligence agent is sent back into action.

After allegedly bungling a counter-espionage mission in Poland and losing his nerve, loner Bernard Samson had been retired to desk duty. Earlier, he had formed a secret agency known as the Brahms Network and, when this was infiltrated by an enemy activist, Samson was called back into the front line to sort it out. He found himself in East Berlin, confronting his long-time friend, Werner Volkmann, and his own KGB-agent wife, Fiona, who headed an underground intelligence unit called Yellow Submarine.

The 13-part series was based on a trilogy of books by Len Deighton, *Berlin Game, Mexico Set* and *London Match*, and was filmed in all three locations.

GANGSTERS
UK (BBC) Crime Drama. BBC 1 1976–8

John Kline .... **Maurice Colbourne**
Khan .... **Ahmed Khalil**
Anne Darracott .... **Elizabeth Cassidy**
Dermot Macavoy .... **Paul Antrim**
Malleson .... **Paul Barber**
Sarah Gant .... **Alibe Parsons**
Rafiq .... **Saeed Jaffrey**
Rawlinson .... **Philip Martin**
Lily Li Tang .... **Chai Lee**
Shen Tang .... **Robert Lee**
Red Stick .... **Kahjoo Chua**
Iqbal Khan .... **Zia Moyheddin**

Writer: **Philip Martin**
Producer: **David Rose**

*The violent face of the underworld in 1970s
Birmingham.*

Gangsters focused on former SAS man John Kline, freed from prison to work for DI6 agent Khan in monitoring and manipulating events in the Birmingham underworld. Installed as the manager of The Maverick nightclub, Kline found himself mixing with all manner of seedy characters, including Chinese triads, pimps, whores, extortionists, terrorists, drug-pushers and illegal-immigrant rings.

Shot on video using a roving camera, *Gangsters* won acclaim for effectively conveying the tension in the city's underworld and the menace of its low life. However, its graphic violence was heavily criticized. The 12-part series resulted from a one-off PLAY FOR TODAY of the same title in 1975, also written by Philip Martin. Chris Farlowe sang the theme song and Dave Greenslade composed the music.

GANNON, LUCY
(1949–)

One-time military policewoman and care worker who has become one of UK television's most prolific screenwriters. Her creations have included SOLDIER, SOLDIER, PEAK PRACTICE, BRAMWELL and *Insiders*. She also wrote *Screen One*'s *Trip Trap* and the single dramas, *Big Cat* and *The Gift*.

GARDEN, GRAEME
(1943–)

Aberdeen-born, Cambridge-educated doctor who began writing for television in the mid-1960s, eventually appearing on screen in a sketch show entitled *Twice a Fortnight* (with Tim Brooke-Taylor, Bill Oddie, *et al.*). This was followed by another sketch show, *Broaden Your Mind*, before Garden and Oddie set about preparing scripts for LWT's DOCTOR IN THE HOUSE and two of its sequels. In 1970 Garden, Brooke-Taylor and Oddie were

offered their own series, based around three crazy do-gooders. In THE GOODIES, Garden, playing an over-the-top version of himself, was the trio's mad scientist. Since then, he has continued writing (for shows such as *Rory Bremner*, SMITH AND JONES, SURGICAL SPIRIT and, with Oddie, the sci-fi spoof, *Astronauts*), straight acting (among his appearances was an episode of STRANGERS), panel gaming (*Tell the Truth*) and presenting TV pop-science programmes (he was one of the hosts of *Bodymatters*).

GARDENERS' WORLD
UK (BBC/Catalyst) Gardening. BBC 2 1968–

Presenters: **Percy Thrower, Peter Seabrook, Clay Jones, Stefan Buczacki, Geoffrey Smith, Geoff Hamilton, Alan Titchmarsh**

Executive Producers: **Stephanie Silk, Tony Laryea**
Producers: **Paul Morby, Bill Duncalf, Barry Edgar, Rosemary Forgan, Laurence Vulliamy, Betty Talks, John Percival, Colette Foster**

Long-running gardening magazine.

This full-colour successor to the highly popular GARDENING CLUB was launched by the much-respected Percy Thrower in 1968, using his own garden as a backdrop. Over the years, reports on shows and garden visits have intercut the sound gardening basics the programme has placed at its core, although the range and scope of plants and plots has expanded considerably, thanks to the garden centre boom of the past 20 years. Alan Titchmarsh took over as host in 1996, following the death of Geoff Hamilton, and he has been supported by presenters like Pippa Greenwood, Gay Search and Stephen Lacey.

GARDENING CLUB
UK (BBC) Gardening. BBC 1 1955–67

Presenter: **Percy Thrower**

Producers: **John Furness, Paul Morby**

Gardening tips and news.

Gardening Club, the forerunner of today's many gardening programmes, was originally screened from a rooftop garden at the BBC's Lime Grove, where Percy Thrower offered useful advice to growers nationwide. Each week he was joined by specialist guests and enthusiastic amateurs. With the arrival of colour television, *Gardening Club* gave way to GARDENERS' WORLD, again hosted by Percy Thrower.

GARDNER, ANDREW
(1932–99)

Tall, respected ITN newscaster, one of the first two presenters of *News at Ten* (with Alastair Burnet), having anchored ITN's earlier offerings: *Dateline, Reporting '66* and *Reporting '67*. His earlier career was in broadcasting in Rhodesia and then with the BBC. After leaving ITN in 1977, he worked for Thames, presenting regional news magazines, before retiring in 1992.

GARNER, JAMES
(James Baumgarner; 1928–)

American actor who entered television in the 1950s, playing small roles in series like CHEYENNE while under contract to Warner Brothers. Warners then gave him his own vehicle, the Western spoof, MAVERICK, which more and more began to reflect Garner's own understated sense of humour. However, tied to a limiting contract, Garner fell into conflict with the studio and walked out in 1960. He remained out of major TV work for 11 years, until he was cast as lead in another *Maverick*-like series entitled *Nichols*, made by his own Cherokee Productions. Three years later he achieved greater success as Jim Rockford, the ex-con private investigator in THE ROCKFORD FILES, before he returned to *Maverick* in a TV movie and a short-lived revamp which went out under the name of *Bret Maverick*. He later played Senator Norman Grant in SPACE and in 1991 he starred in a US sitcom entitled *Man of the People* (politician Jim Doyle).

GARNETT, TONY
(1936–)

British producer and one-time actor whose political sympathies have manifested themselves in plays like *Up the Junction*, CATHY COME HOME, *The Gangster Show* and *The Gamekeeper*, and the series, DAYS OF HOPE and *Law and Order*. He also produced the comedy shorts, *The Staggering Stories of Ferdinand de Bargos*, and the *Screen One* drama, *Born Kicking*. Since the 1990s, as head of World Productions, he has produced major series such as BETWEEN THE LINES, THIS LIFE, *Cardiac Arrest*, THE COPS, BALLYKISSANGEL and *Attachments*.

GASCOIGNE, BAMBER
(1935–)

Erudite Bamber Gascoigne was host of UNIVERSITY CHALLENGE for 25 years (1962–87). He has also presented CINEMA, his own 13-part history of Christianity, *The Christians*, the cultural quiz, *Connoisseur*, and various other high-brow documentaries.

GASCOINE, JILL
(1937–)

London-born actress-turned-novelist, seen in series like THE GENTLE TOUCH and C.A.T.S. EYES (both as female copper Maggie Forbes) and THE ONEDIN LINE (Letty Gaunt). Among her other credits have been parts in DIXON OF DOCK GREEN, DR FINLAY'S CASEBOOK, GENERAL HOSPITAL, RAFFLES, Z CARS, SOFTLY, SOFTLY, WITHIN THESE WALLS, BERYL'S LOT, JUSTICE, BOON,

TAGGART, *Virtual Murder* and EL C.I.D. (opposite her husband, Alfred Molina).

GAUNT, WILLIAM
(1937–)

Yorkshire-born actor whose baby-faced looks made him popular in the late 1950s and 1960s, giving him parts in *Colonel Trumper's Private War* (Lt. Hastings), SERGEANT CORK (Sgt Bob Marriott), HARPERS WEST ONE, PROBATION OFFICER, THE AVENGERS, THE SAINT and SOFTLY, SOFTLY, culminating in the role of Richard Barrett in the supernatural spy series, THE CHAMPIONS. In the 1980s and 90s he resurfaced as foster-parent Tony Hunter in *Claire*, harassed dad Arthur Crabtree in the sitcom, NO PLACE LIKE HOME, solicitor Edward Capstick in *Capstick's Law*, old buffer Aubrey in *A Gentlemen's Club* and grandfather Andrew Prentice in *Next of Kin*. Also in his portfolio are performances in CROWN COURT, *Cottage to Let*, *Holly*, *The Foundation* and *Love and Marriage*.

GBH
UK (GBH Films) Drama. Channel 4 1991

Michael Murray	Robert Lindsay
Jim Nelson	Michael Palin
Barbara Douglas	Lindsay Duncan
Mrs Murray	Julie Walters
Laura Nelson	Dearbhla Molloy
Franky Murray	Philip Whitchurch
Peter	Andrew Schofield
Martin Niarchos	Michael Angelis
Diane Niarchos	Julia St John
Mr Weller	David Ross
Lou Barnes	Tom Georgeson
Mervyn Sloan	Paul Daneman
Bubbles	Peter-Hugo Daly
Geoff	Bill Stewart
Teddy	Alan Igbon
Frank Twist	Colin Douglas
Researcher	Jimmy Mulville

Writer: **Alan Bleasdale**
Executive Producer: **Verity Lambert**
Producers: **Alan Bleasdale, David Jones**

An ambitious council leader and a gentle schoolteacher cross swords against a backdrop of political subversion.

Michael Murray was the newly installed leader of Liverpool City Council. Power, fame and women were the keystones of his life and militancy was his watchword. Jim Nelson, in contrast, was the caring headteacher of a school for children with special needs, a family man whose ambitions were modest. When Nelson's school defied a Murray strike call, the two men became bitter enemies, to the detriment of Murray's career and Nelson's sanity. However, *GBH* was far more complicated than that. This seven-part drama had various sub-plots and undercurrents. It revealed how the two men became pawns in a sinister political game, and Murray's murky past came back to haunt him in the form of the beautiful but mysterious Barbara Douglas. The *GBH* of the title did not stand, as many initially believed, for Grievous Bodily Harm, but for supposedly Great British Holiday, referring to a sequence when Nelson – his mental health breaking up – headed off on vacation, returning to find the family home ransacked.

GBH was a labour of love for Alan Bleasdale. He had already abandoned attempts to script the idea as a film and as a novel. As a tense piece of television drama it won many plaudits although, in established Bleasdale fashion, it ruffled a few feathers at the same time. Former Liverpool Council Deputy Leader Derek Hatton sought legal advice over what he saw as a fictionalization of his time in power, but Bleasdale denied that Michael Murray had been based on anyone in particular. Rather, as star Robert Lindsay explained, *GBH* was a reminder to the public that our lives are manipulated by activists from both left and right. Bleasdale, in the *Radio Times*, described the drama as 'one caring, liberal madman's odyssey through the appalling farce of life in Britain today; trying to make some sense of the place'.

GEE, DUSTIN
(Gerald Harrison; 1942–86)

British comedian and impersonator, for some time partner of Les Dennis, with whom he starred in *Go For It* and *The Laughter Show*. His TV break came with WHO DO YOU DO? in the mid-1970s, and he followed it up with regular appearances in *Russ Abbot's Madhouse*. Among his best-remembered take-offs were Larry Grayson and CORONATION STREET's Vera Duckworth. He died of a heart attack in 1986.

GEMINI MAN
US (Universal) Adventure. BBC 1 1976

Sam Casey .... **Ben Murphy**
Leonard Driscoll .... **William Sylvester**
Dr Abby Lawrence .... **Katherine Crawford**

Executive Producer: **Harve Bennett**
Producer: **Leslie Stevens**

An invisible man works as a secret agent for a Government think-tank.

When NBC's INVISIBLE MAN series, starring David McCallum, was not a success, the company reworked the formula with a new cast and some subtle changes. The result was *Gemini Man*, which fared even worse in the US ratings war. It centred on Sam Casey, an agent for INTERSECT, who had been exposed to underwater radiation and rendered invisible. Thanks to the efforts of his superior, Leonard Driscoll (played by Richard Dysart in the pilot episode), and computer specialist Abby Lawrence, Casey was able to restore his appearance using a special watch-like device. He could, when required, turn the device off and return to invisibility – a very useful ploy for a secret agent; but if he did this for more than 15 minutes in one day, he would die.

GENERAL HOSPITAL
UK (ATV) Drama. ITV 1972–9

Dr Matthew Armstrong .... **David Garth**
Dr William Parker Brown .... **Lewis Jones**
Dr Martin Baxter .... **James Kerry**
Sister Edwards .... **Monica Grey**
Dr Peter Ridge .... **Ian White**
Arnold Capper .... **John Halstead**
Dr Robert Thorne .... **Ronald Leigh-Hunt**
Dr Neville Bywaters .... **Tony Adams**
Sister Ellen Chapman .... **Peggy Sinclair**
Dr Joanna Whitworth .... **Patricia Maynard**
Nurse Hilda Price .... **Lynda Bellingham**
Dr Richard Kirby .... **Eric Lander**
Nurse Katy Shaw .... **Judy Buxton**
Dr Knight .... **Carl Rigg**
Dr Guy Wallman .... **Tom Adams**
Dr Chipapo .... **Jason Rowe**
Sister Washington .... **Carmen Munro**
Staff Nurse/Sister Holland .... **Pippa Rowe**
Nurse Stevens .... **Amber Thomas**
Dr Mayhew .... **Archie Tew**
Dr Helen Sanders .... **Judy Loe**
Staff Nurse Nelson .... **Victoria Burton**

Producers: **Ian Fordyce, Royston Morley**

The day-to-day dramas involving staff and patients at a major hospital.

Although sharing its name with a long-running American soap, *General Hospital* was effectively EMERGENCY – WARD 10 revisited, albeit with a new cast and setting. Having cancelled *Ward 10* in 1967 and living to regret it, Lew Grade and his ATV associates decided to revamp the idea. They wanted an afternoon series to fill space newly made available after restrictions on broadcasting hours had been lifted. The result was a drama set in Midland General Hospital.

While not quite achieving the cult following *Ward 10* had enjoyed, the series still picked up a sizeable audience, enough to earn a transfer to an evening time-slot three years into its run. Episode length increased from a half-hour to a full hour at the same time, and two programmes a week became one. As in its predecessor, it was the lives and loves of the *General Hospital* staff which took centre stage, as well as internal power struggles. Housewives were offered a new generation of heart-throb doctors, most notably Martin Baxter and Neville Bywaters (the latter played by Tony Adams, later Adam Chance in CROSSROADS), while veterans like Drs Armstrong and Parker Brown seldom saw eye to eye and added sparks of tension and excitement.

GENERATION GAME, THE
UK (BBC) Game Show. BBC 1 1971–82; 1990–

Presenters: **Bruce Forsyth, Larry Grayson, Jim Davidson**

Producers: **Alan Tarrant, James Moir, Terry Heneberry,**

Robin Nash, Alan Boyd, Marcus Plantin, David Taylor, Guy Freeman, Jonathan Beazley, Sue Andrew

Family couples compete in silly games and challenges.

The Generation Game has become the number-one game show in British TV history, enjoying two lengthy prime-time runs. Simple in format, it has involved four couples (each composed of an elder and a younger member of a family – father and daughter, aunt and nephew, etc.) competing in two heats and a semi-final. The heats have consisted of two games based on little quizzes and challenges – guessing film themes and miming the answer to a partner, spotting personalities in disguise, etc. Demonstrations by experts (making pots, icing cakes, spinning plates, performing a dance, etc.), which the contestants have had to copy, have proved particularly popular. Points have been awarded for performance and the two heat-winning couples have then competed in a semi-final. This has often taken the form of a comic playlet, with celebrity judges allocating marks for performances. The winning duo have progressed to a final 'conveyor belt' round in which a succession of household goodies (always including a cuddly toy) has passed before their eyes. Everything that they can recall in a set time has been taken home as prizes.

The Generation Game was devised by a Dutch housewife who was inspired by game shows like *Beat the Clock* (part of SUNDAY NIGHT AT THE LONDON PALLADIUM), and when it was televised in Holland as *Een Van De Aacht* (*One From Eight*) it topped the ratings. Former *Beat the Clock* host Bruce Forsyth was the obvious choice to take charge of the UK version and he quickly established the programme as an integral part of Saturday evening viewing. Forsyth revelled in the party game format. With a twinkle in his eye, he bullied and coerced the hapless contestants through each show, combining words of encouragement with false anger and gentle mockery. The contestants loved it. Assisting Bruce was the leggy Anthea Redfern, who was soon to be his second wife.

When Bruce was lured away to ITV in 1978, it seemed that *The Generation Game*'s heyday was over. Camp comedian Larry Grayson was not an obvious replacement, yet he made the show an even bigger hit. Sensibly avoiding Forsyth's aggressive approach, Grayson instead brought his own effete style to proceedings, in which he was assisted by Scottish folk singer Isla St Clair. *The Generation Game* was cancelled in 1982 but was brought back, with Bruce Forsyth again at the helm, in 1990. Once more, his skilful manipulation of the studio audience and his ease with contestants ensured that the programme was as popular as ever. Dancer Rosemarie Ford became his Girl Friday. In 1994, Bruce retired once more, leaving Jim Davidson to take over a year later, supported by Sally Meen and, subsequently, Melanie Stace.

The Generation Game has aired under several titles. In the early days, it was known as *Bruce Forsyth and the Generation Game*. It then became *Larry Grayson's Generation Game*, and the latest incarnation has been called *Bruce Forsyth's Generation Game* or *Jim Davidson's Generation Game*. It has also given us catchphrases galore – from 'Let's meet the eight who are going to generate' and 'Let's see the scores on the doors' to 'Good game, good game' and 'What's on the board, Miss Ford?'. King of the catchphrases, however, has been 'Didn't he do well?' – just like the programme itself.

GENTLE TOUCH, THE
UK (LWT) Police Drama. ITV 1980–4

DI Maggie Forbes	Jill Gascoine
DCI Russell	William Marlowe
DS Jake Barratt	Paul Moriarty
DS Jimmy Fenton	Derek Thompson
DI Bob Croft	Brian Gwaspari
DS Peter Philips	Kevin O'Shea
DI Jack Slater	Michael Graham Cox
Steve Forbes	Nigel Rathbone
DI Mike Turnbull	Bernard Holley
Sgt Sid Bryant	Michael Cronin

Executive Producers: **Tony Wharmby, Nick Elliott**
Producers: **Kim Mills, Jack Williams, Michael Verney-Elliott**

Softly, softly crime-busting with a female police officer.

Maggie Forbes was a former police cadet who had worked her way up through the ranks and was now posted to London's Seven Dials police station, covering the areas of Soho and Covent Garden. As the series began she found herself almost simultaneously promoted to the rank of detective inspector and widowed by the murder of Ray, her PC husband (Leslie Schofield). Despite being ordered to take time off, she dragged herself back into action to pursue her husband's killers but then resigned from the force. Persuaded to rejoin, she found the subsequent months difficult, as problems with Steve, her teenage son, interfered with her progress at the station. Eventually, she and the series settled down into a catalogue of routine crime stories, with the 'gentle touch' of the title always evident in Maggie's investigations.

Maggie Forbes held the distinction of being British TV's first female detective in a starring role. Her colleagues at Seven Dials were Detective Insp. Bob Croft, DS Jake Barratt, DS Jimmy Fenton and, later, DS Peter Philips. Their grouchy boss was DCI Russell. After four years, Maggie left Seven Dials, only to resurface in C.A.T.S. EYES.

GEORGE AND MILDRED
UK (Thames) Situation Comedy. ITV 1976–9

George Roper	Brian Murphy
Mildred Roper	Yootha Joyce
Jeffrey Fourmile	Norman Eshley
Ann Fourmile	Sheila Fearn
Tristram Fourmile	Nicholas Bond-Owen
Ethel	Avril Elgar
Humphrey	Reginald Marsh
Jerry	Roy Kinnear

Writers: **Johnnie Mortimer, Brian Cooke**
Producer: **Peter Frazer-Jones**

*The further adventures of the feuding landlord and
landlady from* MAN ABOUT THE HOUSE.

In this spin-off, George and Mildred Roper had moved
from their ground-floor flat to a middle-class housing
development (46 Peacock Crescent, Hampton Wick).
There, the pushy, man-hungry Mildred strived to be
upwardly mobile and the weedy, shiftless George – with
his motorcycle and sidecar – defiantly proclaimed his
working-class roots. Next door lived the Fourmiles:
snooty Jeffrey, his likeable wife, Ann, and their bespectacled young son, Tristram, who was constantly corrupted by George. The Fourmiles later added baby
Tarquin to their family. Regular visitors, much to Mildred's embarrassment, were her materialistic sister Ethel
and brother-in-law Humphrey. Jerry was George's layabout pal and Truffles Mildred's pampered Yorkshire
Terrier.

Like *Man about the House*, which became *Three's Com-
pany* in the USA, this series was also translated into an
American version. *The Ropers* starred Norman Fell and
Audra Lindley.

GEORGE AND THE DRAGON
UK (ATV) Situation Comedy. ITV 1966–8

George Russell .... **Sid James**
Gabrielle Dragon .... **Peggy Mount**
Col. Maynard .... **John Le Mesurier**
Ralph .... **Keith Marsh**

Creators/Writers: **Vince Powell, Harry Driver**
Producers: **Alan Tarrant, Jack Williams**

*A lecherous chauffeur has his style cramped by a
formidable new housekeeper.*

Randy George Russell was driver and general handyman
to the distinguished Colonel Maynard and enjoyed his
privileged position in the stately household. That all
changed, however, when a new housekeeper was
appointed. George's wandering hands had already seen
off 16 domestics, but when Miss Gabrielle Dragon
arrived, recommended by the Premier Domestic Agency,
there was little chance of George making unwanted
advances to *her*. A bellowing battleaxe of a widow, Gabrielle had reverted to her (appropriate) maiden name on
the death of her husband, and now battle duly commenced between George and the Dragon. Also seen was
Ralph, the smelly, sloppy gardener.

GEORGE BURNS AND GRACIE ALLEN SHOW, THE
See **BURNS AND ALLEN SHOW, THE**.

GEORGESON, TOM
(1941–)

Liverpudlian actor, probably best known as Harry Naylor
in BETWEEN THE LINES, one of the BOYS FROM THE
BLACKSTUFF (Dixie Dean) or DI Howard Jones in LIVER-
POOL ONE. Georgeson's other credits have been many,
with the major offerings being *The Manageress* (Eddie),
WHEN THE BOAT COMES IN, THE BILL, TURTLE'S PRO-
GRESS, *Maybury*, *Les Girls* (Conrad), *Scully*, DEMPSEY AND
MAKEPEACE, STAY LUCKY, *Resnick*, *The Last Place on Earth*,
BRAMWELL, GBH (Lou Barnes) and QED's dramatization,
Cause of Death (bereaved parent Ray Peters).

GERBER, DAVID
(1925–)

Prolific American producer of the 1970s, working on
shows like CADE'S COUNTY, *Nanny and The Professor*,
The Ghost and Mrs Muir, *Born Free*, *Police Story*, POLICE
WOMAN, *Gibbsville*, *David Cassidy – Man Undercover* and
THE QUEST. In 1986 he joined the newly merged MGM
and United Artists, introducing new blood and building
up the company's prime-time share through such series
as THIRTYSOMETHING and IN THE HEAT OF THE NIGHT.
He went on to become head of the MGM Worldwide
Television Group.

GET SMART
US (Talent Associates/Heyday) Situation Comedy. BBC 1
1965–7

Maxwell Smart .... **Don Adams**
Agent 99 .... **Barbara Feldon**
Thaddeus ('The Chief') .... **Edward Platt**
Agent 13 .... **Dave Ketchum**
Prof. Carlson .... **Stacy Keach**
Conrad Siegfried .... **Bernie Kopell**
Starker .... **King Moody**
Hymie, the robot .... **Dick Gautier**
Agent 44 .... **Victor French**
Agent Larrabee .... **Robert Karvelas**
Charlie Watkins .... **Angelique Pettyjohn**
99's mother .... **Jane Dulo**

Creators: **Mel Brooks, Buck Henry**
Executive Producer: **Leonard Stern**

*Spoof on the James Bond/*MAN FROM UNCLE
*espionage capers, featuring an incompetent secret
agent and his ineffective colleagues.*

Maxwell Smart was Agent 86 for CONTROL, an intelligence service with headquarters ten storeys beneath
Main Street in Washington, DC. The offices were entered
through the bottom of a telephone kiosk. Disaster-
prone, but always enthusiastic, Smart operated undercover as a salesman for the Pontiac Greeting Card
Company and wound up in the most embarrassing pre-
dicaments for a spy. He usually blundered his way

through, but not before saying, 'Sorry about that, Chief,' umpteen times to Thaddeus, his long-suffering boss.

CONTROL's adversaries were KAOS, run by the megalomaniac Siegfried and his sidekick, Starker. Against them, Smart worked closely with his attractive and intelligent partner, Agent 99 (her real name was never revealed), who later became his wife and bore him twins. Another colleague was Agent 13, who took his undercover role rather too seriously, hiding in the most unusual places, like mailboxes and vending machines. There were also Agent Larrabee, who was even dimmer than Smart, Charlie Watkins, a spy in drag (but that was some make-up!), and Fang, a dog, code-numbered Agent K13.

Smart was generously supplied with gadgetry to help him perform his duties, although these devices (such as a telephone hidden in his shoe) never functioned quite as intended. For top-secret discussions, CONTROL used an anti-bugging device known as the Cone of Silence, a clear dome which descended from the ceiling. While the intention was that people *outside* the dome would not hear the conversation, unfortunately those *inside* were similarly excluded. In addition, CONTROL had an intelligent robot, Hymie, which took every command literally, with disastrous results.

GET SOME IN!
UK (Thames) Situation Comedy. ITV 1975–8

Cpl. Percy Marsh	**Tony Selby**
Jakey Smith	**Robert Lindsay**
	Karl Howman
Ken Richardson	**David Janson**
Bruce Leckie	**Brian Pettifer**
Matthew Lilley	**Gerard Ryder**
Alice Marsh	**Lori Wells**
Min	**Madge Hindle**
Cpl. Wendy Williams	**Jenny Cryst**

Creators/Writers: **John Esmonde, Bob Larbey**
Producer: **Michael Mills**

Four young lads are drafted into the RAF, where they are bullied by a brainless corporal.

Like THE ARMY GAME before it, *Get Some In!* focused on the National Service years, when thousands of unwilling and often unsuitable young men were conscripted into the forces. This time the action took place in 1955, at RAF Skelton, where the motley draftees included teddy boy Jakey Smith, dim Scotsman Bruce Leckie, wet vicar's son Matthew Lilley and clean-living grammar school boy Ken Richardson. On arrival at the camp, their worst nightmare was realized when they were assigned to the care of Corporal Marsh, a vindictive, cowardly bully-boy who treated his charges like lackeys and made their training period a misery. However, it was usually Marsh who suffered in the end, as the lads, led by 'Poof House' Richardson, easily outwitted their thick NCO.

After subsequent training as nursing assistants at RAF Midham (again alongside Marsh), the lads were posted to Malta but were immediately recalled to RAF Hospital Druidswater. There, they found themselves intimidated yet again by Marsh, who now enjoyed hero status, having allegedly carried a superior officer 84 miles to safety in the snows of Labrador. Marsh's demanding wife, Alice, was also seen, as was NAAFI serving girl Min and Leckie's butch girlfriend and, later, wife, Corporal Wendy.

GHOST

A distortion or double image on a TV picture, generally caused by signals bouncing off another building, or badly positioned aerials.

GHOST SQUAD/GS5
UK (Rank/ATV) Police Drama. ITV 1961–4

Nick Craig	**Michael Quinn**
Sir Andrew Wilson	**Donald Wolfit**
Helen Winters	**Angela Browne**
Tony Miller	**Neil Hallett**
Geoffrey Stock	**Anthony Marlowe**
Jean Carter	**Claire Nielson**
Peter Clarke	**Ray Barrett**

Producers: **Connery Chappell, Antony Kearey, Dennis Vance**

The dangerous adventures of a team of undercover policemen.

The 'Ghost Squad', officially the International Investigation Division of Scotland Yard, operated in total secrecy. Their job was to infiltrate underworld gangs, spy rings or other secret societies, lying low for possibly months at a time and using an alias which only they and their direct superior knew about. They worked in places as far afield as Marseilles and Hong Kong and they could not rely on the regular police force or other governmental agencies for their salvation: their lives were on the line, and this contributed to the suspense of each episode. Number one agent was American Nick Craig, a master of disguise. Tony Miller was his friend and colleague seen later, and their superior was Sir Andrew Wilson, supported by his 23-year-old secretary, Helen Winters. When Wilson and Winters were posted to another department, they were succeeded by Geoffrey Stock and his Scottish secretary, Jean Carter, who also became an agent.

The dangers of the job were poignantly illustrated at the end of the second season, when Craig was killed by an explosion at sea. When the programme returned, he had been replaced by the meeker, more methodical Peter Clarke, who offered quite a contrast to Miller, his tough and physical partner. The programme title also changed, to *GS5*. The series was based on the book, *The Ghost Squad*, an account of real police undercover activity, by former detective John Gosling.

GIDEON'S WAY
UK (ATV) Police Drama. ITV 1965–6

Commander George Gideon .... **John Gregson**
Chief Insp. David Keen .... **Alexander Davion**
Kate Gideon .... **Daphne Anderson**

Producers: **Robert S. Baker, Monty Berman**

Determined detection with a talented Scotland Yard sleuth.

Filmed in documentary fashion, with much location shooting, the gritty, somewhat violent *Gideon's Way* told of the CID investigations of Commander George Gideon and his partner, Chief Inspector David Keen, two men who had worked their way up through the force. The series, transmitted in the USA under the title *Gideon CID*, and based on the novels by John Creasey, aka J. J. Marric, followed a 1958 film version, *Gideon's Day*, starring Jack Hawkins.

GILBERT, JAMES
(1923–)

British producer, with the BBC from the early 1960s, although also in the independent sector later, responsible for comedies like *On the Bright Side*, IT'S A SQUARE WORLD, *Moody in . . .*, THE SEVEN FACES OF JIM, *The Big Noise*, *Barney Is My Darling*, NOT ONLY . . . BUT ALSO . . ., *The Walrus and the Carpenter*, THE FROST REPORT, *The Illustrated Weekly Hudd*, *The Old Campaigner*, ME MAMMY, *Tales from the Lazy Acre*, WHATEVER HAPPENED TO THE LIKELY LADS?, LAST OF THE SUMMER WINE, *Executive Stress*, FRENCH FIELDS, *The Labours of Erica* and *Ain't Misbehavin'*.

GILES, BILL
OBE (1939–)

Devon-born meteorologist, a BBC weather presenter from 1975 and head of the BBC Weather Centre, 1983–2000.

GILL, MICHAEL
(1923–)

British producer/director of documentaries, in charge of Kenneth Clark's CIVILISATION and Alistair Cooke's AMERICA.

GILLIGAN'S ISLAND
US (Gladasaya/United Artists) Situation Comedy. ITV 1965

Gilligan .... **Bob Denver**
Jonas Grumby ('The Skipper') .... **Alan Hale, Jr**
Thurston Howell III .... **Jim Backus**
Mrs Lovey Howell .... **Natalie Schafer**
Roy Hinkley ('The Professor') .... **Russell Johnson**
Ginger Grant .... **Tina Louise**
Mary Ann Summers .... **Dawn Wells**

Creator/Executive Producer: **Sherwood Schwartz**

A group of castaways tries to escape from a tropical island.

A rough time was in store for the motley band of tourists on board the good ship *Minnow*. During their three-hour charter cruise from Honolulu a storm blew up, the boat was lost and they were shipwrecked on a desolate South Pacific island. Their futile attempts to escape and return home provided this sitcom's storylines.

The castaways included two members of the boat's crew, the genial, chubby Skipper and the incompetent First Mate, Gilligan, who was usually responsible for the failure of escape bids. Other members of the party were obnoxious millionaire Thurston Howell III and his dim wife, Lovey; 'The Professor', a science teacher and the group's escape planner; Mary Ann Summers, a simple country girl from Horners Corners, Kansas; and glamorous movie starlet Ginger Grant. However, realism was not *Gilligan's Island*'s strong point. Numerous guest stars turned up to help the party to get off the island, but how these visitors came and went was never explained, nor was the cast's changes of clothes or the presence of a reference library used by The Professor. If the cruise was meant to be only three hours long, how come they were now so far from civilization?

Gilligan's Island enjoyed only a sporadic screening in the UK. As a result, star Alan Hale, Jr has always been better known in Britain as CASEY JONES. Two or three revivals were made for American audiences in the late 1970s and early 1980s.

GILMORE, PETER
(1931–)

German-born, Yorkshire-raised actor, a hit in the 1970s as handsome sea captain James Onedin in THE ONEDIN LINE. Previously, Gilmore had been a singer with the George Mitchell Singers and, in addition to stage and film work, had appeared in TV series like HUGH AND I, as well as having his own song-and-dance act. Since *The Onedin Line* ended, Gilmore's work has become less obvious, though he did play safari park supremo Ben Bishop in ONE BY ONE and starred in the drama, *A Man Called Intrepid*. His two marriages have both been to actresses, to Una Stubbs and Jan Waters.

GIRL FROM UNCLE, THE
US (Arena/MGM) Secret Agent Drama. BBC 1 1966–7

April Dancer .... **Stefanie Powers**
Mark Slate .... **Noel Harrison**
Alexander Waverly .... **Leo G. Carroll**
Randy Kovacs .... **Randy Kirby**

Producer: **Douglas Benton**

A female secret agent and her British partner fight an anarchic global crime syndicate.

In this spin-off from THE MAN FROM UNCLE, The Girl from UNCLE was April Dancer, paired on assignments with British agent Mark Slate (played by Rex Harrison's son, Noel). Like their counterparts in the original series, they took their orders from agency supremo Mr Waverly and worked to combat the efforts of THRUSH to take over the world. Robert Vaughn, as Napoleon Solo, made the odd cross-over appearance; but this series, coming hot on the heels of the campy BATMAN, was even more far-fetched than the original UNCLE adventures and quickly died a death.

Dancer and Slate first appeared in a *Man from UNCLE* episode entitled *The Moonglow Affair*, but the roles were filled at the time by former Miss America Mary Ann Mobley and veteran actor Norman Fell. In the UK, *The Girl from UNCLE* and *The Man from UNCLE* shared the same BBC 1 time-slot, appearing in alternate weeks.

GIRLS ABOUT TOWN
UK (ATV) Situation Comedy. ITV 1970–1

Rosemary Pilgrim	**Julie Stevens**
Brenda Liversedge	**Denise Coffey**
George Pilgrim	**Robin Parkinson**
Harold Liversedge	**Peter Baldwin**
Mrs Pilgrim	**Dorothy Reynolds**

Creator/Writer: **Adele Rose**
Producer: **Shaun O'Riordan**

Two bored housewives try to spice up their lives.

Suffering from a severe case of marriage tedium, housewife friends Rosemary Pilgrim and Brenda Liversedge decided to add some zest to their lives by getting out and about. They hoped to make their husbands sit up and take notice, but with little success. Adding to Rosemary's frustration was her interfering, true-blue mother-in-law.

The series sprang from a 1969 single drama starring Anna Quayle and Barbara Mullaney (later CORONATION STREET's Rita Fairclough), in which Rosemary and Brenda joined an escort agency. When the series began, another future *Street* name, Peter Baldwin (Derek Wilton), was added to the cast, and the roles of Rosemary were filled by former PLAY SCHOOL presenter Julie Stevens and DO NOT ADJUST YOUR SET star Denise Coffey.

GIRLS ON TOP
UK (Witzend/Central) Situation Comedy. ITV 1985–6

Candice Valentine	**Tracey Ullman**
Amanda Ripley	**Dawn French**
Jennifer Marsh	**Jennifer Saunders**
Shelley Dupont	**Ruby Wax**
Lady Carlton	**Joan Greenwood**

Writers: **Dawn French, Jennifer Saunders, Ruby Wax**
Producer: **Paul Jackson**

Four zany, but incompatible, girls share a London flat.

Described by some as a female equivalent of THE YOUNG ONES, *Girls on Top* concerned four wacky girls who shared a comfortably appointed Chelsea flat, owned by Lady Carlton, a batty romantic novelist who lived downstairs. The four were the mendacious Candice (a blonde hypochondriac), domineering feminist Amanda (who worked for a magazine called *Spare Cheeks*), slouchy, slow-witted Jennifer and rich, brash American Shelley (who had come to London to be an actress). When the second season began, Candice was no longer around (actress Tracey Ullman had departed for the USA), and the other three soldiered on without her.

GIVE US A BREAK
UK (BBC) Comedy Drama. BBC 1 1983

Mickey Noades	**Robert Lindsay**
Mo Morris	**Paul McGann**
Tina Morris	**Shirin Taylor**
Ron Palmer	**David Daker**

Creator/Writer: **Geoff McQueen**
Producer: **Terence Williams**

An East End wide boy takes a snooker prodigy under his wing.

Mickey Noades was a 36-year-old waster who had never made anything of his life. For a living, he gambled and did a bit of wheeling and dealing, spending much of his time in Ron Palmer's pub, The Crown & Sceptre, where his girlfriend, Tina, was a barmaid. When Tina's young brother, Mo, arrived from jobless Liverpool, Mickey made him less than welcome, until he realized that Mo was an exceptional snooker player. With plenty of money to be made from hustling in London's snooker halls, Mickey saw his life open up before him and his 'big break' just around the corner.

The series was the first drama written by former carpenter Geoff McQueen, who later went on to create THE BILL. A Christmas special was produced in 1984. Snooker coaching for the series was provided by professional Geoff Foulds.

GIVE US A CLUE
UK (Thames) Game Show. ITV 1979–91

Presenters: **Michael Aspel, Michael Parkinson**

Producers: **Juliet Grimm, David Clark, Robert Reed, Keith Beckett**

Light-hearted celebrity charades game.

Michael Aspel and, from 1984, Michael Parkinson tried to keep order in this TV version of the ancient parlour game, Charades. A team of male celebrities (led by Lionel Blair) took on a team of women (captained by Una Stubbs and, later, Liza Goddard), with each member of the team having to perform a mime in turn, hoping to convey to their colleagues the title of a book, film, TV programme, show, song, etc. To spice things up, a number of risqué titles were dropped in, daring the stars to be a bit cheeky.

GLADIATORS
UK (LWT) Entertainment. ITV 1992 8

Presenters: Ulrika Jonsson, John Fashanu, Jeremy Guscott

Producers: Nigel Lythgoe, Ken Warwick
Executive Producers: John Kaye Cooper, Nigel Lythgoe

Members of the public do battle with superfit athletes in a contest of strength and technique.

Gladiators, recorded at Birmingham's National Indoor Arena, was a mix of IT'S A KNOCKOUT and THE SUPER-STARS, with a lot more muscle and considerably more posing. Body-builders, wrestlers and athletes of all kinds and both sexes were recruited as the resident team of 'Gladiators', all squeezed into leotards and given names like Wolf, Hunter, Nightshade (athlete Judy Simpson), Amazon (swimmer Sharron Davies) and Jet. Their job was to see off the challenges of four daring viewers each week in a series of stamina-sapping contests involving running, climbing, swinging and beating each other with big, cushioned clubs. John Sachs provided the commentary. The series proved surprisingly popular with younger viewers, and international challenge matches were also staged (hosted by Kimberley Joseph and Mike Adamle). The inspiration was the US series, *American Gladiators*.

GLAISTER, GERARD
DFC (1915–)

Former RAF squadron leader and decorated Spitfire pilot who became a BBC drama producer. Much of his work has been in a common vein, namely behind-the-scenes business sagas, as typified by OIL STRIKE NORTH, THE BROTHERS, *Buccaneer*, HOWARDS' WAY and TRAINER, although probably his greatest achievement was COLDITZ, which he devised with Brian Degas. N. J. Crisp has been another of Glaister's collaborators. Other production credits have included *The Men from Room 13*, DR FINLAY'S CASEBOOK, *Moonstrike*, *The Revenue Men*, THE EXPERT, *Codename*, SECRET ARMY and *Kessler*.

GLASER, PAUL MICHAEL
(1943–)

Dark-haired American actor and director whose claim to fame has been the role of Detective Dave Starsky in the 1970s cop series, STARSKY AND HUTCH. Glaser's earliest TV work came in daytime soaps and through guest appearances in shows like THE WALTONS. After hanging up Starsky's chunky cardigans, he turned more to directing, although he has cropped up in a number of TV movies, including *The Great Houdinis*, in which he played escapologist Harry Houdini.

GLESS, SHARON
(1943–)

Blonde American actress, Detective Christine Cagney in CAGNEY AND LACEY. Earlier, Gless had broken into television playing secretaries and other secondary roles. She was Holly Barrett in the detective series, *Faraday and Company*, nurse Kathleen Faverty in MARCUS WELBY, MD, receptionist Maggie in *Switch* and took minor parts in McCLOUD, *Cool Million* and other shows. When Meg Foster was dropped from *Cagney and Lacey* in 1982, Gless was called up to take her place. She later starred in the legal drama series, *The Trials of Rosie O'Neill*, produced, like *Cagney and Lacey*, by Barney Rosenzweig, whom she married in 1991.

GLITTERING PRIZES, THE
UK (BBC) Drama. BBC 2 1976

Adam Morris	Tom Conti
Barbara Morris	Barbara Kellerman
Lionel Morris	Leonard Sachs
Joyce Hadleigh/Bradley	Angela Down
Dan Bradley	Malcolm Stoddard
Barbara Ransome/Parks	Anna Carteret
Mike Clode	Mark Wing-Davey
Anna Cunningham	Emily Richard
Alan Parks	John Gregg
Bill Bourne	Clive Merrison
Stephen Taylor	Eric Porter
Gavin Pope	Dinsdale Landen

Writer: Frederic Raphael
Producer: Mark Shivas

The changing lives of a group of Cambridge students.

Beginning in 1953, when its protagonists were all Cambridge undergraduates, *The Glittering Prizes* followed a group of young intellectuals through to their middle-age in the 1970s, charting the ups and downs in their varied lives. The central character was Adam Morris, a scholarship student who became a wealthy novelist. Taking the form of six 80-minute plays, the series won much critical acclaim. On a similar theme, author Frederic Raphael followed up with *Oxbridge Blues*, seven plays screened in 1984.

GLOVER, BRIAN
(1934–97)

Yorkshire-born actor, presenter and writer, a one-time teacher and professional wrestler (under the name of Leon Arras). A familiar face on television, Glover asked the questions on the science show, DON'T ASK ME, played dimwit Heslop in PORRIDGE, featured as the frightening Tommy Beamish in *Lost Empires* and carried Peter Davison's bags in CAMPION, as the detective's man-servant, Magersfontein Lugg. In addition, he starred as

Edgar Rowley in the comedy, *South of the Border*, appeared as Yorkie in MINDER and Selwyn Price in *Anna Lee*, and was also seen in *Sez Les*, *Sounding Brass*, ALL CREATURES GREAT AND SMALL, WHATEVER HAPPENED TO THE LIKELY LADS?, DIXON OF DOCK GREEN, THE REGIMENT, SECRET ARMY, RETURN OF THE SAINT, FOXY LADY, DOCTOR WHO, BOTTOM and the wrestling drama, *Rumble*, among many offerings. He was the voice of the Tetley teafolk in their various commercials and also wrote scripts for PLAY FOR TODAY and other dramas.

GMTV
(Good Morning Television)

Breakfast television station which – under the consortium name of Sunrise Television – won the early-morning ITV franchise from TV-am in the 1991 auctions with a bid of £34.6 million. Broadcast from London's South Bank television centre, the output is a mixture of news, reaction, general magazine items and cartoons. Transmissions began on 1 January 1993 and the main presenters have included Anthea Turner, Eamonn Holmes, Lorraine Kelly and Penny Smith, with Alastair Stewart fronting Sunday's political programme.

GNOMES OF DULWICH, THE
UK (BBC) Situation Comedy. BBC1 1969

Big .... **Terry Scott**
Small .... **Hugh Lloyd**
Old .... **John Clive**

Creator/Writer: **Jimmy Perry**
Producers: **Sydney Lotterby, Graeme Muir**

Pearls of wisdom from a trio of garden gnomes.

Big, Small and Old were three stone gnomes in a Dulwich garden who spent their time discussing the state of the human race, prompted by the actions (unseen) of people who passed them by. The gnomes also enjoyed a rivalry with their plastic counterparts in the neighbouring gardens.

GOD SLOT

The irreverent term for early Sunday evening when religious programmes have historically been scheduled on British TV. However, the slot has been eroded over the years and ITV has now abandoned it altogether, leaving BBC 1 to uphold the tradition with SONGS OF PRAISE.

GODDARD, LIZA
(1950–)

Smethwick-born actress, some of whose earliest appearances were in Australia alongside SKIPPY THE BUSH KANGAROO (Clancy Merrick). Moving back to the UK, she was Victoria in TAKE THREE GIRLS (and reprised the role for a 1982 update, *Take Three Women*), Lily Pond/Browne in YES – HONESTLY and worked with her future husband, Colin Baker, in THE BROTHERS (April Merroney). In the 1980s she starred as mistress Nellie Bligh in PIG IN THE MIDDLE, Claire in the advertising sitcom, *Watch this Space*, piano teacher Belinda Purcell in ROLL OVER BEETHOVEN and Laurel Manasotti in *That's Love*, as well as being a frequent guest in BERGERAC, playing diamond thief Philippa Vale. Among her many other credits have been parts in *The Befrienders*, *Holding On*, WODEHOUSE PLAYHOUSE, TALES OF THE UNEXPECTED, *Woof!*, DOCTOR WHO and numerous panel games, including GIVE US A CLUE (team captain). Her second husband was pop star Alvin Stardust.

GOING FOR A SONG
UK (BBC) Game Show. BBC 1 1965–77; 1995–

Presenters: **Max Robertson, Michael Parkinson**

Producers: **John Irving, John King, Paul Smith**

Subdued quiz in which panellists attempt to guess the value of an antique.

Produced by the BBC in Bristol, *Going for a Song* was the forerunner to ANTIQUES ROADSHOW but with echoes of the earlier ANIMAL, VEGETABLE, MINERAL?. Chairman Max Robertson offered an intriguing piece of antiquity to his distinguished guests (Customers versus Connoisseurs), who worked out what the item was and then estimated its sales value. Points were awarded for the closest guess. Arthur Negus made his name as a regular pundit and the programme was characterized by the twittering of a caged mechanical bird over the opening and closing credits. The series returned with Michael Parkinson in the chair, expert assistance from Eric Knowles, and team captains Tony Slattery and Leslie Ash (later Mariella Frostrup, Kit Hesketh-Harvey and Penny Smith), at lunchtimes in 1995.

GOING LIVE!
UK (BBC) Children's Entertainment BBC 1 1987–93

Presenters: **Phillip Schofield, Sarah Greene, Kristian Schmid**

Editor: **Chris Bellinger**

Saturday morning children's magazine.

The successor to MULTI-COLOURED SWAP SHOP and *Saturday Superstore*, *Going Live!* brought the Saturday morning TV idea up to date and abandoned the cheesy 'swapping' and 'department store' concepts that had marked its two predecessors. Sarah Greene held her place from the *Superstore* crowd and was now joined, from the Children's BBC's 'broom cupboard', by Phillip Schofield and his puppet pal, Gordon the Gopher. Later, ex-Neighbour Kristian Schmid was roped in to help out when Schofield's West End job as Joseph (he of the *Dreamcoat*) scuppered his early-morning routine.

Regular features included the 'Double Dare' action

trivia quiz with Peter Simon; the chance to ring in and 'Ask the Expert', quiz guests in 'Press Conference', or have your say in 'Soapbox'; plus roving reports from Mark Chase and items from the 'Newsround News-hounds'. Studio 7's odd-job men, Simon Hickson and Trevor Neal, provided the laughs, and imported colour came from a selection of cartoons (*Thundercats*, *Teenage Mutant Hero Turtles*, THE JETSONS, etc.). In later series, slots included 'All About Me' (where kids told their own life-story and discussed their hobbies), 'Greenline' (an ecology slot with Jonathon Porritt), 'Check It Out' (consumerism with Emma Freud), cookery instruction from Emma Forbes, and the new game, 'Run the Risk' (with Peter Simon and Shane Richie). After six years, the series finally relinquished the Saturday morning slot to *Live and Kicking* (1993–).

GOING STRAIGHT
See PORRIDGE.

GOLD ROBBERS, THE
UK (LWT) Police Drama. ITV 1969

Det. Chief Supt. Cradock	**Peter Vaughan**
DS Tommy Thomas	**Artro Morris**
Richard Bolt	**Richard Leech**

Creators: **John Hawkesworth, Glyn Jones**
Producer: **John Hawkesworth**

An aircraft load of gold bullion is stolen in a breathtaking crime. In charge of the investigation is formidable CID man Cradock.

This 13-part serial, created by John Hawkesworth (UPSTAIRS, DOWNSTAIRS) and Glyn Jones, cast Peter Vaughan in an unusual role. Now famed for his arch-criminal performances (especially 'Genial' Harry Grout in PORRIDGE), he found himself on the other side of the law in this earlier outing, with his character totally committed to cracking this dare-devil crime, recovering gold ingots worth £5^1/$_2$ million and, one by one, bringing the perpetrators to book. Not so surprising was George Cole, who appeared as a guest star in one episode, playing a second-rate con-man.

GOLDEN GIRLS, THE
US (Witt-Thomas-Harris/Touchstone) Situation Comedy.
Channel 4 1986–93

Dorothy Zbornak	**Beatrice Arthur**
Blanche Devereaux	**Rue McClanahan**
Rose Nylund	**Betty White**
Sophia Petrillo	**Estelle Getty**
Stanley Zbornak	**Herb Edelman**
Miles Webber	**Harold Gould**

Creator: **Susan Harris**
Executive Producers: **Paul Junger Witt, Tony Thomas, Marc Sotkin, Susan Harris**

Four mature Florida ladies enjoy their 'golden years' together.

The four sparky 'Golden Girls' were out to prove one thing: not only did life begin at 40, but it got better in one's 50s and 60s. The girls shared a roomy bungalow in Miami, owned by Blanche Devereaux, a widowed Southern belle with an enormous appetite for men. Her friends were Dorothy Zbornak, a divorced, level-headed schoolteacher, Rose Nylund, a scatty widow of Scandinavian descent, and Sophia Petrillo, Dorothy's resourceful mother, who had moved in with the others after her Shady Pines retirement home had burned down.

Blanche was the genuine merry widow, openly flirtatious and scandalously brazen, while Dorothy was tall, cynical and a touch domineering. She was visited occasionally by Stan, the hapless husband who had left her after 38 years to live with an air hostess. Naïve Rose was prone to misunderstandings, and the others dreaded her long-winded and pointless tales about her home town, St Olaf, Minnesota. Sicilian-born Sophia, meanwhile, was dry and forthright. Having suffered a stroke which had damaged the tact cells of her brain, she pulled no punches and everyone received the sharp end of her tongue.

Although the girls lived life to the full, the more worrying side of growing old was never forgotten. Grouped around the kitchen table for midnight ice-cream feasts, the foursome openly discussed their feelings and their worries: about men, about their families, about themselves. What came through more than anything was the special relationship they enjoyed, echoed in the theme song, 'Thank You for Being a Friend'.

The Golden Girls came to an end when Dorothy married Blanche's Uncle Lucas (played by Leslie Nielsen) and moved away from Miami. The three others also moved – into a hotel and a spin-off series entitled *The Golden Palace*.

GOLDEN SHOT, THE
UK (ATV) Game Show. ITV 1967–75

Presenters: **Jackie Rae, Bob Monkhouse, Norman Vaughan, Charlie Williams**

Producers: **Colin Clews, John Pullen, Edward Joffe, Mike Lloyd, Les Cocks, Dicky Leeman**

Colourful crossbow-shooting for prizes.

In this popular live game show, contestants fired cross-bows at cartoon targets in an effort to win cash and other prizes. Hosted initially by Canadian SPOT THE TUNE veteran, Jackie Rae, *The Golden Shot* was not an immediate hit. In the hands of Rae's successor, Bob Monkhouse, however, it became one of the biggest shows of its day, notching up large audiences for its Sunday teatime slot (having transferred from Saturday nights). Monkhouse was himself succeeded by Norman Vaughan and then by Charlie Williams, before returning to administer the last rites to a tired and dying show in 1975.

Based on a successful German concept, the programme consisted of a series of shooting games. Viewers at home, by way of telephone, could direct a blindfolded marksman to fire at the target, using basic directions like 'Up a bit, down a bit, left a bit, fire'. Other games involved studio contestants taking over control of the crossbows themselves. They shot at bright, humorous pictures and scored by piercing targets made of apple. The ultimate prize was a treasure chest of gold coins that spilled out on to the studio floor when a slender thread was broken. Celebrities mingled with participants and TV cameras were built into the crossbows to show viewers at home how the contestants were aiming.

Supporting the hosts were the 'Golden Girls', initially Andrea Lloyd, Carol Dilworth (later mother of pop star Chesney Hawkes) and Anita Richardson, but most famously dizzy blonde Anne Aston (whose maths as she added up the target totals always left room for improvement). Aston was later assisted by a guest 'Maid of the Month'. Bernie the Bolt was the silent man who loaded the crossbows, although there were in fact three 'Bernies' employed during the programme's eight-year run (Derek Young, Alan Bailey and, best remembered, Johnny Baker).

GONET, STELLA

British actress, raised in Scotland, best known as Bea in THE HOUSE OF ELIOTT, but also seen in dramas like *The Advocates* (Alex Abercorn), *Screen One*'s *Trip Trap* (abused wife Kate Armstrong), THE CROW ROAD (Fiona), CASUALTY and *Verdict*.

GOOD GUYS, THE

UK (LWT/Haverhall) Comedy Drama. ITV 1992–3

Guy MacFadyean .... **Nigel Havers**
Guy Lofthouse .... **Keith Barron**

Executive Producer: **Nick Elliott**
Producers: **Andrew Montgomery, Michael Whitehall**

Two well-meaning, out-of-work characters join forces to help others, but without much success.

When Guy Lofthouse walked out on both his marriage and his job in Leeds, he found himself in Richmond, Surrey – and somewhat bewildered by life in the south. Meeting his equally unemployed namesake, Guy MacFadyean, the two Guys struck up a friendship and agreed to share a flat. To put some purpose into their empty lives, they set about helping other people, with unpredictable results.

The series was specially created for Nigel Havers and Keith Barron, to enable the two actors to work together. It was made for LWT by Nigel Havers's own production company, Haverhall.

GOOD, JACK

(1930–)

TV's Mr Pop Music. Beginning with SIX-FIVE SPECIAL in 1957, Jack Good revolutionized television coverage of the music scene. At last here was someone (who had joined the BBC as a trainee only in 1956) actually producing programmes for teenage music fans, even if he cautiously sold it to the stuffy Corporation as a young person's magazine. One of its unusual and pioneering features was use of the audience, not ignoring them but bringing them into the proceedings. Controversially sacked a year later, he moved to ABC to produce a rival show, OH BOY!, which ultimately saw the end of the by-now-staid *Six-Five Special*. In 1959 he created *Boy Meets Girls*, a vehicle for Marty Wilde, and, a year later, *Wham!!* Good was a hit even across the Atlantic, devising *Shindig* and numerous other pop successes. *Oh Boy!* was briefly revived in the late 1970s.

GOOD LIFE, THE

UK (BBC) Situation Comedy. BBC 1 1975–8

Tom Good .... **Richard Briers**
Barbara Good .... **Felicity Kendal**
Margo Leadbeatter .... **Penelope Keith**
Jerry Leadbeatter .... **Paul Eddington**

Creators/Writers: **John Esmonde, Bob Larbey**
Producer: **John Howard Davies**

A young couple go self-sufficient in Surbiton.

Tom Good had become tired of the rat race. On his 40th birthday, sick of commuting to his draughtsman's job in the City (where he created cereal gifts for the JJM company), he threw it all in to concentrate on home farming. Ably and inventively assisted by Barbara, his perky wife, the buoyant Tom turned his back garden into an allotment, growing fruit and vegetables and housing chickens, pigs, a cockerel named Lenin and even a goat named Geraldine. For heating and cooking they restored an old cast-iron range, and for power they ran a generator in the cellar. Living off the land, and bartering away the surplus with local shopkeepers, the Goods thrived on the joys of self-sufficiency, even if there were moments of deep despair.

It was at times like these that their true-blue neighbours, Jerry and Margo, came to the rescue. Although they considered Tom and Barbara to be completely insane, and to have brought 'The Avenue' into disrepute, they remained loyal friends. Even if Margo hated donning wellies to feed the pigs, she still did so, and she and Jerry (a former work colleague of Tom's) always took great interest in events next door. In return, the Goods brought a ray of wholesome sunshine into the depressingly snobbish life of their wealthier neighbours.

GOOD MORNING BRITAIN

See TV-AM.

GOOD MORNING TELEVISION

See GMTV.

GOOD OLD DAYS, THE
UK (BBC) Variety. BBC 1 1953–83

Chairmen: **Don Gemmell, Leonard Sachs**

Producer: **Barney Colehan**

The days of the music hall re-created.

Indelibly associated with its loud and wordy compere, Leonard Sachs (who took over from first chairman Don Gemmell), *The Good Old Days* owed just as much to its long-serving producer, Barney Colehan, who was responsible for developing this music-hall revival show. Broadcast (somewhat irregularly) from one of the true surviving music halls, the City Varieties in Leeds, the programme lasted over 30 years and provided older viewers with a happy slice of golden age nostalgia. Its guest stars (the likes of Roy Hudd, Danny La Rue, Ray Alan, Ken Dodd, etc.) performed music-hall acts in the style of Marie Lloyd and others, and dressed for the part in 1890s costume. So did the studio audience, who donned false sideburns and frilly hats and were encouraged to join in the proceedings by singing along or waving a handkerchief. And then there was the polysyllabic Leonard Sachs himself, filled with vociferous verbosity, never using one word when 27 would do, smashing down his gavel and rousing the audience to a rapturous welcome for even the most unheard-of performers. The Players' Theatre Company and the Northern Dance Orchestra were the resident supporting artists and each edition ended with the cast and audience joining together in a chorus of 'The Old Bull and Bush'.

GOOD SEX GUIDE, THE
UK (Carlton) Comedy/Information. ITV 1993–4

Presenter: **Margi Clarke**

Producer: **Vicki Barrass**

Forthright advice on sex, interspersed with personal views and expert opinions, but with humorous sketches to ease embarrassment.

Margi Clarke's colourful commentary added a down-to-earth matter-of-factness to the 'awkward' and intimate subjects considered by this late-night programme, which tackled the taboo subject of 'getting the most out of sex'. Among the actors offering light relief through assorted comedy sketches were Tony Robinson, Linda Robson, Pauline Quirke, Stephanie Cole, Bernard Hill, Roger Lloyd Pack, Julia Hills, Haydn Gwynne and Timothy Spall. Clarke returned with a second series in 1994, with the likes of Leslie Grantham, Nigel Planer and Martin Clunes contributing to the fun.

GOODIES, THE
UK (BBC/LWT) Comedy. BBC 2 1970–7; 1980/ITV 1981–2

Graeme .... **Graeme Garden**
Tim .... **Tim Brooke-Taylor**
Bill .... **Bill Oddie**

Creators/Writers: **Graeme Garden, Tim Brooke-Taylor, Bill Oddie**
Producers: **John Howard Davies, Jim Franklin, Bob Spiers (LWT)**

Zany humour with a trio of do-gooders.

Graeme, Tim and Bill were benefactors to society, available to do anything, anywhere and at any time to help humanity. Taking on the weirdest assignments, they found themselves guarding the Crown Jewels, rescuing London from the advance of a giant kitten, and in other bizarre situations. Sometimes they cooked up their own world improvement schemes and attempted to put them into action. Energetically charging around on a three-seater bicycle (a 'trandem'), the three formed an unlikely team.

Tim was a weedy royalist sporting a Union Jack waistcoat, Graeme was a mad scientist type and Bill was an unkempt, hairy socialist-cum-cynic. They lived in a typical 1970s flat, dominated by portraits of the Queen (for Tim) and Chairman Mao (for Bill), plus Graeme's computer. Their adventures were punctuated with crazy sight gags, slapstick sketches and spoof TV commercials.

There were send-ups galore as the trio took contemporary fads or issues and placed them surreally in different contexts – a North Country spoof on the Kung Fu craze, for instance. Bill Oddie's original music featured prominently and The Goodies had five real life hits in the 1970s (most notably, alas, 'Funky Gibbon' in 1975).

Originally planned as *Super-Chaps Three*, *The Goodies* was one of BBC 2's biggest successes of the 1970s, enjoying repeat showings on BBC 1. However, disillusioned with the Corporation's lack of commitment to the programme, the team moved to LWT for a short run in 1981–2, by which time the concept had dated somewhat.

GOODMAN, JOHN
(1952–)

Giant American comic actor, achieving star status as Dan Conner in the blue-collar sitcom, ROSEANNE. With his film career really taking off, little else has been seen of him on television, save in a few TV movies.

GOODNESS GRACIOUS ME
UK (BBC) Comedy. BBC 2 1998–

Sanjeev Bhaskar, Meera Syal, Kulvinder Ghir, Nina Wadia

Producer: **Anil Gupta**
Executive Producer: **Jon Plowman**

Award-winning cross-cultural sketch show.

Beginning on BBC Radio, *Goodness Gracious Me* soon transferred to television, bringing with it a novel approach to cultural humour. 'Sacred cows' in more than one sense were slaughtered as the four second-generation Indian stars lampooned their own ethnic traditions and at the same time dug away at Britishness and the British treatment of Indians.

Recurring characters included the Coopers (an Indian couple named Kapoor who believed they were pukka English), two Indian mothers who tried to outdo each other in terms of what their respective sons had achieved, a pseudo-Maharishi character who faked his mystic knowledge, two confused youths known as the Bhangramuffins, and an Indian dad who insisted everyone who had achieved anything in this world had been Indian. There were also spoofs of the hyper-dramatic 'Bollywood' films, starring wonderstar Chunky, reports from fading showbiz gossip columnist Smeeta Smitten, and the latest infelicity from the tactless Mr 'Cheque please', who never failed to insult his lady dinner-guests. Memorable sketches included the send-up 'Delhitubbies' and one about a group of young Indians visiting a restaurant for an 'English', boorishly ordering 'something bland'.

GOODNIGHT SWEETHEART

UK (Alomo) Situation Comedy. BBC 1 1993–9

Gary Sparrow	**Nicholas Lyndhurst**
Yvonne Sparrow	**Michelle Holmes**
	Emma Amos
Phoebe Bamford/Sparrow	**Dervla Kirwan**
	Elizabeth Carling
Eric	**David Ryall**
Ron Wheatcroft	**Victor McGuire**
PC Reg Deadman	**Christopher Ettridge**
Noël Coward	**David Benson**

Creators: **Laurence Marks, Maurice Gran**
Executive Producer: **Allan McKeown**
Producers: **John Bartlett, Nic Phillips**

An unhappily married TV engineer wanders through a time warp and picks up a 1940s girlfriend.

London television repair man Gary Sparrow and Yvonne, his personnel officer wife, were going through a sticky patch. She wanted more from life and was heavily involved in her Open University pyschology degree; he had more interest in simpler matters, like the physical side of their relationship. One day, on his rounds, he wandered down Ducketts Passage, an East End alleyway, found himself lost and popped into The Royal Oak pub in Stepney for directions. Having been charged tuppence-farthing for his half-pint, he assumed he had discovered a theme pub but, stepping outside again, realized that he had actually slipped back in time to 1940. Taking a shine to Phoebe, the landlord's daughter, Gary soon made a habit of popping back to the war years, where the locals (and particularly Phoebe's dad, Eric) distrusted this strange young man with weird ideas who claimed to be a songwriter (his hits included 'Your Song', 'I Can't Get No Satisfaction' and 'When I'm Sixty-Four'). Meanwhile Yvonne was increasingly bemused by

Gary's new interest in wartime nostalgia. Gary's only confidant was his printer pal, Ron.

After the death of her dad, Phoebe ran the pub with the help of inept local bobby PC Deadman (actor Christopher Ettridge was also seen occasionally as Deadman's grandson, a 1990s policeman). Gary married Phoebe and a son, Michael, was born. They moved to a plush West End flat for security, where one of their neighbours was Noël Coward. There were changes in the 20th century, too. Gary opened a wartime nostalgia shop ('Blitz and Pieces'), on the site of the now-developed Ducketts Passage, to provide a cover for his time-travelling activities, while Yvonne first joined a Korean company, then set up a holistic cosmetics business that made her a fortune and earned her a peerage from the Blair government. In the finale to the series, Gary saved the life of Prime Minister Clement Attlee, and then found his time portal permanently blocked, implying that he had now fulfilled the mission for which he had been allowed to travel through time. Trapped in 1945, he scribbled a note beneath the wallpaper of his West End flat, explaining his predicament to Yvonne and Ron, knowing it would be discovered during decorating work in 1999.

GOODSON, MARK

MBE (1915–92)

Prolific American inventor of TV quizzes and panel games, often in conjunction with his partner, Bill Todman. Together they were responsible for the likes of WHAT'S MY LINE?, *I've Got a Secret*, *Beat the Clock*, CALL MY BLUFF, THE PRICE IS RIGHT and FAMILY FORTUNES. Goodson-Todman Productions was their company, formed after Goodson had worked as a radio announcer and Todman as a scriptwriter. Their ventures into drama productions were not so successful.

GOODYEAR, JULIE

MBE (1942–)

Inseparable from bold, brassy Bet Lynch/Gilroy, her character in CORONATION STREET until 1995, Lancashire-born Julie Goodyear arrived in Weatherfield in 1966, although it wasn't until 1970 that she became a Rover's Return regular. Among her other TV credits have been Granada series like PARDON THE EXPRESSION (the 1966 *Street* spin-off), A FAMILY AT WAR, *City '68*, *The War of Darkie Pilbeam*, THE DUSTBINMEN and NEAREST AND DEAREST.

GOOLDEN, JILLY

Sussex-born TV wine and drinks expert, first gaining recognition on FOOD AND DRINK for her much-mimicked 'over the top' tasting descriptions, and later extending into other programming, including as host of *The Great Antiques Hunt*.

GORDON, HANNAH
(1941–)

Scottish actress seen in both dramatic and comedy roles. Among her best-remembered performances have been as Suzy Bassett, with John Alderton, in MY WIFE NEXT DOOR; as Victoria Jones, Richard Briers's landlady, in Goodbye Mr Kent; Peter Barkworth's wife (Sylvia Telford) in TELFORD'S CHANGE; and as Belinda Braithwaite in another banking series, Joint Account, with Peter Egan. She played Virginia Hamilton, Lord Bellamy's second wife, in UPSTAIRS, DOWNSTAIRS and her other credits have included parts in THE RAT CATCHERS, Ladykillers, Middlemarch, DR FINLAY'S CASEBOOK, HADLEIGH, THE PERSUADERS!, Miss Morrison's Ghosts, THE PROTECTORS, My Family and Other Animals and some Dickens adaptations. She was also seen with Morecambe and Wise, as one of their harassed guests, and has presented the series, Watercolour Challenge.

GORDON, NOELE
(1923–85)

CROSSROADS proprietor Meg Richardson/Mortimer, and one-time Queen of the Soaps, Noele Gordon became a household name after a long and varied career on stage and television. She first appeared in a BBC play way back in 1938 and shortly afterwards assisted John Logie Baird by appearing in one of his colour TV experiments. In the 1950s, with a string of stage plays and musicals to her name, Gordon formally studied the new medium of television in the USA and returned to the UK to work for the embryonic ATV as an adviser on women's programmes. This led to on-screen presentation work on programmes such as Tea with Noele Gordon, Fancy That and Hi-T!, some sports shows, the admag, About Homes and Gardens, a part in the sitcom, The Most Likely Girl (Eve Edwards), and, in 1957, the well-remembered magazine, Lunch Box. In 1964 she was cast as the queen bee of the company's new daily soap opera, and she remained with Crossroads until being surprisingly axed in 1981.

GORDON-SINCLAIR, JOHN
(1962–)

Scottish comedy actor, starring in series such as HOT METAL (Bill Tytla), Your Cheatin' Heart (journalist Frank McClusky), Snakes and Ladders (Gavin), An Actor's Life for Me (hopeful thespian Robert Neilson), Nelson's Column (reporter Gavin Nelson), Loved by You (newly wed film-maker Michael Adams) and the single comedy, My Summer with Des (Cameron). He also played Macbeth in the Shakespeare Shorts series of extracts.

GORING, MARIUS
CBE (1912–98)

Isle of Wight-born actor with a flair for accents and dialects. A prolific film performer, Goring's first television appearance came in a Chekhov play in 1938. In 1956 he became TV's master of disguise, Sir Percy Blakeney, alias THE SCARLET PIMPERNEL, saver of aristocratic French souls, in a series which he also co-produced. Goring's next starring role came 13 years later and was in quite a different vein. On this occasion he played Midlands pathologist John Hardy in THE EXPERT. He resurfaced in 1983 as Dr Emile Englander, one of the Old Men at the Zoo, and among his other credits were episodes of series as varied as EDWARD AND MRS SIMPSON (King George V), The Fall of Eagles (Paul von Hindenburg), MAN IN A SUITCASE and WILDE ALLIANCE, plus many single dramas.

GOWER, DAVID
(1957–)

Former England batsman and Test captain, retiring in 1993 and now one of the leading commentators on the sport, working for both the BBC and Sky Sports, and for a while presenting GRANDSTAND's Cricket Focus and BBC 2's Gower's Cricket Monthly. Gower has also been a team captain in the comedy quiz, THEY THINK IT'S ALL OVER.

GRACE AND FAVOUR
See ARE YOU BEING SERVED?.

GRADE, Lord LEW
(Louis Winogradsky; 1906–98)

Born in the Ukraine, Lew Grade's showbiz career began in the world of dance (he was World Charleston Champion in 1926) but then moved into talent-spotting and management. He set up the Lew and Leslie Grade agency with his younger brother and took care of many of the world's finest acts of the 1940s and 1950s. In 1955 he formed a consortium to bid for one of the ITV franchises. The resulting company, Associated Television (ATV), was given the Midlands weekday and the London weekend ITV contracts. Grade and his colleagues also established ITC (Incorporated Television Production Company) at the same time, with a view to producing films for television. The company was responsible for such dramas as THE ADVENTURES OF ROBIN HOOD, THE SAINT, JESUS OF NAZARETH and the Gerry Anderson puppet series, all aimed purposefully at the American market. Throughout ATV's time on air and ITC's time in production, Grade's influence was enormous, and his personality and presence ensured his programmes were never short of publicity. His ventures into the movie business, primarily in the 1970s and 1980s, proved less lucrative. He was the uncle of TV executive Michael Grade (Leslie's son) and brother of the late Lord Bernard Delfont.

GRADE, MICHAEL
CBE (1943–)

British TV executive with experience on both sides of the Atlantic. Grade began as a sports writer, before joining his family's theatrical agency and subsequently moving into television. At LWT, he was Head of Light Entertainment and Director of Programmes and, crossing to the States, spent some time with Embassy Television. He became Controller of BBC 1 in 1984 and, later, Director of Programmes, and during his four years at the Corporation was given credit for rejuvenating both BBC television networks, with his scheduling expertise widely acclaimed. He repositioned existing shows to their greater benefit (drawing on his intimate knowledge of ITV competition) and was responsible for commissioning and nurturing a host of new ideas. EAST-ENDERS was a classic case, with Grade firmly committed to its early success. EDGE OF DARKNESS, *The Late Show*, TUTTI FRUTTI and THE SINGING DETECTIVE were other notable achievements. Grade's BBC years were not without controversy, however. In 1986 he added to the storm over THE MONOCLED MUTINEER by passing a press release which wrongly stated that all the facts were authentic; and, a year earlier, he had angered sci-fi fans by postponing a season of DOCTOR WHO and cancelling THE TRIPODS two-thirds of the way through. From 1988–97 he was chief executive of Channel 4, controversy following him back into the independent sector. Grade is the son of talent agent the late Leslie Grade and nephew of the late Lord Lew Grade.

GRAMMER, KELSEY
(1955–)

American actor, born in the US Virgin Islands. After minor roles in soaps, Grammer made the decisive move from stage to small screen when offered the part of psychiatrist Frasier Crane in CHEERS, a character who was then spun off into his own even more successful series, FRASIER, making Grammer an international star.

GRAMPIAN TELEVISION

Taking to the air on 30 September 1961, Grampian Television is the independent television contractor for North Scotland (basically from Fife north to Shetland and west to the Hebrides – the largest of all ITV franchise regions). Its main production centre is in Aberdeen, but the company also operates smaller studios in Stornoway, Dundee and Inverness. Since 1976 some regional programmes have been made in Gaelic, but, while the company has a good reputation for local news and current affairs, it is not renowned for contributions to the ITV national network. Grampian is now part of Scottish Media Group, which also owns Scottish Television and has a share in GMTV.

GRAN, MAURICE
(1949–)

British comedy scriptwriter, in collaboration with partner Laurence Marks. Together Marks and Gran, whose early work included writing for Marti Caine, have been responsible for some of the most popular sitcoms and comedy-dramas since the 1980s, many produced by their own company, Alomo (part of Pearson Television since 1996). These have included SHINE ON HARVEY MOON, *Roots*, HOLDING THE FORT, *Relative Strangers*, THE NEW STATESMAN, ROLL OVER BEETHOVEN, *Young, Gifted and Broke, Snakes and Ladders, So You Think You've Got Troubles*, BIRDS OF A FEATHER, LOVE HURTS, GOODNIGHT SWEETHEART, *Get Back, Unfinished Business, Dirty Work* and *Men of the World* (as producers). After setting up the premiss in early episodes, Marks and Gran have often passed the writing of their comedies into other hands. In contrast, the duo also scripted the drama, *Mosley*.

GRANADA TELEVISION

Granada Television was formed in 1955 by Sidney (later Lord) Bernstein and his brother, Cecil, to operate the North of England ITV weekday franchise (ABC was given the weekends). Following the London ITV companies on to the air, its first programmes went out on 3 May 1956. With restructuring and the arrival of Yorkshire Television in 1968, its transmission area was recentred on the north-west, but for the full seven days a week.

Granada has always occupied a hallowed position among ITV companies, managing to combine commercial astuteness with a commitment to high-quality programming, an attribute not often recognized in commercial broadcasting. The company has fostered young writers and producers in all areas of programming, from the mass-market appeal of CORONATION STREET to the weaker audience potential of award-winning documentaries like WORLD IN ACTION and DISAPPEARING WORLD. Granada has also shown itself to be a rival to the BBC in classic drama. BRIDESHEAD REVISITED and THE JEWEL IN THE CROWN were lavish productions in the early 1980s, and equal acclaim has since been afforded to productions such as THE ADVENTURES OF SHERLOCK HOLMES, PRIME SUSPECT and CRACKER. However, the company has also been happy to exploit cheap and cheerful, viewer-spinning concepts, including THE COMEDIANS, BUSMAN'S HOLIDAY, STARS IN THEIR EYES, YOU'VE BEEN FRAMED and THE KRYPTON FACTOR. In the 1980s Granada opened up its studios to the public, instantly creating one of Britain's major tourist attractions.

Despite its impressive record, there were fears that Granada would lose its franchise in the 1991 auctions, when Phil Redmond's Mersey Television outbid it by several millions. This was one decision which went in favour of quality instead of cash, however, and Granada survived. Since then, Granada – the longest surviving ITV company – has taken overall control of its fellow ITV franchisees, LWT, Yorkshire, Tyne Tees, Anglia and

Meridian, with an option to buy Border from Capital Radio. The company also has shares in Scottish Media, ITN, GMTV and BSkyB, and has launched its own satellite channels through Granada Sky Broadcasting: Granada Men and Motors, Granada Breeze and the archive-raiding Granada Plus. The company has also begun producing programmes for the BBC, notably WHAT THE PAPERS SAY, UNIVERSITY CHALLENGE and THE ROYLE FAMILY.

The name Granada was dreamt up by Sidney Bernstein for his theatre business in the 1920s, following a breathtaking visit to the Spanish city of the same name.

GRANDSTAND

UK (BBC) Sport. BBC 1 1958–

Presenters: **Peter Dimmock, David Coleman, Frank Bough, Desmond Lynam, Steve Rider**

The BBC's Saturday afternoon sports showcase.

Now past its 40th birthday, *Grandstand*, the world's longest-running live sports programme, is a national institution, and Saturday afternoons would not be the same without it – despite the BBC's loss of many major sporting events in recent years. Its format has changed little over the years. Live horse racing has been mixed with boxing, rugby union, rugby league, cricket, motor sports and occasional other events, and all the day's soccer and rugby details have been rounded up to provide a full results service at the end, including reports from the major matches. The final scores, as they happen, have been reported on the Teleprinter and, in latter years, its replacement, the Videprinter.

Peter Dimmock was the first host but quickly gave way to David Coleman. Frank Bough took over in 1968, and from the 1980s Desmond Lynam and Steve Rider shared the honours, until Lynam's departure to ITV in 1999. Other presenters have been drafted in as relief cover over the years, including Harry Carpenter, Harry Gratian, Bob Wilson and, more recently, Helen Rollason (first female presenter), Sue Barker, Ray Stubbs, Dougie Donnelly, John Inverdale and Hazel Irvine. The main specialist commentators have been as follows: boxing, Harry Carpenter and Jim Neilly; rugby union, Cliff Morgan, Bill McLaren and Nigel Starmer-Smith; rugby league, Eddie Waring and Ray French; racing, Peter O'Sullevan, Clive Graham, Julian Wilson, Jimmy Lindley, Richard Pitman, Peter Scudamore, Clare Balding, Willie Carson and Jim McGrath; motor sports, Murray Walker and Barry Nutley; winter sports, Alan Weeks, David Vine and Julian Tutt; golf, Henry Longhurst and Peter Alliss; swimming, Alan Weekes and Hamilton Bland; cricket, Richie Benaud, Jim Laker, Peter West and Tony Lewis; darts, Sid Waddell and Tony Green; snooker, Ted Lowe, Clive Everton and Ray Edmonds; tennis, Dan Maskell and John Barrett; athletics, Ron Pickering, Stuart Storey, David Coleman and Brendan Foster. *Football Preview*, the look ahead to the day's soccer, was hosted for many years by Sam Leitch. *Football Focus*, its successor, was fronted by Bob Wilson until his departure to ITV in 1994 and his replacement by Ray Stubbs and Gary Lineker.

The sports results have been read by the famous voices of the late Len Martin (soccer) and Tim Gudgin (most of the others).

Variations on the *Grandstand* theme have included *Sunday Grandstand* (inaugurated in 1981) and extended versions for the Olympic Games, the World Cup, etc.

GRANGE HILL

UK (BBC) Children's Drama. BBC 1 1978–

Peter 'Tucker' Jenkins	**Todd Carty**
Mr Tony Mitchell	**Michael Percival**
Justin Bennett	**Robert Craig Morgan**
Benny Green	**Terry Sue Patt**
Trisha Yates	**Michelle Herbert**
David Lewis	**Gary Fetterplace**
Jackie Heron	**Miriam Mann**
Thomas Watson	**James Jebbia**
Hughes	**Donald Waugh**
Mr Foster	**Roger Sloman**
Ann Wilson	**Lucinda Duckett**
Penny Lewis	**Ruth Davies**
Judy Preston	**Abigail Brown**
Alan Hargreaves/Humphries	**George Armstrong**
Lucinda	**Letitia Dean**
Mr Graham Sutcliffe	**James Wynn**
Mr Baxter	**Michael Cronin**
Mr Llewellyn	**Sean Arnold**
Simon Shaw	**Paul Miller**
Andrew Stanton	**Mark Chapman/Eadie**
Michael Doyle	**Vincent Hall**
Cathy Hargreaves	**Lyndy Brill**
Mary Johnson	**Kim Benson**
Karen Stanton	**Carey Born**
Susi McMahon	**Linda Slater**
Clare Scott	**Paula Ann Bland**
Sudhamani Patel	**Sheila Chandra**
Tommy Watson	**Paul McCarthy**
Matthew Cartwright	**Nicholas Pandolfi**
Mr Hopwood	**Brian Capron**
Mrs Bridget McCluskey	**Gwyneth Powell**
Mr Keating	**Robert Hartley**
Pogo Patterson	**Peter Moran**
Michael Green	**Mark Bishop**
'Gripper' Stebson	**Mark Savage**
Duane Orpington	**Mark Baxter**
'Stewpot' Stewart	**Mark Burdis**
Pamela Cartwright	**René Alperstein**
Annette Firman	**Nadia Chambers**
Anita Unsworth	**Joanne Boakes**
Precious Matthews	**Dulice Liecier**
Suzanne Ross	**Susan Tully**
Samuel 'Zammo' McGuire	**Lee MacDonald**
Roland Browning	**Erkan Mustafa**
Miss Mooney	**Lucinda Gane**
Mr 'Scruffy' McGuffy	**Fraser Cains**
Mr Bronson	**Michael Sheard**
Jonah Jones	**Lee Sparke**
Mr Smart	**Simon Haywood**
Janet St Clair	**Simone Nylander**
Fay Lucas	**Alison Bettles**
Jimmy Flynn	**Terry Kinsella**

Julie Marchant	**Lisa York**
Sarah Wilks	**Joanne Bell**
Jackie Wright	**Melissa Wilks**
Robbie Wright	**John Alford**
Diane Cooney	**Julie-Ann Steel**
Mandy Firth	**Anita Savage**
Ronnie Birtles	**Tina Mahon**
Miss Booth	**Karen Ford**
Gonch Gardner	**John Holmes**
Cheryl Webb	**Amma Asante**
Imelda Davis	**Fleur Taylor**
'Hollo' Holloway	**Bradley Sheppard**
Mrs Reagan	**Lucinda Curtis**
Vince Savage	**Steve West**
'Mauler' McCaul	**Joshua Fenton**
Helen Kelly	**Ruth Carraway**
Georgina Hayes	**Samantha Lewis**
Danny Kendall	**Jonathan Lambeth**
Ted	**Ian Congdon-Lee**
Matthew Pearson	**Paul Adams**
Ant Jones	**Ricky Simmonds**
Ziggy Greaves	**George Wilson/Christopher**
Mr Mackenzie	**Nicholas Donnelly**
Mr Griffiths	**George A. Cooper**
Mr Max Hargreaves	**Kevin O'Shea**
Mr Geoff Hankin	**Lee Cornes**
Mr Peter Robson	**Stuart Organ**
Caroline 'Calley' Donnington	**Simone Hyams**
Chrissy Mainwaring	**Sonya Kearns**
'Tegs' Ratcliffe	**Sean Maguire**
Mrs Keele	**Jenny Howe**
Trevor Cleaver	**John Drummond**
Mrs Monroe	**Anna Quayle**
Fiona Wilson	**Michelle Gayle**
Natasha Stevens	**Clare Buckfield**
Natalie Stevens	**Julie Buckfield**
Becky Stevens	**Natalie Poyser**
Justine Dean	**Rachel Roberts**
Maria	**Luisa Bradshaw-White**
Jacko Morgan	**Jamie Lehane**
Robyn	**Nina Fry**
Miss Jayne Carver	**Sally Geoghegan**
Julie Corrigan	**Margo Selby**
Anna Wright	**Jenny Long**
Gordon	**Andrew Henry**
Wendy Wright	**Amelda Brown**
Con	**Daniel O'Grady**
Mrs Jenkins	**Madelaine Newton**
Sarah-Jane Webster	**Laura Hammett**
Dudley	**Steven Hammett**
Kevin Jenkins	**George Stark**
Poppy Silver	**Ayesha Antoine**
Wayne Sutcliffe	**Peter Morton**
Colin Brown	**Colin Ridgewell**
Sam	**Kevin Bishop**
Delia 'Dill' Lodge	**Rochelle Gadd**
Josh Davis	**Jamie Groves**
Joe Williams	**Martino Lazzeri**
Lucy Mitchell	**Belinda Crane**
Dennis Morris	**Alan Cave**
Jessica Arnold	**Amy Simcock**
James 'Arnie' Arnold	**Aidan J. David**
Jerome	**Nicholas Pinnock**
Mr Mitchell	**Tim Bentinck**
Chris Longworth	**Ben Freeman**
Mr Brisley	**Adam Ray**
Mr Parrot	**Peter Leeper**
Paula	**Abigail Hart**
Lauren	**Melanie Joseph**
Judi Jeffries	**Laura Sadler**
Mrs Margaret Holmes	**Rachel Bell**
Mr Phillips	**Don Warrington**
Mr Dai 'Hard' Jones	**Clive Jones**
Laurie Watson	**Sian Welsh**
Joanna	**Fiona Wade**
Andy	**Ashley Walters**
Tom 'Speedy' Smith	**Oliver Elmidoro**
Sam 'Cracker' Bacon	**Jonathon Marchant-Heatley**
Lisa West	**Charlotte McDonagh**
Alec Jones	**Thomas Carey**
Matt Singleton	**Robert Stuart**
Rachel	**Francesca Martinez**
Adam Hawkins	**Sam Bardens**
Gemma Lyons	**Maggie Mason**
Franco Savi	**Francesco Bruno**
Carlene	**Lorraine Woodley**
Max Abassi	**Michael Obiora**
Sean Pearce	**Iain Robertson**
Nathan Charles	**Marcel McCalla**
Darren Clarke	**Adam Sopp**
Amy Davenport	**Lindsey Ray**
Becky	**Emma Pierson**
Zoe	**Jade Williams**
Ben Miller	**Daniel Lee**
Ian Hudson	**John Hudson**
Kamal	**Taylor Scipio**
Spencer Hargreaves	**Colin White**
Ray	**Kelly George**
Calvin Braithwaite	**Arnold Oceng**
Anika Modi	**Jalpa Patel**
Evelyn Wright	**Diana Magness**
Kelly Bradshaw	**Kate Bell**
Tracey Long	**Sally Morton**
Miss Fraser	**Judith Wright**
Simon	**Dominic Power**

Creator: **Phil Redmond**
Executive Producers: **Anna Home, Richard Callanan**
Producers: **Colin Cant, Susi Hush, Kenny McBain, Ben Rea, Ronald Smedley, Albert Barber, Christine Secombe**

Realistic tales of life in a London comprehensive school.

In the days when the nearest thing to unruly behaviour on children's television was an elephant wetting itself in the BLUE PETER studio, it would have been quite unthinkable to have switched on at five o'clock and watched a schoolboy trying to kick his heroin addiction. But times move on and kids' TV certainly caught up with its viewers when the BBC launched *Grange Hill* in 1978.

The brainchild of Liverpudlian writer Phil Redmond (later to take BROOKSIDE to Channel 4), *Grange Hill* (screened twice a week as a children's soap opera) was school as it really was, with none of the jolly japes and wizard wheezes of Billy Bunter's days. The action took place at Grange Hill Comprehensive and, to make its intended audience feel at home, low, kid-height camera-angles were used. The series showed pupils (mostly Form I Alpha) out of control, insulting teachers, truanting, bullying weaklings, smoking and shoplifting. It covered subjects as intense as child abuse, racism, sex, pregnancy, job hunting and, yes, drugs; and, while it received no thanks from Mary Whitehouse, its audience, aged between six and 16, loved it. Critics also failed to note that no one ever benefited from any of the hell-raising. Punishments were suitably doled out and the moral angles were well publicized. The programme's educational value was equally overlooked. In 1986, on the back of pupil Zammo's fight with heroin addiction, the cast released a hit record, 'Just Say No', and the relevant episode of the series was followed by a special factual programme on the subject. Within the unfolding drama, one other major turn of events involved the merger of Grange Hill with arch-rival schools Brookdale and Rodney Bennett in 1981.

Although lead and supporting characters have come and gone as pupils have progressed through school (the major players are listed above), the best remembered is Tucker Jenkins (played by future *EastEnder* Todd Carty), who also earned his own spin-off series, *Tucker's Luck* (1983–5), on leaving school. Carty's EASTENDERS sister, Susan Tully, was another early star, playing Suzanne Ross, and several other members of the prime-time soap cut their TV teeth in the classrooms of *Grange Hill*. Oscar-winning writer Anthony Minghella was the series' script editor, 1983–8.

GRANT, ROB

British comedy writer, most often in collaboration with partner Doug Naylor. Undoubtedly, Grant and Naylor's biggest success has been with the space sitcom, RED DWARF, although they have also been major contributors to THREE OF A KIND, SPITTING IMAGE, ALAS SMITH AND JONES, CARROTT'S LIB and numerous radio series. Another sitcom product of theirs was *The 10%ers*.

GRANT, RUSSELL
(1952–)

Bouncy TV astrologer and contributor to magazine programmes, an early star of the BBC's BREAKFAST TIME.

GRANTHAM, LESLIE
(1947–)

London-born actor who shot to fame as EASTENDERS' Dirty Den Watts. During his time in the series, it was revealed that Grantham had spent 11 years in prison for a murder he had committed while a soldier in Germany. In confinement he took up acting and, on release, he trained at drama school. His earliest TV roles came with minor parts in THE JEWEL IN THE CROWN, DOCTOR WHO and BULMAN. On leaving *EastEnders*, capitalizing on his new-found status as a TV sex-symbol, Grantham moved on to star in *Winners and Losers* (boxing promoter Eddie Burt), THE PARADISE CLUB (nightclub manager Danny Kane), *99–1* (undercover cop Mick Raynor), CLUEDO (Colonel Mustard), *The Uninvited* (Chief Supt. Gates, also as creator and executive producer) and Sky One's *The Stretch* (Terry Greene). He has also co-hosted the game show, *Fort Boyard*, and was seen in *Time Keepers of the Millennium*.

GRAVES, PETER
(Peter Aurness; 1925–)

Tall American actor, the brother of GUNSMOKE star James Arness. The brothers' TV breaks came at about the same time. In the mid-1950s, while James was beginning a long career in the guise of Dodge City lawman Matt Dillon, Peter launched into a five-year run as Jim Newton, the father figure in the horsey kids' series, *Fury*. In 1960 Graves starred as Chris Cobb, an American stage-coach owner, in the Australian Western, WHIPLASH, and, five years later, appeared in the drama series, COURT MARTIAL. Around this time he also popped up in series like ALFRED HITCHCOCK PRESENTS and *Route 66*. However, it is as Jim Phelps, team leader of the Impossible Missions Force in MISSION: IMPOSSIBLE, that he is best remembered. Moving on to TV movies and mini-series, Graves later played Fred 'Palmer' Kirby in the blockbusters, THE WINDS OF WAR and *War and Remembrance*.

GRAY, LINDA
(1942–)

Model turned actress whose earliest TV credits came in such series as MARCUS WELBY, MD and McCLOUD. From 1978 to 1989 Gray starred as Sue Ellen, JR Ewing's boozy wife in DALLAS, also trying her hand at directing some episodes. When Ian McShane guested in the Texan super soap, Gray repaid the compliment by accepting a part in his somewhat less flashy LOVEJOY series. Her most prominent role since has been as Hillary Michaels in *Melrose Place* and its spin-off, *Models Inc*. She has also been seen in numerous TV movies and a few American programmes that were not screened in the UK, most notably the comedy show, *All That Glitters*.

GRAYSON, LARRY
(William White; 1923–95)

Camp British comedian, once a music-hall drag performer known as Billy Breen. With stories of friends like Everard, Apricot Lil and Slack Alice, Grayson earned himself TV celebrity status in the early 1970s through one-off guest performances (on shows like *Saturday Variety*) and his own ITV series, *Shut That Door* (named after his catchphrase). A close friend of Noele Gordon, he made a famous cameo appearance in CROSSROADS in 1973, playing a disgruntled motel guest, and returned two years later to act as chauffeur at Noele's TV wedding to John Bentley, when Meg married Hugh Mortimer.

However, the high spot of his career came when Bruce Forsyth moved to ITV in 1978 and Grayson was chosen to succeed him as host of the hugely popular GENERATION GAME. With Isla St Clair as his partner, Grayson matched Forsyth's success, and the series continued for another three years. A tell-the-truth guessing game, *Sweethearts*, in 1987, proved less durable and little was seen of Grayson afterwards. His last TV appearance was in the 1994 Royal Variety Performance.

GREATOREX, WILFRED

British scriptwriter and editor, responsible for creating series like THE PLANE MAKERS (later *The Power Game*), *Front Page Story* (with Rex Firkin), HINE, *The Man from Haven*, SECRET ARMY (with Gerald Glaister), 1990 and AIRLINE. In 1987 Greatorex tried unsuccessfully to sue advertising agency J. Walter Thompson over the use of *Airline* star Roy Marsden in a look-alike TV commercial for the British Airports Authority.

GREEN, HUGHIE
(1920–97)

Canadian showman, talent spotter and quiz show host, one of ITV's earliest stars. After a career in radio and on stage and screen as a child performer (among his film credits were *Midshipman Easy* and *Tom Brown's School-days*), Green spent the war as a pilot in the Canadian air force, continuing in civil aviation after the hostilities. He also returned to radio, hosting OPPORTUNITY KNOCKS for both the BBC and Radio Luxembourg and then DOUBLE YOUR MONEY for the latter. Both shows transferred to television with the arrival of ITV, *Opportunity Knocks* running for a marathon 21 years from 1956 and *Double Your Money* for 13 years from 1955. In 1971 Green hosted the quiz's natural successor, *The Sky's the Limit*, which was, effectively, *Double Your Money* with air miles. In the early days, Green also compered SUNDAY NIGHT AT THE LONDON PALLADIUM. His contrived gags and his catchphrase, 'I mean that most sincerely, folks', were much mimicked. On his death in 1997, it was revealed that he was the real father of TV presenter Paula Yates.

GREEN, ROBSON
(1964–)

Northumberland-born, Byker-raised, one-time shipyard draughtsman who entered television via a local theatre company. His major roles have included Jimmy Powell in CASUALTY, Dave Tucker in SOLDIER, SOLDIER, Rory Connor in CATHERINE COOKSON's *The Gambling Man*, Owen Springer in *Reckless*, DI Dave Creegan in TOUCHING EVIL, Eric Trapp in AIN'T MISBEHAVIN', Joe Purvis in *Grafters*, John Close in *Close and True* and Barry Grimes, Michael Flynn, Steve McTear and Richard Thomas in the single productions, *The Student Prince*, *Rhinoceros*, *The Last Musketeer* and *Blind Ambition*, respectively. He runs his own company, Coastal Productions, and has

often appeared alongside his acting (and singing) partner, Jerome Flynn.

GREENE, HUGH CARLETON
Sir Hugh Greene (1910–87)

The brother of novelist Graham Greene and one of the BBC's most famous directors-general. Greene, a former *Daily Telegraph* journalist, was editor of the BBC's German Service during the war and, when hostilities ceased, helped to reorganize broadcasting in Germany. He became the BBC's Director of News and Current Affairs and then was appointed Director-General in 1960, holding the post for over nine years. During this period, a decade of technological advances and social change, Greene was credited with allowing the BBC to move with the times. Under his guidance, the Corporation drifted away from the starchy proprieties of the 1950s and floated into innovative, more permissive waters. The Hugh Greene era was the era of THAT WAS THE WEEK THAT WAS, STEPTOE AND SON, CATHY COME HOME and TILL DEATH US DO PART. It was also the era that prompted Mary Whitehouse's first criticisms of broadcasting standards, although Greene quite happily shrugged off complaints from her fledgling Clean-up TV campaign. However, on one notable occasion Greene did err on the side of caution, refusing to screen the realistic nuclear war drama, THE WAR GAME, in 1966, fearing it would alarm the public (it was eventually shown in 1985). Although, generally, Greene remained steadfast in his protection of the independence of the BBC, his postponement of an episode of *Steptoe and Son* on election night in 1964, allegedly at the request of Harold Wilson, did rather tarnish his reputation with observers. Greene was knighted the same year, but his relationship with the Labour Party later deteriorated. When Wilson appointed Lord Hill, Chairman of the Independent Television Authority, to the position of Chairman of the BBC in 1967, it was seen as a means of keeping Greene in check and a response to some perceived anti-Labour programming controversies. Greene eventually left his post in 1969, but became the first ex-DG to take a seat on the board of Governors, a seat he maintained until 1971.

GREENE, LORNE
(1915–87)

Whether as a roving merchant seaman, a reassuring father-figure in the Wild West or an intergalactic space commander, Lorne Greene won the respect of more than one generation of TV viewers. Born in Ottawa, Lorne Greene's first field of expertise was radio. Failing to find much acting work, he became an announcer for CBC and during the war established himself as the authoritative 'Voice of Canada'. Moving south to the USA in the 1950s, he began to pick up small TV roles, in programmes like ALFRED HITCHCOCK PRESENTS, WAGON TRAIN and CHEYENNE, and then, in 1957, in the UK, won the part of Captain Grant 'Mitch' Mitchell in the adventure series, SAILOR OF FORTUNE. However, it was his next major role which proved definitive. He was cast as Ben Cartwright,

patriarch of the Ponderosa in the classic Western, BON-
ANZA, which ran for 14 years up to 1973. He moved into
police work with the short-lived detective drama, *Griff*,
the same year, added his voice to two long-running
nature series, *Lorne Greene's Last of the Wild* and *Lorne
Greene's New Wilderness*, and in 1978 was launched into
outer space to be the Moses-like Commander Adama in
the *Star Wars* clone, BATTLESTAR GALACTICA. His last
starring role was in a fire-fighting caper called *Code Red*.
Among his other credits were TV movies and mini-series
such as ROOTS (slave-owner John Reynolds).

GREENE, RICHARD
(1918–85)

Plymouth-born leading man in Hollywood films of the
1930s, who found new fame as the swashbuckling Robin
Hood in THE ADVENTURES OF ROBIN HOOD, an early ITV
success. The show's 143 episodes proved such a hit that
Greene made few TV appearances afterwards, choosing
to settle down to a retirement of horse breeding in
Ireland.

GREENE, SARAH

London-born presenter, a former child actress/model,
the daughter of TV DIY man and actor Harry Greene
and actress Marjie Lawrence, and now the wife of pre-
senter/DJ Mike Smith. Greene's TV break came with
BLUE PETER in 1980, from which she progressed to SATUR-
DAY SUPERSTORE, GOING LIVE!, *Posh Frocks and New
Trousers*, the game show, *Happy Families*, the swap shop,
The Exchange, *Good Morning Summer*, PEBBLE MILL, Sky
One's afternoon chat show, programmes for Carlton
Food Network, and numerous documentary specials.
She also once guested in DOCTOR WHO. Her sister is
weather presenter Laura Greene.

GREGSON, JOHN
(1919–75)

British actor who, after many film appearances (most
notably in *Genevieve*), took the role of Commander
George Gideon in the police series, GIDEON'S WAY, in
1965. Six years later he resurfaced in Shirley MacLaine's
photojournalist sitcom, *Shirley's World*, playing her
editor, Dennis Croft, and in 1976 he was Kirby, the risk-
taking insurance agent, in Southern's thriller serial,
Dangerous Knowledge, a series screened a year after his
death.

GRIFFITHS, LEON
(1928–92)

British scriptwriter, best remembered as the creator of
MINDER. Griffiths's early TV writing included episodes
of THE FOUR JUST MEN, OUT OF THE UNKNOWN, TALES
OF MYSTERY and NO HIDING PLACE, plus the Roy Kinnear
sitcom, *A Slight Case of . . .* While working on single plays

such as the boxing drama, *Dinner at the Sporting Club*, in
the 1970s he was advised to adapt one of his stories so
that it concentrated on just two of its characters, a dodgy
wheeler-dealer and his jailbird bodyguard. *Minder* was
born and with it one of TV's classic creations, Arthur
Daley. (Ironically, Daley's fluent Cockney patter was
provided by a writer who had been born in Sheffield and
brought up in Glasgow.) Griffiths, however, suffered a
stroke and the second season had to be written by others,
although the Writers' Guild award that the programme
won was still presented to him personally. Inspired, Griffiths fought his way back to work and resumed his
involvement, right up to his death in 1992. His other
contributions included the six-part adaptation of *Piece
of Cake*, plus scripts for series like THE RACING GAME.

GRIFFITHS, RICHARD
(1947–)

Versatile Cleveland-born actor, star of the sitcom,
Nobody's Perfect (Sam Hooper, alongside Elaine Stritch),
the bizarre comedy, WHOOPS APOCALYPSE (Soviet leader
Dubienkin), the thriller, BIRD OF PREY (snoopy civil servant Henry Jay), the wine comedy, *Ffizz* (Jack Mowbray),
and the unsuccessful historical drama, THE CLEOPATRAS
(the grotesque Potbelly). Griffiths has also starred as
Trevor Beasley in another comedy, *A Kind of Living*,
appeared as the porter in the murder-mystery, *Mr Wakefield's Crusade*, played the policeman-chef Henry Crabbe
in PIE IN THE SKY, and took the parts of Geoffrey Crichton Potter in *In the Red*, Swelter the cook in *Gormenghast*
and Leo Wheeldon in *Hope and Glory*. Among his many
guest appearances have been parts in WHEN THE BOAT
COMES IN, BERGERAC and MINDER.

GRIFFITHS, TREVOR
(1935–)

Manchester-born playwright, one of TV's most political
dramatists, espousing left-wing causes, particularly in
his notable series, BILL BRAND. His first contribution was
Adam Smith (written under the pen name of Ben Rae)
and among his other offerings have been *Occupations,
Comedians, Through the Night, Country, The Last Place
on Earth* (the story of Captain Scott) and the skinhead
drama, *Oi for England*. He has also adapted D. H. Lawrence's *Sons and Lovers* for the small screen.

GRIMLEYS, THE
UK (Granada) Situation Comedy. ITV 1999–

Gordon Grimley	James Bradshaw
Miss Geraldine Titley	Amanda Holden
Mr Doug Digby	Brian Conley
Mr Neville Holder	Noddy Holder
Darren Grimley	Ryan Cartwright
Lisa Grimley	Corrieann Fletcher
Janet Grimley	Jan Ravens
Baz Grimley	Nigel Planer
Nan	Barbara Keogh

Shane Titley	**Simon Lowe**
Reg Titley	**Paul Angelis**
	John Arthur
Miss Thing	**Ruby Snape**

Writer: **Jed Mercurio**
Producer: **Spencer Campbell**

Retro-comedy reflecting on adolescence in the West Midlands in the 1970s.

Riding the wave of 1970s nostalgia that broke at the end of the 1990s, *The Grimleys* was set on the Jericho Council Estate, Dudley, in 1975. Young Gordon Grimley hoped to go to university one day (against the wishes of his slobby dad, Baz) but, in the meantime, had visions of a romance with his attractive English teacher, Miss Titley, who also happened to be a neighbour. As if this ambition was not already too great, standing obstinately in the way was his sadistic gym teacher, Doug Digby. More amenable was Mr Holder, the music teacher whom thirtysomething viewers thought bore more than a passing resemblance to the former lead singer of pop group, Slade. Littered with 1970s references, from Vauxhall Vivas to Angel Delight, *The Grimleys* was a nostalgic wallow for anyone who had been a teenager at the time and followed a 1997 pilot episode in which Samantha Janus played Miss Titley and Jack Dee played Doug Digby. Apart from the aforementioned Mr Holder, there were also cameo appearances by 1970s figures Alvin Stardust (as a barman), William Woollard (science teacher), Frank Bough (newsreader), Jim Bowen (shop steward), Stephen Lewis (bus-driver), Patrick Mower (hero), Johnny Ball (teacher) and Tony Blackburn (swinger).

GRIP

The technician responsible for production hardware like props, camera mountings, dollies and cranes. Where a large crew is involved, the head man is known as the key grip.

GROSSMAN, LOYD

(1950–)

Boston, Massachusetts-born presenter working on British TV. Grossman's first attempts to enter the entertainment business came as a member of the punk band, Jet Bronx and the Forbidden, but he has achieved far greater success snooping around celebrities' homes in THROUGH THE KEYHOLE and dissecting amateur cooks' dinners in MASTERCHEF. Other credits have included various food programmes, the quiz, *Relative Knowledge*, and the shopping documentary series, *Off Your Trolley with Loyd Grossman*.

GROUND FORCE

UK (Bazal/BBC) Lifestyle. BBC 2/BBC 1 1997–

Presenters: **Alan Titchmarsh, Charlie Dimmock, Tommy Walsh, Will Shanahan**

Producer: **John Thornicroft**
Executive Producer: **Carol Haslam**

Garden make-overs for unsuspecting householders.

Inviting viewers to nominate gardens that could do with a make-over (and whose owners probably wouldn't mind) was the basis of this CHANGING ROOMS-meets-GARDENERS' WORLD cross. The unsuspecting owner would then be summoned away, leaving Alan Titchmarsh and his team two days in which to transform an ugly patch of land into a domestic paradise. Titchmarsh provided the designs, Charlie Dimmock (soon to become a cult figure because, always bra-less, she displayed a cult figure) specialized in water features, and landscaping builder Tommy Walsh organized the infrastructure with the help of Will Shanahan. With a budget of no more than £1,000, the team set about creating dream gardens and then waited anxiously for the bewildered owner to return. On one famous occasion in 1999, the team set off for South Africa and surprised ex-President Nelson Mandela by redeveloping his back yard.

Like its sister programme, *Changing Rooms*, *Ground Force* began quietly on BBC 2, moving into the BBC 1 limelight after two years. The two programmes merged for a special in 2000 entitled *When Changing Rooms Met Ground Force*, in which the interior decorating and gardening specialists switched jobs.

GROVE FAMILY, THE

UK (BBC) Drama. BBC 1954–7

Bob Grove	**Edward Evans**
Gladys Grove	**Ruth Dunning**
Pat Grove	**Sheila Sweet**
	Carole Mowlam
Jack Grove	**Peter Bryant**
Daphne Grove	**Margaret Downs**
Lenny Grove	**Christopher Beeny**
Gran	**Nancy Roberts**

Writers: **Michael Pertwee, Roland Pertwee**
Producer: **John Warrington**

Ups and downs in the life of Britain's first soap family.

The Grove Family was the BBC's first attempt at a grown-up soap, although the Corporation had already produced a children's equivalent in THE APPLEYARDS. The Groves (named after the BBC's Lime Grove studios) were lower middle class, just about comfortably off, and had come through the post-war shortages like most other 'ordinary' families. This enabled viewers to relate to the characters and made the series very popular.

The family lived in Hendon and consisted of dad Bob, a jobbing builder, housewife Gladys, elder daughter and assistant librarian Pat, Jack, who was doing National Service and was a bit of a lad, teenage schoolgirl Daphne and cheeky young Lenny (a youthful Christopher Beeny). Completing the household was the hunched, crotchety Gran, a grumble forever on her lips. Cousin

Rodney was added for youth interest as the younger Groves grew up.

Drawing heavily on the likes of *Mrs Dale's Diary* and *The Archers* in style, there was very little drama in *The Grove Family*. Reassuringly British (with no intruding US culture), its action focused instead on petty squabbles and occasional domestic strife, but a 'public service' element was also built in. Viewers were made acutely aware of the need to purchase a TV licence, for example, or to protect themselves from burglaries. One story even warned of the dangers of sailing! Scripts were provided by father and son Roland and Michael Pertwee and, when they asked for a short break after three years of solid writing, the BBC declined and, much to viewers' dismay, closed down the series altogether.

Little footage of the series is known to exist today, although there was a film spin-off, entitled *It's a Great Day*, in 1955. Also, as part of the BBC's Lime Grove commemorations in 1991, modern-day soap stars stepped in to re-create extracts from original scripts. Mum was played by Sue Johnston, Dad by Leslie Grantham, Gran by Anna Wing, Pat by Sally Ann Matthews, Jack by Nick Berry, Daphne by Kellie Bright and Lenny by Paul Parris.

GROWING PAINS OF ADRIAN MOLE, THE
See **THE SECRET DIARY OF ADRIAN MOLE, AGED 13³/₄.**

GROWING PAINS OF PC PENROSE, THE
See **ROSIE.**

GRUFFUDD, IOAN
(1973–)

Welsh actor noted for his lead roles in dramas like HORNBLOWER (Horatio Hornblower), *Great Expectations* (Pip) and *Warriors* (Lt. John Feeley). Gruffudd has also been seen in *Love in the 21st Century* (Jack), the 1996 sequel to POLDARK (Jeremy Poldark), plus Welsh-language dramas.

GS5
See **GHOST SQUAD.**

GUINNESS, Sir ALEC
CBE (1914–2000)

Distinguished British film actor whose television work came late in life. By far his most acclaimed role was as spycatcher George Smiley in John Le Carré's TINKER, TAILOR, SOLDIER, SPY and *Smiley's People*. Among his other credits were *Caesar and Cleopatra*, *Conversations at Night*, *Gift of Friendship*, *Little Lord Fauntleroy*, *Monsignor Quixote* and the *Screen One* presentations, *A Foreign Field* (war veteran Amos) and *Eskimo Day* (academic James Poole).

GUN LAW
See **GUNSMOKE.**

GUNSMOKE/GUN LAW
US (CBS) Western. ITV 1956–

Marshal Matt Dillon	**James Arness**
Kitty Russell	**Amanda Blake**
Dr Galen ('Doc') Adams	**Milburn Stone**
Chester Goode	**Dennis Weaver**
Quint Asper	**Burt Reynolds**
Sam	**Glenn Strange**
Festus Haggen	**Ken Curtis**
Thad Greenwood	**Roger Ewing**
Newly O'Brien	**Buck Taylor**
Mr Jonas	**Dabbs Greer**
Hank	**Hank Patterson**
Louie Pheeters	**James Nusser**
Barney	**Charles Seel**
Howie	**Howard Culver**
Ed O'Connor	**Tom Brown**
Percy Crump	**John Harper**
Ma Smalley	**Sarah Selby**
Miss Hannah	**Fran Ryan**

Creators: **Norman Macdonnell, John Meston, Charles Marquis Warren**
Producers: **Norman Macdonnell, Philip Leacock, John Mantley**

A strong and virtuous marshal maintains law and order in a Wild West town.

Gunsmoke focused on the fictional figure of Matt Dillon, the strong, no-nonsense marshal of Dodge City in 1870s Kansas. Standing six and a half feet tall, he was a giant physically and inspirationally, a man of great integrity and principle. He was tough but fair, and outlaws quickly realized that they were not welcome on his patch. But Dillon was not flawless. A rather intense and occasionally uncertain man, he was seen to worry and anguish over the right course to take, and he didn't always make the correct decision. However, Dillon knew he could rely on the support of the Dodge City townsfolk. His closest confidants were Doc Adams and Kitty Russell, proprietress of the Longbranch Saloon. Adams was tetchy but kind; Russell was tough, with a soft centre, an early tart with a heart who seemed to have a crush on Dillon, although the relationship was never taken any further. Dillon was also assisted by his deputies, Chester Goode (who brought a touch of comic relief with his limp) and, later, Festus Haggen (a drawling hillbilly). Also seen at various times were the rugged half-Indian blacksmith, Quint Asper, gunsmith Newly O'Brien and Dillon's friend, Thad Greenwood. Other Dodge City residents included shopkeeper Jonas; rancher O'Connor; Percy Crump, the undertaker; a hotel clerk called Howie; Hank, the stable keeper; Ma Smalley, who ran the boarding house; Barney, the telegraph man; and the local drunkard, Louie Pheeters. A year before the series ended, Kitty Russell was replaced in the saloon by a new landlady, Miss Hannah.

Dillon himself did not appear in many later episodes, leaving the stage to the townsfolk and one-off guest stars, although the series always stayed true to its principles of portraying the realistic side of Wild West life. That's what John Wayne had promised when he introduced the very first episode, even though he himself declined the role of the marshal. With William Conrad (who had provided Dillon's voice for years on radio) lacking the looks the part demanded, Wayne recommended the relatively unknown actor, James Arness.

When *Gunsmoke* arrived in the UK, as an early ITV import, it was screened under the title of *Gun Law*, although later episodes and re-runs carried the original programme name.

GUTTERIDGE, REG
OBE (1924–)

Long-serving ITV boxing commentator, a one-time amateur champion himself before his career was ended by the loss of a leg during the Normandy campaign. He turned instead to journalism and eventually to boxing writing. Gutteridge has also dabbled in coverage of greyhound racing. In the 1990s, he was paired with his old commentating 'rival', Harry Carpenter, for a nostalgic sports series on satellite TV.

GUYLER, DERYCK
(1914–99)

Deep-voiced, Cheshire-born radio comedian who moved into television as a foil for Eric Sykes. Playing the part of policeman Corky, Guyler stayed with SYKES for many years. He is also remembered as the Desert Rat school caretaker, Norman Potter, in PLEASE SIR! and was much seen on television playing his specialist musical instrument, the washboard. Among his other credits were supporting roles for the likes of Charlie Chester, Fred Emney, Dick Emery and Eric Barker, plus the Michael Bentine shows, IT'S A SQUARE WORLD and *All Square*, and the sitcoms, *Something in the City*, HERE'S HARRY, *Three Live Wires*, *Room at the Bottom* and *The Best of Enemies*.

GWYNNE, FRED
(1926–93)

Tall (6 foot 5 inch) American comic actor, forever remembered as Herman, the lumbering Frankenstein's monster look-alike in THE MUNSTERS. Previously Gwynne had starred in another successful sitcom, playing inept cop Francis Muldoon in CAR 54, WHERE ARE YOU?. That role followed appearances in THE PHIL SILVERS SHOW and other series, plus films like *On the Waterfront*. Gwynne also made a living writing and illustrating children's books and was once a copywriter for the J. Walter Thompson advertising agency, a position which gave him financial security while he worked his way into acting in his spare time.

HADLEIGH

UK (Yorkshire) Drama. ITV 1969–73; 1976

James Hadleigh .... **Gerald Harper**
Jennifer Caldwell/Hadleigh .... **Hilary Dwyer**
Charles Caldwell .... **Gerald James**

Creator: **Robert Barr**
Executive Producers: **Peter Willes, David Cunliffe**
Producers: **Terence Williams, Jacky Stoller**

The life and times of a laid-back Yorkshire squire.

James Hadleigh was the classic smoothie, a refined country gentleman who occasionally had to stoop as low as work to finance his rich tastes. A former civil servant, who had inherited his wealth and his mansion, Melford Park in the West Riding of Yorkshire, from his father, Hadleigh still farmed himself out to the Treasury now and again when times grew 'hard' – when his race-horse stable was threatened with closure, for example. At first a most eligible bachelor with a flat in Knightsbridge, the suave, charming Hadleigh finally succumbed to marriage when the attractive (and independently wealthy) Jennifer Caldwell came his way. The series was a spin-off from a 1968 series called *Gazette*, the story of a weekly newspaper owned by Hadleigh's father.

HAGMAN, LARRY

(1931–)

The son of musical star Mary Martin, Larry Hagman broke into showbiz in the early 1950s, finding work in New York's theatreland. He appeared with his mother in London as an extra in *South Pacific* in 1951 and spent some time in the USAF before working his way into television. His first prominent role was in the US daytime serial, *The Edge of Night*, in 1961 and then in 1965 Hagman was chosen to play genie master Tony Nelson in the sitcom, I DREAM OF JEANNIE. The show was a hit and ran for five years, and Hagman followed it with film roles and two other US comedies, *The Good Life* and *Here We Go Again*, both of which failed to take off. Then, just when it seemed his career had peaked and was on the slide, up popped the part of TV's all-time Mr Nasty, JR Ewing, in the hugely successful DALLAS. Hagman soon became vital to the series. He directed as well as starred in it, also becoming joint executive producer; and when JR was shot in 1980 the world stopped to find out who had pulled the trigger. The series ran until 1991.

HALE, ALAN, JR

(1918–90)

Cheerful American light and comic actor, best remembered by British TV audiences as CASEY JONES in the 1950s railroad Western. In the 1960s he was a stalwart of the farce, GILLIGAN'S ISLAND, playing Jonas Grumby, the skipper of the shipwrecked cruise ship. His dad,

whom Alan Jr resembled physically, was a silent movie star.

HALE, GARETH
(1953–)

London-born former teacher who turned comedian and formed a successful, if at times controversial, double act with another ex-teacher, Dudley-born Norman Pace. After writing for THREE OF A KIND and appearances in THE YOUNG ONES, *The Entertainers*, *The Laughter Show*, *Pushing Up Daisies*, *Coming Next . . .*, *Saturday Live* and *Saturday Gang*, the duo were given their own series by LWT. Never afraid to put pressure on the boundaries of taste, they found themselves at the centre of a storm over a sketch involving a cat and a microwave oven. Their act also included an impersonation of a pair of Cockney gangster bodyguards, the two Rons (who gained their own series, *The Management*, in 1988), and a parody of kids' TV (as Billy and Johnny, the patronizing presenters). Hale and Pace also tried their hand at straight acting in DOCTOR WHO and the three-part crime drama, *A Pinch of Snuff* (an ITV forerunner of DALZIEL AND PASCOE). Moving to the BBC, they took the challenges presented by the documentary series, *Jobs for the Boys*, starred in the silent comedy, *Oddbods*, and hosted their own comedy/variety series, *h&p@bbc*.

HALL, ROBIN
(1937–98)

Popular Scottish folksinger of the 1950s and 1960s, in partnership with Jimmie MacGregor. Their big break came on TONIGHT, for which they performed a number every week. They were then given the chance to branch out in THE WHITE HEATHER CLUB and were also seen on the ITV series, *Hullabaloo*. After their partnership broke up in 1979 Hall became an occasional folk performer back in Scotland. MacGregor has since worked for Radio Scotland and Scottish television.

HALL, WILLIS
(1929–)

British scriptwriter, often in collaboration with Keith Waterhouse. Among their many joint credits have been BUDGIE, *Billy Liar*, INSIDE GEORGE WEBLEY, QUEENIE'S CASTLE, *The Upper Crusts*, *Our Kid* and WORZEL GUMMIDGE, plus sketches for THAT WAS THE WEEK THAT WAS, BBC-3 and THE FROST REPORT, and shows starring Dick Emery, Dora Bryan, Millicent Martin and Roy Hudd. They also contributed plays for anthologies like *The Sunday Play* and *Studio '64*. Additionally, Hall has worked solo on the sitcoms, *The Fuzz* and *The Bright Side*, written episodes of SECRET ARMY, THE CREZZ, MINDER and other series, and penned notable single dramas like *The Villa Maroc*.

HAMILTON, ANDY

British actor, producer, director and comedy writer, often in conjunction with Guy Jenkin, with whom he worked on NOT THE NINE O'CLOCK NEWS, ALAS SMITH AND JONES, WHO DARES, WINS . . ., SHELLEY and *Kit Curran* and, most notably, created DROP THE DEAD DONKEY. Hamilton's solo work has included the soccer comedy, *Eleven Men against Eleven*, and the comedy-thriller, *Underworld*, plus sketches for *The Dawson Watch* and *The Marti Caine Show*. On screen, he played editor Robin Sanders in Guy Jenkin's *Screen One* drama, *The Lord of Misrule*.

HAMISH MACBETH
UK (Zenith) Drama. BBC 1 1995–7

Hamish Macbeth	**Robert Carlyle**
TV John McIver	**Ralph Riach**
Lachlan	**Jimmy Yuill**
	Billy Riddoch
Lachie Jr	**Stuart Davids**
Alex MacLaine	**Valerie Gogan**
Rory Campbell	**Brian Pettifer**
Esme	**Anne Lacey**
Doc Brown	**Duncan Duff**
Barney	**Stuart McGugan**
Agnes	**Barbara Rafferty**
Jimmy Soutar	**Rab Christie**
Major Roddy Maclean	**David Ashton**
Isobel Sutherland	**Shirley Henderson**
Neil the Bus	**Iain McColl**

Producers: **Deirdre Keir, Charles Salmon**

Unconventional policing with a Highland bobby.

Hamish Macbeth was the unambitious community copper in the dozy, eccentric-populated Highland village of Lochdubh (pronounced 'Lochdoo' – real-life Plockton). Laid back about most things (salmon poaching never exercised him, pub lock-ins were community events, pirate radio was a service not a felony, and he liked to smoke a bit of pot himself now and again), he nevertheless proved more than a handful for any prospective criminals (usually outsiders up to no good). Stories reflected the timeless, parochial nature of the village where key characters included Doc Brown, grocer Rory Campbell and the second-sighted TV John (so named for having the first set in the village). However, Macbeth's best pal was his West Highland terrier, Wee Jock (real name Zippy) who, to much grief, did not survive the first series after a hit-and-run incident. Wee Jock Two (real name Fraoch, later replaced by Dex) was appointed for future episodes. Human love for the lawman came from journalist Isobel and Alex, a former girlfriend.

The series, a first starring role for Robert Carlyle, was based on the novels by M. C. Beaton (Marion Chesney), in which Macbeth's dog was a mongrel called Towser. Less twee than HEARTBEAT, with more bite than BALLY-

KISSANGEL, and not far removed from a Wild West drama – sheriff rounding up invading outlaws, etc. – this darkly humorous series appealed to more than the usual Sunday night light-drama crowd.

HAMMER HOUSE OF HORROR
UK (ATV/Hammer/Chips/Cinema Arts) Thriller Anthology.
ITV 1980

Producer: **Roy Skeggs**

A collection of suspense tales produced in conjunction with the cinema horror specialists.

The gory one-hour films grouped together as *Hammer House of Horror* featured guest stars like Diana Dors, Denholm Elliott and Hammer favourite, Peter Cushing. The 13 stories (under the control of Hammer directors such as Peter Sasdy, Don Sharp and Alan Gibson) revolved around such subjects as voodoo, cannibalism, werewolves, witchcraft and other manifestations of the supernatural.

HAMNER, EARL, JR
(1923–)

American writer whose own life story formed the basis of THE WALTONS, which he created. Hamner acted as narrator on the series and later created and produced the glossy soap, FALCON CREST. Among his other work were the scripts of some episodes of THE TWILIGHT ZONE.

HAMPSHIRE, SUSAN
OBE (1937–)

British actress whose TV debut came as Andromeda in *The Andromeda Breakthrough*, the sequel to the sci-fi classic, A FOR ANDROMEDA, thanks to Julie Christie's decision to leave the role. However, most people's earliest recollection of Hampshire is as the headstrong Fleur in THE FORSYTE SAGA. She followed it up with Forsyte look-alikes THE FIRST CHURCHILLS (Sarah Churchill) and THE PALLISERS (Lady Glencora Palliser). She has also starred in *The Barchester Chronicles* (Madeline), *Vanity Fair* (Becky Sharp), *The Grand* (Esme Harkness), *Coming Home* and *Nancherrow* (Miss Catto in both), and *Monarch of the Glen* (Molly), plus a musical version of *Dr Jekyll and Mr Hyde*, as well as taking the lead in the Carla Lane sitcom, *Leaving* (Martha Ford), and the Roy Clarke comedy, *Don't Tell Father* (Natasha Bancroft). She has numerous guest appearances to her name, in programmes as diverse as THE TIME TUNNEL and THE MORECAMBE AND WISE SHOW. Hampshire has been an active campaigner for dyslexia awareness (she is a sufferer herself).

HANCOCK, NICK
(1962–)

Stoke-on-Trent-born actor and comedian, once a Cambridge Footlights member. He was the original host of ROOM 101, fronts the biographical comedy, *You Only Live Once*, and is chairman of the comedy quiz, THEY THINK IT'S ALL OVER. He was star of the series of comedy shorts called *Nights* (Bob), and the sitcoms, *Me, You and Him* (John, as well as co-writer) and *Holding the Baby* (Gordon Muir), plus the soccer drama, *Bostock's Cup* (Mike Tonker). Guest appearances take in series as diverse as *Great Railway Journeys* and MR BEAN. Hancock also co-wrote the sitcom *Blind Men* and, in contrast, presented *Sex and Stopping: A History of Contraception*.

HANCOCK, SHEILA
OBE (1933–)

Isle of Wight-born actress, the wife of John Thaw and mother of actress Melanie Thaw. Among her sitcom credits have been THE RAG TRADE (Carole), THE BED-SIT GIRL (Sheila), MR DIGBY DARLING (devoted secretary Thelma Teesdale), *Now Take My Wife* (Claire Love), *Gone to Seed* (Mag), and *Brighton Belles* (Frances). Hancock has also proved her versatility through serious dramas with 1989's *Jumping the Queue*, in which she played suicidal widow Matilda in an adaptation of Mary Wesley's book (which Sheila herself sold to the BBC). Other credits have included *Entertaining Mr Sloane*, the 1972 version of Waugh's *Scoop*, *Horizontal Hold*, *The Mating Machine*, *God Our Help*, *But Seriously – It's Sheila Hancock*, *The Buccaneers* (Duchess of Trevenick), *Dangerous Lady* (Sarah Ryan), *Alice in Wonderland* (Cook) and *The Thing about Vince . . .* (Pat Skinner).

HANCOCK, TONY
(1924–68)

'The lad himself', as he was dubbed, Birmingham-born Tony Hancock has been widely acclaimed as one of Britain's funniest ever comedians and a pioneer of TV situation comedy. A member of *Ralph Reader's Gang Show* during the war, Hancock remained on the stage when the hostilities ceased, becoming resident comic at the Windmill and touring other theatres. In 1951 he joined the cast of radio's *Educating Archie* and was such a success that he began appearing on TV (in series like KALEIDO-SCOPE) and was given his own radio show, HANCOCK'S HALF HOUR, in 1954. Two years later the series transferred to television, although not before Hancock had made a couple of sketch series for ITV under the banner of *The Tony Hancock Show*. *Hancock's Half Hour* (finally just known as *Hancock*) ran until 1961, making Hancock the country's number-one comic. He even turned his hand to straight drama, appearing in the 1958 play, *The Government Inspector* (part of the *Television World Theatre* anthology). In 1963 he switched to ITV, leaving behind him his scriptwriters, Ray Galton and Alan Simpson, and with them the peak of his success. A career in film fizzled out and Hancock grew more and more depressed. His drink problem was well documented and, always highly self-critical, he took his own life while working on a series for Australian TV in 1968. His last British offering had been *Hancock's* in 1967, in which he played a nightclub owner. In 1991 Alfred Molina starred in a *Screen One* production, *Hancock*, which dramatized his tragic last seven years.

HANCOCK'S HALF HOUR/HANCOCK

UK (BBC/ATV) Situation Comedy. BBC 1956–60/1961; ITV 1963

Anthony Aloysius Hancock .... **Tony Hancock**
Sidney James .... **Sidney James** (*Half Hour*)

Creators/Writers: **Ray Galton, Alan Simpson**
Producers: **Duncan Wood (BBC), Tony Hancock (ATV)**

The highs and lows in the life of a perpetual dreamer.

Hancock's Half Hour, its title announced in breathless, stammering fashion by 'the lad himself', was one of Britain's first major comedy series and remains in the eyes of many a true classic. Beginning on radio in 1954, it quickly transferred to television and introduced to viewers the complex personality of Anthony Aloysius Hancock, inhabitant of 23 Railway Cuttings, East Cheam. The character was a moody, bumptious type, sporting a Homburg hat and a heavy overcoat, a man prone to constant questioning of the whys and wherefores of the world and a gloomy ponderer of his personal circumstances. Life's petty injustices and annoyances were guaranteed to generate a torrent of observations and criticisms. For instance, what could be worse than reading a thriller novel only to find the last page torn out? Similarly frustrating was the way in which his ambitious plans to improve his station always ended in failure and humiliation, as prophesied by his cynical roommate, played by Sid James.

James, the man who pricked Hancock's bubbles, left the series in 1960 to pursue his own starring roles, and the last season went out simply under the title of *Hancock*, the star having moved to a new address. These episodes included such classics as *The Radio Ham* and *The Blood Donor* (with its oft-quoted exclamation: 'A pint? That's very nearly an armful!'). Hancock subsequently broke up his partnership with writers Galton and Simpson and moved to ITV, where he produced himself one (notably less successful) series of *Hancock*.

In 1996–7, Galton and Simpson revamped some of the classic scripts (including the above-mentioned) for the ITV series, *Paul Merton in Galton & Simpson's . . .*, with the deadpan HAVE I GOT NEWS FOR YOU panellist filling the Hancock role.

HANDL, IRENE
(1901–87)

Cheerful Cockney character actress, in her latter years well versed in daffy old lady parts. She did not begin acting until she was 40 but soon secured herself plenty of film, stage and radio work. On television in the 1950s she was seen in variety shows like CHELSEA AT NINE and in the screen version of *Educating Archie*, as well as in HANCOCK'S HALF HOUR and in *Laughter in Store* and

Drake's Progress (both with Charlie Drake). However, her biggest TV success was opposite Wilfred Pickles in the OAP sitcom, FOR THE LOVE OF ADA (Ada Cresswell). Among her other major roles were *Barney Is My Darling* (Ramona Pank), *Mum's Boys* (Mrs Crystal Pallise), *Maggie and Her* (Julia McKenzie's nosy neighbour, Mrs Perry), METAL MICKEY (the granny) and *Never Say Die* (Dorothy). Handl also enjoyed scores of guest appearances, ranging from THE ADVENTURES OF ROBIN HOOD and THE RAG TRADE to SUPERGRAN.

HANLEY, JIMMY
(1918–70)

Former child star Jimmy Hanley was a versatile showman, notching up a series of films for Rank in the 1940s and becoming a hit on radio and TV in the 1950s. His most prominent role was as the landlord of *Jim's Inn*, a fictitious pub that he ran with his second wife, Maggie. The series was TV's most popular admag, a vehicle for promoting various goods and services. Customers used to stroll in to discuss their latest bargains at the bar. The series started in 1957, but in 1963 admags were banned by Parliament and Hanley was out of a job, although he was later seen on the kids' series, FIVE O'CLOCK CLUB, talking about hobbies. His first wife was actress Dinah Sheridan, with whom he had two children, actress/presenter Jenny and Conservative politician Jeremy.

HANNAH, JOHN
(1962–)

Scottish actor with numerous starring and supporting parts to his name. He played the title roles of both *McCallum* (pathologist Iain McCallum) and *Rebus* (detective John Rebus), shared the limelight as DS Franky Drinkall in *Out of the Blue*, and appeared in Steve Coogan's *Three Fights, Two Weddings and a Funeral* (comically echoing his role in the film, *Four Weddings and a Funeral*). Other credits have included *Civvies* (Don Walker), BETWEEN THE LINES (DC Mellis), *Faith* (Nick Simon), *Circles of Deceit* (Jason Sturden) and *Screen One*'s *Truth or Dare* (Nick), as well as narration work on *Predators* and *The Natural World*. He is married to actress Joanna Roth.

HANNAY

UK (Thames) Drama. ITV 1988–9

Richard Hannay .... **Robert Powell**
Count Von Schwabing .... **Gavin Richards**

Executive Producer: **Lloyd Shirley**
Producers: **Richard Bates, Robert Banks Stewart**

An Edwardian adventurer confronts agents of Imperial Germany.

Reprising the role he played in the 1978 cinema version of *The Thirty-Nine Steps*, Robert Powell once again stepped into the shoes of Richard Hannay, John

Buchan's daring adventurer. On this occasion, timed as 1912, Hannay had returned from 30 years in South Africa to confront the might of Imperial Germany and the attentions of Count Von Schwabing in particular. Various escapades followed for the dashing hero in the tweed suit.

HANRAHAN, BRIAN
(1949–)

British journalist, who joined BBC TV News as a reporter in 1980. After notable achievements alongside ITN's Michael Nicholson in the Falklands conflict (in one memorable report he declared that, while he couldn't comment on British aircraft losses, he had 'counted them all out and counted them all back in'), Hanrahan became the BBC's Far East Correspondent, 1983–6, and Moscow Correspondent, 1986–8. Since 1989 he has been the BBC's Diplomatic Correspondent.

HAPPY DAYS
US (Paramount/Miller-Milkis) Situation Comedy. ITV
1976–85

Richie Cunningham .... **Ron Howard**
Arthur Fonzarelli ('Fonzie') .... **Henry Winkler**
Howard Cunningham .... **Tom Bosley**
Marion Cunningham .... **Marion Ross**
Joanie Cunningham .... **Erin Moran**
Warren 'Potsie' Webber .... **Anson Williams**
Ralph Malph .... **Donny Most**
Chuck Cunningham .... **Gavan O'Herlihy**
                                                     Randolph Roberts
Arnold (Matsuo Takahashi) .... **Pat Morita**
Alfred Delvecchio .... **Al Molinaro**
Charles 'Chachi' Arcola .... **Scott Baio**
Lori Beth Allen/Cunningham .... **Linda Goodfriend**
Jenny Piccalo .... **Cathy Silvers**
Roger Phillips .... **Ted McGinley**
K. C. Cunningham .... **Crystal Bernard**
Ashley Pfister .... **Linda Purl**
Heather Pfister .... **Heather O'Rourke**

Creator: **Garry K. Marshall**
Executive Producers: **Thomas L. Miller, Edward K. Milkis, Garry K. Marshall**
Producers: **Tony Marshall, Jerry Paris**

Nostalgic sitcom based around a middle-class Milwaukee family and their teenage children.

Laced with contemporary pop hits, *Happy Days* followed the Cunningham family throughout the late years of the 1950s and into the 1960s, with particular focus on their teenage son, Richie, and his pals. The Cunninghams lived in Milwaukee, Wisconsin, where chubby, hapless dad Howard owned a hardware store. His red-haired wife, Marion, was a typical housewife of the time, bringing up the children and supporting her husband, but always with a youthful spring in her step. Son Richie was the classic all-American boy, complete with apple-pie looks, and viewers shared his growing pains as he

started dating girls and progressed through school. Apart from Richie, there were two other Cunningham kids, Chuck and Joanie. Chuck, however, appeared in only the earliest episodes before moving off to college, to be strangely forgotten by everyone in the cast, including his own mother and father. Joanie, on the other hand, genuinely grew up with the show. At the start, she was just a freckly little kid with only a few lines, but by the end of the run she had developed into one of the star names and even had her own spin-off series, *Joanie Loves Chachi*.

The show was originally intended to focus on Richie and his chum Potsie as they negotiated teenage life in the rock'n'roll era. While Richie remained central to the show, the rather slow-witted Potsie was gradually pushed into the background, alongside wisecracking red-head Ralph Malph, as an unexpected star was born. That star was Fonzie, the show's leather-jacketed hell-raiser, who cruised the streets on a cherished motorcycle. There was always something special about 'The Fonz'. He was cool with a capital C, an expert mechanic with a magic touch and the dream date of every girl in Milwaukee. He moved into the flat above the Cunninghams' garage and, as the series developed, his rough edges became considerably smoother.

Richie, Potsie, Ralph and Fonzie were all regulars at Arnold's, a drive-in diner and soda store run initially by Japanese proprietor Arnold, then by the sad-faced but kind-hearted Al Delvecchio. The boys attended Jefferson High School, before graduating and moving on to the University of Wisconsin in Milwaukee. As they grew older, the emphasis switched to kids of Joanie's generation. Richie and Ralph joined the army and were dispatched to Greenland (Ron Howard and Donny Most had left the series), while Potsie took a job at the Cunningham hardware store. New faces included Fonzie's cousin, Chachi, who was to become Joanie's boyfriend, and Roger, Marion's nephew, the school's new basketball coach. Howard's niece, K. C., lived with the family for a while and Joanie's much-talked-about, boy-mad friend, Jenny Piccalo, was eventually seen (played by Cathy Silvers, daughter of comedian Phil Silvers). Other characters introduced over the years included Fonzie's divorcée girlfriend, Ashley Pfister, and her little daughter, Heather. Rock singer Leather Tuscadero, played by Suzi Quatro, was an occasional guest.

Richie eventually married his college sweetheart, Lori Beth (by telephone, with Fonzie acting as proxy groom), and a Richie Junior appeared on the scene. Fonzie joined Al as a partner in Arnold's and even taught at the High School. In the final episode, Joanie and Chachi were married, the whole family (except Chuck) reassembled and Howard thanked viewers for being part of their lives for over ten years.

Apart from *Joanie Loves Chachi*, *Happy Days* led to two other spin-offs, LAVERNE AND SHIRLEY and MORK AND MINDY. The programme was not, as often surmised, based on the film, *American Graffiti* (in which Ron Howard had starred), but on an episode of LOVE, AMERICAN STYLE entitled *Love and the Happy Day*, which had featured Howard and Anson Williams as 1950s school-kids. The original series theme music was Bill Haley's 'Rock Around The Clock', although an original title track soon superseded it, becoming a minor hit itself for a group called Pratt and McLain with Brotherlove.

HAPPY EVER AFTER
UK (BBC) Situation Comedy. BBC 1 1974–8

Terry Fletcher .... **Terry Scott**
June Fletcher .... **June Whitfield**
Aunt Lucy .... **Beryl Cooke**
Susan Fletcher .... **Pippa Page**
Debbie Fletcher .... **Caroline Whitaker**

Creators: **John Chapman, Eric Merriman, Christopher Bond, John Kane**
Producer: **Peter Whitmore, Ray Butt**

A middle-aged couple are saddled with a geriatric aunt.

Middle-class suburban couple Terry and June Fletcher were just settling down to life on their own after 23 years of marriage. Their two daughters had, at last, flown the nest. Then, out of the blue, June's frail, 73-year-old Aunt Lucy arrived, looking for somewhere to put up for two weeks. With her squawking pet mynah bird (Gunga Din) also in attendance, Lucy put down roots and made sure the Fletchers' burdensome days were not over. The daughters, Susan and Debbie, paid occasional visits to cheer up their patient, resilient mum and blustering, hapless dad.

The series, which was spun off a 1974 COMEDY PLAYHOUSE pilot, eventually evolved into TERRY AND JUNE, in which the old bird (and the mynah) had disappeared and the Fletchers were known as the Medfords.

HAPPY FAMILIES
UK (BBC) Situation Comedy. BBC 1 1985

Edith/Joyce/Cassie/Roxanne/Madelaine Fuddle ....
.... **Jennifer Saunders**
Guy Fuddle .... **Adrian Edmondson**
Cook .... **Dawn French**
Dr De Quincy .... **Stephen Fry**
Flossie .... **Helen Lederer**

Writer: **Ben Elton**
Producer: **Paul Jackson**

A crazy, crotchety grandmother summons her grandchildren to her deathbed.

Barmy Edith Fuddle, being about to pop her clogs, demanded the presence of her four granddaughters at her bedside. Unfortunately, they were now scattered around the world. To bring them together, their imbecile brother, Guy, was dispatched on his travels. Despite constantly losing his way, Guy eventually tracked them all down, one per episode. Cassie was working as a Hollywood soap actress, Madelaine was living with a randy poet in a French artists' commune, Joyce was a novice nun inspired by *The Sound of Music* and Roxanne was in jail.

All the sisters and the grandmother were played by Jennifer Saunders, and the series, made by the BBC in Manchester, cleverly varied its camera techniques to reflect the granddaughters' situations. The Hollywood scenes were shot in soap style, arty pastels were used for France, a jolly 1940s style was employed for the convent episode and a hard documentary edge pervaded the prison sequences.

HARBEN, PHILIP
(1906–70)

A familiar face on British television from the 1940s through the 1960s, small, bearded Philip Harben was one of the UK's first TV cooks. Presenting in his striped butcher's apron, his major series were *Cookery*, *Cookery Lesson* (a back-to-basics guide), *Man in the Kitchen* (cookery tips for men), *What's Cooking*, *Headway* (cookery theory) and *The Tools of Cookery*.

HARDING, GILBERT
(1907–60)

British TV celebrity of the 1950s, earning a reputation for acute rudeness through appearances on panel games like WHAT'S MY LINE?. A one-time schoolmaster and police officer, Harding had used his skill at languages to enter the BBC's monitoring service. From there, via service overseas, he became host of the radio quizzes, *Round Britain Quiz*, *The Brains Trust* and *Twenty Questions*. Initially earmarked to host *What's My Line?* on alternate weeks, Harding found being a panel member infinitely more suitable and allowed Eamonn Andrews to keep the chairman's job full time. In one famous television moment in 1960, Harding appeared on FACE TO FACE, only to admit readily that his bad manners and temper were 'quite indefensible'. In the same interview, he broke down when interrogator John Freeman inadvertently touched on the recent death of Harding's mother. Harding died the same year.

HARDY, ROBERT
CBE (1925–)

Cheltenham-born actor whose most prominent TV roles have been as Dudley, Earl of Leicester, in ELIZABETH R, Siegfried Farnon in ALL CREATURES GREAT AND SMALL and the title part in WINSTON CHURCHILL – THE WILDERNESS YEARS. He also played Fred Potter in the sitcom, *If the Crown Fits*, Alec Stewart in THE TROUBLESHOOTERS, Abwehr Sergeant Gratz in MANHUNT, Prince Albert in EDWARD THE SEVENTH, *Daily Crucible* editor Russell Spam (and its proprietor, Twiggy Rathbone) in HOT METAL, Arthur Brooke in MIDDLEMARCH, Sir Herbert Hamilton in BRAMWELL, and Dr Parnell in *Gulliver's Travels*. In addition, since the early 1960s, Hardy has been seen in many other single dramas and series such as MYSTERY AND IMAGINATION, THE BARON, *Supernatural*, UPSTAIRS, DOWNSTAIRS, THE DUCHESS OF DUKE STREET, THE CLEOPATRAS, THE FAR PAVILIONS, *Jenny's War*,

The Shooting Party and *War and Remembrance* (again as Winston Churchill).

HARGREAVES, JACK
OBE (1911–94)

Yorkshire-raised Jack Hargreaves was one of TV's gentler personalities. Whether it was explaining scientific facts to kids on HOW! or delving into the wonders of nature and practising rural crafts in his series, *Out of Town*, he was a presenter who moved at his own pace, drawing calmly on his pipe and offering (usually adlibbed) opinions in a relaxed, natural, unhurried way. A former vet's assistant and journalist, his first TV series was *Gone Fishing* for Southern, for whom he was also Deputy Programme Controller in the late 1960s and early 1970s. When Southern lost its franchise in 1981, *Gone Fishing*'s successor, *Out of Town*, was cancelled, although Hargreaves did follow it up with a similar effort, *Old Country*, for Channel 4.

HARK AT BARKER/HIS LORDSHIP ENTERTAINS
UK (LWT/BBC) Situation Comedy. ITV 1969–70/ BBC 2 1972

Lord Rustless	**Ronnie Barker**
Badger	**Frank Gatliff**
Mildred Bates	**Josephine Tewson**
Dithers	**David Jason**
Cook	**Mary Baxter**
Effie	**Moira Foot**

Producer: **Humphrey Barclay** (*Hark*), **Harold Snoad** (*Entertains*)

The misadventures of a lecherous old peer of the realm and his inept staff.

Hark at Barker was based on Alun Owen's single play, *Ah, There You Are*, which was screened as part of *The Ronnie Barker Playhouse* in 1968. It featured the lusty, opinionated, cigar-puffing Lord Rustless, as he meandered around his stately home, Chrome Hall. His staff consisted of Badger the butler, Dithers the gardener, Mildred the secretary, Effie the maid and Cook. Other occasional characters were also played by Ronnie Barker. After two seasons on ITV, Rustless and his employees switched to BBC 2 in 1972 to star in the series, *His Lordship Entertains*, in which the old buffer's stately pile had been turned into a hotel. These seven episodes were written by Barker himself under the pseudonym, Jonathan Cobbald.

HARKER, SUSANNAH
(1965–)

London-born actress, the daughter of actress Polly Adams and sister of actress Caroline Harker. Her major TV credits have included *The Fear* (Linda Galton), *Chancer* (Jo Franklyn), HOUSE OF CARDS (Mattie Storin), PRIDE AND PREJUDICE (Jane Bennet) and *Ultraviolet* (Angie). She is married to actor Iain Glen.

HARLECH TELEVISION
See HTV.

HARPER, GERALD
(1931–)

Smooth-talking actor and radio presenter, the epitome of a country gent when portraying HADLEIGH, a character given his own series after appearances in *Gazette*. Earlier, Harper had been the more flamboyant ADAM ADAMANT, a frozen Edwardian adventurer reawakened in the Swinging Sixties. Although a number of smaller TV roles had come his way pre-*Adamant* (in series such as SKYPORT), and Harper had also guested in action series like THE AVENGERS and THE CHAMPIONS, since *Hadleigh* he has concentrated on radio and stage work.

HARPERS WEST ONE
UK (ATV) Drama. ITV 1961–3

Mike Gilmore	**Tristram Jellinek**
Edward Cruickshank	**Graham Crowden**
Harriet Carr	**Jan Holden**
Aubrey Harper	**Arthur Hewlett**
Albert Fisher	**Frederick Peisley**
Jackie Webb	**Pauline Stroud**
Julie Wheeler	**Vivian Pickles**
Roger Pike	**Norman Bowler**
Oliver Backhouse	**Philip Latham**
Philip Nash	**Bernard Horsfall**
Frances Peters	**Jayne Muir**
Jeff Tyson	**Gordon Ruttan**
Susan Sullivan	**Wendy Richard**

Creators: **John Whitney, Geoffrey Bellman**
Producers: **Hugh Rennie, Rex Firkin, Royston Morley**

Behind the scenes at a fictional London department store.

'Shopping with the lid off', as the programme blurb put it, *Harpers West One* focused on events in the lives of the team at Harpers department store in the West End. From customer liaison to personal liaisons, this series looked at all aspects of life in the store, but lasted a mere two seasons. Among the major players were PR man Mike Gilmore, staff controller Edward Cruickshank, personnel officer Harriet Carr, chairman Aubrey Harper and, in later episodes, secretary Susan Sullivan. It was co-created by future IBA Director-General John Whitney. *Harpers West One* was also responsible for one of 1961's biggest hit singles, 'Johnny Remember Me' by John Leyton, who turned up in the series playing the character Johnny St Cyr.

HARRIOTT, AINSLEY
(1957–)

Flamboyant, London-born TV chef fronting series like *Can't Cook, Won't Cook, Ainsley's Barbecue Bible, Ainsley's Meals in Minutes, Ainsley's Big Cook Out, Party of a Lifetime* and *Ainsley's Gourmet Express*, after making his TV cooking debut on *Good Morning with Anne and Nick* and following this up with spots on FOOD AND DRINK. He has also been a regular competitor on *Ready, Steady, Cook*. His lively presentation recalls his previous part-time career as a stand-up comedian at The Comedy Store while working shifts as a sous-chef (which led to his supporting Bobby Davro in the series, *Davro*). In his catering past, Harriott was head chef at Lord's cricket ground's famous Long Room for nine years. He is the son of pianist Chester Harriott.

HARRIS, ROLF
OBE (1930–)

Bearded Australian TV personality, a musician, a singer, a comedian and a painter rolled into one. Former Junior Backstroke Champion of Australia, Harris arrived in the UK in 1952 to study art but soon took up showbiz as a career, making his TV debut in *Whirligig*. In 1959 he appeared with Tony Hancock in HANCOCK'S HALF HOUR and in the same year continued in children's TV with *Musical Box*, an animated nursery rhyme show, made with Peter Firmin. During the early 1960s Rolf's regular partner was Coojee Bear, a koala puppet. From 1967 Harris starred in his own Saturday night variety show, inevitably conjuring up a giant painting (using large pots of paint and decorating brushes) to illustrate one of his novel songs. Viewers could also count on odd musical instruments, be they didgeridoos, wobble boards, piano accordions or Stylophones. In the 1980s he hosted *Rolf Harris's Cartoon Time* and in the 1990s he began a new lease of life as presenter of ANIMAL HOSPITAL, *Zoo Watch Live* and *Rolf's Amazing World of Animals*. Among his other credits have been *Rolf's Walkabout, Rolf on Saturday, OK?, Hey Presto, It's Rolf, Rolf's Here! OK?* and *Rolf's Cartoon Club*.

HARRIS, SUSAN

American comedy writer (on sitcoms like ALL IN THE FAMILY and THE PARTRIDGE FAMILY) who broke through in the 1970s by creating SOAP and its spin-off, *Benson*. In the 1980s and 1990s she was responsible for THE GOLDEN GIRLS, *The Golden Palace, Nurses* and *Empty Nest*, all made by Witt-Thomas-Harris, the production company she founded with her husband, Paul Junger Witt, and another partner, Tony Thomas.

HARRISON, KATHLEEN
(1892–1995)

Veteran British actress, fond of Cockney charlady roles, even though she was born in Lancashire. Her big TV success came in 1966, after a lengthy career in films (most notably in the *Huggett* series), when she was cast as MRS THURSDAY, a cleaner who inherited a fortune and a controlling interest in a large company. After that, her appearances were confined to guest spots in series like DANGER UXB and a couple of Dickens adaptations (including the 1978 version of *Our Mutual Friend* as Henrietta Boffin), having turned down the part of *Edna, The Inebriate Woman*, which won Patricia Hayes much acclaim.

HARRY O
US (Warner Brothers) Detective Drama. BBC 1 1974–7

Harry Orwell	**David Janssen**
Det. Lt Manny Quinlan	**Henry Darrow**
Lt. K. C. Trench	**Anthony Zerbe**
Sgt Don Roberts	**Paul Tulley**
Lester Hodges	**Les Lannom**
Dr Fong	**Keye Luke**

Creator: **Howard Rodman**
Executive Producer: **Jerry Thorpe**
Producers: **Robert E. Thompson, Robert Dozier, Buck Houghton, Alex Beaton**

A retired cop lives in a beach shack but still works as a private detective.

Former marine Harry Orwell had been pensioned out of the police force after being shot in the back. Despite constant pain from a bullet lodged in his body, he took to working as a private detective, taking on cases that both aroused his interest and supplemented his income. A drop-out among detectives, the grumpy, whisky-swilling Orwell was, all the same, a lot more dependable than his temperamental car, which forced him to make good use of public transport. Based in San Diego, and living in a beach-front house, he worked closely with his by-the-book former colleague, Lt. Manny Quinlan, of the local police; but when Quinlan was killed off Orwell moved to Santa Monica. Here, life was even less comfortable, as Harry had to deal with the sarcastic Lt. Trench.

Actress Farrah Fawcett made her TV debut in this series, appearing as Orwell's next-door neighbour.

HARRY'S GAME
UK (Yorkshire) Thriller. ITV 1982

Capt. Harry James Brown	**Ray Lonnen**
Davidson	**Benjamin Whitrow**
Bannen	**Nicholas Day**
Billy Downes	**Derek Thompson**
Theresa McCorrigan	**Linda Robson**

Seamus Duffryn .... **Charles Lawson**
Minister of Defence .... **Denys Hawthorne**
Col. George Frost .... **Geoffrey Chater**
Capt. Arthur Fairclough .... **Andy Abrahams**
Insp. Howard Rennie .... **Sean Caffrey**
Mrs Downes .... **Margaret Shevlin**
Josephine Laverty .... **Gil Brailey**
Frankie .... **Christopher Whitehouse**

Writer: **Gerald Seymour**
Executive Producer: **David Cunliffe**
Producer: **Keith Richardson**

An army captain infiltrates terrorist ranks to track down a killer.

This three-part thriller, screened on consecutive nights, centred on 34-year old Captain Harry Brown, a specialist called up on the orders of the Prime Minister (against the advice of military and local experts) to go undercover in Northern Ireland. Born in Portadown (and therefore knowing the territory) and with wide military experience under his belt, Brown's mission was to mingle with the IRA and to hunt down the assassin of government minister Henry Danby. The tense, cat-and-mouse action was penned by former ITN reporter Gerald Seymour from his own novel, with the haunting theme song a hit for Clannad in 1982.

HART TO HART
US (Aaron Spelling) Detective Drama. ITV 1980–5

Jonathan Hart .... **Robert Wagner**
Jennifer Hart .... **Stefanie Powers**
Max .... **Lionel Stander**

Creator: **Sidney Sheldon**
Executive Producers: **Aaron Spelling, Leonard Goldberg**

A self-made millionaire and his journalist wife spice up their life by chasing crooks.

Jonathan Hart, head of Hart Industries, and his wife, Jennifer (a former world-famous journalist), lived in a mansion in Bel-Air, where they had everything they needed – except excitement. They didn't need to work, so, to add some zest to their sad, pampered lives, they spent most of their time dashing around the world in a private jet, acting as a pair of amateur sleuths. They were supported by Max, their gruff, wrinkled chauffeur, and their dog, Freeway.

The series was created by novelist Sidney Sheldon and borrowed heavily from *The Thin Man* films of the 1930s and 1940s, which starred William Powell and Myrna Loy as Nick and Nora Charles.

HART, TONY
(1925–)

Maidstone-born children's TV artist and presenter of VISION ON, the programme for youngsters with hearing difficulties. He subsequently gained his own series, *Take*

Hart, HARTBEAT and *The Artbox Bunch*, although some of his early work was as operator of *Quackers* in Ray Alan's *Tich and Quackers*. He also appeared in the long-running series, *Whirligig* and *Playbox*, and drew the Packi adventures for BLUE PETER in the late 1950s (as well as designing the *Blue Peter* ship logo).

HARTBEAT
See VISION ON.

HARTNELL, WILLIAM
(1908–75)

London-born actor, for ever remembered as the first DOCTOR WHO, playing the role as a mysterious, tetchy, headstrong old man in an Edwardian frock-coat. He stayed with the series from its beginnings in 1963 to 1966, when a combination of dissatisfaction with the series and illness saw him leave. He made one further appearance in the series, in the story called 'The Three Doctors', in which Jon Pertwee's version was given the assistance of his previous incarnations. Previously, Hartnell had starred in THE ARMY GAME, as the blustery Sgt Major Bullimore, a similar performance to his Sgt Grimshaw in the film, *Carry On Sergeant* (just one of over 60 films he made). One of Hartnell's last TV performances was in the anthology series, CRIME OF PASSION.

HARTY, RUSSELL
(1934–88)

Northern presenter and chat show host who worked his way from schoolteaching and producing BBC radio arts programmes to national status through shows such as *Russell Harty Plus* and *Harty*. Along the way, his distinctive 'you are, are you not?' style of questioning was much mimicked. One of his earliest production (and presentation) successes was AQUARIUS in 1969, and Harty continued in front of the cameras for a series of chat shows for LWT (*Eleven Plus*, which became *Russell Harty Plus*). He switched channels in 1980 and gained his own peak-time slot on BBC 2 with the show, *Russell Harty*. In one famous instance, model/singer Grace Jones whacked him about the head, believing he was ignoring her. Among his other credits were *Saturday Night People* (with Janet Street-Porter and Clive James, for the London ITV region), *All About Books*, SONGS OF PRAISE, *Harty Goes to Hollywood*, *Russell Harty at the Seaside* and *Favourite Things*. Harty died in 1988 of hepatitis, an illness he picked up while filming a series on the Grand Tour of Europe.

HASS, HANS
(1919–) and **LOTTE** (1929–)

Austrian husband-and-wife diving team who pioneered underwater filming for television in the 1950s and 1960s. In 1956 they brought the wonders of the deep to BBC viewers in *Diving to Adventure*, although their longer-running series was *The Undersea World of Adventure*. Their films were dubbed into German, as well as English, to cover both markets. In 1966 Hans presented a different kind of nature programme. Entitled *Man*, it looked at the behaviour of the human race as if observed by outsiders.

HASSELHOFF, DAVID
(1952–)

American actor who shot to fame as co-star (with a car!) of KNIGHT RIDER, playing do-gooder Michael Knight. After four years behind the wheel of the world's cleverest motor, Hasselhoff moved to the seaside to star in the hugely popular BAYWATCH, as lifeguard Lt. Mitch Buchannon. When the network decided to drop the series, Hasselhoff used his own money to produce more episodes under the title of *New Baywatch* and sold them into syndication. These were followed by a detective spin-off, *Baywatch Nights*. His earlier TV career included guest spots in THE LOVE BOAT and *Police Story*, as well as a seven-year run in a US daytime soap, *The Young and the Restless*.

HAVE GUN WILL TRAVEL
US (CBS) Western. ITV 1959–64

Paladin .... **Richard Boone**
Hey Boy .... **Kam Tong**
Hey Girl .... **Lisa Lu**

A mysterious Wild West troubleshooter hires himself out to those seeking justice.

This series centred on the enigmatic Paladin, a cultured, well-educated former West Point student who now lived at the classy Hotel Carlton in San Francisco. A loner, dressed menacingly in black, he appeared cynical and somewhat threatening, but he was also warm and sensitive at the same time, a good man at heart. His work, after all, involved righting wrongs – even if it was for a fee. His love of the good things in life meant that he needed to earn his keep, and he operated as a bodyguard, a courier, a private detective, or whatever was asked of him. But, although his gun was for hire, the inscrutable Paladin was a man of principle and was even known to turn on his employers if it appeared that they were the real bad guys. He was a slick operator and far removed from the other, rough-and-ready ranch-bound TV cowboys of his time.

'Paladin' means 'knightly hero' and is a name given to the knight chess piece, which appeared in white on Paladin's holster and also on his calling-card, which bore the words 'Have Gun, Will Travel . . . Wire Paladin, San Francisco'. Any wires received were delivered by Hey Boy, the Chinese hotel hand (who was replaced by Hey Girl for a short period). Duane Eddy had a UK hit with an instrumental version of the theme song, 'The Ballad of Paladin', in 1962.

HAVE I GOT NEWS FOR YOU
UK (Hat Trick) Comedy. BBC 2/BBC 1 1990–

Angus Deayton, Paul Merton, Ian Hislop

Producers: **Harry Thompson, Colin Swash, Richard Wilson, Giles Pilbrow**

Ultra-topical current affairs satire/quiz.

The television version of Radio 4's *The News Quiz*, *Have I Got News For You* has been a contest between comedian Paul Merton (for one season replaced by stand-in captains due to other commitments) and *Private Eye* editor Ian Hislop, each accompanied by celebrity guests from the worlds of entertainment, journalism or politics. The format has relied heavily on the speed of thought and quick wit of its contestants (not to mention a little forward planning) as they have adlibbed answers and jokes to various clips of the week's events. Blacked-out words in newspaper headlines, odd ones out and a caption competition have been regular features. Comics such as Alexei Sayle, Vic Reeves and Frank Skinner have been called in as team members, as have writers like Andrew Morton and Will Self, and TV folk like Anne Robinson, Jonathan Ross and Trevor McDonald. Among the political guests have been Neil Kinnock, Cecil Parkinson, Charles Kennedy, Ken Livingstone and Sir Rhodes Boyson. When Roy Hattersley failed to show up, his place alongside Paul Merton was taken by a tub of lard. Even though scoring has been totally haphazard, it is Hislop's team that has always seemed to lose. Events have been chaired by Angus Deayton, who has contributed as much ribald and risqué humour as the panellists themselves. Thankfully, by pre-recording the show the night before transmission, the libellous bits have been cut out – allegedly.

HAVERS, NIGEL
(1949–)

One of TV's aristocratic smoothies, Nigel Havers, son of the late former Attorney-General, Sir Michael Havers, has seldom been short of television work. From early appearances in dramas such as UPSTAIRS, DOWNSTAIRS, *Shabby Tiger* and *Nicholas Nickleby*, Havers moved on to THE GLITTERING PRIZES, PENNIES FROM HEAVEN, NANCY ASTOR (Bobbie Shaw) and WINSTON CHURCHILL – THE WILDERNESS YEARS (Randolph Churchill). He starred as Paul Craddock in A HORSEMAN RIDING BY, Roy in *Strangers and Brothers* and Dr Tom Latimer in DON'T WAIT UP. He also took the title role (Ralph Gorse) in THE CHARMER, played one of THE GOOD GUYS (Guy McFadyean), was Hugh Fleming in *A Perfect Hero* and Richard in the thriller, *Element of Doubt*, and in 1998 succeeded Nigel Le Vaillant as star of DANGERFIELD (Dr Jonathan Paige). He has also hosted *OK! TV*, and among his other credits have been *A Raging Calm*, *An Englishman's Castle*, *Coming Out*, *Unity*, *Goodbye Darling*, *After the Party*, CATHERINE COOKSON's *The Glass Virgin* and MURDER MOST HORRID.

HAWAII FIVE-O
US (CBS/Leonard Freeman) Police Drama. ITV 1970–82

Det. Steve McGarrett .... **Jack Lord**
Det. Danny 'Danno' Williams .... **James MacArthur**
Det. Chin Ho Kelly .... **Kam Fong**
Det. Kono Kalakaua .... **Zulu**
Governor Philip Grey .... **Richard Denning**
Wo Fat .... **Khigh Dhiegh**
Det. Ben Kokua .... **Al Harrington**
Che Fong .... **Harry Endo**
Doc Bergman .... **Al Eben**
May .... **Maggi Parker**
Jenny Sherman .... **Peggy Ryan**
Duke Lukela .... **Herman Wedemeyer**
Attorney General John Manicote .... **Glenn Cannon**
James 'Kimo' Carew .... **William Smith**
Lori Wilson .... **Sharon Farrell**
Tom 'Truck' Kealoha .... **Moe Keale**

Creator/Executive Producer: **Leonard Freeman**
Producers: **Bill Finnegan, Bob Sweeney, Philip Leacock,
Richard Newton, Douglas Green, B. W. Sandefur**

*The cases of a special police unit and its
tight-lipped, self-righteous leader on the paradise
islands of Hawaii.*

Five-O was not your normal police force. These guys (a special division of the Hawaiian State Police) worked separately from the Honolulu Police Department and were directly answerable to the Governor. They operated from the Iolani Palace, the supposed seat of the Hawaiian Government, and their tough, no-nonsense boss was Steve McGarrett.

The blue-suited McGarrett loathed crooks and seemed to have no other passion in life. He was ably supported by his main men, 'Danno' Williams ('Book 'em, Danno' became a catchphrase) and Chin Ho Kelly. Another original colleague, Kono Kalakaua, was written out after a few years, although most of the cast stayed with the show for much of its very long run. When Williams and Kelly eventually left, new officers like Lori Wilson, Truck Kealoha and 'Kimo' Carew were added to see the series through to its close (1980 in its native USA).

Five-O, being independent, was able to avoid the petty bureaucracies of normal police work. Its brief was to keep this tropical paradise clean, to mop up vermin that disrupted the life of Honolulu and the other islands. Consequently, McGarrett and his boys targeted the spivs, the hoodlums and, more purposefully, the organized underworld, especially an elusive oriental villain by the name of Wo Fat.

As well as taking the star role, Jack Lord was also heavily involved behind the scenes of the series. He became a Hawaiian resident and, to many viewers, became synonymous with the islands.

HAWK, JEREMY
(Cedric Lange; 1918–)

A former music-hall straight man to stars like Arthur Askey, Arthur Haynes and Norman Wisdom, Jeremy Hawk also supported Benny Hill and American comic Sid Caesar on TV, but he found his niche in the early days of television as a quiz master. As host of CRISS CROSS QUIZ and *Junior Criss Cross Quiz* from 1957 to 1962, he was a familiar face in most households. He then presented the improvisation comedy, *Impromptu*, but found little TV work later (save a memorable Cadbury's Whole Nut commercial in the 1970s: 'Nuts Who-ole Ha-azelnuts; Cadbury's take 'em and they cover 'em in chocolate') and returned to the stage. Hawk is the father of actress Belinda Lang.

HAWKESWORTH, JOHN
(1920–)

British writer/producer, a one-time Rank film scriptwriter, chiefly remembered for period pieces such as UPSTAIRS, DOWNSTAIRS and THE DUCHESS OF DUKE STREET (also as creator). In addition, he produced and co-scripted THE GOLD ROBBERS and the sitcom, *In for a Penny*, created/adapted *The Short Stories of Conan Doyle*, BY THE SWORD DIVIDED, DANGER UXB and *The Flame Trees of Thika*, and worked on episodes of THE ADVENTURES OF SHERLOCK HOLMES and CRIME OF PASSION.

HAWKEYE AND THE LAST OF THE MOHICANS
Canada (Normandie) Adventure. ITV 1957

Nat 'Hawkeye' Cutler .... **John Hart**
Chingachgook .... **Lon Chaney Jr**

Producer: **Sigmund Neufeld**

*Escapades in the American wilderness with a
trapper and his Indian comrade.*

This drama series, loosely based on the novel by James Fenimore Cooper, featured Nat Cutler, known familiarly as 'Hawkeye', a trapper, fur trader and scout for the US cavalry. His adventures in the northern frontierland, and encounters with the Huron Indians during the 1750s, were shared by his redskin blood-brother, Chingachgook, the 'Last of the Mohicans'. Star John Hart had previously enjoyed brief TV fame when temporarily taking over the role of the LONE RANGER from Clayton Moore.

HAWKINS, PETER
(1924–)

British actor best known for voicing children's animated characters. His vocal talents were put to good use in programmes like FLOWER POT MEN, THE WOODENTOPS,

CAPTAIN PUGWASH, TIN TIN, *Noah and Nelly* and *The Perishers*; and Hawkins also spoke for DOCTOR WHO's Daleks and Cybermen. In vision, he appeared in *Whirligig*, among other programmes.

HAWTHORNE, Sir NIGEL
CBE (1929–)

Coventry-born actor, acclaimed for his tongue-twisting performances as Sir Humphrey Appleby in YES, MINISTER and *Yes, Prime Minister*. Hawthorne also played Pierre Curie in *Marie Curie*, Dr Grantly in *The Barchester Chronicles* and the sadistic examiner of would-be taxi-drivers in Jack Rosenthal's play, *The Knowledge*. Among his other credits have been EDWARD AND MRS SIMPSON (Walter Monckton), *Warrior Queen*, *The Hunchback of Notre Dame*, *A Tale of Two Cities*, *The World Cup – A Captain's Tale*, *Jenny's War*, *Mapp and Lucia*, *The Miser*, *The Fragile Heart* (heart surgeon Edgar Pascoe) and the *Everyman* documentary, *Canterbury* (presenting a history of Canterbury Cathedral).

HAYES, MELVYN
(1935–)

Diminutive English actor. As a teenager he played one of the boys in BILLY BUNTER OF GREYFRIARS SCHOOL in the 1950s and appeared in QUATERMASS II, plus other dramas. He was the Artful Dodger in BBC's 1962 adaptation of *Oliver Twist*, and in 1971 he was seen as Albert, the grown-up, in HERE COME THE DOUBLE DECKERS. Hayes was also cast as Gregory in the Jimmy Edwards comedy, *Sir Yellow*, and played Melvyn Didsbury in the kids' series, *Potter's Picture Palace*, as well as providing the voice of Skeleton for the *SuperTed* cartoons. Other early roles included assorted crooks in DIXON OF DOCK GREEN and Z CARS, and supporting roles in *Mr Pastry* and THE SEVEN FACES OF JIM. However, by far his most successful part has been as Bombardier 'Gloria' Beaumont, the drag artist in IT AIN'T HALF HOT MUM. His second wife was actress Wendy Padbury and they are the parents of actress Charlie Hayes (Ruth in WYCLIFFE).

HAYES, PATRICIA
OBE (1909–98)

London-born actress, on stage from the age of 12 and generally seen as a foil or support to comedians like Arthur Askey, Tony Hancock, Arthur Haynes, Eric Sykes, Ken Dodd and Benny Hill. In contrast, her dramatic skills were brought to the fore in the award-winning PLAY FOR TODAY, *Edna, The Inebriate Woman*. Hayes was also seen as neighbour Griselda Wormold in HUGH AND I, Lillian in *The Trouble with Lillian*, Mrs Basket in *Last of the Baskets*, traffic warden Mrs Cantaford in SPOONER'S PATCH, mother Alice Tripp in *Marjorie and Men*, Old Pat in *The Lady Is a Tramp* and in programmes as varied as *Educated Evans*, TILL DEATH US DO PART (Min), *The World of Beachcomber*, *The Corn Is Green*, THE AVENGERS, *The*

Very Merry Widow, *Mr Pye* and CASUALTY. Her son is actor Richard O'Callaghan.

HAYGARTH, TONY
(1945–)

Liverpudlian actor seen in scores of dramas and comedies, particularly ROSIE (PC Wilmot), KINVIG (Des Kinvig), OUR FRIENDS IN THE NORTH (Roy Johnson) and WHERE THE HEART IS (Vic Snow). Other credits have come in WHATEVER HAPPENED TO THE LIKELY LADS?, I, CLAUDIUS, SHOESTRING, *Hardwicke House* (Harry Savage), LOVEJOY, *Farrington of the FO* (Fidel Sanchez), *All Change* (Brian Oldfield), *Scully*, EL C.I.D. (Frank), *The Borrowers* (Mildeye), MAKING OUT (Kip), A TOUCH OF FROST, PRESTON FRONT, BETWEEN THE LINES, SHARPE, PIE IN THE SKY, INSPECTOR MORSE and KAVANAGH QC.

HAYNES, ARTHUR
(1915–66)

One of TV's first star comedians, former radio comic Arthur Haynes specialized in social nuisance characters like the manipulative, silent Oscar Pennyfeather and a disgruntled, bemedalled tramp. These appeared in *The Arthur Haynes Show* (written by Johnny Speight and co-starring Nicholas Parsons as his straight man) which was launched in 1956 after Haynes had stolen the spotlight in a series called *Strike a New Note* and had appeared in *The Charlie Chester Show*. He was still starring in his own series when he died suddenly in 1966.

HAZELL
UK (Thames) Detective Drama. ITV 1978–80

James Hazell	Nicholas Ball
'Choc' Minty	Roddy McMillan
Cousin Tel	Desmond McNamara

Creators: **Terry Venables, Gordon Williams**
Producers: **June Roberts, Tim Aspinall**

A crooked London policeman becomes a private eye.

When James Hazell was forced to retire from the police force in his early 30s because of a damaged ankle, he turned to drink and destroyed his marriage. Reformed and dried out, he became a private investigator, helped by his cousin Tel, with his main sparring partner a Scottish CID officer named 'Choc' Minty.

Even if the series erred on the violent side, Hazell was a fun character, a Jack the Lad with a flair for the telling phrase. A true Cockney, he enjoyed the glamour of his profession and bustled along in life, mixing it with the best, but not always coming out on top. In spoof *film noir* fashion, Hazell provided a commentary voice-over for each episode. The series was based on books by football manager Terry Venables and Gordon Williams, who also contributed to the TV version.

HEALY, TIM
(1952–)

Geordie actor, familiar from a number of light comedy-dramas. It was as Denis in AUF WIEDERSEHEN, PET that Healy first grabbed the viewers' attention, although he had already appeared in programmes like CORONATION STREET, EMMERDALE FARM, MINDER, *The World Cup – A Captain's Tale* and WHEN THE BOAT COMES IN. His other credits have included *A Kind of Living* (Brian Thompson), *A Perfect Spy*, CRACKER, *Tom Jones* (Mr Nightingale Sr), CATHERINE COOKSON's *A Dinner of Herbs* (Mr Mulcaster) and the kids' show, *Tickle on the Tum*. Healy also head-lined as expatriate Cockney, Reg Toomer, in THE BOYS FROM THE BUSH, Foxy in the dustbinmen comedy, COMMON AS MUCK, Mr Collins in *The Grand*, seedy hotelier Harry Springer in *Heartburn Hotel* and Bertie Masson in *Bostock's Cup*. He is married to actress Denise Welch.

HEARNE, RICHARD
OBE (1909–79)

Acrobatic Richard Hearne was one of British TV's first clowns, playing the part of a nimble but accident-prone old man in numerous slapstick sketches. The character was Mr Pastry, complete with walrus moustache, long coat-tails and gold-rimmed spectacles perched half-way down the nose. Mr Pastry first appeared in one of Hearne's many stage performances and arrived on tele-vision in 1946. He went on to star in series such as *Mr Pastry's Progress*, *Leave It to Mr Pastry*, *Ask Mr Pastry* and *Mr Pastry's Pet Shop*, as well as guesting on CRACKERJACK and SUNDAY NIGHT AT THE LONDON PALLADIUM. Pre-Pastry, Hearne had featured in a number of early BBC comedy programmes. He also starred in several films.

HEARTBEAT
UK (Yorkshire) Drama. ITV 1992–

PC/Sgt Nick Rowan	**Nick Berry**
Dr Kate Rowan	**Niamh Cusack**
Sgt Oscar Blaketon	**Derek Fowlds**
Claude Jeremiah Greengrass	**Bill Maynard**
Dr Alex Ferrenby	**Frank Middlemass**
PC Alf Ventress	**William Simons**
PC Phil Bellamy	**Mark Jordon**
George Ward	**Stuart Golland**
Gina Ward	**Tricia Penrose**
Maggie Bolton	**Kazia Pelka**
Eileen	**Anne Stallybrass**
Jo Weston/Rowan	**Juliette Gruber**
Bernie Scripps	**Peter Benson**
Dr Neil Bolton	**David Michaels**
PC Mike Bradley	**Jason Durr**
Sgt Raymond Craddock	**Philip Franks**
Auntie Mary	**Arbel Jones**
Jackie Lambert/Bradley	**Fiona Dolman**
Andy Ryan	**Martin Ledwith**

Executive Producer: **Keith Richardson**
Producers: **Stuart Doughty, Steve Lanning, Keith Richardson, Carol Wilks, Gerry Mill**

Nostalgic drama about a constable patrolling a Yorkshire moorland beat.

Beginning in 1964, *Heartbeat* was the story of PC Nick Rowan and his doctor wife, Kate. Having left their London base to return to Kate's home area of the North Yorkshire moors, the Rowans took up residence in the police house in the village of Aidensfield, where Nick became the village bobby. He reported to the grouchy Sgt Blaketon at the Ashfordly police station, and his PC colleagues were the skiving, chain-smoking veteran, Alf Ventress, and the somewhat reckless Phil Bellamy. Kate became a partner in the Aidensfield general practice headed by old friend Alex Ferrenby and, following his death, she became the village's only doctor. Tragedy struck, however, when Kate died shortly after giving birth to a daughter, Katie. Bane of Rowan's life was the lovable rogue, Claude Jeremiah Greengrass, who, with his loyal mutt, Alfred, was usually at the heart of some scam or other. George Ward, assisted by Gina, his trendy Liverpudlian niece, ran The Aidensfield Arms, the local pub. Later arrivals were district nurse Maggie Bolton, Nick's Auntie Eileen and schoolteacher Jo Weston, the new girl in the PC's life. Following their marriage, Nick's promotion to sergeant (when Blaketon retired to run the post office) and the Rowans' subsequent departure from Aidensfield (Nick went to Canada to become a Mountie, taking his family with him), attention focused on new copper Mike Bradley, freshly dispatched from the Met aboard a Triumph Bonneville motorbike to learn about rural policing. Also new was Dr Neil Bolton, Maggie's former husband; Nick's replacement, Sgt Raymond Craddock; and Jackie Lambert, Mike's girlfriend.

Heartbeat was based on the *Constable* novels by Nicholas Rhea, the pen-name of former Yorkshire policeman Peter Walker. With its liberal use of contemporary pop hits and careful selection of period furniture and other items, this gentle, nostalgic drama attracted a huge audi-ence. Buddy Holly's 'Heartbeat', sung by Nick Berry, was the programme's theme song. As a series cash-in, Nick Rowan's transatlantic adventure was chronicled in a one-off video production entitled *Heartbeat: Changing Places*, which was eventually screened by ITV in June 1999.

HECTOR'S HOUSE
France (Europe 1/Télécompagnie) Children's Entertainment. BBC 1 1968–70

Creator: **Georges Croses**

The domestic adventures of a dog, a cat and a frog.

In this five-minute pre-news filler the Hector in question was a large, sensible-looking dog with floppy ears who shared his home with Zaza, a cat dressed in a red pina-fore. Their next-door neighbour (forever nipping over the fence by ladder) was Mrs Kiki, a giggly frog in a gingham overall, who displayed a talent for weather forecasting. The trio enjoyed mild mirth around the house and garden, the two females playing silly jokes on the gullible hound and Hector never failing to act gallantly as a true gentleman, courteously assisting his friends at every turn. His catchphrase was a variation on 'I'm just a big, silly old Hector', adapted according to circumstance into 'big sensible old Hector', 'big sad old Hector', etc. The only other regular was a bird that twittered in a tree at the start and finish of each programme. The series was known in its native France as *La Maison de Tu Tu*.

HEDLEY, JACK
(Jack Hawkins; 1930–)

Solid British actor whose starring status in the Francis Durbridge thriller, *The World of Tim Frazer*, in 1960 was not followed up with another lead role until COLDITZ in 1972, in which he played Lt. Colonel Preston. However, he did play Corrigan Blake in the 1962 Alun Owen play, *You Can't Win 'Em All*, which led to the *Corrigan Blake* series (although John Turner then assumed the title role). Hedley was also seen in KATE, as Kate Graham's editor, the TV movie of *Brief Encounter* and scores of other series, from *Who Pays the Ferryman?*, ONE BY ONE and REMINGTON STEELE to the dramas, *Gentlemen and Players*, *A Quiet Conspiracy* and *Hard Cases*.

HEINEY, PAUL
(1949–)

Yorkshire-born TV reporter and presenter, the husband of broadcaster Libby Purves. He first came to light as one of Esther Rantzen's supporting crew on THAT'S LIFE and THE BIG TIME, before sharing the limelight with Chris Serle in IN AT THE DEEP END. He presented *The Travel Show* for BBC 2 and once stepped in as host of FOOD AND DRINK while Chris Kelly took a season off.

HELEN – A WOMAN OF TODAY
UK (LWT) Drama. ITV 1973

Helen Tulley	Alison Fiske
Frank Tulley	Martin Shaw
Carole	Sharon Duce

Producer: **Richard Bates**

A wife and mother divorces her cheating husband and seeks a new life of her own.

Reflecting the increasingly feminist mood of the time, and for once making the woman in a broken marriage the centre of attention, *Helen – A Woman of Today* related the story of Helen Tulley, a middle-class, thirtysomething mother of two who decided to strive for more from life. It all began with an affair between Frank, her husband, and another woman, Carole. Despite being urged by friends and families to stand by her man, Helen turned instead to study, becoming self-reliant and

battling her own way through a cold world. There were 13 episodes.

HELLO GIRLS, THE
UK (BBC/Diverse Fiction) Drama. BBC 1 1996–8

Chris Cross	Letitia Dean
Sylvia Sands	Amy Marston
Ronni Ferrari	Helen Sheals
Val Pepper/Latimer	Samantha Seager
Susi Simmons	Samantha Hardcastle
Pamela Heath	Kate Lonergan
Miss Annie Armitage	Stephanie Turner
Miss Dolly Marriott	Maggie McCarthy
Dick Mandeville	Colin Wells
Rick Hollister	Daniel Newman
Jim	Paul Parris
Dave Curtis	Mark Aiken
Mike Simmons	Stephen Lord

Writers: **Ruth Carter, Jo O'Keefe, David Ashton, Julie Rutterford**
Producers: **Laurence Bowen, Jacinta Peel**

Fun and games with a team of switchboard girls at the turn of the 1960s.

Based on the novel, *Switchboard Operators* by Carol Lake, this light drama was based around the lives of a rather naïve group of teenage GPO employees in Derby. Ringleader of the switchboard girls was confident blonde Chris Cross, who took under her wing new girl Sylvia Sands. For Sylvia – nicknamed 'Fruity' – it was the first job and the start of a learning curve about adult life. Also in the team were streetwise Ronni Ferrari, who joined Chris and Sylvia as part of a singing group called The Teletones; married, former hairdresser Pam Heath; union rep Val Pepper; and gossipy farmer's daughter Susi Simmons. Overseeing their work – and underlining the generation chasm that was opening up at the time – were dowdy Miss Marriott and prim Miss Armitage. Also seen were Dick Mandeville, Chris's boyfriend ('a thousand-a-year man' at Rolls-Royce), who was engaged to another girl; telegraph boy Jim; and Sylvia's young Marxist friend, Rick Hollister.

Beginning in 1959, stories followed everyday dramas at the exchange, friendly rivalry with the male engineers, and events after work at the Locarno ballroom. A second series, set two years later, saw the girls coming to terms with the new liberation of the 1960s and, at work, battling against job losses through automation. New characters included journalist Mike Simmons and engineer Dave Curtis.

HENDERSON, DICKIE
OBE (1922–85)

Versatile British entertainer, the son of Dick Henderson, a Yorkshire-born vaudeville comic. Dickie's peak television years were undoubtedly the mid-1950s to the early 1970s. After a decade and a half on the stage, he broke into television alongside Arthur Askey in *Before Your Very*

Eyes and was given his own series, *The Dickie Henderson Show*. He then compered SUNDAY NIGHT AT THE LONDON PALLADIUM, starred in *The Dickie Henderson Half-Hour* and in 1960 embarked on the long-running *The Dickie Henderson Show*. In this song-and-dance sitcom he played himself, with June Laverick (later Isla Blair) cast as his wife. This was followed by another comedy entitled *A Present for Dickie*, in which he found himself entrusted with an Indian elephant. His other notable TV credits were in *I'm Bob, He's Dickie* (with Bob Monkhouse) and *I'm Dickie – That's Showbusiness*.

HENDERSON, DON
(1932–)

Softly spoken British actor, the glove-wearing, inhaler-sniffing star of BULMAN and other series. His character of George Bulman first appeared in THE XYY MAN and then in STRANGERS, with his ever-present scarf employed to hide scars left by Henderson's cancer surgery. His weak voice, often put down to a cold in the series, was another by-product of Henderson's illness. Post-Bulman, Henderson moved into THE PARADISE CLUB (ex-priest Frank Kane) alongside Leslie Grantham. Among Henderson's many other appearances have been parts in POLDARK, CROSSROADS, DICK TURPIN, NEW SCOTLAND YARD, DIXON OF DOCK GREEN, VAN DER VALK, THE ONEDIN LINE, WARSHIP (Master-at-Arms Heron), RIPPING YARNS, DOCTOR WHO, *Knights of God*, HOT METAL, MINDER, *Dead Head* and 2 POINT 4 CHILDREN (Frank, Ben's dad). He is married to actress Shirley Stelfox, with whom he appeared in MAKING OUT (Mr Beachcroft).

HENDRY, IAN
(1931–84)

Determined-looking British actor whose showbusiness debut was as stooge to Coco the clown. After some notable stage performances, he broke into films in the 1950s, then secured himself some minor roles in such series as THE INVISIBLE MAN, PROBATION OFFICER and EMERGENCY – WARD 10. His first starring part was as Dr Geoffrey Brent in POLICE SURGEON, a series which quickly evolved into THE AVENGERS, the character becoming Dr David Keel and linking up with Patrick McNee's John Steed, as a couple of crime fighters. Hendry left *The Avengers* in 1962, to be replaced eventually by Honor Blackman, triggering a major change of direction for the series. He waited four years for his next major role, which arrived in THE INFORMER, when he played disbarred barrister Alex Lambert, who worked as a police informer, and he was then cast as astronaut Captain Don Quick in the sci-fi fantasy comedy, *The Adventures of Don Quick*, in 1970. THE LOTUS EATERS, in which he took the part of alcoholic expatriate Erik Shepherd, followed in 1972. Among Hendry's other credits were guest spots in series like THE PROTECTORS and *Supernatural*. His most prominent last roles were in *For Maddie with Love*, opposite Nyree Dawn Porter, and a stint in BROOKSIDE as hard-drinking sailor Davey Jones.

HENRY, LENNY
CBE (Lenworth Henry; 1958–)

Dudley-born comedian whose rise to fame began on NEW FACES (and appearances in *The Summer Show*, a showcase for the best finds of the series) in 1975. Majoring initially on gags and impressions, Henry graduated to sitcom in the short-lived THE FOSTERS (Sonny Foster). Then came TISWAS and its late-night offspring, *OTT*, before Henry joined Tracey Ullman and David Copperfield in the sketch show, THREE OF A KIND. He appeared on *Saturday Live* and THE YOUNG ONES and secured his own BBC series, *The Lenny Henry Show*, which fluctuated between stand-up comedy, sketches and sitcom, allowing him to develop characters like Fred Dread, Minister for Reggae; Algernon the Rasta; Theophilus P. Wildebeeste; Deakus the old Jamaican; Reverend Nat West; PC Ganja and his dog, Selassie; and the 'crucial' Brixton pirate radio DJ, Delbert Wilkins (who enjoyed a later series all to himself). A series of comedy playlets, *Lenny Henry Tonite*, followed. Soon Henry became a linchpin of the COMIC RELIEF appeals and was also seen as the temperamental Gareth Blackstock in CHEF. In 1996 he provided the voice for cartoon cat *Famous Fred*. In 1997 he headed into the jungle for *Lenny Henry's Big Amazon Adventure*, and a year later he took his humour on the road for a series of shows from provincial theatres in *Lenny Henry Goes to Town*. Later he played superhead-teacher Ian George in the drama series, *Hope and Glory*, and sailed the ocean for the documentary, *Lenny's Big Atlantic Adventure*. In 2000 he returned to character comedy with *Lenny Henry in Pieces*. He is married to comedienne Dawn French and runs the Crucial Films independent production company.

HENSON, JIM
(1936–90)

American puppeteer and TV executive, the man responsible for the Muppets (a combination of marionettes and hand puppets). Henson's puppetry was first featured on television in Washington, DC, through a series called *Sam and Friends*, which ran for six years from 1955. This gave him the exposure to send his creations on to national programmes like *The Tonight Show* and *The Ed Sullivan Show*. In 1969 his Muppet empire really began to move, thanks to a starring role in the new educational kids' series, SESAME STREET. Creatures like Big Bird, Oscar the Grouch and Kermit the Frog helped youngsters worldwide to learn their numbers and letters. However, in order to win his puppets a prime-time slot, Henson was forced to move to the UK, where Lord Grade put up funds for the phenomenally successful THE MUPPET SHOW. Henson himself voiced some of the characters, including the show's emcee, Kermit. On the back of the Muppets Henson created *Fraggle Rock* and the award-winning THE STORYTELLER, starring John Hurt. *Dinosaurs* was his last completed project before he died prematurely in 1990. Jim's son, Brian Henson, is now at the helm of Jim Henson Productions.

HEPTON, BERNARD
(1925–)

Stern-looking British actor whose performance as Archbishop Thomas Cranmer in THE SIX WIVES OF HENRY VIII was followed by a spell in COLDITZ as the kind Nazi Kommandant. He switched sides to play café owner/Resistance fighter Albert Foiret in SECRET ARMY, was Pallus in I, CLAUDIUS, played estate agent Donald Stimpson, trying to nail down Nigel Havers, in THE CHARMER, and was Mr Woodhouse in *Jane Austen's Emma*. Hepton has also taken to comedy in THE SQUIRRELS (Mr Fletcher) and *Sadie It's Cold Outside* (Norman Potter). His other credits have included THE TROUBLESHOOTERS, TINKER, TAILOR, SOLDIER, SPY, *Blood Money*, BERGERAC and *The Woman in Black*.

HERBS, THE
UK (Filmfair) Children's Entertainment. BBC 1 1968

Narrator: **Gordon Rollings**

Creator/Writer: **Michael Bond**
Executive Producer: **Graham Clutterbuck**

Fragrant happenings in an English country garden, with its herbs as the stars.

Relating the surreal happenings in the garden of Sir Basil and Lady Rosemary, *The Herbs* featured such characters as Constable Knapweed, schoolteacher Mr Onion, the Chives (his pupils), Bayleaf the gardener, Aunt Mint, Sage the owl, Tarragon the dragon, Pashana Bedi the snake-charmer and Belladonna. However, the undoubted stars were a manic, tail-chasing dog called Dill and a 'very friendly' lion, Parsley – later to gain his own spin-off series, *The Adventures of Parsley* (1970). 'Herbidacious' was the magic word which opened the gate to the garden. The action was narrated by Gordon Rollings (Arkwright in the John Smith's beer commercials) and the series aired under the WATCH WITH MOTHER banner.

HERE COME THE DOUBLE DECKERS
UK (Twentieth Century-Fox/Century Films) Children's Entertainment. BBC 1 1971

Scooper	**Peter Firth**
Billie	**Gillian Bailey**
Brains	**Michael Audreson**
Doughnut	**Douglas Simmonds**
Spring	**Brinsley Forde**
Sticks	**Bruce Clark**
Tiger	**Debbie Russ**
Albert	**Melvyn Hayes**

Creators: **Roy Simpson, Harry Booth**
Producer: **Roy Simpson**

A group of do-gooder kids stumble into musical adventures.

Using a disused double-decker bus housed in a London junkyard as their HQ, the Double Deckers were a bunch of game kids who found themselves wrapped up in a series of zany escapades. Leader of the gang was Scooper (played by Peter Firth, who later earned an Academy Award nomination for his role in *Equus*) and the other members were the swotty Brains (usually inventing something), the chubby Doughnut, the American Sticks (so named after his drumming skills), Billie (played by Gillian Bailey, later Jinny Martin in POLDARK), Spring (future Aswad reggae group-member and VH-1 presenter Brinsley Forde) and tiny Tiger. Albert was their grown-up friend. With its jaunty 'Get on board' theme song, the series, made in the UK, was screened first in the USA before being bought by the BBC.

HERE'S HARRY
UK (BBC) Situation Comedy. BBC 1960–5

Harry Worth	**Harry Worth**
Mrs Williams	**Vi Stevens**
Mrs Benson	**Doris Gambell**
Tommy	**Reginald Marsh**
Alf	**Joe Gladwin**

Producers: **John Ammonds, John Street**

A well-meaning bumbler tackles bureaucracy.

Playing himself, trilby-hatted Harry Worth starred as a clumsy, ineffective, dithering complainer who ended up confusing all around him. Living with his cat, Tiddles, in the northern town of Woodbridge, Harry made plenty of references to his aunt, Mrs Amelia Prendergast, but she was never seen. However, he did have a housekeeper, Mrs Williams (later replaced by Mrs Benson), and two old friends, Tommy and Alf. *Here's Harry* was the series for which Worth created his famous shop-window opening sequence in which he waved one arm and one leg in the air and, because of the reflection in the glass, made it look as if he was completely off the ground.

HERE'S LUCY
US (CBS/Lucille Ball) Situation Comedy. BBC 1 1969–71

Lucy Carter	**Lucille Ball**
Harrison Carter	**Gale Gordon**
Mary Jane Lewis	**Mary Jane Croft**
Kim Carter	**Lucie Arnaz**
Craig Carter	**Desi Arnaz, Jr**

Producer: **Gary Morton**

Lucille Ball's third family sitcom, with the action now set in California.

Here's Lucy was in many ways no more than a name change for THE LUCY SHOW, with Lucy still aided in her slapstick routines by Mary Jane Croft, and Gale Gordon still around to provide the foil. However, Lucy had now moved to Los Angeles and her surname had become Carter, although she was still a widow. Her new children, Kim and Craig, were played by her own son and daughter, while Gale Gordon this time played Uncle Harry, Lucy's brother-in-law and owner of the Unique Employment Agency, where she worked as a secretary.

HERGÉ'S ADVENTURES OF TINTIN
France (Télé-Hachette) Animation. BBC 1 1962–4

Narrator: **Peter Hawkins**

Producer (UK): **Peggy Miller**

A young reporter and his pet dog lurch from scrape to scrape.

Created in 1929 and first seen as a comic strip in the Belgian weekly, *Le Petit Vingtième*, Tintin was the brainchild of Hergé, alias cartoonist George Rémi. Over the years, the character appeared in over 20 books and made his TV bow in France in 1961 in this series of episodic adventures. Dubbed into English, Tintin arrived in the UK a year later, and British viewers were treated to the hair-raising (in more ways than one, considering his tufty locks) escapades of the red-headed cub reporter. Loyally at Tintin's side was his white fox-terrier, Snowy (Milou in the original French), and also lending a hand was the grog-sodden Captain Haddock, the black-bearded skipper of the ship *Karaboudjan*. Other characters seen from time to time were the bowler-hatted Thompson Twins (who gave their name to the 1980s pop group), the deaf and forgetful Professor Calculus and the conspiratorially minded General Alcazar.

With each adventure chopped up into breathless five-minute episodes, complete with cliffhanger endings, Tintin was forever immersed in investigations like *The Crab with the Golden Claw*, *Star of Mystery*, *Red Rackham's Treasure*, *Black Island*, *Objective Moon* and *The Calculus Case*. With so many repeat showings over the years, who could now forget the announcer's booming voice heralding another instalment of *Hergé's Adventures of . . . Tintin*?

HETTY WAINTHROPP INVESTIGATES
UK (BBC) Drama. BBC 1 1996–8

Hetty Wainthropp .... **Patricia Routledge**
Robert Wainthropp .... **Derek Benfield**
Geoffrey Shawcross .... **Dominic Monaghan**
DCI Adams .... **John Graham Davies**
Janet .... **Suzanne Maddock**

Creators: **John Bowen, David Cook**
Producer: **Carol Parks**
Executive Producer: **Jo Wright**

A pensioner housewife turns private detective.

Set in deepest Lancashire (as the mournful cornet theme music pre-warned), this unusual series of investigations featured redoubtable 60-year-old Hetty Wainthropp, the happily married, but rather bored, wife of redundant Robert. Donning her worn beret and raincoat, and using her natural talent for snooping to the full, she began to dig into more serious matters than local tittle-tattle,

starting her own Wainthropp Detective Agency with the help of her young sidekick, Geoffrey, a reformed shoplifter, who carried his boss pillion on a red scooter. Her first case arose from an instance of fraud involving the post office where she worked part-time; and from then on, by infiltrating knitting circles or posing as a dinner lady, she constantly bemused the local constabulary's DCI Adams with her success rate. A fifth regular character, Geoffrey's girlfriend Janet, was introduced in later episodes.

The series was co-devised by David Cook, who had created the character of Hetty in his novel, *Missing Persons*.

HI-DE-HI!
UK (BBC) Situation Comedy. BBC 1 1981–8

Ted Bovis .... **Paul Shane**
Gladys Pugh .... **Ruth Madoc**
Jeffrey Fairbrother .... **Simon Cadell**
Spike Dixon .... **Jeffrey Holland**
Peggy Ollerenshaw .... **Su Pollard**
Fred Quilley .... **Felix Bowness**
Mr Partridge .... **Leslie Dwyer**
Yvonne Stewart-Hargreaves .... **Diane Holland**
Barry Stewart-Hargreaves .... **Barry Howard**
Sylvia .... **Nikki Kelly**
Betty .... **Rikki Howard**
Mary .... **Penny Irving**
Squadron Leader Clive Dempster, DFC ... **David Griffin**
The Twins (Bruce and Stanley) .... **The Webb Twins**
Tracey .... **Susan Beagley**
April .... **Linda Regan**
Dawn .... **Laura Jackson**
Julian Dalrymple-Sykes .... **Ben Aris**
Uncle Sammy Morris .... **Kenneth Connor**

Creators/Writers: **David Croft, Jimmy Perry**
Producers: **David Croft, John Kilby, Mike Stephens**

High jinks in a British holiday camp at the turn of the 1960s.

Beginning in the summer of 1959, this thinly veiled send-up of Butlins, Pontins and the like focused on events at Maplins holiday camp at Crimpton-on-Sea, progressing season by season into the early 1960s. The pilot programme (screened in 1980) saw the arrival of the members of staff. The new Entertainments Officer was the ineffective Jeffrey Fairbrother, a Cambridge archaeologist who decided to seek pastures new when his wife left him. Also new was young camp comic Spike Dixon, quickly corrupted when taken under the wing of wily camp host Ted Bovis. Fairbrother's assistant was valleys girl Gladys Pugh who tripled up as sports organizer and Radio Maplin announcer (rousing campers from their slumbers with a lilting 'Morning, campers'). Fairbrother instantly warmed her frigid heart, although her smouldering advances were never welcomed. Other members of the entertainments team were bent jockey Fred Quilley, now in charge of the camp horses, grouchy, boozy Punch-and-Judy man Mr Partridge ('Jolly Uncle Willie' to the kids he hated), snooty, fading ballroom stars Yvonne and Barry Stewart-Hargreaves, and a small group of Yellowcoats, whose job it was to cajole the campers into having fun, whether they liked it or not. Desperate to get in the thick of the action was daffy chalet maid Peggy Ollerenshaw, who longed to abandon her dustpan and brush in favour of a yellow jacket. Always in the background, issuing edicts but never showing his face, was the all-powerful but illiterate boss man, Joe Maplin. In later series, ex-RAF man Clive Dempster replaced Fairbrother in the entertainments hot seat.

Action centred on the glorious coarseness of everyday holiday-camp life. In the daytime, campers gathered around the Olympic-sized swimming pool to witness beauty contests and various slapstick competitions. In the evening they repaired to the Hawaiian Ballroom to be entertained by Ted's vulgar jokes and Spike's silly costumes. Unfortunately for real-life holiday camps, who were trying to live down their primitive past, the series was a huge hit and ran for eight years. Nostalgia was a key to its success, but so was authenticity, with co-writer Jimmy Perry drawing inspiration for the series from his time as a Butlins Red Coat. Perry also composed the theme song, 'Holiday Rock'.

HICKSON, JOAN
OBE (1906–98)

Although synonymous with Agatha Christie's geriatric sleuth MISS MARPLE, Northants-born Joan Hickson didn't arrive in St Mary Mead until she was nearly 80 years old. Her earlier TV credits included the roles of the receptionist in the 1950s series, *The Royalty*, housekeeper Mrs Peace in OUR MAN AT ST MARK'S, Mrs Morrow in *Good Girl* and Lady Harriet in *Poor Little Rich Girls*, plus a host of appearances in series like THE INVISIBLE MAN, BACHELOR FATHER, NANNY and *Time for Murder*.

HIGH CHAPARRAL, THE
US (NBC/David Dortort) Western. BBC 2 1967–71

Big John Cannon .... **Leif Erickson**
Buck Cannon .... **Cameron Mitchell**
Billy Blue Cannon .... **Mark Slade**
Manolito Montoya .... **Henry Darrow**
Victoria Cannon .... **Linda Cristal**
Don Sebastian Montoya .... **Frank Silvera**
Sam Butler .... **Don Collier**
Reno .... **Ted Markland**
Pedro .... **Roberto Contreras**
Joe .... **Robert Hoy**
Vasquero .... **Rodolfo Acosta**
Wind .... **Rudy Ramos**

Creator/Producer: **David Dortort**

A family struggles to make a living from its ranch.

In BONANZA the Cartwrights had their Ponderosa in Nevada. The Cannons in this series lived on The High Chaparral in Arizona Territory, some time in the 1870s. Head of the family was gritty, hard-working Big John

Cannon, assisted in his efforts to establish a cattle ranch by his blond son, Billy Blue, and by Buck, John's gruff but fun-loving younger brother. John's first wife was killed by Apaches in the first episode, but he then married Victoria Montoya, daughter of Mexican nobleman Don Sebastian Montoya. When she moved to The High Chaparral, so did her brother, Manolito.

Despite constant Indian attacks, wrangles with Mexicans and hassles from rustlers and other outlaws, Big John and his family never flinched from their fight with the land. Reno, Pedro and Joe were their ranch hands, working under the supervision of Sam Butler. When the naïve Blue was written out of the series towards its close, he was replaced by Wind, a half-breed who came to live with the Cannons. The programme's creator, David Dortort, was also the man behind *Bonanza*.

HIGHWAY
UK (Various) Religion. ITV 1983–93

Presenter: **Harry Secombe**

Executive Producer: **Bill Ward**

Easy-going Sunday evening hymns and chat from various locations around the British Isles.

Hosted by Harry Secombe from a different venue each week, *Highway* was a roving version of STARS ON SUNDAY, produced in turn by all the different ITV companies for the network. Harry (later Sir Harry) invited guests to sing religious songs, give readings or just chat about their lifestyles and spiritual feelings. Secombe himself provided a number of the songs in every programme. For the last series, in 1993, the programme was displaced to early afternoons, as ITV looked for bigger audiences at Sunday teatimes. Secombe returned with a new series, *Sunday Morning with Secombe*, in 1994, in which he chatted to guests at the venue for the week's *Morning Worship*, which then followed.

HIGHWAY PATROL
US (Ziv) Police Drama. ITV 1956–62

Chief Dan Mathews .... **Broderick Crawford**
Narrator .... **Art Gilmore**

Executive Producer: **Vernon E. Clark**

No-nonsense crimebusting with an American squad car officer.

There was only one regular in *Highway Patrol* and that was Chief Dan Matthews. Matthews, a chunky, determined, fast-talking police officer with a broken nose, worked for an unnamed force in an unnamed state (the emblems on the patrol cars read simply 'Highway Patrol'). His targets were criminals of all kinds – murderers, bank robbers, smugglers, hijackers and petty thieves – and by posting all-points bulletins, yelling 'Ten-Four' ('Message received and understood') and 'Ten-Twenty' ('Report your position') into his car intercom, the gravel-voiced Matthews always got his man.

With nearly all the action taking place out on the road, involving bikes and occasionally helicopters as well as cars, little was seen of Matthews's office base.

Highway Patrol was one of the founding fathers of TV cop shows, even though it came together on a minuscule budget. Over 150 half-hour episodes were made between 1955 and 1959.

HIGHWAY TO HEAVEN
US (NBC) Drama. ITV 1987–90

Jonathan Smith .... **Michael Landon**
Mark Gordon .... **Victor French**

Creator/Executive Producer: **Michael Landon**

An angel in training is sent to Earth to help people in trouble.

When Arthur Morton died, he went to Heaven and was groomed as an angel. With his name changed to Jonathan Smith, he was sent back to Earth to gain some experience of helping sad and worried people. He travelled the globe as a wandering labourer, accompanied by one of his first converts, a cynical cop named Mark Gordon. Smith opted for counselling, moral support and leadership by example as means of lightening the loads of others, but he could always call upon his angelic powers, if required. Both lead actors had previously appeared in Michael Landon's earlier success, LITTLE HOUSE ON THE PRAIRIE.

HILL, BENNY
(Alfred Hawthorne Hill; 1925–92)

Celebrated British funnyman whose saucy postcard style of humour made him a favourite around the world. Benny Hill was one British comedy export who made even the Americans laugh, and his cheeky grin and feigned air of innocence enabled him to get away with smutty jokes and innuendoes that would have died in the hands of other comics. They certainly wouldn't have been aired in peak hours. The hallmarks of his shows were send-ups of other TV personalities (whether they were Moira Anderson, Fanny Cradock or Jimmy Hill), comic creations like the saluting half-wit, Fred Scuttle, bawdy songs that exhibited his skill with words – such as his number-one hit, 'Ernie (The Fastest Milkman in the West)' – and, most provocatively, slapstick chases involving scantily clad women. Most of the time he was ably supported by stooges like Bob Todd, Henry McGee and Jack Wright. Hill's career began in music hall (including a period as a straight man to Reg Varney) and progressed to television via the radio comedy, *Educating Archie*. His TV debut came in 1949 and his first series for the BBC was shown in 1955. In 1964 he won plaudits for his portrayal of Bottom in *A Midsummer Night's Dream* and then, in 1969, Hill switched to Thames TV, where he stayed until his show was axed amid rows over sexism in 1989 (even though he had already toned down the voyeurism and ditched the steamy Hill's Angels dance troupe). Central was prepared to give him another bite

of the cherry three years later but Hill died of a heart attack before he could finish the series.

HILL, BERNARD
(1944–)

Manchester-born actor who won acclaim for his portrayal of Yosser 'Gissa Job' Hughes in BOYS FROM THE BLACKSTUFF. Previously Hill had played Gratus in I, CLAUDIUS and appeared in FOX (Vin Fox). He later starred as Lech Walesa in Channel 4's *Squaring the Circle* and as Mike in *Olly's Prison*, and appeared as DS Gavin Douglas in *Telltale*, Uncle Fred in LIPSTICK ON YOUR COLLAR, and Joe in the *Stages* presentation, *Speaking in Tongues*. He also played Len Tollit in the sitcom, *Once Upon a Time in the North*, Frank Nickle in CATHERINE COOKSON'S *The Gambling Man*, Edward Tulliver in *The Mill on the Floss* and Magwitch in *Great Expectations*. He has been seen in many single dramas and presented a factual series, *The Real History Show*.

HILL, HARRY
(Matthew Hall; 1964–)

Kent-born, bespectacled, surreal/off-beat comedian, a qualified doctor, who has made an obsession with badgers his trademark (along with pointy-collared shirts and pockets full of pens) and created a catchphrase out of 'What are the chances of that happening, eh?'. His first TV series, *Harry Hill's Fruit Fancies*, was a collection of six 15-minute, silent monochrome films, but vocal lunacy has since been re-established with the series, *Harry Hill*, in which he has been supported by Al Murray, Bert Kwouk and others.

HILL, JIMMY
OBE (1928–)

British soccer pundit, a former Brentford and Fulham footballer, and later manager of Coventry City, who broke into television with LWT, for which he became Head of Sport and Deputy Controller of Programmes. Via *On the Ball* (part of WORLD OF SPORT) and *The Big Match*, Hill arrived at the BBC, becoming its football expert during the 1970s and 1980s, and hosting MATCH OF THE DAY and other major events. He retired from the Corporation in 1998 and has since worked for Sky Sports. In the mid-1960s Hill was a consultant on the soccer soap, UNITED!.

HILL, Lord CHARLES
(1904–89)

Fondly remembered from the war years as the Radio Doctor, Charles Hill, one-time secretary of the British Medical Association, became Member of Parliament for Luton in 1950, serving in the Ministries of Food, Housing and Local Government, and Welsh Affairs, as well as occupying the positions of Postmaster-General and

Chancellor of the Duchy of Lancaster. He left Parliament in 1963 (he was a victim of Macmillan's 'Night of the Long Knives') and took over as Chairman of the Independent Television Authority. At the ITA he insisted that the ITV companies offered more time to ITN (a move that resulted in *News at Ten*) and oversaw the important 1967 franchise reviews. Surprisingly, he was transferred virtually overnight to the chairmanship of the BBC in the same year. This appointment was seen as an attempt by Prime Minister Harold Wilson to discipline the BBC's Director-General, Sir Hugh Greene (Greene and Wilson had fallen out). Hill remained with the Corporation until 1972, before becoming Chairman of Abbey National Building Society and Laporte Industries. During his time as BBC Chairman he was criticized for unhinging the delicate relationship between the Director-General and the Chairman, intervening in day-to-day decisions and concentrating greater power in the hands of the Governors.

HILL STREET BLUES

US (MTM) Police Drama. ITV/Channel 4 1981–9

Capt. Frank Furillo	**Daniel J. Travanti**
Sgt Phil Esterhaus	**Michael Conrad**
Officer Bobby Hill	**Michael Warren**
Officer Andy Renko	**Charles Haid**
Joyce Davenport	**Veronica Hamel**
Det. Mick Belker	**Bruce Weitz**
Lt. Ray Calletano	**Rene Enriquez**
Det. Johnny 'JD' LaRue	**Kiel Martin**
Det. Neal Washington	**Taurean Blacque**
Lt. Howard Hunter	**James B. Sikking**
Sgt/Lt. Henry Goldblume	**Joe Spano**
Officer/Sgt Lucy Bates	**Betty Thomas**
Grace Gardner	**Barbara Babcock**
Fay Furillo	**Barbara Bosson**
Det./Lt. Alf Chesley	**Gerry Black**
Officer Leo Schnitz	**Robert Hirschfield**
Officer Joe Coffey	**Ed Marinaro**
Chief Fletcher P. Daniels	**Jon Cypher**
Officer Robin Tataglia/Belker	**Lisa Sutton**
Assistant DA Irwin Bernstein	**George Wyner**
Jesus Martinez	**Trinidad Silva**
Det. Harry Garibaldi	**Ken Olin**
Det. Patricia 'Patsy' Mayo	**Mimi Kuzyk**
Mayor Ozzie Cleveland	**J. A. Preston**
Sgt Stanislaus Jablonski	**Robert Prosky**
Lt. Norman Buntz	**Dennis Franz**
Celeste Patterson	**Judith Hansen**
Sidney Thurston ('Sid the Snitch')	**Peter Jurasik**
Officer Patrick Flaherty	**Robert Clohessy**
Officer Tina Russo	**Megan Gallagher**
Officer Raymond	**David Selburg**

Creators/Executive Producers: **Steven Bochco, Michael Kozoll**
Producers: **Gregory Hoblit, David Anspaugh, Anthony Yerkovich**

Life with the officers of a busy police station on the seedier side of town.

The Hill Street Station was based in the wrong side of a large, unnamed eastern American city (the exteriors were done in Chicago). Surrounded by the worst elements – drug-pushers, prostitutes, racketeers, and more – the policeman's lot at Hill Street was not a happy one. This series revealed how the motley band of law-enforcers struggled to cope with daily trauma, and witnessed its effect on their personal lives and working relationships.

In semi-serial form, the programme followed a day's events in Hill Street, from the morning roll-call to last thing at night. The show's own roll-call was as follows. Head of the station was Captain Frank Furillo, a patient, quietly spoken, firm commander. Dedicated and responsible, he found himself dealing not only with events on the streets but also with police bureaucracy and turmoil in his personal life. Plagued for alimony by his ex-wife, Fay, he struck up an affair with defence attorney Joyce Davenport which turned into marriage. At work, however, they remained professional adversaries.

Beneath Furillo was Sgt Phil Esterhaus, a fatherly head sergeant who urged his troops, 'Let's be careful out there.' When actor Michael Conrad died, three years into the run, Esterhaus was written out (having had a heart attack while making love to widow Grace Gardner). Then there was scruffy undercover detective Mick Belker (known to bite those he arrested), SWAT squad lieutenant Howard Hunter, toothpick-chewing plainclothesman Neal Washington, his alcoholic partner J. D. LaRue, Detective Alf Chesley and the sensitive community affairs officer, Henry Goldblume. Completing the team were the station's hispanic second-in-command, Ray Calletano, the black/white patrolman team of Bobby Hill and Andy Renko (who were shot in the opening episode), and Lucy Bates, with her partner, Joe Coffey. Leo Schnitz was the desk officer and Fletcher Daniels was the smarmy, ambitious police chief who later ran for mayor.

Added over the years were Robin Tataglia (an officer who married Belker), Detective Harry Garibaldi, Sgt Stan Jablonski (Esterhaus's replacement), Detective Patsy Mayo, Officer Tina Russo, Officer Pat Flaherty, Officer Raymond and the abrasive Lt. Norman Buntz, on the face of it a lout, but in fact nobody's fool. The local underworld was also represented, by informer Sid the Snitch and cocky Jesus Martinez, leader of the Diablos gang, as were the city's legal eagles by prosecutor Irwin Bernstein (as well as by Joyce Davenport).

Hill Street Blues was applauded by critics but was not a hit in the ratings. Nevertheless, it won eight Emmys in one season (a record) and attracted a dedicated following. Its success came from its subtle juxtaposition of humour and human drama, and from its realistic characterizations. The storylines were equally true to life. The cops did not always come out on top. Sometimes the cases were never resolved. On other occasions, the cops themselves were seen to be the bad guys. Handheld, news-style camerawork added to the realism. In short, the '*Blues*' changed the face of American cop shows: car chases and shoot-outs were no longer enough after this series. The poignant theme music, by Mike Post, was a UK hit in 1982. Buntz and Sid the Snitch eventually went on to a short-lived spin-off, *Beverly Hills Buntz*.

HINE
UK (ATV) Drama. ITV 1971

Joe Hine .... **Barrie Ingham**
Walpole Gibb .... **Colin Gordon**
Astor Harris .... **Paul Eddington**
Sir Christopher Pendle .... **Michael Goodliffe**

Creator/Producer: **Wilfred Greatorex**

The tough, grimy world of an international arms-dealer.

Joe Hine sold weapons for a living and made enemies along the way. A lone trader, he battled against giant corporations, chancing his arm in a multi-billion-pound undercover market in defence equipment. His chief rivals were Walpole Gibb and Astor Harris, men who set out to destroy him. Sick of the hypocritical business, Hine always sought to pull off the last big deal that would allow him to retire in style.

HINES, FRAZER
(1944–)

Yorkshire-born actor, best known as EMMERDALE's Joe Sugden, a role he played off and on for over 20 years. His TV debut came as Jan in *The Silver Sword*, and he also played Tim in *Smugglers' Cove* and Tim Birch in EMERGENCY – WARD 10, before travelling with DOCTOR WHO as Highland warrior Jamie McCrimmon. Among his other credits have been appearances in COMPACT, Z CARS, CORONATION STREET and DUTY FREE. His first wife was actress Gemma Craven and his second wife is sportswoman Liz Hobbs.

HIRD, Dame THORA
OBE (1913–)

Morecambe-born actress Thora Hird has become a national institution. Although much of her work has fallen into the comedy vein, she has proved herself possibly even more adept in straight drama, as evidenced by her moving monologues, *A Cream Cracker under the Settee* and *Waiting for the Telegram* for Alan Bennett's TALKING HEADS series. In the world of sitcoms, Hird will be remembered, to a lesser and greater degree, for her performances as disgruntled housewife Thora Blacklock in MEET THE WIFE, boarding-house proprietor Thora Parker in *Ours is a Nice House*, funeral director Ivy Unsworth in IN LOVING MEMORY, Salvation Army Captain Emily Ridley in *Hallelujah!* and Edie Pegden, the tutting ringleader of the ladies, in LAST OF THE SUMMER WINE. Among her many other credits have been the hymn series, *Praise Be* (host), and roles in series as varied as THE ADVENTURES OF ROBIN HOOD, ALL CREATURES GREAT AND SMALL, *The First Lady* (councillor Sarah Danby), *Flesh and Blood* (Mabel Brassington) and *Goggle Eyes* (Mrs

Harrington). There have also been numerous single dramas like *A Kind of Loving* in 1962, *Memento Mori* in 1992 and *Lost for Words* in 1999, in which she returned to the part of the mother (this time a stroke victim) of writer Deric Longden that she had first played in the *Screen One* presentation, *Wide-Eyed and Legless*, in 1993. Her daughter is actress Janette Scott.

HIS LORDSHIP ENTERTAINS
See HARK AT BARKER.

HISLOP, IAN
(1960–)

English humorist, comic writer and satirist. Editor of *Private Eye* for over a decade and a team captain on HAVE I GOT NEWS FOR YOU. Hislop's other TV work has included scripts for THREE OF A KIND and, with Nick Newman, *About Face*, SPITTING IMAGE, *Harry Enfield and Chums* and MURDER MOST HORRID. He and Newman also penned the *Screen One* comedy, *Gobble*. In quite a different vein, Hislop also presented *Canterbury Tales*, Channel 4's review of the Church of England in the 20th century.

HITCHCOCK, Sir ALFRED
(1899–1980)

Celebrated British film director whose television work, although limited, is listed among TV's all-time classics. In the US-made ALFRED HITCHCOCK PRESENTS (later extended into *The Alfred Hitchcock Hour*) he gave viewers an anthology of thrillers, not all directed but at least all overseen by the Master of Suspense himself. He also appeared on screen to top and tail each story, mostly with short quirky or bizarre anecdotes which had little to do with the main feature. In the mid-1980s, after his death, he resurfaced as host of a new run of *Alfred Hitchcock Presents*, his appearances coming courtesy of colourized old footage from the original series.

HITCH-HIKER'S GUIDE TO THE GALAXY, THE
UK (BBC) Situation Comedy. BBC 2 1981

Arthur Dent .... **Simon Jones**
Ford Prefect .... **David Dixon**
The Book .... **Peter Jones** (*voice only*)
Zaphod Beeblebrox .... **Mark Wing-Davey**
Trillian .... **Sandra Dickinson**
Marvin .... **David Learner**
Stephen Moore (*voice*)

Creator/Writer: **Douglas Adams**
Producer: **Alan J. W. Bell**

An intergalactic-guidebook compiler and his human friend flee Earth's destruction and hitch rides across the universe.

Ford Prefect had been a researcher for the electronic *Hitch-Hiker's Guide to the Galaxy*, the ultimate universal reference book. With the book badly needing an update, he had been dispatched to Earth to gather information, remaining there for 15 years and making friends with Arthur Dent. One day, learning that the Earth was in imminent danger of demolition to make way for a hyperspace bypass, Prefect revealed that he was not from Guildford after all and urged Dent to escape with him aboard the demolition spacecraft. Unfortunately, the ship was manned by the ugly, sadistic Vogons, a race of green aliens who terrorized others with appalling poetry. Fleeing their clutches, Prefect and Dent joined the *Heart of Gold*, a spaceship in the hands of two-headed former con-man and part-time Galactic President, Zaphod Beeblebrox, who was heading for the lost planet of Magrathea. His crew consisted of pilot Trillian (actually a former Earthling named Trisha McMillan) and a manic-depressive robot, Marvin the Paranoid Android, who suffered from pains in his diodes.

As the duo thumbed their way around the galaxy, and the bemused Arthur hunted for a good cup of tea, they encountered Slartibartfast (architect of the fjords), the Golgafrinchians (former middle-managers and telephone operatives who had been banned from their planet because of their uselessness) and pan-dimensional beings dressed up as white mice who were desperately seeking the Ultimate Question to Life, the Universe and Everything. They already knew the answer: it was 42. The hitch-hikers also visited Milliways, the Restaurant at the End of the Universe, and were entertained by the talking Dish of the Day and galactic rock star Hotblack Desiato, before ending up on prehistoric Earth, contemplating the events that were to engulf the planet in the aeons ahead.

A mixture of fantasy, satire and pun, the series employed some innovative special effects, including the use of video games to stage space battles and mock-computer graphics to show pages from the book. It needed such efforts, since the original Radio 4 version – with that medium's decidedly cheaper advantage of mere suggestion – had enjoyed a cult following.

HMS BRILLIANT
See **SAILOR**.

HOBLEY, McDONALD
(Dennys Jack Valentine McDonald-Hobley; 1917–87)

One of Britain's earliest on-screen TV announcers, McDonald Hobley, complete with bow tie and dinner jacket, first appeared on the BBC in 1946, sharing announcing shifts with Jasmine Bligh, Sylvia Peters and, later, Mary Malcolm. During the same period he also presented the magazine programme, KALEIDOSCOPE, and appeared with Mr Pastry (Richard Hearne), this coming after a pre-war stint in the theatre, and radio work in the Far East during the hostilities. After ten years with the BBC, Hobley moved to ABC. Born in the Falkland Islands, one of Hobley's last TV contributions

came in a Channel 4 programme about the South Atlantic dependencies.

HODGE, PATRICIA
(1946–)

British actress, cast in comedy as well as straight drama roles. Among her TV highlights have been the part of the plummy barrister, Phyllida Trant, in RUMPOLE OF THE BAILEY, Mary Fisher in THE LIFE AND LOVES OF A SHE DEVIL, TV presenter/detective Jemima Shore in JEMIMA SHORE INVESTIGATES, Lady Julia Verinder in *The Moonstone*, and the title role in THE CLONING OF JOANNA MAY. Hodge played Sybilla Howarth in THE OTHER 'ARF, starred as Penny Milburn in HOLDING THE FORT and as Julia Merrygrove in *Rich Tea and Sympathy*, and appeared as solicitor Geraldine Hackstraw in THE LEGACY OF REGINALD PERRIN. She has also popped up in episodes of SOFTLY, SOFTLY, EDWARD AND MRS SIMPSON, THE PROFESSIONALS, NANNY, ROBIN OF SHERWOOD, THE ADVENTURES OF SHERLOCK HOLMES, INSPECTOR MORSE and more, and was seen in the dramas, THE NAKED CIVIL SERVANT and *The One and Only Phyllis Dixey*, among others.

HOGAN, PAUL
(1939–)

Australian comedian, a former construction-worker who hit the box office big time in the 1980s with the film, *Crocodile Dundee*. In between, *The Paul Hogan Show* was extremely popular Down Under and was imported to the UK by Channel 4. Supported by the likes of Delvene Delaney and John Cornell, Hogan used the 'Benny Hill'-type sketch show to introduce a range of wacky characters like Leo Wanker and Hoges, a 'no-poofters' man-of-the-world, always dressed in sleeveless shirts, shorts and football socks. It helped put Foster's lager and Vegemite on the UK map. Hogan married actress Linda Kozlowski in 1990.

HOGAN'S HEROES
US (Bing Crosby) Situation Comedy. ITV 1967–71

Col. Robert Hogan	**Bob Crane**
Col. Wilhelm Klink	**Werner Klemperer**
Sgt Hans Schulz	**John Banner**
Cpl. Louis LeBeau	**Robert Clary**
Cpl. Peter Newkirk	**Richard Dawson**
Cpl. James Kinchloe	**Ivan Dixon**
Sgt Andrew Carter	**Larry Hovis**
Helga	**Cynthia Lynn**
Hilda	**Sigrid Valdis**

Creators: **Bernard Fein, Albert S. Ruddy**
Producer: **Ed Feldman**

Allied soldiers rule the roost at a Nazi POW camp.

Somewhere in the Nazi empire was Stalag 13, a prisoner-of-war camp nominally commanded by the monocled

Colonel Klink and his inept, fat sidekick, Sgt Schultz. In actuality, although their captors didn't realize it, the camp was run by its inmates and the true supremo was the shrewd, wisecracking American, Colonel Robert Hogan. Hogan was ably supported by a troop of versatile Allied soldiers. These were LeBeau, a Frenchman with culinary skills, Newkirk, a brash Cockney, Sgt Carter, the skilful but slow farmboy, and a black electronics genius, Corporal Kinchloe. Between them, the prisoners ran a useful Allied operational base. They supplied intelligence, they assisted refugees and they printed counterfeit money, but, above all, they had a wonderful time. This was more of a hotel than a prison. By lifting the wire fence in garage door style, they could pop out to take the air or seek entertainment in the town. They also had their own sauna in which to sweat off the delights of LeBeau's wonderful Gallic cuisine. Little wonder they never sought to escape.

The series echoed the far more serious Billy Wilder film, *Stalag 17*, which was released in 1953, starred William Holden and blended humour with moments of drama and realism.

HOLDING THE FORT
UK (LWT) Situation Comedy. ITV 1980–2

Russell Milburn .... **Peter Davison**
Penny Milburn .... **Patricia Hodge**
Fitzroy 'Fitz' .... **Matthew Kelly**

Creators/Writers: **Laurence Marks, Maurice Gran**
Producer: **Derrick Goodwin**

A husband and wife try role-reversal.

Young married couple Russell and Penny Milburn had a baby daughter, Emma. However, instead of Russell being the breadwinner, it was Penny who returned to work, reclaiming her old job as a captain with the army. Russell stayed at home, looked after Emma and dabbled with his own brewery, housed in the basement, generally hindered by his lifelong pal, Fitz. With Russell and Fitz both ardent pacifists, Penny's source of income was a cause of constant friction.

When *Holding the Fort* ended, after three seasons, Fitz was given his own spin-off, *Relative Strangers* (Channel 4 1985–7), in which he was surprised by John, his 18-year-old son (played by Mark Farmer), a child he had never known about.

HOLIDAY
UK (BBC) Travel. BBC 1 1969–

Presenters: **Cliff Michelmore, Joan Bakewell, Anne Gregg, Frank Bough, John Carter, Desmond Lynam, Eamonn Holmes, Anneka Rice, Jill Dando, Craig Doyle**

Long-running holiday magazine.

A tourism brochure of the air, *Holiday* is now the oldest travel review programme on British television. Initially its title incorporated the year in question, beginning with *Holiday 69*, but that idea has now been dropped. Throughout, its concept has been quite simple: holiday destinations at home and abroad have been featured and appraised in pre-filmed reports, with plaudits given to the best features and less generous comments made about the limitations of each resort. The very first programme included an item on Torremolinos; however, some destinations over the years have been attacked as being too fanciful and beyond the limits of the ordinary viewer's pocket. To complement the recorded inserts, *Holiday* has also offered general advice for travellers, publicized last-minute bargains and investigated tourist complaints.

Holiday was once a stalwart of BBC 1's Sunday evening schedules and its Gordon Giltrap theme music, 'Heartsong', led nicely into the God slot during the dark winter months. It has since moved to a peak-time weeknight position. Cliff Michelmore was the chief presenter for 17 years, but his successors have proved less durable, some, like Desmond Lynam and Anneka Rice, lasting only one or two seasons. Anne Gregg spent ten years with the programme, enjoying varying degrees of prominence; and among the show's many contributing reporters have been Fyfe Robertson, Kieran Prendiville, Sarah Kennedy, Bill Buckley, John Pitman, Kathy Tayler, Kevin Woodford, Sankha Guha and Monty Don. John Carter was one of the 'experts' in the first series and remained close to the programme for many years. From 1988 Carter was involved with Thames TV's rival programme, *Wish You Were Here . . . ?*, which began in 1974. *Wish You Were Here . . . ?* was introduced chiefly by Judith Chalmers, who was partnered over several series by Chris Kelly. Mary Nightingale has been its latest anchor.

Since 1994, *Holiday* has been joined by a sister programme, *Summer Holiday*, providing more topical information during the summer season. There was also a budget version, *Holiday on a Shoestring*, in 1999. Another spin-off was *Holiday: Fasten Your Seatbelt* (1996–8), in which the programme's presenters and other celebrities attempted to perform holiday jobs such as air stewardess, chalet maid or cast member at Walt Disney World.

HOLLAND, JEFFREY
(1946–)

Midlands-born comedian and comic actor, much seen in company with Russ Abbot on his *Madhouse* shows and on *The Les Dennis Laughter Show*. Holland played up-and-coming holiday-camp comedian Spike Dixon in HI-DE-HI! and remained with the Perry/Croft repertory company for YOU RANG, M'LORD?, taking the role of head of the household James Twelvetrees, and OH, DOCTOR BEECHING!, as station master Cecil Parkin.

HOLLAND, JOOLS
(Julian Holland; 1958–)

London-born presenter, formerly keyboards player with the group, Squeeze. Holland moved into television as host of the controversial rock show, THE TUBE, following this up with the more eclectic *Later with Jools Holland* and its New Year extension, *Jools's Annual Hootenanny*. Holland has also chaired a relaunch of JUKE BOX JURY, played himself in the comedy, *The Groovy Fellers*, hosted the music and comedy show, *The Happening*, supported Chris Evans on DON'T FORGET YOUR TOOTHBRUSH, introduced the musical travelogue, *Beat Route*, and contributed to the architectural series, *Building Sites*.

HOLLAND, MARY

British actress famed not for a television series but for her role in a long-running commercial. As Katie, Mary was TV's Oxo mum for 18 years from 1958. When the advert was eventually dropped in 1976, Holland was snapped up by Electrolux and later made a commercial for Oxo rivals, Bovril.

HOLLYOAKS

UK (Mersey) Drama. Channel 4 1995–

Kurt Benson	Jeremy Edwards
Ollie Benson	Paul Leyshon
Lucy Benson	Kerrie Taylor
Natasha Andersen	Shebah Ronay
Greg Andersen	Alvin Stardust
Sarah Andersen	Anna Martland
Louise Taylor	Brett O'Brien
Maddie Parker	Yasmin Bannerman
Tony Hutchinson	Nick Pickard
Jambo Bolton	William Mellor
Lisa Bolton	Isabel Murphy
Dawn Cunningham	Lisa Williamson
Angela Cunningham	Liz Stooke
Max Cunningham	Matthew Littler
Jude Cunningham	Davinia Taylor
Cindy Cunningham	Stephanie Waring
Bazz	Toby Sawyer
Lewis Richardson	Ben Hull
Mandy Richardson	Sarah Dunn
Ruth Osborne/Benson	Terri Dwyer
Jack Osborne	James McKenna
Mrs Osborne	Lynda Rooke
Julie Matthews	Julie Buckfield
Rob Hawthorn	Warren Derosa
Dermot Ashton	Lauren Beales
Susi Harrison	Deborah Chad
Carol Groves	Natalie Casey
Benny Stringer	Matthew Morgan
Sol Patrick	Paul Danan
Kate Patrick	Natasha Symms
Gina Patrick	Dannielle Brent
Mr Richardson	David McAlister
Mrs Richardson	Kathryn George
Finn	James Redmond
Jasmine Bates	Elly Fairman
Sean Tate	Daniel Pape
Sam 'OB' O'Brien	Darren Jeffries
Emily Taylor	Lorna Pegler
Adam Morgan	David Brown
Luke Morgan	Gary Lucy
Beth Morgan	Elizabeth O'Grady
Zara Morgan	Kelly Greenwood
Andy Morgan	Ross Davidson
Sue Morgan	Eve White
Darren Osborne	Ashley Taylor-Dawson
Paul Millington	Zander Ward
Sam Smallwood	Tim Downie
Nikki Sullivan	Wendy Glenn
Anna Green	Lisa Kay
Mark Gibbs	Colin Parry
Alex Bell	Martino Lazzeri
Geri Hudson	Joanna Taylor
Ben Davies	Marcus Patrick
Izzy Cornwell	Elize du Toit
Taylor James	Michael Price
Lorraine Wilson	Jo-Anne Knowles
Victoria Hutchinson	Fiona Mollison
Jacqui Hudson	Julie Peasgood

Creator: **Phil Redmond**
Producers: **Phil Redmond, Jo Hallows**

Teen soap set in a comfortable northern suburb.

Unlike creator Phil Redmond's earlier angst-ridden offerings, GRANGE HILL and BROOKSIDE, *Hollyoaks* initially played on the lighter side of life, following the social scene among a group of middle-class kids in a pleasant suburb of Chester. The thrust of the action centred on teen crushes, clothes, cars and other adolescent worries; but darker themes emerged as the series progressed, with broken marriages, law-breaking, drugs, death and other less wholesome activities getting into the picture.

The main characters at the outset were motor-mad Kurt Benson, confident Natasha Andersen (soon to meet a sad end), theatrically-minded Louise Taylor, trendy Maddie Parker, social struggler Tony Hutchinson, rebellious joker Jambo Bolton, and interior-design shopworker Dawn Cunningham. New kids arrived on the block as the series advanced to twice a week (sometimes more). Among the more mature members of the cast was Greg Andersen, Natasha's dad, who was landlord of the local boozer, The Dog and Pond, and who (in keeping with his actor's glitzy past) was well into 1960s and 1970s music. In autumn 2000 some 'adult' episodes, screened later in the evening, were shown.

HOLLYWOOD

UK (Thames) Historical Documentary. ITV 1980

Narrator: **James Mason**

Writers/Producers: **Kevin Brownlow, David Gill**

A detailed study of the age of the silent movie.

Subtitled *A Celebration of the American Silent Film* when shown in the USA, *Hollywood* won much acclaim as a well-researched, thoughtful history of the great days of the US film industry. Project masterminds Kevin Brownlow and David Gill took the trouble to explore in depth the background to the world of the silent movie, explaining the context of certain films and, most importantly, screening them in the best possible condition, with appropriate music and at the proper speed. This revealed how these early pieces of cinema were really artistic jewels and not the jumpy, jerky bits of footage most people thought them to be. The contributions of the directors, writers, cameramen and performers of the day were also evaluated in this 13-part documentary. Carl Davis supplied the grand theme music.

HOLLYWOOD GREATS, THE
UK (BBC) Documentary. BBC 1 1977–85; 1999

Narrators: **Barry Norman, Ian McShane**

Producers: **Margaret Sharp, Richard Downes**

Warts-and-all documentary portraits of Hollywood's legendary film stars.

Intermittently, over eight years, BBC film critic Barry Norman compiled a collection of biographies of the biggest names in the movie world. Using film clips and interviews to illustrate his points, Norman was not afraid to destroy a few myths in his interpretation of the stars' work and private lives. Among those featured were Judy Garland, Charles Laughton, Ronald Coleman, Joan Crawford, Clark Gable, Errol Flynn, Spencer Tracy, Jean Harlow, Humphrey Bogart, Groucho Marx, Charlie Chaplin, Marilyn Monroe, Edward G. Robinson, John Wayne, Henry Fonda and Steve McQueen. The last contribution by Norman was a one-off film on Bing Crosby, shown in January 1985.

In 1999 the series was resurrected as simply *Hollywood Greats* for profiles of Cary Grant, Bette Davis, Robert Mitchum and Katharine Hepburn. Barry Norman having departed for Sky TV, the narration was handled by Ian McShane.

HOLM, Sir IAN
(Ian Holm Cuthbert; 1932–)

British actor, largely on stage and screen but also prominent on television, including as narrator on series like TELEVISION and SURVIVAL. The highlight to date has been the part of disgraced spy Bernard Samson in GAME, SET AND MATCH, which Holm accepted having already supported Alec Guinness in another drama of subterfuge, TINKER, TAILOR, SOLDIER, SPY. Holm also starred in *Frankenstein* (a MYSTERY AND IMAGINATION story), played Paul Presset in the intense drama, *We, the Accused*, and took the parts of Napoleon in *Napoleon and Love* and Himmler in HOLOCAUST. He appeared as Michael in the trilogy, *Conjugal Rites*, assumed the guise of J. M. Barrie in the *Play of the Week* trilogy, *The Lost Boys*, played Hercule Poirot in a one-off thriller, *Murder by the Book*, and was seen as Pod in *The Borrowers* and Patrick in *Last of the Blonde Bombshells*, in addition to parts in a host of heavyish dramas and classics like *Uncle Vanya*, *The Misanthrope* and *King Lear* (Lear himself). He married his third wife, actress Penelope Wilton, in 1991.

HOLMES, EAMONN
(1959–)

Belfast-born presenter of current affairs, sport and magazine programmes, chiefly associated with GMTV. His TV career began with Ulster Television, where he covered farming and sport after training as a journalist. He took over as host of *Good Evening Ulster* from Gloria Hunniford and followed her to the UK mainland to host *Open Air*, *Pot Black Timeframe*, HOLIDAY, *Oddballs*, *How Do They Do That?* and THE NATIONAL LOTTERY LIVE among other programmes.

HOLNESS, BOB
(1928–)

Radio and television personality, beginning his career in his native South Africa in 1955. After a number of years with Radios 1 and 2, Radio Luxembourg and LBC in London, Holness found himself an unlikely cult figure among teenagers in the 1980s, thanks to his long-running quiz show, BLOCKBUSTERS. He later hosted another quiz, *Raise the Roof*, and the revival of CALL MY BLUFF. Among his earlier TV credits were the game shows, *Take a Letter* and *Junior Criss Cross Quiz*, and, more seriously, WORLD IN ACTION and WHAT THE PAPERS SAY.

HOLOCAUST
US (NBC/Titus) Drama. BBC 1 1978

Dr Josef Weiss	**Fritz Weaver**
Berta Weiss	**Rosemary Harris**
Karl Weiss	**James Woods**
Inga Helms/Weiss	**Meryl Streep**
Rudi Weiss	**Joseph Bottoms**
Anna Weiss	**Blanche Baker**
Moses Weiss	**Sam Wanamaker**
Erik Dorf	**Michael Moriarty**
Marta Dorf	**Deborah Norton**
Kurt Dorf	**Robert Stephens**
Reinhard Heydrich	**David Warner**
Heinrich Himmler	**Ian Holm**
Adolf Eichmann	**Tom Bell**

Writer: **Gerald Green**
Executive Producer: **Herb Brodkin**
Producer: **Robert Berger**

Controversial dramatization of the persecution of the Jews by the Nazis.

This grim, four-part drama, screened on consecutive nights by the BBC, recounted the atrocities of World War II, with particular focus on the plight of European Jews and their persecution and extermination by the Nazis. The Weiss family from Berlin, headed by Dr Josef Weiss, represented the Judaic race, and the character of lawyer Erik Dorf was seen as a manifestation of Nazi ambition. Their respective lives were charted from the year 1935 to the end of hostilities. Despite criticism for turning one of the most horrific periods in history into a semi-soap opera, with sentimental music, pointless dialogue and inevitably subdued horrors, the series became a moving experience for most viewers and won numerous awards.

HOME AND AWAY
Australia (Network 7) Drama. ITV 1989–2000/Channel 5 2001–

Tom Fletcher	Roger Oakley
Pippa Fletcher/Ross	Vanessa Downing
	Debra Lawrance
Celia Stewart	Fiona Spence
Alf Stewart	Ray Meagher
Ruth 'Roo' Stewart	Justine Clarke
Ailsa Hogan/Stewart	Judy Nunn
Donald Fisher	Norman Coburn
Lance Smart	Peter Vroom
Sally Keating/Fletcher	Kate Ritchie
Carly Morris/Lucini	Sharyn Hodgson
Lynn Davenport/Fletcher	Helena Bozich
Al Simpson	Terence Donovan
Bobby Simpson/Morgan	Nicolle Dickson
Sophie Simpson	Rebekah Elmaloglou
Martin Dibble	Craig Thompson
Viv	Mouche Phillips
Morag Bellingham	Cornelia Frances
Frank Morgan	Alex Papps
Steven Matheson	Adam Willits
Matt Wilson	Greg Benson
Marilyn Chambers/Fisher	Emily Symons
Emma Jackson	Dannii Minogue
Grant Mitchell	Craig McLachlan
Ben Lucini	Julian McMahon
Adam Cameron	Mat Stevenson
Michael Ross	Dennis Coard
Blake	Les Hill
Karen	Belinda Jarrett
Nick Parrish	Bruce Roberts
Simon	Richard Norton
Haydn	Andrew Hill
David Croft	Guy Pearce
Lucinda Croft	Dee Smart
Ryan	Alastair MacDougall
Shane Parrish	Dieter Brummer
Damian Roberts	Matt Doran
Sam Marshall	Ryan Clark
Greg	Ross Newton
Finlay Roberts	Tina Thomsen
Irene Roberts	Lynne McGranger
Luke Cunningham	John Adam
Tug O'Neale	Tristan Bancks
Roxanne Miller	Lisa Lackey
Sarah Taylor	Laura Vazquez
Angel Brooks/Parrish	Melissa George
Jack Wilson	Daniel Amalm
Rob Storey	Matthew Lilley
Shannon Reed	Isla Fisher
Curtis Reed	Shane Ammann
Donna Bishop	Nicola Quilter
Selina Cook	Tempany Deckert
Travis Nash	Nic Testoni
Joel Nash	David Woodley
Natalie Nash	Antoinette Byron
Tom Nash	Graeme Squires
Gypsy Nash	Kimberley Cooper
Rebecca Nash	Belinda Emmett
Jesse McGregor	Ben Unwin
Peta Janossi	Aleetza Wood
Hayley Smith	Rebecca Cartwright
Will Smith	Zac Drayson
Justine Welles	Bree Desborough
Vinnie Patterson	Ryan Kwanten
Chloe Fraser	Kristy Wright
James Fraser	Michael Piccirilli
Duncan Stewart	Brendan McKensy
Mitch McColl	Cameron Welsh
Harry Keller	Justin Melvey
Shauna Bradley	Kylie Watson
Nick Smith	Chris Egan
Colleen Smart	Lyn Collingwood

Creator/Executive Producer: **Alan Bateman**

Life with troubled kids in the fictitious Australian resort of Summer Bay.

Home and Away was broadcast by Australia's Seven Network, the station which gave away NEIGHBOURS in 1985. It was perceived as a rival to that series not only in its native country but also in the UK, where it was purchased by ITV to run head to head with *Neighbours* at lunchtimes and in the early evening.

Set in the coastal town of Summer Bay (it was *always* summer), near Sydney, *Home and Away* initially focused on foster-parents Tom and Pippa Fletcher, who had moved to a run-down caravan park after Tom had lost his job. Tom died of a heart attack in his car early on, and his wife, Pippa, then soldiered on alone (albeit with a different actress in the role) before marrying Michael Ross. Among the other prominent citizens of Summer Bay were local headmaster Donald Fisher, know-all grocer/bait-shop owner Alf Stewart, his wife Ailsa, and teacher Grant Mitchell (played by Craig McLachlan, poached from *Neighbours*). The kids were initially headed by Bobby Simpson (one-time co-owner with Ailsa of the local restaurant, The Summer Bay Diner), Carly Morris (later married to former soldier Ben Lucini), orphan Adam Cameron and the studious Steven Matheson, but new generations of youngsters made their way to Summer Bay over the years as, melodramatically, the series mingled tales of romance, death, family secrets and other scandals. One episode was filmed in Ironbridge, Shropshire.

HOME TO ROOST
UK (Yorkshire) Situation Comedy. ITV 1985–90

Henry Willows	John Thaw
Matthew Willows	Reece Dinsdale
Enid Thompson	Elizabeth Bennett
Fiona Fennell	Joan Blackham

Writer: **Eric Chappell**
Producers: **Vernon Lawrence, David Reynolds**

A father's life is turned upside down when his grown-up son returns home.

With his parents divorced, 17-year-old Matthew Willows had lived with his mother – until she threw him out. In him she recognized the same stubbornness and other character traits that had led to her separation from his father, Henry, and when Matthew decided to move in with his dad the sparks began to fly. Henry had long been accustomed to living life at his own pace, in his own grumpy way and only for himself. Now there was a cuckoo in the nest, and what's more this cuckoo was a younger version of himself. The result was a series of generation-gap conflicts, as father and son did domestic battle. Enid was Henry's housekeeper (actress Elizabeth Bennett reprised the role for the American version, *You Again*, starring Jack Klugman), replaced in later editions by the new daily, Fiona Fennell. Rebecca Lacey occasionally dropped in as Julie, Matthew's sister.

HONEY LANE

See **MARKET IN HONEY LANE.**

HONEYCOMBE, GORDON
(1936–)

Versatile Gordon Honeycombe is remembered by most viewers as one of ITN's longest-serving newscasters, joining the network in 1965. Honeycombe entered broadcasting in radio in Hong Kong and then became a member of the Royal Shakespeare Company. After 12 years at ITN, he left after a dispute over a firefighters' strike, which he publicly supported, and concentrated instead on his successful writing career. He has had a number of books published and has scripted three TV plays. A keen genealogist, he hosted *Family History* for the BBC in 1979 and also acted as narrator on *Arthur C. Clarke's Mysterious World* for YTV. In 1984 he resumed newsreading with TV-am, staying five years before returning to the stage.

HONG KONG BEAT, THE
UK (BBC) Documentary. BBC 1 1978

Producer: **John Purdie**

A nine-part study of policing in the cramped colony of Hong Kong.

Focusing on the activities of the British Colonial Force as they provided law and order in Hong Kong's busy, lively streets, *The Hong Kong Beat* won much acclaim and also gave rise to its fair share of controversy. It watched as local policemen rounded up the illegal immigrants, drug-pushers and other social nuisances which made policing this part of the world so complicated, hazardous and unique. The programme's theme music was a Top 30 hit for Richard Denton and Martin Cook in 1978.

HONG KONG PHOOEY
US (Hanna-Barbera) Cartoon. BBC 1 1975

Voices:

Penrod 'Penry' Pooch/Hong Kong Phooey	**Scatman Crothers**
Sgt Flint	**Joe E. Ross**
Rosemary	**Kathy Gory**
Spot	**Don Messick**

Executive Producers: **William Hanna, Joseph Barbera**
Producer: **Iwao Takamoto**

The clumsy canine janitor at a police station is actually a superhero trained in the martial arts.

Penrod Pooch (or Penry as he was known to Rosemary, the switchboard operator) worked as the flunky in a big city police station. Unknown to his colleagues, especially the grouchy Sgt Flint, this was no ordinary dog but a crimebuster extraordinaire who operated under the guise of Hong Kong Phooey. Leaping into a filing cabinet, Penry donned his oriental superhero costume before dashing out in the Phooeymobile (garaged in a rubbish bin behind the station) to confront the weirdest criminals in the world. By banging a gong, he could convert his vehicle into other forms of transport, or even into hiding places. Phooey was accompanied only by Spot, the station's striped cat. Once in action, our hero demonstrated the martial arts he had learned from a correspondence course, dipping into the *Hong Kong Book of Kung Fu* to attempt manoeuvres like the slow-motion Hong Kong Phooey Chop (much to the exasperation of his feline companion). Among the Mutt of Steel's adversaries were Mr Tornado, the Gum Drop Kid and Professor Presto.

HOPALONG CASSIDY
US (William Boyd) Western. BBC 1955–6

Hopalong Cassidy	**William Boyd**
Red Connors	**Edgar Buchanan**

Producer: **William Boyd**

A cowboy samaritan rides to the rescue on his snow-white charger.

The character of Hopalong Cassidy was created by Clarence E. Mulford around the turn of the century. But that was a different Hopalong from the one the kids knew and loved in the 1950s. Mulford had portrayed Cassidy as a rough, mean vagabond with a bad limp, a man who drank, swore and smoked. Actor William Boyd turned him into a faultless hero, an idol for the children, immaculately turned out in black to contrast dramatically with his silver hair, his silver spurs, his pearl-handled revolvers and his white steed, Topper. No longer troubled by the limp, he lived at the Bar 20 ranch and was accompanied in his adventures by Red Connors.

William Boyd had already played the role in the

cinema, and he picked up the rights to these old B-movies when no one else was interested. He and his associate, Toby Anguish, re-edited them and re-packaged them for TV. The first TV Hopalong, therefore, was actually the cinema version revisited. Eventually Boyd produced this new series specifically for television. It became an instant hit with younger viewers and went on to be one of the first great merchandising successes of the small screen.

HOPKINS, Sir ANTHONY
(1937–)

Welsh cinema grandee who, before Hollywood beckoned, focused on television, appearing in work as varied as *War and Peace* (Pierre), *QB VII* (Dr Adam Kelno), *The Lindberg Kidnapping Case*, *Kean* (Edmund Kean), *Victory at Entebbe*, *Othello* (the Moor himself), *A Married Man*, *The Bunker* (Hitler), *The Hunchback of Notre Dame* (Quasimodo), *Hollywood Wives* and *Across the Lake* (Donald Campbell), most of which were mini-series. Guest appearances in series like DEPARTMENT S characterized Hopkins's early career.

HOPKINS, JOHN
(1931–98)

Acclaimed London-born writer, the first script editor on Z CARS, a series for which he himself penned over 50 episodes. His work on the programme (and an earlier thriller series, *A Chance of Thunder*, in 1961) was followed by a couple of notable TV plays, *Fable* (1965) and *Horror of Darkness* (1966), before he contributed a four-part series entitled *Talking to a Stranger* (also 1966), which depicted the break-up of a family from various viewpoints. It was bestowed with praise and led to a growing involvement in the cinema, although Hopkins continued to script television material, including the hugely expensive *Divorce His, Divorce Hers* for HTV and *Smiley's People* (with John Le Carré). Other credits included episodes of DETECTIVE and two early CAMPION serials, *Dancers in Mourning* (1959) and *Death of a Ghost* (1960). His second wife was actress Shirley Knight.

HORDERN, Sir MICHAEL
CBE (1911–95)

Grand old man of the English stage and screen, whose television work was occasional but notable, if focused at the heavier end of the drama market. His small-screen work stretched back to the 1940s (he appeared in a production of *Rebecca* in 1947, for instance) and his major roles were as Willie in *Cakes and Ale*, Friar Domingo in SHOGUN and the Reverend Simeon Simcox in *Paradise Postponed*, with other credits including EDWARD THE SEVENTH (Gladstone), *The History Man*, *Ivanhoe*, *Mistress of Suspense*, TALES OF THE UNEXPECTED, *Scoop*, *The Green Man*, the ghost story, *Whistle, and I'll Come to You*, for OMNIBUS, the *Screen Two* presentation, *Memento Mori* (Godfrey Colston) and MIDDLEMARCH (Peter Feather-

stone). Hordern also performed Shakespeare for television, including *King Lear*, *Romeo and Juliet* and *The Tempest*. At the other end of the scale, he appeared with Richard Briers in the sketch anthology, *Tall Stories*, acted as narrator for PADDINGTON, voiced the part of Badger in the 1980s animation of THE WIND IN THE WILLOWS and told stories on JACKANORY.

HORIZON
UK (BBC) Science Documentary. BBC 2 1964–

Award-winning popular-science programme.

Beginning monthly but now seen more frequently, *Horizon* has been a centrepiece of BBC 2's schedules since the channel's inception. Its brief has been science, but the scope has been broad and the treatment flexible. The usual pattern has been to devote a whole programme to one particular issue. Often using remarkable footage, the programme has discussed a topic of general scientific interest or reviewed the latest scientific advance. On occasions, dramatizations have been used, perhaps to illustrate events in the life of an inventor or chemist. Topics in recent years have included ice mummies, mosquitoes, asteroid impacts and the lost city of Atlantis.

HORNBLOWER
UK (United/Meridian/A&E) Drama ITV 1998–

Midshipman/Lt. Horatio Hornblower	**Ioan Gruffudd**
Captain Pellew	**Robert Lindsay**
Matthews	**Paul Copley**
Styles	**Sean Gilder**
Oldroyd	**Simon Sherlock**
Lt. Bracegirdle	**Jonathan Coy**
Master Bowles	**Colin McClachlan**
Finch	**Chris Barnes**
Midshipman Archie Kennedy	**Jamie Bamber**
Midshipman Cleveland	**Frank Boyce**

Producer: **Andrew Benson**
Executive Producers: **Vernon Lawrence, Delia Fine, Michele Buck**

Rousing tales of life on the high seas.

This series of four two-hour films was based on the book, *Mr Midshipman Hornblower*, by C. S. Forester and featured the exploits of one Horatio Hornblower. A callow, seasick, 17-year-old youth new on board HMS *Justinian* in the first film – set in 1794 – Hornblower matured into a more than able seaman and worked his way up the naval ladder to the rank of lieutenant. Taking the raw recruit under his wing, and recognizing his talent, was the redoubtable Captain Pellew, skipper of Hornblower's second ship, HMS *Indefatigable*. Guest stars included Denis Lawson as Captain Foster, Cherie Lunghi as the Duchess of Wharfedale and Peter Vaughan as Admiral Lord Hood. The series, costing £12 million, was filmed off the coasts of Yalta in the Ukraine and Portugal, using two authentic vessels – a Baltic trader called the *Julia* and the newly built 22-gun *Grand Turk*. These and some 11 scale models were employed to re-create some of the fiery battles of the late 18th century. But, as well as the glory, the often sheer misery and discomfort of life at sea were also shown.

The four films were screened over autumn 1998 and spring 1999. More films, covering some of the ten other *Hornblower* books, have been planned.

HORSEMAN RIDING BY, A
UK (BBC) Drama. BBC1 1978

Paul Craddock .... **Nigel Havers**
John Rudd .... **Glyn Houston**
Grace Lovell/Craddock .... **Fiona Gaunt**
Claire Derwent/Craddock .... **Prunella Ransome**
Rose Derwent .... **Valerie Phillips**
Dr O'Keefe .... **Glyn Owen**
Dr Maureen O'Keefe/Rudd .... **Gillian McCutcheon**
Arabella Codsall .... **Madge Ryan**
Martin Codsall .... **Joby Blanshard**
Will Codsall .... **David Delve**
Sydney Codsall .... **Kevin Cope**
.... **Terence Budd**
Elinor Willoughby/Codsall .... **Sarah Porter**
Lord Gilroy .... **Jack May**
Tamer Potter .... **Forbes Collins**
Meg Potter .... **Pam St Clement**
Smut Potter .... **Martin Fisk**
Cissie Potter .... **Valerie Holloway**
Violet Potter .... **Wendy Holloway**
Arthur Pitts .... **Robert Vahey**
Martha Pitts .... **Maryann Turner**
Gloria Pitts .... **Christine Hargreaves**
Henry Pitts .... **Christopher Reeks**
Mrs Ada Handcock .... **Julie May**
James Grenfell .... **Frank Moorey**
Revd Horsey .... **Milton Johns**

Writer: **Arden Winch**
Producer: **Ken Riddington**

A young invalid soldier becomes the liberal new squire of a Devon estate.

In 1902 young, well-to-do Paul Craddock, a former Boer War lieutenant suffering from a shrapnel wound to his leg, arrived on the Devon coast to view an estate which was on the market. He wanted a new role in life and had money to invest after inheriting his father's scrap business in London. The Shallowford Estate on the River Sorrel had been badly run by its previous owners, the Lovells; but Craddock liked what he saw and, encouraged by very capable estate manager John Rudd, he accepted the challenge and became the new squire. His new title involved keeping a close eye on the various farming families who rented property in 'The Valley'. These included rough-and-ready poachers the Potters, the pushy Codsalls, the modest Pitts family and the very pleasant Derwents (particularly pleasant was daughter Claire, who became Paul's assistant and eventually his second wife). Craddock impressed the locals with his fairness and liberality, but these traits were not so popular with his Conservative neighbour, Lord Gilroy.

The story – based on the novel by R. F. Delderfield – progressed in 13 parts through various personal ups and downs and through times of difficulty and happiness in the estate right up to and beyond World War I, when many of the men were called away to duty, with tragic consequences.

HORTON, ROBERT
(Mead Howard Horton; 1924–)

Rugged American leading man of the 1950s and 1960s, seen to best effect as trail scout Flint McCullough in WAGON TRAIN, following a year in an American soap called *King's Row*. After five years in *Wagon Train*, Horton left the series, allegedly because he was fed up with Westerns. All the same, his next – and, to date, last – starring role was in another Western, the short-lived A MAN CALLED SHENANDOAH in 1965. Among Horton's other TV credits have been episodes of ALFRED HITCHCOCK PRESENTS and another US soap, *As the World Turns*.

HOT METAL
UK (LWT) Situation Comedy. ITV 1986–8

Terence 'Twiggy' Rathbone/Russell Spam ....
.... **Robert Hardy**
Harry Stringer .... **Geoffrey Palmer**
Greg Kettle .... **Richard Kane**
Bill Tytla .... **John Gordon-Sinclair**
Max .... **Geoffrey Hutchings**
Father Teasdale .... **John Horsley**
Richard Lipton .... **Richard Wilson**

Writers: **Andrew Marshall, David Renwick**
Producer: **Humphrey Barclay**

An ailing tabloid newspaper falls victim to an unscrupulous media baron.

The Daily Crucible, a flabby newspaper at the tabloid end of the market, was being strangled by its competitors and its circulation was plummeting. Its proprietors, Rathouse International, a global media conglomerate headed by the ruthless 'Twiggy' Rathbone, consequently took remedial action, installing a new editor, Rathbone's lookalike, Russell Spam. Spam radically altered the nature of the paper, introducing sex exposés, majoring on political scandals and adding titillation to page three, much to the disgust of managing editor Harry Stringer. But it worked, and circulation roared ahead. Stringer (mysteriously lost in a flying incident) was replaced by a new MD, Richard Lipton, in the second and last series.

HOTEL
US (Aaron Spelling) Drama. ITV 1983–9

Victoria Cabot .... **Anne Baxter**
Peter McDermott .... **James Brolin**
Christine Francis .... **Connie Sellecca**
Mark Danning .... **Shea Farrell**
Billy Griffin .... **Nathan Cook**

Dave Kendall .... **Michael Spound**
Megan Kendall .... **Heidi Bohay**
Julie Gillette .... **Shari Belafonte-Harper**

Executive Producers: **Aaron Spelling, Douglas S. Cramer**

The lives and loves of visitors to a swish San Francisco hotel.

From the creators of THE LOVE BOAT, this series adopted a similar format – introducing guest stars to supply the main action in each episode, with a small supporting permanent cast to provide the background. Events centred around the St Gregory Hotel and the regulars were manager Peter McDermott, his attractive assistant, Christine Francis, Mark Danning, the hotel's PR executive, and Billy Griffin, an ex-con turned security officer. Bette Davis was scheduled to star in the series, playing hotel owner Laura Trent but, through illness, she appeared in only the first episode. Anne Baxter was brought in to take over in the guise of her sister-in-law, Victoria Cabot. The series was based on the novel by Arthur Hailey.

HOUSE OF CARDS/TO PLAY THE KING/THE FINAL CUT
UK (BBC/WGBH Boston) Drama. BBC 1 1990/1993/1995

Francis Urquhart .... **Ian Richardson**
Mattie Storin .... **Susannah Harker** (*Cards*)
Elizabeth Urquhart .... **Diane Fletcher**
Tim Stamper .... **Colin Jeavons** (*Cards/King*)
Roger O'Neill .... **Miles Anderson** (*Cards*)
Henry Collingridge .... **David Lyon** (*Cards*)
Anne Collingridge .... **Isabelle Amyes** (*Cards*)
Penny Guy .... **Alphonsia Emmanuel** (*Cards*)
Lord Billsborough .... **Nicholas Selby** (*Cards*)
Charles Collingridge .... **James Villiers** (*Cards*)
Patrick Woolton .... **Malcolm Tierney** (*Cards*)
John Krajewski .... **William Chubb** (*Cards*)
Stephen Kendrick .... **Tommy Boyle** (*Cards*)
The King .... **Michael Kitchen** (*King*)
Sarah Harding .... **Kitty Aldridge** (*King*)
David Mycroft .... **Nicholas Farrell** (*King*)
Chloe Carmichael .... **Rowena King** (*King*)
John Stroud .... **Leonard Preston** (*King*)
Ken Charterhouse .... **Jack Fortune** (*King*)
Lord Quillington .... **Frederick Treves** (*King*)
Princess Charlotte .... **Bernice Stegers** (*King*)
Sir Bruce Bullerby .... **David Ryall** (*King/Cut*)
Commander Corda .... **Nick Brimble** (*King/Cut*)
Claire Carlsen .... **Isla Blair** (*Cut*)
Tom Makepeace .... **Paul Freeman** (*Cut*)
Geoffrey Booza Pitt .... **Nickolas Grace** (*Cut*)

Writer: **Andrew Davies**
Producer: **Ken Riddington**
Executive Producer: **Michael Wearing**

A scheming Government whip aims to become Prime Minister – by hook or by crook.

House of Cards, a four-part tale of political intrigue and in-fighting, was dramatized by Andrew Davies from the novel by Conservative Party Chief of Staff Michael Dobbs and benefited from being originally screened at the time of Mrs Thatcher's downfall. It went on to become the BBC's best-selling drama of the early 1990s, with sales to some 24 countries.

The drama focused on Government Chief Whip Francis Urquhart ('FU'), a highly ambitious but untrustworthy man (his stock answer to a leading question was: 'You might think that, but I couldn't possibly comment'). The viewer was taken into the character's confidence and left in no doubt about his unscrupulous behaviour through regular asides to the camera. The story picked up with the demise of Margaret Thatcher and her replacement with a wimpy male successor. This gave Urquhart all the motivation he needed to put his Machiavellian plans into action, ably assisted by devious whip Tim Stamper. By the end of the serial Urquhart was installed in Number 10, at the expense of the life of investigative journalist (and FU's lover) Mattie Storin.

Urquhart's troubles were just beginning, however. In a sequel, *To Play the King*, produced by the same team from another Michael Dobbs novel, Urquhart found himself under pressure from a newly enthroned monarch with liberal tendencies. He employed opinion pollster Sarah Harding as his adviser (and lover) and battled with the King and his PR team led by covert homosexual David Mycroft. Stamper, elevated only as far as party chairman, though deeming himself worthy of greater reward, sought to blackmail his mentor over the death of Mattie Storin.

The Final Cut provided the last instalment in the FU saga. Despite having seen off the King and Stamper, Urquhart was now clinging on to power, beleaguered by memories of his military past in Cyprus, where he had callously murdered two local men. Among his pursuers were Foreign Secretary Tom Makepeace and his lover, backbencher Claire Carlsen, who became FU's Parliamentary Private Secretary.

Michael Dobbs, unhappy at Andrew Davies's adaptation of this series, had his name removed from *The Final Cut* credits.

HOUSE OF ELIOTT, THE
UK (BBC) Drama. BBC 1 1991–4

Beatrice Eliott .... **Stella Gonet**
Evangeline Eliott .... **Louise Lombard**
Lady Lydia Eliott .... **Barbara Jefford**
Arthur Eliott .... **Peter Birch**
Jack Maddox .... **Aden Gillett**
Penelope Maddox .... **Francesca Folan**
Sebastian Pearce .... **Jeremy Brudenell**
Peregrine 'Piggy' Garstone .... **Robert Daws**
Tilly Watkins/Foss .... **Cathy Murphy**
Lady Dolly Haycock .... **Jill Melford**
Mr Duroque .... **Colin Jeavons**
Victor Stride .... **Anthony Valentine**
Daphne Haycock .... **Kelly Hunter**
Sir Desmond Gillespie .... **David De Keyser**
Madge Howell/Althorpe .... **Judy Flynn**
Gerry Althorpe .... **Jamie Foreman**

Betty Butcher .... **Diana Rayworth**
Agnes Clarke .... **Victoria Alcock**
Chalmers .... **Kate Paul**
Florence Ranby .... **Maggie Ollerenshaw**
Ralph Saroyan .... **Michael Culver**
Lord Alexander Montford .... **Rupert Frazer**
Lady Elizabeth Montford .... **Elizabeth Garvie**
Alice Burgoyne .... **Kate Fahy**
Joseph Wint .... **Stephen Churchett**
Charles Quance .... **Bill Thomas**
Grace Keeble .... **Melanie Ramsey**
Larry Cotter .... **Ian Redford**
Miles Bannister .... **Robert Hands**
Daniel Page .... **Richard Lintern**
Katya Beletsky .... **Caroline Trowbridge**
Norman Foss .... **Toby Whitehouse**

Creators: **Jean Marsh, Eileen Atkins**
Producers: **Jeremy Gwilt, Ken Riddington**

*Two impoverished sisters set up their own fashion
house in the 1920s.*

When their 'respectable' doctor father suddenly died in
1920, leaving a host of debts and a mistress to boot,
Beatrice (Bea) and Evangeline (Evie) Eliott were shaken
out of their somewhat sheltered existence in Highgate
by the need to find their own way in the world. Thirty-
year-old Bea took a job with photographer Jack Maddox,
while Evie (12 years her junior) became an apprentice
dressmaker. Despite the hindrance of their devious solicitor cousin Arthur, their efforts culminated in the
setting-up of their own London fashion company, The
House of Eliott. Their battles to survive in a competitive
world, to see off their unscrupulous banker, Ralph
Saroyan, and to meet head-on the social prejudices facing independent women at that time provided the focus
for later episodes. The personal lives of the girls and their
workshop assistants also came to the fore. In the second
series, the sisters briefly moved to Paris to learn about
international fashion. Bea married Jack but, as his film-
making/journalistic/political career began to take off,
cracks developed in their relationship. A third series saw
the birth of Bea's baby, Lucy, and Evie's liaison with
portrait painter Daniel Page.

Costing some £6 million in its first series alone, *The
House of Eliott* was devised by UPSTAIRS, DOWNSTAIRS
creators Jean Marsh and Eileen Atkins and bore many of
the hallmarks of that popular period drama. Costumes
featured in the series were exhibited at the Victoria and
Albert Museum in 1992.

HOW!/HOW 2
UK (Southern/TVS/Meridian/Scottish) Children's
Entertainment. ITV 1966–81/1990–

Presenters: (*How!*/*How 2*) Fred Dinenage; (*How!*) Jack
Hargreaves, Jon Miller, Bunty James, Marian Davies;
(*How 2*) Carol Vorderman, Gareth Jones, Sian Lloyd,
Gail Porter, Gail MacKenna

*Educational children's series explaining how
things happen.*

Always popular, *How!* was a series that managed to combine science with humour. Its four studio-bound presenters took turns to explain the scientific reasons why
certain things happened. These could be of vital importance or of the most trivial nature. Tricks and experiments involving matchsticks, coins and water were
favourite items. The four hosts (palms raised in Red
Indian greeting at the beginning and end of each programme) were jokey Fred Dinenage, thoughtful Jack
Hargreaves, gadget-minded Jon Miller and Bunty James,
who was later replaced by Marian Davies. The series
was revived in 1990 under the title of *How 2*. Dinenage
returned for the relaunch and was joined by
COUNTDOWN girl Carol Vorderman (with various later
replacements) and kids' TV presenter Gareth 'Gaz Top'
Jones.

HOWARD, RON
(1954–)

American child actor, today one of Hollywood's most
successful directors. Following early appearances in
shows like *Dennis the Menace* and THE TWILIGHT ZONE,
Ron (or Ronny) Howard's TV career began to move at
the age of six when he was cast in the part of Opie Taylor,
Andy's son in the extremely popular US sitcom, *The
Andy Griffith Show*. The series ran from 1960 to 1968 and,
in between episodes, Howard took time off to appear in
dramas such as THE FUGITIVE. In the early 1970s he was
a member of *The Smith Family* (Bob Smith), another US
comedy, which starred Henry Fonda, before he secured
his biggest TV role, that of Richie Cunningham in HAPPY
DAYS. Howard had played the role of the fresh-faced
1950s teenager in a pilot episode, seen as part of LOVE,
AMERICAN STYLE, and he stayed with *Happy Days* for six
years, making occasional return appearances later while
establishing himself in the movie world. He has since
worked on the TV version of his feature film, *Parenthood*.

HOWARD, RONALD
(1918–)

A former journalist and the son of Leslie Howard, Ronald
Howard was a familiar face in two diverse series, a 1954
version of *Sherlock Holmes* (in the title role) and the
action adventure, *Cowboy in Africa* (Wing Commander
Howard Hayes), more than a decade later.

HOWARDS' WAY
UK (BBC) Drama. BBC 1 1985–90

Tom Howard .... **Maurice Colbourne**
Jan Howard .... **Jan Harvey**
Jack Rolfe .... **Glyn Owen**
Avril Rolfe .... **Susan Gilmore**
Ken Masters .... **Stephen Yardley**
Leo Howard .... **Edward Highmore**
Lynne Howard/Dupont .... **Tracey Childs**
Polly Urquhart .... **Patricia Shakesby**
Abby Urquhart/Hudson .... **Cindy Shelley**

Gerald Urquhart .... **Ivor Danvers**
Kate Harvey .... **Dulcie Gray**
Charles Frere .... **Tony Anholt**
Bill Sayers .... **Robert Vahey**
Sir John Stevens .... **Willoughby Grey**
Davy .... **Kulvinder Ghir**
Dawn .... **Sally Farmiloe**
Claude Dupont .... **Malcolm Jamieson**
Richard Shellet .... **Oscar Quitak**
Admiral Redfern .... **Michael Denison**
David Lloyd .... **Bruce Bould**
Orrin Hudson .... **Ryan Michael**
                                                                    Jeff Harding
Sarah Foster .... **Sarah-Jane Varley**
Mark Foster .... **Graham Pountney**
Curtis Jaeger .... **Dean Harris**
Sir Edward Frere .... **Nigel Davenport**
Robert McIntyre .... **Fraser Kerr**
Amanda Parker .... **Francesca Gonshaw**
Anna Lee .... **Sarah Lam**
Emma Neesome .... **Sian Webber**
Richard Spencer .... **John Moulder-Brown**
Michael Hanley .... **Michael Loney**
Vanessa Andenberg/Rolfe .... **Lana Morris**
Laura Wilde .... **Kate O'Mara**
Vicki Rockwell .... **Victoria Burgoyne**
James Brooke .... **Andrew Bicknell**
Robert Hastings .... **Paul Jerricho**
Jenny Richards .... **Charmian Gradwell**

Creators: **Gerard Glaister, Allan Prior**
Producer: **Gerard Glaister**

Glossy soap centring on boats, boardrooms and bedrooms.

Redundant 44-year-old aircraft designer Tom Howard decided to take the plunge and bought into a boat-building business, inspired by the work he had done on his own yacht, *The Flying Fish*. His wife, Jan, having given her life to establishing the family and home, and fearing for the future, was less than impressed with Tom's new venture. Tom's partner in the struggling Mermaid Yard, where they perfected swish boats like the *Barracuda*, was boozy craftsman Jack Rolfe. Rolfe's obsolete business knowledge was supplemented with advice from his shrewd daughter, Avril, soon to be Tom's new lover. In response, Jan became manageress of a fashion house and embarked on affairs with her posing boss Ken Masters and ageing businessman Sir Edward Frere, father of smarmy tycoon Charles Frere. Tom's racing-mad but kind-hearted mother-in-law, Kate Harvey, lent a hand whenever called upon, but the Howards' children, the drop-out student Leo and the spoilt, sailing-obsessed Lynne, caused more than a few headaches. Lynne married Frenchman Claude Dupont, but he was killed while water-skiing. Languid Leo's on/off girlfriend was the prickly Abby Urquhart, whose squabbling parents were also featured.

Howards' Way, set on the River Hamble in fictional Tarrant (real-life Bursledon), was a series about dodgy business deals, gaudy lifestyles, brave men and flashy women. It has been described as the 'first Thatcherite soap' and survived not only the years of boom and bust

but also the tragic death of its main star. When Maurice Colbourne died of a heart attack in 1989, Tom Howard was written out and the rest of the cast bravely soldiered on for one more year. Singer Marti Webb, backed by the Simon May Orchestra, took the programme's theme song, 'Always There', into the Top 20 in 1986.

HOWERD, FRANKIE
OBE (Francis Howard; 1917–92)

British comedian, known for his 'oohs', 'aahs', 'please yourselves' and stuttering, bumbling delivery (caused by a natural childhood stammer, which he exaggerated for effect). Eventually breaking into showbiz at the end of the war, and making a name for himself on radio shows like *Variety Bandbox*, Howerd was given his first TV show in 1952. It was entitled *The Howerd Crowd* and was followed by numerous variety spots and guest turns over the years. Although his popularity faltered at the turn of the 1960s, and Howerd appeared not to be moving with the times, he was thrown a lifeline with an appearance on THAT WAS THE WEEK THAT WAS which resulted from a successful appearance in Peter Cook's Establishment Club. Howerd never looked back. He went on to star in a London stage version of *A Funny Thing Happened on the Way to the Forum*, which led to a TV lookalike, UP POMPEII!, in 1969. In this, as Lurcio the slave, Howerd meandered his way through *double entendres* and innuendoes (some allegedly too strong for the man himself), trying to deliver a prologue. The series led to a run of film spin-offs, as well as a similar TV outing set in the Middle East, *Whoops Baghdad!*, in 1973. In all, Howerd was seldom off TV screens in the 1960s and 1970s, thanks to programmes such as *The Frankie Howerd Show*, *The Howerd Confessions*, *Frankie Howerd Strikes Again* and *A Touch of the Casanovas* (the pilot for a never-realized series). His wartime sitcom, *Then Churchill Said to Me*, made in 1982, was not broadcast (because of the Falklands conflict) until UK Gold screened it 11 years later. One of his last series was the kids' comedy, *All Change*, in 1989, in which he played the ghostly Uncle Bob.

HOWMAN, KARL
(1953–)

British comic actor, well versed in Jack the Lad-type roles. Howman succeeded Robert Lindsay in the guise of Jakey Smith in the RAF sitcom, GET SOME IN!, before securing his own series, BRUSH STROKES, playing the gentle womanizer/decorator Jacko. He went on to star with Geraldine McEwan as the mysterious MULBERRY, as villainous barman Wayne Todd in *Bad Boys*, and as Charlie in *Babes in the Wood*. Among his other credits have been episodes of ANGELS, MINDER, THE SWEENEY, HAZELL, FOX, SHELLEY, THE PROFESSIONALS, A FINE ROMANCE, JULIET BRAVO, DEMPSEY AND MAKEPEACE and BOON. He was also in the play, THE FLIPSIDE OF DOMINICK HIDE. He is the father of *Family Affairs* actress Chloe Howman.

HR PUFNSTUF
US (Krofft) Children's Comedy. ITV 1970

Jimmy .... **Jack Wild**
Witchiepoo .... **Billie Hayes**

Writers: **Lennie Weinrib, Howard Morris**
Producers: **Sid Krofft, Marty Krofft**

A young boy is lured to a magic island by an evil witch.

This lively musical cross between *Robinson Crusoe* and *The Wizard of Oz* told the story of Jimmy, a young lad who owned a talking golden flute named Freddie. To steal the flute, a nasty sorceress by the name of Witchiepoo lured Jimmy to her island home, enticing him into a boat then leaving him shipwrecked. Thankfully, HR Pufnstuf, the genial dragon mayor of Living Island (as the theme song said: 'He's your friend when things get rough') spotted the boy in distress and brought him ashore. Thereafter, Jimmy shared the company of Pufnstuf and his humorous friends – Judy the Frog, Cling and Clang, Ludicrous Lion and Dr Blinky (a white owl). Also seen were Horsey and Grandfather and Grandmother Clock, and the voices of the Four Winds were heard from time to time. Living with Witchiepoo in her spooky castle were her three sidekicks: a yellow spider named Seymour, a green vulture called Orson and the grey Stupid Bat. She also controlled the Evil Trees and Mushrooms in the Evil Forest and darted around on her rocket-powered Vroom Broom. With the help of her cronies, and by spying on events around the island through her Image Machine, Witchiepoo scuppered all Jimmy's attempts to return home, but she never gained control of the magic flute.

The programme's non-human characters were represented by colourful, lifelike puppets, with voices supplied by Joan Gerber, Felix Silla and Walker Edmiston, among others. Seventeen episodes were made and a feature-film version was released in 1970.

HTV
(Harlech Television)

HTV has been the ITV contractor for Wales and the west of England since 4 March 1968, after winning the franchise from TWW. Initially Harlech Television, the name of the successful bidding consortium, which included Lord Harlech, was used on air, but this was soon shortened to HTV. The company has since retained its franchise on two occasions and offers two separate services for viewers. HTV West (based in Bristol) covers the west of England, with specifically targeted news, sports and features programmes dropped into the general output, while HTV Cymru/Wales (based in Cardiff) does the same for Welsh viewers. The Welsh side of the company also produces Welsh-language programmes. These are now screened on S4C, but before the Welsh fourth channel was established in 1982 Welsh programmes replaced certain English-language programmes in the HTV Wales schedules. HTV West made a name for itself for innovative children's science fiction in the 1970s. Programmes such as *The Georgian House*, *Sky* and *The Children of the Stones* all made it to the national network. It also contributed game shows like MR AND MRS, *Definition*, *Cuckoo in the Nest* and *Three Little Words*. The adventure series *Robin of Sherwood* was another network success. HTV is now owned by Carlton.

HUCKLEBERRY HOUND SHOW, THE
US (Hanna-Barbera/Screen Gems) Cartoon. ITV 1960–4

Voices:

Huckleberry Hound .... **Daws Butler**
Pixie .... **Don Messick**
Dixie .... **Daws Butler**
Mr Jinks .... **Daws Butler**
Yogi Bear .... **Daws Butler**
Boo Boo .... **Don Messick**
Hokey Wolf .... **Daws Butler**
Ding-a-Ling .... **Doug Young**

Creators/Executive Producers: **William Hanna, Joseph Barbera**

The adventures of an easy-going, never-flustered Southern pooch.

Huckleberry Hound took things as they came. He always saw the good things in life and made little criticism of the bad – and this despite the cruellest of luck, which invited trees to fall on him and bombs to blow up beneath him. He just carried on cheerfully singing 'Clementine'. Painfully slow in thought and speech, this was a dog with all the time in the world and the spirit to give anything a go. The baggy-eyed bloodhound assumed various guises throughout his successful series. He was seen as a French legionnaire, a professor, a fireman and also the dashing Purple Pumpernickel, and became one of the small screen's first cartoon heroes. Sharing his limelight, in their own segments of the show, were *Pixie and Dixie* and YOGI BEAR. Pixie and Dixie were two Southern mice who tormented Mr Jinks, the cat (who hated 'those meeces to pieces'). Yogi, in conjunction with his sidekick, Boo Boo, was the perennially hungry picnic-snatcher of Jellystone National Park who became so popular that he was given his own series. His replacement was the Bilko-like Hokey Wolf, a sharp-talking conwolf, aided and abetted by the fox, Ding-a-Ling.

The Huckleberry Hound Show was the programme that launched former TOM AND JERRY animators William Hanna and Joseph Barbera into the TV bigtime. Their first offering had been a cat-and-dog series called *Ruff and Reddy*, but after Huckleberry Hound they were in a position to produce THE FLINTSTONES, THE JETSONS, SCOOBY DOO – WHERE ARE YOU?, WACKY RACES and countless other children's favourites.

HUDD, ROY
(1936–)

Croydon-born entertainer in the music-hall tradition, whose TV career kicked off with guest appearances in sitcoms like OUR HOUSE but really progressed through regular work on NOT SO MUCH A PROGRAMME, MORE A WAY OF LIFE. His own series for the BBC and ITV followed, including *Hudd*, *The Illustrated Weekly Hudd* and *The Roy Hudd Show*, all of which exhibited his versatility and demonstrated his fondness for the music-hall greats. These days, whenever a nostalgic programme is on the air, Roy Hudd is never far away. Hudd's dramatic skills were also given the chance to shine when, in 1993, he played Harold Atterbow in Dennis Potter's LIPSTICK ON YOUR COLLAR. He followed this with the parts of John Parry in COMMON AS MUCK, Beach in *P. G. Wodehouse's Heavy Weather* and Ben Baglin in Potter's swan-song, KARAOKE. Hudd has been just as familiar on radio, thanks to his long-running series, *The News Huddlines*.

HUDSON, ROCK
(Roy Scherer; 1925–85)

Hollywood heart-throb of the 1950s and 1960s, whose television work was reserved until the end of his career (save for the odd guest appearance on shows like I LOVE LUCY and ROWAN AND MARTIN'S LAUGH-IN). In 1971 (the same year as he allegedly turned down the Tony Curtis role in THE PERSUADERS!), Hudson starred in a TV movie, *Once Upon a Dead Man*, which proved to be the pilot for the MYSTERY MOVIE series, McMILLAN AND WIFE, in which he appeared with Susan Saint James. The series ran for six years and, when it ended, Hudson stayed with TV, taking roles in an assortment of mini-series, including *Wheels* (Adam Trenton) and *The Martian Chronicles* (Colonel John Wilder). In 1982 he was cast as another detective, Brian Devlin, in a short-lived series entitled *The Devlin Connection* (it was cancelled because Hudson underwent heart surgery), before he resurfaced as Daniel Reece in DYNASTY in 1984. It proved to be Hudson's last major role before his well-publicized death from an AIDS-related illness a year later.

HUGGINS, ROY
(1914–)

Prolific American producer and writer, the creator of series like MAVERICK, 77 SUNSET STRIP, THE FUGITIVE, *Run for Your Life* and THE ROCKFORD FILES. He has also produced CHEYENNE, THE VIRGINIAN, ALIAS SMITH AND JONES and *Baretta* among numerous other action series. His own production company was known as Public Arts.

HUGH AND I
UK (BBC) Situation Comedy. BBC 1962–6

Terry Scott	**Terry Scott**
Hugh Lloyd	**Hugh Lloyd**
Mrs Scott	**Vi Stevens**
Mr Crispin	**Wallas Eaton**
Mrs Crispin	**Mollie Sugden**
Norma Crispin	**Jacquie Wallis**
	Jill Curzon
Arthur Wormold	**Cyril Smith**
	Jack Haig
Griselda Wormold	**Patricia Hayes**

Creator/Writer: **John Chapman**
Producers: **David Croft, Duncan Wood**

Two friends seek to improve their lot, with disastrous results.

Lobelia Avenue, Tooting, was the home of Mrs Scott, her troublesome, unemployed son, Terry, and their lodger, Hugh Lloyd, a worker at a local aircraft factory. Forming a Laurel-and-Hardy-like double act, the two lads constantly found themselves in hot water, with the bumptious, over-ambitious Terry leading the timid, fretful Hugh astray. Usually 'get rich quick' schemes were to blame. Next to the Scotts, on one side, lived the Crispins, he a loud-mouth, she a snob, and their daughter, Norma, an object of lust for the boys. On the other side were the Wormolds. For their final fling in 1966, the lads were sent on a cruise to the Far East, paid for out of the £5,000 Hugh had won with a Premium Bond. Terry and Hugh then embarked on more adventurous escapades in the murky world of espionage in their 1968 follow-up series, *Hugh and I Spy*, in which each episode was given a cliffhanger ending.

HUGHES, GEOFFREY
(1944–)

Liverpudlian actor often cast in slobby, layabout roles. For eight years he was kind-hearted bin man Eddie Yeats in CORONATION STREET, with more recent highlights being Onslow, Hyacinth Bucket's vest-wearing brother-in-law, in KEEPING UP APPEARANCES, and iffy-goods dealer Twiggy in THE ROYLE FAMILY. He also played Mr Lithgow in the Channel 4 sitcom, *The Bright Side*, Ray Hartley in *Coasting* and Dilk in MAKING OUT, and he has popped up in a range of other series from Z CARS, THE LIKELY LADS, YOU RANG, M'LORD? and CURRY AND CHIPS to THE MIND OF MR J. G. REEDER, NO – HONESTLY, DOCTOR WHO and SPENDER. He provided the voice for Paul McCartney's character in the cartoon film, *Yellow Submarine*.

HUGHES, NERYS
(1941–)

Welsh actress most notable on TV as Sandra Hutchinson in THE LIVER BIRDS and Megan Roberts in THE DISTRICT NURSE. She played Maisie, the barmaid, in the comedy drama, *The Flying Swan* in 1965, Beth Jenkins in a short-lived YTV sitcom called *Third Time Lucky* in 1982, Diana in Ruth Rendell's *Gallowglass*, and has also appeared in *How Green Was My Valley*, presented kids' series like PLAY

AWAY, *Alphabet Zoo* and JACKANORY, guested in DOCTOR WHO and hosted the practical magazine programme, *Bazaar*. One of her earliest starring roles was in the 1964 serial, *Diary of a Young Man*.

HULL, ROD
(1935–99)

British entertainer with Australian connections, not least his aggressive, giant Emu puppet, which Hull first spotted in 1969 when working on a children's TV show in Australia. Armed with this uncontrollable beast, Hull returned to the UK a year later and was, throughout the 1970s and 1980s, a big name in children's television. He devised and hosted the first *Children's Royal Variety Performance* and starred in series like *Rod Hull and Emu*, EBC (Emu's Broadcasting Company), *Emu's World* and *Emu's Pink Windmill Show*. On one celebrated appearance on *Parkinson*, Emu very clearly ruffled the interviewer's feathers, violently attacking Parky and pushing him on to the floor. Hull also enjoyed success across the Atlantic.

HUMAN BODY, THE
UK (BBC/Learning Channel) Documentary. BBC 1 1998

Presenter: **Prof. Robert Winston**

Producer: **Richard Dale**

A journey through the life of the human body in seven instalments.

Professor (now Lord) Robert Winston was the host of this acclaimed series which explored the changes that take place in the body during the course of a lifetime. Beginning with ovulation and showing the very moment of conception – the actual fusion of sperm and ovum – and continuing through birth, infancy, puberty and beyond, right up to the point of death (the series controversially filmed the death of a 63-year-old man), it aimed to provide viewers with a new insight into how the body works. With the aid of some brave volunteers and ground-breaking camerawork, the series provoked thought and won awards.

HUMAN JUNGLE, THE
UK (Independent Artists/ABC) Medical Drama. ITV 1963–5

Dr Roger Corder	**Herbert Lom**
Dr Jimmy Davis	**Michael Johnson**
Jennifer Corder	**Sally Smith**
Nancy Hamilton	**Mary Yeomans**

Creator: **Julian Wintle**
Producers: **Julian Wintle, Leslie Parkyn**

The professional and domestic troubles of a London psychiatrist.

Widower Dr Roger Corder was a specialist in emotional distress and his counselling helped many disturbed patients back to health. He enjoyed a good relationship with his junior colleague, Dr Jimmy Davis, and his supportive secretary, Nancy Hamilton, and stories revolved around the various cases they undertook, with Corder heading out and about to meet his patients in their own surroundings (where he could understand them better). However, the workaholic doctor was less successful in his private life, seldom being able to communicate with his determined teenage daughter, Jennifer.

HUMPHRIES, BARRY
(1934–)

Australian entertainer, the creator of larger-than-life housewife megastar Dame Edna Everage and boozy cultural attaché Sir Les Patterson. His first TV appearances came in comedies like NOT ONLY . . . BUT ALSO . . . and *The Late Show*, and his own series have included *Barry Humphries' Scandals*, *The Dame Edna Experience* and *Dame Edna's Neighbourhood Watch*. Humphries has also organized more than one *Audience with Dame Edna*. Additionally, he was seen in the single drama, *Doctor Fischer of Geneva* and the serial, *Selling Hitler* (as Rupert Murdoch).

HUMPHRYS, JOHN
(1943–)

Cardiff-born seasoned journalist, newsreader and presenter, one of the Radio 4 *Today* team since 1987 but still active on television. After a grounding in newspapers, Humphrys entered television with HTV and then, in 1970, became a BBC foreign correspondent, working in the USA and South Africa up to 1980. He then took over as diplomatic correspondent, before joining the new-look *Nine O'Clock News* team as one of its chief presenters a year later. He stayed with the news until 1986 and still occasionally works as a newsreader on the BBC's main bulletins. Humphrys has also hosted the Sunday political programme, *On the Record*, and chaired numerous debates and discussion programmes. His brother Bob is a sports presenter with BBC Wales.

HUNNIFORD, GLORIA
(1940–)

Northern Ireland-born radio and TV presenter. Hunniford's showbusiness career began in singing (she made her debut at the age of nine), before progressing into radio work in Canada and Northern Ireland, then television (*Good Evening Ulster*). From a base as a Radio 2 presenter in the early 1980s, she moved into UK TV, hosting shows like *Sunday, Sunday*, SONGS OF PRAISE, *We Love TV*, *Wogan*, *Gloria*, *Family Affairs* (with her daughter, Caron Keating), *Gloria Live*, *Sunday Live*, *Good Fortune*, *Ladies of the House*, CHILDREN IN NEED, PEBBLE MILL and *Open House with Gloria Hunniford*. She was also a regular panellist on *That's Showbusiness*.

HUNT, GARETH
(1943–)

London-born actor who came to light as Frederick, the footman, in UPSTAIRS, DOWNSTAIRS and later headlined in THE NEW AVENGERS, playing Mike Gambit. He then turned to comedy and starred in the sitcom, *That Beryl Marston*, playing Gerry Bodley, and, later, *Side by Side*, as plumber Vince Tulley. Hunt has also appeared in MINDER and DOCTOR WHO, plus countless coffee commercials.

HUNTER'S WALK
UK (ATV) Police Drama. ITV 1973–6

DS Smith	Ewan Hooper
Sgt Ken Ridgeway	Davyd Harries
PC Fred Pooley	Duncan Preston
DC 'Mickey' Finn	David Simeon
PC Harry Coombes	Charles Rea
Betty Smith	Ruth Madoc

Creator: **Ted Willis**
Producer: **John Cooper**

A small police force keeps the peace in a provincial town.

Set in the modest Midlands settlement of Broadstone (actually Rushden, Northants), *Hunter's Walk* focused on the team at the local police station, namely po-faced DS 'Smithy' Smith, 'Mickey' Finn, his junior detective colleague, PCs Pooley and Coombes, and station officer Ken Ridgeway. Faced with routine police investigations, mostly of a domestic nature, they successfully patrolled the streets in steady, DIXON OF DOCK GREEN fashion (not surprisingly, as this was also created by Lord Ted Willis). Smith's wife was played by future HI-DE-HI! star Ruth Madoc.

HURT, JOHN
(1940–)

Award-winning Derbyshire-born actor who, after appearances in series like GIDEON'S WAY and THE SWEENEY, shot to fame as Quentin Crisp in Thames TV's THE NAKED CIVIL SERVANT in 1975. He followed this with the roles of Caligula in I, CLAUDIUS and Raskolnikov in *Crime and Punishment* and was THE STORYTELLER in Jim Henson's acclaimed children's series. Other credits have included the VJ Day drama, *Prisoners in Time* (Eric Lomax).

HYLTON, JACK
(1892–1965)

British bandleader who became one of ITV's earliest light entertainment producers, working with Tony Hancock, Alfred Marks, Dickie Henderson, Anne Shelton and others.

IBA

See ITC.

I, CLAUDIUS

UK (BBC/London Films) Historical Drama. BBC 2 1976

Claudius	Derek Jacobi
Livia	Siân Phillips
Augustus	Brian Blessed
Tiberius	George Baker
Drusus	Ian Ogilvy
Marcellus	Christopher Guard
Julia	Frances White
Antonia	Margaret Tyzack
Agrippa	John Paul
Lucius	Simon MacCorkindale
Caligula	John Hurt
Germanicus	David Robb
Livilla	Patricia Quinn
Agrippina	Fiona Walker
Postumus	John Castle
Herod	James Faulkner
Sejanus	Patrick Stewart
Piso	Stratford Johns
Messalina	Sheila White
Drusilla	Beth Morris
Nero	Christopher Biggins
Castor	Kevin McNally
Gratus	Bernard Hill
Marcus	Norman Eshley
Narcissus	John Cater
Pallas	Bernard Hepton
Caractacus	Peter Bowles

Writer: **Jack Pulman**
Producer: **Martin Lisemore**

The power struggles of Imperial Rome as seen through the eyes of an innocent.

Depicting the debauchery and duplicity of life in ancient Rome, *I, Claudius*, directed by Herbert Wise, was a 12-part dramatization of two novels by Robert Graves: *I, Claudius* and *Claudius the God*. It focused on Emperor Claudius, who related events in his lifetime via flashbacks, taking up the story in the time of the Emperor Augustus (24 BC) when the stammering, limping Claudius was a sickly child. It progressed through the reigns of the despotic Tiberius and the deranged Caligula to reveal how, quite against his desires, Claudius himself became ruler of the empire. Murder and manoeuvring lay at every turn, interspersed with perverse orgies and gluttonous feasts, with the chief manipulator Claudius's cruel grandmother, the arch-poisoner Livia.

The snake that writhed across the mosaic in the opening titles aptly set the tone for this colourful, often gory series which won much acclaim, not least for the performance of Shakespearean actor Derek Jacobi.

I DIDN'T KNOW YOU CARED

UK (BBC) Situation Comedy. BBC 1 1975–9

Uncle Mort	**Robin Bailey**
Les Brandon	**John Comer**
Annie Brandon	**Liz Smith**
Carter Brandon	**Stephen Rea**
	Keith Drinkel
Pat Partington/Brandon	**Anita Carey**
	Liz Goulding
Uncle Staveley	**Bert Palmer**
	Leslie Sarony
Linda Preston	**Deirdre Costello**
Mrs Partington	**Vanda Godsell**
Sid Skelhorn	**Ray Dunbobbin**
	Bobby Pattinson

Creator/Writer: **Peter Tinniswood**
Producer: **Bernard Thompson**

The battle of the sexes in a morose northern household.

The Brandons were a miserable-go-unlucky Yorkshire family living in an industrial town. They consisted of Les and Annie (unhappily married for 25 years), their son, Carter, his wife, Pat, and Annie's mufflered brother, Mort, who 'served all through First World War' and who was forced to move in when his wife, Edna, died. While the womenfolk harassed and bullied, the men tried desperately to slink away to the pub or Mort's allotment, where he hoisted a Union Jack above his converted railway-carriage shed. There Les and Mort aimed to protect young Carter from his socially ambitious new wife over a brew of tea and a hand of dominoes. Carter's response was usually a hesitant 'Aye . . . Well . . . Mmm . . .' Visits by the terrifying Three Great-Aunts From Glossop, much-dreaded works outings and encounters with Unsworth's lively pork pies gave the family plenty to battle over, with only funerals and opposition to 'London beer' likely to bring any harmony. Also seen was senile army veteran Uncle Staveley, who carried the ashes of his 'oppo', Cpl. Parkinson, in a box around his neck and whose best conversation was, 'I heard that, pardon?' Linda Preston was the local Jezebel who aimed to seduce Carter at every turn.

Creator Peter Tinniswood had earlier introduced the Brandons in a trilogy of novels, and Uncle Mort and Carter have also been heard on BBC Radio.

I DREAM OF JEANNIE

US (Sidney Sheldon/Screen Gems) Situation Comedy. ITV 1966–71

Jeannie	**Barbara Eden**
Capt./Major Tony Nelson	**Larry Hagman**
Capt./Major Roger Healey	**Bill Daily**
Dr Alfred Bellows	**Hayden Rorke**
Gen. Martin Peterson	**Barton MacLane**
Amanda Bellows	**Emmaline Henry**

Creator/Executive Producer: **Sidney Sheldon**

An astronaut is the master of a beautiful young genie.

When his test mission was aborted, NASA astronaut Tony Nelson parachuted back to Earth and found himself marooned on a desert island. There, he picked up a bottle, uncorked it and let loose a beautiful genie, appropriately named Jeannie, who promised him his every wish. Naturally, the first thing he called for was a rescue helicopter and then returned home to his base at Cocoa Beach, Florida, taking Jeannie along for the ride.

The fun of this series came from the fact that only Tony and his playboy buddy, Roger Healey, knew about Jeannie and only they could see her. NASA's psychiatrist, Alfred Bellows, thought Tony was nuts, of course, and looked for every opportunity to prove it. With Jeannie supposedly being 2,000 years old, she had some difficulty interpreting 20th-century expressions and figures of speech, and this led to even more confusion and chaos whenever she stepped in to 'help' her master. She was also in love with Tony, and took every opportunity to spoil his chances with other women. Somewhat ironically, it was Jeannie whose wish finally came true, when she and Tony were married towards the end of the series.

I LOVE LUCY

US (CBS/Desilu) Situation Comedy. ITV 1955–61

Lucy Ricardo	**Lucille Ball**
Ricky Ricardo	**Desi Arnaz**
Ethel Mertz	**Vivian Vance**
Fred Mertz	**William Frawley**
Little Ricky Ricardo	**Richard Keith**

Writers: **Jess Oppenheimer, Madelyn Pugh, Bob Carroll**
Producers: **Jess Oppenheimer, Desi Arnaz**

A dance-band leader's patience is sorely tried by his scatterbrained wife.

I Love Lucy was a pioneer among TV programmes. It set the pattern for the 'domestic' sitcom and was the first series to be filmed (before a live audience), rather than transmitted live. This has also contributed to its longevity, since all the original programmes are still available in good condition. It centred on the life of Lucy Ricardo (née MacGillicuddy), a zany, rather immature redhead of Scottish descent, for whom nothing would go right. Her Cuban husband, Ricky, was a dance-band leader and Lucy longed to follow him into showbusiness, despite her lack of talent. Failing this, she at least wanted to be more than an ordinary housewife and consequently cooked up endless hare-brain schemes to make money or to improve life around the home, most of them prone to disaster. But, as the programme's title revealed, Ricky really did love Lucy and, although extremely annoyed, he was remarkably forgiving, considering the amount of hassle she caused him.

The Ricardos lived in an apartment on the East Side of Manhattan, where their frumpy landlord and landlady were Fred and Ethel Mertz. Lucy found a willing ally and accomplice in Ethel, who was years younger than her wisecracking, irascible husband, and the two girls often waged a battle of the sexes with the guys. But they were all good friends at heart. In one season, Ricky found fame in Hollywood and the foursome set off on a famous car trek across America; in another, they toured Europe with Ricky's band.

One of the highlights of the series was the birth of Little Ricky in the second season, an event planned to coincide with Lucille Ball's own second pregnancy (the episode was screened the night that Ball's real baby was born). Other developments included Ricky moving on from the Tropicana Club, where he worked, to owning his own nightspot, the Babaloo Club, and then starring in his own TV show.

Lucille and Desi Arnaz were married in real life and owned the programme's production company, Desilu. After their divorce, Lucille developed another two successful comedies in the same vein, THE LUCY SHOW and HERE'S LUCY, while Desi went on to produce THE UNTOUCHABLES, among other programmes.

I'M THE LAW
US (Cosman) Police Drama. BBC 1954–5

Lt. George Kirby .... **George Raft**

Executive Producer: **Pat Costello**
Producer: **Jean Yarborough**

Very early American cop show set in New York City.

Gangster actor George Raft swapped sides for this half-hour foray into primitive TV policing. Taking on the mantle of Lt. George Kirby of the NYPD, Raft's beat was the Big Apple and he patrolled the city streets in search of thugs, murderers and thieves, dishing out knuckle sandwiches and bullets aplenty. Raft also acted as narrator. Lou Costello's brother, Pat, was the show's executive producer, maintaining a very tight budget.

IDENT BOARD

A board displaying details of the programme being recorded. Often incorporating a countdown clock, it is shown to the camera or imposed on the screen at the start of recording to confirm the title, episode, scene, date, etc.

IDIOT BOARD

A cue card, displaying lines or instructions, held next to the camera to help forgetful presenters and actors.

IDLE, ERIC
(1943–)

British comedy actor and writer, best known for his work as part of the MONTY PYTHON team. Previously, Idle had scripted sketches for THE FROST REPORT with Tim Brooke-Taylor and other Pythons. He had also written

episodes of the Ronnie Corbett comedy NO – THAT'S ME OVER HERE and been seen in AT LAST THE 1948 SHOW, *We Have Ways of Making You Laugh* and the children's comedy, DO NOT ADJUST YOUR SET. He later worked as script editor on early episodes of THE LIVER BIRDS, wrote for THE TWO RONNIES, created and starred in RUTLAND WEEKEND TELEVISION and its spin-off, *The Rutles*, and headlined as Grant Pritchard in the short-lived American sitcom, *Nearly Departed*. Idle also wrote and sang the theme song for ONE FOOT IN THE GRAVE.

IMRIE, CELIA
(1952–)

British actress in dramatic and comedy roles. Apart from scores of guest appearances, her many credits have included BERGERAC (Marianne Bellshade), *A Question of Guilt*, ORANGES ARE NOT THE ONLY FRUIT (Miss Jewsbury), THE RIFF RAFF ELEMENT (Joanna Tundish), *A Very Open Prison*, *A Dark Adapted Eye* (Vera Hillyard), *Black Hearts in Battersea* (Duchess of Battersea), *Wokenwell* (June Bonney), *Tom Jones* (Mrs Miller), *The Writing on the Wall* (Kirsty), *Into the Blue* (Nadine), *Mr White Goes to Westminster* (Victoria), *Gormenghast* (Lady Gertrude), and various Victoria Wood offerings, including DINNERLADIES (Philippa Moorcroft).

IN AT THE DEEP END
UK (BBC) Documentary. BBC 1 1982–4; 1987

Presenters: **Chris Serle, Paul Heiney**

Executive Producer: **Edward Mirzoeff**
Producer: **Nick Handel**

Two reporters take crash courses in other people's professional skills.

THAT'S LIFE presenters Chris Serle and Paul Heiney alternated as stars of this light-hearted series which saw them attempting to acquire professional skills and put them to the test – all within a matter of weeks. For instance, Serle was called upon to partner snooker star Steve Davis in a doubles match against Tony Meo and Alex Higgins after receiving coaching from the likes of Ray Reardon, Terry Griffiths and Cliff Thorburn. He also underwent intense training to become a press photographer and then covered a royal assignment for the *Daily Mirror*. Between them Serle and Heiney tried their hand at numerous occupations, including auctioneer, actor, shepherd, opera singer, bookmaker and fashion designer.

IN LOVING MEMORY
UK (Yorkshire) Situation Comedy. ITV 1979–86

Ivy Unsworth	**Thora Hird**
Billy Henshaw	**Christopher Beeny**
Amy Jenkinson	**Avis Bunnage**
Ernie Hadfield	**Colin Farrell**
Mary Braithwaite/Henshaw	**Sherrie Hewson**

Writer: **Dick Sharples**
Producer: **Ronnie Baxter**

*A widow and her hapless nephew run a northern
undertaker's.*

When Jeremiah Unsworth died in the first episode of
this series, he left his wife, Ivy, as sole proprietor of his
funeral director's business in the Lancashire mill-town
of Oldshaw. The year was 1929. To help in running the
business, Ivy enlisted her gormless nephew, Billy. Other
local characters, like bachelor Ernie Hadfield, were also
on the scene.

The pilot for this series had been screened some ten
years earlier (and indeed topped the ratings). Written
by Dick Sharples and produced by Ronnie Baxter, this
one-off comedy for Thames cast Edward Chapman and
Marjorie Rhodes in the lead roles of Jeremiah and Ivy.

IN SICKNESS AND IN HEALTH
See TILL DEATH US DO PART.

IN THE HEAT OF THE NIGHT
US (MGM) Police Drama. ITV 1988–90

Chief Bill Gillespie .... **Carroll O'Connor**
Chief of Detectives Virgil Tibbs .... **Howard Rollins**
Althea Tibbs .... **Anne-Marie Johnson**
Sgt Bubba Skinner .... **Alan Autry**
Deputy Parker Williams .... **David Hart**
Deputy Lonnie Jamison .... **Hugh O'Connor**
Deputy Willson Sweet .... **Geoffrey Thorne**
Deputy Junior Abernathy .... **Christian Le Blanc**

Creator: **James Lee Barrett**
Executive Producers: **Fred Silverman, Juanita Bartlett,
David Moessinger, Jeri Taylor, Carroll O'Connor, Hugh
Benson, Ed Ledding**

*TV version of the Oscar-winning film of the same
name.*

Reprising the roles played by Rod Steiger and Sidney
Poitier in the classic movie, Carroll O'Connor, formerly
of ALL IN THE FAMILY, became Police Chief Bill Gillespie
and Howard Rollins black cop Virgil Tibbs. Together
they aimed to fight crime in the small town of Sparta,
Mississippi. Tibbs was a native of the town but had only
just returned home, having worked in the high-tech
police circles of Philadelphia. He found himself
appointed to the role of Chief of Detectives, alongside
Gillespie, although the crusty old cop resented the
appointment, which had been made by a black mayor
seeking black votes. His resentment was not racial (the
series had little of the tension of the original film) but
centred on his dislike of the modern police methods
Tibbs introduced. It was the familiar experience-versus-
youth argument. However, as a team they achieved
results and a healthy mutual respect developed between
the two men.

Carroll O'Connor was forced to withdraw from a few
episodes because of ill-health, and his place was taken
by Joe Don Baker in the guise of Acting Chief Tom
Dugan. Actor Hugh O'Connor, who played Deputy Jamison, was Carroll O'Connor's son.

INCORPORATED TELEVISION
PRODUCTION COMPANY
See ITC.

INCREDIBLE HULK, THE
US (Universal) Science Fiction/Adventure. ITV 1978–82

Dr David Banner .... **Bill Bixby**
The Incredible Hulk .... **Lou Ferrigno**
Jack McGee .... **Jack Colvin**

Executive Producers: **Glen A. Larson, Kenneth Johnson**
Producers: **James D. Parriott, Chuck Bowman**

*A mild-mannered scientist turns into an angry
green monster when provoked.*

Scientist David Banner had become a victim of his own
experiments on human strength by accidentally exposing himself to a massive dose of gamma rays. The effects
of the radiation meant that he turned into a raging green
giant whenever he felt angry. Banner could feel the
change coming on but, after the Hulk had indulged in
an orgy of violence and then reverted to his true self,
Banner could never remember what had happened 'during his absence'.

With the world believing him to be dead, Banner ran
from town to town in search of a cure for his weird
malady. On his tail was *National Register* reporter Jack
McGee, who had guessed Banner's secret and was looking for concrete evidence to back up his suspicions.
Inevitably, something always managed to irk the docile
Dr Jekyll, releasing the shirt-busting, roaring Mr Hyde
figure of the Hulk.

Lou Ferrigno, who played the monster, was a former
Mr Universe, and the series was based on the early 1960s
Marvel comic strip by Stan Lee, in which Banner's Chris-
tian name was Bruce, not David.

INDEPENDENT TELEVISION
COMMISSION
See ITC.

INDEPENDENT TELEVISION NEWS
(ITN)

ITN was established by the 1954 Television Act as a news-
gathering organization jointly owned by the various
ITV companies. Its first news bulletin was aired on 22
September 1955, when Christopher Chataway read the
headlines in a 12-minute programme. Following the
introduction of new regulations in the 1990 Broadcasting
Act, ITN was refounded as a profit-making news business
with commercial contracts to the ITV companies and
other broadcasters. It is now owned by a consortium
made up of Associated Newspapers, Carlton Communi-

cations, the Granada Group, Reuters, and United News and Media. Also in 1990, ITN moved to new purpose-built headquarters in London's Gray's Inn Road. ITN now provides news 24 hours a day, with the main bulletins being *Lunchtime News* at 12.30 (launched in 1972 under the title *First Report* and now monitoring the day's developing stories), *ITV Evening News* at 6.30 (a 30-minute review of the day's events so far), *Channel 4 News* (the 7 p.m. in-depth bulletin), *5 News* (Channel 5 at 6 p.m.) and a late bulletin at 10 or 11 p.m., since 1999 the successor to the highly regarded *News at Ten* (Britain's first 30-minute news programme when introduced in 1967). In addition to these, ITN offers news headlines through the night and a half-hour round-up at 5.30 a.m. known as *ITV Morning News*. The company also provides news services for other broadcasters. *ITN Euronews*, compiled in Lyon, France, supplies world news 20 hours a day in six languages for channels in 43 countries. A bouncy, headline-only format is supplied to Channel 4's THE BIG BREAKFAST, and ITN also compiles radio news bulletins for IRN (Independent Radio News) and Classic fM. Over and above formal news reports, ITN has also produced a number of feature programmes, which have been broadly news and current affairs based. Between 1957 and 1964, for instance, ROVING REPORT was a series of topical documentaries compiled by ITN correspondents around the world. More recently, *House to House*, fronted by Maya Even on Channel 4, reported the business of the day from the Houses of Commons and Lords. There have been programmes on royalty, elections, budgets and other state occasions, too. In August 2000 the 24-hour, digital ITN News Channel was launched. See also NEWS.

INFORMER, THE
UK (Rediffusion) Adventure. ITV 1966–7

Alex Lambert .... **Ian Hendry**
Janet Lambert .... **Heather Sears**
Sylvia Parrish .... **Jean Marsh**
DS Piper .... **Neil Hallett**
Cass .... **Tony Selby**

Creators: **John Whitney, Geoffrey Bellman**
Executive Producer: **Stella Richman**
Producers: **Stella Richman, Peter Collinson, John Whitney**

The risky life of a professional informer.

Disgraced and disbarred barrister Alex Lambert had begun to rebuild his life and his shaky marriage. Using the excellent contacts he had made over the years on both sides of the law, he branched out into a new career as a paid informer. Passing on information to Piper, his police contact, Lambert lived off the substantial rewards offered by insurance companies. But secrecy was vital and his life was continually under threat. Not even his wife was party to his true profession and he masqueraded under the guise of a business consultant.

INHERITED AUDIENCE

An audience that a programme gains from the previous show on the same channel, with viewers not bothering to switch over. Planners make use of inherited audiences to give new series a launch-pad.

INIGO PIPKIN/PIPKINS
UK (ATV) Children's Entertainment. ITV 1973–81

Inigo Pipkin .... **George Woodbridge**
Johnny .... **Wayne Laryea**
Hartley Hare .... **Nigel Plaskitt**
Tortoise .... **Nigel Plaskitt**
Topov .... **Heather Tobias**
                                                           Loraine Bertorelli
                                                           Elizabeth Lindsay
Pig .... **Heather Tobias**
                                                           Loraine Bertorelli
                                                           Anne Rutter
                                                           Alex Knight
Octavia Ostrich .... **Heather Tobias**
                                                           Loraine Bertorelli
                                                           Elizabeth Lindsay
Fred Pipkin .... **Royce Mills**
Mrs P .... **Diana Eden**
Charlie .... **Charles McKeown**
Bertha .... **Jumoke Debayo**
Tom .... **Jonathan Kydd**
Peter .... **Paddy O'Hagan**
Uncle .... **Nigel Plaskitt**
Pigeon .... **Loraine Bertorelli**
Moony .... **Nigel Plaskitt**
Narrator .... **Nigel Plaskitt**

Writers: **Susan Pleat, Anna Standon, David Cregan**
Producer: **Michael Jeans**

Comical adventures in a puppeteer's workshop.

This long-running, pre-school entertainment was set in the workshop of one Inigo Pipkin, a craftsman who specialized in glove puppets called Pipkins. But these were no ordinary puppets: they could sing, dance and behave like humans, and stories followed their adventures in and around the workshop and the fun they had with the items therein. Most fondly remembered were the toothy Hartley Hare, Topov the monkey and Pig. Initially titled *Inigo Pipkin*, the series was renamed *Pipkins* for most of its eight years on air.

INMAN, JOHN
(1935–)

Preston-born actor, a stage pantomime dame, known for his camp roles of menswear assistant Mr Humphries in ARE YOU BEING SERVED? (through which 'I'm free!' became his catchphrase), rock factory proprietor Neville Sutcliffe in *Odd Man Out* and male secretary Graham Jones in *Take a Letter, Mr Jones*. The character of Mr

Humphries resurfaced in the *Are You Being Served?* revival, *Grace and Favour*, in 1992.

INNES BOOK OF RECORDS, THE
UK (BBC) Comedy/Music. BBC 2 1979–81

Host: **Neil Innes**

Producer: **Ian Keill**

Sketches and musical parodies with the former Bonzo Dog man.

In the late 1960s Neil Innes mixed easily with the new breed of alternative comedians, working with the MONTY PYTHON team and inspiring the wacky pop group, The Bonzo Dog Doo Dah Band. In this, his own series, a decade later, he demonstrated his talent for deadpan humour and his flair for uncannily accurate musical send-ups. Anyone who saw *The Rutles* would vouch for this rare ability.

INSIDE GEORGE WEBLEY
UK (Yorkshire) Situation Comedy. ITV 1968–70

George Webley .... **Roy Kinnear**
Rosemary Webley .... **Patsy Rowlands**

Creators/Writers: **Keith Waterhouse, Willis Hall**
Producers: **Bill Hitchcock, John Duncan**

A man's life is dominated by worry.

Bank clerk George Webley was one of life's know-alls and the archetypal worryguts. He fretted over the silliest matters and, in his mind, something was always about to go wrong. Had he left the gas on, for example? His dozy, ever-hungry wife, Rosemary, was far more relaxed.

There was more than an echo of *Inside George Webley* in Paul Smith and Terry Kyan's comedy, COLIN'S SANDWICH, 20 years later.

INSPECTOR ALLEYN MYSTERIES, THE
UK (BBC) Detective Drama. BBC 1 1993–4

Chief Insp. Roderick Alleyn .... **Patrick Malahide**
Insp. Brad Fox .... **William Simons**
Agatha Troy .... **Belinda Lang**

Creator: **Ngaio Marsh**
Producer: **George Gallaccio**

A well-bred, academically brilliant detective works for Scotland Yard in the late 1940s.

New Zealand author Dame Ngaio Marsh's toff detective was first brought to television in the 1960s as part of the DETECTIVE anthology in which he was played by Michael Allinson. Simon Williams donned Alleyn's trilby for a 90-minute special in 1990, but when a series was cast in 1993 it was Patrick Malahide – already familiar as MINDER's Sgt Chisholm – who was offered the role. He portrayed Roderick Alleyn as a true gentleman, unfailingly polite but a steely adversary for law-breakers. A man with a double first in Classics from Oxford, Alleyn was a policeman almost out of a sense of duty. He moved in aristocratic circles but was never a snob. He was supported in his work by the loyal Inspector Fox and in his private life by his artistic lady friend, Agatha Troy (both William Simons and Belinda Lang had taken the same roles in the 1990 offering).

In the original novels, Alleyn's cases covered the period 1933 to 1980 (two years before his creator's death). For this television rendition, the action was confined to 1948. After a run of five mysteries, Alleyn returned in 1994, not in another series but in the first of a collection of one-off investigations.

INSPECTOR MORSE
UK (Zenith/Central/Carlton) Police Drama. ITV 1987–2000

Chief Insp. Endeavour Morse .... **John Thaw**
DS Robbie Lewis .... **Kevin Whately**
Max .... **Peter Woodthorpe**
Dr Grayling Russell .... **Amanda Hillwood**
Chief Supt. Bell .... **Norman Jones**
Chief Supt. Strange .... **James Grout**
Dr Laura Hobson .... **Clare Holman**
Adele Cecil .... **Judy Loe**

Executive Producer: **Ted Childs**
Producers: **Kenny McBain, Chris Burt, David Lascelles, Deirdre Keir**

The complicated cases of a cerebral Oxford detective.

Chief Inspector Morse (first name concealed for many years) of the Thames Valley Police was an Oxford graduate and a lover of culture. Poetry, Wagnerian opera and cryptic crosswords were his passions, along with gallons of real ale to oil the cogs of his brilliant detective mind. Somewhat squeamish for a copper, and always with an eye for the ladies (although seldom a success with the opposite sex), Morse cruised the dreaming-spired streets of Oxford in his 1960 Mark 2 red Jaguar, accompanied by his ingenuous sergeant, Lewis, a Geordie making his way up the CID ladder. Unlike the crotchety bachelor Morse, genial Lewis was a family man, and the contrast between the two was well contrived. The pair enjoyed a good working relationship, even if Morse was cruelly patronizing at times.

The investigations were unfailingly multidimensional and Morse always needed time to collar his man, or woman. His theories regularly went awry, and one murder would turn into two or three before he finally pieced together the solution (often with the help of a chance remark from Lewis), much to the dissatisfaction of his boss, Chief Supt. Strange. Indeed, seldom was there an episode when pathologists like Max or Dr Russell did not have to appear more than once.

With each beautifully photographed episode lasting two hours, there was bags of scope for both character and plot development. Stories initially came from the original novels by Oxford academic Colin Dexter, who endowed Morse with his own love of classics, culture, crosswords and booze. Indeed, Morse's name was derived from Sir Jeremy Morse, then Chairman of Lloyds Bank and one of Dexter's crossword rivals. Lewis, too, was christened after a crossword setter, although in the books he was Welsh and nearing retirement age. When the novels ran out, Dexter penned a series of new plots for TV, before finally handing over the invention to other writers. His involvement with the series continued, however – as an extra, walking on in every episode, as Hitchcock used to do.

The series of *Inspector Morse* ended in 1993, but one-off specials (generally following new books by Colin Dexter) were produced in each of the years 1995–8, with the last-ever episode, based on Dexter's *The Remorseful Day*, being aired in 2000. In the 1997 story, *Death Is Now My Neighbour*, Morse's Christian name was finally revealed as being 'Endeavour'. The programme's sweeping theme music by Barrington Pheloung was cleverly based on the Morse Code beat for the letters M-O-R-S-E.

INSPECTOR WEXFORD

See **RUTH RENDELL MYSTERIES, THE.**

INTERCEPTOR

See **TREASURE HUNT.**

INTERFERENCE

Sound or picture distortion caused by external electrical signals.

INTERNATIONAL DETECTIVE

UK (Delfry/ABC) Detective Drama. ITV 1959–61

Ken Franklin .... **Arthur Fleming**

Producer: **Gordon L. T. Scott**

The adventures of a calm, systematic detective-agency man.

Ken Franklin worked for the William J. Burns International Detective Agency in New York and jetted around the world on various assignments. Given his briefing by W. J. Burns himself (a character never properly seen), Franklin then used intellect rather than brute force to bring home results. Each episode was entitled *'The . . . Case'* (fill in the blank) and was shot in documentary style.

The series was supposedly based on the files of a real William J. Burns agency. Star Arthur (Art) Fleming went on to host one of American TV's most popular quiz shows, *Jeopardy.*

INTERPOL CALLING

UK (Rank/Wrather/ATV) Police Drama. ITV 1959–60

Insp. Paul Duval .... **Charles Korvin**
Insp. Mornay .... **Edwin Richfield**

Executive Producer: **F. Sherwin Green**
Producers: **Anthony Perry, Connery Chapell**

Cases from the files of the International Criminal Police Organization, Interpol.

Inspectors Duval and Mornay, two detectives operating out of Interpol's Paris headquarters, investigated murders, foiled blackmailers, arrested hijackers, duped drug-pushers and apprehended would-be assassins all around the world in this half-hour series. Each episode opened with a speeding car crashing through a checkpoint, setting the pace for the action to follow. Thirty-nine stories were filmed.

INVADERS, THE

US (Quinn Martin) Science Fiction. ITV 1967

David Vincent .... **Roy Thinnes**
Edgar Scoville .... **Kent Smith**
Narrator .... **William Conrad**

Creator: **Larry Cohen**
Executive Producer: **Quinn Martin**
Producer: **Alan A. Armer**

An architect tries to alert the world to an alien invasion.

Most people thought David Vincent was paranoid: he believed the world was under threat from a race of aliens whose planet was dying. In the style of Richard Kimble in THE FUGITIVE, he moved from town to town, attempting to warn the human race, but at the same time keeping himself clear of the Invaders' clutches.

Vincent, an architect, had been driving down a deserted country road and had pulled over to get some sleep. He had been awakened by the arrival of a spaceship and the realization that an invasion was taking place. He had run to bring help, but the police discovered only a young courting couple who denied everything Vincent had said. It was the first of many brick walls to confront him during the course of the series.

Because the Invaders assumed human form, Vincent had great difficulty persuading people to believe his story. Usually, those in whom he placed his trust turned out to be aliens themselves, as even he had problems spotting them. He soon gathered, though, that they were not complete human clones and that they had some strange defects, most notably a crooked little finger. Another giveaway was the fact that, having no hearts, they had no pulse or emotions.

After many narrow escapes, Vincent managed to convince a small group of citizens that his story was true, and he was thus given seven colleagues (known as 'The Believers') to finance and support his mission to save the planet. The leader of the group was Edgar Scoville, a millionaire electronics executive.

The story never was brought to a climax, but Vincent did have his successes. He thwarted various alien plans and killed a number of Invaders during the course of the series, seeing them glow red then evaporate, leaving behind just a burnt outline on the ground. But the aliens, too, were killers, using either ray guns or a small disc device which, when applied to the back of the neck, gave the victim heart failure. Only once was the Invaders' true likeness revealed, and even then it was blurred, leaving the viewer truly mystified about these sinister spacemen. The series was rerun on BBC 2 in 1984 and 1992.

INVERDALE, JOHN
(1957–)

Devon-born sports presenter, moving from Radio 5 Live to front programmes like *On Side*, *Rugby Special* and GRANDSTAND for the BBC.

INVISIBLE MAN, THE
UK (Official Films/ITP/ATV) Science Fiction. ITV 1958–9

Dr Peter Brady .... **Tim Turner** (*voice only*)
Diane Brady .... **Lisa Daniely**
Sally Brady .... **Deborah Watling**
Col. Ward .... **Ernest Clarke**

Producer: **Ralph Smart**

An invisible scientist works for the secret service.

Dr Peter Brady had become a victim of his own experiments into light refraction and had lost his visibility. Unable to reverse the process and condemned to a life of transparency, he became an intelligence agent and worked for the UK Government in places where more obvious spies literally could not tread. He also helped out friends, the police and other needy persons who learned of his unusual attribute while, at the same time, always seeking an antidote for his affliction. Often bandaged up and wearing sunglasses to give him some recognizable form, he was supported by his sister, Diane, and niece, Sally. Colonel Ward was the man at the Ministry.

The series was acclaimed for some of its special effects, which included a self-smoking cigarette and self-drinking glass of wine. The man who played Brady was never credited, although the voice turned out to belong to actor Tim Turner.

INVISIBLE MAN, THE
US (Universal) Science Fiction. BBC 1 1975

Dr Daniel Westin .... **David McCallum**
Walter Carlson .... **Craig Stevens**
Dr Kate Westin .... **Melinda Fee**

Executive Producer: **Harve Bennett**
Producer: **Leslie Stevens**

An invisible scientist undertakes covert missions for a West Coast think-tank.

Dr Daniel Westin had perfected the means of making things invisible, but when he heard that the Government wished to use his achievement for military purposes, he destroyed all his equipment, memorized the formula and made himself invisible in order to escape.

However, with the reversing procedure ineffective, he was stranded in invisibility.

In an effort to pursue a normal life, Westin had a wig, a realistic face mask and rubber hands created, which he pulled off in times of trouble. So that he could continue his experiments and find a way back to normality, he and his wife, Kate, went to work for the KLAE Corporation (a Californian research unit), occasionally performing undercover missions for his boss, Walter Carlson. KLAE financed Westin's attempts to resume normality, and Westin used the codename 'the KLAE Resource' whenever he was in action.

IRELAND: A TELEVISION HISTORY
UK/Ireland (BBC/RTE) Historical Documentary. BBC 2
1980–1

Presenter/Writer: **Robert Kee**

Producers: **Jeremy Isaacs, Jenny Barraclough**

A 13-part account of the development of Ireland.

Bravely attempting to portray the history of this country on television for the first time, Robert Kee's Irish documentary began 800 years earlier, at the point when the English first became involved with their island neighbour. It progressed through to the recent troubles and the days of violence, using eye-witness accounts and old film footage to analyse the underlying causes of the unrest. For its efforts, the series won the BAFTA Best Documentary Series award. Kee also supplied an accompanying book.

IRISH RM, THE
UK (James Mitchell/Rediffusion Films/Ulster/RTE) Drama.
Channel 4 1983–5

Major Sinclair Yeates .... **Peter Bowles**
Philippa Butler/Yeates .... **Doran Godwin**
Florence Macarthy 'Flurry' Knox .... **Bryan Murray**
Sally Knox .... **Lise-Ann McLaughlin**
Mrs Knox .... **Beryl Reid**

Executive Producer: **James Mitchell**
Producer: **Adrian Hughes**

An army major resigns his commission to become a Resident Magistrate in colonial Ireland at the turn of the century.

Prim and proper Major Sinclair Yeates had retired to the rural west coast of Ireland in the hope of enjoying peace in his new role of local magistrate, helping to administer British rule. But his hopes of pastoral calm were rudely shattered by parochial disputes, arguments over livestock and sheer, unfathomable blarney, leaving the rather gullible Yeates deep in hot water, especially if his mischievous landlord, Flurry Knox, was involved. The series was based on the 1899 book *Some Experiences of an Irish RM*, by Somerville and Ross (Edith Somerville and Violet Florence Martin).

IRON HORSE

US (Screen Gems) Western. BBC 1 1967–8

Ben Calhoun .... **Dale Robertson**
Dave Tarrant .... **Gary Collins**
Barnabas Rogers .... **Bob Random**
Nils Torvald .... **Roger Torrey**
Julie Parsons .... **Ellen McRae**

Producers: **Fred Freiberger, Matthew Rapf**

A playboy-gambler becomes a railroad pioneer in the 1880s.

Ben Calhoun had won the Buffalo Pass, Scalplock and Defiance railroad line in a poker game. However, the line was in difficulty, only half constructed and on the verge of bankruptcy. Undaunted, Ben, together with his pet racoon, Ulysses, construction engineer Dave, brawny crewman Nils and Barnabas, an orphan clerk, set about reviving the company's fortunes and getting the trains to run on time through the untamed West. Julie Parsons was introduced later as proprietor of the Scalplock General Store. (Actress Ellen McRae found greater success after changing her name to Burstyn; she picked up an Oscar for *Alice Doesn't Live Here Anymore* in 1974.)

IRONS, JEREMY

(1948–)

Isle of Wight-born actor, now a Hollywood name but successful on TV first in such series as *Notorious Woman* (Franz Liszt), THE PALLISERS (Frank Tregear), *Love for Lydia*, Pinter's adaptation of *Langrishe, Go Down* and BRIDESHEAD REVISITED. In the last, his portrayal of Charles Ryder was widely acclaimed. Early exposure was gained in the children's series, PLAY AWAY. His second wife is actress Sinead Cusack.

IRONSIDE

See MAN CALLED IRONSIDE, A.

ISAACS, Sir JEREMY

(1932–)

Scottish-born producer and TV executive, initially with Granada working on programmes like WHAT THE PAPERS SAY and ALL OUR YESTERDAYS, and then with the BBC (PANORAMA, etc.) and Thames. Among the highlights of his television career have been the acclaimed THE WORLD AT WAR and Robert Kee's IRELAND: A TELEVISION HISTORY (both as producer). He later became Programme Controller at Thames and was the first Chief Executive of Channel 4. Isaacs has also been seen in front of the cameras, as the inquisitor in the revival of FACE TO FACE. After becoming General Director of the Royal Opera House in Covent Garden, 1988–97, he returned to television production with his own company, creating the factual series, *Cold War* and *Millennium: A Thousand Years of History*.

IT AIN'T HALF HOT MUM

UK (BBC) Situation Comedy. BBC 1 1974–81

RSM B. L. Williams .... **Windsor Davies**
Gunner/Bombardier 'Gloria' Beaumont **Melvyn Hayes**
Bombardier 'Solly' Solomons .... **George Layton**
Rangi Ram .... **Michael Bates**
Gunner 'Lofty' Sugden .... **Don Estelle**
Col. Reynolds .... **Donald Hewlett**
Capt. Ashwood .... **Michael Knowles**
Gunner 'Paderewski' Graham .... **John Clegg**
Gunner Mackintosh .... **Stuart McGugan**
Gunner 'Nobby' Clark .... **Kenneth MacDonald**
Gunner Nigel Parkin .... **Christopher Mitchell**
Gunner 'Nosher' Evans .... **Mike Kinsey**
Char Wallah Muhammed .... **Dino Shafeek**
Punka Wallah Rumzan .... **Babar Bhatti**

Creators/Writers: **Jimmy Perry, David Croft**
Producers: **David Croft, Graeme Muir**

Life with an army concert party in the Indian subcontinent.

Set during World War II, *It Ain't Half Hot Mum* focused on the exploits of the Royal Artillery Concert Party as they entertained the active men, and took its name from the content of letters written home by one of its recruits, Gunner Parkin. Joining Parkin in the troupe were Bombardier Solomons (written out after the early episodes), drag artist Gunner Beaumont (known to all as Gloria), intellectual pianist Gunner Graham, diminutive chief vocalist Gunner 'Lofty' Sugden, Scotsman Gunner Mackintosh, and Gunners Clark and Evans. Their out-of-touch COs were the snooty Colonel Reynolds and his idiotic sidekick, Captain Ashwood, but bane of their lives was the Welsh Sgt Major Williams. 'Old Shut Up', as they knew him, considered the concert party to be a bunch of 'pooftahs' (especially Gloria and 'Mr Lah-de-dah Gunner Graham'). He did, however, have more respect for young Parkin, a Colchester lad who, in the Sgt Major's eyes, had a fine pair of shoulders and always set a good example to the rest of the unit (Williams thought he was the boy's father). The local wallahs, genuinely considering themselves to be true Brits, provided the racial humour. The late Michael Bates was blacked up as the comical Rangi Ram and, on Bates's death, Dino Shafeek's loyal char wallah gained more prominence, warbling 'Land of Hope and Glory' after each programme's closing credits. The show opened to the troupe's rousing theme song, inviting viewers to 'Meet the gang 'cos the boys are here, the boys to entertain you'.

Windsor Davies and Don Estelle capitalized on their roles for a spin-off single, 'Whispering Grass', which surprisingly topped the UK charts in 1975.

IT TAKES A THIEF

US (Universal) Spy Drama. ITV 1968–71

Alexander Mundy .... **Robert Wagner**
Noah Bain .... **Malachi Throne**
Wallie Powers .... **Edward Binns**
Alister Mundy .... **Fred Astaire**

Creator: **Collier Young**
Producer: **Jack Arnold**

An expert thief is freed from jail to work for the Government.

Sophisticated, handsome Al Mundy was the perfect cat-burglar, yet, somehow, he had been caught and confined in San Jobel prison. Realizing his potential, the US Government offered him a degree of liberty, inviting him to steal for the SIA intelligence agency. Between missions, Mundy was forced to return to custody, but when he was out he certainly made the most of it, travelling all round the world and making contact with hordes of glamorous women, most of whom fell for his style and charm. His father, Alister, another master thief, was introduced later. He had taught his son the tricks of the trade and now found himself joining Alexander on certain missions. Mundy's SIA chief in the early days was Noah Bain. In later episodes (when Mundy was no longer locked up between assignments), Wallie Powers was his agency contact. Running from 1968 to 1970 in its native USA, the programme received only sporadic screenings around the ITV network in the UK.

IT'LL BE ALRIGHT ON THE NIGHT

UK (LWT) Comedy. ITV 1977–

Presenter/Writer: **Denis Norden.**

Producers: **Paul Smith, Paul Lewis**

Sporadic collections of out-takes and bloopers from the worlds of film and TV.

When the clipboard-clutching Denis Norden, in an avalanche of puns and corny wisecracks, launched *It'll Be Alright on the Night* in 1977, he tapped into a new vein of television comedy. Previously, fluffs and foul-ups by professional actors and TV presenters had been discreetly kept away from the viewing public (although, for years, they had been mischievously edited together by TV technicians for private viewing). Now everything came out into the open and the public loved seeing their word-perfect announcers and performers brought crashing down to earth by a Freudian slip of the tongue or the lapse of an imperfect memory. Clips of actors 'corpsing' (creasing up into uncontrollable laughter) were particularly popular. Because such infelicities are everyday occurrences in TV and film production, Norden has been able to gather up the best scraps from the cutting-room floor at least once every couple of years since, and the best bits have been recycled into various compilation programmes to fill the gaps between new

episodes. The BBC has withheld its own out-takes for use in its similar offering, *Auntie's Bloomers* (1991–), hosted by Terry Wogan, which spawned its own spin-off series, *Auntie's Sporting Bloomers* (1995–7).

IT'S A KNOCKOUT/JEUX SANS FRONTIERES

UK (BBC/Ronin) Game Show. BBC 1 1966–82/Channel 5 1999–

Presenters: **David Vine, Eddie Waring, Stuart Hall, Keith Chegwin, Frank Bruno**

Producers: **Barney Colehan, Cecil Korer, Geoff Wilson, Richard Hearsey, Robin Greene**

Inter-town silly games contests.

Greasy poles, daft costumes, giant beach balls and impossible obstacle courses were the order of the day in *It's a Knockout*. Very loosely based on a 1950s series called *Top Town*, in which amateur entertainers competed for their home town, this series pitched willing and athletic citizens into combat for the right to represent the United Kingdom in the European finals. These finals went out under the title of *Jeux Sans Frontières*.

Each *It's a Knockout* contest consisted of a variety of races and battles in which teams struggled to jump through hoops, climb sticky slopes or splash through water while dressed as outsize cartoon figures. There was usually a theme (often medieval) to link events, and a 'joker' could be played to double the points won in any one game. Interspersed throughout was the Mini-Marathon (the Fil Rouge in the Euro-edition), a drawn-out, multi-element game presided over by rugby league's Eddie Waring. Hosting proceedings initially was David Vine, but he gave way to laugh-a-minute Stuart Hall in 1972. Veteran announcer McDonald Hobley and Katie Boyle were also involved in the very early days, and Arthur Ellis acted as tournament referee for the duration.

Jeux Sans Frontières began in 1967 and was hosted by a different country each week, but always in the presence of international arbiters Gennaro Olivieri and Guido Pancaldi. After a series of international heats, a grand final was held, featuring the top-scoring team from each country. The UK's first representatives were Bridlington, who took on the rest of the Continent in France.

There were numerous *It's a Knockout* celebrity specials, the most notable being *The Grand Knockout Tournament* in 1987, when the four teams competing for charity were captained by HRH the Prince Edward, HRH the Princess Anne, HRH the Duke of York and HRH the Duchess of York. *It's a Knockout* also transferred to the USA in 1975, where it was renamed *Almost Anything Goes*. This survived only one year before being superseded by a celebrity series entitled *All-Star Anything Goes*.

Back in the UK, Channel 5 resurrected the series in summer 1999, with Keith Chegwin the excitable host, assisted by guffawing referee Frank Bruno and scorers Lucy Alexander and Nell McAndrew.

IT'S A SQUARE WORLD
UK (BBC) Comedy. BBC 1960–4

Michael Bentine, Clive Dunn, Frank Thornton, Benny Lee, Len Lowe, Dick Emery, Leon Thau, Ronnie Barker, Louis Mansi, Anthea Wyndham, Janette Rowselle, John Bluthal, Freddie Earlie, Joe Gibbons

Creator: **Michael Bentine**
Writers: **Michael Bentine, John Law**
Producers: **G. B. Lupino, James Gilbert, John Street, Joe McGrath**

Madcap, surreal, early sketch show.

Collating fictitious reports from the four corners of the world and adding much more besides, *It's a Square World* was a direct ancestor of MONTY PYTHON and other bizarre comedies. Former Goon Michael Bentine was the brains behind the project, and he and an extensive supporting cast starred in a series of zany visual sketches which pushed back the boundaries of TV comedy. Bentine had a penchant for scale models, using them to weird effect. Boats were a favourite: he caused the Woolwich Ferry to sink in one stunt, and in another famous episode sent a Chinese junk to attack the House of Commons. Bentine also planted a 40-foot whale outside the Natural History Museum, much to the dismay of local drivers, and, on another occasion, sent the BBC Television Centre into space.

A follow-up series, *All Square*, appeared courtesy of ATV in 1966–7 and there was a one-off *It's a Square World* revival back on BBC 1 in 1977.

IT'S DARK OUTSIDE
UK (Granada) Police Drama. ITV 1964–5

DI Charles Rose	**William Mervyn**
DS Swift	**Keith Barron**
Anthony Brand	**John Carson**
Alice Brand	**June Tobin**
DS Hunter	**Anthony Ainley**
Claire	**Veronica Strong**
Fred Blaine	**John Stratton**
Sebastian	**Oliver Reed**

Producer: **Derek Bennett**

The return of the sharp-tongued detective, Mr Rose.

It's Dark Outside formed the middle segment of a trilogy of series featuring the acerbic Inspector Rose. He had first appeared in THE ODD MAN six months earlier, as did the character of Detective Sgt Swift, a soft-hearted, pensive copper. Now they were joined by Anthony and Alice Brand, a barrister and his journalist wife, though not for long. By the second season the Brands and Swift were gone, leaving the calm, cold Rose in prime position, supported by newcomers DS Hunter (Anthony Ainley, a future DOCTOR WHO Master), his girlfriend, Claire, and her boozy reporter friend, Fred Blaine. A young actor

named Oliver Reed appeared in some episodes as Sebastian, the ringleader of a bunch of tearaways. The programme gained a cult following for its grim, tense, almost *film noir* atmosphere and it also generated a chart-topping single, Jackie Trent's 'Where Are You Now (My Love)'. For more adventures with the refined investigator, see MR ROSE.

IT'S GARRY SHANDLING'S SHOW
US (Showtime) Situation Comedy. BBC 2 1987–90

Garry Shandling	**Garry Shandling**
Mrs Ruth Shandling	**Barbara Cason**
Nancy Bancroft	**Molly Cheek**
Pete Schumaker	**Michael Tucci**
Jackie Schumaker	**Bernadette Birkett**
Grant Schumaker	**Scott Nemes**
Leonard Smith	**Paul Willson**
Phoebe Bass	**Jessica Harper**

Creators: **Garry Shandling, Alan Zweibel**
Executive Producers: **Bernie Brillstein, Brad Grey, Garry Shandling**

Unusual comedy series in which the star played himself and talked directly to the studio audience.

This show was based around the fictitious life of neurotic comic Garry Shandling, with the set modelled around his real-life sitting-room. There was a plot (of sorts) in each episode, usually centring on Garry's lack of success with women or other paranoia. He confided in viewers and positively encouraged the studio audience to welcome the guest stars he introduced. Other members of the cast also engaged the audience, and the whole show was put together so that it parodied the techniques and conventions of television.

Regular droppers-by to his Sherman Oaks condominium were his mother, his friend Nancy Bancroft and neighbours the Schumakers, with intelligent young son, Grant. Nosy Leonard Smith, manager of the building, also appeared. Just before the series ended, Garry married his girlfriend, Phoebe Bass.

This break-all-the-rules type of television was not new. The inspiration was very clearly THE BURNS AND ALLEN SHOW in the 1950s, in which George Burns drew himself aside from the plots to discuss the show with viewers. This technique has become known as 'breaking the fourth wall'.

ITA
See ITC (Independent Television Commission).

ITC
(Incorporated Television Programme Co.)

ITC was the company founded in 1954 by theatrical businessmen Lew and Leslie Grade, Prince Littler and Val Parnell to bid for one of the first ITV franchises. Initially unsuccessful, ITC turned instead to independent production and distribution, with THE

ADVENTURES OF ROBIN HOOD the first commissioned programme. However, the group were soon asked to join another consortium, which had won a franchise but was having difficulty getting on air. The resulting company became ATV. To avoid conflicts of interest between the broadcasting company and the production company, ATV took over full control of ITC in 1957, making it a wholly owned subsidiary. ITC went on to specialize in action series like DANGER MAN, THE SAINT, THE CHAMPIONS, RANDALL AND HOPKIRK (DECEASED) and THE PRISONER, as well as most of the Gerry Anderson puppet series and, in the 1970s, THE MUPPET SHOW. ITC was sold to Australian businessman Robert Holmes à Court in 1982, who in turn sold it to another Australian, Alan Bond. A management buy-out later conferred control into yet newer hands. In 1995 it was taken over by Polygram, and today it is owned by Carlton Communications.

ITC
(Independent Television Commission)

The ITC is the public organization that is responsible for licensing and regulating commercially funded television services in the UK. However, the Government has set out proposals for its role to be taken over by a new super-regulator called Ofcom from 2003.

The ITC replaced both the IBA (Independent Broadcasting Authority) and the Cable Authority on 1 January 1991. It not only grants broadcasting licences to Channel 3 (ITV) companies, Channel 4, Channel 5, cable channels and satellite services but also monitors their progress, ensuring they adhere to the strict standards and guidelines it lays down for programming and advertising. Those failing to do so are liable to penalties. The Chairman, Deputy Chairman and the eight Members of the Commission are all appointed by the Secretary of State for Culture, Media and Sport, and the ITC is funded by licence fees payable by contracting broadcasters.

The ITC's predecessor, the IBA, was responsible for both independent television and independent radio. It had a greater 'hands-on' approach to programme monitoring, with the various contractors needing to agree schedules with the IBA (in accordance with the Broadcasting Act). As a result, the IBA was the legally accountable broadcaster. Under the new system it is the programme company which is legally accountable. The IBA, inaugurated in 1971, was a descendant of the ITA (Independent Television Authority), which was established by Parliament under the Television Act of 1954 and concerned itself solely with the appointment and output of ITV companies in the days before the advent of independent radio.

ITN
See INDEPENDENT TELEVISION NEWS.

ITV
(Channel 3)

Independent television arrived in the UK in 1955 after years of debate. There were widespread fears that commercial television would turn out to be a vulgar and gimmicky concept, fears that were stimulated by the American experience, where sponsors and game shows ruled the airwaves. Nevertheless, the Television Act of 1954 bravely opened up the television market to an advertising-led channel.

This channel was controlled and regulated by a public body, the Independent Television Authority (ITA), who owned the transmitters, oversaw programme standards and monitored advertising. A federal system was conceived for broadcasters. For coverage, the UK was carved up into regions; independent companies then applied for sole transmission rights, selling advertising to generate revenue and paying a levy to the ITA for their licences. The first ITV region to go on air was London, where the franchise was split into weekdays and weekends. Associated-Rediffusion was awarded the Monday-to-Friday contract, with ATV handling Saturday and Sunday. The first transmission was on 22 September 1955, when Associated-Rediffusion and ATV jointly held a Gala Opening Night, beginning with a formal inauguration ceremony at London's Guildhall. The new channel was known by a number of names, the most common being CTV, Channel 9 or ITA.

Piecemeal, the other elements of the ITV network fell into place until, by 1962, nearly all of the UK, including the Channel Islands, was covered (the one exception, the Isle of Man, followed in 1965). The ITV companies were closely monitored for performance and over the years several franchise reviews were held. In 1964 all the companies passed muster (except for Wales West and North, which had gone out of business). In 1967 there were several changes. ATV was given the Midlands on a seven-day-a-week basis, and Associated-Rediffusion and ABC (the contractor for the Midlands and the north at weekends) were asked to merge to take on the London weekday franchise. This they did under the name of Thames Television. London at weekends was given to London Weekend Television (LWT). In Wales and the west TWW lost its licence to Harlech Television, and in the north Granada was allowed to extend its transmission times from five to seven days a week, but had to relinquish the area east of the Pennines to a new franchisee (ultimately Yorkshire Television). In 1980 there were more changes. Out went Westward Television (the contractor for the south-west) and Southern (southern England), to be replaced by TSW and TVS respectively. At the same time ATV was obliged to reconstitute itself as Central Independent Television to hang on to the Midlands area.

For the next round of franchise renewals a new system was brought into play by the Conservative Government. Instead of merely applying for the licence to broadcast, prospective ITV companies were asked to bid for the franchise. This was designed to extract more money from ITV companies, which the Government felt were operating advertising monopolies in their individual areas. Under the new system, the highest bidder would get the franchise, provided that the new regulatory body, the ITC, was happy with the business plan and the commitment to programme quality. In highly controversial circumstances, Thames was outbid by Carlton Communications and lost its franchise. However, Granada was outbid by Mersey Television but retained its franchise. Other losers were TVS and TSW (both deemed to have overbid) and these gave way to Meridian and Westcountry respectively. TV-am, the breakfasttime contractor appointed in 1980, lost out to Sunrise Television (soon to be renamed GMTV). The farcicality of the situation was further outlined when it was revealed that Central (unopposed in its application) secured the profitable Midlands area with a bid of just £2,000. Since this restructuring, ITV has been officially known as Channel 3. There has also been much consolidation in the industry, with the effect that there are now only two major players on the ITV stage – Granada (owner of LWT, Tyne Tees, Yorkshire, Anglia, Meridian and some of GMTV) and Carlton (owner of Central, Westcountry, HTV and also part of GMTV). Some commentators believe that it is only a matter of time before ITV becomes just one big company.

ITV 2

Launched on 7 December 1998, ITV 2 is the digital sister channel to Channel 3. It majors on youth appeal, with a strong sports emphasis (including alternative live football coverage to matches shown on ITV) and repeats of the week's big ITV programmes like CORONATION STREET and EMMERDALE, plus re-runs of major dramas from further back. The channel – known as S2 in Scotland – was initially available only via ONdigital and some cable networks, and not via digital satellite.

IVANHOE

UK (Sydney Box) Adventure. ITV 1958

Ivanhoe .... **Roger Moore**
Gurth .... **Robert Brown**
Bart .... **John Pike**
Prince John .... **Andrew Keir**
King Richard .... **Bruce Seton**

Executive Producer: **Peter Rogers**
Producer: **Herbert Smith, Bernard Coote**

The chivalrous hero of Sir Walter Scott's novel takes on a 'Robin Hood' mantle.

Ivanhoe returned home after the Crusades to find that good King Richard had been usurped by his wicked brother, Prince John, who was now tyrannizing the people. Having freed Gurth and Bart, two doomed serfs who became his squires, he set about righting wrongs and helping those in distress. This swashbuckling series was Roger Moore's first starring role and he bravely performed his own stunts. Its executive producer, Peter Rogers, went on to develop the *Carry On* series of films.

The original *Ivanhoe* tale has since been dramatized twice by the BBC, in 1970 starring Eric Flynn (father of Jerome), and again in 1997, starring Steven Waddington.

IVOR THE ENGINE

UK (Smallfilms) Cartoon. ITV 1962–4/BBC 1 1976–9

Narrators: **Oliver Postgate, David Edwards, Anthony Jackson, Olwen Griffiths**

Writer: **Oliver Postgate**
Producer: **Oliver Postgate**

The homely adventures of a little Welsh steam train.

'In the top left-hand corner of Wales there was a railway called the Merioneth and Llantissily Rail Traction Company Ltd', so viewers of this animation were told before being introduced to the railway's star employee, Ivor the Engine. Bearing the M&LRT Co. Ltd livery, the little green puffer was driven by Jones the Steam, who worked in conjunction with colleagues like Owen the Signal and Dai Station, the man who looked after Llaniog Station. Ivor's boiler was fired by Idris, a small dragon with a high-pitched voice who took up residence when his volcano home was rendered uninhabitable. In a series of quaint little adventures, Ivor and Jones chugged around the mountainous landscape of Wales helping out citizens in trouble and longing to sing in the choir, like Ivor's friend, Evans the Song.

Ivor the Engine was produced by the Smallfilms partnership of Oliver Postgate and Peter Firmin, with Firmin drawing all the pictures. It was first screened at lunchtime on ITV via Associated-Rediffusion, before transferring to the BBC in 1976.

JACKANORY
UK (BBC) Children's Entertainment. BBC 1/BBC 2
1965–96

Executive Producers: **Anna Home, Angela Beeching**
Producers: **Joy Whitby, David Coulter, Anna Home,
Daphne Jones, David Turnball, Angela Beeching,
Christine Secombe, Margie Barbour, Roger
Singleton-Turner, Nel Romano**

Celebrity storytime for younger viewers.

Jackanory took its name from the nursery rhyme which
begins 'I'll tell you a story of Jackanory . . .', and that
effectively sums up what the programme was about –
simple storytelling. The success and longevity of the
programme stemmed from this most basic of formats,
with just a few illustrations and the narrative skills of
the guest reader as embellishments.

Characterized in its golden age by twirling kaleidoscope images in its opening and closing credits, *Jackanory*
usually presented just one book a week, its contents
abridged to fit over five 15-minute editions with the same
reader employed for the duration (later episodes were
shown on BBC 2 on Sunday mornings). The first story
to be featured was *Cap of Rushes*, told by Lee Montague.
Over the years, more than 700 books were read, by over
400 storytellers. Bernard Cribbins holds the record for
most appearances, followed by the late Kenneth Williams. Many children's favourites were aired, some more
than once, with Roald Dahl recognized as the viewers'
top author (his *Charlie and the Chocolate Factory* was
voted number one in a poll on the occasion of *Jackanory*'s
20th birthday). In 1979, Tolkien's *The Hobbit* was read to
celebrate the programme's 3,000th edition. In 1984, HRH
the Prince of Wales narrated his own story, *The Old Man
of Lochnagar*.

A sister programme of playlets, *Jackanory Playhouse*,
was also developed (1972–85).

JACKSON, GLENDA
MP, CBE (1936–)

Birkenhead-born actress and latterly Labour MP for
Hampstead and Highgate, whose television highlight
was her Emmy-award-winning title role in ELIZABETH R,
though a later appearance as Cleopatra with Morecambe
and Wise in a play 'wot Ernie wrote' ironically is just as
well remembered by viewers. One of Jackson's last TV
performances before taking her seat in the House came
in the 1991 John Le Carré drama, *A Murder of Quality*. She
has since returned to narrate the documentary series,
Boss Women.

JACKSON, GORDON
OBE (1923–90)

With his soft Scottish burr and impeccable com-
portment, Gordon Jackson became one of TV viewers'
favourite personalities in the early 1970s in his guise of

the reliable butler, Hudson, in UPSTAIRS, DOWNSTAIRS. His next starring role, however, was in quite a different vein, as George Cowley, the demanding boss of Bodie and Doyle in THE PROFESSIONALS. All this came after a lengthy career as a character actor in the British film and theatre industries and television appearances in plays and series like DR FINLAY'S CASEBOOK and MYSTERY AND IMAGINATION. Jackson was one of the hosts of STARS ON SUNDAY and also popped up in programmes and TV movies such as *Spectre*, *The Last Giraffe*, THE NEW AVENGERS, *Noble House* (Supt. Armstrong), *My Brother Tom* and *A Town Like Alice* (Noel Strachan).

JACKSON, KATE
(1948–)

American actress, one of the original three CHARLIE'S ANGELS, a role she was awarded after appearing in the supernatural daytime soap, *Dark Shadows*, and another US action series, *The Rookies*. Jackson stayed with *Charlie's Angels*, playing the part of team leader Sabrina Duncan, for three years, eventually leaving to concentrate on film work and TV movies. She returned to US prime-time TV in 1983, playing secret agent Amanda King in *Scarecrow and Mrs King*, a role which lasted four years. In 1988 she played the lead in the TV series version of the film, *Baby Boom*.

JACOBI, Sir DEREK
CBE (1938–)

Distinguished British thespian who won the plaudits of TV viewers with his portrayal of the stammering, bumbling Claudius in I, CLAUDIUS. Previously, Jacobi had appeared in THE STRAUSS FAMILY (Josef Lanner) and THE PALLISERS (Lord Fawn), and post-Claudius he has starred as spy Guy Burgess in *Philby, Burgess and Maclean*, Mr Pye, George Salisbury in the *Screenplay* presentation, *The Vision Thing*, Alan Turing in *Breaking the Code*, Squire Fairfield in *The Wyvern Mystery* and as the monastic sleuth, CADFAEL. He also contributed to THE BBC TELEVISION SHAKESPEARE (Richard II). In TV movies, Jacobi was seen as Frollo in *The Hunchback of Notre Dame* and Hitler in *Inside the Third Reich*.

JACOBS, DAVID
CBE (1926–)

Silken-voiced, London-born radio and television personality, one of the original presenters of TOP OF THE POPS when it started in 1964, although Jacobs had already been host of the successful JUKE BOX JURY since 1959. Jacobs also chaired *Tell the Truth* in the 1950s, hosted a brief revival of WHAT'S MY LINE? in 1973, and compered COME DANCING. He is the younger brother of drama director John Jacobs and the father of actress Emma Jacobs.

JACOBS, DAVID

American writer/producer, creator of DALLAS and its spin-off, KNOTS LANDING, among other prime-time TV credits.

JACQUES, HATTIE
(Josephina Edwina Jacques; 1924–80)

Kent-born actress and comedienne, seen most often in matronly roles in the cinema (particularly in *Carry On* films) and as a foil for Eric Sykes on TV. She played Eric's sister in SYKES for many years from 1960, having previously worked with him on the radio series, *Educating Archie*. However, Hattie did once have a series of her own, MISS ADVENTURE in 1964, in which she played investigator Stacey Smith who haplessly stumbled into global escapades. She also starred as Georgina Ruddy in the communal comedy, OUR HOUSE, in 1960, played Miss Manger in the shortlived sitcom, *Charley's Grants*, in 1970, and appeared in HANCOCK'S HALF HOUR, *The World of Beachcomber* and as a guest on THAT WAS THE WEEK THAT WAS as well as many other shows. She was once married to John Le Mesurier.

JAFFE, SAM
(1893–1984)

American actor seen in many series, from ALFRED HITCHCOCK PRESENTS to ALIAS SMITH AND JONES and BUCK ROGERS IN THE 25TH CENTURY, as well as numerous TV movies and mini-series, though he is chiefly remembered as the distinguished Dr Zorba in BEN CASEY.

JAMES, CLIVE
(1939–)

Perceptive, wry Australian journalist, commentator and TV personality, one-time member of the Cambridge Footlights. His series, *Saturday Night People*, *Clive James on Television*, *The Late Clive James*, *Postcard From . . .*, *Saturday Night Clive*, *The Talk Show with Clive James*, CLIVE JAMES – FAME IN THE TWENTIETH CENTURY and *The Clive James Show*, as well as regular New Year's Eve parties, have amply demonstrated his self-effacing wit, droll humour and keenness to poke gentle fun (particularly at foreign television programmes). In addition, James was a regular on *Up Sunday* and has contributed numerous single features (such as *Clive James and the Calendar Girls*, *Clive James Meets Roman Polanski* and *Clive James Finally Meets Frank Sinatra*). He also presented the film magazine, CINEMA, for a while and has his own production company, Watchmaker Productions.

JAMES, GERALDINE
(1950–)

English actress seen in a variety of prominent dramas. These have included *Dummy* (Sandra X), *The History Man* (Barbara Kirk), THE JEWEL IN THE CROWN (Sarah Layton), *I Remember Nelson* (Emma Hamilton), BLOTT ON THE LANDSCAPE (Lady Maud Lynchwood), *Stanley and the Women* (Dr Trish Collings), *The Healer* (Dr Mercedes Honeysett), *Over Here* (Lady Beatrice Billingham), BAND OF GOLD (Rose Garrity), *Drovers' Gold* (Ruth), KAVANAGH QC (Eleanor Harker) and *The Sins* (Gloria Green), plus *Screen One*'s *Ex* (Alice), *Losing Track* (Mrs Dewey) and *Doggin' Around* (Sarah Williams), and *Performance*'s *A Doll's House* (Mrs Linde).

JAMES, P. D.
See P. D. JAMES.

JAMES, SID
(1913–76)

South African comic actor, a stalwart of the *Carry On* films. On television (and radio) in the 1950s, James was the perfect foil for Tony Hancock in HANCOCK'S HALF HOUR, which led to his own sitcom, *East End – West End*, in 1958. From this base, he went on to star in a succession of comedies. These included CITIZEN JAMES (champion of the underdog Sid James), TAXI (cabbie Sid Stone), GEORGE AND THE DRAGON (chauffeur George Russell), TWO IN CLOVER (rat race escapee Sid Turner) and BLESS THIS HOUSE (frustrated family man Sid Abbott), all of which gave him ample opportunity to exercise his trademark dirty chuckle. James's earliest contributions came in single dramas in the 1940s.

JAMESON, LOUISE
(1951–)

London-born actress with a number of prominent roles to her name. These have included Leela in DOCTOR WHO, Dr Anne Reynolds in *The Omega Factor*, Blanche Simmons in TENKO, Susan Young, Jim's girlfriend, in BERGERAC and, most recently, Rosa di Marco in EASTENDERS. Jameson has also appeared in Z CARS, EMMERDALE FARM, CASUALTY, THE SECRET DIARY OF ADRIAN MOLE AGED 13¾, THE GENTLE TOUCH, *Cider With Rosie*, *The Boy Dominic*, THE BILL and *Rides* (Janet), among other series.

JANE
UK (BBC) Comedy. BBC 2 1982

Jane .... **Glynis Barber**

Producer: **Ian Keill**

Ten-minute short based on the wartime cartoon heroine.

Featuring a pre-DEMPSEY AND MAKEPEACE Glynis Barber, this inventive filler placed live actors and actresses against cartoon backgrounds to re-create the adventures of the *Daily Mirror*'s forces favourite. Jane, originally drawn by Norman Pett, had a disconcerting habit of losing her outer clothing, which left her struggling through various escapades in nothing but her underwear. The episodes were screened on five consecutive nights and an omnibus edition was shown the following weekend. Two years later, Jane returned in another five episodes entitled *Jane in the Desert*.

JANSSEN, DAVID
(David Meyer; 1930–80)

For four years in the 1960s, TV audiences worldwide sweated with David Janssen in his guise of Dr Richard Kimble, aka THE FUGITIVE, as his nemesis, Lt. Philip Gerard, closed in time and again. It was a role that made Janssen one of TV's biggest stars and followed another lead role as *Richard Diamond, Private Detective*, between 1957 and 1960. All the same, Janssen had to wait nearly ten years after *The Fugitive* ended for a series to approach the success of his 1960s hit. That was HARRY O, in which he played wounded private eye Harry Orwell, one of the 1970s' quirky investigators. In between had come a largely unnoticed drama, *O'Hara, US Treasury*. Janssen's last dramatic contribution to television was the expensive mini-series, *Centennial*, in which he played Paul Garrett. He died of a heart attack just before his 50th birthday.

JANUS, SAMANTHA
(1972–)

British actress whose TV highlights have included *Demob* (Hedda), PIE IN THE SKY (Nicola), GAME ON (Mandy Wilkins), the pilot for *The Grimleys* (Geraldine Titley), *Imogen's Face* (Imogen), *Babes in the Wood* (Ruth) and LIVERPOOL ONE (DC Isobel De Pauli). Other credits have come in *Sharman* and MINDER. In 1991 she represented the UK in the EUROVISION SONG CONTEST, singing 'A Message to Your Heart' and finishing tenth.

JARVIS, MARTIN
(1941–)

British actor seen in dramas like *Nicholas Nickleby* (title role), *Breakaway* (Sam Harvey), DOCTOR WHO, CRIME OF PASSION, THE RIVALS OF SHERLOCK HOLMES, THE PALLISERS, WITHIN THESE WALLS, JULIET BRAVO, ENEMY AT THE DOOR, RUMPOLE OF THE BAILEY, MURDER MOST HORRID, INSPECTOR MORSE and *Sex 'n' Death* (Neil Biddle). His major roles have been in THE FORSYTE SAGA (Jon Forsyte) and the sitcom, RINGS ON THEIR FINGERS (Oliver Pryde). He also played Godfrey Ablewhite in the BBC's 1972 adaptation of *The Moonstone*, Uriah Heep in its 1975 *David Copperfield*, M. de Rênal in its 1993 *Scarlet and Black* and Baron de Whichehalse in *Lorna Doone* in 2000. As narrator, his voice has added authority to such series as SURVIVAL and HORIZON. He is married to actress Rosalind Ayres.

JASON, DAVID
OBE (David White; 1940–)

One of British television's biggest stars since the 1980s, Finchley-born David Jason came late into the acting world, having first trained as an electrician. He was discovered in a play on Bournemouth pier by producer Humphrey Barclay and his TV break arrived in 1968, in the bizarre children's comedy, DO NOT ADJUST YOUR SET. One role he played in the series was 'superhero' Captain Fantastic, who also appeared later in MAGPIE. From there he moved into sitcom, with the kids' series, *Two Ds and a Dog* (chauffeur Dingle Bell), and then with Ronnie Barker in HARK AT BARKER, *His Lordship Entertains* (both as Dithers the gardener) and *Six Dates with Barker*. He appeared in the Richard Gordon '*Doctor*' series, was a gardener in CROSSROADS, guested in Z CARS and then gained his own vehicles, THE TOP SECRET LIFE OF EDGAR BRIGGS, playing an inept spy, and *Lucky Feller*, as shy plumber Shorty Mepstead. As the wily old lag Blanco in PORRIDGE and the hapless and frustrated shop boy Granville in OPEN ALL HOURS Jason almost became Ronnie Barker's protégé, but was then given another series of his own, playing Peter Barnes for three years in *A Sharp Intake of Breath*. In 1981 Jason was offered a role which took him to the top of his trade, that of wideboy Del Boy Trotter in ONLY FOOLS AND HORSES. After this, Jason never looked back and branched out into straight(er) drama as the porter Skullion in PORTERHOUSE BLUE, Ted Simcock in A BIT OF A DO, chirpy Pop Larkin in THE DARLING BUDS OF MAY, Billy Mac in the *Screen One* presentation, *The Bullion Boys*, and the morose copper, Jack Frost, in A TOUCH OF FROST (which also featured his real-life brother, Arthur White). He starred in the one-off dramas, *March in Windy City* (Steven March) and *All the King's Men* (Captain Frank Beck), and, in contrast, took viewers on scuba tours of the Caribbean Sea in *David Jason: in His Element* and the Pacific in *David Jason in Search of Paradise*, and looked at Australian wildlife in *David Jason with Killers and Koalas*. He also voiced the part of Toad in the 1980s animation of *The Wind in the Willows*, the DANGERMOUSE and *Count Duckula* cartoon characters, and Rola Pola Bear in the kids' series, *The Adventures of Dawdle*.

JASON KING
UK (Scoton/ITC) Detective Drama. ITV 1971–2

Jason King	Peter Wyngarde
Nicola Harvester	Ann Sharp
Sir Brian	Dennis Price
Ryland	Ronald Lacey

Creators: **Dennis Spooner, Monty Berman**
Producer: **Monty Berman**

Light-hearted DEPARTMENT S *spin-off featuring novelist Jason King.*

Jason King had been the prominent member of the *Department S* team. This was not surprising, given the extravagant lifestyle he enjoyed and the outrageous 1970s fashions he favoured. Now out on his own, he continued writing his 'Mark Caine' mysteries and indulging in investigations of his own, usually surrounded by beautiful girls. Nicola Harvester was his publisher, and Sir Brian, together with his assistant, Ryland, were civil servants who blackmailed King (over tax evasion) into working for the Government from time to time. His assignments were considerably more down-to-earth than the baffling *Department S* cases, despite being set in exotic locations.

JAY, Sir ANTONY
(1930–)

Former TONIGHT journalist who helped launch THAT WAS THE WEEK THAT WAS in 1962 and later wrote for THE FROST REPORT. He also served on the Annan Committee, which looked into the future of British broadcasting in the 1970s. However, Jay's greatest success came in collaboration with Jonathan Lynn when he created and wrote YES, MINISTER (and, later, *Yes, Prime Minister*). The show became a firm favourite with politicians, and Jay picked up a knighthood in 1987.

JAY, PETER
(1937–)

British journalist, currently the BBC's Economic Editor. The son of Labour cabinet minister Douglas Jay, he worked in the Treasury and then became Economics Editor of *The Times*. From 1972 Jay was the presenter of WEEKEND WORLD, ITV's Sunday political programme, until leaving in 1977 to take up an appointment as British Ambassador to the USA, bestowed on him by his father-in-law, premier James Callaghan. He returned to television in 1983 as head of TV-am, bringing with him a 'mission to explain', as the new station set out to provide news and information to early morning viewers. However, with audiences and advertising woefully low, Jay was forced to leave after six weeks, and with his departure the tone of the programming became less serious. Other credits have included *A Week in Politics*.

JAYSTON, MICHAEL
(Michael James; 1935–)

British stage and screen actor whose television work has majored on adaptations of classics (he was Edward Rochester in the BBC's 1980 version of *Jane Eyre*) but also extends to comedy, as well as dramas like THE POWER GAME and CALLAN. He took the part of Charles Rolls in THE EDWARDIANS episode, *Mr Rolls and Mr Royce*, and then, in 1975, starred as *Quiller* in a TV version of the 1966 George Segal film, *The Quiller Memorandum*. Among his later credits have been parts in *About Face*, TINKER, TAILOR, SOLDIER, SPY (Peter Guillam), A BIT OF A DO (Neville Badger), *Haggard* (Sir Joshua), DOCTOR WHO, THE DARLING BUDS OF MAY, THE GOOD GUYS and OUTSIDE EDGE (Bob Willis).

JEEVES AND WOOSTER
UK (Granada/Picture Partnership) Comedy Drama.
ITV 1990–3

Jeeves	Stephen Fry
Bertie Wooster	Hugh Laurie
Aunt Agatha	Mary Wimbush
	Elizabeth Spriggs
Aunt Dahlia	Brenda Bruce
	Vivian Pickles
	Patricia Lawrence
	Jean Heywood
Roderick Spode	John Turner
Madeline Bassett	Francesca Folan
	Diana Blackburn
	Elizabeth Morton
Gussie Fink-Nottle	Richard Garnett
	Richard Braine
Oofy Prosser	Richard Dixon
Sir Watkyn Bassett	John Woodnutt
Tuppy Glossop	Robert Daws
Barmy Fotheringay Phipps	Adam Blackwood
	Martin Clunes
Stiffy Byng	Charlotte Attenborough
	Amanda Harris

Writer: **Clive Exton**
Executive Producer: **Sally Head**
Producer: **Brian Eastman**

An aristocratic airhead is bailed out by his savvy butler.

This adaptation of P. G. Wodehouse's tales of upper-class twit Bertie Wooster and his redeeming valet, Jeeves, was tailor-made for the comedy double act of Stephen Fry and Hugh Laurie, who donned period costume for their 1930s roles. As the socializing Wooster stumbled from social disaster to social disaster, sometimes in trepidation of his London aunts Agatha and Dahlia, it was the calm, resourceful Jeeves who rode to the rescue. Later episodes were set in New York.

An earlier (1965–7) BBC version, entitled *The World of Wooster*, starred Ian Carmichael as Wooster and Dennis Price as Jeeves.

JEMIMA SHORE INVESTIGATES
UK (Thames) Detective Drama. ITV 1983

Jemima Shore	Patricia Hodge

Creator: **Antonia Fraser**
Producer: **Tim Aspinall**

A TV reporter discovers blackmail and murder among the upper classes.

Jemima Shore was a TV reporter, the writer and presenter of Megalith Television's *Jemima Shore Investigates*. In her spare time, as well as indulging her love of music, her inquiring mind led her into amateur detective work, prowling around her own high-class social circles and sniffing out crime amid the aristocracy and the *nouveaux riches*. The stories were based on the novels by Antonia Fraser.

Shore made her TV bow as early as 1978 when, portrayed by Maria Aitken, she appeared in an *Armchair Thriller* presentation entitled *Quiet as a Nun*.

JENKIN, GUY

British producer, director and comedy writer, often in conjunction with Andy Hamilton (see Hamilton's entry for joint credits). Jenkin's solo work has included sketches for A KICK UP THE EIGHTIES, SPITTING IMAGE, *Saturday Live* and *Now – Something Else*, plus an episode of *Look at the State We're In!*. He also wrote *Screen Two*'s *A Very Open Prison* and *Crossing the Floor*, *Screen One*'s *The Lord of Misrule*, and Channel 4's *Mr White Goes to Westminster*.

JENNIE, LADY RANDOLPH CHURCHILL
UK (Thames) Historical Drama. ITV 1974

Jennie Jerome/Lady Randolph Churchill	Lee Remick
Lord Randolph Churchill	Ronald Pickup
Duchess of Marlborough	Rachel Kempson
Duke of Marlborough	Cyril Luckham
Count Kinsky	Jeremy Brett
George Cornwallis-West	Christopher Cazenove
Mrs Patrick Campbell	Siân Phillips
Winston Churchill	Warren Clarke
Mr Leonard Jerome	Dan O'Herlihy
Mrs Jerome	Helen Horton
Aunt Leonie	Barbara Parkins

Writer: **Julian Mitchell**
Executive Producer: **Stella Richman**
Producer: **Andrew Brown**

The life and career of the mother of Sir Winston Churchill.

This seven-part drama was produced as part of the celebrations to mark the centenary of Churchill's birth, and it focused on the life of his mother, an American born into a wealthy family. It followed her rise into aristocratic circles after meeting her future husband, Lord Randolph Churchill, at a party off Cowes in 1873. It showed the daring, flirtatious lady campaigning politically on her husband's behalf, giving birth to Winston and progressing her own career by launching a literary magazine. Scripts were vetted by Lady Spencer Churchill, Sir Winston's widow, and filming took place at family homes, including Blenheim Palace. Warren Clarke, playing Winston, was required to age from 16 to 47 during the series.

JESUS OF NAZARETH
UK (ITC/RAI) Drama. ITV 1977

Jesus Christ	Immad Cohen (*boy*)
	Robert Powell (*adult*)
Virgin Mary	Olivia Hussey
Joseph	Yorgo Voyagis
Mary Magdalene	Anne Bancroft
Simon	Peter James Farentino
Judas Iscariot	Ian McShane
John the Baptist	Michael York
Nicodemus	Laurence Olivier
Simeon	Ralph Richardson
Herodias	Valentina Cortese
Balthazar	James Earl Jones
Melchior	Donald Pleasence
Gaspar	Fernando Rey
Joseph of Arimathea	James Mason
Herod the Great	Peter Ustinov
Salome	Isabel Mestres
Herod Antipas	Christopher Plummer
Caiaphas	Anthony Quinn
Pontius Pilate	Rod Steiger
Barabbas	Stacy Keach
The Adulteress	Claudia Cardinale
Yehuda	Cyril Cusack
Amos	Ian Bannen
Elizabeth	Marina Berti
Anna	Regina Bianchi
Joel	Oliver Tobias

Writers: **Anthony Burgess, Suso Cecchi d'Amico, Franco Zeffirelli**
Executive Producer: **Bernard J. Kingham**
Producer: **Vincenzo Labella**

The life of Jesus as seen by Franco Zeffirelli and Lord Lew Grade.

This much-publicized epic centred on Jesus as a man, not a myth. By playing down the supernatural, Lew Grade's ITC hoped to present the life of Christ to all religions, and not just to Christians. And, although chock-full of star names, the production was not simply a vehicle for celebrities, with the glitzy sensationalism of early Hollywood versions steadfastly avoided.

The story (in two two-hour episodes) followed Christ from his boyhood (with plenty of footage devoted to his time with Joseph in the carpentry shop), through the inspirational, public part of his life (with the gathering of the disciples and the delivering of the sermons and parables) and on to the crucifixion and resurrection. In line with the Gospels, the miracles were featured, but special effects were minimal and it was the words, not the spectacular deeds, of Jesus which became the focus of his greatness.

In conjunction with Italy's RAI network, the film was shot on location in Tunisia and Italy at great expense over three years, and the attention to detail in costumes and backdrops was much applauded. The idea for the epic allegedly came from Pope Paul, who had mentioned it to Lew Grade at an audience some years earlier.

JETSONS, THE
US (Hanna-Barbera/Screen Gems) Cartoon. ITV 1963–4

Voices:

George Jetson	George O'Hanlon
Jane Jetson	Penny Singleton
Judy Jetson	Janet Waldo
Elroy Jetson	Daws Butler
Astro	Don Messick
Cosmo G. Spacely	Mel Blanc
Rosie	Jean Vander Pyl

Executive Producers: **William Hanna, Joseph Barbera**

THE FLINTSTONES *inverted: an animation taking 20th-century lifestyles and applying them to the future, instead of the past.*

The Jetsons lived in the 21st century, in the push-button world of Orbit City. Head of the household was 35-year-old George Jetson, who worked at Spacely Space Sprockets, owned by Cosmo Spacely, where the three-hour day was still far too long. With his shopping-mad wife, Jane, and two children, George lived in the Skypad Apartments, which could be conveniently raised above the clouds to avoid bad weather. George also owned a nuclear-powered space car, while Jane had the assistance of a sarcastic robot maid named Rosie to help with the housework. The Jetsons' two children were 15-year-old Judy, a teenybopper, and nine-year-old Elroy, an electronics whizzkid who travelled to school (the Little Dipper School) down a pneumatic tube. The family's Scooby-Doo-like dog was called Astro.

Whereas the Flintstones enjoyed 20th-century comforts *à la* Stone Age, the Jetsons had high-tech benefits which could only have been imagined when the series was created in the 1960s. Some, such as the video phone, are already now in use, but devices like the 'Foodarackacycle', which provided a selection of meals at the touch of a button, are still a little ahead of us.

The Jetsons' voices sounded familiar: Penny Singleton played Blondie in the 1940s films, Daws Butler was the voice behind Yogi Bear, and Don Messick went on to further canine success when voicing Scooby-Doo. Jean Vander Pyl was Wilma Flintstone. New episodes were produced in 1985, and a full-length cinema version was released a few years later.

JEUX SANS FRONTIERES
See IT'S A KNOCKOUT.

JEWEL IN THE CROWN, THE
UK (Granada) Drama. ITV 1984

Ronald Merrick	Tim Pigott-Smith
Hari Kumar	Art Malik
Daphne Manners	Susan Wooldridge
Sgt Guy Perron	Charles Dance
Dr Anna Klaus	Renee Goddard

Lady Lili Chatterjee	**Zohra Segal**
Pandit Baba	**Marne Maitland**
Barbie Batchelor	**Peggy Ashcroft**
Sarah Layton	**Geraldine James**
Susan Layton/Bingham/Merrick	**Wendy Morgan**
Capt. Teddie Bingham	**Nicholas Farrell**
Mildred Layton	**Judy Parfitt**
Lady Ethel Manners	**Rachel Kempson**
Mabel Layton	**Fabia Drake**
Fenny Grace	**Rosemary Leach**
Major/Col. Arthur Grace	**James Bree**
Count Dimitri Bronowsky	**Eric Porter**
Cpl. 'Sophie' Dixon	**Warren Clarke**
Capt. Nigel Rowan	**Nicholas Le Prevost**
Major Gen. Rankin	**Bernard Horsfall**

Writer: **Ken Taylor**
Producer: **Christopher Morahan**

Race and class conflict in wartime India.

Based on *The Raj Quartet*, four books by Paul Scott, *The Jewel in the Crown* (the title of the first book – the 'jewel' allegorically standing for India) traced growing unrest in the Indian subcontinent during World War II, by following the lives of certain Britons and locals. The story began in Mayapore in 1942 and continued in various Indian locations, including Mirat, Pankot and Calcutta. At the forefront was the sadistic Ronald Merrick, a devious, bigoted police officer (later army officer) who framed Hari Kumar, an English-raised Indian reporter for the *Mayapore Gazette*, for the rape of Daphne Manners, an ungainly orphan-girl hospital worker who had shunned Merrick's advances. Although the rape outrage happened early on in the story, and Hari and Daphne were soon written out, the incident – and its consequences – came to symbolize the cauldron of race hatred and distrust which was boiling up in India at that time. The plot then switched to the Layton family (particularly level-headed Sarah Layton), ageing missionary Barbie Batchelor and other associates, and the series rolled steadily, dramatically and colourfully on to 1947 and the eve of Indian independence, all the while introducing new facets of the cultural problem, particularly growing Muslim/Hindu conflicts.

Drawing obvious comparisons with the contemporary feature film, *A Passage to India* (which also starred Art Malik and Peggy Ashcroft), *The Jewel in the Crown* was made in both India and the UK, at great expense, but not without a catalogue of production problems, from freak weather conditions in India to a fire at the TV studio in Manchester. Its TV inspiration had been a 1982 Granada play, *Staying On*, featuring Trevor Howard and Celia Johnson. Newsreel footage was used to help establish the context for the complicated storyline.

JEWEL, JIMMY
(James Marsh; 1909–95)

Sheffield-born music-hall comedian who successfully took his double act with cousin Ben Warriss into radio and then on to the small screen in the early 1950s. Variety series like *Re-turn It Up* and *The Jewel and Warriss Show*, the sitcoms, *Double Cross* and *It's a Living*, and appearances on SUNDAY NIGHT AT THE LONDON PALLADIUM made the duo popular and wealthy, keeping them at the forefront of TV comedy until the 1960s, when their act began to seem rather dated. Jewel left showbusiness but was tempted back by Frank Muir with a part in a BBC comedy in 1967. This encouraged him to look away from gags and sketches and more seriously at acting roles, and he secured the part of pickle factory owner Eli Pledge in the popular sitcom, NEAREST AND DEAREST, in 1968. He followed up with guest spots in series like THE AVENGERS and two further sitcoms, *Thicker than Water* (widower father Jim Eccles) and SPRING AND AUTUMN (pensioner Tommy Butler). Among his later credits were WORZEL GUMMIDGE, ONE FOOT IN THE GRAVE, *Look at It This Way*, CASUALTY and the 1981 13-part drama, *Funny Man*, which was based around the life of Jimmy's comedian father (also known as Jimmy Jewel) in the 1920s.

JIM'LL FIX IT
UK (BBC) Children's Entertainment. BBC 1 1975–94

Presenter: **Jimmy Savile**
Producer: **Roger Ordish**

Long-running children's programme which made viewers' dreams come true.

A favourite with adults as well as youngsters, *Jim'll Fix It* was a popular segment of Saturday evening viewing for 19 years. Its premiss was simple: children (and some adults) wrote in with a special wish and the BBC, fronted by Jimmy Savile from a gadget-loaded armchair, fulfilled the most enterprising requests. The dreams-made-reality varied from meeting favourite pop stars to piloting Concorde and interviewing the Prime Minister. The Osmonds and Pan's People were among the first guests. Featured viewers were presented with a 'Jim Fixed It For Me' medallion to commemorate the occasion.

JIMMY'S
UK (Yorkshire) Documentary. ITV 1987–96

Executive Producer: **Chris Bryer**
Producers: **Richard Handford, Irene Cockcroft**

The stresses, the strains, the tears and the smiles at a major general hospital.

This fly-on-the-wall documentary series lasted longer than most critics would have dared to suggest. Centring on events at St James's Hospital in Leeds (the largest general hospital in Europe), it witnessed highs and lows in the lives of its numerous patients, doctors and nurses. With its delicate observation of the skill and care of staff, and the heartaches and joys of inmates, *Jimmy's*, originally only a daytime programme, so intrigued viewers that it soon earned itself an evening slot. Over the years, the production crew became almost part of the hospital team. No patient was obliged to appear and, even if giving initial consent, all had the right to pull out halfway through filming or to ask for edits to be made. Later series were screened by Sky One.

JIM'S INN
See ADMAGS.

JOE 90
UK (Century 21/ITC) Children's Science Fiction. ITV
1968–9

Voices:
Joe McClaine/Joe 90 .... **Len Jones**
Prof. Ian McClaine .... **Rupert Davies**
Commander Shane Weston .... **David Healy**
Sam Loover .... **Keith Alexander**
Mrs Ada Harris .... **Sylvia Anderson**

Creators: **Gerry Anderson, Sylvia Anderson**
Executive Producer: **Reg Hill**
Producer: **David Lane**

*The top agent of a global protectorate is a
nine-year-old boy brainwashed with expert skills.*

Brilliant scientist Professor Ian 'Mac' McClaine had developed a machine which allowed the transfer of people's brain-patterns. Known as BIG RAT – Brain Impulse Galvanoscope, Record And Transfer – the equipment was tested and then regularly used on Mac's nine-year-old adopted son, Joe, who became the Most Special Agent for World Intelligence Network (WIN), an agency dedicated to keeping peace around the globe. Furnished with the expert knowledge of an airline pilot, an astronaut, an explosives specialist or even a brain surgeon, Joe McClaine became Joe 90, a special operative whose schoolboy looks enabled him to venture where other agents feared to tread. To activate the new brain-patterns and pick up the specialist skills or knowledge he needed, Joe simply donned a pair of scientific glasses, making him look more like the class swot than a secret agent. To help him on his assignments, he was equipped with a special 'school bag', containing a transmitter, a gun and, of course, his magic glasses. Contacts at WIN were its deputy head, Commander Weston, and Weston's assistant, Sam Loover. Mrs Harris was the McClaines's housekeeper.

The programme's opening titles showed BIG RAT at work, with Joe's chair lifted into a metal cage which revolved at high speed. Around him, sophisticated computers whizzed and sparkled as they transferred brain-patterns into the boy's mind. *Joe 90* was Gerry Anderson's ninth puppet series, but was considerably less successful than the three which immediately preceded it, STINGRAY, THUNDERBIRDS and CAPTAIN SCARLET AND THE MYSTERONS. Among the actors lending their vocal cords were MAIGRET'S Rupert Davies and Keith Alexander, formerly the voice of the Italian mouse puppet, Topo Gigio.

JOHN CRAVEN'S NEWSROUND
See NEWSROUND.

JOHNS, STRATFORD
(1925–)

South African actor, best remembered in the guise of Charlie Barlow of Z CARS, SOFTLY, SOFTLY and BARLOW AT LARGE fame, following early guest appearances in series like THE AVENGERS. Later he was cast as Piso, the head of the guards, in I, CLAUDIUS, union-boss-turned-peer Lord Mountainash in the sitcom, *Union Castle*, the evil killer in Channel 4's *Brond* and Abbé Pirard in *Scarlet and Black*, among many other roles in series like MINDER and MURDER MOST HORRID. He also played Barlow in *Jack the Ripper*, a 1973 investigation into the mysterious case of the Victorian murderer, which led to the series, SECOND VERDICT, in 1976, with Barlow and his colleague John Watt (Frank Windsor) taking a look at other unsolved crimes.

JOHNSON, DON
(1950–)

Despite appearing in films as early as 1970, Don Johnson failed to make TV inroads (apart from failed pilots, some guest appearances and one role in a version of *From Here to Eternity*) until 1984, when he was cast as Detective James 'Sonny' Crockett in the all-action cop series, MIAMI VICE. Running for five years, it made Johnson one of the biggest names of the 1980s, his ultra-casual dress, stubbled chin and permanent scowl inspiring a generation of look-alikes. In the 1990s he returned to the limelight as star (and executive producer) of the cop show, *Nash Bridges*. He has twice married (and divorced) actress Melanie Griffith.

JOHNSTON, SUE
(1943–)

Warrington-born actress who gained national prominence through her portrayal of BROOKSIDE matriarch Sheila Grant. Previously, Johnston had played Mrs Chadwick in CORONATION STREET among other smaller TV roles. Since leaving Brookside Close, she has been cast as Barbara Grade in *Goodbye Cruel World,* was the mother in a celebratory remake of THE GROVE FAMILY, starred as Miriam Johnson in *Screenplay*'s *Bitter Harvest,* took the part of Grace Robbins in the limousine drama, *Full Stretch,* and featured as rich but frustrated housewife Terese Craven in LUV. Starring roles have kept coming and she has headlined in MEDICS (Ruth Parry), *Into the Fire* (Lyn Candy), CRIME TRAVELLER (Grisham), *Duck Patrol* (Val), *The Jump* (Maeve Brunos), THE ROYLE FAMILY (Barbara Royle), *Sex, Chips and Rock 'n' Roll* (Irma), *Waking the Dead* (DI Grace Foley) and *Face* (Alice), as well as appearing in series like INSPECTOR MORSE and A TOUCH OF FROST.

JOKING APART

UK (Pola Jones/Peter Jones/BBC) Situation Comedy. BBC2
1993–5

Mark Taylor .... **Robert Bathurst**
Becky Johnson/Taylor .... **Fiona Gillies**
Tracy Glazebrook .... **Tracie Bennett**
Robert Glazebrook .... **Paul Raffield**
Trevor .... **Paul-Mark Elliott**

Writer: **Steven Moffat**
Producer: **Andre Ptaszynski**

A stand-up comic recalls his failed marriage.

'My wife left me,' drily declared comedian and TV script-writer Mark Taylor. This preluded a series of flashbacks which recalled his fleeting marriage to Becky Johnson. Having met at a funeral (which Mark had gatecrashed by accident), their romance developed apace, but then fell apart just as quickly, as Mark's stand-up humour took over their relationship. When he cracked one joke too many, Becky left him, tired of being his 'lawfully wedded straight man'. Mark's efforts to win her back from boring estate agent Trevor formed the basis of the rest of the first series and all the second (shown in 1995). Also involved in this farcical comedy of errors were Robert and Tracy, their increasingly bizarre and totally dim friends. Chris Rea's 'Fool If You Think It's Over' (sung by Kenny Craddock) provided the theme music. *Joking Apart* was developed from a one-off *Comic Aside*, screened in July 1991.

JONATHAN CREEK

UK (BBC) Comedy Drama. BBC 1 1997–

Jonathan Creek .... **Alan Davies**
Madelaine 'Maddy' Magellan .... **Caroline Quentin**
Adam Klaus .... **Anthony Head**
                                            Stuart Milligan

Creator/Writer: **David Renwick**
Producers: **Susan Belbin, Verity Lambert**

Lateral-thinking detective work from a stage magician's assistant and his journalist girlfriend.

Nerdy Jonathan Creek lived in an East Anglian windmill, had wild, curly hair, wore a duffel coat and worked for smarmy top illusionist Adam Klaus. In fact, he was the brains behind Klaus's act, devising all the tricks and building the elaborate equipment needed to perform the 'magic'. It turned out that the sort of mind which excelled at this work was also pretty good at solving baffling crimes – bodies in a sealed room, etc. – a fact that was immediately grasped by devious journalist Maddy Magellan. Using Creek to supply her with great copy, Maddy manipulated him into obscure investigations where logic seemed to go out of the window and only the impossible seemed possible. Thus began not only their sparky working relationship but also a 'will they, won't they' romantic scenario, all laced together with a

wry humour viewers associated more with writer David Renwick. Renwick claims to have plucked the name of his hero from a place he visited in Kentucky.

JONES, CAROLYN

(1929–83)

American actress in films from the late 1940s. On television, after some early appearances in shows like DRAGNET, Jones was cast as Morticia Addams, the sultry wife in THE ADDAMS FAMILY, in 1964. A few years later, she was also seen in BATMAN, playing Marsha, the Queen of Diamonds. Later in her career, Jones focused on daytime soaps, TV movies and mini-series, including ROOTS. At one time, she was the wife of TV executive Aaron Spelling.

JONES, CHUCK

(Charles M. Jones; 1915–)

American animation producer/director, for 24 years with Warner Brothers, where he created the characters of Roadrunner and Pepe Le Pew among others, and contributed to Daffy Duck, Sylvester and Tweety Pie, Porky Pig and Bugs Bunny adventures. He also worked on later TOM AND JERRY cartoons and became head of children's programmes at the USA's ABC network.

JONES, DAVY

(David Jones; 1945–)

Diminutive Manchester-born actor, a would-be jockey but tempted on to the stage instead. One of his first TV breaks came with CORONATION STREET, in which he played Ena Sharples's grandson, Colin Lomax, in 1961. Moving to America, he starred on Broadway as the Artful Dodger in *Oliver* and took a guest part in BEN CASEY. However, global fame awaited. In 1966 he successfully auditioned for a role in a new zany comedy about a pop group, becoming the lead singer of THE MONKEES and embarking on a few years of frenzied touring and filming. Since those days, Jones has resurfaced only sporadically, appearing in TV movies and series such as LOVE, AMERICAN STYLE and *The Brady Bunch*, as well as occasionally piecing together *The Monkees* for nostalgia tours. He is the father of actress Sarah Jones.

JONES, ELWYN

(1923–82)

British screenwriter and producer, with contributions to *Jacks and Knaves*, Z CARS, SOFTLY, SOFTLY and *Jack the Ripper* among other scripting credits. He also produced Alun Owen's 1963 sitcom, *Corrigan Blake*, and created the police series, PARKIN'S PATCH.

JONES, FREDDIE
(1927–)

Versatile British actor whose television work has varied between the classics, general drama, sitcom and kids' programmes. These have included *Treasure Island, Uncle Vanya, Vanity Fair* (Sir Pitt Crawley), THE CAESARS (Claudius), MYSTERY AND IMAGINATION (Sweeney Todd), THE DISTRICT NURSE (Dr Emlyn Isaacs), THE AVENGERS, *Menace*, THE RETURN OF SHERLOCK HOLMES, INSPECTOR MORSE, PENNIES FROM HEAVEN, IN LOVING MEMORY (pilot episode), THE SECRET DIARY OF ADRIAN MOLE, *Sob Sisters* (Leo), *Screen One's Adam Bede* (Squire), *The True Adventures of Christopher Columbus* (Herald), MR WROE'S VIRGINS (Tobias), *Cold Comfort Farm* (Adam Lambsbreath), *Drovers' Gold* (Moc) and *The Ghosts of Motley Hall* (Sir George Uproar).

JONES, GEMMA
(1942–)

As the gruff cook and proprietress of The Bentinck Hotel, Louisa Trotter, British actress Gemma Jones found instant fame in THE DUCHESS OF DUKE STREET in 1976. Since that time she has made the odd guest appearance in series like INSPECTOR MORSE and appeared as Mrs Fairfax in *Jane Eyre*, Beatrice Kyle in *An Evil Streak*, and Elizabeth Harrison in *Longitude*. Previously, she had played Fleda Vetch in the Henry James drama, *The Spoils of Poynton*, and Princess Victoria in *The Fall of Eagles*.

JONES, GRIFF RHYS
(1953–)

Cardiff-born comedian and actor, partner of Mel Smith. A Cambridge Footlights performer (alongside the likes of Rory McGrath and Clive Anderson), Jones was working as a radio producer before he joined Smith, Pamela Stephenson and Rowan Atkinson in NOT THE NINE O'CLOCK NEWS in 1980, replacing Chris Langham, who had left the series after one year. In 1984, Griff and Mel branched out into ALAS SMITH AND JONES, their own sketch show, which later became simply *Smith and Jones*. They also presented *The World According to Smith and Jones* (voicing over old film clips) for ITV and a series of semi-dramas entitled *Smith and Jones in Small Doses* for BBC 2. Jones also played Bamber Gascoigne in one memorable episode of THE YOUNG ONES and, while always a stalwart of COMIC RELIEF, he has also turned his hand to straight drama, playing Cornelius Carrington in PORTERHOUSE BLUE and Ian Deasey in *Demob*. Other credits are as host of the literary review, *Bookworm*, and the annual *Nation's Favourite Poem* contest, and as narrator of the children's series, *Tales From the Poop Deck*. With Smith, Jones founded Talkback, the production company responsible for some of their series, plus other comedy hits.

JONES, KEN
(1930–)

Liverpudlian comic actor and writer, often cast in shifty working-class roles. He played prison officer Leslie Mills in *Her Majesty's Pleasure*, Detective Sgt Arnold Nixon in *The Nesbitts are Coming*, 'Orrible Ives in PORRIDGE, Archangel Derek in *Dead Ernest*, boxing trainer Dave Locket in SECONDS OUT, park-keeper Tom in *Valentine Park*, Whistle Willy in the kids' comedy, *Behind the Bike Sheds*, and, more memorably, Rex in THE SQUIRRELS, Billy Clarkson in *The Wackers* and Clifford Basket in LAST OF THE BASKETS. Jones has also been seen in THE LIVER BIRDS, *Struggle*, THE BOUNDER, BOON, WATCHING and HUNTER'S WALK, among numerous series.

JONES, PETER
(1920–2000)

Shropshire-born comedy actor and writer, on television from the 1950s. He is probably best remembered as Mr Fenner in THE RAG TRADE, although he was also seen as Gerald Garvey in BEGGAR MY NEIGHBOUR, Roland Digby in MR DIGBY, DARLING, Clive Beauchamp in the airline sitcom, *From a Bird's Eye View*, Sidney in the busking comedy, *Kindly Leave the Kerb*, Eddie, the petty crook, in *Mr Big* (also as co-writer), Gerald, the frustrated dad, in the shortlived *I Thought You'd Gone* (again with writing credits), mad Prime Minister Kevin Pork in WHOOPS APOCALYPSE and the Voice of The Book in THE HITCH-HIKER'S GUIDE TO THE GALAXY. Jones also appeared in *Mild and Bitter, Q6* and *One-Upmanship* and had a wealth of guest appearances in his portfolio, in series as diverse as C.A.T.S. EYES, THE GOODIES, RUMPOLE OF THE BAILEY, *Holby City* and MIDSOMER MURDERS.

JONES, STEVE
(1945–)

Bespectacled radio and television presenter, concentrating largely on game shows, notably hosting *The Pyramid Game, Jeopardy* and *Search for a Star*. He has also been heard as an announcer and commentator on awards events.

JONNY QUEST
US (Hanna-Barbera) Cartoon. BBC 1 1965

Voices:

Jonny Quest	**Tim Matthieson**
Dr Benton Quest	**John Stephenson**
	Don Messick
Roger 'Race' Bannon	**Mike Road**
Hadji	**Danny Bravo**
Bandit	**Don Messick**

Creator/Writer: **Doug Wildey**
Executive Producers: **William Hanna, Joseph Barbera**

*Four scientific adventurers travel the world
explaining away natural phenomena.*

Jonny Quest was the bright 11-year-old son of bearded scientist Dr Benton Quest, leader of a small team of intelligence specialists. With Jonny, an Indian chum named Hadji, their pilot-cum-bodyguard Race Bannon, and miniature bulldog Bandit, Dr Quest whizzed around the globe in a supersonic plane, following up reports of strange happenings and unearthing rare treasures in the style of Indiana Jones. Whether it was the sighting of an alien creature or another bizarre event, Quest and his crew soon got to the bottom of it, more often than not battling against the clock in the process. They usually concluded their adventures by explaining the scientific reasons for the phenomena encountered.

This sensibly constructed, well-liked, educational cartoon was aired during evening prime time in the USA, just like its Hanna-Barbera predecessors, THE FLINTSTONES, THE JETSONS and TOP CAT.

JONSSON, ULRIKA
(1967–)

Swedish TV personality, branching out from a position as secretary at TV-am to become one of the station's weather presenters. She has since moved into light entertainment, hosting GLADIATORS, the 1998 EUROVISION SONG CONTEST, THE NATIONAL LOTTERY *Dreamworld* and the game show, *Mother Knows Best*, and acting as a team captain in the spoof quiz SHOOTING STARS. Her *Shooting Stars* colleagues, Vic Reeves and Bob Mortimer, then wrote her a one-off sketch show called *It's Ulrika!*. She has also ventured into politics, interviewing John Major prior to the 1997 election and fronting *Ulrika in Euroland*.

JOSEPH, LESLEY
(1946–)

British actress, most familiar as the man-hungry Dorien Green in BIRDS OF A FEATHER, but with other credits including *Sadie*, *It's Cold Outside*, *Les Girls*, AND MOTHER MAKES FIVE, MINDER, HORIZON, *Roots* (Melanie Goldblatt in the ITV comedy, not the US mini-series), the wrestling comedy, *Rumble* (Ma Pecs), and the schools drama, *Spywatch* (Miss Millington).

JOURNEY TO THE CENTER OF THE EARTH
US (Filmation/Twentieth Century-Fox) Cartoon. BBC 1
1968–9

Voices:
Prof. Oliver Lindenbrook .... **Ted Knight**
Cindy Lindenbrook .... **Jane Webb**
Alec McEwen .... **Pat Harrington, Jr**
Lars .... **Pat Harrington, Jr**
Count Saccnuson .... **Ted Knight**
Torg .... **Pat Harrington, Jr**

Executive Producers: **Louis Scheimer, Norman Prescott**

*A party of explorers tries to reach the legendary
centre of the Earth.*

In an attempt to retrace the steps of explorer Arnie Saccnuson, archaeologist Professor Oliver Lindenbrook gathered together a small team of adventurers, consisting of his niece, Cindy, student Alec McEwen, a guide, Lars, and Gertrude, Cindy's pet duck. Entering a cavern to look for clues, they found themselves trapped when an explosion blocked the entrance. They soon discovered the blast to be the work of the malevolent Count Saccnuson, the last living descendant of the renowned explorer who, with Torg, his dim henchman, had his own plans for the Earth's core. For the Professor and his team there was no alternative: they just had to follow Arnie's trail (marked 'AS') and hope to find a way back to the surface. As they did so, not only were they hindered by the Count and Torg (who had also been trapped by the bungled explosion), but they also encountered a variety of prehistoric monsters, lost civilizations and assorted natural phenomena. The series was based very loosely on Jules Verne's 1865 novel and the 1959 film starring James Mason.

JOURNEY TO THE UNKNOWN
UK (Hammer/Twentieth Century-Fox) Drama. ITV 1968–9

Producer: **Anthony Hinds**
Executive Producers: **Joan Harrison, Norman Lloyd**

An anthology of supernatural suspense tales.

Financed by Twentieth Century-Fox but produced in Britain by Hammer, this anthology of 17 stories embraced both science fiction and psychological horror with its varied tales of murder, twisted minds, sorcery, ESP, medical experimentation and the afterlife. The tone was set by sinister opening titles, which depicted a spooky abandoned fairground. American stars usually took the lead (the likes of Joseph Cotten, Julie Harris, Barbara Bel Geddes, Roddy McDowall and Stefanie Powers were seen), with familiar UK faces in support. Producers Joan Harrison and Norman Lloyd had both worked on ALFRED HITCHCOCK PRESENTS and the influence of the Master of Suspense was very apparent. Unfortunately, the progamme did not enjoy a steady run on ITV, appearing first in London and then only sporadically around the network.

JOYCE, YOOTHA
(1927–80)

British comic actress, imprinted in viewers' minds as the sex-starved Mildred Roper in MAN ABOUT THE HOUSE and GEORGE AND MILDRED. Joyce came to the role on the back of a run of guest appearances in the 1960s (in programmes like THE AVENGERS and in the comedies, BROTHERS IN LAW and *Corrigan Blake*). She had also starred in the Milo O'Shea sitcom, ME MAMMY, in which she played his willing secretary, Miss Argyll, and ON THE BUSES, as Jessie the clippie. She was once married to actor Glynn Edwards.

JUKE BOX JURY

UK (BBC/Noel Gay) Pop Music. BBC 1 1959–67; 1979;
BBC 2 1989–90

Presenters: **David Jacobs, Noel Edmonds, Jools Holland**

Creator: **Peter Potter**

A celebrity panel reviews new record releases.

Along with DOCTOR WHO and DIXON OF DOCK GREEN, *Juke Box Jury* was one of the stalwarts of Saturday teatime television in the early 1960s. The name of its instrumental theme music, 'Hit and Miss' (a Top Ten entry for the John Barry Seven in 1960), summed up what the programme was all about. Host David Jacobs played a selection of brand-new records to a panel of four knowledgeable personalities, who then declared whether the records would be 'hits' or 'misses'. While the records played, the cameras focused on the faces of the studio audience, gauging their reaction to the new discs. If the jury's overall conclusion was a 'hit', Jacobs rang a bell; if it was a 'miss' he sounded a klaxon. To add to the excitement, a mystery guest usually lurked in the background, waiting to confront pundits who gave their record the thumbs down.

The very first panel consisted of disc jockey Pete Murray, singers Alma Cogan and Gary Miller, and 'typical teenager' Susan Stranks (later wife of Robin Ray and presenter of MAGPIE). In December 1963, a massive audience was generated by the fact that The Beatles filled all four pundits' chairs and, a year later, the jury was temporarily increased to five, to accommodate the Rolling Stones. Although cancelled in 1967 (when the last panel again included Murray and Stranks, as well as Eric Sykes and Lulu), *Juke Box Jury* was briefly revived with Noel Edmonds as chairman in 1979, and once more in 1989, when former THE TUBE presenter Jools Holland became host.

JULIET BRAVO

UK (BBC) Police Drama. BBC 1 1980–5

Insp. Jean Darblay	**Stephanie Turner**
Tom Darblay	**David Hargreaves**
Sgt Joseph Beck	**David Ellison**
Sgt George Parrish	**Noel Collins**
PC Roland Bentley	**Mark Drewry**
Supt. Hallam	**James Grout**
PC Gallagher	**Gerard Kelly**
DCI Logan	**Tony Caunter**
PC Sims	**David Gillies**
PC Helmshore	**David Straun**
Insp. Kate Longton	**Anna Carteret**
PC Brian Kelleher	**C. J. Allen**
PC Danny Sparks	**Mark Botham**
DCI Perrin	**Edward Peel**
DS Maltby	**Sebastian Abineri**

Creator: **Ian Kennedy Martin**
Producers: **Terence Williams, Jonathan Alwyn, Geraint Morris**

Community policing with a female inspector.

Reminiscent of Z CARS in its setting, tone and content, *Juliet Bravo* focused on Jean Darblay and Kate Longton, female police inspectors in the small, fictional town of Hartley in Lancashire. Darblay, career copper and housewife, battled against sexism from the start. Her arrival was greeted by distrust and resentment from her fellow officers (especially the obnoxious CID mob), but she rapidly earned respect, enjoying particular support from her solid, dependable sergeants, Joe Beck and George Parrish, as well as her husband, Tom, a social worker. Juliet Bravo was her police call-sign. When, after three years, Darblay took promotion and moved on, she was replaced by Kate Longton, who took over not only her patch but also the headaches that went with it.

Cosy and reassuring, with an emphasis on human drama rather than sensational crime, *Juliet Bravo* was written by Ian Kennedy Martin, creator of THE SWEENEY. He brought Stephanie Turner with him (she had played George Carter's wife and, incidentally, was once a WPC in *Z Cars*). The series proved particularly popular with female viewers.

JUNKIN, JOHN
(1930–)

British actor and comedy writer, also working as a programme consultant/script editor. On screen he has been seen supporting stars like Tommy Cooper and Marty Feldman, and in sitcoms, as Wally, Alf Garnett's milkman, in TILL DEATH US DO PART, boozy husband Sam Marshall in *Sam and Janet*, Bert Ryding in the Stanley Holloway comedy, *Thingumybob*, building foreman Charlie Cattermole in *On the House*, Odius in UP POMPEII!, Tim Brooke-Taylor's flatmate, Harold King, in *The Rough with the Smooth* (also as co-writer), Tommy Wallace in SHARON AND ELSIE and legal clerk Steven in *Law and Disorder*. Junkin has also revealed his skill in straight drama in the crime thriller, OUT, and in series like *Penmarric*, DICK TURPIN, *All for Love* and ALL CREATURES GREAT AND SMALL. Other credits have included BLOTT ON THE LANDSCAPE, *Looking for Clancy*, *Scoop* and SHELLEY, while his own comedy series, *Junkin*, ran for four seasons and his radio show, *Hello Cheeky*, also transferred to TV for a while. Junkin's many writing credits have included episodes of *The World of Beachcomber, Mr Aitch, Langley Bottom, Paradise Island*, QUEENIE'S CASTLE and the sketch show, *What's on Next?*, plus scripts for many top comedians, including Ted Ray, Bob Monkhouse, Morecambe and Wise, Leslie Crowther, Jim Davidson and Mike Yarwood.

JUST GOOD FRIENDS

UK (BBC) Situation Comedy. BBC 1 1983–6

Vince Pinner	**Paul Nicholas**
Penny Warrender	**Jan Francis**
Daphne Warrender	**Sylvia Kay**
Norman Warrender	**John Ringham**
Rita Pinner	**Ann Lynn**

Les Pinner	**Shaun Curry**
Clifford Pinner	**Adam French**
Georgina Marshall	**Charlotte Seely**

Creator/Writer: **John Sullivan**
Producer: **Ray Butt**

A jilted girl meets up with her former fiancé and they embark on a new on-off romance.

Jack-the-Lad Vincent Pinner had met prim-and-proper Penny Warrender at a Rolling Stones concert in Hyde Park. Romance had blossomed and they had decided to get married. But, on the day, Vince chickened out. Five years later, he and Penny met by accident in a pub and found themselves drawn into a new love-hate relationship, exasperated by their different class roots and chosen professions. Cheeky, working-class Vince was assistant manager at Eddie Brown's Turf Accountants, while prissy, middle-class Penny worked for the Mathews, Styles and Lieberman advertising agency. Other major characters were Penny's snooty mum, Daphne, her unemployed, hen-pecked dad, Norman, and Vince's gloriously vulgar parents, Rita, a keen rock'n'roll fan, and Les, a scrap-metal merchant. Also seen was Vince's accident-prone younger brother, Cliffy. After numerous false dawns, Vince (now in charge of his dad's business) and Penny (now working in Paris) did indeed manage to tie the knot.

A letter from a girl in the same situation as Penny, published on the problems page of a women's magazine, allegedly inspired John Sullivan to create the series.

JUST JIMMY
UK (ABC) Situation Comedy. ITV 1964–8

Jimmy Clitheroe	**Jimmy Clitheroe**
Mrs Clitheroe	**Mollie Sugden**
Danny	**Danny Ross**

Producer: **Ronnie Baxter**

The misadventures of an unruly schoolboy.

Translated from BBC Radio, *Just Jimmy* was the television manifestation of *The Clitheroe Kid*, in which 4-foot 3-inch Lancastrian comedian Jimmy Clitheroe performed his naughty-schoolboy routines. He was supported in this series by Mollie Sugden as his over-the-top mum and by Danny Ross as Danny, his older, girls- and motorbikes-mad cousin.

JUST WILLIAM
UK (LWT) Situation Comedy. ITV 1977–8

William Brown	**Adrian Dannatt**
Mr Brown	**Hugh Cross**
Mrs Brown	**Diana Fairfax**
Ethel Brown	**Stacy Dorning**
Robert Brown	**Simon Chandler**
Violet Elizabeth Bott	**Bonnie Langford**

Mrs Bott	**Diana Dors**
Mr Bott	**John Stratton**
Douglas	**Tim Rose**
Ginger	**Michael McVey**
Henry	**Craig McFarlane**

Writer: **Keith Dewhurst**
Executive Producer: **Stella Richman**
Producer: **John Davies**

A mischievous schoolboy is a constant handful for his parents.

Richmal Crompton's colourful adventures of trying schoolboy William Brown were first brought to the screen by the BBC in *William* in 1962–3, with Dennis Waterman and then Dennis Gilmore in the title role. Fifteen years later, William was back, with Adrian Dannatt filling Master Brown's shoes.

William was the mischievous type, fond of pranks and tricks and never far from trouble. His band of followers, known as the Outlaws, consisted of Douglas, Ginger and Henry. William had a sister, Ethel, and an older brother, Robert, though his arch-enemy was the dreadful, lisping Violet Elizabeth Bott. She had set her heart on marrying him and promised to scream until she made herself sick whenever she failed to get her way.

Just William made yet another return to the small screen in 1994–5, when the BBC cast young Oliver Rokison in the lead role. Over two series, he was joined by Polly James, Lindsay Duncan and Joan Sims, among other stars.

JUSTICE
UK (Yorkshire) Legal Drama. ITV 1971–4

Harriet Peterson	**Margaret Lockwood**
Sir John Gallagher	**Philip Stone**
Dr Ian Moody	**John Stone**
James Eliot	**Anthony Valentine**

Creators/Writers: **James Mitchell, Edmund Ward**
Executive Producer: **Peter Willes**
Producers: **James Ormerod, Jacky Stoller**

The cases of a junior barrister.

Middle-aged Harriet Peterson was a devoted, dedicated lawyer doing the rounds of the courtrooms of northern England. After the first 13 episodes, and following encouragement from her boss, Sir John Gallagher, she moved to London, where she ultimately discovered a rival in barrister James Eliot, whom she regularly upstaged. With the scripts checked by a real lawyer, the programme was careful in its detail and depicted the legal system in all its colours. Harriet, for instance, was no Perry Mason and was certainly not infallible.

The role provided a triumphant return to the small screen for Margaret Lockwood, who had previously been seen as lawyer Julia Stanford in a one-off play, *Justice Is a Woman*, in 1969.

KALEIDOSCOPE
UK (BBC) Magazine. BBC 1946–53

Host: **McDonald Hobley**

Producer: **John Irwin**

Easy-going magazine programme calling on viewer involvement.

This television manifestation of the 1930s radio series, *Monday Night at Eight*, comprised a variety of light-hearted items, from competitions and puzzles to comedy and games. Among the features were Word Play (an early version of GIVE US A CLUE), Be Your Own Detective (an observation game), Collectors' Corner (antiques with Iris Brooke), contributions from Memory Man Leslie Welch and Puzzle Corner with Ronnie Waldman (with viewers asked to spot the deliberate mistake). Anyone at home wishing to take part in the 'which year' tune medley competition had to place a copy of the *Radio Times* in their window by noon on broadcast day in order to be spotted and selected. Assisting host McDonald Hobley with events were the likes of Max Kester, Dorothy Ward, Lind Joyce, Garry Miller, John Slater, Diana Decker, Elizabeth Welch and Carole Carr. *Kaleidoscope* was screened once a fortnight.

KARAOKE/COLD LAZARUS
UK (Whistling Gypsy/BBC/Channel 4) Drama. BBC1/Channel 4 1996

Daniel Feeld	Albert Finney
Nick Balmer	Richard E. Grant
Arthur 'Pig' Mailion	Hywel Bennett
Sandra Sollars	Saffron Burrows
Ben Baglin	Roy Hudd
Linda Langer	Keeley Hawes
Anna Griffiths	Anna Chancellor
Mrs Baglin	Liz Smith (*Karaoke*)
Oliver Morse	Ian McDiarmid
Lady Ruth Balmer	Julie Christie (*Karaoke*)
Mrs Haynes	Alison Steadman
Peter (*movie*)	Neil Stuke (*Karaoke*)
Waiter (*movie*)	Steven Mackintosh (*Karaoke*)
Prof. Emma Porlock	Frances de la Tour (*Cold Lazarus*)
Martina Masdon	Diane Ladd (*Cold Lazarus*)
Fyodor Glazunov	Ciaran Hinds (*Cold Lazarus*)
David Siltz	Henry Goodman (*Cold Lazarus*)
Luanda	Ganiat Kasumu (*Cold Lazarus*)
Tony Watson	Grant Masters (*Cold Lazarus*)
Kaya	Claudia Malkovich (*Cold Lazarus*)

Writer: **Dennis Potter**
Executive Producers: **Peter Ansorge, Michael Wearing**
Producers: **Kenith Trodd, Rosemarie Whitman**

Two linked, four-part dramas depicting the dying days of a writer and the exploitation of his mind in the future.

In an unprecedented display of collaboration, the BBC

and Channel 4 jointly brought the final works of acclaimed TV playwright Dennis Potter to the screen. It was Potter who had instigated the arrangement. Speaking in his last TV interview, with Melvyn Bragg, the pain-racked author requested on air that the two broadcasting companies should come together and co-produce his final two, linked works, *Karaoke* and *Cold Lazarus*. They were dramas that Potter had fought hard to finish as his death from pancreatic cancer loomed large. With a determination few authors possess, he ground away at his scripts, often forgoing painkillers to keep his head clear, and completed the works just weeks before he died. Potter chose the director, Renny Rye, and the two producers with whom he had enjoyed greatest success over the years, Kenith Trodd and Rosemarie Whitman, to see the project through. *Karaoke* was screened first on BBC1, with a repeat a day later on Channel 4. *Cold Lazarus* aired first on Channel 4, with BBC1 offering the re-run the next day.

Karaoke concerned a writer named Daniel Feeld, a man suffering from a serious illness and alcoholism who found his written lines suddenly issuing from the mouths of real people and his fiction becoming fact. Comic relief was provided by his spoonerizing agent, Ben Baglin. The serial was resonant in Potter themes: an author – a thinly disguised version of Potter himself – haunted by his work and his past; repressed sexuality; a beautiful girl (nightclub hostess Sandra Sollars); some particularly nasty villains (the vile Arthur 'Pig' Mailion); and, of course, no shortage of strong language.

Cold Lazarus took the action way into the future, to the year AD 2368. There, scientists at the Masdon Science Centre in London, headed by Professor Porlock, were successfully reviving the head of Daniel Feeld, which had been preserved cryogenically. They managed to release memories of the 20th century and extracts from Feeld's life and work that soon became of interest to international media tycoon David Siltz – a final attack by Potter on the manipulation of authors and their work by commercial media. In this future age, people moved around the lab in thought-powered, semi-organic wheelchairs called auto-cubes and drove hovering bubble cars down the streets, while a terrorist group known as RON (Reality or Nothing) waged war on the way the world was now run.

KARLIN, MIRIAM
OBE (Miriam Samuels; 1925–)

London-born actress who satirized militant trade-unionists in her portrayal of Paddy, the whistle-blowing shop steward in THE RAG TRADE. Earlier, Karlin had appeared in the 1946 production of *Alice* and then starred with Sid James in his first (post-Hancock) sitcom, *East End – West End*. She returned to television in the 1990s in the sitcom, SO HAUNT ME, playing Jewish ghost Yetta Feldman.

KARLOFF, BORIS
(William Pratt; 1887–1969)

Although a master of the horror genre in the cinema, Boris Karloff's major television role was quite different. He played COLONEL MARCH OF SCOTLAND YARD in 1956, head of the Department of Queer Complaints. In a more familiar vein, he also hosted OUT OF THIS WORLD, an anthology of science-fiction stories in the early 1960s, and he continued to make guest appearances, in series like THE GIRL FROM UNCLE and *Route 66*, until his death in 1969.

KATE
UK (Yorkshire) Drama. ITV 1970–2

Katherine 'Kate' Graham	**Phyllis Calvert**
Donald Killearn	**Jack Hedley**
Wenda Padbury	**Penelope Keith**
Stephen Graham	**Marcus Hammond**
Mr Winch	**Preston Lockwood**
Ellen Burwood	**Elizabeth Baker**
Bruce Rogers	**Tony Anholt**
Lillian Coates	**Barbara Markham**

Producers: **Stanley Miller, Pieter Rogers**

An agony aunt has problems of her own.

Kate Graham, aged around 50, the widowed mother of teenage son Stephen, worked as the 'Dear Monica' problem-page editor for *Heart and Home* magazine. But, as well as dispensing advice to her readers, Kate found herself in demand among her colleagues, particularly her friend, editor Donald Killearn, the boss of Killearn Enterprises, who had encouraged Kate to take the job. Furthermore, her own home life in Chelsea – where housekeeper Ellen Burwood kept things ship-shape – was far from settled. Also prominent in the office was Wenda Padbury, the heiress daughter of Lord Padbury, who had turned to journalism as a hobby and was at times quite insufferable; respected company secretary Mr Winch; features editor Lillian Coates; and new-blood journalist Bruce Rogers. As the series unfolded, Donald moved on up, and Kate and Wenda went on to share the editor's chair.

KAVANAGH QC
UK (Carlton) Drama. ITV 1995–

James Kavanagh QC	**John Thaw**
Lizzie Kavanagh	**Lisa Harrow**
Julia Piper/Piper-Robinson	**Anna Chancellor**
Peter Foxcott QC	**Oliver Ford Davis**
Jeremy Aldermarten QC	**Nicholas Jones**
Tom Buckley	**Cliff Parisi**
Kate Kavanagh	**Daisy Bates**
Matt Kavanagh	**Tom Brodie**
Alex Wilson	**Jenny Jules**
Helen Ames	**Arkie Whiteley**

| Emma Taylor | **Valerie Redmond** |
| Eleanor Harker QC | **Geraldine James** |

Producer: **Chris Kelly**
Executive Producer: **Ted Childs**

The cases of a brilliant lawyer with a complicated personal life.

Fresh from playing INSPECTOR MORSE and a less successful excursion in A YEAR IN PROVENCE, John Thaw grew his hair and became battling barrister James Kavanagh, a talented, working-class, liberal-minded, Mancunian brief with a penchant for defending the underdog. However, in tried and tested TV fashion, his own personal life was less well organized. His wife, Lizzie, was having an affair with another lawyer and his teenage kids were up to the usual adolescent tricks. His free time was devoted to his hobby of sailing. Julia Piper was Kavanagh's junior colleague at work.

As the series progressed, Julia moved to the States (once recruiting her old boss to help with a trial in Florida) and Lizzie died, leaving Kavanagh mournful but free to build a sparky new working relationship with Scots colleague Emma Taylor and a romantic liaison with fellow barrister Eleanor Harker. The series was applauded for its legal accuracy and co-creator Chris Kelly (of FOOD AND DRINK) has admitted that certain aspects of the lead character were inspired by real-life defence barrister Michael Mansfield QC.

KAYE, GORDEN
(1941–)

British comedy actor, much seen on TV, especially as the reluctant Resistance hero, René Artois, in 'ALLO 'ALLO. Previously, Kaye had popped up in a host of other comedies, including TILL DEATH US DO PART, ARE YOU BEING SERVED?, IT AIN'T HALF HOT MUM, THE GROWING PAINS OF PC PENROSE, *Oh Happy Band* and COME BACK MRS NOAH. He was Ray Benge in the black comedy, *Born and Bred*, the neighbour, Mr Chatto, in *Just Liz* and was also seen in LAST OF THE SUMMER WINE as Maynard Lavery, a TV presenter, and in dramas like the *Screen One* presentation, *Bullion Boys* (Nickson), SHOESTRING, ALL CREATURES GREAT AND SMALL, *The Foundation*, *Fame Is the Spur* and CORONATION STREET (Bernard Butler, Elsie Tanner's nephew). In 1987 he narrowly escaped death in the gales which ravaged southern England, sustaining severe head injuries, but made a full recovery.

KEACH, STACY
(1941–)

American cinema and television actor, known for Shakespearean roles in the 1960s, but famous as the tough detective, MIKE HAMMER, in the 1980s. Previously, Keach had starred in the shortlived detective series, *Caribe*, and in the Civil War drama, *The Blue and the Grey*, as well as playing Barabbas in JESUS OF NAZARETH. He later appeared in the mini-series, *Mistral's Daughter* and *Hemingway*. Unfortunately, his big-time period in Mickey

Spillane's *Mike Hammer* was punctuated by a much-publicized spell in Reading prison for drugs offences. His father, Stacy Keach Sr, played Professor Carlson in GET SMART.

KEE, ROBERT
(1919–)

British journalist, a reporter on PANORAMA and THIS WEEK in the 1950s and 1960s, who joined ITN in the mid-1970s to present the novel lunchtime news bulletin, *First Report*. In 1980 he wrote and presented IRELAND: A TELEVISION HISTORY and in 1983 was a member of TV-am's 'Famous Five', presenting *Daybreak*, the station's news and information reveillé.

KEEL, HOWARD
(Harold Leek; 1917–)

American musical star for whom television celebrity arrived late. His earliest TV appearances were as a guest in series like HERE'S LUCY and THE QUEST, but it wasn't until he arrived in DALLAS in 1981, as silver-haired Clayton Farlow, that Keel became an established TV performer.

KEEN, DIANE
(1946–)

British actress coming to light as Fliss Hawthorne in THE CUCKOO WALTZ sitcom, though she had already enjoyed credits in SOFTLY, SOFTLY, CROSSROADS (Sandra Gould), PUBLIC EYE, THE SWEENEY, CROWN COURT, *The Fall of Eagles* and a BBC version of *The Legend of Robin Hood* (Maid Marian) among other programmes. During and after *The Cuckoo Waltz*, Keen played Empress Chimalma in *The Feathered Serpent*, Laura Dickens in THE SANDBAGGERS, Sandy Bennett in RINGS ON THEIR FINGERS, Sally Higgins in SHILLINGBURY TALES, provincial newspaper editor Daisy Jackson in FOXY LADY and novelist-housewife Alice Hammond in *You Must Be the Husband*. More recently, she has been seen as Jenny Burden in THE RUTH RENDELL MYSTERIES, Connie French in SEPTEMBER SONG and Molly Marchbank in BROOKSIDE.

KEEP IT IN THE FAMILY
UK (Thames) Situation Comedy. ITV 1980–3

Dudley Rush	**Robert Gillespie**
Muriel Rush	**Pauline Yates**
Duncan Thomas	**Glyn Houston**
Susan Rush	**Stacy Dorning**
Jacqui Rush	**Jenny Quayle**
	Sabina Franklyn

Creator: **Brian Cooke**
Producers: **Mark Stuart, Robert Reed**

Upstairs-downstairs, generation-gap comedy.

This series centred on the Rush family, who lived in Highgate Avenue, Highgate. Nominal head of the household was Dudley, a slightly eccentric, professional cartoonist (drawer of the 'Bionic Bulldog' cartoon). His caricature family consisted of dutiful wife Muriel and problematic daughters Susan (aged 17) and Jacqui (21), who were constantly tapping him for cash, bringing home unsuitable boyfriends and indulging in reckless pursuits. When the Rushes' old lodger died and his downstairs flat became vacant, the girls took it over, giving themselves more independence and their parents more grey hairs. Duncan was Dudley's Welsh boss, who also moved in with the family, and another regular was the old glove-puppet Dudley talked to while drawing.

The series gave rise to an American cover version entitled *Too Close for Comfort*, starring Ted Knight.

KEEPING UP APPEARANCES
UK (BBC) Situation Comedy. BBC1 1990–5

Hyacinth Bucket .... **Patricia Routledge**
Richard Bucket .... **Clive Swift**
Elizabeth .... **Josephine Tewson**
Emmet Hawksworth .... **David Griffin**
Daisy .... **Judy Cornwell**
Onslow .... **Geoffrey Hughes**
Rose .... **Shirley Stelfox**
                                                               Mary Millar
Vicar .... **Jeremy Gittins**
Daddy .... **George Webb**

Creator/Writer: **Roy Clarke**
Producer: **Harold Snoad**

A socially climbing housewife lives in fear of letting herself down.

Only one thing mattered to Hyacinth Bucket (pronounced 'bouquet') and that was what other people thought of her. From her suburban base in Blossom Avenue, she moved heaven and earth to mix with the right crowd and to ensure that her image remained intact. Sadly, her council-house sisters, the slutty Daisy and the tarty Rose, plus her shirtless brother-in-law, Onslow, ensured it was a battle she was doomed to lose. They looked after Hyacinth's loopy old dad and were always likely to pop round in Onslow's S-reg Cortina (complete with furry dice). Undaunted, Hyacinth badgered her meek, long-suffering husband, Richard, into helping with her candlelight suppers and other socially aspirant schemes and talked up the brilliance of her son, Sheridan (who was away at polytechnic), to all who would listen. She answered the telephone with a ringing 'The Bucket residence: the lady of the house speaking', and hounded Elizabeth, her nervous neighbour, and Elizabeth's divorced brother, Emmet, to the point where they became prisoners in their own home. Generally, though, it was Hyacinth's own social gaffes that scuppered her rise to the top.

KEITH, PENELOPE
OBE (1939–)

British comedy actress often in plummy, snooty parts. Having appeared in series like *Six Shades of Black*, HADLEIGH, KATE (Wenda Padbury) and THE PALLISERS (Mrs Hittaway), it was as the socially-paranoid Margo Leadbeatter, neighbour of the self-sufficient Goods, in THE GOOD LIFE, that Keith found her forte. This led to a series of her own, TO THE MANOR BORN, in which she played Audrey fforbes-Hamilton, cruelly ejected from her stately home on the death of her husband. Her later sitcom work has included *Moving* (would-be house mover Sarah Gladwyn), *Sweet Sixteen* (Helen Walker, a love-struck owner of a building firm), *Executive Stress* (publisher Caroline Fairchild), NO JOB FOR A LADY (novice Labour MP Jean Price), *Law and Disorder* (barrister Phillippa Troy) and *Next of Kin* (stressed grandmother Maggie Prentice). Other credits have included *The Norman Conquests*, SPYDER'S WEB, *On Approval* and JACKANORY. She briefly hosted WHAT'S MY LINE? on the death of Eamonn Andrews, was Aunt Louise in the drama, *Coming Home*, and, in complete contrast, provided the voice of the bear in TELETUBBIES.

KELLY, BARBARA
(1923–)

Canadian actress and television personality, a familiar face in the 1950s as a panellist on WHAT'S MY LINE?. With her husband, the late Bernard Braden, Kelly moved to Britain in 1949 and, together, they made a name for themselves on BBC Radio and then TV, including the shortlived sitcom *B and B*. Kelly was also seen in assorted plays and in programmes like CRISS CROSS QUIZ and *Kelly's Eye*. She returned to the screen in the 1984 revival of *What's My Line?*. Kelly is the mother of actress Kim Braden.

KELLY, CHRIS
(1940–)

Cheshire-born presenter, writer and producer, for many years at Granada, and previously at Anglia, working on programmes like WORLD IN ACTION (narrator), CINEMA and the children's series, ZOO TIME, *Junior Criss Cross Quiz*, CLAPPERBOARD and *Anything You Can Do*. He was Judith Chalmers's partner on WISH YOU WERE HERE . . . ? for many years and host of BBC2's FOOD AND DRINK for another lengthy period. He is also a published writer, wrote the dramas, *Zero Option* and *Saracen*, and produced the dramas, SOLDIER, SOLDIER and KAVANAGH QC.

KELLY, HENRY
(1946–)

Irish journalist turned presenter of game shows, whose major TV break came with GAME FOR A LAUGH in 1981.

Since then, he has appeared on TV-am and *Monkey Business* and also hosted the inter-European quiz, *Going for Gold*. Kelly's 'day job' is as a presenter on Classic fM.

KELLY, LORRAINE
(1959–)

Breakfast TV presenter who joined TV-am as its Scottish correspondent after working in local newspapers and as a researcher at BBC Scotland. She went on to become one of the anchors of *Good Morning Britain* from 1988, before joining GMTV when it acquired the breakfast franchise in 1993.

KELLY, MATTHEW
(1950–)

Tall, bearded British presenter and actor, coming to the fore through GAME FOR A LAUGH and subsequently host of *Kelly's Eye*, YOU BET! and STARS IN THEIR EYES. Kelly earlier appeared in the drama, *Funny Man*, the hotel sitcom, *Room Service* (Dick Sedgewick), and the comedy, HOLDING THE FORT, playing the part of Fitz, which was later spun off into another series, *Relative Strangers*, in which he starred. Other credits have included *The Rather Reassuring Programme*, *The Critic*, *Madabout*, *Quandaries*, *The Sensible Show*, *Adventures of a Lifetime* and *Give a Pet a Home*.

KELLY, SAM
(1943–)

British actor, often seen in incompetent or slightly stupid parts, such as the illiterate Warren in PORRIDGE and the inept Captain Hans Geering in 'ALLO 'ALLO. Among his earliest opportunities were episodes of EMERGENCY – WARD 10 and THE LIVER BIRDS. He played Norman Elston in the flashback sitcom, *Now and Then*, Les Brooks in the unemployment comedy, *We'll Think of Something*, Grunge in *Haggard*, Sam the chauffeur in ON THE UP and he supported *Paul Merton in Galton & Simpson's* . . . He has also been seen in more serious roles in INSPECTOR MORSE, BOYS FROM THE BLACKSTUFF and *Christabel*, and other credits have included CORONATION STREET (decorator Bob Challis), *Thin Air*, THE BILL, MAKING OUT, STAY LUCKY, *Martin Chuzzlewit* (Mr Mould), *Oliver Twist* (Giles), *Where There's Smoke* (DI Collins) and *Barbara* (Ted).

KEMP, ROSS
(1964–)

English actor, best known as the bullish Grant Mitchell in EASTENDERS (for ten years from 1989). Previously, Kemp had played Graham Lodsworth, the son of Dolly Skilbeck, in EMMERDALE FARM and had been seen in various programmes, including BIRDS OF A FEATHER, LONDON'S BURNING, *The Manageress* and THE CHIEF. More recently, he has ventured into the wild for the

survival documentary, *Ross Kemp Alive in Alaska*, and starred in the security guard story, *Hero of the Hour* (Richie Liddle), the legal drama *In Defence* (Sam Lucas), as DC Jack Mowbray in *Without Motive* and in *A Christmas Carol* (Eddie Scrooge). Other credits have included *One Foot in the Past*, a cameo in *City Central* (as a transvestite), and the docu-soap, *Paddington Green* (narrator).

KENDAL, FELICITY
CBE (1946–)

British actress, born into a showbiz family. She proved particularly popular in the 1970s and 1980s, playing whimsical, independent females, beginning with Barbara Good in THE GOOD LIFE and continuing with Gemma Palmer in SOLO and Maxine in THE MISTRESS. Among her earliest TV work were episodes of MAN IN A SUITCASE, THE PERSUADERS, CRIME OF PASSION, LOVE STORY and EDWARD THE SEVENTH. In 1978 she appeared as Dorothy Wordsworth in *Clouds of Glory*, Ken Russell's biopic of the Lakeland poets. In the 1990s she was seen in *The Camomile Lawn* (Aunt Helena) and played Nancy Belasco, an American widow in Cambridge, in the sitcom, *Honey for Tea*.

KENDALL, KENNETH
(1924–)

A teacher immediately after the war, Kenneth Kendall joined the BBC in 1948 and became one of the Corporation's first three 'on-screen' newsreaders in 1955. He stayed until 1961, when he left to go freelance and made rare guest appearances in dramas like THE TROUBLE-SHOOTERS, DOCTOR WHO and ADAM ADAMANT LIVES!. He returned to the BBC in 1969 and left again 12 years later, after a shake-up of the main news bulletins, soon resurfacing in regional television and as host of Channel 4's popular TREASURE HUNT series. After retiring from television, he opened a restaurant on the Isle of Wight.

KENNEDY, SARAH
(1950–)

Blonde British presenter of GAME FOR A LAUGH, BUSMAN'S HOLIDAY, *Classmates*, *Daytime* and various animal series. She was one of the shortlived *Sixty Minutes* team which took over from NATIONWIDE, and also broadcasts regularly on radio.

KENNEDY, Sir LUDOVIC
(1919–)

British writer, journalist and presenter, one of ITN's first newscasters back in 1956. In 1958 and 1959 Kennedy stood unsuccessfully as Liberal parliamentary candidate for Rochdale (the first occasion being a by-election). In the 1960s he became a reporter on PANORAMA and also worked on TONIGHT, 24 HOURS, THIS WEEK and *Midweek*.

He was the first host of the review programme, DID YOU SEE . . . ? and has also presented QUESTION TIME. In 1972 he chaired the controversial debate, *A Question of Ulster*, and, in 1979, he secured a frank interview with Lord Mountbatten only weeks before his untimely death. Kennedy also contributed to the BBC's *Great Railway Journeys of the World* (New York–Los Angeles). He married ballerina Moira Shearer in 1950, has written numerous books (including the exposé of the Christie murders, *10 Rillington Place*) and has been a campaigner against miscarriages of justice and for voluntary euthanasia.

KERR, GRAHAM
(1934–)

As host of *Entertaining with Kerr: The Galloping Gourmet* in the late 1960s, Graham Kerr became a housewives' favourite and made swilling wine part of a TV cook's repertoire long before Keith Floyd raised a glass in anger. His 'Galloping Gourmet' nickname came from his maddash cooking style and the fact that he tore around the set.

KEY GRIP
See GRIP.

KICK UP THE EIGHTIES, A
UK (BBC) Comedy. BBC2 1981; 1984

Richard Stilgoe, Tracey Ullman, Ron Bain, Miriam Margolyes, Roger Sloman, Rik Mayall, Robbie Coltrane

Producers: **Tom Gutteridge, Colin Gilbert**

Comedy sketch show introducing a host of new talent.

A product of BBC Scotland's comedy department, which was later to contribute NAKED VIDEO among other programmes, *A Kick Up the Eighties* featured humorist Richard Stilgoe anchoring a series of offbeat sketches. Tracey Ullman, Miriam Margolyes and Robbie Coltrane (who replaced Stilgoe in the second series) all gained valuable early exposure from the series, as did Rik Mayall, billed under his alter ego of Kevin Turvey, a boring Brummie who delivered a pointless monologue each week. Turvey was also featured in a one-off spoof documentary, *Kevin Turvey – The Man Behind the Green Door* (1982).

KILLER
See TAGGART.

KILROY-SILK, ROBERT
(1942–)

Former Labour MP who, after the publication of his book, *Hard Labour*, branched out into daytime TV talk shows with *Day by Day*, which was quickly renamed *Kilroy*.

KING, LARRY
(Lawrence Zeiger; 1933–)

American journalist and radio and TV presenter, since 1985 host of the influential *Larry King Live* for CNN, which attracts all the top political names and allows viewers telephone access to them.

KINGSTON, ALEX
(1963–)

English Shakespearean actress seen in series like *The Knock* and CROCODILE SHOES, but making her mark in the title role of *Moll Flanders*. She then moved to America to take the part of Dr Elizabeth Corday in ER. Her first husband was actor Ralph Fiennes.

KINNEAR, ROY
(1934–88)

Wigan-born comedian and actor, originally a member of the THAT WAS THE WEEK THAT WAS team and later moving on to star in his own sitcoms, usually portraying breathless, sweaty types. The highlights were *A Slight Case of* . . . (smooth talker H. A. Wormsley), *A World of his Own* (daydreamer Stanley Blake), INSIDE GEORGE WEBLEY (George, a perpetual worrier), *Cowboys* (building-firm manager Joe Jones), *The Clairvoyant* (title character Arnold Bristow), *No Appointment Necessary* (greengrocer/hairdresser Alf Butler) and the ill-fated *Hardwicke House* (headmaster Mr R. G. Wickham). Kinnear also supported hosts of other actors (such as Dick Emery and then Willie Rushton in *Rushton's Illustrated*) in their series. His credits included TILL DEATH US DO PART, THE AVENGERS, THE GOODIES, THE SWEENEY, CASUALTY, MINDER (Whaley), GEORGE AND MILDRED (George's friend, Jerry), *The Incredible Mr Tanner* (Sidney) and the animation, *Bertha* (narrator). Kinnear died in 1988 while shooting the film, *The Return of the Musketeers*, in Spain, when his horse slipped and fell, throwing him to the ground.

KINVIG
UK (LWT) Situation Comedy. ITV 1981

Des Kinvig	**Tony Haygarth**
Netta Kinvig	**Patsy Rowlands**
Jim Piper	**Colin Jeavons**
Miss Griffin	**Prunella Gee**
Mr Horsley	**Patrick Newell**
Buddo	**Simon Williams**

Creator/Writer: **Nigel Kneale**
Producer: **Les Chatfield**

An electrical repairman is whisked off to Mercury by a sexy spacewoman.

Des Kinvig led a mundane life. Running a back-street electrical repair shop in Bingleton, married to the suffocating Netta and sharing his home with a giant dog named Cuddley, this was one man in urgent need of excitement. It arrived in the form of shapely alien Miss Griffin, who persuaded Des to join her on trips to Mercury. There, they and the 500-year-old Buddo teamed up against an ant-like race called the Xux, who aimed to take over Earth by giving humans the power to bend cutlery and by flooding the planet with humanoid robots.

Played for laughs, the storyline left viewers wondering whether it had all been a figment of Des's imagination, sparked off by UFO discussions with his anoraky friend, Jim Piper. Creator Nigel Kneale was the writer of 1984 and QUATERMASS in the 1950s.

KIRWAN, DERVLA
(1971–)

Dublin-born actress who appeared in the series, *Troubles*, as a teenager but whose first major role was in Melvyn Bragg's controversial drama, *A Time to Dance* (Bernadette Kennedy). She then starred as Phoebe Bamford in GOODNIGHT SWEETHEART and as Assumpta Fitzgerald in BALLYKISSANGEL, quitting both roles before the series ended. She has also featured in *The Dark Room* (Jinx Kingsley), *Mr White Goes to Westminster* (Pam), *Eureka Street* (Aoirghe), *The Flint Street Nativity* (Gabriel), *The Greatest Store in the World* (Geraldine) and *Happy Birthday Shakespeare* (Kate Green).

KLUGMAN, JACK
(1922–)

American actor, star of TV's version of THE ODD COUPLE (Oscar Madison) and even better known as the grouchy pathologist, QUINCY. In a long television career, Klugman has appeared in kids' shows, plays and early cult series like THE TWILIGHT ZONE, NAKED CITY, BEN CASEY and THE DEFENDERS. His first starring role was in a comedy not seen in the UK, *Harris Against the World*. Klugman also played Henry Willows in *You Again?*, a US translation of the sitcom, HOME TO ROOST.

KNEALE, NIGEL
(1922–)

Isle of Man-born BBC staff writer and script reader who helped shift the goal posts of TV drama through his adventurous 1953 thriller, THE QUATERMASS EXPERIMENT. A year later, Kneale was responsible for the graphic adaptation of Orwell's 1984, which caused a storm in Parliament. His next major work was QUATERMASS II in 1955, joined by QUATERMASS AND THE PIT in 1958. Kneale continued to lean on the boundaries of acceptability with plays like *The Year of the Sex Olympics* (a *Theatre 625* presentation, 1968) and *Wine of India* (a *Wednesday Play*, 1970), before leaving the BBC in 1975 to work for ITV. *Beasts*, an anthology of chillers involving animals, was aired in 1976, and QUATERMASS was revived for Euston Films in 1979, before Kneale attempted comedy with the sci-fi sitcom, KINVIG, in 1981. Among his recent works have been *The Woman in Black*, *Stanley and the Women* and one episode of SHARPE, with other notable credits over the years including an adaptation of *Wuthering Heights* (1953), *The Creature* (1955), *The Road* (part of the *First Night* anthology, 1963), *The Crunch* (from *Studio '64*, 1964), *The Chopper* (for *Out of the Unknown* in 1971) and *The Stone Tape* (1972).

KNIGHT ERRANT
UK (Granada) Adventure. ITV 1959–61

Adam Knight	John Turner
Liz Parrish	Kay Callard
Peter Parker	Richard Carpenter
Toby Hollister	William Fox
Stephen Drummond	Hugh David
Frances Graham	Wendy Williams
Gregory Wilson	Stephen Cartwright
Col. Cope-Addams	Alan Webb

Creator: **Philip Mackie**
Producers: **Warren Jenkins, Kitty Black**

A newspaper advertisement leads to a life of adventure for a modern-day crusader.

Adam Knight, a meanderer between jobs, bit the bullet and decided to work for himself, placing a newspaper advert which read: 'Knight Errant '59. Quests undertaken, dragons defeated, damsels rescued. Anything, anywhere, for anyone, so long as it helps. Fees according to means.' The result was a series of interesting and diverse cases, revolving around other people's problems.

Joining Adam in his Knight Errant agency were ex-*Daily Clarion* journalist Liz Parrish and young writer Peter Parker. A later addition to the team was Adam's new business consultant, Toby Hollister, a spirits tycoon. When Adam left for Canada to run his uncle's farm, he was replaced as agency boss by Stephen Drummond, a publisher with little time for his true profession. Drummond's secretary, Frances Graham, also arrived. Peter Parker then returned to his writing and was substituted by Greg Wilson and a retired army man, Colonel Cope-Addams, added military experience to the set-up.

The first series was entitled *Knight Errant '59*, becoming *Knight Errant '60* when the year changed. After Adam Knight's departure, the programme was renamed *Knight Errant Limited*. Richard Carpenter, who played Peter Parker, switched career himself, from acting to writing, moving on to create series like CATWEAZLE and DICK TURPIN.

KNIGHT RIDER
US (Universal/Glen A. Larson) Science Fiction. ITV 1983–7

Michael Knight	David Hasselhoff
Devon Miles	Edward Mulhare
Bonnie Barstow	Patricia McPherson
April Curtis	Rebecca Holden

KITT .... **William Daniels** (*voice*)
Reginald Cornelius III ('RC3') .... **Peter Parros**

Creator/Producer: **Glen A. Larson**

An ex-cop rights wrongs with the help of a supercar.

Michael Long, a young police officer, was shot in the face and left for dead. To his rescue came Wilton Knight, a millionaire industrialist (played in the opening episode by Richard Basehart) who himself had little time to live. Long underwent plastic surgery to repair his features and, in respect for his saviour, changed his name to Michael Knight. When the millionaire died, he left his estate to Michael for the benefit of the fight against crime, and Michael accepted the bequest with relish.

As part of the inheritance, Michael took possession of an amazing, computerized black car, known as the Knight Industries Two Thousand, or KITT for short. KITT was not only capable of speeds over 300 m.p.h. and equipped with an armoury of lethal weapons, it also talked, had a moody personality and came whenever Michael needed it. With such a trusty steed, Knight, not surprisingly, often succeeded in his fight for justice.

Knight's helpers were Devon Miles, manager of the dead millionaire's estate, and a mechanic, Bonnie Barstow, who was temporarily replaced by April Curtis and then the laid-back RC3. They operated from a base known as the Foundation for Law and Government in California and followed KITT and Knight in a large support van. KITT, despite its flashy appearance, was no more than a souped-up Pontiac Trans Am.

KNOCK, THE
UK (LWT/Bronson/Knight) Drama. ITV 1994–

Bill Adams .... **Malcolm Storry**
Gerry Birch .... **David Morrissey**
George Webster .... **Anthony Valentine**
Nicki Lucas .... **Suzan Crowley**
Barry Christie .... **Steve Toussaint**
Jo Chadwick .... **Tracy Whitwell**
Arnie Rheinhardt .... **Marston Bloom**
George Andreotti .... **Enzo Squillino, Jr**
Diane Ralston .... **Caroline Lee Johnson**
Eddie Barton .... **Jack Ellis**
Kevin Butcher .... **Andrew Dunn**
Tommy Maddern .... **Ian Burfield**
Katherine Roberts .... **Alex Kingston**
Allan Montfort .... **Oliver Tobias**
Alex Murray .... **Daniel Brown**
Jake Munro .... **Daniel O'Grady**
David Ancrom .... **Mark Lewis Jones**
Lynn Hickson .... **Sarah Malin**
Glen Vaughan .... **Peter O'Brien**
Rob Maguire .... **Jonathan Kerrigan**
Jessica Haworth .... **Michelle Morris**

Executive Producer: **David Newcombe**
Producers: **Anita Bronson, Paul Knight, Philip Leach**

A team of customs officers go undercover to foil smuggling rackets.

The Knock focused on the London-based City and South team of Customs and Excise officers, whose job was to root out the most sophisticated attempts to bring drugs, arms, jewellery and other illegal or counterfeit goods into the UK. Head of the squad was Bill Adams, later replaced by David Ancrom. In a selection of mostly three- and four-part stories, the team travelled the world in search of their prey, hoping to nail such villains as gold smuggler George Webster, gangster Tommy Maddern and wheeler-dealer Allan Montfort. Other guest criminals were played by Dennis Waterman, Cherie Lunghi and Michael Brandon. In 2000 a new task force was introduced. Codenamed Indigo, it featured stalwarts Diane Ralston, Barry Christie and Alex Murray, alongside new colleagues, under new, hard-line boss Glen Vaughan. The series was supposedly inspired by the documentary series, *The Duty Men*.

KNOTS LANDING
US (Lorimar/Roundlay/MF) Drama. BBC1 1980–3; 1986–94

Gary Ewing .... **Ted Shackleford**
Valene Ewing/Gibson/Waleska .... **Joan Van Ark**
Sid Fairgate .... **Don Murray**
Karen Fairgate/MacKenzie .... **Michele Lee**
Richard Avery .... **John Pleshette**
Laura Avery/Sumner .... **Constance McCashin**
Kenny Ward .... **James Houghton**
Ginger Ward .... **Kim Lankford**
Diana Fairgate .... **Claudia Lonow**
Michael Fairgate .... **Pat Petersen**
Eric Fairgate .... **Steve Shaw**
Jason Avery .... **Justin Dana**
Danny Gellis
Danny Ponce
Matthew Newmark
Abby Cunningham/Ewing/Sumner .... **Donna Mills**
Brian Cunningham .... **Bobby Jacoby**
Brian Austin Green
Olivia Cunningham/Dyer .... **Tonya Crowe**
Roy Lance .... **Steven Hirsch**
Lilimae Clements .... **Julie Harris**
Amy .... **Jill Cohen**
Joe Cooper .... **Stephen Macht**
M. Patrick (Mack) MacKenzie .... **Kevin Dobson**
Ciji Dunne .... **Lisa Hartman**
Chip Roberts .... **Michael Sabatino**
Ben Gibson .... **Douglas Sheehan**
Gregory Sumner .... **William Devane**
Cathy Geary/Rush .... **Lisa Hartman**
Mary-Frances Sumner .... **Danielle Brisebois**
Stacy Galina
Joshua Rush .... **Alec Baldwin**
Paul Galveston .... **Howard Duff**
Ruth Galveston .... **Ava Gardner**
Peter Hollister .... **Hunt Block**
Linda Martin .... **Leslie Hope**
Jill Bennett .... **Teri Austin**

Paige Matheson	**Nicollette Sheridan**
Tina	**Tina Lifford**
Peggy	**Victoria Ann-Lewis**
Marsha	**Marcia Solomon**
Anne Winston/Matheson	**Michelle Phillips**
Jean Hackney	**Wendy Fulton**
Russell Winston	**Harry Townes**
Al Baker	**Red Buttons**
Bobby Gibson	**Joseph Cousins**
	Christian Cousins
Betsy Gibson	**Kathryn and Tiffany Lubran**
	Emily Ann Lloyd
Carlos	**Carlos Cantu**
Jody Campbell	**Kristy Swanson**
Charles Scott	**Michael York**
Barbara	**Ronne Troup**
Ana	**Movita Castenada**
Johnny Rourke	**Peter Reckell**
Patricia Williams	**Lynne Moody**
Frank Williams	**Larry Riley**
Julie Williams	**Kent Masters-King**
Harold Dyer	**Paul Carafotes**
Bob Phillips	**Zane Lasky**
Mort Tubor	**Mark Haining**
Danny Waleska	**Sam Behrens**
Linda Fairgate	**Lar Park-Lincoln**
Virginia Bullock	**Betsy Palmer**
Paula Vertosick	**Melinda Culea**
Ted Melcher	**Robert Desiderio**
Amanda Michaels	**Penny Peyser**
Claudia Whittaker	**Kathleen Noone**
Kate Whittaker	**Stacy Galina**
Nick Schillace/Dimitri Pappas	**Lorenzo Caccialanza**
Jason Lochner	**Thomas Wilson Brown**
Dick Lochner	**Guy Boyd**
Tom Ryan	**Joseph Gian**
Steve Brewer	**Lance Guest**
Charlotte Anderson	**Tracy Reed**

Creator: **David Jacobs**
Executive Producers: **Lee Rich, Michael Filerman, David Jacobs**

Life, love, death and deception in a Californian cul-de-sac.

Having fled the excesses of DALLAS, Gary Ewing, his family's alcoholic black sheep, arrived in the small town of Knots Landing in California. Remarried to his estranged wife, Val, he settled down in a pleasant cul-de-sac, taking a job at Knots Landing Motors, a classic car dealership owned by one of his neighbours, Sid Fairgate. Sid and his wife, Karen, lived with their three teenage children, Diana, Michael and Eric. Also on the close were scheming, lecherous attorney Richard Avery and Laura, his estate agent wife, as well as music executive Kenny Ward and his partner, Ginger. Soon to arrive was Sid's divorcée sister, Abby Cunningham. She moved into the cul-de-sac with her two children, Brian and Olivia, and quickly began to spread gossip and seduce the menfolk.

So the scene was set, and against this backdrop the usual soap storylines developed, pitting the characters against each other in romance, business and intrigue. Typically, there were murders, scandals, adulterous affairs and bitchy in-fighting, but *Knots Landing* didn't stray too far off what was realistically possible, unlike its glossier contemporaries. Characters came, made a big splash and then disappeared. Gregory Sumner stayed longer than most. He was a dodgy senator with underworld connections who married both Laura (divorced from Richard) and, later, Abby. The Williamses were other new arrivals, a black family hiding out under a witness protection scheme. Gradually, the neighbourhood's younger generation pushed their way to the fore, especially Michael Fairgate, Olivia Cunningham and Paige Matheson, the illegitimate daughter of Karen's new husband, attorney Mack MacKenzie (Sid had been killed when his car drove off a cliff). Gary's brothers from *Dallas* popped into some episodes, and Gary and Val returned the compliment by occasionally visiting Texas to see their wayward daughter, Lucy.

Despite winning praise for its 'ordinariness' (well, at least when compared with DYNASTY), *Knots Landing* didn't really catch on in the UK. The series was dropped by the BBC after just a few years and, when picked up again in 1986, it was given only an afternoon time-slot, not the Saturday evening prime time with which it began.

KNOX, BARBARA
(1938–)

Oldham-born actress, CORONATION STREET's Rita Littlewood/Fairclough/Sullivan. Pre-Weatherfield, Knox (as Barbara Mullaney) had appeared in rep and on radio, as well as in series like EMERGENCY – WARD 10 (Nurse Fulton), MRS THURSDAY, THE DUSTBINMEN, NEVER MIND THE QUALITY, FEEL THE WIDTH, A FAMILY AT WAR and the pilot play for GIRLS ABOUT TOWN. Mullaney changed her name on marrying businessman John Knox in the late 1970s.

KOJAK
US (Universal) Police Drama. BBC1 1974–8

Lt. Theo Kojak	**Telly Savalas**
Capt. Frank McNeil	**Dan Frazer**
Lt. Bobby Crocker	**Kevin Dobson**
Det. Stavros	**George Savalas**
Det. Rizzo	**Vince Conti**
Det. Saperstein	**Mark Russell**
Det. Prince	**Borah Silver**

Creator: **Abby Mann**
Executive Producer: **Matthew Rapf**

Unorthodox police work with a no-nonsense, plain-clothes cop in New York City.

Theo Kojak was a distinctive kind of police officer. For starters, he sucked lollipops and wore fancy waistcoats. He called people 'Pussycat' and, even more unusually, when he lifted his trilby, he revealed a magnificent shaven head. Once seen, he was never forgotten.

His policing methods were rather unconventional, too. He worked in the Manhattan South, 13th Precinct of the New York Police Department, where his boss, Frank McNeil, had once been his partner. Kojak's refusal to play the police game by the book meant that promotion had never come his way. Dry and cynical, he was always too ready to bend the rules, which needled his superiors. On the streets, Kojak was supported by another plain-clothes cop, Bobby Crocker, though his sharpest banter was reserved for Stavros, the overweight, bushy-haired detective played by Telly Savalas's brother, George (originally credited as 'Demosthenes', his middle name).

Kojak became a cult figure in the UK. Lollipop sales boomed and bald became beautiful. Kids strolled around asking, 'Who loves ya, baby?' echoing Kojak's catchphrase. Telly Savalas, although already an established character actor, was propelled to international stardom by the series and even broke into the pop charts, mumbling his way to number one in 1975 with a depressing rendition of David Gates's 'If'. After a couple of sequels in the mid-1980s, the character returned to the screens in a series of TV movies in 1989, by which time he had at last gained promotion to inspector.

KOSSOFF, DAVID
(1919–)

Softly spoken British actor, prominent in the 1950s as hen-pecked Alf in THE LARKINS and in the 1960s as Marcus Lieberman, boss of the family furniture company, in A LITTLE BIG BUSINESS. Kossoff also took the role of the Sheriff of Nottingham in a 1953 version of *Robin Hood* and appeared in the very first ARMCHAIR THEATRE production, *The Outsider*, in 1956, among other plays. Much later, he was seen giving Bible readings on STARS ON SUNDAY. He was the father of the late Paul Kossoff, guitarist with the rock band, Free.

KRYPTON FACTOR, THE
UK (Granada) Quiz. ITV 1977–95

Presenters: **Gordon Burns, Penny Smith**

Creator: **Jeremy Fox**
Producers: **Jeremy Fox, Stephen Leahy, David Jenkins, Geoff Moore, Patricia Pearson, Rod Natkiel, Kieran Roberts, Caroline Gosling, Wayne Garvie**

Physical and mental contest to find Britain's 'superperson'.

Taking its name from Superman's home planet, *The Krypton Factor* aimed to find Britain's brainiest and fittest quiz show contestant. Four contenders took part in each heat, progressing to semi-finals and then the Grand Final, in which *The Krypton Factor* champion was declared. They were subjected to tests of mental agility, intelligence, general knowledge and observation (using film clips and, for many years, an identity parade). An army assault course was used to assess physical strength and fitness (age and sex handicaps levelled the playing field), and a flight simulator was employed to gauge 'response'. Each contestant's final score was known as

his or her Krypton Factor. Gordon Burns presented the show throughout its long run and was joined by Penny Smith as co-presenter in the final series in 1995.

A number of celebrity specials were produced over the years, as well as a few international challenge editions (this was the first UK quiz format to be sold to America). Ross King hosted a short-lived junior version, *Young Krypton*, in 1988.

KUNG FU
US (Warner Brothers) Western. ITV 1973–6

Kwai Chang Caine	**David Carradine** (*adult*)
	Radames Pera (*boy*)
Master Po	**Keye Luke**
Master Kan	**Philip Ahn**

Creator: **Ed Spielman**
Executive Producer: **Jerry Thorpe**
Producers: **Herman Miller, Alex Beaton**

A Chinese half-breed wanders through the Wild West avoiding bounty-hunters and looking for his long-lost brother.

A man of few words, the peace-loving Kwai Chang Caine had been born in Imperial China, son of an American sea-captain and a local woman. He had grown up in a strict Buddhist temple, becoming a Shaolin priest and benefiting from the wisdom of great sages. There, he had also learnt the martial art of Kung Fu. Having killed a member of the Chinese royal family (in self-defence), he fled to America in the 1870s to seek out his half-brother. However, with a price on his head, he was pursued from town to town by oriental hitmen and other bounty-hunters.

The softly spoken, somewhat spaced-out drifter enjoyed the freedom of his own company and the pleasure of his own thoughts. He found himself helping folk in trouble at every turn, but he was a reluctant hero and always the last to resort to violence, turning the other cheek as often as possible. However, a half-breed stumbling around in the violent Wild West was an easy target for bullies. So, when the situation called for it (every episode), he was forced to draw on his fighting skills. With much of the action filmed in slow motion for effect, Caine effortlessly kicked and chopped down his aggressors, often more than one at a time.

Intercut with flashbacks to his childhood, the programme also showed Caine learning his philosophical approach to life from Master Kan and the blind Master Po, the Buddhist priests who called him 'Grasshopper'. Each episode began by recalling the tortuous initiation ceremony at the temple, Caine lifting a burning-hot cauldron with his wrists and so branding them with the mark of the dragon. The series stemmed from the success of the Kung Fu films made by master of the art Bruce Lee. The concept was revived in 1993, in *Kung Fu: The Legend Continues*. Carradine this time played Caine's modern-day grandson, also called Kwai Chang Caine.

KYDD, SAM
(1915–82)

British character actor, a supporting player for many big names (from Arthur Askey to Tony Hancock) and a star in his own right on more than one occasion. Probably the highlight of his television career was the 1960s children's series, ORLANDO, in which he played former smuggler Orlando O'Connor, a character first seen in the drama series, CRANE. Among his earliest contributions was a 1950 version of *Toad of Toad Hall*. Kydd went on to appear in Harry Worth's first sitcom, *The Trouble with Harry*, play Bosun 'Croaker' Jones in *Mess Mates*, take the part of Smellie in the controversial Johnny Speight comedy, CURRY AND CHIPS, and star as Herbert Quince, valet to Jimmy Edwards, in *The Fossett Saga*. He was Sam Weller in *The Pickwick Papers*, was seen in the kids' comedy, *Tottering Towers*, and one of his last appearances was as Mike Baldwin's father in CORONATION STREET. He was the father of actor Jonathan Kydd.

KYTV
UK (BBC) Situation Comedy. BBC2 1990–3

Mike Channel	**Angus Deayton**
Mike Flex	**Geoffrey Perkins**
Anna Daptor	**Helen Atkinson Wood**
Martin Brown	**Michael Fenton Stevens**
various characters	**Philip Pope**

Writers: **Angus Deayton, Geoffrey Perkins**
Producer: **Jamie Rix**

Mock satellite broadcasting with a fictitious TV station.

KYTV was a spoof on the emerging satellite TV networks, satirizing their programming, poking fun at their technical problems and parodying their broadcasters. The station was named after Sir Kenneth Yellowhammer, its founder and chairman, and the main presenters were Mike Channel, Mike Flex, Anna Daptor and the bumbling Martin Brown. Phil Pope provided the music as well as appearing as continuity announcer. The team sent up every aspect of programming, from travelogues and crime reports to God slots and election coverages. The one-off special, *The Making of David Chizzlenut*, gave viewers the chance to look behind the scenes of a TV classic.

KYTV was a follow-up to the same team's Radio 4 series, *Radio Active*, in which they mocked the standard of programming at some commercial radio stations.

LA FRENAIS, IAN
(1937–) See CLEMENT, DICK.

LA LAW
US (Twentieth) Legal Drama. ITV 1987–92

Leland McKenzie	**Richard Dysart**
Douglas Brackman, Jr	**Alan Rachins**
Michael Kuzak	**Harry Hamlin**
Arnie Becker	**Corbin Bernsen**
Grace Van Owen	**Susan Dey**
Ann Kelsey	**Jill Eikenberry**
Stuart Markowitz	**Michael Tucker**
Victor Sifuentes	**Jimmy Smits**
Abby Perkins	**Michele Greene**
Roxanne Melman	**Susan Ruttan**
Benny Stulwicz	**Larry Drake**
Jonathan Rollins	**Blair Underwood**
Dave Meyer	**Dann Florek**
Rosalind Shays	**Diana Muldaur**
Cara Jean (C. J.) Lamb	**Amanda Donohoe**
Tommy Mullaney	**John Spencer**
Zoey Clemmons	**Cecil Hoffman**

Creators: **Steven Bochco, Terry Louise Fisher**
Executive Producers: **David Kelley, Gregory Hoblit**

The cases of a prominent Los Angeles law firm.

LA Law has been described as HILL STREET BLUES in a courtroom. Indeed, there were many similarities between the two programmes, not least because *Law*'s co-creator, Steven Bochco, had also been one of the brains behind the *Blues*. He brought with him much the same format: a large, well-defined cast, interweaving storylines and the ability to mix serious business with the lightest of humour. His collaborator on this series was former CAGNEY AND LACEY producer, Terry Louise Fisher, herself a former Deputy District Attorney.

The law firm in question was that of McKenzie, Brackman, Chaney and Kuzak. McKenzie was the paternal senior partner, Brackman the penny-pinching, balding son of one of the founding partners, and Kuzak the hard-working, compassionate litigation partner. Chaney died in the opening episode. Working with them were Ann Kelsey (another litigation partner), Stuart Markowitz (the tax partner and Ann's future husband), and the philandering divorce partner, Arnie Becker. Also in the team were their associates, the hispanic Victor Sifuentes, new arrival Abby Perkins and Roxanne Melman, Becker's secretary. Grace Van Owen was Kuzak's Deputy DA girlfriend who sometimes had to oppose him in the courtroom. Black lawyer Jonathan Rollins and mentally retarded office boy Benny Stulwicz were added later.

Political and romantic ambitions punctuated the legal activities of the company, with associates vying to become partners and workmates trying to become bedmates. Abby set up on her own but found life hard away from the practice and soon returned. New litigator Roz Shays was brought in and proved too disruptive, before she fell into an empty elevator shaft and was killed, and Grace became a judge, but decided she preferred attorney work and packed it in to join the firm. Later, Kuzak left to form his own company, resulting in a name change for the firm to McKenzie, Brackman, Chaney and Becker, and the arrival of three new attorneys. They were freelancer Tommy Mullaney, his former wife, Zoey, and English litigation lawyer, C. J. Lamb.

Combining soapy storylines with responsible handling of touchy subjects like AIDS and racial abuse, *LA Law* also proved that TV lawyers were not infallible. Like the cops on Hill Street, the legal eagles in LA were not always successful. In the UK, the series was dropped by ITV in 1992, but further episodes were seen on Sky One.

LA PLANTE, LYNDA
(Lynda Titchmarsh; 1946–)

Liverpudlian actress turned dramatist, making a major impression with her first TV offering, WIDOWS. She followed this up with *Widows 2* and then the highly acclaimed PRIME SUSPECT series of police dramas. Her other work has included *The Lifeboat*, *Framed*, *Civvies*, *Comics*, *She's Out* (the revival of *Widows*), *Supply and Demand*, *The Governor* – the first major series from her own production company, La Plante Productions – *Trial and Retribution* (which introduced revolutionary split-screen imagery), and the Internet thriller, *Killer Net*.

LA RUE, DANNY
(Daniel Patrick Carroll; 1927–)

Britain's most famous drag artist, Danny La Rue (actually born in Cork, Ireland) was almost a regular on THE GOOD OLD DAYS and other variety shows in the 1960s and 1970s. His other TV work has been confined to guest appearances and adaptations of his stage shows.

LADD, CHERYL
(Cheryl Stoppelmoor; 1951–)

American leading lady, wife of Alan Ladd's son, David. Her first television work involved providing one of the singing voices for the cartoon, *Josie and the Pussycats* (under the name Cherie Moore). She later appeared on US TV under her maiden name of Cheryl Stoppelmoor, before, as Cheryl Ladd, she was cast as Kris Munroe, sister of Farrah Fawcett-Major's character, Jill, in CHARLIE'S ANGELS. After the series ended, Ladd moved into films and TV movies but returned to US prime time in 1994 in the detective series, *One West Waikiki*.

LAKES, THE
UK (BBC/Company) Drama. 1997–9

Danny Kavanagh	**John Simm**
Emma Quinlan/Kavanagh	**Emma Cunniffe**
Bernie Quinlan	**Mary Jo Randle**
Peter Quinlan	**Paul Copley**
Pete Quinlan	**James Thornton**
Annie/Jessica Quinlan	**Jessica Perry**
Grandad	**Tony Rohr**
Sheila Thwaite	**Elizabeth Rider**
Arthur Thwaite	**David Westhead**
Paula Thwaite	**Jenna Scruton**
Father Matthew	**Robert Pugh**
Gary Alcock (Chef)	**Charles Dale**
John Parr/Fisher	**Kevin Doyle**
Simone Parr/Fisher	**Clare Holman**
Ruth Alcock	**Elizabeth Berrington**
Mr Archer	**Nicholas Day**
Lucy Archer	**Kaye Wragg**
Doreen Archer	**Elizabeth Bennett**
Joey	**Robin Laing**
Tharmy	**Lee Oakes**
Albie	**Matt Bardock**
Robert	**Ryan Pope**
Sgt Eddie Slater	**Bob Mason**
Dr Sarah Kilbride	**Barbara Wilshere**
Juliet Bray	**Sally Rogers**
Susan Charles	**Sam Hall**
Jo Jo Spiers	**Amanda Mealing**
Ged Hodson	**Marshall Lancaster**
Charles Kilbride	**Robert Morgan**
Beverly	**Annabelle Apsion**
Thomas Alcock	**Joel Philimore**
Billy Jennings	**Justin Brady**

Writer: **Jimmy McGovern**
Executive Producer: **George Faber**
Producers: **Charles Pattinson, Matthew Bird**

An unemployed Liverpool lad moves to Cumbria and becomes the catalyst for local tensions.

Poetry-loving tearaway Danny Kavanagh was on the dole, addicted to gambling and becoming less welcome at home. He decided to make a new life in the Lake District, meeting local girl Emma on the coach journey north. He took a job as a kitchen slave under a brutal, bigoted chef in an Ullswater hotel and proceeded to make Emma pregnant. After marriage, a brief return to Liverpool, and a period in jail for theft, inspired by gambling-induced poverty, Danny returned to the Lakes to find Emma, hoping to repair their relationship and promising never to gamble again. A family accident on the lake led to the finger being pointed again at Danny and a spotlight being trained on the hypocrisy, deceit, wavering Catholicism and sexual profligacy that permeated the tight-knit local community.

Semi-autobiographical, in that writer Jimmy McGovern had himself been a gambler in youth, had taken a job in a lakeside hotel kitchen and met his wife along the way, *The Lakes* was promoted as 'a Britpop serial for the nineties', and featured music from bands like Stone Roses and Primal Scream. Although the series won rave reviews, Lake District inhabitants were not impressed with the image it portrayed of Cumbrian life.

More controversy followed the second series, which focused less on Danny and more on characters like flirty hotelier's daughter Lucy Archer, Emma's mother (Bernie) and the local priest. Police complained of similarities between a real crime and events in the programme and, while producers declared the circumstances to be purely coincidental, the names of two characters, local headteacher John Parr and his wife Simone, were changed to reflect sensitivities.

LAMARR, MARK
(Mark Jones; 1967–)

Swindon-raised comedian and presenter, the host of the pop quiz, NEVER MIND THE BUZZCOCKS, *Mark Lamarr Leaving the 20th Century* and *Lamarr's Attacks*. Previously he was seen as team captain in SHOOTING STARS, presenter of THE WORD and interviewer on THE BIG BREAKFAST.

LAMBERT, VERITY
(1935–)

Verity Lambert was one of Britain's earliest female producers. She was the first producer (1963–5) of DOCTOR WHO and was fundamental in establishing the series as a popular 'bug-eyed monster' show, instead of the educational series its creator, Sydney Newman, intended. Lambert was also the first producer of THE NEWCOMERS, then, in 1966, she co-created and produced ADAM ADAMANT LIVES!. In 1968 she worked on DETECTIVE and in 1969 produced *W. Somerset Maugham,* a series of stories by the famous author, before moving to LWT, where she was responsible for BUDGIE. Later Head of Drama at Thames and an executive with Euston Films, Lambert nurtured MINDER from its shaky beginnings into a classic and had other hits with series like ROCK FOLLIES and HAZELL, and the trilogy, *The Norman Conquests*. She now runs her own independent production company, Cinema Verity, makers of *Coasting*, BOYS FROM THE BUSH, GBH, MAY TO DECEMBER, *Sleepers, Class Act, She's Out, A Perfect State* and the ill-fated ELDORADO.

LAME DUCKS
UK (BBC) Situation Comedy. BBC 2 1984–5

Brian Drake	**John Duttine**
Tommy	**Patric Turner**
Angie	**Lorraine Chase**
Maurice	**Tony Millan**
Ansell	**Brian Murphy**
Mrs Drake	**Primi Townsend**
Mrs Kelly	**Cyd Hayman**

Creator/Writer: **Peter J. Hammond**
Producer: **John B. Hobbs**

A man on the brink of divorce sells his house and moves to the country, taking a motley band of losers with him.

Brian Drake, hit by a lorry and convalescing in hospital, was told by his wife that she wanted a divorce. On release, he sold his house and took off with the proceeds to find a new home in the country. Accompanying him was a reformed arsonist, Tommy, whom he met in hospital, and soon they were joined by the promiscuous Angie and by Maurice, a postman who wanted to walk round the world on a 6-foot ball. Completing this collection of lame ducks was Ansell, the incompetent private eye sent by Drake's wife to track him down. They all moved into a cottage in the village of Scar's Edge, where Mrs Kelly was their glamorous but somewhat unpredictable neighbour. For the second series, the setting had changed to a disused railway station at Stutterton Stop.

Lame Ducks was the first venture into comedy by drama writer P. J. Hammond, the creator of SAPPHIRE AND STEEL among other programmes.

LANCASHIRE, SARAH
(1964–)

Blonde English actress, the daughter of CORONATION STREET scriptwriter Geoffrey Lancashire, and it was in the soap that she became famous, playing Raquel Wolstenhulme/Watts. Since leaving the *Street*, she has won acclaim for a number of roles, including the parts of Liz Deakin in *Bloomin' Marvellous*, Ruth Goddard in WHERE THE HEART IS, Anne Cloves QC in *Verdict*, Yvonne Kolakowski in *Clocking Off*, Coral Atkins in *Seeing Red*, Ruth Quirke in *Chambers* and Trina Lavery in *My Fragile Heart*.

LAND OF THE GIANTS
US (Twentieth Century-Fox/Irwin Allen) Science Fiction.
ITV 1968–72

Capt. Steve Burton	**Gary Conway**
Mark Wilson	**Don Matheson**
Barry Lockridge	**Stefan Arngrim**
Dan Erickson	**Don Marshall**
Commander Alexander Fitzhugh	**Kurt Kasznar**
Valerie Scott	**Deanna Lund**
Betty Hamilton	**Heather Young**
Insp. Kobrick	**Kevin Hagen**

Creator/Executive Producer: **Irwin Allen**

The crew and passengers of a stricken airliner find themselves stranded on a planet inhabited by giants.

On 12 June 1983, a sub-orbital commercial flight from America to London flew through a mysterious cloud and crash-landed on a planet resembling Earth but which was home to people 12 times normal height. The series followed the space castaways' efforts to repair their ship, the *Spindrift*, and return home, while fending off monster insects and animals, or fleeing from the giants, who wanted them for experiments.

The crew were Captain Steve Burton, his co-pilot, Dan Erickson, and stewardess Betty Hamilton. The passengers were engineering executive Mark Wilson, wealthy heiress Valerie Scott, 12-year-old Barry Lockridge and Barry's dog, Chipper. There was one joker in the pack, however: the intriguing, unscrupulous Commander Fitzhugh, who was wanted by the police. Their adversaries in the Land of the Giants were headed by Inspector Kobrick, who worked for the SIB security service.

The series was noted for its elaborate special effects (particularly the use of giant-size props) and was created by Irwin Allen, the inspiration behind VOYAGE TO THE BOTTOM OF THE SEA, THE TIME TUNNEL and the similar LOST IN SPACE. It was repeated on Channel 4 from 1989.

LANDAU, MARTIN
(1928–)

American actor, the husband of Barbara Bain, who starred with him in his two big successes, MISSION: IMPOSSIBLE (in which he played Rollin Hand) and SPACE: 1999 (Commander John Koenig). Previously, Landau had guested on episodes of THE TWILIGHT ZONE, BONANZA, *I Spy* and *The Wild, Wild West*, but has found little TV work of note in recent years, save the odd movie.

LANDEN, DINSDALE
(1932–)

British actor in comedy as well as straight drama. The highlights of his TV career have been the part of Pip in *Great Expectations* and the title roles in *Mickey Dunne* and *Devenish*. He also starred as Barty Wade in PIG IN THE MIDDLE and Lord Brightlingsea in *The Buccaneers*, and appeared in *World in Ferment*, *The Mask of Janus*, THE GLITTERING PRIZES and *Arms and the Man*.

LANDON, MICHAEL
(Eugene Orowitz; 1936–91)

American actor, writer, director and producer, who entered the business through bit parts in the 1950s, an injury having brought to an end a promising sports career. He starred in the cult movie, *I Was a Teenage Werewolf*, and took parts in series like *Wanted Dead or Alive* and WELLS FARGO, before he was spotted by David Dortort, creator of BONANZA, and pitched into the role of Little Joe Cartwright, which was to last for 14 years. When *Bonanza* ended, Landon (who had already gained behind-the-camera experience in the series) created a programme of his own, LITTLE HOUSE ON THE PRAIRIE, in which he also starred (dad Charles Ingalls). When *Little House* finished after eight years, Landon's versatility proved itself yet again as he launched into another of his own productions, HIGHWAY TO HEAVEN, playing probationary angel Jonathan Smith. The series ended in 1988 and Landon, the producer, followed it with the prime-time series, *Father Murphy*, plus a few TV movies.

LANE, CARLA
OBE (Romana Barrack; 1937–)

Liverpudlian comedy writer whose first major success was THE LIVER BIRDS, created with her former scripting partner, Myra Taylor. With Taylor, Lane also contributed numerous episodes to BLESS THIS HOUSE before embarking on a string of hits of her own. These have included *No Strings*, *The Last Song*, SOLO, THE MISTRESS, BUTTERFLIES, *Leaving*, *I Woke Up One Morning*, BREAD, *Screaming*, LUV and *Searching*. Much of her work has focused on mid-life crises and, in particular, the pressures on a woman, with pathos mixing readily with humour throughout.

LANG, BELINDA
(Belinda Lange; 1955–)

London-born actress, the daughter of former quiz show host Jeremy Hawk and actress Joan Heal. Among her more prominent roles have been Kate in DEAR JOHN, Liza in SECOND THOUGHTS, Agatha Troy in THE INSPECTOR ALLEYN MYSTERIES and Bill Porter in 2 POINT 4 CHILDREN. Other credits have included *To Serve Them All My Days*, *The Cabbage Patch* (Susie), *The Bretts*, *Bust* (Sheila Walsh), *Making News*, STAY LUCKY (Lady Karen) and an acclaimed portrayal of Christine Hamilton in the drama, *Justice in Wonderland*. She is married to actor Hugh Fraser (*Poirot*'s Captain Hastings).

LANGFORD, BONNIE
(Bonita Langford; 1964–)

Flame-haired singer, dancer and actress, a former child star seen on OPPORTUNITY KNOCKS (aged six), *Junior Showtime* and as Violet Elizabeth Bott in JUST WILLIAM. Later credits have included *The Saturday Starship*, *The Hot Shoe Show* and DOCTOR WHO, in which she played Mel, one of his assistants. She is married to actor Paul Grunert.

LANGRISHE, CAROLINE
(1958–)

British actress probably best known as auctioneer Charlotte Cavendish in LOVEJOY but with a TV career stretching back to the mid-1970s. She appeared in THE GLITTERING PRIZES, *Anna Karenina* and THE BROTHERS, as well as playing Jane in the PLAY FOR TODAY productions, THE FLIPSIDE OF DOMINICK HIDE and *Another Flip for Dominick*. She was also Kate in *Pulaski*, Bella Niculesco in FORTUNES OF WAR and Jane Bewley in *Mosley*. THE RETURN OF SHELLEY, BOON, *Chancer*, TRAINER, PEAK PRACTICE, SHARPE and CLUEDO have been other credits.

LANSBURY, ANGELA
CBE (1925–)

British actress enjoying a late lease of life as novelist-cum-amateur-sleuth Jessica Fletcher in MURDER, SHE WROTE. Lansbury's showbusiness debut came after she was evacuated out of England in 1940. Three years later, she caught the eye in *Gaslight* and embarked on a successful film career. Television work beckoned in the

1950s, with appearances in assorted plays and anthology series, but she soon moved on to the stage instead, notching up hits on Broadway, breaking off in between for more film work. She returned to the small screen in the 1980s, taking parts in some TV movies before being offered her most celebrated role to date, as the perceptive Miss Fletcher, in 1984.

LARAMIE
US (Revue) Western. BBC 1959–64

Slim Sherman	John Smith
Andy Sherman	Bobby Crawford, Jr
Jess Harper	Robert Fuller
Jonesy	Hoagy Carmichael
Mike Williams	Dennis Holmes
Daisy Cooper	Spring Byington
Gandy	Don Durant
Mort Corey	Stuart Randall

Two friends run a ranch and trading post in the Wild West.

In the 1870s Slim Sherman and his 14-year-old brother, Andy, were orphaned by an outlaw who shot their father on their Wyoming ranch. Rather than leave, they decided to keep up the estate and, with the help of an old friend, Jonesy (played by songwriter Hoagy Carmichael), and Jess Harper, a drifter who put down roots, they set about scratching out a living from the never-too-fruitful property. Andy was eventually written out, and Jonesy left after a year or so, leaving Slim and Jess as partners. As well as raising cattle, they offered a staging-post for traffic on the Great Overland Mail Stage Line, which ensured that a host of interesting and troublesome characters passed their way. Later additions to the cast were young Mike Williams, who had been orphaned by Indians, housekeeper Daisy Cooper and ranch-hand Gandy. The town sheriff, Mort Corey, was also seen on a regular basis.

LARBEY, BOB

British comedy writer, often in conjunction with John Esmonde (see Esmonde's entry for joint work). Larbey, singly, has also penned A FINE ROMANCE, AS TIME GOES BY, ON THE UP, AIN'T MISBEHAVIN' and episodes of THE DARLING BUDS OF MAY.

LARGE, EDDIE
(Eddie McGinnis; 1942–)

As his stage name suggests, the bigger half of the Manchester comedy duo Little and Large, with Syd Little. Discovered on OPPORTUNITY KNOCKS in 1971, the pair later worked on CRACKERJACK, the impressionists' show, WHO DO YOU DO?, and their own prime-time series for Thames (*The Little and Large Tellyshow*) and then the BBC (*The Little and Large Show*). They have also been guest stars in numerous variety programmes and game shows.

LARKINS, THE
UK (ATV) Situation Comedy. ITV 1958–60; 1963–4

Alf Larkins	David Kossoff
Ada Larkins	Peggy Mount
Eddie Larkins	Shaun O'Riordan
Joyce Rogers	Ruth Trouncer
Jeff Rogers	Ronan O'Casey
Sam Prout	George Roderick
Hetty Prout	Barbara Mitchell
Myrtle Prout	Hilary Bamberger
Vicar	Charles Lloyd Pack
Major Osbert Rigby-Soames	Hugh Paddick
Mrs Gannett	Hazel Coppen
Georgie	Hugh Walters

Creator/Writer: **Fred Robinson**
Producers: **Bill Ward, Alan Tarrant**

Life with a lively Cockney family.

The Larkins were hen-pecked but shrewd dad Alf, his battleaxe wife Ada, unemployable son Eddie, daughter Joyce, and her American husband, Jeff Rogers, an out-of-work writer of cowboy comics. They lived at 66 Sycamore Street, somewhere in the London suburbs, and Alf worked in the canteen at a plastics factory. Also seen were snoopy neighbour Hetty Prout, her husband, Sam, and their daughter, Myrtle. Together they found themselves in a variety of farcical situations that proved popular with viewers at the turn of the 1960s (so much so that a spin-off film, *Inn for Trouble*, was released in 1959 and saw the Larkins in charge of a country pub). In the last series, shown three years after the main run, Sycamore Street had been demolished, Alf and Ada (now alone) took over a nearby café and gained a lodger, Osbert Rigby-Soames.

Shaun O'Riordan, who played Eddie Larkins, went on to be one of ATV's major drama and comedy producers.

LARRY SANDERS SHOW, THE
US (Brillstein-Grey/Columbia Tristar) Comedy. BBC 2 1993–9

Larry Sanders	Garry Shandling
Arthur	Rip Torn
Hank Kingsley	Jeffrey Tambor
Jeannie Sanders	Megan Gallagher
Jerry	Jeremy Piven
Phil	Wallace Langham
Paula	Janeane Garofalo
Darlene	Linda Doucett
Beverly	Penny Johnson
Francine	Kathryn Harrold
Brian	Scott Thompson

Executive Producers: **Garry Shandling, Brad Grey**

A revealing glimpse behind the scenes of a late-night talk show.

After the success of the innovative *It's Garry Shandling's Show*, its star became a popular replacement host of Johnny Carson's *Tonight Show*, and was once in the running to take the place of David Letterman. The experience gave Shandling the idea for a sitcom based on the late-night chat show concept, in which he was cast as the host of such a show.

The Larry Sanders Show was split between on- and off-air action. On air, the programme (shot on videotape) played like a real-life chat show, featuring genuine celebrity guests like Roseanne and David Duchovny. Off air (shot on film), the backroom business revealed the bickering, bad language and cynicism behind making such a programme, and these segments were recorded without the customary US laugh-track to emphasize the difference between the two worlds. Sanders himself was a perfectionist and smarmily self-absorbed. His confident, generous on-screen persona contrasted with his insecure, demanding real personality. His team included a devious producer-cum-protective-manager, Artie; guest booker Paula; chief writer Jerry and his scripting colleague, Phil; and Sanders's dim, sycophantic stooge, Hank, whose catchphrase 'Hey, now!' caught on big in the States.

Although winning critical acclaim, the series was never given a fair crack of the whip in the UK, being shunted into late-night slots on BBC 2.

LARSON, GLEN A.
(1937–)

Highly successful American writer, producer and director, working on such hits as IT TAKES A THIEF, THE VIRGINIAN, ALIAS SMITH AND JONES, McCLOUD, THE SIX MILLION DOLLAR MAN, THE FALL GUY, QUINCY, BATTLESTAR GALACTICA, BUCK ROGERS IN THE 25TH CENTURY, *Manimal*, MAGNUM PI and KNIGHT RIDER, many as creator. In the 1950s he was a member of the Four Preps vocal group, who had three UK hits, most notably 'Big Man'.

LASSIE
US (Lassie Television) Children's Adventure. ITV 1956–75

Jeff Miller	**Tommy Rettig**
Ellen Miller	**Jan Clayton**
Gramps Miller	**George Cleveland**
Sylvester 'Porky' Brockway	**Donald Keeler**
Matt Brockway	**Paul Maxey**
Timmy Martin	**Jon Provost**
Doc Weaver	**Arthur Space**
Ruth Martin	**Cloris Leachman**
	June Lockhart
Paul Martin	**Jon Shepodd**
	Hugh Reilly
Uncle Petrie Martin	**George Chandler**
Boomer Bates	**Todd Ferrell**
Cully Wilson	**Andy Clyde**
Corey Stuart	**Robert Bray**
Bob Erickson	**Jack De Mave**
Scott Turner	**Jed Allan**
Garth Holden	**Ron Hayes**
Ron Holden	**Skip Burton**
Mike Holden	**Joshua Albee**
Dale Mitchell	**Larry Wilcox**
Keith Holden	**Larry Pennell**
Lucy Baker	**Pamelyn Ferdin**
Sue Lambert	**Sherry Boucher**

Executive Producers: **Robert Maxwell, Jack Wrather**
Producers: **Rudy Abel, Sherman Harris, Bob Golden, William Beaudine Jr, Bonita Granville Wrather**

An intelligent and heroic collie dog saves lives and averts disasters.

In this long-running series, based on the 1943 film, *Lassie Come Home*, starring Elizabeth Taylor and Roddy McDowall, the lovable Lassie moved from owner to owner. Initially, she lived with young Jeff Miller and his widowed mother and grandfather on a farm near the town of Calverton. When the Millers moved to the city, Lassie was taken in by the Martin family, who had bought the farm, with Lassie's best friend now Timmy, an adopted orphan. The next home for Lassie was provided by oldtimer Cully Wilson, after the Martins had emigrated to Australia, but he suffered a heart attack and Lassie's new master became ranger Corey Stuart. After a few years, Corey was hurt in a fire and care of the collie was handed on to two of his colleagues, Scott Turner and Bob Erickson, though Lassie was already beginning to find her own freedom. Eventually, she became a real loner and took to wandering across the USA. At one point, she gave birth to a litter of pups. The last *Lassie* series saw the dog at home with a new family, the Holdens, whose friends were Sue Lambert, a vet, and deaf girl Lucy Baker.

An animated version, *Lassie's Rescue Rangers*, was also produced, before a revival, *The New Lassie*, appeared in 1989. In this series Lassie lived in California with the McCulloch family, whose Uncle Steve was really young Timmy from the earliest episodes (actor Jon Provost), now grown up and using his real name (Timmy had been a name given to him as an orphan).

Throughout the run, the storylines were always much the same: heartwarming tales of Lassie saving the day, looking after the injured and raising the alarm in times of trouble. Despite her name (and the birth of the pups), Lassie was always played by a male collie. She was created by author Eric Knight.

LAST OF THE BASKETS, THE
UK (Granada) Situation Comedy. ITV 1971–2

Bodkin	**Arthur Lowe**
Clifford Basket	**Ken Jones**
Mrs Basket	**Patricia Hayes**

Creator/Writer: **John Stevenson**
Producer: **Bill Podmore**

A factory worker inherits an earldom and all its debts.

When the 12th Earl of Clogborough decided to abdicate after 93 years of holding the title, an heir to the earldom had to be found. It turned out to be Clifford Basket, a boiler-tender in a northern factory and as unlikely a peer as ever there was. Sadly, what the uncouth Clifford inherited was a run-down mansion and an ever-increasing mound of unpaid bills. At least Bodkin, the Earl's last remaining servant, was still around to guide the unfortunate Basket and his mother through their new, demanding lifestyle. The setting was the fictitious Little Clogborough-in-the-Marsh, and two series were produced.

LAST OF THE SUMMER WINE

UK (BBC) Situation Comedy. BBC 1 1973–

Norman Clegg	**Peter Sallis**
William 'Compo' Simmonite	**Bill Owen**
Cyril Blamire	**Michael Bates**
Foggy Dewhurst	**Brian Wilde**
Seymour Utterthwaite	**Michael Aldridge**
Nora Batty	**Kathy Staff**
Wally Batty	**Joe Gladwin**
Sid	**John Comer**
Ivy	**Jane Freeman**
Crusher (Milburn)	**Jonathan Linsley**
Wesley Pegden	**Gordon Wharmby**
Edie Pegden	**Thora Hird**
Howard	**Robert Fyfe**
Marina	**Jean Fergusson**
Pearl	**Juliette Kaplan**
Glenda	**Sarah Thomas**
Barry	**Mike Grady**
Eli	**Danny O'Dea**
Clem 'Smiler' Hemingway	**Stephen Lewis**
Auntie Wainwright	**Jean Alexander**
Herbert 'Truly' Truelove	**Frank Thornton**
Tom	**Tom Owen**

Creator/Writer: **Roy Clarke**
Producers: **James Gilbert, Bernard Thompson, Sydney Lotterby, Alan J. W. Bell**

Geriatric delinquents while away their retirement in a series of childish games and pranks.

Last of the Summer Wine is the world's longest-running sitcom. It began as a COMEDY PLAYHOUSE presentation in 1973 and then emerged as a series in its own right the same year. Filmed in the Yorkshire village of Holmfirth, it focused for most of its life on three mischievous but lovable pensioners who passed their twilight years energetically engaging themselves in a second childhood of assorted romps and antics. The original trio were the seedy, tramp-like Compo, laconic widower (and lifelong Co-op furniture operative) Cleggy and former Royal Signals sergeant Cyril Blamire. When actor Michael Bates was taken ill, Blamire was replaced by another ex-military man, army sign-writer Foggy Dewhurst, who, in turn, was substituted for a few years by schoolteacher turned crackpot inventor Seymour Utterthwaite. More recently, former policeman Herbert Truelove ('Truly of the Yard') was the third man behind Compo and Clegg.

As the men lurched from scrape to scrape, desperately trying to keep them in check were the town's disapproving womenfolk, particularly the redoubtable Nora Batty, the object of Compo's desires. Also seen in this battle of the sexes have been Wally, Nora's hen-pecked late husband, Seymour's sister, Edie, and her mechanic husband, Wesley, and fiery Pearl and her wimpy husband, Howard (with the brassy Marina as his fancy woman). Auntie Wainwright, the junk-shop owner who never misses a sale, has also been in the action, as have café-proprietor Ivy and her late husband, Sid. Edie's daughter, Glenda, and her husband, Barry, the short-sighted Eli, and the inappropriately named Smiler have also contributed as the character ensemble has extended over the years.

The spring 2000 series was a tribute to actor Bill Owen, who died after filming only three episodes. His character suffered a fatal seizure after seeing Nora Batty not in her usual wrinkled stockings but in black tights. Compo's funeral was shown, and other episodes revealed how his ageing chums coped with his loss, with Owen's own son, Tom, playing Compo's long-lost offspring.

In 1988, the series spawned a prequel, which showed the old folk in their formative years. Entitled *First of the Summer Wine*, it featured Peter Sallis as Cleggy's dad, with David Fenwick as the young Norman, Paul Wyett as Compo, Richard Lumsden as Foggy and Paul McLain as Seymour.

LATE, LATE BREAKFAST SHOW, THE

UK (BBC) Entertainment. BBC 1 1982–6

Presenters: **Noel Edmonds, Mike Smith**

Producer: **Michael Hurll**

Saturday evening collection of silly stunts, pranks and gags.

A halfway house between MULTI-COLOURED SWAP SHOP and NOEL'S HOUSEPARTY, *The Late, Late Breakfast Show* represented Noel Edmonds's successful transition from children's TV to adult programming. Despite becoming popular for regular features like The Hit Squad (hidden-camera jokes staged by former CANDID CAMERA man Peter Dulay), bizarre contests like Mr Puniverse and a feature on out-takes entitled The Golden Egg Awards, the series is unfortunately now best remembered for the death of a member of the public in one of the show's action sequences. In a section entitled Give It a Whirl, a willing viewer was chosen each week to attempt (with prior training) a daredevil stunt for a live outside broadcast hosted by Mike Smith. Sadly, one 'Whirly Wheeler' was killed during practice for a high-rise escapology trick. This led to major ructions within the BBC and the inevitable cancellation of the series after four years on air. The programme's theme music was provided by Gary Kemp of the pop group, Spandau Ballet.

LATE NIGHT LINE-UP

See LINE-UP.

LATHAM, PHILIP

(1929–)

British actor, familiar in the 1960s and 1970s through his portrayals of Willy Izard in MOGUL and THE TROUBLESHOOTERS and Plantagenet Palliser in THE PALLISERS. Among his many other credits have been *The Cedar Tree*, MAIGRET, SERGEANT CORK, JUSTICE, *Love Story*, *Killers*, HAMMER HOUSE OF HORROR, DOCTOR WHO, *No. 10*, NANNY and THE PROFESSIONALS.

LAUGH TRACK

Also known as canned laughter. Pre-recorded audience laughter that is added to programmes (particularly filmed programmes) to provide atmosphere. Studio-produced shows generally have live audiences which are 'warmed up' before recording starts.

LAURIE, HUGH

(1959–)

Eton- and Cambridge-educated actor who rowed in the 1980 Boat Race and starred alongside Emma Thompson, Tony Slattery and others in the 1981 Footlights Revue. It was at Cambridge that Laurie joined forces with Stephen Fry, with whom he entered television in the sketch show, ALFRESCO. There followed appearances in THE YOUNG ONES, GIRLS ON TOP, FILTHY RICH AND CATFLAP, HAPPY FAMILIES, *Saturday Live*, *Look at the State We're In!* and, most prominently, BLACKADDER (Prince George in *Blackadder the Third* and Lt. George in *Blackadder Goes Forth*). The duo also appeared in their own sketch show, *A Bit of Fry and Laurie*, and in Granada's dramatization of JEEVES AND WOOSTER (with Laurie as Bertie Wooster). Laurie has also been seen in serious parts, as in the drama, *All or Nothing at All*.

LAURIE, JOHN

(1897–1980)

As Mr Frazer, the gloomy, penny-pinching undertaker in DAD'S ARMY, John Laurie became a household name, 'We're doomed' becoming his catchphrase. But this eye-rolling Scottish actor had already enjoyed decades of showbusiness success by the time the small screen beckoned. Some viewers will recall him in the classic Hitchcock version of *The Thirty-Nine Steps* back in 1935, just one of dozens of film roles, in addition to extensive stage work. Laurie was also seen on television in the 1930s, though his first major role didn't arrive until 1961, when he played the thriller writer Algernon Blackwood in hosting the anthology series TALES OF MYSTERY. Later in the 1960s he was the mad scientist, McTurk, in the

kids' adventure series, *The Master*, and he also appeared in DR FINLAY'S CASEBOOK.

LAVENDER, IAN

(1946–)

British actor, usually in comic roles, and easily best remembered for his portrayal of mummy's boy Frank Pike in DAD'S ARMY. As Clive Cunliffe, he was stranded in space with Mollie Sugden in COME BACK MRS NOAH, and he also played Ginger in *Mr Big*, gormless Ron in the revival of the radio series, *The Glums*, for *Bruce Forsyth's Big Night* (and later in their own short series), Denis Ailing, the failing salesman, in *The Hello Goodbye Man*, and Tom, the dentist, in the sitcom, *Have I Got You . . . Where You Want Me?*.

LAVERNE AND SHIRLEY

US (Paramount/Miller-Milkis) Situation Comedy.
ITV 1977–84

Laverne De Fazio	**Penny Marshall**
Shirley Feeney	**Cindy Williams**
Carmine Ragusa	**Eddie Mekka**
Frank De Fazio	**Phil Foster**
Andrew 'Squiggy' Squigman	**David L. Lander**
Lenny Kosnowski	**Michael McKean**
Edna Babish/De Fazio	**Betty Garrett**
Sonny St Jacques	**Ed Marinaro**
Rhonda Lee	**Leslie Easterbrook**

Creator: **Garry K. Marshall**
Executive Producers: **Thomas L. Miller, Edward K. Milkis, Garry K. Marshall**
Producers: **Lowell Ganz, Tony Marshall, Mark Rothman**

Two incident-prone girl flatmates work at a brewery but long for something better.

Laverne De Fazio and Shirley Feeney worked in the bottling section of the Shotz brewery in Milwaukee in the late 1950s. They also roomed together in the basement of a town house. They were ambitious, sought fun and fame, but were always short of cash. Tall Laverne (sporting a large, looping 'L' on her sweater) was rather loud, but very insecure. Petite, dark-haired Shirley was naïve and easily taken in. Together they lurched from scrape to scrape.

Their friends featured prominently, particularly the womanizing Carmine, Shirley's on-off boyfriend who liked to be known as 'The Big Ragu' and was always liable to burst into his signature song, 'Rags To Riches'. There were also the well-meaning but very dim brewery truck-drivers, Squiggy and Lenny. Laverne's father, Frank, owned the Pizza Bowl, the hangout where the girls bowled and danced. He later married Mrs Babish, Laverne and Shirley's landlady.

Well into its run, *Laverne and Shirley* changed location. It was now the early 1960s and the action had moved to California, where Laverne and Shirley were seeking a career in films. True to form, they ended up working only as shop assistants, in Bardwell's Department Store.

All the friends moved with them, and a couple of new neighbours, Rhonda, a dancer and model, and Sonny, a stuntman, were introduced. Laverne's father and new stepmother took over a restaurant, Cowboy Bill's. A couple of years later, after a dispute over working hours, actress Cindy Williams asked to be written out and Shirley was married off to army doctor Walter Meany. The show continued for one last season with just Penny Marshall starring and Laverne now working at the Ajax Aerospace Company.

Laverne and Shirley was a very successful spin-off from HAPPY DAYS, in which the girls had made a couple of fleeting appearances. Penny Marshall was the sister of *Happy Days* creator Garry Marshall and has since made a name for herself as a Hollywood director. 'Making Our Dreams Come True', the theme song performed by Cyndi Grecco, was an American hit single in 1976. The series, originally seen sporadically around the ITV network, has also been rerun on the BBC as a daytime filler.

LAWFORD, PETER
(1923–84)

British leading man in Hollywood, a former child actor and the star of numerous films from the 1930s. His major television role was as Nick Charles in THE THIN MAN, though he also appeared in a US comedy entitled *Dear Phoebe* and was seen as Dr Peter Lawrence in *The Doris Day Show*. He was once married to President John F. Kennedy's sister, Pat.

LAWLEY, SUE
OBE (1946–)

Midlands-born journalist and current affairs presenter, originally seen on NATIONWIDE and *Tonight*. She has also chaired QUESTION TIME, the BBC right-to-reply programme, *Biteback*, and other debates, stood in for Terry Wogan on his chat show, read the main BBC news bulletins, presented some interview shows for ITV and fronted *Hospital Watch*, *Review of the Year* and the news magazine, *Here and Now*. In 1995 she anchored the special 50th anniversary BBC news programmes which commemorated events leading up to VE and VJ Day. Lawley is also host of the radio series, *Desert Island Discs*.

LAWRENCE, JOSIE
(Wendy Lawrence; 1959–)

British actress and comedienne, one of the stars of the improvisation series, WHOSE LINE IS IT ANYWAY?. Previously, Lawrence had been seen on *Friday Night Live* (with her Florence from Cradley characterization) and among her other appearances have been parts in POIROT, *Campaign* (film-maker Linda Prentice), Harry Enfield's *Norbert Smith – A Life*, *The Green Man* (Lucy), the kids' comedy, *Jackson Pace: The Great Years* (Ryveeta Tusk), and *Paul Merton in Galton & Simpson's . . .* She was Janet Wilkins in the apocalyptic comedy, *Not with a*

Bang, Lottie in the *Screen Two* film, *Enchanted April*, Maggie Costello in the cricketing comedy, OUTSIDE EDGE, Sophie in *Downwardly Mobile*, Mary in *The Flint Street Nativity* and fitness guru Julia Fleshman in *Fat Friends*. She has also starred in her own series, *Josie*, and appeared in THE COMIC STRIP PRESENTS.

LAWSON, DENIS
(1947–)

Glaswegian actor seen on TV as DJ Kit Curran in *The Kit Curran Radio Show*, Eddie Cass in the thriller, *Dead Head*, Rossi in *The Justice Game*, John Stone in AMBASSADOR, Greg in *Bob Martin* and Tom in *Other People's Children*. Other credits include BERGERAC, *That Uncertain Feeling*, EL C.I.D., *Screen One*'s *Born Kicking*, *Natural Lies*, CATHERINE COOKSON's *The Round Tower* and HORNBLOWER. He is the uncle of actor Ewan McGregor.

LAYTON, GEORGE
(1943–)

British actor, comedian and writer, his earliest appearances coming as striker Jimmy Stokes in the soccer soap, UNITED!, and as Paul Collier in the various *Doctor* series (some episodes of which he also wrote, initially under the name of Oliver Fry). Layton was one of the first three presenters of THAT'S LIFE (with Esther Rantzen and Bob Wellings) and played Bombardier Solomons in the earlier seasons of IT AIN'T HALF HOT MUM. He was Brian Booth in *My Brother's Keeper* (again also as writer), popped up now and again as Des in MINDER and as the Aussie crook, Ray, in THE SWEENEY, and hosted the quiz show, *Pass the Buck*. More recently, Layton played Alan Brooks in *Sunburn*. Among his other writing credits have been DON'T WAIT UP and *Executive Stress*, and episodes of ON THE BUSES, ROBIN'S NEST and *My Name is Harry Worth*.

LE MESURIER, JOHN
(John Elton Halliley; 1912–83)

Elegant British actor, immortalized as the ineffective Sgt Wilson in DAD'S ARMY but a prominent performer on TV for four decades. In the 1950s he starred on children's television and went on to be a regular guest on HANCOCK'S HALF HOUR, appeared as Colonel Maynard in GEORGE AND THE DRAGON, and headlined as the hard-up aristocrat, Lord Bleasham, in *A Class by Himself*. His performance in the Dennis Potter play, *Traitor*, based on the spy, Kim Philby, was much acclaimed. Le Mesurier (his stage name was his mother's maiden name) was also seen in such programmes as THE AVENGERS, THE TROUBLESHOOTERS, THE GOODIES, DOCTOR AT LARGE, WORZEL GUMMIDGE and BRIDESHEAD REVISITED and his voice was as familiar as his face, thanks to numerous Homepride flour commercials and the children's animation, *Bod*, for which he was narrator. His second wife was comedienne Hattie Jacques.

LE VAILLANT, NIGEL

British actor born in Pakistan. Oxford-educated, Le Vaillant has performed Shakespeare on stage, and on television he is best known as Drs Julian Chapman in CASUALTY and Paul Dangerfield in DANGERFIELD. Other credits have included BRIDESHEAD REVISITED, JEMIMA SHORE INVESTIGATES, *Christabel*, *Call Me Mister*, WISH ME LUCK, AGATHA CHRISTIE'S POIROT, MINDER, HANNAY, *Ladies in Charge*, *Poor Little Rich Girls* and *Honey for Tea* (Professor Simon Latimer). He married actress Nicola Jeffries in 1995.

LEACH, ROSEMARY
(1935–)

Shropshire-born actress much seen on television as a supporting player in sitcoms and straight drama, but also with some notable starring parts to her name. She appeared with Ronnie Corbett in NO – THAT'S ME OVER HERE, NOW LOOK HERE . . . and *The Prince of Denmark*, was Sadie Potter in *Sadie, It's Cold Outside*, Queen Victoria in *Disraeli*, Katy Bunting, a late first-time mother, in *Life Begins at Forty*, Fenny Grace in JEWEL IN THE CROWN, Joan Craddock in *Growing Pains*, swindled widow Joan Plumleigh-Bruce in THE CHARMER, Lady Brightlingsea in *The Buccaneers* and Nanny Collins in *Berkeley Square*. The 1971 version of *Cider with Rosie* gave her another chance to shine, and among other credits have been parts in ARMCHAIR THEATRE productions and other plays, THE POWER GAME, RUMPOLE OF THE BAILEY, JACKANORY, *The Roads to Freedom*, *When We Are Married*, *Summer's Lease*, *Titmuss Regained*, *Blood and Peaches* and various TV adaptations of classics.

LEAGUE OF GENTLEMEN, THE
UK (BBC) Comedy. BBC 2 1999–

Mark Gatiss, Steve Pemberton, Reece Shearsmith

Writers: **Jeremy Dyson, Mark Gatiss, Steve Pemberton, Reece Shearsmith**
Producers: **Sarah Smith, Jemma Rodgers**

Darkly comic goings-on in a bleak northern town.

Having secured awards at the Edinburgh Festival and then enjoyed success on BBC Radio, *The League of Gentlemen* team switched seamlessly to television in 1999. Their surreal series, set in the bleak northern town of Royston Vasey ('You'll Never Leave') and involving sketches plus a continuing storyline, focused on the in-bred local townsfolk, all seemingly hiding a deep, dark, desperate secret. Among the oddball creations – all played by the trio of Steve Pemberton, Mark Gatiss and Reece Shearsmith – were sadistic, pen-obsessed careers adviser Pauline; dim, unemployed lad Mickey; Edward and Tubbs, whose shop is only for the use of locals; Barbara, the transsexual taxi-driver; Mr Chinnery, the lethal vet; dubious butcher Hilary Briss; gun-toting businessman

Geoff and his colleagues, Mike and Brian; alcoholic vicar Bernice; German exchange teacher Herr Lipp; forgotten pop star Les McQueen and his band, Crème Brûlée; and inept theatre group Legz Akimbo. The only sanity came from outsiders like back-packer Benjamin, whose local aunt and uncle, Harvey and Val Denton, had some peculiar domestic rules concerning bodily functions. A guest character, foul-mouthed Mayor Vaughan, was played by comedian Roy 'Chubby' Brown, whose real name is Royston Vasey. The series was filmed in the Derbyshire town of Hadfield.

LEAR, NORMAN
(1926–)

Influential American producer, a former scriptwriter who, in the 1970s, was responsible for introducing a more adult attitude to American situation comedy. The break came with ALL IN THE FAMILY and its outspoken lead character, Archie Bunker, based on TILL DEATH US DO PART and Alf Garnett. The series was a huge hit and broke new ground in exploring what was acceptable in American television. Its spin-offs, *Maude* and *The Jeffersons*, were just as challenging to the 'Honey, I'm home' tradition of US comedies, as was *Sanford and Son* (another UK clone, this time of STEPTOE AND SON). Lear was also responsible for the cult comedies, *Mary Hartman, Mary Hartman* and *Diff'rent Strokes*, and became a shrewd media businessman. Much of his early TV (and film) work was in collaboration with Bud Yorkin.

LEGACY OF REGINALD PERRIN, THE
See FALL AND RISE OF REGINALD PERRIN, THE.

LEIGH, MIKE
OBE (1943–)

British writer and director, noted for comedies derived from social observation (particularly of the middle classes) with a strong leaning on his actors' improvisational skills, including those of long-time wife Alison Steadman (they are now separated). His most acclaimed works have been *Nuts in May* (1976) and ABIGAIL'S PARTY (1977), with other credits including *Hard Labour* (1973), *Kiss of Death* (1977), *Grown-Ups* (1980) and *Home Sweet Home* (1982).

LENNY THE LION SHOW, THE
UK (BBC) Children's Entertainment. BBC 1956–63

Producer: **Ronald Eyre, Johnny Downes, Peter Whitmore**

Fun, games and pop music with a soppy ventriloquist's lion.

Ventriloquist Terry Hall and his Lenny the Lion puppet were one of the hottest properties in children's television in the late 1950s and early 1960s. Somewhat languid in appearance, failing to pronounce his 'r's, and prone to burying his maned head in his paw, the wide-eyed Lenny was unusual in being an animal dummy rather than the run-of-the-mill talking boy. He was also one of the first dummies to be given arm-movements, which added to his novelty factor. As well as gags, Lenny's programmes (first seen under the *Children's Television* banner), had a strong pop-music element. Indeed, his 1962 series was entitled *Pops and Lenny* and listed The Beatles as guests on one occasion.

LENSKA, RULA
(Roza Maria Lubienska; 1947–)

Tall, flame-haired, British actress of noble Polish descent who first came to light in ROCK FOLLIES (playing 'Q' – or Nancy Cunard de Longchamps – of The Little Ladies rock band) and has since been seen in programmes like *Take a Letter, Mr Jones* (Mrs Warner, John Inman's boss), *Family Pride*, PRIVATE SCHULZ, MINDER, ROBIN OF SHERWOOD, BOON, *An Actor's Life for Me*, CLUEDO (Mrs Peacock), the kids' series, *Kappatoo*, and STAY LUCKY. Earlier credits included DIXON OF DOCK GREEN, THE BROTHERS, EDWARD THE SEVENTH, THE SAINT and SPECIAL BRANCH. Her second husband was Dennis Waterman.

LETTERMAN, DAVID
(1947–)

American comedian and talk show host, a former announcer, weatherman, children's presenter and writer who, after working with Mary Tyler Moore, eventually broke into the big time courtesy of Johnny Carson's *Tonight* (as a regular guest and stand-in host). This led indirectly to his own series, *Late Night with David Letterman*, in 1982. This cult chat show, famous for its offbeat stunts and camera trickery, has been screened occasionally in the UK.

LEVINSON, RICHARD
(1934–87)

American executive, a writer and producer, working closely with William Link to create action series like COLUMBO, *Ellery Queen*, MANNIX, BANACEK, *Tenafly* and MURDER, SHE WROTE, as well as many TV movies. They also contributed episodes to ALFRED HITCHCOCK PRESENTS, THE FUGITIVE, BURKE'S LAW and other dramas.

LEWIS, MARTYN
CBE (1945–)

Prominent Welsh newsreader and presenter, formerly with the BBC in Northern Ireland, HTV Wales and ITN but for many years from 1986 back at the BBC as one of its main frontmen. He has also hosted special reports, SONGS OF PRAISE, *Crime Beat* and the daytime game show, *Today's the Day*, and, after leaving BBC News in 2000, fronted the retrospective *News 40: the Battle of Britain*.

LEWIS, SHARI
(Shari Hurwitz; 1934–98)

New York-born ventriloquist who had her own show on British television in the 1960s and 1970s, featuring her glove puppets, Lamb Chop (first seen on US TV in 1957), Hush Puppy and Charlie Horse. She also wrote dozens of children's books.

LIBERACE
(Wladziu Valentino Liberace; 1919–1987)

Flamboyant American pianist and entertainer whose variety shows were very popular in the 1950s and 1960s. Although he had been classically trained, 'Lee' Liberace forwent all the starchy trappings of a concert pianist and, instead, he made brightly sequined costumes, shiny candelabra and a sparkling toothy smile his trademarks. He may have been panned by the critics, but he was loved by his audience and was so unperturbed by all the flak that he coined the memorable phrase, 'I cried all the way to the bank.' Fully aware of his outrageous persona, Liberace was happy to camp it up in BATMAN, playing the villain, Chandell. His later television work was focused on specials and guest appearances.

LIBRARY FILM

Stock footage used to illustrate a news item or another feature.

LICENCE FEE

The annual fee payable to the Government for the use of radio and television receivers in the UK. This provides the funding for the BBC. The licence (initially wireless only, of course) was introduced at ten shillings (50p) in 1922. The fee remained static until 1946, when it was doubled to £1. It has gradually increased over the years and a two-tier licence fee, for monochrome or colour viewing, was instigated in 1967, on the arrival of colour television.

LIFE AND LEGEND OF WYATT EARP, THE
US (Louis F. Edelmann/Wyatt Earp Enterprises) Western.
ITV 1956–62

Wyatt Earp	**Hugh O'Brian**
Bat Masterson	**Mason Alan Dinehart III**
Ben Thompson	**Denver Pyle**
Abbie Crandall	**Gloria Talbot**
Doc Fabrique	**Douglas Fowley**
Marsh Murdock	**Don Haggerty**
Jim 'Dog' Kelly	**Paul Brinegar**
	Ralph Sanford

Doc Holliday .... **Douglas Fowley**
                                                      Myron Healey
Shotgun Gibbs .... **Morgan Woodward**
Morgan Earp .... **Dirk London**
Virgil Earp .... **John Anderson**
Nellie Cashman .... **Randy Stuart**
Old Man Clanton .... **Trevor Bardette**
Sheriff John Behan .... **Lash La Rue**
                                                      Steve Brodie
Doc Goodfellow .... **Damian O'Flynn**

Producer: **Robert F. Sisk**

*Early Western in almost serial form, depicting the
colourful life of the famous Marshal Wyatt Earp.*

Broadly based on fact, this series followed Wyatt Earp's
career and catalogued his encounters with the famous
outlaws of the Wild West. It began with the murder of
his friend, Marshal Whitney, and Earp agreeing to take
on his badge in Ellsworth, Kansas. The rugged lawman
later moved to Dodge City, where he confronted the infamous Doc Holliday and was assisted by his deputy, Bat
Masterson. The mayor, Jim 'Dog' Kelly, was also a friend,
and Earp's brothers Virgil and Morgan appeared now and
again (but not Matt Dillon who, according to GUNSMOKE,
was also Marshal of Dodge City at that time).

In his last posting, Earp took over as Marshal of Tombstone, Arizona, meeting some of his most fearsome
adversaries, the Clanton 'Ten Percent Gang'. With the
Tombstone sheriff, Johnny Behan, in the pocket of Old
Man Clanton, Earp was forced to call up frontiersman
Shotgun Gibbs, a friend from Dodge City, to be his new
deputy. Doc Holliday also showed up, and the series
came to a conclusion with the celebrated 'Gunfight at
the OK Corral'. Nellie Cashman, owner of the Birdcage
Saloon, was Earp's romantic attachment. Throughout
the series, Earp's trademark was a pair of 'Buntline
Special' pistols with extended barrels. They allowed him
to shoot his enemies from a long distance – very useful
when dealing with such a bad crowd.

LIFE AND LOVES OF A SHE DEVIL, THE
UK (BBC) Drama. BBC 2 1986

Ruth .... **Julie T. Wallace**
Bobbo .... **Dennis Waterman**
Mary Fisher .... **Patricia Hodge**
Mrs Fisher .... **Liz Smith**
Nurse Hopkins .... **Miriam Margolyes**
Father Ferguson .... **Tom Baker**

Writer: **Ted Whitehead**
Producer: **Sally Head**

*A spurned wife uses supernatural powers to wreak
revenge on her husband and his mistress.*

Ruth was a pathetic specimen. Hideously ugly and
devoid of self-confidence, she discovered that her
accountant husband, Bobbo, had only married her out
of pity and simply used her to look after the kids and
run the home. When one day he walked out to live with
Mary Fisher, a best-selling authoress, in her luxurious
converted lighthouse, Ruth's hurt and anger manifested
itself supernaturally. Remembering his parting words,
in which he dubbed her a 'she devil', Ruth burned down
the family home and set out on the road of revenge.
Using a selection of disguises and identities to weave her
spell, Ruth manipulated other people into destroying
Bobbo's life and career. Along the way, she struck a
powerful blow for womankind.

The Life and Loves of a She Devil, directed by Philip
Saville and adapted by Ted Whitehead in four parts
from Fay Weldon's novel, gave unknown actress Julie T.
Wallace her big break. 'Uglified' to fit the bill, Wallace
stole the show but wasn't asked to appear in the 1989 US
film version, *She Devil*, which starred Roseanne Barr.

LIFE AND TIMES OF GRIZZLY ADAMS, THE
US (Sunn Classic) Adventure. ITV 1978–9

James Capen 'Grizzly' Adams .... **Dan Haggerty**
Mad Jack .... **Denver Pyle**
Nakuma .... **Don Shanks**
Robbie Cartman .... **John Bishop**

Executive Producer: **Charles E. Sellier, Jr**
Producers: **Leonard B. Kaufman, Jim Simmons, Art
Stolnitz**

*Accused of a crime he did not commit, a man flees
to a satisfying life in the western American
wilderness.*

The Life and Times of Grizzly Adams was based on the
exploits of a real 19th-century refugee who lived in the
Sierra Nevada and struck up a rapport with animals. In
the TV version, Grizzly lived in a log cabin, at one with
nature, wearing only cloth garments. He fished to eat
but never hunted. He was befriended by Mad Jack (also
the show's narrator), an Indian named Nakuma and a
young lad, Robbie Cartman, who lived on a nearby farm.
Adams's constant companion was a wild bear named
Ben which he had rescued as a cub. Their heartwarming
adventures were built around the call of the wild, the
trials of nature and the disruptive visits of strangers.
The real Adams died in 1860 while touring with P. T.
Barnum's circus.

The series, which first aired in the USA in 1977, enjoyed
a sporadic screening around the ITV network. The
theme song, 'Maybe', was a UK hit for Tom Pace in 1979.

LIFE OF BLISS, A
UK (BBC) Situation Comedy. BBC 1960–1

David Bliss .... **George Cole**
Zoe Hunter .... **Sheila Sweet**
Tony Fellows .... **Colin Gordon**
Anne Fellows .... **Isabel Dean**
Pam Batten .... **Frances Bennett**
Bob Batten .... **Hugh Sinclair**

Creator/Writer: **Godfrey Harrison**
Producers: **Graeme Muir, Godfrey Harrison**

A shy and confused young bachelor's life is riddled with misunderstanding.

It's hard to imagine George Cole playing a bashful young bachelor prone to verbal gaffes, but that was his role in this long-running radio series which enjoyed some television exposure in 1960 and 1961. As the constantly confused David Bliss, he stumbled from one mishap to another, finding solace in the company of Psyche, his wire-haired fox-terrier (barked for by Percy Edwards). Also seen were Bliss's girlfriend, Zoe, and his sister and brother-in-law, Anne and Tony Fellows, the last two replaced by Pam and Bob Batten (also Bliss's sister and brother-in-law) in the second series.

LIFE ON EARTH

UK (BBC/Warner Brothers) Documentary. BBC 2 1979

Host/Writer: **David Attenborough**

Producers: **Christopher Parsons, John Sparks, Richard Brock**

Painstaking insight into how life-forms developed on our planet.

Reflecting on the geological development of the Earth from the earliest times to the present day, naturalist/broadcaster David Attenborough lucidly explained in this ambitious series how different species of plants and animals came into being and evolved as the planet changed climate. Assisted by spectacular photography (over a million feet of film were shot) and visits to more than 30 countries in three years, Attenborough's colourful history of 3,500 million years of nature won acclaim from all quarters, with probably the best-remembered scene his frolics with friendly gorillas in a tropical jungle.

Life on Earth was, at the time, the biggest project ever undertaken by the BBC's Natural History Unit in Bristol, and it prompted four sequels, THE LIVING PLANET in 1984, TRIALS OF LIFE in 1990, *The Private Life of Plants* in 1995 and *The Life of Birds* in 1998.

LIFE WITH THE LYONS

UK (BBC/Associated-Rediffusion) Situation Comedy. BBC 1955–6; ITV 1957–60

Ben Lyon	**Ben Lyon**
Bebe Daniels Lyon	**Bebe Daniels Lyon**
Barbara Lyon	**Barbara Lyon**
Richard Lyon	**Richard Lyon**
Aggie Macdonald	**Molly Weir**
Florrie Wainwright	**Doris Rogers**

Producers: **Bryan Sears (BBC), Barry Baker (ITV)**

At home with an American family in Britain.

The Lyons family of entertainers – dad Ben, his wife Bebe Daniels, son Richard and daughter Barbara – endeared themselves to the British public by staying on in the UK during the war years, instead of fleeing back to their native USA. They remained popular in the 1950s through their BBC radio sitcom, in which they played themselves. *Life with the Lyons* then transferred to television, initially on the BBC and then on ITV. Assisting the Lyons was their Scottish housekeeper, Aggie, with Florrie their nosey neighbour. Their dog was called Skeeter. Many of the scripts were penned by Bebe.

LIFE WITHOUT GEORGE

UK (BBC) Situation Comedy. BBC 1 1987–9

Jenny Russell	**Carol Royle**
Larry Wade	**Simon Cadell**
Amanda	**Rosalind March**
	Elizabeth Estensen
Ben Morris	**Michael Thomas**
Sammy	**Kenny Ireland**
	Campbell Morrison
Carol	**Cheryl Maiker**
Mr Harold Chambers	**Ronald Fraser**
Josie	**Selina Cadell**

Writers: **Penny Croft, Val Hudson**
Executive Producer: **Robin Nash**
Producer: **Susan Belbin**

Love on the rebound for a dance instructor and an estate agent.

When George Stanton, her live-in lover of five years' standing, walked out, Jenny Russell, owner of Russell's dance and fitness studio, was distraught. Then a one-night stand with drippy, Marmite-drinking estate agent Larry Wade set her on course for a new on–off love affair. Larry, a partner in Morris, Morris and Wade, was divorced and lived with his dog, Napoleon. Although his intentions towards Jenny were transparent, he was constantly frustrated by her memories of George, and this led him to binge on cheese-and-onion crisps. Jenny's best friend was her neighbour, Amanda, who was having trouble with her womanizing husband, Patrick. They consoled each other. Larry's friend and business partner, Ben, was altogether more ruthless when it came to women and never failed to give Larry worthless advice. Carol was Jenny's receptionist at the studio, where senile Mr Chambers played the piano and country girl Josie was an assistant. The main social rendezvous was the local singles bar, run by gay barman Sammy. The setting was Primrose Hill.

Co-writer Penny Croft (daughter of comedy producer David Croft) also wrote and sang the programme's theme song.

LIFT OFF/LIFT OFF WITH AYSHEA

UK (Granada) Pop Music. ITV 1969–74

Presenters: **Ayshea Brough, Graham Bonney, Wally Whyton**

Producer: **Muriel Young**

Pop-music magazine for younger viewers.

Airing as part of ITV's children's programming, *Lift Off*

was no rival to TOP OF THE POPS but was still one of the few outlets for pop on TV in the early 1970s. Although co-hosted initially by Graham Bonney and later by Wally Whyton, the programme's star was actress Ayshea Brough (also seen in UFO) and, from 1972, the programme's title was changed to reflect this, becoming *Lift Off with Ayshea*. Ayshea also kept youngsters in touch with the latest pop news via a weekly column in the 'Junior *TV Times*', *Look-in*. As well as highlighting the top bands of the day, *Lift Off* also featured a resident team of dancers. It was produced, like other similar Granada pop shows – *Discothèque*, *Get It Together*, *Shang-A-Lang*, *Arrows* and *45* – by former FIVE O'CLOCK CLUB hostess Muriel Young.

LIGHT ENTERTAINMENT

The generic term given to programmes like variety shows, quizzes and comedies.

LIKELY LADS, THE/WHATEVER HAPPENED TO THE LIKELY LADS?

UK (BBC) Situation Comedy. BBC 2 1964–6/BBC 1 1973–4

Bob Ferris .... **Rodney Bewes**
Terry Collier .... **James Bolam**
Audrey Collier .... **Sheila Fearn**
Thelma Chambers/Ferris .... **Brigit Forsyth**

Creators/Writers: **Dick Clement, Ian La Frenais**
Producers: **Dick Clement** (*The Likely Lads*), **James Gilbert, Bernard Thompson** (*Whatever Happened To*)

Life in the 1960s and 1970s with a couple of North-eastern lads-about-town.

Bob Ferris and Terry Collier were two young pals who worked in a factory making electrical parts. Bob was ingenuous, ambitious and keen to see the good side of people (especially those in authority). Terry was a cynic, proud of his working-class roots and a true Jack the Lad figure. Theirs was an unusual but solid friendship which saw them tour the pubs of Newcastle in search of beer and birds, chewing the fat over several pints of brown ale and ending up in all manner of scrapes, usually at Terry's instigation and against Bob's better judgement. The series became a surprise hit, even though only screened on BBC 2, but it ended after just two years. Bob, disillusioned with his lot, decided to join the army and Terry resolved to keep him company. But Bob's flat feet kept him in civvy street and he and Terry parted company.

The duo were back together again seven years later, thanks to a remarkably successful revival entitled *Whatever Happened to the Likely Lads?*. With the turn of the 1970s, Bob's bourgeois dreams had begun to be realized. Now an executive on the point of marriage to his boss's daughter, Thelma (seen at the end of *The Likely Lads*), he owned his own house and had taken to holidays on the Costa Brava and Saturday nights in the trattoria. Terry, on the other hand, escaping a disastrous marriage in Germany, had not changed, except perhaps to bury

himself even further into his proletarian origins and deep-rooted chauvinism. The two met up by chance on a train, inadvertently chatting to each other in the dark when the train's lighting failed, before each suddenly realizing who the other was. Their revived friendship was just as loyal, if more strained than before, with Bob and the fierce Thelma cosseting themselves with middle-class comforts and Bob kicking his heels like some latter-day Andy Capp. The lads' altered relationship echoed the social changes that had swept Britain between the 1960s and the 1970s, changes stressed time and again as they reminisced about their heyday and paid dispiriting visits to old stamping grounds that were sadly now unrecognizable or even demolished.

A feature-film version was released in 1976.

LILLIE

UK (LWT) Drama. ITV 1978

Lillie Le Breton/Langtry .... **Francesca Annis**
Edward Langtry .... **Anton Rodgers**
William Le Breton .... **Anthony Head**
Dean Le Breton .... **Patrick Holt**
Clement Le Breton .... **Adam Bareham**
Mrs Le Breton .... **Peggy Ann Wood**
Reggie Le Breton .... **Simon Turner**
Arthur Jones .... **David Gwillim**
Prince Louis of Battenberg .... **John Castle**
Dominique .... **Catherine Feller**
Frank Miles .... **Brian Deacon**
Oscar Wilde .... **Peter Egan**
James Whistler .... **Don Fellows**
Morten Frewen .... **Philip York**
Edward, Prince of Wales .... **Denis Lill**
Princess/Queen Alexandra .... **Ann Firbank**
Patsy Cornwallis-West .... **Jennie Linden**
King Leopold of Belgium .... **Derek Smith**
Crown Prince Rudolf .... **Patrick Ryecart**
Sarah Bernhardt .... **Cheryl Campbell**
Henrietta Labouchere .... **Annette Crosbie**
Agnes Langtry .... **Stephanie Cole**
Jeanne Marie .... **Joanna David**
Sir Hugo De Bathe .... **James Warwick**

Writers: **David Butler, John Gorrie**
Executive Producer: **Tony Wharmby**
Producer: **Jack Williams**

The colourful life of actress Lillie Langtry.

From her birth as the daughter of a clergyman in the Channel Islands, the life of the beautiful 'Jersey Lily' was always eventful. The highlight was her scandalous relationship with Edward, Prince of Wales ('Bertie'), although she was known to have dallied with other royals, while being married to the weak-willed Edward Langtry. In true rags-to-riches style, she rose determinedly from humble beginnings to become one of the most glamorous women of her time (late 19th–early 20th century), along the way having the honour of being the first celebrity to promote a commercial product (Pears soap). She became the darling of America and socialized closely with the likes of Oscar Wilde and James Whistler, conceiving an illegitimate daughter, Jeanne Marie, and eventually marrying for a second time, to Hugo De Bathe.

For this biopic, actress Francesca Annis reprised the role she had played in ATV's EDWARD THE SEVENTH three years earlier. Over the 13 parts, she was called upon to age from 16 to 70. The series was based on the book, *The Prince and the Lily*, by James Brough.

LIMBO

The use of no scenery in the studio. Plain white/black flooring combines with a plain white/black background to give an infinity effect.

LINDSAY, ROBERT
(1949–)

Derbyshire-born actor whose television break came in 1975 with the sitcom, GET SOME IN!, in which he played teddy-boy Jakey Smith. Lindsay was then signed up to star as Tooting's Che Guevara, Wolfie Smith, in CITIZEN SMITH. He was later cast as boxer Pete Dodds in SECONDS OUT, played wheeler-dealer Mickey Noades in GIVE US A BREAK and took the part of Carter in Channel 4's security guard comedy, *Nightingales*, as well as topping the bill as rising political star Michael Murray in Alan Bleasdale's GBH. Jack Higgins's drama, *Confessional*, was another of his credits, as were the *Screen Two* presentation, *Genghis Cohn* (former SS man Otto Schatz), the comedy-drama, *The Wimbledon Poisoner* (Henry Farr), the feature-length comedy, *Brazen Hussies* (Billy Bowmans), the drama-doc, *Goodbye My Love* (Derek Humphry), Bleasdale's *Jake's Progress* (Jamie Diadoni), *Oliver Twist* (Fagin), HORN-BLOWER (Captain Pellew) and the sitcom, *My Family* (Ben). Lindsay has also been seen in numerous Shake-spearean roles. His first wife was actress Cheryl Hall (also seen in *Citizen Smith*).

LINEKER, GARY
(1960–)

Former England soccer captain (and his country's second-highest goal-scorer) turned TV sports presenter, the host of MATCH OF THE DAY and GRANDSTAND's *Football Focus* slot. He has also been a team captain in the comedy quiz, THEY THINK IT'S ALL OVER.

LINE-UP/LATE NIGHT LINE-UP
UK (BBC) Arts Magazine. BBC 2 1964–72

Presenters: **Denis Tuohy, John Stone, Michael Dean, Joan Bakewell, Nicholas Tresilian, Sheridan Morley, Tony Bilbow**

Late-night magazine programme covering most aspects of the arts and popular culture.

Beginning as no more than a ten-minute preamble to the evening's programmes on the fledgling BBC 2, *Line-Up* was soon extended and moved to a new, end-of-the-evening time-slot. In doing so, it became a popular arts magazine and a lively talking shop, looking at films, literature and music of all kinds on most nights of the week. Segments of the programme became series in their own right. *Film Night* began as a strand called *The Film World Past and Present*, and the adventurous late-1960s rock show, *Colour Me Pop*, was another *Late Night Line-Up* spin-off. *Disco 2* (a progressive rock show, despite its name) arrived via the same route and eventually led to the durable OLD GREY WHISTLE TEST.

LINK, WILLIAM
(1933–) See LEVINSON, RICHARD.

LIP MIKE

A hand-held microphone for use in noisy environments like sports arenas. The mike is pressed against the mouth to eliminate much of the outside sound.

LIPMAN, MAUREEN
CBE (1946–)

Yorkshire-born actress, usually in comedy parts (often scripted by her husband, Jack Rosenthal). Her earliest credits include roles in *Up the Junction*, THE LOVERS, *Rooms*, CROWN COURT, THE SWEENEY, the dramas, *Rogue Male*, *The Evacuees*, *The Knowledge*, *Absent Friends* and *Absurd Person Singular*, and the sketch show, *Don't Ask Us*. After taking the part of Alison Holmes in the short-lived sitcom, *A Soft Touch*, in 1978, Lipman was given her own series, AGONY, playing Jane Lucas, an agony aunt (revived in 1995 as *Agony Again*). She then starred as Miriam Dervish in the original production of OUTSIDE EDGE and hard-up landlady Sheila Haddon in *All at No. 20*, played 12 different roles in the series, *About Face*, and was cast as Shani Whittle in Rosenthal's *Screen One* film, *Eskimo Day*. Ironically, greatest praise came after her commercials for British Telecom and her characteriz-ation of the classic worry-ridden Jewish mother (Beattie). Lipman's stage tribute to Joyce Grenfell, *Re-Joyce!*, has also reached the small screen. Away from acting, she is a successful writer of books and a magazine columnist.

LIPSTICK ON YOUR COLLAR
UK (Whistling Gypsy) Musical Drama. Channel 4 1993

Pte. Francis Francis	Giles Thomas
Pte. Mick Hopper	Ewan McGregor
Sylvia Berry	Louise Germaine
Cpl. Peter Berry	Douglas Henshall
Col. Harry Bernwood	Peter Jeffrey
Major Wallace Hedges	Clive Francis
Major Archie Carter	Nicholas Jones
Major Johnnie Church	Nicholas Farrell
Lt. Col. 'Truck' Trekker	Shane Rimmer
Aunt Vickie	Maggie Stead

Uncle Fred .... **Bernard Hill**
Harold Atterbow .... **Roy Hudd**
Lisa .... **Kymberley Huffman**

Writer: **Dennis Potter**
Producer: **Rosemarie Whitman**

The final part of Dennis Potter's
semi-autobiographical, musical trilogy which
began with PENNIES FROM HEAVEN *and*
continued with THE SINGING DETECTIVE.

Lipstick on Your Collar focused on the social changes
sweeping Britain in the 1950s, and particularly on the
growing awareness among young people of their own
identities. At the heart of the story was Pte. Mick Hopper,
a national serviceman working in War Office boredom,
having to seek permission to speak and spending his
days translating Russian documents as the Cold War
gathered momentum. In the background the Suez Crisis
was breaking and the atom bomb proliferating. But the
younger generation were now looking to the west and
the exciting, glitzy possibilities off-loaded by an influential USA. While his days remained dreary, Hopper
broke free in the evenings to play drums in a rock'n'roll
band. A new sexual promiscuity was pervading the
country and Hopper fell for the beautiful, dark-haired
Lisa, while his Welsh friend, Francis, was dangerously
drawn to Sylvia, the blonde bombshell who was badly
abused by her bullying husband, Corporal Berry, and
agitated by the odious Harold Atterbow.

LISEMORE, MARTIN
(1940–77)

British TV executive, the producer of classics like THE
PALLISERS and I, CLAUDIUS, and other adaptations such
as *How Green Was My Valley* and *Murder Most English*.

LITTLE BIG BUSINESS, A
UK (Granada) Situation Comedy. ITV 1964–5

Marcus Lieberman .... **David Kossoff**
Simon Lieberman .... **Francis Matthews**
Lazlo .... **Martin Miller**
Charlie .... **Billy Russell**
                                                                        Jack Bligh
Naomi Lieberman .... **Diana Coupland**
                                                                Constance Wake
Basil Crane .... **David Conville**
Miss Stevens .... **Joyce Marlowe**

Writer: **Jack Pulman**
Producer: **Peter Eton**

Business and family conflicts coincide at a
furniture factory.

Marcus Lieberman was the proprietor of a furniture
workshop and a stubborn traditionalist at heart. However, when he introduced Simon, his educated and
ambitious son, into the business, he was forced to
modernize his ways. Such innovation didn't please

craftsmen Lazlo and Charlie either. On Simon's side was
colleague Basil Crane. This series, with its light Jewish
humour, followed a pilot screened in 1963, in which the
role of Simon was played by James Maxwell.

LITTLE HOUSE ON THE PRAIRIE/ LITTLE HOUSE: A NEW BEGINNING
US (NBC) Drama. BBC 1 1975; ITV 1976–84

Charles Ingalls .... **Michael Landon**
Caroline Ingalls .... **Karen Grassle**
Laura Ingalls/Wilder .... **Melissa Gilbert**
Mary Ingalls/Kendall .... **Melissa Sue Anderson**
Carrie Ingalls .... **Lindsay Greenbush**
                                                                Sidney Greenbush
Isaiah Edwards .... **Victor French**
Grace Edwards .... **Bonnie Bartlett**
Nels Oleson .... **Richard Bull**
Harriet Oleson .... **Katherine MacGregor**
Nellie Oleson/Dalton .... **Alison Arngrim**
Willie Oleson .... **Jonathan Gilbert**
Lars Hanson .... **Karl Swenson**
Dr Baker .... **Kevin Hagen**
Revd Robert Alden .... **Dabbs Greer**
Eva Beadle/Simms .... **Charlotte Stewart**
Ebenezer Sprague .... **Ted Gehring**
Jonathan Garvey .... **Merlin Olsen**
Alice Garvey .... **Hersha Parady**
Andy Garvey .... **Patrick Laborteaux**
Adam Kendall .... **Linwood Boomer**
Albert Ingalls .... **Matthew Laborteaux**
Grace Ingalls .... **Wendy Turnbeaugh**
                                                                Brenda Turnbeaugh
Hester Sue Terhune .... **Ketty Lester**
Almanzo Wilder .... **Dean Butler**
Eliza Jane Wilder .... **Lucy Lee Flippin**
Percival Dalton .... **Steve Tracy**
James Cooper .... **Jason Bateman**
Cassandra Cooper .... **Missy Francis**
Nancy Oleson .... **Allison Balson**
Jenny Wilder .... **Shannen Doherty** (*New Beginning*)
John Carter .... **Stan Ivar** (*New Beginning*)
Sarah Carter .... **Pamela Roylance** (*New Beginning*)
Jeb Carter .... **Lindsay Kennedy** (*New Beginning*)
Jason Carter .... **David Friedman** (*New Beginning*)
Etta Plum .... **Leslie Landon** (*New Beginning*)

Creator: **Michael Landon**
Executive Producers: **Michael Landon, Ed Friendly**

A family struggles to make a living on the
American plains in the late 19th century.

Here was a Western with a difference. Instead of engaging in squabbles with Indians and bandits, the main
protagonists of this series enjoyed a peaceful existence,
their only fight being with nature in an effort to maintain a comfortable home. *Little House on the Prairie* was
based on the autobiographical books by Laura Ingalls
Wilder. She appeared as a character in the series and,
acting as narrator, led viewers through the changes
taking place in the Ingalls household.

The family lived on a smallholding in Walnut Grove,

Plum Creek, Minnesota, in the 1870s. Head of the household was Charles Ingalls, hardworking and trustworthy. His wife, Caroline, had borne him three children: Laura, her elder sister Mary, and little Carrie, and the family owned a dog, Jack. In their efforts to scratch out a living they were supported by their friends, the tough-looking Mr Edwards, Mr Hanson, who owned the mill, and Nels Oleson, the local shopkeeper. Edwards was later replaced by Jonathan Garvey, his wife Alice, and son Andy.

Over the years, the Ingalls had their ups and downs, leading to numerous cast changes. They were blessed with a fourth daughter, Grace, but tragedy struck when Mary lost her sight and was forced to attend a special blind school. There she met up with blind tutor Adam Kendall, later to be her husband. As times grew even harder, the Ingalls were forced to sell up and move temporarily to Winoka, Dakota, where they adopted a young orphan, Albert. Mary gave birth to a baby boy, who was tragically killed in a fire which also took the life of Alice Garvey.

Laura married Almanzo Wilder, after becoming a teacher, and Nels Oleson's spiteful daughter, Nellie, was also married, to a Jew named Isaac Cohen who hid his religion under the name of Percival Dalton. Adam miraculously regained his sight and headed for New York to work for his father's law company, taking Mary with him. The Ingalls took in two more orphans, Charles and Caroline Cooper; and another orphan, Nancy, was adopted by Mrs Oleson and proved to be as dislikeable as her own daughter, Nellie. Meanwhile, Laura gave birth to a daughter, Rose.

In the programme's final season, its star and executive producer, Michael Landon, decided to call it a day, and much rejigging was required before the show could continue. It was renamed *Little House: A New Beginning* and centred on Laura, Almanzo and little Rose. Charles sold the Little House and moved to a job in Burr Oak, Iowa, leaving the homestead to local newspaper proprietors John and Sarah Carter and their two sons.

These heartwarming tales of honest labour and strong family values were similar in flavour to those seen in THE WALTONS, but *Little House* was very much Michael Landon's baby. Not only did he star and produce, he also directed and wrote some of the episodes. The series lasted only one year after his departure. The programme, somewhat unusually, changed channels in the UK, from BBC 1 to ITV, during the course of its initial run. It was re-run on Channel 4 in the 1990s.

LITTLE, SYD

(Cyril Mead; 1942–) See LARGE, EDDIE.

LIVE

A programme transmitted as it takes place; not prerecorded.

LIVE AID

UK (BBC) Music. BBC 2/BBC 1 1985

Presenters: **Janice Long, Richard Skinner, David Hepworth, Andy Batten-Foster, Mike Smith, Mark Ellen, Andy Kershaw, Paul Gambaccini, Steve Blacknell**
Producers: **John Burrowes, Trevor Dann**

Legendary big-name pop concert in aid of the African famine appeal.

Following the success of Band Aid's chart-topping charity single, 'Do They Know It's Christmas?', 'Feed the World' campaigner Bob Geldof conjured up the idea for a globally transmitted live concert. This came to fruition on Saturday, 13 July 1985. Beginning at noon (UK time) at Wembley Stadium and continuing through to 4 a.m. from JFK Stadium in Philadelphia, *Live Aid* was simply the biggest rock festival ever to be staged over one day. Satellites beamed pictures from one stadium to the other so that the live audiences could view the staggered events on both sides of the Atlantic. On television, DJs interviewed the stars, who urged viewers to ring in with cash pledges. A total of over £60 million was raised as a result. Status Quo set the ball rolling with a rendition of 'Rocking All Over the World', Phil Collins appeared at both stadia, courtesy of Concorde, and the full list of acts billed to appear was as follows: at Wembley, Status Quo, Style Council, Ultravox, Boomtown Rats, Adam Ant, Spandau Ballet, Elvis Costello, Nik Kershaw, Sade, Sting, Phil Collins, Julian Lennon, Howard Jones, Bryan Ferry, Paul Young, Alison Moyet, U2, Dire Straits, Queen, David Bowie, The Who, Elton John, Wham and Paul McCartney; at Philadelphia, Bryan Adams, The Beach Boys, Tears For Fears, Simple Minds, The Pretenders, Santana, Pat Metheny, The Thompson Twins, Nile Rodgers, Madonna, Tom Petty, The Cars, Kenny Loggins, Neil Young, Power Station, Eric Clapton, Phil Collins, Robert Plant, Jimmy Page, Paul Martinez, Duran Duran, Patti Labelle, Hall and Oates, The Temptations, Mick Jagger, Tina Turner and Bob Dylan. Not originally billed, but appearing, were Kiki Dee, George Michael, INXS and B. B. King (Wembley), and George Thorogood and the Destroyers (Philadelphia).

LIVER BIRDS, THE

UK (BBC) Situation Comedy. BBC 1 1969–79; 1996

Beryl Hennesey	**Polly James**
Dawn	**Pauline Collins**
Sandra Hutchinson/Paynton	**Nerys Hughes**
Carol Boswell	**Elizabeth Estensen**
Mrs Hutchinson	**Mollie Sugden**
Mr Hutchinson	**Ivan Beavis**
Mrs Hennesey	**Sheila Fay**
	Carmel McSharry
Mr Hennesey	**Cyril Shaps**
	Bill Dean
Paul	**John Nettles**
Robert	**Jonathan Lynn**

Mrs Boswell	**Eileen Kennally**
	Carmel McSharry
Lucien Boswell	**Michael Angelis**
Grandad	**Jack Le White**
Mr Boswell	**Ray Dunbobbin**
Father O'Leary	**Patrick McAlinney**
Derek Paynton	**Tom Chadbon**
Rex	**Geoffrey Leesley**
Gwyn	**Lee Oakes**

Creators: **Carla Lane, Myra Taylor, Lew Schwarz**
Producers: **Sydney Lotterby, Douglas Argent, Roger Race, Philip Kampff**

The ups and downs in the life of two Liverpudlian flatmates.

Seen by some as a female version of THE LIKELY LADS, *The Liver Birds* centred on two perky single girls who shared a bedsit in Huskisson Street, Liverpool, where their life revolved around romance, finance and family troubles. Initially, the two girls were wacky Beryl and prim Dawn, but that first series (resulting from a 1969 COMEDY PLAYHOUSE pilot) ran to only four episodes. When *The Liver Birds* returned in 1971, Dawn had disappeared and in her place was the naïve and ingenuous Sandra. A year later, the girls moved to a more spacious apartment and, when Beryl left (to marry Robert, a Londoner played by Jonathan Lynn) at the end of the fourth season, Sandra gained a new flatmate, Carol, whose voice and dress sense both needed volume controls. Also seen over the years were Sandra's boyfriend, Paul (a pre-*Bergerac* John Nettles), her snooty mother and various members of Beryl's and Carol's families. Possibly best remembered was Carol's brother, Lucien, who kept and loved rabbits, but her Catholic mother was another notable creation, as she proved to be a forerunner of BREAD's Nellie Boswell (writer Carla Lane even gave her the same surname). Before the series ended, Sandra had married Derek, her vet boss, and Carol had moved in as their lodger.

Although very much associated with Carla Lane, the series was in fact co-created with her former writing partner, Myra Taylor, and Lew Schwarz, and the early episodes were script-edited by Eric Idle. From the fourth season, however, Lane was in sole charge. The jaunty theme song, with its 'You dancing? You asking? I'm asking. I'm dancing' tag, was performed by The Scaffold.

In 1996, BBC 1 revived the series, bringing back Beryl as a lodger in Sandra's house. Beryl had been married three times, while Sandra was now looking after her demanding mother and trying to maintain a relationship with boyfriend Rex. Also seen was Beryl's son, Gwyn. Somewhat confusingly, actress Carmel McSharry was brought back to play Beryl's mum (she had played Carol's mum previously), and Michael Angelis returned as Lucien, this time Beryl's brother.

LIVERPOOL ONE
UK (Lime Street) Drama. ITV 1998–

DC Isobel De Pauli	**Sam Janus**
DC Mark Callaghan	**Mark Womack**
DI Howard Jones	**Tom Georgeson**
DC Joanna McMullan	**Katy Carmichael**
DC Frank White	**Paul Broughton**
Ch. Insp. Graham Hill	**Eamon Boland**
John Sullivan	**Paul Usher**
DC Tomaszewski	**Simon O'Brien**

Writer: **Simon Burke**
Producer: **Colin McKeown**

An attractive, intelligent policewoman finds life hard on the streets of Liverpool.

Moving from the Metropolitan Police to the Merseyside Police's vice squad was not a soft option for DC Isobel De Pauli. De Pauli – a psychology graduate – discovered that her new patch in Liverpool was tough and violent, with gangsters, drugs and prostitutes the everyday fare. Working for boss DI Jones and partnered by DC 'Cally' Callaghan, she found herself in close pursuit of the Sullivan family in particular, a hard-nosed family of drug-pushers headed by the devious John Sullivan who, to complicate matters, was also Cally's cousin. But her arrival also caused resentment in the force, possibly not helped by her glamorous looks and the rather skimpy tops she wore. Typical of what is now known as a 'gritty drama', *Liverpool One* was well received by viewers and critics.

LIVING

One-time sister channel to UK Gold – when it was known as UK Living – Living is a satellite/cable/digital channel dedicated to women's interests. As a result, programming has majored on cookery (repeats of Keith Floyd, Delia Smith, etc.), fashion, agony aunts, romance, gardening, health and female-orientated game shows. Any imports shown have also had a female bias and have included the American series, CAGNEY AND LACEY, *Kate and Allie*, CHARLIE'S ANGELS and ALLY MCBEAL. Feature films have usually been of the emotional type.

LIVING PLANET, THE
UK (BBC) Documentary. BBC 1 1984

Host: **David Attenborough**

Executive Producer: **Richard Brock**
Producer: **Ned Kelly**

The exhaustive follow-up to LIFE ON EARTH.

Employing the same brilliant photography and imbued with the same infectious enthusiasm as in *Life on Earth*, David Attenborough now turned his attention away from the evolution of plants and animals and fixed his gaze instead on the way life-forms have learned to live in the modern world. Again, there was no stinting on travel – the team filmed at the edge of volcanic craters, in the baking heat of the Sahara and in the freezing wastes of the Arctic – to graphically portray just how well flora and fauna have learned to adapt to today's

Earth with all its diverse environments. It revealed that nowhere on the planet was devoid of life.

LLOYD, INNES
(1925–91)

Innovative British drama producer, for many years with the BBC, initially in outside broadcasts and then working on series like DOCTOR WHO (in the Patrick Troughton era) and the anthology, *Dead of Night*, as well as many one-off plays. Lloyd also contributed the mini-series, *Waugh on Crime*, for the *Thirty-Minute Theatre* collection, and among other offerings were *The Snow Goose* (1971), *The Stone Tape* (1972), *Sunset Across the Bay* (1974), *Orde Wingate* (1976), *An Englishman's Castle* (1978), *Speed King* (1979), *Fothergill* and *Going Gently* (both 1981). His last production was Alan Bennett's *A Question of Attribution* (1991), telling the story of an encounter between spy Anthony Blunt and the Queen. Lloyd had previously produced many of Bennett's works, including *A Day Out* (1972), *An Englishman Abroad* (1983), *The Insurance Man* (1985) and the series, TALKING HEADS.

LLOYD, JEREMY
(1932–)

British comedy actor and scriptwriter, once a cast member of ROWAN AND MARTIN'S LAUGH-IN and also seen in the comedy, *It's Awfully Bad for Your Eyes, Darling*. On the writing side, in conjunction with David Croft, Lloyd was responsible for ARE YOU BEING SERVED? (and its sequel, *Grace and Favour*), COME BACK MRS NOAH, *Oh Happy Band!* and 'ALLO 'ALLO. Earlier collaboration with Jimmy Grafton resulted in scripts for *The Dickie Henderson Show*, the sketch show, *New Look*, and the sitcoms, *Vacant Lot* and *Mum's Boys*. Lloyd also co-devised the panel game, WHODUNNIT?, with Lance Percival. He was once married to Joanna Lumley.

LLOYD, JOHN
(1951–)

Radio-producer-turned-TV-producer, responsible for some of the major TV comedies since the 1980s. These have included NOT THE NINE O'CLOCK NEWS, SPITTING IMAGE and the BLACKADDER series.

LLOYD, KEVIN
(1949–98)

Best known as THE BILL's DC 'Tosh' Lines, Derby-born actor Kevin Lloyd was a familiar face on British television for some 20 years. He was Oscar in *Misfits* and Ricky in DEAR JOHN, and other credits came in programmes as varied as AUF WIEDERSEHEN, PET, BY THE SWORD DIVIDED, Z CARS, *All in Good Faith*, *Sounding Brass*, THE BORGIAS, MINDER, HAZELL, *Andy Capp*, DEMPSEY AND MAKEPEACE, BOON and CORONATION STREET (Don

Watkins). He was the brother of ITN journalist Terry Lloyd.

LLOYD PACK, ROGER
(1944–)

British actor immortalized as the slow-witted Trigger in ONLY FOOLS AND HORSES. However, Lloyd Pack (the son of actor Charles Lloyd Pack and father of actress Emily Lloyd) has been much seen on TV. He was David Irving in *Selling Hitler*, Jimmy Ryan in *Moving*, Albert Mason in SPYDER'S WEB, Beckett in BYKER GROVE, Rex Regis in HEALTH AND EFFICIENCY, Owen Newitt in THE VICAR OF DIBLEY, Sir Baldwin De'Ath in the kids' comedy, *Knight School*, Ken Thompson in *The Missing Postman*, Anderson in *Tom Jones*, Mr Sowerberry in *Oliver Twist*, and Captain Man in *Longitude*, as well as appearing in series like PRIVATE SCHULZ, STAY LUCKY, MR BEAN, BOON, INSPECTOR MORSE, THE CHIEF, *Paul Merton in Galton & Simpson's . . .*, and 2 POINT 4 CHILDREN (practical joker/plumber Jake).

LOACH, KEN
(1936–)

British drama director, fond of the documentary style, noted for his realism and responsible for emotive pieces like *Up the Junction* (1965), CATHY COME HOME (1966), *In Two Minds* (1967), *The Rank and File* (1971), *The Price of Coal* (1977) and the series, DAYS OF HOPE, among other offerings. Earlier he had worked on Z CARS and the serial, *Diary of a Young Man*.

LOCKWOOD, MARGARET
CBE (Margaret Mary Lockwood Day; 1916–90)

British actress for whom television success arrived late. After a long and respectable career in the movies, dating back to the 1930s, Margaret Lockwood only really found her TV niche in 1971, when she donned the wig of barrister Harriet Peterson in JUSTICE. Seven years earlier she had starred in the pub series, *The Flying Swan*, playing landlady Mollie Manning, and before that, in 1957, she played a similar role as Mollie Miller, proprietress of the Royalty Hotel in the drama series, *The Royalty*. Lockwood also enjoyed numerous other TV drama credits, including *Pygmalion*, as early as 1948.

LOE, JUDY
(1947–)

British actress, seen in comedy as well as straight drama roles. She was Lulli in the children's series, ACE OF WANDS, Celia Kemp in the game-show sitcom, *Good Night and God Bless*, abandoned wife Alison Reynolds in *Missing from Home*, Pam in SINGLES and Dr Elizabeth Stafford in THE CHIEF. Among her numerous other credits have been Z CARS, MAN AT THE TOP, EDWARD THE SEVENTH, WHEN THE BOAT COMES IN, *Yesterday's Dreams*,

The Upchat Line, *Couples*, MISS JONES AND SON, RIPPING YARNS, *Heartland*, PEAK PRACTICE, *Eurocops*, *Revelations* and CASUALTY. She was married to the late Richard Beckinsale and is the mother of actress Kate Beckinsale.

LOGAN'S RUN
US (MGM) Science Fiction. ITV 1978

Logan	**Gregory Harrison**
Jessica	**Heather Menzies**
Rem	**Donald Moffat**
Francis	**Randy Powell**

Executive Producers: **Ivan Goff, Ben Roberts**
Producer: **Leonard Katzman**

In the 24th century, two refugees flee from certain death.

This series, based on the book by William F. Nolan and George Clayton Johnson, and the film starring Michael York, was set in the year 2319 on an Earth devastated by nuclear war. No longer one civilization, the planet existed only as a series of individual cities, separated by stretches of wilderness. In one such settlement, the City of Domes, all the citizens had a wonderful lifestyle – they lived only for fun. However, there was one drawback: life was terminated at the age of 30.

Logan, a high-ranking police officer, or a Sandman as they were known, had reached the critical age and was about to undergo the 'Carousel' death ceremony when he decided to make a run for it. He was assisted by Jessica, a young rebel girl, and a humorous android, Rem, whom they met early on in their travels. Together, they sought a legendary haven known as Sanctuary, but they were pursued all the way by another Sandman, Logan's former partner, Francis, as they braved the outside world and its hostile inhabitants.

LOLLIPOP LOVES MR MOLE/ LOLLIPOP
UK (ATV) Situation Comedy. ITV 1971–2

Maggie Robinson	**Peggy Mount**
Reg Robinson	**Hugh Lloyd**
Bruce Robinson	**Rex Garner**
Violet Robinson	**Pat Coombs**

Creator/Writer: **Jimmy Perry**
Producer: **Shaun O'Riordan**

A husband and wife's happy little life is disrupted by their close family.

Although she was big, bold and domineering, Maggie Robinson was the perfect partner for her meek and timid husband, Reg. They gave each other the soppy nick-names referred to in the programme's title and their life together in Fulham was a peaceful one. Then, out of the blue, Reg's brother, Bruce, returned from Africa with his wife, Violet, supposedly for a few days' holiday. However, the visitors outstayed their welcome and soon upset Lollipop and Mr Mole's domestic bliss. The second

series – with Bruce and Violet still *in situ* – aired under the truncated title of *Lollipop*.

LOMBARD, LOUISE
(Louise Perkins; 1970–)

Essex-born actress best known for her role as Evie in THE HOUSE OF ELIOTT, although with several other TV parts to her name. Her earliest credits came in dramas like CAPITAL CITY (Louise), *Chancer* (Anna) and CATHERINE COOKSON's *Black Velvet Gown*, and more recently she has starred in *Shakespeare Shorts* (Lady Macbeth) and *Bodyguards* (Liz Shaw).

LONDON WEEKEND TELEVISION
See LWT.

LONDON'S BURNING
UK (LWT) Drama. ITV 1988–

Roland 'Vaseline' Cartwright	**Mark Arden**
Mike 'Bayleaf' Wilson	**James Hazeldine**
Station Officer Sidney Tate	**James Marcus**
Sub-Officer John Hallam	**Sean Blowers**
Tony Sanders	**Treva Etienne**
Malcolm Cross	**Rupert Baker**
Bert 'Sicknote' Quigley	**Richard Walsh**
Leslie 'Charisma' Appleby	**Gerard Horan**
Josie Ingham	**Katharine Rogers**
George Green	**Glen Murphy**
Kevin Medhurst	**Ross Boatman**
David	**George Costigan**
Donna	**Paddy Navin**
Clare	**Valerie Holliman**
Jean Quigley	**Amanda Dickinson**
Marion Cartwright	**Helen Blizard**
Sandra Hallam	**Kim Clifford**
Scase	**Cliff Howells**
Colin Parrish	**Stephen North**
Maggie	**Shirley Greenwood**
Kate Stevens	**Samantha Beckinsale**
Nick Georgiadis	**Andrew Kazamia**
Stuart 'Recall' Mackenzie	**Ben Onwukwe**
Kelly	**Vanessa Pett**
Laura MacKenzie	**Ona McCracken**
Geoff 'Poison' Pearce	**Michael Garner**
Billy Ray	**John Alford**
Ariadne	**Katerina Jugati**
Ben	**Gordon Calliste**
Jack Morgan	**Clive Wood**
Clingfilm	**Chris Larner**
Jaffa	**Alan Talbot**
Cyril	**Frederick Warder**
Pitbull	**Al Hunter Ashton**
Skip	**Brad Clayton**
Carole Webb	**Zoë Hayes**
Gregg	**Steven Houghton**
Beattie	**Christine Ellerbeck**
Nanny Ray	**Pamela Lyne**
Evgenia	**Sonia Graham**

Costas .... **Peter Birrel**
Marcus Katsantonis
DO Chapman .... **Graham Sinclair**
Tiggy .... **Anouka Brook**
Nancy .... **Kim Taylforth**
Nicky .... **Katy Stephens**
Jo .... **Natalie Ratcliff**
Marianne .... **Minna Aaltonen**
Sally 'Gracie' Fields .... **Heather Peace**
Daniel Barratt .... **Brad Gorton**
Joe Walker .... **Jim Alexander**
Chris Hammond .... **Jonathan Guy Lewis**
Yvonne Bradley .... **Jane Hazlegrove**
Lisa Hammond .... **Melanie Barker**
Jacqui Parker .... **Sharon Gavin**
Fiona .... **Helen Anderson**
Rob 'Hyper' Sharpe .... **Connor Byrne**
Ronnie 'Hi-Ho' Silver .... **Fuman Dar**
DO Griggs .... **Simon Merrells**

Creator: **Jack Rosenthal**
Executive Producers: **Linda Agran, Nick Elliott, Sarah Wilson**
Producers: **Paul Knight, Gerry Poulson, David Shanks, David Newcombe**

High drama with the chirpy crew of a London fire station.

The firefighters of Blue Watch B25, Blackwall, made their bow in Jack Rosenthal's 1986 TV film, *London's Burning*. It focused on the brave men and women of this undervalued emergency service. Watching them at home and at work, the play introduced such lively characters as Vaseline (a slippery customer), Charisma (who had none) and Sicknote (always ill). The public took to this motley crew of loafers and mickey-takers who selflessly risked life and limb, irrespective of personal problems, and a series was commissioned in 1988.

Other members of Blue Watch – a mixture of senior firefighters and rookies – were Sidney Tate (the father figure), Bayleaf (the mess manager who dreamt of opening a restaurant), Josie and Kate (women in a predominantly man's world), Tony, Malcolm, Kevin, George and Colin. Recall (because of his photographic memory), the motorbike-loving Nick, Geoff 'Poison' Pearce, wide-boy Billy Ray, sub-officer Carole Webb and temporary station officer Chris Hammond have been among the later additions. Incidents have been based on real-life events and have included plane crashes, petrol-tanker explosions, tube disasters and hostel fires. The stunts have been spectacular and carefully choreographed. Actor James Hazeldine (Bayleaf) also directed a number of episodes.

LONE RANGER, THE

US (Apex/Lone Ranger Television) Western. BBC 1956–62

The Lone Ranger .... **Clayton Moore**
John Hart
Tonto .... **Jay Silverheels**
Dan Reid .... **Chuck Courtney**
Jim Blaine .... **Ralph Littlefield**

Creators: **George W. Trendle, Fran Striker**
Executive Producers: **Jack Chertok, Jack Wrather**
Producers: **Harry Poppe, Sherman Harris**

Cult Western series featuring a mysterious masked hero and his Indian companion.

The Lone Ranger's story began when a group of six Texas Rangers was ambushed by a band of outlaws known as the Butch Cavendish Hole in the Wall gang. Only one survived, John Reid, and he was nursed back to health by an Indian, Tonto, whose life Reid had already saved. Swearing to avenge the death of his colleagues, who included his own brother, Reid tracked down the killers. He then began a life as an intriguing Robin Hood character, dedicated to helping those in trouble. He wore a white hat and a black mask to conceal his identity and he rode a white stallion named Silver. His loyal companion, Tonto (who rode a horse called Scout), knew him as 'Kemo Sabe', meaning 'trusty scout'.

The Lone Ranger's identity was never revealed and, as he wandered from town to town routing villains, people were left to wonder, 'Who was that masked man?' as he let out a cry of 'Hi-yo Silver' and sped away, refusing payment and gratitude for the help he had provided. The Lone Ranger did have one base which he touched from time to time: the silver mine he had owned with his dead brother. Looked after by old Jim Blaine, this provided him with the wealth to continue his travels and also the silver bullets that he used in his pistol (although the squeaky-clean Lone Ranger never shot to kill; the outlaws usually shot each other or died by accident). Occasionally, Dan Reid, John's nephew, joined the duo, riding a horse called Victor.

The Lone Ranger was played for most of its run by Clayton Moore, though John Hart took over the role for a couple of years. Jay Silverheels, the one and only TV Tonto, was a real Mohawk Indian, who later spoke out against the humbling way Indians had always been portrayed on television. The TV series followed the success of *The Lone Ranger* on American radio in the 1930s. A cartoon version was produced in the 1960s, using the same William Tell Overture by Rossini as its theme music.

LONG JOHN SILVER

See **ADVENTURES OF LONG JOHN SILVER, THE**.

LONGTHORNE, JOE

(1957–)

British singer and impressionist, well known for his take-offs of Shirley Bassey, Johnny Mathis and other vocalists. Longthorne was a regular on the kids' variety series, *Junior Showtime*, while a teenager in the early 1970s and emerged into the adult market via the talent show, *Search for a Star*. He then joined *The Les Dennis Laughter Show*, before being given his own ITV series in the late 1980s.

LOOK

UK (BBC) Natural History. BBC 1 1955–69

Host: **Peter Scott**

Producers: **Brandon Acton-Bond, Tony Soper, Eileen Molony, Jeffrey Boswell**

Innovative British wildlife series.

This pioneering, long-running, in-depth view of the natural world was presented for most of its life by the famous naturalist Peter Scott, founder of the Severn Wildfowl Trust at Slimbridge. Pre-dating Anglia's SURVIVAL by six years, *Look* was produced by the BBC's wildlife specialists in Bristol, and a children's version was also aired. Repeats were at one time shown under the title of *Look Again*. When Scott travelled to Oceania and the Galapagos Islands, the series briefly took the title of *Faraway Look*.

LORD, JACK

(John Joseph Ryan; 1920–98)

New York-born leading man who found his niche (and fortune) as Steve McGarrett, the no-nonsense head of detectives on HAWAII FIVE-O. He played McGarrett for 12 years, making Hawaii his home in the process. An exhibited artist, Lord's other TV work was confined to guest appearances (usually as baddies) in series like THE UNTOUCHABLES, THE FBI, HAVE GUN WILL TRAVEL, NAKED CITY, RAWHIDE, GUNSMOKE, THE FUGITIVE, DR KILDARE, BONANZA, THE MAN FROM UNCLE and A MAN CALLED IRONSIDE, as well as the lead role in an early 1960s Western series, *Stoney Burke*.

LORD PETER WIMSEY

UK (BBC) Drama. BBC 1 1972–5

Lord Peter Wimsey	**Ian Carmichael**
Bunter	**Glyn Houston**
	Derek Newark
DCI Charles Parker	**Mark Eden**

Producers: **Richard Beynon, Bill Sellars**

Classy crime-solving with an elegant aristocrat.

Lord Peter Wimsey was the scourge of all murderers in the 1920s. Created in novels by Dorothy L. Sayers, he came to life in this period-TV outing through the monocled impersonation of Ian Carmichael. Wimsey was prim, proper and always a gentleman, and tended to appear a bit of an upper-class twit, but this was a deliberate ploy to fool his adversaries. In truth, he possessed a sharp analytical mind, enhanced by an encyclopaedic knowledge of classical music. He loved cricket, enjoyed good conversation and savoured the best food and drink, just part of the *bon viveur* lifestyle he pursued at his home in Piccadilly.

With never a financial worry, and desperate to restore order to an untidy world, Wimsey was regularly on hand to pick up the pieces of a murder mystery in the most unusual of settings. Invaluable on these occasions was his loyal manservant, Bunter (a former army sergeant colleague), a man who could easily mix with the lower classes and exact information denied to his employer. Police presence was provided by Wimsey's brother-in-law, Inspector Parker (played by future CORONATION STREET villain Mark Eden).

Five of Sayers's novels were dramatized for this TV version: *Clouds of Witness, The Unpleasantness at the Bellona Club, Murder Must Advertise, The Nine Tailors* and *Five Red Herrings*. Three more – *Strong Poison, Have His Carcase* and *Gaudy Night* – were adapted for a series entitled *A Dorothy L. Sayers Mystery*, screened on BBC 2 in 1987, with Edward Petherbridge as Wimsey, Richard Morant as Bunter and David Quiller as Parker. Also featured in this revamp was Harriet Walter as Harriet Vane, Wimsey's crime-writer friend.

LOST IN SPACE

US (Twentieth Century-Fox/Irwin Allen) Science Fiction. ITV 1965–9

Prof. John Robinson	**Guy Williams**
Maureen Robinson	**June Lockhart**
Dr Zachary Smith	**Jonathan Harris**
Major Don West	**Mark Goddard**
Judy Robinson	**Marta Kristen**
Will Robinson	**Billy Mumy**
Penny Robinson	**Angela Cartwright**
The Robot	**Bob May**
	Dick Tufeld (*voice*)

Creator/Executive Producer: **Irwin Allen**
Producers: **Jerry Briskin, William Faralla**

A pioneering family finds itself stranded in outer space.

In 1997 an over-populated Earth sent the Space Family Robinson on a five-year mission to a planet in the Alpha Centauri system to plan for colonization. But their spaceship was sabotaged and they became *Lost in Space*.

The family consisted of father John Robinson, an astrophysicist, his biochemist wife, Maureen, and children Judy, Will and Penny. Geologist Don West was the pilot of their spaceship, the *Jupiter II*, and a genial, somewhat sarcastic robot provided scientific expertise and controlled the spacecraft. The joker in the pack was Dr Zachary Smith, a foreign agent who had sabotaged the mission by interfering with the robot, but who found himself trapped on board when the ship took off. He was forced to wake the family from their suspended animation to try to rectify the situation.

For most of the first season, the Robinsons survived on a barren planet on which their ship had crash-landed. Stories revolved around their attempts to repair the *Jupiter II* and to find a way home, but each week some strange alien intelligence arrived to throw them into danger. The aliens were always treacherously assisted by the cowardly, work-shy Dr Smith, whose sole aim was to find a quick way back to civilization, preferably without the Robinsons. His plans consistently backfired and, just as you thought all was well, the programme ended with another sinister turn of events, a cliffhanger to be resolved next time. In later seasons, the Robinsons did manage to take off, but still Earth eluded them.

At first, *Lost in Space* was straight science fiction, but it became very lighthearted when it was forced into competition with BATMAN on American TV. The plots were somewhat predictable, with the arrogant Dr Smith constantly bringing trouble to the extremely accommodating and surprisingly forgiving family. His closest friend, nine-year-old Will, a wholesome, electronics whizz-kid, often ruined Smith's indulgent schemes by staying loyal to his family. Will's blonde sister, Judy, spent much of her time romantically entwined with action man Don West, while his other sister, the dark-haired, 11-year-old Penny, doted on her pet space monkey, which was known as 'The Bloop'.

The character of Dr Smith was scheduled for only six episodes, but actor Jonathan Harris, a late addition to the cast, quickly became the show's star and Smith stayed. Guy Williams had previously starred as the swashbuckling ZORRO, and Angela Cartwright was one of the Von Trapp children in *The Sound of Music*. Child actor Billy Mumy has more recently been seen (grown up) in another sci-fi series, *Babylon 5*. The robot, which had no name, closely resembled Robbie the robot in the 1956 Walter Pidgeon film, *Forbidden Planet*.

LOTTERBY, SYDNEY

Prolific British comedy producer/director, working for the BBC on series of varying success, like *Broaden Your Mind*, THREE OF A KIND (1967 version), THE LIVER BIRDS, THE GNOMES OF DULWICH, ME MAMMY, UP POMPEII, SYKES, *Now Take My Wife*, SOME MOTHERS DO 'AVE 'EM, PORRIDGE, *Going Straight*, LAST OF THE SUMMER WINE, OPEN ALL HOURS, BUTTERFLIES, YES, MINISTER (and *Yes, Prime Minister*), *Coming Home*, *The Last Song*, EVER DECREASING CIRCLES, THE MAGNIFICENT EVANS, BRUSH STROKES, *Foreign Bodies*, MAY TO DECEMBER, *A Gentleman's Club*, AS TIME GOES BY, *Bloomin' Marvellous* and, for Central, *Old Boy Network*.

LOTUS EATERS, THE

UK (BBC) Drama. BBC 2 1972–3

Erik Shepherd	**Ian Hendry**
Ann Shepherd	**Wanda Ventham**
Nestor Turton	**Maurice Denham**
Major Edward Woolley	**Thorley Walters**
Mrs Miriam Woolley	**Sylvia Coleridge**
Donald Culley	**James Kerry**
Ruth Stewart	**Cyd Hayman**
Capt. Krasakis	**Stefan Gryff**
Philip Mervish	**Karl Held**
Leigh Mervish	**Carol Cleveland**
Nikos	**Antony Stamboulieh**
Katerina	**Karan David**
Gerald Mace	**Timothy Carlton**

Dr Dartington	**Ronald Howard**
Sam Webber	**Paul Maxwell**
Imogen Lundqvist	**Susan Engel**
Cotton	**Frank Duncan**
Ariadne Mazonaki	**Calliope Petrohilos**

Creator/Writer: **Michael J. Bird**
Producers: **Anthony Read, Michael Glynn**

Expatriate drama set in the sunny climes of Crete.

'To eat the fruit of the lotus is to lose the desire to return home. But everyone who does has a reason.' So read the promotional blurb for this 15-part drama over two series. Focusing on a little tavern (Shepherd's Bar) in the Cretan resort of Aghios Nikolaos, *The Lotus Eaters* told tales of its proprietors, Erik (an alcoholic) and Ann Shepherd, and the various emigrants who used the bar as a home from home. These included a crusty old major and his wife, scrounging hobo Nestor Turton and squabbling American siblings Philip and Leigh Mervish. Their lives and secrets unfolded as the series progressed. It was revealed for instance that Erik had once been acquitted of the murder of a 15-year-old schoolgirl but was still haunted by the experience.

LOU GRANT

US (MTM) Drama. ITV 1979–83

Lou Grant	**Edward Asner**
Charlie Hume	**Mason Adams**
Joe Rossi	**Robert Walden**
Billie Newman/McCovey	**Linda Kelsey**
Margaret Pynchon	**Nancy Marchand**
Art Donovan	**Jack Bannon**
Dennis 'Animal' Price	**Daryl Anderson**
Adam Wilson	**Allen Williams**
Carla Mardigian	**Rebecca Balding**
Reuben Castillo	**Emilio Delgado**

Executive Producers: **Gene Reynolds, James L. Brooks, Allan Burns**

Dramas unfold in the newsroom of a Los Angeles daily newspaper.

Lou Grant was a spin-off from the highly successful sitcom, THE MARY TYLER MOORE SHOW, but it was far more serious than its predecessor. Its lead character, Lou Grant, had been News Director at WJM-TV in Minneapolis, in the Mary Tyler Moore series. However, when that show finished, Grant and the other members of the news team were fired. At the age of 50, knowing little else but news, he took a job as City Editor of the *Los Angeles Tribune*, working under Managing Editor Charlie Hume but often in conflict with the paper's outspoken proprietor, widow Margaret Pynchon.

Colleagues at the newspaper were investigative reporter Joe Rossi, Art Donovan the Assistant City Editor, and photographer 'Animal'. Also featured was independent young reporter Billie Newman. As an informative, crusading team, they covered all manner of news stories, including sensitive issues such as Vietnamese refugees, child abuse and gun control. It is believed that Ed Asner's outspoken views on such matters may have contributed to the cancellation of the series after five years.

LOVE, AMERICAN STYLE
US (Paramount) Comedy. ITV 1970–5

Creators: **Douglas S. Cramer, Tom Miller**
Executive Producers: **Arnold Margolin, Jim Parker**

An anthology of comedy skits (three or four per show) characterizing love and the American way of life.

There were no regular stars of *Love, American Style*. Guest artistes were called in to perform all the sketches. Each sketch was titled '*Love and . . .*' (fill in the blank with the subject-matter), and romance of all kinds was featured: among old people, among young people, extra-marital, intra-marital, and in all sorts of settings. The only familiar faces belonged to a repertory company that performed short comic interludes. One other regular feature was 'Lovemate of the Week' (an attractive bathing beauty).

Guest stars attracted to the series included the likes of Sonny and Cher, Tiny Tim and Burt Reynolds, and one episode proved particularly fruitful. *Love and the Happy Day*, starring Ron Howard and Anson Williams, was the pilot for the 1950s nostalgia comedy, HAPPY DAYS. *Love, American Style* proved to be a useful filler programme for numerous ITV regions. It first aired in the USA in 1969.

LOVE BOAT, THE
US (Aaron Spelling) Comedy. ITV 1978–87

Capt. Merrill Stubing	**Gavin MacLeod**
Burl 'Gopher' Smith	**Fred Grandy**
Dr Adam Bricker	**Bernie Kopell**
Isaac Washington	**Ted Lange**
Julie McCoy	**Lauren Tewes**
Vicki Stubing	**Jill Whelan**
Ashley Covington ('Ace') Evans	**Ted McGinley**
Judy McCoy	**Pat Klous**

Executive Producers: **Aaron Spelling, Douglas S. Cramer**

Romantic sketches set aboard a luxurious cruise ship.

Three years after LOVE, AMERICAN STYLE (in its native USA) came *The Love Boat*, another anthology series centring on romance. The setting this time was the *Pacific Princess* cruise liner, with the storylines provided by each week's passengers. Like its predecessor, *The Love Boat* attracted a wealth of Hollywood talent as guest stars: Jane Wyman, Raymond Burr and Greer Garson, for instance; but it also had a cast of regulars as the ship's crew, and they featured in the various playlets. Headed by Captain Stubing, the staff included the ship's doctor, Adam Bricker, purser Gopher Smith, bartender Isaac Washington, photographer Ace and social director Julie McCoy, later replaced by Judy McCoy. The Captain's 12-year-old daughter, Vicki, was also introduced. The

Love Boat Mermaids, a troupe of female singers and dancers, were added to the show later, performing a different musical number each week. Much of the series was filmed on real cruises, with fare-paying passengers performing as extras. The series closed when Captain Stubing married a lady called Emily Heywood, played by Marion Ross of HAPPY DAYS fame. The theme song, 'The Love Boat', was sung by Jack Jones (by Dionne Warwick in the last series). A revamp, *The Love Boat: the Next Wave*, began on US TV in 1998, with Robert Urich as Captain Jim Kennedy.

LOVE, GEOFF
(1917–91)

British bandleader, seen in support of many TV stars, particularly Max Bygraves. Among his theme tune credits was BLESS THIS HOUSE. Love also recorded under the pseudonym of Manuel and His Music of the Mountains and was the father of the late radio personality, Adrian Love.

LOVE HURTS
UK (Alomo) Drama. BBC 1 1992–4

Frank Carver	**Adam Faith**
Tessa Piggott	**Zoe Wanamaker**
Diane Warburg	**Jane Lapotaire**
Hugh Marriner	**Stephen Moore**
Max Taplow	**Tony Selby**
Mrs Piggott	**Hilary Mason**
Dr Piggott	**Richard Pearson**
Bob Pearce	**John Flanagan**
Jade Carver	**Robin Weaver**
Malcolm Litoff	**Richard Cordery**
Grace Taplow	**Edna Doré**
Simon Friedman	**David Horovitch**
Anthony Friedman	**Ben Fisher**
Jonathan Friedman	**Laurence Amias**
Sandra	**Belinda Davison**
Alex Friedman	**Carl Morris**
Marshall Baumblatt	**Olivier Pierre**
David Ben-Ari	**Sasson Gabi**
Sam Levison	**Rolf Saxon**
Mirav Levison	**Suzanne Bertish**

Creators: **Laurence Marks, Maurice Gran**
Producers: **Guy Slater, Tara Brem, Irving Teitelbaum**

A disillusioned businesswoman and a millionaire plumber try to make a relationship work.

Forty-one and single, Tessa Piggott was a high-flyer in the City. But, seeking pastures new, she ditched her boss/lover, moved into her own flat and became a director of the Seed aid agency. At the same time, she met up with rough-diamond divorcé Frank Carver, on the face of it a lowly plumber but in fact a millionaire businessman. They, somewhat inconveniently, fell in love, with all its emotional consequences. *Love Hurts* traced the development of Tessa and Frank's relationship, as work pressures and time apart took their toll. In the second series, they got married while on business together in Russia, but married life proved just as difficult, since Tessa continued her development work, this time for the Baumblatt Foundation. By the third and final season, she was pregnant, giving birth to baby Alice. Juggling work and parenthood was equally fraught with tension.

LOVE STORY

UK (ATV) Drama Anthology. ITV 1963–9; 1972–4

Single dramas in the romantic vein.

Love Story was the umbrella title for a collection of one-off plays that had romance as their linchpin. Among its most prominent contributing writers were Robert Muller, Edna O'Brien, Doris Lessing, Mordecai Richler, Robert Holles, Alfred Shaughnessy, Roman Polanski and the French novelist and screenwriter, Marguérite Duras. Judi Dench, Patrick Macnee, Vanessa Redgrave, Jeremy Kemp, Dudley Moore, Julia Foster and Robert Hardy were some of the featured performers.

LOVE THY NEIGHBOUR

UK (Thames) Situation Comedy. ITV 1972–6

Eddie Booth	**Jack Smethurst**
Joan Booth	**Kate Williams**
Bill Reynolds	**Rudolph Walker**
Barbie Reynolds	**Nina Baden-Semper**
Arthur	**Tommy Godfrey**
Jacko Jackson	**Keith Marsh**
Nobby Garside	**Paul Luty**

Creators/Writers: **Harry Driver, Vince Powell**
Producers: **Stuart Allen, Ronnie Baxter, Anthony Parker, William G. Stewart**

A bigot's life is turned upside down when a black man moves in next door.

There have been few more controversial sitcoms than *Love Thy Neighbour*. It told the story of white trade-unionist Eddie Booth whose new next-door neighbour in Maple Terrace, Bill Reynolds, was a true-blue Tory and, even worse, a black man. It was intended, according to its producers, to take the sting out of racial conflict. Others saw it as a barrage of cheap colour jokes that reinforced racial stereotypes. It is quite true, however, that the bigot always lost out. Eddie was never prepared to give Bill a chance, yet Bill always came up trumps, delighting in humiliating Eddie and always giving as good as he got. Meanwhile, to underline the futility of it all, the two wives, Joan and Barbie, became good friends. Arthur, Jacko ('I'll have a half') and Nobby were their pals down at the Jubilee Social Club. Remarkably, the series was a huge ratings success. The theme song was sung by Stuart Gillies. A feature-film version was released in 1973, and the series was revamped in 1980 in Australia. *Love Thy Neighbour in Australia*, as it was titled when screened in the UK two years later, depicted Eddie embroiled in the same racial conflict on his emigration Down Under. There was also a short-lived American version, starring Ron Masak and Harrison Page, in 1973.

LOVEJOY

UK (Tamariska/Witzend/McShane) Comedy Drama.
BBC 1 1986; 1991–4

Lovejoy	**Ian McShane**
Tinker Dill	**Dudley Sutton**
Eric Catchpole	**Chris Jury**
Lady Jane Felsham	**Phyllis Logan**
Lord Felsham	**Pavel Douglas**
Charlie Gimbert	**Malcolm Tierney**
Dandy Jack	**Geoffrey Bateman**
Beth	**Diane Parish**
Charlotte Cavendish	**Caroline Langrishe**

Creator: **Ian La Frenais**
Producers: **Robert Banks Stewart, Richard Everitt, Emma Hayter, Jo Wright, Colin Schindler**

A shady antiques dealer stumbles into intrigue in the East Anglian countryside.

Dubbed by some 'The Antiques Rogue Show', *Lovejoy* was based on the novels of Jonathan Gash and concerned a slightly dodgy dealer in antiquities. Lovejoy's patch was East Anglia and, more specifically, rural Essex and Suffolk, which he combed for underpriced treasures to sell on with a nice mark-up. Being what is known as a 'divvie', he instinctively knew when an antique was rare and valuable. At his side were Tinker, his tweedy, beret-hatted old friend, and young gopher Eric Catchpole. When Eric left to run his uncle's pub, he was replaced by Beth, another 'trainee'. Leather-jacketed Lovejoy (who lived in a picturesque country cottage and drove a battered Morris Minor affectionately named Miriam) enjoyed the company of local aristocrat Lady Jane Felsham and, though flirtation was the name of the game, wedding bells never chimed. On Lady Jane's departure, in came university-educated auctioneer Charlotte Cavendish, and she almost succeeded in getting the lovable wheeler-dealer to the altar in the very last episode of the series.

Played in humorous-thriller style, *Lovejoy* also employed the television technique known as 'breaking the fourth wall'. As seen earlier in programmes like THE GEORGE BURNS AND GRACIE ALLEN SHOW and IT'S GARRY SHANDLING'S SHOW, this called on Lovejoy, in an aside to the camera, to explain events directly to the viewers.

LOVERS, THE

UK (Granada) Situation Comedy. ITV 1970–1

Geoffrey Scrimgeor	**Richard Beckinsale**
Beryl Battersby	**Paula Wilcox**
Mrs Battersby	**Joan Scott**
Roland Lomax	**Robin Nedwell**

Creator: **Jack Rosenthal**
Writers: **Jack Rosenthal, Geoffrey Lancashire**
Producers: **Jack Rosenthal, Les Chatfield**

Two teenagers have different hopes for their relationship.

Geoffrey (or 'Geoffrey Bubbles Bon Bon', as Beryl, his girlfriend, liked to call him) was very concerned with the physical side of their romance – or, more precisely, with the fact that there was no physical side. No matter how hard he tried to consummate their relationship (egged on by his pal, Roland, with whom he worked at Westland Bank), the scheming Beryl (watched over by her prudish widowed mum) was always too virtuous to give in. 'Percy Filth', as she knew it, was not for her, despite the permissive age in which they lived. Marriage, in her eyes, was a far better objective.

The Lovers proved to be the break that both Paula Wilcox and Richard Beckinsale needed in their fledgling careers. A feature-film version followed in 1972.

LOWE, ARTHUR
(1915–82)

Derbyshire-born actor, for ever the bumptious Captain Mainwaring in DAD'S ARMY, but the star of numerous other sitcoms. These included POTTER (Redvers Potter), BLESS ME FATHER (Father Duddleswell) and A. J. WENTWORTH, BA (schoolmaster Wentworth, his last TV role). In the 1960s he was draper Leonard Swindley, the man jilted by Emily Nugent at the altar in CORONATION STREET – a character which he took into the spin-off series, PARDON THE EXPRESSION and *Turn Out the Lights*. Lowe also voiced the *Mr Men* cartoons, starred with Richard Briers in *Ben Travers Farces*, appeared in Harold Pinter's first TV play (an ARMCHAIR THEATRE production called *A Night Out*) and was Dr Maxwell in DOCTOR AT LARGE, Bodkin in LAST OF THE BASKETS, Micawber in a 1975 BBC version of *David Copperfield* and Louis Pasteur in *Microbes and Men*. Lowe was also seen in the dramas, *Philby, Burgess and Maclean* and *A Voyage Around My Father*, and appeared as a guest in THE AVENGERS, among other series. He was married to actress Joan Cooper, who was cast as Godfrey's sister, Dolly, in *Dad's Army*.

LUCY SHOW, THE
US (CBS/Desilu) Situation Comedy. BBC 1 1962–8; ITV 1964–5

Lucy Carmichael	**Lucille Ball**
Vivian Bagley	**Vivian Vance**
Chris Carmichael	**Candy Moore**
Jerry Carmichael	**Jimmy Garrett**
Mr Barnsdahl	**Charles Lane**
Theodore J. Mooney	**Gale Gordon**
Harry Conners	**Dick Martin**
Sherman Bagley	**Ralph Hart**
Harrison Cheever	**Roy Roberts**
Mary Jane Lewis	**Mary Jane Croft**

A bored widow seeks a new husband and thinks up hare-brained schemes to improve her life.

In this follow-up to I LOVE LUCY, Lucille Ball starred without her husband, Desi Arnaz. Having said that, the format was essentially much the same, with Lucy playing Lucy Carmichael, a scatterbrained widow living with her two children, Chris and Jerry, in Danfield, Connecticut. She was once again supported by Vivian Vance, this time in the guise of Vivian Bagley, a divorcée friend who, with her son, Sherman, shared a house with the Carmichaels. Lucy's main aspiration was to find herself a new husband, but, as ever, all her best plans crumbled around her. Lucy found a perfect foil for her slapstick antics in her no-nonsense boss, Mr Mooney, who succeeded the cantankerous Mr Barnsdahl seen in the earliest episodes. Mooney was President of the Danfield First National Bank and she was his part-time secretary.

After a few seasons, the location of the series was switched to San Francisco, with major cast-changes. Lucy still worked for Mr Mooney, who was now Vice-President of the Westland Bank, under boss Harrison Cheever, but her daughter, Chris, was no longer featured. Also gone was Vivian Bagley, to appear only occasionally as a visitor. Lucy's new accomplice was neighbour Mary Jane Lewis.

See also *I Love Lucy* and HERE'S LUCY.

LUMLEY, JOANNA
OBE (1946–)

British actress and former model, born in India and typically seen in classy, sophisticated roles, though offering a game alternative as Patsy in the comedy, ABSOLUTELY FABULOUS. Lumley's TV career has veered between lead roles and strong supporting parts, with the highlights being the athletic Purdey in THE NEW AVENGERS and the mysterious Sapphire in SAPPHIRE AND STEEL. She was Samantha Ryder-Ross in Jilly Cooper's sitcom, *It's Awfully Bad for Your Eyes, Darling*, played Elaine Perkins, a girlfriend of Ken Barlow, in CORONATION STREET, and starred as Mrs Smiling in *Cold Comfort Farm*, Kate Swift in *Class Act*, Diana Carey-Lewis in *Coming Home* and *Nancherrow*, and Donna Sinclair in *Dr Willoughby*. One of her earliest performances was in EMERGENCY – WARD 10 and other credits have included parts in STEPTOE AND SON, THE PROTECTORS, *Oxbridge Blues*, *The Glory Boys*, *Mistral's Daughter*, *A Perfect Hero* (Loretta Stone), LOVEJOY, CLUEDO (Mrs Peacock) and the cartoon, *The Forgotten Toys*. In 1989 she stood in as host of *Wogan*; in 1994 she appeared in the documentary, *Girl Friday*, which recounted her nine-day 'survival' on the uninhabited island of Tsarabajina, off Madagascar. In 1997 she retraced her grandparents' trek through the Himalayas in *Joanna Lumley in the Kingdom of the Thunder Dragon*. Her first husband was comedy actor/writer Jeremy Lloyd.

LUNGHI, CHERIE
(1952–)

Nottingham-born actress, as Gabriella Benson the star of the football drama, *The Manageress*, but also seen as Dorothy in THE MONOCLED MUTINEER, Margaret Van de Merwe in *Master of the Game*, Laura Testvalley in *The Buccaneers*, Mrs Steerforth in *David Copperfield*, Merle

Kirschman in *A Likeness in Stone*, and also in TALES OF THE UNEXPECTED, *Praying Mantis*, *Strangers and Brothers*, *Harem* and THE RUTH RENDELL MYSTERIES, among other dramas.

LUV
UK (BBC) Situation Comedy. BBC 1 1993–4

Harold Craven	**Michael Angelis**
Terese Craven	**Sue Johnston**
Lloyd	**Peter Caffrey**
Hannah Craven	**Sandy Hendrickse**
Victor Craven	**Russell Boulter**
	Stefan Escreet
Darwin Craven	**Stephen Lord**
Bernie	**Jackie Downey**
Carro	**Debbie Andrews**
Eden	**Julie Peasgood**
Martinique	**Jan Ravens**
Antonio	**Zubin Varla**
Tone	**Gerard O'Hare**
Arthur	**Raymond Coulthard**
Chezz	**Akim Mogaji**

Creator/Writer: **Carla Lane**
Producer: **Mike Stephens**

A successful Liverpool businessman finds that money can't buy him love or peace at home.

Harold Craven, self-made proprietor of Craven's Ornamental Garden Requisites (mostly plastic flowerpots), cared deeply for his wife and children and showered them with gifts. Nevertheless, he found himself head of a family that struggled to express their need for each other. His wife, Terese, was a bored housewife who wanted only one thing – for her husband to say he loved her – and their adopted children brought even more heartache into their stressed lives. Elder son Victor was gay and lived with his boyfriend in an 'out of the way' cottage Harold had bought for them. Daughter Hannah endured a stormy marriage with a dim Italian named Antonio, and whining younger son Darwin still lived at home, dossing his way through life, espousing the animal rights cause and indulging in pseudo-paramilitary manoeuvres to free livestock. Away from the bedlam of home life, Harold relaxed in the company of Lloyd, his perceptive Irish chauffeur, and in the arms of Eden, a beautiful blonde whom he employed as his secretary. Bernie and Carro were the workers who gave Harold a hard time on the factory floor, especially when he insisted on playing them classical music.

In the second series, Harold abandoned Eden, only to find his former mistress bent on revenge, and the factory went through financial difficulties that had repercussions for all the Craven family.

LWT

LWT (formerly London Weekend Television) won the ITV franchise for London weekends in 1967 (under the application name of London Television Consortium),

and went on air on 2 August 1968. It retained its franchise in 1980 and again in 1992 and now broadcasts to London from 5.15 p.m. on Friday to closedown on Sunday, as well as making many programmes for the ITV network at its South Bank studios. Among its most notable contributions over the years have been sitcoms like DOCTOR IN THE HOUSE and ON THE BUSES, arts programmes like AQUARIUS and THE SOUTH BANK SHOW, drama such as UPSTAIRS, DOWNSTAIRS and BOUQUET OF BARBED WIRE, current affairs series like WEEKEND WORLD and game shows such as GAME FOR A LAUGH and PLAY YOUR CARDS RIGHT. LWT is now part of Granada.

LYNAM, DESMOND
(1942–)

Laid-back Irish-born sports frontman whose charm and style have led him into other presentation work. Beginning his broadcasting career in radio sport, working particularly on boxing commentaries, Lynam's TV break came in the late 1970s with NATIONWIDE's Friday night sports segment and led to GRANDSTAND, *Sportsnight*, MATCH OF THE DAY and all the BBC's major sporting events coverage, before he defected to anchor ITV's soccer coverage in 1999. He tried one season as presenter of HOLIDAY and was also seen as co-host of *How Do They Do That?*.

LYNCH, JOE
(1925–)

Irish comedy actor, chiefly recalled as the tailor Patrick Kelly in NEVER MIND THE QUALITY, FEEL THE WIDTH. He was later seen as Paddy O'Brien in another sitcom, *Rule Britannia*, and was narrator of the children's series, *Chorlton and the Wheelies*.

LYNDHURST, NICHOLAS
(1961–)

Although widely recognized as plonker Rodney Trotter from the hugely successful ONLY FOOLS AND HORSES, Nicholas Lyndhurst's showbiz career began as a child actor. He was seen in numerous kids' dramas, including *Anne of Avonlea* (Davy Keith), *Heidi* and THE TOMORROW PEOPLE, and took the dual lead roles in *The Prince and the Pauper*. He was one of the hosts of the Saturday morning magazine, *Our Show* (along with Susan Tully and others), and played Fletch's son, Raymond, in *Going Straight*, before maturing into adult parts through BUTTERFLIES, in which he was Ria's son, Adam. Since *Only Fools and Horses* began, Lyndhurst has not looked back and has been a popular choice for sitcom producers. He was Ashley in THE TWO OF US, Peter Chapman in *The Piglet Files* and Gary Sparrow in GOODNIGHT SWEETHEART. Among his other credits have been *Round and Round*, *Spearhead*, *Slimming Down*, *To Serve Them All My Days*, *Stalag Luft*, *Gulliver's Travels* (Clustril), *David Copperfield* (Uriah Heep) and *Thin Ice* (Graham Moss).

LYNN, JONATHAN
(1943–)

British actor, writer and director, a Cambridge Footlights graduate, acclaimed in particular for YES, MINISTER and *Yes, Prime Minister*, which he scripted in collaboration with Antony Jay. In front of the cameras, he appeared in the sketch show, *Twice a Fortnight*, and played Danny Hooley in DOCTOR IN THE HOUSE, Beryl's husband (Robert) in THE LIVER BIRDS and Pete Booth in *My Brother's Keeper* (also as writer). Other acting parts have come in *Bar Mitzvah Boy*, *Turnbull's Finest Hour* (Roddy Cheever-Jones), OUTSIDE EDGE (Kevin Costello) in the 1982 one-off, *The Knowledge* and *Diana*. Among Lynn's other writing credits (usually with George Layton) have been episodes of the '*Doctor*' series, ON THE BUSES and *My Name is Harry Worth*.

LYTTON'S DIARY
UK (Thames) Drama. ITV 1985–6

Neville Lytton	**Peter Bowles**
Henry Field	**Bernard Lloyd**
Ian	**Bernard Archard**
Catherine Lytton	**Fiona Mollison**
Laura Gray	**Anna Nygh**
Colin	**Lewis Fiander**
David Edding	**Adam Norton**
Dolly	**Holly de Jong**
Norman	**David Ryall**
Pandora	**Jane Laurie**
Henry Field	**Bernard Lloyd**
Wayne Munroe	**John Stride**
Mark	**James Aubrey**
Helena	**Barbara Kellerman**
Trevor Bates	**Joseph Young**
Jenny	**Harriet Keevil**

Creators: **Peter Bowles, Philip Broadley**
Writer: **Ray Connolly**
Producers: **Chris Burt, Derek Bennett**
Executive Producer: **Lloyd Shirley**

Incidents in the life of a newspaper diarist.

Partly created by its star, Peter Bowles, *Lytton's Diary* began life as part of Thames Television's anthology series, *Storyboard*, in 1983. Two years later, it became a series. Bowles starred as Neville Lytton, the gossip columnist for *The Daily News*. His investigations into society scandals provided ample titbits for his features and drew him into intrigue. Office colleagues included editors Ian and Mark, and lawyer Colin. His Fleet Street rival was Henry Field, who also lived with Lytton's wife, Catherine. Lytton's girlfriend was Laura Gray.

McANALLY, RAY
(1926–89)

Irish actor who, after years of supporting roles in the cinema and on TV, became a star late in life. Although he had appeared as gangster Alec Spindoe in *Spindoe* in 1968, and was seen in ME MAMMY, it was as Rick, Peter Egan's deceitful dad, in *A Perfect Spy* that he began to steal the show, and he capped that with a BAFTA award-winning performance as left-wing Labour Prime Minister Harry Perkins in Channel 4's *A Very British Coup*. Other early appearances had been as a guest in series like THE AVENGERS and MAN IN A SUITCASE.

McCALL, DAVINA
(1967–)

London-born presenter of light-entertainment series such as *Streetmate, The Real Holiday Show, Don't Try This at Home, The Brit Awards* and BIG BROTHER.

McCALLUM, DAVID
(1933–)

Blond Scottish actor, busy on both sides of the Atlantic and once a heart-throb as secret agent Illya Kuryakin in THE MAN FROM UNCLE. *UNCLE* followed his arrival in the USA in the early 1960s and roles in series like PERRY MASON and THE OUTER LIMITS. Later, he was airman Simon Carter in COLDITZ, Dr Daniel Westin aka THE INVISIBLE MAN, Steel in SAPPHIRE AND STEEL, Alan Breck in *Kidnapped*, Alex Vesey in MOTHER LOVE, John Grey in TRAINER, Professor Plum in CLUEDO, Billy Fawcett in *Coming Home*, and Dr Joseph Bloom in the US sci-fi series, *VR.5*. McCallum has also been in demand for TV movies and guest appearances, and has, at times, turned his hand to directing. His first wife was actress Jill Ireland.

McCASKILL, IAN
(1938–)

Quirky Scottish meteorologist who joined the BBC forecasting team in 1978 and quickly attracted the attentions of impressionists. He worked for a while at Central Television in the early 1980s and has also been seen as a guest on numerous other programmes. He retired from the BBC in the late 1990s.

McCLAIN'S LAW
US (MGM) Police Drama. BBC 1 1982

Det. Jim McClain	James Arness
Det. Harry Gates	Marshall Colt
Det. Jerry Cross	Carl Franklin
Lt. Edward DeNisco	George DiCenzo
Vangie Cruise	Conchata Ferrell

Creator: **Eric Bercovici**
Producers: **Mark Rafters, Robert H. Justman**

A retired detective rejoins the police to hunt for his friend's killer.

Forced to leave the police force in San Pedro, California, some 13 years earlier because of a leg injury, Jim McClain was dragged back into detective work when his fishing partner was brutally murdered. Convinced that only he was capable of tracking down the killer, McClain – now aged 52 – persuaded the authorities to take him back into the force, even though detection methods had changed dramatically in his absence. But, with excellent support from colleagues Harry Gates and Jerry Cross, McClain quickly dropped back into the routine. Even though his rough-and-tumble ways seemed rather archaic at times (and wound up his boss, Lt. DeNisco), he proved reasonably effective. Off duty, Jim returned to his waterside hang-out, Vangie Cruise's bar.

A welcome change in direction for James Arness, after his 20-odd years in GUNSMOKE, this series was partly inspired by a 1952 film in which he had starred with John Wayne. Called *Big Jim McLain*, it featured Wayne in the title role as a right-wing special agent rooting out communists in Hawaii.

McCLANAHAN, RUE
(1934–)

After plenty of supporting roles, Rue McClanahan was at last able to claim some of the limelight when she was cast as the man-hungry southern belle, Blanche Devereaux, in THE GOLDEN GIRLS and *The Golden Palace*. The former brought her back into contact with Bea Arthur, with whom she had appeared in the ALL IN THE FAMILY offshoot, *Maude*. Among McClanahan's other credits have been parts in LOU GRANT, THE LOVE BOAT and numerous TV movies, as well as the US sitcoms, *Apple Pie* and *Mama's Family* (neither screened in the UK).

McCLOUD
US (Universal) Police Drama. ITV 1972–6

Sam McCloud .... **Dennis Weaver**
Peter B. Clifford .... **J. D. Cannon**
Sgt Joe Broadhurst .... **Terry Carter**
Chris Coughlin .... **Diana Muldaur**
Sgt Grover .... **Ken Lynch**

Creator/Executive Producer: **Glen A. Larson**

A cowboy becomes a cop in New York City.

Deputy Marshal Sam McCloud had arrived in New York in pursuit of a refugee prisoner. Having caught his man, he decided to stick around for a while and learn the ways of a big city police force, operating in a world far removed from his usual beat of Taos, New Mexico. Riding a horse through the New York traffic and sporting a sheepskin jacket, cowboy boots and a stetson, he joined

Manhattan's 27th Precinct, working alongside Sgt Joe Broadhurst. Although McCloud was meant to be the learner, it was Broadhurst who had the greater education, as the determined western lawman dragged him into the thick of the action, shunning the subtler approach to policing usually employed in the city. This did little to endear either of them to their superior, Chief Clifford. But, as our hero would have put it, 'There you go.' Chris Coughlin was McCloud's writer girlfriend.

Based on the Clint Eastwood film, *Coogan's Bluff*, and derived from a pilot called *Who Killed Miss USA* (aired as *Who Killed Merri-Ann* in the UK), the series was part of ITV's MYSTERY MOVIE package. A TV movie, *The Return of Sam McCloud*, was made in 1989, with McCloud having become a US senator.

McCLURE, DOUG
(1935–95)

American actor, Trampas in THE VIRGINIAN for nine years, but otherwise unfamiliar to British audiences, except for TV movies and mini-series like ROOTS (in which he played Jemmy Brent). In the States, McClure enjoyed several short-run series, but nothing to match *The Virginian*.

MacCORKINDALE, SIMON
(1952–)

Successful British actor, now focusing on behind-the-scenes work. His most notable TV performances have been as Lucius in I, CLAUDIUS, Joe Kapp in the 1979 revival of QUATERMASS, Jonathan Chase, hero of the sci-fi detective series, *Manimal*, and Greg Reardon in FALCON CREST (also with directing credits). Other appearances have come in JUST WILLIAM, JESUS OF NAZARETH, *Beasts*, WILL SHAKESPEARE, *The Mannions of America* and THE DUKES OF HAZZARD. MacCorkindale is currently married to Susan George (his first wife was Fiona Fullerton) and together they run the Amy International production company.

McCOY, SYLVESTER
(James Kent-Smith; 1943–)

Scottish actor, dealing in both comic and straight drama roles. Undoubtedly his most famous character has been DOCTOR WHO (the seventh incarnation, 1987–9). Previously (often under the name of Sylveste McCoy) he had been seen in children's offerings like VISION ON, TISWAS, *Jigsaw*, *Dramarama* and *Eureka*, sitcoms like *Big Jim* and *The Figaro Club* (Turps, the painter) and dramas like *The Last Place on Earth* (Birdie Bowers).

McCUTCHEON, MARTINE
(1976–)

London-born actress who shot to fame as Tiffany Raymond/Mitchell in EASTENDERS, using her success to branch out into a singing career (beginning with the hit, 'Perfect Moment').

McDONALD, Sir TREVOR
OBE (1939–)

Trinidadian newscaster, for years the main anchor for *News at Ten*. He joined ITN in 1973 and, after working as a reporter and sports correspondent, became its diplomatic correspondent and diplomatic editor, also spending seven years with *Channel 4 News*. McDonald had previously worked in radio and television in the West Indies and for the BBC World and Caribbean Services in London. His most recent work includes *Tonight – with Trevor McDonald*.

McDOWALL, RODDY
(1928–98)

London-born actor/celebrity photographer, formerly a Hollywood child star (particularly remembered with Lassie and Flicka), whose most memorable TV role was as Galen in THE PLANET OF THE APES. His earliest TV credits were in episodes of THE TWILIGHT ZONE, NAKED CITY, ARREST AND TRIAL, ALFRED HITCHCOCK PRESENTS and THE INVADERS, and he also played The Bookworm in BATMAN. After *The Planet of the Apes*, McDowall enjoyed a run of US dramas and TV movies, such as *The Rhinemann Exchange*, *Fantastic Journey* and *Tales of the Gold Monkey* (Bon Chance Louie), and guest spots in series like WONDER WOMAN.

McEWAN, GERALDINE
(Geraldine McKeown; 1932–)

English actress much seen on television in roles like Miss Farnaby in MULBERRY, Anne Dickens in *Tears Before Bedtime*, Mrs Proudie in *The Barchester Chronicles*, Jess's religious mother in ORANGES ARE NOT THE ONLY FRUIT, Emmeline Lucas (aka Lucia) in *Mapp and Lucia*, and the title character in *The Prime of Miss Jean Brodie*, plus many single dramas, including *Thin Ice* (Mrs Violet Jerome).

McGANN, JOE
(1958–), PAUL (1959–), MARK (1961–), STEPHEN (1963–)

Four acting brothers much seen on British TV since the 1980s. Joe has starred in ROCKLIFFE'S BABIES as PC Gerry O'Dowd and in THE UPPER HAND as Charlie Burrows, and appeared in *Harry Enfield's Television Programme* (one of 'The Scousers'); Paul has been Mo Morris in GIVE US A BREAK, Percy Toplis in THE MONOCLED MUTINEER, Joe Thompson in *Nice Town*, Cpl. Chris Ryan in the SAS drama, *The One That Got Away*, the eighth DOCTOR WHO, Eugene Wrayburn in *Our Mutual Friend* and Jonathan Vishnevski in *Fish* (he was also pencilled in for the title role in SHARPE but missed out through injury); Mark

has played Mad Dog in *Scully*, Detective C. J. Brady in *Yellowthread Street*, Halliwell in *The Manageress* and Marcus Bannerman in *The Grand*; and Stephen has taken the roles of Bob in *Streetwise*, Tex in *Help!* and Sean Reynolds in EMMERDALE. All four have many other credits to their names and appeared together (as the Phelan brothers) in the 1995 drama series, *The Hanging Gale*.

McGEE, HENRY
(1929–)

British actor and straight man to leading comics, particularly Benny Hill, Tommy Cooper, Dick Emery, Frankie Howerd, Reg Varney and Charlie Drake (Mr Pugh in THE WORKER). In sitcom, he was Lt. Raleigh in TELL IT TO THE MARINES, appeared with Ronnie Corbett in NO – THAT'S ME OVER HERE, and played Dicky Bligh in *Up the Workers* and Dennis in *Let There Be Love*. His other credits have included parts in THE GOODIES, RISING DAMP, SYKES and *Doctor at Large*.

McGOOHAN, PATRICK
(1928–)

American-born, British-raised actor whose earliest television credits were in action series like THE ADVENTURES OF SIR LANCELOT and *The Vise*. He became a big name in the 1960s thanks to his starring roles as John Drake in DANGER MAN and Number 6 in his own cult series, THE PRISONER (he created it and wrote and directed some episodes). At one point, it is claimed, McGoohan was the richest man on TV and allegedly turned down the part of THE SAINT, before it was offered to Roger Moore, because Simon Templar was too promiscuous. In the 1970s he returned to the small screen as medical man *Rafferty* and in TV movies, but he also worked behind the scenes, directing an episode of COLUMBO, for instance (as well as guest starring in the series).

McGOVERN, JIMMY
(1949–)

Acclaimed, Liverpool-born dramatist, known for tackling difficult subjects and for creating gritty characters. After working as a bus conductor and in insurance, he qualified as a teacher, but then started writing for local theatre. He was given a chance to write for BROOKSIDE and stayed for six years. Since then his major works have included CRACKER, *Hearts and Minds*, Screen Two's *Priest*, *Hillsborough*, THE LAKES and *Dockers*.

McGOWAN, ALISTAIR

British actor/comedian/impressionist, specializing in take-offs of sports personalities like Alan Hansen, David Beckham and Naseem Hamed, but also successful with innovative characterizations, such as newsreader Huw Edwards, actor Nigel Havers and interior designer

Laurence Llewellyn-Bowen. All of these were high-lighted in his own series, *Alistair McGowan's Big Impression*, in which he was supported by Ronni Ancona. Previously, McGowan had provided voices for SPITTING IMAGE, *The Staggering Stories of Ferdinand de Bargos* and *Klinik!* (Dr Werther) and, as an actor, appeared in PRESTON FRONT (Spock), *Spark* (Mike) and *Dark Ages* (Redwald).

McGRATH, RORY
(1956–)

British comedian, writer and presenter, a member of Cambridge Footlights troupe before becoming a writer for BBC Radio comedy programmes and then scripting for NOT THE NINE O'CLOCK NEWS (and its spin-off, ALAS SMITH AND JONES). He later appeared in WHO DARES, WINS . . . and co-founded Hat Trick Productions (for whom he co-wrote – and played Badvoc in – *Chelmsford 123*). He has also taken part in WHOSE LINE IS IT ANY-WAY?, fronted *Rory McGrath's Commercial Breakdown*, hosted the quizzes, *Trivial Pursuit* and *Sports Anorak of the Year*, and, most prominently, been a regular on THEY THINK IT'S ALL OVER.

MacGREGOR, JIMMIE
See HALL, ROBIN.

McINNERNY, TIM
(1956–)

British actor whose most prominent roles have been as Lord Percy and, later, Captain Darling in BLACKADDER. However, he has also been seen in programmes as varied as EDGE OF DARKNESS (Terry Shields), THE ADVENTURES OF SHERLOCK HOLMES, *Shadow of the Noose*, *A Very British Coup*, THE COMIC STRIP PRESENTS and *Longitude* (Christopher Irwin). He is the brother of actress Lizzie McInnerny.

McINTIRE, JOHN
(1907–91)

John McIntire's craggy looks were very familiar to viewers in the 1950s and 1960s, courtesy of his starring roles in NAKED CITY (Lt. Dan Muldoon) and WAGON TRAIN (Christopher Hale). A few years later, McIntire turned up in another Western, THE VIRGINIAN, taking the role of Clay Grainger, new owner of the Shiloh Ranch. With guest appearances in the 1970s in series like LOVE, AMERICAN STYLE and THE LOVE BOAT, plus roles in prime-time American series right up to 1981, McIntire enjoyed a remarkable television career, especially if you consider that he didn't start working in the medium until he was nearly 50, having concentrated earlier on radio acting.

MACKAY, FULTON
OBE (1922–87)

Scottish actor, PORRIDGE's by-the-book prison officer, Mr Mackay. Previously, he was Willie in *Mess Mates*, a regular guest as Jamie in DR FINLAY'S CASEBOOK, played Det. Supt. Inman in SPECIAL BRANCH and featured in the sketch show, *Between the Lines*. Among his later work were roles in the kids' sci-fi adventure, KING OF THE CASTLE (Hawkspur, a mad scientist), the single dramas, *Going Gently* and *A Sense of Freedom*, a Channel 4 sitcom, *Mann's Best Friends* (lodger Hamish Ordway), and *Fraggle Rock* (the Captain). Other appearances over the years were in series such as THE EDWARDIANS, THE TROUBLESHOOTERS, *The Foundation*, SOME MOTHERS DO 'AVE 'EM, CROWN COURT and *Going Straight*.

McKEE, GINA
(1964–)

British actress who holds the rare distinction of appearing in the first ever TV advertisement for condoms, playing a chemist's shop assistant. Her TV debut came as teenager Jane in *Quest of Eagles*, but, much more significantly, she went on to win acclaim for her portrayal of Mary Cox in OUR FRIENDS IN THE NORTH (ageing from 18 to 52). She has also been seen as kidnap victim Stephanie Slater in *Beyond Fear*, insecure wife Beth Murray in *Element of Doubt*, Mary Leslie in *The Treasure Seekers*, drunken single mum Caroline in *Screen Two's Mothertime*, and Ellie, the older woman in love with a young man (Paul Nicholls), in *The Passion*. McKee also featured in the comedies, *Brass Eye* and *The Chest*, and played Julie and Sue Bishop in the sitcoms, *The Lenny Henry Show* and *An Actor's Life for Me*, respectively.

McKENZIE, JULIA
(1941–)

Middlesex-born actress, star of the sitcoms, *Maggie and Her* (Maggie), *That Beryl Marston . . . !* (Georgie Bodley) and FRESH/FRENCH FIELDS (Hester Fields). She was Mrs Forthby in BLOTT ON THE LANDSCAPE and her singing voice has occasionally been heard in series like *Song by Song*. Among her numerous other credits have been appearances in *Battle of the Sexes*, *Frost's Weekly*, *Adam Bede*, *Absent Friends*, *Fame Is the Spur*, *Hôtel du Lac*, THE TWO RONNIES and *The Stanley Baxter Show*, as well as her own programme, *Julia and Company*.

McKENZIE, ROBERT
(1917–81)

Enthusiastic Canadian political commentator who brought his 'Swingometer' into BBC election coverages. Though chiefly an academic, his other work included pieces for PANORAMA, TONIGHT and 24 HOURS, as well as a series of his own, *The Pursuit of Power*, shortly before he died.

McKERN, LEO
(Reginald McKern; 1920–)

Australian actor, identified by most viewers as the irascible legal rogue, RUMPOLE OF THE BAILEY. However, McKern's TV appearances have been many. He was one of the actors to play the mysterious Number 2 in the cult series, THE PRISONER, popped up in early series like THE ADVENTURES OF ROBIN HOOD, played Zaharov in REILLY – ACE OF SPIES, has numerous guest appearances and TV films to his name and has earned acclaim in single dramas like *The Tea Party*, Jonathan Miller's *Alice In Wonderland*, *The Sun Is God* (playing the artist Turner), *On the Eve of Publication*, Screen One's *A Foreign Field* (Cyril), and Screen Two's *The Last Romantics* (Sir Arthur Quiller-Couch). He was a familiar face in the 1980s, advertising Lloyds Bank.

MACKIE, PHILIP
(1918–85)

British playwright and producer whose long career's highlights (the later ones as writer) were *Maupassant*, *The Victorians*, MR ROSE, *The Liars*, *Saki*, *Paris 1900*, THE CAESARS, *Napoleon and Love*, *Good Girl*, THE NAKED CIVIL SERVANT, RAFFLES, *An Englishman's Castle*, *The Organisation*, *Thérèse Raquin*, *Conjugal Rites*, THE CLEOPATRAS and *Praying Mantis*. A former documentary-maker, Mackie joined the BBC as a contract writer in 1954 and later worked for Granada, among other companies.

McLACHLAN, CRAIG
(1965–)

Australian actor who shot to fame as Henry Ramsay in NEIGHBOURS before switching soaps and taking on the role of Grant Mitchell in HOME AND AWAY. He had earlier appeared in *Sons and Daughters*. Later credits have included the mini-series, *Heroes II*, and the part of Ed in BUGS. McLachlan has had some hit singles in the UK, most notably 'Mona'.

McMANUS, MARK
(1940–94)

Scottish actor, a former boxer, whose first major role was as the eponymous lead in the northern mining saga, SAM, although in his latter years he was known to viewers as the gritty Glasgow detective, TAGGART, making 30 episodes of the series from 1983. McManus was another policeman, DCI Jack Lambie, in STRANGERS and also appeared in COLDITZ, THE BROTHERS, CROWN COURT, *The Foundation*, TARGET, *Union Castle* and other dramas. The late Brian Connolly, lead singer of The Sweet pop group, was his foster-brother.

McMILLAN AND WIFE
US (Universal) Police Drama. ITV 1972–9

Commissioner Stewart McMillan	**Rock Hudson**
Sally McMillan	**Susan Saint James**
Sgt/Lt. Charles Enright	**John Schuck**
Mildred	**Nancy Walker**
Agatha	**Martha Raye**
Sgt Steve DiMaggio	**Richard Gilliland**
Maggie	**Gloria Stroock**

Creator/Executive Producer: **Leonard B. Stern**
Producer: **Jon Epstein**

A San Francisco police chief and his wife stumble across crime at every turn.

Loosely based on *The Thin Man* series of films, *McMillan and Wife* concerned a hapless police commissioner who was continually dragged into detective work by his attractive wife. Stewart and Sally McMillan had a successful marriage, a witty rapport and a nose for crime, which meant that there was no chance of this policeman leaving his work at the office. Whether they were doing the shopping, going to a party or taking a holiday, *something* was bound to arouse their curiosity. Even in bed all they talked about was murder. Little wonder they needed the sharp-tongued Mildred to do their housework.

McMillan and Wife was part of the MYSTERY MOVIE collection of crime capers and was derived from a pilot movie called *Once Upon a Dead Man*. When, after five years, Susan Saint James and Nancy Walker decided to leave the series, Rock Hudson soldiered on alone, with the title shortened to *McMillan*. Sally was killed off in a plane crash and Stewart was furnished with a new assistant, in the shape of Sgt Steve DiMaggio, who replaced the well-intentioned but slow-witted Sgt Charles Enright, now promoted to lieutenant. Mildred's sister, Agatha, arrived to be his housekeeper, and Maggie was his new secretary. The new format didn't last long, however.

MacMURRAY, FRED
(1908–91)

Although primarily a big-screen actor, Fred MacMurray was one of America's sitcom greats in the 1950s, thanks to his hit series, *My Three Sons*, which was also aired on ITV in the UK. His other television work was concentrated into TV movies.

MACNEE, PATRICK
(1922–)

Old Etonian Patrick Macnee will probably be remembered for one television role – debonair, gentleman agent John Steed in THE AVENGERS and THE NEW AVENGERS – although he has contributed to numerous TV movies and mini-series since. He played the head of

UNCLE in the one-off *Return of the Man from UNCLE* in 1983, was cast in the US series, *Empire* (Calvin Cromwell), *Gavilan* (Milo Bentley) and *Thunder in Paradise* (Edward Whitaker), and appeared as a guest in dramas like BATTLESTAR GALACTICA, DICK TURPIN, MAGNUM PI and MURDER, SHE WROTE. A cousin of David Niven, most of Macnee's earliest television work was gained in Canada and the USA (including one role in RAWHIDE), following some stage and film work in Britain.

McPARTLIN, ANTHONY
(1975–)

One half of Ant and Dec, the popular kids' TV presenters, hosting series like *The Ant and Dec Show*, *Ant and Dec Unzipped*, *SM:TV* and *Friends Like These*, after they both came to fame in BYKER GROVE, in which Ant played PJ and Dec played Duncan. These roles also took them into the record charts with a series of PJ and Duncan hits like 'Let's Get Ready to Rhumble' and 'Stuck on U'.

McQUEEN, GEOFF
(1947–94)

British scriptwriter, a former manager with an electrical company who broke into television with the snooker-room drama, GIVE US A BREAK. Soon afterwards, McQueen penned a single play for Thames TV's STORYBOARD anthology. Entitled *Woodentop*, it proved to be the pilot for THE BILL. McQueen's later offerings included the light-hearted dramas, BIG DEAL and STAY LUCKY, and episodes of *Up the Elephant and Round the Castle* and *Home James*. His last TV work was *Rules of Engagement* (shown posthumously).

McSHANE, IAN
(1942–)

British actor, prominent on both sides of the Atlantic. McShane starred as Heathcliff in a 1967 version of *Wuthering Heights*, appeared in the Joe Orton play, *Funeral Games*, in 1968, played Judas in JESUS OF NAZARETH, Sir Eric Russell in ROOTS, Benjamin Disraeli in *Disraeli* and Bert in *Dirty Money*. His other major credits have been in WILL SHAKESPEARE and plays and miniseries like *Grand Larceny*, *The Pirate*, *War and Remembrance*, *Bare Essence* and *Evergreen*. From 1986 he became familiar as the roguish antiques dealer, LOVEJOY, a series which he also co-produced through his own company, McShane Productions. The company was also responsible for the two-part drama, *Soul Survivors*, in which McShane played DJ Otis Cooke, and the legal series, *Madson*, with McShane, who devised the series, as prisoner-turned-lawyer John Madson. Narration work on SURVIVAL, *The Natural World* and HOLLYWOOD GREATS, plus guest appearances in series like MINDER, COLUMBO, PERRY MASON and DALLAS (Don Lockwood) add to his varied portfolio. He is married to actress Gwen Humble.

MADELEY, RICHARD
(1956–)

British presenter, largely associated with daytime television where, with his wife, Judy Finnigan, he has presented *This Morning* on ITV (they also hosted the evening chat show, *Tonight with Richard Madeley and Judy Finnigan*). Madeley has also chaired the quizzes, *Runway* and *Connections*, plus the panel game, CLUEDO, and previously worked as a journalist, reporting for Border, Yorkshire and Granada TV news.

MADIGAN
US (Universal) Police Drama. ITV 1973

Sgt Dan Madigan .... **Richard Widmark**

Executive Producer: **Frank Rosenberg**
Producers: **Dean Hargrove, Roland Kibbee**

An abrasive New York cop prefers his own company.

Madigan was one of TV's great loners, one of the quirky cops of the 1970s. Living in a spartan one-room flat, he worked for the NYPD during the day, but had little social life at night. Perhaps it was his hard, cool indifference that put people off, with his genuinely soft centre just too well concealed. At least, having no attachments, he was free to travel, and his work took him a long way from the busy streets of New York City.

The concept was inspired by a 1968 film of the same name. After a pilot movie called *Brock's Last Case*, *Madigan* became part of the MYSTERY MOVIE crime anthology series, showing in feature-length episodes. However, only six were ever made, each known by its setting, for example *The Manhattan Beat*, *The Naples Beat* and *The Lisbon Beat*.

MADOC, PHILIP
(1934–)

Welsh actor normally cast in somewhat sombre or menacing roles. He was Magua in the BBC's 1972 version of *Last of the Mohicans*, Det. Chief Supt. Tate in TARGET, Lloyd George in *The Life and Times of David Lloyd George*, newspaper baron Fison in *A Very British Coup*, TV producer George in *Hilary* and Lancing in FIRST BORN. Madoc was also seen in both BOUQUET OF BARBED WIRE and its sequel, *Another Bouquet*, plus the lifeboat drama, *Ennal's Point*, and has enjoyed guest roles in TV movies and series like THE AVENGERS, DOCTOR WHO, THE BARON, MAN IN A SUITCASE, RANDALL AND HOPKIRK (DECEASED), DEPARTMENT S, MANHUNT, FORTUNES OF WAR, SINGLES, CAPITAL CITY, BROOKSIDE and DAD'S ARMY, often playing a villain. He was once married to actress Ruth Madoc.

MADOC, RUTH
(1943–)

British actress, popular in the 1980s as HI-DE-HI!'s Welsh camp announcer, Gladys Pugh. Previously, Madoc had appeared in HUNTER'S WALK, as policeman's wife Betty Smith, and in the series, *Leave It to Charlie* and *The Life and Times of David Lloyd George* (alongside her first husband, Philip Madoc). She has since been seen in the dramas, *Oliver's Travels* (Mrs Evans) and *Jack of Hearts* (Jean Pryce), and as presenter of SONGS OF PRAISE.

MAGAZINE

A programme made up of assorted features of various lengths and on numerous topics, some inserted on film or video, others presented in the studio.

MAGIC ROUNDABOUT, THE
France (Serge Danot) Children's Entertainment. BBC 1
1965–71; 1974–7/Channel 4 1992

Creator: **Serge Danot.**
Narrators/Writers: **Eric Thompson, Nigel Planer**

A girl and her friends enjoy surreal adventures in a magic garden.

Few series are more fittingly described as 'cult' than *The Magic Roundabout*. Although each episode was just five minutes long and, almost as an afterthought, tagged on to the end of children's hour, this animation became a firm favourite not only with kids but also with adult audiences. Consequently, there were howls of protest when transmission was switched to an earlier time-slot.

The Magic Roundabout was produced in France by Serge Danot and shown first on French television in 1963. When the series arrived in the UK, the narration was drily and wittily redubbed by Eric (father of Emma) Thompson, who also rewrote the scripts for British consumption. Effectively, the storyline went as follows. Florence would arrive at a carousel owned by the ancient, bewhiskered Mr Rusty, a man whose barrel-organ provided the show's theme music. Zebedee, a strange, freckle-faced creature with a waxed moustache and a bedspring for feet, then bounced into the picture and, in a cascade of harp strings, the 'real' nature of life around the roundabout disappeared and all manner of odd things began to happen. New characters drifted into the action, primarily a sleek-haired dog known as Dougal, a quirky snail called Brian and a laid-back rabbit named Dylan. There was also Ermintrude, a flower-chewing cow, the manic cyclist, Mr McHenry, a talking train and, occasionally, Florence's friend Paul, plus one or two other chums. When it all got a bit too frenetic, up would bounce Zebedee to declare it was 'Time for bed'.

Children loved the series for its visual humour. Adults enjoyed Thompson's 'in' references to topical issues and personalities of the day. With the arrival of colour tele-vision, the surreality of it all became even more apparent, and some viewers began to question just what lay behind the series. Fingers were pointed at the almost hallucinogenic nature of the concept, with The Magic Roundabout itself declared to be an allegory for a 'trip' and Mr Rusty some kind of drug-peddler. It may seem ludicrous, but there was plenty of evidence to support this theory. After all, everything was perfectly normal until Florence arrived at the roundabout, Dylan was always spaced out and Dougal's favourite food was sugar cubes (with all their LSD connections)! But even if you dismiss the 'drug culture' theory, *The Magic Roundabout* will still be fondly remembered by today's parents and grandparents as a cheerful part of everyday life in the 1960s.

A cinema version, *Dougal and the Blue Cat*, was released in the UK in 1972 and the series was revived by Channel 4 in 1992, with previously unscreened episodes adapted (very much in the Eric Thompson vein) for British audiences by Nigel Planer.

MAGIC WANDS

The flippant term used for programmes that make viewers' dreams and wishes come true. One of the first such programmes in the UK was *Ask Pickles* in the 1950s, but the longest-running example was JIM'LL FIX IT, which notched up 20 years of giving kids the chance to meet pop stars, drive trains, interview politicians, etc. Some adults' hopes were also fulfilled. Esther Rantzen's THE BIG TIME was another such vehicle, and among more recent offerings has been the heavily sentimental *Noel's Christmas Presents*. Screened on Christmas Day, it has featured Noel Edmonds rewarding brave, sick or deserving folk with their ultimate Christmas gift, usually a visit back to a distant and forgotten homeland or a meeting with a long-lost son or daughter.

MAGICIAN, THE
US (Paramount) Adventure. ITV 1974–5

Anthony Blake	**Bill Bixby**
Max Pomeroy	**Keene Curtis**
Dennis Pomeroy	**Todd Crespi**
Jerry	**Jim Watkins**
Dominick	**Joseph Sirola**

Executive Producer: **Lawrence Heath**

An illusionist uses his talents to assist the cause of justice.

Conjuror Tony Blake had been wrongfully convicted of a crime early in his life. Bitter about the experience, he had left prison vowing to make sure that the same thing couldn't happen to other innocent people. He aimed to help folk in trouble or under threat, preventing crime wherever he could, making full use of the sleight-of-hand and other illusionary skills he employed in his stage act. His assistants in his crusade were journalist Max Pomeroy (who gave Blake his leads) and Max's wheelchair-bound son, Dennis. Jerry was the pilot of

Blake's private plane, *The Spirit*. Later, the setting switched to the Magic Castle, a Hollywood nightclub where Blake had a residency.

The series received a sporadic screening around the ITV network, after premièring in its native USA in 1973. Actor Bill Bixby performed many of the illusionist's tricks himself.

MAGILL, RONALD

(1920–)

With his mutton-chop sideburns, in his guise of Amos Brearly, Ronald Magill was the distinctive landlord of EMMERDALE FARM's Woolpack for over 17 years. Previously Magill had focused on stage work, with just a handful of TV appearances to his name. These included episodes of the police series, SPECIAL BRANCH, and *Parkin's Patch*. He left *Emmerdale* in 1991, but has made return visits to Beckindale.

MAGNIFICENT EVANS, THE

UK (BBC) Situation Comedy. BBC 1 1984

Plantagenet Evans	**Ronnie Barker**
Rachel	**Sharon Morgan**
Willie	**Dickie Arnold**
Bron	**Myfanwy Talog**
Probert	**William Thomas**
Home Rule O'Toole	**Dyfed Thomas**

Creator/Writer: **Roy Clarke**
Producer: **Sydney Lotterby**

Shameless philandering with a flamboyant Welsh photographer.

Plantagenet Evans, modestly describing himself as a 'genius, photographer and man of letters', was the most colourful character in a sleepy Welsh town. So colourful, in fact, that the local chapel folk openly disapproved. Just one of his many scandalous activities was his relationship with Rachel, a local beauty who, as his fiancée and assistant, had her own apartment at his home/studio, much to the concern of her sister, Bron, and Bron's husband, Probert. While modest Rachel played down their affair, Evans himself, dressed in flowing cape and wide-brimmed hat, never shirked attention. As the local franchise-holder for Scandinavian log stoves and a part-time antiques dealer, he was also a man of many means, devoted to the cause of making money. Bullying Willie, his loyal but silent sidekick, into doing all the donkey work, he paraded around in his vintage motor, leering at girls, defying the local gossips, plying his artistic trade and disparaging his customers. Also seen from time to time was the town's fervent nationalist, Home Rule O'Toole.

MAGNUM PI

US (Universal/Bellisario/Glen A. Larson) Detective Drama.
ITV 1981–7

Thomas Sullivan Magnum	**Tom Selleck**
Jonathan Quayle Higgins III	**John Hillerman**
Theodore 'TC' Calvin	**Roger E. Mosley**
Orville 'Rick' Wright	**Larry Manetti**
Robin Masters	**Orson Welles** (*voice only*)
Mac Reynolds	**Jeff MacKay**
Lt. Maggie Poole	**Jean Bruce Scott**
Lt. Tanaka	**Kwan Hi Lim**
Agatha Chumley	**Gillian Dobb**
Francis Hofstetler ('Ice Pick')	**Elisha Cook, Jr**
Assistant DA Carol Baldwin	**Kathleen Lloyd**

Creators: **Donald P. Bellisario, Glen A. Larson**

A private eye looks after the Hawaiian estate of a mysterious millionaire.

Womanizing Thomas Sullivan Magnum (TS to his friends) was a former naval intelligence officer turned private investigator. He was based on the Hawaiian islands, where his main contract was to protect the estate of writer Robin Masters, who was perpetually away from home and, hence, never seen, only heard. In return, Magnum was provided with luxurious accommodation on the Oahu seafront and the use of his employer's Ferrari. However, all was not plain sailing, thanks to the presence of Jonathan Quayle Higgins III, Masters's crusty English manservant. A former sergeant major, his strict military background jarred with Magnum's easygoing approach to life and, while a professional respect developed over the years, there was always much friction between them. Higgins particularly disliked Magnum's abuse of the millionaire's generosity, but he did have the consolation of knowing that his two Doberman Pinscher guard-dogs, Zeus and Apollo, shared his feelings about the private investigator.

Magnum also took on other assignments, many thrust upon him by Assistant DA Carol Baldwin. For these, he was assisted by two Vietnam veteran colleagues, TC and Rick, but the cases seldom paid their way and Magnum often fouled up. TC ran the Island Hoppers helicopter company, while Rick (real name Orville, which he refused to use) was owner of a bar based on Rick's Café in the film, *Casablanca*. He later moved to the exclusive King Kamehameha Beach Club, in joint ownership with Robin Masters. Rick also had some handy connections in the local underworld, such as the dodgy businessman, Ice Pick.

With the end of the series in sight, the studio shot a two-hour special in which the hero was killed off and went to Heaven. However, the show continued for one more season and so it had to be explained away as a dream. When the finale did eventually come, Magnum rediscovered a lost daughter and rejoined the navy. But a degree of ambiguity veiled the denouement. Robin Masters, it was suggested, was none other than Higgins himself but, as this was never properly confirmed, the audience was left in some doubt.

Magnum PI, most often billed in the UK simply as *Magnum*, used the same production facilities as HAWAII FIVE-O and the scripts often referred to the Five-O police unit and its leader, Steve McGarrett.

MAGNUSSON, MAGNUS
KBE (Hon.) (Magnus Sigursteinnson; 1929–)

Icelandic TV presenter, famous for his 'I've started so I'll finish' role as questionmaster on MASTERMIND. He is also a keen historian and an expert on Viking matters, resulting in series like *Vikings!*, CHRONICLE, *Unsolved Mysteries*, *BC: The Archaeology of the Bible Lands*, *Living Legends* and *The Balloon Game*. His earliest TV work was on TONIGHT, after a journalistic career in Scotland, where he was raised. Magnusson has also worked on Icelandic television. He is the father of news presenter Sally Magnusson.

MAGPIE
UK (Thames) Children's Magazine. ITV 1968–80

Presenters: **Susan Stranks, Pete Brady, Tony Bastable, Douglas Rae, Mick Robertson, Jenny Hanley, Tommy Boyd**

Executive Producer: **Lewis Rudd**
Producers: **Sue Turner, Tony Bastable, David Hodgson, Randal Beattie, Tim Jones, Leslie Burgess**

Lively children's-hour magazine.

Transmitted live twice a week from Thames TV's Teddington studios, *Magpie* was conceived as a rival to the BBC's well-established BLUE PETER. Its trendy trio of presenters, Susan Stranks, Tony Bastable and former Radio 1 DJ Pete Brady, set out to bring kids' TV up to date, with features on pop music (even the theme music was rock-based), fashions and genuinely interesting pastimes. Specialist educational segments like *A Date with Tony* (a regular in-depth look at a historical event), the *ABC of Football*, and items of space news with ITN's Peter Fairley were introduced and, for humour, the zany Captain Fantastic character (David Jason) from DO NOT ADJUST YOUR SET was given a five-minute slot. *Magpie* also had a motor-launch (called *Thames Magpie* – the Thames studios were at the side of Teddington Lock). All this might have been viewed as radical, given the wholesome, almost puritan, fare served up by its BBC competitor, but, having said that, the format of the two programmes was remarkably similar and many ideas were shared.

There were plenty of making and cooking projects, animals featured strongly (*Magpie* had its own pony, Puff) and, each Christmas, *Magpie* annuals accompanied *Blue Peter* books on the newsagents' shelves. Both programmes offered badges as prizes and both organized yearly appeals. *Magpie*, however, offered ten different badges, awarded for various achievements or contributions, and the *Magpie* appeal was subtly different, too. Instead of calling for used paperback books or milk bottle tops, it asked directly for cash, and the totals raised were indicated by a red line that ran around the entire Thames studio complex. Early efforts were modest in their ambitions and were known as *Magpie Sixpence* appeals, kids being asked to donate a tanner ($2\frac{1}{2}$p) out of their pocket money.

However, *Magpie* and *Blue Peter* seemed to grow further apart over the years. While the BBC show seemed firmly rooted in the 1960s, *Magpie* became more 'with it' by the day and enjoyed a far more relaxed studio atmosphere. Captain Fantastic was quickly dropped and new presenters were gradually drafted in. Quiet Scotsman Douglas Rae, mop-haired Mick Robertson, actress Jenny Hanley and disc jockey Tommy Boyd were later recruits. When *Magpie* ended in 1980, Robertson went on to present a similar, leisure-based series entitled *Freetime* (1980–5; 1988).

The *Magpie* name was derived from the old rhyme which featured in the theme music – 'One for sorrow, Two for joy, Three for a girl and Four for a boy, Five for silver, Six for gold, Seven is a secret never to be told. Eight's a wish and Nine a kiss, Ten is a bird you must not miss'. The programme's fat magpie mascot was known as Murgatroyd.

MAID MARIAN AND HER MERRY MEN
UK (BBC) Children's Comedy. BBC 1 1989–90; 1993–4

Maid Marian	**Kate Lonergan**
Robin Hood	**Wayne Morris**
Sheriff of Nottingham	**Tony Robinson**
Barrington	**Danny John-Jules**
Rabies	**Howard Lew Lewis**
Little Ron	**Mike Edmonds**
King John	**Forbes Collins**
Gary	**Mark Billingham**
Graeme	**David Lloyd**

Creator/Writer: **Tony Robinson**
Producer: **Richard Callanan**

Robin Hood with a difference: now Maid Marian is in charge and Robin is a wimp.

This off-beat, award-winning children's comedy, penned by BLACKADDER star Tony Robinson, turned the tales of Sherwood Forest inside out. It cast Robin Hood as an ineffective yuppie figure (known as Robin of Islington) and gave command of the Merry Men to the bold Maid Marian, who egged them on like a school hockey captain. In her ineffective troupe were the midget Little Ron, the Rastafarian Barrington and Rabies. Tony Robinson himself appeared as the Sheriff of Nottingham.

MAIGRET
UK (BBC/Winwell) Police Drama. BBC 1960–3

Chief Insp. Maigret	**Rupert Davies**
Lucas	**Ewen Solon**
Madame Maigret	**Helen Shingler**

Creator: **Georges Simenon**
Executive Producer: **Andrew Osborn**

The investigations of the celebrated French detective.

Hero of some 150 stories by Belgian novelist Georges Simenon, and already played in the cinema by Jean Gabin, Maigret, the Paris detective, reached the TV screen in 1960. Produced not by a French company but by the BBC, whom Simenon had approached because of its reputation for drama, this hugely successful series made a star – if a chronically typecast one – out of Rupert Davies.

Maigret was an officer with the Sûreté, the Parisian equivalent of Scotland Yard. Renowned for his pipe, raincoat and trilby trademarks, like Morse and company over 20 years later, he was a thinking man's detective. He solved cases by analysing the characters and personalities of his suspects, and by visiting them at home, where he could learn more about them, rather than calling them into the sterile atmosphere of his office (where a photograph of his beloved Madame Maigret held pride of place on his desk). In his investigations, he was assisted by a young sidekick, Lucas.

Although it failed as a stage play, and despite a disastrous attempt to film the character (Rupert Davies walked off the set), *Maigret* has lingered pleasantly in viewers' minds. Ron Grainer's theme music and the classic opening sequence, showing Maigret striking a match against a wall to light his pipe, are particularly fondly remembered. Davies returned for a one-off 90-minute production, *Maigret at Bay*, in 1969; Richard Harris took over for an HTV film in 1988; and a new TV adaptation, produced by Granada with Michael Gambon in the lead role and Geoffrey Hutchings as Lucas, ran 1992–3. On this occasion, filming took place in Budapest, rather than Paris (it was cheaper and looked more like 1950s Paris than the real thing).

MAIN CHANCE, THE
UK (Yorkshire) Legal Drama. ITV 1969–72; 1975

David Main .... **John Stride**
Julia Main .... **Kate O'Mara**
Sarah Courtenay/Lady Radchester .... **Anna Palk**
Margaret Castleton .... **Margaret Ashcroft**
Henry Castleton .... **John Wentworth**

Creator/Writer: **Edmund Ward**
Executive Producers: **Peter Willes, David Cunliffe, John Frankau, Derek Bennett**

A successful young lawyer strives to reach the top.

David Main, in his early 30s, was brash, keen and hungry for success. He shopped around for the best cases, hoping to pocket a share of the profitable legal business, and yet also found himself drawn to the defence of the most humble. His impetuosity led him into precarious situations, but his energy and knowledge of the law carried him through. A stickler for efficiency, Main's high-tech office suite boasted all the latest electrical gadgets. Julia, his wife, appeared only in the first series, but his 23-year-old little-rich-girl secretary, Sarah Courtenay, later to become Lady Radchester, stayed with him throughout the show's lengthy run.

MAISIE RAINE
UK (BBC/Fair Game) Police Drama. BBC 1 1998–9

DI Maisie Raine .... **Pauline Quirke**
Chief Supt. Jack Freeman .... **Ian McElhinney**
DCI Susan Askey .... **Anna Patrick**
TI/DC George Kyprianou .... **Steve John Shepherd**
Kelvin Raine .... **Paul Reynolds**
DC Stephen Holmes .... **Brian Bovell**
DC Helen Tomlin .... **Rakie Ayola**
DS Mickey Farrel .... **Richard Graham**
TI Chris Mallory .... **Dean Lennox Kelly**
Joan .... **Stella Moray**

Producers: **Irving Teitelbaum, Ian Scaife**

A no-nonsense female detective finds her methods questioned by her graduate boss.

Allotment-digging widow Maisie Raine was a down-to-earth London copper who had risen through the ranks to the position of detective inspector, answerable to station boss Jack Freeman, an old friend. However, life in the Bessomer Street nick was never straightforward, thanks to her direct superior, Susan Askey, a yuppie-ish fast-track recruit with modern methods. Into the same bracket fell trainee detective George Kyprianou, who initially rubbed Maisie up the wrong way but soon gained her respect, while in the background were the other team members, Holmes, Farrel and Tomlin. Maisie's private life was similarly eventful, as her slightly shifty brother, Kelvin, kept filling her flat with dodgy goods.

Based on the experiences, if not precisely the career, of real-life policewoman Carol Bristow, this series abandoned car chases and sensationalism in favour of the human approach to policing, with Maisie always seeking a reason for a crime and taking time to consider the consequences for all those involved. The second series saw Kyprianou promoted to detective constable, the arrival of a new recruit named Chris Mallory for Maisie to knock into shape, Askey and Kelvin both safely out of Maisie's hair, and a maternal new cleaner, Joan, for our heroine to confide in.

MAJORS, LEE
(Harvey Lee Yeary II; 1940–)

American actor Lee Majors has seldom been short of a prime-time TV role since making his TV debut in 1965. After appearances in series like *The Alfred Hitchcock Hour* and GUNSMOKE, he was cast as Heath Barkley, Barbara Stanwyck's third son, in THE BIG VALLEY. The series ran for four years and, when it ended, Majors quickly moved on to another Western, THE MEN FROM SHILOH. In this revamped version of THE VIRGINIAN he played Roy Tate. A less notable series, *Owen Marshall, Counselor at Law*, followed and then, in 1974, came his biggest role, that of bionic man Colonel Steve Austin in THE SIX MILLION DOLLAR MAN. In 1981 Majors was THE FALL GUY, stuntman Colt Seavers, in a series that ran for five years and for which Majors also sang the theme song. In 1990, he joined the Vietnam drama series, *Tour of Duty* ('Pop' Scarlet), moving on to the martial arts action series, *Raven* (Herman Jablonski, or 'Ski'). He has also appeared in numerous TV movies and was once married to actress Farrah Fawcett.

MAKING OUT
UK (BBC) Comedy Drama. BBC 1 1989–91

Queenie	Margi Clarke
Jill	Melanie Kilburn
Rex	Keith Allen
Carol May	Shirley Stelfox
Stella	Sheila Grier
Pauline	Rachel Davies
Chunky	Brian Hibbard
Norma	Tracie Bennett
Bernie	Alan David
Donna	Heather Tobias
Gordon	Jonathan Barlow
Ray	Tim Dantay
Klepto	Moya Brady
Bella Grout	Deborah Norton
Simon	Gary Beadle
Frankie	John Forgeham
Mr Beachcroft	Don Henderson
Nicky	William Ash
Colin	David Hargreaves
Sharon	Claire Quigley
Gavin	John Lynch
Kip	Tony Haygarth
Rosie	Jane Hazlegrove
Avril	Susan Brown
Maureen	Alexandra Pigg
Dilk	Geoffrey Hughes
Hetty	Pat Mills

Creator: **Franc Roddam**
Writer: **Debbie Horsfield**
Producers: **John Chapman, Carol Wilks**

Ups and downs in the lives of a group of factory workers.

Set in a converted Manchester mill, home of New Lyne Electronics, *Making Out* revolved around the tumultuous lives of the company's shop-floor workers as they battled against bosses, fought with their menfolk and generally tried to make more of their lives. Nominal shop steward was Pauline, but the group's ringleader was the fiery Queenie, whose petty-criminal husband, Chunky, was always looking for a quick buck. Carol May was the lady-like granny who chased sexy boss Rex, well-educated fellow worker Donna longed for a baby and Klepto was a teenage romantic in conflict with her Orthodox Greek family. Then there was Jill, the new girl, who embarked on an affair with Gavin, a Northern Irish Manchester United footballer, while her husband, Ray, became involved with Rosie, a hairdresser. Among the New Lyne bosses were the ineffective Bernie, secretary Norma and chairman Mr Beachcroft. By the time the series ended after three runs, new management had

taken over and the company was known as Shangri-La Electronics. Music for the programme was provided by New Order.

MALAHIDE, PATRICK
(Patrick G. Duggan; 1945–)

Berkshire-born actor/writer featured as DS Chisholm in MINDER, Raymond/Mark Binney/Finney in THE SINGING DETECTIVE and Arthur Starkey in the kids' fantasy, *News at Twelve*. In 1988, he starred in the sci-fi series, *The One Game*, in 1992 he was both the Assistant Commissioner in *The Secret Agent* and Robert Dangerfield in *The Blackheath Poisonings*, and in 1993 he became Inspector Roderick Alleyn in THE INSPECTOR ALLEYN MYSTERIES. He has since played Reverend Edward Casaubon in MIDDLEMARCH and Bailie Creech in *Screen One*'s *Deacon Brodie*. Other credits have included episodes of SHOESTRING, INSPECTOR MORSE, BOON, LOVEJOY, THE RUTH RENDELL MYSTERIES and the *Performance* presentation of *A Doll's House* (Dr Rank). He runs the production company, Ryan Films, and writes under his real name of P. G. Duggan – his works have included the *Screen Two* offering, *Reasonable Force*, and the thriller series, *The Writing on the Wall*.

MALCOLM, MARY
(1918–)

Former radio announcer who became one of the BBC's on-screen continuity announcers after the war. In 1958 she left to go freelance and later worked for German television (making programmes about Britain). Malcolm was the granddaughter of actress Lily Langtry.

MALDEN, KARL
(Karl Mladen Sekulovich; 1914–)

American actor of Yugoslav descent whose television career did not take off until the early 1970s, despite having first appeared on the Broadway stage in the 1930s and in the movies in 1940. It was his role as Det. Lt. Mike Stone in a TV movie called THE STREETS OF SAN FRANCISCO which proved the catalyst, with a full-blown series following and running for five years. Malden has since been seen in numerous TV movies, though a second series of his own, entitled *Skag*, proved to be a flop.

MALLENS, THE
UK (Granada) Drama. ITV 1979–80

Thomas Mallen	John Hallam
Donald Radlet	John Duttine
Dick Mallen	David Rintoul
Jane Radlet	Gillian Lewis
Michael Radlet	John Southworth
Mary Peel	Mary Healey
Barbara Farrington	Pippa Guard

Constance Farrington/Radlet .... **Julia Chambers**
June Ritchie
Anna Brigmore .... **Caroline Blakiston**
Matthew Radlet .... **Ian Saynor**
Barbara Mallen .... **Juliet Stevenson**
Michael Radlet .... **Gerry Sundquist**

Writer: **Jack Russell**
Producer: **Roy Roberts**

A rogue Victorian squire is the father of numerous bastard children.

Ruthless Thomas Mallen was the lord of High Banks Hall, set amid the Northumberland moors (filming actually took place in Dovedale, Derbyshire). Living with his weak-willed gambler son Dick, he was a man with scant regard for women and, having lusted and raped most of his life, was now the father of several illegitimate sons, all easily identified by the trademark Mallen white streak in their hair. As the feuding children began to emerge from the woodwork, and his fortunes became intertwined with the Radlet family of Wolfbur Farm, so Thomas's troubles increased. He eventually moved in with his nieces, Barbara and Constance Farrington, and their governess (soon to be his latest lover), Anna Brigmore.

The first seven episodes were based on the novels *The Mallen Litter* and *The Mallen Streak* by Catherine Cookson. These were followed by a second series (entitled *Catherine Cookson's The Mallens*) which focused on Barbara Mallen (the illegitimate, deaf daughter of Thomas and Barbara Farrington) and her lover, Michael Radlet (the illegitimate son of Constance). These episodes were derived from another Cookson novel, *The Mallen Girl*.

MAN ABOUT THE HOUSE
UK (Thames) Situation Comedy. ITV 1973–6

Robin Tripp .... **Richard O'Sullivan**
Chrissy Plummer .... **Paula Wilcox**
Jo .... **Sally Thomsett**
George Roper .... **Brian Murphy**
Mildred Roper .... **Yootha Joyce**
Larry Simmons .... **Doug Fisher**

Creators/Writers: **Johnnie Mortimer, Brian Cooke**
Producer: **Peter Frazer-Jones**

Two girls and a boy share a flat at a time when co-habitation was a novelty.

Needing a third sharer to help pay the rent on their Earl's Court flat, two young, attractive girls, the dark-haired Chrissy and the blonde, toothy Jo, had planned to find another girl. But when Robin Tripp, a catering student, was found sleeping in the bath the morning after a party, they decided to let him move in, especially as he could cook. The new arrangement understandably raised a few eyebrows, particularly with the girls' landlords, George and Mildred Roper, who lived downstairs.

Although there was much mock-sexual bravado, this *ménage à trois* was definitely not of the murky kind, despite Robin's attempts to bed the far too sensible Chrissy. The well-signalled humour came from domestic squabbles (like hogging the bathroom), their respective boyfriends/girlfriends, and Robin and Chrissy's attempts to follow Jo's weird logic. There were also nosy interruptions from the Ropers, he a work-shy weakling, she a man-devouring social climber with an eye on young Robin.

Two spin-offs followed: ROBIN'S NEST, in which Robin opened his own bistro, and GEORGE AND MILDRED, following the Ropers' new life on a middle-class housing estate. The series also spawned a feature film of the same title and was translated for American audiences in a less subtle version called *Three's Company*.

MAN ALIVE
UK (BBC) Current Affairs. BBC 2 1965–82

Producer: **Michael Latham**

Social pains and pleasures examined through the lives of ordinary people.

This long-running documentary series took an interest in the problems and sometimes the happier experiences of ordinary citizens, tackling awkward and difficult subjects in the process. Each film focused on one topic, which could be as varied as agoraphobia and child molesting. Its production team, originally headed by Michael Latham, comprised such notables as Desmond Wilcox, Trevor Philpott, Esther Rantzen, John Pitman and Harold Williamson. Variations on the theme included *The Man Alive Report* in 1976 and *The Man Alive Debate* in 1982.

MAN AT THE TOP
UK (Thames) Drama. ITV 1970–2

Joe Lampton .... **Kenneth Haigh**
Susan Lampton .... **Zena Walker**
Margaret Brown .... **Avice Landon**

Creator: **John Braine**
Producers: **George Markstein, Lloyd Shirley, Jacqueline Davis**

An unscrupulous businessman fights to stay ahead of the game.

Picking up the story told in John Braine's novel, *Room at the Top*, and the 1958 Laurence Harvey film of the same name (plus its 1965 sequel, *Life at the Top*), *Man at the Top* concerned Joe Lampton, a pushy, aggressive northerner who had battled his way up the ladder to relative prosperity. Thirteen years on, Lampton now lived in Surrey's stockbroker belt, working as a management consultant. He was determined to stay there and was prepared to pull any stroke to do so. He was also keen on pulling women, as his wife, Susan, was only too aware. In 1973 the series spawned a feature film of its own, also called *Man at the Top* and starring Kenneth Haigh.

MAN CALLED IRONSIDE, A
US (Harbour/Universal) Police Drama. BBC 1 1967–76

Chief Robert T. Ironside	**Raymond Burr**
DS Ed Brown	**Don Galloway**
Officer Eve Whitfield	**Barbara Anderson**
Mark Sanger	**Don Mitchell**
Officer Fran Belding	**Elizabeth Baur**
Commissioner Dennis Randall	**Gene Lyons**
Lt. Carl Reese	**Johnny Seven**
Diana Sanger	**Joan Pringle**

Creator: **Collier Young**
Executive Producers: **Joel Rogosin, Cy Chermak**

A wheelchair-bound cop still gets his man.

Raymond Burr followed up his enormously successful PERRY MASON role with this series about a top detective who faced early retirement after receiving a crippling injury. Robert T. Ironside had been Chief of Detectives in the San Francisco Police Department, but his career was placed on the line when, at the age of 46, he was badly injured by a bullet from a would-be assassin. He was expected to quit the force but, although confined to a wheelchair, he persuaded his superior, Commissioner Randall, to allow him to stay on in a consultative capacity.

So it was that, paralysed from the waist down, the grouchy Ironside was still able to put his 25 years of experience to good use. Living and working from a converted attic above the police department, he travelled to the scenes of crime in a modified police van, assisted and minded by Mark Sanger. Sanger had been a juvenile delinquent, a street rebel, but he mellowed so much during the series that he had even graduated from law school before it ended. Two other colleagues, Sgt Ed Brown and policewoman Eve Whitfield, helped put Ironside's ideas into action, with Eve replaced after a few seasons by new policewoman Fran Belding. In America, the show was known simply as *Ironside*. In the UK, some episodes aired under the umbrella title of *The Detectives*.

MAN CALLED SHENANDOAH, A
US (MGM) Western. ITV 1966–7

Shenandoah	**Robert Horton**

Creator/Executive Producer: **E. Jack Neuman**
Producer: **Fred Freiberger**

A cowboy with amnesia wanders the Wild West looking for his true identity.

Some time after the American Civil War ended, a man wounded in a gunfight was found by two buffalo-hunters, who took him to the nearest town in the hope of claiming a bounty. As it happened, he was not on the wanted list, but no one actually knew who he was. He recovered but continued to suffer from memory loss. He adopted the name of Shenandoah and set out to find his real self. Drifting from town to town, he searched in vain for clues that would help him discover his identity. Fortunately, star Robert Horton was no stranger to travelling the prairies, having previously appeared in WAGON TRAIN. The series was screened in its native USA from 1965, but was shown only sporadically around the ITV network in the UK.

MAN FROM ATLANTIS
US (Solow) Science Fiction. ITV 1977–8

Mark Harris	**Patrick Duffy**
Dr Elizabeth Merrill	**Belinda J. Montgomery**
C. W. Crawford	**Alan Fudge**
Mr Schubert	**Victor Buono**
Brent	**Robert Lussier**

Executive Producer: **Herbert F. Solow**
Producer: **Herman Miller**

An underwater man works for the secret services.

When a half-man, half-fish was washed up on the California shore, it was believed that he was the last survivor of the lost continent of Atlantis. Nursed back to health by naval doctor Elizabeth Merrill, Mark Harris (as she christened him) stayed on to work with her and the Foundation for Oceanic Research in their efforts to learn more about the seas. He was also employed by the US Government to help combat marine crime (and, on occasion, even space aliens).

Green-eyed Mark looked human but benefited from extra-sharp senses and superhuman strength. His webbed feet and hands allowed him to swim faster than a dolphin. He also had gill tissue instead of lungs, which forced him to return to the sea to breathe every 12 hours. Mark and Elizabeth used a submersible known as the *Cetacean* on their sea patrols and worked for Foundation head C. W. Crawford. Their biggest adversaries were the mad scientist, Mr Schubert, and his inept sidekick, Brent.

MAN FROM INTERPOL, THE
UK (Danziger) Police Drama. ITV 1960–1

Commander Anthony Smith	**Richard Wyler**
Supt. Mercer	**John Longden**

Producers: **Edward J. Danziger, Harry Lee Danziger**

The cases of a top Interpol agent.

Anthony Smith was one of Interpol's leading men. His investigations took him all around the world, tracking down international criminals and, occasionally, spies. He specialized in cases where crime crossed national borders, pursuing his targets from country to country. The low-budget productions have gained a reputation for being somewhat unexciting.

MAN FROM UNCLE, THE
US (MGM/Arena) Secret Agent Drama. BBC 1 1965–8

Napoleon Solo	**Robert Vaughn**

Illya Kuryakin .... **David McCallum**
Mr Alexander Waverly .... **Leo G. Carroll**
Lisa Rogers .... **Barbara Moore**

Creators: **Norman Felton, Sam Rolfe**
Executive Producer: **Norman Felton**

*The counter-conspiracy assignments of a secret
agent and his partner.*

The 'Man from UNCLE' was Napoleon Solo, a suave, relaxed American agent working for an undercover, international, anti-crime organization. UNCLE stood for United Network Command for Law and Enforcement, and head of its agents was elderly Englishman Alexander Waverly. Solo was accompanied on most of his missions by Illya Kuryakin, a sullen blond Russian. Their efforts chiefly centred on foiling the ambitious plans of THRUSH, an eccentric global crime syndicate. Each episode was entitled '*The . . . Affair*' (fill in the blank as appropriate).

UNCLE headquarters was located in Manhattan, with a secret entrance behind the Del Floria tailor's shop. Agents entered the shop and the tailor lifted a clothes press to open a hidden door in a changing cubicle. Once inside, the agents donned special triangular badges to allow them to pass through the corridors of the office. Each agent had his own numbered badge: Solo's was 11, Waverly's 1 and Kuryakin's 2. Solo and Kuryakin never went into action without their collection of electronic gadgetry, including two-way radios concealed in fountain pens. 'Open Channel D' paved the way for a message back to HQ. Yet, for all this technology, the pair constantly required help from ordinary civilians (often a beautiful girl falling for Solo's charms) in achieving their goals.

The Man from UNCLE came to TV on the back of the James Bond craze. The name Napoleon Solo was actually borrowed from a gangster in *Goldfinger*, and producer Norman Felton consulted Bond author Ian Fleming before developing the series. Catching the secret agent wave, *The Man from UNCLE* was, all the same, played with tongues firmly in cheeks (more so even than the Bond originals). However, a couple of years later, following criticism of its spoofiness, the series was firmed up, and a new character, that of Mr Waverly's secretary, Lisa Rogers, was introduced. The show also spawned a spin-off, THE GIRL FROM UNCLE (with which it alternated weekly in the UK), and a series of eight full-length movies, collated from the TV footage.

The acronym 'UNCLE' was given its meaning only after the series had started, in response to viewers' requests for an explanation of the letters. THRUSH was never spelt out.

MAN IN A SUITCASE
UK (ITC) Detective Drama. ITV 1967–8

McGill .... **Richard Bradford**

Creators: **Richard Harris, Dennis Spooner**
Producer: **Sidney Cole**

A discredited CIA agent turns to detective work.

McGill was a grim, tough man of few words. A former US intelligence agent, he had been wrongly accused of allowing a top scientist to defect to the USSR. Framed and sacrificed in the name of international diplomacy, he had been dismissed from his post, his reputation in tatters. With only a battered suitcase and a gun to his name, he now operated as a private detective and bounty-hunter in Britain and on the Continent, never relenting in his search for the evidence which would clear his name.

McGill (whose first name was supposedly John but was never used) charged $500 a day (plus expenses) for his work, although he was sometimes cheated by shady employers. Having a dodgy past himself, and lacking friends in authority, there was very little he could do about it. And that was not the only complication. His former CIA colleagues were always lurking in the background, blackmailing him into doing jobs or threatening to drop him in it at any moment.

MAN IN ROOM 17, THE
UK (Granada) Detective Drama. ITV 1965–6

Oldenshaw .... **Richard Vernon**
Dimmock .... **Michael Aldridge**
Imlac Defraits .... **Denholm Elliott**
Sir Geoffrey Norton .... **Willoughby Goddard**

Creator: **Robin Chapman**
Producer: **Richard Everitt**

*Two top criminologists solve the most baffling
crimes without even leaving their room.*

Room 17, based near the Houses of Parliament, had been set up by the Government to house the Department of Social Research, a secret unit for investigating the criminal mind. The actual 'Man' was Oldenshaw, a barrister, ex-war correspondent and crime specialist, who recruited as his partner the younger Dimmock, a former student of the Ohio University Institute of Criminology. Together the two men out-thought the most experienced police and counter-intelligence brains in the country. If Scotland Yard or the Government found themselves in need of assistance, they called upon this far-from-dynamic duo, whose brain power always delivered the goods. Civil servant Sir Geoffrey Norton was their link with the outside world.

In the second season, Dimmock was replaced by a new specialist, Defraits, but the original pairing were reunited when a follow-up series, THE FELLOWS, came to the screen. To firmly detach the 'Men' and their cerebral work from the nitty-gritty of street detection, two film crews with different directors were employed. One handled the scenes inside the Room, the other the rest of the action.

MAN OF THE WORLD
UK (ATV) Adventure. ITV 1962–3

Mike Strait .... **Craig Stevens**
Maggie .... **Tracey Reed**
Hank .... **Graham Stark**

Producer: **Harry Fine**

The adventurous life of a globe-trotting photo-journalist.

American Mike Strait enjoyed a glamorous lifestyle. His freelance assignments (mostly for fashion magazines) took him to the four corners of the world. However, instead of merely photographing or reporting his story, Strait unfailingly became involved in the action, finding himself up to his neck in murder, blackmail, espionage and intrigue of all kinds. *Man of the World* gave rise to a spin-off series, THE SENTIMENTAL AGENT, drawn from an episode of the same title, in which Carlos Thompson played the part of import-export agent Carlos Varela.

MANHUNT
UK (LWT) Drama. ITV 1970

Jimmy Porter .... **Alfred Lynch**
Vincent .... **Peter Barkworth**
Nina .... **Cyd Hayman**
Adelaide .... **Maggie Fitzgibbon**
Abwehr Sgt Gratz .... **Robert Hardy**
Lutzig .... **Philip Madoc**

Creator/Executive Producer: **Rex Firkin**
Producer: **Andrew Brown**

Heroic tales of French Resistance activity during World War II.

Using Beethoven's Fifth Symphony as its theme tune (echoing its use as a wartime code by the Allies), *Manhunt* told of the daring exploits of Resistance workers who sought to sabotage German activities and smuggle stranded airmen or vital supplies to Britain from occupied France. The principals were agents Vincent and Nina, plus downed RAF pilot Jimmy. Together, they were on the run from the Nazis, headed by Abwehr Sgt Gratz. Fear, conscience, loyalty and suspicion competed for control of their minds, and a tense atmosphere pervaded all 26 episodes.

MANNIX
US (Paramount) Detective Drama. ITV 1968–76

Joe Mannix .... **Mike Connors**
Lou Wickersham .... **Joseph Campanella**
Peggy Fair .... **Gail Fisher**
Lt. Adam Tobias .... **Robert Reed**
Lt. George Kramer .... **Larry Linville**
Lt. Art Malcolm .... **Ward Wood**

Creators: **Richard Levinson, William Link**

Executive Producer: **Bruce Geller**
Producers: **Ivan Goff, Ben Roberts**

A private eye prefers fists to computers when trying to get results.

Joe Mannix worked for Lou Wickersham, head of an enterprising, high-tech Los Angeles detective firm known as Intertect. Despite being equipped with the latest crime-prevention technology (including a car computer that transmitted and received photographs and fingerprints of the suspects), Mannix was more at home using the tried and tested combination of his own detective nous and the good, old-fashioned knuckle sandwich.

After leaving Intertect he became his own boss, setting up a detective agency on the first floor of his apartment block at 17 Paseo Verdes in West LA, and employing widow Peggy Fair as his personal assistant. Her husband (a police officer and a friend of Mannix's) had been killed in action and she turned out to be more than just a secretary herself, lending a hand in investigations and often being held hostage for her pains. Several LA cops also chipped in from time to time, most notably Lieutenants Adam Tobias, Art Malcolm and George Kramer (the last played by the late Larry Linville, better known as Frank Burns in M*A*S*H).

MARCHANT, TONY

British dramatist whose most acclaimed work has included *Take Me Home*, *Goodbye Cruel World*, *Into the Fire*, *Great Expectations* and *Never, Never*.

MARCUS WELBY, MD
US (Universal) Medical Drama. ITV 1969–77

Dr Marcus Welby .... **Robert Young**
Dr Steven Kiley .... **James Brolin**
Consuelo Lopez .... **Elena Verdugo**
Myra Sherwood .... **Anne Baxter**
Kathleen Faverty .... **Sharon Gless**
Janet Blake/Kiley .... **Pamela Hensley**

Creator/Executive Producer: **David Victor**

Doctors-and-patients drama, a kind of DR KILDARE *or* BEN CASEY *in reverse.*

Thoroughly dedicated, silver-haired GP Marcus Welby ran a practice from his home in Santa Monica, California. After suffering a heart attack, he was forced to take on a younger doctor to help with the workload. That younger man was Steven Kiley, a motorcycling student neurologist. He signed up for a year's experience but never left. Unlike previous medical dramas, in which revered old docs had to keep young hothead physicians in check, this series turned the youngster into the level-headed one and made the older man a bit of a maverick. Kind, reassuring Welby employed an unusual technique in dealing with sickness. He believed in treating the whole patient, not just the precise ailment, convinced that psychological and other factors had some bearing in each case. This was all new to the outspoken Kiley, who played it by the book.

Both men led a bachelor existence, though there was a romantic liaison early on for Welby in the form of Myra Sherwood, and Kiley eventually married Janet Blake, a PR director at the local Hope Memorial Hospital. Other cast regulars were nurses Consuelo Lopez and Kathleen Faverty (the latter played by Sharon Gless, later famous as Chris Cagney in CAGNEY AND LACEY).

MARINE BOY
Japan (Japan Telecartoons/Seven Arts) Cartoon. BBC 1
1969–70

Voices:

Marine Boy	Corinne Orr
Dr Mariner	Jack Curtis
Bulton	Peter Fernandez
Piper	Jack Grimes
Neptina	Corinne Orr
Cli Cli	Corinne Orr

Producer: **Hinoru Adachi**

The adventures of a young aquatic hero.

Marine Boy was the son of Dr Mariner, head of Ocean Patrol, an international body dedicated to preserving peace beneath the waves. But Marine Boy was also one of the organization's top agents. Diving into danger, he battled it out with a host of sea foes, including Captain Kidd and Dr Slime, keeping his air-supply alive by chewing Oxygum, a revolutionary oxygen-generating bubblegum. This amazing gum had been invented by oceanographer Dr Fumble, who also created Marine Boy's other gadgets, which included an electric boomerang, a bullet-proof wetsuit and jet-propelled flying boots. Assisting our hero were Bulton and Piper, his colleagues in the flying submarine known as the P-1, as well as a pet white dolphin called Splasher, a fishy friend called Cli Cli and a mermaid, Neptina (possessor of a magic pearl).

MARK SABER/SABER OF LONDON
UK (Danziger) Detective Drama. ITV 1957–9/1959–61

Mark Saber	Donald Gray
Barny O'Keefe	Michael Balfour
Judy	Teresa Thorne
Stephanie Ames	Diana Decker
Peter Paulson	Neil McCallum
	Gordon Tanner
Bob Page	Robert Arden
Eddie Wells	Jerry Thorne
Ann Summers	Jennifer Jayne
Insp. Brady	Patrick Holt
Insp. Chester/Parker	Colin Tapley

Producers: **Edward J. Danziger, Harry Lee Danziger**

The cases of a one-armed Scotland Yard detective turned private eye.

Mark Saber has had a chequered TV history. The character first reached the small screen in the USA as a British detective in the New York Police Department (in series entitled *Mystery Theatre* and *Inspector Mark Saber – Homicide Squad*, both with Tom Conway in the title role). However, when he came to Britain in a production called simply *Mark Saber*, things had changed considerably. For a start he only had one arm! He now worked as a private detective, supported by sidekick Barny O'Keefe, briefly by a girl named Judy and by his blonde secretary, Stephanie Ames. Two police officers were also prominent, Inspectors Chester and Brady. This series was retitled *The Vise* for US consumption.

To add to the confusion, after a couple of years the concept was reworked yet again, with the title switched to *Saber of London* and our hero now undertaking assignments on the Continent. O'Keefe was replaced by Canadian Pete Paulson, who was in turn replaced by Bob Page and then by Eddie Wells, a reformed crook. Ann Summers was introduced as Saber's girlfriend.

The programme's star, Donald Gray, was a former BBC announcer who had lost an arm in World War II. He later provided the voice for Colonel White in CAPTAIN SCARLET AND THE MYSTERONS.

MARKET IN HONEY LANE/ HONEY LANE
UK (ATV) Drama. ITV 1967–9

Billy Bush	John Bennett
Sam English	Michael Golden
Dave Sampson	Ray Lonnen
Mike Sampson	Iain Gregory
Jacko Bennet	Peter Birrel
Jimmy Bentall	Jack Bligh
Polly Jessel	Pat Nye
Danny Jessel	Brian Rawlinson
Harry Jolson	Ivor Salter
Gervase Lorrimer	Gabriel Woolf
Carol Frazer	Veronica Hurst
Al Dowman	Derren Nesbitt
Tom Mount	Michael Ripper
Alf Noble	James Culliford
Stella Noble	Patricia Denys
Dawn	Julie Samuel

Creator: **Louis Marks**
Producer: **John Cooper**

Events in the lives of London market stall-holders.

Set in London's East End, *Market in Honey Lane* challenged CORONATION STREET's supremacy in the ratings for a while. It focused on the vibrant Cockney workers at the fictitious Honey Lane market, with a different character highlighted in each episode. The protagonists included fruit-and-veg merchant Billy Bush and the mother and son duo of Polly and Danny Jessel. In September 1968 the title was shortened to *Honey Lane* and transmission was switched to afternoons. The series was cancelled a year later.

The programme was staged and recorded at ATV's Elstree studios. When the BBC took over Elstree, it, too, produced a drama series centred chiefly around London market folk. EASTENDERS, however, has been considerably more resilient than its 1960s predecessor.

MARKS, ALFRED
OBE (1921–96)

London-born comedian and comic actor, big in the 1950s and 1960s through series like *Don't Look Now*, *Alfred Marks Time* and SUNDAY NIGHT AT THE LONDON PALLADIUM (which he compered). He was Charlie, the fire chief, in the farce, FIRE CRACKERS, in 1964 and starred as Albert Hackett in another sitcom, *Albert and Victoria*, in 1970. Marks was also a regular on panel games and appeared in the dramas, *Paris 1900*, *Funny Man* and *Maybury*. One of his last appearances came in *The All New Alexei Sayle Show*.

MARKS, LAURENCE
(1948–)
See GRAN, MAURICE.

MARKS, LOUIS
(1928–)

British writer, script editor and producer, working prominently on science fiction and thriller series like DOCTOR WHO, *Dead of Night* and DOOMWATCH, and the soap, MARKET IN HONEY LANE (which he created). He has also produced a number of other single and serial dramas, such as *The Lost Boys*, *Bavarian Night*, *The Trial*, *Silas Marner*, MIDDLEMARCH and *Plotlands*.

MARLOWE – PRIVATE EYE
See PHILIP MARLOWE.

MARRIAGE LINES, THE
UK (BBC) Situation Comedy. BBC 1 1963–6

George Starling	**Richard Briers**
Kate Starling	**Prunella Scales**
Peter	**Ronald Hines**
Norah	**Christine Finn**

Creator/Writer: **Richard Waring**
Producers: **Graeme Muir, Robin Nash**

The highs and lows of newly-wed life.

Recently married George and Kate Starling lived in a flat in Earl's Court. George worked in the City as a lowly paid clerk and Kate had been his secretary, but, in keeping with the mood of the times, she now stayed at home. This series focused on their domestic and financial problems, with their compatibility severely tested by endless petty rows that usually saw George heading for the pub. Two neighbours, Peter and Norah, were around for the first season, before they moved away and up market, leaving the Starlings depressingly stuck on the first rung of the property ladder. Kate later gave birth to a baby daughter, Helen, whom George described as 'The Cuckoo', because her presence added to his domestic duties and interfered with his already restricted social life.

The Marriage Lines was specifically created by writer Richard Waring for the talents of young Richard Briers, who had appeared with him in BROTHERS IN LAW.

MARSDEN, ROY
(Roy Mould; 1941–)

British actor now best known as detective Adam Dalgliesh in the P. D. JAMES mysteries. Previously, Marsden played George Osborne in the BBC's 1972 version of *Vanity Fair*, Neil Burnside in THE SANDBAGGERS, Jack Ruskin in AIRLINE, Charles Edward Chipping, the eponymous hero of another BBC adaptation, *Goodbye Mr Chips*, and Blick in FRANK STUBBS. He also appeared in the series of dramatic reconstructions of real events, *Against All Odds*, and played Sir William Boyd-Templeton in *Dangerous Lady*. Marsden was once married to *Airline* co-star Polly Hemingway and is the brother of actor/director Michael Mould.

MARSH, JEAN
(1934–)

English actress, best remembered as parlourmaid Rose in UPSTAIRS, DOWNSTAIRS, a series she created with Eileen Atkins in 1971. Twenty years later, Marsh and Atkins also devised THE HOUSE OF ELIOTT. On screen, Marsh has also been seen in the TV version of the film, *9 to 5*, playing Roz Keith, in the Sidney Sheldon drama, *Master of the Game* (Mrs Talley), the *Screen One* adaptation of *Adam Bede* (Lisbeth Bede) and *The All New Alexei Sayle Show*, as well as starring as Rosie Tindall in the short-lived sitcom, *No Strings*. She was an early guest in DOCTOR WHO (Sara Kingdom) and appeared in other 1960s series such as *Blackmail* and THE INFORMER (Sylvia Parrish). Marsh was once married to actor Jon Pertwee.

MARSH, REGINALD
(1926–2001)

London-born actor, often in sitcoms as someone's boss. Marsh appeared in CORONATION STREET (Dave Smith), GEORGE AND MILDRED (Mildred's brother-in-law, Humphrey), with Harry Worth in HERE'S HARRY and *My Name Is Harry Worth*, and with Les Dawson in *The Loner*. Among his many other credits were CROSSROADS, THE PLANE MAKERS, THE POWER GAME, *The Handy Gang*, *The Old Campaigner* ('LB'), *How's Your Father* (Mr Winterbottom), *Never Say Die* (Mr Hebden), THE RATCATCHERS, BLESS THIS HOUSE, TERRY AND JUNE (Sir Dennis Hodge), THE GOOD LIFE ('Sir'), CROWN COURT, WHODUNNIT?,

BARLOW, THE SWEENEY, *Searching* (Chancy's dad) and *Help!*. He also starred in Joe Orton's play, *The Erpingham Camp*, and in Nigel Kneale's *The Stone Tape*, as well as his own drama, *The Man Who Came to Die*.

MARSHALL, ANDREW
(1954–)

British comedy writer, for many years in collaboration with David Renwick. Together they worked on BBC Radio before moving into television and providing scripts for NOT THE NINE O'CLOCK NEWS, *Russ Abbot's Madhouse*, *Alexei Sayle's Stuff*, *There's a Lot of It About*, *The Steam Video Company* and *The Kenny Everett Television Show*, as well as creating *End of Part One*, WHOOPS APOCA-LYPSE and HOT METAL. While Renwick has since scored solo with ONE FOOT IN THE GRAVE and JONATHAN CREEK, Marshall has developed *Sob Sisters*, 2 POINT 4 CHILDREN, *Health and Efficiency* and *Dad*. They joined forces again in 1993 for the Richard Briers comedy, *If You See God Tell Him*.

MARSHALL, GARRY K.
(Gary Masciarelli; 1934–)

American writer, director and producer with a string of TV hits behind him and now active in the cinema. After working as a writer on THE DICK VAN DYKE SHOW and THE LUCY SHOW in the 1960s, Marshall went on to greater things in the 1970s, producing THE ODD COUPLE, then creating and producing series like HAPPY DAYS and its spin-offs, LAVERNE AND SHIRLEY, MORK AND MINDY and *Joanie Loves Chachi*, plus *Makin' It* and the poorly received *Me and the Chimp*. He is the brother of actress/director Penny Marshall, who appeared in *The Odd Couple* and *Laverne and Shirley* (Laverne).

MARTIN, DAVE
(1935–) See BAKER, BOB.

MARTIN, DICK
(1923–)

American comedian, the writing and performing part-ner of Dan Rowan from 1952. A stand-in spot for Dean Martin in the summer of 1966 proved to be their big break. As a result, they were given their own gag-and-sketch show, LAUGH-IN, which became a massive inter-national hit. Martin (the dumb one) had earlier been seen in THE LUCY SHOW, playing Lucy's friend, Harry Conners, and, post-*Laugh-in*, he made guest appearances in series like THE LOVE BOAT as well as involving himself in production. Rowan decided upon retirement when *Laugh-in* ended after five years, but died in 1987.

MARTIN, IAN KENNEDY
(1936–)

British screenwriter, usually on crime series, and the creator of THE SWEENEY, JULIET BRAVO, THE CHINESE DETECTIVE and *King and Castle*. Among his other writing credits have been episodes of THE TROUBLESHOOTERS, *This Man Craig*, *Parkin's Patch*, COLDITZ, THE ONEDIN LINE and *Madson*. He was also story editor of REDCAP and is the brother of fellow writer Troy Kennedy Martin.

MARTIN KANE, PRIVATE INVESTIGATOR
UK (Towers of London/ABC) Detective Drama. ITV 1957–8

Martin Kane .... **William Gargan**
Supt. Page .... **Brian Reece**

Producer: **Harry Alan Towers**

An American private eye moves to London.

Martin Kane had been an investigator in New York City. Now taking up residence in England, he brought his transatlantic talents to bear in the capture of British and European criminals, working closely with Supt. Page of Scotland Yard. Although this odd combination of wise-cracking gumshoe and staid English copper rarely strayed outside the office, they still got results.

William Gargan had been the first actor to portray Kane on US television and radio at the turn of the 1950s, and had himself been a private investigator before turn-ing to the stage. He didn't stay with the show for the whole of its US run (three other Martin Kanes – Lloyd Nolan, Lee Tracy and Mark Stevens – were introduced) but, being the original and best, he was brought back for this British version. Ironically, considering the American series had been sponsored by a tobacco company, Gar-gan later underwent surgery for throat cancer and sub-sequently dedicated his life to warning others about the dangers of smoking. He died in 1979. The real Martin Kane had not been a detective at all, but was an advertis-ing executive for the J. Walter Thompson agency, pro-ducers of the American version.

MARTIN, MILLICENT
(1934–)

Essex-born singer seen as a guest on numerous variety and comedy shows (including with Morecambe and Wise) but chiefly remembered for her contributions (and particularly her topical intros) to THAT WAS THE WEEK THAT WAS. She was later given her own series, *Mainly Millicent*, *Millicent* and *The Millicent Martin Show*, and starred as stewardess Millie Grover in the airline sitcom, *From a Bird's Eye View*. She returned to UK TV in 1992, starring as clairvoyant Gladys Moon in the thriller series, *Moon and Son*, and made a prominent cameo appearance as Daphne's mum in FRASIER several years later. Her first husband was singer Ronnie Carroll and her second actor Norman Eshley.

MARTIN, QUINN
(Martin Cohn; 1922–87)

American producer, initially with Desilu, for whom he produced THE UNTOUCHABLES. Branching out on his own, Martin founded QM Productions and was responsible for some of the biggest hits of the 1960s and 1970s, including THE FUGITIVE, THE FBI, THE INVADERS, CANNON, DAN AUGUST, *Most Wanted*, THE STREETS OF SAN FRANCISCO and BARNABY JONES.

MARTIN, TROY KENNEDY
(1932–)

British writer, the creator of Z CARS, although he left after three months, allegedly concerned at the direction the series was taking. He did, however, return to write the last episode. Among his other notable credits have been *Diary of a Young Man* (with John McGrath), REILLY – ACE OF SPIES, the acclaimed EDGE OF DARKNESS, *The Fourth Floor*, *The Old Men at the Zoo* and episodes of OUT OF THE UNKNOWN, COLDITZ and THE SWEENEY. Martin has also worked as a writer in Hollywood. He is the brother of writer Ian Kennedy Martin.

MARY TYLER MOORE SHOW, THE
US (MTM) Situation Comedy. BBC 1 1971–2

Mary Richards .... **Mary Tyler Moore**
Lou Grant .... **Edward Asner**
Ted Baxter .... **Ted Knight**
Murray Slaughter .... **Gavin MacLeod**
Rhoda Morgenstern .... **Valerie Harper**
Phyllis Lindstrom .... **Cloris Leachman**
Bess Lindstrom .... **Lisa Gerritsen**
Gordon 'Gordy' Howard .... **John Amos**
Georgette Franklin/Baxter .... **Georgia Engel**
Sue Ann Nivens .... **Betty White**

Creators/Writers/Executive Producers: **James L. Brooks, Allan Burns**
Producers: **Ed Weinberger, Stan Daniels**

Life at work and at home with an independent single girl.

This award-winning sitcom was set in the newsroom of a fictitious Minneapolis TV station, WJM-TV, Channel 12, and focused on the working and domestic lives of Mary Richards, the assistant producer of its news programme. Mary, single, friendly, level-headed and very genuine, was also independently minded, a sensible career woman of the 1970s. She arrived at WJM-TV following a break-up with her boyfriend. Her boss at the station was Lou Grant, the blustering news producer, with other staff members including the chief newswriter, Murray Slaughter, weatherman Gordy Howard, and Ted Baxter, the dim, conceited anchorman. The

newsroom was a real family, even if it was the worst TV news set-up in America.

Mary's best friend was window-dresser Rhoda Morgenstern, a girl far more in fear of being left on the shelf than Mary. She was eventually written out into her own series, RHODA. Another spin-off was *Phyllis*, based around Mary's highly strung, nosey landlady, Phyllis Lindstrom, who moved to San Francisco with her daughter, Bess, after the death of her never-seen husband, Lars. A later addition to the cast was Sue Ann Nivens, the man-eating hostess of the station's *Happy Homemaker Show*.

When Mary Tyler Moore decided to call it a day, the series was concluded by introducing new management who sacked virtually all the staff. Only bumbling newsreader Ted kept his job. Lou Grant was another survivor, moving on to Los Angeles and his own drama series, LOU GRANT. After success in the 1960s as Laura Petrie in THE DICK VAN DYKE SHOW, Mary Tyler Moore confirmed her star status with this role. Not only that, but the programme established her powerful MTM production company and provided valuable early experience for the creators and performers of many top sitcoms of the 1980s (including producer James L. Brooks, the brains behind TAXI and THE SIMPSONS).

MASCHWITZ, ERIC
OBE (1901–69)

Versatile British light entertainment producer, with the BBC from 1926 and holding various posts, including Editor of *Radio Times*, Head of Light Entertainment (1958–61) and Assistant and Adviser to Controller of Television Programmes (1961–3). Maschwitz also worked as a novelist, writing thrillers with Val Gielgud (Sir John's brother) under the pen-name of Holt Marvell. He was an accomplished dramatist and, wearing his lyricist's hat, wrote the words to the songs 'These Foolish Things' and 'A Nightingale Sang in Berkeley Square'. Away from the BBC, he worked for MGM in Hollywood, on films like *Goodbye Mr Chips*, before surprisingly returning to the Corporation in 1958. Those who thought he was of the wrong generation for the new era were quickly proved wrong when he commissioned, among other successes, JUKE BOX JURY, THE BLACK AND WHITE MINSTREL SHOW, WHACK-O! and STEPTOE AND SON. He left the BBC for Associated-Rediffusion in 1963, where he became producer of special projects and worked on programmes like OUR MAN AT ST MARK'S. His first wife was actress Hermione Gingold.

M*A*S*H
US (Twentieth Century-Fox) Situation Comedy. BBC 2 1973–84

Capt. Benjamin Franklin 'Hawkeye' Pierce ... **Alan Alda**
Capt. 'Trapper John' McIntyre .... **Wayne Rogers**
Major Margaret 'Hot Lips' Houlihan .... **Loretta Swit**
Major Frank Burns .... **Larry Linville**
Cpl. Walter 'Radar' O'Reilly .... **Gary Burghoff**
Lt. Col. Henry Blake .... **McLean Stevenson**

Father Francis Mulcahy .... **William Christopher**
Cpl./Sgt Maxwell Klinger .... **Jamie Farr**
Col. Sherman T. Potter .... **Harry Morgan**
Capt. B. J. Hunnicut .... **Mike Farrell**
Major Charles Emerson Winchester III ....
.... **David Ogden Stiers**
Dr Sidney Freedman .... **Alan Arbus**
Gen. Clayton .... **Herb Voland**
Nurse Kellye .... **Kellye Nakahara**
Igor Straminsky .... **Jeff Maxwell**
Nurse Bigelow .... **Enid Kent**
Sgt Zale .... **Johnny Haymer**
Sgt Luther Rizzo .... **G. W. Bailey**
Roy .... **Roy Goldman**
Soon-Lee .... **Rosalind Chao**

Creator: **Larry Gelbart**
Executive Producers: **Gene Reynolds, Burt Metcalfe**

*Life with an anarchic army hospital during the
Korean War.*

M*A*S*H was based on the film of the same name, starring Donald Sutherland and Elliott Gould. It is rare for a TV spin-off to achieve the success of a mother film, let alone surpass it, but *M*A*S*H* was an exceptional series, as nearly all TV critics agreed. Many have paid tribute to the writing, acting and production skills that enabled it to extract laughter from the most unlikely scenario of a blood-sodden war.

The series was set in the early 1950s, when the American involvement in Korea resulted in the draft not only of soldiers but also of medical men and women, most serving in MASH (Mobile Army Surgical Hospital) units. It followed everyday events in the fictitious 4077th MASH, reflecting and never neglecting the tragedy and futility of war and the seemingly needless loss of life. It was, indeed, an unusual setting for a comedy, but in such numbing circumstances as these, where a sense of humour is vital, it was very apt.

Bringing mirth out of madness was Captain Benjamin Franklin Pierce, commonly known as 'Hawkeye'. Drafted from his home town of Crabapple Cove, Maine, where he lived with his father, he was Chief Surgeon and was desperately sickened by the pointless bloodshed. Diligent and dedicated to his vocation, at the same time he spurned military discipline and refused to doff his cap to the powers that be. Master of the wisecrack and the quick retort, Hawkeye could also bring tears to viewers' eyes with his human reflections on the carnage around him.

His roommate, in a tent known as 'The Swamp', was 'Trapper John' McIntyre. Together they alleviated the heaviness of war by playing practical jokes, making advances to the nurses and distilling their own liquor. Butt of their humour was the self-centred, by-the-book jerk, Frank Burns, who tried to pull rank but never succeeded. Someone who had more time for Frank was Chief Nurse Margaret 'Hot Lips' Houlihan, a gutsy blonde with a voice like a foghorn. Despite Frank's well-publicized marriage, the two conducted a covert love affair that was the worst-kept secret of the whole war.

In charge of this mayhem was easy-going commanding officer Lt. Colonel Henry Blake. His only concern was discipline within the operating theatre and he was admirably supported by his shy company clerk, Walter O'Reilly, nicknamed 'Radar' after his uncanny clairvoyance, especially when choppers bearing wounded soldiers were due to arrive. Cuddly, bespectacled Radar brought out mothering instincts in all the nurses. He slept with a teddy bear and drank only Grape Nehis on his visits to the well-frequented Rosie's Bar. Spiritual comforter to the unit was chaplain Francis Mulcahy, mild-mannered but never afraid to speak his mind.

After the first season, a new arrival added extra colour. He was Corporal Max Klinger, a reluctant soldier of Lebanese extraction from Toledo, Ohio. In an effort to wangle a 'Section Eight' (a discharge for madness) he dressed in women's clothing.

M*A*S*H also saw other important cast-changes over the years. Colonel Blake was discharged and left for home, only for his plane to be shot down over the Sea of Japan with no survivors. His replacement was the horse-loving, ex-cavalry officer, Colonel Sherman Potter. Potter was a genial commander with plenty of bark, but his bite was reserved, like Blake's, for medical discipline, allowing the madness instigated by Hawkeye and Trapper John to continue – at least until Trapper shipped out. Actor Wayne Rogers left the series to be replaced by Mike Farrell as B. J. Hunnicut, Hawkeye's new accomplice. B. J. (the initials were never explained) was a real family man, shunning all advances and longing to rejoin his wife, Peg, and their little daughter, Erin. Nevertheless, he was as much a joker as Hawkeye, so Frank Burns found no respite here.

Indeed, Frank's days were numbered. The beginning of the end came when Margaret married Lt. Colonel Donald Penobscot. Although he was seldom seen and the marriage was short-lived, it brought her involvement with Frank to an end. After the break-up of her marriage, Margaret mellowed somewhat and found herself more in tune with the rest of the camp; but by this time Frank had gone AWOL and then been dispatched to another unit, to be replaced by an aristocratic Bostonian, Major Charles Emerson Winchester III. Pompous Winchester, like Frank, found himself rooming with Hawkeye and B. J. and he was just as easy a victim. He genuinely believed his blue blood placed him in a higher circle than his army colleagues, and he bitterly resented the waste of his enormous medical talents in the 'patch-up' operating theatres of a MASH unit. He did, however, earn a modicum of respect which sly, sneaky Frank could never have done.

When Radar was allowed home to help his elderly mother run their country smallholding, his place as clerk went to Klinger, who abandoned his female wardrobe and switched back to traditional military attire. In addition to these primary characters, *M*A*S*H* also saw the comings and goings of many temporary personnel, including psychiatrist Sidney Freedman, who paid occasional visits to check the mental health of both patients and staff.

M*A*S*H was deliberately conceived to shame Americans over their involvement in the Vietnam War, which was still under way when the programme started. But its tactics changed over the years and the last episodes were quite different in style from the first. The blatant anarchy had gone and the show had become less a comedy with dramatic moments and more a drama with comic touches. In its two-hour-special finale (which gained America's biggest-ever TV audience), Hawkeye harrowingly suffered a nervous breakdown, Winchester was gutted by the senseless killing of the POW musicians he had befriended, and, while everyone else returned home, Klinger, ironically, decided to stay in Korea, having met and married beautiful local girl Soon-Lee. It wasn't quite the end, though. Potter, Mulcahy and Klinger resurfaced in the spin-off series, *AfterMASH*. There had been an earlier spin-off, too, entitled *Trapper John MD*, but not featuring Wayne Rogers (it was set 28 years later).

Gary Burghoff was the only leading member of the cast to star in the film version, and Jamie Farr was the only cast member actually to have served in the Korean War. In the pilot for the TV series, the unit chaplain was Father *John* Mulcahy, played by George Morgan. More notable is the fact that Alan Alda won Emmy awards for his contributions as actor, writer and director in the series – a unique achievement. The concept was based on Richard Hooker's novel, *M*A*S*H*, which drew on his own experience as a medic in the Korean War. A cover version of the theme tune, 'Suicide Is Painless', was a UK number one hit for a group called The MASH in 1981.

MASSEY, RAYMOND
(1896–1983)

Canadian actor remembered by many viewers as the crusty old Dr Leonard Gillespie, mentor of DR KILDARE. Previously, Massey had enjoyed a film career stretching back to the late 1920s and also starred in an early US anthology series called *I Spy* (not the Robert Culp/Bill Cosby version). However, after *Dr Kildare* finished in 1966, not much was seen of him, save the odd TV movie, before he retired. He was the father of actors Daniel and Anna Massey.

MASTERCHEF
UK (Union Pictures/BBC) Cookery. BBC 1 1990–

Presenter: **Loyd Grossman**

Creator: **Franc Roddam**
Executive Producers: **Bradley Adams, Richard Kalms**
Producers: **Phillippa Robinson, Richard Bryan**

Long-running contest for amateur chefs.

This annual knock-out tournament showcased the very best in home cooking, inviting the viewing public to don their aprons and prove to the experts that top cuisine was not just the preserve of the professional chef. Three contestants each week individually planned and executed a menu to a budget (in an edited-down two and a half hours) which would be tasted and reviewed by Grossman and a pair of celebrity guests (top chefs and showbiz stars). The anxious contenders to the *Masterchef* title waited patiently while the judges 'deliberated, cogi-

tated and digested'. Regional heats led to an end-of-series grand final. One of the 1993 finalists, Ross Burden, has since progressed to TV chefdom. A spin-off version for 10–15-year-olds, *Junior Masterchef* (1994–), followed.

MASTERMIND
UK (BBC) Quiz. BBC 1 1972–97

Presenter: **Magnus Magnusson**

Creator: **Bill Wright**
Producers: **Bill Wright, Roger Mackay, Peter Massey, David Mitchell**

High-brow quiz tournament.

Mastermind proved to be one of television's most unlikely hits. Initially airing late at night, because schedulers considered it too academic for the viewing masses, it quickly gained a cult following. When it was brought into peak hours as a short-term replacement, it clocked up huge audience figures, so there it remained.

Each programme (usually staged at a university) featured four contenders (never 'contestants'), all taking turns to answer questions on a nominated specialist subject and then facing a round of general knowledge posers. The highest scorer (and sometimes the highest-scoring loser) progressed to a semi-final, in which a different specialist subject had to be chosen. On reaching the four-contender grand final, the participants were able to revert to their original or second-choice topics or opt for a brand-new subject. Chosen topics over the years varied from British Moths, The Works of Dorothy L. Sayers and Old Time Music Hall to Drama in Athens, 500–388 BC, English Cathedrals and the Sex Pistols and Punk Rock. The relentless questioning of host Magnus Magnusson was likened to interrogation. Indeed, creator Bill Wright brought his World War II past into play by echoing the standard interrogation procedure – 'Name, Rank, Serial Number' – in the series' 'Name, Occupation, Specialist Subject' contender introductions. With the lights dimmed, the contender (spot-lit in a lonely black leather chair) was faced with a barrage of notoriously difficult questions for a keenly timed two minutes.

Mastermind was responsible for a couple of over-used catchphrases in the English language. 'Pass' (used to skip a question and save time) became a common reply when someone didn't know an answer to something, and 'I've started so I'll finish' (Magnus's quip when interrupted by the time-up buzzer) was open to all sorts of interpretation. The programme's threatening theme music was called 'Approaching Menace', by Neil Richardson. On its retirement from television in 1997, *Mastermind* switched to Radio 4, installing Peter Snow as question-master.

Probably the best-remembered *Mastermind* champions were taxi-driver Fred Housego and train-driver Christopher Hughes, but the following all won the cut-glass *Mastermind* trophy:

1972	**Nancy Wilkinson**
1973	**Patricia Owen**
1974	**Elizabeth Horrocks**

1975	John Hart
1976	Roger Prichard
1977	Sir David Hunt
1978	Rosemary James
1979	Philip Jenkins
1980	Fred Housego
1981	Leslie Grout
1982	No contest
1983	Christopher Hughes
1984	Margaret Harris
1985	Ian Meadows
1986	Jennifer Keaveney
1987	Jeremy Bradbrooke
1988	David Beamish
1989	Mary Elizabeth Raw
1990	David Edwards
1991	Stephen Allen
1992	Steve Williams
1993	Gavin Fuller
1994	Dr George Davidson
1995	Kevin Ashman
1996	Richard Sturch
1997	Anne Ashurst

MATCH OF THE DAY
UK (BBC) Football. BBC 2/BBC 1 1964–6/1966–

Presenters: **Kenneth Wolstenholme, David Coleman, Jimmy Hill, Bob Wilson, Desmond Lynam, Gary Lineker**
Commentators: **Kenneth Wolstenholme, David Coleman, Wally Barnes, John Motson, Barry Davies, Idwal Robling, Tony Gubba, Alan Parry, Gerald Sinstadt, Clive Tyldesley, Jon Champion**

Recorded highlights, and occasional live action, from the day's top football matches.

In these days, when soccer is a prized commodity among TV stations, it is hard to believe that regular football coverage did not begin until 1964, and even then was relegated to BBC 2, the minority-interest channel. However, once England had won the World Cup in 1966, the mood changed and *Match of the Day* was switched to BBC 1.

The original format involved the playback of highlights of just one of the day's top games. Not to deter spectators, details of the match being covered were not publicized in advance. The first game televised was Liverpool versus Arsenal at 6.30 p.m. on 22 August 1964 (Liverpool won 3–2, Roger Hunt scored the first *Match of the Day* goal and only 50,000 viewers bothered to tune in). Over the years, a second and then a third match were added, with eventually all the important goals scored in the Premiership reviewed as well. During the late 1960s and 1970s, a regional format was pioneered whereby, after the main match, some BBC studios around the country broadcast highlights of local interest.

The programme's chief commentator for many years was Kenneth Wolstenholme, with other contributors including Wally Barnes, David Coleman, Alan Weeks and Idwal Robling (who primarily covered Welsh action). Since 1971 John Motson and Barry Davies have taken charge of matches, supported by the likes of Tony Gubba, Alan Parry, Gerald Sinstadt and Clive Tyldesley. The programme's presenters have varied, too, the current frontman being Gary Lineker, and expert analysts have been introduced to highlight the key moments. Jimmy Hill (as well as anchoring the programme for many years) was one. Others have included Alan Hansen, Trevor Brooking and Mark Lawrenson.

The title *Match of the Day* has also been used by the BBC for highlights of the Wimbledon tennis championships.

MATT HOUSTON
US (Aaron Spelling/Warner Brothers) Detective Drama.
BBC 1 1983–7

Matlock 'Matt' Houston	**Lee Horsley**
C. J. Parsons	**Pamela Hensley**
Bo	**Dennis Fimple**
Lamar Pettybone	**Paul Brinegar**
Lt. Vince Novelli	**John Aprea**
Rosa 'Mama' Novelli	**Penny Santon**
Det. Lt. Michael Hoyt	**Lincoln Kilpatrick**
Chris	**Cis Rundle**
Roy Houston	**Buddy Ebsen**

Creator: **Lawrence Gordon**
Executive Producer: **Aaron Spelling**
Producer: **Michael Fisher**

A super-rich playboy tracks criminals in his spare time.

Matt Houston hailed from a wealthy family, a very wealthy family. Having managed their cattle and oil empire in Texas, he moved to California to look after the family's off-shore exploration rigs. However, Matt spent less and less time in the job once he discovered a new, more exciting hobby: detective work. He proved to be an effective semi-professional sleuth. With the help of his beautiful lawyer friend, C. J., and an amiable Los Angeles cop, Lt. Novelli (whose mama often invited Matt for dinner), Matt revelled in this new adventure. With Bo and Lamar, a couple of squabbling Texan ranch-hands, also in tow, Houston Investigations was never going to be a lucrative enterprise, but what did that matter to a loaded young guy like Matt, who was surrounded by gorgeous women and all the trappings of a playboy lifestyle, including a luxurious penthouse, his own private helicopter and flashy cars (an Excalibur, a Rolls or a Mercedes)?

In later seasons, Matt gave up his oil interests and devoted himself full time to his hobby. Lt. Hoyt was the new police officer on the scene, and Matt's uncle, Roy, also turned up. A retired detective, he joined his nephew back on the streets, linking up with C. J. and the team's state-of-the-art computer (known as Baby), in pursuit of villains.

MATTHEWS, FRANCIS
(1930–)

British actor, star of the late 1960s/early 1970s detective series, PAUL TEMPLE, and the voice of Captain Scarlet in CAPTAIN SCARLET AND THE MYSTERONS. He also appeared in the sitcoms, *My Man Joe* (Lord Peregrine Hansford), A LITTLE BIG BUSINESS (Simon Lieberman), *A Roof Over My Head* (Jack Askew), *Tears Before Bedtime* (Geoffrey Dickens) and DON'T FORGET TO WRITE (Tom Lawrence). He starred as Eric the Prologue in Alan Plater's TRINITY TALES, was seen in *Brat Farrar*, and made guest appearances in THE AVENGERS, THE MORECAMBE AND WISE SHOW, CROWN COURT and THE DETECTIVES, among other series.

MAUGHAN, SHARON
(Sharon Mughan; 1952–)

British actress as well known for her coffee commercials as for her programme credits, which have included BY THE SWORD DIVIDED (Anne Lacey/Fletcher), *The Flame Trees of Thika*, *Shabby Tiger*, *Dombey and Son*, HANNAY, THE RETURN OF THE SAINT, INSPECTOR MORSE and THE RUTH RENDELL MYSTERIES (billed in some under her real name of Sharon Mughan). She is married to Trevor Eve.

MAVERICK

US (Warner Brothers) Western. ITV 1959–63

Bret Maverick	James Garner
Bart Maverick	Jack Kelly
Samantha Crawford	Diane Brewster
Cousin Beauregard Maverick	Roger Moore
Brent Maverick	Robert Colbert

Creator: **Roy Huggins**
Producers: **Roy Huggins/William L. Stewart**

Two cowardly brothers are professional poker-players in the Wild West.

Maverick was a Western with a difference – it was played for laughs. It featured wisecracking Texan Bret Maverick, a full-time card-shark who earned a living by preying on losers. It began as a traditional cowboy series but soon turned into a spoof on the Old West, despite the introduction of Bret's more serious younger brother, Bart. (Bart was actually added to ease production problems. With two film crews and two stars alternating as leads, twice as many programmes could be produced.)

The Mavericks were wanderers, stumbling into towns with ridiculous names like Bent Fork and Ten Strike. Unlike other cowboy heroes, these guys were true yellowbellies. When in trouble they followed their pappy's advice: 'Run!' Both were lazy, untrustworthy and self-centred, yet they often found time to help people in trouble. They generally didn't cheat at cards and, in case things turned nasty during a game, they kept a $1,000 bill pinned inside their jackets. For a while, Bret had a female rival, attractive swindler Sam Crawford, and the duo spent several episodes trying to out-con each other.

Maverick's gentle mockery of the conventional Western was highlighted when guest stars like Clint Walker (from CHEYENNE) and Ty Hardin (from BRONCO) dropped by. Some episodes were also parodies of BONANZA and GUNSMOKE. Like Clint Walker, James Garner fell out with Warner Brothers and was replaced by Roger Moore as Cousin Beau who, unusually for a Maverick, had won a commendation in the Civil War before moving to England to soak up the culture. A third Maverick brother, Brent, arrived later but, without Garner, it wasn't long before the series came to an end. A few revivals were attempted in the 1970s and 1980s, none with the success of the original.

MAY TO DECEMBER
UK (Cinema Verity) Situation Comedy. BBC 1 1989–94

Alec Callender	Anton Rodgers
Zoe Angell/Callender	Eve Matheson
	Lesley Dunlop
Jamie Callender	Paul Venables
Miles Henty	Clive Francis
Vera Flood/Tipple	Frances White
Hilary	Rebecca Lacey
Dot Burgess	Kate Williams
Debbie Burgess	Chrissie Cotterill
Roy Morgan-Jones	Paul Raynor
Simone	Carolyn Pickles
Mr Burgess	Ronnie Stevens
Rosie MacConnachy	Ashley Jensen

Creator/Writer: **Paul A. Mendelson**
Executive Producer: **Verity Lambert**
Producers: **Sydney Lotterby, Sharon Bloom**

Generation-gap romance between a middle-aged lawyer and a young schoolteacher.

When 26-year-old games mistress Zoe Angell arrived in the Pinner offices of Semple, Callender and Henty to make arrangements for her divorce, little did she know that she would eventually marry Alec Callender, the 53-year-old senior partner (and ardent Perry Mason fan) who handled her case. For sprightly Zoe and lumbering Alec, it wasn't love at first sight but, seeing each other out of business hours, their relationship began to blossom, much to the surprise of Zoe's greengrocer mum, Dot, and her frustrated sister, Debbie. Even more shocked were Alec's prim daughter, Simone, his wise-cracking son, Jamie (who worked with him in the office), and the other members of the office staff. These were frumpy secretary Miss Flood and over-familiar typist Hilary. While Zoe and Alec moved on to marriage and its inherent difficulties, plus the birth of their daughter, Fleur, so changes took place at the law firm. Jamie was made a partner after the departure of Miles Henty (the company name changed to Semple, Callender and Callender), Miss Flood secured herself a husband, hospital plasterer Gerald Tipple, and Hilary, as daffy as ever, eventually made way for an eccentric Scots girl by the name of Rosie MacConnachy.

MAYALL, RIK
(Richard Mayall; 1958–)

Anarchic Essex-born comedian/comic actor/writer, whose reputation was established by his role as Rick in THE YOUNG ONES (also co-writer) and its echoes in FILTHY RICH AND CATFLAP (Richie Rich) and BOTTOM (Richie Richard; again co-writer). Earlier, Mayall (once part of an act called 20th-Century Coyote with Adrian Edmondson) had established the character of boring Brummie Kevin Turvey in the sketch series, A KICK UP THE EIGHTIES, and also featured in THE COMIC STRIP PRESENTS. He then starred as MP Alan B'Stard in THE NEW STATESMAN and played Lord Flashheart in assorted episodes of BLACKADDER. With Edmondson, he appeared as one of the Dangerous Brothers on *Saturday Live*, and among his numerous other credits have been the showcase anthology, *Rik Mayall Presents*, *Grim Tales*, *The Lenny Henry Show*, JACKANORY, HAPPY FAMILIES, *In The Red* (Dominic De'Ath), THE BILL, JONATHAN CREEK, *How to Be a Little S*d* (voice only) and, in complete contrast, the musical *Horse Opera*.

MAYNARD, BILL
(Walter Williams; 1928–)

Yorkshire-born actor, primarily in comic roles. His TV career was launched in the 1950s, when he shared top billing with Terry Scott in *Great Scott – It's Maynard!*, and then gained his own series, *Mostly Maynard*. After a career downturn, he resurfaced in the 1970s and early 1980s, and was much in demand as Frank Riley in *The Life of Riley*, Stan the Fryer in TRINITY TALES and the accident-prone Selwyn Froggitt in OH NO! IT'S SELWYN FROGGITT and *Selwyn*. He was also the Reverend Alexander Goodwin in the sitcom, *Paradise Island*, and Fred Moffat, otherwise known as *The Gaffer*. More recently, he has been seen as the petty crook Claude Jeremiah Greengrass in HEARTBEAT. Maynard also has plenty of guest appearances to his name, in series as varied as UP POMPEII!, WORZEL GUMMIDGE and CORONATION STREET (music agent Micky Malone), and has made his mark in single dramas (particularly *Kisses at Fifty* in 1973).

ME & MY GIRL
UK (LWT) Situation Comedy. ITV 1984–8

Simon Harrap	Richard O'Sullivan
Derek Yates	Tim Brooke-Taylor
Nell Cresset	Joan Sanderson
Samantha Harrap	Joanne Ridley
Madeleine 'Maddie' Dunnock	Leni Harper
Isobel McClusky	Sandra Clarke
Liz	Joanne Campbell

Creator: **John Kane**

Writers: **Colin Bostock-Smith, John Kane, Bernard McKenna**
Executive Producer: **Humphrey Barclay**
Producers: **John Reardon, Malcolm Taylor**

A widower struggles to bring up his teenage daughter.

Simon Harrap, an executive at the Eyecatchers advertising agency in Covent Garden, found himself alone and in sole charge of adolescent daughter Samantha when his wife passed away (she had died when Samantha was three). To help him cope, his snooty mother-in-law, Nell Cresset, joined the household (and became a director of his company), and they also took on a housekeeper. Initially, this was the goofy Scots girl, Maddie, later replaced by fellow-Scot Isobel. Humour came from Simon's attempts to set an example and to keep Samantha on the straight and narrow (particularly with regard to homework and boys) while, at the same time, failing to curb his own recklessness. His friend and work-colleague was the heavily married-with-three-kids Derek Yates, and Liz was his secretary. The theme song was sung by Peter Skellern.

ME MAMMY
UK (BBC) Situation Comedy. BBC 1 1969–71

Bunjy Kennefick	Milo O'Shea
Mrs Kennefick	Anna Manahan
Miss Argyll	Yootha Joyce
Cousin Enda	David Kelly
Father Patrick	Ray McAnally

Creator/Writer: **Hugh Leonard**
Producers: **James Gilbert, Sydney Lotterby**

An Irishman's style is cramped by his clinging mother.

Forty-year-old Bunjy Kennefick was an Irishman living and working in London. An executive with a large West End company, he drove a flash car and lived in an expensive Regent's Park flat. His secretary, Miss Argyll, was also his girlfriend. Unfortunately, his widowed mother had also crossed the Irish Sea and, being a devout Catholic, was reluctant to give up her innocent son to the heady delights of the English capital – and Miss Argyll in particular. A later addition to the cast was Bunjy's Cousin Enda, another exile from the Emerald Isle. The series began life as a COMEDY PLAYHOUSE pilot in 1968.

MEDICS
UK (Granada) Drama. ITV 1990–5

Prof. Geoffrey Hoyt	Tom Baker
Ruth Parry	Sue Johnston
Dr Robert Nevin	James Gaddas
Dr Claire Armstrong	Francesca Ryan
Jess Hardman	Penny Bunton
Dr Gail Benson	Emma Cunningham
Dr Alison Makin	Teddie Thompson

Dr Jay Rhaman	**Jimmi Harkishin**
Toby Maitland-Evans	**Jo Stone-Fewings**
Dr Alex Taylor	**Peter Wingfield**
	Edward Atterton
Dr Tom Carey	**Hugh Quarshie**
Gavin Hall	**Ian Redford**
Helen Lomax	**Dinah Stabb**
Dr Sarah Kemp	**Patricia Kerrigan**
Billy Cheshire	**Clarence Smith**
Derek Foster	**Nick Dunning**
Diana Hardy	**Gabrielle Drake**
Janice Thornton	**Susan McArdle**
Stuart Bevan	**Rupert Frazer**
Peter Vance	**Ian Shaw**

Executive Producer: **Sally Head**
Producers: **Tony Dennis, Alison Lumb, Louise Berridge**

The pressures of work on the doctors and staff at a busy general hospital.

Described by Tony Dennis, one of the show's producers, as a programme 'about people doing an impossible job', *Medics* focused on the staff of fictitious Henry Park Hospital, examining the stresses and strains of their intense employment. At the heart of much of the action were Geoffrey Hoyt and Ruth Parry. Hoyt was the flamboyant and eccentric professor of surgery and Parry the embattled chief executive. Contemporary NHS politics thrust their way to the top of the agenda, and personal problems, like the death of Hoyt's wife and his near-fatal car accident, also came to the fore. Increasing attention was also paid to the younger members of staff, like student doctor Alex Taylor, house officer Jess Hardman, new mother Claire Armstrong and lesbian doctors Sarah Kemp and Alison Makin, as the series progressed.

MEET THE WIFE
UK (BBC) Situation Comedy. BBC 1 1964–6

Thora Blacklock	**Thora Hird**
Freddie Blacklock	**Freddie Frinton**

Creators/Writers: **Ronald Wolfe, Ronald Chesney**
Producers: **John Paddy Carstairs, Graeme Muir, Robin Nash**

A northern couple bicker their way through married life.

Thora and Freddie Blacklock were not unhappily married: they just didn't always see eye to eye. Thora was bossy and domineering and Freddie, a plumber by profession, liked to rebel now and again; but whatever divided them was soon forgotten. It was a marriage much like many others, really, allowing viewers to feel comfortable with the characters. *Meet the Wife* was, consequently, a popular series. It stemmed from a 1963 COMEDY PLAYHOUSE presentation entitled *The Bed*, in which the Blacklocks, having just celebrated their silver wedding anniversary, argued over whether to buy twin beds to replace their lumpy and uncomfortable matrimonial double.

MELLOR, KAY

English writer, a former actress, whose works have included BAND OF GOLD, PLAYING THE FIELD and *Jane Eyre*, as well as episodes of BROOKSIDE and CORONATION STREET. She is the mother of actress Gaynor Faye (the *Street*'s Judy Mallet), who starred in her series, *Fat Friends*, and also appeared in *Playing the Field*.

MEMOIRS OF SHERLOCK HOLMES, THE
See ADVENTURES OF SHERLOCK HOLMES, THE.

MEN BEHAVING BADLY
UK (Hartswood/Thames) Situation Comedy. ITV 1992; BBC 1 1994–8

Dermot Povey	**Harry Enfield**
Gary Strang	**Martin Clunes**
Tony Smart	**Neil Morrissey**
Deborah	**Leslie Ash**
Dorothy	**Caroline Quentin**
Les	**Dave Atkins**
George	**Ian Lindsay**
Anthea	**Valerie Minifie**
Ken	**John Thomson**

Creator/Writer: **Simon Nye**
Producer: **Beryl Vertue**

Two friends flatshare in typically squalid bachelor fashion.

In this series, based on writer Simon Nye's own novel, Dermot and Gary, a pair of overgrown adolescents, were the *Men Behaving Badly*. This involved sharing a flat in South London, neglecting the washing-up, using colourful language, ogling the girl upstairs (Deborah), drooling over aerobics videos, swilling beer and having limited success with women. After the first season, Dermot left to travel the world and was replaced by the drippy, unemployed Tony, who instantly fell in love with Deborah. Also seen was Dorothy, Gary's cynical girlfriend (a nurse), Les, slovenly landlord of the local boozer, The Crown (later replaced by the dim, stone-faced Ken), and George and Anthea, Gary's limp colleagues at the security firm where he worked. Although initially an ITV sitcom, from the third season the programme was screened on BBC 1, at a later transmission time. This allowed the men to behave just that little bit more badly. The final three episodes were shown over Christmas 1998 and explored Gary and Dorothy's attempts to conceive a child.

MEN FROM SHILOH, THE
See VIRGINIAN, THE.

MEN INTO SPACE
US (United Artists/CBS) Science Fiction. BBC 1960

Col. Edward McCauley .... **William Lundigan**

Producer: **Lewis Rachmil**

The adventures of early space-pioneers.

One of TV's first 'space race' series, reaching American screens less than two years after the first Sputnik was launched, *Men into Space* centred on the exploits of brave astronaut Colonel Edward McCauley, who travelled the solar system, landing on other planets, working at the moon base and orbiting Earth in a space station. Dramas and crises revolved around equipment failure or personal problems, rather than alien attacks or visits from bug-eyed monsters. Although many of the series' ideas have yet to come to fruition, this was generally regarded as a sensible, realistic science-fiction series and was produced in semi-documentary style in conjunction with the US armed forces.

MEN'S ROOM, THE
UK (BBC) Drama. BBC 2 1991

Charity Walton	**Harriet Walter**
Prof. Mark Carleton	**Bill Nighy**
James Walton	**Patrick Drury**
Jane Carleton	**Mel Martin**
Sally	**Amanda Redman**
Margaret Lacey	**Charlotte Cornwell**
Mavis McDonald	**Cheryl Hall**
Alan Pascoe	**David Ryall**
Tessa Pascoe	**Kate Hardie**
Dr Ivan Swinhoe	**Bill Stewart**
Mack MacKinnon	**Philip Croskin**
Steve Kirkwood	**James Aubrey**
Delia	**Tilly Vosburgh**
Shelley	**Victoria Scarborough**
Eric	**Ian Redford**

Writer: **Laura Lamson**
Producer: **David Snodin**

Steamy saga of academic adultery.

Beginning in 1980 and spanning most of the Thatcher years (to 1989), *The Men's Room* was the story of sociologist Charity Walton, a mother of four whose life was turned upside down by an affair with Mark Carleton, the deceitful, womanizing new head of department at Queen's College, University of London, where she worked as a researcher. Sex and betrayal were the hallmarks of this acclaimed five-part drama, which also featured Charity's best friend, Sally, a publisher; Margaret, an outspoken feminist; Swinhoe, a shoplifting criminologist; and Mavis, Carleton's boozy secretary. It was adapted by Laura Lamson from the novel by Ann Oakley.

MERCER, DAVID
(1928–80)

Prolific British socialist playwright, one of the so-called 'angry young men' of 1960s drama. Mercer brought his own political experiences, his criticisms of the failures of Communist Bloc regimes and a fascination with psychiatry to his many television dramas (some seen as WEDNESDAY PLAYS). He began with a trilogy (now known as *The Generations*), comprising the plays, *Where the Difference Begins* (1961), *A Climate of Fear* (1962) and *The Birth of a Private Man* (1963), interrupted by *A Suitable Case for Treatment* (1962) and *The Buried Man* (1963). He later penned another trilogy made up of *On the Eve of Publication* (1968), *The Cellar and the Almond Tree* and *Emma's Time* (both 1970). Among other memorable works over the years were *And Did Those Feet?* (1965), *In Two Minds* (1967), *The Parachute* (1968), *Let's Murder Vivaldi* (1968) and *Huggy Bear* (1976). His last offering was *Rod of Iron* for Yorkshire TV in 1979.

MERCIER, SHEILA
(Sheila Rix; 1919–)

Yorkshire-born actress, sister of farce star Brian Rix but known to most viewers as EMMERDALE's Annie Sugden, a role she played for well over 20 years. She had previously appeared with her brother in his series, *Dial RIX*.

MERIDIAN TELEVISION

Meridian is the ITV franchise-holder for the South and South-east of England, winning the contract from TVS in 1991 and taking to the air on 1 January 1993. Meridian operates from three studios, in Southampton, in Newbury and near Maidstone. The most notable contributions to the ITV network so far have been the dramas, *Harnessing Peacocks*, *Under the Hammer* and THE RUTH RENDELL MYSTERIES, the comedy, *Tracey Ullman: A Class Act* and the travelogue, *Coltrane in a Cadillac*. Meridian is now part of the Granada Media group.

MERTON, PAUL
(Paul Martin; 1957–)

South London-born comedian, a former civil servant. Merton is best known as one of the regulars in the topical quiz, HAVE I GOT NEWS FOR YOU, although he has also been seen on WHOSE LINE IS IT ANYWAY?, in two series of his own surreal sketch show for Channel 4, in the comedy, *An Evening with Gary Lineker* (Ian), in *Paul Merton in Galton & Simpson's . . .* (two series reworking classic *Hancock* and other scripts), and as host of ROOM 101. In 1994 he presented a history of the London Palladium for the BBC and a year later hosted *Paul Merton's Life of Comedy*. He was once married to actress Caroline Quentin.

MERVYN, WILLIAM
(William Mervyn Pickwoad; 1912–76)

British actor whose earliest TV parts (after years on the stage) included Captain Crocker-Dobson in the naval comedy, *The Skylarks*, in 1958 and Sir Hector in *Saki* in 1962. In 1963 he adopted the guise of Chief Inspector Charles Rose in THE ODD MAN, which led to a rather weird spin-off, IT'S DARK OUTSIDE, in 1964 and finally to the character's own series, MR ROSE, in 1967. A year earlier, Mervyn played Sir Gerald in *The Liars* and embarked on a five-year clerical career as the Bishop in ALL GAS AND GAITERS. In 1971 he starred as the 43rd Duke of Tottering in the kids' comedy, *Tottering Towers*.

MESSICK, DON
(1926–)

American cartoon voicer, specializing in canine creations, including SCOOBY-DOO, Muttley in WACKY RACES and the JETSONS' dog, Astro. He was also Bamm Bamm in THE FLINTSTONES, Dr Benton Quest in JONNY QUEST, Boo Boo in YOGI BEAR, Snorky in THE BANANA SPLITS, Aramis in *The Three Musketeers*, Multi Man in FRANKENSTEIN JR AND THE IMPOSSIBLES, Spot the cat in HONG KONG PHOOEY, Pixie in *Pixie and Dixie*, plus Atom Ant, Touché Turtle and many more characters. Messick was originally a ventriloquist, then a radio actor in the 1940s and 1950s.

METAL MICKEY
UK (LWT) Children's Comedy. ITV 1980–3

Mr Wilberforce	**Michael Stainton**
Mrs Wilberforce	**Georgina Melville**
Granny	**Irene Handl**
Ken Wilberforce	**Ashley Knight**
Haley Wilberforce	**Lucinda Bateson**
Janey Wilberforce	**Lola Young**
Steve Wilberforce	**Gary Shail**

Writer: **Colin Bostock-Smith**
Producer: **Michael Dolenz**

A family's home life is disrupted by a zany robot.

Invented by boy scientist Ken Wilberforce to help out around the home, Metal Mickey brought nothing but chaos to Ken's family. A five-foot tall, magical robot in the R2D2 (*Star Wars*) vein, Mickey spouted the catchphrase 'Boogie boogie' and turned the household upside down with his space-age antics, which included trips to the future, teleportation and conversations with aliens. There were also more mundane happenings, like Mickey trying to become a pop star or Mickey finding himself kidnapped. The show is possibly best remembered, however, for another Mickey – its producer/director was the former Monkee, Mickey Dolenz.

MIAMI VICE
US (Universal) Police Drama. BBC 1 1985–90

Det. James 'Sonny' Crockett	**Don Johnson**
Det. Ricardo Tubbs	**Philip Michael Thomas**
Lt. Martin Castillo	**Edward James Olmos**
Det. Gina Navarro/Calabrese	**Saundra Santiago**
Det. Trudy Joplin	**Olivia Brown**
Det. Stan Switek	**Michael Talbott**
Det. Larry Zito	**John Diehl**
Izzy Moreno	**Martin Ferrero**
Caitlin Davies	**Sheena Easton**

Creators: **Michael Mann, Anthony Yerkovich**
Executive Producer: **Michael Mann**

Two trendy cops patrol the glitzy but drug-poisoned streets of Miami.

Very much a 1980s programme in its feel, with generous use of contemporary rock music, *Miami Vice* delved behind the cool, pastel shades of this glamorous Florida city and unearthed a seedier side, heavily dependent on the drug culture. Its stars were cops Crockett and Tubbs. Stubble-chinned, heavy-smoking Crockett was an ex-football star, aggressive and straight-talking. He worked under the street name of Sonny Burnett and lived on a houseboat called *St Vitus' Dance*, which he shared with a pet alligator named Elvis. Separated from his wife, Caroline, Crockett now enjoyed the attentions of many of the city's beautiful women, although most of his girlfriends tended to meet a grisly end. Even one he married, rock star Caitlin Davies (played by real-life singer Sheena Easton), bought it.

Dressed in a crumpled light jacket and a T-shirt, Crockett's casual scruffiness contrasted sharply with the silk-shirted, double-breasted, sartorial elegance of his hip partner, Tubbs, a black New York cop, who had come to Miami to flush out the drugs-pusher who murdered his brother. Tubbs's undercover identity was Rico Cooper and the duo cruised the tropical streets in Crockett's flash Ferrari Spider, or the Testarossa that replaced it. They were assisted by undercover policewomen Trudi Joplin and Gina Calabrese and detectives Stan Switek and Larry Zito, and their boss was the temperamental Lt. Castillo.

Miami Vice was conceived as a sort of MTV cops show, hence the rock-video-style photography and the liberal helpings of chart music. The pounding theme tune, by Jan Hammer, became a hit on both sides of the Atlantic in 1985 and numerous guest stars from the rock world dropped in for cameo roles, including Phil Collins, Ted Nugent, James Brown, Glenn Frey and Little Richard. Also featured were celebrities like Bianca Jagger, boxer Roberto Duran and comedian Tommy Chong.

MICHELL, KEITH
(1926–)

Australian Shakespearean actor, a former art teacher, whose finest hour came in 1970 as the legendary king in

THE SIX WIVES OF HENRY VIII, ageing and fattening up as the series progressed (it was a role he resumed in 1996 for the BBC's adaptation of *The Prince and the Pauper*). Michell also starred in the 1972 film version, *Henry VIII and His Six Wives*, and took up singing on the back of his acting success, notching up one minor hit in 1971 with 'I'll Give You The Earth' and then resurfacing with the novelty single, 'Captain Beaky', in 1980. Later credits have been few, apart from appearances in some TV movies, although his earliest parts date from 1951 (a production of R. L. Stevenson's *The Black Arrow*) and 1962 (Heathcliff in *Wuthering Heights*).

MICHELMORE, CLIFF
CBE (1919–)

British presenter, on TV from the 1950s when he fronted *Highlight* and, more notably, TONIGHT, as well as contributing some early sports commentaries. He joined the BBC after working for British Forces radio on *Family Favourites* (through which he met his wife, the late Jean Metcalfe), and moved into television to write, direct and produce children's programmes like ALL YOUR OWN. His other notable credits have included PANORAMA, 24 HOURS, *Talkback*, *Wheelbase*, *Chance to Meet*, STARS ON SUNDAY, *Home on Sunday*, SONGS OF PRAISE and the charity programme, *Lifeline*. He was the first presenter of HOLIDAY, in 1969, worked on the nightly magazine, *Day by Day*, for Southern Television and hosted the BBC's space and election coverages, as well as the occasional information panel game, *So You Think . . . ?* He is the father of TV presenter Guy Michelmore.

MICKEY SPILLANE'S MIKE HAMMER
See MIKE HAMMER.

MIDDLEMARCH
UK (BBC/WGBH Boston) Drama. BBC 2 1994

Dorothea Brooke	Juliet Aubrey
Arthur Brooke	Robert Hardy
Dr Tertius Lydgate	Douglas Hodge
Peter Featherstone	Michael Hordern
Nicholas Bulstrode	Peter Jeffrey
Revd Edward Casaubon	Patrick Malahide
Rosamond Vincy	Trevyn McDowell
Will Ladislaw	Rufus Sewell
Celia Brooke	Caroline Harker
Revd Camden Farebrother	Simon Chandler
Sir James Chettam	Julian Wadham
Fred Vincy	Jonathan Firth
Mrs Dollop	Pam Ferris
Mrs Vincy	Jacqueline Tong
Mary Garth	Rachel Power
Mayor Vincy	Stephen Moore
Mrs Cadwallader	Elizabeth Spriggs
Mr Standish	Ronald Hines
Caleb Garth	Clive Russell
Raffles	John Savident
Voice of George Eliot	Judi Dench

Writer: **Andrew Davies**
Producer: **Louis Marks**
Executive Producers: **Rebecca Eaton, Michael Wearing**

Acclaimed, six-part dramatization of George Eliot's best-known work.

Costing £6 million to produce, *Middlemarch* was a risky enterprise for the BBC, but the corporation had no need to worry, as this venture into elaborate costume drama was exceptionally well received. Indeed, it acted as a catalyst for a host of other 1990s period-pieces, including PRIDE AND PREJUDICE.

Opening in 1829, at a time of political and industrial change, the story centred on the idealistic, well-meaning Dorothea Brooke, who mistakenly married the mean-minded Revd Edward Casaubon and then fell for his artist cousin, Will Ladislaw. Other prominent characters included the feckless Rosamond Vincy and her future husband, Tertius Lydgate, a forward-thinking young doctor. Members of the old establishment, like Dorothea's landowning uncle, Arthur Brooke, Rosamund's father, Mayor Vincy, and unscrupulous banker Nicholas Bulstrode exemplified the generation gap that was beginning to grow in this era of social upheaval. The series was filmed in Stamford, Lincolnshire. The BBC had previously adapted the novel for the small screen in 1968.

MIDNIGHT CALLER
US (December 3rd/Lorimar) Detective Drama. BBC 1
1989–92

Jack 'Nighthawk' Killian	Gary Cole
Devon King	Wendy Kilbourne
Billy Po	Dennis Dun
Lt. Carl Zymak	Arthur Taxier
Deacon Bridges	Mykel T. Williamson
Nicky Molloy	Lisa Eilbacher

Creator: **Richard Di Lello**
Executive Producer: **Robert Singer**
Producer: **John F. Perry**

An ex-cop becomes a radio presenter but can't leave his former life behind.

When Jack Killian accidentally killed his patrol partner while pursuing a crook, his life turned upside down. Although officially cleared of all blame by the police, he decided to quit the force. At a loose end, he accepted the offer of working for beautiful Devon King, as a late-night phone-in host on her radio station, KJCM (98.3 FM) in San Francisco. There (using the nickname of 'Nighthawk') he found himself in contact with all manner of shady people who called him up and left him intriguing cases to solve, which he either passed on to his policeman friend, Carl Zymak, or to a newspaper contact, Deacon Bridges, or, more likely, set out to handle himself, often at great personal danger. The phone-in also covered intense moral issues like AIDS and drugs, and Killian proved to be a thoughtful but straight-talking host, if a touch too moody and flip outside the studio.

On the other side of the glass was engineer Billy Po. Nicky Molloy later took over as Nighthawk's boss.

MIDSOMER MURDERS

UK (Bentley/A&E) Police Drama. ITV 1997–

DCI Tom Barnaby	**John Nettles**
DS Gavin Troy	**Daniel Casey**
Joyce Barnaby	**Jane Wymark**
Cully Barnaby	**Laura Howard**

Producers: **Brian True-May, Betty Willingale**

Murder investigations in picture-postcard England.

Overtly aimed at the American audience with its overdose of traditional English village imagery (rose gardens, churches, cricket, pubs, hunts, red phone-boxes, etc.), *Midsomer Murders* was a two-hour detective series steeped in the colours of INSPECTOR MORSE, but without the forensic and intellectual complexity. It centred on easygoing DCI Tom Barnaby, a more than competent career copper – strangely bereft of quirky traits and personal problems – based in the town of Causton. With the level-headed, though still a little wet behind the ears, Sgt Troy at his side, Barnaby was called out into the beautiful English countryside to solve heinous crimes involving eccentric folk in villages with provocative names like Badger's Drift, Midsomer Mallow and Morton Fendle. Providing moral support, if rather resigned to disrupted mealtimes and abandoned social evenings, were Barnaby's wife Joyce and his theatrically minded daughter Cully, increasingly the object of Troy's attentions. The series, filmed in and around Aylesbury, Buckinghamshire, was based on the novels by Caroline Graham.

MIKE HAMMER

US (Columbia) Detective Drama. ITV 1984–6

Mike Hammer	**Stacy Keach**
Velda	**Lindsay Bloom**
Capt. Pat Chambers	**Don Stroud**
Assistant DA Lawrence Barrington	**Kent Williams**
Ozzie the Answer	**Danny Goldman**
Jenny	**Lee Benton**
The Face	**Donna Denton**

Executive Producer: **Jay Bernstein**
Producer: **Lew Gallo**

Violent, macho and leering private eye series, based on the colourful books by Mickey Spillane.

Spillane's Mike Hammer was a hard New York detective fighting crime in a tough city. His investigations into the underworld, among drug-pushers, murderers, kidnappers and other such lively characters, were glossily depicted in this series. Assisted by his buxom secretary, Velda, the chain-smoking Hammer could also call on the help of his friend, Pat, a captain in the New York Police Department. On the streets, he had several contacts, including Ozzie the Answer, and among the parade of shapely females on view was Jenny, the bartender at Hammer's regular drinking hole, the Light 'n' Easy bar. Lawrence Barrington, Hammer's legal adversary, was an assistant district attorney who operated by the book and disliked the brawling gumshoe's unorthodox methods. The most intriguing character, however, was a beautiful brunette known as 'The Face'. Hammer caught sight of her in nearly every episode but never managed to meet her. Finally, it was revealed that she was a writer looking to use his exploits as the basis for a series of novels.

When criticism of the show's sexist attitude grew too heavy, the glamorous women were 'toned down'; but the violence, if anything, increased, with Hammer's hatred of the criminal fraternity exposed in an orgy of killings and maimings. It says it all that Hammer gave a pet name – Betsy – to his hand-gun.

Ironically, filming of the series was interrupted for a year or so because of real-life crime matters, when actor Stacy Keach spent time in Reading Jail for a drugs offence. Keach resumed the role in 1997 in a short-lived series entitled *Mike Hammer: Private Eye*. He was not TV's first Mike Hammer, however. This honour went to Darren McGavin, star of an American adaptation in the 1950s.

MILES, MICHAEL

(1919–71)

New Zealand-born 'quiz inquisitor' of TAKE YOUR PICK, conducting the quickfire 'yes/no interlude' and asking contestants to 'take the money or open the box' from the very start of ITV broadcasts in 1955. Miles had brought the show over from Radio Luxembourg, where it had been a hit for three years. It proved extremely popular on television, too, and ran for 13 years. Undaunted by its cancellation in 1968, Miles returned with a similar format in *Wheel of Fortune* a year later, but died in 1971. He was the father of radio presenter Sarah Lucas.

MILLER, JONATHAN

CBE (1934–)

Multi-talented British writer, director and producer, who is also a qualified doctor. A product of the Cambridge Footlights troupe that included the likes of David Frost and Peter Cook, Miller arrived in television via the *Beyond the Fringe* revue. Among other TV contributions, he edited MONITOR, produced a version of Plato's *Symposium* and an acclaimed adaptation of *Alice in Wonderland*, worked on OMNIBUS, took charge of the BBC's ambitious Shakespeare project in 1980 and merged his medical and television knowledge in *The Body in Question* in 1978 (writer and presenter). In 1997 he hosted *Jonathan Miller's Opera Works*, a series of workshops for aspiring singers.

MILLIGAN, SPIKE
KBE (Hon.) (Terence Milligan; 1918–)

Offbeat British comedian, born in India. Through his work with The Goons on radio in the 1950s, Milligan established a reputation for bizarre, quirky humour, which later translated to television in the form of the animated TELEGOONS. He also starred with fellow Goon Peter Sellers in *Idiot Weekly, Price 2d* in 1956, and wrote its sequels, A SHOW CALLED FRED and *Son of Fred*. He guested in NOT ONLY . . ., BUT ALSO . . . in the mid-1960s, and then, in 1968, appeared in *The World of Beachcomber*, before launching into his run of innovative Q programmes in 1969, beginning with *Q5* and working his way up to *Q9*. The early episodes predated even MONTY PYTHON with their free-form sketches, often lacking beginnings and proper endings. Less successful was his interpretation of Pakistani Kevin O'Grady (Paki-Paddy) in Johnny Speight's controversial sitcom, CURRY AND CHIPS (Milligan had previously popped up in Speight's TILL DEATH US DO PART). He wrote the mini-saga, *The Phantom Raspberry-Blower of Old London Town* (first seen as one of *Six Dates for Barker*) for THE TWO RONNIES, and was a regular on *The Marty Feldman Comedy Machine*. Among Milligan's numerous other contributions have been *Milligan's Wake, Muses with Milligan, Oh in Colour, The Last Turkey in the Shop Show, There's a Lot of It About, Gormenghast* (headmaster De'Ath) and voices for the children's puppet series, *Wolves, Witches and Giants* and *The Great Bong*.

MILLS, ANNETTE
(1894–1955)

The sister of John Mills, Annette Mills was a children's favourite in the 1940s and 1950s when introducing popular puppets like Prudence and Primrose Kitten, Sally the Sealion, Oswald the Ostrich, Louise the Lamb, Monty the Monkey, Mr Peregrine the Penguin and, most famous of all, MUFFIN THE MULE. As Muffin danced on top of her piano, Mills sang and played. They first appeared together in 1946, as part of the BBC's *For the Children* series, after Mills had been forced to give up her song-and-dance career following a couple of bad accidents. She died just eight days after her last appearance with Muffin in 1955.

MILLS, Sir JOHN
CBE (1908–)

Stalwart of the British cinema John Mills has enjoyed relatively few television credits. Most notable have been the offbeat Western, *Dundee and the Culhane* (as barrister Dundee), the Resistance revival, *Zoo Gang* (Tommy Devon or 'The Elephant'), the 1979 version of QUATERMASS (Professor John Quatermass), the retirement sitcom, *Young at Heart* (Albert Collyer), the mini-series, A WOMAN OF SUBSTANCE (Henry Rossiter), the single drama, *Harnessing Peacocks* (Bernard), and *Martin*

Chuzzlewit (Mr Chuffey). Mills has also guested on numerous shows, most famously with *Morecambe and Wise*. He is the father of actresses Juliet and Hayley Mills.

MILLS, ROGER

Award-winning British documentary producer and editor, working for the BBC on programmes like *Inside Story*, SAILOR, HONG KONG BEAT, *Strangeways*, FORTY MINUTES and Michael Palin's extravagant voyages, AROUND THE WORLD IN 80 DAYS, *Pole to Pole* and *Full Circle*.

MILNE, ALASDAIR
(1930–)

BBC current affairs producer and director in the 1950s and 1960s, working on programmes like *Highlight*, TONIGHT and THAT WAS THE WEEK THAT WAS, who later became the Corporation's Director of Programmes, Managing Director and Director-General (1982–7). Milne was the first Director-General to come from a production background, and under his auspices the BBC opened up its breakfast television and daytime television services. His resignation in January 1987, at the behest of the Chairman, led to a period of upheaval and change at the BBC.

MILNE, PAULA

British dramatist whose most acclaimed work has included ANGELS (creator), the 1982 play, *John David*, and the serials, *The Politician's Wife, The Fragile Heart* and *Second Sight*. Her other credits have included *A Bunch of Fives* and episodes of CORONATION STREET, CROSSROADS, Z CARS, JULIET BRAVO, *Girl Talk* and THE RUTH RENDELL MYSTERIES.

MIND OF MR J. G. REEDER, THE
UK (Thames) Detective Drama. ITV 1969–71

Mr J. G. Reeder	**Hugh Burden**
Sir Jason Toovey	**Willoughby Goddard**
Mrs Houchin	**Mona Bruce**
Miss Belman	**Gillian Lewis**

Executive Producer: **Lloyd Shirley**
Producers: **Kim Mills, Robert Love**

In the 1920s a gentle DPP office clerk solves crimes in his own unassuming way.

Mr J. G. Reeder worked for the Department of Public Prosecutions. Although his everyday appearance was quite innocuous (bespectacled, slightly downmarket in dress, and totally unthreatening in manner), he nevertheless possessed a mind capable of cracking the most enigmatic of crimes. As he himself put it, he saw evil in everything, much to the misfortune of crooks up and down the country. Sir Jason Toovey was his department head, and Reeder was assisted first by Mrs Houchin and later by Miss Belman. The series was based on the stories of Edgar Wallace, published in 1925.

MIND YOUR LANGUAGE

UK (LWT) Situation Comedy. ITV 1977–9

Jeremy Brown	**Barry Evans**
Miss Courtney	**Zara Nutley**
Danielle Favre	**Françoise Pascal**
Ali Nadim	**Dino Shafeek**
Jamila Ranjha	**Jamila Massey**
Anna Schmidt	**Jacki Harding**
Juan Cervantes	**Ricardo Montez**
Giovanni Cupello	**George Camiller**
Chung Su-Lee	**Pik-Sen Lim**
Taro Nagazumi	**Robert Lee**
Maximillian Papandrious	**Kevork Malikyan**
Ranjeet Singh	**Albert Moses**
Sid	**Tommy Godfrey**
Zoltan Szabo	**Gabor Vernon**
Ingrid Svenson	**Anna Bergman**
Henshawe	**Harry Littlewood**
Gladys	**Iris Sadler**

Creator/Writer: **Vince Powell**
Producer: **Stuart Allen**

Mayhem and misunderstanding in an English-for-foreigners class.

English teacher Jeremy Brown bit off more than he could chew when enrolling as instructor of a night-school class for mature foreign students. His multinational pupils included amorous French girl Danielle Favre, humourless German Anna Schmidt, Italian romeo Giovanni Cupello, and other similarly well-defined racial stereotypes, all of whom had clearly never considered the concept of ethnic tolerance. Misunderstanding and abuse were rife, leading to constant aggression and turning the naïve, inoffensive Brown into a quivering, frustrated wreck. Miss Courtney was the dragon-like principal who had the knack of entering the classroom at just the wrong moment, and Sid (later replaced by Henshawe) was the Cockney caretaker.

MINDER

UK (Euston Films/Thames/Central) Comedy Drama. ITV 1979–85; 1988–94

Arthur Daley	**George Cole**
Terry McCann	**Dennis Waterman**
Dave	**Glynn Edwards**
Des	**George Layton**
DS Albert 'Charlie' Chisholm	**Patrick Malahide**
Sgt Rycott	**Peter Childs**
Maurice	**Anthony Valentine**
DC Jones	**Michael Povey**
Ray Daley	**Gary Webster**
DS Morley	**Nicholas Day**
DC Park	**Stephen Tompkinson**
DC Field	**Jonty Stephens**

Creator: **Leon Griffiths**
Executive Producers: **Verity Lambert, Lloyd Shirley, Johnny Goodman**
Producers: **Lloyd Shirley, George Taylor, Ian Toynton**

The dodgy dealings of one of London's great survivors and his beefy assistant.

Arthur Daley is a name that has become synonymous with shady deals, for this cowardly but lovable rogue specialized in less than reliable, marginally hooky produce dished out at a bargain price. Whether it was mutton-dressed-as-lamb motors from his used-car showroom or crates of *appellation noncontrollée* from his lock-up, Arthur had the knack of twisting suckers' arms and getting them to buy. Of course, they soon returned the goods, or the law intervened to ensure that Daley's pockets were once again as empty as when they started. But this trilby-sporting, cigar-chewing master of cockney slang was never far away from another 'nice little earner'.

Arthur's right hand was Terry McCann, a former professional boxer and occasional jailbird. Now on the straight and narrow (as far as Arthur would allow), McCann – one of life's losers – was easy meat for Daley, who paid him a pittance and promised him the earth. Hired out as a commodity by Arthur to be a bodyguard, bouncer, fetcher or carrier, Terry nevertheless was always there to protect his guv'nor from someone with a grievance – and such people were not hard to find. The wonderful repartee between Daley and his uncomfortable, generally kind-hearted 'minder' as they worked their way around the fringes of the underworld was even more important than the stories themselves.

Off duty, the pair could be found in the Winchester Club, run by its genial steward, Dave. This refuge from ''er indoors' (as Daley referred to his wife) was also the setting for many 'business' meetings. On the side of justice were policemen Chisholm, Rycott and Jones. Just like Wyle E. Coyote and the Road Runner, their sole aim was to catch up with Arthur Daley, the crook with the Teflon finish.

The series was nearly brought to a close on many occasions, as both George Cole and Dennis Waterman contemplated a way out. But when Waterman finally called it a day in 1991, Gary Webster was introduced in the role of Arthur's second cousin's son, Ray, and Daley's schemes and scams continued apace. Pursuit this time came from coppers Morley and Park.

Dennis Waterman also co-wrote (with Gerard Kenny) and performed the theme song, 'I Could Be So Good For You', which he took to number three in the charts in 1980. Cole joined him on a novelty hit, 'What Are We Gonna Get 'Er Indoors' at Christmas 1983, and the partnership was celebrated in a hit for The Firm, 'Arthur Daley ('E's Alright)', in 1982.

MINI-SERIES

A term generally given to glossy dramas (often adaptations of blockbuster novels) spread over a handful of episodes, which are usually scheduled on consecutive nights. The genre was initiated in the 1970s by concepts like RICH MAN, POOR MAN and others in the *Best Sellers* collection.

MINOGUE, KYLIE
(1968–)

Australian actress and singer, shooting to fame as Charlene Robinson in NEIGHBOURS before quitting the series to concentrate on a pop music and film career. Previously Minogue had appeared in series like THE SULLIVANS and *The Henderson Kids*. Her sister, Dannii, is also an actress/singer.

MIRREN, HELEN
(Ilynea Lydia Mironoff; 1946–)

London-born actress who scored some notable TV successes with the PRIME SUSPECT mini-series, playing DCI Jane Tennison. Earlier, she was Valerie in the 1972 adaptation of *Cousin Bette*, took roles in numerous classic plays and single dramas, like *The Duchess of Malfi* and THE BBC TELEVISION SHAKESPEARE (*As You Like It*), and also appeared in Dennis Potter's acclaimed *Blue Remembered Hills*. *Mrs Reinhard, Behind the Scenes*, THRILLER, *Miss Julie, The Serpent Son, After the Party, Coming Through* and JACKANORY number among her other credits. More recent work includes the mini-series, *Painted Lady* (blues singer Maggie Sheridan).

MISFIT, THE
UK (ATV) Situation Comedy. ITV 1970–1

Basil 'Badger' Allenby-Johnson	**Ronald Fraser**
Ted Allenby-Johnson	**Simon Ward**
Alicia Allenby-Johnson	**Susan Carpenter**
Stanley Allenby-Johnson	**Patrick Newell**

Creator/Writer: **Roy Clarke**
Producer: **Dennis Vance**

An expat returns from the Far East and finds Britain has changed for the worse.

Fifty-year-old Basil Allenby-Johnson, nicknamed 'Badger' during his many years of rubber planting in Malaya, returned to live with his son, Ted, and daughter-in-law, Alicia, in 1970s London. While in the Orient, the permissive society had by-passed Badger, rendering him shocked and bewildered on arrival back in the old country. The liberal and open-minded attitudes of his hosts were equally baffling. In the second series he linked up with his brother, Stanley, but, wherever he went, Badger was the complete *Misfit* of the title. Written by LAST OF THE SUMMER WINE and OPEN ALL HOURS creator Roy Clarke, episodes were one hour in length.

MISS ADVENTURE
UK (ABC) Detective Drama. ITV 1964

Stacey Smith	**Hattie Jacques**
Henry Stanton	**Jameson Clark**

Creators: **Peter Yeldham, Marjorie Yeldham**
Producer: **Ernest Maxin**

A female investigator finds herself constantly in hot water.

Lively Stacey Smith worked for the hard-up, London-based Stanton Detective Agency, run by Henry Stanton. Henry sent her off on rather tepid assignments, but these always offered more excitement than they promised. For instance, when she boarded a number 22 London bus for her first mission, she somehow ended up in Greece, confronting blackmailers, murderers and jewel thieves. But what she was really looking for was a man. This was an unusual role for distinguished comedy actress Hattie Jacques and one which lasted only 13 episodes and three investigations.

MISS JONES AND SON
UK (Thames) Situation Comedy. ITV 1977–8

Elizabeth Jones	**Paula Wilcox**
Mrs Jones	**Charlotte Mitchell**
	Joan Scott
Mr Jones	**Norman Bird**
Geoffrey	**Christopher Beeny**
Rose Tucker	**Cass Allen**
David	**David Savile**
Penny	**Catherine Kirkwood**
Roly Jones	**Luke Steensil**

Creator/Writer: **Richard Waring**
Producer: **Peter Frazer-Jones**

A young, unmarried mum struggles to bring up her baby.

Elizabeth Jones was shocked when her boyfriend left her after a four-year relationship. She was even more surprised to discover she was pregnant. Despite failing to make the appropriate arrangements for claiming benefit, and consequently finding herself short of income, she happily gave birth to a baby son whom she christened Roland Desmond Geoffrey Jones. Her prudish parents were less than pleased with the situation at first but soon rallied round to support their daughter, as did her neighbour, Geoffrey, and friend, Rose Tucker. This daring (for the time) comedy focused on Elizabeth's attempts to make ends meet and do the best by her son. In the second series, Geoffrey moved out and a new neighbour, David (a widower), and his daughter, Penny, moved in. David, a writer, and Elizabeth, an illustrator, began to pool their talents and gradually their relationship became less platonic and rather more intimate.

MISS MARPLE

UK (BBC) Detective Drama. BBC 1 1984–92

Miss Jane Marple .... **Joan Hickson**
DI/DCI Slack .... **David Horovitz**

Producers: **Guy Slater, George Gallaccio**

The cases of Agatha Christie's celebrated female sleuth.

In an interpretation far removed from the blustery character portrayed by Margaret Rutherford in 1960s films, Joan Hickson played the role of geriatric detective Miss Marple much closer to the written original, dressed heavily in tweed, with a crocodile-skin handbag draped over her arm. Frail, gentle and self-effacing, she relied on a softly spoken investigative technique with a well-chosen query, followed by intense periods of listening. This, combined with a flair for analysing personality traits and an uncanny skill of spotting the out-of-the-ordinary, endowed this elderly, gardening-loving spinster with the talent to suss out even the cleverest murderer. In doing so, she suitably embarrassed the police force in her home of St Mary Mead and other picturesque 1930s villages. In true Christie tradition, the gory side of murder and the cruelty involved was always quickly overlooked, as each case developed into a complex, mind-bending puzzle which only our heroine could solve.

The first adaptation to be screened was *The Body in the Library*, with *The Mirror Crack'd from Side to Side* concluding the sporadic, drawn-out series at Christmas 1992, when Joan Hickson retired at the tender age of 86.

MISS WORLD

UK (BBC/Thames) Beauty Contest. BBC/ITV/Channel 5
1951–79/1980–8/1999–

Producers: **Bryan Cowgill, Humphrey Fisher, Philip Lewis, Michael Begg, Ken Griffin (BBC), Steve Minchin (Thames), Lisa Chapman (Channel 5)**

Long-running beauty pageant aiming to discover the world's most attractive girl.

Miss World was one of the television highlights of the year in the UK for over three decades until being dropped from the schedules in 1988 as political correctness gathered speed. After a revival on Sky One in the late 1990s, the beauty pageant returned to terrestrial TV in 1999, televised from London Olympia by Channel 5.

Conceived by Eric and Julia Morley of Mecca in 1951, its unashamed purpose has been to choose the most beautiful and charming girl from a collection of national representatives to reign (tiara and all) as *Miss World* for the next 12 months. Vital statistics have been quoted, tears have been shed, there has been much talk of working with children and animals, and, in the contest's heyday, the British public backed their fancies like horses in the Grand National. There have been contro-versial moments, too. For instance, Helen Morgan (UK), *Miss World* 1974, was forced to resign only days later when newspapers revealed she was actually the mother of a young child. Miss Sweden, Kiki Haakonson, won the first contest, and among the other well-remembered *Miss World*s are Eva Reuber-Staier (Austria, 1969), Marjorie Wallace (USA, 1973), Wilnelia Merced (Puerto Rico, 1975 – later wife of Bruce Forsyth), Cindy Breakspeare (Jamaica, 1976) and Mary Stavin (Sweden, 1977). Rosemarie Frankland (1961), Ann Sydney (1964), Lesley Langley (1965) and Sarah-Jane Hutt (1983) were other UK winners.

The venue in the early days was London's Lyceum Ballroom, with music supplied by the Joe Loss Orchestra but, from 1964, the Royal Albert Hall hosted proceedings and the Phil Tate Orchestra provided accompaniment. Among the main comperes (some for just single years) were David Coleman, Peter West, David Jacobs, Michael Aspel, Simon Dee, Keith Fordyce, Pete Murray, David Vine, Terry Wogan, Ray Moore, Patrick Lichfield, Andy Williams, Paul Burnett, Sacha Distel and Esther Rantzen. When coverage was transferred to ITV via Thames TV from 1980, Judith Chalmers, Peter Marshall, Anne Diamond, Mary Stavin and Alexandra Bastedo were seen in charge at various times. Jerry Springer hosted the 2000 event from the Millennium Dome.

MISSION: IMPOSSIBLE

US (Paramount) Spy Drama. BBC 1 1970–5

Daniel Briggs .... **Steven Hill**
Jim Phelps .... **Peter Graves**
Cinnamon Carter .... **Barbara Bain**
Rollin Hand .... **Martin Landau**
Barney Collier .... **Greg Morris**
Willy Armitage .... **Peter Lupus**
Voice on the tape .... **Bob Johnson**
Paris .... **Leonard Nimoy**
Dr Doug Lane .... **Sam Elliott**
Dana Lambert .... **Lesley Ann Warren**
Casey .... **Lynda Day George**
Mimi Davis .... **Barbara Anderson**

Creator/Executive Producer: **Bruce Geller**

A highly skilled task force undertakes ridiculously dangerous assignments.

These tales of international intrigue featured the Los Angeles-based IMF (Impossible Missions Force). This was a team of remarkable individuals, each renowned for his or her distinctive skills, and it was led by Jim Phelps, who took over from Daniel Briggs, the man seen in charge in the very earliest episodes. It was Phelps who collected the team's briefings, which arrived in a parcel containing a self-destructing audio tape. The tape burst into flames five seconds after delivering its message. Along with the tape came a series of photographs to help with the mission, but, beyond these, the team knew they were always on their own. The secret government body issuing the assignment offered no assistance whatsoever and even promised to deny all knowledge of the agents.

Although the tape didn't order the team into action (it always stated 'Your mission, should you choose to accept it . . .'), Phelps always agreed to take on the job. He then devised a complicated plan of attack and chose his task force from a sheaf of possible agents. However, with the exception of occasional guest stars, he always chose the same team. The agents were strong man Willy Armitage, electronics wizard Barney Collier (who created most of their high-tech gadgets), master of disguise Rollin Hand, and fashion model Cinnamon Carter, whose main function was distraction. The last two left after a couple of years and were replaced by Dana Lambert in the glamour role and new disguise expert Paris (played by 'Mr Spock', Leonard Nimoy).

The ultra-cool squad's outrageous missions usually centred on thwarting Communist plots in banana republics and tiny European states, although they did also work against more conventional crime in the United States. By restricting dialogue and characterization to a minimum, and by the use of snappy editing, the producers turned out a series of high-paced, all-action adventures.

Mission: Impossible (mostly billed as *Mission Impossible* – without the colon – in the UK) was revived briefly in 1988 to fill gaps in US TV schedules caused by a Hollywood writers' strike. Filmed in Australia, it again starred Peter Graves as head of a new team of operators, with the self-destructing audio tape now updated to a digital disc. A film version, starring Tom Cruise, was released in 1996.

MR AND MRS
UK (HTV/Border/Action Time) Quiz. ITV 1969–88; 1999

Presenters: **Alan Taylor** (HTV), **Derek Batey** (Border),
Julian Clary (Action Time)

Creator: **Roy Ward Dickson**
Producers: **Derek Clark** (HTV), **Derek Batey, William Cartner** (Border), **Jo Sargent** (Action Time)

Couples win money by answering questions about their partners.

'Which shoe does your husband put on first?' and 'Does your wife carry a handbag – always, sometimes or never?' were typical *Mr and Mrs* questions. This quiz, which had been running in the HTV area before being networked, demanded no more of married couples than that they know their partner's little habits and foibles. Three questions were put to the husband and three to the wife. While one was answering questions, the spouse was asked to leave the studio. He/she was then brought back to put the record straight and give the correct answers themselves. Each right response earned the couple some cash and all six correct answers won the jackpot. Three couples were usually featured in each programme.

The series was produced alternately by HTV and Border (it has been one of the latter company's few contributions to the ITV network). Alan Taylor hosted the HTV programmes and Derek Batey those from Border. A Welsh-language version, *Sion a Sian*, was also made. The idea returned to television in the early 1990s when the satellite channel, UK Living, broadcast *The New Mr and Mrs Show*. In 1999 ITV presented *Mr and Mrs* with *Julian Clary*, in which the couples no longer needed to be married to participate. Stacey Young was Clary's assistant.

MR BEAN
UK (Thames/Central/Tiger) Comedy. ITV 1990–5

Mr Bean .... **Rowan Atkinson**

Writers: **Rowan Atkinson, Richard Curtis, Robin Driscoll**
Producers: **John Howard Davies, Sue Vertue, Peter Bennett-Jones**

The virtually silent adventures of a walking disaster zone.

Effectively a vehicle for Rowan Atkinson's mime skills, this near-silent comedy revolved around the accident-prone Mr Bean, a gormless, friendless, brainless little chap with a flair for causing havoc. A trip to the sales, a spot of DIY or a day at the seaside, all were likely to bring threats to life and limb to Mr Bean or those around him. Numerous specials were made, as well as regular series. Such was the international appeal of this modern-day Monsieur Hulot that a feature film, *Bean – the Ultimate Disaster Movie*, was produced in 1997.

MR BENN
UK (Zephyr) Children's Entertainment. BBC 1 1971–2

Narrator: **Ray Brooks**

Creator/Writer: **David McKee**

A man discovers magical adventures at the back of a costume shop.

Mr Benn, inhabitant of 52 Festive Road, London, enjoyed escapism. In each episode, he indulged his hobby by walking to a local fancy-dress shop, where he was greeted by a shopkeeper who arrived 'as if by magic' and escorted him through to the changing rooms. Donning the outfit of the day, Mr Benn then exited through a special door and into a land of adventure, which was always related to the clothes he was wearing. He was seen as a caveman, a spaceman, a pirate, a cowboy and a hunter, among other guises. Inevitably, the courteous and genial Mr Benn was able to provide some valuable assistance to the people he met before the shopkeeper suddenly popped up to lead him back into the changing room. Switching back into his business suit and bowler hat, Mr Benn then strolled off home, taking with him a souvenir of his day's work.

Although the series has been repeated endlessly on the BBC, only 13 episodes of this WATCH WITH MOTHER animation were ever produced.

MR DIGBY, DARLING
UK (Yorkshire) Situation Comedy. ITV 1969–71

Roland Digby .... **Peter Jones**
Thelma Teesdale .... **Sheila Hancock**

Mr Trumper	**Brian Oulton**
Olive	**Beryl Cooke**
Mr Bailey	**Peter Stephens**
Joyce	**Janet Brown**
Norman Stanhope	**Michael Bates**

Creators/Writers: **Ken Hoare, Mike Sharland**
Producers: **Christopher Hodson, Bill Hitchcock**

An executive is cosseted by his loyal and devoted secretary.

Thelma Teesdale worked for the Rid-O-Rat pest extermination company as secretary to Mr Roland Digby. From the time he arrived in the morning until he left for home in the evening, Thelma catered for his every need, pulling out all the stops to protect him from the outside world. However, her ambitious plans to secure his advancement were usually ill advised and doomed to failure. Thelma's colleagues included Norman Stanhope.

MISTER ED
US (Filmways) Situation Comedy. ITV 1962–5

Wilbur Post	**Alan Young**
Carol Post	**Connie Hines**
Roger Addison	**Larry Keating**
Kay Addison	**Edna Skinner**
Gordon Kirkwood	**Leon Ames**
Winnie Kirkwood	**Florence MacMichael**
Mister Ed's Voice	**Allan 'Rocky' Lane**

Creator: **Al Simon**
Executive Producers: **Al Simon, Arthur Lubin**
Producer: **Herbert W. Browar**

A talking horse gives his master headaches.

When architect Wilbur Post decided to give up the city in favour of the countryside around Los Angeles, little did he know what awaited him. With his newly-wed wife, Carol, he bought a large country house and discovered in the barn an eight-year-old palomino, named Mister Ed (played by a horse called Bamboo Harvester). However, this was no ordinary horse: this one could talk and, to prove the point, he introduced every programme with the whinnied words, 'Hello, I'm Mister Ed.'

But Mister Ed would talk only to Wilbur, since Wilbur (or 'Buddy Boy', as the horse nicknamed him) was the only human being Ed had found worth talking to. Predictably, this tended to land his master in hot water, particularly when he was overheard talking to the horse. As if that wasn't enough, the cynical and grumpy Mister Ed was also keen on giving Wilbur advice (from the horse's mouth, so to speak), which usually led to even more trouble.

The cast was completed by the Posts' bemused next-door neighbours, Roger and Kay Addison. When actor Larry Keating died, his screen wife, Edna Skinner, continued alone for a while until she was replaced with a new couple, the Kirkwoods. The series was created by Arthur Lubin, who had directed the *Francis* (the talking mule) films, starring Donald O'Connor, in the 1950s.

MR MAGOO
US (UPA) Cartoon. BBC 1962–4

Voices:

Mr Quincy Magoo	**Jim Backus**
Waldo	**Jerry Hausner**
	Daws Butler
Millie	**Julie Bennett**

Executive Producer: **Henry G. Saperstein**

The misadventures of a short-sighted old codger.

Created in the 1940s, myopic Mr Magoo appeared in various TV packages, from half-hour compilations to this series of five-minute shorts. Most of the mirth came from the fact that he couldn't tell a telephone box from a police officer, or an ugly woman from a moose – although, with his surly, irascible manner and bulbous nose, there was more than an echo of W. C. Fields. Whereas Fields disliked children intensely, Magoo hated dogs, for instance. (Indeed, it is reputed that Fields used the name Primrose Magoo when checking into hotels.)

Semi-regulars in these short TV animations were Magoo's stupid nephew, Waldo, and Waldo's girlfriend, Millie, although other relatives did appear from time to time. In the longer programmes made later, Magoo sometimes appeared in a historical or literary guise, such as Rip Van Winkle or William Tell. Assorted cinema versions were also produced, beginning in 1949 with *Ragtime Bear*, which saw Magoo in a supporting role.

MR PALFREY OF WESTMINSTER
UK (Thames) Spy Drama. ITV 1984–5

Mr Palfrey	**Alec McCowen**
The Co-ordinator	**Caroline Blakiston**
Blair	**Clive Wood**

Executive Producer: **Lloyd Shirley**
Producer: **Michael Chapman**

The cases of a master spycatcher.

Mr Palfrey (first name never given) worked for a secret Government department from an office close to the Houses of Parliament. His 'Iron Lady' boss was the similarly unnamed Co-ordinator, and his leg work was done by vicious action man Blair. Through the studious, inquisitorial Mr Palfrey viewers learned much about the mysterious world of counter-espionage. The ten-episode series was spun off *The Traitor*, a play in Thames TV's STORYBOARD anthology, shown in 1983, and Mr Palfrey was also seen in another *Storyboard* production called *A Question of Commitment* in 1989.

MR ROSE
UK (Granada) Detective Drama. ITV 1967–8

Mr Rose	**William Mervyn**

John Halifax	**Donald Webster**
Drusilla Lamb	**Gillian Lewis**
Jessica Dalton	**Jennifer Clulow**
Robert Trent	**Eric Woolfe**

Creator: **Philip Mackie**
Producers: **Philip Mackie, Margaret Morris**

A retired police officer can't escape from his previous life.

Chief Inspector Rose, formerly of THE ODD MAN and IT'S DARK OUTSIDE, had inherited the wealth of two maiden aunts and taken retirement from the force to concentrate on his cottage garden in Eastbourne and the writing of his memoirs. Having kept copies of all his case files, he had a personal library of crime, and the fear that he was about to reveal all brought some of his former adversaries – and colleagues – back into his life. Gratefully picking up the scent and rejecting the boredom of his retirement years, Mr Rose lurched once again from investigation to investigation. Rose's assistants were his manservant, former detective John Halifax, and his attractive secretary, Drusilla Lamb. Drusilla was later replaced by Jessica Dalton, and Robert Trent became Rose's sidekick for the last series.

MR WROE'S VIRGINS
UK (BBC) Drama. BBC 2 1993

John Wroe	**Jonathan Pryce**
Joanna	**Lia Williams**
Leah	**Minnie Driver**
Hannah	**Kerry Fox**
Martha	**Kathy Burke**
Dinah	**Moya Brady**
Rachel	**Catherine Kelly**
Rebekah	**Ruth Kelly**
Tobias	**Freddie Jones**
Moses	**Nicholas Woodeson**
Samuel Walker	**Stefan Escreet**

Writer: **Jane Rogers**
Producer: **John Chapman**

A self-styled prophet of doom demands seven virgins from the local community.

Broadly based on a true-life incident, this drama was set in the mill town of Ashton-under-Lyne, near Manchester. The central figure was John Wroe, founder of a Christian Israelite church in readiness for an impending apocalypse. In 1830 he asked the townsfolk to give him seven virgins for his 'comfort and succour', and the unfolding events were then seen through the eyes of four of the women, one per episode. They were Joanna, a woman of absolute religious conviction and the spiritual leader of the commune, whom Wroe chose to father a new messiah; Leah, beautiful, shapely and sexually precocious, who joined Wroe to escape from everyday life but who found herself rejected by him; Hannah, the educationally liberated, socialist-minded member of the group, who was greatly attracted to the grotesque Wroe; and Martha, a devastated, badly beaten mute who had

been treated like an animal on her father's farm and whom Wroe transformed through care and attention. The other girls were Dinah, Rachel and Rebekah. The drama was set against the backdrop of great industrial change and religious impropriety, tempered by an epidemic of cholera.

The series was adapted by Jane Rogers from her own novel.

MISTRESS, THE
UK (BBC) Situation Comedy. BBC 2 1985–7

Maxine	**Felicity Kendal**
Luke Mansel	**Jack Galloway**
	Peter McEnery
Helen Mansel	**Jane Asher**
Jenny	**Jenny McCracken**
Simon	**Tony Aitken**
Jamie	**Paul Copley**

Creator/Writer: **Carla Lane**
Producer: **Gareth Gwenlan**

The pitfalls of an extra-marital affair.

The Mistress was more a situation tragedy than a situation comedy, dealing, as it did, with the touchy subject of adultery and all its drawbacks and dangers. At the apex of this particular eternal triangle was Maxine, an independent, single-minded woman who lived alone (apart from her pet rabbits) in a comfortable pink flat. Her lover was Luke Mansel, a married businessman, torn between the demanding Maxine and his suspecting wife, Helen. Secret meetings, snatched moments of passion and longed-for dirty weekends were balanced by pangs of guilt and desperate attempts to keep the illicit affair under wraps. Jenny was an old school friend with whom Maxine owned the Flora florist's shop, while Simon was Luke's envious work-colleague and confidant who suffered chronically from marital boredom.

MITCHELL, DENIS
(1912–)

Pioneering British documentary-maker, noted for his impressionistic studies of human life, the highlights of his career being *In Prison* (1957), *On Tour* (1958), *Morning in the Streets*, *A Soho Story* (both 1959), *The Wind of Change* (1960), *Chicago – Portrait of a City* (1961), *A Wedding on Saturday* (1964), *Seven Men* (1971), *European Journey* (1972 and 1973) and *Private Lives* (1975). His first contribution (after beginning in BBC radio) was *On the Threshold* in 1955, and he also worked on *This England* and WORLD IN ACTION.

MITCHELL, JAMES
(1926–)

North-eastern English scriptwriter, the creator of CALLAN and WHEN THE BOAT COMES IN and the co-creator of JUSTICE, but also contributor to THE

TROUBLESHOOTERS and THE AVENGERS, among other series.

MITCHELL, LESLIE
(1905–85)

British television's first regular announcer, Leslie Mitchell opened up the BBC service from Alexandra Palace in 1936, welcoming viewers to 'the magic of television'. As a sideline in those early days, he also interviewed guests for PICTURE PAGE. The Scots-born former actor and radio presenter turned freelance after the war (during which he had worked for British Movietone News), commentating on state and political events for the BBC, but also working for ITV. He was the first presenter of THIS WEEK, in 1956, briefly Head of Talks at Associated-Rediffusion and, in the 1970s, resurfaced as chairman of the Tyne Tees nostalgia quiz, *Those Wonderful TV Times*.

MITCHELL, WARREN
(Warren Misell; 1926–)

RADA-trained British actor, infamous as the bigoted Alf Garnett in TILL DEATH US DO PART. Mitchell's showbusiness career began on the stage and progressed via radio (Radio Luxembourg, plus BBC shows like *Educating Archie*) to television, where some of his first roles were to support Tony Hancock in HANCOCK'S HALF HOUR and Charlie Drake in *Drake's Progress*. He also appeared as Cromwell in the 1955 adaptation of *The Children of the New Forest* and starred in an early sitcom, *Three Tough Guys*. In 1961 Mitchell played Pan Malcov in a short-lived Granada sitcom called *Colonel Trumper's Private War*. More successfully, in 1965 he was cast as the outspoken Alf Ramsey in a COMEDY PLAYHOUSE episode which proved to be the pilot for *Till Death Us Do Part*. Ramsey became Garnett and the series ran from 1966 to 1968 and returned for another three years in 1972. It was briefly revived as *Till Death...* by ATV in 1981, and then revamped as IN SICKNESS AND IN HEALTH by the BBC for seven years from 1985. *The Thoughts of Chairman Alf* were still being broadcast as recently as 1998. Mitchell's other TV work has included performances in classic dramas such as *The Caretaker*, *The Merchant of Venice* and *Death of a Salesman*, *Screen One*'s *Wall of Silence* (Hassidic Jew Schmuel Singer), *Screen One*'s *Gobble* (Waterboard Chairman), and two further sitcoms – an early sort of YES, MINISTER called *Men of Affairs* (Sir William) in 1973, and *So You Think You've Got Troubles* (Ivan Fox, a Jew in Northern Ireland) in 1991– plus smaller roles in many series like OUT OF THE UNKNOWN, THE AVENGERS, THE SAINT, THE SWEENEY, AIN'T MISBEHAVIN' (Ray Smiles), *Gormenghast* (Barquentine) and *A Christmas Carol* (Eddie Scrooge's dad).

MIXED BLESSINGS
UK (LWT) Situation Comedy. ITV 1978–80

Thomas Simpson	**Christopher Blake**
Susan Lambert/Simpson	**Muriel Odunton**
Aunt Dorothy	**Joan Sanderson**
Edward Simpson	**George Waring**
Annie Simpson	**Sylvia Kay**
William Lambert	**Stefan Kalipha**
Matilda Lambert	**Carmen Munro**
Winston Lambert	**Gregory Munroe**
Mrs Beasley	**Pauline Delany**
Mr Huntley	**Ernest Clark**

Creator: **Sid Green**
Writers: **Sid Green, Derrick Goodwin**
Producer: **Derrick Goodwin**

A racially mixed couple struggle to make their marriage acceptable to others.

This adventurous comedy focused on two university graduates, Thomas Simpson and Susan Lambert. It saw them getting engaged, being married and then starting a family; but what made this relationship unusual (for the time) was that Thomas was white and Susan was black. Both sets of parents were convinced the marriage would not work, other relatives disapproved and only Thomas's Aunt Dorothy had confidence in the liaison. Realizing that money was scarce (Susan was a social worker, but Thomas was initially unemployed), Dorothy even offered them a home in her basement flat. The programme's theme music – sung by star Christopher Blake – was written by actor Peter Davison.

MOGUL/THE TROUBLESHOOTERS
UK (BBC) Drama. BBC 1 1965–72

Brian Stead	**Geoffrey Keen**
Willy Izard	**Philip Latham**
Peter Thornton	**Ray Barrett**
Alec Stewart	**Robert Hardy**
Robert Driscoll	**Barry Foster**
Derek Prentice	**Ronald Hines**
Steve Thornton	**Justine Lord**
Jane Webb	**Philippa Gail**
Roz Stewart	**Deborah Stanford**
Mike Szabo	**David Baron**
Eileen O'Rourke	**Isobel Black**
Charles Grandmercy	**Edward De Souza**
Claire Cooke	**Camilla Brockman**
Julie Serres	**Virginia Wetherell**
Ginny Vickers	**Jayne Sofiano**
Miss Jenkins	**Beryl Cooke**
Ghislaine Foss	**Dora Reisser**
James Langely	**John Carson**
Britte Langely	**Anna Matisse**
Lita Perez	**Barbara Shelley**

Creator: **John Elliot**
Producers: **Peter Graham Scott, Anthony Read**

Power struggles and other excitement in the oil industry.

Mogul International was a major oil production company, headed by managing director Brian Stead and his financial controller, Willy Izard. In the first series, which was simply entitled *Mogul*, much of the action took place at executive level but, as attention shifted to the younger and more dynamic members of staff, the title was changed to *The Troubleshooters* and the drama moved out of the office and on to the rigs scattered around the world. The key, globetrotting 'troubleshooters' were Peter Thornton and Alec Stewart.

The 'soapy' boardroom and bedroom elements apart, the series was much respected in the real oil world for its attention to detail and accuracy in technical matters. Issues covered in the storylines, such as explosions, earthquakes, racial tension, company takeovers and the discovery of new oilfields, uncannily foretold real events, and this no doubt contributed to its seven-year residence on UK screens. The Mogul company was allegedly based on BP.

MOLINA, ALFRED
(1953–)

British actor, the husband of Jill Gascoine, with whom he guested in C.A.T.S. EYES. He has also been seen in CASUALTY, played Nigel the wrestler in the Leonard Rossiter comedy, *The Losers*, musician John Ogden in the drama, *Virtuoso*, and retired crook Hamish in *Alan Bleasdale Presents Requiem Apache*. He also appeared in the TV movies, *The Accountant*, *Drowning in the Shallow End*, *Trust Me*, *A Very Polish Practice*, *Hancock* ('the lad himself'), *The Trial* and *Nervous Energy*. Probably his most prominent role has been as the retired copper, Blake, in EL C.I.D.

MONITOR

A television display showing camera output. Monitors are used by the director to line up and select the next shot and also by presenters to see what is going out while they are on air.

MONITOR
UK (BBC) Arts Magazine. BBC 1 1958–65

Hosts: **Huw Wheldon, Jonathan Miller**

Producers: **Peter Newington, Nancy Thomas, Humphrey Burton**

Britain's first successful arts programme.

During its seven-year run, *Monitor* became a Sunday night institution for the learned classes. Screened at around 10 p.m., and presented for the most part in relaxed, authoritative fashion by its editor, Huw Wheldon, the programme spanned all artistic fields and laid the foundations for later successes like OMNIBUS, AQUARIUS and THE SOUTH BANK SHOW. *Monitor* also broke new ground by commissioning film profiles of artists from emerging film-makers like Ken Russell and John Schlesinger. These have since become archive classics. Russell, for instance, made biopics of Elgar, Debussy, Rousseau and Bartók, while Schlesinger contributed pieces on Britten and others. Melvyn Bragg co-scripted some of Russell's work.

MONKEES, THE
US (Raybert/Screen Gems) Situation Comedy. BBC 1
1966–8

Davy	Davy Jones
Mickey	Mickey Dolenz
Peter	Peter Tork
Mike	Mike Nesmith
Miss Purdy	Jesslyn Fax
Mr Babbitt	Henry Corden

Creators/Producers: **Bert Schneider, Robert Rafelson**

Zany humour with a quartet of pop musicians.

In the wake of the success of The Beatles and, particularly, their madcap films, *A Hard Day's Night* and *Help!*, a couple of American producers, Bert Schneider and Robert Rafelson, developed an idea for a TV version and advertised for four young lads to fashion into a pop group. The advert called for 'Four insane boys, aged 17–21'. After auditioning over 400 applicants, they settled on three Americans and one Englishman. Davy Jones was an actor from Manchester who had appeared briefly in CORONATION STREET as Ena Sharples's grandson. He was joined by another actor, Mickey Dolenz, formerly Mickey Braddock of CIRCUS BOY fame, and the group was completed by Peter Tork and Michael Nesmith, both of whom did have some musical experience, albeit in the folk medium. Stephen Stills, later of supergroup Crosby, Stills and Nash, was one of the hopefuls turned down for the series.

Musically, their early recordings were made by session musicians, masterminded by producer Don Kirschner, and the series spawned some huge hits on both sides of the Atlantic. 'Last Train To Clarksville', 'I'm A Believer', 'Daydream Believer', 'Pleasant Valley Sunday' and 'A Little Bit Me, A Little Bit You' were the group's biggest successes, and all premièred on the TV show. In the group, the calm, bobble-hatted Nesmith and lankhaired, dozy Tork were the guitarists, the manic Dolenz sang and played the drums, and the hopeless romantic Jones mainly sang but sometimes tapped a tambourine or rattled a maracca.

The series, although borrowing heavily from Dick Lester's Beatles films in concept, was quite original in its own way. This was the first time that comedy had been treated to unusual camera-angles (often hand-held), blurred focuses, cranked-up or overexposed film and really snappy editing. The plots were less remarkable and featured the band getting into various scrapes and nearly always ending up in some kind of chase sequence.

After the break-up of the band and the end of the series, the most musically active was Nesmith, who became a respected performer/producer in the country rock sphere. Dolenz went on to produce and direct the METAL MICKEY series, Jones also returned to acting, but little was heard of Tork. The band re-formed for a major concert tour in the late 1990s.

MONKEY

See WATER MARGIN, THE.

MONKHOUSE, BOB

OBE (1928–)

Quick-witted British comedian, actor, writer, presenter and game show host. Monkhouse's showbiz career began to take off when he sold a joke to Max Miller in 1943, while still a schoolboy. With his partner, Denis Goodwin, he worked in radio and then broke into television. Their first series, *Fast and Loose*, in 1954, was an instant success and they also worked together on the sitcom, *My Pal Bob*, and *The Bob Monkhouse Hour*. Monkhouse, heading off solo, compered SUNDAY NIGHT AT THE LONDON PALLADIUM and fronted CANDID CAMERA. His love of silent films led to his own retrospective, *Mad Movies*, and he also tackled another sitcom, playing Bob Mason, a disc jockey, in *The Big Noise* in 1964. A few years later, Monkhouse replaced Jackie Rae as host of THE GOLDEN SHOT and turned it into a huge Sunday teatime hit. He went on to chair CELEBRITY SQUARES in 1975 (and its revival in 1993), did three years in charge of FAMILY FORTUNES from 1980, and switched to the BBC to host the bingo quiz, *Bob's Full House*, and the revived talent show, *Bob Says* OPPORTUNITY KNOCKS, in the middle of that decade. Back on ITV, he was the questionmaster on *The $64,000 Question* and star of the newlywed game show, *Bob's Your Uncle*. Among his other contributions have been *I'm Bob, He's Dickie* (with Dickie Henderson), the slapstick show, *Bonkers!*, the cartoon contest, *Quick on the Draw*, a BBC 2 chat show majoring on top comics, the fast-moving joke panel-game, *Gagtag*, the quick recall quiz, *Monkhouse's Memory Masters*, the audience-inspired *Bob Monkhouse on the Spot*, periods hosting both NATIONAL LOTTERY LIVE and THE BIG BREAKFAST, and the quiz, *Wipeout*. Straight drama credits include parts in *All or Nothing at All* and JONATHAN CREEK.

MONOCLED MUTINEER, THE

UK (BBC) Drama. BBC 1 1986

Percy Toplis	Paul McGann
Charles Strange	Matthew Marsh
Cruikshank	Nick Reding
Geordie	Billy Fellows
Brigadier Gen. Thomson	Timothy West
Lady Angela Forbes	Penelope Wilton
Strachan	Ron Donachie
Guiness	Anthony Calf
Dorothy	Cherie Lunghi
Woodhall	Philip McGough

Writer: **Alan Bleasdale**
Producer: **Richard Broke**

A rebellious private leads a coup on the eve of a World War I battle.

Based on true events recalled in a book by William Allison and John Fairley, *The Monocled Mutineer* was the story of dashing rogue Percy Toplis. The cynical Nottinghamshire miner, a private in the British army, was stationed at the Etaples training camp in France and, on the night before the Battle of Passchendaele in 1917, instigated a mutiny among his harshly treated fellow recruits. His partner in the action was Charles Strange, a political idealist. This four-part dramatization by Alan Bleasdale (whose own grandfather had died at Passchendaele) added fiction to the bare facts and depicted how Toplis escaped into the French hills, took to impersonating an army officer and led a group of renegades in the taking of a bridge. He then returned to England and fell in love with Dorothy, a young widow, before being captured in the Lake District and 'executed' for his crimes by MI5 assassin Woodhall.

The series proved to be the most provocative of Bleasdale's works to date and roused the ire of Establishment figures and old soldiers. The suggestion that deserters were executed by their own side (exemplified in the drama by the shooting of an officer named Cruikshank) was heavily condemned. The fact that Michael Grade, the BBC's Director of Programmes, had passed a press release stating that the story was totally factual only made matters worse. According to Grade, the fuss detracted from the quality of the drama itself.

MONTGOMERY, ELIZABETH

(1933–95)

Betty Grable insured her legs, so perhaps Elizabeth Montgomery should have sought cover for her nose, for, as winsome witch Samantha Stephens in BEWITCHED, she relied on its twitching to cast her benign spells. Samantha was a role she played for eight years from 1964 and the series was produced by her husband, William Asher. Keeping it in the family, it was her dad, actor Robert Montgomery, who, somewhat reluctantly, gave Elizabeth her TV break, offering her a part in his anthology series, *Robert Montgomery Presents*, in the early 1950s. She followed this with appearances in dozens of other series but, after leaving *Bewitched*, Montgomery was generally seen only in TV movies.

MONTY PYTHON'S FLYING CIRCUS

UK (BBC) Comedy. BBC 2 1969–74

John Cleese, Michael Palin, Eric Idle, Graham Chapman, Terry Jones, Terry Gilliam, Carol Cleveland

Writers: **John Cleese, Michael Palin, Eric Idle, Graham Chapman, Terry Jones, Terry Gilliam**
Producers: **John Howard Davies, Ian MacNaughton**

Innovative comedy show, combining cerebral wit, visual humour and slapstick in an atmosphere of virtual anarchy.

When it first reached the TV screen in 1969, filling a former religious slot, late on Sunday night, *Monty Python's Flying Circus* understandably met with some bemusement. However, it soon acquired a fervent global following and genuine cult status. Each programme was well endowed with sketches and held together with animation and one-liner humour; but, essentially, anything went in this manic collage of comedy styles.

The sketches relied heavily on off-beat domestic situations and spoof TV interviews or documentaries, although the series seldom lacked invention. Swaying between incomprehensibility and bad taste, it was a show that shocked and confused, but was always inspired. The Oxbridge background of its writers/performers surfaced in the show's literary and artistic allusions, yet there was always room for juvenile pranks, vulgar asides and general silliness. Among the highlights were skits like *The Dead Parrot*, in which John Cleese confronted Michael Palin, a shopkeeper, with the corpse of a bird he had just purchased. Another classic was *The Lumberjack Song*, a rousing Canadian chorus of machismo which unravelled into a celebration of transvestism. There was also *The Argument Clinic, Upper Class Twit of the Year, The Ministry of Silly Walks, Spam, The Spanish Inquisition, The Fish-Slapping Dance*, and *Blackmail* (a sadistic game show). Classic characters included Graham Chapman's stuffy army officer, Terry Jones's piercingly vocal women, Eric Idle's seedy men, and the cerebrally challenged Gumby, complete with knotted handkerchief on head.

Wrapped around the sketches were Terry Gilliam's chaotic, surreal cartoons which 'stole' images from classical art. Sometimes they picked up from the end of the previous sketch (which seldom had a punchline), in the same way that sketches themselves occasionally merged when a character from an earlier skit wandered into the action. Snappily cut together, it was a programme without a beginning and without an end which broke all the rules of television structure. Its opening titles, bouncing along on the music of Sousa's *Liberty Bell*, could appear anywhere in the show, even after the closing credits, and along the way there was plenty of time for developing catchphrases, from Michael Palin's succinct 'It's' to John Cleese's 'And now for something completely different'.

Yet if *Monty Python* broke new ground, it could at the same time be seen as the culmination of the unconventional comedy trend that had begun with THAT WAS THE WEEK THAT WAS, and developed through THE FROST REPORT, NOT ONLY ... BUT ALSO, AT LAST THE 1948 SHOW and DO NOT ADJUST YOUR SET. The Pythons had all learned their craft in such programmes, a craft which was to stand them in good stead in individual projects long after *Monty Python* was laid to rest. John Cleese did not appear in the final season (which went out under the simple title of *Monty Python*).

A series of stage shows and feature films was also produced, the earliest films reprising the best of the TV sketches but the later ones taking the Python manic humour to new bounds in mock epics like *Monty Python and the Holy Grail* and the notorious *Life of Brian*.

MOODY, RON
(Ronald Moodnick; 1924–)

British actor whose television work has, by general consensus, not matched his cinema and stage performances. Indeed, his TV outlets have been few. These have included a 1961 BBC series entitled *Moody in . . .* (various contrived 'lands', such as *Storeland*), a show for YTV in 1968 entitled *Moody*, and the odd single drama (such as Jack Rosenthal's *Mr Ellis Versus the People* in 1974). There have also been TV movies, a couple of kids' series (*Into the Labyrinth*, playing sorcerer Rothgo, and *Mike and Angelo*, as Angelo's father), plus a sitcom, HART OF THE YARD (DI Roger Hart, a London detective working in San Francisco – the series was called *Nobody's Perfect* in the US). Moody has, however, guested in numerous other programmes, including THE AVENGERS.

MOONLIGHTING
US (Picturemaker) Comedy Drama. BBC 2 1986–9

Maddie Hayes	**Cybill Shepherd**
David Addison	**Bruce Willis**
Agnes Dipesto	**Allyce Beasley**
Herbert Viola	**Curtis Armstrong**
Virginia Hayes	**Eva Marie Saint**
Alex Hayes	**Robert Webber**
MacGilicuddy	**Jack Blessing**

Creator/Executive Producer: **Glenn Gordon Caron**
Producer: **Jay Daniel**

Off-beat sleuthing with a squabbling but romantically linked pair of investigators.

When top fashion model Maddie Hayes was swindled by her financial manager, she found that one of the few investments she still owned was the City of Angels Detective Agency, a private investigation company set up to make a loss to offset against her tax bills. Head of the agency was cocky David Addison, a flippant, streetwise young private eye. Although Maddie intended to sell off the company, Addison ensured that she held on to it, renaming the business the Blue Moon Detective Agency, after the Blue Moon shampoo she used to market. With her modelling career now behind her, Maddie decided to take a hand in the running of the business and the aloof, classy blonde and the smirking, stubble-chinned punk became unlikely partners.

From the start, their relationship was electric. They came from widely differing backgrounds and they had different ways of working, yet they also had chemistry. Although they sparred and fought their way through investigations, there was always a restrained romance behind their bickering. Maddie toyed with other suitors (even marrying a stranger on a train) and David played the field, but the two eventually caved in and came together. All the same, even while pregnant with his child (later miscarried), the animosity between the partners remained and exploded into violent verbal exchanges (the sharp repartee was the highlight of the programme).

At work, they were successful, taking on a variety of unusual cases and usually gaining positive results, at the same time turning the Blue Moon Detective Agency into a viable business. They were assisted by their scatty receptionist, Agnes Dipesto, who answered the telephone with a little rhyme, and Herbert Viola, the object of Agnes's desires, who joined the team as a clerk but longed to be a detective. His office rival was MacGilicuddy. Maddie's parents, Alex and Virginia, were also seen.

With its witty dialogue style gleaned from the 1940 film, *His Girl Friday*, starring Cary Grant and Rosalind Russell, *Moonlighting* was one of those programmes that broke every law of television. Characters spoke to camera, out-takes were shown over the closing credits and actors dropped out of character and addressed the audience as themselves. The surreal air was enhanced with episodes like *Atomic Shakespeare*, based on *The Taming of the Shrew* and written in iambic pentameters, which was performed in period and in costume. However, the programme was plagued with production problems, and re-runs had to be inserted when the latest episodes failed to arrive on time. Stars Shepherd and Willis didn't always see eye to eye, and this all contributed to a rather scrappy finish to the series. It faded away rather than going out with a bang. The theme song was a UK hit for Al Jarreau in 1987, and Bruce Willis followed up with hits of his own.

MOORE, BRIAN
(1932–)

Experienced British soccer commentator and general sports presenter, whose main credits have been *The Big Match*, WORLD OF SPORT (the *On the Ball* segment), *Who's the Greatest?*, *Midweek Sports Special* and other major sport coverage. Before joining ITV, Moore worked as a journalist for *The Times* and BBC radio. He retired after the 1998 soccer World Cup finals, but has since been seen on satellte TV.

MOORE, CLAYTON
(Jack Carlton Moore; 1914–99)

Television's LONE RANGER, Clayton Moore began his movie career in 1938 as a stuntman (he was previously a circus performer). He was offered the part of the masked Western hero ten years later and, as soon as the series hit US TV screens, Moore became a huge celebrity. After three years, he fell out of favour with the show's producers over contractual matters and John Hart was brought in as a replacement for 52 episodes, before Moore returned to the role he now felt to be his own. In 1979, the Wrather Corporation, which owned the rights to the character, took legal action to prevent Moore from continuing to wear the *Lone Ranger* mask. He adopted mask-shaped sunglasses instead.

MOORE, DUDLEY
(1935–)

Oxford-educated classical pianist, jazz performer, actor and comedian, in the early days in collaboration with Peter Cook. Moore, together with Cook, Alan Bennett and Jonathan Miller, was one of the *Beyond the Fringe* team in 1960–1. TV work soon followed. When the BBC asked him to do a special, he enrolled Cook to compile a couple of sketches. The BBC liked what it saw and gave them their own series NOT ONLY . . . BUT ALSO . . . Among Moore's other credits were assorted variety shows, an episode of the drama anthology, *Love Story*, and his own *Not To Mention Dudley Moore*. In the 1970s, however, Moore concentrated mainly on film work, becoming a Hollywood name through his role in *10*. Recent TV work has been confined to two unsuccessful US sitcoms, *Dudley* and *Daddy's Girls*, and to providing the voice for Oscar the piano in the cartoon, *Oscar's Orchestra*. Moore's first wife was actress Suzy Kendall; his second was actress Tuesday Weld.

MOORE, MARY TYLER
(1936–)

American actress and television executive whose MARY TYLER MOORE SHOW was one of the USA's biggest successes in the 1970s. A former dancer, her TV break came in unusual circumstances. After a few commercials and small roles, she was cast as Sam, the secretary, in David Janssen's 1959 series, *Richard Diamond, Private Detective*, although the only parts of her that viewers saw were her legs. She quit after three months in favour of appearances in dramas like *Hawaiian Eye*. Two years later, her role as Laura Petrie, the wife in THE DICK VAN DYKE SHOW, established Moore as a major sitcom star, but her career seemed to be going no further when the series ended in 1966. After a few stage and film disappointments, she was given another chance to shine in her own *Mary Tyler Moore Show* in 1970 and this time didn't let the opportunity pass. It was a ratings hit and its portrayal of an independent, career-minded female (Mary Richards) matched the general mood of the 1970s. Moore and her then husband, Grant Tinkler, founded the production company MTM (Mary Tyler Moore Enterprises, responsible for such series as LOU GRANT, REMINGTON STEELE and HILL STREET BLUES), which was later sold to the UK's TVS. She has since returned to the small screen in the unsuccessful 1985 and 1988 sitcoms, *Mary* and *Annie McGuire*, and the 1995 drama series, *New York News*.

MOORE, Sir PATRICK
CBE (Patrick Caldwell-Moore; 1923–)

Britain's number one stargazer, Patrick Moore has been presenting his monthly series, THE SKY AT NIGHT, since 1957, making it one of the BBC's longest-running programmes. His fascination with astronomy began at an early age and he became a member of the British Astronomical Association when just 11. After working as a navigator in the wartime RAF, Moore was commissioned to write his first books on space and set up his own observatory. All this led to a call from the BBC and, eventually, *The Sky at Night*. He also hosted the series about eccentrics, *One Pair of Eyes*, in 1969, hosted a kids' astronomy series, *Seeing Stars*, in 1970, and was the resident expert on the BBC's coverage of the lunar missions in the 1960s and 1970s. In the 1990s Moore was seen as *The Gamesmaster* in Channel 4's computer game contest. Additionally, he has been a popular guest in numerous light entertainment shows, often exhibiting his prowess on the xylophone.

MOORE, ROGER

CBE (1927–)

London-born leading man who arrived on television in 1958, wearing the chain mail of Sir Walter Scott's IVANHOE, having already made one film in Hollywood and others in England. In 1959 he played Silky Harris in the gold rush caper, *The Alaskans*, and a year later was cast as Cousin Beauregard in MAVERICK. He even introduced SUNDAY NIGHT AT THE LONDON PALLADIUM. Then, in 1962, came his most celebrated TV characterization, that of Simon Templar, debonair hero of THE SAINT. The series ran for seven years and made Moore – a former film cartoonist and model – an international star. Although he didn't really capitalize on the situation with his next TV outing, THE PERSUADERS! (Lord Brett Sinclair), in 1971, he soon made up for it by making seven films as James Bond. Apart from guest appearances, that put paid to Moore's television career, as he fixed his quizzical gaze (and much-mimicked raised eyebrows) firmly on the movie world. Moore's second wife was the late singer Dorothy Squires.

MORE, KENNETH

(1914–82)

British actor, a 1950s cinema favourite who also enjoyed a couple of notable TV roles. These came in 1967, as Jolyon Forsyte in THE FORSYTE SAGA, and seven years later as G. K. Chesterton's cleric-detective, FATHER BROWN. More also starred in *The White Rabbit*, a 1967 dramatization of the heroics of resistance fighter Wing-Commander Yeo-Thomas, and took the part of Peter Ingram in *An Englishman's Castle* in 1978. However, one of his earliest small-screen performances came in 1946 as Badger in *Toad of Toad Hall* and he enjoyed numerous other single-drama credits, too. More's third wife was actress Angela Douglas.

MORECAMBE, ERIC

OBE (Eric Bartholomew; 1926–84)

Possibly Britain's most popular comedian to date, Eric Morecambe took his stage name from his home town.

His career began in variety theatres before the war and, when auditioning for a new-talent show in 1941, he met a young entertainer from Leeds by the name of Ernest Wiseman, otherwise known as Ernie Wise. They forged an enterprising double-act, but their progress was shattered by war service. However, meeting again by chance in 1947, they were able to resume their joint career. Their first television forays came in the early 1950s and led, in 1954, to their own disastrous series called *Running Wild*, which set back their hopes of stardom. Undaunted, the pair continued to improve their act on stage and radio and were chosen to support Winifred Atwell in her TV series, this resulting in another short series of their own, *Double Six*, and appearances on SUNDAY NIGHT AT THE LONDON PALLADIUM, which encouraged ATV to give them *The Morecambe and Wise Show* in 1961, scripted by Sid Green and Dick Hills. This time they didn't miss their chance and quickly established themselves and the characteristics of their act – Ernie's pomposity, Eric's boyish anarchy, their Abbot-and-Costello-like exchanges, all underscored by impeccable comic timing. Viewers took to their many sight gags: Eric slipping his glasses askew, for instance, slapping Ernie around the face or pretending to be strangled behind the stage curtain. The public began to refer to Ernie as Little Ern and 'the one with the short, fat, hairy legs'. Unfortunately, their attempts to make it in the movies proved fruitless. Their films, *The Intelligence Men*, *That Riviera Touch* and *The Magnificent Two*, flopped. In 1968, after Eric had suffered a heart attack, they were tempted over to the BBC where, by common consent, they produced their best work (most scripted by Eddie Braben). A regular feature of their shows was a play 'wot Ernie wrote' which never failed to attract a big-name guest star. Among those who giggled their way through proceedings were Glenda Jackson, Diana Rigg, John Mills, Eric Porter, Peter Cushing (to return many times still looking for payment) and Hannah Gordon. Angela Rippon danced and Shirley Bassey sang in a hobnail boot. The duo were seen in domestic situations (even innocently sharing a double bed). They cruelly disparaged Des O'Connor's singing and were constantly upstaged at the end by the outsize Janet Webb or Arthur Tolcher with his mouth-organ. Ernie's alleged hairpiece ('you can't see the join') provided many gags and Eric flicked non-existent pebbles into a paper bag. Most shows closed with a neck-slapping rendition of 'Bring Me Sunshine' (their ITV theme song had been 'Two of a Kind'). *The Morecambe and Wise Christmas Show* became a national institution and, if Eric had put one of his catchphrases, 'What do you think of it so far?', to the nation, he would not have received the usual reply of 'Rubbish!' The partners switched back to ITV in 1978 with less success, while the BBC countered by screening repeats of their best material. However, they soon knew they would have to start treading carefully. Eric's heart problems resurfaced in 1979 and, after surgery, he was forced to take things somewhat easier. The partnership was brought to an end when Eric suffered another, this time fatal, heart attack in 1984. Their last work together was the TV movie, *Night Train to Murder*, which was aired in 1985. Ernie soldiered on alone, making stage and television appearances, becoming a member of the revived WHAT'S MY LINE? panel and even writing on gardening for the *News of the World*. He died in 1999.

MORGAN, ELAINE
(1920–)

Welsh dramatist whose most notable works have included *A Matter of Degree* (1960 – and a spin-off sitcom, *Lil*, five years later), *Epitaph for A Spy* (1963), *A Pin to See the Peepshow* (1972), *Joey* (1974), *How Green Was My Valley* (1976), an adaptation of Vera Brittain's *Testament of Youth* (1979), *The Life and Times of David Lloyd George* (1981) and episodes of DR FINLAY'S CASEBOOK, THE DOCTORS, THE ONEDIN LINE and THE BROTHERS.

MORGAN, HARRY
(Harry Bratsburg; 1915–)

American actor who arrived in television in the early 1950s, after acting in films (as Henry Morgan) since 1942. In the USA, he has notched up plenty of prime-time roles, beginning with the part of Pete Porter in the comedy, *December Bride*, which was spun off into its own series, *Pete and Gladys*. For UK viewers, however, Morgan will be remembered for two roles in particular. In 1967 he joined Jack Webb in a revival of DRAGNET, becoming Officer Bill Gannon. Then, in 1974, he made a one-off guest appearance in M*A*S*H and proved such a hit that he was asked back as the unit's new CO, Colonel Sherman Potter. Morgan's character lived on in the sequel, *After M*A*S*H*. Viewers may also recall him as Phil Jensen in the sitcom, *My World and Welcome to It*, Doc. Amos B. Coogan in *Hec Ramsey*, Bob Campbell in ROOTS: THE NEXT GENERATIONS and as a guest star in numerous series, from GUNSMOKE to THE PARTRIDGE FAMILY.

MORK AND MINDY
US (Miller-Milkis/Henderson/Paramount) Situation
Comedy. ITV 1979–81

Mork	**Robin Williams**
Mindy McConnell	**Pam Dawber**
Frederick McConnell	**Conrad Janis**
Cora Hudson	**Elizabeth Kerr**
Orson	**Ralph James** (*voice only*)
Eugene	**Jeffrey Jacquet**
Exidor	**Robert Donner**
Franklin Delano Bickley	**Tom Poston**
Nelson Flavor	**Jim Staahl**
Remo Da Vinci	**Jay Thomas**
Jean Da Vinci	**Gina Hecht**
Glenda Comstock	**Crissy Wilzak**
Mearth	**Jonathan Winters**
Miles Sternhagen	**Foster Brooks**

Creators: **Garry K. Marshall, Joe Glauberg, Dale McRaven**
Executive Producers: **Garry K. Marshall, Tony Marshall**
Producers: **Bruce Johnson, Dale McRaven**

A naïve alien arrives on Earth and pals up with a pretty young girl.

Fifteen years after MY FAVORITE MARTIAN had created comedy from an alien–human friendship, *Mork and Mindy* came to the TV screen and did the same thing – in subject-matter, at least. This time the style was much more frenetic and the alien far less predictable than Uncle Martin in the early series. Mork came from the planet Ork, bleems and bleems away from Earth (as he put it). There, he was considered odd because he had a sense of humour and, when he went too far and poked fun at Orson, their leader, the Orkans sent him to our planet as a punishment, to file reports on the weird lifestyles of Earth's inhabitants. He arrived in a large eggshell-like spacecraft near Boulder, Colorado, and was discovered by Mindy McConnell, an attractive single girl who worked in her dad's music store. She found him intriguing and amusing, was entertained by his child-like ways and touched by his kindness. Consequently, Mork took up residence in Mindy's attic, much to the consternation of her crusty father.

Although he looked human, Mork was prone to talking gibberish and doing wacky things like wearing a suit back to front, sitting on his head or drinking water with his fingers. There were always aspects of Earth life that he just could not comprehend and, at the end of every episode, he reported back his experiences to the unseen Orson, before signing off, twisting his ears and saying 'Nanu Nanu', the Orkan for goodbye.

In later episodes, Mindy's father, Fred, her hip grandmother, Cora Hudson, and Eugene, a black youth who frequented the music store, were written out. Fred later returned and some new characters were introduced when a brother and sister, Remo and Jean Da Vinci, arrived from the Bronx. He worked at the New York Deli and paid for Jean to attend medical school. Also new were Mindy's politically ambitious cousin, Nelson, and Mork's UFO-prophet friend, Exidor, leader of the invisible Friends of Venus clan. Mr Bickley, the crotchety neighbour who wrote greeting cards for a living, came into the action a little more, and Mindy took a job in the newsroom of a television station, KTNS, working for boss Mr Sternhagen.

Mork and Mindy's friendship grew deeper and deeper until they eventually married, taking a honeymoon on Ork. Soon after, Mork gave birth by releasing a tiny egg from his navel. The egg grew in size until it burst open to reveal the baby, a fully grown, middle-aged man. He, in the Orkan tradition, would grow younger, not older, and would never want for love and care in his later years. They called the 'baby' Mearth; he called Mork 'Mommy' and Mindy 'Shoe'.

Mork and Mindy was a spin-off from an episode of HAPPY DAYS where, in a dream, Mork arrived in Milwaukee and tried to kidnap Richie Cunningham. It made a star out of the relatively unknown Robin Williams, whose unpredictably quirky humour was perfect for the character of Mork. One of his childhood heroes had been comedian Jonathan Winters, and Williams was able to pay his mentor a tribute by helping to cast him as Mearth.

MORLEY, KEN
(1943–)

British actor, a former teacher who became a cult hero with his portrayal of self-important supermarket manager Reg Holdsworth in CORONATION STREET from 1990, but whose TV career has also encompassed programmes like 'ALLO 'ALLO (the German Flockenstuffen), YOU RANG, M'LORD?, THE FALL AND RISE OF REGINALD PERRIN, BULMAN, *Who Dares, Wins . . .*, *All Passion Spent*, *Les Girls*, WATCHING, *The Return of the Antelope* and *The Grand*.

MORRIS, COLIN
(1916–96)

British writer and producer, creator of *Jacks and Knaves*, THE NEWCOMERS and THE DOCTORS. Among his other contributions were drama-documentaries like *The Wharf Road Mob* (1957), *Who, Me?* (1959) and *Walk with Destiny* (a Winston Churchill biography, 1974), plus episodes of series like WHEN THE BOAT COMES IN. He also produced a number of editions of Z CARS.

MORRIS, JOHNNY
OBE (1916–99)

Fondly remembered for making animals talk, Welsh-born Johnny Morris presented ANIMAL MAGIC for 21 years from 1962. Before moving into television, he had managed a farm in Wiltshire and presented a radio series, in which he did other people's jobs for a day and travelled around the South-west. On TV, he appeared as *The Hot Chestnut Man*, which made full use of his flair for telling a tale. When *Animal Magic* came along, Morris donned a zoo-keeper's uniform and spent many days at Bristol Zoo, adding a whimsical vocal track to the films he made, putting casual quips in the mouths of his animal subjects. It was a trick he used when narrating another children's favourite, the Canadian series, TALES OF THE RIVERBANK. In 1970 Morris took a journey through South America for a series entitled *A Gringo's Holiday* and followed this with *Series in the Sun*, a look at Captain Cook's Pacific. In 1976 he presented *Oh to Be in England*, a tourist's-eye view of the country. He was working on a new animal series, *Wild Thing*, for ITV when he was taken ill and died in 1999.

MORRIS, JONATHON
(John Morris; 1960–)

Manchester-born actor whose most prominent role has been as the poetic Adrian Boswell in BREAD but who has had plenty of other TV credits to his name since the early 1980s, among them *Beau Geste* (John), *That Beryl Marston . . . !* (Phil), *The Prisoner of Zenda*, *Hell's Bells*, *The Consultant*, THE AGATHA CHRISTIE HOUR and *The Practice*. For kids, Morris has presented JACKANORY and chaired the quiz, *The Movie Game*.

MORRIS, JULIET
(1965–)

English factual programme presenter, beginning in BBC regional news in the West Country and moving on to front NEWSROUND, *BBC Breakfast News*, *The Six O'Clock News*, *Here and Now*, *999*, *The House Detectives*, *The Heaven and Earth Show* and *The Travel Show*, among other offerings.

MORRISSEY, NEIL
(1962–)

Midlands-born actor, usually in comic roles, such as Rocky Cassidy in BOON and Tony in MEN BEHAVING BADLY. He featured regularly on NOEL'S HOUSE PARTY as window cleaner Sammy the Shammy, played art student David in *A Woman's Guide to Adultery*, John Croft and Martin in the one-off comedies, *The Chest* and *My Summer with Des*, respectively, Paul Rochet in *Paris*, Phil in the pilot of ROGER ROGER, the New Romantic transsexual Charlie/Charlotte in *Hunting Venus*, Nick Cameron aka *The Vanishing Man*, and bus-driver Will Green in *Happy Birthday Shakespeare*. He has also supplied voices for the animations, *Bob the Builder* and *Maisy*, and donned an oxygen tank to present *Dive to Shark City*. Other credits have included the mini-series, *Ellis Island*, JULIET BRAVO, FAIRLY SECRET ARMY, ROLL OVER BEETHOVEN, C.A.T.S. EYES, *Pulaski*, *Gentlemen and Players*, *The Flint Street Nativity* (a Wise Man), *The Morph Files* (narrator) and *Men Down Under*.

MORSE, BARRY
(1919–)

London-born actor who made his name on the Canadian stage before moving into television. He has enjoyed major roles on both sides of the Atlantic, not least as the relentless Lt. Philip Gerard on the trail of Dr Richard Kimble, THE FUGITIVE. Later, Morse took on the role of Mr Parminter in the secret agent caper, THE ADVENTURER, and played Alec Marlowe (The Tiger) in THE ZOO GANG, Professor Victor Bergman in SPACE: 1999, Adam Verver in an adaptation of Henry James's *The Golden Bowl*, Wolf Stoller in THE WINDS OF WAR, Murgatroyd in A WOMAN OF SUBSTANCE, Dr Harley in *Master of the Game* and the US President, former actor Johnny Cyclops, in WHOOPS APOCALYPSE.

MORTIMER, BOB
(1959–) See REEVES, VIC.

MORTIMER, Sir JOHN
CBE (1923–)

British barrister, writer and dramatist, the creator of RUMPOLE OF THE BAILEY. Among his other offerings have been WILL SHAKESPEARE, *A Voyage Round My Father*, *Paradise Postponed*, *A Summer's Lease*, *Under the Hammer* and the hugely successful adaptation of Evelyn Waugh's BRIDESHEAD REVISITED. Mortimer also contributed to the 1965 satire show, BBC-3. He is the father of actress Emily Mortimer.

MORTIMER, JOHNNIE
(1930–)

British comedy scriptwriter, usually in collaboration with Brian Cooke. Together they created series such as FATHER, DEAR FATHER, MAN ABOUT THE HOUSE, GEORGE AND MILDRED, ROBIN'S NEST, *Alcock and Gander*, *Full House*, *Let There Be Love*, *Tom, Dick and Harriet*, *Kindly Leave the Kerb* and *The Incredible Mr Tanner* (the last two extensions of an episode they penned for *The Ronnie Barker Playhouse*). The duo also wrote episodes of the sitcoms, AND MOTHER MAKES FIVE, *Bernie*, *Life with Cooper* and *Cribbins*. In addition, Mortimer created NEVER THE TWAIN.

MOSLEY, BRYAN
OBE (1931–99)

Leeds-born actor, a former stunt-fight choreographer and keen fencer who was best known as Alf Roberts in CORONATION STREET, a part he first played in 1961. Not being a long-term contract-holder, Mosley was forced to leave the series the same year, during an actors' strike, but returned in 1968 and was in Weatherfield continuously until his character died of a heart attack just 40 days before Mosley himself died of the same cause. His other TV work included *The Villains'* episode, *Bent*, ARMCHAIR THEATRE, IT'S A SQUARE WORLD, Z CARS, THE PLANE MAKERS, THE SAINT, THE AVENGERS, NO HIDING PLACE, A FAMILY AT WAR, THE WORKER, QUEENIE'S CASTLE, DOCTOR WHO and CROSSROADS (Denis Rutledge).

MOTHER LOVE
UK (BBC) Drama. BBC 1 1989

Helena Vesey .... **Diana Rigg**
Kit Vesey .... **James Wilby**
Alex Vesey .... **David McCallum**
Angela .... **Fiona Gillies**
Ruth .... **Isla Blair**
George .... **James Grout**

Writer: **Andrew Davies**
Producer: **Ken Riddington**

A mother's overbearing love for her son ruins their lives.

Helena Vesey was the ultra-possessive mother cited in the title of this four-part tale of deception and revenge, adapted by Andrew Davies from the novel by Domini Taylor. Her suffocating affection for her son, Kit, a recently qualified barrister who still lived at home in Wimbledon, allied to her loathing for her estranged husband, famous musical conductor Alex, were the catalysts for the disruption of all their lives. Drawn into the tangled web was Angela, an art gallery assistant from rural Berkshire whom Kit had agreed to marry after only three weeks' acquaintance. Diana Rigg picked up a BAFTA for her sinister performance.

MOTSON, JOHN
(1945–)

Salford-born, long-serving BBC soccer commentator (covering well over 1,000 matches). He is known and much mimicked for his sheepskin coat and endless supply of match trivia.

MOUNT, PEGGY
OBE (Margaret Mount; 1916–)

Powerful Essex-born actress, usually seen as a domineering wife or colleague. Her first major TV role set the trend. In THE LARKINS, first seen in 1958, she played Ada, battleaxe wife of David Kossoff's Alf Larkins. In 1961 she was Martha, one of the *Winning Widows*, and in 1966 she teamed up with Sid James as the appropriately named Gabrielle Dragon in GEORGE AND THE DRAGON. Somewhat changing tack, Mount played sleuth Virginia Browne in 1969's *John Browne's Body*, but was back on form in 1971, as Maggie in LOLLIPOP LOVES MR MOLE. From brow-beating men she made the weedy Pat Coombs her next target when playing Flora Petty in *You're Only Young Twice* but, since that series ended in 1981, Mount has largely been seen in straight roles. She has taken guest spots in dramas like INSPECTOR MORSE, CASUALTY and DOCTOR WHO, although, as if to prove that old habits die hard, she did also appear as Aunt Fanny in the kids' sitcom, *All Change*, in 1991.

MOWER, PATRICK
(1940–)

British actor, a 1970s favourite following his roles as lecturer Michael West in *Haunted*, agent Cross in CALLAN, DCI Tom Haggerty in SPECIAL BRANCH, Det. Supt. Steve Hackett in TARGET, and many panel game appearances (WHODUNNIT?, WHAT'S MY LINE?, etc.). In addition to the above, Mower also appeared as reporter John Brownhill in the newspaper drama, *Front Page Story*, the biography of *Marco Polo* and guested in series like DIXON OF DOCK GREEN, THE AVENGERS, THE PROTECTORS, UFO, THE SWEENEY and STRANGERS. In 2000 he returned to the small screen as Rodney Blackstock in EMMERDALE.

MRS THURSDAY
UK (ATV) Comedy Drama. ITV 1966–7

Alice Thursday .... **Kathleen Harrison**
Richard B. Hunter .... **Hugh Manning**

Creator: **Ted Willis**
Producer: **Jack Williams**

A charlady inherits a fortune.

When millionaire tycoon George Dunrich died, he left his estate not to his four grasping ex-wives but to his long-serving and loyal charlady, Alice Thursday. Inheriting his wealth, his multinational property empire, his Rolls-Royce and his Mayfair mansion, Mrs Thursday moved out of her Mile End home and into the privileged classes. But, until the kind-hearted char learned to distinguish her friends from her enemies, she was chaperoned and protected by the genial Richard Hunter, her aide and business adviser.

Allegedly created by Ted Willis specifically as a vehicle for Kathleen Harrison (cinema's Mrs Huggett), *Mrs Thursday* was a surprise hit, knocking shows like CORONATION STREET off the top of the ratings and giving Harrison a late taste of TV stardom.

MTV

MTV, or Music Television, was established as a cable channel in the USA in 1981 by Warner Amex Satellite Entertainment, with the aim of focusing on the rock and pop markets. During its first decade on air it helped establish the music video as a major source of entertainment for the teens and twenties, and coined a new term, VJ (video jockey), for the presenter linking each item. The first video seen (on 1 August 1981) was 'Video Killed The Radio Star' by Buggles. MTV Europe (kicking off on 1 August 1987 with the video 'Money For Nothing' by Dire Straits) became part of a series of global stations comprising also MTV Japan, MTV Brasil, MTV Internacional and MTV Latino, and in 1997 MTV UK and Ireland was launched. MTV has been broadcast from the Astra satellites since 1989 and it now has several sister channels. Foremost is VH-1, which was started in 1985 to cater specifically for older, thirtysomething music fans. There are also MTV Extra, M2, MTV Base and VH-1 Classic, all reflecting different shades of the rock and pop spectrum. As well as music videos, MTV features interviews, concert news, items on film and fashion, and original programming including an upbeat version of BLIND DATE called *Singled Out*. Among the channel's biggest successes have been the cartoon characters, *Beavis and Butthead*, and the *Unplugged* series, in which rock stars play without electronic amplification. The company is currently owned by Viacom, which took control in 1987.

MUFFIN THE MULE

UK (BBC) Children's Entertainment. BBC 1946–55

Presenters/Writers: **Annette Mills, Jan Bussell**

Producers: **David Boisseau, Joy Harington, Peter Thompson, Dorothea Brooking, Nan McDonald, John Warrington, Gordon Murray, Peggy Bacon**

Song and dance with a puppet mule.

One of the earliest favourites of children's television, the legendary Muffin the Mule made his TV debut in 1946, in a five-minute FOR THE CHILDREN slot in which he danced atop a grand piano while his co-star, Annette Mills, sang. Muffin and Mills (sister of actor John Mills) were subsequently given their own series and other puppets were introduced, like Oswald the ostrich, Mr Peregrine the penguin, Prudence and Primrose Kitten, Sally the sealion, Louise the lamb and Monty the monkey. The strings were pulled by puppeteer Ann Hogarth from behind a screen on top of the piano (Hogarth had bought the piebald mule for just 15 shillings (75p)). Muffin's last TV appearance with Annette Mills came in 1955, just days before she died. Muffin then briefly moved to ITV, before returning for one last series at the BBC in 1957, accompanied in vision by Jan Bussell.

MUGGERIDGE, MALCOLM
(1903–90)

London-born journalist and commentator, working as an interviewer for PANORAMA in the 1950s and later for Granada. Much of his work involved spiritual matters, initially as a sceptic in many instances, but later as a firm Catholic, gaining the nickname of St Mugg. Muggeridge was never afraid to bring important people, historical and modern, down to earth, and his documentaries included *The Thirties, Pilgrimage to Lourdes, Twilight of Empire* (about India), *Ladies and Gentlemen, It Is My Pleasure* (reflecting on his own US lecture-tour), *A Socialist Childhood* (his own), *Remembering Virginia* (Woolf), *Lord Reith Looks Back, A Life of Christ, A Quest for Gandhi, Something Beautiful for God* (about Mother Teresa) and *Tolstoy: Rags to Riches*. He was also seen on *Press Conference*, THE BRAINS TRUST, *Appointment With . . .*, *Let Me Speak*, BBC-3, *The Late Show*, Jonathan Miller's *Alice in Wonderland* and his own retrospective, *Muggeridge Ancient and Modern*. Outside of broadcasting, Muggeridge had been a teacher in India and Egypt, reporter for the *Manchester Guardian* and the *Daily Telegraph*, and Editor of *Punch*.

MUIR, FRANK
CBE (1920–98)

To many viewers, Frank Muir is best remembered as a team captain on the BBC 2 word game, CALL MY BLUFF, the one in the bow tie who couldn't sound his 'r's. However, Muir's TV background was far more complex than that. With his writing partner, Denis Norden (having already scripted *Take It from Here* and other comedies for radio), Muir penned Dick Bentley's sitcom, *And So to Bentley*, the Jimmy Edwards series, WHACK-O! and THE SEVEN FACES OF JIM, Richard Briers's first major outlet, BROTHERS IN LAW (and its spin-off, *Mr Justice Duncannon*), and the Bob Monkhouse comedy, *The Big Noise*, as well as episodes of *Early to Braden* and material for THE FROST REPORT. He presented a talent show entitled *New to You* way back in 1946, two decades later guested in NOT ONLY . . . BUT ALSO . . ., and over the years brought his wit and wisdom to numerous panel games. In 1964, with Norden, he wrote and presented the sketch show, *How to Be an Alien*, and they joined forces again to revive their *Take It from Here* creations, *The Glums*, for *Bruce Forsyth's Big Night* in 1978. Behind the scenes, Muir was, at one time, Assistant Head of Comedy at the BBC and, later, Head of Light Entertainment at LWT (where he also fronted *We Have Ways of Making You Laugh*). In 1992 he plundered the small-screen archives for 13 weeks of *TV Heaven* on Channel 4.

MULBERRY

UK (BBC) Situation Comedy. BBC 1 1992–3

Mulberry	**Karl Howman**
Miss Rose Farnaby	**Geraldine McEwan**
Bert Finch	**Tony Selby**
Alice Finch	**Lill Roughley**
	Mary Healey
The Stranger	**John Bennett**

Creators/Writers: **John Esmonde, Bob Larbey**
Producer: **John B. Hobbs**

A mysterious manservant enriches the life of a dowdy spinster.

Cantankerous Rose Farnaby lived alone in her musty family home, Farnaby Manor, with only her well-entrenched, conniving servants, Bert and Alice Finch, for company. Then, one day, an enigmatic new figure arrived. Mulberry instantly brightened up the household, sweet-talking the frumpy Miss Farnaby into making more of her life, adding zest to each day and encouraging her to break habits of a lifetime and try her hand at unusual pursuits. He genially ensured that the Finches knew their place and also protected Miss Farnaby from other detractors like her scheming sisters, Adele and Elizabeth. Where the lovable Mulberry came from no one seemed to know, but his paranormal connections with a figure known only as The Stranger made the mystery even deeper.

MULLARD, ARTHUR

(Arthur Mullord; 1913–95)

Cockney comic actor – a former professional boxer – popular for his down-to-earth, working-class roles in the 1970s. In particular, he was Wally Briggs in ROMANY JONES and its sequel, *Yus My Dear*. Additionally, Mullard guested in HANCOCK'S HALF HOUR, played Mr Rossiter, the neighbour, in *The Arthur Askey Show*, supported Alfie Bass and Bill Fraser in *Vacant Lot*, appeared in the kids' comedies, *On the Rocks* and *Whizzkid's Guide*, and backed up Spike Milligan in *Oh in Colour*. At his peak, he was a popular panellist on programmes like CELEBRITY SQUARES.

MULLER, ROBERT

(1925–98)

British screenwriter, born in Germany and an escapee, with his family, from the Nazis in 1938. Not surprisingly, Nazism featured prominently in his work, although his later efforts also focused on Gothic horror and history. He wrote pieces for ARMCHAIR THEATRE in the early 1960s, as well as the anthologies, MYSTERY AND IMAGINATION and OUT OF THE UNKNOWN, penned some episodes for COLDITZ in the 1970s and also worked for German television. Other credits included *Supernatural* and the plays, *Russian Night 1941* and *Secrets*.

MULTI-COLOURED SWAP SHOP

UK (BBC) Children's Entertainment. BBC 1 1976–82

Presenters: **Noel Edmonds, Keith Chegwin, Maggie Philbin, John Craven**

Producer: **Rosemary Gill**

Live, interactive kids' magazine.

Opening a new front in Saturday-morning children's programming, and allowing younger viewers to actually participate in events for once, *Multi-Coloured Swap Shop* was a light-hearted magazine which bound together cartoons, pop music, sport, phone-ins and competitions with a loose 'swapping' theme. Kids were encouraged to ring in with details of toys, books, clothes, etc. (but definitely no pets), they wished to swap, naming the item they were looking for in return. The most interesting exchanges were highlighted in the list of Top Ten Swaps. Celebrity guests were also asked to donate a 'swap' as a competition prize, and John Craven organized the 'News Swap', which gave viewers the chance to air their opinions on news items of the day. Maggie Philbin helped out around the studio, Delia Smith dropped in for a spot of cooking, and Keith Chegwin was out on the road, secretly visiting a different venue each week and calling on locals to turn out in force and bring along their swaps. However, *Multi-Coloured Swap Shop* was very much a vehicle for Noel Edmonds, who relished this early opportunity to show off his live-TV skills. (For the record, Edmonds's co-star, the *Swap Shop* dinosaur mascot, was called Posh Paws and the unseen studio crane operator was Eric.)

The series was initially intended as a six-week filler. But it was only after six *years*, when Edmonds decided to move on, that the *Multi-Coloured Swap Shop* came to an end (for the last two years it was known simply as *Swap Shop*). It was replaced by the similarly styled *Saturday Superstore* (1982–7). This was hosted by 'General Manager' Mike Read, assisted by Chegwin (still out and about, this time in the 'Delivery Van') and John Craven, plus 'Saturday Girl' Sarah Greene. Vicky Licorish and David Icke held court in the 'Coffee Shop' and the 'Music and Sports Departments'. Also seen was the puppet, Crow.

MULTIPLEX

The name given to a collection of digital channels, six services that use up only the same space as one old analogue channel. When Digital Terrestrial Television was launched in the UK, six multiplexes were developed: one for the BBC; one for ITV, Channel 4 and Teletext; one for Channel 5, S4C and Scottish Gaelic programming; and three for new service provider, ONdigital.

MULVILLE, JIMMY
(1955–)

Liverpool-born actor, comedian and TV executive, a former Cambridge Footlights performer and co-founder of Hat Trick Productions. He was a member of *The Steam Video Company* and the WHO DARES, WINS . . . teams, co-wrote and appeared as Aulus Paulinus in the Roman spoof, *Chelmsford 123*, took the part of Donald Redfern in the sitcom *That's Love* and played the researcher in GBH and Monica's husband in *Jake's Progress*. Mulville has also been programme consultant on HAVE I GOT NEWS FOR YOU, a writer/producer on ALAS SMITH AND JONES, producer of the sitcom, *The Big One*, and Simon Mayo's series, *Confessions*, host of *The Brain Game* and contributed reports for HOLIDAY. Other credits include producing or directing one-off dramas like *Eleven Men Against Eleven*, *Lord of Misrule* and *Gobble*.

MUNSTERS, THE
US (Universal) Situation Comedy. BBC 1 1965–7

Herman Munster	**Fred Gwynne**
Lily Munster	**Yvonne De Carlo**
Grandpa	**Al Lewis**
Eddie Munster	**Butch Patrick**
Marilyn Munster	**Beverly Owen**
	Pat Priest

Creators: **Joe Connelly, Bob Mosher**

A ghoulish family scare the living daylights out of their neighbours.

The Munsters hit the TV screen at the same time as THE ADDAMS FAMILY and there were many similarities between the two series. If anything, *The Munsters* was less subtle than its rival, for while the Addams family looked more or less normal and just acted odd, the Munsters were real monsters, although of the friendly, kind-hearted type.

Nominal head of the household was timid giant Herman, a Frankenstein's monster look-alike, complete with bolted-on head and leaden boots. His wife, Lily, was a vampire who walked around the house in shrouds, wearing a bat necklace. Her father, Grandpa, sometimes known as 'The Count', was an experimental magician who conjured up potions in his cellar laboratory and then struggled to find an antidote. He was known to disappear and hide, or even change into a bat. The Munsters' son was Eddie (actually Edward Wolfgang), a werewolf with a pronounced V-shaped haircut and pointed ears. He was often seen playing with his wolf-man doll. With the family lived Herman's niece, Marilyn, pitied by all for her plainness (in fact, she was an attractive blonde and the only human-looking member of the household).

Stories revolved around the family's contacts with the outside world and the misconception that they were normal and everyone else was strange. Visitors to their rambling Gothic mansion at 1313 Mockingbird Lane, Mockingbird Heights, were at first bemused and then terrified by its contents: heavy cobwebs, suits of armour, secret passages, an electric chair, a coffin telephone-booth, and a black cat that roared like a lion. For the Munsters, life was seen in reverse. They talked about noises 'loud enough to wake the living', were worried when the shutters didn't creak at night and adorned the house with weeds instead of flowers. They cruised around town in a souped-up hearse. At night, Lily slept like a corpse, with her arms crossed over her chest, clutching a flower to her bosom. In the day, Herman worked for a funeral home, Gateman, Goodbury & Graves. At all times, Grandpa longed for the Old Country (Transylvania).

Beverly Owen, who played Marilyn, left after the first series and was replaced by Pat Priest. Fred Gwynne, Yvonne De Carlo and Al Lewis reprised their roles in a one-off TV movie entitled *The Munsters' Revenge*, made in 1981, before new actors took over for a limp revival in 1988 (from 1990 in the UK) called *The Munsters Today*.

MUPPET SHOW, THE/ MUPPETS TONIGHT!
UK (*Show*: ITC/Henson; *Tonight!*: Henson) Variety. ITV 1976–81/BBC 1 1996

Voices:

Kermit the Frog	**Jim Henson**
	Steve Whitmire (*Tonight!*)
Miss Piggy Lee	**Frank Oz**
Fozzie Bear	**Frank Oz**
Zoot	**Dave Goelz**
Gonzo	**Dave Goelz**
Statler	**Richard Hunt**
	Jerry Nelson (*Tonight!*)
Waldorf	**Jim Henson**
	Dave Goelz (*Tonight!*)
Sweetums	**Richard Hunt**
Sam the Eagle	**Frank Oz**
The Swedish Chef	**Jim Henson**
Dr Teeth	**Jim Henson**
Sgt Floyd Pepper	**Jerry Nelson**
Rowlf	**Jim Henson**
Animal	**Frank Oz**
Capt. Link Hogthrob	**Jim Henson**
Dr Julius Strangepork	**Jerry Nelson**
Dr Bunsen Honeydew	**Dave Goelz**
Beaker	**Richard Hunt**
	Steve Whitmire (*Tonight!*)
Scooter	**Richard Hunt**
Beauregard	**Dave Goelz**

Pops .... Jerry Nelson
Lew Zealand .... Jerry Nelson
Janice .... Richard Hunt
Rizzo the Rat .... Steve Whitmire
Robin the Frog .... Jerry Nelson
Spamela Hamderson .... Leslie Carrara
Bill the Bubble Guy .... Dave Goelz
Clifford .... Kevin Clash
Sal .... Brian Henson
Pepe .... Bill Barretta
Seymour .... Brian Henson
Bob .... Bill Barretta
Randy .... Dave Goelz
Andy .... Steve Whitmire
Johnnie Fiama .... Bill Barretta

Creators: **Jim Henson, Frank Oz**
Executive Producer: **David Lazer**
Producers: **Jack Burns, Jim Henson**

A wacky troupe of puppet animals tries to stage a variety show.

The Muppets were devised and christened by Jim Henson in America in the 1950s. They were half marionette and half glove-puppet, hence their name, and they appeared intermittently on US TV for more than a decade before coming to the fore in the children's educational series, SESAME STREET. The chance of a major show of their own eluded them in America, but Lew Grade put his trust in their abilities and financed the production of *The Muppet Show* in Britain.

The premiss of each programme was that the Muppets would organize and perform a variety show, before a live audience. Master of Ceremonies was Kermit the Frog, operated and voiced by Henson himself. He was supported (or hindered) by a large cast of weird animal and humanoid performers and stage-hands. Fozzie Bear was a stand-up comedian with a pointed head, small hat and lame jokes. Rowlf was a shaggy dog piano-player, and other music came from Dr Teeth and the Electric Mayhem, featuring Animal on drums and laid-back guitarist Floyd. Gonzo was a hook-beaked stuntman and trumpeter whose instrument exploded at the start of each show.

Soon to become co-star with Kermit was blonde Miss Piggy. Her unrequited love for the frog meant she was constantly trying to ensnare him, and anyone who stood in the way of her success felt the power of her left hook. Other notable protagonists were mad scientist Dr Bunsen Honeydew, a crazy Swedish Chef, and a pair of crotchety old men, Statler and Waldorf, who heckled the show from their box seats. More barracking came from Sam, the right-wing American eagle. A regular slot in the show was given to the serial, *Pigs in Space*, which pitted Captain Link Hogthrob, commander of the starship *Swinetrek*, against the evil Dr Strangepork.

A host of famous stars also appeared as the Muppets' guests, Elton John, Peter Sellers, George Burns, Peter Ustinov, Raquel Welch and Rudolf Nureyev among them, and, apart from the technical mastery of the puppet form, the show's success came from the human nature of its characters, their attempts to succeed and their tendency to fail. The inventiveness of the musical numbers also played a part. Buffalo Springfield's 'For What It's Worth', for instance, was performed with pathos against a field sports backdrop, and the show spawned a couple of chart hits, 'The Muppet Show Music Hall EP' and A. A. Milne's 'Halfway Down the Stairs' (by Kermit's nephew, Robin).

The Muppets also made a couple of feature films before returning to the small screen in 1996. In *Muppets Tonight!* (made and screened first in the US), the manic creatures had abandoned their variety theatre in favour of a local TV station, K-MUP TV. Among the characters added to the troupe were mob-linked lounge crooner Johnny Fiama and his bodyguard monkey, Sal; Bob, a security bear; elevator flunkies Seymour and Pepe, an elephant and a prawn; Miss Piggy's stupid nephews, Randy and Andy; and Bill the Bubble Guy, whose party-piece was blowing bubbles out of the top of his head. The new host was allegedly streetwise Clifford and the *Bay of Pigs Watch* saga featured curvy porker Spamela Hamderson. Guest stars like Michelle Pfeiffer, Pierce Brosnan and John Goodman flocked to appear.

MUPPETS TONIGHT!
See MUPPET SHOW, THE.

MURDER BAG
UK (Associated-Rediffusion) Police Drama. ITV 1957–9

Det. Supt. Tom Lockhart .... **Raymond Francis**

Creator: **Glyn Davies**
Producer: **Barry Baker**
Writers: **Barry Baker, Peter Ling**

Half-hour detective series that introduced viewers to the snuff-taking Detective Superintendent Lockhart.

In this early series, Tom Lockhart was assisted in his investigations by different police officers each week, but always present was the 'Murder Bag' of the title. This black briefcase, seen in close-up behind the opening titles, provided Lockhart with the equipment needed to gather forensic evidence. Over 70 items were held in the case, ranging from airtight jars to tweezers, and each week it was called into play in pursuit of yet another murderer. The first 30 episodes had not separate titles but case numbers, and were listed as *Murder Bag – Case One*, etc. All subsequent programmes carried titles such as *Lockhart Sets a Trap* and *Lockhart Misses a Clue*, and all transmissions were live. From here, the character of Lockhart went on to CRIME SHEET (where he could investigate more than murder) and then his *pièce de résistance*, NO HIDING PLACE.

MURDER MOST HORRID

UK (Talkback/BBC) Comedy Anthology. BBC 2 1991;
1994–6; 1999

Dawn French

Producers: **Jon Plowman, Sophie Clarke-Jervoise**
Executive Producers: **Peter Fincham, Jon Plowman**

Series of spoof murder playlets.

Dawn French starred in this colourful pastiche of the TV mystery/thriller genre. Adopting a new character every episode – kids' TV presenter Bunty Breslaw, social worker Tina Mellish, secretary Sally Fairfax, surgeon Kate Marshall, abattoir-worker Daisy Talwinning, policewoman Greaves-turned-gangster Whoopi Stone, dinner lady Tiffany Drapes, etc. – French found herself embroiled in the most grisly and gruesome situations yet always managed to prove that murder is a funny business. Among the major guest stars were Nigel Havers, Timothy Spall, Amanda Donohoe, Timothy West, Jim Carter, Sarah Lancashire and Frances Barber. Scripts were penned by writers such as Anthony Horowitz, Ian Hislop and Nick Newman, Paul Smith and Terry Kyan, and Steven Moffat.

MURDER ONE

US (Steven Bochco Productions/Twentieth Century-Fox) Drama. BBC 2 1996–7

Theodore 'Teddy' Hoffman	**Daniel Benzali**
Justine Appleton	**Mary McCormack**
Richard Cross	**Stanley Tucci**
Neil Avedon	**Jason Gedrick**
Chris Docknovich	**Michael Hayden**
Lisa Gillespie	**Grace Phillips**
Miriam Grasso	**Barbara Bosson**
Arnold Spivak	**J. C. Mackenzie**
Arthur Polson	**Dylan Baker**
Lila Marquette	**Vanessa Williams**
Julie Costello	**Bobbie Phillips**
Annie Hoffman	**Patricia Clarkson**
Louis Heinsbergen	**John Fleck**
Francesca Cross	**Donna Murphy**
Det. Raymond Velacek	**Joe Spano**
Dr Graham Lester	**Stanley Kamel**
Judge Beth Bornstein	**Linda Carlson**
DA Roger Garfield	**Gregory Itzin**
James Wyler	**Anthony LaPaglia**
Det. Vince Biggio	**Clayton Rohner**
Aaron Mosely	**D. B. Woodside**
Sharon Rooney	**Missy Crider**
Caroline Van Allen	**Romy Walthall**
Malcolm Dietrich	**Ralph Waite**
Rickey Latrell	**Rick Worthy**
Clifford Banks	**Pruitt Taylor Vince**
Lynette Banks	**Karen Austin**
Gary Blondo	**John Pleshette**

Creators: **Steven Bochco, Charles H. Eglee, Channing Gibson**

Executive Producers: **Steven Bochco, Charles H. Eglee**

The cases of a rich person's law firm, exploring all aspects of the American justice system.

Murder One broke new ground when, for its first series, all 23 episodes focused on just one criminal trial. In the dock was Neil Avedon, a young film star with a serious attitude problem, pleading not guilty to the murder of teenager Jessica Costello. However, before even reaching the trial, the series looked at preliminary police inquiries, jury selection and other important background details, as well as the effect on the personal lives of those involved, and it didn't end when the verdict was announced. Head of the defending team from Hoffman & Associates was bald-headed, bespectacled Teddy Hoffman, a brilliant advocate with enormous respect in the business. Sadly, his marriage was falling apart. Joining Teddy in the firm were reliable Chris Docknovich, ambitious Lisa Gillespie, impetuous Justine Appleton, quirky Arnold Spivak and gay PA Louis Heinsbergen. On the other side of the bench was hard-nosed Assistant District Attorney Miriam Grasso, an old friend of Teddy's, and vengeful local cop Arthur Polson. Key figures in the case were slimy businessman Richard Cross, dubious doctor Graham Lester and untrustworthy District Attorney Roger Garfield.

Despite winning rave notices from viewers and critics, the series failed in the US ratings, thanks to being allocated the suicide slot against ER. It was, however, given a second bite of the cherry and returned a year later with a new lead man. Teddy had been written out (to work on his marriage) and had handed over control of the firm to his junior partners, who had brought on board slick but devious lawyer James Wyler to give their image a bit more clout. Lisa had also left, to be replaced by Aaron. This time there were three separate trials under the microscope during the season's run, involving the murder of the Californian governor and his mistress, the future of a serial murderer and an O. J. Simpson-style case concerning a basketball star.

MURDER, SHE WROTE

US (Universal) Detective Drama. ITV 1985–97

Jessica Fletcher	**Angela Lansbury**
Sheriff Amos Tupper	**Tom Bosley**
Grady Fletcher	**Michael Horton**
Dr Seth Hazlitt	**William Windom**
Mayor Sam Booth	**Richard Paul**
Sheriff Mort Metzger	**Ron Masak**

Creators: **Richard Levinson, William Link, Peter S. Fischer**
Executive Producer: **Peter S. Fischer**
Producers: **Robert F. O'Neill, Robert E. Swanson**

A middle-aged novelist solves murder cases in her spare time.

Widow Jessica Beatrice Fletcher lived in Cabot Cove, Maine, and had been a substitute teacher until writing brought her fame and wealth. Her first book, a detective thriller called *The Corpse Danced at Midnight*, was submitted to a publisher by Grady, her accountant nephew, and became a huge success. However, when one of her relatives was suspected of murder, Jessica was able to bring her own detective skills into play. She cleared his name and thus began her investigative career.

Jessica became a sort of American Miss Marple. Travelling the world to promote her books or to visit her many relations, she found herself constantly embroiled in murder mysteries that the local police could not resolve. Piecing together the clues in often very complicated plots, Jessica proved to be a thorough and quick-witted sleuth, bringing many a culprit to book, much to the amazement of the local law-enforcers. When not travelling, her acquaintances in Cabot Cove (which itself had more than its fair share of murders) included the local sheriff, Amos Tupper (later replaced by Sheriff Mort Metzger), Mayor Sam Booth and Dr Seth Hazlitt. In later episodes, Jessica moved part-time to New York, living weekdays in a Manhattan apartment while teaching criminology at Manhattan University. On some occasions, Jessica herself did not appear, other than to introduce the week's 'guest sleuth'.

MURDOCH, RUPERT
(1931–)

One of the world's media barons, Australian-born Rupert Murdoch, the head of the News International empire, has left his mark on the television world as well as in newspapers and publishing. In 1985 he became an American citizen for business reasons and took control of Twentieth Century-Fox and a string of regional TV stations in order to establish a fourth US television network (Fox). Then, in 1989, he pre-empted the launch of British Satellite Broadcasting (BSB), the official UK satellite station, by opening up his own Sky network, which, in 1990, merged with (in many ways absorbed) BSB, becoming British Sky Broadcasting. News International also owns the Asian satellite station, Star TV.

MURNAGHAN, DERMOT
(1957–)

Devon-born ITN newscaster, who also read the news for *Channel 4 Daily* and has presented series like *Police Action Live* and *The Big Story*. He is married to journalist/producer Maria Keegan.

MURPHY, BEN
(1941–)

American actor, in television since 1968, initially guesting in series like IT TAKES A THIEF, THE VIRGINIAN and *The Name of the Game*. He waited until 1971 to earn a starring role, which came as Thaddeus Jones (aka Kid Curry) in ALIAS SMITH AND JONES, a bigger hit in the UK than in its native USA, leaving Murphy still looking for a TV breakthrough back home. He followed it with a

series of similarly prominent but not overwhelming parts, including the title role in THE GEMINI MAN (Sam Casey). Among other dramas, Murphy was also seen in THE WINDS OF WAR (Warren Henry), and in the series, *Griff* and *The Chisholms*.

MURPHY, BRIAN
(1933–)

Isle of Wight-born comic actor chiefly remembered as the hen-pecked, work-shy George Roper in MAN ABOUT THE HOUSE and GEORGE AND MILDRED. However, Murphy has also starred in other comedies: *Sez Les*, *The Incredible Mr Tanner* (busker Ernest Tanner), *L for Lester* (hapless driving instructor Lester Small), and LAME DUCKS (inept private eye Ansell). In 1995 he was seen as con-man George Manners in BROOKSIDE and in 1999 played Arthur Capstick in *Mrs Merton and Malcolm*.

MURRAY, BRIAN
(1949–)

Irish actor seen in a variety of series, usually in 'dodgy' roles. The highlights have been THE IRISH RM (Flurry Knox), BREAD (Shifty), PERFECT SCOUNDRELS (con-man Harry Cassidy) and BROOKSIDE (wife-beater Trevor Jordache).

MY FAVORITE MARTIAN
US (Jack Chertok) Situation Comedy. ITV 1963–4

Uncle Martin	**Ray Walston**
Tim O'Hara	**Bill Bixby**
Lorelei Brown	**Pamela Britton**
Angela Brown	**Ann Marshall**
Mr Harry Burns	**J. Pat O'Malley**
Det. Bill Brennan	**Alan Hewitt**

Creator: **John L. Greene**
Producer: **Jack Chertok**

A journalist befriends a Martian who has crash-landed on Earth.

Los Angeles Sun reporter Tim O'Hara was on the way to an assignment when he discovered a crashed spacecraft and its occupant, a Martian anthropologist who had been studying Earthmen. Seeing the alien was stunned and in need of help, Tim took him home and made him comfortable in his boarding-house room, while he worked on the amazing story for his boss, Mr Burns. But, being almost human-like and speaking English, the Martian made a strong impression on Tim, who scrapped the story and decided to keep the alien's identity a secret. He passed him off as his Uncle Martin and found him a room in the house, to give Martin time to repair his ship. No one else knew Martin's secret, though Bill Brennan, a police officer, who arrived in the second series, was always fishing around. He was also Martin's rival for the attentions of their landlady, Mrs Brown.

Her teenage daughter, Angela, appeared in the first season.

Preceding MORK AND MINDY by a decade and a half, *My Favorite Martian* had many similarities. Martin was not as zany as Mork but he did have unusual powers, such as telepathy and the ability to make himself invisible. He could move objects by pointing at them, was a technological genius, could talk to animals and had little retractable antennae on his head.

MY FRIEND FLICKA

US (Twentieth Century-Fox) Children's Adventure. ITV 1957–8

Ken McLaughlin .... **Johnny Washbrook**
Rob McLaughlin .... **Gene Evans**
Nell McLaughlin .... **Anita Louise**
Gus Broeberg .... **Frank Ferguson**
Hildy Broeberg .... **Pamela Beaird**

Executive Producer: **Buddy Adler**
Producers: **Alan A. Armor, Peter Packer, Sam White, Herman Schlom**

A boy's best friend is his horse.

Eleven-year-old Ken McLaughlin lived with his parents, Rob and Nell, ranch-hand Gus and, most importantly, his horse, Flicka, on the Goose Bar Ranch near Coulee Springs in turn-of-the-century Montana. In the LASSIE vein, boy and horse fell into all manner of adventures, although the drama was not always as intense, and much of the action centred on the family's struggles on the northern American frontier. Hildy was Gus's niece.

My Friend Flicka (which was one of the first children's series to be filmed in colour) was based on the book by Mary O'Hara and the 1943 film starring Roddy McDowall. It was shown intermittently around the ITV network after debuting in its native USA in 1956. 'Flicka' is Swedish for 'little girl', and the equine star was a horse called Wahama.

MY GOOD WOMAN

UK (ATV) Situation Comedy. ITV 1972–4

Clive Gibbons .... **Leslie Crowther**
Sylvia Gibbons .... **Sylvia Syms**
Philip Broadmore .... **Keith Barron**
Bob Berris .... **Glyn Houston**
Revd Martin Hooper .... **Richard Wilson**

Creator/Writer: **Ronnie Taylor**
Producers: **Les Chatfield, William G. Stewart, Ronnie Baxter**

A husband suffers because his wife is a compulsive charity-worker.

Antiques dealer Clive Gibbons was a charity widower. His wife, Sylvia, was so concerned with raising money for good causes and helping out the less fortunate that their life together was rather barren. Despite his efforts to convince her that charity began at home, the hapless Clive was forced to seek solace in the company of his neighbour, Philip Broadmore, and then, in later episodes, his darts colleague, Bob Berris, as Sylvia arranged yet another jumble sale. Martin Hooper was the vicar benefiting from most of Sylvia's worthy deeds.

MY MOTHER THE CAR

US (United Artists/Cottage Industries/NBC) Situation Comedy. ITV 1965

Dave Crabtree .... **Jerry Van Dyke**
Abigail Crabtree .... **Ann Sothern** (*voice only*)
Barbara Crabtree .... **Maggie Pierce**
Cindy Crabtree .... **Cindy Ellbacher**
Randy Crabtree .... **Randy Whipple**
Capt. Bernard Mancini .... **Avery Schreiber**

Creators: **Allan Burns, Chris Hayward**
Producer: **Rod Amateau**

A man buys a vintage motor car, only to find it is his mother reincarnated.

When lawyer Dave Crabtree visited a second-hand car lot in his small Californian town to look for a cheap new car, he found himself inexplicably drawn to a rickety 1928 Porter. He soon discovered why: the car was actually a reincarnation of his late mother. Understandably, he bought the car and restored it, much to the disgust of his wife, Barbara, and two children, Cindy and Randy, who really wanted a station-wagon. They couldn't understand why he was so protective of the old bone-shaker and why he resisted the villainous attempts by classic-car dealer Captain Mancini to take the Porter off his hands. Of course, *they* couldn't hear his mother's voice bellowing out of the car radio, nagging and domineering him just as she had done when she was still alive.

Jerry Van Dyke is Dick Van Dyke's brother, but he failed to achieve the same kind of success. *My Mother the Car* was almost universally panned by critics and lasted only one season. For some, it was the worst US sitcom of the 1960s.

MY WIFE NEXT DOOR

UK (BBC) Situation Comedy. BBC 1 1972

George Bassett .... **John Alderton**
Suzy Bassett .... **Hannah Gordon**

Creators: **Brian Clemens, Richard Waring**
Writer: **Richard Waring**
Producer: **Graeme Muir**

A freshly divorced couple live side by side in the country.

When George Bassett was divorced by his wife, Suzy, he decided to make a fresh start. He moved out of London and into the countryside. Unfortunately for George, Suzy had also escaped from the city and they found themselves living as next-door neighbours in numbers 1 and 2 Copse Cottages, near Stoke Poges. To preserve their independence they drew up an 'Atlantic Charter' of rules and regulations which they attempted to follow on a day-by-day basis, while all the time prying into each other's affairs (domestic and romantic). They were clearly still in love but were terrified to admit it, to their mutual cost.

MYSTERY AND IMAGINATION
UK (ABC/Thames) Thriller Anthology. ITV 1966–70

Richard Beckett .... **David Buck**

Creators: **Jonathan Alwyn, Terence Feely**
Producer: **Jonathan Alwyn**

Dramatizations of Victorian chillers.

Hosted by David Buck in the guise of Victorian adventurer Richard Beckett (who also appeared in some of the stories), *Mystery and Imagination* presented three series of 19th-century thrillers. These included works by Robert Louis Stevenson and Edgar Allan Poe, as well as lesser-known writers, but most were in the spine-tingling Gothic tradition. The classics, *Frankenstein* and *Dracula*, were both featured, as were *Sweeney Todd*, *The Canterville Ghost* and *The Fall of the House of Usher*. Episodes until 1968 were produced by ABC, with Thames taking over after ABC lost its ITV franchise.

MYSTERY MOVIE
US (Universal) Mystery. ITV 1972–8

Rotating series of TV movies featuring various sleuths and law-enforcers.

The *Mystery Movie* umbrella title covered the adventures of COLUMBO, McCLOUD, McMILLAN AND WIFE, MADIGAN, QUINCY, *The Snoop Sisters*, *Hec Ramsey*, *Faraday and Company*, *Tenafly*, AMY PRENTISS, *Cool Million*, *McCoy* and BANACEK, which aired in sequence on ITV. The most successful concepts (like *Columbo*, *McMillan and Wife*, *Quincy* and *McCloud*) were later billed simply under their own titles, whereas others (like *McCoy* and *Cool Million*) faded away very quickly. In the USA, the series was broken down into *Sunday Mystery Movie* and *Wednesday Mystery Movie* blocks for airing on NBC.

MYSTIC MEG
(Meg Lake; 1942–)

Accrington-born astrologer who, after working as a sub-editor on the *Daily Telegraph* and *Woman's Realm*, was given her own horoscope column. From this, she graduated to resident soothsayer on THE NATIONAL LOTTERY LIVE and countrywide fame for her dramatic predictions about the week's numbers.

NAIL, JIMMY
(James Bradford; 1954–)

Geordie actor, writer, producer and singer, coming to fame as Oz in AUF WIEDERSEHEN, PET and later turning to his own ideas for starring roles. These have come in SPENDER, as the maverick Newcastle copper, and CROCODILE SHOES, playing singer/songwriter Jed Shepperd. He now runs his own production company, Big Boy. Nail has also been seen in BLOTT ON THE LANDSCAPE, *Shoot for the Sun*, MINDER and *Spyship*. His stage name allegedly comes from an accident when he worked in a glass factory: he stood on a six-inch nail and gained the nickname 'Jimmy the Nail'.

NAKED CITY
US (Shelle/Screen Gems) Police Drama. ITV 1959–64

Det. Lt. Dan Muldoon	**John McIntire**
Det. Jim Halloran	**James Franciscus**
Janet Halloran	**Suzanne Storrs**
Patrolman/Sgt Frank Arcaro	**Harry Bellaver**
Lt. Mike Parker	**Horace McMahon**
Det. Adam Flint	**Paul Burke**
Libby	**Nancy Malone**

Creator: **Sterling Silliphant**
Executive Producer: **Herbert B. Leonard**

Grimy, realistic police dramas set in New York City.

'There are eight million stories in the Naked City', the narrator of this programme revealed. Most of them, it seemed, revolved around crime, as the city's police officers (by no means all of them angels) came under the spotlight, combing the seedy streets in search of muggers, murderers and other assorted felons. Veteran cop Dan Muldoon of the 65th Precinct was the programme's first main man, but he was killed off early on when his car crashed into a petrol tanker. His younger partner, Jim Halloran, and Jim's wife, Janet, didn't last much longer and were also written out after only one season. Muldoon was replaced by Mike Parker, a tough, determined operator, who was later assisted by Detective Adam Flint and Sgt Frank Arcaro (promoted from his patrolman status in the earlier episodes). Flint's girlfriend, Libby, was also seen. But, in many ways, the real star of the programme was the city itself. The series was filmed entirely on location, with long shots drawing the attention of the viewer away from the personalities and focusing it instead on the bustling metropolis, the hub of all this villainous activity. The jazzy score by Billy May added to the moody atmosphere.

Naked City also specialized in weird episode titles. Examples included *The King of Venus Will Take Care of You*, *Howard Running Bear Is a Turtle* and *No Naked Ladies in Front of Giovanni's House*. Guest stars abounded, most just fledgling actors at the time. Dustin Hoffman, Robert Redford, Jon Voight, Gene Hackman, Peter Falk, George Segal and Peter Fonda were the most notable. The story on which *Naked City* was based was written by Broadway columnist Mark Hellinger, and an Oscar-winning film version, starring Barry Fitzgerald and Don Taylor, appeared in 1948.

NAKED CIVIL SERVANT, THE
UK (Thames) Drama. ITV 1975

Quentin Crisp .... **John Hurt**

Writer: **Philip Mackie**
Producer: **Barry Hanson**

The biography of an outspoken homosexual.

This 90-minute dramatization by Philip Mackie of Quentin Crisp's revealing autobiography was initially turned down by the BBC before being accepted, with caution, by Thames and the IBA. It portrayed events in the life of Crisp, a prominently homosexual government employee and former art school model (hence the title), from the late 1920s to the mid-1970s. John Hurt played the lead with flamboyant effeminism, and the work proved influential in opening stubbornly closed eyes to the predicament of gay men in society, thanks to its balanced combination of humour and tenderness. Viewers were shocked; critics doled out awards.

NAKED VIDEO
UK (BBC) Comedy. BBC 2 1986–91

Helen Lederer, Gregor Fisher, Tony Roper, Ron Bain, Andy Gray, Elaine C. Smith, Jonathan Watson, John Sparkes, Louise Beattie

Producers: **Colin Gilbert, Philip Differ**

Pot-pourri of comic sketches from north of the border.

A comedy offering from BBC Scotland, *Naked Video* helped establish the careers of Helen Lederer and Gregor Fisher in particular and also gave the world a handful of well-defined new comic characters. These included Rab C. Nesbitt, the aggressive, Glaswegian street philosopher, and the follically-challenged Baldy Man (both played by Fisher and later graduating to their own series). Another innovation was Siadwell, the simple-minded Welsh poet, portrayed by John Sparkes. These appeared amid a collection of running sketches, some of which satirized topical issues. *Naked Video* was derived from a radio programme entitled *Naked Radio*.

NAME THAT TUNE
See **SPOT THE TUNE.**

NANCY ASTOR
UK (BBC) Drama. BBC 2 1982

Nancy Langhorne/Shaw/Astor .... **Lisa Harrow**
Chillie Langhorne .... **Dan O'Herlihy**

Nanaire Langhorne .... **Sylvia Syms**
Phyllis Langhorne/Brand .... **Lise Hilboldt**
Robert Gould Shaw .... **Pierce Brosnan**
Waldorf Astor .... **James Fox**
Lord Revelstoke .... **Julian Glover**
Philip Kerr .... **David Warner**
Robert Brand .... **Bernard Brown**
Bobbie Shaw .... **Nigel Havers**
Wissie Astor .... **Marsha Fitzalan**

Writer: **Derek Marlowe**
Producer: **Philip Hinchcliffe**

Biography of Britain's first female MP.

In nine episodes, this series traced the ups and downs in the life of Nancy Langhorne, an ambitious southern belle, the daughter of a tobacco auctioneer from Virginia. It followed her marriage to Robert Gould Shaw, a wealthy Boston playboy, and its subsequent collapse; her move to Europe with her sister, Phyllis; and her new romance with a British millionaire politician, Waldorf Astor, proprietor of *The Observer*, whom she went on to marry and with whom she set up home at Cliveden. When he was elevated to the House of Lords in 1919, Nancy took his place in the House of Commons, thereby carving herself a niche in history as the first woman to take her seat as a Member of Parliament. In the House, her sharp American tongue earned many enemies.

NANNY
UK (BBC) Drama. BBC 1 1981–3

Barbara Gray/Taverner .... **Wendy Craig**
Donald Gray .... **Colin Douglas**
Mrs Sackville .... **Patricia Hodge**
Mrs Rudd .... **Anna Cropper**
Mr Rudd .... **Frank Mills**
Duke of Broughton .... **Richard Vernon**
Duchess of Broughton .... **Judy Campbell**
Lord Somerville .... **John Quayle**
Lady Somerville .... **Jane Booker**
Twomey .... **Jim Norton**
Lillian Birkwith .... **Jayne Lester**
Sam Taverner .... **David Burke**
Frank Hailey .... **Stephen Sweeney**
Major Fancombe .... **Geoffrey Chater**
Capt. Marsh .... **Allan Cuthbertson**

Creator: **Wendy Craig**
Producers: **Guy Slater, Bernard Krichefski**

The life of a children's nurse in the 1930s.

Dreamt up by actress Wendy Craig, who submitted the idea under the pen-name of Jonathan Marr, *Nanny* was the story of Barbara Gray, a traditional children's carer, working in the homes of the rich and noble. She began her new career in 1932, having trained as a nanny after the break-up of her marriage. Her enlightened approach made her a popular and trustworthy choice for wealthy parents, although she regularly moved from home to home. On her marriage to Sam Taverner, Barbara was generally expected to give up her vocation but, contrary to the mood of the times, she preferred to continue in her profession. Craig's idea was developed into three series of scripts, most penned by the NO – HONESTLY husband-and-wife writing team of Charlotte Bingham and Terence Brady.

NARDINI, DANIELA
(1967–)

Scottish actress coming to the fore as Anna in THIS LIFE, after small parts in series like TAKE THE HIGH ROAD, TAGGART and DR FINLAY. Her later credits have included *Reckless* (Viv Reid), *Big Women* (Layla), *Undercover Heart* (Lois Howarth) and *Rough Treatment* (Eve Turner).

NATION, TERRY
(1930–97)

Welsh comedy scriptwriter (sometimes in collaboration with John Junkin), working in BBC Radio in the 1950s, then on Tony Hancock's ITV series in 1963. Nation then switched more to drama and, in particular, to science fiction, with significant results. He will undoubtedly go down in television history as the man who invented the Daleks, the pepperpot megalomaniacs from DOCTOR WHO, but he also created the 1970s sci-fi classics, SURVIVORS and BLAKE'S 7. In addition, Nation contributed to NO HIDING PLACE, THE BARON, DEPARTMENT S, THE SAINT, THE CHAMPIONS, THE AVENGERS, THE PERSUADERS!, THE PROTECTORS, OUT OF THE UNKNOWN, OUT OF THIS WORLD and other anthologies, and dramatized Isaac Asimov's *The Caves of Steel* for BBC 2 in 1964.

NATIONAL LOTTERY LIVE, THE
UK (BBC) BBC 1 1994–

Presenters: **Anthea Turner, Gordon Kennedy, Bob Monkhouse, Ulrika Jonsson, Dale Winton, Carol Smillie, Terry Wogan, Patrick Kielty, Bradley Walsh, Brian Conley, Angela Griffin, Simon Mayo, Claudia Winkelman, Eamonn Holmes, Lulu, Terry Alderton, Des O'Connor, Suzi Perry, Shauna Lowry**

Light entertainment around the week's National Lottery draws.

Launched with much fanfare on 19 November 1994, The National Lottery was an immediate TV hit, as viewers switched on in millions to check their tickets. The first draw was wrapped up in the glitz of a lively game show, hosted by Noel Edmonds, supported by former ABSOLUTELY comic, Gordon Kennedy, and (as she was then known) ex-BLUE PETER girl Anthea Turner. Kennedy and Turner took over the show from the second week, visiting places of interest around the UK where the draw would take place (first port of call was the Rhondda Heritage Park in South Wales). Kennedy was the first to move on, while Turner continued to use the draw as a springboard to TV stardom, as did the resident psychic predictor, Mystic Meg.

The introduction of a midweek draw on Wednesdays on 5 February 1997 produced a shorter equivalent of the Saturday show. The formats of both editions have been revamped regularly since, to incorporate new quizzes, games, music and other entertainment, adopting titles like *The National Lottery Big Ticket* (Anthea Turner and Patrick Kielty), *The National Lottery on Tour* (Bradley Walsh; concert venues around the UK), *The National Lottery Dreamworld* (Ulrika Jonsson making people's dreams come true; midweek), *The National Lottery: Amazing Luck Stories* (Carol Smillie and, later, Shauna Lowry; midweek), *The National Lottery Greatest Hits* (Angela Griffin; midweek, from Manchester), *The National Lottery: Local Heroes* (Carol Smillie; championing charitable individuals around the country), *The National Lottery – We've Got Your Number* (Brian Conley), *National Lottery Winning Lines* (Simon Mayo; produced by the WHO WANTS TO BE A MILLIONAIRE? team), *National Lottery Love Songs* (Claudia Winkelman; midweek), *The National Lottery Stars* (Dale Winton and big names), *National Lottery Third Degree* (Eamonn Holmes and a quiz for charities; midweek), *Red Alert with the National Lottery* (Lulu and Terry Alderton), *Dale's All Stars with the National Lottery* (Dale Winton with music and chat; midweek), *The National Lottery: UK 2000* (Carol Smillie looking at lottery-funded projects; midweek) and *The National Lottery – on the Spot* (Des O'Connor and Suzi Perry).

In addition to the regular hosts mentioned above, Alan Dedicoat has acted as announcer ('the Voice of the Balls'), interviews have been conducted by the likes of Krishnan Guru-Murthy and Toby Anstis, and there have been many guest presenters, including Jimmy Tarbuck, Adam Woodyatt, Gary Barlow, Carol Vorderman, Ainsley Harriott, Michael Ball, Bruce Forsyth, Ronnie Corbett, Hale and Pace, Shirley Bassey and Rolf Harris.

NATIONWIDE
UK (BBC) Current Affairs. BBC 1 1969–83

Presenters: **Michael Barratt, Bob Wellings, Sue Lawley, Richard Stilgoe, Frank Bough, Dilys Morgan, Brian Widlake, Glyn Worsnip, Valerie Singleton, John Stapleton, Hugh Scully, Sue Cook, Richard Kershaw, Laurie Mayer, Fran Morrison, David Dimbleby**

Creator: **Derrick Amoore.**
Producers/Editors: **Derrick Amoore, Michael Bunce, Phil Sidey, Ron Neil, Andrew Clayton, Tim Gardam, Paul Corley, Richard Tait, John Gau, Paul Woolwich, Hugh Williams, Roger Bolton**

Light-hearted early-evening news magazine.

For a decade and a half *Nationwide* was an integral part of British teatime. Following on from the main early-evening news bulletin, Monday to Friday, the 50-minute programme was a mixed bag of newsy items, political discussions, consumer affairs and light entertainment. After the introductory headlines, viewers were sent 'nationwide', i.e. the BBC regions opted out to present their own 20-minute or so local news round-ups (*Points West, Look North, Wales Today*, etc.). When these programmes finished, they handed back to London and the

Nationwide studio, although the regions stayed 'live' to feed back reports and local reactions to the day's news, and to allow interviews to take place across the network. Technical problems abounded, with sound or vision going down on a regular basis.

Nationwide seemed to be obsessed with the great British eccentric and was always looking for unusual stories about skateboarding ducks or men who claimed they could walk on eggs. Regular features included the programme's Consumer Unit (headed behind the scenes by Bernard Wiggins who, as Bernard Cornwell, later wrote the SHARPE novels) which developed into a separate series called WATCHDOG, and Price Check, which monitored the cost of living. Richard Stilgoe performed topical songs, Susan Stranks took a stroll down Memory Lane and numerous politicians were put On The Spot. On Fridays, the weekend sporting action was previewed by Desmond Lynam, Peter Walker and other sports presenters in Sportswide and, most Decembers, there was a *Nationwide* Carol Competition.

Michael Barratt, Sue Lawley and Bob Wellings were the mainstays of the programme for many years, with Valerie Singleton and Frank Bough joining from BLUE PETER and GRANDSTAND later. A young John Stapleton and David Dimbleby also acted as anchors. *Nationwide*'s best-remembered reporters included Jack Pizzey, Bernard Falk, Philip Tibenham, Bernard Clarke, Martin Young, and Pattie Coldwell, and among the frequent contributors from the regional studios were Tom Coyne and Alan Towers (Birmingham), Mike Neville (Newcastle), Bruce Parker (Southampton), Stuart Hall (Manchester), Ian Masters (Norwich) and Hugh Scully (Plymouth). In all, 3,131 editions were produced before *Nationwide* gave way to a look-alike programme entitled *Sixty Minutes* in 1984. Hosted by Desmond Wilcox, Sally Magnusson, Nick Ross, Beverly Anderson and Sarah Kennedy, it lasted only one year.

NAYLOR, DOUG
(1955–)
See GRANT, ROB.

NBC

America's NBC, standing for National Broadcasting Company, was established by RCA to help sell the radio (and later television) equipment it manufactured. Its first radio broadcast came in 1926, with a regular TV service following in 1939, and NBC's history remained indelibly linked to the fortunes of RCA for decades. In the 1950s, for instance, the network became the first to broadcast all its programmes in colour, in an effort to boost sales of the newly developed RCA colour system. Among the company's most influential early executives was David Sarnoff, powerful head of RCA for 40 years.

As a network, NBC has nearly always run behind its great rival, CBS, but all that has changed in recent years, thanks to huge success with series like ER, SEINFELD, FRIENDS and FRASIER. Earlier hits included DRAGNET, BONANZA, DR KILDARE, THE MAN FROM UNCLE, THE COSBY SHOW and CHEERS. Of the three main US broadcasters, NBC has also been the most innovative. It launched the first dual-anchor news programme, for example, and also developed the TV movie concept.

NBC, which was sold to General Electric in 1985, took a majority holding in the European satellite station Super Channel in 1993. However, NBC Super Channel, as it became known, has since been replaced on the Astra satellite and in digital packages by CNBC, a business and financial channel, set up in the USA in 1989.

NEAREST AND DEAREST
UK (Granada) Situation Comedy. ITV 1968–73

Nellie Pledge	**Hylda Baker**
Eli Pledge	**Jimmy Jewel**
Lily	**Madge Hindle**
Walter	**Edward Malin**
Stan	**Joe Gladwin**
Bert	**Bert Palmer**
Grenville	**Freddie Rayner**

Creators: **Vince Powell, Harry Driver**
Producers: **Peter Eckersley, Bill Podmore**

A middle-aged brother and sister grudgingly share control of a northern pickle factory.

Eli and Nellie Pledge, bachelor and spinster, were brought back together on the death of their father, who bequeathed them his Pledge's Purer Pickles business. Bickering and fighting, the pair somehow managed to keep the company afloat, although there was just as much vinegar in their relationship as in the pickle jars. The plots often played second fiddle to the boundless insults they traded, which ranged from 'big girl's blouse' to 'knock-kneed knackered old nosebag'. The show was essentially a vehicle for Hylda Baker's distinctive line in comedy, littered with malapropisms and *doubles entendres*. It allowed her a few gems along the way, such as when Nellie remarked that Eli reminded her of that beautiful song from *The Sound of Music*. 'Which one,' responded Eli, ' "My Favourite Things?" ' 'No,' came back the put-down, ' "Idleswine." '

The Pledges were ably supported in the factory by their down-to-earth but rather decrepit foreman, Stan, and often had to play host at home to cousin Lily and her silent, quivering husband, Walter, who was plagued with waterworks trouble. The burning question was always 'Has he been?', although we were all assured that 'He knows, you know' (one of Baker's oldest catchphrases). A cinema version was made in 1972. Hylda Baker moved on to another sitcom in a similar vein. Entitled *Not on Your Nellie* (ITV 1974–5), it saw her cast as Fulham publican Nellie Pickersgill.

NEDWELL, ROBIN
(1946–99)

Birmingham-born comic actor, popular in the 1970s as the hero of most of the DOCTOR series (Duncan Waring). Nedwell also appeared in THE LOVERS, playing Geoffrey's friend Roland and, when John Alderton left the role of Mike Upchat in *The Upchat Line*, Nedwell stepped in for the sequel, *The Upchat Connection*. He was also pop musician Peter Higgins in SHILLINGBURY TALES, Fiddler in the shortlived comedy, *West End Tales*, and Harry Lumsdon, *The Climber*, in the 1983 BBC sitcom. Nedwell returned to the small screen in the 1991 Doctors revival, *Doctor at the Top*.

NEGUS, ARTHUR
OBE (1903–85)

Amiable, silver-haired antiques expert, prominent in GOING FOR A SONG, ANTIQUES ROADSHOW and the travelogue, *Arthur Negus Enjoys*. His gentle, informative manner encouraged viewers to regard their family heirlooms in quite a different light.

NEIGHBOURS
Australia (Grundy) Drama. BBC 1 1986–

Helen Daniels	**Anne Haddy**
Jim Robinson	**Alan Dale**
Paul Robinson	**Stefan Dennis**
Julie Robinson/Martin	**Vikki Blanche**
	Julie Mullins
Scott Robinson	**Darius Perkins**
	Jason Donovan
Lucy Robinson	**Kylie Flinker**
	Sasha Close
	Melissa Bell
Max Ramsay	**Francis Bell**
Maria Ramsay	**Dasha Blahova**
Shane Ramsay	**Peter O'Brien**
Danny Ramsay	**David Clencie**
Tom Ramsay	**Gary Files**
Eileen Clarke	**Myra De Groot**
Des Clarke	**Paul Keane**
Daphne Lawrence/Clarke	**Elaine Smith**
Mike Young	**Guy Pearce**
Dr Clive Gibbons	**Geoff Paine**
Madge Mitchell/Ramsay/Bishop	**Anne Charleston**
Charlene Mitchell/Robinson	**Kylie Minogue**
Henry Mitchell/Ramsay	**Craig McLachlan**
Rosemary Daniels	**Joy Chambers**
Nell Mangel/Worthington	**Vivean Gray**
Zoe Davis	**Ally Fowler**
Jane Harris	**Annie Jones**
Susan Cole	**Gloria Ajenstat**
Rob Lewis	**Ernie Bourne**
Gail Lewis/Robinson	**Fiona Corke**
Harold Bishop	**Ian Smith**
Bronwen Davies	**Rachel Friend**
Sharon Davies	**Jessica Muschamp**
Nick Page	**Mark Stevens**
Sally Wells	**Rowena Mohr**
Todd Landers	**Kristian Schmid**
Katie Landers	**Sally Jensen**
Lou Carpenter	**Tom Oliver**
Josh Anderson	**Jeremy Angerson**
Melissa Jarrett	**Jade Amenta**
Joe Mangel	**Mark Little**
Toby Mangel	**Finn Greentree Keene**
	Ben Guerens
Kerry Bishop/Mangel	**Linda Hartley**
Melanie Pearson/Mangel	**Lucinda Cowden**
Sky Bishop/Mangel	**Mirander Fryer**
Gemma Ramsay	**Beth Buchanan**
Hilary Robinson	**Anne Scott-Pendlebury**
Matthew Williams/Robinson	**Ashley Paske**
Dr Beverly Marshall	**Lisa Armytage**
	Shaunna O'Grady
Caroline Alessi	**Gillian Blakeney**
Christina Alessi/Robinson	**Gayle Blakeney**
Ryan McLachlan	**Richard Norton**
Eddie Buckingham	**Bob La Castra**
Doug Willis	**Terence Donovan**
Pam Willis	**Sue Jones**
Adam Willis	**Ian Williams**
Cody Willis	**Amelia Frid**
	Peta Brady
Brad Willis	**Scott Michaelson**
Gaby Willis	**Rachel Blakely**
Dorothy Burke	**Maggie Dence**
Glen Donnelly	**Richard Huggett**
Brenda Riley	**Genevieve Lemon**
Guy Carpenter	**Andrew Williams**
Phoebe Bright/Gottlieb	**Simone Robertson**
Cameron Hudson	**Benjamin Mitchell**
Beth Brennan/Willis	**Natalie Imbruglia**
Marco Alessi	**Felice Arena**
Rick Alessi	**Dan Falzon**
Philip Martin	**Ian Rawlings**
Hannah Martin	**Rebecca Ritters**
Debbie Martin	**Marnie Reece-Wilmore**
Benito Alessi	**George Spatels**
Cathy Alessi	**Elspeth Ballantyne**
Stephen Gottlieb	**Lochie Daddo**
Lauren Carpenter	**Sarah Vandenbergh**
Michael Martin	**Troy Beckwith**
Mark Gottlieb	**Bruce Samazan**
Annalise Hartman	**Kimberley Davies**
Wayne Duncan	**Jonathan Sammy-Lee**
Cheryl Stark	**Caroline Gillmer**
Dannielle 'Danni' Stark	**Eliza Szonert**
Brett Stark	**Brett Blewitt**
Darren Stark	**Todd MacDonald**
Sam Kratz	**Richard Grieve**
Marlene Kratz	**Moya O'Sullivan**
Serendipity 'Ren' Gottlieb	**Raelee Hill**
Karl Kennedy	**Alan Fletcher**
Susan Kennedy	**Jackie Woodburne**
Billy Kennedy	**Jesse Spencer**
Libby Kennedy	**Kym Valentine**
Malcolm Kennedy	**Benji McNair**
Kevin 'Stonefish' Rebecchi	**Anthony Engleman**
Jarrod 'Toadfish' Rebecchi	**Ryan Moloney**
Jen Handley	**Alyce Platt**
Luke Handley	**Bernard Curry**
Mike Healey	**Andrew Blackman**
Bianca Zanotti	**Anne Gagliardi**
Joanna Hartman/Evans	**Emma Harrison**
Angie Rebecchi	**Lesley Baker**
Louise Carpenter	**Jiordan Anna Tolli**

Drew Kirk	**Dan Paris**
Teresa Bell	**Krista Vendy**
Joel Samuels	**Daniel MacPherson**
Ruth Wilkinson/Martin	**Ailsa Piper**
Anne Wilkinson	**Brooke Satchwell**
Lance Wilkinson	**Andrew Bibby**
Ben Atkins	**Brett Cousins**
Caitlin Atkins	**Emily Milburn**
Amy Greenwood	**Jacinta Stapleton**
Sarah Beaumont	**Nicola Charles**
Paul McClain	**Jansen Spencer**
Wayne 'Tad' Reeves	**Jonathon Dutton**
Joe Scully	**Shane Connor**
Lyn Scully	**Janet Andrewartha**
Stephanie Scully	**Carla Bonner**
Felicity Scully	**Holly Valance**
Michelle Scully	**Katie Keltie**

Creator/Executive Producer: **Reg Watson**

Middle-class ups and downs for the residents of a Melbourne cul-de-sac.

From shaky beginnings, *Neighbours* has become one of the success stories of Australian TV. Created by former CROSSROADS producer Reg Watson, it initially aired in 1985 on the country's Seven Network but dwindling audiences resulted in its cancellation after only six months. The programme's producers, Grundy, however, decided to fight on and sold the show to the rival Ten Network. With a complete facelift, including new sets and new, predominantly younger, actors (only five remained from the Seven Network episodes), *Neighbours* slowly began to take off. The series arrived in the UK in 1986, as one of the BBC's first daytime offerings. It was originally scheduled at 10 a.m. and 1.30 p.m. each day but, on the advice of his schoolgirl daughter, BBC 1 Controller Michael Grade moved the 10 a.m. showing to 5.35 p.m. There it captured a massive children, house-wives and home-from-work audience and never looked back.

Neighbours is set in Ramsay Street, a semi-affluent cul-de-sac in the fictitious Melbourne suburb of Erinsborough. The street took its name from the ancestors of one of its most prominent families, the Ramsays, who dominated the action in the early days along with the Robinsons and the Clarkes. The most noteworthy characters over the years have been widower Jim Robinson, his supportive mother-in-law, Helen Daniels, and his assorted kids, including the pompous Paul and teenager Scott (a role which launched Jason Donovan into celebrity status). The rival Ramsays were at first headed by Max, a plumber, but he quickly gave way to his sister, Madge Mitchell, and her wayward children, former jailbird Henry and car mechanic Charlene (Kylie Minogue's big break). The Clarkes were primarily hapless bank manager Des and his ex-stripper wife, Daphne. These families have been expanded in the course of time to bring in various errant children, ex-wives, forgotten parents, etc., and numerous other residents have come and gone, too. Tittle-tattling Mrs Mangel and her loud son, Joe, the twins Christina and Caroline Alessi, dithery Harold Bishop (Madge's new husband), and the Willis brood are representative of these newcomers.

The concerns of Ramsay Street residents have varied from the life-threatening to the banal, but the sun has always shone and things have generally turned out well. The younger element (the kids of Erinsborough High School) and their middle-aged parents and grandparents have happily shared the limelight, ensuring interest for viewers old and young, and, apart from the school and the close itself, the main focal point has been the Lassiters complex and, in particular, its bar (formerly The Waterhole and latterly Lou's Place), coffee shop and hairdresser's. The programme's theme song was composed by Tony Hatch and Jackie Trent, and sung by Barry Crocker.

NESBITT, JAMES
(1965–)

Northern Irish actor whose major role has been as Adam Williams in COLD FEET, although he has also been seen in *Searching* (Duncan), BALLYKISSANGEL (Leo), PLAYING THE FIELD (John Dolan), TOUCHING EVIL (Laney) and the TV film, *Hear My Song*.

NESMITH, MICHAEL
(1942–)

American actor and musician, one of The Monkees. When the series ended, Nesmith drifted off into ambitious musical projects with his First National Band, writing the song, 'Different Drum', for Linda Ronstadt, plus other tracks, mostly in a country rock vein. He became a pioneer in rock videos which, ironically, brought him back to TV in *Michael Nesmith in Television Parts* in 1985. Its combination of avant-garde humour and music videos proved familiar to Monkees fans.

NETTLES, JOHN
(1948–)

Cornish actor John Nettles's earliest television performances came in series like A FAMILY AT WAR (Ian Mackenzie) and THE LIVER BIRDS (Paul, Sandra's boyfriend). Via appearances in series like THE ADVENTURES OF BLACK BEAUTY and some single dramas, he arrived in 1981 at his TV *pièce de résistance*, the part of Jim BERGERAC, the Jersey detective with a drink problem and a gammy leg. It was a role Nettles played for over ten years, making Jersey his home in the process and doing wonders for its tourist trade. He has since become known as another detective, the sanguine DCI Tom Barnaby in MIDSOMER MURDERS. Nettles has also narrated the documentaries, AIRPORT and *Disaster*.

NETWORK

A chain of TV stations linked by cable or satellite in order to broadcast programmes over a larger area. The term is given to the USA's big stations (NBC, ABC, CBS, Fox, UPN and WB) which are able to transmit their programmes across the country via the transmitters of their affiliated independent stations. In the UK, a programme transmitted by all the ITV companies (as opposed to only one or two regions) is described as being 'networked'.

NEVER MIND THE BUZZCOCKS
UK (Talkback/BBC) Quiz. BBC 2 1996–

Presenter: **Mark Lamarr**

Producers: **Jim Pullin, Richard Wilson**
Executive Producer: **Peter Fincham**

Comedy quiz show based around pop and rock music.

Combining in its title a controversial 1977 Sex Pistols album and the name of a Manchester-based New Wave band, *Never Mind the Buzzcocks* was a logical progression from HAVE I GOT NEWS FOR YOU and its sports follow-up, THEY THINK IT'S ALL OVER. The subject this time was the world of rock and pop. Mark Lamarr saw fair and unfair play, and installed as team captains were comedians Sean Hughes and Phill Jupitus. These, together with guests from the music business and comedy, did light-hearted battle over rounds that included guessing hummed record introductions, working out obscure words in a well-known hit, spotting faded stars in an identity parade and adding the next line to a given lyric.

NEVER MIND THE QUALITY, FEEL THE WIDTH
UK (ABC/Thames) Situation Comedy. ITV 1967–71

Emmanuel 'Manny' Cohen	**John Bluthal**
Patrick Kelly	**Joe Lynch**
Rabbi Levy	**Cyril Shaps**
Father Ryan	**Eamon Kelly**

Creators: **Vince Powell, Harry Driver**
Producers: **Ronnie Baxter, Stuart Allen**

Genial ethnic comedy set in an East End tailor's shop.

Manny Cohen and Patrick Kelly were partners in a small tailoring enterprise in the East End of London. Their religious differences provided the chief source of conflict and comedy, as coat-maker Manny, the Jew, always considered Patrick, the trouser-maker, to be a bigoted Catholic. Similar sentiments flowed in the opposite direction and often the local rabbi and priest needed to intervene. The series stemmed from a one-off ARMCHAIR THEATRE production in 1967, in which Frank Finlay took the part of Patrick Kelly. Thames TV took over production of the series in 1968, when ABC lost its ITV franchise. A film version was released in 1972.

NEVER THE TWAIN
UK (Thames) Situation Comedy. ITV 1981–91

Simon Peel	**Donald Sinden**
Oliver Smallbridge	**Windsor Davies**
David Peel	**Robin Kermode**
	Christopher Morris
Lyn Smallbridge/Peel	**Julia Watson**
	Tracy Kneale
Veronica Barton	**Honor Blackman**
Aunt Eleanor	**Zara Nutley**
Ringo	**Derek Deadman**

Creator: **Johnnie Mortimer**
Writers: **Johnnie Mortimer, Vince Powell, John Kane**
Producers: **Peter Frazer-Jones, Anthony Parker**

Two neighbouring antiques dealers are the best of enemies.

Simon Peel and Oliver Smallbridge were old adversaries. Despite the fact that Simon's son, David, and Oliver's daughter, Lyn, were in love, the squabbling antiques experts could never patch up their quarrel. Not even when David and Lyn were married. Nor when Martin, their mutual grandson, was born. Exacerbating their rivalry was the occasional appearance of Veronica Barton, the lady both men wanted in their lives. When David and Lyn emigrated to Canada, Simon's Aunt Eleanor arrived to keep the two old fools in check.

NEW ADVENTURES OF CHARLIE CHAN, THE
UK (ITC) Detective Drama. ITV 1957–8

Charlie Chan	**J. Carrol Naish**
Barry Chan	**James Hong**
Insp. Duff	**Rupert Davies**
Insp. Marlowe	**Hugh Williams**

Executive Producer: **Leon Fromkess**
Producers: **Sidney Marshall, Rudolph Flothow**

Tales of the oriental detective created by Earl Derr Biggers.

Charlie Chan originally found fame in the cinema (played by the likes of Warner Oland, Sydney Toler and Roland Winters) as a smart, proverb-quoting detective from Honolulu who had numerous children. In this series, he had moved to London, but was still supported by his ever-eager 'Number One Son', Barry. As before, the oriental investigator was polite, calm, diligent and very successful.

Earl Derr Biggers's character was allegedly based on Chang Apana, a real Hawaiian police detective. He re-appeared in cartoon form in the 1970s, in a series called *The Amazing Chan and the Chan Clan*.

NEW ADVENTURES OF WONDER WOMAN, THE
See WONDER WOMAN.

NEW AVENGERS, THE
UK (Avengers Enterprises/IDTV) Adventure. ITV 1976–7

John Steed	**Patrick Macnee**

Purdey .... **Joanna Lumley**
Mike Gambit .... **Gareth Hunt**

Producers: **Albert Fennell, Brian Clemens**

*The further adventures of John Steed and his
daring assistants.*

In *The New Avengers*, John Steed was called up once more
to thwart extravagant plots by the world's most eccentric
saboteurs and assassins. Working undercover for the
British Secret Service, as in THE AVENGERS, Steed, however, now spent more time on his private stud-farm,
where he indulged his hobbies of breeding horses and
entertaining beautiful women. Ageing a little, but as
suave and sophisticated as ever, he was typically supported by a glamorous female, but also, this time, by a
tough young male, someone to do the running around.

The newcomers were Purdey and Gambit. Purdey, a
former ballerina with a much-copied page-boy haircut,
was classy, elegant and as hard as nails. Like her predecessors Gale, Peel and King, she knew how to fight. Her
strength was in her kick, and many an assailant felt the
power of her long, shapely legs. She was also a good shot
and extremely fit. Mike Gambit provided the muscle
which Steed now lacked. A former mercenary, he was a
weapons specialist and a practitioner of kung fu. Both
young colleagues showed Steed the respect he deserved
and relied on his wealth of experience and knowledge.

Produced in association with a French TV company
and also with some Canadian input, three episodes were
filmed in France and four in Canada, with the majority
made in the UK.

NEW FACES
UK (ATV/Central) Talent Show. ITV 1973–8/1986–8

Hosts: **Derek Hobson, Nicky Martin, Marti Caine**

Producers: **Les Cocks, Albert Stevenson, Richard
Holloway**

*Talent show in which hopefuls are openly
criticized by a professional panel.*

Branded as cruelly frank and downright insensitive, *New
Faces* was OPPORTUNITY KNOCKS with bite. It aimed to
feature artists who had never appeared on television
before, and those who dared to participate found their
acts subjected to the views of four 'experts'. These
included established showbusiness names, record producers, DJs, agents and critics. Among regular pundits
were Mickie Most, Clifford Davis, Alan A. Freeman,
Martin Jackson, Ted Ray, Tony Hatch, Hilary Kingsley,
George Elrick, Ed Stewart, John Smith and Peter Prich-
ard. Awarding marks out of ten in categories such as
Presentation, Content and Star Quality, the panel's
forthright comments were known to reduce artists to
tears at times. Some were awarded no points at all. Arthur
Askey, on the other hand, thought every act was fantastic. Some were, indeed, good enough to make the grade:
Lenny Henry, Les Dennis, Jim Davidson, Victoria Wood,
Showaddywaddy, Patti Boulaye and Gary Wilmot
were the most prominent. EMMERDALE star Malandra

Burrows (using the name of Malandra Newman)
appeared as a singer at the age of nine and became the
series' youngest winner. Like other heat-winners, she
progressed to the grand final, where the series winner
was decided.

One *New Faces* champion, Marti Caine, went on to
host a revival of the series, entitled *New Faces of 86*
(then *87* and *88*). Among the new celebrity critics was
newspaper columnist Nina Myskow. The Johnny Patrick
Orchestra provided musical support in the early days,
with Harry Rabinowitz's Orchestra taking over in the
1980s. The show's original 'You're a Star' theme song was
performed by former Move vocalist Carl Wayne.

NEW SCOTLAND YARD
UK (LWT) Police Drama. ITV 1972–4

Det. Chief Supt. John Kingdom .... **John Woodvine**
DS Alan Ward .... **John Carlisle**
Det. Chief Supt. Clay .... **Michael Turner**
DS Dexter .... **Clive Francis**

Executive Producer: **Rex Firkin**
Producer: **Jack Williams**

*Two CID officers investigate serious crimes in
London.*

Kingdom and Ward were two quietly efficient detectives,
working from New Scotland Yard. Kingdom was the
more thoughtful, Ward the tougher, less approachable
partner. Together – and not without friction – they
inquired into cases of murder, blackmail, extortion and
the new, violent crimes of the 1970s. After two years,
they were replaced for one more series by the experienced Chief Supt. Clay and his junior colleague, DS
Dexter, but, throughout, the series avoided the plain
'cops-and-robbers' stereotype of many police series, and
depicted police work, more truthfully, as hard and personally distressing.

NEW STATESMAN, THE
UK (Yorkshire) Situation Comedy. ITV 1987–92

Alan Beresford B'Stard .... **Rik Mayall**
Sarah B'Stard .... **Marsha Fitzalan**
Piers Fletcher-Dervish .... **Michael Troughton**
Bob Crippen .... **Nick Stringer**
Norman Bormann .... **R. R. Cooper**
Beatrice Protheroe .... **Vivien Heilbron**
Sir Stephen Baxter .... **John Nettleton**
Sir Greville .... **Terence Alexander**
Roland Gidleigh-Park .... **Charles Gray**
Mrs Thatcher .... **Steve Nallon**
Neil Kinnock .... **Johnny More**
Sidney Bliss .... **Peter Sallis**

Creators/Writers: **Laurence Marks, Maurice Gran**
Producers: **David Reynolds, Tony Charles, Andrew
Benson, Bernard McKenna**

The unscrupulous manoeuvrings of an ambitious MP.

Alan B'Stard was the Conservative Member of Parliament for the North Yorkshire constituency of Haltemprice. Styling himself as a country squire, he was not so much a confirmed Thatcherite as a rampant right-winger, a man who had maimed his electoral opponents in a car crash to win a 27,000-vote majority and become the youngest MP in the House. Riding roughshod over all who stood in his way (physically as well as metaphorically), sleaze meant nothing to the mean and vicious B'Stard, who lined his own pockets, cynically hid behind his parliamentary scapegoat, Piers Fletcher-Dervish, and wriggled his way up the ladder. B'Stard's lesbian wife, Sarah, daughter of the odious Roland Gidleigh-Park, was heiress to a fortune and only stayed with her husband for appearances' sake. Also seen was B'Stard's sex-changing business consultant, Norman Bormann, (actress Rowena Cooper was billed as R. R. Cooper so as not to give the game away too early). Eventually leaving Parliament, B'Stard found himself imprisoned in a Russian gulag before returning to the political fray as a Euro MP.

Although the series – which used Mussorgsky's 'Pictures At An Exhibition' as its theme music – ended in 1992, a one-off special in which B'Stard was interviewed by Brian Walden was screened on BBC 1 at Christmas 1994.

NEWCOMERS, THE
UK (BBC) Drama. BBC 1 1965–9

Ellis Cooper	Alan Browning
Vivienne Cooper	Maggie Fitzgibbon
Gran Hamilton	Gladys Henson
Philip Cooper	Jeremy Bulloch
Maria Cooper	Judy Geeson
Lance Cooper	Raymond Hunt
Janet Langley/Cooper	Sandra Payne
Jeff Langley	Michael Collins
Arnold Tripp	Gerald Cross
Arthur Huntley	Tony Steedman
Cornwallis	Philip Ray
George Harbottle	Glynn Edwards
Tom Lloyd	Michael Standing
Betty Lloyd	Helen Cotterill
Peter Connolly	Patrick Connor
Dick Alderbeach	Keith Smith
Ted Rumble	Anthony Wager
Mrs Katie Heenan	Vanda Godsell
Andrew Heenan	Jonathan Bergman
Celia Blatchford	Barbara Keogh
Sydney Huxley	Anthony Verner
Eunice Huntley	Sally Lahee
Amelia Huntley/Malcolm	Naomi Chance
Paul Bose	Mahav Sharma
Frank Claw	Thomas Heathcote
Cora Brassett	Eileen Way
Bert Harker	Robert Brown
Vera Harker	June Bland
Joyce Harker	Wendy Richard
Jimmy Harker	David Janson
James Neal	David Knight
Charlie Penrose	Victor Platt
Mary Penrose	Megs Jenkins
Prudence Penrose	Eileen Helsby
Jacob Penrose	George Woodbridge
Herbert Button	J. G. Devlin
Celia Stuart/Murray	Beryl Cooke
Henry Burroughs	Campbell Singer
Sally Burroughs	Alysoun Austin
William Pargeter	Julian Somers
Gordon Pargeter	Colin Stepney
Rufus Pargeter	Michael Redfern
Minnie Pargeter	Cindy Wright
Andrew Kerr	Robin Bailey
Caroline Kerr	Heather Chasen
Kirsty Kerr	Jenny Agutter
	Maggie Don
Margot Kerr	Sally-Jane Spencer
Charles Turner	Neil Hallett
Robert Malcolm	Conrad Phillips
Eric Crutchley	John Kidd
Peter Metcalfe	Gil Sutherland
Hugh Robertson	Jack Watling
Olivia Robertson	Mary Kenton
Julie Robertson	Deborah Watling
Michael Robertson	Robert Bartlett
Adrian Robertson	Paul Bartlett

Creator: **Colin Morris**
Producers: **Verity Lambert, Morris Barry, Ronald Travers, Bill Sellars**

A London family are uneasy about their new life in the country.

The Newcomers, a twice-weekly soap, centred around the Coopers, a London family who moved out of the Smoke into the sticks and set up home in the fictitious Suffolk village of Angleton (real-life Haverhill). The series' petty dramas revolved around life at work with dad Ellis (a supervisor at Eden Brothers' computer parts factory – boss: Arthur Huntley) and at home, on a new housing estate, as well as other focal points of the town, including the pubs The Crown and primarily The Bull (landlord: Peter Connolly, then Henry Burroughs), Burroughs' Supermarket and St Peter's Church. Mum Vivienne struggled to cope with their three teenage children (17-year-old Philip, 16-year-old Maria and 13-year-old troublemaker Lance), as well as her glum, live-in mum, as the difficulties of settling into a new neighbourhood and integration with locals like the Langleys and the indigenous farming community became all too evident. Throughout, the problems facing the fast-developing town – such as the need for a by-pass – were prominently reported in the *Angleton Advertiser* (editor: Arnold Tripp). Among the Coopers' later neighbours was brash, 20-year-old Cockney Joyce Harker, played by a pre-EASTENDERS Wendy Richard. Another actress gaining experience in the series was Jenny Agutter, as Kirsty Kerr, young daughter of another new family. Ellis Cooper was written out in 1968, dying of a heart attack, and Vivienne emigrated to New Zealand with new lover Charles Turner. Another family, the Robertsons, subsequently took over the role of 'the newcomers'.

NEWMAN, ANDREA
(1938–)

British novelist and TV writer, known for controversial series (often exploring middle-class mores) such as BOUQUET OF BARBED WIRE, *Another Bouquet*, A SENSE OF GUILT, *Imogen's Face* and *An Evil Streak*. She has also contributed single dramas to anthologies like *Tales of Unease* and *The Frighteners*.

NEWMAN, NANETTE
(1934–)

British actress and presenter who is probably better known for her detergent commercials than her programme credits. Among her TV contributions have been the dramas, *Stay With Me Till Morning* (Robin Lendrick) and *Jessie* (title role), and the comedies, *Let There Be Love* (widow Judy) and *Late Expectations* (middle-aged mother-to-be Liz Jackson). Newman also appeared in *Prometheus* and *The Endless Game*, and has guested on numerous series, including THE SAINT. She is married to film director Bryan Forbes and is the mother of TV presenter Emma Forbes.

NEWMAN, SYDNEY
(1917–97)

Canadian drama specialist who joined ABC in 1958 to produce the influential ARMCHAIR THEATRE series of plays. While there, as Head of Drama, Newman was also co-creator of THE AVENGERS (and its forerunner, POLICE SURGEON), as well as the *Target Luna*/PATHFINDERS sci-fi adventures for kids. Five years later, he was enticed over to the BBC, where he became its Head of Drama and gained a reputation as a tough overseer. Among the BBC's most notable achievements under his auspices were DOCTOR WHO (creator), THE WEDNESDAY PLAY (including classics like *Up the Junction* and CATHY COME HOME) and THE FORSYTE SAGA. His own productions over the years included Alun Owen's *Lena, O My Lena* (1960), John Wyndham's *Dumb Martian* (1962) and Harold Pinter's *Tea Party* (1965). He subsequently returned to Canada to work in film and TV.

NEWS

Television presentation of the news was initially a voice-only affair. Announcers simply regurgitated radio bulletins. While BBC TELEVISION NEWSREEL, which began in 1948, was an advance into moving pictures (if not up-to-the-minute stories), it took until 1954 for the first television news bulletin as we now know it to reach the air. Richard Baker was the first presenter of *BBC Television News*, on 5 July, although, for a further 14 months, no newsreader was seen in vision while delivering the news. It was feared that their facial expressions would detract from their impartiality. Kenneth Kendall became the

first newsreader in shot, in September 1955, but, in those days before autocues, he and his colleagues (Baker and Robert Dougall) were forced to read, head down, from a script. The same month, not coincidentally, ITV took to the air, bringing with it the more dynamic forces of ITN (Independent Television News). It was ITN who pioneered the American two-presenter format in the UK when it launched the half-hour *News at Ten* on 3 July 1967. The programme was a huge success, being axed – amid great controversy – only on 5 March 1999. The first presenters were Alastair Burnet and Andrew Gardner. The last (with the bulletin now back to single-presenter format) was Trevor McDonald. The name *ITV News at Ten* has since been revived for some late-evening bulletins.

Over the years, technical developments have changed the face of television news presentation. Satellites have provided instant international coverage, computer graphics have added colour and variety to dull items and brightened up studio sets, and Electronic News Gathering (ENG) has enabled reporters and cameramen to send on-the-spot reports directly back to the studio, with small, lightweight camera equipment allowing access to hitherto impossible situations. Non-stop satellite and digital news channels have been established to provide information on breaking events around the clock. At the forefront of these was CNN, followed by Sky News and, later, BBC News 24.

It is believed by many that Angela Rippon was the first national female newsreader, but in fact there were others before her. Barbara Mandell appeared on ITN's lunchtime news as early as 1955, and Nan Winton was seen on the BBC for six months from 1960. Other prominent newsreaders (or newscasters, as ITN has traditionally called them) have been Michael Aspel, Corbett Woodall, Bob Langley, John Edmunds, Richard Whitmore, Peter Woods, John Humphrys, John Simpson, Andrew Harvey, Sue Lawley, Jan Leeming, Michael Buerk, Philip Hayton, Nicholas Witchell, Jeremy Paxman, Chris Lowe, Moira Stuart, Jennie Bond, Debbie Thrower, Laurie Mayer, Jill Dando, John Tusa, Edward Stourton, Justin Webb, Huw Edwards, Jon Sopel, George Alagiah, Sian Williams and Fiona Bruce (all for the BBC); Christopher Chataway, Robin Day, Anthony Brown, Ludovic Kennedy, Andrew Gardner, Reginald Bosanquet, Sandy Gall, Gordon Honeycombe, Alastair Burnet, Leonard Parkin, Ivor Mills, Peter Snow, Robert Kee, Trevor McDonald, Rory MacPherson, Michael Nicholson, Alastair Stewart, Selina Scott, Pamela Armstrong, Fiona Armstrong, John Suchet, Carol Barnes, Jon Snow, Sue Carpenter, Dermot Murnaghan, Anne Leuchars, Nicholas Owen, Anya Sitaram, Denis Tuohy, Katie Derham, Mark Austin and Andrea Catherwood (for ITN). Martyn Lewis, Peter Sissons, Anna Ford and Julia Somerville are four newsreaders who have worked for both channels. Peter Sissons was also an early anchor of Channel 4 News, but Jon Snow has been in that hot seat since 1989, supported by Zeinab Badawi, Shahnaz Pakravan, Cathy Smith, Jane Bennett-Powell, Phil Gayle, Daljit Dhaliwal, Tanya Sillem, Krishnan Guru-Murthy, Sue Turton, Alex Thomson and Kirsty Lang. The newest national service, Channel 5 News, was launched by Kirsty Young, who was backed up by Rob Butler and Charlie Stayt and eventually succeeded, when she left for ITN's ITV news, by Andrea Catherwood.

NEWS AT TEN
See NEWS.

NEWSNIGHT
UK (BBC) Current Affairs. BBC 2 1980–

Presenters: **Peter Snow, Peter Hobday, Charles Wheeler, John Tusa, Olivia O'Leary, Jenni Murray, Donald MacCormick, Gavin Esler, Jeremy Paxman, Francine Stock, Kirsty Wark, Jeremy Vine**

Editors: **Ron Neil, Sian Keevil**

Late-night current affairs round-up.

Much acclaimed, *Newsnight* (initially four nights a week, later five) has performed the task of reviewing in detail the major news stories of the day, with special emphasis on political and foreign affairs. After industrial disputes had postponed the launch on various occasions, the original team of presenters comprised Peter Snow (with the programme until 1997), Peter Hobday, Charles Wheeler and John Tusa, with news bulletins read by Fran Morrison and sports reports from David Davies (later David Icke). The format was later changed to incorporate just one host/interviewer. Jeremy Paxman, Kirsty Wark and Jeremy Vine have held this position in recent years, relieved occasionally by Sue Cameron, John Simpson, James Cox, Huw Edwards, Gordon Brewer, Sarah Montague and Martha Kearney.

Newsnight's challenging interviewing techniques have made it both admired and feared by politicians, some of whom openly questioned the programme's 'patriotism' during international conflicts such as the Falklands and Gulf Wars, when presenters deliberately aimed to present a balanced picture of events. One of the most memorable moments in the programme's history came when Jeremy Paxman unsuccessfully pressed the then Home Secretary Michael Howard 14 times for an answer to the question, 'Did you threaten to overrule him?', referring to Howard's dispute with Prison Chief Derek Lewis.

NEWSROUND
UK (BBC) Children's News. BBC 1 1972–

Presenters: **John Craven, Lucy Mathen, Roger Finn, Helen Rollason, Paul McDowell, Juliet Morris, Krishnan Guru-Murthy, Julie Etchingham, Chris Rogers, Kate Sanderson**

A bulletin of topical news for juniors.

This innovative series has aimed to make important news stories more accessible to younger viewers. Lasting just five or ten minutes and dropped into the children's schedule on weekday evenings (just two to start, now five nights), *Newsround* (*John Craven's Newsround* until 1987, Craven eventually leaving in 1989) has presented snippets of real news, explaining the background in fine detail for young minds to grasp. There has always been an emphasis on subjects of youth interest, but the programme has never been patronizing. On some occasions, *Newsround* has even beaten adult news programmes to the punch with breaking stories, such as the *Challenger* space-shuttle disaster. The first programme on 4 April 1972 was intended to be the start of only a six-week trial. In the early days, the programme carried details of an earthquake in Iran and the build-up to the launch of *Apollo 16*. More recent initiatives have included mock elections for children in the run-up to a general election and the introduction of the monthly Doc Slot, in which Dr David Bull has discussed children's health.

A round-up programme, *Newsround Weekly* (presented by Lucy Mathen), was added in 1977 and the longer *Newsround Extra* (an investigative series introduced in 1975) has been aired on some Fridays.

NICE TIME
UK (Granada) Comedy. ITV 1968–9

Presenters: **Germaine Greer, Jonathan Routh, Kenny Everett, Sandra Gough**

Producer: **John Birt**

Anarchic and bizarre sketch show.

Originally a programme just for the Granada region, *Nice Time* proved so popular that it was extended to the ITV network. It comprised a collection of wacky sketches and inventive stunts, built around viewers' requests for favourite moments from comedy films. However, it is best remembered today for giving young DJ Kenny Everett his TV break, for promoting the then Warwick University lecturer Germaine Greer, and for being produced by future BBC Director-General John Birt. Sandra Gough (ex-CORONATION STREET) joined the team in series two.

NICHOLAS, PAUL
(Paul Beuselinck; 1945–)

British singer and actor who used his charm to good effect as Vince Pinner in the sitcom, JUST GOOD FRIENDS, in the 1980s. Before that, his biggest role was in a short-lived 1979 BBC comedy entitled *Two Up, Two Down* in which, as Jimmy, he starred with Su Pollard. Nicholas had also guested in numerous series (like Z CARS and *Lady Killers*), appeared in assorted films and stage musicals, and notched up a few pop chart hits (also hosting *Paul*, his own kids' pop show). He was later seen as the financially embarrassed Neil Walsh in *Bust* (1987) and as vet James Shepherd in the comedy, *Close to Home* (1989), as well as singing and dancing in variety shows. He returned to the small screen in 2000, as David Janus in *Sunburn*. Nicholas was also the narrator of the *Spot* cartoons.

NICHOLLS, PAUL
(1979–)

Bolton-born actor coming to light in the kids' series, *Earthfasts* (David Wix) and *The Biz* (drama student Tim), and then being cast as Joe Wicks in EASTENDERS. His next move was into the police series, *City Central* (PC Terry Sydenham), and he has followed this with the drama, *The Passion* (passion play actor Daniel). Nicholls has also guested in *Out of the Blue* and *Fully Booked*.

NICHOLLS, SUE
(Susan Harmar-Nicholls; 1943–)

Known today as Audrey Roberts in CORONATION STREET (a role she has played since 1979), Sue Nicholls's TV appearances have been many and varied. Some viewers may recall her in CROSSROADS, as waitress Marilyn Gates, a part which gave her a hit single, 'Where Will You Be?', in 1968. Others may recall her performances as Joan Greengross, Reggie Perrin's devoted secretary, or as Wanda Pickles, Jim Davidson's neighbour in *Up the Elephant and Round the Castle*. Her other credits have included *Not on Your Nellie* (barmaid Big Brenda), RENTAGHOST (Nadia Popov), THE DUCHESS OF DUKE STREET, *Village Hall*, *Heartland*, THE PROFESSIONALS, DOCTOR ON THE GO, THE GENTLE TOUCH and WODE-HOUSE PLAYHOUSE. She is the daughter of one-time Conservative MP Lord Harmar-Nicholls and is married to former *Street* bad guy Mark Eden.

NICHOLS, DANDY
(Daisy Nichols; 1907–86)

British actress, famous for one role, that of Else, Alf Garnett's much-abused wife in TILL DEATH US DO PART and *In Sickness and in Health*. Her one other major part was as Madge in the 1971 sitcom, *The Trouble with Lillian* (opposite Patricia Hayes), although she also appeared in series like *Ask Mr Pastry*, EMERGENCY – WARD 10, DIXON OF DOCK GREEN, NO HIDING PLACE, MRS THURSDAY, MAN IN A SUITCASE, BERGERAC and the kids' comedy, *The Bagthorpe Saga* (Mrs Fosdyke).

NICHOLS, PETER
(1927–)

British stage and television dramatist whose earliest TV work dates from the late 1950s. Among his most notable offerings (generally in a light, socially observational vein) have been *Promenade* (1959), *The Continuity Man* (1963), *The Hooded Terror* (1963), *The Gorge* (1968), *Hearts and Flowers* (1968), *The Common* (1973), *Forget-Me-Not Lane* (1975) and the *Ben Spray* mini-series of dramas (spread over two decades from 1961). He has also contributed to INSPECTOR MORSE.

NICHOLSON, MICHAEL
OBE (1937–)

Award-winning ITN journalist, with the company since 1963, having previously worked as a political writer with D. C. Thompson. Nicholson has the distinction of covering more wars than any other British TV reporter. These have included the conflicts in Vietnam, Biafra (eastern Nigeria), the Falklands and in the Gulf. He was ITN's Southern Africa correspondent, 1976–81, and presenter of *News at 5.45* for three years from 1982. He is currently the chief foreign affairs correspondent.

NICKELODEON

Children's channel originating on cable TV in the USA in 1979 when it was founded by the Warner Amex company. It was later taken over by Viacom. From the start, the focus of its programming has been on variety for younger viewers, combining cartoons with live programming, youth drama and game shows. Since 1993 it has broadcast to Europe from the Astra satellite system, and is also now available via cable companies and digital. Its programming remains heavily American, with hit series like *Sabrina the Teenage Witch* and *Rugrats* to the fore, but there is also UK input in the form of 'Children's BBC for Nickelodeon', complete with TELETUBBIES reruns. A younger children's service is provided by sister channel, Nick Jr. In the USA, Nickelodeon's daytime service is complemented by Nick at Night, a grown-ups channel which features vintage TV shows.

NIELSENS

The all-important US league table of TV audiences, collated by the AC Nielsen company (using a technical device known as the 'Audimeter' which is attached to television receivers). The term has become synonymous with 'ratings' in America. AC Nielsen was also active in the UK TV industry for a while in the 1950s.

NIMMO, DEREK
(1932–99)

Liverpudlian actor often seen in rather dithery roles. He enjoyed great success with his clerics, Reverend Mervyn Noote in ALL GAS AND GAITERS, Brother/Father Dominic in OH BROTHER and *Oh Father*, and Dean Selwyn Makepeace in *Hell's Bells*. He also played David in THE BED-SIT GIRL, Frederick in the comedy, *Blandings Castle*, Bingo Little in *The World of Wooster*, David in another sitcom, *Sorry I'm Single*, Henry Prendergast in the political comedy, *My Honourable Mrs*, Chris Bunting in *Life Begins at Forty* and George Hutchenson in *Third Time Lucky*. Nimmo also made a well-publicized cameo appearance in NEIGHBOURS and, in the 1970s, was host of the chat shows, *If It's Saturday, It Must Be Nimmo* and *Just a Nimmo*.

NIMOY, LEONARD
(1931–)

American actor who will always be STAR TREK's pointy-eared Vulcan, Mr Spock, even though he has enjoyed plenty of other TV work. Nimoy's TV debut came in the 1950s, with parts in series like DRAGNET and LARAMIE. More guest appearances came in the 1960s, including in THE MAN FROM UNCLE and GET SMART, before he was cast as Spock, which he followed with the role of Paris, master of disguise, in MISSION: IMPOSSIBLE. Nimoy has since been seen in TV movies and mini-series (such as *Marco Polo*) and has also worked as a programme narrator.

1984
UK (BBC) Science Fiction. BBC 1954

Winston Smith	Peter Cushing
O'Brien	André Morell
Julia	Yvonne Mitchell
Syme	Donald Pleasence
Emmanuel Goldstein	Arnold Diamond
Parsons	Campbell Gray

Writer: **Nigel Kneale**
Producer: **Rudolph Cartier**

Highly controversial adaptation of George Orwell's portentous novel.

Variously criticized and praised by the politicians of the day, this one-off drama shocked the nation. As its title suggested, it focused on life in 1984 (30 years ahead), at a time when a totalitarian regime known as Big Brother was watching over all of Britain. Society was divided into clearly defined groups. First there was the Inner Party, then came the Outer Party. Beyond these 'privileged' citizens were the ordinary masses, the Proles. Language had been eroded away, limiting individual expression by the abolition of words, and videoscreens watched people as they went about their everyday chores, checking for signs of dissent.

At the heart of the action was Winston Smith, a member of the Outer Party who worked as a rewriter of history in the Ministry of Truth. It was his growing rebellion, encouraged by a girlfriend, Julia, and then viciously curbed by the devious O'Brien in the dreaded Room 101, which exemplified the control of the authorities and the nightmare of life under such a regime. The torture sequence involving live rats is well remembered.

Transmitted live on a Sunday night, *1984* was repeated – again live – four days later, drawing the biggest audience since the Coronation (largely as a result of the clamour which followed the first showing). The play was written by Nigel Kneale and produced by Rudolph Cartier, two adventurous BBC men who, a year or so earlier, had created the ground-breaking QUATERMASS EXPERIMENT. Kneale revived *1984* in 1965, with David Buck, Jane Merrow and Joseph O'Connor in the lead

roles of Smith, Julia and O'Brien, but, unlike its predecessor, it passed virtually unnoticed.

1990
UK (BBC) Drama. BBC 2 1977–8

Jim Kyle	Edward Woodward
Faceless (Maudsley)	Paul Hardwick
Herbert Skardon	Robert Lang
Dave Brett	Tony Doyle
Delly Lomas	Barbara Kellerman
Dan Mellor	John Savident
Henry Tasker	Clifton Jones
Greaves	George Murcell
Jack Nichols	Michael Napier Brown
Kate Smith	Yvonne Mitchell
Lynn Blake	Lisa Harrow
PCD Insp. MacRae	David McKail
Tony Doran	Clive Swift

Creator: **Wilfred Greatorex**
Producer: **Prudence Fitzgerald**

An Orwellian vision of the future, in all its depressing glory.

This drama centred on the hypothesis that at the end of the 20th century Britain would be ruthlessly controlled by a government that suppressed all resistance in the name of the common good. Looking just 13 years into the future, *1990* foresaw a Britain where rationing and identity cards were back on the agenda and where *emi*gration, not *immi*gration, was the problem, as scientists and other dissidents sought to flee the totalitarian state. Overseeing the oppression was a Home Office division known as the Public Control Department (PCD), with the cruel Herbert Skardon at its head, supported by a deputy, Delly Lomas (later replaced by Lynn Blake). Opposing them was resistance leader Jim Kyle, a Home Affairs reporter for one of the three surviving newspapers. With his colleagues, Kyle aimed to smuggle dissidents out of the country and subvert the powers of the PCD by operating an underground press and hindering their every movement.

NIXON, DAVID
(1919–78)

Popular British conjuror and game show panellist of the 1950s–1970s. A former stage partner of Norman Wisdom, Nixon became one of UK TV's earliest celebrities, appearing on the children's show, *Sugar and Spice*, and using his charm to good effect as a regular panellist on shows like WHAT'S MY LINE? and *My Wildest Dream*. In the late 1950s he starred in *It's Magic* and went on to host *Showtime* and *Comedy Bandbox*. In the late 1960s and 1970s, he was given his own shows, *Nixon at Nine-Five, Now for Nixon, The Nixon Line, David Nixon, Tonight with David Nixon, The David Nixon Show* and *David Nixon's Magic Box*, some of which helped introduce an aristocratic foxy puppet by the name of Basil Brush to an enthusiastic audience.

NO HIDING PLACE

UK (Associated-Rediffusion) Police Drama. ITV 1959–67

Det. Chief Supt. Tom Lockhart .... **Raymond Francis**
DS Harry Baxter .... **Eric Lander**
DS Russell .... **Johnny Briggs**
DS Perryman .... **Michael McStay**
DS Gregg .... **Sean Caffrey**

Producers: **Ray Dicks, Richard Matthews, Jonathan Goodman, Peter Willes, Geoffrey Hughes, Ian Fordyce, Michael Currer-Briggs**

More adventures with top detective Lockhart.

Detective Chief Superintendent Lockhart of Scotland Yard, after earlier exploits in the programmes, MURDER BAG and CRIME SHEET, returned to the screen in this long-running series in which he was assisted by keen young DS Baxter. Baxter's popularity was so great that he was later given his own spin-off series, ECHO FOUR TWO, before returning to Lockhart's side when that programme failed to take off. When Baxter moved on yet again, replacement sergeants Russell and Perryman were introduced, with DS Gregg eventually added as the final partner for this genial, snuff-taking sleuth.

The series was popular with both the public and the police, particularly for its authenticity. Over 230 episodes were produced, many of them transmitted live. When it was taken off in 1965, such was the furore that the producers were forced to extend Lockhart's career by a couple more years. One 1962 episode saw a guest appearance by Patrick Cargill in the guise of TOP SECRET's Miguel Garetta. Supporting actor Johnny Briggs, of course, has since found fame as CORONATION STREET's Mike Baldwin, but for the part of Russell the rather short actor had to wear built-up shoes. The *No Hiding Place* theme music, performed by Ken Mackintosh and his orchestra, entered the pop charts in 1960.

NO – HONESTLY

UK (LWT) Situation Comedy. ITV 1974–5

Charles 'CD' Danby .... **John Alderton**
Clara Burrell/Danby .... **Pauline Collins**

Writers: **Terence Brady, Charlotte Bingham**
Producer: **Humphrey Barclay**

A couple look affectionately back to the early days of their courtship and marriage.

Clara and CD Danby were a well-matched, romantic couple. She was a children's novelist, the daughter of peer Lord Burrell and author of the 'Ollie the Otter' books. He was a comic actor and together they had become a success. But life hadn't always been so generous. Their early relationship (ten years before) had been pitted with minor disasters, and these were introduced in flashback form in each episode, after the couple's introductory chat to the camera. Their whimsical approach to life and their fondness for social pranks formed a backdrop to most of the plots, as did Clara's scatty, convoluted logic which bemused and amused her patient, caring husband. The duo then wrapped up each episode with another piece to camera.

This was very much a 'married couples' series, as both the writers, Terence Brady and Charlotte Bingham, and the stars, John Alderton and Pauline Collins, were real-life husbands and wives. With its pieces to camera and Clara's weird logic, it owed more than a little to THE BURNS AND ALLEN SHOW. When Alderton and Collins called it a day, Donal Donnelly and Liza Goddard were brought in as Matt Browne and Lily Pond, a songwriter and his secretary, and the title became 'Yes – Honestly' (it was screened 1976–7). The *No – Honestly* theme song, by Lynsey De Paul, reached the Top Ten in 1974, but 'Yes – Honestly' by Georgie Fame was not a hit.

NO JOB FOR A LADY

UK (Thames) Situation Comedy. ITV 1990–2

Jean Price .... **Penelope Keith**
Sir Godfrey Eagan .... **George Baker**
Ken Miller .... **Paul Young**
Norman .... **Garfield Morgan**
Geoff Price .... **Mark Kingston**
Harry .... **Nigel Humphreys**
Richard .... **Michael Cochrane**

Creator/Writer: **Alex Shearer**
Producer: **John Howard Davies**

A new, ambitious female MP discovers the House of Commons is a bit of a jungle.

When newly elected Labour MP Jean Price took her seat at Westminster, she quickly learned that its operations were far from straightforward. In dealings with her Tory opposite number, Sir Godfrey Eagan, and her Labour whip, Norman, she soon learned to pick her friends carefully. Principles and practicality, she found, were not always compatible. Advising her was her office share, Scottish MP Ken Miller, while hubby Geoff provided support at home.

NO PLACE LIKE HOME

UK (BBC) Situation Comedy. BBC 1 1983–7

Arthur Crabtree .... **William Gaunt**
Beryl Crabtree .... **Patricia Garwood**
Nigel Crabtree .... **Martin Clunes**
                                     Andrew Charleson
Paul Crabtree .... **Stephen Watson**
Tracy Crabtree .... **Dee Sadler**
Lorraine Codd .... **Beverley Adams**
Raymond Codd .... **Daniel Hill**
Vera Botting .... **Marcia Warren**
                                        Ann Penfold
Trevor Botting .... **Michael Sharvell-Martin**
Roger Duff .... **Roger Martin**

Creator/Writer: **Jon Watkins**
Producer: **Robin Nash**

A middle-aged couple plan for a quiet life once their children have left home. Sadly, it is not to be.

Arthur and Beryl Crabtree had raised four children and looked forward to the day when their time, once again, would be their own. A second honeymoon was planned as the last of their offspring finally left home. However, their hopes were soon dashed as one by one the fledglings returned to the nest, disillusioned with life in the outside world. For the children, there simply was no place like home. Eldest of the kids was Lorraine, who had married Raymond Codd but quickly cast him aside. There were also Nigel, Paul and Tracy (and their assorted boy- and girlfriends), while the Crabtrees' domestic bliss was also disturbed by their nosey neighbours, the Bottings, particularly the shrieking, animal-loving Vera. Arthur and Vera's husband, Trevor, often escaped to the greenhouse when things became unbearable, seeking solace in a glass of home-made sherry.

Actress Beverley Adams, who played Lorraine, is the daughter of former CRACKERJACK hostess Jillian Comber.

NO – THAT'S ME OVER HERE
UK (Rediffusion/LWT) Situation Comedy. ITV 1967–70

Ronnie .... **Ronnie Corbett**
Laura .... **Rosemary Leach**
Henry .... **Henry McGee**
Secretary .... **Jill Mai Meredith**

Writers: **Graham Chapman, Eric Idle, Barry Cryer**
Executive Producer: **David Frost**
Producers: **Bill Hitchcock, Marty Feldman**

A middle-class commuter seeks social status.

Life was never straightforward for Ronnie. The little man, smartly attired in three-piece suit, bowler hat, brolly and briefcase, aimed high, but somehow always fell well short. This was particularly the case when he strove to outdo his patronizing next-door neighbour, Henry, who commuted alongside him to their City offices. Laura was Ronnie's long-suffering wife.

Although dropped after one season in 1968 when Rediffusion lost its ITV franchise, the series was picked up two years later by LWT. Corbett went on to play numerous other 'little man' roles, often accompanied, as here, by Rosemary Leach (see NOW LOOK HERE . . . !).

NOAKES, JOHN
(1934–)

Yorkshire-born actor whose greatest role was as the resident daredevil in BLUE PETER. Noakes joined the series in 1966, after acting in a number of TV series and working on stage as a 'feed' to Cyril Fletcher. He stayed with *Blue Peter* for 12 years, forming part of the series' golden-age trio with Valerie Singleton and Peter Purves. Accompanied by his playful collie, Shep ('Get down, Shep' became a catchphrase), he even secured his own spin-off series, GO WITH NOAKES, in which he continued his hair-raising stunts such as climbing chimneys, leaping out of aircraft and tearing around in racing cars. Later, he worked for YTV and then for TV-am, on their Saturday morning show, but more or less retired to Majorca thereafter. In 1994 he was reunited with Valerie Singleton to present the over-50s afternoon magazine, *Next*, and returned again in 1999 as host of *Mad About Pets*.

NOBBS, DAVID
(1935–)

British novelist and screenwriter, responsible for series like THE FALL AND RISE OF REGINALD PERRIN, *The Legacy of Reginald Perrin*, FAIRLY SECRET ARMY, A BIT OF A DO and *The Life and Times of Henry Pratt*. Among his other TV work have been scripts for THAT WAS THE WEEK THAT WAS, *The Roy Hudd Show*, THE FROST REPORT and *The Dick Emery Show* (all with Peter Tinniswood), *Sez Les*, THE TWO RONNIES, and the series, *Lance at Large* (for Lance Percival), *Shine a Light* (with David McKellar and Peter Vincent), *Keep It in the Family* (with Peter Vincent), *Whoops Baghdad!* (with Sid Colin and David McKellar), *Dogfood Dan and the Carmarthen Cowboy*, *The Glamour Girls*, *The Hello Goodbye Man*, *The Sun Trap*, *Rich Tea and Sympathy* and adaptations of *Love on a Branch Line* and Malcolm Bradbury's *Cuts*.

NODDY

A familiar, contrived shot in news interviews where the interviewer is seen to nod in acknowledgement to the interviewee's answers. These shots are usually recorded at the end of the interview and then dropped in between questions during editing, to smooth over ugly breaks.

NOEL'S HOUSE PARTY
UK (BBC) Entertainment. BBC 1 1991–9

Presenter: **Noel Edmonds**

Executive Producer: **Michael Leggo**
Producers: **Michael Leggo, Jonathan Beazley, Guy Freeman, John McHugh, Philip Kampff**

Live Saturday-evening mélange of gags and silly games.

Following the demise of THE LATE, LATE BREAKFAST SHOW in 1986, Noel Edmonds returned to Saturday teatime telly in 1988 with *Noel Edmonds' Saturday Road Show*, in which he pretended to present each programme from a different and exotic location. The emphasis was on silly games, lots of laughs and a few hidden-camera tricks. Some elements he then took on to *Noel's House Party*, based at a mock stately home in the fictitious village of Crinkley Bottom. The show went from strength to strength, benefiting from Edmonds's coolness with live television. Among the favourite features were the Gotcha Oscars (in which a celebrity was conned into making a spoof TV programme or personal appearance), Grab A Grand (celebrities clutching at banknotes in a wind machine to earn money for a lucky viewer),

NTV (hidden cameras in people's homes), The Pork Pie (a member of the audience trying to deny a shameful incident in his/her life), Wait Till I Get You Home (precocious kids telling secrets about their parents), and My Little Friend (where an inanimate object started talking to children). There were also little quizzes like The Lyric Game, surprise guests, psychedelic drenchings courtesy of the gunge tank, and the show's own soap opera, *Crinkley Bottom*, featuring the Weeks family, headed by Liszt and Newt publican George Weeks (played by Brian Croucher). Veteran DJ Tony Blackburn was seen as the butler on many occasions. One newcomer introduced by the show – Mr Blobby, a bloated pink dummy with yellow spots – went on to take the country by storm.

The last series of *Noel's House Party* were not happy ones for Noel Edmonds. In January 1998, he demanded that the show did not go out, as the quality was well below what he considered suitable (compilation programmes filled the slot for two weeks). Nevertheless, the *House Party* returned the following autumn, only to be finally cancelled in March 1999.

NOGGIN THE NOG

See SAGA OF NOGGIN THE NOG, THE.

NORDEN, DENIS
CBE (1922–)

British comedy writer, the former partner of Frank Muir and with him responsible for many TV scripts (see Frank Muir for their joint credits). Norden was also seen on the satire show, BBC-3, and, in the 1970s, hosted the nostalgia game, *Looks Familiar*. Since 1977 he has become best known for presenting television out-takes under the title IT'LL BE ALRIGHT ON THE NIGHT, as well as one-off specials involving nostalgic/funny TV clips.

NORMAN, BARRY
CBE (1933–)

The son of British film director Leslie Norman, Barry Norman was born into the world of cinema. Since leaving a position with the *Daily Mail*, he has brought his love of the silver screen into TV via programmes such as THE HOLLYWOOD GREATS and the long-running FILM series, which he quit in 1999 to work for Sky. He was, for a while in 1982, presenter of OMNIBUS and hosted the Olympic Games for Channel 4 in 1988. His other series have included *The British Greats*, *The Rank Charm School* and *Barry Norman's Hong Kong*, *Barry Norman on Broadway/in Chicago/in Celebrity City*, plus work on LATE NIGHT LINE-UP. Trivia buffs will know that he once appeared with Morecambe and Wise and that he also directed an episode of THE SAINT. He is the father of fellow film critic Emma Norman and TV presenter Samantha Norman.

NORTHERN EXPOSURE
US (Finnegan-Pinchuk/Falahey/Austin Street/Cine-Nevada/Universal) Drama. Channel 4 1992–7

Dr Joel Fleischman	**Rob Morrow**
Maggie O'Connell	**Janine Turner**
Maurice Minnifield	**Barry Corbin**
Chris Stevens	**John Corbett**
Ed Chigliak	**Darren E. Burrows**
Holling Vincoeur	**John Cullum**
Shelly Tambo	**Cynthia Geary**
Marilyn Whirlwind	**Elaine Miles**
Ruth-Anne Miller	**Peg Phillips**
Dr Phillip Capra	**Paul Provenza**
Michelle Capra	**Teri Polo**

Creators: **Joshua Brand, John Falsey**
Executive Producers: **John Falsey, Andrew Schneider**

Events in the off-beat life of an isolated Alaskan town.

Set in the fictional settlement of Cicely, Alaska, miles from civilization, *Northern Exposure* focused on the interrelationships of its mildly eccentric townsfolk. At the forefront was Jewish New Yorker Joel Fleischman, a newly qualified doctor whose arrival heralded the start of the series. Much against his will, but obliged because the Alaskan state had subsidized his college fees, Fleischman moved to the town to take over the vacant local practice. His escape attempts were always thwarted, but Fleischman's real reason for staying on (though never admitting it) was his love-hate relationship with his landlady, Maggie O'Connell, the air-taxi pilot. However, messing with O'Connell was fraught with danger, as her five previous boyfriends had all died in tragic circumstances. Others in the cast were Ed Chigliak, a young Red Indian film-buff, and Maurice Minnifield, former NASA astronaut and the town's patriarch. One-time adventurer Holling Vincoeur was proprietor of the local bar/restaurant (The Brick), which he ran with his teenage girlfriend, Shelly (whom he had stolen from Maurice). Chris 'In The Morning' Stevens was the town's philosophizing radio DJ and part-time minister, sensible Ruth-Anne ran the all-purpose shop and Marilyn was Fleischman's unflappable, monosyllabic Eskimo assistant. Occasional visitors to town were Adam, a sort of missing-link backwoodsman with a talent for *cordon bleu* cookery, his hypochondriac wife, Eve, Bernard, Chris's black half-brother, and Mort, a moose that wandered down the main street during the titles and credits.

Star Rob Morrow left the series after five years and was replaced by Paul Provenza and Teri Polo, as new doctor Phillip Capra and his journalist wife, Michelle. The series ended a few months later. With its stunning scenery and quirky feel, *Northern Exposure* was often likened to the spooky TWIN PEAKS, but with a much more wholesome atmosphere.

NORTON, GRAHAM
(Graham Walker; 1963–)

Camp Irish comedian and chat show host whose big break came after standing in as presenter of *The Jack Docherty Show*, which led to his own talk show, *So Graham Norton*. He has also hosted the quiz, *Bring Me the Head of Light Entertainment*, and played Father Noel Furlong in FATHER TED.

NOT IN FRONT OF THE CHILDREN
UK (BBC) Situation Comedy. BBC 1 1967–70

Jennifer Corner .... **Wendy Craig**
Henry Corner .... **Paul Daneman**
Ronald Hines
Trudi Corner .... **Roberta Tovey**
Verina Greenlaw
Robin Corner .... **Hugo Keith-Johnston**
Amanda Corner .... **Jill Riddick**
Mary .... **Charlotte Mitchell**

Creator/Writer: **Richard Waring**
Producer: **Graeme Muir**

A mother tries to cope with her troublesome family.

Beginning as a 1967 COMEDY PLAYHOUSE presentation called *House in a Tree*, *Not in Front of the Children* was Wendy Craig's first excursion into the daffy, harassed-housewife role she was to perfect in later series like AND MOTHER MAKES THREE/FIVE and BUTTERFLIES. Here she held together a middle-class household comprising her husband, Henry, and growing children, Trudi, Robin and Amanda, trying all the while to moderate between disagreeing parties. The series also ran on BBC radio.

NOT ONLY . . . BUT ALSO . . .
UK (BBC) Comedy. BBC 2 1965–6; 1970

Peter Cook, Dudley Moore

Creators: **Peter Cook, Dudley Moore**
Producers: **Joe McGrath, Dick Clement, James Gilbert**

Innovative comedy revue, renowned for its offbeat humour.

Not Only . . . But Also . . . resulted from a one-off show that the BBC commissioned from musician/comedian Dudley Moore. Enlisting the help of his *Beyond the Fringe* partner, Peter Cook, for a couple of sketches, Moore came up with a formula that worked, and the duo were rewarded with this series which initially ran on BBC 2 but was quickly repeated on BBC 1 to much acclaim. Mixing manic comedy with jazzy interludes, each programme began in the most unusual of settings, including underwater. One regular insert was Poets Cornered, an opportunity for comics like Spike Milligan and Barry Humphries to show off their spontaneous rhyming skills on pain of being dropped into a gunge tank (long before TISWAS popularized this form of punishment). For many viewers, however, the highlights were Cook and Moore's Pete and Dud routines, the so-called 'Dagenham Dialogues', in which they played two ordinary but rather dim blokes who discussed issues of the day, cultural matters and flights of fantasy over a sandwich or a pint. Although largely scripted, these sequences were prone to bouts of adlibbing, particularly from Cook. Like Poets Cornered, Pete and Dud found their echo in later comedy work, especially in Mel Smith and Griff Rhys Jones's head-to-head dialogues. Programmes ended with the closing song, 'Goodbye-ee', which, when released as a single, reached number 18 in the 1965 charts.

Although the series ended in 1966 after just two seasons, *Not Only . . . But Also . . .* was revived in 1970 as part of BBC 2's *Show of the Week* showcase, and in 1971 two programmes recorded in Australia were also screened by the BBC.

NOT SO MUCH A PROGRAMME, MORE A WAY OF LIFE
UK (BBC) Comedy BBC 1 1964–5

John Bird, Eleanor Bron, Michael Crawford, John Fortune, David Frost, Roy Hudd, P. J. Kavanagh, Cleo Laine

Producer: **Ned Sherrin**

Direct descendant of THAT WAS THE WEEK THAT WAS.

The ground-breakingly irreverent *That Was The Week That Was* was taken off the air in advance of the 1964 general election, and was eventually replaced by this similar show of topical satire, running three times a week. Equally aggressive in its sardonic treatment of politics and current affairs, it, in turn, gave way to a successor series, BBC-3, in 1965.

NOT THE NINE O'CLOCK NEWS
UK (BBC) Comedy. BBC 2 1979–82

Mel Smith, Griff Rhys Jones, Pamela Stephenson, Rowan Atkinson, Chris Langham

Producers: **Sean Hardie, John Lloyd**

Topical satire with a new generation of Fringe *comedians.*

Squared up against BBC 1's main bulletin, as its title suggested, this was BBC 2's spoof of current events, presented from a very familiar, newsy studio set. Interspersed with the 'headlines' were topical send-ups of anything from the proposed Advanced Passenger Train to MISS WORLD, providing the young stars of *Not the Nine O'Clock News* with ample opportunity to show off the talents that were to make them household names in the decade to follow.

The team consisted of Pamela Stephenson (with her astute Angela Rippon take-offs), Rowan Atkinson (flexing his facial muscles in portrayals of aliens and other odd-bods), Mel Smith and fourth partner, Chris Langham. By series two, Langham had left for a chequered TV future in writing and stand-up comedy, to be replaced by Griff Rhys Jones, who quickly forged a successful liaison with Smith.

Throughout, the humour ranged from honest, TWO RONNIES-ish gags to the positively outrageous. Dubbing spoof headlines over existing news footage was one running theme, mocking pop videos was another, and there was also biting satire, wicked parody and skits on other TV programmes like UNIVERSITY CHALLENGE, POINTS OF VIEW and even MONTY PYTHON'S FLYING CIRCUS. Among the writers were Richard Curtis, David Renwick, Clive Anderson, Andy Hamilton and Guy Jenkin. A selection of books, records and concerts followed to capitalize on the show's enormous success.

NOW LOOK HERE . . .
UK (BBC) Situation Comedy. BBC 1 1971–3

Ronnie	**Ronnie Corbett**
Mother	**Madge Ryan**
	Gillian Lind
Laura	**Rosemary Leach**
Keith	**Richard O'Sullivan**
Col. Sutcliffe	**Donald Hewlett**

Writers: **Graham Chapman, Barry Cryer**
Producers: **Bill Hitchcock, Douglas Argent**

A mummy's boy finds himself at odds with the world.

Seen off to work by his mum each morning, bachelor Ronnie lived in the suburban town of Bramley and worked in an office where he railed against everything in sight (while, at the same time, pretending to be liberal-minded). His chief adversary was his colleague, Keith. In the second and last series, Ronnie finally fled the nest (though not entirely his mother's attentions) by marrying a girl called Laura. The story resumed in a spin-off series called *The Prince of Denmark* (1974), in which he and his new wife ran a pub she had inherited.

NTSC

Standing for National Television System Committee (the body which introduced it as standard), NTSC is the system of television transmission used in the USA. It is based on 525 lines, unlike the British PAL system which operates on 625 lines. NTSC is also standard in Canada and Japan, among other countries.

NYE, SIMON
(1958–)

British novelist and comedy writer, a former translator and the creator of MEN BEHAVING BADLY, FRANK STUBBS

PROMOTES, *Is it Legal?*, the one-off comedy drama, *True Love* – which led to the series, *My Wonderful Life – How Do You Want Me?* and *Beast*.

NYPD BLUE
US (Steven Bochco) Police Drama. Channel 4 1994–

Det. John Kelly	**David Caruso**
Det. Andy Sipowicz	**Dennis Franz**
Lt. Arthur Fancy	**James McDaniel**
Laura Hughes Kelly	**Sherry Stringfield**
Officer Janice Licalsi	**Amy Brenneman**
Officer/Det. James Martinez	**Nicholas Turturro**
Asst District Attorney Sylvia Costas	**Sharon Lawrence**
Det. Greg Medavoy	**Gordon Clapp**
Donna Abandando	**Gail O'Grady**
Det. Bobby Simone	**Jimmy Smits**
Det. Diane Russell	**Kim Delaney**
Det. Adrienne Lesniak	**Justine Miceli**
Jill Kirkendall	**Andrea Thompson**
John Irvin	**Bill Brochtrup**
Danny Sorenson	**Rick Schroder**
James Sinclair	**Daniel Benzali**
Baldwin Jones	**Henry Simmons**

Creators: **Steven Bochco, David Milch**
Executive Producers: **Steven Bochco, David Milch, Mark Tinker, Bill Clark**

The stresses and strains of policing the Big Apple.

This classy police drama devoted as much attention to the personal lives of the featured cops as to their heroic anti-crime activities. At the front of the action was red-haired, fast achiever John Kelly, who still had a soul despite 15 years of gritty police work and continued to carry a torch for his ex-wife, Laura, a lawyer, even though he became dangerously involved with fellow cop Janice Licalsi. Under Kelly's wing was streetwise trainee cop James Martinez. Kelly was partnered by overweight alcoholic Andy Sipowicz, who was forced to reappraise his life after being shot while in the company of a prostitute and who eventually married assistant DA Sylvia Costas. In the background was the by-the-book station boss, Lt. Fancy, unreliable officer Greg Medavoy and attractive clerk Donna Abandando. Kelly left in the second season and was replaced by Bobby Simone, a sensitive cop still grieving after the death of his wife. Simone was kicked off the force for a while but returned, cleared of the accusations made against him, before sensationally dying of a heart attack. His replacement was youthful Danny Sorenson, a keen ex-drugs cop, who became a surrogate son for Sipowicz, whose own son had been murdered.

Hand-held camerawork added an air of authenticity to recordings, and the series received a record 26 Emmy nominations for its first year, this despite being boy-cotted by dozens of TV stations because of its much-touted bad language and graphic sex (neither of which proved heavy by British standards).

OATER

A familiar term for a television Western, much in use in the 1960s when series like BONANZA, RAWHIDE, WAGON TRAIN and LARAMIE were the order of the day. Another nickname is 'horse opera'.

O'BRIEN, RICHARD
(1942–)

British actor, writer and presenter with a trademark shaven head. He is probably best known for his work as host of Channel 4's game show, THE CRYSTAL MAZE, though he has also been seen in series like *Rushton's Illustrated*, ROBIN OF SHERWOOD (the druid Gulnar) and the kids' fantasy, *The Ink Thief*. O'Brien also wrote the 1977 *Premiere* film, *A Hymn from Jim*. The theatre remains important, and among the plays and musicals he has scripted has been *The Rocky Horror Show*.

O'CONNOR, CARROLL
(1922–)

In his guise of bigot Archie Bunker in ALL IN THE FAMILY, American actor Carroll O'Connor was the USA's Alf Garnett. The role came in O'Connor's middle age, after decades of treading the boards in Europe as well as America. His first TV appearances came in series like THE RIFLEMAN, BONANZA, VOYAGE TO THE BOTTOM OF THE SEA and *I Spy*, playing rather modest roles. But in 1968 he starred in a risky pilot for *All in the Family*, which became a full series three years later and, with its sequel, *Archie Bunker's Place*, ran for 12 years in all. In contrast, in 1988, O'Connor was cast as Bill Gillespie, Chief of Police, in the TV version of IN THE HEAT OF THE NIGHT. He has also been seen in TV movies.

O'CONNOR, DES
(1932–)

London-born singer, comedian, presenter and talk show host who came to the fore in the 1950s in series like SPOT THE TUNE. *The Des O'Connor Show* (for ATV, featuring comic Jack Douglas in support) ran through most of the 1960s (a time when Des was notching up a string of hit singles) and O'Connor's other series for ITV in the 1960s and 1970s included *Des* and *Des O'Connor Entertains*. O'Connor then switched to the BBC for *Des O'Connor Tonight*, a chat/variety show, but that, too, transferred to ITV. He was once compere of SUNDAY NIGHT AT THE LONDON PALLADIUM and, in recent years, has hosted a revival of TAKE YOUR PICK, the talent show, *Pot of Gold*, and *The National Lottery – on the Spot*. Despite being mercilessly pilloried for his singing by Morecambe and Wise, O'Connor has remained one of the UK's favourite entertainers.

O'CONNOR, TOM
(1939–)

Liverpudlian comic who found his niche as a variety and game show presenter in the 1970s and 1980s. A former teacher, O'Connor broke out of the nightclub circuit and into the big time after winning OPPORTUNITY KNOCKS. He also appeared on THE COMEDIANS before hosting *Wednesday at Eight* and *London Night Out*. One element of these was the NAME THAT TUNE quiz, which soon became a series in its own right, with O'Connor at the helm. He has also had his own series, *Tom O'Connor*, compered *Night Out at the London Casino* and has been seen on numerous panel games, including *Zodiac*, *Password*, *Gambit*, *I've Got a Secret* and *Cross Wits*.

ODD COUPLE, THE
US (Paramount) Situation Comedy. ITV 1971–3

Felix Unger	Tony Randall
Oscar Madison	Jack Klugman
Murray Greshner	Al Molinaro
Speed	Garry Walberg
Vinnie	Larry Gelman
Roy	Ryan McDonald
Dr Nancy Cunningham	Joan Hotchkis
Gloria Unger	Janis Hansen
Blanche Madison	Brett Somers
Myrna Turner	Penny Marshall
Miriam Welby	Elinor Donahue

Executive Producers: **Garry K. Marshall, Sheldon Keller**
Producer: **Tony Marshall**

Two incompatible friends share an apartment and get on each other's nerves.

Felix Unger and Oscar Madison had been childhood friends. They were brought together again when both were divorced, and they decided to share Oscar's apartment in Manhattan. The only trouble was that the two were totally incompatible. Felix was a hard-working, cultured photographer, a hypochondriac with an over-the-top need to see everything in its place and lead an organized life. In contrast, Oscar was a slobbish sportswriter for the *New York Herald*. He lived sloppily, ate messily and littered his room with empty beer cans and dirty laundry. Not surprisingly, there was a great deal of friction between the two 'friends'.

Other regulars were Oscar's Thursday night poker partners, Murray the inept cop, Speed and Vinnie. Myrna was Oscar's secretary, and Nancy Cunningham was his sporty girlfriend in the early episodes. Felix's girlfriend was Miriam Welby, who lived in the same building, but he was later reunited with his wife, Gloria, and when he moved out to live with her again the series ended, leaving Oscar to revel in his regained squalid freedom.

Based on Neil Simon's successful comedy, and the 1968 film starring Jack Lemmon and Walter Matthau, the series also generated a cover version of its own, entitled *The New Odd Couple*, with the same characters now played by black actors. There was also an animated adaptation, featuring a tidy cat and a lazy dog, entitled *The Oddball Couple*.

ODD MAN, THE
UK (Granada) Police Drama. ITV 1962–3

Steve Gardiner	Edwin Richfield
Chief Insp. Gordon	Moultrie Kelsall
Chief Insp. Rose	William Mervyn
DS Swift	Keith Barron
Judy Gardiner	Sarah Lawson
Anne Braithwaite	Sarah Lawson
South	Christopher Guinee

Creator: **Edward Boyd**
Producer: **Stuart Latham**

Weirdly atmospheric detective series, famous for introducing the character of Chief Inspector Rose.

The Odd Man initially centred on five main characters, all involved in or around the murky world of crime. These were Steve Gardiner, a theatrical agent and part-time private eye, his wife, Judy, the grim Chief Inspector Gordon, his amiable colleague, DS Swift, and a mysterious villain named South. Although each programme was self-contained, the episodes ran in a serial format, culminating in the murder of Judy by South, and Steve's pursuit of her killer.

Although this series is credited with bringing Inspector Rose (later of IT'S DARK OUTSIDE and MR ROSE) to our screens, in fact he did not appear until the second season, taking over from Gordon and teaming up with Swift. He was also a rather different character from the one seen later, considerably more unpleasant. Actress Sarah Lawson, although written out in the first season, returned in the third as Judy's twin sister, and the cult series continued its bizarre tales of crime and intrigue.

Creator Edward Boyd specialized in husband-and-wife sleuths, having written such stories for BBC Radio before moving to television.

ODDIE, BILL
(1941–)

Cambridge Footlights graduate, a contemporary of his writing partners, Tim Brooke-Taylor and Graeme Garden. Lancashire-born Oddie broke into television through appearances on BBC-3 and then, more significantly, AT LAST THE 1948 SHOW, *Twice a Fortnight* and *Broaden Your Mind*. He also contributed scripts to HARK AT BARKER, but it was when he joined Brooke-Taylor and Garden in THE GOODIES in 1970 that viewers really began to take notice. Oddie was seen as the hairy, aggressive, cynical member of the trio of do-gooders. He also wrote the music for the show. With Garden, Oddie had already scripted episodes of DOCTOR IN THE HOUSE (he went on to write for some of its sequels) and when *The Goodies* ended, the two penned the short-lived sitcom, *Astronauts*. Oddie has since brought his love of bird watching to TV in series like *Birding with Bill Oddie*. He also co-wrote (with wife Laura Beaumont) and starred in the comedies, *From the Top* (William Worthington) and *The Bubblegum Brigade* (William), fronted the kids' show, *The Saturday Banana*, and hosted the religious celebration, *Festival*. Other credits have included the drama, *Titmuss Regained* (Hector Bolitho Jones). He is the father of actress Kate Hardie.

OFFICE OF STRATEGIC SERVICES

See OSS.

OGILVY, IAN

(1943–)

British actor whose major TV role has been as Simon Templar in THE RETURN OF THE SAINT. Ogilvy was also seen as Rupert in *The Liars*, Lawrence Kirbridge in UPSTAIRS, DOWNSTAIRS, Drusus in I, CLAUDIUS and Richard Maddison in the comedy, *Tom, Dick and Harriet*, and featured in dramas like *The Spoils of Poynton*, *Moll Flanders*, *Anna Karenina*, and the three-part thriller, *Menace Unseen*. Other credits include the US series, *Generations* (Reginald Hewitt), and RIPPING YARNS.

O'GRADY, PAUL

(1955–)

British drag comedian, the real identity of Lily Savage, the towering peroxide bombshell from Birkenhead. As his brassy, ex-prostitute creation, which he launched in a London pub, acquiring his mother's maiden name, he has appeared in countless TV programmes, including THE BIG BREAKFAST, *The Lily Savage Show*, BROOKSIDE (guest), *Lily Live* and as host of the revival of BLANKETY BLANK. Out of his famous disguise, O'Grady fronted the documentary series, *Paul O'Grady's Orient*.

OH BOY!

UK (ABC/ATV) Pop Music. ITV 1958–9; 1979–80

Hosts: **Tony Hall, Jimmy Henny**

Creator: **Jack Good**
Producers: **Jack Good, Ken O'Neill**
Executive Producer: **Richard Leyland**

Britain's first total rock'n'roll programme.

Oh Boy! was created by TV pop pioneer Jack Good after a dispute had led him to pull out of his earlier success, SIX-FIVE SPECIAL. Whereas the latter had featured magazine items and intrusions of other kinds of music, *Oh Boy!* was pure rock'n'roll and, as direct competition on Saturday nights, hastened *Six-Five Special*'s demise. It was the programme that made a star out of Cliff Richard, who had been installed by Good as the featured artist; and other regular contributions came from Marty Wilde, the Vernons Girls, the Dallas Boys, Cherry Wainer, Red Price, Tony Hall, Ronnie Carroll and Neville Taylor and the Cutters. Harry Robinson's band (which provided the

music) was remodelled by Good into Lord Rockingham's XI and went on to have chart hits of its own (most notably 'Hoots Mon' in 1958). All programmes were staged at the Hackney Empire. The programme was briefly revived by ATV in 1979–80, with Les Gray of Mud, Alvin Stardust, Freddie 'Fingers' Lee, Joe Brown and Shakin' Stevens among the regulars.

OH BROTHER!/OH FATHER!

UK (BBC) Situation Comedy. BBC 1 1968–70/1973

Brother/Father Dominic	**Derek Nimmo**
Father Anselm	**Felix Aylmer**
Father Matthew	**Derek Francis**
Master of the Novices	**Colin Gordon** (*Oh Brother!*)
Father Harris	**Laurence Naismith** (*Oh Father!*)
Mrs Carr	**Pearl Hackney** (*Oh Father!*)
Walter	**David Kelly** (*Oh Father!*)

Writers: **David Climie, Austin Steele**
Producers: **Duncan Wood, Harold Snoad, Johnny Downes (*Oh Brother!*), Graeme Muir (*Oh Father!*)**

A bumbling novice is accepted into a priory.

Oh Brother! saw the return of Derek Nimmo's plummy but good-hearted cleric character, first exhibited as Noote in ALL GAS AND GAITERS. This time his identity was Brother Dominic, a sincere but hapless novice at Mountacres Priory. Dominic was eventually 'promoted' to Father Dominic for a follow-up series, *Oh Father!*, in which he left the monastery to become curate to Father Harris.

OH DOCTOR BEECHING!

UK (BBC) Comedy. BBC 1 1996–7

Jack Skinner	**Paul Shane**
Ethel Schumann	**Su Pollard**
Cecil Parkin	**Jeffrey Holland**
May Skinner	**Julia Deakin**
Vera Plumtree	**Barbara New**
Harry Lambert	**Stephen Lewis**
Arnold	**Ivor Roberts**
Ralph	**Perry Benson**
Percy	**Terry John**
Gloria Skinner	**Lindsay Grimshaw**
Wilfred Schumann	**Paul Aspden**
Amy Matlock	**Tara Daniels**
Mr Orkindale	**Richard Spendlove**

Creators: **David Croft, Richard Spendlove**
Producers: **David Croft, Charles Garland**

The staff of a steam railway station fight for its survival.

Set at rural Hatley station (real-life Arley, on the Severn Valley Railway), *Oh Doctor Beeching!* was another of David Croft's nostalgic ensemble comedies, this time penned in collaboration with former railwayman Richard Spendlove. The time was 1963, with Beeching's swingeing cuts to the railway network about to come into force. Fearful for their jobs, the station crew did their best to keep things alive. They were headed by new-broom station master Cecil Parkin; ticket collector/ announcer Jack Skinner, whose days of scamming were coming to an end; Skinner's wife, May, who ran the station buffet and, it seemed was one of Cecil's old flames; the Skinners' teenage daughter (possibly Cecil's), Gloria; and ticket clerk Ethel Schumann. Ethel's dim son, Wilfred (his US serviceman dad having long disappeared), lent a hand here and there, while miserable Harry Lambert (a revival of Stephen Lewis's Blakey character from ON THE BUSES) manned the signal box, cut the men's hair and grew vegetables all at the same time. Engine-driver's widow Vera Plumtree lived in one of the cottages behind the station, next door to Ethel and Wilfred. Regular callers at the station were engine-driver Arnold, his hopeless fireman, Ralph, and guard, Percy.

The series followed a 1995 pilot episode, in which May was played by Sherrie Hewson. Partly re-recorded, it was transmitted again as the first episode of series one a year later.

OH NO IT'S SELWYN FROGGITT/ SELWYN
UK (Yorkshire) Situation Comedy. ITV 1976–7/1978

Selwyn Froggitt	**Bill Maynard**
Mrs Froggitt	**Megs Jenkins**
Maurice Froggitt	**Robert Keegan**
Ray	**Ray Mort**
Clive	**Richard Davies**
Jack	**Bill Dean**
Harry	**Harold Goodwin**
Vera Parkinson	**Rosemary Martin**
	Lynda Baron
Mervyn Price	**Bernard Gallagher** (*Selwyn*)

Creator/Writer: **Alan Plater (not *Selwyn*)**
Producer: **Ronnie Baxter**

The misadventures of an irrepressible but inept handyman.

Bachelor Selwyn Froggitt lived with his long-suffering mum and brother Maurice (whose girlfriend was the much-married Vera Parkinson) in the fictitious Yorkshire town of Scarsdale. Employed by the local council in its Public Works department, Froggitt fancied himself as a handyman, but his self-confidence was tragically misplaced. Every job he undertook ended in disaster. Froggitt also considered himself a bit of an intellectual, reading the *Times Literary Supplement* for fun, and was secretary of the Scarsdale Workingmen's Club and Institute where he drank pints of 'cooking' and socialized with the likes of Clive, Jack and Ray, the barman. A thumbs-up cry of 'Magic' and an inane grin became his trademarks.

After three seasons of mayhem in Scarsdale, Froggitt was uprooted for a spin-off series simply called *Selwyn*. This pitched him into the role of Entertainments Officer at the Paradise Valley holiday camp on the Yorkshire coast, where the predictable consequences were witnessed by manager Mervyn Price. Alan Plater created the character of Selwyn Froggitt for a one-off play in 1974

and continued to write most of the scripts for the resultant series (but not *Selwyn*). Actor Bill Dean wrote the topical lyrics for each programme's theme song.

O'HANLON, ARDAL
(1965–)

Irish stand-up comedian and comic actor, the son of a former Irish Health Minister. It was as the idiotic Father Dougal Maguire in FATHER TED that O'Hanlon made his name, following the role with the parts of journalist Eamon Donaghy in *Big Bad World* and George Sunday (alias superhero Thermoman) in *My Hero*. He has also hosted *The Stand-Up Show*.

OIL STRIKE NORTH
UK (BBC) Drama. BBC 1 1975

Jim Fraser	**Nigel Davenport**
Frank Ward	**Michael Whitney**
Julie Ward	**Angela Douglas**
Elaine Smythe	**Barbara Shelley**
Angus Gallacher	**Callum Mill**
Shona Campbell	**Angela Cheyne**
Charles Wayman	**Richard Hurndall**
Donald Cameron	**Andrew Robertson**
Jack Mullery	**Glyn Owen**

Creators: **N. J. Crisp, Gerard Glaister**
Producer: **Gerard Glaister**

High drama in the North Sea with the crew of an oil-rig.

This 13-part serial featured the company Triumph Oil, which was battling against the elements to extract oil from the cold and bleak North Sea, using rig *Nelson One*. Three months before its Government concession expired, the company discovered that there just might be oil in an area it hadn't yet considered, so the race was on to find the black gold. Episodes tended to involve helicopters and divers, usually with a heightened sense of danger, and attention was also paid to the pressures facing the 70 men cooped up on the rig, as well as the commercial side of the venture.

The top men were Fraser, the Operations Area Manager, and Frank Ward, the American drilling superintendent. Ward's wife Julie was also seen. Angus Gallacher was Editor of the local *Muirport Gazette*, campaigning against the environmental and cultural damage being wreaked on this part of Scotland. After creators Gerard Glaister and N. J. Crisp had spent two years in research, filming took place in Peterhead.

OLD GREY WHISTLE TEST/ WHISTLE TEST
UK (BBC) Rock Music. BBC 2 1971–88

Presenters: **Ian Whitcomb, Richard Williams, Bob Harris, Anne Nightingale, David Hepworth, Mark Ellen, Richard Skinner, Andy Kershaw, Ro Newton**

Producer: **Michael Appleton**

Cult rock-music programme.

Taking its name from the old adage that if the grey-haired doorman whistles your tune you've a hit on your hands, *Old Grey Whistle Test* developed out of a progressive-rock programme called *Disco 2*, which in turn was a derivative of LATE NIGHT LINE-UP. Unlike TOP OF THE POPS, *Whistle Test* did not pander to the pop charts but focused instead on developments in the album and live-music worlds. Two bands generally played live in the (unfurnished) studio, with interviews, film inserts and gig news completing the package. Its initial hosts were Ian Whitcomb and Richard Williams, but it was under the guidance of 'Whispering' Bob Harris that the programme's glory years arrived. Harris's laid-back, understated intros and genuine feel for the music added an air of authenticity and authority to proceedings and helped to ensure that the programme became a must for every self-respecting rock-music fan. A succession of other DJs and journalists, beginning with Anne Nightingale, filled the presenter's chair in the 1980s and, from 1983, the title was officially shortened to *Whistle Test*. The jaunty theme music, played over the 'star-kicker' opening titles, was 'Stone Fox Chase', by Area Code 615.

OLIVER, JAMIE
(1975–)

If cookery is the new rock 'n' roll, as some people rather unimaginatively claim, then Jamie Oliver must be the new Mick Jagger. Oliver was born in Southend and gained his culinary experience in the kitchen of his parents' pub in Clavering, Essex. He went on to catering college and then took jobs in two top London restaurants. He was spotted working at the River Café and offered his own TV series, *The Naked Chef*, in 1999, so named because of his down-to-earth enthusiasm for a simple style of cooking in which he claimed to take everyday ingredients and make them more tasty, stripping food back to its fundamentals. Supermarket adverts followed, as did a recording contract for his band, Scarlet Division, in which he plays drums.

OLIVIER, LORD LAURENCE
(1907–89)

Lord Olivier's glorious theatrical and cinematic biography has been well presented in other publications, but his television work, though sparse, was no less well received. His first contribution was a play, *John Gabriel Borkman*, in 1958. Fifteen years later, he was narrator on the award-winning WORLD AT WAR and then appeared in JESUS OF NAZARETH as Nicodemus. In the 1980s he starred in a series of dramas, all of which attracted high praise. He was Lord Marchmain in BRIDESHEAD REVISITED, played *King Lear* for Channel 4 and starred in *A Voyage Round My Father* (Clifford Mortimer) and *The Ebony Tower*. There were also TV movies and mini-series,

with his last TV role coming in *Lost Empires*, as fading comedian Harry Burrard. His wives were actresses Jill Esmond, Vivien Leigh and Joan Plowright.

OLSEN, GARY
(1958–2000)

British comedy actor, best known as dad Ben Porter in 2 POINT 4 CHILDREN, but also star of *Wilderness Road* (Keith), THE BILL (PC Dave Litten), *Health and Efficiency* (Dr Michael Jimson) and *Pilgrim's Rest* (café owner Bob Payne). He also appeared in Steve Coogan's *Three Fights, Two Weddings and a Funeral*.

O'MARA, KATE
(1939–)

British actress who appeared in numerous drama series (THE AVENGERS, THE TROUBLESHOOTERS, THE SAINT, Z CARS, NO HIDING PLACE, DANGER MAN, MARKET IN HONEY LANE, COURT MARTIAL, PAUL TEMPLE, THE CHAMPIONS, DEPARTMENT S, THE PROTECTORS, THE MAIN CHANCE, etc.) while building a career in the British cinema (particularly in Hammer horror films). In the 1970s and 1980s, however, she gradually made TV her forte with roles like air-freight magnate Jane Maxwell in THE BROTHERS, Katherine Laker in TRIANGLE, The Rani (a renegade Time Lord) in DOCTOR WHO, Caress Morell in DYNASTY and Laura Wilde in HOWARDS' WAY. O'Mara has also appeared on panel games, with comedians like THE TWO RONNIES and Morecambe and Wise, and as a guest in ABSOLUTELY FABULOUS. The daughter of actress Hazel Bainbridge and sister of actress Belinda Carroll, she is married to actor Richard Willis.

OMNIBUS
UK (BBC) Arts. BBC 1 1967–

Long-running BBC arts programme.

The natural successor to MONITOR, *Omnibus* – with its declared aim of providing 'television to remember' – has proved even more durable than its predecessor. Its creative weekly films and essays have won much acclaim, among the best recalled being Ken Russell's *Dante's Inferno* (about Dante Gabriel Rossetti) in 1967, Tony Palmer's pop-music critique, *All My Loving*, in 1968, and the spooky Jonathan Miller adaptation of M. R. James's *Whistle, and I'll Come to You* in the same year. In 1993, to commemorate the programme's silver jubilee, a series of the best films was repeated on BBC 1. These included works on Kathleen Ferrier, David Bowie, Leonard Bernstein's *West Side Story*, cinematographer Vittorio Storaro, the Brothers Grimm and Ken Russell's 1968 profile of Frederick Delius. More recent subjects have included Reeves and Mortimer, Darcey Bussell, Mrs Gaskell, Sir Norman Foster, Roddy Doyle, Deborah Harry and Stephen King. Henry Livings was the programme's first presenter, though other hosts have included

Humphrey Burton, Richard Baker and Barry Norman (who briefly chaired proceedings in the early 1980s).

ON AIR/OFF AIR

Terms denoting when a programme is/is not being transmitted.

ON SAFARI

See DENIS, ARMAND AND MICHAELA.

ON THE BRADEN BEAT

UK (ATV) Consumer Affairs. ITV 1962–7

Presenter: **Bernard Braden**

Producers: **Jock Watson, Francis Coleman**

Consumer affairs and light entertainment magazine.

On the Braden Beat was ITV's Saturday night answer to THAT WAS THE WEEK THAT WAS. However, this programme combined general entertainment and topical humour with consumer investigations and battles against bureaucracy. After five years with ITV, Braden took the show to the BBC, creating BRADEN'S WEEK, in which he was assisted by reporter/researcher Esther Rantzen. Its clear descendant, THAT'S LIFE (without Braden), followed in 1973.

ON THE BUSES

UK (LWT) Situation Comedy. ITV 1969–73

Stan Butler	**Reg Varney**
Mrs Butler	**Cicely Courtneidge**
	Doris Hare
Olive	**Anna Karen**
Arthur	**Michael Robbins**
Jack Harper	**Bob Grant**
Insp. Cyril Blake	**Stephen Lewis**

Creators: **Ronald Chesney, Ronald Wolfe**
Producers: **Stuart Allen, Derrick Goodwin, Bryan Izzard**

A bus-driver and his conductor lark about on their travels.

Stan Butler was a driver for the London-based Luxton Bus Company, usually working with his conductor mate Jack on the number 11 route to the cemetery gates. Bane of his life was the humourless Inspector Blake, who was always desperate to catch the chirpy pair up to no good. Blakey's catchphrase, 'I 'ate you, Butler,' was quickly adopted by the viewing public.

Stan lived with his widowed mother, his dowdy sister, Olive, and her gruff, layabout husband, Arthur, but life was brighter at the depot, where there were always busty clippies to chase and jokes to play on the much-maligned Blakey. In keeping with the humour of the time, leering and innuendo dominated the series,

although there was seldom any serious sexual activity – living with his mum, Stan never had the opportunity, much to his frustration.

Cicely Courtneidge was the first actress to play Stan's mum, although Doris Hare is best remembered in the role, while Stephen Lewis, who played Blakey, took his character into a spin-off series. Entitled *Don't Drink the Water* and shown in 1974–5, it saw Blakely moving into a retirement home in Spain with his spinster sister (Pat Coombs).

Three feature film versions (*On the Buses, Mutiny on the Buses* and *Holiday on the Buses*) were released in the 1970s, reflecting the popularity of this cheerfully vulgar comedy, and a US copy, set in New York and entitled *Lotsa Luck*, was also produced.

ON THE MOVE

UK (BBC) Education. BBC 1 1975–6

Alf	**Bob Hoskins**
Bert	**Donald Gee**

Writer: **Barry Took**
Producer: **David Hargreaves**

Light-hearted attempt to encourage illiterate viewers to learn to read and write.

This series of award-winning 10-minute programmes, shown at Sunday teatimes, featured Bob Hoskins and Donald Gee as removals men Alf and Bert, who travelled around Britain and, with the help of famous guest stars in each episode, remarked on strange words in the English language. The aim was to stimulate people who couldn't read to do something about it. *On the Move* was partly inspired by an Italian series from the 1950s and 1960s, *Non E Mai Troppo Tardi* (*It's Never Too Late*), which tackled that country's chronic illiteracy problem.

ON THE UP

UK (BBC) Situation Comedy. BBC 1 1990–2

Tony Carpenter	**Dennis Waterman**
Sam	**Sam Kelly**
Mrs Fiona Wembley	**Joan Sims**
Ruth Carpenter	**Judy Buxton**
Maggie	**Jenna Russell**
Stephanie Carpenter	**Vanessa Hadaway**
Dawn	**Michelle Hatch**
Mrs Carpenter	**Dora Bryan**
	Pauline Letts

Creator/Writer: **Bob Larbey**
Producer: **Gareth Gwenlan**

A self-made millionaire has wife and domestic-staff troubles.

East Ender Tony Carpenter was somewhat ill at ease with the sumptuous trappings of wealth, even though his own graft had made them possible. Forced to live in a posh Surrey neighbourhood (Esher) by Ruth, his socially superior wife of 16 years' standing (who kept walking out on him), he employed a trio of home-based assistants who also gave him a few headaches (but remained his only true friends). These were Sam, a childhood pal, who had become his butler and chauffeur; widow Mrs Wembley, his tipsy, old-movie-loving housekeeper; and Maggie, the Scottish personal assistant who helped with his car hire company (TC Luxury Cars). Tony struggled to justify his extravagant lifestyle, especially to his own mum, an avowed socialist who did her best to disown him. Adding to the conflict were Stephanie, Tony's problematic, public school-based daughter, and Dawn, the rather dim model Tony dated in later episodes.

Star Dennis Waterman also wrote and sang the programme's closing theme song.

ONDIGITAL

ONdigital is the UK's Digitial Terrestrial Television provider, operating three multiplexes and broadcasting a wide range of channels through a normal domestic aerial, although not as many as supplied by Digital Satellite Television broadcaster BSkyB or Digital Cable Television operators. ONdigital, the first company in the world to offer terrestrial digital TV, won its licence to transmit from the ITC under the consortium name of British Digital Broadcasting, but changed its name prior to launching its service on 15 November 1998 (shortly after its satellite rival, but ahead of cable competitors). The company is jointly owned by Carlton Communications and Granada Media Group.

ONE BY ONE
UK (BBC) Drama. BBC 1 1984–7

Donald Turner	Rob Heyland
Maurice Webb	Peter Jeffrey
Paddy Reilly	James Ellis
Gran Turner	Liz Smith
Howard Rundle	Garfield Morgan
Ethel Ledbetter	Sonia Graham
Jenny Blount	Rosie Kerslake
Peter Raymond	Jack Hedley
Maggie Raymond	Heather James
Ben Bishop	Peter Gilmore
Lady Ann	Catherine Schell
Jock Drummond	Andrew Robertson
Liz Collier	Christina Nagy

Producer: **Bill Sellars**

A newly qualified vet transforms the treatment of exotic animals.

Donald Turner, fresh from veterinary school, returned to his home town to become assistant to the local practitioner, Maurice Webb. However, most of his time seemed to be spent at the local zoo, and his first case involved treating an elephant with the 'skitters'. This was an era (the 1960s) when exotic creatures were little understood. The vet's job was no more than to keep them alive, rather than assisting in their general well-being. Dedicated medications were unheard of and the

animals were treated with human or domestic pets' drugs. Turner recognized the problems and gradually became a specialist in the care of exotic beasts. Paddy Reilly was the resident head zookeeper.

In the second series, set eight years later, Turner was a full partner in the practice (Webb soon left altogether) and the action switched to a safari park – supposedly Britain's first – run by new character Ben Bishop. The final instalments in this ALL CREATURES GREAT AND SMALL-type, amusing drama were fixed in 1971, with Turner now set up as freelance international vet, handling exotic species. The programme was based on the experiences recalled by vet David Taylor in his *Zoo Vet* books.

ONE FOOT IN THE GRAVE
UK (BBC) Situation Comedy. BBC 1 1990–7; 2000

Victor Meldrew	Richard Wilson
Margaret Meldrew	Annette Crosbie
Mrs Jean Warboys	Doreen Mantle
Patrick Trench	Angus Deayton
Pippa Trench	Janine Duvitski
Mr Nick Swaney	Owen Brenman

Creator/Writer: **David Renwick**
Producers: **Susan Belbin, Esta Charkham, Jonathan P. Llewellyn**

An accident-prone pensioner is the world's greatest whinger.

Unceremoniously retiring from his job as a security guard, 60-year-old amateur ventriloquist Victor Meldrew settled down to long days at home, much to the distress of his Scottish wife, Margaret. For Victor was the world's number one complainer. Litter in his front garden was one of his pet hates; the failure of mail order firms to supply the correct goods was another. His curmudgeonly attitude to life was soon recognized by their new neighbours when the Meldrews moved from their demolished home at 37 Wingate Drive to 19 Riverbank, a more modern development. On one side lived bus-driver Pippa and her cynical, professional husband, Patrick – proud master of the tiny dog Denzil – who, from the strange happenings next door, was firmly convinced that Victor was insane. On the other side lived the very cheerful but very boring Mr Swaney and his invalid mother. The insensitive Mrs Warboys – whose unseen husband, Chris, deserted her – was another close associate (rather too close at times).

Although the series centred on ridiculous misunderstandings and gentle forms of farce, *One Foot in the Grave* also had its surreal elements and more than a touch of pathos (it was once barely mentioned that the Meldrews had long before lost a young son named Stuart). Tender moments intermingled with Victor's yells of outrage ('I don't believe it!') and Margaret's cries of despair. All this made *One Foot in the Grave* the BBC's most popular sitcom in the early 1990s. For Christmas 1993, a feature-length special, *One Foot in the Algarve*, was produced, and after January 1995 only Christmas specials were made for a couple of years. In the last, Patrick and Pippa had finally escaped and the Meldrews' new neighbours were Derek and Betty McVitie (played by Tim Brooke-Taylor and Marian McLoughlin). Patrick and Pippa were back for the final series, screened in 2000, when Victor was – unusually for a sitcom character – killed off.

The theme song for the series was written and sung by Eric Idle. An American version, beginning in 1996, starred Bill Cosby and was simply entitled *Cosby*.

100%
UK (Grundy) Quiz. Channel 5 1997–

Announcer: Robin Houston

Creator: **Tom Atkinson**
Producer: **Mark Noades**

Quiz show without a host.

Three contestants have taken part in each edition of this 100-question general knowledge daily (weekdays) quiz, a stalwart of Channel 5's schedules from its first week on air. There have been a number of novelty factors to capture the viewer's attention. Firstly, there has been no visible host, just the voice of Robin Houston to introduce the contestants and read the questions and scores. Secondly, each contestant's score has been given as a percentage of correct answers against the total number of questions asked. Thirdly, for the latter half of the game, contestants have not been able to see who has been leading. All questions have been displayed on the screen, together with three possible answers, some of which have been included for humour. Subject categories have helped to break up the 100 questions. A modest £100 has been awarded to the daily winner, but he/she has been able to return to accumulate more money.

The simple format has been easily applied to spin-off series and specials. A mid-afternoon quiz called *100% Gold* included questions aimed at the 50+ age-group, while *100% Sex* was a late-night variation for the younger generation. Specials have been devised to slot into Channel 5 'theme days' and have included quizzes dedicated to the likes of Abba, Queen and Elvis Presley.

ONE MAN AND HIS DOG
UK (BBC) Sheep Dog Trials. BBC 2 1976–

Presenters: **Phil Drabble, Robin Page**

Producers: **Philip S. Gilbert, Ian Smith, Joy Corbett**

Shepherds and their faithful hounds round up flocks in a contest for the BBC Television Trophy.

An unlikely hit, *One Man and His Dog* was hosted by flat-capped Phil Drabble for 18 years, before he handed over his crook and wellies to new presenter Robin Page. Loyal viewers on a Sunday teatime appreciated the traditional, rural skills of dog-handling, epitomized by shepherds who, with just a few whistles, could instruct their charges to herd the most unruly sheep through gates, round posts and into wooden pens. No doubt the beautiful rural landscapes, with its rolling fields and

dry-stone walls, added to the attraction. Trials experts Eric Halsall, Ray Ollerenshaw and Gus Dermody also contributed over the years.

ONEDIN LINE, THE
UK (BBC) Drama. BBC 1 1971–80

Capt. James Onedin	**Peter Gilmore**
Robert Onedin	**Brian Rawlinson**
	James Garbutt
Elizabeth Onedin/Frazer/Lady Fogarty	**Jessica Benton**
Anne Webster/Onedin	**Anne Stallybrass**
Capt. Baines	**Howard Lang**
Sarah Onedin	**Mary Webster**
Mr Callon	**Edward Chapman**
Capt. Webster	**James Hayter**
Emma Callon/Fogarty	**Jane Seymour**
Matt Harvey	**Ken Hutchison**
Albert Frazer	**Philip Bond**
Daniel Fogarty	**Michael Billington**
	Tom Adams
Mr Jack Frazer	**John Phillips**
Charlotte Onedin	**Laura Hartong**
	Victoria Thomas
Leonora Biddulph	**Kate Nelligan**
Caroline Maudslay	**Caroline Harris**
Margarita Juarez/Onedin	**Roberta Iger**
Mr Dunwoody	**John Rapley**
Letty Gaunt/Onedin	**Jill Gascoine**
Samuel Onedin	**Timothy Slender**
	Christopher Douglas
William Frazer	**Marc Harrison**
Josiah Beaumont	**Warren Clarke**
Max Van Der Rheede	**Frederick Jaeger**
Caroline	**Jenny Twigge**
Tom Arnold	**Keith Jayne**

Creator: **Cyril Abraham**
Producers: **Peter Graham Scott, Peter Cregeen, Geraint Morris**

The saga of a Liverpool shipping line.

Twenty-eight-year-old James Onedin was a determined, hard-driving ship's captain. On returning from a voyage in 1860, he learned of his shopkeeper father's death and that he had inherited little of his estate. The business went instead to his elder brother, Robert, but James didn't really mind as his heart remained at sea. Unhappy at his treatment by his boss, Mr Callon, and brim-full of enterprise, he set out to start his own rival business, acquiring the decrepit three-masted schooner, *Charlotte Rhodes*, from the penniless, boozy Captain Webster, largely in return for marrying Webster's sour-faced, determined daughter, Anne (played by Sheila Allen in the pilot), who immediately involved herself in the business as an active partner.

The late 1800s were precarious times and running a merchant ship was not a comfortable business, even with a whiskery old sea-dog like Captain Baines (who constantly objected to his master's methods) as first mate. The series followed the commercial and personal exploits of the quick-tempered Onedin, as well as his life on the cruel sea. In the background, adding domestic and business complications, were his wealthy, but penny-pinching brother – whom James had roped in as partner – and his attractive sister, Elizabeth. Later problems were provided by his troublesome daughter, Charlotte, and his next two wives (when Anne died in childbirth, James married Charlotte's governess, Letty Gaunt, who also died, before he wed a Spanish widow, Margarita Juarez).

Running for nine years (and taking the period up to 1886), *The Onedin Line* was derived from a one-off *Drama Playhouse* presentation in 1970 and became a stalwart of BBC 1's Sunday nights. Its evocative theme music came from Khachaturyan's 'Spartacus', intended for a situation far removed from the Dartmouth docksides where this series was filmed.

O'NEILL, MAGGIE

(1964–)

British actress whose major TV credits have included *Take Me Home* (Kathy), *Friday on My Mind* (Louise Ross), *The Life and Times of Henry Pratt* (Auntie Doris), *Killing Me Softly* (Sara Thornton), *Invasion: Earth* (Dr Amanda Tucker), *Births, Marriages and Deaths* (Alex) and *Hero of the Hour* (Alison Liddle), plus *Screen One's Blore – MP* and *Screen Two's Defrosting the Fridge*. In 2000 she joined the cast of PEAK PRACTICE as Dr Alex Redman.

ONLY FOOLS AND HORSES

UK (BBC) Situation Comedy. BBC 1 1981–93; 1996

Derek 'Del Boy' Trotter	**David Jason**
Rodney Trotter	**Nicholas Lyndhurst**
Grandad Trotter	**Lennard Pearce**
Uncle Albert Trotter	**Buster Merryfield**
Raquel Slater/Turner	**Tessa Peake-Jones**
Cassandra Parry/Trotter	**Gwyneth Strong**
Aubrey 'Boycie' Boyce	**John Challis**
Marlene Boyce	**Sue Holderness**
Trigger	**Roger Lloyd Pack**
Mike Fisher	**Kenneth MacDonald**
Mickey Pearce	**Patrick Murray**
Denzil	**Paul Barber**
Jevon	**Steven Woodcock**
Sid	**Roy Heather**
Roy Slater	**Jim Broadbent**
Alan Parry	**Denis Lill**
Pam Parry	**Wanda Ventham**

Creator/Writer: **John Sullivan**
Producers: **Ray Butt, Gareth Gwenlan**

The misadventures of a flashy London spiv and his hapless brother.

Only Fools and Horses was *the* British sitcom of the 1980s. From humble beginnings as a slow-moving idea for a series called *Readies*, it grew into one of the best-loved comedies the BBC has ever produced, ranking alongside STEPTOE AND SON, TILL DEATH US DO PART, HANCOCK'S HALF HOUR and FAWLTY TOWERS. Testimony to its popularity is the fact that its Christmas Day specials were the highlight of the BBC's festive season.

Taking its name from the old adage that 'only fools and horses work', the series was constructed around Derek 'Del Boy' Trotter, a market fly-pitcher with an endless supply of hooky goods fresh off the back of a lorry. Ever the optimist ('this time next year, we'll be millionaires' and 'he who dares, wins' became his catchphrases), Del Boy was the sole provider for his close-knit family, which consisted of his lanky 'plonker' of a brother, Rodney, and his dim old Grandad. Together they shared a high-rise council flat (368 Nelson Mandela House) on the Nyerere estate in Peckham. Swathed in gold, heavily splashed with Brut and puffing a chunky cigar, Del enjoyed the good life, which effectively meant a night down The Nag's Head drinking Drambuie-and-grapefruit cocktails, followed by a Ruby Murray (a curry). Lovely jubbley, as he would have put it. His choice of women left a lot to be desired, although occasionally he would stumble across a classier girl, which warranted a trip to a Berni Inn for a steak meal.

Rodney, left orphaned when his mother died and his dad cleared off, relied on Del for his wellbeing, although this effectively scuppered any hopes he harboured of a life of his own. It was Rodney who, despite having two GCEs (Maths and Art), was the dogsbody of Trotter's Independent Trading (Titco), and the driver of the firm's decrepit, yellow three-wheeled van (emblazoned with Del's dreams of empire: 'New York, Paris, Peckham'). Grandad was the silly old sod who ran the home and did the (bad) cooking, in between bouts of sulking or simultaneously watching two TV sets. When actor Lennard Pearce died, Grandad also passed away and in his place his equally wily brother, the boys' Uncle Albert, was introduced. An old sea-dog with a Captain Birdseye beard, Albert could instantly break up any party with the ominous words 'During the war . . .'

The Trotters were also well blessed with friends and associates. These included dense road-sweeper Trigger (so named not because he carried a gun but because he looked like a horse), who always thought Rodney's name was Dave; flashy car salesman Boycie and his flirty wife, Marlene; Mike, landlord of the pub; Denzil, a lorry driver; and Sid, the unhygienic café owner. Rodney's pals included the brainless Mickey Pearce and the snappy-dressing Jevon. The Trotters' nemesis was bent copper Roy Slater.

Writer John Sullivan allowed his characters to mature as the series progressed and moments of pathos were introduced – such as when Rodney married yuppie banker Cassandra and Del was left isolated and, for once, alone. However, Del's momentary introspection soon gave way to love for actress/stripogram girl Raquel, who bore him a son, portentously named Damien, much to Rodney's terror.

After a three-year hiatus, *Only Fools and Horses* returned at Christmas 1996 with a three-part story that revealed how Del and Rodney did, at last, become millionaires by rediscovering a watch in their lock-up garage that was worth £6 million. It was a universally acclaimed revival that many considered to be a glorious finale. With the death of actor Buster Merryfield in 1999, it now seemed that the Trotters had done their last dodgy deal but there were plans in place for another short series in 2001.

ONLY WHEN I LAUGH
UK (Yorkshire) Situation Comedy. ITV 1979–82

Roy Figgis	**James Bolam**
Archie Glover	**Peter Bowles**
Norman Binns	**Christopher Strauli**
Dr Gordon Thorpe	**Richard Wilson**
Staff Nurse Gupte	**Derrick Branche**

Creator/Writer: **Eric Chappell**
Producer: **Vernon Lawrence**

The petty squabbles of a trio of long-term hospital patients.

Bolshy lorry-driver Roy Figgis, snooty, upper-class hypochondriac Archie Glover and naïve young Norman Binns were the long-stay patients in this hospital comedy. They battled over the best beds, put the wind up new patients, complained about the hospital radio service and wrangled with the medical staff. These included haughty, irascible surgeon Gordon Thorpe and frustrated male Indian nurse Gupte. The ironic 'H.A.P.P.Y.' theme song set the tone.

OPEN ALL HOURS
UK (BBC) Situation Comedy. BBC 2 1976; BBC 1 1981–2; 1985

Arkwright	**Ronnie Barker**
Granville	**David Jason**
Nurse Gladys Emmanuel	**Lynda Baron**
Milkwoman	**Barbara Flynn**
Mrs Delphine Featherstone	**Stephanie Cole**

Creator/Writer: **Roy Clarke**
Producer: **Sydney Lotterby**

Penny-pinching with a North Country shopkeeper and his ha-ha-hapless nephew.

Adopting yet another characterization that showed off his comic gifts to great effect, Ronnie Barker in this series introduced viewers to Arkwright, the tightest grocer in the North of England. Constantly battling with an entrenched stammer and the advances of 1970s shopkeeping, Arkwright was mean, devious and conniving. He was particularly hard on his young nephew, Granville, the son of Arkwright's sister by an unnamed Hungarian, who had grown up as the grocer's errand boy, shop assistant and general skivvy. But Granville was also a daydreamer and pictured himself in better situations, usually in the arms of some beautiful woman.

Arkwright, too, had romantic aspirations, in his case to fall into the bosom of buxom Gladys Emmanuel, the Morris Minor-driving nurse who lived across the street with her ailing mother. Although she needed to fend off Arkwright's wandering hands and turn a deaf ear to his practised innuendo, she nevertheless harboured a genuine affection for the stingy old grocer.

The days were long in this shop. From well before dawn to well after dusk the lights were on and the door was open. Each programme began with Arkwright setting out his special offers on stalls at the front, winding up with his taking them back in again. In between, confused customers came and went (usually with goods Arkwright had conned them into buying), and Granville had suffered another day of abuse and frustration. But it never prevented him from answering back to his mentor or smirking whenever Arkwright caught his fingers in the shop's temperamental till.

The characters first appeared in the Ronnie Barker anthology of pilot shows, *Seven of One*, in 1973 (with Sheila Brennan in the role of Nurse Emmanuel) but three years passed before a series followed (on BBC 2). This was repeated on BBC 1 in 1979 and new episodes eventually appeared in 1981 and 1982. However, the last series was not transmitted until 1985, four years after David Jason had switched trading places to Peckham market, and taken on the role of Del Boy in ONLY FOOLS AND HORSES. An American version of *Open All Hours* was also made, entitled *Open All Night*.

OPENING TITLES

The (often pre-recorded) sequence of film, text and music which identifies a programme, sometimes giving key credits like performers and writers.

OPPORTUNITY KNOCKS/BOB SAYS 'OPPORTUNITY KNOCKS'
UK (Associated-Rediffusion/ABC/Thames/BBC) Talent Show. ITV 1956–78; BBC 1 1987–90

Hosts: **Hughie Green, Bob Monkhouse, Les Dawson**

Producers: **Peter Dulay, Milo Lewis, Royston Mayoh, Robert Fleming, Keith Beckett, Stewart Morris**

Long-running talent show in which viewers at home elect the top act.

Beginning on Radio Luxembourg in the early 1950s, *Opportunity Knocks* and its ebullient host, Hughie Green, were brought to television soon after ITV began. There had been talent shows on TV before – *Carroll Levis Discoveries* was one – but none proved to have the stamina of *Opportunity Knocks*, which not only survived the ITV franchise swap of 1968 but was resurrected by the BBC in 1987, having been cancelled by Thames in 1978.

The format was simple. Green introduced half-a-dozen acts per week ('Friends, we want to hear them,' Green declared), each 'sponsored' by a studio guest who offered background information about the performers. At the end of the show, all the acts gave a short reprise of their routine which the studio audience evaluated by applauding. The highest scorers on the 'clapometer' were declared the studio winners, but this counted for nothing. What mattered ('And I mean that most sincerely, folks,' Green was known to swear) were the votes of viewers at home, expressed by the mailing in of postcards. At the start of the following week's programme, the winners were announced and were given the chance to repeat their success. A winning contestant could return literally week after week and, at the end of each series, an all-winners show was put together. Telephone voting replaced postal votes when the BBC revived the show under the title of *Bob Says 'Opportunity Knocks'* (the new host being Bob Monkhouse). Les Dawson, himself probably the programme's greatest find, presented the final season, with the title reverting to *Opportunity Knocks*.

Other notable performers given their showbusiness break by *Opportunity Knocks* were Russ Abbot (as part of the Black Abbots group), Freddie Starr, The Bachelors, Frank Carson, Mary Hopkin, Little and Large, Paul Daniels, Freddie Davies, Peters and Lee, Lena Zavaroni, Ken Goodwin, Pam Ayres, Bonnie Langford, Paul Melba, Tom O'Connor and Paper Lace. But whatever happened to perennial winners like Bobby Crush, Neil Reid, Gerry Monroe, Millican and Nesbitt, Stuart Gillies, Berni Flint and 1960s muscle man Tony Holland? There were hard-luck stories, too. Su Pollard was allegedly beaten by a singing dog and a singer called Gerry Dorsey even failed the audition. He changed his name to Englebert Humperdinck and did rather better for himself.

OPT OUT

The term given to the practice by regional TV stations of leaving national output and screening local programmes/inserts instead.

ORANGES ARE NOT THE ONLY FRUIT
UK (BBC) Drama. BBC 2 1990

Jess	**Emily Aston**
	Charlotte Coleman
Mother	**Geraldine McEwan**
Pastor Finch	**Kenneth Cranham**
May	**Elizabeth Spriggs**
Mrs Green	**Freda Dowie**
Elsie	**Margery Withers**
Miss Jewsbury	**Celia Imrie**
Cissy	**Barbara Hicks**
Mrs Arkwright	**Pam Ferris**
Melanie	**Cathryn Bradshaw**

Writer: **Jeanette Winterson**
Producer: **Phillippa Giles**

A young Lancashire girl rebels against her mother's religious ambitions.

Adapted for television in three parts by Jeanette Winterson from her own Whitbread Prize-winning novel, *Oranges Are Not the Only Fruit* was the story of Jess, an adopted northern lass who refused to yield to her mum's religious fanaticism. Earmarked as a future missionary, Jess was subjected to oppressive preaching from the bigoted Pastor Finch and made to join in thunderous hymn-singing with her mother's geriatric friends. A lesbian encounter with Melanie, a teenage acquaintance, provoked the wrath of the assembled Pentecostals, but their primitive efforts to drive the Devil out of the girl backfired and she was lost to them for ever.

Despite seeming a risky undertaking by the BBC, as neither the director, Beeban Kidron, nor the producer, Phillippa Giles, had conducted a TV drama before, the serial was widely acclaimed and went on to collect several awards.

ORLANDO
UK (Associated-Rediffusion) Children's Adventure. ITV 1965–8

Orlando O'Connor	**Sam Kydd**
Steve Morgan	**David Munro**
Jenny Morgan	**Judy Robinson**

Producer: **Ronald Marriott**

Spin-off for children from the adult series, CRANE.

Orlando O'Connor had been Crane's right-hand man in the earlier tales of smuggling and petty crime on the North African coast. Now he had returned to Britain and, after failing to establish a boat-building business, had sought out an old Navy friend. His friend, however, had been killed and Orlando, with the help of Steve and Jenny Morgan, two teenagers who had inherited their uncle's detective agency, set about finding his murderer. This was the first of many adventures for the trio, in which Orlando's life was saved on many an occasion by a magical Arabic charm called a 'Gizzmo', which doubled up as a homing device. The action took place mostly around London's docklands.

OSMONDS, THE
ALAN (1949–), WAYNE (1951–), MERRILL (1953–), JAY (1955–), DONNY (1957–), MARIE (1959–) and JIMMY (1963–)

American singing family, possibly the world's most famous Mormons, who first found TV fame in the 1960s on *The Andy Williams Show*. In the 1970s they were extremely popular, both on television and in the pop charts, with *Donny and Marie* their longest-lasting series. They also sang the theme song for the Western, *The Travels of Jaimie McPheeters*, a series in which they once guested. In 1995 Marie starred with Betty White in the sitcom, *Maybe This Time*.

OSOBA, TONY

British actor with some memorable supporting roles behind him. He was the Scottish heavy, McLaren, in PORRIDGE, DS Chas Jarvis in DEMPSEY AND MAKEPEACE, Freddie in *Making News* and rag-trade boss Peter Ingram in CORONATION STREET. Among his other credits have been *The Flame Trees of Thika*, THE PROFESSIONALS, DOCTOR WHO, MINDER, THE CLEOPATRAS, *Churchill's People*, BERGERAC, THE BILL, *Crown Prosecutor*, *Arabian Nights*, BROOKSIDE and *A Dance to the Music of Time*.

OSS/OFFICE OF STRATEGIC SERVICES
UK (Buckeye/ITC) Spy Drama. ITV 1957–8

Capt. Frank Hawthorne .... **Ron Randell**
The Chief .... **Lionel Murton**
Sgt O'Brien .... **Robert Gallico**

Producers: **Jules Buck, William Eliscu**

World War II espionage tales, based on true events.

OSS stood for Office of Strategic Services, the USA's precursor to the CIA, whose top man was Captain Frank Hawthorne. Against a wartime backdrop, Hawthorne and his colleague, Sgt O'Brien, worked on the Continent to expose foreign spies, rescue stranded personnel and mount sabotage missions, often in conjunction with the French Resistance. The stories were drawn from the files of the real OSS, which had been disbanded after the war, and authenticity was ensured by co-producer William Eliscu, who had himself served in the agency. In the UK the series was often billed in full as *Office of Strategic Services*. Each episode was entitled 'Operation . . .' (fill in the blank).

O'SULLEVAN, Sir PETER
CBE (1918–)

Irish-born horse-racing commentator, the voice of the BBC's racing coverage for over 50 years. O'Sullevan called the horses for the Corporation from 1947 to 1997, initially while racing correspondent for the Press Association. He later wrote for the *Daily Express*.

O'SULLIVAN, RICHARD
(1944–)

British actor, once a child performer and seen on TV since the 1950s in series like *Little Lord Fauntleroy*, *All Aboard*, DIXON OF DOCK GREEN and THE ADVENTURES OF ROBIN HOOD (Prince Arthur). In 1966 he played mailroom boy Taplow in the sitcom, *Foreign Affairs*, and in the early 1970s played the sneaky Dr Bingham in DOCTOR AT LARGE and DOCTOR IN CHARGE, which led to other sitcom roles, most notably that of Robin Tripp in MAN ABOUT THE HOUSE and ROBIN'S NEST. He appeared with Ronnie Corbett in NOW LOOK HERE! (Keith), and was Richard Gander with Beryl Reid in *Alcock and Gander*. Switching briefly to drama, O'Sullivan starred as DICK TURPIN in the series of the same name in 1979, but was tempted back to comedy with ME AND MY GIRL in 1984, playing widower Simon Harrap. In 1991 he was psychiatrist Adam Charlesworth in *Trouble in Mind*. Other credits have included FATHER, DEAR FATHER.

OTHER 'ARF, THE
UK (Witzend/ATV/Central) Situation Comedy. ITV 1980–4

Lorraine Watts .... **Lorraine Chase**
Charles Latimer MP .... **John Standing**
Brian Sweeney .... **Steve Adler**
Sybilla Howarth .... **Patricia Hodge**
George Watts .... **John Cater**
Lord Freddy Apthorpe .... **James Villiers**
Bassett .... **Richard Caldicot**
Mrs Lilley .... **Sheila Keith**

Creator: **Terence Howard**
Writers: **Terence Howard, Paul Makin**
Executive Producer: **Allan McKeown**
Producers: **Tony Charles, Douglas Argent**

A Tory MP has an affair with a Cockney model.

The course of love never did run smooth for upper-class Tory MP Charles Latimer and the Cockney model, Lorraine Watts, whom he met in a restaurant. Sybilla Howarth and Brian Sweeney, the partners they ditched, remained on the scene to make life uncomfortable, and ultimately Charles lost his parliamentary seat, forcing him and Lorraine to open up his home, Dormer House, to paying guests. Bassett and Mrs Lilley were his domestic staff, George was Lorraine's dad and Lord Freddy Apthorpe an aristocratic chum of Charles's.

The Other 'Arf capitalized on model Lorraine Chase's success as the Cockney girl in adverts for Campari. When asked by her smoothie suitor, 'Were you truly wafted here from Paradise?' she responded, 'No. Luton Airport', and so launched her acting career.

OUR FRIENDS IN THE NORTH
UK (BBC) Drama. BBC 2 1996

Nicky Hutchinson .... **Christopher Eccleston**
Mary Soulsby/Cox .... **Gina McKee**
Tosker Cox .... **Mark Strong**
Geordie Peacock .... **Daniel Craig**
Felix Hutchinson .... **Peter Vaughan**
Austin Donohue .... **Alun Armstrong**
Florrie Hutchinson .... **Freda Dowie**
Eddie Wells .... **David Bradley**
John Edwards .... **Geoffrey Hutchings**
Benny Barratt .... **Malcolm McDowell**
Deputy Chief Constable Roy Johnson . **Tony Haygarth**
Commissioner Colin Blamire .... **Peter Jeffrey**
Commander Harold Chapple .... **Donald Sumpter**
DI/Det. Chief Supt. John Salway .... **David Schofield**
DS Ron Conrad .... **Danny Webb**
Julia Allen .... **Louise Salter**
Claud Seabrook .... **Julian Fellowes**
Anthony Cox .... **Matthew Baron**
 Adam Pearson
 Daniel Casey
Elaine Craig/Cox .... **Tracey Wilkinson**
Claudia Seabrook .... **Saskia Wickham**

Writer: **Peter Flannery**

Producer: **Charles Pattinson**

Socio-political change in Britain illustrated by the lives of four friends from Newcastle.

The widely acclaimed *Our Friends in the North* was the nine-part story of four teenage friends, beginning in 1964 and tracing their vastly differing lives through to the 1990s, providing an insight into the social and political developments that shaped the country along the way. The foursome were idealistic young socialist Nicky Hutchinson, who gave up his education to work for local politician Austin Donohue at a time when a Labour government was being elected and new hope was spreading through the working classes. His girlfriend, Mary Soulsby, a university student, was forced to abandon academia when she fell pregnant to Tosker Cox, an objectionable 'pal' of Nicky's who had unrealistic pretensions of becoming a pop star. The fourth member of the gang was Geordie Peacock, Nicky's best mate, who was destined to run away from home and his violently abusive father.

Progressing through the 1960s and 1970s, the drama unfolded as Nicky angrily walked out on corrupt local politics and turned to anarchy; the self-sacrificing Mary and the self-centred Tosker became unhappily married parents of two kids, living in an uninhabitable new tower block; and Geordie found himself living the high life in the pay of London vice baron Bennie Barratt.

Things came to a head in the Thatcherite 1980s. Nicky unsuccessfully returned to the political arena as a parliamentary candidate and then made his mark as a photojournalist, Mary found her own voice and was voted on to the council, womanizing Tosker joined the 'me first' band of wealth-gatherers, buying council houses and running his own businesses, and sad Geordie slid into a miserable spiral of prison and homelessness. Nicky finally married, and then cheated on, Mary, and Tosker found himself a new wife, too.

In the more harmonious 1990s there was an air of reconciliation. Now in their middle ages, the four friends had experienced the trauma of raising kids and watching parents grow old and die. The idealism and hopes of youth had been transformed into scepticism born out of bitter experience. And, though the four continued on their individual paths in life – Nicky again solo, Mary riding high in politics, Tosker scrabbling back up from near-bankrupcy and buying a boat nightclub on the Tyne, and Geordie, the loner, resignedly walking away from it all yet again, they did at least seem to have learned to understand each other.

As intriguing as its personal storylines were, the serial was also recognized for the way in which it explored social upheavals in the late 20th century – from political and police corruption in the 1960s and union militancy in the 1970s to uncompromising Thatcherism (especially concerning the miners' strike) in the 1980s and the more subdued, post-recession 1990s. It began life as a stage play, in which events ended in 1979 at the start of the Thatcher years. When its writer, Peter Flannery, was eventually commissioned to develop it for television (after 15 years), he extended the action up to 1995 and the threshold of another new political era.

OUR HOUSE

UK (ABC) Situation Comedy. ITV 1960–1

Georgina Ruddy	**Hattie Jacques**
Simon Willow	**Charles Hawtrey**
Daisy Burke	**Joan Sims**
Capt. Iliffe	**Frank Pettingell**
Mrs Iliffe	**Ina de la Haye**
Gordon Brent	**Norman Rossington**
Herbert Keene	**Frederick Peisley**
Stephen Hatton	**Trader Faulkner**
Marcia Hatton	**Leigh Madison**
William Singer	**Bernard Bresslaw**
Henrietta	**Hylda Baker**
Marina	**Eugenie Cavanagh**

Writers: **Norman Hudis, Brad Ashton, Bob Block**
Producer: **Ernest Maxin**

Comic capers with the oddball residents of a large house.

Carry On Under One Roof may have been a more appropriate title for this farcical comedy, partly written by *Carry On* scriptwriter Norman Hudis and starring several of the big-screen performers. It featured a rag-bag of nine people who met in an estate agent's office and, by pooling their funds, managed to buy a house big enough to accommodate them all. The cohabitors were librarian Georgina Ruddy, council official Simon Willow, unemployable Daisy Burke, the artistic, newly-wed Hattons, Yorkshire sea-dog Captain Iliffe and his French violinist wife, bank clerk Herbert Keene and law student Gordon Brent. When the second series began, some new house-sharers, including William Singer, Marina and Henrietta, were added.

After the introductory first episode, which was billed as *Moving in to Our House*, not all the characters appeared each week.

OUR MAN AT ST MARK'S/ OUR MAN FROM ST MARK'S

UK (Associated-Rediffusion) Situation Comedy. ITV 1963–5/1966

Revd Andrew Parker	**Leslie Phillips**
Revd Stephen Young	**Donald Sinden**
Mrs Peace	**Joan Hickson**
Anne Gibson	**Anne Lawson**
Harry the Yo Yo	**Harry Fowler**

Creators/Writers: **James Kelly, Peter Miller**
Producer: **Eric Maschwitz**

Humorous happenings in the daily life of a country vicar.

St Mark's, a rural parish centring around the village of Felgate, was blessed with the Reverend Andrew Parker as its slightly eccentric vicar. This series focused on his day-to-day exploits, taking in the amusing incidents and, occasionally, the sentimental. He was assisted by his girlfriend, Anne Gibson, and his housekeeper, Mrs Peace. When St Mark's gained a new vicar, Stephen Young, a year later, Mrs Peace remained *in situ* and a reformed crook by the name of Harry the Yo Yo (on account of the fact that he was in and out of prison) was employed as sexton/gravedigger. Stephen also brought with him a Scottie dog named Mr Robertson. The title changed slightly for the fourth and final season. Becoming *Our Man from St Mark's*, it saw Stephen promoted to archdeacon and transferred to a cathedral.

Our Man at St Mark's began a year after a similar series had aired in the USA. Entitled *Going My Way*, it starred Gene Kelly and was a small-screen version of the classic 1944 Bing Crosby film.

OUR WORLD
UK (BBC) Entertainment. BBC 1 1967

Presenter: **Cliff Michelmore**

Producer: **Ray Colley**

Satellite link-up featuring contributions from TV companies around the world.

This celebration of satellite technology, sponsored by the European Broadcasting Union, was broadcast between 8 and 10 p.m. on the evening of Sunday, 25 June 1967. Hosted by Cliff Michelmore, it employed four satellites and over a million miles of cabling to bring together live pictures from most parts of the globe (the Soviet Union and Poland were notable exceptions, having pulled out because of the Israeli Six-Day War earlier in the month). In all, 18 countries contributed a (non-political) televisual message or other item. The BBC's offering was a live performance of The Beatles singing 'All You Need Is Love'.

OUT
UK (Thames/Euston Films) Drama. ITV 1978

Frank Ross	**Tom Bell**
Anne Ross	**Lynne Farleigh**
Evie	**Pam Fairbrother**
DI Bryce	**Norman Rodway**
Rimmer	**Robert Walker**
Cimmie	**Katharine Schofield**
Ralph Veneker	**John Junkin**
Chris Cottle	**Brian Croucher**
Vic Lee	**Frank Mills**
Bernie Machen	**Oscar James**
Pretty Billy Binns	**Peter Blake**

Writer: **Trevor Preston**
Executive Producer: **Johnny Goodman**
Producer: **Barry Hanson**

A vicious, bitter criminal is released from jail and looks for revenge.

Tough, intense bank-robber Frank Ross, a hardman among hardmen, had only one aim in life. Now back on the streets after eight years in prison, he was looking for the person who had shopped him. Nothing got in his way in his quest for the informer, and his obsessed meanderings through London's underworld were punctuated by encounters with numerous sad and evil characters. The violence was heavy and the police Ross confronted were as grubby and miserable as the villains they set out to catch. Frank's wife, mentally wrecked by his bleak life of crime, was also seen. A powerful, six-part drama, *Out* won much acclaim.

OUT OF THE UNKNOWN
UK (BBC) Science Fiction. BBC 2 1965–71

Producers: **Irene Shubik, Alan Bromly**

Well-respected sci-fi anthology series.

Initially taking works by renowned science-fiction authors like John Wyndham, Ray Bradbury and Isaac Asimov, this collection of spooky tales proved to be Britain's definitive answer to THE TWILIGHT ZONE. It employed skilled TV writers like Troy Kennedy Martin, Terry Nation and Leon Griffiths as adaptors, and was masterminded by former ARMCHAIR THEATRE story editor Irene Shubik, who had already attempted a similar concept when working on ABC's OUT OF THIS WORLD. The tales were not all thrillers, some were satires and comedies, but fantastic space creatures and bug-eyed monsters were steadfastly avoided. The series also attracted some of the best contemporary acting talents – the likes of Marius Goring, George Cole, Warren Mitchell, Donald Houston, David Hemmings and Rachel Roberts – as well as aspiring directors like Ridley Scott, later of *Alien* and *Blade Runner* fame. In 1969, after a two-year gap, the series was revived in colour and the emphasis switched from pure sci-fi to horror and psychological suspense, as new producer Alan Bromly took over the reins.

OUT OF THIS WORLD
UK (ABC) Science Fiction. ITV 1962

Host: **Boris Karloff**

Producer: **Leonard White**

An innovative British series of hour-long science-fiction plays.

Produced by ABC, already highly successful with its ARMCHAIR THEATRE collection of single dramas, this series was British TV's first attempt at a science-fiction anthology. Many of the trends it set, such as using the works of established sci-fi authors, employing first-rate adaptors and leading performers, and varying the style of each play from pure suspense to black comedy, were continued through to its natural successor, the BBC's OUT OF THE UNKNOWN. Thirteen episodes were made, and were shown on Saturday nights, with introductions by the softly sinister Boris Karloff.

OUTER LIMITS, THE

US (Daystar/United Artists) Science Fiction. ITV 1964;
BBC 2 1995–9

The Control Voice .... **Vic Perrin**
Kevin Conway

Creator/Executive Producer: **Leslie Stevens**
Producers: **Joseph Stefano, Ben Brady**

Stylish anthology of sci-fi thriller stories.

In the 1950s and 1960s, video static and picture distortion
were annoyingly familiar to TV viewers. However, there
was always an announcer at hand to confirm that normal programming would resume as soon as possible –
unless you happened to be watching *The Outer Limits*.
Playing on the poor reliability of TV signals and television equipment, *The Outer Limits* set out to frighten
viewers from the start, opening with the loss of the
picture and a voice that declared ominously: 'There is
nothing wrong with your television set. Do not attempt
to adjust the picture. We are controlling transmission.
We will control the horizontal. We will control the vertical. For the next hour, sit quietly and we will control all
you see and hear. You are about to experience the awe
and mystery that reaches from the inner mind to the
Outer Limits.'

What followed was one of the 49 sci-fi thrillers that
made up *The Outer Limits* anthology. Most concerned
Earth invasions by extraterrestrial life-forms and are best
remembered for their catalogue of terrifying aliens,
which varied from giant insects to intelligent rocks and
invisible parasites. But there was much more to *The Outer
Limits* than bug-eyed monsters. The camerawork applied
a stark, *film noir* veneer to the imaginative stories and,
though the monsters took centre stage, it was the
humans – or, rather, human nature – that stole the
show, with a moral always drawn from proceedings.
Thankfully, the announcer – or Control Voice (the
person was never seen) – then restored normality, concluding with the words: 'We now return control of your
television set to you, until next week at the same time,
when the Control Voice will take you to . . . the Outer
Limits.'

The show's first producer, Joseph Stefano, certainly
knew how to chill; he had already written the screenplay
for Hitchcock's *Psycho*. Being an anthology series, *The
Outer Limits* called upon guest artists every week, with
stars like Leonard Nimoy, William Shatner, Martin
Sheen, Donald Pleasence and David McCallum taking
on lead roles. BBC 2 re-ran the entire series in 1980–1. A
new version aired sporadically on BBC 2 from 1995, with
Kevin Conway assuming the Control Voice role.

OUTSIDE BROADCAST

Abbreviated to OB, an outside broadcast is a programme
or part of a programme that takes place outside the
controlled environment of a television studio. An OB at
a major sporting event or state occasion, for example, is
a complex operation, involving numerous strategically
placed cameras and microphones, all co-ordinated by a
director and his/her team working from a mobile control
room.

OUTSIDE EDGE

UK (Central) Situation Comedy. ITV 1994–6

Miriam (Mim) Dervish .... **Brenda Blethyn**
Roger Dervish .... **Robert Daws**
Maggie Costello .... **Josie Lawrence**
Kevin Costello .... **Timothy Spall**
Dennis Broadley .... **Denis Lill**
Bob Willis .... **Jeremy Nicholas**
Michael Jayston
Alex Harrington .... **Ben Daniels**
Christopher Lang
Nigel .... **Nigel Pegram**
Ginnie Willis .... **Tracy Brabin**
Shirley Broadley .... **Hilary Crane**

Writer: **Richard Harris**
Producer: **Paula Burdon**

*Middle-class tensions run high at an English
cricket club.*

While the concept of early-middle-aged men playing
cricket at weekends, supported by their tea-making
wives, formed the hub of this popular ITV comedy, the
real focus was on class, sex and marital harmony. The
major players – an otherwise incompatible foursome –
at Brent Park Cricket Club were stuffy chauvinist Roger
Dervish (club captain) and his frustrated, mousy wife,
Mim, and the more earthy Maggie and Kevin Costello,
she an ever-practical nymphomaniac who thought her
husband the best thing since sliced bread, he enjoying
their lusty relationship but also slobbishly indulging in
real kitchen activities, not to mention a good few pints
with the rest of the lads.

The series was spun off a stage play which had already
been made into a TV drama in 1982, starring Paul Eddington and Prunella Scales as the Dervishes and Maureen
Lipman and Jonathan Lynn as the Costellos.

OUT-TAKES

Material shot but not used in the finished programme,
often because of gaffes and blunders. These have proved
particularly popular with viewers when grouped in
humorous collections like IT'LL BE ALRIGHT ON THE
NIGHT and *Auntie's Bloomers*.

OWEN, ALUN

(1925–94)

Liverpudlian dramatist, one of British TV's major early
playwrights. For ARMCHAIR THEATRE he penned *No
Trams to Lime Street* in 1959, quickly followed by *After the
Funeral, Lena, O My Lena* (both 1960) and *The Rose Affair*
(1961). *The Strain* (1963) and *Shelter* (1967) were among

other acclaimed 1960s offerings, as was *You Can't Win 'Em All* (1962), which led to a six-part series, *Corrigan Blake*, the following year. Similarly, another play, *Ah – There You Are* (part of *The Ronnie Barker Playhouse* collection), created the character of Lord Rustless and resulted in the series, HARK AT BARKER, in 1969. The same year, his trilogy comprising *MacNeil*, *Cornelius* and *Emlyn* aired under the *Saturday Night Theatre* banner. His later work included *Norma* (1974), *Forget-Me-Not* (1976) and *Kisch, Kisch* (1983). Owen also wrote the screenplay for The Beatles' film, *A Hard Day's Night*.

OWEN, BILL
MBE (Bill Rowbotham; 1914–99)

Few actors have held down the same television role for over 20 years, but Bill Owen was one of them, thanks to his marathon stint as the seedy Compo in LAST OF THE SUMMER WINE. Owen's TV career, however, stretched way back. In 1951 he played Inspector Lestrade in an ambitious BBC adaptation of the SHERLOCK HOLMES mysteries. In 1963 he starred as Fred Cuddell, alongside Sid James, in TAXI and, eight years later, played the conniving Sgt Sam Short in *Copper's End*. Among his other credits were WHATEVER HAPPENED TO THE LIKELY LADS?, TALES OF THE UNEXPECTED, BRIDESHEAD REVISITED and CORONATION STREET. Owen also wrote several plays and the lyrics for numerous songs.

OWEN, CLIVE
(1966–)

Midlands-born actor, the star of *Chancer* (Stephen Crane), *Sharman* (Nick Sharman), *Split Second* (Michael Anderson) and *Second Sight* (DCI Ross Tanner), as well as *An Evening with Gary Lineker* (Bill), and *Screen Two's Bad Boy Blues*. His dad, Jess, once won NEW FACES with his country band, The Gingerbreads. Owen is married to actress Sarah-Jane Fenton.

OWEN, MD
See DOCTORS, THE.

OWEN, NICHOLAS
(1947–)

ITN newscaster and reporter, working on all the main bulletins (including *Channel 4 News*) and at times the company's royal correspondent.

OWEN, NICK
(1947–)

Berkhamsted-born journalist and presenter, coming to the fore as host of TV-am's GOOD MORNING BRITAIN in 1983, following work as a news and sports frontman for ATV and Central (as well as TV-am). Owen has also hosted the quizzes, *Sporting Triangles* and *Hitman*, *Midweek Sports Special* and other sporting events. His breakfast-time partnership with Anne Diamond was poached by the BBC for *Good Morning with Anne and Nick* in the 1990s.

PACE, NORMAN

(1953–) See HALE, GARETH.

PADDINGTON

UK (Filmfair) Animation. BBC 1 1976; 1979

Narrator: **Michael Hordern**

Creator/Writer: **Michael Bond**
Producer: **Graham Clutterbuck**

The adventures of a somewhat disorientated
Peruvian bear in London.

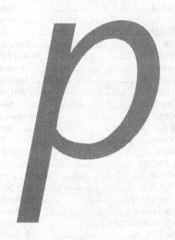

Paddington, the hero of books by Michael Bond since 1958, finally arrived on television in 1976. As a result, a new generation of youngsters was able to appreciate the cuddly bear in the blue duffle coat, floppy hat and wellies who loved marmalade sandwiches and lived with the Brown family at 32 Windsor Gardens. Mr Henry Brown was the head of the family, along with his wife and children Jonathan and Judy. Mrs Bird was the family cook.

The Browns had found the bear at Paddington station (hence his name) wearing a tag reading 'Please look after this bear'. Looking after this bear, however, proved increasingly difficult, as the rather bemused but always inquisitive Paddington stumbled from mishap to mishap. Paddington's best friend was antiques dealer Mr Gruber, like Paddington a refugee from his own country.

These five-minute episodes, shown in the 'MAGIC ROUNDABOUT slot' just before the early evening news, featured a model Paddington animated by Ivor Wood against a static drawn background. One-off specials followed the two series, in 1983, 1986 and 1987. A more advanced, technically superior, updated series entitled *Paddington Bear* was seen on ITV in 1990 but failed to charm audiences like the original series.

PAGETT, NICOLA

(Nicola Scott; 1945–)

Cairo-born actress, popular on TV in the 1970s in particular, during which time she played Miss Elizabeth in UPSTAIRS, DOWNSTAIRS and took the title role in *Anna Karenina*. In the 1980s she was Adele Fairley in A WOMAN OF SUBSTANCE and Liz Rodenhurst in A BIT OF A DO. In 1994 she starred as hairdresser Sonia Drysdale in *Ain't Misbehavin'* and in 2000 she took the part of Sally Kegworth in *Up Rising*. Among her other credits have been THE CAESARS, THE PERSUADERS!, BARLOW AT LARGE, THE SWEENEY, THE RIVALS OF SHERLOCK HOLMES, *War and Peace*, *French Without Tears*, LOVE STORY, *Shadow on the Sun*, *Scoop* and the Dennis Potter play, *Visitors*. She is married to playwright Graham Swannell.

PAL

Phase Alternate Line colour-television system, developed in Germany and now in use throughout western Europe, except for France, which uses its own SECAM system. PAL, an adaptation of the American NTSC system (using 625 lines in the UK instead of the USA's 525, and with built-in colour correction), is also the standard in Brazil and China.

PALIN, MICHAEL
CBE (1943–)

Sheffield-born actor, comedian, writer and presenter, famously one of the MONTY PYTHON troupe but with many other strings to his bow. Among his first writing credits were sketches for THE FROST REPORT, which brought Palin and his writing partner, Terry Jones, in touch with John Cleese, Graham Chapman and Eric Idle. They also scripted for John Bird's comedy, *A Series of Bird's*, *The Late Show*, *Broaden Your Mind* and *Marty*. In 1967 Palin appeared in *Twice a Fortnight*, a late-night sketch show, and was then given the chance to shine in the wacky children's comedy, DO NOT ADJUST YOUR SET. This led to *The Complete and Utter History of Britain*, a spoof history series he compiled and presented with Jones in 1969. *Monty Python's Flying Circus*, the same year, was a natural progression. While a serving Python, Palin continued to write elsewhere, with one of his regular outlets THE TWO RONNIES, and, when the Python team decided to call it a day in 1974, his next TV project was RIPPING YARNS, a send-up of *Boy's Own* tales, again in collaboration with Terry Jones. In the 1980s Palin drifted away from the small screen and focused more on cinema work. He was tempted back by the chance to emulate Phileas Fogg's attempt to go AROUND THE WORLD IN 80 DAYS, for a 1988 BBC documentary series. It proved to be an enormous success and the accompanying book sold over half a million copies – enough to call for two sequels, *Pole to Pole* and *Full Circle*, plus another travelogue, *Michael Palin's Hemingway Adventure*, celebrating the centenary of Ernest Hemingway's birth. Palin also demonstrated his dramatic skills with an acclaimed performance as schoolteacher Jim Nelson in Alan Bleasdale's GBH. Among his other credits have been *Great Railway Journeys of the World* and the scripts for the TV films, *East of Ipswich* and *Number 27*. Palin was also a founder director of Meridian Television, for whom he compiled *Palin's Column*, a series about the Isle of Wight, and starred in *A Class Act* (alongside Tracey Ullman).

PALLISERS, THE
UK (BBC) Drama. BBC 2 1974

Lady Glencora M'Cluskie/Palliser ..... **Susan Hampshire**
Plantagenet Palliser MP .... **Philip Latham**
Duke of Omnium .... **Ronald Culver**
Burgo Fitzgerald .... **Barry Justice**
Countess of Midlothian .... **Fabia Drake**
Alice Vavasor/Grey .... **Carole Mortimer**
George Vavasor .... **Gary Watson**
Laura Kennedy .... **Anna Massey**
Lady Dumbello .... **Rachel Herbert**
Marie Goesler/Finn .... **Barbara Murray**
Marchioness of Auld Reekie .... **Sonia Dresdel**
John Grey .... **Bernard Brown**
Dolly Longstaffe .... **Donald Pickering**
Duke of St Bungay .... **Roger Livesey**
Lord Chiltern .... **John Hallam**
Phineas Finn .... **Donal McCann**
Lord Fawn .... **Derek Jacobi**
Lizzie Eustace/Emilius .... **Sarah Badel**
Barrington Erle .... **Moray Watson**
Robert Kennedy .... **Derek Godfrey**
Lawrence Fitzgibbon .... **Neil Stacy**
Collingwood .... **Maurice Quick**
Mr Monk .... **Bryan Pringle**
Violet Effingham/Chiltern .... **Mel Martin**
Mrs Bunce .... **Brenda Cowling**
Mary Flood/Finn .... **Máire Ní Ghráinne**
Mrs Hittaway .... **Penelope Keith**
Lord Brentford .... **Lockwood West**
Revd Emilius .... **Anthony Ainley**
Frank Greystock .... **Martin Jarvis**
Lord George .... **Terence Alexander**
Mr Gresham .... **Robin Bailey**
Mr Bonteen .... **Peter Sallis**
Mrs Bonteen .... **June Whitfield**
Adelaide Palliser .... **Jo Kendall**
Gerard Maule .... **Jeremy Clyde**
Frank Tregear .... **Jeremy Irons**
Earl of Silverbridge .... **Anthony Andrews**
Lady Mabel Grex .... **Anna Carteret**
Emily Wharton/Lopez .... **Sheila Ruskin**
Abel Wharton .... **Brewster Mason**
Ferdinand Lopez .... **Stuart Wilson**
Quintus Slide .... **Clifford Rose**
Isabel Boncasson .... **Lynne Frederick**
Sir Orlando Drought .... **Basil Dignam**

Writer: **Simon Raven**
Producer: **Martin Lisemore**

Six of Anthony Trollope's novels merged into one TV series.

Tracing the rise to power of snooty Plantagenet Palliser, his arranged marriage to the flighty Lady Glencora, and ending with the political emergence of his son, the Earl of Silverbridge, this series followed the ups and downs of the wealthy Palliser family and their associates in Victorian times. This was a family of near-noble birth that strove for power under the Liberal banner, echoing Trollope's own parliamentary yearnings. Dwelling also on personalities, social conflicts and the battle for family supremacy, this dramatization became a reflection of life in Trollope's time. However, made up of 26 episodes, the series was badly disrupted by a BBC labour dispute in July 1974. When filming was finally completed, the Corporation was forced to repeat five earlier episodes in order to enable viewers to catch up on events. Consequently, although the first part went out in January, the long-awaited finale did not arrive until November.

PALMER, GEOFFREY
(1927–)

London-born actor, in a range of supporting and starring roles, usually of a lugubrious nature. In the 1970s, he played Jimmy, Reggie's brother-in-law, in THE FALL AND RISE OF REGINALD PERRIN (also in the 1990s revival, *The Legacy of Reginald Perrin*) and Ben, Ria Parkinson's husband, in BUTTERFLIES. Later, Palmer starred as Leo Bannister in Carla Lane's *The Last Song* and loony right-winger Harry Truscott in FAIRLY SECRET ARMY. He also appeared as Donald Fairchild in *Executive Stress* and as Lionel Hardcastle in AS TIME GOES BY. In addition, Palmer has been seen in *Bulldog Breed*, THE AVENGERS, FAWLTY TOWERS, DOCTOR WHO, BERGERAC, INSPECTOR MORSE and Dennis Potter's *Christabel*, as well as taking the roles of Field Marshal Haig in BLACKADDER GOES FORTH, Harry Stringer in HOT METAL, the Foreign Secretary in WHOOPS APOCALYPSE and Robert Crane in *Reckless: The Sequel*. He also narrated *The 1940 House*.

PALMER, TONY
(1935–)

British writer, director, rock-music critic and documentary-maker. His early contributions included the sketch show, *Twice a Fortnight*, and teenage pop shows like *How It Is* and *How Late It Is*. These changed the way pop was presented on TV, using music as a background to arts features, politics and other world events. He produced *All My Loving* for OMNIBUS in 1968, which aimed to dispel the myth that rock stars were all delinquents, and has also supplied profiles of Benjamin Britten, Peter Sellers, William Walton, Stravinsky and Richard Burton. Palmer's ALL YOU NEED IS LOVE, a 13-part history of popular music, was screened in 1977.

PAN

The movement of a camera horizontally from left to right or vice versa, as opposed to tilt which is its up-and-down manoeuvre.

PANORAMA
UK (BBC) Current Affairs. BBC 1 1953–

Presenters: **Patrick Murphy, Max Robertson, Richard Dimbleby, James Mossman, Robin Day, Alastair Burnet, David Dimbleby, Charles Wheeler, Fred Emery, Robert Kee**

Editors: **Dennis Bardens, Michael Barsley, Rex Moorfoot, Michael Peacock, Paul Fox, David Wheeler, Jeremy Isaacs, John Grist, David J. Webster, Brian Wenham, Frank Smith, Christopher Capron, Roger Bolton, George Carey, Peter Ibbotson, David Dickinson, Tim Gardam, Robert Rowland, Peter Pagnamenta, Mark Thompson, Glenwyn Benson, Steve Hewlett, Peter Horrocks**

The world's longest-running current affairs programme.

Although noted today for its hard-hitting investigations and reports into matters of political and social concern, *Panorama* began in quite a different vein. It was launched in 1953 as a fortnightly magazine programme with newspaper journalist Patrick Murphy, who quickly made way for Max Robertson, as host. Malcolm Muggeridge was the resident interviewer, Denis Mathews was the art critic, Nancy Spain reviewed books and Lionel Hale discussed events in the theatre. After two years, however, *Panorama* was completely revamped to become a 'window on the world'. In came respected commentator Richard Dimbleby, and he fronted the programme through its glory days in the late 1950s and early 1960s. Other notable anchormen are listed above (although the studio has lately been abandoned in favour of prerecorded reports). Dimbleby's team included John Freeman (later of FACE TO FACE) and Christopher Chataway. Later contributors included Michael Barratt, Trevor Philpott, Michael Charlton and Leonard Parkin.

As well as being noted for its longevity, *Panorama* has also provided some memorable items for the TV archives. In 1961 the Duke of Edinburgh became the first member of the royal family to be interviewed on television when quizzed by Richard Dimbleby. Four years earlier, on 1 April 1957, Dimbleby and his crew sprang a celebrated April Fools' prank on the viewing public, when it presented a documentary on the spaghetti harvest in southern Switzerland. A massive audience was attracted in November 1995 for the (then unknown) Martin Bashir's explosive interview with Diana, Princess of Wales.

PARA HANDY – MASTER MARINER
UK (BBC) Comedy Drama. BBC 1959–60

Para Handy McFarlane .... **Duncan Macrae**
Dan Macphail .... **John Grieve**
Dougie .... **Roddy McMillan**
Sunny Jim (Davey Green) .... **Angus Lennie**

Writer: **Duncan Ross**
Producer: **Pharic MacLaren**

Easy-going tales of a roguish merchant seaman.

The *Para Handy* stories written by Neil Munro (initially under the pen-name of Hugh Foulis in 1905 editions of the *Glasgow Evening News*) have become some of the most televised pieces of literature. This series from the turn of the 1960s featured Duncan Macrae as Captain Peter 'Para Handy' McFarlane, the wily skipper of the tiny Clyde steamer known as *The Vital Spark*, which plied its trade along the lochs and channels of western Scotland, delivering goods to isolated communities. Para Handy was notoriously unreliable and his crew were equally inept.

Under the name of *The Vital Spark*, Para Handy was revived for a COMEDY PLAYHOUSE presentation in 1965, and a series with the same title followed in 1966–7. Roddy McMillan took the lead role in both, and John Grieve was once again cast as Macphail, the chief engineer. Walter Carr took the part of Dougie the mate and cabin boy/cook Sunny Jim was played by Alex McAvoy. The series was revived again in 1974 and then completely recast for a 1994–5 version, *The Tales of Para Handy*, starring Gregor Fisher as the boozy old sea-dog. Rikki Fulton was seen as Macphail, Sean Scanlan as Dougie and Andrew Fairlie as Sunny Jim. The stories were now set in the 1930s.

PARADISE CLUB, THE
UK (Zenith) Drama. BBC 1 1989–90

Danny Kane	**Leslie Grantham**
Father Frank Kane	**Don Henderson**
DI Rosy Campbell	**Kitty Aldridge**
Carol Kane	**Barbara Wilshere**
Jonjo O'Brady	**Peter Gowen**
Polish Joe	**Leon Herbert**
Ginger	**Jack Ellis**
Eddie Cleary	**Peter Gunn**
DS Tommy Cooper	**Malcolm Raeburn**
DC Webster	**Ben Daniels**
DI Sarah Turnbull	**Caroline Bliss**
DS Nesbit	**Jack Galloway**
Peter Noonan	**Philip Martin Brown**

Creator/Writer: **Murray Smith**
Producer: **Selwyn Roberts**

Two dodgy brothers run a seedy dance-hall.

Francis (Frank) and Danny Kane were two brothers who had drifted apart. Frank, a one-time boxing champ, had run away to the Foreign Legion and then become a priest, but was troubled by gambling addiction; Danny lived a yuppie lifestyle with his young family in Docklands, his earnings enhanced by his position in the family 'firm' (their dad was the infamous 'Hatchet Jack' Kane). They were brought together for the first time in eight years by the death of their mother, the vicious head of 'The Paradise Mob', who bequeathed Frank her Paradise Club, in Paradise Street, Rotherhithe. Having just left his seamen's mission in Liverpool, following false accusations of theft against him, Frank decided to make a go of running the club, with Danny as his partner. As proprietors of this drinking and dancing den, they became further immersed in the activities of the East End underworld. Two series were made of their murky adventures.

PARAMOUNT COMEDY CHANNEL

Satellite/cable/digital channel specializing in re-runs of sitcoms, drawing on a major catalogue of past hits. A typical evening's viewing might consist of US series like CHEERS, *Ellen*, THE LARRY SANDERS SHOW, FRASIER, SEINFELD and *Married with Children*, supported by British contributions like *Harry Hill*, FATHER TED, WHOSE LINE IS IT ANYWAY? and DROP THE DEAD DONKEY. There is also room for US comedies that have not aired on UK terrestrial networks, such as *Mad About You*, *Becker* and

Clueless. Jointly owned by Viacom and BSkyB, the channel was launched in the UK in 1995 as simply The Paramount Channel, acquiring the word 'Comedy' when it narrowed down its content from general entertainment to pure humour.

PARAS, THE
UK (BBC) Documentary. BBC 1 1983

Presenter/Writer: **Glyn Worsnip**

Executive Producer: **David Harrison**
Producer: **Bill Jones**

Fly-on-the-wall documentary featuring recruits to the Parachute Regiment.

This gruelling, seven-part look at military life focused on 41 newcomers to 480 Recruit Platoon of the Parachute Regiment. Recorded over 22 weeks, it monitored the rookies as they endured possibly the world's toughest military training regime to obtain the right to wear the famous red beret. The series witnessed the initial 41 being reduced in number week by week.

PARDON THE EXPRESSION
UK (Granada) Situation Comedy. ITV 1965–6

Leonard Swindley	**Arthur Lowe**
Ernest Parbold	**Paul Dawkins**
Miss Sinclair	**Joy Stewart**
Mrs Edgeley	**Betty Driver**
Walter Hunt	**Robert Dorning**

Executive Producer: **H. V. Kershaw**
Producers: **Harry Driver, Derek Granger**

A pompous draper joins a large chain store and assumes extra responsibility.

A spin-off series from CORONATION STREET, *Pardon the Expression* followed the fortunes of Leonard Swindley, the teetotal, lay-preaching, one-time proprietor of Weatherfield's Gamma Garments boutique. Mr Swindley was now assistant manager of a branch of the Dobson and Hawks chain store, a position guaranteed to exaggerate his pomposity. Ernest Parbold was his buck-passing boss, Miss Sinclair was the staff manageress and Mrs Edgeley (played by Betty Driver, the *Street's* future Betty Turpin) was in charge of the canteen. When Mr Parbold left after the first series, Walter Hunt took his place.

Pardon the Expression, taking its name from Mr Swindley's catchphrase of 'If you'll pardon the expression', gave birth to a spin-off series of its own, *Turn Out the Lights* (1967), in which Swindley and Hunt teamed up as a duo of amateur ghost-hunters.

PARKER, FESS
(1925–)

American actor, an instant hit as Disney's DAVY CROCKETT. Enjoying his American hero status, Parker followed up with tales of another pioneer, DANIEL BOONE, ten years later. In between he starred as Senator Eugene Smith in *Mr Smith Goes to Washington*.

PARKIN, LEONARD
(1929–93)

British reporter and newscaster, with ITN for many years. Initially working as a newspaper journalist in his native Yorkshire, Parkin joined the BBC news team in 1954, later becoming its Canadian and then Washington correspondent. As such, he was the first British reporter to break the news of President Kennedy's assassination. For the BBC, he also worked on PANORAMA and 24 HOURS. In 1967, the year that *News at Ten* was launched, he switched to ITN, for whom he also presented election programmes and, later, the lunchtime news (*First Report* and *News at One*) and *News at 5.45*, eventually leaving in 1987.

PARKINSON, MICHAEL
CBE (1935–)

Undoubtedly king of the chat shows in the 1970s, Barnsley-born Michael Parkinson's career began in newspaper journalism, graduating to work for Granada, where he contributed to local news magazines, WORLD IN ACTION, WHAT THE PAPERS SAY and CINEMA. He then joined the BBC's 24 HOURS team, produced sports documentaries for LWT and ventured into talk shows with *Tea Break*, before, in 1971, embarking on his 11-year run as host of *Parkinson*. BBC 1's extremely popular Saturday night series specialized in featuring the biggest names in Hollywood and elsewhere, providing memorable moments such as Muhammad Ali at his verbal best, some classic early exposure for Billy Connolly and, much to the host's displeasure, a rough-and-tumble encounter with Rod Hull's Emu. In 1983 he became one of TV-am's 'Famous Five', largely working on the weekend output, and later sharing the limelight with his wife, Mary. Parkinson has since chaired the game shows, GIVE US A CLUE, *All Star Secrets* and GOING FOR A SONG, worked on *The Help Squad*, written and narrated the animation for *The Woofits*, presented a history of rugby league in *A League Apart*, and resurrected *Parkinson* with some success.

PARSONS, NICHOLAS
(1928–)

Grantham-born actor and presenter, first seen on TV in guest roles in series like THE ADVENTURES OF ROBIN HOOD, sketch shows like *Look at It This Way* and *Here and Now*, and, more prominently, as stooge to Arthur Haynes, Eric Barker and, later, Benny Hill. At around the same time he was providing the voice for Gerry Anderson's puppet cowboy, Tex Tucker, in FOUR FEATHER FALLS, and pursuing a bright career in British film comedies. In the late 1960s Parsons appeared in the American sitcom, *The Ugliest Girl in Town*. More successfully, in the 1970s, Parsons hosted the remarkably

popular quiz show, SALE OF THE CENTURY. In the 1990s, he chaired TV versions of his successful radio series, *Just a Minute*. His has also been a familiar face on other panel games, and Parsons has never been afraid to mock his own smoothie image with cameo roles in THE COMIC STRIP PRESENTS, THE NEW STATESMAN and other comedies, plus the late-night game show, *The Alphabet Quiz*. His first wife was actress Denise Bryer.

PARTRIDGE FAMILY, THE
US (Screen Gems) Situation Comedy. BBC 1 1971; ITV 1972–4

Shirley Partridge	**Shirley Jones**
Keith Partridge	**David Cassidy**
Laurie Partridge	**Susan Dey**
Danny Partridge	**Danny Bonaduce**
Christopher Partridge	**Jeremy Gelbwaks** **Brian Forster**
Tracy Partridge	**Suzanne Crough**
Reuben Kinkaid	**Dave Madden**

Creator: **Bernard Slade**
Executive Producer: **Bob Claver**

Life at home and on the road with a family pop group.

When suburban widow Shirley Partridge casually joined her children's band as a singer, little did she know that a career as a pop star beckoned. Putting together a song called 'I Think I Love You' in the family's garage-cum-rehearsal room, the group sold the track to a record company. It became a hit and turned the family into top performers. Climbing aboard a painted-up old school bus, Shirley and her kids then headed off on tour across America from their home in San Pueblo, California. Apart from Mom, the family consisted of 16-year-old Keith, 15-year-old Laurie, freckly Danny, aged ten (who organized the band), Chris, aged seven, and five-year-old Tracy. Their agent (who disliked children) was Reuben Kinkaid. The family had a dog called Simone.

Like The Monkees before them, The Partridge Family grew into a real-life pop group and had hits on both sides of the Atlantic. However, they never claimed to perform on the actual recordings, apart from vocals by Shirley Jones and David Cassidy. Their biggest hits in Britain were cover versions of 1960s classics like 'Breaking Up Is Hard To Do', 'Looking Through the Eyes of Love' and 'Walking In The Rain'. David Cassidy quickly outgrew the series, branching out on his own and becoming one of the 1970s' first teenage idols. Shirley Jones was his real-life stepmother. *The Partridge Family* was inspired by the experiences of the Cowsills, a Rhode Island family of a mom and her kids who had American hits in the 1960s.

PASTRY, MR
See HEARNE, RICHARD.

PATHFINDERS IN SPACE/ PATHFINDERS TO MARS/ PATHFINDERS TO VENUS

UK (ABC) Children's Science Fiction. ITV 1960/1960–1/ 1961

Prof. Wedgwood	**Peter Williams**
Conway Henderson	**Gerald Flood**
Geoffrey Wedgwood	**Stewart Guidotti**
Valerie Wedgwood	**Gillian Ferguson**
Jimmy Wedgwood	**Richard Dean**
Prof. Mary Meadows	**Pamela Barney**
Harcourt Brown	**George Coulouris**
Margaret Henderson	**Hester Cameron**
Ian Murray	**Hugh Evans**
Capt. Wilson	**Graydon Gould**

Creators: **Malcolm Hulke, Eric Paice**
Producer: **Sydney Newman**

Escapades in outer space with the pioneering Wedgwood family.

Following on from an adventure in six parts, which went out under the programme title, *Target Luna* (1960), this series featured three more adventures for an early space family: *Pathfinders in Space*, *Pathfinders to Mars* and *Pathfinders to Venus* were all broadcast as part of ITV's Sunday *Family Hour*.

In *Target Luna* (incidentally with a completely different cast), Professor Wedgwood had successfully managed to send his son, Jimmy, and pet hamster, Hamlet, into lunar orbit and back. In the first of the *Pathfinders* stories, the scientist and his family went a step further and actually landed on the moon. Despite being stranded on the surface and facing alien threats, they eventually escaped back home. In the second story the destination was Mars. Again fraught with danger, and despite unexpected outside interference, the expedition was once more a success. The third tale picked up from the return journey to Earth and involved the rescue of a rival astronaut from the planet Venus under the gaze of menacing pterodactyls and an erupting volcano. As well as members of the Wedgwood family, the adventures involved several other transient characters, in particular science reporter Conway Henderson and Professor Meadows, the leading female authority on space.

Pathfinders was produced by future DOCTOR WHO creator, Sydney Newman, and partly devised by Malcolm Hulke, writer of *Doctor Who* and CROSSROADS stories among other TV work. Although somewhat crude, the series was itself a pathfinder for children's science-fiction television.

PAUL TEMPLE

UK (BBC/Taurus) Detective Drama. BBC 1 1969–71

Paul Temple	**Francis Matthews**
Steve Temple	**Ros Drinkwater**
Kate Balfour	**June Ellis**
Eric	**Blake Butler**

Creator: **Francis Durbridge**
Producers: **Alan Bromly, Peter Bryant, Derrick Sherwin**

A writer of detective novels is also a part-time private eye.

Paul Temple, aged 30, impeccably bred, suave, cool and sophisticated, was also amazingly wealthy. Living in a swish Chelsea apartment with his 25-year-old wife, Steve, he needed to write only one book a year (three months' work) to maintain his extravagant lifestyle. Consequently, the couple spent the rest of their time touring Britain and Europe, using Paul's finely honed analytical mind to root out international criminals. Temple drove a Rolls-Royce Silver Shadow Coupé and thoroughly enjoyed his opulent existence, but he abhorred violence of all kinds.

The character of Paul Temple was created by writer Francis Durbridge back in the 1930s, and the inspiration is said to have been a fellow passenger on a train, who looked like a private detective. By 1938 Paul Temple had appeared on BBC Radio, conceived as a Canadian-born, Rugby School- and Oxford-educated son of an army officer. With some three dozen novels to his name, Temple had turned to amateur detection, helping out Scotland Yard with some of their more baffling crimes, and had met up with Steve Trent, a Fleet Street journalist whom he went on to marry. Six actors played the role on radio but some critics have suggested that the TV version (one of the BBC's first colour productions) was tailor-made for the urbane Francis Matthews.

PAXMAN, JEREMY
(1950–)

Leeds-born journalist and presenter, frontman of NEWS-NIGHT since 1989 and previously a reporter in Northern Ireland. Among his credits have been PANORAMA, TONIGHT, BREAKFAST TIME, *The Six O'Clock News* and regional programmes. Paxman took over from Ludovic Kennedy as chairman of the review programme, DID YOU SEE . . . ? and has since been questionmaster in the revival of UNIVERSITY CHALLENGE, as well as chairing the debate show, *You Decide*.

PAY PER VIEW

A system devised to allow viewers to watch certain additional programmes (films, sporting events, etc.) on the payment of an on-the-spot fee. Whereas the primitive concept looked at coins and slots as a method of payment, today's sophisticated technology uses telephones, credit cards, invoices and interactive digital networks.

P. D. JAMES

UK (Anglia) Police Drama. ITV 1983–5; 1988; 1991–8

Chief Supt./Commander Adam Dalgliesh	**Roy Marsden**

John Massingham .... **John Vine**

Producers: **John Rosenberg, Hilary Bevan Jones, Andrew Benson, Martyn Auty**

The assignments of pensive Scotland Yard detective Adam Dalgliesh.

Unlike Jim Taggart or Inspector Morse, Adam Dalgliesh never had his name in lights. All his adventures, adaptations of P. D. James's novels, aired under their individual book titles, but everyone knew he was the star. In fact, he had only one regular companion, the ambitious copper, John Massingham, and that was just for the first three investigations.

A Scotland Yard chief superintendent, Dalgliesh found himself promoted to commander in the story entitled *The Black Tower* and held the rank thereafter. He lived partly in London and partly in Norfolk, where the country lanes were leafy and the seaside towns quiet, but where, nevertheless, murders came thick and fast.

His first TV case, *Death of an Expert Witness*, aired in seven parts in 1983 (pre-dating his fellow cerebral cops Morse, Taggart and Wexford). Then followed *Shroud for a Nightingale, Cover Her Face, The Black Tower, A Taste for Death, Devices and Desires, Unnatural Causes, Mind to Murder, Original Sin* and *A Certain Justice*, most in serial form and filled with guest stars like Joss Ackland, Phyllis Calvert, Pauline Collins, Maurice Denham and Susannah York. They also all featured more than one murder for the tall, confident, morally sound detective to tackle and, true to the books, the plots were complicated and involved. Furthermore, in the best tradition of TV cops, Dalgliesh was not denied his quirks. Behind his rather formal, stuffy image, he was a competent poet, the son of an Anglican vicar. He was also a widower and lived alone in a converted windmill.

PEACOCK, MICHAEL
(1929–)

British news and current affairs producer (PANORAMA, etc.) who joined the BBC as a trainee in 1952 and was given the responsibility of launching BBC 2 in 1964. He later became Controller of BBC 1 and then was LWT's managing director in the late 1960s. After some time as an independent producer and consultant, Peacock joined Warner Brothers for a few years in the 1970s. Since 1989 he has been chairman of the production company, Unique Broadcasting.

PEAK PRACTICE
UK (Central/Carlton) Drama. ITV 1993–

Dr Jack Kerruish .... **Kevin Whately**
Dr Beth Glover .... **Amanda Burton**
Dr Will Preston .... **Simon Shepherd**
Sarah Preston .... **Jacqueline Leonard**
Dr Daniel Acres .... **Tom Beard**
Dr John Reginald .... **Andrew Ray**
Kim Beardsmore .... **Esther Coles**
Ellie Ndebala .... **Sharon Hinds**

Isabel de Gines .... **Sylvia Syms**
James White .... **Richard Platt**
Chloe White .... **Hazel Ellerby**
Sandy .... **Melanie Thaw**
Trevor Sharpe .... **Shaun Prendergast**
Alice North .... **Margery Mason**
Francine Sinclair .... **Veronica Quilligan**
Dr Andrew Attwood .... **Gary Mavers**
Dr Erica Matthews .... **Saskia Wickham**
Kate Webster .... **Shelagh McLeod**
Kirsty Attwood .... **Sukie Smith**
Russ Skinner .... **James Kerr**
Laura Elliott .... **Veronica Roberts**
Dr Pat Hewland .... **Elisabeth Sladen**
Dr David Shearer .... **Adrian Lukis**
Clare Shearer .... **Yolanda Vazquez**
                                                                Fiona Gillies
Emma Shearer .... **Jenni Gallagher**
Tom Shearer .... **Nicholas Harvey**
Norman Shorthose .... **Clive Swift**
Dawn Rudge .... **Sarah Parish**
Dr Joanna Graham .... **Haydn Gwynne**
Patricia Davey .... **Annette Ekblom**
Dr Sam Morgan .... **Joseph Millson**
Bridgit Mellors .... **Siobhan O'Carroll**
Rita Barratt .... **Anne Reid**
Dr Tom Deneley .... **Gray O'Brien**
Kate Turner .... **Lynsey Baxter**
Richard Turner .... **David Mallinson**
Kerri Davidson .... **Susannah Corbett**
Dr Alex Redman .... **Maggie O'Neill**

Creator: **Lucy Gannon**
Producers: **Tony Virgo, Michele Buck, Damien Timmer, Mervyn Gill-Dougherty, Phil Collinson**

Professional and personal problems for the staff of a Derbyshire general practice.

Dr Jack Kerruish was disillusioned with city life and city medicine. Having enjoyed a fulfilling three years establishing a medical centre in Africa, he returned to London in search of a new career direction. He wanted to join a country practice and was eventually accepted into a somewhat wobbly partnership in the Peak District village of Cardale (real-life Crich). His colleagues were Beth Glover and Will Preston, two local doctors who had decided to keep their independence and fight on in their dilapidated Beeches surgery when threatened by competition from a new, flashy health-centre. Kerruish's financial input was important, but he also brought new technology and dynamism to the practice. However, Kerruish soon found that, if the city had its problems, so did the country, as he came face to face with the everyday hardships of rural life and the emotional problems of the local community. There was also the practice to re-establish, the bank to stave off, and the rival health-centre to keep an eye on.

Kerruish was very much his own man. Sometimes selfish and insensitive, he often found himself at odds with his partners, even though he became romantically linked with Beth and, by the end of the second series, they had been married. In the third series, Kerruish's wanderlust had returned, and he and Beth eventually left Cardale for Africa. From the next series, their places alongside senior partner Will Preston were taken by newly qualified former electrician Andrew Attwood, a Liverpudlian, and the idealistic Erica Matthews, both of whom brought new inner-city ideas – and with them no shortage of friction – into the country backwater. A series later, Attwood temporarily left for Manchester and was replaced by Preston's friend, David Shearer, whose wife, Clare, suffered from manic depression. Attwood later returned to replace Preston and began a romance with Erica, which ended with her jilting him at the altar. Her replacement was hospital surgeon Joanna Graham. Joining the Beeches after the death of the adulterous Shearer was Sam Morgan, and another new arrival was ex-army medic Alex Redman.

PEAK TIME / PRIME TIME

The hours when TV audiences are at their greatest, and so the time of day of particular importance to advertisers. Known generally as peak time in the UK, the hours are 7.00–10.30 p.m. Prime time in the USA covers 7.30–11 p.m.

PEARSON, NEIL
(1959–)

London-born actor, best known as hot-headed CIB detective Tony Clark in BETWEEN THE LINES and newsroom romeo Dave Charnley in DROP THE DEAD DONKEY. Other credits have included *Submariners* ('Cock' Roach), *Chelmsford 123* (Mungo), *That's Love* (Gary), *Les Girls*, *This is David Lander*, the single drama, *Oi For England*, *Rhodes* (Dr Jameson), *Screen Two's Crossing the Floor* (New Labour leader Tom Peel), *See You Friday* (Greg), *Bostock's Cup* (Gerry Tudor), *The Magician's House* (Jack Green) and *Dirty Work* (Leo Beckett).

PEARSON TELEVISION

Pearson – part of the global media group, Pearson plc, which also owns Penguin Books and the *Financial Times* – has come from nowhere to become one of the world's major players in the television industry, largely by acquiring other production companies. First into the portfolio was Thames Television, the former ITV franchisee for London weekdays and still manufacturer of important series like THE BILL and THIS IS YOUR LIFE. More recent acquisitions have included Alomo (BIRDS OF A FEATHER, GOODNIGHT SWEETHEART), Witzend (AUF WIEDERSEHEN, PET), Grundy (NEIGHBOURS, *Going for Gold*) and Regent Television (FIFTEEN TO ONE). Pearson is also a major shareholder in Channel 5 and owns various other TV companies and distribution agencies around the world.

PEASGOOD, JULIE

Blonde British actress with a host of drama and sitcom credits to her name. Among the most notable parts have been Fran Pearson in BROOKSIDE, Roxy in SEPTEMBER SONG, Eden in LUV and Anne in FIRST BORN. Others have included SURVIVORS, *Seven Faces of Woman*, *Clayhanger*, LORD PETER WIMSEY, BOON, TAGGART, BRUSH STROKES, 2 POINT 4 CHILDREN, VAN DER VALK, *The 10%ers*, SPENDER, CHANDLER & CO., *A Woman's Guide to Adultery* (Sandra), PERFECT SCOUNDRELS and THE RUTH RENDELL MYSTERIES. She was TV critic for *Good Morning with Anne and Nick*, team captain in GIVE US A CLUE, and has been heard on many commercials.

PEBBLE MILL AT ONE / PEBBLE MILL
UK (BBC) Magazine. BBC 1 1972–86; 1991–6

Presenters: **Bob Langley, Tom Coyne, Marian Foster, David Seymour, Donny MacLeod, Jan Leeming, Bob Hall, Tony Francis, Philip Tibenham, Jonathan Fulford, Marjorie Lofthouse, David Freeman, Paul Gambaccini, Anna Ford, Paul Coia, Josephine Buchan, Magnus Magnusson; (1991–6) Judi Spiers, Alan Titchmarsh, Gloria Hunniford, Ross King, Sarah Greene**

Producers/Editors: **Terry Dobson, Roy Ronnie, Roger Ecclestone, Roger Laughton, Malcolm Nisbet, Jim Dumighan, Peter Hercombe**

Light-hearted early-afternoon magazine.

This frivolous lunchtime filler was the BBC's response to ITV's new afternoon series like CROWN COURT and EMMERDALE FARM. Broadcast live from the foyer of Pebble Mill, the BBC's Birmingham TV centre, it featured, among other items, music, celebrity interviews, fashion news, gardening with Peter Seabrook, keep fit with Eileen Fowler, *Collectors' Corner* with Arthur Negus, and cookery with Michael Smith and Glyn Christian. The title was shortened to *Pebble Mill* in later years and a few spin-off programmes were created. *Saturday Night at the Mill* ran from 1976, Norman Vaughan hosted *Pebble Mill Showcase* in 1978 and *Pebble Mill on Sunday* appeared in 1979. Although cancelled in 1986 to make way for the *One O'Clock News* and programmes like NEIGHBOURS, the series was revived as part of the BBC's daytime package in 1991, becoming more of a chat show, broadcast from a studio rather than the entrance hall.

PECK, BOB
(1945–99)

English Shakespearean actor whose major TV credit came in EDGE OF DARKNESS (Ronald Craven). He also appeared in dramas like *An Ungentlemanly Act* (Major Mike Norman), *After Pilkington*, *Who Bombed Birmingham?*, *Natural Lies* (Andrew Fell), *Deadly Summer* (Donald Hardcourt) and *The Scold's Bridle* (DS Cooper). He was married to actress Jill Baker.

PENHALIGON, SUSAN

(1950–)

British actress born in the Philippines who has enjoyed a number of prominent roles on television. Most notably, she was Prue Sorenson in A BOUQUET OF BARBED WIRE in 1976 and in 1987 starred in *Heart of the Country*. She was Helen in A FINE ROMANCE, guested in PUBLIC EYE, UPSTAIRS, DOWNSTAIRS, COUNTRY MATTERS, REMINGTON STEELE and BERGERAC, and has also appeared in single dramas like Jack Rosenthal's *Polly Put the Kettle on* and the BBC's 1977 adaptation of *Count Dracula*. In the 1990s Penhaligon was seen as Julia Charlesworth in *Trouble in Mind* and also in THE RUTH RENDELL MYSTERIES, among other series.

PENNIES FROM HEAVEN

UK (BBC) Drama. BBC 1 1978

Arthur Parker	Bob Hoskins
Eileen	Cheryl Campbell
Joan Parker	Gemma Craven
The Accordion Man	Kenneth Colley
Tom	Hywel Bennett
The Headmaster	Freddie Jones
The Inspector	Dave King

Writer: **Dennis Potter**
Producer: **Kenith Trodd**

An unhappily married sheet-music salesman finds life is not as kind as his songs make out.

Arthur Parker, an itinerant song-plugger and music salesman, really loved his music. Given the chance, he would drift away from his fractious marriage and into the fantasy world of song lyrics. A meeting with a young teacher named Eileen led him to be unfaithful to his wife, Joan, but the consequences of his actions came home to haunt him in a nightmare of abortion and prostitution set against the backdrop of the 1930s Depression.

What was innovative about *Pennies from Heaven* was the use of contemporary 1930s tunes to underpin the plot, their banal words given new meaning when contrasted with the various goings-on. As in Hollywood pictures, the actors suddenly broke into song and dance, but this time merely mimed to the original recordings. Sometimes, men mimed to women's voices and vice versa. It was a technique that Dennis Potter re-employed in THE SINGING DETECTIVE eight years later and again in the third part of his musical trilogy, LIPSTICK ON YOUR COLLAR, in 1993. A film version of *Pennies from Heaven*, also scripted by Potter and starring Steve Martin and Bernadette Peters, was made in 1981.

PENTELOW, ARTHUR

(1924–91)

Northern actor known to viewers as EMMERDALE's Henry Wilks for 19 years, having previously been seen in the football soap, UNITED! (supporters' club chairman Dan Davis) and plenty of other series, including EMERGENCY – WARD 10, Z CARS, THE TROUBLESHOOTERS, ARMCHAIR THEATRE, HADLEIGH, BUDGIE and CORONATION STREET (park-keeper George Greenwood).

PEPPARD, GEORGE

(1928–94)

American actor, popular in the cinema in the 1960s, after making his TV debut a decade earlier, in series like ALFRED HITCHCOCK PRESENTS. In the 1970s Peppard returned to the small screen, taking the role of MYSTERY MOVIE detective BANACEK. Two years into the series, he moved on to another prime-time drama, *Doctors' Hospital*, but left a year later. He then played Blake Carrington in the pilot for DYNASTY but was not given the series role and, just when it seemed that his career was petering out, up popped the character of cigar-chomping A-TEAM leader, Colonel John 'Hannibal' Smith, which made him a favourite with youngsters all over the world. Peppard was also seen in numerous TV movies.

PERFECT SCOUNDRELS

UK (TVS) Comedy Drama. ITV 1990–2

Guy Buchanan	Peter Bowles
Harry Cassidy	Bryan Murray

Creators: **Peter Bowles, Bryan Murray**
Executive Producer: **Graham Benson**
Producers: **Tim Aspinall, Terence Williams, Tony Virgo**

Two sophisticated con-men team up to swindle shadier members of society.

Meeting at the funeral of a master con-man, suave Guy Buchanan and rough diamond Harry Cassidy were coaxed into joining forces to avenge the death of their old ally. Executing an elaborate sting on the alleged murderer, the two lovable rogues discovered themselves swindled when the 'dead' man took care of the proceeds. However, realizing how well they performed in tandem, Guy and Harry made their double act permanent, despite personal differences which threatened their partnership. For instance, Harry, an Irish parrot-fancier, lacked vital discipline, which angered the smooth-talking Guy, and an element of mutual distrust pervaded their business dealings. They worked as latter-day Robin Hoods, for the most part picking only on those who ripped off others. The third and final season, though, showed the perfect scoundrels in a new light, as they occasionally targeted less deserving victims.

Actors Peter Bowles and Bryan Murray, who had worked together in THE IRISH RM, devised this series as a vehicle for their own talents.

PERRIE, LYNNE
(Jean Dudley; 1931–)

Pint-sized, Yorkshire-born actress and cabaret performer who played Ivy Tilsley/Brennan in CORONATION STREET from 1971 until written out in 1994. Previously, Perrie (sister of comic/actor Duggie Brown) had been seen in series like QUEENIE'S CASTLE (Mrs Petty), CROWN COURT and FOLLYFOOT, as well as in a number of single dramas, such as *Leeds United* and *Slattery's Mounted Foot.*

PERRY, JIMMY
OBE (1923–)

British actor and comedy scriptwriter, usually in collaboration with David Croft, with whom he created the doyen of British sitcoms, DAD'S ARMY (based on his own misadventures as a youth in the Home Guard). With Croft, Perry went on to script other comedy favourites like IT AIN'T HALF HOT MUM (echoing his time as a Royal Artillery concert-party manager), HI-DE-HI! (Perry was a Butlins redcoat) and YOU RANG, M'LORD?. Perry also penned THE GNOMES OF DULWICH, LOLLIPOP LOVES MR MOLE, *Room Service* and, with Robin Carr, wrote the shopkeeping sitcom, *High Street Blues.*

PERRY MASON
US (Paisano) Legal Drama. BBC 1 1961–7

Perry Mason	Raymond Burr
Della Street	Barbara Hale
Paul Drake	William Hopper
Hamilton Burger	William Talman
Lt. Arthur Tragg	Ray Collins
Lt. Anderson	Wesley Lau
Lt. Steve Drumm	Richard Anderson

Creator: **Erle Stanley Gardner**
Executive Producers: **Gail Patrick Jackson, Arthur Marks**
Producers: **Ben Brady, Art Seid, Sam White**

The cases of an almost invincible Los Angeles defence lawyer.

Created by writer-lawyer Erle Stanley Gardner in 1933, defence attorney Perry Mason was remarkable. His brilliant analytical mind, his vast experience in the legal field and his finely honed powers of advocacy enabled him to succeed in even the most hopeless cases. With any other attorney, dozens of defendants would have gone straight to the electric chair. With Perry Mason, not only were they acquitted but the real culprits were unearthed. It's true that he did, in fact, lose three cases, but all had mitigating circumstances, such as the defendant who refused to give evidence to clear her name.

Mason's technique was based on methodical, painstaking collation of all the evidence, relying heavily on Drake's ability to dig up some new facts. Very often the vital clues did not arrive until the last minute, with Drake charging into the courtroom to pass the information to his burly boss. It was then that Mason's verbal skills were put to the test, to extract a confession from one of the witnesses, or even one of the spectators. All this was particularly frustrating for prosecuting attorney Hamilton Burger, Mason's chief adversary, and the testifying police officer, Lt. Tragg (later replaced by Lt. Drumm). And just in case the audience had not been able to keep up with events, Perry, Paul and Della gathered together in the finale to talk through and explain each case.

In the very last episode, *The Case of the Final Fade-out*, creator Erle Stanley Gardner guest-starred as the judge. However, the series was revived in 1973 under the title of *The New Perry Mason*, with Monte Markham in the lead role. It bombed, but Raymond Burr picked up the reins again for a 1985 TV movie that saw Della accused of murder and Perry leaving his new-found place on the judges' panel to defend her. An intermittent run of feature-length episodes followed, in which Mason was assisted by Della and Paul Drake Jr, son of the original investigator (actor William Hopper had died and Barbara Hale's real-life son, William Katt, was drafted in to do the running around). Drake was later replaced by Ken Malansky, played by William R. Moses. William Talman, who had played Ham Burger, had also died and Mason now encountered a new opponent in Michael Reston, played by M*A*S*H's Major Winchester, David Ogden Stiers.

PERSUADERS!, THE
UK (Tribune/ITC) Adventure. ITV 1971–2

Danny Wilde	Tony Curtis
Lord Brett Sinclair	Roger Moore
Judge Fulton	Laurence Naismith

Creator/Producer: **Robert S. Baker**

Two playboys tackle corruption among the jet-set.

Danny Wilde was a rough diamond, a fun-loving American from the streets of Brooklyn. But he was also rich. Through skilful buying and selling of oil stocks, he had made himself into a multi-millionaire. In contrast, Lord Brett Sinclair had found things rather easy. Born into the English aristocracy and heir to a fortune, he had never needed to work. Together, they comprised an unlikely team of investigators, tracking down villains in the glamour spots of the world.

Their liaison stemmed from a party on the French Riviera at which they had both been guests. There they were coerced by a retired judge named Fulton into joining his fight for justice. He wanted them to use their spare time and many millions to help him catch those criminals who fell through the usual legal nets, realizing that they could work in places where conventional detectives could not go. Wilde and Sinclair took up the challenge as a bit of a lark, enjoying visiting Europe's high spots, wining and dining in all the best places and meeting scores of beautiful women along the way. As they came from totally different backgrounds and upbringings, the rapport between the two stars was one of the keystones of the programme.

Glossy and expensively produced, *The Persuaders!* was deliberately aimed at the American market. Sadly, it failed to take off in the States and as a result didn't last long in Britain. The theme music, by John Barry, was a Top 20 hit in the UK in 1971.

PERTWEE, BILL
(1926–)

British actor, usually in comic roles and best remembered as the obnoxious ARP Warden, Hodges, in DAD'S ARMY. He has also been seen in other Jimmy Perry and David Croft productions, including YOU RANG, M'LORD?, as the scrounging policeman, PC Wilson. He had earlier played another policeman, in the Sid James/Victor Spinetti sitcom, TWO IN CLOVER and among his other credits are roles in *The Norman Vaughan Show*, *Frost's Weekly*, *The World of Beachcomber*, SYKES, *Billy Liar*, *Chance in a Million* and *Tom, Dick and Harriet*. Bill was the cousin of the late Jon Pertwee.

PERTWEE, JON
(John Pertwee; 1919–96)

British actor, much heard in BBC Radio comedy in the post-war years and also making a few inroads into the cinema. However, it was television that gave Pertwee his finest hours. In 1970 he took over one of the classic roles on UK TV, namely that of DOCTOR WHO, succeeding Patrick Troughton. It was a part he played for four years. Pertwee was largely responsible himself for his next major series. He recalled Barbara Euphan Todd's WORZEL GUMMIDGE books and sold the concept of a series to Southern Television, securing himself the role of the famous talking scarecrow in the process. His other credits were as varied as the panel game, WHODUNNIT? (host), SIX-FIVE SPECIAL, JACKANORY, THE AVENGERS, THE GOODIES, a 1946 version of *Toad of Toad Hall*, and the early comedies, *Round the Bend* and *Evans Abode*. He was the son of writer Roland Pertwee, cousin of actor Bill Pertwee, brother of playwright Michael Pertwee and father of actor Sean Pertwee and actress Dariel Pertwee. Jon's first wife was UPSTAIRS, DOWNSTAIRS star Jean Marsh.

PETERS, SYLVIA

British television personality of the 1940s and 1950s, working as one of the BBC's on-screen continuity announcers (in rota with Mary Malcolm and McDonald Hobley). She joined the Corporation in 1947, making use of her talents as a former dancer to also introduce TELEVISION DANCING CLUB with Victor Sylvester and COME DANCING in its formative years. For children's television she read the *Bengo* stories. Peters eventually left the BBC to freelance for commercial television.

PETROCELLI
US (Paramount) Legal Drama. BBC 1 1978–9

Tony Petrocelli	**Barry Newman**
Maggie Petrocelli	**Susan Howard**
Pete Ritter	**Albert Salmi**
Lt. John Ponce	**David Huddleston**

Creators: **Sidney J. Furie, Harold Buchman, E. Jack Neuman**
Executive Producers: **Thomas L. Miller, Edward J. Milkis**

A Harvard-educated lawyer of Italian descent opens a legal practice for ranchers.

Tony Petrocelli and his wife, Maggie, had given up their lucrative city life and moved west into the fictitious town of San Remo, setting up home in a camper-van. Having hired ranch-hand Pete Ritter as an investigator, Petrocelli opened up a legal practice, providing help for the local cattle-farmers. Unfortunately, his sophisticated eastern methods were not always appreciated and many clients could not afford to pay him at the end of the day. As a result, the Petrocellis were not the richest attorney family in America. Lt. Ponce was Tony's friend, despite being the police officer who worked against him on many cases.

Based on the 1970 film, *The Lawyer*, in which Barry Newman played the part of Petrocelli, the series was innovative in using flashback sequences to show how crimes had occurred from the viewpoints of various characters. It was filmed in Tucson, Arizona.

PETTIFER, JULIAN
(1935–)

Wiltshire-born journalist and presenter, working for programmes like TONIGHT, PANORAMA and 24 HOURS after appearing on Southern Television. As well as award-winning reports from the Vietnam War and a raft of documentaries and nature programmes (including narrating *The Natural World* and presenting *Safari UK*), Pettifer has also hosted *Biteback* (the BBC viewers' response programme) and the quiz, BUSMAN'S HOLIDAY, and contributed to *Assignment*.

PEYTON PLACE
US (Twentieth Century-Fox) Drama. ITV 1965–70

Constance MacKenzie/Carson	**Dorothy Malone**
	Lola Albright
Allison MacKenzie	**Mia Farrow**
Dr Michael Rossi	**Ed Nelson**
Leslie Harrington	**Paul Langton**
Rodney Harrington	**Ryan O'Neal**
Norman Harrington	**Christopher Connelly**
Matthew Swain	**Warner Anderson**
Betty Anderson/Harrington/Cord/Harrington	
	Barbara Parkins
Julie Anderson	**Kasey Rogers**

George Anderson .... **Henry Beckman**
Dr Robert Morton .... **Kent Smith**
Steven Cord .... **James Douglas**
Hannah Cord .... **Ruth Warrick**
Elliott Carson .... **Tim O'Connor**
Eli Carson .... **Frank Ferguson**
Nurse Choate .... **Erin O'Brien-Moore**
Dr Clair Morton .... **Mariette Hartley**
Dr Vincent Markham .... **Leslie Nielsen**
Rita Jacks/Harrington .... **Patricia Morrow**
Ada Jacks .... **Evelyn Scott**
Mrs Dowell .... **Heather Angel**
Stella Chernak .... **Lee Grant**
Gus Chernak .... **Bruce Gordon**
Dr Russ Gehring .... **David Canary**
DA John Fowler .... **John Kerr**
Marian Fowler .... **Joan Blackman**
Martin Peyton .... **George Macready**
                                                        Wilfred Hyde-White
Sandy Webber .... **Lana Wood**
Chris Webber .... **Gary Haynes**
Lee Webber .... **Stephen Oliver**
Rachael Welles .... **Leigh Taylor-Young**
Jack Chandler .... **John Kellogg**
Adrienne Van Leyden .... **Gena Rowlands**
Eddie Jacks .... **Dan Duryea**
Carolyn Russell .... **Elizabeth 'Tippy' Walker**
Fred Russell .... **Joe Maross**
Marsha Russell .... **Barbara Rush**
Revd Tom Winter .... **Bob Hogan**
Susan Winter .... **Diana Hyland**
Dr Harry Miles .... **Percy Rodriguez**
Alma Miles .... **Ruby Dee**
Lew Miles .... **Glynn Turman**
Jill Smith/Rossi .... **Joyce Jillson**

Creator/Producer: **Paul Monash**

The inhabitants of a small New England town
have many dark secrets to hide.

Based on the novel by Grace Metalious, which had
already been adapted for two feature films, *Peyton Place*
found its way to the small screen courtesy of the success
of CORONATION STREET in the UK. Realizing that a TV
soap opera could be sustained in prime time on a twice-a-
week basis and was not just worthy of daytime filler
status, producer Paul Monash took up Metalious's tale
of sexual intrigue and closet skeletons to develop this
hugely successful series. It turned out to be the programme which made stars of Ryan O'Neal and Mia
Farrow, and was the first American soap to be sold to
Britain.

The setting for the series was the small, fictitious town
of Peyton Place in New England. The central characters
were bookstore-keeper Constance MacKenzie and her
illegitimate daughter, Allison, who was romantically
involved with Rodney Harrington, the son of wealthy
mill manager Leslie Harrington. There was also handsome, young GP Mike Rossi (Constance's heart-throb),
Betty Anderson (Rodney's wife on two occasions, who,
in between, married drunken lawyer Stephen Cord), and
Elliot Carson (Allison's secret father, who spent 18 years
in prison and who later ran the town newspaper).

Throughout the show's run, well over a hundred actors
and actresses were introduced, and the storyline wandered from trivial family scandals and illicit romances
right through to sensational murders and nail-biting
court cases.

The most significant event in the show's early years
was the disappearance of Allison MacKenzie. When Mia
Farrow left the series, her character was written out, lost
on a foggy night. Other notable storylines saw Rodney
acquitted of murder, the marriage of Norman Harrington (Rodney's younger brother) to Rita Jacks, daughter
of barkeeper Ada Jacks, and the death and funeral of the
town's father figure, Rodney's mill-owning grandfather,
Martin Peyton. When the series ended, Mike Rossi was
in the dock, on trial for murder, and Rodney was confined to a wheelchair.

Viewers of re-runs may be confused by seeing Lola
Allbright as Constance MacKenzie in some early epi-
sodes. She temporarily replaced Dorothy Malone, who
was seriously ill. Wilfred Hyde-White did the same for
George Macready, the actor who played Martin Peyton.
Return to Peyton Place, a daytime sequel employing differ-
ent actors, reached US screens in 1971, and several
members of the original cast resurfaced in a couple of
TV movies, *Murder in Peyton Place* (1977) and *Peyton Place:
The Next Generation* (1985).

PHIL SILVERS SHOW, THE
US (CBS) Situation Comedy. BBC 1957–60

M/Sgt Ernest T. Bilko .... **Phil Silvers**
Cpl. Rocco Barbella .... **Harvey Lembeck**
Cpl. Henshaw .... **Allan Melvin**
Col. John Hall .... **Paul Ford**
Pte. Duane Doberman .... **Maurice Gosfield**
Pte. Sam Fender .... **Herbie Faye**
Sgt Rupert Ritzik .... **Joe E. Ross**
Pte. Dino Paparelli .... **Billy Sands**
Pte. Zimmerman .... **Mickey Freeman**
Mrs Nell Hall .... **Hope Sansberry**
Sgt Grover .... **Jimmy Little**
Sgt Joan Hogan .... **Elisabeth Fraser**

Creator/Writer: **Nat Hiken**
Producers: **Nat Hiken, Edward J. Montagne**

A sharp-witted, scheming sergeant is head of a US
Army platoon.

Master Sgt Ernie Bilko was an inmate of the fictitious
Fort Baxter army camp, near Roseville, Kansas (and later
at Camp Freemont, California), although inmate is probably not the right word. Nominal head of the base was
Colonel John Hall, but it was Bilko who pulled all the
strings, certainly as far as his own comfortable lifestyle
was concerned. Not many army sergeants could sleep in
late, come and go as they pleased, avoid physical labour
or drive around in their CO's car. But not every sergeant
was Sgt Bilko.

This balding, bespectacled motor-pool NCO was the
master of the money-making scam. He'd bet on anything, from drill competitions to shooting practices. If a
good singer turned up in his platoon, he'd use him to

win a choir contest or secretly tape his voice to sell to a record company. He had an eagle eye for losers and set out to take them to the cleaners. However, his best-laid plans often backfired, mostly because, behind his brash exterior, Bilko was too kind-hearted and couldn't go through with the kill.

Assisting Bilko with his schemes were his corporals, Barbella and Henshaw, and his inept company of enlisted men, most notably the fat, dozy Doberman (regularly employed as a fall-guy) and the pessimistic Pte. Fender. Although loyal to Bilko, the platoon was also wary of its sergeant, knowing his conniving ways; but, in fairness, Bilko was always very protective of his boys. One of his easier preys was the superstitious Mess Sgt Ritzik, another compulsive gambler.

The series comprised a run of poker games, betting coups and other outrageous money-making ventures, all doomed to failure. But the highlight was quick-thinking, smooth-talking Bilko himself, who could extricate himself from the tightest of corners with a phoney smile, a sackful of charm and a few empty promises. Joan Hogan provided Bilko's romantic interest, although he was not averse to flattering Mrs Hall, the Colonel's wife, if doing so opened a few doors.

Originally titled *You'll Never Get Rich* when first screened in America, *The Phil Silvers Show* has also been billed as *Sgt Bilko*. It has enjoyed re-run after re-run all over the world and helped establish many careers, especially among its writers, who included creator Nat Hiken and future playwright Neil Simon. The show also gave opportunities to up-and-coming young actors like Dick Van Dyke and Alan Alda (the casting director for the series was ex-world boxing champion Rocky Graziano, whose real name, incidentally, was Rocco Barbella, the same as one of Bilko's corporals). Maurice Gosfield, who played Doberman, later provided the voice for Benny the Ball in the Bilko cartoon spoof, BOSS/TOP CAT.

Four years after the series ended, Phil Silvers resurfaced in the role of Harry Grafton, a devious factory foreman, in *The New Phil Silvers Show*, but the programme lasted only one season.

PHILBIN, MAGGIE
(1955–)

Manchester-born presenter, coming to light on MULTI-COLOURED SWAP SHOP, on which she appeared with Keith Chegwin, whom she married (and divorced). Philbin later hosted *The Show Me Show*, TOMORROW'S WORLD, *Hospital Watch* and *Bodymatters Roadshow*, as well as lifestyle programmes such as *Countdown to Christmas*.

PHILIP MARLOWE
US (ABC) Detective Drama. BBC 1960

Philip Marlowe .... **Philip Carey**

Raymond Chandler's famous detective given a rather smoother edge.

This TV portrayal of Chandler's celebrated gumshoe transformed Marlowe from a rough diamond into a softer, more gentlemanly type. His name and his devoutly independent status were the only echoes of the hard-bitten character made famous by Humphrey Bogart. A truer interpretation followed in 1984, in *Marlowe – Private Eye*, a five-episode LWT series starring Powers Boothe. Six more episodes, again featuring Boothe, were made in Canada in 1986.

PHILLIPS, CONRAD
(Conrad Philip Havord; 1925–)

One of British TV's first action heroes, Conrad Phillips played the title role in THE ADVENTURES OF WILLIAM TELL in 1958. Previously, apart from small parts in series like THE COUNT OF MONTE CRISTO and THE NEW ADVENTURES OF CHARLIE CHAN, Phillips had worked in the theatre, and it was to the stage that he returned for most of the 1960s. He resurfaced to play Robert Malcolm in THE NEWCOMERS and, in the 1970s and 1980s, was a guest in numerous series, from SUTHERLAND'S LAW, CRIBB and HOWARDS' WAY to FAWLTY TOWERS, NEVER THE TWAIN and SORRY!. He appeared in the 1973 drama, *The Man Who Was Hunting Himself*, played NY Estates' MD Christopher Meadows in EMMERDALE FARM and was also seen in children's dramas like *Into the Labyrinth*, mini-series like *The Master of Ballantrae* and TV movies such as *Arch of Triumph*. He was back in William Tell country in the late 1980s for a Franco-American version entitled *Crossbow*, in which he played Tell's mentor, Stefan.

PHILLIPS, SIÂN
CBE (1934–)

Welsh actress, winning much acclaim for her portrayal of the manipulative Livia in I, CLAUDIUS. She also played Clemmie in WINSTON CHURCHILL – THE WILDERNESS YEARS, George Smiley's wife Ann in TINKER, TAILOR, SOLDIER, SPY and *Smiley's People*, and appeared in the dramas, *Siwan* (title role), *How Green Was My Valley* (Beth Morgan), *Shoulder to Shoulder* (Emmeline Pankhurst), JENNIE, LADY RANDOLPH CHURCHILL (Mrs Patrick Campbell), *Warrior Queen* (Boudicca), *Crime and Punishment* (Katerina Ivanova), *The Borrowers* (Mrs Driver), *Ivanhoe* (Queen Eleanor), *The Scold's Bridle* (Mathilda Gillespie), ARISTOCRATS (Lady Emily) and *The Magician's House* (Meg Lewis). Among her other offerings have been *The Quiet Man*, *Heartbreak House*, *Off to Philadelphia in the Morning* and *Vanity Fair*, plus guest spots in the likes of JACKANORY and PERFECT SCOUNDRELS. Her second husband was actor Peter O'Toole.

PHILPOTT, TREVOR
(1924–98)

Northampton-born reporter and trend-setting documentary-maker, once with TONIGHT, PANORAMA and MAN ALIVE, but then given his own series, including *The Philpott File* (from 1969).

PHOENIX, PATRICIA
(Patricia Pilkington; 1923–86)

As CORONATION STREET's brassy Elsie Tanner, Irish-born, Manchester-raised Pat Phoenix became one of TV's favourite scarlet women. She joined the series at its outset in 1960, having worked her way through the theatre and performed as a youngster on radio's *Children's Hour*. She had even written scripts for Harry Worth and Terry Hall and Lenny the Lion. Phoenix played the fiery Elsie for 24 years (apart from a few years away in the 1970s) and, when she left the *Street* in 1984, she remained on our screens in the sitcom, *Constant Hot Water* (playing Phyllis Nugent, a seaside landlady), and as an agony aunt for TV-am. Her last TV role was in *Hidden Talents*, a drama in the *Unnatural Causes* anthology series, in which she played a bedridden actress. Phoenix was at one time married to her screen partner, Alan Browning, but they had separated before he died. Shortly before she herself died, of lung cancer in 1986, she wed her companion and old friend, actor Tony Booth.

PICKERING, RON
(1930–91)

London-born athletics coach who became a highly respected BBC sports commentator. Pickering's break came when he discovered young Welsh long-jumper Lynn Davies, whom he coached to a gold medal at the Tokyo Olympics in 1964. He joined the BBC for coverage of the 1968 Olympics and never looked back, becoming the Corporation's main athletics pundit and covering other events such as basketball. Pickering was also seen as host of THE SUPERSTARS and WE ARE THE CHAMPIONS.

PICKLES, WILFRED
OBE (1904–78)

British actor and presenter whose Yorkshire accent caused some consternation when he began reading the news on national radio in the 1940s. Pickles was also popular a decade later, when he hosted (together with his wife, Mabel) *Ask Pickles* for the BBC. A sort of heavily sentimental SURPRISE, SURPRISE of its day, it specialized in reuniting members of families. Pickles also took to acting, gaining guest spots in series like DR FINLAY'S CASEBOOK before securing a starring role in the senior citizens' romantic comedy, FOR THE LOVE OF ADA (grave-digger Walter Bingley). Pickles also hosted STARS ON SUNDAY for a while.

PICTURE BOOK
UK (BBC) Children's Entertainment. BBC 1955–63

Presenters: **Patricia Driscoll, Vera McKechnie**

Writer: **Maria Bird**
Producers: **Freda Lingstrom, David Boisseau**

Early toddlers' magazine programme.

The Monday segment of the WATCH WITH MOTHER strand belonged to *Picture Book* from 1955 to the mid-1960s (including re-runs). Hosted initially by Patricia Driscoll, with stories read by Charles E. Stidwill, the programme was taken over by Vera McKechnie when Driscoll left to star as Maid Marian in THE ADVENTURES OF ROBIN HOOD.

Picture Book was more of a magazine programme than an early JACKANORY, with Driscoll and McKechnie turning the pages to introduce various items. One page showed how to make something – paper lanterns, for instance. Another introduced the puppet adventures of Bizzy Lizzy, a wispy-haired little girl with a magic wishing flower on her dress. Bizzy Lizzy was allowed four wishes by touching the flower, but if she wished a fifth time all her wishes flew away. She later starred in a series of her own. *Picture Book* also had a page for animals, and more puppets, the Jolly Jack Tars, filled another. These sailors in their berets and hooped shirts drifted across the ocean to strange lands like Bottle Island, sometimes in search of the 'Talking Horse'. The principals were the Captain (complete with bushy moustache), Mr Mate, Jonathan the deck-hand and Ticky the monkey. Before the last page was turned and it was time to 'put the *Picture Book* away' for another day, Sausage, the programme's marionette dachshund, was also usually seen.

PICTURE PAGE
UK (BBC) Magazine. BBC 1936–9; 1946–52

Presenters: **Joan Miller, Joan Gilbert, Mary Malcolm**

Creator/Editor: **Cecil Madden**
Producers: **George More O'Ferrall, Royston Morley, Harold Clayton, John Irwin, Stephen McCormack, Michael Mills**

Early magazine programme curiously based around a telephone switchboard.

Canadian actress Joan Miller was the presenter of *Picture Page*, and for this role she took the part of a telephone operator. In very contrived fashion, she called up the guests who had been booked to appear and patched them into vision. As 'The Switchboard Girl', Miller became one of TV's earliest personalities, pre-dating even the official opening of the BBC television service (*Picture Page* began life as an experimental test programme before 'real' programming began). Miller was assisted in proceedings by Leslie Mitchell, who took care of the interviews, and also seen were Jasmine Bligh and John Snagge. About 20 items were packed into each hour-long edition and two programmes a week were transmitted. Among the guests persuaded to appear were Danny Kaye, Maurice Chevalier, Will Hay, Sabu, Dinah Sheridan and Sophie Tucker. When the television service was revived after the war, *Picture Page* came back, too, with Joan Gilbert taking over as presenter.

PIE IN THE SKY
UK (Witzend) Detective Drama. BBC 1 1994–7

Henry Crabbe	**Richard Griffiths**
Margaret Crabbe	**Maggie Steed**
ACC Freddy Fisher	**Malcolm Sinclair**
WPC/Sgt Sophia Cambridge	**Bella Enahoro**
Steve Turner	**Joe Duttine**
Linda	**Alison McKenna**
John	**Ashley Russell**
Henderson	**Nick Raggett**
Nicola	**Samantha Janus**
Gary Palmer	**Nicholas Lamont**
PC Ed Guthrie	**Derren Litten**
PC Jane Morton	**Mary Woodvine**
Sally	**Marsha Thomason**

Creator: **Andrew Payne**
Producers: **Jacky Stoller, David Wimbury, Chrissy Skinns**

A detective-turned-restaurateur is called back into action against his will.

After 25 years in the police force, podgy Det. Inspector Henry Crabbe decided to retire from Barstock CID and pursue a new career based on his hobby, gastronomy (and, in particular, traditional British cooking). Unfortunately, his accountant wife was not so keen, nor was Freddy Fisher, the Assistant Chief Constable who valued Crabbe's investigative skills. Despite opening his own restaurant, named Pie In The Sky, in the fictitious town of Middleton, Henry was not allowed to take full retirement. A little unfortunate incident in his last case was used by Fisher to blackmail Crabbe into staying on part-time, resulting in the rotund chef being constantly dragged away from his kitchen and once again into police matters.

At his restaurant, Crabbe was a perfectionist, carefully choosing his vegetables from Henderson, a small local grower who also worked as washer-up. In addition, Crabbe kept his own chickens, whose nerves he soothed with extracts from Elgar. Steve Turner, an ex-con, and later Gary Palmer were taken on as co-chefs. WPC Cambridge was usually the bringer of bad tidings from the local nick.

In the final series, Crabbe was forced to take charge of the PDS (Public Duties Squad) and against his best instincts was obliged to hire himself out to private companies as a means of raising money for the police. He was joined by two similarly sidelined officers, the upper-class Jane Morton and northerner Ed Guthrie.

The series was created by Andrew Payne specifically for star Richard Griffiths, and Griffiths was closely involved in the development of the programme and its characters. With a recipe or cooking tip included in every episode, *Pie in the Sky* proved popular with foodies as well as crime fans.

PIG IN THE MIDDLE
UK (LWT) Situation Comedy. ITV 1980–3

Nellie Bligh	**Liza Goddard**
Bartholomew 'Barty' Wade	**Dinsdale Landen**
	Terence Brady
Susan Wade	**Joanna Van Gyseghem**

Creators/Writers: **Charlotte Bingham, Terence Brady**
Producer: **Les Chatfield**

A middle-aged man drifts between his wife and his mistress.

Barty and Susan Wade were a middle-class couple living in East Sheen. Sadly, Barty's life was not his own and he was constantly nagged by his fussy wife. At one of Susan's many parties, Barty met up with fun-loving Nellie Bligh and, taking her as his 'other woman', was able to indulge himself in many of the happy pursuits Susan had banned. However, despite Nellie's advances, Barty remained celibate. Even when he eventually walked out on his wife, it was only to move in next door to Nellie. When Dinsdale Landen left the series, the programme's co-writer, Terence Brady, stepped into the lead role.

PIGOTT-SMITH, TIM
(1946–)

British actor, an award-winner for his portrayal of bigot Ronald Merrick in THE JEWEL IN THE CROWN. He also starred in *Fame Is the Spur*, was Brendan Bracken in WINSTON CHURCHILL – THE WILDERNESS YEARS, Hardy in *I Remember Nelson*, Steve Marsh in the sitcom, *Struggle*, King Ferdinand in *The True Adventures of Christopher Columbus*, Hubert in *Screen One*'s *The Bullion Boys*, Chief Constable John Stafford in THE CHIEF and James Wisheart in the drama-doc, *Innocents*. Other appearances have come in classic plays (including Shakespeare) and in dramas like WINGS, THE GLITTERING PRIZES, *North and South*, *The Hunchback of Notre Dame*, *The Lost Boys*, *The Secret Case of Sherlock Holmes*, the HORIZON special, *Life Story*, *Ghosts* and, like many other actors, DOCTOR WHO.

PILGER, JOHN
(1939–)

Award-winning Australian journalist working in the UK since 1958 and specializing in hard-hitting investigations. From a background with the *Daily Mirror* and on WORLD IN ACTION, Pilger has gone on to expose the atrocities of Cambodia in *Year Zero – The Silent Death of Cambodia*, the treatment of Vietnam War veterans back home in the USA, and to compile reports on hidden matters in Nicaragua, Japan and other countries. In 1974 he was given his own series, *Pilger*, and more recent exposés have included *Death of a Nation* (focusing on Indonesian brutality in East Timor); the *Network First* report, *Inside Burma: Land of Fear; Apartheid Did Not Die* (a return to South Africa); and *Paying the Price: the Killing of the Children of Iraq.*

PILOT

A trial programme for a possible series. A pilot is used to see if the idea works, to iron out any previously unforeseen problems and, if aired, to gauge public response. Sometimes the pilot is then used as the first episode of the series or is repeated as a prologue to the series. Pilots are also sometimes aired as part of an anthology, with COMEDY PLAYHOUSE a classic example. This series of pilots has resulted, over the years, in sitcoms like STEPTOE AND SON, TILL DEATH US DO PART and THE LIVER BIRDS. In the 1970s the trend in the USA was to produce feature-length TV movies as pilots. Consequently, *The Marcus Nelson Murders* served as the pilot for KOJAK, *Smile Jenny You're Dead* for HARRY O, etc.

PINK PANTHER SHOW, THE
US (DePatie-Freleng) Cartoon. BBC 1 1970–7

The Inspector .... **Pat Harrington, Jr** (*voice only*)

Executive Producers: **David DePatie, Friz Freleng**

The animated misadventures of a hapless pink cat.

The Pink Panther was originally created for the Blake Edwards film of the same name, starring Peter Sellers as the bungling Inspector Henri Clouseau on the trail of a stolen gemstone called The Pink Panther. The cartoon cat appeared only in the titles sequence, and then for only a few seconds. However, the exposure was enough to earn some cinema releases of his own, before this TV version began in America in 1969.

The series initially contained some puppet sketches and was hosted by comedian Lenny Schultz. More familiar to UK viewers, however, were the 100 per cent cartoon packages which followed, with the series' name changing a number of times as its animated components alternated. The classic combination comprised two Panther cartoons sandwiching the latest case of the Inspector, an inept Clouseau clone. Other notable partners for the Panther were the Ant and the Aardvaark, and Crazylegs Crane. Yet there was only one star, The Pink Panther himself – 'the one and only, truly original panther, Pink Panther, from head to toe'.

Plodding around on his hind legs, the flat-footed pink cat with a long, looping tail was a compulsive do-gooder, a character whose best-laid plans were guaranteed to go awry. Stoically accepting every disaster Nature hurled his way (apart from an occasional gnashing of the teeth or the raising of an eyebrow), the stone-faced, silent feline was completely resigned to the catastrophes in his life. He was so accident-prone that on a bright, sunny day, a single cloud was known to hover over his head, spouting rain. All this as Henry Mancini's 'durrum, durrum' theme music wafted along in the background.

The opening and closing sequences were familiar, too, showing The Panther being ushered in and out of a flashy (real-life) sports car, parked outside the show's theatre. Although it earned some lengthy runs in the BBC's Saturday teatime slot, the show was also well employed as a filler programme, plugging gaps when sporting events overran or another series finished early. In addition, the programme generated an enormous amount of cheap merchandising, ranging from pencil cases to sickly pink chocolate bars.

PINKY AND PERKY
UK (BBC/Thames) Children's Entertainment. BBC/ITV
1957; 1960–8/1970–1

Creators: **Jan Dalibor, Vlasta Dalibor**
Producers: **Trevor Hill, Stan Parkinson**

Pop music and fun with two puppet piglets.

Created by Czech immigrants Jan and Vlasta Dalibor, Pinky and Perky were Britain's favourite string puppets in the late 1950s and early 1960s. The twin pigs were identical in all respects, except that Pinky wore red and Perky wore blue (not much use on black-and-white TV), and that Perky usually donned a beret in front of the cameras. Their repertoire consisted of high-pitched (fast-forwarded tape) jokes and songs, including versions of contemporary pop hits. Their theme song was 'We Belong Together'. The piglets ran their own fictitious television station, PPC TV, which employed some of their animal friends, the likes of Horace Hare, Ambrose Cat, Conchita the cow, Morton Frog, Basil Bloodhound, Bertie Bonkers the baby elephant, Vera Vixen and a bird pop group called The Beakles. The various human straight men keeping them company (at different times) were John Slater, Roger Moffat, Jimmy Thompson, Bryan Burdon and Fred Emney. The prancing porkers' series were given various titles, including *Pinky and Perky's Pop Parade, Pinky and Perky's Island* and *Pinky and Perky Times*.

PINTER, HAROLD
CBE (1930–)

British dramatist, widely applauded for his dialogues but criticized by some for the obscure nature of his plays. He was initially commissioned for stage and radio, but came to the fore via ARMCHAIR THEATRE in 1960 with his first television play, *A Night Out*. After further dramas for ITV – *Night School* (also 1960), *The Collection* (1961) and, more controversially, *The Lover* (1963) – Pinter switched to the BBC. He wrote *Tea Party* for a pan-European anthology series entitled *The Largest Theatre in the World* in 1965, which he followed with *The Basement*, a visually adventurous offering for BBC 2's *Theatre 625* in 1967. Although Pinter then branched out into cinema work, he returned to the small screen in 1973 with a contribution entitled *Monologue* and, three years later, his drama, *The Collection*, was screened in the prestigious anthology, *Laurence Olivier Presents . . .*, with Olivier himself in the cast. Pinter's adaptation of Aidan Higgin's *Langrishe, Go Down* was shown as a *Play of the Week* in 1978 and *The Hothouse* followed in 1982 with, at the end of the decade, *The Heat of the Day*, adapted from Elizabeth Bowen's novel. In

1992 his *Old Times* was a *Performance* presentation, and a year later his adaptation of Kafka's *The Trial* was shown as a *Screen Two* film. Pinter's first wife, Vivien Merchant, starred in some of his earliest works and Pinter himself occasionally appeared, too, under the stage name of David Baron. He was also seen in the 1964 adaptation of Sartre's *In Camera* and in the 1976 drama, *Rogue Male*. Pinter later married novelist/historian Lady Antonia Fraser.

PIPKINS

See INIGO PIPKIN.

PLANE MAKERS, THE/ THE POWER GAME

UK (ATV) Drama. ITV 1963–5/1965–6; 1969

John Wilder	Patrick Wymark
Pamela Wilder	Barbara Murray
	Ann Firbank
Don Henderson	Jack Watling
Arthur Sugden	Reginald Marsh
Kay Lingard	Norma Ronald
Henry Forbes	Robert Urquhart
Sir Gordon Revidge	Norman Tyrrell
James Cameron-Grant, MP	Peter Jeffrey
Sir Gerald Merle	William Devlin
Caswell Bligh	Clifford Evans
Kenneth Bligh	Peter Barkworth

Producers: **Rex Firkin, David Reid**

Friction between unions and bosses at an aircraft factory.

The Plane Makers was set in the hangars and workshops of the fictitious Scott Furlong aircraft factory and focused on industrial strife and management quandaries among the 5,000 staff as they developed the exciting new Sovereign aircraft. In the first series, the cast varied week by week but, from the start of the second season, the company's managing director, John Wilder, was the man everyone was beginning to hate, outshining other characters like works manager Arthur Sugden and chief test pilot Henry Forbes. Wilder was to take on even greater prominence when the series was renamed *The Power Game* after two years. With the action transferred off the shop floor and into the boardroom, more attention was given to Wilder's wheelings and dealings. After the failure of a vertical take-off aircraft (Veetol) project, the bullying businessman left Scott Furlong, took a seat on the board of a bank and picked up a knighthood. He began scheming in pastures new and encountered fresh rivals in the shape of North Country tycoon Caswell Bligh and his son, Kenneth. When the final series was shown in 1969, three years after the previous run, Sir John was ensconced in diplomatic circles as a member of the Foreign Office (Ambassador for Special Situations and Trade), burrowing away for Britain around the world (each episode title was prefixed with his role, 'Special Envoy'). The series ended with the sudden death of its star, Patrick Wymark.

PLANER, NIGEL

(1955–)

British actor and writer, usually in comedy roles. His break came with *The Comic Strip* (which he helped to found with Peter Richardson, his partner in an act called The Outer Limits) and he subsequently appeared in the troupe's run of TV films. He broke into television by writing for NOT THE NINE O'CLOCK NEWS and playing Lou Lewis in SHINE ON HARVEY MOON. Then came THE YOUNG ONES, in which he created the role of the hippy Neil, which won him a cult following. Planer followed this with a more conventional sitcom in ROLL OVER BEETHOVEN (rock'n'roll star Nigel Cochrane), but returned to anarchy as Filthy in FILTHY RICH AND CAT-FLAP. He moved on to light drama in *King and Castle* (debt-collector David Castle) and heavier matters in Dennis Potter's BLACKEYES. Planer was also seen in BLACKADDER, played a pregnant man in the drama, *Frankenstein's Baby*, George Pepperly in *Unnatural Pursuits* and Jocelyn Pride in the single drama, *Cuts*, and offered viewers acting advice in *Nicholas Craig – The Naked Actor* and its various sequels. In 1992 he took over from the late Eric Thompson as writer and narrator of THE MAGIC ROUNDABOUT and a year later starred as hapless French teacher Laurence Didcott in *Bonjour La Classe*. Planer also played Malvolio in the schools' series, *Shakespeare Shorts*, and featured in THE GRIMLEYS (Baz Grimley).

PLANET OF THE APES, THE

US (Twentieth Century-Fox) Science Fiction. ITV 1974–5

Galen	Roddy McDowall
Alan Virdon	Ron Harper
Pete Burke	James Naughton
Urko	Mark Lenard
Zaius	Booth Colman

Executive Producer: **Herbert Hirschman**
Producer: **Stan Hough**

Two astronauts crash-land on a planet ruled by apes, where man is the subservient race.

On 19 August 1980, three American astronauts were approaching the Alpha Centauri system when they ran into radioactive turbulence. Activating an automatic homing device, they were sent spinning back to Earth, but through a time-warp that dumped them over 1,100 years into the future. One of the crew, Jonesy, died on impact but there were two survivors, Alan Virdon and Pete Burke. They discovered an Earth with a remarkably different social structure from the planet they had left. In the year 3085, man was no longer in control. A holocaust had come and gone, during which the monkey race had taken over the planet. Orang-utans were the ruling species, gorillas were the violent law-enforcers and chimpanzees the more gentle intellectuals. The apes talked, wore clothes, rode horses and toted guns. Humans were simply slaves and menial workers.

Virdon and Burke began a life on the run, steering clear of gorilla guerrillas and seeking a way of returning to their own time. Only an inquisitive, peace-loving chimpanzee named Galen afforded them any assistance as they hid from angry Urko, the gorilla chief of security. Zaius was the more rational orang-utan councillor who tried to keep Urko in check. However, the series ended without conclusion after only 14 episodes. It had not been a success in the USA.

The programme was based on the successful film series that began with *Planet of the Apes* and ended with *Battle for the Planet of the Apes*, in which Roddy McDowall played various lead ape roles similar to Galen. The original idea came from Pierre Boulle's book, *The Monkey Planet*.

PLATER, ALAN
(1935–)

North-eastern writer with many credits. Plater has contributed to series like Z CARS, SOFTLY, SOFTLY, CRANE, CRIBB, FLAMBARDS, THE ADVENTURES OF SHERLOCK HOLMES, CAMPION, MAIGRET, MISS MARPLE, FRANK STUBBS and DALZIEL AND PASCOE, as well as presenting his own original series like *The First Lady*, OH NO! IT'S SELWYN FROGGITT, TRINITY TALES, *The Loner*, *Middlemen* and *Oliver's Travels*, plus THE BEIDERBECKE AFFAIR and its two sequels, *The Beiderbecke Tapes* and *The Beiderbecke Connection*. He has also penned original plays like *Ted's Cathedral*, *To See How Far It Is* (a 1968 trilogy for *Theatre 625*), *Close the Coalhouse Door*, *Seventeen Per Cent Said Push Off*, *The Land of Green Ginger* and the 1977 *Premiere* film, *Give Us A Kiss, Christabel*. Plater has also adapted other works for the small screen, like A. J. Cronin's *The Stars Look Down*, Trollope's *The Barchester Chronicles*, Olivia Manning's FORTUNES OF WAR, L. P. Hartley's *Feet Foremost*, J. B. Priestley's *The Good Companions* and Chris Mullin's *A Very British Coup*. Other notable scripts have included *A Day in Summer*, *Misterioso*, *The Referees* and *Orwell on Jura*.

PLAY AWAY
UK (BBC) Children's Entertainment. BBC 2 1971–84

Presenters: **Brian Cant, Derek Griffiths, Chloe Ashcroft, Lionel Morton, Toni Arthur, Julie Stevens, Carol Chell, Rick Jones, Miranda Connell, John Styles, Johnny Silvo, Johnny Ball, Norman Norman, David Wood, Julie Covington, Tony Robinson, Anita Dobson, Floella Benjamin, Nerys Hughes, Alex Norton, Delia Morgan**

Producers: **Cynthia Felgate, Ann Reay, John Smith, Anne Gobey, Jeremy Swan**

Entertainment and education for younger children.

A natural progression from PLAY SCHOOL, *Play Away* was a Saturday afternoon programme aimed at children up to the age of seven. Accordingly, it featured somewhat less infantile games and songs than were seen in its well-established sister programme and also threw in a few jokes. The series did, however, share many of the same presenters (the most prominent mentioned above), although some new faces were also introduced (including a young Jeremy Irons). A studio audience added to the fun. Music was provided by pianist Jonathan Cohen and the Play Away Band, and the theme song was written by Lionel Morton.

PLAY FOR TODAY
UK (BBC) Drama Anthology. BBC 1 1970–84

Influential collection of single dramas.

Play for Today was effectively THE WEDNESDAY PLAY under a different name (the transmission day having moved to Thursday) and what the latter had contributed to 1960s TV drama, the former emulated in the 1970s and early 1980s. The *Play for Today* collection featured tragedies, comedies and fantasies, with, among its most celebrated offerings, Jim Allen's *The Rank and File*, Jeremy Sandford's *Edna, The Inebriate Woman* (both 1971), Hugh Whitemore's *84 Charing Cross Road* (1975), Mike Leigh's *Nuts in May* (1976) and ABIGAIL'S PARTY (1977), Jack Rosenthal's *Bar Mitzvah Boy* (1976), Dennis Potter's *Blue Remembered Hills* (1979) and Jeremy Paul and Alan Gibson's THE FLIPSIDE OF DOMINICK HIDE and *Another Flip for Dominick* (1980 and 1982). The series also introduced RUMPOLE OF THE BAILEY in 1975 and won notoriety for two plays that were initially banned: Dennis Potter's *Brimstone and Treacle* (1976, eventually screened in 1987) and Roy Minton's *Scum* (1977, screened in 1991).

PLAY OF THE MONTH
UK (BBC) Drama Anthology. BBC 1 1965–79; 1982–3

Sunday-night collection of old and new plays.

Airing originally once a month, as its title suggests, but then more sporadically, this anthology of single dramas won much acclaim for its treatment of established works and also for its new commissions. Noted offerings included John Osborne's *Luther* in 1965, Rudolph Cartier and Reed de Rouen's *Lee Oswald – Assassin* in 1966, Arthur Miller's *Death of a Salesman* also in 1966, David Mercer's *The Parachute* in 1968, and adaptations of E. M. Forster's *A Passage to India* in 1965 and *A Room with a View* in 1973, by Santha Rama Rau and Pauline Macauley, respectively.

PLAY SCHOOL
UK (BBC) Children. BBC 2 1964–88

Presenters: **Patrick Abernethy, Bruce Allen, Mike Amatt, Nigel Anthony, Stan Arnold, Toni Arthur, Chloe Ashcroft, Johnny Ball, Janine Barry, Ben Bazell, Floella Benjamin, Stuart Bradley, Christopher Bramwell, Brian Cant, Stephen Cartwright, Carol Chell, Gordon Clyde, John Colclough, Miranda Connell, Kate Copstick, Hilary Crane, Brian Croucher, Paul Danquah, Simon Davies, Ray C. Davis, Jonathan Dennis, Susan Denny, Marian Diamond, Diane Dorgan, Heather Emmanuel, Sheelagh Gilbey, Jon Glover, John Golder, Gordon**

Griffin, Derek Griffiths, Elvi Hale, Jane Hardy, David Hargreaves, Fred Harris, Maggie Henderson, Terence Holland, Wayne Jackman, Emrys James, Brian Jameson, Colin Jeavons, Kerry Jewell, Lloyd Johnson, Jona Jones, Rick Jones, Dawn Keeler, Judy Kenny, Robin Kingsland, Robert Kitson, Marla Landi, Ian Lauchlan, Phyllida Law, Carole Leader, Sarah Long, Bridget McCann, Stuart McGugan, Nigel Makin, Michael Mann, Dibbs Mather, Nick Mercer, Elizabeth Millbank, Mary Miller, Delia Morgan, Ann Morrish, Lionel Morton, Susan Mosco, Carmen Munroe, Libby Murray, Jennifer Naden, Lesley Nightingale, Janet Palmer, Angela Piper, Valerie Pitts, Karen Platt, Peter Reeves, Gordon Rollings, Beryl Roques, Sheila Rushkin, Dev Sagoo, Michael Scholes, Andrew Secombe, Shireen Shah, Johnny Silvo, Lucie Skeaping, Evelyn Skinner, Jon Skolmen, Don Spencer, Julie Stevens, Virginia Stride, Ben Thomas, Eric Thompson, Christopher Tranchell, Valerie Turnbull, Miguel Villa, Carole Ward, Liz Watts, John White, Mela White, Wally Whyton, Rod Wilmott, Heather Williams, Barry Wilsher, Fraser Wilson, Rosalind Wilson, Lesley Woods, Sam Wyse, Lola Young

Creator: **Joy Whitby**

Fun and games for the pre-school age.

'Here is a house. Here is a door. Windows: one, two, three, four. Ready to knock? Turn the lock. It's *Play School*.' These were the words that introduced the under-fives to *Play School*, the first programme seen on BBC 2. It wasn't meant to be the first, but a celebration outside broadcast from Paris the night before had been wiped out by a power cut and the honour of opening up Britain's third TV channel fell to the first programme in the next day's schedule (*Play School* went out at 11 a.m.).

A mixture of songs, mimes and stories, *Play School* provided a daily dose of mild education and entertainment for the youngest viewers for 24 years. In its heyday there were two presenters per programme (one male, one female), aided by William Blezard on piano, and each pair worked for a whole week before giving way to two of their colleagues. They were ably assisted by the *Play School* toys: two bears, Little Ted and Big Ted; two dolls, the staid Hamble (retired and replaced in 1986 by Poppy, a black doll) and raggy Jemima; and the villain of the piece, Humpty, a stuffed egg with arms, legs and a face. Dressed up and bounced on many a knee, these toys became known to every child in the land. The show also had a rocking horse, Dapple, and real animals. Katoo, the cockatoo, was the best known, alongside rabbits George and Peter, a guinea-pig called Elizabeth, Henry and Henrietta mice and two goldfish, Bit and Bot.

The programme opened with a study of the calendar, with the day, month and date carefully spelled out, and each day had a theme. Monday was Useful Box Day, Tuesday was Dressing-up Day, Wednesday was Pets Day, Thursday was Ideas Day, and Friday Science Day. A central feature was the glance at the clock and a chance to tell the time, using the 'big hand, little hand' system, followed by a look at the models at the base of the clock that set the scene for the daily story (sometimes told by a guest reader: the first tale was *Little Red Hen*, read by Athene Seyler). After all this came the dilemma of which window to look through – the arched, the square or the round – before a film about some outside activity or workplace. All these features were held together by a series of songs, dances, mimes and games of pretend, led by presenters who tended to overuse the prompt: 'Can you do that?' Songs about catching fishes alive and wibbly, wobbly walks were used over and over again, and some renditions were more tuneful than others.

The programme brought to light many notable performers whose talents were only hinted at by their monosyllabic duties here. The first show's presenters were Virginia Stride and Gordon Rollings (later Arkwright in the John Smith's beer commercials), and among other fondly remembered hosts were the whimsical Brian Cant, mime specialist Derek Griffiths, ex-Four Pennies vocalist Lionel Morton, quirky Johnny Ball and dreadlocked Floella Benjamin. Emma Thompson's parents, Phyllida Law and Eric (MAGIC ROUNDABOUT) Thompson, were also prominent in the show's early days, as was musician Rick Jones, subsequently presenter of *Fingerbobs*.

PLAY UK

Dedicated to the youth market, the cable/digital channel Play UK combines music with comedy, mixing new programming with repeat showings. Part of the UKTV group of channels.

PLAY YOUR CARDS RIGHT
UK (LWT/Talbot) Game Show. ITV 1980–7; 1994–

Presenter: **Bruce Forsyth**

Creator: **Chester Feldman**
Producers: **David Bell, Alasdair Macmillan, Paul Lewis**

Game show involving some general knowledge and a lot of luck with cards.

A 'higher or lower' card game, *Play Your Cards Right* combined knowledge of public opinion with a little gambling technique. Contestant couples guessed how many people out of a survey sample of 100 believed this or that. The first couple's guess was used as a marker by the second couple, who then simply stated 'higher' or 'lower'. The winners took control of the card game and progressed along a board, turning over playing cards, guessing whether the next card would be higher or lower than the one before. A wrong answer gave control to their opponents. For contestants successfully negotiating the final card round, and amassing enough points by gambling along the way, the prize was a new car. Enthusiastically hosted as ever by Bruce Forsyth, the series generated plenty of new Brucie catchphrases, most notably 'You get nothing for a pair – not in this game', 'What do points make? Prizes!' and 'It could still be a big night, if you play your cards right.'

Under the name of *Bruce Forsyth's Play Your Cards Right*, the show returned to the screen in 1994, after an absence of seven years. The concept was derived from the US game show, *Card Sharks*.

PLAYING THE FIELD

UK (Tiger Aspect/BBC) Drama. BBC 1 1998–

Theresa Mullen	**Lesley Sharp**
Jo Mullen	**Jo McInnes**
Luke Mullen	**Ralph Ineson**
Matthew Mullen	**Chris Walker**
Mrs Mullen	**Elizabeth Spriggs**
Mr Mullen	**James Ellis**
Eddie Ryan	**John Thomson**
Rita Dolan	**Melanie Hill**
John Dolan	**James Nesbitt**
Geraldine Powell	**Lorraine Ashbourne**
Dave Powell	**Tim Dantay**
Diane Powell	**Debra Stephenson**
Rick Powell	**Nicholas Gleaves**
Sharon 'Shazza' Pearce/Mullen	**Marsha Thomason**
Gabrielle Holmes	**Saira Todd**
Angie Gill	**Tracey Whitwell**
Jim Pratt	**Ricky Tomlinson**
Francine Pratt	**Brigit Forsyth**
Garry McGreer	**Dorian Healy**
Kate Howard	**Olivia Caffrey**
Mikey	**Emma Rydal**
Ryan Pratt	**Lee Ross**
Scott Bradley	**James Thornton**
Holly	**Gaynor Faye**
Pauline Pearce	**Annette Bentley**
Kelly Powell	**Claudie Blakley**

Creator: **Kay Mellor**
Executive Producers: **Charles Brand, Tessa Ross**
Producers: **Greg Brenman, Hugh Warren, Kathleen Hutchison**

More off- than on-the-field drama with a team of women footballers.

Although a South Yorkshire women's football team lay at the heart of this emotional drama, most of the action took place away from the pitch and inside the personal lives of the players and their families. In the first episode, for instance, Theresa Mullen was due to marry long-time lover Eddie Ryan, but the weak-willed Ryan bailed out at the last minute. All this while Theresa was summoning up the courage to tell her young sister, Jo, that she was really her natural mother, and while Theresa's mum struggled against agoraphobia. Captain of the Castlefield Blues was Geraldine Powell, battling to get out of an extra-marital affair with her brother-in-law, Rick; and also prominent was mother-of-two Rita Dolan, whose husband John, an ex-pro, was coerced into taking the job of team coach by sponsor Jim Pratt. Pratt's company, J. P. Electrics, funded the team against the wishes of his snooty wife, Francine. Other players included Rick's glamorous wife Diane, lesbian Angie Gill, drug-taker Shazza and policewoman-goalkeeper Gabby Holmes. In later series, new players like Irish midwife Kate Howard, loner Mikey and firewoman Holly, plus a new coach, Scott Bradley, were introduced, as was the Pratts' untrustworthy son, Ryan.

PLEASE SIR!

UK (LWT) Situation Comedy. ITV 1968–72

Bernard Hedges	**John Alderton**
Norman Potter	**Deryck Guyler**
Miss Doris Ewell	**Joan Sanderson**
Mr Cromwell	**Noel Howlett**
Mr Price	**Richard Davies**
Mr 'Smithy' Smith	**Erik Chitty**
Eric Duffy	**Peter Cleall**
Frankie Abbott	**David Barry**
Dennis Dunstable	**Peter Denyer**
Maureen Bullock	**Liz Gebhardt**
Sharon Eversleigh	**Penny Spencer**
	Carol Hawkins
Peter Craven	**Malcolm McFee**
Penny Wheeler/Hedges	**Jill Kerman**
Mr Dix	**Glynn Edwards**
Mr David Ffitchett-Brown	**Richard Warwick**
Miss Petting	**Vivienne Martin**
Gobber	**Charles Bolton**
Terry Stringer	**Barry McCarthy**
Daisy	**Rosemary Faith**
Des	**Billy Hamon**
Celia	**Drina Pavlovic**

Creators/Writers: **John Esmonde, Bob Larbey**
Producers: **Mark Stuart, Phil Casson**

A hesitant, naïve teacher's first job is in a rough inner-city school.

Recent graduate Bernard Hedges secured his first appointment as English and History teacher at Fenn Street Secondary Modern, under the auspices of headmaster Mr Cromwell. From the start, his unruly class, 5C, went out of their way to make life difficult for him, but they soon came to respect the bashful yet dedicated master, whom they nicknamed 'Privet'.

Behind the desks the youths included loudmouth Frankie Abbot, who acted hard but always ran to his mother; slow-witted Dennis, who came from a deprived home; brash class-leader Eric Duffy; flirtatious Penny; and Maureen, the evangelical Christian who had a crush on her teacher. The staff were just as unhelpful. Apart from the incompetent headmaster, there was thick-skinned Welshman Pricey teaching maths and science; formidable deputy-head Doris Ewell; dithery old Smithy; and former Desert Rat caretaker Norman Potter, who was terrified of the kids but enjoyed great influence with the headmaster. After a couple of years, Hedges acquired a girlfriend, Penny Wheeler, who went on to become his wife.

Please Sir!, LWT's first big comedy success, was inspired by the 1967 film, *To Sir, with Love*. Its own feature film was released in 1971 and a spin-off, *The Fenn Street Gang*, followed on TV, tracing the lives of the teenagers after leaving school. *Please Sir!* continued simultaneously for one more year, but the new kids and teachers introduced failed to catch on. The American version was *Welcome Back Kotter*, featuring a young John Travolta among the pupils.

PLEASENCE, DONALD
(1919–95)

British actor, a specialist in macabre and sinister roles. In addition to his long film career, Pleasence was seen in numerous TV dramas, including Dennis Potter's *Blade on the Feather*, Joe Orton's *The Good and Faithful Servant*, the tabloid satire, *Scoop*, and Gerald Savory's adaptation of *Double Indemnity*. He was Syme in the classic Nigel Kneale version of 1984, Prince John in THE ADVENTURES OF ROBIN HOOD, Melchior in JESUS OF NAZARETH, Reverend Septimus Harding in *The Barchester Chronicles* and also starred in THE RIVALS OF SHERLOCK HOLMES, in which he played Carnacki, the ghost-hunter. He made a number of mini-series and TV movies (one of his last appearances was as Victor in *Screen Two's Femme Fatale*) and was seen as a guest in THE OUTER LIMITS, DICK TURPIN and COLUMBO. Occasionally, he appeared with his actress daughter, Angela Pleasence.

PLOWRIGHT, DAVID
CBE (1930–)

Distinguished British TV executive, closely associated with Granada Television, which he joined in 1957 having previously been a newspaper journalist. With Granada, he worked on regional news magazines before moving up to edit WORLD IN ACTION. In 1968 he was made the station's Programme Controller, in 1975 its Managing Director and in 1987 Chairman of the company. He has also been an important figure in the ITV network and was once Chairman of the Independent Television Companies Association and a director of ITN. In his time at Granada, Plowright – brother of actress Joan Plowright – was widely respected and involved himself closely in programming matters. He even produced episodes of CORONATION STREET. However, in 1992, to the dismay of many of his colleagues, he left in controversial circumstances, reputedly concerned at the company's lack of commitment to, and investment in, quality programming. From then until 1997 he was deputy chairman of Channel 4.

POGLES' WOOD
UK (Smallfilms) Children's Entertainment. BBC 1 1966–7

Voices: **Oliver Postgate, Olwen Griffiths, Steve Woodman**

Creator/Writer/Producer: **Oliver Postgate**

The fairy-tale adventures of a woodland family.

Originally entitled *The Pogles* (BBC1 1965), *Pogles' Wood* focused on the day-to-day happenings in the yokel life of the industrious Mr Pogle, his domesticated wife, their son Pippin and pet squirrel Tog, all of whom lived in a tree in the heart of the forest. Their magic bean plant was also closely monitored. However, the witch who added a touch of menace in *The Pogles* had long since departed by the time *Pogles' Wood* began. Film footage of the countryside was cut into each episode and the wonders of nature were admired. This WATCH WITH MOTHER contribution, with puppets by Peter Firmin, proved so popular that it gave birth to a children's comic, *Pippin*.

POINTS OF VIEW
UK (BBC) Viewer Response. BBC 1 1961–71; 1979–

Presenters: **Robert Robinson, Kenneth Robinson, Barry Took, Anne Robinson, Carol Vorderman, Terry Wogan**

Fast-moving viewer-response programme.

This sprightly little offering was originally conceived as a five-minute filler for dropping in before the news, but it has become one of the BBC's longest-running programmes. It has consisted chiefly of viewers' moans and groans about the Corporation's output, though not all feedback has been negative. Extracts from letters have been read out on air by announcers and, strangely, most contributions seem to have begun with the words 'Why, oh why, oh why?'. Critics have knocked the programme for offering only token criticism of the BBC and for being of little constructive benefit. The presenters' cheery put-downs have perhaps fostered this idea.

Robert Robinson was the original host, followed by Kenneth Robinson. Barry Took picked up the reins in the late 1970s and Anne Robinson was in the hot seat for a number of years. Having the name Robinson obviously helps if you want to host *Points of View* (Tony Robinson was also once a stand-in – one of many guest presenters).

Robert Robinson also presented a children's version, *Junior Points of View* (1963–70), a job he shared with Sarah Ward and Gaynor Morgan Rees.

POIROT
See AGATHA CHRISTIE'S POIROT.

POLDARK
UK (London Films/BBC) Drama. BBC 1 1975–7

Capt. Ross Poldark	Robin Ellis
Elizabeth Chynoweth/Poldark	Jill Townsend
George Warleggan	Ralph Bates
Francis Poldark	Clive Francis
Verity Poldark	Norma Streader
Charles Poldark	Frank Middlemass
Demelza Carne/Poldark	Angharad Rees
Caroline Penvenen/Enys	Judy Geeson
Jud Paynter	Paul Curran
Prudie	Mary Wimbush
Nicholas Warleggan	Nicholas Selby
	Alan Tilvern
Dr Dwight Enys	Richard Morant
	Michael Cadman
Sir Hugh Bodrugan	Christopher Benjamin
Lady Constance Bodrugan	Cynthia Grenville
Capt. Malcolm McNeil	Donald Douglas

Mr Nat Pearce	**John Baskcomb**
Pascoe	**Ralph Nossek**
Zacky Martin	**Forbes Collins**
Paul Daniel	**Pip Miller**
Sam Carne	**David Delve**
Drake Carne	**Kevin McNally**
Revd Osborne Whitworth	**Christopher Biggins**
Morwenna Chynoweth/Whitworth	**Jane Wymark**
Rowella Chynoweth	**Julie Dawn Cole**

Producers: **Morris Barry, Anthony Coburn, Richard Beynon, Colin Tucker**

An 18th-century Cornish squire fights to keep his estate in order and his emotions in check.

Returning home (believed dead) from doing battle with the Americans in their War of Independence, dashing Cornish squire Ross Poldark discovered his late father's estate in ruin, the tin mines up for sale and the love of his life, Elizabeth, betrothed to his cousin Francis. Determined to rectify matters, Ross set about tackling the local powers that be, especially the loathsome George Warleggan. He aimed to re-establish the Poldark name and to bring justice to his workers and other oppressed Cornish folk. He even took on the invading French. However, one battle he struggled to win was with his heart over the fair Elizabeth, even after she was married to Francis and he to Demelza, the fiery, nit-ridden, urchin servant-girl he had made pregnant.

Winston Graham's novels were adapted by the BBC into 29 serial episodes and, thanks in no small part to the good looks of its leading man, *Poldark* was one of the most popular dramas of its time. The story was revived by HTV in 1996 in a two-hour sequel costing around £1.5 million and set ten years after the close of the BBC serial. John Bowe and Mel Martin took over the roles of Ross and Demelza in the Winston Graham story, *Strangers from the Sea.*

POLE TO POLE
See **AROUND THE WORLD IN 80 DAYS.**

POLICE
UK (BBC) Documentary. BBC 1 1982

Editor: **John Shearer**

Out and about with the officers of the Thames Valley Police.

This warts-and-all documentary series focused on E Division of the Thames Valley Police as they patrolled the streets of Reading and its environs over a nine-month period. Among various incidents, it showed the force organizing a stake-out for a planned robbery and, at the other extreme, saw officers accused of beating up a drunk. One detective broke down in tears after being demoted, but the most controversial of the 11 episodes dealt with a rape case in which police treatment of the victim brought howls of protest. The series was directed by Roger Graef and Charles Stewart.

POLICE FIVE
UK (ATV/LWT) Factual. ITV 1962–90

Presenter: **Shaw Taylor**

Short filler programme in which police request help in solving crimes.

With questions like 'Were *you* in the neighbourhood', host Shaw Taylor appealed for viewers' assistance in tracking down criminals and preventing future incidents. Produced in conjunction with New Scotland Yard, this series focused on crimes in the capital, although regional equivalents were also shown in other ITV areas. Taylor's parting advice was, 'Keep 'em peeled.' LWT also produced *Junior Police Five* in the 1970s.

POLICE SQUAD!
US (Zucker/Zucker/Abrahams/Paramount) Situation Comedy. ITV 1983

Frank Drebin	**Leslie Nielsen**
Capt. Ed Hocken	**Alan North**
Ted Olson	**Ed Williams**
Johnny the Snitch	**William Duell**
Officer Norberg	**Peter Lupus**
Al	**John Wardell**

Creators/Executive Producers: **Jerry Zucker, David Zucker, Jim Abrahams**
Producer: **Bob Weiss**

Ridiculous satire on all established cop shows.

Police Squad!, from the team that produced the cinema hit, *Airplane*, was a zany, over-the-top collection of word-plays and sight gags that parodied every cliché and action sequence of 'serious' police programmes. Its star, Leslie Nielsen, played the stone-faced Frank Drebin, whose rank varied from lieutenant down to sergeant. Gathered around him were his boss, Captain Hocken, lecherous lab technician Ted Olson, Officer Norberg, and Johnny the Snitch, a shoeshine boy with all the latest words on the street (in fact he could answer questions on anything, as long as someone was paying). There was also Al, an officer so tall his face never fitted on the screen. Old TV gimmicks were ripe for the picking: the narrator read out a different episode title from that shown on the screen, 'Tonight's Guest Star' was instantly murdered and forgotten for the rest of the show, and the programme ended with the classic freeze-frame finish seen in many early series, only this time it was the actors themselves who did the freezing, struggling to hold their poses as the credits rolled by.

Only six episodes of *Police Squad!* were made, however, and its ratings were low, probably because the programme demanded so much attention from viewers with its many puns and background jokes. All the same, the series did spawn a few successful feature films, *The Naked Gun: From the Files of Police Squad!, The Naked Gun*

$2^1/_2$: *The Smell of Fear* and *The Naked Gun* $33^1/_3$: *The Final Insult*, not to mention a collection of Red Rock cider advertisements.

POLICE SURGEON
UK (ABC) Police Drama. ITV 1960

Dr Geoffrey Brent	**Ian Hendry**
Insp. Landon	**John Warwick**
Amanda Gibbs	**Ingrid Hafner**

Producers: **Julian Bond, Leonard White**

A police doctor gets too involved in his cases.

Geoffrey Brent was a doctor with the Bayswater police who had the knack of solving cases which baffled his detective colleagues. The programme was seen by many as the basis for THE AVENGERS, as Ian Hendry soon went on to fill the similar role of Dr David Keel in the first episodes of that long-running series. This British-made *Police Surgeon* should not to be confused with the Canadian series of the same name, starring Sam Groom.

POLICE WOMAN
US (David Gerber/Columbia) Police Drama. ITV 1975–9

Sgt Suzanne 'Pepper' Anderson	**Angie Dickinson**
Lt. Bill Crowley	**Earl Holliman**
Det. Joe Styles	**Ed Bernard**
Det. Pete Royster	**Charles Dierkop**
Cheryl	**Nichole Kallis**
Lt. Paul Marsh	**Val Bisoglio**

Creator: **Robert Collins**
Executive Producer: **David Gerber**
Producer: **Douglas Benton**

A glamorous policewoman works undercover for the Los Angeles Police Department.

Blonde divorcée Pepper Anderson worked for the criminal conspiracy bureau of the LAPD, as part of the vice squad, taking on unusual undercover roles. Posing as a prostitute, a stripper, a gangster's moll and other ladies of the underworld, she infiltrated the seamier side of LA society, backed up by her colleagues, Joe Styles and Pete Royster. The drama came from the highly risky (and risqué) situations in which she was placed. The squad chief, and Pepper's best friend, was Lt. Bill Crowley. In the earliest episodes, Pepper's autistic sister, Cheryl, a student at a special school, was occasionally seen.

Police Woman was a spin-off from an American anthology series called *Police Story*, in which Angie Dickinson once appeared as an officer named Lisa Beaumont.

POLLARD, SU
(1949–)

British actress, comedian and singer, specializing in daffy females. It was as Peggy, the ambitious chalet maid in HI-DE-HI!, that she made her name, having earlier appeared on OPPORTUNITY KNOCKS and with Paul Nicholas in a short-lived sitcom entitled *Two Up, Two Down*. She played Peggy for eight years and followed it with virtually the same role in YOU RANG, M'LORD?, this time in the guise of parlourmaid Ivy Teasdale, and again in OH DOCTOR BEECHING!, as ticket clerk Ethel Schumann. Pollard also sang the theme song ('Starting Together') for the fly-on-the-wall documentary series, *The Marriage*, and other credits have included the kids' comedy, *Clock on*, THE COMEDIANS, *Summer Royal* and *Get Set for Summer*.

PORRIDGE
UK (BBC) Situation Comedy. BBC 1 1974–7

Norman Fletcher	**Ronnie Barker**
Lennie Godber	**Richard Beckinsale**
Mr Mackay	**Fulton Mackay**
Mr Barrowclough	**Brian Wilde**
Ingrid Fletcher	**Patricia Brake**
Harry Grout	**Peter Vaughan**
Lukewarm	**Christopher Biggins**
McLaren	**Tony Osoba**
Warren	**Sam Kelly**
Mr Geoffrey Venables	**Michael Barrington**
Blanco Webb	**David Jason**
Harris	**Ronald Lacey**
Cyril Heslop	**Brian Glover**
Ives	**Ken Jones**
Judge Stephen Rawley	**Maurice Denham**

Writers: **Dick Clement, Ian La Frenais**
Producer: **Sydney Lotterby**

Fun behind bars with a wise old lag and his ingenuous young cell-mate.

Norman Stanley Fletcher was a habitual criminal who accepted imprisonment as an occupational hazard, according to his trial judge. So it was that this Muswell Hill wide-boy with a heart of gold was sentenced to a five-year term in HMP Slade, an isolated prison in deepest Cumbria. Much against his wishes, he was forced to share a cell with young Lennie Godber, a first-time offender from Birmingham, embarking on a two-year stretch for breaking and entering. Fletch became a father-like figure to the amiable Godber, helping him to weather his first period of confinement, showing him the tricks of survival and leading him through the vagaries of prison etiquette.

Fletcher's considerable experience in incarceration brought him respect from most of the criminals around him, the likes of 'Bunny' Warren, illiterate and easily led; decrepit Blanco; 'Black Jock' McLaren, the Glaswegian heavy; and Lukewarm, the gay cook. But there were also less agreeable inmates like 'Orrible' Ives, the slimy Harris and 'genial' Harry Grout, the wing's Mr Big, who ran all the rackets and enjoyed life's little luxuries in his own comfortably appointed private room. On the other side of the fence was Mr Mackay, the chief warder. Despairing of the ineffective governor, Mr Venables, he longed to regiment the prisoners and rule the prison with an iron jackboot. But, like his easily conned, hen-pecked assistant, Mr Barrowclough, he was never a match for our hero.

Laced together with Fletcher's sparkling wit and skilful repartee, *Porridge* extolled the ironies and paradoxes of prison life, never glorifying life inside but cleverly commenting on the difficulties and pressures endured by convicted criminals. The series – which grew out of a play called *Prisoner and Escort*, seen as part of the *Seven of One* Ronnie Barker anthology in 1973 – became a firm favourite in jails all across Britain. However, a short-lived TV sequel, *Going Straight* (1978), featuring Fletcher's life back on the outside, failed to reach the heights of the original. A cinema version of *Porridge* was released in 1979.

PORTER, ERIC
(1928–95)

London-born actor who won acclaim for his TV portrayal of Soames in THE FORSYTE SAGA. He was later seen in dramas like *Churchill and the Generals* (Sir Alan Brooke), *Anna Karenina* (Alexei Karenin), WINSTON CHURCHILL – THE WILDERNESS YEARS (Neville Chamberlain), *Oliver Twist* (Fagin), THE ADVENTURES OF SHERLOCK HOLMES (Moriarty) and THE JEWEL IN THE CROWN (Count Dimitri Bronowski). His television appearances dated back to the 1950s.

PORTER, NYREE DAWN
OBE (1940–2001)

New Zealand-born actress seen on British TV in single dramas and series like *Madame Bovary* (title role), THE FORSYTE SAGA (Irene), *The Liars* (Hermione), *Never a Cross Word* (Deirdre Baldock) and THE PROTECTORS (the Contessa di Contini). Lesser roles came in DOCTOR IN CHARGE and *Anne of Green Gables*, among other programmes.

PORTERHOUSE BLUE
UK (Picture Partnership) Comedy. Channel 4 1987

Skullion	David Jason
Sir Godber Evans	Ian Richardson
The Dean	Paul Rogers
Senior Tutor	John Woodnutt
The Bursar	Harold Innocent
The Praelector	Ian Wallace
Cornelius Carrington	Griff Rhys Jones
Lionel Zipser	John Sessions
Prof. Siblington	Willoughby Goddard
Sir Cathcart D'eath	Charles Gray
Mrs Biggs	Paula Jacobs
Lady Mary Evans	Barbara Jefford

Writer: **Malcolm Bradbury**
Producer: **Brian Eastman**

A new principal attempts to drag an ancient college into the modern world and finds his efforts resisted.

Porterhouse, the most archaic of Cambridge colleges, found itself in the hands of a new Master, Sir Godber Evans. Evans wanted to abandon many college traditions and bring procedures up to date, but was resisted chiefly by the old head-porter, Skullion, who was summarily sacked after 45 years' service. This four-part adaptation of Tom Sharpe's black comedy depicted the ensuing developments, including a famous scene in which thousands of inflated condoms were released up the college chimneys, floated around the elegant spires and settled in the college grounds.

POSTLETHWAITE, PETE
(1945–)

Northern English actor whose recent success in the cinema has overshadowed his TV work. On the small screen his major roles have included parts in *The Muscle Market* (Danny), *Martin Chuzzlewit* (Montague Tigg), SHARPE (Obadiah Hakeswill), *Lost for Words* (Deric Longden), *Butterfly Collectors* (DI John McKeown) and *The Sins* (Len Green).

POSTMAN PAT
UK (BBC/Woodlands Animation) Animation. BBC 1
1981–2; 1991–2; 1995–7

Narrator: **Ken Barrie**

Creator/Writer: **John Cunliffe**
Producer: **Ivor Wood**

The daily rounds of a rural postman.

Accompanied by Jess, his black-and-white cat, Postman Pat did the rounds of the countryside around Greendale (based on the Lake District), providing assistance above and beyond the call of duty to the local residents. These included postmistress Mrs Goggins; Reverend Peter Timms; the bike-riding, posh Miss Hubbard; Granny Dryden; farmers George Lancaster and Alf Thompson; builder Ted Glen; mobile shopkeeper Sam Waldron; lady doctor Sylvia Gilbertson; PC Selby; and Major Forbes, who lived at Garner Hall. Pat's family was also seen: wife Sarah and son Julian. His red post-van bore the registration number PAT 1. The stories were written by John Cunliffe, best remembered as the canalboat-owning master of ROSIE AND JIM. Bryan Daly provided the music and narrator Ken Barrie's rendition of the catchy theme song entered the UK charts no fewer than three times between 1982 and 1983, but on no occasion climbing higher than number 44. However, when the song was played as a joke on Terry Wogan's radio show, it brought the programme to the attention of a wider audience and sparked a merchandising boom on which the real-life Post Office capitalized with glee.

POST-PRODUCTION

The work done on a programme after the recording has finished. This principally involves editing and sound dubbing.

POT BLACK/POT BLACK TIMEFRAME
UK (BBC/White Rabbit) Snooker. BBC 2 1969–86; 1991–3

Creator/Commentator: **Ted Lowe**
Presenters: **Keith Macklin, Alan Weeks, David Icke, Eamonn Holmes, David Vine**

Producers: **Philip Lewis, Reg Perrin, David Kenning, John G. Smith**

Innovative TV snooker championship.

An ideal exhibition vehicle for colour television, *Pot Black*, a popular, one-frame, annual snooker tournament, was devised by 'whispering' commentator Ted Lowe. The series, unexpectedly, ran and ran but was eventually overshadowed by the extensive televising of 'real' snooker. As such, it became a victim of its own success and was taken off in 1986. *Junior Pot Black* was produced instead. *Pot Black* returned, hosted by Eamonn Holmes, in 1991. A year later it was revamped as *Pot Black Timeframe*, and saw players having to pocket the balls in a set time. The original format was revived in 1993, with David Vine as emcee. The theme tune was entitled 'Ivory Rag'.

POTTER
UK (BBC) Situation Comedy. BBC 1 1979–80; 1983

Redvers Potter	**Arthur Lowe**
	Robin Bailey
Aileen Potter	**Noël Dyson**
The Vicar	**John Barron**
'Tolly' Tolliver	**John Warner**
Diana	**Honor Shepherd**
Harry Tooms	**Harry H. Corbett**
Jane	**Brenda Cowling**

Creator/Writer: **Roy Clarke**
Producers: **Peter Whitmore, Bernard Thompson**

A cantankerous former businessman can't help interfering in other people's affairs.

Redvers Potter, former MD of Pottermints ('the hotter mints'), a firm founded by his grandfather, was in need of new horizons after selling his share in the company. He took up jogging, nosed his way into other people's business and struck up friendships with Tolly, his antiques dealer neighbour, and the local vicar, who seemed as out of touch with reality as the bumbling Potter himself. Potter's independent wife, Aileen (though she preferred to be called Madge), took regular rollockings from her pedantic husband but remained defiant, while the Vicar's largely silent wife, Jane, was no more than an unpaid housekeeper. Also seen was a sad local villain, Harry Tooms, who tried to reinvent his life in the company of the curmudgeonly old buffers.

The title role unfortunately had to be recast when Arthur Lowe died between series. Into the breach stepped Robin Bailey.

POTTER, DENNIS
(1935–94)

Controversial but innovative British playwright, responsible for some of the most acclaimed dramas seen on television, but also for some of the most criticized. Much of Potter's writing had autobiographical undertones, echoing a childhood in the Forest of Dean and a life dogged by illness (psoriatic arthropathy, later exemplified in THE SINGING DETECTIVE). The susceptibility of youth, patriotism, the power of religion and nostalgia of all kinds (particularly musical) pervaded his bold screenplays, and he seldom shunned multi-layered storylines and frank sexual content. An Oxford graduate, Potter once stood as Labour parliamentary candidate, wrote for THAT WAS THE WEEK THAT WAS and worked on the *Daily Herald* in the early 1960s as a reporter and TV critic. His understanding of television matters was exhibited in his own screenwriting, as he sought to move the barriers of TV convention. His first offering was a WEDNESDAY PLAY, *The Confidence Course*, in 1965. The same year he contributed *Alice, Stand Up, Nigel Barton* and *Vote, Vote, Vote for Nigel Barton*. His *Son of Man* (1969), in which he humanized Christ, brought howls of disapproval from the Establishment and, in a way, his CASANOVA (1971), with its nudity, was not unexpected by those who raised the clamour. *Brimstone and Treacle*, made in 1976, was deemed to be too upsetting with its rape of a handicapped girl and was not screened until 1987; but Potter won new fans with his PENNIES FROM HEAVEN in 1978. *Blue Remembered Hills* (1979) famously put actors like Colin Welland, Michael Elphick and Helen Mirren into children's clothing, but it is THE SINGING DETECTIVE, shown in 1986, which many consider to be his most fitting memorial. Later efforts such as BLACKEYES (1989) and LIPSTICK ON YOUR COLLAR (1993) were not as well received, although still attracting their share of protest. Among Potter's many other works were *Emergency – Ward 9* (1966), *Message for Posterity* (1967), *A Beast with Two Backs* (1968), *Angels Are So Few* (1970), *Traitor* (1971), *Double Dare* (1976), *The Mayor of Casterbridge* (adaptation, 1978), *Rain on the Roof, Cream in My Coffee, Blade on the Feather* (all 1980), F. Scott Fitzgeralds's *Tender Is the Night* (1985), *Visitors* (1987) and *Christabel* (1988). He also set up his own production company, Whistling Gypsy. Potter's last dramas, KARAOKE and COLD LAZARUS, were chiselled out under great strain in his dying days, and were screened, according to the author's wishes, consecutively on BBC 1 and Channel 4 in spring 1996. To the end he expressed his love of television and his sadness at increased commercialization which, he felt, was ruining the medium.

POWELL, ROBERT
(1944–)

Salford-born actor whose first major TV role was as Toby Wren in DOOMWATCH in 1970. He soon followed it with the lead in Thomas Hardy's *Jude the Obscure*, but it wasn't until he played Christ in the blockbuster JESUS OF NAZARETH in 1977 that Powell became a major star. His other credits have included *Pygmalion*, THE EDWARDIANS' episode, *Mr Rolls and Mr Royce* (as Royce), *The Four Feathers*, *Looking for Clancy* (Frank Clancy), *The First Circle* and *Merlin of the Crystal Cave*. He was Dr Henry Fynn in the mini-series, *Shaka Zulu*, and was cast as John Buchan's hero, HANNAY, having already taken the role in a film version of *The Thirty-Nine Steps*. In the 1990s Powell was seen in company with Jasper Carrott, playing inept copper Dave Briggs in *Canned Carrott* and its spin-off, THE DETECTIVES. His wife, Barbara 'Babs' Lord, is a former Pan's People dancer.

POWELL, VINCE

Prolific British scriptwriter, for many years in collaboration with his former comedy partner, Harry Driver (see entry for Driver for their work together). Since Driver's death in 1973, Powell has devised and written *The Wackers*, *Rule Britannia*, *Home Sweet Home*, *My Son Reuben*, MIND YOUR LANGUAGE, *Odd Man Out*, *Young at Heart*, *Father Charlie* and *Bottle Boys*, and contributed episodes of *Paradise Island*, *A Sharp Intake of Breath*, NEVER THE TWAIN, SLINGER'S DAY and *Full House*, among other series.

POWER GAME, THE
See PLANE MAKERS, THE.

POWERS, STEFANIE
(Stefania Federkiewicz; 1942–)

American actress who shot to international stardom as April Dancer, THE GIRL FROM UNCLE, in 1966, after just a few small roles in series like BONANZA. The fame didn't last, however, when the series was cancelled after just one year, and Powers was forced to climb her way back to the top in the theatre and through guest spots in programmes like LOVE, AMERICAN STYLE and MARCUS WELBY, MD. It worked and, though one prime-time drama, *The Feather and Father Gang*, was not a huge success, Powers did find her métier as millionairess adventurer Jennifer Hart in HART TO HART. She has also been seen in numerous mini-series and TV movies, notably *Mistral's Daughter* and WASHINGTON: BEHIND CLOSED DOORS.

PRAED, MICHAEL
(1960–)

British actor seen in series like THE PROFESSIONALS and THE GENTLE TOUCH before hitting the big time as ROBIN OF SHERWOOD, which in turn led to his being cast (after a stint on the Broadway stage) as Prince Michael of Moldavia in DYNASTY. In 1993 Praed played Jake Lovell in *Jilly Cooper's Riders* and in 1995 was seen as Marty James in the legal drama series, *Crown Prosecutor*.

PREQUEL

Follow-up to a drama in which the action pre-dates that in the original programme, often introducing younger versions or ancestors of the original's main characters. Examples have included *First of the Summer Wine* and *Dallas: The Early Years*.

PRESENTATION CONTROLLER

The technician who presses the buttons to send programmes, trailers and commercials to air.

PRESS GANG
UK (Richmond Films/Central) Children's Adventure. ITV
1989–93

Lynda Day	Julia Sawalha
Spike Thomson	Dexter Fletcher
Kenny Phillips	Lee Ross
Sarah Jackson	Kelda Holmes
Matt Kerr	Clive Ward
Danny McColl	Charlie Creed-Miles
Tiddler	Joanna Dukes
Billy Homer	Andy Crowe
Julie Craig	Lucy Benjamin
Frazz Davis	Mmoloki Chrystie
Sam Black	Gabrielle Anwar
Colin Mathews	Paul Reynolds
Jennie Eliot	Sadie Frost

Creator: **Bill Moffat**
Writer: **Steven Moffat**
Producer: **Sandra C. Hastie**

The trials and tribulations of running a school newspaper.

In this acclaimed children's drama, the GCSE pupils of Norbridge High ran a youth newspaper called the *Junior Gazette*, an offshoot of the local press. Its hard-nosed editor was Lynda Day. American Spike Thomson was the number-one reporter, genial Kenny Phillips the deputy editor, and slippery Colin Mathews the advertising manager. Adopting a far more adult approach than previous efforts in the same vein (*Adventure Weekly*, *A Bunch of Fives*, etc.), *Press Gang* drew comparisons with HILL STREET BLUES, LOU GRANT and other thoughtful US dramas, thanks to its realism and its level-headed treatment of touchy subjects like child abuse, drugs and even local politics and corruption. Serious press issues like censorship, morality and privacy were prominent, too. The series also explored relationships between its protagonists, particularly the Lynda and Spike will-they, won't-they tease, and allowed its characters to mature season by season. Filmed cinematically, it also dabbled in dream sequences, flashbacks and fantasies. Both its stars, Julia Sawalha and Dexter Fletcher, have moved on to bigger things, while former teacher Steven Moffat, who made his TV writing debut with *Press Gang*, later scripted the sitcoms, JOKING APART and *Coupling*.

PRESTON FRONT
UK (BBC) Comedy Drama. BBC 1 1994–7

Dave Gadd ('Hodge')	**Colin Buchanan**
Wayne Disley ('Eric')	**Paul Haigh**
Simon Matlock ('Spock')	**Stephen Tompkinson**
	Alistair McGowan
Ally	**Kate Gartside**
Tony Lloyd ('Lloydy')	**Adrian Hood**
Des Moyle ('Diesel')	**Tony Marshall**
Dawn Lomax	**Caroline Catz**
Laura	**Lucy Akhurst**
Peter Polson	**David MacCreedy**
Carl Rundle	**Kieran Flynn**
Bob Betty	**Mark Fletcher**
Lennox	**Sam Graham**
Doyle	**Darren Brown**
Jeanetta	**Susan Wooldridge**
	Caroline Pickles
Mr Wang	**Ozzie Yue**
Kirsty	**Holly Grainger**
Greg Scarry	**Nicky Henson**
Mel	**Angela Lonsdale**
Declan	**Oliver Cotton**
Mrs Ruddock	**Maytelock Gibbs**

Writer: **Tim Firth**
Executive Producers: **Barry Hanson, Chris Parr**
Producers: **Chris Griffin, Bernard Krichefski**

Ups and downs in the lives of a group of Territorial Army soldiers.

As this series humorously revealed, the Territorial Army, the UK's reserve force, takes its recruits from all walks of life. Butchers, bakers and candlestick-makers during the week are transformed into a fighting unit at weekends. *All Quiet on the Preston Front* (simply *Preston Front* in its second and third series) focused on a reserve unit in Roker Bridge, Lancashire. It exposed how a bickering squad of twenty-something civilians became brothers and sisters in arms in their spare time, and followed each individual's (often wayward) attempts at life fulfilment.

The main characters were teenage father Hodge – his nickname derived from his middle names of Howard Roger – who lived in a caravan and worked at Roker Bridge Garden Centre; his best mate, Wayne Disley, known only as Eric, who lived with his elderly parents; Spock, a nerdy history teacher, who provided the brains for the unit; the hapless Lloydy, whose occupation was deemed to be 'classified' but who at one time bred koi carp for a millionaire, and then invented a successful boardgame called Gurkha Tank Battle; Dawn, Eric's student-hating, student-teacher girlfriend; Ally, an unhappily married solicitor's wife; the optimistic Diesel, who ran a garage but was always looking for a new venture; mean corporal Polson; and Laura, Hodge's ingenuous girlfriend, who sang (badly) in a Chinese restaurant and worked in a wholefood shop.

In the interests of accuracy, the cast was made to endure a five-day training exercise with the real-life TA so that they knew how to ford rivers, load a rifle and generally act like real soldiers. However, as writer Tim Firth conceded, the army was only a device to introduce the characters, and increasingly TA activity was pushed into the background in favour of a closer look at the personal lives of the protagonists. Comparisons were drawn with the US series, FRIENDS, as relationships between the characters grew ever stronger.

PRICE IS RIGHT, THE/ BRUCE'S PRICE IS RIGHT
UK (Central/Talbot/Yorkshire) Game Show. ITV 1984–8/ 1995–

Presenters: **Leslie Crowther, Bruce Forsyth**

Producers: **William G. Stewart, Howard Huntridge**

Manic game show in which contestants win prizes by knowing the price of goods in the shops.

'Come on down' was the gimmicky catchphrase employed by Leslie Crowther when hosting this all-action game show. Selecting contestants at random from a hyped-up studio audience, Crowther urged the chosen ones to join him in a series of games that shared one theme – guessing the value of household items. The contestants with the closest guesses picked up the prizes. After a gap of seven years, the series was brought back as *Bruce's Price Is Right*, with Bruce Forsyth calling the shots. Before arriving in the UK, *The Price Is Right* had been one of America's most popular game shows, first airing in 1956.

PRIDE AND PREJUDICE
UK (BBC/A&E) Drama. BBC 1 1995

Fitzwilliam Darcy	**Colin Firth**
Elizabeth Bennet	**Jennifer Ehle**
Mrs Bennet	**Alison Steadman**
Lydia Bennet	**Julia Sawalha**
Mr Bennet	**Benjamin Whitrow**
Jane Bennet	**Susannah Harker**
Kitty Bennet	**Polly Maberly**
Mary Bennet	**Lucy Briers**
Miss Bingley	**Anna Chancellor**
Mr Bingley	**Crispin Bonham-Carter**
Mr Hurst	**Rupert Vansittart**
Mrs Louisa Hurst	**Lucy Robinson**
Sir William Lucas	**Christopher Benjamin**

Lady Lucas .... **Norma Streader**
Charlotte Lucas .... **Lucy Scott**
Maria Lucas .... **Lucy Davis**
George Wickham .... **Adrian Lukis**
Mr Collins .... **David Bamber**
Lady Catherine de Bourgh .... **Barbara Leigh-Hunt**
Anne de Bourgh .... **Nadia Chambers**
Georgiana Darcy .... **Emilia Fox**
Mr Gardiner .... **Tim Wylton**
Mrs Gardiner .... **Joanna David**

Writer: **Andrew Davies**
Producer: **Sue Birtwistle**

An eligible bachelor and a bright young woman's mutual attraction is confounded by bad first impressions and social etiquette.

Universally acclaimed as one of the BBC's most successful costume romps, *Pride and Prejudice*, remarkably, became cult viewing. Jane Austen's 19th-century story of the lowly but respectable Bennet sisters, their ambitions to marry into higher society and the various husbands they courted along the way caught the public imagination. However, much of the attraction must have come from the engaging lead couple of Jennifer Ehle and Colin Firth and their celebrated mix of coy glances, smouldering looks, heaving bosoms and skin-tight wet shirts.

The stars assumed the identities of Miss Elizabeth Bennet and Mr Fitzwilliam Darcy, she level-headed, intelligent but of rather rustic origins; he restrained, seemingly arrogant and much more wealthy. Although their relationship had a rocky start, their mutual attraction grew by the episode. Pemberley, Darcy's stately pile, was destined to be shared with the independent-minded Miss Bennet.

Other characters who added depth to the tale included the excitable Mrs Bennet, the stoical Mr Bennet and Elizabeth's sisters Jane (kind, but shy), Lydia (flirty and reckless), Kitty and Mary. The first two married Darcy's rich friend, Mr Bingley (who rented Netherfield Hall near the Bennets' home in Longbourne), and the caddish ex-army officer, Mr Wickham, respectively. Unctuous, sycophantic ecclesiast, Mr Collins, also hoped for the hand of Elizabeth, while Bingley's sister – another contender for the key to Pemberley – did everything she could to discredit Elizabeth.

Hot on the heels of the immensely successful MIDDLE-MARCH, *Pride and Prejudice* continued the 1990s revival in costume dramas. It had been dramatized by the BBC on four previous occasions.

PRIME SUSPECT
UK (Granada) Police Drama. ITV 1991–6

DCI/Supt. Jane Tennison .... **Helen Mirren**
DS Bill Otley .... **Tom Bell** (*1* and *3*)
Det. Chief Supt. Mike Kernan ....
.... **John Benfield** (*1*, *2* and *series*)
George Marlow .... **John Bowe** (*1*)
Tim Woodward (*series*)
Moyra Henson .... **Zoe Wanamaker** (*1*)

DI Muddiman .... **Jack Ellis** (*1*, *2* and *series*)
DI Burkin .... **Craig Fairbrass** (*1* and *2*)
DI Richard Haskons .. **Richard Hawley** (*1*, *2*, *3* and *series*)
DCI John Shefford .... **John Forgeham** (*1*)
Peter Rawlins .... **Tom Wilkinson** (*1*)
DS Oswalde .... **Colin Salmon** (*2*)
DC Lillie .... **Philip Wright** (*2* and *3*)
DC Jones .... **Ian Fitzgibbon** (*2*)
Det. Supt. Rosper .... **Andrew Tiernan** (*2*)
Vera Reynolds .... **Peter Capaldi** (*3*)
Jimmy Jackson .... **David Thewlis** (*3*)
Commander Chiswick .... **Terrence Hardiman** (*3*)
Insp. Larry Hall .... **Mark Strong** (*3*)
WPC Norma Hastings .... **Karen Tomlin** (*3*)
Supt. Halliday .... **Struan Rodger** (*3*)
WPC Kathy Bibby .... **Liza Sadovy** (*3*)
DI Dalton .... **Andrew Woodall** (*3*)
DI Ray Hebdon .... **Mark Drewry** (*3*)
DS Rankine .... **David O'Hara** (*5*)
DI Devanney .... **Julia Lane** (*5*)
DC Henry Adeliyeka .... **John Brobbey** (*5*)
Det. Chief Supt. Ballinger .... **John McArdle** (*5*)
The Street .... **Steven Mackintosh** (*5*)

Creator: **Lynda La Plante**
Executive Producer: **Sally Head**
Writers: **Lynda La Plante** (*1* and *3*), **Allan Cubitt** (*2*),
Paul Billing (*series*), **Eric Deacon** (*series*), **Guy Hibbert**
(*series*), **Guy Andrews** (*5*)
Producers: **Don Leaver** (*1*), **Paul Marcus** (*2*, *3* and *series*),
Brian Park (*series*), **Lynn Horsford** (*5*)

An ambitious woman detective fights sexism within the force.

Jane Tennison was a single-minded, career policewoman whose progress through the ranks had been impeded by male prejudice – until, that was, she won the battle to take charge of an intriguing murder case. At long last her abilities were given the chance to shine through, though there was still plenty of resentment from colleagues like Sgt Bill Otley.

Such was the success of the two-part original *Prime Suspect* that *Prime Suspect 2* followed a year later. A second sequel, *Prime Suspect 3*, shown in 1993, saw Tennison moving from her base at Southampton Row to Soho's vice squad. A subsequent series of three single dramas (entitled simply *Prime Suspect*) was screened in 1995, and then a final two-parter, *Prime Suspect 5*, in 1996, in which Tennison had been transferred to Manchester and was dealing with drug crime.

Taking the role of this hard-nosed copper signalled a major change in career direction for former Shakespearean actress Helen Mirren. Her new severe haircut and sober suits were a world away from the roles she once enjoyed on stage. But Mirren had little difficulty in convincing viewers and went on to collect the BAFTA Best Actress award for three consecutive years. It was not enough for Hollywood, however, and when Universal bought the film rights to *Prime Suspect*, she was not considered for the lead role.

PRIME TIME

See PEAK TIME.

PRINCE REGENT

UK (BBC) Historical Drama. BBC 1 1979

George, Prince of Wales	Peter Egan
King George III	Nigel Davenport
Mrs Maria Fitzherbert	Susannah York
Charles James Fox	Keith Barron
Queen Charlotte	Frances White
Frances, Lady Jersey	Caroline Blakiston
William Pitt	David Collings
Princess Caroline	Dinah Stabb
Isabella, Lady Hertford	Barbara Shelley
Princess Charlotte	Cherie Lunghi

Producer: **Colin Tucker**

Eight-part biopic of the future King George IV.

Spanning 37 years, this costume romp took the lead character from being a vibrant, young prince up to his days as an old, gout-ridden ruler. The tale began in 1782, as drunkard, waster, lecher George Augustus Frederick, the Prince of Wales, came of age. He considered himself to be witty, a lover of fine things and a talented, sensitive soul; his father believed otherwise. The Prince fell in love with widow Mrs Fitzherbert, who was quite an unsuitable match, being both older and a Catholic, but he nevertheless married her in secret. The marriage not being officially recognized, the Prince then wed Princess Caroline, whom he grew to hate. His wait for the throne was almost terminal. Despite becoming Prince Regent, he ascended to the throne himself only in 1820, by which time he was fat and sick. Carl Davis provided the music.

PRINGLE, BRYAN

(1935–)

Staffordshire-born actor, a familiar face in situation comedies. He was Cheese and Egg in THE DUSTBINMEN and Sgt Flagg in THE GROWING PAINS OF PC PENROSE. He has also been seen in *Room Service* (Charles Spooner), AUF WIEDERSEHEN, PET, *The Good Companions*, LOVE STORY, *The Management* (Mr Crusty), *Paradise Postponed*, *Blind Justice*, *Once Upon a Time in the North* (Mr Bebbington), *King and Castle*, *Flying Lady*, INSPECTOR MORSE, ALL CREATURES GREAT AND SMALL, AFTER HENRY, PRIME SUSPECT, PERFECT SCOUNDRELS, RUMPOLE OF THE BAILEY, BOON, *P. G. Wodehouse's Heavy Weather* (Pirbright), *A Prince Among Men* (Vince), *Tess of the D'Urbervilles* (Kail), *Vanity Fair* (Raggles), *Wokenwell* (Sadly Stan Potter), and plenty more series.

PRISONER, THE

UK (Everyman/ATV) Adventure. ITV 1967–8

The Prisoner (Number 6)	Patrick McGoohan
The Butler	Angelo Muscat

Creator/Executive Producer: **Patrick McGoohan**
Producer: **David Tomblin**

A secret agent is held captive in a mysterious Italianate village.

In the opening titles of *The Prisoner*, a sports car was seen to race through the streets of London beneath a thundery sky. An unnamed British intelligence agent stepped out and burst into a Whitehall office, abruptly handing in his resignation. Returning home to pack a suitcase, he was overcome by a puff of gas, waking up in a quaint, turreted village, surrounded by mountains and sea. As each episode then made clear, the agent was trapped. There was no escape from the village and he was constantly pumped for information, mostly about his sudden resignation. He had even lost his identity and was now known simply as Number 6, though he continued to claim, 'I am not a number. I am a free man.'

And that, on the face of it, was all *The Prisoner* was about: a man held against his will, subjected to interrogation and attempting to escape. But there was far more to this series and so many questions were left unanswered. Who were his captors? Why were they holding him? Indeed, who was our hero? And would he ever be able to get away? All that viewers knew was that head of the village was Number 1, and he was never seen, leaving his chief operative, Number 2, to deal with Number 6. But even Number 2 changed from episode to episode and the only face Number 6 could always recognize was that of the silent, dwarf butler.

Number 6 was not the only captive, but he was the only one who still had the will to break out. The others had already been brainwashed, going through the motions of their everyday life, playing human chess on the giant board in the village square, saying 'Be seeing you' and staggering on with their purposeless existence. And who were they anyway? In contrast, Number 6's mind was firmly set on escape, slipping away from the village's penny-farthing bicycles, its golf-cart taxis, piped blazers, closed-circuit security cameras and the floating, bouncing, white balloon-like guard known as Rover. Inevitably, his plans were foiled.

Enigmatic to the end, *The Prisoner* concluded with a story that saw Number 6 being invited to take over the community and at last revealing the face of Number 1 – it was his own. A missile was launched to destroy the village, and Number 6 fled with the butler and two other inmates. As he raced through London in his sports car, with the skies once again thundery, a certain familiarity shone through. With the doors of his house slamming closed behind him, could it have been that the nightmare really was over, or had it just begun again?

Many conclusions have been drawn from this classic series. Was the village a sort of retirement home for burned-out secret agents, or was it some kind of enemy intelligence centre? Or could it have been that The Prisoner was really trapped only in his own mind, a victim of a severe nervous breakdown, a theory supported by the circular pattern of events, including the conclusion, and the revelation of Number 1's face as his own.

Certainly there were statements about democracy, personal freedom and social engineering in there, but the surreal nature of the series made it difficult for anyone to pin it all down.

The star of the series, Patrick McGoohan, was also the creator and driving force. Many fans believed *The Prisoner* to be a sequel to his previous success, DANGER MAN, although this was never stated. Instead, McGoohan has subsequently agreed that the programme was an allegorical conundrum. Not for nothing was his independent production company called Everyman, in direct reference to medieval morality plays.

Actors who played Number 2 included Leo McKern, Anton Rodgers, Peter Wyngarde and Patrick Cargill. The village used for filming was Portmeirion in North Wales, created as an Italian fantasy by architect Sir Clough Williams-Ellis.

PRISONER: CELL BLOCK H
Australia (Grundy) Drama. ITV 1979–87

Lynn Warner	Kerry Armstrong
Bea Smith	Val Lehman
Vera Bennett	Fiona Spence
Freida 'Franky' Doyle	Carol Burns
Karen Travers	Peita Toppano
Jeanette 'Mum' Brooks	Mary Ward
Erica Davidson	Patsy King
Meg Jackson/Morris	Elspeth Ballantyne
Dr Greg Miller	Barry Quin
Doreen Anderson/Burns	Collette Mann
Marilyn Mason	Margaret Laurence
Elizabeth Birdsworth	Sheila Florance
Eddie Cook	Richard Moir
Jim Fletcher	Gerard Maguire
Pat O'Connell	Monica Maughan
Chrissie Latham	Amanda Muggleton
Noeline Burke	Jude Kuring
Steve Wilson	Jim Smillie
Jean Vernon	Christine Amor
Barbara Davidson	Sally Cahill
Jock Stewart	Tommy Dysart
Judy Bryant	Betty Bobbit
Margo Gaffney	Jane Clifton
Helen Smart	Caroline Gillmer
Colleen Powell	Judith McGrath
Steve Faulkner	Wayne Jarratt
Maxine Daniels	Lisa Crittenden
Joan Ferguson	Maggie Kirkpatrick
Pixie Mason	Judy McBurney
Myra Desmond	Ann Phelan
Joyce Barry	Joy Westmore
Lexie Patterson	Pepe Trevor
Ann Reynolds	Gerda Nicholson
Rita Connors	Glenda Linscott

Creator/Executive Producer: **Reg Watson**
Producers: **Phil East, Marie Trevor, Ian Bradley, John McRae, Sue Masters**

Low-budget, far-from-glitzy soap set in an Australian women's jail.

The Wentworth Detention Centre housed some of Melbourne's toughest female criminals and, through a series of rather far-fetched plots, the programme examined the inter-relationships of the prisoners, their warders, and fringe characters such as partners on the outside, prison doctors and other officials. The series dealt openly with issues such as lesbianism and wanton assault (by both prisoners and guards) and in its own melodramatic way stripped the front off hard-bitten inmates to reveal personal tragedies that had led them to a life of crime. It showed how some matured to rehabilitate themselves successfully on their release, although it also made it clear that, for others, prison life was the only option.

Principal characters early on were Governor Erica Davidson, her deputy Jim Fletcher, brutal warder Vera Bennett and the more sympathetic guard, Meg Jackson. Ringleader of the prisoners was Bea Smith (doing time for the murder of her husband), and other protagonists were the lesbian biker and armed robber, Franky Doyle, Karen Travers, a deeply religious ex-schoolteacher (also convicted of the murder of her husband), and dumb blonde Lynn Warner, a convicted nanny. Thumb-sucking Doreen Anderson was the easily led unmarried-mother-turned-forger, Marilyn Mason was a prostitute and the prison nympho, 'Mum' Brooks the gentle, well-respected gardening lover (yet another imprisoned for killing her husband), and Lizzie Birdsworth the alcoholic, chain-smoking mass-murderer who was hell-bent on escape. Greg Miller was the prison doctor.

The show, originally entitled simply *Prisoner*, was renamed *Prisoner: Cell Block H* to avoid confusion with Patrick McGoohan's cult series of the 1960s in the UK and USA. Its creator, Reg Watson (a former CROSSROADS producer), and one of its producers, Marie Trevor, later moved on to the rather more successful NEIGHBOURS. Maggie Kirkpatrick, who played Joan Ferguson, appeared with Lily Savage in the London spoof stage version, which began in 1995.

PRIVATE INVESTIGATOR
UK (BBC) Detective Drama. BBC 1958–9

John Unthank	Campbell Singer
Bill Jessel	Douglas Muir
James Wilson	Allan McClelland
Peter Clarke	Ian White
Mrs Layton	Ursula Camm

Creator/Producer: **Arthur Swinson**

The cases of an unspectacular private eye.

Keeping himself to himself, with a view to avoiding attention and preserving his cover, Scottish private investigator John Unthank was rolled out by the BBC for two pieces of detective work, spread over nine weeks. The first concerned French currency fraud, the second a job for the National Canine Defence League on the Mediterranean. His restrained approach was an ocean apart from that of the wisecracking American sleuths of his era.

PRIVATE SCHULZ

UK (BBC) Comedy Drama. BBC 2 1981

Pte. Gerhard Schulz	**Michael Elphick**
Major Neuheim	**Ian Richardson**
Bertha Freyer	**Billie Whitelaw**
Iphraim 'Solly' Solikoff	**Cyril Shaps**
Schumacher	**Terence Suffolk**
Gertrude Steiner	**Rula Lenska**
Prof. Bodelschwingh	**David Swift**

Writer: **Jack Pulman**
Producer: **Philip Hinchcliffe**

A German fraudster reluctantly works for the SS.

Cowardly, small-time wheeler-dealer Gerhard Schulz had spent two spells in Spandau prison for fraud. In summer 1939 he applied for a role in the Postal Censorship department, so he could use his knowledge of five languages, but was seconded instead to SS Counter Espionage. Headed by mad Major Neuheim, the division was charged with developing novel ideas that would be useful in war – schemes like dropping forged £5 notes on Britain. Although masterminded by Schulz, it was Neuheim who took the credit. Solly was the master forger Schulz employed to make his plans work, while the Dietrich-esque Bertha Freyer was the good-time girl at Salon Kitty, where the stoical Schulz listened in to bugged bedroom conversations. Schulz's lively war also saw him on duty undercover in England. In addition to Neuheim, actor Ian Richardson played a number of other roles in the series. Each episode opened with newsreel footage highlighting the stage of the war that had been reached at the time.

PROBATION OFFICER

UK (ATV) Drama. ITV 1959–62

Philip Main	**John Paul**
Jim Blake	**David Davies**
Iris Cope	**Honor Blackman**
Margaret Weston	**Jessica Spencer**
Stephen Ryder	**Bernard Brown**

Creator: **Julian Bond**
Producers: **Antony Kearey, Rex Firkin**

Drama in the lives of a team of probation officers.

Charged with the welfare of delinquents, criminals and other social unfortunates, members of the probation service constantly find themselves dragged into the affairs of others. This series depicted – in semi-documentary style – some of the typical problems faced by a team from inner London, and originally featured Philip Main, Jim Blake and Iris Cope as its protagonists. Numerous other characters were introduced during the programme's three-year run and the cast lists changed frequently.

PRODUCER

The executive in charge of a programme, taking the original idea and drawing together the resources to make it happen. These resources include the budget and the crew, from the director and camera team to the performers. Sometimes, particularly in non-drama programming, the producer may provide more 'hands-on' creative input. Otherwise, he or she delegates this to the director but still assumes overall responsibility for the finished project.

PRODUCTION ASSISTANT

The production assistant, or PA, is the producer and director's right-hand person. PAs work on a programme from its very earliest days, helping in the planning and staging, and continue their involvement through to the eventual recording or live transmission.

PROFESSIONALS, THE

UK (Avengers Mark 1/LWT) Spy Drama. ITV 1977–83

George Cowley	**Gordon Jackson**
William Bodie	**Lewis Collins**
Ray Doyle	**Martin Shaw**
Murphy	**Steve Alder**

Creator: **Brian Clemens**
Executive Producers: **Albert Fennell, Brian Clemens**
Producers: **Sidney Hayers, Raymond Menmuir**

The violent activities of a secret crime-busting unit.

'The Professionals' were the men and women of CI5 (Criminal Intelligence 5), a covert agency set up by the Government to specialize in criminal intelligence in the way that MI5 centred on military intelligence. The aim was to pre-empt trouble and so nip crime in the bud. Head of the section was no-nonsense, ex-MI5 man George Cowley. He assembled around him a team of the toughest operatives, none more resilient and respected than Bodie, a former SAS and Parachute Regiment hero brimming with confidence. Bodie's partner was Doyle, an ex-copper with a much-derided curly perm. Fresh from an East End CID division, he was calm on the outside but harboured a rage within which threatened to burst out at any second. The pair were affectionately known as 'The Bisto Kids' to Cowley, whom they knew as 'The Cow'.

The programme was created by Brian Clemens, the brains behind some of THE AVENGERS' best adventures, although this all-action, macho series did not share the light-hearted, tongue-in-cheek, quirky qualities of his earlier work. It was parodied by members of *The Comic Strip* in a one-off satire, *The Bullshitters*. In 1999, Sky One launched an updated version of *The Professionals*. Entitled *CI5: the New Professionals*, it starred Edward Woodward, Kal Weber, Colin Wells and Lexa Doig.

PROMPTER
See AUTOCUE.

PROPERTIES OR PROPS

Studio or set furnishings/decorations intended to provide realism or convey a certain atmosphere.

PROTECTORS, THE
UK (ABC) Adventure. ITV 1964

Ian Souter	**Andrew Faulds**
Robert Shoesmith	**Michael Atkinson**
Heather Keys	**Ann Morrish**

Producer: **Michael Chapman**

Three professional troubleshooters nip crime in the bud.

'We sell security. Object: To prevent crime.' This was the motto of The Protectors, a trio of crime specialists working from a swish London office. The three were former insurance claims inspector Ian Souter, ex-policeman Robert Shoesmith and their girl Friday, Heather Keys. Operating in the twilight zone between the underworld and the security services, this determined trio acted to prevent crimes from taking place. The bearded, relaxed Souter, a Scotsman, was intelligent, experienced and decisive, Shoesmith had an understanding of the criminal mind which bordered on admiration, and Keys had an expert's eye for art forgeries. After placing an advertisement in newspapers, encouraging potential clients to 'Call Welbeck 3269', they found themselves protecting people in fear of an imminent crime, or those who had already fallen victim. They called themselves SIS, standing for Specialists In Security, and their assignments led them into murder, espionage and other forms of intrigue.

Two of the stars headed off in rather different career directions when this short-lived series came to an end. Andrew Faulds became a Member of Parliament and Ann Morrish went on to present PLAY SCHOOL, among other television roles.

PROTECTORS, THE
UK (Group Three/ITC) Adventure. ITV 1972–4

Harry Rule	**Robert Vaughn**
Contessa di Contini	**Nyree Dawn Porter**
Paul Buchet	**Tony Anholt**
Suki	**Yasuko Nagazami**
Chino	**Anthony Chinn**

Producers: **Gerry Anderson, Reg Hill**

Three top investigators join forces to save the world from international crime.

The Protectors were Harry Rule, the Contessa di Contini and Paul Buchet. Together they blazed around Europe's top resorts, darting from flashy cars into private jets and meeting crime head on. They tackled spies, drug-pushers, smugglers, thieves and murderers. Rule was their leader, an ultra-cool American working from a high-tech office in London. He lived in a country mansion with an Irish wolfhound named Gus and was looked after by his au pair, Suki (a martial arts expert). The Contessa di Contini was Lady Caroline Ogilvy, an elegant English widow whose late Italian husband had left her a villa in Rome. Her speciality was art and antiques fraud, and she was chauffeured around by a karate-chopping driver named Chino. Fresh-faced Paul Buchet was an amorous Frenchman who operated out of a Paris apartment. Their glossy, rather violent adventures were produced by puppet-master Gerry Anderson. Tony Christie belted out the closing theme song, 'Avenues and Alleyways', a UK chart hit in 1973.

PUBLIC EYE
UK (ABC/Thames) Detective Drama. ITV 1965–75

Frank Marker	**Alfred Burke**
Mrs Helen Mortimer	**Pauline Delany**
DI Firbank	**Ray Smith**
Ron Gash	**Peter Childs**

Creators: **Roger Marshall, Anthony Marriott**
Executive Producers: **Lloyd Shirley, Robert Love**
Producers: **Don Leaver, John Bryce, Richard Bates, Michael Chapman, Kim Mills, Robert Love**

The poorly paid investigations of a grimy private detective.

Frank Marker was an unambitious detective, a sad character who dipped in and out of the murky underworld pond. He worked for next to nothing, sometimes not even getting paid for his troubles; but his satisfaction came from a job well done and the escapism it provided from his own drab world. He operated out of seedy, backstreet offices, firstly in London, then Birmingham and, finally, Brighton. He was a one-man band whose professional trust was often abused. On one occasion he went to jail for handling stolen jewellery, even though he was only acting as a go-between for the insurers and the thieves.

Marker was joined later in the series by Mrs Mortimer, his landlady, as well as by Inspector Firbank, a copper whose feathers Marker repeatedly ruffled. Ron Gash was a fellow detective who wanted Marker to join him in a partnership. The first three seasons (with quirkily named episode titles like *They Go Off in the End, Like Fruit* and *I Went to Borrow a Pencil, and Look What I Found*) were produced by ABC TV but, when it lost its ITV franchise, production was taken over by its successor, Thames Television.

PULMAN, JACK
(1925–80)

British writer, first on TV in the 1950s with his own dramas, but later better known for his adaptations. The highlights were I, CLAUDIUS, *War and Peace* and *Crime and Punishment*. Of his own creations, PRIVATE SCHULZ and the David Kossoff sitcom, A LITTLE BIG BUSINESS, were among the most notable, as well as the plays, *A Book with Chapters in It*, *Nearer to Heaven* and *You Can't Have Everything*.

PURSUERS, THE
UK (Crestview/ABC) Police Drama. ITV 1961–2

DI John Bollinger .... **Louis Hayward**
DS Steve Wall .... **Gaylord Cavallaro**

Executive Producer: **Donald Hyde**

The cases of two Scotland Yard detectives and a loyal Alsatian police dog.

Middle-aged Detective Inspector John Bollinger patrolled the streets of London, assisted by Detective Sgt Wall and, usually, a large, black German Shepherd dog named Ivan. Its human star, the South African Louis Hayward, arrived on television, having been a Hollywood actor since the 1930s. Thirty-nine episodes were made of this half-hour series.

PURVES, PETER
(1939–)

Northern English actor/presenter, undoubtedly best known as one of the three presenters, along with John Noakes and Valerie Singleton, of BLUE PETER's 'golden age'. However, he also has the rare distinction of playing two separate parts in one story of DOCTOR WHO, the latter being space pilot Steven Taylor, who went on to become one of the Doctor's regular companions. Since leaving *Blue Peter*, Purves has hosted series like *Stopwatch* and *Kick Start*, as well annual events like darts tournaments, Crufts and other animal shows.

PYKE, DR MAGNUS
OBE (1908–92)

British scientist turned TV presenter in the 1970s, thanks to the YTV series, DON'T ASK ME and *Don't Just Sit There*, on which he was the resident pundit. His natural enthusiasm, fast talking and flailing arms made him an instant celebrity.

QED

UK (BBC) Documentary. BBC 1 1982–98

Editors: **David Filkin, Simon Campbell-Jones, Susan Spindler, Lorraine Heggessey, Michael Mosley**

Wide-ranging documentary series with a scientific bent.

Spontaneous combustion, overcoming drug addiction, the intense training of children to be sporting superstars, the effect of smoking on the human body and the chemistry of sexual attraction were all typical subjects aired in this ambitious series of sometimes light-hearted science documentaries. Occasional dramatizations helped sugar the scientific pill. In 1999, the series was replaced with the similar *Living Proof,* from the same production team. The logic was that – even after 16 years – the public did not understand the significance of the abbreviation QED.

QUANTUM LEAP

US (Bellisarius) Science Fiction. BBC 2 1990–4

Dr Sam Beckett .... **Scott Bakula**
Al Calavicci .... **Dean Stockwell**

Creator/Producer: **Donald Bellisario**

A time-travelling scientist is stranded in the past.

Scientist Sam Beckett was heavily involved in a secret time-travel project known as Quantum Leap. One day, turning himself into a human guinea-pig, he used the machine to go spinning back in time. But there he became stranded, thrown forwards and backwards to different eras within a period of 30 years of his own birth (1953). In each episode, he found himself trapped in the body of another person which could have been male or female. One week he was a trapeze artist who had to prevent his sister suffering a tragic fall, another week a high school quarterback trying to stop two team-mates from throwing an important game. While he was allowed to meddle with time in such minor instances, Sam was prohibited from altering anything major, such as Kennedy's assassination. In his temporary persona, though he looked the part to all concerned, to viewers he still appeared as the same old Sam.

While waiting to be returned to his own time, Sam's only hope was to fulfil his temporary roles as flawlessly as possible, trying not to arouse suspicions and aiming to win the day for the person concerned. To this end, he was aided by the hologrammatic image of a colleague, a cigar-chewing admiral called Al. Al (seen only by Sam) brought news of the efforts to return Sam home, as well as assorted tit-bits about the people and the times in which he had been stranded, using a hand-held terminal linked to a computer named Ziggy. But Al's information was always incomplete, with the key details left out until the last possible moment. Having averted disaster, or at least having carried off his historical impersonation without too much distress, Sam, with a tremulous 'Oh boy!', was whisked away into another time zone and another body. Unfortunately, the final episode did not make happy viewing for fans of Sam Beckett. He learned that there was simply no way back to the present day. This was one hero who wasn't coming home.

QUATERMASS
UK (BBC/Thames/Euston Films) Science Fiction. BBC
1953; 1955; 1958–9; ITV 1979

The Quatermass Experiment (BBC, 1953)

Prof. Bernard Quatermass	**Reginald Tate**
Judith Carroon	**Isabel Dean**
Victor Carroon	**Duncan Lamont**
John Paterson	**Hugh Kelly**
James Fullalove	**Paul Whitsun-Jones**
Dr Gordon Briscoe	**John Glen**
Chief Insp. Lomax	**Ian Colin**
DS Best	**Frank Hawkins**

Quatermass II (BBC, 1955)

Prof. Bernard Quatermass	**John Robinson**
Paula Quatermass	**Monica Grey**
Dr Leo Pugh	**Hugh Griffiths**
Capt. John Dillon	**John Stone**
Vincent Broadhead	**Rupert Davies**

Quatermass and the Pit (BBC, 1958–9)

Prof. Bernard Quatermass	**André Morell**
Barbara Judd	**Christine Finn**
Dr Matthew Roney	**Cec Linder**
Sladden	**Richard Shaw**
Col. Breen	**Anthony Bushell**
Capt. Potter	**John Stratton**
James Fullalove	**Brian Worth**

Quatermass (ITV, 1979)

Prof. Bernard Quatermass	**John Mills**
Joe Kapp	**Simon MacCorkindale**
Clare Kapp	**Barbara Kellerman**
Kickalong	**Ralph Arliss**
Caraway	**Paul Rosebury**
Bee	**Jane Bertish**
Hettie	**Rebecca Saire**
Marshall	**Tony Sibbald**
Sal	**Toyah Willcox**
Annie Morgan	**Margaret Tyzack**

Writer: **Nigel Kneale**
Executive Producer: **Verity Lambert (Thames)**
Producers: **Rudolph Cartier (BBC), Ted Childs (Thames)**

The alien-thwarting adventures of Professor Bernard Quatermass, grandfather of all TV science-fiction heroes.

The name 'Quatermass' has become synonymous with early TV sci-fi, yet relatively few viewers would have seen the original ground-breaking series. Transmitted live in 1953, when homes with TVs were few and repeats impossible, it nevertheless managed to set the trend for TV horror-fantasy leading to three follow-ups, the last 26 years later. The brains behind the project was Nigel Kneale, a BBC staff-writer given the chance to branch out with his own ideas. What he foresaw in *The Quatermass Experiment* was a new kind of TV thriller, adventurous in both its subject-matter and presentation. It concerned astronaut Victor Carroon, who returned to Earth contaminated by an alien life-form. As the alien vegetable gradually took over Carroon's body and threatened to reproduce in vast quantities, to devastating effect, it was left to level-headed space scientist Professor Quatermass to track him down. Cornering Carroon at Westminster Abbey, Quatermass appealed to what remained of his human nature, urging Carroon to destroy himself and save the planet.

When Quatermass resurfaced, two years later, production techniques had advanced somewhat and this time the Professor was called upon to protect Earth from aliens which had infiltrated people's minds and bodies. The invaders had been using a chemical plant as a secret acclimatization centre. Identifying the alien base as being an asteroid on the other side of the planet, Quatermass and his colleague, Dr Pugh, set off in the Professor's own latest space rocket to destroy it. The original Quatermass, Reginald Tate, died just weeks before this second series, leaving John Robinson to take over the character.

The third element in the saga, *Quatermass and the Pit*, was the most sophisticated of the BBC versions, concentrating on the idea that Martians had arrived on Earth millions of years earlier and had imparted certain attributes to man's ancestors, a process that explained away phenomena like ghosts, demons and ESP. This came to light as the last traces of blitzed London were being redeveloped and a five-million-year-old skull was discovered next to an alien capsule in a deep pit. The Professor (now played by André Morell), aided by palaeontologist Matthew Roney, was brought in to restore order.

No more was heard of Quatermass until Thames and Euston Films picked up the reins in 1979. In a story Kneale had first penned around ten years earlier, John Mills became the fourth actor to play the scientist, who returned to London from a Scottish retirement to look for his missing granddaughter, Hettie. Once again, aliens were at the heart of the problem, bringing chaos to society and harvesting and taking away hordes of young people (hippies known as 'Planet People') at places as diverse as Wembley Stadium and ancient stone circles. Teaming up with Joe Kapp, a young Jewish astronomer, Quatermass not only foiled the aliens but retrieved Hettie along the way.

The first three *Quatermass* stories were also filmed by Hammer and released on the cinema circuit, two with Brian Donlevy in the title role. The films were given new titles for American audiences: *The Creeping Unknown*, *Enemy from Space* and *Five Million Years to Earth* (starring Andrew Keir), respectively.

QUAYLE, Sir ANTHONY
CBE (1913–89)

Anthony Quayle's finest hours definitely came on the stage and in the cinema, but he made his contribution to television's archives as well. He starred as criminologist Adam Strange in the 1968 series, STRANGE REPORT, acted as narrator for many series, and appeared in numerous TV movies, plays and mini-series, including *QB VII* (Tom Bannister), *Moses the Lawgiver* (Aaron), *Masada* (Rubrius Gallus), *The Last Days of Pompeii* and THE BBC TELEVISION SHAKESPEARE (*Henry IV* parts I and II).

QUEENIE'S CASTLE
UK (Yorkshire) Situation Comedy. ITV 1970–2

Queenie Shepherd .... **Diana Dors**
Raymond Shepherd .... **Freddie Fletcher**
Douglas Shepherd .... **Barrie Rutter**
Bunny Shepherd .... **Brian Marshall**
Jack .... **Tony Caunter**
Mrs Petty .... **Lynne Perrie**

Creators: **Keith Waterhouse, Willis Hall**
Producers: **Graham Evans, Ian Davidson**

A Yorkshire matriarch runs her family with a rod of iron.

Queenie Shepherd was the undoubted head of the impoverished Shepherd clan. Dominating her motley trio of sons (Raymond, Douglas and Bunny), she lived in the Buckingham flats, a Yorkshire housing development. Also part of the household was Queenie's brother-in-law, Jack, and poking her nose in – and risking Queenie's ready wrath – was her neighbour, Mrs Petty (a pre-CORONATION STREET Lynne Perrie). Another *Street* star, Bryan Mosley, was seen as their landlord.

QUENTIN, CAROLINE
(1960–)

Surrey-born actress whose major TV series have included MEN BEHAVING BADLY (Dorothy), *Don't Tell Father* (Kate Bancroft), *All or Nothing at All* (Rebecca), JONATHAN CREEK (Maddy Magellan) and *Kiss Me Kate* (Kate Salinger), as well as the comedy-drama, *An Evening with Gary Lineker* (Monica). Quentin also presented the first series of the interior design programme, *Home Front*, and has been seen in many other series, from WHOSE LINE IS IT ANYWAY? and MR BEAN to *This Is David Lander* and *Harry Enfield's Television Programme*. She was once married to comedian Paul Merton and was part of the chorus in the original stage production of *Les Misérables*.

QUEST, THE
US (Columbia) Western. BBC 1 1976–7

Morgan Beaudine .... **Kurt Russell**
Quentin Beaudine .... **Tim Matheson**

Creator: **Tracy Keenan Wynn**
Executive Producer: **David Gerber**
Producers: **Mark Rodgers, James H. Brown**

In the Wild West of the 1880s, two brothers set out to find their long-lost sister.

Morgan Beaudine and his sister, Patricia, had been taken captive when children by Cheyenne Indians, but they had become separated. Morgan had been raised by the Indians and given the name of 'Two Persons' and, although he had now returned to white society, he still trusted Indians more than his own kind. He also dressed like a Redskin and spoke their language – a useful asset in the Wild West. His brother, Quentin, had enjoyed a quite different upbringing, living with an aunt and being educated in San Francisco. He planned to be a doctor, but first things first. Their sister was still missing, so the brothers hit the road in an attempt to track her down and reunite the family. Their 'Quest' proved long and largely fruitless.

QUESTION OF SPORT, A
UK (BBC) Quiz. BBC 1 1970–

Presenters: **David Vine, David Coleman, Sue Barker**

Producers: **Nick Hunter, Mike Adley, Kieron Collins, Carl Doran**

Light-hearted quiz featuring sporting personalities.

A Question of Sport has achieved an audience appeal that reaches beyond the realms of traditional sports fans. The relaxed, jokey atmosphere and flippant banter have made the series into a popular light entertainment show, with high viewing figures to boot. Two teams of three sporting celebrities (each containing a resident captain) have worked their way through several rounds of sporting teasers, answering questions on their own individual events as well as general sporting matters. Favourite rounds have included the picture board (identifying the personality from an obscure picture), what happened next? (guessing the sequence of events after the film has stopped), the mystery personality (revealed only in short glimpses through unusual camera-angles) and the 60-second rapid-fire section (worth up to nine points).

David Vine was the first host, succeeded in 1979 by David Coleman, who in turn gave way to Sue Barker in 1997. Excluding guest captains, *A Question of Sport* teams have been led by Cliff Morgan, Henry Cooper, Fred Trueman, Brendan Foster, Gareth Edwards, Emlyn Hughes, Willie Carson, Bill Beaumont, Ian Botham, Ally McCoist and John Parrott. In 1987 the programme achieved a rare coup, when HRH the Princess Anne was recruited on to Emlyn Hughes's team to celebrate the 200th edition.

QUESTION TIME
UK (BBC) Debate. BBC 1 1979–

Presenters: **Robin Day, Peter Sissons, David Dimbleby**

Studio-audience-led political debate.

Question Time has been based on a simple formula: take three politicians of different persuasions, plus one 'neutral' – often an industrialist or academic – and throw them to the lions (in the form of a studio audience of mixed political views). Without pre-knowledge, the panellists have to answer tricky, topical questions put to them by the gathered masses. Keeping order, and helping to put the panellists on the spot, was initially Robin Day, whose inimitably gruff style helped establish the series. When he retired in 1989, his seat was taken, amid much publicity, by then Channel 4 newscaster Peter Sissons. Sissons has subsequently handed over control to David Dimbleby. Over the years, several fill-in hosts have also been employed to cover for sickness. These have included Sue Lawley and Ludovic Kennedy. The idea for *Question Time* was based on Radio 4's *Any Questions*.

QUILLEY, DENIS
(1927–)

British actor seen in a variety of series from the kids' sci-fi thriller, TIMESLIP (Commander Traynor), to the sitcom, *Rich Tea and Sympathy* (biscuit magnate George Rudge). He played Richard Shelton in a 1951 version of R. L. Stevenson's *The Black Arrow*, Gladstone in *No. 10*, Quadratus in the mini-series, *Masada*, Peter in another mini-series, *AD*, and among his other credits have been DIXON OF DOCK GREEN, *Clayhanger*, *The Bretts*, *After the War* and *Family Album*, plus single dramas.

QUINCY
US (Universal/Glen A. Larson) Detective Drama. ITV
1977–85

Quincy ME	**Jack Klugman**
Lt. Frank Monahan	**Garry Walberg**
Sam Fujiyama	**Robert Ito**
Danny Tovo	**Val Bisoglio**
Lee Potter	**Lynette Mettey**
Dr Robert J. Asten	**John S. Ragin**
Sgt Brill	**Joseph Roman**
Eddie	**Ed Garrett**
Marc	**Marc Scott Taylor**
Diane	**Diane Markoff**
Dr Emily Hanover	**Anita Gillette**

Creators: **Glen A. Larson, Lou Shaw**
Executive Producer: **Glen A. Larson**
Producers: **Lou Shaw, Peter Thompson, Robert F. O'Neill, Michael Star**

An inquisitive pathologist keeps unearthing new clues and frustrating the local police.

Widower Quincy worked for the Los Angeles County Coroner's Office as a medical examiner and had abandoned a profitable medical practice in order to take on this demanding job. But he was born to it. The quick once-over of the corpse was not for Quincy. He went into every detail and, just when the cops thought they had a 'natural causes' case on their hands, the pushy pathologist unearthed something more suspicious. Indeed, so pushy was Quincy that the police could hardly ignore him. But, just in case they did, much to the consternation of his boss, Dr Asten, Quincy often turned detective himself and went out looking for clues, assisted by his young colleague, Sam Fujiyama.

In his private life, Quincy had a girlfriend, Lee Potter, though such was his dedication to his job, their romance never quite took off. He therefore lived alone, on a boat moored near a bar called Danny's Place, where he spent whatever free time he had. Lee soon left the scene, but Quincy later met psychiatrist Emily Hanover, whom he subsequently married. Quincy's Christian name was never given, though a once-seen business card did give his initial as R.

The series (known in the USA as *Quincy, ME*) began life as a part of the MYSTERY MOVIE anthology, but proved so popular in the USA that it was given its own regular slot.

QUIRKE, PAULINE
(1959–)

A teenage performer in the 1970s, Pauline Quirke has now developed into an adult star, thanks largely to roles in ANGELS (Vicki Smith), SHINE ON HARVEY MOON (Veronica), BIRDS OF A FEATHER (Sharon), *The Sculptress* (murderess Olive Martin), REAL WOMEN (Mandy), the police series, MAISIE RAINE (title role), and the rural drama, *Down to Earth* (Faith Addis). With her *Birds* co-star, Linda Robson, she also featured in the challenge series, *Jobs for the Girls*; and other notable credits have included the dramas, *Deadly Summer* (Linda Topping), *The Canterville Ghost* (medium Madame Murielle), *Our Boy* (Sonia) and *David Copperfield* (Peggotty). She appeared in DIXON OF DOCK GREEN as a child, and worked in all manner of kids' shows for Thames, including *You Must Be Joking!* and her own series, *Pauline's Quirkes* and *Pauline's People*. She has also been seen in THE DUCHESS OF DUKE STREET, CROWN COURT, *Lovely Couple*, GIRLS ON TOP, ROCKLIFFE'S BABIES, THE GOOD SEX GUIDE and CASUALTY, and narrated the docu-soap, *Lakesiders*.

QUIZ BALL
UK (BBC) Quiz. BBC 1 1966–72

Presenters: **David Vine, Barry Davies, Stuart Hall**

Producers: **Bill Wright, Mary Evans**

Light-hearted soccer quiz involving football league teams.

Quiz Ball was a game show in the QUESTION OF SPORT vein, but with its sporting content confined to association football. In each match, two professional soccer teams competed for the right to advance through the knock-out tournament. Arsenal played Nottingham Forest in the very first programme. Teams were composed of players, management and celebrity supporters and they answered questions of varying degrees of difficulty to progress along an electronic scoreboard (designed like a football pitch) towards goal. A hard question was the equivalent of a 'long ball', catapulting the team into their opponents' penalty box if answered correctly, whereas easier questions could be pieced together like a passing game for a slower approach. The team with the most goals won the match. There was even an international element to the tournament, with special Home International matches taking place between England, Wales, Scotland and Northern Ireland. David Vine was the first chairman and questionmaster, followed by Barry Davies and, finally, Stuart Hall.

R3
UK (BBC) Science Fiction. BBC 1 1964–5

Sir Michael Gerrard	**John Robinson**
Miss Brooks	**Brenda Saunders**
Dr George Fratton	**Moultrie Kelsall**
Dr May Howard	**Elizabeth Sellars**
Dr Peter Travers	**Richard Wordsworth**
Dr Jack Morton	**Simon Lack**
Betty Mason	**Janet Kelly**
Pomeroy	**Edwin Richfield**
Tom Collis	**Derek Benfield**
Porter	**Maxwell Foster**
Phillip Boult	**Michael Hawkins**
Dr Richard Franklin	**Oliver Reed**

Creator: **N. J. Crisp**
Producers: **Andrew Osborn, John Robins**

*Drama centring on the private and professional
lives of a team of scientists.*

Focusing on the staff of R3 (short for Research Centre
No. 3, a division of the Ministry of Research), this series
examined how scientists cope with the responsibilities
and demands of their jobs, and how these affect their
domestic lives. Effectively, it took eggheads and boffins
and gave them a human dimension. Sir Michael Gerrard
(played by former Professor Quatermass, John Robinson) was director of the unit, supported by his number
two, Dr George Fratton. Beneath him worked a team of
dedicated scientists, struggling to cope with the morality
of certain experiments and the social consequences of
new discoveries. In the second season the focus moved
to the department's trouble-shooting agency, a specialist
team geared up to solving problems beyond normal
human knowledge. It was led by Phillip Boult, aided by
a young Oliver Reed in the role of Dr Richard Franklin.

RAB C. NESBITT
UK (BBC) Situation Comedy. BBC 2 1990–

Rab C. Nesbitt	**Gregor Fisher**
Mary Nesbitt	**Elaine C. Smith**
Gash Nesbitt	**Andrew Fairlie**
Burney Nesbitt	**Eric Cullen**
Jamesie Cotter	**Tony Roper**
Ella Cotter	**Barbara Rafferty**
Andra	**Brian Pettifer**
Dodie	**Iain McColl**
Norrie	**John Kazek**
Bridie	**Nicola Park**
Natalie	**Elaine Ellis**
Screech Nesbitt	**David McKay**
Mr Grogan	**Jimmy Logan**

Creator/Writer: **Ian Pattison**
Producer: **Colin Gilbert**

*The downs and downs of tenement life with a
Glasgow street-philosopher.*

Sporting a string vest and a grubby headband, and brandishing a rolled-up newspaper, Rab C. Nesbitt made his name in the NAKED VIDEO sketch show, taking the Establishment to task in an opinionated drunken stupor. Following a New Year's special in 1989 (*Rab C. Nesbitt's Seasonal Greet*), this series was launched and showed the aggressive waster at home and at play, battling with his wife, Mary, and obnoxious kids, Gash and Burney, squabbling with his drinking chums (including his best mate, Jamesie) and bamboozling the forces of law and order with unfathomable Scottish gibberish. Bouts of prison, illness and family strife allowed the giro-king to reflect on his unhappy lot.

RACING GAME, THE
UK (Yorkshire) Detective Drama. ITV 1979–80

Sid Halley .... **Mike Gwilym**
Chico Barnes .... **Mick Ford**

Executive Producer: **David Cunliffe**
Producer: **Jacky Stoller**

A disabled jockey turns to private detective work.

Horse racing has never fared well in TV drama. Like the much-criticized TRAINER a decade later, this attempt to bring the colour of the sport of kings into viewers' living rooms was doomed to failure. Based on the hugely successful novels by former Royal jockey Dick Francis, this six-part series focused on one Sid Halley, a jump jockey who had suffered a bad riding accident and lost a hand. Denied a return to his true vocation, Halley did the next best thing – he hovered around the fringes of racing society, setting himself up as a private investigator and mingling with some of the murkier characters in the racing world. Despite successes against dopers and nobblers, betting-coup merchants and horsenappers, he and his assistant, Chico Barnes, failed to win over viewers, and a second series didn't come under starter's orders.

RAFFLES
UK (Yorkshire) Crime Drama. ITV 1977

L. J. Raffles .... **Anthony Valentine**
Bunny Manders .... **Christopher Strauli**
Insp. Mackenzie .... **Victor Carin**

Writer: **Philip Mackie**
Executive Producer: **David Cunliffe**
Producer: **Jacky Stoller**

Audacious robberies performed with aplomb by a turn-of-the-century gentleman thief.

A first-class cricketer, man-about-town and a general good egg, Raffles had but one excitement in life: the buzz that came from pulling off risky thefts from his upper-class associates, often under the noses of the authorities. Part of the pleasure lay in seeing his police adversary, Inspector Mackenzie, humiliated time and again. From his first daring theft of a £10,000 diamond necklace at a stately home, Raffles was loyally supported by reliable Bunny Manders, his former public school fag and the only man in the world who knew of his old friend's escapades.

The series was based on the original stories of E. W. Hornung, with the pilot episode, *Raffles – The Amateur Cracksman*, screened as a one-off in 1975. In this pilot, Mackenzie was played by James Maxwell.

RAG TAG AND BOBTAIL
UK (BBC) Children's Entertainment. BBC 1953–5

Narrators: **Charles E. Stidwill, David Enders, James Urquhart**

Writer: **Louise Cochrane**
Producers: **Freda Lingstrom, David Boisseau**

The hedgerow adventures of a trio of country animals.

Rag Tag and Bobtail was the Thursday segment of the WATCH WITH MOTHER strand and featured the little escapades of glove puppets Rag (a hedgehog), Tag (a mouse) and Bobtail (a clover-chewing buck rabbit). The puppets were created and controlled by Sam and Elizabeth Williams, and 26 episodes were made. Episodes one and two were never screened, but the remaining 24 were repeated endlessly until the programme was replaced in 1965.

RAG TRADE, THE
UK (BBC/LWT) Situation Comedy. BBC 1961–3; ITV 1977–8

Mr Fenner .... **Peter Jones**
Reg .... **Reg Varney**
Paddy .... **Miriam Karlin**
Carole .... **Sheila Hancock**
Little Lil .... **Esma Cannon**
Judy .... **Barbara Windsor**
Shirley .... **Wanda Ventham**
Janet .... **Amanda Reiss**
Sandra .... **Sheena Marshe**
Betty .... **Patricia Denys**
Myrtle .... **Claire Davenport**
Olive .... **Stella Tanner**
Gloria .... **Carmel Cryan**
Tony .... **Christopher Beeny** (*LWT*)
Olive .... **Anna Karen** (*LWT*)
Kathy .... **Diane Langton** (*LWT*)
Lyn .... **Gillian Taylforth** (*LWT*)
Jojo .... **Lucita Lijertwood** (*LWT*)
Mabel .... **Deddie Davies** (*LWT*)

Creators/Writers: **Ronald Chesney, Ronald Wolfe**
Producers: **Dennis Main Wilson** (*BBC*), **Bryan Izzard, William G. Stewart** (*LWT*)

Union strife at a clothing factory.

Set in the East End dressmaking workshop of Fenner Fashions, *The Rag Trade* focused on the him-and-us relationship between the unscrupulous, scheming boss, Mr Fenner, and his work-shy employees, with militant

Paddy, the shop steward, always ready to blow her whistle and order, 'Everybody out!' Carole was the shop treasurer, with Little Lil the buttonholer and tea-maker. Other girls came and went during the series' two-year run, but always stuck in the middle was Reg, the factory foreman.

A huge hit in the early 1960s, *The Rag Trade* was revived with less success in 1977. Only Peter Jones and Miriam Karlin survived from the original cast, and newcomers like Christopher Beeny (as foreman Tony) and Anna Karen (reprising her ON THE BUSES role of Olive) were added to the roll-call of workers. Lynsey de Paul provided the updated theme song.

RAINBOW/RAINBOW DAYS
UK (Thames/HTV/Tetra Films) Children's Entertainment.
ITV 1972–92; 1996–7

Presenters: **David Cook, Geoffrey Hayes, Dale Superville**

Executive Producers: **Charles Warren, Alan Horrox**
Producers: **Pamela Lansdale, Vic Hughes, Charles Warren, Lesley Burgess, Sheila Kinany, Paul Cole**

Education and entertainment for the pre-school age.

Although effectively ITV's answer to PLAY SCHOOL, *Rainbow* was more a British SESAME STREET. It was hosted originally by David Cook but more famously by former Z CARS actor Geoffrey Hayes (from 1973). Judi Dench was occasionally seen as a storyteller in the early days, and Stephanie Beacham filled the same role later, but better remembered are the *Rainbow* puppet characters. Taught and instructed as if they were kids (indeed they acted as surrogate children to convey the educational angle), the first puppets were Moony, a sad-looking mauve creature, and his antithesis, Sunshine, a livelier, yellow one. For many years, however, the puppet cast comprised Zippy, an oval-headed, wide-eyed creation with a painful-looking zip for a mouth, George, a pink hippopotamus, and Bungle, a good-natured bear originally played by actor John Leeson. Music was provided by the trio of Rod (Burton), Jane (Tucker) and Matthew (Corbett of Sooty fame), with Freddy (Marks) later taking the place of Matthew. Roger Walker was also once a member of the musical team. The singers were later given their own spin-off series, appropriately entitled *Rod, Jane and Freddy* (1981–5; 1989–91). The programme ended its long lunchtime run when Thames TV lost its franchise, although it later returned minus Geoffrey and with a new female puppet called Cleo in an afternoon slot. New host Dale Superville joined up when the show was revamped as *Rainbow Days* (1996–7).

RANDALL AND HOPKIRK (DECEASED)
UK (ITC) Detective Drama. ITV 1969–70

Jeff Randall	**Mike Pratt**
Marty Hopkirk	**Kenneth Cope**
Jean Hopkirk	**Annette Andre**
Insp. Large	**Ivor Dean**

Creator: **Dennis Spooner**
Producer: **Monty Berman**

Unorthodox investigations by a private eye and his partner, a ghost.

Jeff Randall and Marty Hopkirk were partners in a private detection agency – or, rather, they had been, until Marty was murdered in a hit-and-run incident. Returning as a ghost, he helped Jeff bring his killers to book, but, from that time onward, Marty was obliged to remain on Earth (for 100 years), having broken a rule of the afterlife by staying down here after daybreak. As the old rhyme went: *Afore the sun shall rise anew / Each ghost unto his grave must go. / Cursed be the ghost who dares to stay / And face the awful light of day. / He shall not to the grave return / Until a hundred years be gone.*

Being a ghost, Marty was visible to only one person, Jeff. Not even his bemused widow, Jean, who was Jeff's secretary, knew of his presence. But this rendered him remarkably useful in the detection game, as a valuable source of information, despite the fact that he could not get physically involved. Sadly, he was also rather unreliable and very frustrating: many a time Jeff was left waiting for his white-suited, deceased partner to show up with a vital clue, or to warn him of impending danger. Inspector Large was the programme's token grumpy copper.

The series, played with a generous slice of humour, was shown in the USA under the title *My Partner the Ghost* but was not a great success across the Atlantic. BBC 2 re-ran the series in 1994.

RANDALL AND HOPKIRK (DECEASED)
UK (Working Title) Detective Drama. BBC 1 2000–

Jeff Randall	**Bob Mortimer**
Marty Hopkirk	**Vic Reeves**
Jeannie Hurst	**Emilia Fox**
Wyvern	**Tom Baker**

Writer/Producer: **Charlie Higson**
Executive Producer: **Simon Wright**

Humorous update of the classic 1960s series.

Stylishly and colourfully shot for the digital age, the new *Randall and Hopkirk* was not a simple retread of the earlier series. For a start it starred Reeves and Mortimer and so, as straight as they hoped to play it, the revamp was never likely to be taken too seriously. Secondly, Charlie Higson, a long-time associate of Vic and Bob and best known for his work on THE FAST SHOW, was drafted in to write the scripts (with a little help from Paul Whitehouse), which again meant that humour was unlikely to be far away. The third major point was that special effects had come a long way in 30 years and the producers now had the opportunity to play around a lot more with the supernatural world inhabited by the deceased Marty. To explore this dimension further, a new character, Wyvern – a sort of ghostly godfather for the newly dead – was introduced. In all, there was more fantasy fun and less hard detective work, classier production values and a flippancy that even the original series couldn't match.

RANDALL, JOAN AND LESLIE

One of TV's first husband-and-wife couples, the Randalls starred in their own mid-1950s sitcom, appropriately titled *Joan and Leslie* but later changed to *The Randall Touch*, which evolved from a series called *Leslie Randall Entertains*. They later appeared as investigators Jane and Dagobert Brown in the DETECTIVE anthology and advertised Fairy Snow for nine years before splitting up. Leslie headed off for TV work in the USA and Australia, but returned in the 1970s to write plays and work in radio. Joan was often billed under her maiden name of Joan Reynolds.

RANGE RIDER, THE
US (Flying A) Western. BBC 1955

The Range Rider .... **Jock Mahoney**
Dick West .... **Dick Jones**

Executive Producer: **Armand Schaefer**
Producer: **Louis Gray**

A mysterious do-gooder and his friend roam the West, helping folk in trouble.

This early Western featured the exploits of the honest, principled and tough Range Rider and his boyish side-kick, Dick West. Together they drifted across the Wild West of the 1860s, putting outlaws in their place, rescuing helpless civilians and assisting the forces of law and order in their own unconventional way. They must have been the two most athletic cowboys around, for rarely did they spurn the chance to leap from their horses, rope in the criminals and perform whatever heroic feat was required. This was largely because the two stars were fit and brawny themselves and were willing to do their own stuntwork (actor Jock Mahoney later went on to play Tarzan).

Dressed in a fringed buckskin shirt and a white stetson, The Range Rider wore no boots, only Indian moccasins. His horse was called Rawhide. Dick, sporting a dark, military-style shirt and a black hat, rode a steed called Lucky. The theme song for the show was 'Home On The Range'.

RANTZEN, ESTHER
(1940–)

Doyenne of TV consumerists, Esther Rantzen began her career in radio production, arriving in television as a production assistant on BBC-3, MAN ALIVE and as a researcher/reporter on BRADEN'S WEEK. She moved on to produce and present her own series, which looked at the quirks of everyday life and stood up for the embattled consumer. Entitled THAT'S LIFE, it ran for 21 years from 1973, making Rantzen a household name. It also gave her the opportunity to expand into other programmes.

These included THE BIG TIME, *Hearts of Gold* and CHILDREN IN NEED (associated with her main charity concern, Childline). Since the end of *That's Life*, she has presented a BBC 2 topical discussion show called *Esther* and an ITV series, *That's Esther*. She was married to the late TV presenter and producer, Desmond Wilcox.

RAPHAEL, FREDERIC
(1931–)

British screenwriter, author of THE GLITTERING PRIZES and its sequel, *Oxbridge Blues*. His other credits have included *Rogue Male* (1976), *The Serpent Son*, *School Play* (both 1979), *After the War* (1989) and the 1978 *Premiere* film, *Something's Wrong* (also as director). He also hosted FILM 72 for a while.

RAT CATCHERS, THE
UK (Associated-Rediffusion) Spy Drama. ITV 1966–7

Peregrine Smith .... **Gerald Flood**
Brigadier Davidson .... **Philip Stone**
Richard Hurst .... **Glyn Owen**

Producer: **Cyril Coke**

The assignments of a top-secret counter-espionage team.

The Rat Catchers were based in Whitehall but officially had no name or number; their existence was denied by the highest authorities and they worked in the greatest secrecy. Their role was to defend the country from foreign threats and to obey orders without question. As a result, they lived and operated in a violent, hazardous world.

The three members of the team were wealthy playboy Peregrine Smith, cold, analytical Brigadier Davidson (the brains of the team) and newcomer Richard Hurst, a former Scotland Yard superintendent. It was with Hurst's arrival that viewers first learned about the squad, and his uncertain start revealed just how unsavoury this profession could be. Indeed, it was a far cry from the glitzy world of James Bond, their cinema contemporary.

RATINGS

The audience figures enjoyed by television programmes, arranged in order of popularity. These are of particular value to advertisers but are also a useful pointer for programme-makers when gauging the success of their projects. The statistics are compiled using various means, from simple consumer surveys and viewer diaries to electronic devices attached to television receivers. Numerous companies have collated the information in the UK over the years. The American giant, AC Nielsen, was active in the 1950s, but also involved have been Gallup, Pulse, TAM (Television Audience Measurement) and AGB (Audits of Great Britain), the last producing figures for the Joint Industry Committee for Television Audience Research (JICTAR), a committee representing the interests of ITV companies and their advertisers. In 1981, at the behest of the 1977 Annan Committee's review of broadcasting in the UK, the separate BBC and JICTAR ratings systems were amalgamated into the Broadcasters' Audience Research Board (BARB). The collation method in use today is complex and involves drawing data by meter from sample households that are selected to provide a cross-section of ages, sex and economic and social status.

RAVEN, SIMON
(1927–2001)

British novelist and screenwriter, initially scripted his own plays like *Royal Foundation*, *The Scapegoat* and *A Soirée at Bossom's Hotel* in the 1960s, before he turned to adaptations like *The Way We Live Now* and THE PALLISERS and series dramas such as EDWARD AND MRS SIMPSON in the 1970s. Among his later work was the dramatization of *The Blackheath Poisonings* in 1992.

RAWHIDE
US (CBS) Western. ITV 1959–67

Gil Favor	**Eric Fleming**
Rowdy Yates	**Clint Eastwood**
Wishbone	**Paul Brinegar**
Pete Nolan	**Sheb Wooley**
Jim Quince	**Steve Raines**
Joe Scarlett	**Rocky Shahan**
Harkness 'Mushy' Mushgrove	**James Murdock**
Hey Soos Patines	**Robert Cabal**
Clay Forrester	**Charles Gray**
Jed Colby	**John Ireland**
Ian Cabot	**David Watson**

Creator/Producer: **Charles Marquis Warren**

The adventures of a cattle-driving team as they cross the Wild West.

Chiefly remembered for being the show that gave Clint Eastwood his first taste of stardom, *Rawhide* was a Western for men by men, a kind of WAGON TRAIN with cows and precious few women. It revolved around a team of cattle-drovers, trying to lead a herd from San Antonio, Texas, up to Sedalia, Missouri, some time in the 1860s, well before the railroad arrived to alleviate this chore. Gil Favor was the head of the team, with Eastwood's Rowdy Yates the second-in-command, later to assume control when Favor was written out. Also in the troop were trail scout Pete Nolan, cook Wishbone, Mushy, the drover, and a Mexican, Hey Soos (Jesus). Their men-against-the-elements voyage was constantly interrupted by encounters with intriguing strangers, so much so that when the series ended seven years later, they still hadn't reached the end of the trail.

The 'Keep them doggies rollin'' theme song was a UK hit for Frankie Laine in 1959. Sheb Wooley, who played Pete Nolan, was also a comedian-cum-country-singer and had already broken into the UK Top 20 in 1958 with 'The Purple People Eater' (a number one in the USA).

RAY, ROBIN
(Robin Olden; 1935–98)

London-born actor/presenter, first seen on TV in the 1956 play, *The Guv'nor*, and then alongside his father, comedian Ted Ray. He went on to appear in the comedy show, *Dig This Rhubarb*, and then began to indulge his interest in the arts and, in particular, music and the cinema. Among his credits were *Film Buff of the Year* (questionmaster), CALL MY BLUFF (first chairman) and FACE THE MUSIC (panellist). Robin was the brother of actor Andrew Ray and was married to former MAGPIE presenter Susan Stranks.

RAY, TED
(Charles Olden; 1905–77)

Music-hall comedian/violinist who came to television following success with *Ray's a Laugh* on the radio. His *Ted Ray Show* was popular in the 1950s, and he also compered SPOT THE TUNE on some occasions. In the 1970s he was back on the small screen as a regular panellist on the gag show, *Jokers Wild*, and the talent show, NEW FACES. He was the father of actors Andrew and Robin Ray.

RAYNER, CLAIRE
OBE (1931–)

One of Britain's leading agony aunts, former nurse Claire Rayner is a familiar face on UK TV. She has answered problems and proffered advice on TV-am and in her own series, *Claire Rayner's Casebook*, as well as appearing as a guest on many magazine programmes. She is also a published novelist.

READY, STEADY, GO!
UK (Associated-Rediffusion) Pop Music. ITV 1963–6

Presenters: **Keith Fordyce, David Gell, Michael Aldred, Cathy McGowan**

Producers: **Frances Hitching, Vicki Wickham**
Executive Producer: **Elkan Allan**

Influential British pop-music show, a focal point of the beat boom.

'The Weekend Starts Here' was the slogan of this lively pop showcase that opened up each week to the sound of Manfred Mann's '5-4-3-2-1', and later the same band's 'Hubble Bubble Toil and Trouble'. Airing early on a Friday evening, the weekend really did begin here for many teenagers, particularly those outside London, for whom this was one of the few opportunities to savour the heady years of British beat. The kids took their lead from *RSG!* in dance, in fashion and, of course, in musical taste.

Technically advanced for its era, particularly in the innovative camerawork, *RSG!* enjoyed the patronage of nearly all the leading acts – from The Beatles and The Rolling Stones to Stevie Wonder and Little Richard – who seldom missed the chance to appear. But it also bravely introduced lesser-known artists, including obscure bands, some from across the Atlantic (who now remembers Glenda Collins and the Orchids, Van Dyke and the Bambies or Bobby Shafto?). Far more lively than the rather static TOP OF THE POPS, *RSG!* boasted a tiny studio, crammed full with excited youths enjoying a club-like atmosphere, nudging and pressing against the featured artists as they bopped to the music.

The hosts (at various times) were Keith Fordyce, David Gell, Michael Aldred and Cathy McGowan, a young discovery who quickly mastered the art of presenting TV pop. She had answered an advertisement calling for a 'typical teenager' to act as an adviser on the show, but she was soon pushed in front of the cameras. Her success lay in the fact that she was one of the fans; the viewers could identify with her as she fluffed her lines, grinned at inappropriate moments and panicked during interviews with celebrities. She was one of the teenagers, not a long-in-the-tooth broadcaster, and she soon became a style leader herself. When the programme switched to a larger studio and bands were obliged to perform live instead of miming, McGowan was kept on as solo presenter.

The series drew to a close just as the beat boom came to an end. The fact that it was axed at the height of its popularity has clearly helped maintain its respected status as a TV pop classic. Compilations were shown on Channel 4 in the 1980s, courtesy of drummer-turned-entrepreneur Dave Clark, who now owns the rights to the tapes.

REAL LIVES

UK (BBC) Documentary. BBC 1 1984–5

Executive Producers: **Peter Pagnamenta, Edward Mirzoeff**

A series of close inspections of how people live today.

This documentary series looked at the lives of people from all parts of society, examining what made them tick. Among those featured were a defecting Russian violinist, drug-pushers, Los Angeles street-gang members, finalists in a 'True Romances' contest and a British army unit going back to Northern Ireland as civilians. One programme due for transmission in the second series caused a major stir. Entitled *At the Edge of the Union*, it focused on two individuals at opposite extremes in the Northern Ireland troubles. The two were Gregory Campbell and Martin McGuinness. The fact that McGuinness was said to have been an IRA supporter enraged the Government, which felt that terrorists should not have been given the oxygen of publicity. Home Secretary Leon Brittan intervened (without seeing the programme) and called for it to be withdrawn. This led to a dispute between the BBC's Board of Governors (who agreed with his sentiments) and the BBC Management (who wanted it to be screened). The programme was not transmitted and, in protest at what they viewed

as interference in the BBC's independence, journalists from both BBC and ITN staged a one-day strike. With some changes, the programme was finally shown in October 1985, two months late.

REAL WOMEN

UK (BBC) Drama. BBC 1 1998–

Mandy	**Pauline Quirke**
Susie	**Michelle Collins**
Karen	**Lesley Manville**
Janet	**Gwyneth Strong**
Anna	**Frances Barber**
Chris	**Jane Gurnett**
Steve	**Gary Webster**
Pete	**Richard Graham**
Barry	**Peter Hugo-Daly**
Doreen	**Toni Palmer**
Bobby	**Tony Selby**
Jonathan Bell	**Mark Moraghan**
Lyndsay	**Debbie Arnold**
Jo	**Con O'Neil**
Frank	**Brian Protheroe**
Richard Scholes	**Peter Lindford**
Barrett	**Aaron White**
Derek Johnson	**Dave Hill**
Michael	**Ray Stevenson**
Jackie	**Juliet Cowan**

Writer: **Susan Oudot**
Executive Producer: **Jane Tranter**
Producer: **Debbie Shewell**

A wedding brings old schoolfriends together and exposes crises in their personal lives.

Five London women in their late thirties were the focus of this earthy three-part drama, written by Susan Oudot and based on her own novel of the same title. At the centre of the action was flighty Susie, about to get married to Jo but clearly having second thoughts. The four former schoolfriends who joined her for the hen night began with Mandy, the downtrodden family woman whose husband, Pete, and sons never showed her any appreciation. She had now embarked on an affair with estate agent Jonathan. Then there was Janet, a bank clerk who was desperate to have her own child, but whose efforts with her husband Steve came to nothing; lonely-heart Anna, a features writer who had moved into more sophisticated circles since leaving school and was now recovering from a broken relationship; and Karen, a teacher, who was scared to introduce her lesbian lover, Chris, to the rest of the gang. Also seen was Susie's sister, Lyndsay, married with four kids.

From the first drunken night out, through the eve of the wedding to the wedding day itself, secrets began to leak out and the individual problems facing the women began to unfold. The drama resumed in a second four-part series – based on the sequel novel, *All That I Am* – in 1999. Set 18 months further on, with Susie about to give birth, it picked up the girls' stories as they headed for the landmark age of 40.

RECORD BREAKERS
UK (BBC) Children's Entertainment. BBC 1 1972–

Presenters: **Roy Castle, Ross McWhirter, Norris McWhirter, Dilys Morgan, Fiona Kennedy, Julian Farino, Cheryl Baker, Ron Reagan Jr, Kriss Akabusi, Mark Curry, Dan Roland, Linford Christie, Jez Edwards, Kate Sanderson, Sally Gray**

Producers: **Alan Russell, Eric Rowan, Greg Childs**

The tallest, the shortest, the latest and the greatest: TV's answer to the Guinness Book of Records.

Record Breakers is one programme which is unlikely to run out of ideas. After all, there is always someone about to break a record, however brave or daft it may be. For nearly 30 years this series has been featuring some of the world's wackiest record-setters and even claiming a few firsts of its own, by arranging record-breaking attempts in the studio (over 300). Its host, until his untimely death in 1994, was Roy Castle, a man who was a record-breaker on many occasions in his own right. In the very first programme he created the world's biggest one-man band, with over 40 instruments at his disposal. He also set records for the world's fastest tap-dance (24 beats a second) and for wing-walking across the Channel, not to mention riding on top of a 39-man motorcycle pyramid and leaping from the top of the Blackpool Tower. For such achievements, as he sang in the theme song, 'You need dedication'. The *Guinness Book of Records* founders, Norris and the late Ross McWhirter, assisted Roy in the early days, and Norris has continued to make appearances from time to time. Cheryl Baker was Castle's partner from 1987 and then she remained in charge alongside ex-athlete Kriss Akabusi, former BLUE PETER man Mark Curry and, for two seasons, Ron Reagan Jr (son of the former US President). Baker and Akabusi also presented *Record Breakers Gold* (1997–8), a compilation series of greatest moments. The programme was revamped in 1998 and retitled *Linford's Record Breakers*, when athlete Linford Christie took control.

RED DWARF
UK (Paul Jackson/Grant Naylor/BBC) Situation Comedy. BBC 2 1988–93; 1997–

Arnold J. Rimmer, BSc, SSC	**Chris Barrie**
Dave Lister	**Craig Charles**
Cat	**Danny John-Jules**
Holly	**Norman Lovett**
	Hattie Hayridge
Kryten	**David Ross**
	Robert Llewellyn
Christine/Kristine Kochanski	**Clare/C. P. Grogan**
	Chloë Annett
Capt. Hollister	**Mac McDonald**

Creators: **Rob Grant, Doug Naylor**
Executive Producers: **Paul Jackson, Rob Grant, Doug Naylor**

Producers: **Ed Bye, Hilary Bevan Jones, Justin Judd**

Space-age sitcom featuring the last survivor on a spaceship and his annoying non-human companions.

When Technician Third-Class Dave Lister was sentenced to a period in suspended animation (or 'stasis'), some time in the 24th century, for smuggling a pregnant cat aboard his spaceship, little did he know that he would wake up three million years later and be the sole survivor of a radiation leak. Resigned to roaming the cosmos in the five-mile-long, three-mile-wide mining ship, *Red Dwarf*, Lister discovered that all 168 other crew members had died and his only companions were Holly, the ship's computer, Cat, a hybrid life-form evolved from his pet, and a hologram of his obnoxious former roommate and supervisor, Arnold J. (Judas) Rimmer.

While the deadpan Holly (seen only as a face on a TV screen) was a bit of a practical joker (for a computer), the overzealous Rimmer was devoid of humour and was the exact opposite of Lister in every way. Their incompatibility was central to the series. Desperately ambitious, Rimmer, sadly, was also a coward and unfailingly inept (it had been his error that led to the fatal radiation leak). Being a hologram, he couldn't touch anything and relied on Holly for his existence and wellbeing. Lister, on the other hand, whiled away his time eating curry, watching videos, slagging off 'smegging' Rimmer and lounging on his bunk, perhaps dreaming of Christine Kochanski, another dead crewmate (played initially in flashbacks by one-time Altered Images singer Clare Grogan but then made flesh by Chloë Annett). However, it was Cat who proved to be the most intriguing character. Portrayed as a narcissistic, black dude in snappy dress, Cat looked human (except for his fangs and six nipples) but possessed feline instincts. Lining his stomach and looking good were paramount. He toyed with a roast chicken as a cat would a bird, took 'cat naps', licked his laundry clean and sprayed perfume from an aerosol to mark out his territory.

In later seasons, a new Holly was introduced, with comedian Hattie Hayridge replacing Norman Lovett as the dry, lugubrious computer (Lovett returned in the seventh series), and an android, Kryten, was added to the cast. Discovered working as a manservant to three human girls (who had long since perished), the angular robot temporarily joined *Red Dwarf* in the second series; but, with a new actor in the role, he took up permanent residence the following year. The only other regular characters were a couple of silent robot helpers called scutters and a few talking appliances, like an outspoken toaster. However, by dipping into parallel universes, or whizzing forward to the future or back to the past, there was no shortage of new situations for the mismatched crew to encounter. When the mining ship was somehow stolen, the team were stranded for a while in space in the pokey *Starbug* shuttle.

More than three years separated series six and seven and Chris Barrie committed to only part of that seventh series but, contrary to fans' fears, *Red Dwarf* did return in 1997, with an eighth series following in 1999. In the latter, the original *Red Dwarf* had been re-created by nanobots, complete with real human crew.

Red Dwarf, though slow to pick up audiences, rapidly gained cult status. Each series' title included a number, with the second series called Red Dwarf II, etc. Its creators, Rob Grant and Doug Naylor, had previously worked with Chris Barrie on SPITTING IMAGE. Grant, however, was not involved after Red Dwarf VI.

REDCAP
UK (ABC) Police Drama. ITV 1964–6

Sgt John Mann .... **John Thaw**

Creator: **Jack Bell**
Producer: **John Bryce**

Investigations into crime in the armed forces, conducted by a tough, no-nonsense military policeman.

John Mann was a sergeant in the Special Investigation Branch of the Royal Military Police – the 'Redcaps' – and a thorough one at that. His forceful, demanding investigations rooted out army crooks all over the world, from Malaya and Borneo to Aden and Cyprus; and, although he reserved a softer side of his character for those in genuine distress, his fuse was short and regularly lit. The series provided good training for John Thaw, with John Mann's bluster carried through to Jack Regan in THE SWEENEY and his sullen solitude resurfacing in INSPECTOR MORSE.

REDIFFUSION
See **ASSOCIATED-REDIFFUSION**.

REDGRAVE, JEMMA
(Jemima Redgrave; 1965–)

British actress, the daughter of Corin Redgrave. Her major TV credits have included *The Buddha of Suburbia* (Eleanor), BRAMWELL (Eleanor Bramwell), *Mosley* (Cynthia Curzon/Mosley), *Blue Murder* (Gale Francombe), *Cry Wolf* (Dr Wolf) and *Fish* (Joanna Morgan).

REDMAN, AMANDA
(1958–)

British actress seen in a number of high-profile roles, in series such as THE MEN'S ROOM (Sally), *Streets Apart* (Sylvia), EL C.I.D. (Rosie Bromley), *Body and Soul* (Lynn Gibson), *Demob* (Janet Deasey), DANGERFIELD (Dr Joanna Stevens), *Beck* (title role), *Close Relations* (Prudence), THE RUTH RENDELL MYSTERIES (Susan Townsend), *The Blonde Bombshell* (Diana Dors), *Hope and Glory* (Debbie Bryan) and *At Home with the Braithwaites* (Alison Braithwaite). Other credits have come in *Richard's Things*, BERGERAC, *To Have and to Hold*, SPENDER and *Screen Two*'s *The Lorelei*. Redman also runs a theatre school in Ealing and was once married to actor Robert Glenister.

REDMOND, PHIL
(1949–)

Liverpudlian writer whose early efforts included episodes of DOCTOR IN CHARGE, DOCTOR AT SEA, *The Kids From 47A*, *Potter's Picture Palace* and THE SQUIRRELS. In 1976 he changed direction and took an idea for a realistic schooldays programme to the BBC. The idea was commissioned and GRANGE HILL was born. Redmond followed this up with *Going Out*, a programme about struggling school-leavers, for Southern Television and then began work on a major project for the BBC. Entitled *County Hall*, it aimed to dramatize the workings of a major local authority but ran for only one series. Somewhat disillusioned, Redmond moved into the independent sector. He set up Mersey Television and sold an idea for a vibrant, down-to-earth soap opera to Channel 4. As BROOKSIDE, it aired on the station's first night and has proved to be one of its major successes. Among Redmond's other work has been the police series, *Waterfront Beat*, and the teen soap, HOLLYOAKS. He has also been a consultant for EMMERDALE (the plane crash was his idea). Mersey Television, meanwhile, unsuccessfully challenged Granada for the ITV North-west England franchise in 1991.

REDMOND, SIOBHAN
(1959–)

Scottish actress, probably best known for her role as Det. Sgt Maureen Connell in BETWEEN THE LINES. Earlier, Redmond had appeared in the Granada comedy, ALFRESCO, before joining Don Henderson in BULMAN, playing his sidekick, Lucy McGinty. Redmond was also seen in *The Advocates* (Janie Naismith), THE BILL, the sitcom *The High Life* (air stewardess Shona Spurtle), *Screen One*'s *Deacon Brodie* (Jean Brodie), *Screen Two*'s *Nervous Energy* (Joyce), the Alexei Sayle comedy, *Sorry About Last Night* (Julie Cordova), *In the Red* (Ms Sin), *Wokenwell* (Cheryl Cappler) and *Every Woman Knows a Secret* (Jess Arrowsmith).

REES, ROGER
(1944–)

Welsh actor who has enjoyed TV work on both sides of the Atlantic, most notably as Malcolm in SINGLES and millionaire Robin Colcord in CHEERS. He was also the lead in the RSC's screen version of *The Life and Adventures of Nicholas Nickleby*, appeared with Laurence Olivier in *The Ebony Tower* and has other credits like BOUQUET OF BARBED WIRE, *Under Western Eyes*, *Saigon – Year of the Cat*, *Imaginary Friends* and *The Voysey Inheritance*, plus TV Shakespeare. Among his most recent work has been the US adventure series, *M.A.N.T.I.S.*

Maud Slingsby	Shirley Dixon
Pte. Hodge	John Hallett
Lt. Henry Percival	Michael Elwyn

Creators: **Jack Gerson, Nick McCarty**
Producers: **Royston Morley, Terence Dudley**

The fortunes of an army regiment as seen through the eyes of two families.

Beginning as a single play (part of the DRAMA PLAYHOUSE collection in 1970), *The Regiment* focused on the years 1895–1904 and the events that unfolded around the Cotswold Regiment. With the Boer War in the first series and then the days of the Raj in India in the second as backdrops, the series particularly looked at members of two families, the Gaunts and the Brights, and their varied positions in the greater scheme of things.

REID, BERYL
OBE (1920–96)

British actress/comedienne who enjoyed her own series (*The Beryl Reid Show* and *Beryl Reid*), plus a host of guest parts. Her earliest credits were with Vic Wise in the comedy, *Vic's Grill*, and as Arethusa Wilderspin in a sitcom called *The Most Likely Girl* in 1957. She then starred as Bessie Briggs in the comedy, *Bold as Brass*, played Rene Jelliot and Marigold Alcock in the sitcoms, *Wink to Me Only* and *Alcock and Gander*, respectively, took the part of Mrs Knox in THE IRISH RM and appeared as Grandma in THE SECRET DIARY OF ADRIAN MOLE. Her cameo role as Connie Sachs in TINKER, TAILOR, SOLDIER, SPY won her a BAFTA award, and she went on to act in the follow-up, *Smiley's People*. Reid was also seen in *A–Z*, THE GOOD OLD DAYS, MINDER, DOCTOR WHO, THE BEIDERBECKE TAPES, THE COMIC STRIP PRESENTS, CRACKER and *A Perfect Spy*, among numerous other series spanning four decades.

REID, MIKE
(1940–)

Cockney comedian and actor, coming to the fore in THE COMEDIANS with his 'Terr-i-fic' catchphrase and aggressive style of joke-telling. He moved into children's TV to 'manage' the hectic game show, *Runaround*, and later played Arthur Mullard's brother, Benny Briggs, in YUS MY DEAR, as well as appearing in the drama, BIG DEAL. More recently he has been better known as Frank Butcher in EASTENDERS. Reid has also hosted his own variety series, *Mike Reid's Mates and Music* and *Entertainment Express*.

REILLY – ACE OF SPIES
UK (Euston Films/Thames) Spy Drama. ITV 1983

Sidney Reilly	Sam Neill
Major Fothergill	Peter Egan
Bruce Lockhart	Ian Charleson
Cummings	Norman Rodway

REEVES, GEORGE
(George Brewer; 1914–59)

TV's first Superman, George Reeves at one time looked to have a promising film career ahead of him. He appeared in *Gone with the Wind* in 1939, but then things gradually headed downhill. Turning to television, he landed the role which was, at last, to make him a household name, that of the 'Man of Steel' in THE ADVENTURES OF SUPERMAN, which began in the USA in 1951. He played Superman for six years, suffering cruelly from typecasting when it ended. Two years later he was found shot dead, but the official suicide verdict has been challenged by those close to him.

REEVES, VIC
(Jim Moir; 1959–)

North-eastern comedian, partner of Bob Mortimer. Both having failed as punk rockers, Reeves was managing an alternative comedy venue in London where Mortimer, a solicitor, was a regular heckler. Joining forces, they took the *Vic Reeves Big Night Out* act on a tour of universities. It then secured its own slot on Channel 4 in 1990, where it gained a cult following for its absurd humour, catchphrases like 'You wouldn't let it lie' and novel characters like The Man With The Stick, The Ponderers, Les, and Wavy Davy. Subsequently the duo moved to the BBC with a similarly off-beat show entitled *The Smell of Reeves and Mortimer* and new characters such as The Bra Men and a chance to visit pop group Slade at home. A departure from their 'norm' was the spoof celebrity quiz, SHOOTING STARS, and they also devised a one-off showcase for team captain Ulrika Jonsson. The next outings for their anarchic, but increasingly slapstick, humour (large frying pans in the face, etc.) were *Bang, Bang, It's Reeves and Mortimer* and a surreal Saturday tea-time game show, *Families at War*. The pair were also seen in the single comedies, *The Weekenders* and *The Honeymoon's Over*. In 2000 they starred in the revamp of the detective caper, RANDALL AND HOPKIRK (DECEASED).

REGIMENT, THE
UK (BBC) Drama. BBC 1 1972–3

Lt./Capt. Richard Gaunt	Christopher Cazenove
Lt. Col. Gaunt-Seymour	Richard Wordsworth
Lt. James Willoughby	John Hallam
Hon. Alice Gaunt	Wendy Williams
Charlotte Gaunt	Wendy Allnutt
Capt./Major Rupert Saunders	Bernard Brown
Dorothy Saunders	Maria Aitken
Capt./Major Alfred Slingsby	Denis Lill
Lt./Capt. Jeffrey Sissons	Roy Herrick
RSM William Bright	Michael Brennan
Col. Cranleigh-Osborne	Frederick Treves
Mrs Cranleigh-Osborne	Virginia Balfour
Dr Mary Mitcheson/Gaunt	Penelope Lee
Cpl. Ernest Bright	James Bate

Dzerzhinsky	**Tom Bell**
Stalin	**David Burke**
Lenin	**Kenneth Cranham**
Basil Zaharov	**Leo McKern**
Margaret Thomas/Reilly	**Jeananne Crowley**
Insp. Tsientsin	**David Suchet**
Baldwin	**Donald Morley**
Count Massino	**John Castle**

Writer: **Troy Kennedy Martin**
Executive Producer: **Verity Lambert**
Producer: **Chris Burt**

Dramatization of the life of one of Britain's first secret agents.

In early Revolutionary Russia, Sidney Reilly, born in Odessa and raised by an aristocratic Russian family, operated as a British agent, aiming to topple the Bolshevik regime and install a new, British-approved government with himself at its head. His attempt failed, however, and Reilly was executed at the hands of the Supreme Soviet Revolutionary Tribunal.

This lavish 12-part drama was based on the biography of the real Reilly by Robin Bruce Lockhart. Although the character was artistically spiced up for TV, Reilly was himself a colourful and intriguing personality: suave, cool and daring, with a keen eye for the ladies. The series' acclaimed, sweeping theme music was written by Harry Rabinowitz.

REITH, Lord JOHN
(1889–1971)

Lord Reith was effectively the BBC's founding father. Born in Scotland, Reith had served in World War I and had managed a large engineering works in Coatbridge before being appointed to the job of General Manager of the newly inaugurated British Broadcasting Company in 1922. (While this may seem a surprising background, it has to be considered that there were few people at the time with experience of broadcasting in any form.) In 1927 he became what was by then the British Broadcasting Corporation's first Director-General and was knighted the same year. He left the Corporation in 1938 to become Chairman of Imperial Airways and later a government minister during the war, having set the course of public-service broadcasting the BBC was to follow successfully for decades. Reith's view of broadcasting was as more than mere entertainment for the masses. He insisted that the new media of radio and television also contributed to the intellectual and moral fabric of society – the mission was to inform and educate as well as to entertain. He was made a baron in 1940 and, in his honour, the BBC founded the prestigious annual Reith Lectures in 1948.

RELATIVE STRANGERS
See **HOLDING THE FORT.**

REMINGTON STEELE
US (MTM) Detective Drama. BBC 1/Channel 4 1983–4/ 1986–7

Remington Steele	**Pierce Brosnan**
Laura Holt	**Stephanie Zimbalist**
Murphy Michaels	**James Read**
Bernice Foxe	**Janet De May**
Mildred Krebs	**Doris Roberts**

Creators: **Michael Gleason, Robert Butler**
Executive Producers: **Michael Gleason, Gareth Davies**
Producers: **Glenn Gordon Caron, Lee Zlotoff**

An ambitious blonde opens a detective agency, names it after a man and then finds someone to play the part.

When Laura Holt set up the Laura Holt Investigations detective agency, she found that work was hard to come by. The problem was that no one seemed to trust a female detective. So she created an imaginary male boss for herself, renaming the company Remington Steele Investigations. At last the business began to pay. Although it was easy at first to make excuses for her absent chief, Laura soon realized that there would have to be a real Remington Steele to keep the customers happy. As chance would have it, a suitable candidate conveniently turned up on her doorstep. He was actually a con-man, trying to get his hands on some jewels Laura was protecting. But the couple hit it off from the start. He was suave, handsome and just the job, so they agreed that he should become Remington Steele, and he joined the agency as a partner.

Nothing much was ever revealed about this dark, handsome stranger of Irish descent, least of all his real name. There were occasional hints about his murky past, but he developed into a more than useful detective and the business boomed. His encyclopaedic knowledge of classic Hollywood movies proved particularly handy, enabling him to solve cases by re-creating memorable scenes from films like *The Third Man*, *Casablanca* and *Key Largo*. He and Laura flirted with each other, though it took some time for the full-blown affair to take off, and even then it was not properly consummated until the final season. The romantic tension between the duo helped give the show some buzz, and their sparkling repartee introduced a comic dimension to the plot, but it was never at the same level witnessed later in MOON-LIGHTING (created by one of *Remington Steele*'s producers, Glenn Gordon Caron).

Also seen were Murphy Michaels, Laura's first partner, who left to form his own agency, and secretary Bernice Foxe, who was replaced by former tax inspector Mildred Krebs. All the episodes had titles containing 'Steele' puns, such as *Steele Crazy After All These Years*, *Thou Shalt Not Steele* and *You're Steele the One for Me*.

Stephanie Zimbalist was the daughter of THE FBI and 77 SUNSET STRIP star Efrem Zimbalist Jr, who guest-starred in one episode. Although Pierce Brosnan became a Hollywood name as a result of this series, he also found it to be an impediment to future success. It was an open secret that his name had been pencilled in as the next James Bond when Roger Moore retired, but, because of his contractual commitments to *Remington Steele*, the part was given to Timothy Dalton. When Dalton eventually quit the Bond role in 1994, Brosnan was free and promptly signed up as 007.

RENALDO, DUNCAN
(Renaldo Duncan; 1904–80)

American actor, busy in the 1930s and 1940s in a variety of film roles, including that of THE CISCO KID, a part that he brought to television in 1950. As the Western rogue with the heart of gold, he became one of TV's earliest stars.

RENTAGHOST
UK (BBC) Children's Comedy. BBC 1 1976–84

Timothy Claypole	**Michael Staniforth**
Mr Harold Meaker	**Edward Brayshaw**
Fred Mumford	**Anthony Jackson**
Hubert Davenport	**Michael Darbyshire**
Mr Mumford	**John Dawson**
Mrs Mumford	**Betty Alberge**
Mrs Ethel Meaker	**Ann Emery**
Hazel the McWitch	**Molly Weir**
Tamara Novek	**Lynda Marchal**
Nadia Popov	**Sue Nicholls**
Rose Perkins	**Hal Dyer**
Arthur Perkins	**Jeffrey Segal**
Adam Painting	**Christopher Biggins**
Catastrophe Kate	**Jana Sheldon**
Queen Matilda	**Paddie O'Neill**
Susie Starlight	**Aimi Macdonald**
Bernie St John	**Vincent White**

Creator/Writer: **Bob Block**
Producers: **Paul Ciani, Jeremy Swan**

*A trio of hapless ghosts try to help those still
living, with disastrous consequences.*

Recently deceased Fred Mumford was finding it hard coming to terms with being a ghost, but helping him adjust to the afterlife were Victorian spectre Hubert Davenport and mischievous medieval jester Timothy Claypole. Their earthly associates included their landlord, Mr Meaker, and Fred's middle-aged mum and dad. The fun and games derived from the ghosts' hopeless efforts to make themselves useful by setting up the Rentaghost agency, through which they could be hired to tackle all sorts of 20th-century activities, like running a restaurant or becoming newspaper reporters.

Later additions to the cast included a wife for Mr Meaker (who became the ghosts' manager); constantly bemused new neighbours Rose and Arthur Perkins; department store manager Adam Painting; and assorted new ghosts. These included Hazel the McWitch, American Catastrophe Kate, nanny Tamara Novek (played by future screenwriter Lynda La Plante under the stage name of Lynda Marchal), her replacement, Nadia Popov,

and fairy godmother Susie Starlight. Adding to the confusion was Dobbin, the pantomime horse, and Bernie St John, a dragon that lived in the cellar. Star Michael Staniforth also sang the theme song.

RENWICK, DAVID
(1951–)

British comedy writer, for many years in partnership with Andrew Marshall (see Marshall's entry for joint work). Renwick, without Marshall, provided gags for THE TWO RONNIES, Mike Yarwood, Little and Large, Dick Emery, Janet Brown and Les Dawson earlier in his career, and since going solo he has enjoyed his greatest success through ONE FOOT IN THE GRAVE and JONATHAN CREEK.

REPEAT

The second or subsequent showing of a TV programme, usually to fill gaps in the schedule, to cover holiday periods (when low audiences do not merit new productions) or, occasionally and increasingly, because the quality of the original warrants another screening. The new interest in classic television has made repeats (once the bane of viewers' lives, or at least claimed to be) a growing segment of the TV market. In the USA, repeats are known as re-runs and have always enjoyed a regular place in the schedules. With new programmes generally aired in the States between September and May, re-runs have traditionally come into their own from June to August. Furthermore, once a national network has exhausted its contract for running and re-running a series, its producers have often sold it into syndication, giving independent stations across the country the chance to buy old episodes of popular series for screening locally. That is why viewers can always find episodes of classics from the 1950s onwards doing the rounds of the USA's smaller TV stations.

RE-RUN
See REPEAT.

RESEARCHER

A member of the production team whose job is to look into possible issues and subjects for programming, to brief presenters on background information, to investigate locations prior to shooting and to contact and vet potential contributors, be they experts, interviewees or game show contestants.

RETURN OF SHELLEY, THE
See SHELLEY.

RETURN OF SHERLOCK HOLMES, THE
see ADVENTURES OF SHERLOCK HOLMES, THE.

RETURN OF THE SAINT, THE
UK (ITC) Adventure. ITV 1978–9

Simon Templar .... **Ian Ogilvy**

Executive Producer: **Robert S. Baker**
Producer: **Anthony Spinner**

A revival of the charming 1960s international adventurer.

Nine years after Roger Moore hung up Simon Templar's halo, lookalike Ian Ogilvy tried it on for size. Similar in many ways, although critically less well received, this regeneration of Leslie Charteris's dashing, confident hero once again saw our hero whizzing around the globe, relaxing in the company of beautiful women and escaping from many life-threatening situations – all against a backdrop of international intrigue.

REYNOLDS, BURT
(1936–)

American actor who served his apprenticeship in television before becoming a Hollywood star. His breaks came in the 1950s, primarily in a series called *Riverboat*, in which he shared the lead for one season. There followed guest spots in programmes like ALFRED HITCHCOCK PRESENTS, *Route 66* and THE TWILIGHT ZONE before Reynolds joined the cast of GUNSMOKE, playing half-breed blacksmith Quint Asper. He left after three years to star in his own vehicle, *Hawk*, a police series about an Indian detective in New York. In 1970 he was cast as DAN AUGUST, another cop, this time in California, and, returning to the small screen after movie success, he was retired lawman, *B. L. Stryker*, in a MYSTERY MOVIE series in 1989. A year later Reynolds starred as football coach Wood Newton in the rustic sitcom, *Evening Shade* (also as director/executive producer), and around the same time was providing the voice for the alien Troy in the comedy, *Out of This World*. He was married to LAUGH-IN girl Judy Carne for three years in the 1960s and in 1988 married actress Loni Anderson.

REYNOLDS, DEBBIE
(Mary Frances Reynolds; 1932–)

Popular American actress and singer, star of the sitcom, *The Debbie Reynolds Show*, in the late 1960s (playing scatterbrained housewife Debbie Thompson) and later seen in the impressionists' show, *Kopykats*, and the US comedy, *Alohi Paradise* (Sydney Chase). She had previously been married to American singer Eddie Fisher and is the mother of actress Carrie Fisher.

REYNOLDS, JOAN
See **RANDALL, JOAN AND LESLIE.**

RHODA
US (MTM) Situation Comedy. BBC 2 1974–81

Rhoda Morgenstern/Gerard	**Valerie Harper**
Brenda Morgenstern	**Julie Kavner**
Joe Gerard	**David Groh**
Ida Morgenstern	**Nancy Walker**
Martin Morgenstern	**Harold J. Gould**
Carlton the Doorman	**Lorenzo Music** (voice only)
Donny Gerard	**Todd Turquand**
Myrna Morgenstein	**Barbara Sharma**
Gary Levy	**Ron Silver**
Sally Gallagher	**Anne Meara**
Johnny Venture	**Michael Delano**
Jack Doyle	**Ken McMillan**
Ramon Diaz, Jr	**Rafael Campos**

Creators: **James L. Brooks, Allan Burns**
Executive Producers: **James L. Brooks, Allan Burns, Charlotte Brown**
Producers: **David Davis, Lorenzo Music**

Life with a single Jewish girl in New York City.

A spin-off from THE MARY TYLER MOORE SHOW, *Rhoda* followed the fortunes of Mary's best friend, Rhoda Morgenstern. Back in her native New York, Rhoda had lost some weight and generally had a more positive outlook on life. She now lived with her podgy bank clerk sister, Brenda, after failing to settle down with her parents, Martin and Ida. Brenda, like Rhoda, was on the lookout for a husband, but Rhoda found hers first, in the shape of Joe Gerard, divorced father of ten-year-old Donny and boss of the New York Wrecking Company.

Rhoda and Joe took an apartment in Brenda's block, where Carlton was the doom-laden doorman viewers never saw. But Joe went out to work and Rhoda was stuck at home, frustrated and bored. Not surprisingly, the marriage was doomed to failure, especially after Rhoda formed her own window-dressing business with old schoolfriend Myrna Morgenstein. Joe and Rhoda divorced and she returned to the singles bars, accompanied by Brenda and some new acquaintances, air hostess Sally Gallagher and boutique-owner Gary Levy. Also seen was Rhoda's on-off boyfriend, a Vegas lounge singer named Johnny Venture. In the final series, Rhoda went to work with Jack Doyle and Ramon Diaz at the struggling Doyle Costume Company.

Rhoda, like *The Mary Tyler Moore Show*, was very much a 1970s series. It was also richly ethnic, applauded for its abundant Jewishness (despite the fact that neither Valerie Harper nor Nancy Walker, who played Rhoda's mother, were Jewish themselves).

RHODES, GARY
(1960–)

London-born TV chef with a trademark spiky haircut. His series have included *Rhodes Around Britain*, *More Rhodes*, *Open Rhodes*, *Gary Rhodes* and *Gary Rhodes's New British Classics*.

RICE, ANNEKA
(Annie Rice; 1958–)

British presenter, born in Wales but initially working on radio and TV in Hong Kong. After a time as personal assistant to Anna Home, at BBC's children's programmes, her UK break came with Channel 4's adventurous game show, TREASURE HUNT, in 1983, in which she did much leaping from helicopters and running about looking for clues. She then became known for CHALLENGE ANNEKA, a charity-orientated programme involving unlikely feats like publishing a book or building an orphanage in a matter of days. Rice also worked on TV-am's *Good Morning Britain*, contributed to WISH YOU WERE HERE . . . ? and presented one season of HOLI-DAY. She hosted *Sporting Chance* and the exotic game show, *Passport*, and has been seen on various panel games and special reports.

RICH, LEE
(1926–)

Former advertising executive who founded Lorimar Productions (with Merv Adelson) in 1968. The company achieved several prime-time hits, including THE WALTONS, DALLAS, KNOTS LANDING, FALCON CREST and FLAMINGO ROAD, before it was eventually taken over by Warner Brothers. Rich moved on to MGM/United Artists (as Chairman and Chief Executive) but left in 1988 to go back into independent production.

RICH MAN, POOR MAN
US (Universal/Harve Bennett) Drama. ITV 1976

Rudy Jordache	**Peter Strauss**
Tom Jordache	**Nick Nolte**
Julie Prescott/Abbott/Jordache	**Susan Blakely**
Axel Jordache	**Edward Asner**
Mary Jordache	**Dorothy McGuire**
Willie Abbott	**Bill Bixby**
Duncan Calderwood	**Ray Milland**
Teddy Boylan	**Robert Reed**
Virginia Calderwood	**Kim Darby**
Harold Jordache	**Bo Brundin**
Teresa Sanjoro	**Talia Shire**
Bill Denton	**Lawrence Pressman**
Kate Jordache	**Kay Lenz**
Asher Berg	**Craig Stevens**
Joey Quales	**George Maharis**
Linda Quales	**Lynda Day George**
Marsh Goodwin	**Van Johnson**
Irene Goodwin	**Dorothy Malone**
Arthur Falconetti	**William Smith**
Clothilde	**Fionnuala Flanagan**

Writer: **Dean Reisner**
Executive Producer: **Harve Bennett**
Producer: **Jon Epstein**

Two brothers grow up in very different ways and achieve contrasting success and happiness.

Rich Man, Poor Man was one of the television events of the 1970s. With a cast list littered with big names, this adaptation of Irwin Shaw's mammoth 1970 novel of the same name can be viewed today as the original blockbuster mini-series. It captivated world audiences and led to a boom in dramatizations of popular novels, which were screened under the *Best Sellers* umbrella title (usually on consecutive nights). These included Taylor Caldwell's *Captains and Kings*, Robert Ludlum's *The Rhinemann Exchange*, Arthur Hailey's *Wheels*, John Jakes's *The Bastard* and Harold Robbins's *79 Park Avenue*.

Rich Man, Poor Man was the story of the Jordache brothers, sons of an impoverished immigrant family (dad Axel was a hard-working baker in Port Phillip, New York), and followed their lives and relationships from 1945 through to the mid-1960s. The intelligent one, Rudy, broke free from his deprived roots to become a successful businessman and politician. Julie Prescott was the girl he loved. The brawny one, Tom, meandered from scrape to scrape, taking up boxing for a while, dabbling in crime and always likely to meet an unhappy end.

Two sequels followed. *Rich Man, Poor Man – Book II*, picking up the story in 1965, focused on the now Senator Rudy Jordache, his fight against corporate greed and the family feuds that still engulfed him. A new generation of rich and poor men were seen in the form of his surrogate kids, Wesley Jordache (Tom's son) and Billy Abbott (son of Julie). *Beggarman, Thief*, set in the late 1960s, switched attention to the boys' sister, Gretchen, a film-maker who had previously not been seen.

RICHARD THE LIONHEART
UK (Danziger) Adventure. ITV 1962–3

King Richard	**Dermot Walsh**
Prince John	**Trader Faulkner**
Lady Berengaria	**Sheila Whittington**
Blondel	**Iain Gregory**
Sir Gilbert	**Robin Hunter**

Producers: **Edward J. Danziger, Harry Lee Danziger**

King Richard returns from the Crusades to stop Prince John stealing the English throne.

Prince Richard was away with his army when news reached him of the death of his father, King Henry. Worse still, his younger brother, John, had designs on the throne that was legally Richard's, and so Lionheart returned home to put an end to the plot. It was not to be a quick affair, however, as John and his knaves proved elusive and determined, resulting in a series of swashbuckling adventures in which Richard's life was always in danger. His other enemies included Leopold and Philip of France, as well as the Saracen, Saladin, and some of the action took place back in the Holy Land.

RICHARD, WENDY
MBE (1946–)

Middlesbrough-born actress, in TV since the early 1960s. Her major roles have been as blouse-busting Miss Brahms in ARE YOU BEING SERVED? (and *Grace and Favour*) and, in total contrast, dowdy Pauline Fowler in EASTENDERS. However, she also played supermarket manageress Joyce Harker in THE NEWCOMERS, appeared with Dora Bryan in *Both Ends Meet* (Maudie) and Hylda Baker in *Not on Your Nellie* (Doris), and was Doreen, one of the ON THE BUSES clippies, as well as Pearl in the kids' series, *Hogg's Back*. Among her many other credits have been parts in HARPERS WEST ONE, DIXON OF DOCK GREEN, Z CARS, DANGER MAN, NO HIDING PLACE, PLEASE SIR! and DAD'S ARMY. At the start of her career, she was the girl on the Mike Sarne chart-topper, 'Come Outside' (1962).

RICHARDS, STAN
(Stan Richardson; 1930–)

Yorkshire-born actor, a former musical-comedy entertainer on the nothern clubs circuit, seen in programmes like CORONATION STREET, CROWN COURT, THE CUCKOO WALTZ, ALL CREATURES GREAT AND SMALL, LAST OF THE SUMMER WINE and various dramas (such as *The Price of Coal*), before taking the role of poacher/gamekeeper Seth Armstrong in EMMERDALE FARM in 1977.

RICHARDSON, IAN
CBE (1934–)

Scottish actor whose portrayal of the devious Francis Urquhart in Michael Dobbs's HOUSE OF CARDS, *To Play the King* and *The Final Cut* was highly acclaimed. In a long and varied TV career, Richardson has also played Bill Haydon in TINKER, TAILOR, SOLDIER, SPY, Major Neuheim in PRIVATE SCHULZ, Ramsay MacDonald in *No. 10*, (Uncle) Frederick Fairlie in *The Woman in White*, Nehru in *Lord Mountbatten: The Last Viceroy*, Michael Spearpoint in *The Gravy Train* and *The Gravy Train Goes East*, Anthony Blunt in the 1987 play about the British traitor, Rex Hunt in the Falklands drama, *An Ungentlemanly Act*, Sir Godber Evans in PORTERHOUSE BLUE, Stephen Tyler in *The Magician's House* and Lord Groan in *Gormenghast*. He has also been seen in programmes as varied as HORIZON, BRASS, SORRY!, *Mistral's Daughter*, *A Voyage Round My Father*, *Churchill's Generals*, *The Master of Ballantrae*, *Charlie Muffin* and *Star Quality*, as well as Shakespearean offerings.

RICHARDSON, MIRANDA
(1958–)

Versatile British actress seen in comedies like THE COMIC STRIP PRESENTS, SMITH AND JONES and *The True Adventures of Christopher Columbus* (Queen Isabella), plus dramas such as *After Pilkington*, the *Performance* presentation, *Old Times* (Anna), *Redemption*, THE STORYTELLER, *Snapshots*, A WOMAN OF SUBSTANCE (Paula), *Mr Wakefield's Crusade* (Sandra), *A Dance to the Music of Time* (Pamela Flitton), *The Scold's Bridle* (Dr Sarah Blakeney), *Merlin* (Mab) and *Alice in Wonderland* (Queen of Hearts). However, she is still remembered for her naughty schoolgirl interpretation of Queen Elizabeth I in BLACKADDER *II*. She was also seen in *Blackadder the Third* (highwaywoman Amy Hardwood) and *Blackadder Goes Forth* (Nurse Mary).

RICHIE, SHANE
(Shane Roche; 1964–)

Former Pontin's Blue Coat who arrived on television in sketch shows like *Up to Something* and *You Gotta Be Jokin'*. He then hosted the home video show, *Caught in the Act*, and was seen in *Live and Kicking* (fronting the *Run the Risk* game), *Win, Lose or Draw*, *Lucky Numbers* and *The Shane Richie Experience* (later reworked as *Love Me Do*). He is married to Coleen Nolan, of the Nolans vocal group.

RIDER, STEVE
(1950–)

Unflappable British sports anchorman, the main presenter of the BBC's GRANDSTAND, following work for ITV on *Midweek Sports Special* and other programmes.

RIDLEY, ARNOLD
OBE (1896–1984)

Bath-born actor and writer, fondly remembered as the incontinent Private Godfrey in DAD'S ARMY, a role he assumed at the tender age of 72. Previously, he had played a vicar in CROSSROADS and two roles in CORONATION STREET. By far his greatest achievement, however, was his penning, in 1923, of the famous stage play, *The Ghost Train* (televised as early as 1937), among other theatre scripts.

RIFF RAFF ELEMENT, THE
UK (BBC) Drama. BBC 1 1993–4

Joanna Tundish	Celia Imrie
Petula Belcher	Mossie Smith
Roger Tundish	Ronald Pickup
Carmen	Jayne Ashbourne
Declan	Cal Macaninch
Acky Belcher	Trevor Peacock
Granny Grogan	Brenda Bruce
Boyd Tundish	Nicholas Farrell
Mortimer Tundish	Richard Hope
Phoenix	Pippa Guard
Nathan Tundish	Ashley Wright
Dearbhla	Kate Binchy
Alister	Greg Wise

Vincent .... **George Costigan**
Oliver Tundish .... **Stewart Pile**
Nelson .... **Dicken Ashworth**
Maggie Belcher .... **Susan Brown**
Father Casper .... **Lionel Guyett**

Creator/Writer: **Debbie Horsfield**
Producer: **Liz Trubridge**

*Families from different class backgrounds share a
stately home.*

Roger Tundish, recently recalled ambassador to San
Andres, upset his family on arrival home at Tundish Hall
in Lancashire. With the house falling into disrepair and
finances tight, he was forced to advertise for new tenants
for one wing. 'The riff raff element need not apply', he
stated. However, that was precisely what he got when
his daughter-in-law, Joanna, employed Petula Belcher
as resident cook, and the rest of the common-as-muck
Belcher family took up residence. Not just class friction
but adultery, pregnancy and crime, including murder,
ensued. Much acclaimed, a second series of this light
drama followed in 1994.

RIFLEMAN, THE

US (Four Star/Sussex) Western. ITV 1959–64

Lucas McCain .... **Chuck Connors**
Mark McCain .... **Johnny Crawford**
Marshal Micah Torrance .... **Paul Fix**
Milly Scott .... **Joan Taylor**
Lou Mallory .... **Patricia Blair**
Sweeney .... **Bill Quinn**
Eddie Holstead .... **John Harmon**
Hattie Denton .... **Hope Summers**

Producers: **Arthur Gardner, Arnold Laven, Jules Levy**

*A Wild West rancher helps keep order with the aid
of a specially adapted gun.*

Dour, level-headed Lucas McCain had arrived in New
Mexico after the death of his wife. He had purchased the
Dunlap Ranch, four miles south of North Fork, and was
now struggling to make it pay. At the same time, he was
trying to raise his 12-year-old son, Mark, teaching him
lessons in life and showing him right from wrong. But
Lucas also had a third job to do. Whenever outlaws
arrived in town or there was a threat to law and order,
he was always called upon to save the day, bailing out
the town's helpless marshal, Micah Torrance. He did
have some assistance, however, in the form of his converted .44 Winchester rifle that allowed rapid fire. It gave
Lucas a distinct advantage over his adversaries.

Like most cowboys, Lucas was provided with a little
romantic interest, first with shopkeeper Milly Scott and
then with Lou Mallory, ambitious proprietress of the
Mallory House Hotel. Other townsfolk included Eddie
Holstead, owner of the Madera House Hotel, shopkeeper
Hattie Denton and Sweeney, bartender at the Last
Chance Saloon. All in all, though, this was a rather
heavy, sombre half-hour Western, screened between

1958 and 1963 in the USA and then sporadically around
the ITV network in the UK.

RIGG, Dame DIANA
(1938–)

Doncaster-born actress leaping to fame as the karate-
chopping Emma Peel in THE AVENGERS in 1965, having
already made appearances in programmes like ARM-
CHAIR THEATRE. She played Mrs Peel for three years, and
later credits have included her own US sitcom, entitled
Diana, in which she played divorcée and fashion co-
ordinator Diana Smythe, plus *The Diana Rigg Show*, the
sketch show, *Three Piece Suite*, *Bleak House* (Lady Ded-
lock), the thriller, MOTHER LOVE (Helen Vesey), *Screen
Two's Genghis Cohn* (Frieda von Stangel), *Moll Flanders*
(Mrs Golightly), *Rebecca* (Mrs Danvers) and *The Mrs Bradley Mysteries* (title role).

RILEY, LISA
(1976–)

Bury-born actress, EMMERDALE's Mandy Dingle. She has
also fronted the home video show, YOU'VE BEEN
FRAMED, and appeared in the drama, *Blood and Peaches*.

RIN TIN TIN
See ADVENTURES OF RIN TIN TIN, THE.

RINGS ON THEIR FINGERS

UK (BBC) Situation Comedy. BBC 1 1978–80

Oliver Pryde .... **Martin Jarvis**
Sandy Bennett/Pryde .... **Diane Keen**
Victor .... **Tim Barrett**
Mr Gordon Bennett .... **John Harvey**
Mrs Bennett .... **Barbara Lott**
Mr Pryde .... **Keith Marsh**

Creator/Writer: **Richard Waring**
Producer: **Harold Snoad**

*Shall-we, shan't-we marriage dilemmas for a
young couple.*

Oliver Pryde had been happy sharing six years of his life
and his West Acton flat with his winsome girlfriend,
Sandy Bennett, but he still valued his independence.
Sandy, on the other hand, was desperately keen on marriage. With the occasional interference of relatives and
workmates, the two ditherers attempted to find a way
forward, with wedding bells, unfortunately for Oliver,
the ultimate answer. Subsequent episodes centred on
their marital strife and preparations for the birth of their
first child. With its traditionalist hubby-at-work, little-
lady-at-home stance, feminists loathed it.

RIPCORD

US (United Artists) Adventure. BBC 1 1964–5

Ted McKeever	**Larry Pennell**
Jim Buckley	**Ken Curtis**
Chuck Lambert	**Paul Comi**
Charlie Kern	**Shug Fisher**

Producers: **Maurice Unger, Leon Benson**

The all-action adventures of a pair of crime-fighting skydivers.

Ted McKeever and Jim Buckley, proprietors of Ripcord Inc., were parachuting teachers who doubled up as crime-busters. Although they often hired themselves out for dangerous rescue and recovery work, they were more usually found apprehending criminals, dropping from the skies like avenging angels. Sometimes their battles took place in mid-air. They were supported in their work by their pilot, Chuck Lambert, later replaced by Charlie Kern.

RIPPING YARNS

UK (BBC) Comedy. BBC 2 1977–9

Michael Palin, Terry Jones

Writers: **Michael Palin, Terry Jones**
Producer: **Alan J. W. Bell**

Over-the-top Boys' Own *adventures satirized.*

Tongue-in-cheek escapism lay at the heart of this series of playlets by Michael Palin and Terry Jones that glorously parodied classic schoolboy literature. These dashing tales of exploration, sporting excellence, wartime heroics and more celebrated every exaggeration and cliché of the Victorian and Edwardian originals. Ridiculous in the true MONTY PYTHON way, the lead characters – Palin starred in all episodes, Jones only in one – bounded with youthful exuberance and naïvety, with their creators taking an almost cruel pleasure in sending up this uniquely British form of fiction. Two series were produced, two years apart, following a one-off comedy, *Tomkinson's Schooldays*, in 1976, each episode lavishly shot on film for the highest production values. The eight other stories were: *The Testing of Eric Olthwaite*, *Escape from Stalag Luft 112B*, *Murder at Moorstones Manor*, *Across the Andes by Frog*, *The Curse of the Claw*, *Whinfrey's Last Case*, *Golden Gordon* and *Roger of the Raj*.

RIPPON, ANGELA

(1944–)

British presenter, a former newspaper journalist, generally considered to have been the UK's first female newsreader, although this honour actually belongs to Barbara Mandell, who read the ITN news way back in 1955. Rippon arrived on national TV in 1973 via news magazines in the South-west. Working initially as a reporter, she went on to front *News Review* and then *The Nine O'Clock News*. On the 1976 *Morecambe and Wise Christmas Show*, she revealed new talents, pushing aside the news desk and kicking her way through 'Let's Face The Music And Dance'. Not surprisingly, she was later recruited to present COME DANCING. In 1983 she became one of TV-am's 'Famous Five' presenters, although her time at the station was, as for the others, somewhat brief. She has never been short of radio or television work, however, and has also presented THE EUROVISION SONG CONTEST, ANTIQUES ROADSHOW, *Masterteam*, *Matchpoint*, WHAT'S MY LINE?, TOP GEAR, *The Entertainers* and *Open House with Gloria Hunniford* among many other programmes, and has read the news occasionally on THE BIG BREAKFAST.

RISING DAMP

UK (Yorkshire) Situation Comedy. ITV 1974–8

Rupert Rigsby	**Leonard Rossiter**
Ruth Jones	**Frances de la Tour**
Alan Moore	**Richard Beckinsale**
Philip Smith	**Don Warrington**
Brenda	**Gay Rose**

Creator/Writer: **Eric Chappell**
Producers: **Ronnie Baxter, Vernon Lawrence, Len Lurcuck**

The inhabitants of a seedy boarding house suffer the intrusions of its even seedier owner.

Rupert Rigsby, grubby, lecherous, ignorant, nosey and tight-fisted (and those were just his good points) was the owner of a horribly run-down northern boarding house that was home to an odd mix of lodgers. Rigsby lived on the ground floor with his cat, Vienna. Upstairs, long-haired Alan, a medical student, shared one room with Philip, the son of an African tribal chief, and another room was taken by frustrated spinster Miss Jones, a university administrator. Although liberally treated to decrepit furnishings and the eponymous rising damp, the one thing Rigsby's paying guests did not receive was privacy. Given the opportunity to catch his lodgers 'at it', the snooping Rigsby would barge in. Whatever secrets lay in their personal lives, Rigsby prised them out into the open. However great their hopes and dreams, Rigsby would sneer and jeer at them. His own ambition, though, was to share a night of torrid passion with Miss Jones but, like his other plans, it was never realized. Brenda was one of Rigsby's later lodgers.

The series sprang from a one-off play entitled *The Banana Box* (in which the landlord was called Rooksby) and gave Leonard Rossiter the first chance to show off his acclaimed comic timing. Indeed, most of the series' humour came from his sharp, glib delivery. A film version was released in 1980.

RIVALS OF SHERLOCK HOLMES, THE
UK (Thames) Detective Drama. ITV 1971–3

Dr Thorndyke	John Neville
	Barrie Ingham
Horace Dorrington	Peter Vaughan
Jonathan Pride	Ronald Hines
Arthur Hewitt	Peter Barkworth
Prof. Van Dusen	Douglas Wilmer
Max Carrados	Robert Stephens
Simon Carne	Roy Dotrice
Carnacki	Donald Pleasence
Dixon Druce	John Fraser
Lady Molly	Elvi Hale
Romany Pringle	Donald Sinden
Bernard Sutton	Robert Lang
Polly Burton	Judy Geeson
Insp. Lipinzki	Barry Keegan
Laxworthy	Bernard Hepton
Monsieur Valmont	Charles Gray
Lt. Holst	John Thaw
Dabogert Trostler	Ronald Lewis
William Drew	Derek Jacobi
Mr Horrocks	Ronald Fraser
Hagar	Sara Kestelman

Executive Producers: **Lloyd Shirley, Kim Mills**
Producers: **Robert Love, Jonathan Alwyn,
Reginald Collin**

*Series of literary adaptations which revealed that
Sherlock Holmes was not the only great detective
of Victorian times.*

The self-contained episodes of this period anthology
featured investigations from the casebooks of various
literary sleuths. One or two cropped up more than once.
Authors whose work was featured included Arthur
Morrison (Horace Dorrington, Arthur Hewitt and Jonathan Pride), R. Austin Freeman (Dr Thorndyke), Baroness
Orczy (Polly Burton) and Jacques Futrelle (Professor Van
Dusen). Notable performances came from John Thaw as
Danish detective Lt. Holst, Robert Stephens as blind
detective Max Carrados, Donald Pleasence as Carnacki,
a ghost-hunter, and Sara Kestelman as Hagar, a gypsy
detective. The series was based on a literary collection
put together by one-time BBC Director-General Sir
Hugh Greene.

RIVER, THE
UK (BBC) Situation Comedy. BBC 1 1988

Davey Jackson	David Essex
Sarah McDonald	Katy Murphy
Aunt Betty	Vilma Hollingbery
Tom Pike	Shaun Scott
Col. Danvers	David Ryall

Creator/Writer: **Michael Aitkens**
Producer: **Susan Belbin**

*An ex-con lock-keeper and a young Scots girl fall
in love on the riverbank.*

Set in the fictitious rustic settlement of Chumley-on-the-
Water, *The River* focused on London-born lock-keeper
Davey Jackson, revealing how his idyllic existence was
thrown into turmoil by the arrival of a wayward Scots
girl. Sarah McDonald, a refugee from society, was forced
to call on Davey's help when the propeller on her
narrowboat was damaged in an accident. While the relevant repairs were made, Davey took the aggressive
Sarah into his cottage and a romance slowly developed,
despite the best efforts of Davey's grumpy Aunt Betty
(an active Marxist). It was subsequently revealed that
Davey had retired to this rural backwater after serving
six months in prison for allegedly forging banknotes.
Tom Pike was Davey's assistant lock-keeper and Colonel
Danvers the local nob and snob. Some of the action took
place in the local boozer, The Ferret, presided over by an
unconscious landlord, Jim.

Star David Essex also wrote and performed the programme's theme song.

RIVIERA POLICE
UK (Associated-Rediffusion) Police Drama. ITV 1965

Insp. Legrand	Brian Spink
Lt. Col. Constant Sorel	Frank Lieberman
Supt. Adam Hunter	Geoffrey Frederick
Supt. Bernie Johnson	Noel Trevarthen

Producer: **Jordan Lawrence**

Crime fighting on the Côte d'Azur.

Legrand, Sorel, Hunter and Johnson were four determined police officers plying their trade against such
glamorous backdrops as the Cannes Film Festival, the
Monaco Grand Prix and the Nice Flower Festival. They
usually worked separately (except for the opening episode) to put the block on killers, thieves and other
exponents of crime in the South of France. However,
despite its sun, sea, sand and scantily clad beauties, the
series never took a hold, not even when following CORO-
NATION STREET in the transmission schedules.

RIX, Lord BRIAN
(1924–)

Yorkshire-born actor, Britain's number one farceur,
largely in the theatre but seen to lose his trousers on TV
on many occasions, too. Rix has also had his own series,
Dial RIX, and presented a programme for handicapped
viewers, *Let's Go* (he later became Chairman of Mencap).
Rix starred with Warren Mitchell in an early form of YES,
MINISTER entitled *Men of Affairs* (playing MP Barry Ovis)
in 1973, and played James, opposite Lynda Baron, in the
house-buying comedy, *A Roof Over My Head*, in 1977. Rix
is the brother of EMMERDALE's Sheila Mercier, husband
of actress Elspet Gray, and father of actress Louisa Rix.

ROACHE, WILLIAM
MBE (1932–)

CORONATION STREET's Ken Barlow, William Roache has been with the series since its inception, back in 1960, making him the longest surviving cast member. His previous TV experience was confined to small parts in Granada series like *Skyport* and KNIGHT ERRANT and a single drama, *Marking Time*, and, since being in the *Street*, he has had little opportunity to work elsewhere on television. He is the father of actor Linus Roache (who once played Ken's son, Peter).

ROBBINS, MICHAEL
(1930–92)

Former straight man to comics like Dick Emery and Tommy Cooper, British actor Michael Robbins hit the big time when he was cast as Arthur, Reg Varney's layabout brother-in-law, in the hit sitcom, ON THE BUSES, in 1969. His previous TV work had largely consisted of plays and guest spots in series like CALLAN, but thereafter Robbins was known as a solid comedy actor. Among his later credits were THICK AS THIEVES, *How's Your Father* (Eddie Cropper), *The Fuzz* (DS Marble), FAIRLY SECRET ARMY (Sgt Major Throttle), *Devenish*, THE NEW STATESMAN, Dick Emery's *Legacy of Murder* and the drama, *Adam Bede*.

ROBERTSON, DALE
(1923–)

One of TV's Western heroes, rugged Dale Robertson was the star of TALES OF WELLS FARGO (Jim Hardie) and IRON HORSE (Ben Calhoun). He also hosted the long-running anthology series, *Death Valley Days*, in the late 1960s and early 1970s and resurfaced in 1981 as Walter Lankershim in DYNASTY. A 1987 adventure series, *J. J. Starbuck*, proved short-lived.

ROBERTSON, FYFE
(1902–87)

Much-mimicked, distinctive Scottish roving reporter, a former newspaper journalist who was seen on TONIGHT and 24 HOURS in the 1950s and 1960s but remained on TV up to the turn of the 1980s. Some of his last contributions were nostalgic documentaries broadcast under the title of *Robbie* in the 1970s.

ROBIN HOOD
See ADVENTURES OF ROBIN HOOD, THE.

ROBIN OF SHERWOOD
UK (HTV/Goldcrest) Adventure. ITV 1984–6

Robin of Loxley	**Michael Praed**
Robert of Huntingdon	**Jason Connery**
Little John	**Clive Mantle**
Will Scarlet	**Ray Winstone**
Maid Marion	**Judi Trott**
Much	**Peter Llewellyn-Williams**
Friar Tuck	**Phil Rose**
Nasir	**Mark Ryan**
Sheriff of Nottingham	**Nickolas Grace**
Guy of Gisburne	**Robert Addie**
Abbot Hugo	**Philip Jackson**
Herne the Hunter	**John Abineri**
Edward of Wickham	**Jeremy Bulloch**
Lord Owen	**Oliver Cotton**
Sir Richard of Leaford	**George Baker**
Gulnar	**Richard O'Brien**
Baron Simon de Belleme	**Anthony Valentine**

Creator: **Richard Carpenter**
Executive Producer: **Patrick Dromgoole**
Producers: **Paul Knight, Esta Charkham**

The Robin Hood legend, boosted with a dose of magic.

In this imaginative version of the famous 12th-century legend, Robin Hood (Robin of Loxley) was said to have possessed deep spiritual powers which assisted him in his fight with the Sheriff of Nottingham. His adventures began when his home at Loxley Mill was destroyed by Norman soldiers. Swearing revenge, Robin encountered the mystical Herne the Hunter, who appeared to him in the form of a man with a stag's head. He endowed Robin with the sword *Albion*, and Robin then assumed the mantle of the Hooded Man, legendary hero of the oppressed Saxon folk ('Robin in the Hood' becoming 'Robin Hood'). Maid Marion (Lady Marion of Leaford), Little John, Will Scarlet, Friar Tuck and all the familiar names joined Robin in his struggle, as the episodes combined various facets of the Robin Hood legend with the zest of pagan sorcery. The cast was predominantly young and the action suitably brisk as they fought to free the people of England.

After two seasons, Michael Praed left for the USA, Broadway and eventually DYNASTY, and was replaced by Sean Connery's son, Jason. The storyline had it that Robin of Loxley was killed in an ambush but his revolutionary spirit was assumed by a new Hooded Man, the blond-haired Robert of Huntingdon, a lad of noble birth who, like his predecessor, had been inspired by Herne the Hunter.

ROBIN'S NEST
UK (Thames) Situation Comedy. ITV 1977–81

Robin Tripp	**Richard O'Sullivan**
Victoria Nicholls/Tripp	**Tessa Wyatt**
James Nicholls	**Tony Britton**
Albert Riddle	**David Kelly**
Marion Nicholls	**Honor Blackman**
	Barbara Murray
Gertrude	**Peggy Aitchison**

Creators: **Johnnie Mortimer, Brian Cooke**

Producer: **Peter Frazer-Jones**

A recent catering graduate opens his own bistro with the help of his girlfriend.

Fresh from the successful MAN ABOUT THE HOUSE, Robin Tripp had now left his two female flatmates and teamed up with his live-in lover, air hostess Vicky Nicholls. They lived above their own Fulham restaurant – Robin's Nest – where they were not-so-ably assisted by their one-armed washer-up, Albert Riddle, an Irish ex-con with an endless line in blarney. The fly in the ointment was Vicky's disapproving dad, James Nicholls, a far from sleeping partner in the business, although her divorced mother, Marion, was far more sympathetic about her daughter's co-habitation with a long-haired cook. Tensions were eventually eased with a marriage and, eventually, the birth of twins. Also seen in later episodes was restaurant help Gertrude.

Star Richard O'Sullivan also wrote the synthesizer theme music.

ROBINSON, ANNE
(1944–)

Red-haired, Liverpudlian presenter, a national newspaper journalist who was given her television break on BREAKFAST TIME as TV critic and then hosted POINTS OF VIEW. Since then, Robinson has also presented the consumer affairs programme, WATCHDOG, and the quiz show, THE WEAKEST LINK.

ROBINSON CRUSOE
See ADVENTURES OF ROBINSON CRUSOE, THE.

ROBINSON, ROBERT
(1927–)

British journalist and presenter, a specialist in panel games, thanks to long spells as chairman of CALL MY BLUFF and ASK THE FAMILY. Robinson also hosted POINTS OF VIEW and *The Book Programme*, and worked on *Picture Parade*, MONITOR and ALL OUR YESTERDAYS. Occasionally, he has presented his own travelogues. As interviewer on BBC-3 in 1965, it was Robinson who faced Kenneth Tynan when he famously became the first person to use the 'F' word on British TV. He is the father of actress Lucy Robinson.

ROBINSON, TONY
(1946–)

British comedian, actor, presenter and writer, chiefly remembered for his portrayal of Baldrick, the most menial of manservants, in the various BLACKADDER manifestations. Robinson has also been a member of the WHO DARES, WINS . . . team, a guest presenter of POINTS OF VIEW and host of the cartoon series, *Stay Tooned*, and the archaeology series, *Time Team*. He wrote and

appeared in the kids' comedy, MAID MARIAN AND HER MERRY MEN (playing the Sheriff of Nottingham), was the headmaster in *Teenage Health Freak*, the storyteller in *Blood and Honey* and Alan in *My Wonderful Life*. On Sunday mornings, Robinson fronted the Biblical series, *The Good Book Guide*. He has also been seen in programmes as diverse as PLAY AWAY, *Big Jim and the Figaro Club*, THE GOOD SEX GUIDE, THE YOUNG ONES, BERGERAC, *Virtual Murder*, *A Woman's Guide to Adultery* and *Knight School* (also as script consultant) and, in 1994, made one of the BBC's *Great Journeys*.

ROBSON, LINDA
(1958–)

Cockney actress, a former child performer. Although she is well known today as Tracey Stubbs in BIRDS OF A FEATHER (alongside her lifelong friend, Pauline Quirke), Robson's TV career stretches back to the 1970s. As a 12-year-old she appeared in *Jackanory Playhouse* and went on to pop up in numerous Thames TV series, including *Pauline's Quirkes*, *Pauline's People* and *You Must Be Joking!*, as well as the teenage drama, *Going Out* (Gerry), for Southern. Moving into adult TV, Robson was seen in WITHIN THESE WALLS, CRIBB, AGONY, THE OTHER 'ARF, *L for Lester*, HARRY'S GAME (Theresa McCorrigan), *Up the Elephant and Round the Castle*, THE BILL, *South of the Border* and plenty of other dramas, including SHINE ON HARVEY MOON, in which she played Harvey's daughter, Maggie. With Quirke, she took part in the challenge series, *Jobs for the Girls*, and THE GOOD SEX GUIDE.

ROCK FOLLIES
UK (Thames) Drama. ITV 1976–7

Anna Wynd	**Charlotte Cornwell**
Devonia 'Dee' Rhoades	**Julie Covington**
Nancy 'Q' Cunard de Longchamps	**Rula Lenska**
Derek Huggin	**Emlyn Price**
Harry Moon	**Derek Thompson**
Kitty Schreiber	**Beth Porter**
Rox	**Sue Jones-Davies**

Writer: **Howard Schuman**
Executive Producer: **Verity Lambert**
Producer: **Andrew Brown**

Life on the road with an ambitious female rock group.

The Little Ladies were a struggling girl rock band, lurching from gig to gig, striving to rise out of the sordid lower reaches of the rock-music business. This series followed their ups and downs (mostly downs), as they fought to avoid exploitation – often sexual – and establish themselves as genuine musicians. Derek Huggin was their less than helpful manager.

Busby Berkeley-inspired fantasy sequences added extra colour to this six-part drama. The music was original and penned by Roxy Music guitarist Andy Mackay, leading to two soundtrack albums and a hit single, 'OK?', which also featured Sue Jones-Davies whose character, Rox, joined the band in the second series. Also new was pushy American agent Kitty Schreiber. This second series was entitled *Rock Follies of '77*.

ROCK 'N' ROLL YEARS, THE
UK (BBC) Documentary. BBC 1 1985–7; 1994

Producers: **Ann Freer, Sue Mallinson**

Historical review of events year by year played over a soundtrack of contemporary pop hits.

Beginning in 1956, at the birth of the age of rock'n'roll, this innovative series used old newsreel and TV clips to illustrate world events year by year. To add to the period feel, rock and pop records of the day provided the soundtrack. Each track was carefully selected to ensure that its lyrics tied in with the theme of the archive footage, and some concert performances were also relived. The years up to 1979 were reviewed in 1985–7 and, after a one-off special entitled *The Years That Rocked the Planet*, part of BBC 2's *One World* six-week season on ecological matters to coincide with the Rio Earth Summit in 1992, the programme returned in 1994 to update coverage to the end of the 1980s.

ROCKFORD FILES, THE
US (Universal/Cherokee/Public Arts) Detective Drama.
BBC 1 1975–82

Jim Rockford	**James Garner**
Joseph 'Rocky' Rockford	**Noah Beery, Jr**
DS Dennis Becker	**Joe Santos**
Beth Davenport	**Gretchen Corbett**
Evelyn 'Angel' Martin	**Stuart Margolin**
John Cooper	**Bo Hopkins**
Lt. Alex Diehl	**Tom Atkins**
Lt. Doug Chapman	**James Luisi**
Gandolph Fitch	**Isaac Hayes**
Lance White	**Tom Selleck**

Creators: **Roy Huggins, Stephen J. Cannell**
Executive Producers: **Stephen J. Cannell, Meta Rosenberg**
Producers: **Roy Huggins, Charles Johnson, David Chase**

An ex-con turns private investigator, taking on cases of rough justice.

Jim Rockford had been imprisoned in San Quentin for five years for a robbery he did not commit and, when new evidence exonerated and freed him, he devoted his life to investigating other dodgy cases on which the police had closed their books. He formed the Rockford Private Detective Agency, of which he was the sole employee. Having been a jailbird himself, he could call upon his crooked connections to gather vital information (especially his weasely ex-cellmate, Angel Martin). But, because he was treading on their toes and undermining their work, he was not popular with the local cops.

Jim's chief rival (but also a good friend) was Det. Sgt Dennis Becker. John Cooper was his legal ally (albeit disbarred), and Rocky, his retired truck-driver father,

also lent a hand, though he was always trying to talk his son into finding a real job. Jim's one-time girlfriend, Beth Davenport, also proved useful. She was the attorney who bailed him out whenever he found himself behind bars again.

Rockford lived on a Los Angeles beach in a scruffy caravan and, unlike TV's more sophisticated private eyes, he didn't have a fancy office or a sexy secretary. All he had was a crummy answerphone, which switched itself on at the start of each episode. Rockford charged $200 a day for his work (plus expenses), but often ended up unpaid and usually much the worse for wear. He hated violence and seldom carried a gun, so he was always looking nervously over his shoulder, relying on his wry sense of humour to carry him through the murky business of private detection. But he knew how to play dirty, too, and, if the end justified the means, he was not averse to donning a disguise, slipping a few bribes or playing the con-man.

In the final series, Jim gained another rival, in the form of private eye Lance White, who irked Jim by solving cases with the minimum of effort and, usually, a huge slice of luck. Played by Tom Selleck, it presaged his star role as MAGNUM PI.

ROCKLIFFE'S BABIES/ ROCKLIFFE'S FOLLY
UK (BBC) Police Drama. BBC 1 1987–88/1988

DS Alan Rockliffe	**Ian Hogg**
PC David Adams	**Bill Champion** (*Babies*)
PC Keith Chitty	**John Blakey** (*Babies*)
PC Steve Hood	**Brett Fancy** (*Babies*)
PC Gerry O'Dowd	**Joe McGann** (*Babies*)
PC Paul Georgiou	**Martyn Ellis** (*Babies*)
WPC Karen Walsh	**Susanna Shelling** (*Babies*)
WPC Janice Hargreaves	**Alphonsia Emmanuel** (*Babies*)
DI Charlie Flight	**Edward Wilson** (*Babies*)
Det. Supt. Munro	**Malcolm Terris** (*Babies*)
Chief Supt. Barry Wyatt	**Brian Croucher** (*Babies*)
DI Derek Hoskins	**James Aubrey** (*Folly*)
Insp. Leslie Yaxley	**Ian Brimble** (*Folly*)
DC Paul Whitmore	**Aaron Harris** (*Folly*)
WPC/Sgt Rachel Osborne	**Carole Nimmons** (*Folly*)
PC Guy Overton	**Craig Nightingale** (*Folly*)
WPC Hester Goswell	**Elizabeth Morton** (*Folly*)
PC Alfred Duggan	**John Hartley** (*Folly*)

Creator: **Richard O'Keefe**
Producers: **Leonard Lewis** (*Babies*), **Ron Craddock** (*Folly*)

An experienced police sergeant takes a team of rookie detectives under his wing.

Rockliffe's Babies followed the progress of seven young police officers as they trained to become detectives. It showed them venturing into some of London's seediest areas as part of the Met.'s Victor Tango division, coming to terms with the stresses and strains of the job and coping with their demanding, and less than perfect, supervisor, DS Alan Rockliffe. His 'babies' consisted of two WPCs, Hargreaves and Walsh, plus five male officers, Adams, Chitty, Hood, O'Dowd and Georgiou, men and women of diverse backgrounds now forced to work together.

After two successful seasons, the teetotal Rockliffe was given his own spin-off series, *Rockliffe's Folly*, in which he moved out of the capital and took up a new appointment in Wessex, believing it to be a softer option. He soon discovered that hard crime still existed, even in this rural backwater.

RODDENBERRY, GENE
(Eugene Roddenberry; 1921–91)

American TV executive, one-time writer for series like HIGHWAY PATROL, NAKED CITY, DR KILDARE and particularly HAVE GUN WILL TRAVEL, but whose claim to fame was always STAR TREK, which he created and produced. Roddenberry was also responsible for STAR TREK: THE NEXT GENERATION. He was married to actress Majel Barrett, who played Nurse Christine Chapel in *Star Trek*.

RODGERS, ANTON
(1933–)

Cambridgeshire-born actor seen on television since the late 1950s, although his major roles have been since the 1980s, primarily as William Fields in FRESH/FRENCH FIELDS, Alec Callender in MAY TO DECEMBER, vet Noah Kirby in *Noah's Ark* and Ronald Kegworthy in *Up Rising*. Rodgers played Lt. Gilmore in *The Sky Larks*, a 1958 comedy, was one of the actors to appear as Number 2 in THE PRISONER, took the part of Stanley Featherstonehaugh Ukridge in the P. G. Wodehouse series, *Ukridge*, and was policeman David Gradley in the psychic series, *Zodiac*. He played Edward Langtry in LILLIE, appeared in Roy Clarke's *Pictures*, was DI Purbright in *Murder Most English*, and starred in Frederic Raphael's 10-part drama, *After the War*, as well as guesting in series such as THE PROTECTORS, RANDALL AND HOPKIRK (DECEASED), *The Organisation*, UPSTAIRS, DOWNSTAIRS, RUMPOLE OF THE BAILEY and assorted single dramas like the *Performance* presentation of *After the Dance* (David Scott-Fowler).

ROGER ROGER
UK (BBC) Comedy Drama. BBC 1 1998–

Sam	Robert Daws
Dexter	Keith Allen
Phil	Philip Glenister
Reen	Pippa Guard
Baz	David Ross
Marlon	Ricci Harnett
Barry	John Thomson
	Jonathan Moore
Rajiv	Paul Sharma
André	Terence Maynard
Cambridge	Chris Larkin
Henry	Jude Akuwudike
Tina	Barbara Durkin
Chrissie	Helen Grace
Marilyn	Joan Hodges

Creator/Writer: **John Sullivan**
Producer: **Gareth Gwenlan**

Misadventures in the life of the harassed boss of a minicab firm.

Sam, a widower, was the co-proprietor of Cresta Cabs, a London-based minicab company. His partner, Dexter, was unreliable to say the least and proved it by throwing himself into the Thames and bequeathing a host of debts to the beleaguered business. His bimbo widow, Tina, failed to see the difficulty in the situation and, with as incompetent a crew of drivers as it was possible to hire, Sam was left to tear out his hair.

In the usual style of writer John Sullivan, the cast-list was large and finely honed. Among the cabbies was Phil, a frustrated rock musician whose relationship with waitress Chrissie (children Cher and Madonna) was on the rocks. The character had featured even more prominently in the 1996 pilot episode, in which he was played by Neil Morrissey and his wife by Lesley Vickerage. Ever-optimistic part-timer Baz also worked as a postman and spent his social hours taking his latest dating-agency acquaintance to his favourite Chinese restaurant. The presence of his dopey step-son, Marlon, only made his life more difficult. Of the other characters, André was the black stud, with children all over the place; Rajiv, the intelligent one who helped with the firm's books; Cambridge, the easily duped graduate; Barry, the loudmouth; Henry, the African who could never find his way; and Reen, the unhappily married radio operator who still had feelings for old flame Sam.

With 18 months between pilot and series one, and the same time-span between series one and two, not to mention the major cast-changes, *Roger Roger* was slow to catch on, despite securing a peak-hour Saturday evening time-slot.

ROGERS, ROY
(Leonard Slye; 1911–98)

'King of the Cowboys' Roy Rogers began his career in Country and Western music. He performed for a while under the name of Dick Weston before legally changing his name to Roy Rogers in 1942. In the late 1930s Rogers was groomed as a Hollywood cowboy, taught to ride and pitched into a series of Westerns, beginning with *Under Western Skies* in 1938. He became one of kids' TV's first favourites when he drifted on to the small screen, in THE ROY ROGERS SHOW, accompanied by his wife, Dale Evans (Frances Octavia Smith; 1912–2001 – the 'Queen of the West'), and his trusty steed, Trigger. Some of Rogers's old movies were also edited down for TV consumption. 'Happy Trails' was his theme song.

ROGERS, TED
(1935–2001)

Twinkly-eyed, fast-talking British comic whose finest hour arrived with the game show, 3-2-1, on which he was the finger-twiddling host for nine series. Previously,

Rogers had been seen in numerous variety shows, from the *Billy Cotton Band Show* to SUNDAY NIGHT AT THE LONDON PALLADIUM, and his own brief series, *And So To Ted*.

ROLL OVER BEETHOVEN
UK (Central) Situation Comedy. ITV 1985

Belinda Purcell .... **Liza Goddard**
Nigel Cochrane .... **Nigel Planer**
Oliver Purcell .... **Richard Vernon**
Lem .... **Desmond McNamara**
Marvin .... **Emlyn Price**

Creators/Writers: **Laurence Marks, Maurice Gran**
Executive Producer: **Allan McKeown**
Producer: **Tony Charles**

A famous rock star and a demure music teacher fall in love.

Crusty retired headmaster Oliver Purcell was not amused to hear that legendary rock star Nigel Cochrane had decided to give up touring and was intending to move into his staid, peaceful village. He was even more disturbed when his own daughter, Belinda, began to give Nigel piano lessons, and when they fell in love he very nearly needed oxygen. It was an unlikely romance. Belinda, usually the dutiful, demure daughter, hardly seemed the type to turn a rock legend's head, but turn it she did. Belinda also supported Nigel by writing songs with his pal, Marvin. Eventually she cut her own album and dad, despite his bluster, was really quite pleased. The two series were screened virtually back to back.

ROLLASON, HELEN
MBE (1956–99)

London-born sports presenter whose brave fight against cancer proved inspiring to many. A former PE teacher, Rollason entered broadcasting with Essex Radio before joining Channel 4 to cover various sports, including the 1988 Olympics. She moved to the BBC and fronted NEWSROUND and then, in 1990, she became the first woman to present the BBC's GRANDSTAND, going on to anchor numerous other sports programmes and the sports sections of news bulletins. As her illness became widely known, she was featured in a BBC documentary, *Hope for Helen*, in 1998. Her courage in sickness was recognized with a new award for inspiration at the BBC's SPORTS REVIEW OF THE YEAR ceremony in 1999.

ROMANY JONES
UK (LWT) Situation Comedy. ITV 1973–5

Bert Jones .... **James Beck**
Betty Jones .... **Jo Rowbottom**
Wally Briggs .... **Arthur Mullard**
Lily Briggs .... **Queenie Watts**
Jeremy Crichton-Jones .... **Jonathan Cecil**
Susan Crichton-Jones .... **Gay Soper**

Creators: **Ronald Chesney, Ronald Wolfe**
Producer: **Stuart Allen**

Neighbour versus neighbour on a run-down campsite.

Work-shy Bert Jones lived with his wife, Betty, in a battered, leaky, ant-ridden caravan on a grotty campsite. Their nearest neighbours were bluff Cockneys Wally and Lily Briggs and, needless to say, they didn't always see eye to eye. Beginning as a one-off play in 1972, the series had just completed one successful run, with another in the can, when actor James Beck died. Recasting was necessary and snooty Jeremy and Susan Crichton-Jones were introduced as Wally and Lily's new neighbours. The Briggses were later given their own spin-off show, *Yus My Dear* (1976), in which Wally took a job as a bricklayer and they were transferred to the comfort of a council house. Wally's sponging brother, Benny (played by Mike Reid), was thrown in for company.

ROOBARB
UK (Bob Godfrey) Children's Entertainment. BBC 1
1974–5

Narrator: **Richard Briers**

Creator/Writer: **Grange Calveley**
Producer: **Bob Godfrey**

Cat and dog one-upmanship.

Drawn in dazzling colours and in a distinctive, half-finished, wobbly style (making a virtue out of a low budget), *Roobarb* concerned the daily battles of an ambitious green dog named Roobarb and a cynical, laid-back pink cat called Custard. Producer Bob Godfrey likened the relationship to the one shared by Tony Hancock and Sid James. Events took place in a back garden, with a fenceful of smirking birds taking sides with the winner. Quirkily narrated by Richard Briers and filled with adult wit, it became a favourite with all ages, although it was aimed squarely at the children's market.

ROOM 101
UK (Hat Trick) Comedy. BBC 2 1994–

Presenters: **Nick Hancock, Paul Merton**

Producers: **Lissa Evans, Toby Stevens**

Celebrities name the things they detest most in life.

Taking its cue from George Orwell's *1984*, in which Room 101 was the place of ultimate torture, this series (which began on Radio 5) comically explored the *bêtes noires* of its famous guests. Choosing irritating pop songs, useless domestic tools, corny books, nauseating TV programmes, or even more abstract items, the participants needed to convince host Nick Hancock (later Paul Merton) that these things they hated most should be consigned to Room 101 where they could do their worst. Each item was illustrated with snippets of music, film clips, cardboard cut-outs, etc. The host then declined or accepted the offer, sending the offending objects along a crematorium-style conveyor-belt and through a sliding door or down a shaft into this bleak TV vision of Hell.

ROOTS

US (ABC/David L. Wolper) Drama. BBC 1 1977

Kunta Kinte	**LeVar Burton**
Toby (Kunta Kinte)	**John Amos**
Binta	**Cicely Tyson**
Omoro	**Thalmus Rasulala**
Nyo Boto	**Maya Angelou**
Kadi Touray	**O. J. Simpson**
The Wrestler	**Ji-Tu Cumbuka**
Kintango	**Moses Gunn**
Fiddler	**Louis Gossett, Jr**
Gardner	**William Watson**
Kizzy	**Leslie Uggams**
Capt. Thomas Davies	**Edward Asner**
Third Mate Slater	**Ralph Waite**
John Reynolds	**Lorne Greene**
Mrs Reynolds	**Lynda Day George**
Dr William Reynolds	**Robert Reed**
Carrington	**Paul Shenar**
Tom Moore	**Chuck Connors**
Ordell	**John Schuck**
Mingo	**Scatman Crothers**
Stephen Bennett	**George Hamilton**
Evan Brent	**Lloyd Bridges**
Tom Harvey	**Georg Stanford Brown**
Irene Harvey	**Lynne Moody**
Sam Bennett	**Richard Roundtree**
Ames	**Vic Morrow**
The Drummer	**Raymond St Jacques**
Missy Anne	**Sandy Duncan**
Squire James	**MacDonald Carey**
Chicken George Moore	**Ben Vereen**
Mrs Moore	**Carolyn Jones**
Sir Eric Russell	**Ian McShane**
Sister Sara	**Lillian Randolph**
Jemmy Brent	**Doug McClure**
Justin	**Burl Ives**
Lewis	**Hilly Hicks**

Writers: **William Blinn, Ernest Kinoy, James Lee, Max Cohen**
Executive Producer: **David L. Wolper**
Producer: **Stan Margulies**

The saga of a black American family, from its roots in slavery to the Civil War.

If RICH MAN, POOR MAN was the mini-series that launched the idea of dramatizing popular novels with a star-studded cast, *Roots* was the serial which ensured the concept stayed well and truly afloat. This 12-hour drama was an enormous success, telling the story of various generations of a black American family, picking up the action around 1750 with the birth of a boy in a Gambian tribe. At the age of 17, the boy, Kunta Kinte, was kidnapped by white slave-traders and taken to America.

Adopting the new name of Toby, he was set to work on the southern plantations, but remained doggedly independent, even losing a foot in an attempt to escape. The series then followed the misfortunes of Kunta Kinte and his clan over a hundred-year period. It saw his daughter, Kizzy, raped by her owner and giving birth to a son later known as Chicken George (because of his prowess with fighting birds), who spent some time in slavery in England. George's son, Tom, fought in the American Civil War and with his family looked forward to the emancipation of slaves that followed it. But, as they embarked on a move to Tennessee and the dream of a better life, they discovered that their new 'freedom', with its grim poverty, poor education and feeble rights, was not the true liberty they had envisaged.

That wasn't the end of the *Roots* saga, however. In 1979, a sequel, entitled *Roots: The Next Generations* (featuring top actors like Henry Fonda, Marlon Brando and Richard Thomas), picked up the story in the 1880s and ran through to the late 1960s. It saw Tom, his daughter and then his granddaughter begin to make inroads in society. At the end of the family line came Alex (played by James Earl Jones), a noted writer who was sufficiently intrigued by his family history that he returned to Africa to learn how his great-great-great-great-grandfather, Kunta Kinte, had been so cruelly robbed of his freedom.

Roots and *Roots: The Next Generations* were adapted from the book by Alex Haley – the Alex of its storyline. The success of the original series (over half the population of America watched the final episode) can be put down partly to its all-star cast, and partly to the fact that the USA was swept by blizzards on the eight consecutive nights on which the series was shown. Some critics have claimed that white Americans gave the series their time in repentance for the sins of their ancestors. Others have simply suggested that sensationalism was the reason for its success, questioning the accuracy of the facts.

ROSE, MONICA
(?–1994)

Chirpy Cockney teenager who sprang to fame as a contestant on DOUBLE YOUR MONEY in 1963. Her personality impressed presenter Hughie Green so much that he made her the permanent hostess. She continued to partner Green on the follow-up quiz, THE SKY'S THE LIMIT, in 1971.

ROSEANNE
(1952–)

Outspoken stand-up comedienne who quickly took control of the TV series named after her. In ROSEANNE, she portrayed a shirty, sarcastic working mum (Roseanne Conner) and led the programme to the top of the US ratings. Her name changed from Barr to Arnold after her second marriage, to comic Tom Arnold, who also worked on the show. However, since that marriage broke down and she remarried, she has preferred to be billed simply as Roseanne. Her own talk show, *The Roseanne Show*, has also been seen in the UK.

ROSEANNE

US (Carsey-Werner/Full Moon & High Tide) Situation
Comedy. Channel 4 1989–97

Roseanne Conner	**Roseanne (Barr/Arnold)**
Dan Conner	**John Goodman**
Jackie Harris	**Laurie Metcalf**
Rebecca 'Becky' Conner/Healy	**Lecy Goranson**
	Sarah Chalke
Darlene Conner	**Sara Gilbert**
David Jacob 'DJ' Conner	**Michael Fishman**
Crystal Anderson/Conner	**Natalie West**
Booker Brooks	**George Clooney**
Ed Conner	**Ned Beatty**
Mark Healy	**Glenn Quinn**
Bonnie	**Bonnie Sheridan**
Leon Carp	**Martin Mull**
Bev Harris	**Estelle Parsons**
Arnie Merchant/Thomas	**Tom Arnold**
Nancy Bartlett	**Sandra Bernhard**
Nana Mary	**Shelley Winters**
David Healy	**Johnny Galecki**
Fred	**Michael O'Keefe**
Scott	**Fred Willard**
Heather	**Heather Matarazzo**

Creator: **Matt Williams**
Executive Producers: **Marcy Carsey, Tom Werner,
Roseanne Barr/Arnold, Tom Arnold**
Producers: **Matt Williams, Jeff Harris**

Down-to-earth comedy of life in Middle America.

Roseanne and Dan Conner, two heavyweight wise-crackers, lived at 714 Delaware Street, in the lacklustre town of Lanford, Illinois. Dan worked as a dry-waller in the building industry, where work was patchy; Roseanne flitted from job to job, abusing her employers and dreaming of the day when the bills would stop arriving. But there was not much chance of that with three demanding kids to support. Eldest was Becky, a typically precocious teenager, anxious to grow up and dismissive of her parents' efforts to keep the family afloat. Next was sports-mad tomboy Darlene, comfortable with her plainness, acerbic in her wit and always her dad's best buddy. Runt of the litter was DJ, a slightly off-beat juvenile, the jewel of his parents' eyes and the bane of his sisters' lives. Well into the programme's run, the Conners produced a fourth child, named Jerry Garcia, after Roseanne's Grateful Dead hero.

Hovering around the comfortable but functional home was Roseanne's unmarried sister, Jackie Harris. Moping between jobs (she was once a cop and then a truck-driver) and boyfriends, she was Roseanne's confidante and disrupter of Dan's mealtimes. Jackie, too, gave birth to a son, fathered by her (brief) husband, Fred. On the fringes was Rosie's half-baked friend, Crystal, who later married Dan's absent father, Ed, and an assortment of work colleagues and bosses from Roseanne's times as plastic factory worker, sweeper-up at a beauty salon and coffee-shop waitress in a shopping mall. The Conners also tried their hand at running a motorbike repair shop

and, when that failed, Roseanne joined Jackie, their grating mum Bev and bisexual friend Nancy in opening The Lunch Box, a loose meat diner.

The novel thing about *Roseanne* was the sheer ordinariness of its lead characters. Here was a family that ate convenience foods, watched TV all day and lived on the telephone. They worked hard yet got nowhere, but the family unit remained whole, even if it did stretch at the seams from time to time, especially when Becky ran off and married her punk boyfriend, Mark, and Darlene also left home for art college and secretly moved in with Mark's brother, David. An enlightened approach to parenthood and an irrepressible sense of humour made the family work, even in the most difficult of times.

In the final series, domestic drudgery was abandoned when Roseanne and Jackie won the state lottery and launched themselves into an unlikely world of luxury hotels and financial wheeler-dealing, which tore the family apart. The fact that the ABSOLUTELY FABULOUS characters Edina and Patsy (Jennifer Saunders and Joanna Lumley) joined them in one episode reveals how far they had strayed from their home in downbeat Lanford. However, this uncharacteristic final season was placed into context in the last, extended episode, in which Darlene and David's baby daughter, Harris, was brought home. In the closing minutes, Roseanne revealed that the crazy events of previous weeks had been a fantasy. Writing her memoirs, she explained that times, in fact, had continued to be hard and announced how much she missed Dan, who had died from a heart attack which viewers had previously been led to believe he had survived.

ROSENTHAL, JACK

CBE (1931–)

Award-winning British screenwriter, creator of the comedy series, THE DUSTBINMEN, THE LOVERS, *Sadie, It's Cold Outside* and *Moving Story*, and writer of many single dramas notable for their wry humour and clever social observation. Among the highlights have been *Pie in the Sky, Green Rub* (both 1963), the *Playhouse* presentation, *There's A Hole In Your Dustbin, Delilah* (1968, which proved to be the pilot for THE DUSTBINMEN), *Another Sunday and Sweet FA* (1972), *Polly Put the Kettle on, Mr Ellis Versus The People* and *There'll Almost Always Be an England* (all 1974, the last two from the *Village Hall* anthology), *The Evacuees* (1975), *Ready When You Are, Mr McGill, Bar Mitzvah Boy* (both 1976), *Spend, Spend, Spend, Spaghetti Two-Step* (both 1977), *The Knowledge* (1979), *P'tang Yang Kipperbang* (1982), *Mrs Capper's Birthday* (1985), *Fools on the Hill* (1986), *And a Nightingale Sang* (1989), *Screen One's Wide-Eyed and Legless* (1993) and *Eskimo Day* (1996), and LONDON'S BURNING (1986, which, again, led to a full series, but with no Rosenthal involvement). Rosenthal also wrote for Maureen Lipman's *About Face* series (she is his wife). His earliest TV work was on CORONATION STREET (well over 100 episodes, plus some as producer) and programmes like THE ODD MAN, *Bulldog Breed*, THAT WAS THE WEEK THAT WAS, *The Villains*, PARDON THE EXPRESSION, MRS

THURSDAY and COMEDY PLAYHOUSE (some with his one-time partner, Harry Driver).

ROSENTHAL, JIM
(1947–)

British sports frontman, formerly in newspapers and then with BBC Radio. For ITV Sport, he has presented coverage of athletics, soccer, boxing, motor racing and other major events.

ROSIE/THE GROWING PAINS OF PC PENROSE
UK (BBC) Situation Comedy. BBC 1 1975–81

PC Michael 'Rosie' Penrose .... **Paul Greenwood**
Sgt Flagg .... **Bryan Pringle** (*Growing Pains*)
PC Buttress .... **David Pinner** (*Growing Pains*)
PC Toombs .... **Alan Foss** (*Growing Pains*)
Insp. Fox .... **Christopher Burgess** (*Growing Pains*)
WPC Dean .... **Catherine Chase** (*Growing Pains*)
PC Wilmot .... **Tony Haygarth**
Gillian Chislehurst .... **Frankie Jordan**
Millie Penrose .... **Avril Elgar**
Patricia Kneale
Uncle Norman .... **Allan Surtees**
Auntie Ida .... **Lorraine Peters**
Bill Chislehurst .... **Don McKillop**
Glenda Chislehurst .... **Maggie Jones**
Chief Insp. Dunwoody .... **Paul Luty**
Sgt West .... **Barry Hart**
WPC Brenda Whatmough .... **Penny Leatherbarrow**
Merv .... **Robert Gillespie**
John Cater

Creator/Writer: **Roy Clarke**
Producers: **Douglas Argent, Bernard Thompson**

The misadventures of a hapless young constable and his associates.

Viewers were introduced to young PC Penrose, or 'Rosie' as he was familiarly known, in the series *The Growing Pains of PC Penrose*. A friendly but exceptionally naïve copper, he was based alongside PCs Toombs and Buttress at the police station in Slagcaster, Yorkshire, where he was cruelly bullied by his superior, the blustering Sgt Flagg. However, when the series' title was shortened to *Rosie*, he was given a compassionate move back to his home town of Ravens Bay, to be near his 'invalid' mother, Millie. He now found himself living with his flighty mum at his Auntie Ida's house, where his Uncle Norman spent most of his time in the garden (whether he liked it or not). At work, Rosie was paired with PC Wilmot, a more experienced but also more reckless bobby whom Rosie often had to bail out of trouble and protect from the clutches of WPC Whatmough. Cigar-puffing Chief Inspector Dunwoody was their no-nonsense boss and Merv their short-sighted, inept super-grass. Rosie also had a girlfriend, the demanding, clinging Gillian, whose snooty, factory-owning dad had little time for her PC boyfriend.

This gentle comedy was written by Roy Clarke (who used to be a policeman himself) and introduced up-and-coming actor Paul Greenwood. Greenwood returned to police ranks a decade later, but this time much further up the ladder, when he took the part of SPENDER's by-the-book boss, Supt. Yelland. Greenwood also co-wrote and sang the theme song for *Rosie*.

ROSIE AND JIM
UK (Ragdoll/Central) Children's. ITV 1990–2; 1995–

Presenters: **John Cunliffe, Pat Hutchins, Neil Brewer**
Creators: **Anne Wood, Doug Wilcox**

Two rag-doll puppets come to life when their bargee companion turns his back.

This long-running infants' favourite was set aboard the narrowboat *Ragdoll*, home of mischievous Rosie and Jim, themselves a couple of rag dolls. The boat's owner – ignorant of their activities and bemused by the inevitable changes they wrought – also took on the guise of presenter of the programme, drawing and telling stories and fronting filmed inserts exploring the neighbourhood where the boat had moored. First host/writer was John Cunliffe (creator of POSTMAN PAT).

ROSLIN, GABY
(1964–)

London-born presenter, the daughter of radio announcer Clive Roslin. She first gained attention in the children's programme, *Motormouth*, after spending time on a cable TV show called *Hippo*, and on the back of this was chosen to be Chris Evans's co-host from the start of THE BIG BREAKFAST. Roslin then hosted the nature series, *Predators*, and her own Channel 4 chat show, and began to co-present the annual CHILDREN IN NEED appeals with Terry Wogan. Her other series have included *The Real Holiday Show, Television's Greatest Hits, Whatever You Want, Watchdog Healthcheck* and *TV Revealed*.

ROSS, JOE E.
(1905–82)

American comic actor, seen as Sgt Rupert Ritzik in THE PHIL SILVERS SHOW and later a star in his own right, playing the podgy Officer Gunther Toody in CAR 54, WHERE ARE YOU?. A later series, *It's About Time* (in which he played a caveman), was less successful and he soon turned to animation voicing as a new career path (among others, he was the voice of Sgt Flint in HONG KONG PHOOEY).

ROSS, JONATHAN
(1960–)

Former TV researcher (on programmes like Channel 4's *Soul Train*) who became an instant hit in the mid-1980s when he hosted his own chat show, *The Last Resort*. His snappy suits and distinctive speech impediment (a soft 'r'), quickly helped ensure celebrity status. He has since hosted *One Hour with Jonathan Ross*, *Tonight with Jonathan Ross* and *The Saturday Zoo*, and sat in for *Wogan*. Ross's other credits have included *The Incredibly Strange Film Show*, *Mondo Rosso* (cult films), *Gagtag* (chairman), *Americana* (a documentary series about American lifestyles), *Fascinating Facts!*, *The Best of Enemies*, *The Big Big Talent Show*, *In Search of Bond*, THEY THINK IT'S ALL OVER, *It's Only TV But I Like It* (questionmaster) and numerous award ceremonies as emcee (especially THE BRITISH COMEDY AWARDS). He set up (and then sold) the Channel X production company and in 1999 took over as host of the FILM series. His brother Paul is also a presenter.

ROSS, NICK
(1947–)

British current affairs anchorman, initially working for the BBC in Northern Ireland. He was once presenter of BREAKFAST TIME and the NATIONWIDE successor, *Sixty Minutes*, but is best known for being at the helm of CRIMEWATCH UK since 1984. Ross has also hosted its associated programmes, *Crimewatch Files* and *Crimestoppers*, plus WATCHDOG, *On the Record*, DID YOU SEE . . . ?, *Westminster with Nick Ross*, *The Search*, *Gridlock: Bank Holiday Hell* and the quiz, *The Syndicate*, as well as presenting and directing *Out of Court* and contributing to series like MAN ALIVE and HORIZON.

ROSSINGTON, JANE
(1943–)

Blonde British actress, Jill Richardson/Harvey/Chance in CROSSROADS throughout the series' entire first run. Indeed, it was Jane who uttered the first words on the programme: 'Crossroads Motel, can I help you?' Her other TV credits have been few, notably the part of nurse Kate Ford in EMERGENCY – WARD 10 before *Crossroads*, and an episode of *Dramarama* since. She returned to *Crossroads* on its revival in 2001.

ROSSITER, LEONARD
(1926–84)

Acclaimed British actor, a viewers' favourite as the seedy landlord Rigsby in RISING DAMP. He proved just as popular when suffering a mid-life crisis as the lead in THE FALL AND RISE OF REGINALD PERRIN. Rossiter did not turn professional until his late 20s and his flair for comedy was even slower to raise its head. When he first arrived on the small screen in the 1960s, after notable stage performances, he was primarily a straight actor. One of his early roles was that of DI Bamber in Z CARS, although he also appeared in the satire show, BBC-3. Among his other credits were the controversial Nigel Kneale play, *The Year of the Sex Olympics*, the HTV movie, *Thick as Thieves*, the Andrew Davies drama, *Fearless Frank*, and the Roy Clarke COMEDY PLAYHOUSE presen-

tation, *Pygmalion Smith*. He also guested in series like THE AVENGERS and STEPTOE AND SON, provided the voice for the dog Boot in *The Perishers*, and was regularly seen spilling Cinzano over Joan Collins in commercials. Rossiter's final sitcoms were *The Losers* (wrestling manager Sydney Foskett) and TRIPPER'S DAY (supermarket manager Norman Tripper). Screened posthumously, his portrayal of King John in a *BBC Shakespeare* offering was a last reminder of his versatility. Both his wives were also in the acting business: Josephine Tewson and Gillian Raine.

ROTHWELL, ALAN
(1937–)

Oldham-born actor on television for over 40 years. Undoubtedly his best-remembered part was that of the ill-fated David Barlow (Ken's brother) in CORONATION STREET, which he played for eight years up to 1968. Taking time out from the *Street*, Rothwell was also seen in the South American spy caper, TOP SECRET (Mike), and he later moved into children's entertainment as presenter of *Picture Box*, *Hickory House* and *Daisy Daisy*. He has been seen in Z CARS, CROWN COURT, ALL CREATURES GREAT AND SMALL, HEARTBEAT and *Children's Ward*, among other series, and also played junkie Nicholas Black in BROOKSIDE.

ROUTH, JONATHAN

The Jeremy Beadle of the early 1960s, Jonathan Routh was CANDID CAMERA's chief prankster – until he became too easily recognized. He also presented the innovative NICE TIME with Kenny Everett and Germaine Greer in 1968.

ROUTLEDGE, PATRICIA
OBE (1928–)

Birkenhead-born actress, much seen in supporting roles until blooming as Hyacinth Bucket (pronounced 'Bouquet') in Roy Clarke's KEEPING UP APPEARANCES and then as the eponymous pensioner sleuth in HETTY WAINTHROPP INVESTIGATES. Other appearances of note have come in 1964's *Victoria Regina* (Queen Victoria, ageing from 18 to 80), the BBC's 1975 version of *David Copperfield* (Mrs Micawber), the comedy, *Marjorie and Men* (divorcée Marjorie Belton), the *Bookmark* presentation, *Miss Pym's Day Out*, and in Alan Bennett's TALKING HEADS. Routledge has also been heard narrating programmes such as *The Natural World* and has been seen in series and single dramas like Z CARS, *Sense and Sensibility*, *Nicholas Nickleby*, STEPTOE AND SON, *The Cost of Loving*, *A Visit from Miss Protheroe*, THE TWO RONNIES, CROWN COURT, AND MOTHER MAKES FIVE, TALES OF THE UNEXPECTED, *First and Last* and *Victoria Wood – As Seen on TV*.

ROVING REPORT
UK (ITN) Documentary. ITV 1957–64

Reporters: **Robin Day, George Ffitch, Tim Brinton, John Hartley, Reginald Bosanquet, Huw Thomas, Lynne Reid Banks, Ian Trethowan, Neville Barker, Elizabeth Kenrick, John Whale**

Creator/Editor: **Geoffrey Cox**
Producers: **Michael Barsley, Robert Verrall**

Series of short documentaries looking at people and places in the news around the world.

Roving Report was ITN's first and more or less only programme that was not exclusively news-based. It consisted of a collection of documentary films of about 20 minutes in length, compiled by ITN reporters as they travelled the world. The films were often by-products of a news-seeking expedition but, nevertheless, had their own distinct character and aimed to paint a picture of the people of a foreign city or country at that time in the news, reflecting their views, thoughts, ways of life, etc. The first programme was recorded atop the Empire State Building. Robin Day was the chief reporter in the early days.

ROWAN, DAN
(1922–87) See MARTIN, DICK.

ROWAN AND MARTIN'S LAUGH-IN
US (Romart) Comedy. BBC 2 1968–71

Dan Rowan, Dick Martin, Gary Owens, Ruth Buzzi, Judy Carne, Goldie Hawn, Arte Johnson, Henry Gibson, Eileen Brennan, Jo Anne Worley, Roddy Maude-Roxby, Larry Hovis, Pigmeat Markham, Charlie Brill, Dick Whittington, Chelsea Brown, Mitzi McCall, Alan Sues, Dave Madden, Jeremy Lloyd, Teresa Graves, Pamela Rodgers, Byron Gilliam, Lily Tomlin, Ann Elder, Dennis Allen, Johnny Brown, Barbara Sharma, Nancy Phillips, Harvey Jason

Executive Producers: **George Schlatter, Ed Friendly**

Hugely popular and influential, fast-moving gag show.

Hosts of *Laugh-In* were Dan Rowan, a smooth straightman, and his grinning fool of a partner, Dick Martin, but they were more than backed up by a large cast of zany comedians who worked around them. The show itself was a cross between slapstick and satire, a sort of Keystone Cops meet THAT WAS THE WEEK THAT WAS, all fused together on bright sets by 1960s TV technology. There were gags galore, not all of them terribly funny, but the weight of numbers meant that the audience just had to find something amusing.

Catchphrases became *Laugh-In*'s speciality. From Dan and Dick's 'You bet your sweet bippy' and 'Look that up in your Funk and Wagnalls', to 'Sock it to me', a cue for Judy Carne to get a thorough soaking. Even Richard Nixon dropped in to say it. Popular features and sketches included 'Letters to *Laugh-In*', the 'Flying Fickle Finger of Fate' (a mock talent show award), and the non-stop joke wall that wound up each programme, with cast members flinging open doors to belt out one-liners. All this came after Rowan and Martin had parodied the old Burns and Allen ending ('Say goodnight, Dick', 'Goodnight Dick').

Also memorable were the man riding a toddler's tricycle; Henry Gibson, the flower-power poet; and Ruth Buzzi as Gladys, the vicious lady on the park bench thrashing Arte Johnson's Tyrone, a dirty old man, with her umbrella. Johnson also popped up from behind a pot plant, as a German soldier muttering 'Very interesting, but stupid'. Lily Tomlin appeared as Ernestine, the sarcastic telephone-operator, and Alan Sues played a gormless sports presenter. Then there was Gary Owens, hand cupped over his ear, bellowing into the microphone to welcome viewers to 'Beautiful Downtown Burbank', Pigmeat Markham, whose 'Here Comes The Judge' was a UK chart hit in 1968, and Goldie Hawn establishing herself as a dumb, giggly blonde.

The jokes were topical, sometimes controversial and generally very silly, but they were held together by slick editing, cameo appearances from guest stars and the hectic pace of the show. *Laugh-In* was the world's favourite comedy programme for two or three years. When it ended, Buzzi and Owens were the only cast members (apart from the hosts) still with it. The show was revived in 1979, but its time had long passed and this version is notable only for the fact that Robin Williams was one of the supporting performers.

ROWLANDS, PATSY
(1934–)

British actress, often seen as a dowdy wife, but enjoying a long and varied TV career. Among her wifely roles have been Rosemary in INSIDE GEORGE WEBLEY, Betty in BLESS THIS HOUSE and Netta in KINVIG. In contrast she was Sally Army Sister Alice Meredith in *Hallelujah!* and also appeared as police officers in the kids' series, *Follow That Dog* (Sgt Bryant), and the sitcom, *The Nesbitts Are Coming* (WPC Kitty Naylor). Rowlands took the roles of Miss Twitty in another children's series, *Tottering Towers*, Susan in THE SQUIRRELS, actress Flossie Nightingale in *Rep*, Mrs Clapton in *Get Well Soon*, Mrs Harty in *Screen Two*'s *Femme Fatale* and Mrs Tinker in *Vanity Fair*. To add to the variety, she has also been seen in dramas like PUBLIC EYE, JULIET BRAVO, *Père Goriot*, KATE, *The History of Mr Polly* and *Crimestrike*, as well as comedies like ROBIN'S NEST, IN LOVING MEMORY, *Carry On Laughing*, *Emery* and GEORGE AND MILDRED.

ROY ROGERS SHOW, THE
US (Roy Rogers) Western. ITV 1955–7

Roy Rogers, Dale Evans, Pat Brady

Executive Producers: **Art Rush, Mike North**

Producers: **Jack C. Lacey, Bob Henry, Leslie H. Martinson**

Clean-cut, modern-day Western with the 'King of the Cowboys' and his wife, Dale Evans, 'Queen of the West'.

Living on the Double R Bar Ranch, near Mineral City, singing cowboy Roy Rogers was an important force in the maintenance of law and order in the neighbourhood. He also owned a diner, the Eureka Café, which was run by Dale Evans, and he was assisted by an incompetent sidekick, Pat Brady, cook at the diner and driver of an unreliable jeep known as Nellybelle. Roy, of course, rode Trigger, alongside Dale on Buttermilk. Bullet the Alsatian dog trotted along in tow, and the Sons of the Pioneers vocal group helped Roy with the musical content.

ROYAL CANADIAN MOUNTED POLICE
Canada/UK (CBC/Crawley Films/BBC) Police Drama. BBC 1960–1

Cpl. Jacques Gagnier .... **Gilles Pelletier**
Constable Scott .... **John Perkins**
Constable Bill Mitchell .... **Don Francks**

Producers: **George Gorman, Harry Horner, Bernard Girard**

Stirring adventures of the RCMP.

As if to prove that a Mountie always got his man, this joint Canadian/UK production brought us heroic tales from the frozen north. It centred on the town of Shamattawa and its Royal Canadian Mounted Police headquarters, following the local officers in their efforts to enforce law and order.

ROYAL VARIETY PERFORMANCE
UK (ATV/BBC) Variety. ITV/BBC 1 1960–

Annual charity concert in the presence of Her Majesty the Queen or other members of the royal family.

A prestigious showbusiness extravaganza, the Royal Variety Performance was instituted in 1912 and became a yearly event in 1921. It was first televised for ITV in 1960 by Lew Grade's ATV, which covered proceedings again the following year. Since 1962, however, the BBC has enjoyed the right to stage the show on alternate years. Among the stars of the first televised show (held at the Victoria Palace theatre) were Norman Wisdom, Harry Worth, Benny Hill, Frankie Howerd, Cliff Richard and The Shadows, Max Bygraves, Russ Conway, Liberace and Nat 'King' Cole. In 1963, The Beatles took the Prince of Wales Theatre by storm and, in 1980, on the occasion of her 80th birthday, the Queen Mother revelled in the tribute to music-hall days paid by Chesney Allen, Arthur Askey, Charlie Chester, Billy Dainty, Charlie Drake, Arthur English, Cyril Fletcher, Stanley Holloway, Roy Hudd, Richard Murdoch, Sandy Powell, Tommy Trinder

and Ben Warriss. Much of 1998's show became a tribute to Frank Sinatra, who had died that year, and in 1999 the show was taken outside London for the first time, with Birmingham's Hippodrome hosting proceedings. Bernard Delfont staged each show from 1961 to 1978.

ROYLE, CAROL
(1954–)

British actress probably best recalled as Jenny in LIFE WITHOUT GEORGE, which she quickly followed with the role of Jessica in Dennis Potter's controversial BLACKEYES. Royle also starred in *Girl Talk*, *Ladies in Charge* (Diana Granville) and in Alan Plater's version of L. P. Hartley's vampire story, *Feet Foremost* (part of the *Shades of Darkness* anthology). Among her other credits have been parts in series like BLAKE'S 7, THE RACING GAME, *The Cedar Tree*, THE PROFESSIONALS, *Heartland*, BERGERAC, *The Outsider*, *Oxbridge Blues* and *Thief Takers*. She is the daughter of actor Derek Royle and sister of actress Amanda Royle.

ROYLE FAMILY, THE
UK (Granada) Situation Comedy. BBC 2/BBC 1 1998–

Jim Royle .... **Ricky Tomlinson**
Barbara Royle .... **Sue Johnston**
Denise Royle/Best .... **Caroline Aherne**
Dave Best .... **Craig Cash**
Antony Royle .... **Ralf Little**
Norma Speakman .... **Liz Smith**
Mary Carroll .... **Doreen Keogh**
Joe Carroll .... **Peter Martin**
Cheryl Carroll .... **Jessica Stevenson**
Twiggy .... **Geoffrey Hughes**

Writers: **Caroline Aherne, Craig Cash, Henry Normal, Carmel Morgan**
Producers: **Glenn Wilhide, Kenton Allen**

The humdrum life of a Manchester family.

When *The Royle Family* took to the air, viewers and critics were equally suspicious about its novel approach to sitcom. However, both were quickly won over and the series became the most talked-about comedy of the late 1990s. The novelty value came from a number of key decisions: to do without a laugh track or studio audience; to film the series rather than videotape it; to keep all events on one set; and, most significantly, to forgo the contrived plots and obvious gag-lines common to other sitcoms. Instead, the series merely peeped behind the council house curtains, fly-on-the-wall style, as a Manchester family went about their daily affairs (it was not that far removed from the 1974 real documentary saga, *The Family*).

The Royle family consisted of layabout dad Jim, wedged in his armchair, for ever scratching his privates, making wisecracks and finding reason for complaint (usually because the immersion had been left on). Mum Barbara worked part-time in a baker's shop and double-time at home, cooking for the family before flopping down with a full ashtray on the sofa. Teenager Antony (known as 'Lurch') was the awkward adolescent incessantly called upon to 'make a brew' and then criticized for his laziness ('Where does he get it from?'). Elder sister Denise was even more static than Jim, unless there was a chance of half-a-dozen glasses of lager, while her fiancé/ husband, Dave, a mobile DJ, gormlessly allowed her constant demands to wash over him. Occasional visitors were Barbara's irritating mother Norma (Nana), hooky-goods merchant Twiggy, and next-door neighbours the Carrolls – taciturn Joe, bubbly Irish Mary and podgy Cheryl, Denise's best friend.

Most of the action – 'action, my arse!' – took place in the evening or on Sunday afternoons, as the family settled down after their evening meal or heavy Sunday lunch to engage in everyday chit-chat, with the television always switched on in the background. Major excitement came from Jim's birthday, Nana's cataract operation or Antony's new girlfriend, although each series did build up to a real climax – Denise and Dave's wedding, for instance, or the birth of their child, Baby David.

As the programme was swiftly switched from BBC 2 to BBC 1 and began to garner the awards, other comedians confessed to being green with envy for not thinking up the concept first. Star Caroline Aherne also directed the third series.

RUMPOLE OF THE BAILEY

UK (Thames) Legal Drama. ITV 1978–80; 1983; 1987–8; 1991–2

Horace Rumpole	**Leo McKern**
Claude Erskine-Brown	**Julian Curry**
Phyllida Trant/Erskine-Brown	**Patricia Hodge**
Guthrie Featherstone	**Peter Bowles**
George Frobisher	**Moray Watson**
Uncle Tom	**Richard Murdoch**
Hilda Rumpole	**Peggy Thorpe-Bates**
	Marion Mathie
Henry	**Jonathan Coy**
Justice Bullingham	**Bill Fraser**
Diane	**Maureen Darbyshire**
Fiona Allways	**Rosalyn Landor**
Marigold Featherstone	**Joanna Van Gyseghem**
Samuel Ballard	**Peter Blythe**
Liz Probert	**Samantha Bond**
	Abigail McKern
Nick Rumpole	**David Yelland**
Judge Graves	**Robin Bailey**

Creator/Writer: **John Mortimer**
Executive Producer: **Lloyd Shirley**
Producers: **Irene Shubik, Jacqueline Davis**

The cases of a gruff old barrister with a zest for justice.

Colourful, middle-aged Horace Rumpole differed from his legal colleagues in his distinct lack of ambition and his genuine interest in clients. His brusque, down-to-earth manner ruffled many a rival's feathers, and he revelled in a joyful lack of respect for authority (he called judges 'Old darling'). Rumpole took defence cases only and his clients came mainly (though not uniquely) from the lower classes. He proved a saviour on most occasions, craftily turning trials in the favour of his clients. Out of the courtroom, he lived at 38 Froxbury Mansions, enjoyed smoking cigars, quoting the *Oxford Book of English Verse*, drinking the Pomeroy's Wine Bar claret ('Château Fleet Street') and disappointing his wife, Hilda, 'She who must be obeyed'. He was retired to Florida after a couple of seasons, but returned in a two-hour special at Christmas 1980. Further series followed intermittently.

Among his more refined legal contemporaries were Samuel Ballard (his Head of Chambers), Erskine-Brown and his future wife, the snobbish Phyllida Trant. The part of junior barrister Liz Probert was eventually filled by Leo McKern's own daughter, Abigail.

The series was written by real-life barrister John Mortimer and the character first appeared in a BBC 1 PLAY FOR TODAY in 1975. When the Corporation declined to take up the option of a series, Mortimer and his producer, Irene Shubik, transferred the irascible old brief to Thames Television.

RUSHTON, WILLIAM
(1937–96)

British satirist and cartoonist, coming to the fore on THAT WAS THE WEEK THAT WAS and its follow-up, NOT SO MUCH A PROGRAMME, MORE A WAY OF LIFE. He went on to host *The New Stars and Garters* with Jill Browne, to guest in NOT ONLY . . . BUT ALSO . . . and to play Plautus in UP POMPEII!, before being given his own series, *Rushton's Illustrated*. He was also seen in programmes like *Grubstreet, Up Sunday, Don't Just Sit There* and *Dawson and Friends*, and was a popular choice for panel games such as CELEBRITY SQUARES and THROUGH THE KEYHOLE. Rushton was one of the founders of *Private Eye* magazine.

RUSSELL, KEN
(1927–)

British director responsible for some outrageous movie moments but more restrained, if just as adventurous, in his television work. Russell began by contributing material for series like MONITOR and OMNIBUS and has given the TV archives some notable documentary-drama portraits of composers like Bartók, Elgar, Wagner, Delius and Debussy, plus other artistic personalities like Isadora Duncan (*Isadora*, 1966), Dante Gabriel Rossetti (*Dante's Inferno*, 1967) and Wordsworth and Coleridge (*Clouds of Glory*, 1978). He returned to TV with his own adaptation of *Lady Chatterley* in 1993 and the musical, *Ken Russell's Treasure Island*, in 1995.

RUTH RENDELL MYSTERIES, THE

UK (TVS/Blue Heaven/United/Meridian) Police Drama. ITV 1987–

DCI Reg Wexford .... **George Baker**

DI Mike Burden .... **Christopher Ravenscroft**
Dora Wexford .... **Louie Ramsay**
Jean Burden .... **Ann Penfold**
Jenny Ireland/Burden .... **Diane Keen**
DS Martin .... **Ken Kitson**
Dr Crocker .... **John Burgess**
Sgt/DS Barry Vine .... **Sean Pertwee**
                                                                Robin Kermode
                                                                Matthew Mills

Executive Producer: **Graham Benson, Michele Buck**
Producers: **John Davies, Neil Zeiger**

The investigations of a slow-speaking but
sharp-thinking country policeman.

Reg Wexford was one of the great thinking coppers of
the 1980s. Like Dalgliesh, Taggart and Morse, he
eschewed the hard-hitting, screaming-tyres kind of
police work much enjoyed by 1970s detectives, in favour
of the painstaking, analytical, working-on-a-hunch sort
of investigation. Created by novelist Ruth Rendell while
on holiday in Ireland (hence the name Wexford, apparently), the Detective Chief Inspector took his first name
from Ruth's uncle, Reg, although most of his character
traits allegedly came from her father, a softly spoken but
firm teacher.

The tales were set in the fictitious Hampshire town of
Kingsmarkham (Romsey was used for filming purposes),
a sleepy backwater which, like Morse's Oxford and
Bergerac's Jersey, quickly witnessed more than its fair
share of murders. Out and about on investigations, the
fatherly Wexford was assisted by the aptly named DI
Mike Burden, a gloomy man with no smile and little to
smile about (his wife had died of cancer). Even when he
remarried, Burden remained rather morose. At home,
Wexford's understanding wife, Dora, proved to be a
rock in support and a source of great encouragement.
Their grown-up daughters were also seen from time to
time.

Like all good TV cops, the affable, well-heeled Wexford had his share of gimmicks, in particular a rich,
Hampshire burr when he spoke, an enjoyment of good
cooking and an evidently well-educated manner, manifested in his quotation from Shakespeare and other
literary greats. And, like all good TV cops, he always got
his man. Sometimes it took two or three episodes, but
his tortoise-like approach ensured the right result
eventually.

By the time production company TVS lost its franchise in 1992, all 13 existing Ruth Rendell novels had been
covered, plus a few of her short stories and a handful of
new scripts (including some from star George Baker).
The Ruth Rendell Mysteries title has since been revived by
Meridian, although these intermittent thrillers have not
usually featured Inspector Wexford. The Kingsmarkham
copper did return, however, in 1996, 1998 and 2000, in
adaptations of new Rendell stories, *Simisola*, *Road Rage*
and *Harm Done* (the last billed simply as *Inspector
Wexford*).

RUTLAND WEEKEND TELEVISION
UK (BBC) Situation Comedy. BBC 2 1975–6

**Eric Idle, David Battley, Neil Innes, Henry Woolf,
Terence Bayler, Gwen Taylor**

Creator/Writer: **Eric Idle**
Producer: **Ian Keill**

*Ambitious programming from Britain's smallest
television network.*

Supposedly based in Rutland, England's smallest county
which had just been swallowed up into Leicestershire,
this spoof series was the brainchild of MONTY PYTHON
star Eric Idle, who cast himself as the programme controller of the financially challenged Rutland Weekend
Television. RWT, for short, presented a variety of programme parodies, some described as 'mini-spectaculars'.
Neil Innes provided the musical content, which reached
its zenith in the one-off, 1978 documentary spin-off, *The
Rutles*. Telling the story of the world's greatest pop band,
known individually as Dirk, Ron, Stig and Barry, but
collectively as The Rutles, it intercut spoof interviews
with celebrities like Mick Jagger with scenes from the
life of the so-called Pre-fab Four. The musical numbers
included all-time classics like 'All You Need Is Lunch',
'W. C. Fields Forever', 'Cheese and Onion' and 'A Hard
Day's Rut', and an accompanying album (with
uncannily Beatle-like vocals and soundtracks) was
released. An EP, headed by the track, 'I Must Be In Love',
made the lower reaches of the UK charts.

RUTLES, THE
See **RUTLAND WEEKEND TELEVISION**.

S4C
(Sianel Pedwar Cymru)

The Welsh fourth channel, S4C was established by the Broadcasting Act 1980 and provides 30 hours a week of Welsh-language programming, ten hours of which are supplied free of charge by the BBC in accordance with its obligations under the Broadcasting Act 1990. The remainder of the Welsh programmes are commissioned by S4C from HTV and other independent producers. Before S4C went on air on 1 November 1982 (a day earlier than Channel 4), BBC Wales and HTV Cymru/Wales mixed Welsh-language programmes with their English-language output. Now they carry only programmes in English. The English-language part of S4C's schedule (around 66 per cent) is made up of programmes also seen on Channel 4, although these are usually rescheduled to give Welsh programmes prominence during peak hours. This practice has not been overly popular with viewers in predominantly English-speaking parts of the Principality.

S4C's Welsh output takes in light entertainment, drama, news, current affairs, sports and children's programmes. Among the most popular has been BBC Wales's *Pobol y Cwm*, a daily soap opera. A subtitled version was shown on BBC 2 in the rest of the UK for a while, under the translated title of *People of the Valley*. The channel has also made a name for itself in the field of animation, commissioning some very successful cartoons from independent producers like Siriol and Bumper Films. These have included *Super Ted*, *Wil Cwak Cwak* and *Fireman Sam*. S4C is funded by a grant from the Treasury and its own advertising sales. It is accountable to a public body known as The Welsh Fourth Channel Authority, whose members are appointed by the Secretary of State for Culture, Media and Sport. In 1998 it launched a digital service, S4C digidol, and a year later added the digital channel S4C-2, which focuses largely on events in the Welsh Assembly and, unlike S4C itself, is accountable to the ITC. The channel's full name, Sianel Pedwar Cymru, means Channel Four Wales.

SABER OF LONDON
See **MARK SABER**.

SACHS, ANDREW
(1930–)

German-born actor whose finest hour came with FAWLTY TOWERS, in which he played the hapless and hopeless Spanish waiter, Manuel. On the back of this success, Sachs has been given the lead role in a few other sitcoms, all of which, sadly, have proved rather short-lived. These have been *Dead Ernest* (the late Ernest Springer), *There Comes a Time* (Tony James, who didn't have long to live) and *Every Silver Lining* (café-owner Nat Silver). Sachs, the father of radio and TV presenter John Sachs, has, however, been seen or heard in plenty of other programmes, from dramas like *The History of Mr Polly*, *The*

Tempest, BERGERAC and CROWN COURT to series as varied as THE WORLD ABOUT US, POINTS OF VIEW (guest presenter), *Supersense* (narrator), *Took and Co.*, RISING DAMP, HORIZON (Albert Einstein), the kids' comedy, *Pirates* (Mr Jones), *Jack of Hearts* (Peter Pryce), and the language lessons, *When in Spain*. He has also presented a programme about his birthplace, *Berliners*.

SACHS, LEONARD
(1909–90)

South African actor who found greater fame as the super-eloquent, gavel-smashing chairman of THE GOOD OLD DAYS, a position he held from 1953 until the series ended in 1983. Among his acting credits were parts in Nigel Kneale's 1984, THE ADVENTURES OF ROBIN HOOD, CROWN COURT, A FAMILY AT WAR, *The Man from Haven*, THE GLITTERING PRIZES, ELIZABETH R (the Count de Feria) and CORONATION STREET (Sir Julius Berlin). His last TV play was entitled *Lost for Words*, something he never was in *The Good Old Days*.

SAGA OF NOGGIN THE NOG, THE
UK (Smallfilms) Children's Entertainment. BBC 1 1959–65; 1982

Narrators: **Oliver Postgate, Ronnie Stevens**

Creator: **Peter Firmin**
Producer: **Oliver Postgate**

The magical adventures of a Norse king.

Using ten-minute episodes in serial form, this characterful animation told the story of Noggin, Prince (later King) of the Nogs, who sailed to the Land of the Midnight Sun to fetch Nooka, Eskimo Princess of the Nooks, to be his queen. His guide on this voyage was Graculus, a great, green talking bird raised from an egg by Nooka, who subsequently became the Royal Bird. Various other adventures befell the brave Noggin, including an encounter with the Ice Dragon and an attempt by his wicked uncle, Nogbad the Bad, to seize his throne. Other characters like Noggin's son, Prince Knut, the mighty Thor Nogson and inventor Olaf the Lofty were also seen.

Noggin the Nog was the second offering (after IVOR THE ENGINE) from the Smallfirms duo of writer/narrator Oliver Postgate and illustrator Peter Firmin. Vernon Elliott wrote the music. In 1982 two colour stories appeared – a remake of *Noggin and the Ice Dragon* and a new story, *Noggin and the Pie*.

SAILOR
UK (BBC) Documentary. BBC 1 1976

Producer: **John Purdie**
Executive Producer: **Roger Mills**

A frank account of life with the crew of HMS Ark Royal.

This ten-part documentary series provided an insight into events in port and at sea with the 2,500 men who crewed the aircraft carrier *Ark Royal*. A camera team lived aboard for ten weeks, capturing the high spots and the low, starting with a boozy last night out in Devonport and continuing to the final disembarkation back home. It saw drunken sailors in disgrace after unruly nights on the town and relived dramas like the winching of a seaman off a submarine for urgent medical treatment. The sailors' antics and their language were both colourful but viewers, generally, loved it. The theme song, 'Sailing', by Rod Stewart, became a Top Three hit for a second time on the back of the series. The programme's format was recalled nearly 20 years later in the documentary series, *HMS Brilliant* (BBC 1 1995).

SAILOR OF FORTUNE
UK (ATV/Michael Sadler) Adventure. ITV 1956–7

Grant Mitchell	**Lorne Greene**
Sean	**Jack MacGowan**
Seamus	**Rupert Davies**
Johnny	**Paul Carpenter**

Writer: **Lindsay Galloway**
Producer: **Michael Sadler**

An honest sea captain finds himself embroiled in other people's murky operations.

American Grant 'Mitch' Mitchell was the skipper of the freighter, *The Shipwreck*. He travelled the world trying to make a living shipping cargo, although intrigue followed him wherever he roamed. There was always someone who needed his help and his ports of call were exotic, even though filming never ventured beyond the bounds of Elstree Studios. All the same, the series provided a springboard for both Lorne Greene and Rupert Davies.

SAINT, THE
UK (ATV/New World/Bamore/ITC) Adventure. ITV 1962–9

Simon Templar	**Roger Moore**
Insp. Claude Eustace Teal	**Ivor Dean**

Creator: **Leslie Charteris**
Producers: **Robert S. Baker, Monty Norman**

A self-supporting amateur sleuth foils crime around the world.

The Saint was Simon Templar (ST being his initials), an independently wealthy adventurer who travelled the globe stumbling into intrigue. Using a business card depicting a matchstick man with a halo, and driving a yellow two-seater Volvo P1800 with the number plate ST1, Templar mingled with the élite and discovered crime at every turn. His devilishly good looks, the twinkle in his eye and his suave manner helped him appear cool in virtually every circumstance, whether it was rescuing blackmail victims or disrupting elaborate robberies. The unruffled, totally self-assured Templar was an unqualified success and proved a wow with the women, including 1960s beauties like Samantha Eggar, Dawn Addams, Julie Christie and Gabrielle Drake. Templar's friendly adversary was Inspector Claude Teal (Teal had been played by three other actors – Campbell Singer, Wensley Pithey and Norman Pitt – before Ivor Dean was confirmed in the role).

The Saint was created by writer Leslie Charteris in 1928 and had already been a hit on radio and in the cinema (most notably starring George Sanders) before the TV series began. Moore, of course, later took his adventurer character into James Bond films, with Ian Ogilvy filling his shoes for a 1970s revival, THE RETURN OF THE SAINT. Simon Dutton was cast in a shortlived 1989 version.

ST ELSEWHERE
US (MTM) Medical Drama. Channel 4 1983–9

Dr Donald Westphall	**Ed Flanders**
Dr Mark Craig	**William Daniels**
Dr Victor Ehrlich	**Ed Begley, Jr**
Dr Jack Morrison	**David Morse**
Dr Ben Samuels	**David Birney**
Dr Annie Cavanero	**Cynthia Sikes**
Dr Wayne Fiscus	**Howie Mandel**
Dr Cathy Martin	**Barbara Whinnery**
Dr Peter White	**Terence Knox**
Nurse Helen Rosenthal	**Christina Pickles**
Dr Daniel Auschlander	**Norman Lloyd**
Dr Hugh Beale	**G. W. Bailey**
Dr Philip Chandler	**Denzel Washington**
Dr V. J. Kochar	**Kavi Raz**
Dr Wendy Armstrong	**Kim Miyori**
Nurse Shirley Daniels	**Ellen Bry**
Luther Hawkins	**Eric Laneuville**
Dr Bob Caldwell	**Mark Harmon**
Dr Michael Ridley	**Paul Sand**
Joan Halloran	**Nancy Stafford**
Mrs Ellen Craig	**Bonnie Bartlett**
Dr Elliot Axelrod	**Stephen Furst**
Nurse Lucy Papandrao	**Jennifer Savidge**
Dr Jackie Wade	**Sagan Lewis**
Warren Coolidge	**Byron Stewart**
Dr Emily Humes	**Judith Hansen**
Nurse Peggy Shotwell	**Saundra Sharp**
Dr Alan Poe	**Brian Tochi**
Mrs Hufnagel	**Florence Halop**
Dr Roxanne Turner	**Alfre Woodard**
Ken Valere	**George Deloy**
Terri Valere	**Deborah May**
Dr Seth Griffin	**Bruce Greenwood**
Dr Carol Novino	**Cindy Pickett**
Dr Paulette Kiem	**France Nuyen**
Dr John Gideon	**Ronny Cox**

Creators: **Joshua Brand, John Falsey**
Executive Producer: **Bruce Paltrow**

Life, death and humanity at a Boston teaching hospital.

St Elegius was a decaying old hospital in one of Boston's roughest suburbs. Run by the city, it was used as a deposi-tory for patients by the more élitist medical centres, hence its nickname of St Elsewhere. In HILL STREET BLUES fashion (the show was by the same production company), *St Elsewhere* took viewers on a journey through hospital life but shunned all the old medical-drama stereotypes. Here the medics were fallible, the patients were nervous and the interactions believable. There were no miracle cures and the seediness of the environment was always apparent.

Realism was a keystone of *St Elsewhere*, with echoes of *Hill Street Blues* in its pace, style and camerawork. But it was also an adventurous show, taking chances with scripts and characters, leaving the viewer wondering what the producers would try next. It became a pro-gramme for baby-boomers, chock-full of references to pop culture, such as tannoy messages for doctors from other TV shows, throw-away allusions to pop songs or gentle parodies of films such as *The Towering Inferno*, all played with a straight face and no explanation. In the final episode, the dénouement of THE FUGITIVE was restaged as, off-camera, a one-armed man climbed an amusement-park water tower.

Chief of staff at the hospital was Daniel Westphall, the widower father of a teenage girl and an autistic son. His heart surgeon was the insensitive Mark Craig, whose loyal junior was Victor Ehrlich. Wayne Fiscus was the emergency specialist, Ben Samuels a randy surgeon; Daniel Auschlander, the hospital's administrator, was a liver expert who, ironically, was suffering from liver cancer. Other members of the team included dedicated but trouble-torn Jack Morrison, psychiatrist Hugh Beale, Annie Cavanero, who tended to get over-involved with her patients, anaesthetist V. J. Kochar, obese Elliot Axel-rod, insecure Philip Chandler and much-married nurse Helen Rosenthal. More tragically, there were also Peter White, who raped pathologist Cathy Martin only to be shot by nurse Shirley Daniels, Wendy Armstrong, who committed suicide, and Bob Caldwell, a promiscuous surgeon who contracted HIV. When the hospital was taken over by a private health-care company, the Ecu-mena Hospitals Corporation, the dirty word 'profit' began to make its presence felt and, as financial pressures grew, the new Chief of Services, Dr John Gideon, forced a showdown with Westphall, who 'mooned' at him and resigned.

Like *Hill Street Blues*, *St Elsewhere* easily won over the critics but failed to gain a big audience. Somehow, though, it clung on for six years, before, in its last epi-sode, the producers wound up the series with a cute little twist. The hospital was seen in miniature, as a model inside a snow globe, held intently by Westphall's autistic son. In the room, Westphall and another cast member were talking but, it appeared, they were no longer doc-tors. As his father took the globe away from the child, viewers were led to believe that *St Elsewhere* had been just a figment of the boy's imagination.

SAINT JAMES, SUSAN
(Susan Miller; 1946–)

American former model who has had three big hit series to her name, principally McMILLAN AND WIFE (as the

'Wife', Sally McMillan) in the 1970s. Her first starring role was in a collection of movies entitled *The Name of the Game* in 1968, which followed guest appearances in series like IT TAKES A THIEF and A MAN CALLED IRONSIDE. In the 1980s, Saint James was seen in *Kate and Allie*, playing Kate McArdle. She has also starred in numerous TV movies.

SALE OF THE CENTURY

UK (Anglia) Quiz. ITV 1971–83

Presenter: **Nicholas Parsons**

Producers: **Peter Joy, Bill Perry**

Quiz in which contestants answer questions, win money and spend it on bargain prizes.

'The Quiz of the Week', as it was billed in the opening announcement, *Sale of the Century* was a remarkably popular quiz game that allowed contestants to use the cash they won to buy prizes at give-away prices. Three contestants took part, answering general knowledge questions on the buzzer. These began at £1 in value, progressing to £3 and then £5. As they began to accumulate cash, the questions were interrupted by bargain offers, tempting contestants to spend some of their winnings on such things as a set of garden furniture for £15. At the end of the game, the person with the most money left could try for the Sale of the Century (a choice of super-bargains) by answering additional questions. Nicholas Parsons was the questionmaster, John Benson acted as announcer and assorted male and female models adorned the prizes. Peter Marshall and Keith Chegwin were the hosts on revivals for satellite TV in the 1990s.

SALLIS, PETER

(1921–)

As LAST OF THE SUMMER WINE's Norman Clegg for 27 years, Twickenham-born Peter Sallis has been a familiar sight on British TV screens. He also appeared in *First of the Summer Wine*, playing Cleggy's father, and was the caretaker, Mr Gudgin, in the children's comedy, *The Ghosts of Motley Hall*, insurance company manager Arthur Simister in the sitcom, *Leave It to Charlie*, and Sidney Bliss in THE NEW STATESMAN. Sallis guested with Patrick Troughton in DOCTOR WHO, and his other credits – varying between serious and humorous work – have included SOFTLY, SOFTLY, BARLOW, *The Culture Vultures*, *The Diary of Samuel Pepys*, PUBLIC EYE, SPYDER'S WEB, *The Moonstone*, THE PALLISERS, RAFFLES, TALES OF THE UNEXPECTED, *Yanks Go Home*, *Ladykillers*, THE RIVALS OF SHERLOCK HOLMES, *Strangers and Brothers* and *The Bretts*. He also provided the voice for Rat in the 1980s animation, THE WIND IN THE WILLOWS, and the voices for the *Wallace & Gromit* films.

SAM

UK (Granada) Drama. ITV 1973–5

Sam Wilson	**Kevin Moreton**
	Mark McManus
Jack Barraclough	**Michael Goodliffe**
Polly Barraclough	**Maggie Jones**
George Barraclough	**Ray Smith**
Ethel Barraclough	**Alethea Charlton**
Toby Wilson	**Frank Mills**
Dora Wilson	**Barbara Ewing**
Frank Barraclough	**James Hazeldine**
Eileen Brady	**Dorothy White**
May Dakin	**Mona Bruce**
Alan Dakin	**John Price**
Sarah Corby/Wilson	**Jennifer Hilary**

Creator/Writer: **John Finch**
Producer: **Michael Cox**

A young lad grows up in a poor mining town in the Pennines.

Ten-year-old Sam Wilson arrived in the Yorkshire town of Skellerton with his mother, Dora, after his dad had sailed off to Canada with another woman. There his life revolved around his grandparents, Toby Wilson, a clothier, and Jack and Polly Barraclough. Proud Jack had been out of work for eight years. Also close at hand were his uncle and aunt, George and Ethel Barraclough. George, unemployed for five years, had just regained a job at the pit. He looked upon Sam as the son he had never had. Dora and George's brother, Frank, was the brainy member of the family, kept out of the mines so he could further his academic studies.

Glumly reflecting the hardships of the 1930s and 1940s, the series saw Sam turn into a man (boy actor Kevin Moreton gave way to future TAGGART Mark McManus). As he grew older, he rebelled against the mining mentality that had forced him into the colliery at the age of 14. Over three series, viewers witnessed Sam venture out to sea and return to work in an engineering factory. He married Sarah Corby and settled in the town of Golwick but, all the while, his poverty-ridden past remained in his mind and the welfare of his family continued to haunt him.

SANDBAGGERS, THE

UK (Yorkshire) Spy Drama. ITV 1978–80

Neil Burnside	**Roy Marsden**
C	**Richard Vernon**
	Dennis Burgess
Willie Caine	**Ray Lonnen**
Sir Geoffrey Wellingham	**Alan MacNaughton**
Laura Dickens	**Diane Keen**
Jeff Ross	**Bob Sherman**
Karen Milner	**Jana Sheldon**
Matthew Peele	**Jerome Willis**
Mike Wallace	**Michael Cashman**
Diane Lawler	**Elizabeth Bennett**

Creator: **Ian MacKintosh**
Executive Producer: **David Cunliffe**
Producer: **Michael Ferguson**

The assignments of a top-secret British security unit.

'The Sandbaggers' was the colloquial title given to the Special Intelligence Force, or SIF, a government-funded counter-espionage squad. Head of the team was tough, determined Neil Burnside. On receiving his team's missions from their boss, C, it was Burnside's decision which of the Sandbaggers to send into action, knowing full well that his colleagues would be risking life and limb in the service of their country. Accordingly, he gave his men and women every assistance he could but remained assured in the knowledge that, if they had to die, the result would still be worth it. That was the pressurized world of the Sandbaggers, depicted in a heavier, less glitzy and gimmicky style than other secret agent programmes.

SANDERSON, JOAN
(1912–92)

British actress, famous for her female dragon roles on television. Sanderson made her name for such characterizations in PLEASE SIR! as the redoubtable Doris Ewell, having already appeared in ALL GAS AND GAITERS and *Wild, Wild Women*, after years on the stage and some TV plays. Later, she took the part of Eleanor, Prunella Scales's mother in AFTER HENRY (radio and television) and Richard O'Sullivan's mother-in-law, Nell Cresset, in ME AND MY GIRL. She also played Mrs Richards, a deaf, never satisfied guest in one memorable episode of FAWLTY TOWERS. In contrast to her battleaxe roles, Sanderson was the benign Aunt Dorothy in the mixed-race comedy, MIXED BLESSINGS, and her other credits included UPSTAIRS, DOWNSTAIRS, RIPPING YARNS, RISING DAMP, *The Ghosts of Motley Hall*, *Full House*, *The Fainthearted Feminist* and Michael Palin's TV movie, *East of Ipswich*. Her last series, screened shortly after her death in 1992, was *Land of Hope and Gloria*, in which she played Nanny Princeton.

SANDFORD, JEREMY
(1934–)

A former journalist with an interest in social campaigning, Jeremy Sandford was a new name to British TV drama when he scripted the provocative and disturbing CATHY COME HOME in 1966. He followed it up five years later with the award-winning *Edna, The Inebriate Woman*.

SAPPHIRE AND STEEL
UK (ATV) Science Fiction. ITV 1979–82

Sapphire .... **Joanna Lumley**
Steel .... **David McCallum**
Silver .... **David Collings**

Creator/Writer: **P. J. Hammond**
Executive Producer: **David Reid**
Producer: **Shaun O'Riordan**

Time-travelling troubleshooters foil agents of chaos and destruction.

In this imaginative series, time was perceived as a tunnel, with different time zones spread along its length. Outside lay dark forces of chaos and destruction which took advantage of any weakness in the tunnel's fabric to enter and wreak havoc. Whenever this happened, Sapphire and Steel were sent to investigate.

Little was revealed about the two protagonists. From the programme's introduction viewers learned that: 'All irregularities will be handled by the forces controlling each dimension. Transuranic heavy elements may not be used where there is life. Medium atomic weights are available: Gold, Lead, Copper, Jet, Diamond, Radium, Sapphire, Silver and Steel. Sapphire and Steel have been assigned.' So, it appeared, Sapphire and Steel were elements sent from above, although their forms were human.

Stunning Sapphire, true to her name, wore bright blue; blond-haired Steel, cold and humourless, dressed in grey. They each had special powers. Sapphire could see through time, gauge the history of an object just by holding it and even turn the clock back for a while. The analytical Steel enjoyed phenomenal strength; he could resist the flow of time and reduce his body temperature to below zero. But sometimes these superhuman attributes were not enough and the pair needed assistance. Usually it came from another element, Silver, but Lead also joined the fray on one occasion.

The nightmarish storylines centred on the pursuit of disruptive forces. In their first outing, Sapphire and Steel were called in to arrest a time warp after the reading of historic nursery rhymes had brought Roundhead soldiers to the 20th century. In another, a haunted railway station was drawn back into the era of World War I. The dark forces were seldom seen, except as faceless beings or globes of light. The longer they were allowed to remain in a dimension of time, the stronger they became, and they tested the dynamic duo to the extreme.

SARNOFF, DAVID
(1891–1971)

Belarus-born American broadcasting pioneer, a former wireless operator who, allegedly, was the first to receive the distress call from the sinking *Titanic* in 1912. Working initially for Marconi, he was employed by RCA when it took over his former company. He eventually rose to be President of the company and created the NBC radio and TV networks as a market for selling RCA receivers. Sarnoff was also one of the earliest proponents of public service broadcasting.

SATELLITE

An orbiting space station used for relaying television signals round the world. In its simplest form, the satellite works by acting as a reflector. Signals can be sent to a satellite and bounced off it like a mirror to another location around the globe that would otherwise (because of the curvature of the planet) be out of direct-transmission contact (such as across the Atlantic). Modern satellites, however, actually take the signals on board, amplify them and retransmit them, carrying news reports, live and recorded programming and other items round the world in a fraction of a second. The receiving station, or household, captures the signal in a dish, which varies in size depending on its location. Nearly all satellites are of the synchronous or geostationary type, that is they maintain a fixed position above the Equator by orbiting at exactly the same speed as the Earth revolves. By so doing, synchronous satellites allow themselves to be used at all times, whereas unfixed satellites in random orbit can be called into use only at certain times of the day. The most famous of satellites have been Telstar, launched in 1962 (in random orbit, but still able to provide the first transatlantic pictures) and Early Bird, otherwise known as Intelsat I, launched in 1965. The Sky satellite network uses the various Astra satellites, beaming signals up from the UK and bouncing them back over most of Europe.

The term 'satellite' also refers to a small TV station that operates by simply retransmitting the output of a larger station (with perhaps a few local-interest programmes added in for community value).

SATURDAY SUPERSTORE
See MULTI-COLOURED SWAP SHOP.

SAUNDERS, JENNIFER
(1958–)

British comedienne, actress and writer, usually seen with Dawn French, her partner since their days with THE COMIC STRIP PRESENTS and before. Saunders went on to star in the Ben Elton sitcom, HAPPY FAMILIES, playing various members of the Fuddle family, and she also appeared as the boring Jennifer in GIRLS ON TOP, a sitcom she co-wrote with French and Ruby Wax. The BBC 2 sketch show, *French and Saunders*, was launched in 1987 and one of its items proved to be the 'pilot' for Saunders's hugely successful series, ABSOLUTELY FABULOUS, in which she starred as the boozy, drug-obsessed, fashion promoter, Edina Monsoon. Again with Dawn French, she featured as Colombine, Comtesse de Vache, in *Let Them Eat Cake*. Saunders has also been seen in THE YOUNG ONES, *Saturday Live* and THE STORYTELLER, and provided the voice of The Rat in *The Magician's House*. She is married to comedian Adrian Edmondson.

SAVAGE, LILY
See O'GRADY, PAUL.

SAVALAS, TELLY
(Aristotle Savalas; 1924–94)

Powerful American actor of Greek descent. Noted for his trademark shaven head, he became one of the 1970s' biggest stars in his guise of New York cop, Lt. Theo KOJAK. Savalas actually took to acting fairly late in life. A war veteran with a Purple Heart, he was Director of News and Special Events for ABC before taking his first on-screen role in 1959. Through guest spots on series like NAKED CITY, THE UNTOUCHABLES, THE FUGITIVE and BURKE'S LAW, he worked his way into the cinema, where he was usually cast as a bad guy. Allegedly, it was for the part of Pontius Pilate in *The Greatest Story Ever Told* that he first shaved his head. His first major TV role was in a series called *Acapulco* in 1961, but it didn't last and he waited until *Kojak* in 1973 for a taste of small-screen stardom. His later work concentrated on mini-series and TV movies.

SAVILE, Sir JIMMY
OBE (1926–)

Yorkshire-born disc jockey and TV presenter, a relentless worker for charitable causes. Savile's working career began as a coal miner and as a professional wrestler, before he branched out into nightclub management. Ever the extrovert, he began broadcasting for Radio Luxembourg and arrived on television as the very first presenter of TOP OF THE POPS, in 1964. He joined Radio 1 in 1968 and continued to expand his TV work. He chaired *Quiz Bingo* and hosted *Clunk Click* (based on his car seatbelt campaigns) and this led to the magic wand series, JIM'LL FIX IT, in 1975. Jim fixed it, in all, for nearly 20 years. In addition, Savile has even hosted SONGS OF PRAISE. His trademark bleached hair, tracksuit, yodel and giant cigar have made him an easy prey for impressionists.

SAVILLE, PHILIP
(1930–)

British director, responsible for many acclaimed dramas. These have included ARMCHAIR THEATRE presentations such as Harold Pinter's *A Night Out* (1960), episodes of OUT OF THE UNKNOWN, plus *Hamlet at Elsinore* (an ambitious 1964 outside broadcast from Denmark), Sartre's *In Camera* (also 1964), Alan Sharp's *The Long Distance Piano Player* (1970), GANGSTERS (the 1976 PLAY FOR TODAY which became a series), and the 1977 version of *Count Dracula*. Saville also directed BOYS FROM THE BLACKSTUFF and THE LIFE AND LOVES OF A SHE DEVIL.

SAWALHA, JULIA
(1968–)

London-born actress coming to the fore in the kids' drama series, PRESS GANG (junior newspaper editor Lynda Day), and then ABSOLUTELY FABULOUS (Saffron). Sawalha has also appeared in numerous other dramas and comedies, including INSPECTOR MORSE, EL C.I.D., CASUALTY, LOVEJOY, SECOND THOUGHTS and *Faith in the Future* (Hannah), *Martin Chuzzlewit* (Mercy Pecksniff), PRIDE AND PREJUDICE (Lydia Bennet), AIN'T MISBE-HAVIN' (Dolly Nightingale) and *The Flint Street Nativity* (Wise Man). She is the daughter of actor Nadim Sawalha and sister of actress Nadia Sawalha.

SAYLE, ALEXEI
(1952–)

Liverpudlian comedian, actor and writer, distinctive in his tight suit and skinhead haircut, whose aggressive, no-nonsense style established him at the forefront of the new stand-up comics of the 1980s. At one time the compere of the Comedy Store and Comic Strip clubs, Sayle moved into television with other members of THE COMIC STRIP, appearing in their Channel 4 films and also taking part in the ill-fated late-night TISWAS spin-off, *OTT*. He was cast as Jerzy Balowski, THE YOUNG ONES' Russian landlord (and the rest of his family), and played another Russian, Commissar Solzhenitsyn, in WHOOPS APOCALYPSE. He has since had his own sketch series, *Alexei Sayle's Stuff, The All-New Alexei Sayle Show* and *Alexei Sayle's Merry-Go-Round*, and has also been seen as Milcic in *The Gravy Train*, a futuristic DJ in DOCTOR WHO, forger Conny Kujau in the drama, *Selling Hitler*, artist Alain Degout in *Paris*, the Puppeteer in *Tom Jones*, Bac Pac in *Arabian Nights*, and Andy Carolides in his own romantic comedy, *Sorry About Last Night*, among other programmes.

SCALES, PRUNELLA
CBE (Prunella Illingworth; 1932–)

Surrey-born actress whose career was launched by MAR-RIAGE LINES, in which she played Kate Starling, in 1963. Scales also appeared with Jimmy Edwards in SIX FACES OF JIM and with Ronnie Barker in *Seven of One*, but she remains best remembered as the grating Sybil Fawlty in FAWLTY TOWERS. She followed this with *Mr Big* (Dolly), *Mapp and Lucia* (Elizabeth Mapp) and AFTER HENRY (widow Sarah France). Earlier she played bus conductress Eileen Hughes in CORONATION STREET, and other credits have come in *The Rector's Wife* (Marjorie Richardson), *Signs and Wonders* (Elizabeth Palmore), TARGET, NEVER THE TWAIN, JACKANORY, BERGERAC, Alan Bennett's play, *Doris and Doreen*, *Searching* (Mrs Tilston), *Breaking the Code* (Sara Turing), *Jane Austen's Emma* (Miss Bates) and the TV films *The Lord of Misrule* (Shirley) and *A Question of Attribution* (the Queen). She is the wife of actor Timothy West and mother of actor Sam West.

SCARLET PIMPERNEL, THE
UK (Towers of London/ITP) Adventure. ITV 1955–6

Sir Percy Blakeney/The Scarlet Pimpernel .... **Marius Goring**	
Chauvelin	**Stanley Van Beers**
Sir Andrew Ffoulkes	**Patrick Troughton**
Lord Richard Hastings	**Anthony Newlands**
The Countess	**Lucie Mannheim**
Prince Regent	**Alexander Gauge**

Producers: **Dennis Vance, David Macdonald, Marius Goring**

The daring escapades of a mysterious hero operating in Georgian England and Revolutionary France.

Although ruthlessly persecuted by the cruel Chauvelin and his followers, the aristocrats of France knew they had an ally to count on: the elusive and intriguing Scarlet Pimpernel, alias English nobleman Sir Percy Blakeney. In contrast to his dashing *alter ego*, Blakeney was weak and foppish, always cleverly deflecting suspicion of his true identity. He was also a master of disguise, and elaborate costume and make-up changes contrived to preserve our hero from a violent death at the guillotine. The series was based on the book by Baroness Orczy. In 1999, Richard E. Grant was cast as Blakeney in a new series of feature-length adventures by the BBC.

SCHOFIELD, PHILLIP
(1962–)

Lancashire-born presenter who gained his first broadcasting experience while living with his family in New Zealand. Moving back to the UK, Schofield won the job of presenting Children's BBC, which led to the Saturday morning magazines, SATURDAY SUPERSTORE and GOING LIVE! He proved such a hit with younger viewers that he was cast as Joseph in the stage musical, *Joseph and the Amazing Technicolor Dreamcoat*. He also presented *The Movie Game* and *Television's Greatest Hits* for the BBC, before being lured over to ITV to present programmes like *Talking Telephone Numbers, Schofield's Quest, Schofield's TV Gold, Schofield in Hawaii* and *One in a Million*. Back with the BBC, after playing Dr Dolittle on stage, he hosted *Schofield's Animal Odyssey* in 1999.

SCOOBY DOO, WHERE ARE YOU?
US (Hanna-Barbera) Cartoon. BBC 1 1970–2

Voices:

Scooby Doo	**Don Messick**
Shaggy	**Casey Kasem**
Freddy	**Frank Welker**
Daphne Blake	**Heather North**
Velma	**Nicole Jaffe**

Creators: **Ken Spears, Joe Ruby**

Executive Producers: **William Hanna, Joseph Barbera**
Producer: **Iwao Takamoto**

The misadventures of a cowardly canine and his teenage pals.

Although his coat was brown with black spots, Great Dane Scooby-Doo had a broad yellow streak right down his back. Far from protecting his human companions, it was Scooby who dashed for cover in times of trouble (leaving his friends to call after him and giving rise to the series' title). Scooby's colleagues were Shaggy, a fumbling youth with a stubbly chin who bribed the ever-ravenous pooch with Scooby Snacks; Velma, the bespectacled, frumpy brains of the unit; Daphne, who was always the first to find trouble; and level-headed, trendy Freddy, the leader of the group. Together they travelled in a transit van known as *The Mystery Machine* and, no matter where the gang arrived, problems were just around the corner. Usually the mysteries involved criminals who dressed up as ghosts in order to commit heinous crimes but, one way or another, the gallant amateur detectives always put an end to their activities (with precious little help from Scooby and Shaggy). In later seasons, Scooby was joined by a pup nephew, Scrappy-Doo, and the lovable hound was also seen in *Laff-a-Lympics* among other animations. Producers Hanna-Barbera obviously liked the concept, because they soon issued another dog-and-teen detective cartoon entitled *Goober and the Ghost Chasers*.

SCOTLAND YARD
See **CASE HISTORIES OF SCOTLAND YARD**.

SCOTT, BROUGH
(1942–)

British National Hunt jockey turned journalist and TV presenter. Brough Scott has worked for ITV and Channel 4 racing since the 1970s, hosting all the major meetings. He has also been seen in other sports coverage.

SCOTT, JACK
(1923–)

British meteorologist who became one of TV's best-known faces through 47 years' service as a weatherman with the Met. Office, appearing on BBC TV (1969–83) and Thames Television (1983–8). On retiring from forecasting, Scott hosted the Channel 4 senior citizens' magazine, *Years Ahead*.

SCOTT, MIKE
(1932–)

British TV executive and presenter, mostly with Granada Television. Scott joined Granada as a floor manager, eventually becoming a director. Behind or in front of the camera, he has worked on local news programmes, WORLD IN ACTION, CINEMA and, when daytime TV arrived, *The Time, The Place*. He was Programme Controller at Granada from 1979 to 1987.

SCOTT, TERRY
(1927–94)

British comic actor, the archetypal hapless husband in cosy, domestic sitcoms. Scott starred alongside Bill Maynard in *Great Scott – It's Maynard!* in 1955 and with Norman Vaughan in *Scott Free* in 1957, but the best remembered of his early screen partners was Hugh Lloyd, with whom he appeared in 1962 in HUGH AND I and, later, *Hugh and I Spy*. They were also seen together in THE GNOMES OF DULWICH. In 1969, in the series *Scott On . . .*, he was teamed for the first time with June Whitfield, who was to be his screen wife for many years. Together, they endured suburban silliness as the Fletchers in HAPPY EVER AFTER and the Medfords in TERRY AND JUNE. Scott was also familiar in the 1970s as the schoolboy in the Curly Wurly commercials and he was cast in *Son of the Bride*, as Mollie Sugden's mummy's boy, in 1973. In the 1980s he provided the voice for the character of Penfold in the DANGERMOUSE cartoons.

SCOTTISH TELEVISION
(STV)

The ITV contractor for Central Scotland, on air continuously since 31 August 1957. It has survived all the franchise reorganizations, despite concerns about its local programming in the mid-1960s. The main broadcasting centre is in Glasgow, with a smaller production base in Edinburgh. Among the company's contributions to the ITV network have been the drama series, TAKE THE HIGH ROAD and TAGGART, and the quiz show, WHEEL OF FORTUNE. Some local programmes have been produced in Gaelic. Scottish is now part of Scottish Media Group, which also owns Grampian Television and has a share in GMTV.

SCRAMBLING
See **ENCRYPTION**.

SCREEN TEST
UK (BBC) Children's Quiz. BBC 1 1970–84

Presenters: **Michael Rodd, Brian Trueman, Mark Curry**

Producers: **John Buttery, David Brown, Tony Harrison**

Observation quiz for kids, based on film clips.

The young contestants on *Screen Test* viewed a series of clips from popular films and were then tested on their observation skills and general knowledge. Interviews and features on the movie world also formed part of this long-running programme, which was hosted for many years by Michael Rodd.

SCRIPT EDITOR

Usually employed on a long-running series, the script editor is responsible for ensuring that scripts supplied by a team of writers conform to the style of the series as a whole, taking into account character continuity, plot developments, etc.

SEA HUNT

US (Ziv/United Artists) Adventure. ITV 1958–62

Mike Nelson .... **Lloyd Bridges**

Producer: **Ivan Tors**

Excitement with an underwater
adventurer-for-hire.

This action series featured former navy diver Mike Nelson, a freelance agent who offered his underwater skills to anyone who wished to employ him. Working from his boat, *The Argonaut*, and travelling the globe, Nelson took on jobs for salvage companies, insurance firms and especially the US Government, swimming into all manner of tight scrapes and always coming up with the goods. Lloyd Bridges was the only regular, though his two young (at the time) sons, Beau and Jeff, also made guest appearances. The real star, however, was the sea itself, with all its underwater glory. The series was briefly revived with little success in 1987, when TV's Tarzan, Ron Ely, donned Nelson's mask and flippers.

SEAGROVE, JENNY
(1958–)

Malaysian-born actress who made her TV name with the lead role (Emma Harte) in the mini-series, A WOMAN OF SUBSTANCE, in 1985 (and its sequel, *Hold That Dream*). Earlier, Seagrove had played Laura in Wilkie Collins's *The Woman in White* and Diana Gaylorde-Sutton in Andrew Davies's adaptation of R. F. Delderfield's *Diana*. She was also seen in the 1987 SHERLOCK HOLMES special, *The Sign of Four*, and has numerous other TV movies and dramas to her name.

SECAM

Séquential Couleur à Mémoire, the system of television transmission developed in and used by France. It operates off 625 lines like the British PAL system, but the two are incompatible. Those countries with a French colonial interest (in Africa and the Middle East, for instance), have also adopted the SECAM system, as have the East European countries (although their SECAM is modified).

SECOMBE, Sir HARRY
CBE (1921–2001)

Swansea-born comedian, singer and presenter, coming to the fore as one of The Goons on BBC Radio (and, later, one of the voices of THE TELEGOONS on TV). The most popular of his series were *The Harry Secombe Show* (on both ITV and BBC), *Secombe and Friends* and *Secombe with Music*, most of them variety shows, although for much of the 1980s and early 1990s, he was strongly associated with the religious travelogue, HIGHWAY, which followed many appearances on STARS ON SUNDAY in the 1970s. He later presented SONGS OF PRAISE.

SECOND THOUGHTS
UK (LWT) Situation Comedy. ITV 1991–4

Bill Macgregor	**James Bolam**
Faith Grayshot	**Lynda Bellingham**
Joe Grayshot	**Mark Denham**
Hannah Grayshot	**Julia Sawalha**
Liza Macgregor	**Belinda Lang**
Richard	**Geoffrey Whitehead**

Creators/Writers: **Jan Etherington, Gavin Petrie**
Producers: **David Askey, Robin Carr**

Two divorcés begin a relationship, despite the
attentions of teenage children and a former wife.

Bill Macgregor was the art editor of a style magazine who began a relationship with divorcée Faith Grayshot. However, the odds were stacked against them, thanks to the interference and the personal problems of Faith's teenage kids, Joe and Hannah, and the devious doings of Bill's promiscuous ex-wife, Liza, who happened to work in the same office as Bill. Suspicion and distrust ruled at home, at work and in Harpo's Wine Bar. Weddings were arranged and postponed, and the course of true love never did run smoothly. Strangely, Faith and Liza never actually met until the very last episode.

The series, which began on BBC Radio in 1988 and ran simultaneously on television for a while, was based on the real-life romance of its creators, *TV Times* journalists Jan Etherington and Gavin Petrie, both of whom had been divorced before beginning a new life together. A sequel series, starring Lynda Bellingham and Julia Sawalha and entitled *Faith in the Future* (1995–8), focused on Faith's attempts to rebuild her life after saying a final goodbye to Bill and gaining a new man-friend named Paul (Jeff Rawle).

SECOND VERDICT
UK (BBC) Drama. BBC 1 1976

Det. Chief Supt. Charlie Barlow	**Stratford Johns**
Det. Chief Supt. John Watt	**Frank Windsor**

Producer: **Leonard Lewis**

Two fictional detectives examine real-life murder mysteries.

Charlie Barlow and John Watt, the Z CARS and SOFTLY, SOFTLY heavyweights, were the stars of this enigmatic series. Having joined forces to re-examine the Jack the Ripper story in 1973, the duo were paired up again to look at six more true-crime mysteries of the past. These included *Who Killed the Princes in the Tower?*, *Lizzie Borden* and *The Lindbergh Kidnapping*.

SECONDS OUT
UK (BBC) Situation Comedy. BBC 1 1981–2

Pete Dodds .... **Robert Lindsay**
Tom Sprake .... **Lee Montague**
Dave Locket .... **Ken Jones**
Hazel .... **Leslie Ash**

Writer: **Bill MacIlwraith**
Producer: **Ray Butt**

A talented amateur boxer turns professional with a wily manager.

Pete Dodds, an amateur boxer with plenty of potential but also a tendency to clown about, turned professional and was taken under the wing of successful manager Tom Sprake. To keep him in line, Sprake paired Dodds with irritating little trainer Dave Locket, relying on the pair's incompatibility to keep Dodds focused on the job. With Locket to nark him at every turn, Dodds began to climb towards the top. First he claimed the British middleweight title and then fought for the European crown. Hazel was Pete's girlfriend.

SECRET ARMY
UK (BBC/BRT) Drama. BBC 1 1977–9

Lisa Colbert ('Yvette') .... **Jan Francis**
Albert Foiret .... **Bernard Hepton**
Squadron Leader John Curtis .... **Christopher Neame**
Sturmbahnführer Ludwig Kessler .... **Clifford Rose**
Monique Duchamps .... **Angela Richards**
Natalie .... **Juliet Hammond-Hill**
Andrée Foiret .... **Eileen Page**
Erwin Brandt .... **Michael Culver**
Max Brocard .... **Stephen Yardley**
Alain .... **Ron Pember**
Dr Pascal Keldermans .... **Valentine Dyall**
Gaston .... **James Bree**
François .... **Nigel Williams**
Madeleine Duclos .... **Hazel McBride**
Reinhardt .... **Louis Sheldon**
　　　　　　　　　　　　　　Terrence Hardiman
Paul Vercors .... **Michael Byrne**
　　　　　　　　　　　　　　　Ralph Bates
Nick Bradley .... **Paul Shelley**
Louise .... **Maria Charles**
Rennert .... **Robin Langford**
Jacques .... **Timothy Morand**
Insp. Delon .... **John D. Collins**

Hauptmann Muller .... **Hilary Minster**
Capt. Durnford .... **Stephan Chase**

Creators: **Gerald Glaister, Wilfred Greatorex**
Producer: **Gerard Glaister**

The daring exploits of the Belgian Resistance.

This series centred on the activities of Lifeline, an underground Resistance movement in Belgium during World War II. This extremely courageous secret army specialized in smuggling trapped Allied servicemen ('evaders') back to Britain, via a number of escape routes and safe houses. Head of the organization was Lisa Colbert, codenamed Yvette, a young teacher who became a Resistance worker after the killing of her parents. She was assisted chiefly by Albert Foiret, proprietor of Le Candide, a Brussels restaurant in the Rue Deschanel which operated as the movement's base. Ironically, it was also a hostelry favoured by German officers, which added to the danger. The other key functionaries were Foiret's mistress, Monique; Natalie; RAF liaison, John Curtis; and, later, forger/pianist Max Brocard. Chief among the Nazis were local head Brandt, his much firmer replacement, Reinhardt, and the cruel Kessler, the local Gestapo leader. Madeleine Duclos was his lover. By the end of the series the war had ended, Brussels was liberated and Kessler had assumed a new identity in order to escape trial. He was to resurface as a German businessman (using the alias Manfred Dorf) in a spin-off series, *Kessler*, in 1981, in which his wartime secrets began to be exposed.

　Secret Army was probably the most unlikely of TV series to earn itself a parody. But it did just that when 'ALLO 'ALLO came along in 1984. Although the setting had been transposed to France, all the other distinctive elements were present, from the long-suffering restaurateur to the Resistance operatives and the pompous Nazis – even some of the actors returned to send themselves up. If anything, the series has been overshadowed by this spoof successor.

SECRET DIARY OF ADRIAN MOLE, AGED 13¾, THE/THE GROWING PAINS OF ADRIAN MOLE
UK (Thames) Situation Comedy. ITV 1985/1987

Adrian Mole .... **Gian Sammarco**
Pauline Mole .... **Julie Walters**
　　　　　　　　　　　　　　　Lulu (*Growing Pains*)
George Mole .... **Stephen Moore**
Grandma Mole .... **Beryl Reid**
Bert Baxter .... **Bill Fraser**
Pandora Braithwaite .... **Lindsey Stagg**
Queenie .... **Doris Hare**
Nigel .... **Steven Mackintosh**
Mr Lucas .... **Paul Greenwood**
Doreen Slater .... **Su Elliot**

Creator/Writer: **Sue Townsend**
Executive Producer: **Lloyd Shirley**
Producer: **Peter Sasdy**

*A teenage boy chronicles his troubles in his diary
as his family self-destructs.*

This series, adapted by Sue Townsend from her own
best-selling novel, *The Secret Diary of Adrian Mole*, was
set in the Midlands and focused on the adolescent woes
which befell young, bespectacled Adrian. In addition
to the usual teenage travails of school, spots, girls and
peer-pressure, Adrian also found himself in the midst of
family turmoil. His mum, Pauline, and dad, George, had
gone their separate ways and now only traded insults.
Also involved was his Grandma and an elderly character
he befriended, Bert Baxter, while Pandora was the girl
Adrian had set his heart on. When the second series
began, using the new name of *The Growing Pains of
Adrian Mole*, and with Adrian aged 15, his (now pregnant)
mum was played by pop singer Lulu.

Ian Dury performed the Adrian Mole theme song,
'Profoundly in Love with Pandora'. A new series, based
on Sue Townsend's 1990s book, *Adrian Mole: The Cappuccino Years*, was due for broadcast in 2001, with Stephen
Mangan as Adrian and Alison Steadman as his mum.

SECRET SERVICE, THE
UK (Century 21/ITC) Children's Science Fiction. ITV 1969

Father Stanley Unwin .... **Stanley Unwin**
Matthew Harding (the gardener) ....
.... **Keith Alexander** (*voice only*)
Matthew Harding (the agent) ...... **Gary Files** (*voice only*)
Mrs Appleby .... **Sylvia Anderson** (*voice only*)
The Bishop .... **Jeremy Wilkin** (*voice only*)

Creators: **Gerry Anderson, Sylvia Anderson**
Executive Producer: **Reg Hill**
Producer: **David Lane**

*Short-lived Gerry Anderson combination of live
action and puppetry.*

Fifty-seven-year-old parish priest Father Unwin was no
ordinary country parson. In fact, he was an undercover
agent for BISHOP (British Intelligence Secret Headquarters, Operation Priest) who possessed a special
device ('The Minimiser') for reducing people and objects
to one-third of their normal size. This device was found
in a book lent to Unwin by one of his late parishioners
and was put to good use on behalf of the security
services. Usually it was the priest's yokel gardener,
Matthew, who was shrunk, in order to take on dangerous
missions on behalf of the country. When minimized,
the priest carried Matthew around in a briefcase. Unwin,
who drove a vintage Model-T Ford named Gabriel, also
had a radio built into his mock deaf-aid, through which
he was given assignments by his commander, 'The
Bishop'. It was also used for contacting other BISHOP
agents. Mrs Appleby was Unwin's blissfully ignorant
housekeeper.

The series provided a stepping stone between the
Supermarionation adventures of STINGRAY, THUNDER-
BIRDS *et al.* and Gerry Anderson's move into live action
with UFO. But it failed to attract a network audience
(being screened only in the Midlands, the South and

the North-West) and was limited to just 13 episodes.
Double-speaking comedian Stanley Unwin played the
priest in long-shots, with a puppet clone used for close-
ups. His gobbledygook was a feature of the series.

SECRET SOCIETY
UK (BBC) Current Affairs. BBC 2 1987

Presenter/Writer: **Duncan Campbell**

Producer: **Brian Barr**

*Highly controversial series about covert British
agencies and operations.*

Although six episodes of this investigative series were
planned, only four made it to the screen on time. One
was eventually shown a year late, and the other was
assigned to the dustbin. This curtailment was a result of
political sensitivity, particularly over an episode
revealing plans for a secret British spy satellite known as
Zircon. On 31 January 1987, the BBC offices in Glasgow
were raided by Special Branch officers and over 30 boxes
of tapes and material relating to the programme were
confiscated. The BBC Chairman, Marmaduke Hussey,
made a strong protest to the Government and there
was uproar in the House of Commons. *The Zircon Affair*
finally aired as a 75-minute special, introduced by Ludovic Kennedy, in 1988, but another edition, entitled *Cabinet* and alleging election dirty tricks, was never
broadcast, being deemed too out of date by the time the
initial fuss had died down. The four episodes which
were screened concerned DHSS computer databanks,
emergency laws in times of national crisis, the influence
of the Association of Chief Police Officers on Government policy, and the UK's radar defence network.

SEINFELD
US (NBC/West-Shapiro/Castle Rock) Situation Comedy.
BBC 2 1993–

Jerry Seinfeld .... **Jerry Seinfeld**
Elaine Benes .... **Julia Louis-Dreyfus**
George Costanza .... **Jason Alexander**
Cosmo Kramer .... **Michael Richards**
Helen Seinfeld .... **Liz Sheridan**
Morty Seinfeld .... **Phil Bruns**
.... **Barney Martin**
Frank Costanza .... **Jerry Stiller**
Estelle Costanza .... **Estelle Harris**
Uncle Leo .... **Len Lesser**
Newman .... **Wayne Knight**

Creators: **Larry David, Jerry Seinfeld**

Four neurotic friends contemplate the minutiae of life.

The widely acclaimed *Seinfeld* – America's supreme 1990s
sitcom – somehow never really gained a foothold in the
UK. The BBC quickly lost faith and consigned it to
the backwaters of late-night BBC 2, at great loss to the
viewers, said the critics. *Seinfeld* was a strange kind of
programme, an eccentric comedy in which nothing

important ever really happened. The basic premiss was that the four self-centred, opinionated lead characters would spend their time working over some utterly trivial aspect of life – the frustration of waiting in line or being stuck in traffic, the impossibility of getting a restaurant table, etc. Plots were therefore negligible, but the dialogue was sharp and perceptive, sometimes pushing back the barriers of taste in its subject-matter.

Nominal star was stand-up Jerry Seinfeld, playing himself, an obsessively fussy man who fell out with girls because of their petty habits. Of equal importance was his ex-girlfriend, Elaine, a book editor, also unlucky in love and destined always to date a weirdo. Then there were their tight-fisted, podgy buddy, George, an insecure estate agent who would tell the most outrageous lies in order to charm a woman, and the semi-crazy Kramer, an unkempt whirlwind figure always with a bright idea for making money, who lived in the same New York apartment block as Jerry. Parents, dates, bosses and other acquaintances – including maligned mailman Newman – were other occasional characters. The 'action' was usually topped and tailed with scenes of Jerry performing his nightclub act, commenting on the same topics that were engaging the characters.

Despite allegedly being offered $5 million a show to continue, Jerry Seinfeld pulled the plug after eight seasons, ensuring the series quit at the top.

SEINFELD, JERRY
(1955–)

Brooklyn-born stand-up comedian who, as star of his own sitcom, SEINFELD (playing himself), became one of US TV's biggest names of the 1990s. Previously, Seinfeld had been occasionally seen in *Benson*, playing joke-writer Frankie.

SELBY, TONY
(1938–)

London-born actor, usually in comic roles. Probably his most memorable creation was the loud-mouthed Corporal Marsh in GET SOME IN!, although he has been seen in numerous other sitcoms. He played Les Robinson in the lighthouse comedy, *Shine a Light*, Norman Lugg in Dick Emery's *Jack of Diamonds* and the scheming handyman, Bert Finch, in MULBERRY. Selby's earliest TV work came in single dramas like Harold Pinter's *A Night Out* and Nell Dunn's *Up the Junction*. He has also been seen in series like *Tom Grattan's War*, DEPARTMENT S, THE INFORMER, *Moody and Pegg*, C.A.T.S. EYES, MINDER, DOCTOR WHO (Glitz), THE SWEENEY, BERGERAC, CASUALTY, LOVEJOY, LOVE HURTS (Max Taplow), REAL WOMEN (Bobby) and *Hero to Zero* (George), and in the 1970s he played Sam in ACE OF WANDS.

SELLECK, TOM
(1945–)

Tall American actor whose ability to combine macho action with a one-of-the-lads type of humour made him one of TV's hottest names in the 1980s, thanks largely to an eight-year stint as MAGNUM PI. Earlier, Selleck had made occasional visits to THE ROCKFORD FILES to play the annoyingly perfect detective, Lance White, although his TV career dates back to the early 1970s and he gained his first small-screen experiences in soap opera (*The Young and the Restless*), TV movies and series like CHARLIE'S ANGELS. His movie career began at about the same time. In 1989 Selleck was executive producer on the Burt Reynolds detective series *B. L. Stryker*.

SELLERS, PETER
CBE (1925–80)

Although he became a major movie celebrity in the 1960s and 1970s, Peter Sellers sadly left little in the TV archives. After graduating from radio work with his fellow Goons, he was seen in the 1950s comedies, *And So to Bentley*, *Idiot Weekly*, *Price 2d*, A SHOW CALLED FRED, *Son of Fred* and *Yes, It's the Cathode-Ray Tube Show*; but, after that, sightings were restricted to occasional variety and chat shows, plus guest spots on series like NOT ONLY . . . BUT ALSO . . . and THE MUPPET SHOW. He was also seen in Jonathan Miller's version of *Alice in Wonderland* and heard on commercials for Kennomeat and PG Tips. Sellers was married to actresses Britt Ekland and Lynne Frederick.

SELWYN
See OH NO! IT'S SELWYN FROGGITT.

SENSE OF GUILT, A
UK (BBC) Drama. BBC 1 1990

Felix Cramer	**Trevor Eve**
Sally Hinde	**Rudi Davies**
Helen Irving	**Lisa Harrow**
Richard Murray	**Jim Carter**
Inge Murray	**Malgoscha Gebel**
Elizabeth Cramer	**Morag Hood**
Carey Hinde	**Philip McGough**
Marsha Hinde	**Kate Duchene**
Karl Murray	**David Chittenden**
Peter Murray	**Charlie Condou**
Jamal Khan	**Kulvinder Ghir**

Writer: **Andrea Newman**
Producer: **Simon Passmore**

Steamy saga of passion and betrayal.

A Sense of Guilt was a drama which set the TV review columns buzzing. 'With more pairing than Noah's Ark', as *Radio Times* put it, this seven-part serial by Andrea (BOUQUET OF BARBED WIRE) Newman focused primarily on selfish, philandering writer Felix Cramer. Returning to London after years overseas, Felix seduced the step-daughter of his best friend, making her pregnant and destroying the lives of those around him. However, there were many other covert and illicit goings-on, too, enough to attract audiences of around nine million viewers.

SENTIMENTAL AGENT, THE
UK (ATV) Adventure. ITV 1963

Carlos Varela .... **Carlos Thompson**
Suzy Carter .... **Clemence Bettany**
Chin .... **Burt Kwouk**
Bill Randall .... **John Turner**

Producer: **Harry Fine**

The adventures of an import-export agent.

Smartly dressed and always charming, Carlos Varela ran an international trading company in London, but was usually seen jetting around the globe on the trail of some criminal. His outward appearance was tough but it concealed a generous heart which often led him into trouble (hence the title). His two main accomplices were secretary Suzy Carter and valet Chin. The character had originally appeared in an episode of MAN OF THE WORLD.

SEPTEMBER SONG
UK (Granada) Drama. ITV 1993–5

Ted Fenwick .... **Russ Abbot**
Billy Balsam .... **Michael Williams**
Cilla .... **Susan Brown**
Arnie .... **Michael Angelis**
Roxy/Jenny .... **Julie Peasgood**
Sarah Fenwick .... **Barbara Ewing**
Katherine Hillyard .... **Diana Quick**
Connie French .... **Diane Keen**
Yannis Alexiou .... **George Savides**
Philip Hathaway .... **Pip Miller**
Vicky .... **Rebecca Callard**
Cyril Wendage .... **Frank Windsor**
Mrs Trigger .... **Jan Waters**
Tom Walker .... **Matt Patresi**

Writer: **Ken Blakeson**
Producers: **Gareth Morgan, Brian Park**

Two unlikely friends seek adventure in Blackpool, with mixed results.

Ted Fenwick and Billy Balsam had known each other for years. Ted, a gentle, sensitive schoolteacher, eased the strains of caring for his sick wife with a nightly drink at the pub where Billy worked as barman. Billy, a chain-smoking, former stand-up comic, then decided to go back on the stage, finding himself a compere's job at a Blackpool strip club, The Magic Cat. When his wife died, Ted agreed to spend the summer sharing Billy's camper van at the seaside. Their fortunes were mixed: Billy met exotic dancer Cilla, was spotted by a talent scout and offered the job he'd always dreamed of, as a TV audience warm-up man. Ted fell in love with a stripper named Roxy, but the feelings were not reciprocated and Billy's indiscretions about Ted's previous love life led to a bitter argument. But when Billy suffered a life-threatening heart attack, it was Ted who returned to keep him out of trouble and ensure his recovery.

In a second series, screened in 1994, Ted took Billy on a Greek island cruise for recuperation. Ted met up with an old flame, Katherine Hillyard, while Billy once again turned to the bottle. For the third series, in 1995, the action switched to Cromer, where Billy found work as a pier comic and Ted tried to come to terms with his uneasy relationship with Katherine.

The series was originally written for Radio 4 in 1991 and some material for the script was provided by the late Tom Mennard, formerly Sam Tindall in CORONATION STREET (the original story was based on Mennard's experiences as a stand-up comic). When it transferred to television, it provided Russ Abbot with his first serious acting role.

SEQUEL

A programme following on from another, taking members of the established cast into new situations.

SGT BILKO
See PHIL SILVERS SHOW, THE.

SERGEANT CORK
UK (ATV) Police Drama. ITV 1963–6

Sgt Cork .... **John Barrie**
Bob Marriott .... **William Gaunt**
Det. Joseph Bird .... **Arnold Diamond**
Supt. Billy Nelson .... **John Richmond**
Supt. Rodway .... **Charles Morgan**

Creator: **Ted Willis**
Producer: **Jack Williams**

The cases of a detective years ahead of his time in Victorian London.

Fortysomething bachelor policeman Sgt Cork lived in Bayswater and worked for the fledgling CID at Scotland Yard. He was a man of vision who deplored bureaucracy and believed in the value of scientific evidence in tracking down criminals. His ideas were pooh-poohed by many of his contemporaries, including his obstructive superior, Detective Joseph Bird. However, he did have Supt. Nelson on his side, as well as his supportive, bright young colleague, Bob Marriott, and, when Bird was removed, another ally was found in Supt. Rodway. The series, characterized by its dark, cobbled streets, swirling cloaks, top hats, and horse-drawn cabs, found an echo in CRIBB in the early 1980s.

SERIAL

Drama broken into a number of episodes with a continuous storyline.

SERIES

A collection of programmes featuring the same cast and situation but with storylines generally confined to one episode, rather than continuing from episode to episode.

SERLE, CHRIS
(1943–)

British actor turned presenter, thanks to a spell as one of Esther Rantzen's assistants on THAT'S LIFE. With Paul Heiney, Serle later shared the limelight in the spin-off series, IN AT THE DEEP END, and has also been seen in *Sixty Minutes*, *People*, *Medical Express*, educational programmes like *Shoot the Video*, the quiz, *Runway*, and the TV archive series, *Windmill*.

SERLING, ROD
(1924–75)

Anyone who has seen the cult series, THE TWILIGHT ZONE, will have soon realized that it was Rod Serling's series. The American writer not only scripted most of the episodes but created it, produced it and top-and-tailed each episode with explanatory dialogue. He began writing in the late 1940s and, in 1956, he joined the staff of CBS's anthology series, *Playhouse 90*. His second script for the series, *Requiem for a Heavyweight*, remains one of the most acclaimed in TV history and won Serling an Emmy. *The Twilight Zone*, his own idea, ran for six years from 1959 and, when it ended, Serling went on to write for numerous other series. He also contributed some notable film screenplays, including *Planet of the Apes*. One of his last TV projects was another suspense anthology, *Night Gallery*, in the early 1970s.

SERPICO
US (Emmet G. Lavery/Paramount) Police Drama. BBC 1
1977

Frank Serpico .... **David Birney**
Lt. Tom Sullivan .... **Tom Atkins**

Executive Producer: **Emmet G. Lavery**
Producers: **Don Ingalls, Barry Oringer**

An undercover cop combats subversion inside and outside the force.

This short-lived series was based on the 1973 film of the same name starring Al Pacino, which, in turn, was derived from the true-life story of a New York cop, as written up by Peter Maas. Frank Serpico worked in New York's 22nd Precinct, where his target was corruption. Ethically unassailable himself, his job was to root out officers on the take and lift the lid on bent officials. Not surprisingly, he made himself many enemies along the way. His investigations took him into the world of organized crime, sniffing around drug-dealers, smugglers and racketeers. When he went undercover, fellow cop Tom Sullivan was his police liaison. The real Frank Serpico was forced to retire from duty after being shot in the face.

SESAME STREET
US (Children's Television Workshop) Children's
Education. ITV 1971–86/Channel 4 1987–

Bob .... **Bob McGrath**
Gordon .... **Matt Robinson**
                                                          Roscoe Orman
Mr Hooper .... **Will Lee**
Susan .... **Loretta Long**
David .... **Northern J. Galloway**
Luis .... **Emilio Delgado**
Maria .... **Sonia Manzano**
Linda .... **Linda Bove**
Gina .... **Alison Bartlett**
Lillian .... **Lillias White**
Uncle Wally .... **Bill McCutcheon**
Mr Handford .... **David Langston Smyrl**
Gabriela .... **Gabriela Rose Reagan**
Miles .... **Miles Orman**
Kermit .... **Jim Henson**
Big Bird .... **Frank Oz**
                                                          Carroll Spinney
Cookie Monster .... **Frank Oz**
Oscar the Grouch .... **Frank Oz**
                                                          Carroll Spinney
The Count von Count .... **Jerry Nelson**
Miss Piggy .... **Frank Oz**
Bert .... **Jim Henson**
Ernie .... **Frank Oz**
Tarah .... **Tarah Lynne Schaeffer**

Creator: **Joan Ganz Cooney**
Executive Producers: **David D. Connell, Jon Stone,
Al Hyslop**

Innovative educational programme for pre-school children.

Acclaimed by some and slated by others, *Sesame Street* was created to address the dearth of pre-school education in the USA. Funded by the non-profit-making Children's Television Workshop, it has introduced kids to numbers, letters and social skills, using a fast-paced, all-action approach to cater for short attention-spans. Heavy repetition of the main points (which have been packaged up like TV commercials) has been another key feature.

The setting has been a fake city backstreet (Sesame Street – the name chosen to convey a hint of magic, as in 'Open, Sesame'), where the residents have provided a degree of continuity. These have included Bob, and Gordon and Susan, a young couple. The sweet shop was run by Mr Hooper in the early days, and Luis and Maria were among later additions to the crew. A row of rubbish bins has lined one side of the road and in one of these has lived a creature called Oscar the Grouch. Oscar was just one of Jim Henson's many Muppet characters which gained important early exposure in the series. Another was Big Bird, a dim, giant canary. Each programme has contained animated inserts, filmed items, sketches, songs and games, and has been 'sponsored' by a number and a letter of the alphabet: 'Today's programme is brought to you by the letter "T" and the number "6".'

Over the years, the scope of *Sesame Street* has been broadened to include other aims, such as teaching cultural diversity, women's roles, health and ecology, and the pace has slowed slightly, to take account of criticism for being overstimulating. The programme was originally aimed at the deprived kids of the inner cities but found favour with most of America and then earned enormous sales all round the world. In the UK, *Sesame Street* was originally screened on ITV, but its most recent airings have been on Channel 4.

SESSIONS, JOHN
(John Marshall; 1953–)

Scottish-born actor/comedian, a specialist in improvisation and mimicry, as evidenced by his many appearances on WHOSE LINE IS IT ANYWAY?. Sessions has also fronted his own series, *John Sessions on the Spot, John Sessions' Tall Tales* and *John Sessions' Likely Stories* and has been seen in programmes as varied as *A History of Psychiatry, Educating Marmalade,* THE NEW STATESMAN, PORTERHOUSE BLUE (Lionel Zipser), GIRLS ON TOP, *Life with Eliza, Tender is the Night,* HAPPY FAMILIES, BOON, *Laugh??? I Nearly Paid My Licence Fee, In the Red* (Hercules Fortescue) and *Gormenghast* (Dr Prunesquallor), and provided some of the voices for SPITTING IMAGE. He appeared as Tippit in the sitcom, *Nice Day at the Office,* played Boswell in *Tour of the Western Isles* and was author Henry Fielding in *Tom Jones.* With Phil Cornwell he starred in the celebrity spoof, *Stella Street.*

SET

The scenic construction on which a programme is presented or a drama performed.

SEVEN FACES OF JIM, THE
UK (BBC) Situation Comedy. BBC 1961

Jimmy Edwards

Writers: **Frank Muir, Denis Norden**
Producers: **James Gilbert, Douglas Moodie**

Anthology comedy series: a Jimmy Edwards showcase.

With the title of each episode beginning *The Face of . . .,* this series covered the subjects of Devotion, Genius, Power, Dedication, Duty, Guilt and Enthusiasm, all in

sitcom fashion, allowing the series' star, Jimmy Edwards, to show off a range of new comic creations. A second series, entitled *Six More Faces of Jim,* ran in 1962. This time the topics were Fatherhood, Renunciation, Wisdom, Perseverance, Loyalty and Tradition. This latter series saw the television première of radio's comic family, The Glums (of *Take It from Here* fame), with Edwards as Mr Glum, Ronnie Barker playing Ron and June Whitfield as Eth. A third and final outing was conceived under the title of *More Faces of Jim.* Airing in 1963, its episodes began 'A Matter of . . .' and featured the topics of Amnesia, Growing Up, Spreadeagling, Upbringing, Espionage and Empire.

77 SUNSET STRIP
US (Warner Brothers) Detective Drama. ITV 1959–64

Stuart Bailey	**Efrem Zimbalist, Jr**
Jeff Spencer	**Roger Smith**
Gerald Lloyd ('Kookie') Kookson III	**Edd Byrnes**
Roscoe	**Louis Quinn**
Suzanne Fabray	**Jacqueline Beer**
Lt. Gilmore	**Byron Keith**
Rex Randolph	**Richard Long**
J. R. Hale	**Robert Logan**
Hannah	**Joan Staley**

Creator: **Roy Huggins**
Executive Producers: **Bill Orr, Jack Webb**
Producers: **Roy Huggins, Howie Horowitz, William Conrad**

A private detective partnership takes on challenges around the world from its Hollywood offices.

77 Sunset Strip, in the nightclub area of Hollywood, was the base for Stu Bailey and Jeff Spencer, college graduates who had turned to private-eye work after experience in undercover government agencies. Bailey was a language expert, Spencer had a law degree, and both were skilled in judo. However, from the outset, their exploits were overshadowed by their association with Kookie, a cool, ambitious youth who ran the car park at the neighbouring Dino's (Dean Martin's) restaurant. His obsessive hair-combing and novel turns of phrase became his trademarks, although British audiences were bemused by such jive talk as 'making the long green' (earning money), 'piling up the Zs' (sleeping) and 'a dark seven' (a bad week).

Kookie soon became the star of the show, upstaging the two leads, and actor Edd Byrnes sought better terms. When he walked out after failing to agree a contract, he was temporarily replaced as parking-lot attendant by Troy Donohue. Byrnes soon settled his differences, however, and Kookie returned as a full member of the detective team, which had briefly taken on another partner, Rex Randolph. Suzanne Fabray was their French receptionist and Roscoe, a racetrack tout from New York, their informant. J. R. Hale was Kookie's new parking-lot replacement and he, like Kookie, had his quirks, one of which was talking in abbreviations.

The final series of the programme featured only Stu Bailey, as a globetrotting private eye. His offices were no longer on Sunset Strip and he had a new secretary, Hannah. This restructuring was the idea of new executive producer Jack Webb, of DRAGNET fame. William Conrad, the future Frank Cannon, was also one of the show's producers.

Edd Byrnes confirmed his teen idol status by making the charts on both sides of the Atlantic in 1960 with a song called 'Kookie Kookie (Lend Me Your Comb)', which he recorded for the series with Connie Stevens. Better remembered is the programme's finger-snapping theme tune.

SEXTON BLAKE

UK (Rediffusion/Thames) Children's Detective Drama. ITV
1967–71

Sexton Blake	**Laurence Payne**
Edward Clark ('Tinker')	**Roger Foss**
Mrs Bardell	**Dorothea Phillips**
Insp. Cutts	**Ernest Clark**
Insp. Van Steen	**Leonard Sachs**
Insp. 'Taff' Evans	**Meredith Edwards**
Insp. Cardish	**Eric Lander**
Insp. Davies	**Charles Morgan**

Producer: **Ronald Marriott**

Whodunnits for kids, featuring a 1920s detective.

Sexton Blake was the great detective of the Roaring Twenties. Like his illustrious predecessor, Sherlock Holmes, he lived in London's Baker Street, had a housekeeper (Mrs Bardell) and enjoyed the company of an assistant, Tinker. However, for Holmes's pipe, substitute a cigar. Solving crimes off their own bat, or called in by various Scotland Yard inspectors to succeed where they had failed, Blake, Tinker and his bloodhound, Pedro, cruised the streets of the capital in a white Rolls-Royce nicknamed 'The Grey Panther'.

The character was created back in the 19th century by Harry Blyth and first appeared in a boys' weekly called *The Halfpenny Marvel*. Blake also featured in several movie versions over the years and resurfaced on TV in 1978 in a BBC serial entitled *Sexton Blake and the Demon God* (with Jeremy Clyde as Blake and Philip Davis as Tinker). This earlier series was initially produced by Rediffusion, but Thames took over production after the 1968 franchise changes.

SEYMOUR, JANE

OBE (Joyce Frankenberg; 1951–)

British actress who has made her name in the cinema but has also been seen in various television offerings, usually glossy TV movies and mini-series. Before moving to Hollywood, Seymour appeared in British series like THE STRAUSS FAMILY, THE ONEDIN LINE (Emma Callon), *The Hanged Man*, *The Pathfinders*, HERE COME THE DOUBLE DECKERS and *Our Mutual Friend* (Bella Wilfer). In the USA, she has starred in *Captains and Kings*, *East of Eden*, *Jack the Ripper*, *War and Remembrance* and *The Woman He Loved* (Mrs Wallis Simpson), among many

dramas, as well as headlining as DR QUINN: MEDICINE WOMAN. Her fourth husband is director James Keach (brother of Stacy).

SHADOW SQUAD

UK (Associated-Rediffusion/Granada) Detective Drama.
ITV 1957–9

Vic Steele	**Rex Garner**
Don Carter	**Peter Williams**
Ginger Smart	**George Moon**
Mrs Moggs	**Kathleen Boutall**

Producer: **Barry Baker**

Two private eyes solve cases with a little help from their charlady.

Detective Vic Steele had resigned from the Flying Squad, tired of the rules and regulations which hampered his work. Sprung from the bureaucratic straitjacket, he set up his own agency, assisted by Londoner Ginger Smart, and named it Shadow Squad. Often calling on the help of their cleaner, Mrs Moggs, the pair investigated all manner of intriguing crimes. After 26 episodes, Steele was mysteriously written out and the agency was handed over to another ex-cop, Don Carter (Steele was sent off on a mission to Australia, never to return). Production, at the same time, switched from Associated-Rediffusion to Granada.

It was the Carter/Smart combination that made this twice-weekly show a success, although a spin-off entitled *Skyport*, featuring Ginger as an airport security man, failed to 'take off' and lasted only one year. The final *Shadow Squad* episode was set in a TV studio, which was revealed to be Granada's own.

SHAFT

US (MGM) Detective Drama. ITV 1974–6

John Shaft	**Richard Roundtree**
Lt. Al Rossi	**Ed Barth**

Executive Producer: **Allan Balter**
Producer: **William Read Woodfield**

The adventures of a smooth, streetwise private eye.

Sharp-talking, straight-shooting John Shaft was based in New York, although his assignments did not confine him to that city. Calm, efficient and ruthless, this slick, trendy, black detective helped clients in all kinds of difficulty, right across America. Lt. Al Rossi was his tame police contact. The series was inspired by the popular *Shaft* film trilogy, which also starred Richard Roundtree and used the same funky theme music by Isaac Hayes. However, with the sex and violence toned down for TV viewing, this television version lacked the edge of the cinema releases. A new feature film, pitching Samuel L. Jackson into the title role, was released in 2000.

SHANE, PAUL
(1940–)

Yorkshire-born comedian and actor, a miner and a comic on the northern clubs circuit before turning professional. It was as holiday camp host Ted Bovis in HI-DE-HI! that he became noticed, playing the role for eight years. As shifty butler Alf Stokes in YOU RANG, M'LORD, two years later, he more or less reprised the role but then went on to star as unscrupulous theatrical agent Harry James in the comedy, *Very Big Very Soon*, before returning to the David Croft comedy troupe as porter Jack Skinner in OH, DOCTOR BEECHING!. Among Shane's early appearances was a spot in CORONATION STREET as postal worker Frank Draper and as one of THE COMEDIANS. He was also seen in TURTLE'S PROGRESS, *Muck and Brass* and *Woof!*, among other series.

SHARON AND ELSIE
UK (BBC) Situation Comedy. BBC 1 1984–5

Elsie Beecroft	Brigit Forsyth
Sharon Wilkes	Janette Beverley
Stanley	John Landry
Roland Beecroft	Bruce Montague
Ivy	Maggie Jones
Elvis Wilkes	Lee Daley
Ike Hepworth	Gordon Rollings
Tommy Wallace	John Junkin

Writer: **Arline Whittaker**
Producers: **Roger Race, Mike Stephens**

Two female workmates don't see eye to eye.

In this generation-gap comedy, early-middle-aged Elsie Beecroft worked as a supervisor in the greetings cards and calendars printing firm of James Blake and Son, based in Manchester. When Sharon Wilkes, a punk school-leaver, was taken on as secretary to the company boss, Elsie did not approve. With the slightly snooty Elsie always ready to act above her station, the scene was set for some healthy workplace conflict. However, this quickly dissolved into friendship and the two girls joined forces in a long-running battle for employee rights. They even socialized outside work hours.

SHARPE
UK (Central/Picture Palace) Drama. ITV 1993–7

Lt./Capt./Major Richard Sharpe	Sean Bean
Hogan	Brian Cox
Sgt Patrick Harper	Daragh O'Malley
Sir Henry Simmerson	Michael Cochrane
Wellesley (Wellington)	David Troughton
	Hugh Fraser
Lawford	Martin Jacobs
Tongue	Paul Trussell
Teresa	Assumpta Serna
Nairn	Michael Byrne
Cooper	Michael Mears
Hagman	John Tams
Harris	Jason Salkey
Perkins	Lyndon Davies
Ramona	Diana Perez
Ducos	Feodor Atkine
Jane Gibbons/Sharpe	Abigail Cruttenden
Major Gen. Ross	James Laurenson
Mungo Munro	Hugh Ross
Lady Anne Camoynes	Caroline Langrishe
Lucille	Cecile Paoli
Rossendale	Alexis Denisof
Obadiah Hakeswill	Pete Postlethwaite
Isabella Farthingdale	Elizabeth Hurley

Producers: **Malcolm Craddock, Simon Lewis, Chris Burt**
Executive Producers: **Ted Childs, Muir Sutherland**

The battlefield and bedroom exploits of an English soldier during the Napoleonic Wars.

Based on the novels by Bernard Cornwell, this sporadic series of feature-length dramas told the story of one Richard Sharpe, a rough-and-ready Londoner who, in 1809, was instantly promoted from the ranks to officer status after saving the life of the Duke of Wellington. Standing out like the proverbial sore thumb among the snooty other commissioned men, he needed to fight prejudice on his own side as well as his country's mortal enemies. His office required him to do his duty in various parts of Europe, often heroically stealing behind enemy lines at the bidding of the Duke himself, but seldom did the unorthodox Sharpe fail to meet with some beautiful women along the way, including Lady Anne Camoynes and Jane Gibbons, who became his wife. The 14 films took the action right up to the Battle of Waterloo in 1815.

Sean Bean – who did his own stunts, including riding and fencing work – was not the first star selected for the role. The original Sharpe was Paul McGann, but a football match injury meant the part had to be recast and all completed scenes reshot. Some episodes were filmed in places like the Crimea and in Turkey.

SHATNER, WILLIAM
(1931–)

Canadian actor who will always be remembered as Captain James T. Kirk, the he-man skipper of the *USS Enterprise* in STAR TREK. Before *Star Trek* began its voyage on America's screens in 1966, Shatner had been seen in numerous drama anthologies, some Westerns and the odd cop series like NAKED CITY. He starred in the pilot of THE DEFENDERS and episodes of THE TWILIGHT ZONE and THE OUTER LIMITS, and allegedly turned down the role of DR KILDARE. Shatner did, however, take a leading part in a legal drama series, *For the People*, in 1965. Because it was cancelled after only three months, he found himself available to take on *Star Trek* a year later (Jeffrey Hunter, who had appeared in the series' pilot, was not free). In the 1970s Shatner was a familiar guest in series like A MAN CALLED IRONSIDE and HAWAII FIVE-O, and also took a role in another ill-fated programme, this time a Western called *The Barbary Coast*. In 1982 he donned the policeman's uniform of Sgt T. J. HOOKER. The series ran for five years and earned Shatner a new generation of fans. In 1989 he began narrating the series, *Rescue 911*, which reconstructed real-life dramas, and in 1994 appeared in the sci-fi series, *Tekwar*, based on his own novels (written with Ron Goulart) .

SHAUGHNESSY, ALFRED
(1916–)

British writer, the script editor of UPSTAIRS, DOWN-STAIRS. Shaughnessy's own aristocratic upbringing was given much of the credit for the historical accuracy in this series. His other major contributions have been the similarly genteel afternoon drama, *The Cedar Tree*, episodes of THE ADVENTURES OF SHERLOCK HOLMES and the pilot for *Ladies in Charge*. One of his earliest offerings was a musical biography of music-hall star Marie Lloyd, *Our Marie* (written with Christopher Barry), which was broadcast in 1953.

SHAW, MARTIN
(1945–)

Versatile British actor seen in series like CORONATION STREET (hippie Robert Croft), DOCTOR IN THE HOUSE (Huw Evans) and HELEN – A WOMAN OF TODAY (Helen's husband, Frank Tulley), before achieving lead status in THE PROFESSIONALS in the role of CI5 agent Ray Doyle. He later played Robert Falcon Scott in *The Last Place on Earth*, starred in the dramas, *The Most Dangerous Man in the World* and *Cream in My Coffee*, and made a guest appearance in ROBIN OF SHERWOOD. Other credits have included parts in *Villains*, SUTHERLAND'S LAW, *Beasts*, Z CARS, THE DUCHESS OF DUKE STREET, THE NEW AVENGERS and Shakespearean plays. More recently, he has been seen as Chief Supt. Mike Barclay in *Screen One's Black and Blue*, Chief Constable Alan Cade in THE CHIEF, Chauvelin in *The Scarlet Pimpernel* and Robert Kingsford in *Always and Everyone*. He is the father of actor Joe Shaw, with whom he shared the lead role in *Rhodes*, and is married to presenter Vicki Kimm.

SHELLEY/THE RETURN OF SHELLEY
UK (Thames) Situation Comedy. ITV 1979–84; 1988–92

James Shelley	**Hywel Bennett**
Frances Smith/Shelley	**Belinda Sinclair**
Mrs Edna Hawkins	**Josephine Tewson**
Gordon Smith	**Frederick Jaeger**
Forsyth	**Kenneth Cope**
Isobel Shelley	**Sylvia Kay**
Paul	**Warren Clarke**
Alice	**Rowena Cooper**
Desmond	**Garfield Morgan**
Carol	**Caroline Langrishe**
Graham	**Andrew Castell**
Phil	**Stephen Hoye**
Ted Bishop	**David Ryall**

Creator: **Peter Tilbury**
Producer: **Anthony Parker**

A university graduate shirks work, battles bureaucracy and bemoans the upheavals of life.

James Shelley, a geography graduate who looked down on those less well educated than himself, wanted more from life, but not if he had to work for it. Living on social security, the 28-year-old shared a flat with his girlfriend, Fran, in Pangloss Road, North London, from where he conducted a permanent war with the taxman and other establishment figures, as well as with Fran's dad, Gordon. Mrs Hawkins was his landlady. Over subsequent series, Shelley did find sporadic work, once as a copywriter and on another occasion with the Foreign Office, but his inability and unwillingness to hold down a job led Fran (now his wife and mother of his daughter, Emma) to kick him out. Shelley moved into his friend Paul's flat and continuously wrangled with Desmond, the building's porter, before deciding to leave for the USA and the Middle East to teach English. Six years later, in 1988, he re-emerged with the same chip on his shoulder and petulant pout on his lips in *The Return of Shelley*. Carol and Graham were his hosts on his comeback, and this time he railed against yuppies and the Americanization of British society. Later episodes reverted to the original title and saw the Hancockian hero lodging with pensioner Ted Bishop.

Shelley was adapted for Radio 2 in 1997, with Stephen Tompkinson taking over the lead role.

SHEPHERD, CYBILL
(1950–)

American actress/singer, star of MOONLIGHTING (Maddie Hayes) and *Cybill* (Cybill Sheridan), as well as a 1980s US soap called *The Yellow Rose* (Colleen Champion) and a few TV movies.

SHEPHERD, JACK
(1940–)

Dour-looking English actor, best known as detective Charles WYCLIFFE, but also star of BILL BRAND in the 1970s. Other credits have included the sketch show, *World in Ferment*, the play, *Ready When You Are Mr McGill*, *The Devil's Crown*, *Count Dracula*, *Blind Justice*, *Sons and Lovers*, *Screen One's Ball-Trap on the Côte Sauvage*, *Shoot to Kill*, BETWEEN THE LINES, LOVEJOY, *Over Here* and *Lorna Doone*.

SHEPHERD, SIMON
(1956–)

Bristol-born actor, familiar as Piers Garfield-Ward in *Chancer*, Duncan McAllister in *Beyond Reason*, Dr Will Preston in PEAK PRACTICE and Dr Sam Bliss in *Bliss*. He has also been seen as Peter Taylor QC in the drama-doc, *A Life for a Life*, Mark Sopwith in CATHERINE COOKSON'S *Tilly Trotter* and Major 'Brick' Stone in *Warriors*.

SHERLOCK HOLMES
UK (BBC) Detective Drama. BBC 1 1965; 1968

Sherlock Holmes .... **Douglas Wilmer** *(1965)*
Peter Cushing *(1968)*
Dr Watson .... **Nigel Stock**
Insp. Lestrade .... **Peter Madden** *(1965)*
William Lucas *(1968)*
Mrs Hudson .... **Mary Holder** *(1965)*
Grace Arnold *(1968)*
Mycroft Holmes .... **Derek Francis** *(1965)*
Ronald Adam *(1968)*

Producer: **David Goddard** *(1965)*, **William Sterling**
(1968)

The BBC's second attempt at televising The Great
Detective.

Having put together an unlikely team of actors for a 1951
version of six Conan Doyle stories, the BBC tried again
14 years later. In the earlier series, Holmes had been
played by Alan Wheatley (the future Sheriff of Nottingham in THE ADVENTURES OF ROBIN HOOD), assisted by
a pre-NO HIDING PLACE Raymond Francis as Watson and
a young Compo, Bill Owen, as Inspector Lestrade. On
this occasion, Douglas Wilmer was handed Holmes's
pipe and magnifying glass and was aided – or, rather,
hindered – by an inept Dr Watson, played by Nigel Stock.
The characters and same actors had originally been seen
in a one-off story, *The Speckled Band*, under the DETEC-
TIVE series banner in 1964. Twelve stories were covered
in the new series.

Stock reprised his role three years later, when Peter
Cushing replaced Wilmer. Taking his lead from the
rather bastardized perception of the great detective as a
thorough do-gooder and an essentially kind man, Peter
Cushing donned the deerstalker and picked up the
hooked pipe. There was no cocaine, no violent mood-
swings and none of the rudeness which Conan Doyle
had perceived and which Jeremy Brett re-introduced in
the 1980s. Fifteen stories comprised this rendition (billed
as *Sir Arthur Conan Doyle's Sherlock Holmes*), including all
the favourites, from *A Study in Scarlet* to *The Hound of*
the Baskervilles. Cushing was already familiar with his
character, having portrayed Holmes in the 1959 Hammer
version of *The Hound of the Baskervilles*.

SHERRIN, NED
CBE (1931–)

Although associated with the Radio 4 series, *Loose Ends*,
these days, Ned Sherrin was one of the BBC's current
affairs team that brought TONIGHT to the screens in the
1950s. He also devised, produced and directed the ground-
breaking THAT WAS THE WEEK THAT WAS in 1962, as well as
its less successful offspring, NOT SO MUCH A PROGRAMME,
MORE A WAY OF LIFE and BBC-3. He later produced the
sketch shows, *Where Was Spring?* and *World in Ferment*,
and in the 1970s, with Caryl Brahms, he adapted French
farces for Patrick Cargill's series, *Ooh La La!*

SHE'S OUT
See WIDOWS.

SHILLINGBURY TALES
UK (ATV) Comedy Drama. ITV 1981

Peter Higgins .... **Robin Nedwell**
Sally Higgins .... **Diane Keen**
Major Langton .... **Lionel Jeffries**
Cuffy .... **Bernard Cribbins**
Jake .... **Jack Douglas**
Harvey .... **Joe Black**
Revd Norris .... **Nigel Lambert**
Mrs Simpkins .... **Diana King**
Mandy .... **Linda Hayden**

Creator/Writer: **Francis Essex**
Producer: **Greg Smith**

Affairs in the life of a picturesque English village.

Shillingbury Tales, set in the fictitious village of Shillingbury, was developed by Francis Essex from his own
one-off play, *The Shillingbury Blowers*, screened in 1980.
In the single drama, the 'Blowers' were members of an
inept local brass band which was kicked into life by pop
musician Peter Higgins. However, when the series began,
other village events came under the microscope. Peter
had married Sally Langton, daughter of the local aristocrat, Major Langton, and had settled into the village.
Also in the action was Cuffy the tinker, a scruffy, mischievous tramp who lived in a run-down caravan. He
was given his own spin-off series, *Cuffy*, in 1983, with
many of the Shillingbury villagers making up the supporting cast.

SHINE ON HARVEY MOON
UK (Central/Witzend/Meridian) Comedy Drama. ITV
1982–5; 1995

Harvey Moon .... **Kenneth Cranham**
Nicky Henson
Rita Moon .... **Maggie Steed**
Maggie Moon/Lewis .... **Linda Robson**
Stanley Moon .... **Lee Whitlock**
Lou Lewis .... **Nigel Planer**
Violet Moon ('Nan') .... **Elizabeth Spriggs**
Veronica .... **Pauline Quirke**
Harriet Wright .... **Fiona Victory**
Erich Gottlieb .... **Leonard Fenton**
Frieda Gottlieb .... **Suzanne Bertish**
Noah Hawksley .... **Colin Salmon**
Helen .... **Wendy Morgan**
Azzopardi .... **Vincenzo Nicoli**

Creators/Writers: **Laurence Marks, Maurice Gran**
Executive Producer: **Allan McKeown**
Producer: **Tony Charles**

Post-war trouble and strife for a former
serviceman and his family.

Returning home to Hackney from wartime service in India as a corporal (stores clerk) in the RAF, former professional footballer Harvey Moon discovered his home destroyed and his family life in tatters. His flighty wife, Rita, had run off with other men, his 17-year-old daughter, Maggie, was seeing his old pal, Lou Lewis, and his mother, Nan, remained as redoubtable as ever. Add to this the problems of rationing, post-war shortages and the constraints of living in a prefab (later demolished by an unexploded bomb), and Harvey's lot was not a happy one. However, he set about making a new life for himself, becoming a Labour councillor, dating Harriet Wright, his worldly son Stanley's headmistress, and taking up residence with Erich Gottlieb and his sister, Frieda. Eventually he and Rita were, somewhat precariously, reunited.

Beginning with six half-hour episodes, *Shine on Harvey Moon*, a nostalgic comedy drama, was later extended into 60-minute instalments and ran for three years, covering the period 1945–8. In 1995 the programme was exhumed, with Nicky Henson replacing Kenneth Cranham in the lead. The story was taken up in 1953, Coronation year, and ran through the 1950s, with immigrants flooding into Britain looking for work and Maggie set to marry Lou (now 'One Lung Lou', having lost the other). In between, creators Laurence Marks and Maurice Gran had returned to the 1940s with another offering, GOODNIGHT SWEETHEART.

SHIVAS, MARK
(1938–)

Successful British executive, one-time film critic and host of CINEMA, but far better remembered for his work as producer on dramas like THE SIX WIVES OF HENRY VIII, CASANOVA, THE GLITTERING PRIZES, *Rogue Male*, *The History Man*, TELFORD'S CHANGE, *The Three Hostages*, *On Giant's Shoulders*, THE BORGIAS, WINSTON CHURCHILL – THE WILDERNESS YEARS, *The Price* and THE STORYTELLER. He also produced the *Black and Blue* series of comedy plays in 1973. In recent years he has been Head of BBC Films.

SHOESTRING
UK (BBC) Detective Drama. BBC 1 1979–80

Eddie Shoestring	**Trevor Eve**
Erica Bayliss	**Doran Godwin**
Don Satchley	**Michael Medwin**
Sonia	**Liz Crowther**

Creator/Producer: **Robert Banks Stewart**

Private detective work with a local radio presenter.

Eddie Shoestring was a radio presenter – but he was also a detective. Working for West Country-based Radio West, Shoestring used his airtime as a springboard for detective work, asking listeners to ring in with investigations he could pursue and information he could use. Usually, the cases were run-of-the-mill affairs, all set in the Bristol area, but occasionally something juicier

turned up to spur the 'private ear' into action. When the crime had been solved, the outcome was related on air, with names changed to protect the innocent.

Shoestring had not always been a broadcaster. He had been egged into the job by the station receptionist, Sonia (played by Leslie Crowther's daughter), after helping the station out on an early investigation. Before that he had been a computer expert but had suffered a nervous breakdown and had spent some time in a mental institution. He now lodged with barrister Erica Bayliss, an occasional girlfriend who joined in some of the sleuthing. Don Satchley was Eddie's station manager.

Although scruffily dressed and prone to drinking sprees, Shoestring was not to be underestimated. He was multi-talented: not only was he a keen sketch artist (sketching was his therapy) and a good mimic, but he enjoyed an excellent, sensitive rapport with his listening public. However, when times were bad, he retreated to his run-down houseboat for moments of reflection. The boat was almost as decrepit as his car, a beaten-up red Ford Cortina estate.

After just two highly successful seasons, Trevor Eve decided to move back into the theatre. It left *Shoestring*'s creator, Robert Banks Stewart, with plenty of unused ideas, so he developed a new series about another rehabilitating detective, this time based in Jersey (see BERGERAC). *Shoestring*'s presence was not quite eradicated, however, as the name Radio West was bought up by the real-life independent radio station set up to serve the Bristol area.

SHOGUN
US (Paramount) Drama. BBC 1 1982

John Blackthorne	**Richard Chamberlain**
Lord Toranaga	**Toshiro Mifune**
Lady Toda Buntaro-Mariko	**Yoko Shimada**
Lord Ishido	**Nobuo Kaneko**
Vasco Rodriguez	**John Rhys-Davies**
Friar Domingo	**Michael Hordern**
Father Alvito	**Damien Thomas**
Omi	**Yuki Meguro**
Yabu	**Frankie Sabai**
Dell' Aqua	**Alan Badel**

Writer/Producer: **Eric Bercovici**
Executive Producer: **James Clavell**

A 17th-century adventurer is captured by the Japanese and adapts to their culture.

Based on the real-life story of Elizabethan seaman Will Adams, *Shogun* told of John Blackthorne, the English pilot of a Dutch vessel that was wrecked on the Japanese coast in the early 1600s. Taken under the wing of the powerful Toranaga, one of the feudal state's great warlords, Blackthorne adopted the name of Anjin-san and quickly acclimatized to the Japanese way of living. The series watched Blackthorne embark on a steamy affair with Lady Mariko (a married noblewoman interpreter), confront western emissaries (traders and Jesuit preachers) and take part in the many bloody conflicts which characterized Japanese life. His quest: to become the first western-born Shogun (a supreme Samurai warrior).

This easy-paced, six-part series was adapted from James Clavell's epic novel of the same name, with Clavell working on the project as executive producer. It was filmed on location in Japan, with much of the dialogue in Japanese.

SHOOTING SCRIPT

A version of a programme script which details all the camera shots required.

SHOOTING STARS
UK (BBC/Channel X) Comedy. BBC 2 1995–7

Presenters: **Vic Reeves, Bob Mortimer, Matt Lucas**

Producer: **Alan Marke**

Spoof celebrity game show.

Shooting Stars was a riotous comedy quiz show in which celebrities – headed by team captains 'Ulrika-ka-ka-ka' Jonsson and 'fifties throw-back' Mark Lamarr – were subjected to a barrage of good-natured abuse and practical jokery by questionmasters Vic Reeves and Bob Mortimer (who also sang the theme song). As one participant, Danny Baker, shrewdly remarked, the guests were not so much contestants as stooges in a sketch.

Questions were divided up into buzzer rounds ('We really want to see those fingers'), a category-board round (or, rather, category bird, being 'the Dove from Above', which the celebs were encouraged to coax down by cooing), an impressions round, a true-or-false round, and a club singer round, in which Vic performed a mystery hit in the style of a club performer. A member of the winning team was called upon to undertake a bizarre challenge in the finale.

Matt Lucas, as drummer George Dawes, usually dressed as a big baby, kept the scores. Graham Skidmore provided the voice-overs. The 'pilot' for the series was a segment of Reeves and Mortimer's 1993 Christmas extravaganza, *At Home with Vic and Bob*.

SHOW CALLED FRED, A
UK (Associated-Rediffusion) Comedy. ITV 1956

Peter Sellers, Valentine Dyall, Graham Stark, Kenneth Connor, Patti Lewis, Max Geldray

Writer: **Spike Milligan**

Off-beat comedy sketch show.

Written by Spike Milligan and also featuring fellow Goon Peter Sellers, assorted comics and Canadian singer Patti Lewis, *A Show Called Fred* was one of TV's first surreal comedies. It followed hot on the heels of another Peter Sellers offering, *Idiot Weekly, Price 2d* (also 1956; both series screened only in London), in which he linked sketches as the editor of a Victorian weekly newspaper.

A sequel, *Son of Fred*, performed by the same team but with Johnny Vyvyan and Cuthbert Harding added to their number, was screened in the same year (including in other parts of the UK). *The Best of Fred* was a 1963 compilation of both series. Future Beatles film director Dick Lester directed proceedings.

SHUBIK, IRENE
(1935–)

British drama producer. Previously a historian, Shubik's first job in television was as story editor to the influential Sydney Newman on programmes like ARMCHAIR THEATRE and OUT OF THIS WORLD at ABC. Moving into production, she switched with Newman to the BBC in 1963 and worked largely on THE WEDNESDAY PLAY and PLAY FOR TODAY, although she was also responsible for the OUT OF THE UNKNOWN science-fiction anthology and the Georges Simenon collection, *Thirteen Against Fate*. She left the BBC in the mid-1970s, when its drama department declined to pursue a series of RUMPOLE OF THE BAILEY, after John Mortimer's one-off play had proved a hit; she took the idea to Thames instead. Later, Shubik was influential in Granada's televising of Paul Scott's *Raj Quartet* as THE JEWEL IN THE CROWN (having produced the single drama, *Staying On*, based on Scott's novel), although she was not involved in the production herself. Among her many credits have been plays like *Mrs Lawrence Will Look After It* (1968), *The Last Train Through the Harecastle Tunnel* (1969), *Hearts and Flowers* (1970), *Edna, The Inebriate Woman* (1971) and *The General's Day* (1973), and the series, *Playhouse* and *Wessex Tales*.

SIANEL PEDWAR CYMRU
See S4C.

SILENT WITNESS
UK (BBC/A&E) Drama. BBC 1 1996–

Dr/Prof. Samantha 'Sam' Ryan	**Amanda Burton**
DI Tom Adams	**John McGlynn**
DS Harriet Farmer	**Clare Higgins**
DC Kerry Cox	**Ruth Gemmell**
Dr Trevor Stewart	**William Armstrong**
Marcia Evans	**Janice Acquah**
Wyn Ryan	**Ruth McCabe**
Beryl Ryan	**Doreen Hepburn**
Ricky Ryan	**Matthew Steer**
PC North	**Milo Twomey**
PC Jarvis	**Ian Keith**
Fred Dale	**Sam Parks**
Det. Supt. Peter Ross	**Mick Ford**
DI Rachel Selway	**Nicola Redmond**
DS Tony Speed	**Richard Huw**
DI Michael Connor	**Nick Reding**
DS Rob Bradley	**Mark Letheren**
Dr James Reynolds	**Michael Siberry**

Creator: **Nigel McCrery**

Executive Producer: **Caroline Oulton**
Producers: **Tony Dennis, Alison Lumb, Anne Pivcevic, Lars Macfarlane, Diana Kyle**

The gruesome cases of a determined female pathologist.

Dr Sam Ryan, born in Belfast, aged 37 and now working in Cambridge, was the lead character in this collection of murder investigations. Almost obsessive in her work, she wasn't the kind of pathologist to jump to conclusions or give up on a case before the truth had been discovered. A sense of justice pervaded her psyche (lightened by a little dry wit) and often placed her at odds with a detective looking for a quick conviction.

Ryan's cases were not pleasant: child abuse, black magic and industrial negligence featured among the storylines, and the nature of her work called for some stomach-churning close-ups of decaying, bloated bodies and dissected organs. Relentlessly lurking in the background was Ryan's complicated family-life: an RUC officer father murdered by terrorists, an Alzheimer's victim mother, a resentful sister, a tearaway nephew and, later, a policeman colleague (Peter Ross) who used to be her lover. In subsequent episodes, Ryan moved out of Cambridge and became a professor of pathology at the University of London, but she was still called out as a consultant to the scenes of grisly events.

SILVERA, CARMEN

Actress born in Canada, primarily recalled as the tuneless Madame Edith in 'ALLO 'ALLO. In the early 1960s, she played Camilla Hope in the magazine soap, COMPACT, and was also seen in one episode of DAD'S ARMY, as Captain Mainwaring's fancy woman. Other credits have included SERGEANT CORK, Z CARS, BEGGAR MY NEIGHBOUR, NEW SCOTLAND YARD, DOCTOR WHO, WITHIN THESE WALLS, LILLIE, WHOOPS APOCALYPSE, TALES OF THE UNEXPECTED and THE GENTLE TOUCH.

SILVERS, PHIL
(Philip Silver; 1912–85)

New York-born, former burlesque comedian, one of TV's early greats. Despite having an up-and-down stage and movie career, and failing to make the grade as a variety compere on *The Arrow Show* in 1948, his later portrayal of the wonderfully devious Sgt Bilko in *You'll Never Get Rich* was so commanding that the programme's title was changed to THE PHIL SILVERS SHOW. Four years into its run (when it was at its peak in 1959), the show was cancelled so that the studio could cash in on syndicated re-runs. An attempt to revive the premiss as *The New Phil Silvers Show* in 1963 (in which he played factory foreman Harry Grafton) flopped, and his TV career never recovered. He was given a semi-regular role (Shifty Shafer) in THE BEVERLY HILLBILLIES in 1969, but otherwise his later appearances were either variety specials or guest spots in series like GILLIGAN'S ISLAND and THE LOVE BOAT. His daughter, Cathy, played flirt Jenny Piccalo in HAPPY

DAYS and Silvers once dropped in to the series as her screen dad.

SIMPSON, ALAN
OBE (1929–) See GALTON, RAY.

SIMPSON, BILL
(1931–86)

One-time Scottish Television announcer Bill Simpson is clearly imprinted in most viewers' minds as the headstrong young GP in DR FINLAY'S CASEBOOK. His later TV work was sparse, the highlight being roles in *Scotch on the Rocks* and *Kidnapped*, but also with guest spots in WHEN THE BOAT COMES IN and *The McKinnons*.

SIMPSON, JOHN
CBE (John Fidler-Simpson; 1944–)

Distinguished British journalist who joined the BBC as a news trainee in 1966. He became its Dublin correspondent four years later, before moving to Brussels in 1975 to cover the increasingly important Common Market business. Simpson was the Corporation's Southern Africa correspondent from 1977 and then took over as diplomatic correspondent in 1978, before holding the position of political editor from 1980 to 1981. Also in the early 1980s, he presented *The Nine O'Clock News* with John Humphrys. From 1982, he was the BBC's diplomatic editor, switching in 1988 to foreign affairs editor.

SIMPSONS, THE
US (Gracie Films/Twentieth Century-Fox) Cartoon.
BBC 1/BBC 2 1996–

Voices:

Homer Simpson	**Dan Castellaneta**
Marge Simpson	**Julie Kavner**
Bart Simpson	**Nancy Cartwright**
Lisa Simpson	**Yeardley Smith**
Patty	**Julie Kavner**
Grampa Simpson	**Dan Castellaneta**
Selma	**Julie Kavner**
Mr Montgomery Burns	**Harry Shearer**
Smithers	**Harry Shearer**
Principal Skinner	**Harry Shearer**
Moe	**Hank Azaria**
Milhouse	**Pamela Hayden**
Krusty the Klown	**Dan Castellaneta**
Apu	**Hank Azaria**

Creator: **Matt Groening**
Executive Producers: **Matt Groening, James L. Brooks, Sam Simon, Bill Oakley, Josh Weinstein, Mike Scully**

The eventful life of a blue-collar American family.

The Simpsons, bug-eyed, yellow-fleshed, four-fingers-per-hand creations of cartoonist Matt Groening, lived in the town of Springfield. Slobbish, doughnut-eating dad Homer ('Doh!') worked for the evil Mr Burns as a safety inspector at the local nuclear power station and drank Duff Beer at Moe's Tavern in his spare time. Mum Marge sported a towering blue beehive, talked hoarsely and tried to keep the house together. Eight-year-old daughter Lisa was a smart achiever who played the sax, while baby Maggie sucked perennially on a dummy. However, key protagonist was the obnoxious, crinkly-headed, ten-year-old Bart ('Eat my shorts!'), a skate-boarding delinquent who drove everyone mad in his pursuit of coolness ('Don't have a cow, man'). Their continual struggle to survive as a unit – they virtually invented the word 'dysfunctional' – reflected some of the worst excesses of American family life. Groening named all but Bart – a thinly disguised anagram of 'brat' – after members of his own family but claimed that was where the similarities ended. The naming of the town 'Springfield' was also deliberate: the same name had been used in the decidedly more wholesome 1950s sit-com, *Father Knows Best*.

Other notable characters included Homer's senile dad, Bart's friend Milhouse, and flawed TV star Krusty the Klown, whose show featured the kids' favourite violent cat-and-mouse cartoon, Itchy and Scratchy. Numerous guest stars' voices also made their mark in the series, including Paul and Linda McCartney, Dustin Hoffman and Elizabeth Taylor (who spoke Maggie's first-ever word).

The Simpsons made their TV debut in *The Tracey Ull-man Show* before they embarked on this series of their own, which became the biggest show on the Fox network. The programme's satirical tone ensured its appeal to adults as well as children, and it became the first successful prime-time animation in the States since THE FLINTSTONES. Extensive merchandising and hit records followed ('Do the Bartman' and 'Deep Deep Trouble'). In the UK, Sky One pre-empted the BBC in airing the show.

SIMS, JOAN
(1930–)

British comedy actress often seen on the small screen, as well as in films. In a long and varied career, she was a guest in THE ADVENTURES OF ROBIN HOOD in the 1950s, Daisy Burke in OUR HOUSE in 1960, Janet with John Junkin in *Sam and Janet* in 1966, and has also enjoyed major roles in the comedies, *Lord Tramp* (Miss Pratt), *Born and Bred* (Molly Peglar), *Cockles* (Gloria du Bois), *Farrington of the FO* (Annie Begley) and ON THE UP (Mrs Wembley). Other credits have included *Here and Now*, *Before The Fringe*, TILL DEATH US DO PART (Gran), SYKES, ONLY FOOLS AND HORSES, *Ladykillers* (Amelia Elizabeth Dyer), *Poor Little Rich Girls*, WORZEL GUMMIDGE (Mrs Bloomsbury-Barton), CROWN COURT, AS TIME GOES BY (Madge), *Martin Chuzzlewit* (Betsy Prig), *My Good Friend* (Miss Byron), *Just William*, *Last of the Blonde Bomb-shells* (Betty), and the kids' series, *Tickle on the Tum* and *Jackanory Playhouse*. Sims has also provided strong support for comics like Dick Emery, Stanley Baxter, Kenneth Williams, Ronnie Barker and Victoria Wood,

and has appeared with her colleagues from the *Carry On* films.

SIMULCAST

A simultaneous broadcast of a programme by a television station and a radio station, usually in order to obtain better sound-quality from the radio's FM frequency. Simulcasts have been used for opera, rock concerts, stereo and quadraphonic experiments and other major events. TOP OF THE POPS was simulcast on BBC 1 and Radio 1 for a few years.

SINDEN, Sir DONALD
CBE (1923–)

Plymouth-born, resonant-voiced actor, generally cast in upright, snooty, typically English parts. On stage since the mid-1930s and in films since the 1950s, Sinden's first TV starring role came in 1964, in the comedy, OUR MAN AT ST MARK'S, as Revd Stephen Young, having already appeared occasionally in the sitcom, A LIFE OF BLISS. Twelve years later he played butler Robert Hiller in TWO'S COMPANY and followed this sitcom with another, NEVER THE TWAIN, in which he played antiques dealer Simon Peel. Sinden has also been seen in *The Organisation* and in numerous single dramas and classic plays, as well as guesting in series like THE PRISONER and with Morecambe and Wise. In 1979, in complete contrast, he presented a series of documentaries, *Discovering English Churches*. He is the brother of actor Leon Sinden, and father of Marc Sinden and the late Jeremy Sinden.

SINGING DETECTIVE, THE
UK (BBC) Drama. BBC 1 1986

Philip E. Marlow	**Michael Gambon**
Nurse Mills/Carlotta	**Joanne Whalley**
Mark Binney/Mark Finney/Raymond Binney	
	Patrick Malahide
Mrs Beth Marlow/Lili	**Alison Steadman**
Philip Marlow (aged 10)	**Lyndon Davies**
Mr Marlow	**Jim Carter**
Nicola Marlow	**Janet Suzman**
Dr Gibbon	**Bill Paterson**
Schoolteacher/Scarecrow	**Janet Henfrey**
Mark Binney (aged 10)	**William Speakman**

Writer: **Dennis Potter**
Producers: **Kenith Trodd, John Harris**

A hospitalized thriller writer hallucinates into paranoia.

This highly complex, six-part musical drama was the story of a man suffering. Philip Marlow was an author of pulp fiction, confined to hospital with a debilitating skin disease. As his sickness worsened, paranoia over-whelmed him, leading him to conjure up images of the people around him as alien to his well-being. The story meandered through time back to the 1930s; it looked at the patient as a young boy, examining his formative years; and it infiltrated the pages of fiction, as people became characters from one of his own books, *The Singing Detective*. It confused reality and fantasy, and offered a weird psychoanalytical insight into the lead character.

Claustrophobically interned in a hospital's Sherpa Tensing ward, tortured by unbearable psoriasis, the grouchy Marlow found his temperature sweeping up and down, causing his mind to wander. Believing his wife, Nicola, was conspiring with a lover, Mark Finney, to sell his book's film rights, he drifted back to his Forest of Dean childhood to recall a devious classmate called Mark Binney (or was it Finney?). He remembered seeing his mother make love in the woods to her fancy man, Raymond Binney, a Mark Finney look-alike. At other times, he swooned off into the pages of his own novel, picturing himself as the eponymous hero, attempting to solve the mystery of a girl dredged from the Thames, trailed all the while by two shadowy figures, in a nostalgic echo of Chandler's Philip Marlowe tales. Back in reality, the sick author fought desperate verbal battles against a doctor whose opinion he derided, and was then required to restrain his sexuality as the beautiful Nurse Mills worked calming ointment into his suffering, flaking body.

Brilliant to some, outrageous to many and confusing to most (at least until all the pieces fell into place), *The Singing Detective* was in part an autobiographical tale. Potter himself suffered badly from psoriasis, and he had grown up in the Forest of Dean. The evocative 1930s/1940s tunes like 'Cruising Down the River' and 'Dem Bones' were also clearly from Potter's younger days. When all the fuss had subsided, the general reaction was that this was an all-time classic TV drama, skilfully crafted, magnificently produced and highly entertaining. It was shown again shortly after Potter's premature death in 1994.

SINGLES
UK (Yorkshire) Situation Comedy. ITV 1988–91

Malcolm Price	**Roger Rees**
Pamela	**Judy Loe**
Clive Bates	**Eamon Boland**
Jackie Phillips	**Susie Blake**
Dennis Duval	**Simon Cadell**
Di	**Gina Maher**

Creators/Writers: **Eric Chappell, Jean Warr**
Producers: **Vernon Lawrence, Nic Phillips, Graham Wetherell**

Four lonely hearts meet in a singles' bar and embark on a series of duplicitous relationships.

Pamela, married for 20 years but now separated, and her recently divorced friend, Jackie, attended a singles' bar as a step towards finding a new relationship. There they met up with bachelor market-trader Malcolm and hospital porter Clive, whose wife had left him with three children to raise. Malcolm's claim to be 'big in imports' and Clive's fake profession of 'doctor' were exposed by Di, the club's Liverpudlian barmaid, but all the same

the girls and guys struck up a friendship which lasted, through peaks and troughs, for two series. Malcolm and Pamela paired up, as did Clive and Jackie. For the third and final series, Malcolm was replaced by out-of-work thespian Dennis Duval (actor Roger Rees had moved on to play Robin Colcord in CHEERS). *Singles* was derived from a one-hour play screened in 1984, with a completely different cast, including Robin Nedwell as Malcolm.

SINGLETON, VALERIE
OBE (1937–)

Hitchin-born actress turned TV presenter whose first appearances were in ITV admags. She moved to the BBC as an announcer in 1962 and the same year joined BLUE PETER. With Christopher Trace she inaugurated the series' golden age, which continued through her partnership with John Noakes and Peter Purves. Singleton famously joined Princess Anne on the 1971 *Blue Peter Royal Safari to Kenya*, but left *Blue Peter* a year later to work on NATIONWIDE (initially on its Consumer Unit) and later on *Tonight*, *The Money Programme* and BBC Radio. She continued to make occasional visits to the *Blue Peter* studio throughout the 1970s and was sent on *Blue Peter Special Assignment*s. Singleton also presented the series, *Val Meets the VIPs*, in which she interviewed celebrities. She returned to the screen in 1993 as host of *Travel UK* and, the next year, shared the limelight once again with John Noakes in the over-50s afternoon magazine programme, *Next*. She also hosted the quiz, *Backdate*.

SIR ARTHUR CONAN DOYLE'S SHERLOCK HOLMES
See SHERLOCK HOLMES.

SIR FRANCIS DRAKE
UK (ABC/ATV) Adventure. ITV 1961–2

Sir Francis Drake	**Terence Morgan**
Queen Elizabeth	**Jean Kent**
Trevelyan	**Patrick McLoughlin**
John Drake	**Michael Crawford**
Mendoza	**Roger Delgado**

Producer: **Anthony Bushell**

Swashbuckling, maritime adventures with the sailor hero of Queen Elizabeth I.

Sir Francis Drake was Admiral of The Queen's Navy and, from his flagship, *The Golden Hind*, patrolled the oceans for Britain. His travels took him across the Atlantic and into conflict with our continental near-neighbours, although, whenever trouble threatened, Drake would always win through, often showing off his fencing skills in the process. Although accurate in period detail, the programme's storylines were largely fictitious.

The production was especially notable, in hindsight, for its cast, which included in particular a young Michael Crawford, as well as Roger Delgado (the original Master in DOCTOR WHO). Guest stars were noteworthy, too, including David McCallum, Nanette Newman and Warren Mitchell.

SIR LANCELOT
See ADVENTURES OF SIR LANCELOT, THE.

SISSONS, PETER
(1942–)

Senior BBC newsreader who joined ITN in 1964 as a trainee. Working his way up the network's ladder, he became foreign correspondent, industrial editor and presenter of the lunchtime bulletin, *News at One*, and *Channel 4 News*. He moved to the BBC in 1989 as Robin Day's successor in the chair of QUESTION TIME (he stayed for four years) and also to present the Corporation's main bulletins.

SITCOM

Situation comedy, a humorous, episodic series of programmes in which a well-defined cast of characters, confined in one location or set of circumstances, responds predictably to new events.

TV's first comedy offerings were carry-overs from radio or the music hall, but it soon carved its own niche in the world of humour by developing the situation comedy, a type of comedy that made a virtue out of the constraints of early television production. In those primitive days, camera manoeuvrability was limited and dramas and comedies were generally played out entirely within the four walls of a studio set. Consequently, with the situation static, humour had to come from strong characterization.

Most sitcoms have centred around the family. Right from the earliest successes of THE BURNS AND ALLEN SHOW and I LOVE LUCY to today's THE ROYLE FAMILY, the family unit has been the cradle of the action. This is not so surprising, as the family comprises a set number of inter-dependent characters, living in the same location and forced to react with each other to changing events. The workplace has been another popular venue, as typified by programmes like TAXI and ON THE BUSES. However, provided the circumstances are well defined and the characterization is suitably strong, virtually any setting can be used. For THE PHIL SILVERS SHOW it was a US Army base; for CHEERS a Boston bar. As if to prove the point, the most successful of sitcoms have had the most unlikely of settings – M*A*S*H's Mobile Army Surgical Hospital in the Korean War, and the Resistance bar in occupied France in 'ALLO 'ALLO, for instance.

Whereas American sitcoms employ teams of ever-changing writers, many of Britain's most memorable sitcoms have come from a small corps of authors, the likes of Ray Galton and Alan Simpson, Johnny Speight, John Esmonde and Bob Larbey, Dick Clement and Ian La Frenais, Jimmy Perry and David Croft, Vince Powell and Harry Driver, Ronald Chesney and Ronald Wolfe, Johnnie Mortimer and Brian Cooke, Maurice Gran and Lawrence Marks, Roy Clarke, Eric Chappell, John Sullivan, Carla Lane, George Layton, David Nobbs, David Renwick and Andrew Marshall. Many of their works began as pilots in the COMEDY PLAYHOUSE anthology.

SITTING PRETTY
UK (BBC) Situation Comedy. BBC 1 1992–3

Annie Briggs	**Diane Bull**
Tiffany	**Alison Lomas**
Sylvie	**Heather Tobias**
Kitty	**Vilma Hollingbery**
George	**John Cater**

Creator/Writer: **John Sullivan**
Producer: **Susan Belbin**

A 1960s jet-setter, impoverished by her late husband, is driven back to her lowly roots.

Annie Briggs had seen better days. A 1960s good-time girl, once known as 'the Jackie Onassis of Bethnal Green', she had rubbed shoulders with the big names, drifted from party to party and travelled the world on the arms of rich playboys. However, when her husband, Boris, died suddenly, he left her penniless and staring the realities of the 1990s in the face. Her lovely home, her cars and even her dog were repossessed and she was forced to move into her last piece of property, the pokey flat she had given to her daughter, Tiffany. Tiffany, or 'Dumpling' as her mum called her, was a trainee nurse. She had seldom seen her mother while growing up, having been packed off to boarding school while Annie toured the world. Now, claustrophobically trapped within the same four walls, she saw too much of her (and heard too many of Annie's Shirley Bassey tapes). Soon the flat, too, was taken away, and Annie and Tiffany moved in with Annie's mum, Kitty, hypochondriac dad, George, and twin sister, Sylvie, at Sunnyside Farm, a small chicken ranch in the country. Frumpy Sylvie, an ex-hippie with a grown-up air steward son named Lonestar (whose dad, she reckoned, was Bob Marley), particularly resented her sister's presence – or, rather, the fact that she never lifted a finger around the home, unless it was to paint the nail. 'Phenomenal', Annie would have called it.

SITUATION COMEDY
See SITCOM.

SIX ENGLISH TOWNS
UK (BBC) Documentary. BBC 2 1978

Presenter/Writer: **Alec Clifton-Taylor**

Producer: **Denis Moriarty**

An enthusiastic analysis of building styles around England.

Alec Clifton-Taylor, a keen admirer of architecture, took viewers on a ramble through six of the country's most interesting towns in this series for BBC 2. Paying particular attention to houses and terraces, and making clear his views on modern developments, Clifton-Taylor took in visits to Chichester, Richmond (Yorkshire), Tewkesbury, Stamford, Totnes and Ludlow. The series proved so popular that *Six More English Towns* followed in 1981. These were Warwick, Berwick-upon-Tweed, Saffron Walden, Lewes, Bradford-on-Avon and Beverley. *Another Six English Towns* – Cirencester, Whitby, Bury St Edmunds, Devizes, Sandwich and Durham – rounded off the trilogy in 1984.

SIX MILLION DOLLAR MAN, THE

US (Universal/Harve Bennett) Science Fiction. ITV 1974–9

Col. Steve Austin	**Lee Majors**
Oscar Goldman	**Richard Anderson**
Dr Rudy Wells	**Alan Oppenheimer**
	Martin E. Brooks
Peggy Callahan	**Jennifer Darling**
Jaime Sommers	**Lindsay Wagner**
Andy Sheffield	**Vincent Van Patten**

Creator: **Henri Simoun**
Executive Producers: **Glen A. Larson, Harve Bennett, Allan Balter**
Producers: **Michael Gleason, Lee Sigel, Joe L. Cramer, Fred Freiberger, Richard Irving**

An astronaut, rebuilt after a horrendous accident, uses his superhuman powers to work for an intelligence service.

Steve Austin was a NASA astronaut whose lunar landing vehicle crashed on a test flight. The authorities decided to rebuild him at a cost of $6 million, using nuclear-powered technology devised by boffin Dr Rudy Wells. Austin was given a replacement right arm which endowed him with tremendous strength, two new legs which allowed him to run at up to 60 m.p.h., and a left eye with a built-in telescope. He became a cyborg: part-man, part-machine, a superman who was still vulnerable in the usual human ways.

The new 'bionic' man put his amazing abilities to work on behalf of the Office of Scientific Information (OSI), an international secret agency run by the US Government, where his boss was Oscar Goldman. Austin was joined in his adventures by his girlfriend, tennis star Jaime Sommers. She, too, had been rebuilt, following a sky-diving accident. Her first appearance was short-lived, as her body rejected the implants, and she was believed to have died. But doctors and technicians resurrected her from a coma to take part in further bionic adventures alongside Austin, before she was given her own series, THE BIONIC WOMAN. There was also a bionic boy (teenage athlete Andy Sheffield), a bionic dog and even a $7 million man, a racing driver named Barney Miller, rebuilt as Austin's back-up. However, he blew a fuse and Austin had to destroy him.

Also seen in the series was secretary Peggy Callahan, and the brains behind the bionics, Dr Wells (who must have had surgery himself, because he was played by two different actors). The series was based on a handful of

TV movies that had been spun off the book, *Cyborg*, by Martin Caidin.

SIX WIVES OF HENRY VIII, THE

UK (BBC) Historical Drama. BBC 2 1970

Henry VIII	**Keith Michell**
Catherine of Aragon	**Annette Crosbie**
Anne Boleyn	**Dorothy Tutin**
Jane Seymour	**Anne Stallybrass**
Anne of Cleves	**Elvi Hale**
Catherine Howard	**Angela Pleasence**
Catherine Parr	**Rosalie Crutchley**
Cardinal Wolsey	**John Baskcomb**
Duke of Norfolk	**Patrick Troughton**
Thomas Cromwell	**Wolfe Morris**
Archbishop Thomas Cranmer	**Bernard Hepton**
Lady Rochford	**Sheila Burrell**
Sir Thomas Seymour	**John Ronane**
Narrator	**Anthony Quayle**

Creator: **Maurice Cowan**
Producers: **Ronald Travers, Mark Shivas, Roderick Graham**

The life and loves of King Henry VIII.

This award-winning, six-part costume drama told the story of England's celebrated monarch through his relationships with his six wives, one per episode. It saw Henry growing in age (and size) from a slim 17-year-old to an obese 56-year-old at the time of his death. It also helped erode the cinematic Charles Laughton 'glutton' stereotype, introducing further dimensions to the man's character.

As a lead figure, Henry VIII provided much scope for the writers. Although 400 years old, his story made good 1970s TV drama, rich in sex and violence. Here was a man who married six different women, chiefly to give himself an heir, beheaded two, divorced two and saw one die shortly after childbirth. Then there were the whispered conspiracies, the treacherous double-dealing, the bloody murders and the major religious wrangles which were prevalent in those troubled times. It made a star out of a former artist, the Australian Keith Michell, and was reworked with different actresses for a film version, *Henry VIII and His Six Wives* in 1972. Originally screened on BBC 2, the series nevertheless drew huge audiences.

SIX-FIVE SPECIAL

UK (BBC) Youth Magazine. BBC 1957–8

Presenters: **Pete Murray, Josephine Douglas, Freddie Mills, Jim Dale**

Producers: **Jack Good, Josephine Douglas, Dennis Main Wilson**

Pioneering youth music programme.

With its 'Over the points, over the points' theme song (by Johnny Johnson), the *Six-Five Special* rolled into town in February 1957, initially scheduled for a six-week run. Instead it ran for nearly two years. Conceived by the BBC as a means of capturing the youth market, and filling the Saturday 6–7 p.m. vacancy created by scrapping the TODDLERS' TRUCE, it proved to be a major step forward for pop music on TV.

Co-producers Jack Good and Jo Douglas were charged by the BBC with the development of the series, being two of the younger members of staff. Good was undoubtedly the prime mover and pushed the Corporation's conservative instincts to the limit. He wanted spontaneity, movement and energy; the BBC wanted something rather more sedate. Good dragged the clapping and jiving studio audience into shot and whipped up a degree of excitement; the BBC countered by balancing rock'n'roll with skiffle, jazz and even classical music, and filling out the show with wholesome magazine items (spotlights on film stars, comedy, sport, general interest, etc.). Such restrictions proved too much for Good and he left for ITV, where he was given the freedom he needed to produce a real rock'n'roll show, OH BOY!. When this was pitched opposite *Six-Five Special* in the schedules, the latter's days were numbered.

Hosting *Six-Five Special* in its first year were Pete Murray, Jo Douglas and boxer-turned-TV-presenter Freddie Mills. Jim Dale took over in the post-Good days. The resident band were Don Lang and His Frantic Five and among the guest performers were the likes of Tommy Steele and His Steelmen, Adam Faith (making his TV debut) and, to illustrate the wide range of musical styles covered, Lonnie Donegan, Laurie London, Humphrey Lyttelton, Johnny Dankworth and Shirley Bassey. *Six-Five Special*'s early popularity resulted in a spin-off film (of the same name) and two stage shows.

64,000 QUESTION, THE
See DOUBLE YOUR MONEY.

$64,000 QUESTION, THE
See DOUBLE YOUR MONEY.

SIXTY MINUTES
See NATIONWIDE.

SKINNER, FRANK
(Chris Collins; 1957–)

Black Country-born comedian and actor who has a masters degree in English and allegedly 'borrowed' his stage name from a member of his dad's dominoes team. He appeared as the stage manager in *Packet of Three* and *Packing Them In* before starring in his own stand-up and chat shows, writing – and playing Frank in – the semi-autobiographical sitcom, *Blue Heaven*, featuring as a team captain in *Gagtag* and co-hosting *Fantasy Football League* and *Baddiel and Skinner Unplanned* with his pal, David Baddiel.

SKIPPY, THE BUSH KANGAROO
Australia (Norfolk International) Children's Adventure. ITV 1967–9

Matt Hammond	Ed Devereaux
Sonny Hammond	Garry Parkhurst
Mark Hammond	Ken James
Jerry King	Tony Bonner
Clarissa 'Clancy' Merrick	Liza Goddard
Dr Anna Steiner	Elke Neidhardt
Dr Alexander Stark	Frank Thring

Writers: **Ross Napier, Ed Devereaux**
Executive Producers: **John McCallum, Bud Austin**
Producers: **Lee Robinson, Dennis Hill**

Heart-warming tales of a boy and his pet kangaroo.

Set in Australia's Waratah National Park, *Skippy, The Bush Kangaroo*, with its catchy sing-along theme song, related the adventures of Sonny Hammond, son of Chief Ranger Matt Hammond and younger brother of Ranger Mark Hammond, and blonde teenager Clancy Merrick (a young Liza Goddard). But the real star of the show was Sonny's intuitive pet kangaroo, Skippy. Once injured and near to death, Skippy was nursed back to health by Sonny and remained ever loyal thereafter, to the point where the bounding marsupial would even warn its master of impending danger with a distinctive 'tut tut'. Also seen were local pilot Jerry King and hordes of colourful Australian mammals. In 1993 the BBC showed *The New Adventures of Skippy*.

SKY
See BSKYB.

SKY AT NIGHT, THE
UK (BBC) Astronomy. BBC 1 1957–

Presenter: **Patrick Moore**

Producers: **Paul Johnstone, Patricia Owtram, Patricia Wood, Pieter Morpurgo, Ian Russell**

Small-screen astronomy.

Hosted for its entire run of over 40 years by Patrick Moore, *The Sky at Night* – the world's longest-running science programme – has charted events in the space world on a monthly basis. Its first programme went out six months before *Sputnik I*, the first man-made satellite, was launched and so it can justifiably claim to have been ahead of the space race. As well as monitoring the progress of various probes and rockets, the fast-talking, ultra-enthusiastic Moore has also guided viewers on an exploration of the heavens, pointing out unusual phenomena and revealing the location of the various constellations. The dramatic theme music has been 'At The Castle Gate', from *Pelléas et Mélisande*, by Sibelius. A children's version of the programme, under the title of *Seeing Stars*, was screened in 1970.

SKYPORT
See SHADOW SQUAD.

SKY'S THE LIMIT, THE
See DOUBLE YOUR MONEY.

SLATER, JOHN
(1916–75)

British character actor, in TV plays during the 1940s but more familiar in series like Z CARS (as DS Tom Stone). He was also a regular partner of the puppet pigs, PINKY AND PERKY, and, for a number of years, was seen promoting Special K cereal (a not unfamiliar activity to Slater, who had hosted the *Slater's Bazaar* admag in the late 1950s).

SLATTERY, TONY
(1959–)

London-born comedian, actor and presenter who made his name in the improvisation show, WHOSE LINE IS IT ANYWAY?, having already appeared in the late-night comedy, *Saturday Stayback*, and the kids' series, *Tx*. He went on to star in the sitcoms, *That's Love* (Tristan Beasley) and *Just a Gigolo* (Nick Brim), co-wrote the children's series, *Behind the Bike Sheds*, hosted the film magazine, *Saturday Night at the Movies*, shared the limelight with Mike McShane in *S&M* and took over from Stephen Fry in the investigative reporter spoof, *This Is David Lander* (renamed *This Is David Harper* to accommodate the change). He has also been much involved in panel games and quizzes, hosting *Ps and Qs*, *Tibs and Fibs*, *The Music Game* and also *Trivial Pursuit* for satellite TV, and appearing regularly on *Just a Minute* and GOING FOR A SONG. Other credits have included BOON and *Screen Two's Drowning in the Shallow End*.

SLINGER'S DAY
See TRIPPER'S DAY.

SMART, RALPH
(1908–)

British producer/writer/director, working largely for ITC on various action romps. He is chiefly remembered for creating and producing THE INVISIBLE MAN and DANGER MAN, but he also contributed in various ways to THE ADVENTURES OF ROBIN HOOD, THE BUCCANEERS, THE ADVENTURES OF SIR LANCELOT, THE CHAMPIONS, THE PROTECTORS and RANDALL AND HOPKIRK (DECEASED).

SMILLIE, CAROL
(1961–)

Glasgow-born former model now TV 'lifestyle' programme presenter, having previously worked as hostess on the game show, WHEEL OF FORTUNE. Her credits have included CHANGING ROOMS, *The Travel Show*, *Hearts of Gold*, *Smillie's People*, HOLIDAY and THE NATIONAL LOTTERY LIVE.

SMITH AND JONES
See ALAS SMITH AND JONES.

SMITH, DELIA
OBE (1941–)

The modern-day queen of TV cooks, thanks to her 30-part *Delia Smith's Cookery Course* in the 1970s. Smith entered television after preparing food for cookery photographs and then writing a column for the *Evening Standard*. Her first programme for the BBC, *Family Fare*, came in 1973. She was also seen on MULTI-COLOURED SWAP SHOP, and other major contributions have included *One Is Fun*, *Delia Smith's Christmas*, *Delia Smith's Summer Collection*, *Delia Smith's Winter Collection* and *Delia's How to Cook*. The books that have accompanied her series have sold in vast quantities.

SMITH, JACLYN
(1947–)

American actress who played agent Kelly Garrett throughout CHARLIE'S ANGELS' five-year run (even though her partners came and went). Previously, Smith had been seen as a guest in series as varied as McCLOUD and THE PARTRIDGE FAMILY. She later took to TV movies, playing, among other characters, Jackie Kennedy in *Jacqueline Bouvier Kennedy* in 1981 and MYSTERY MOVIE detective *Christine Cromwell* in 1989.

SMITH, JULIA
(?–1997)

British drama producer, script editor and director, chiefly associated with EASTENDERS, which she co-created with Tony Holland, and the much-vaunted but ultimately short-lived ELDORADO. Smith had previously produced ANGELS and THE DISTRICT NURSE (also as creator) and had contributed to BBC programmes from the 1960s, including AN AGE OF KINGS, DOCTOR WHO, *Jury Room*, DR FINLAY'S CASEBOOK, THE NEWCOMERS, *The Railway Children* and Z CARS.

He also adapted the novelist's work for *Frederick Forsyth Presents*.

SMITH, LIZ
(1925–)

English actress, arriving on television in the 1970s after bringing up her children. She has appeared in many single dramas and series (increasingly as grandmothers), with the best-remembered roles being Mrs Brandon in I DIDN'T KNOW YOU CARED, Bette in 2 POINT 4 CHILDREN, Letitia Cropley in THE VICAR OF DIBLEY and Nana in THE ROYLE FAMILY. Other credits have included BOOTSIE AND SNUDGE, THE SWEENEY, NO – HONESTLY, CROWN COURT, IN LOVING MEMORY, *Now and Then*, EMMERDALE FARM, THE LIFE AND LOVES OF A SHE DEVIL, CLUEDO, *King and Castle*, *Bust*, THE BILL, *Valentine Park*, LOVEJOY, EL C.I.D., MAKING OUT, CASUALTY, *The Young Indiana Jones Chronicles*, BOTTOM, *Crapston Villas* (voice), KARAOKE (Mrs Baglin), *Oliver Twist* (Sally), *Alice in Wonderland* (Miss Lory), *Donovan Quick* (Gran), *A Christmas Carol* (Joyce) and the kids' comedy, *Pirates*.

SMITH, MEL
(1952–)

British comedian, actor and director, first coming to prominence as a member of the NOT THE NINE O'CLOCK NEWS team in 1979, in which he forged a partnership with Griff Rhys Jones (see Jones's entry for other joint credits). Smith was also seen with comedian Bob Goody in a children's series, *Smith and Goody*, as ruthless property-developer Tom Craig in the drama, *Muck and Brass*, worryguts Colin Watkins in COLIN'S SANDWICH, and Stephen Milner in *Milner*. He has also guested in THE YOUNG ONES and MINDER.

SMITH, MIKE
(1955–)

Blond-haired British presenter, a former Capital Radio and Radio 1 disc jockey. His credits have included BREAKFAST TIME, THE LATE, LATE BREAKFAST SHOW (with Noel Edmonds) and *Trick or Treat* (with Julian Clary). Smith has also hosted *Transit*, TOP OF THE POPS and the celebrity quiz, *That's Showbusiness*. He once sat in for Terry Wogan on his thrice-weekly chat show and has often been called up to present special programmes on motor fairs, charity events, medical matters, etc. He is married to presenter Sarah Greene, with whom he fronted *The Exchange* in 1995.

SMITH, MURRAY
(1940–)

Former paratrooper turned scriptwriter and novelist. Among Smith's major TV successes have been episodes of MINDER, THE SWEENEY and HAMMER HOUSE OF HORROR. Smith was the major writer on STRANGERS and BULMAN, then moved on to create THE PARADISE CLUB.

SMITH, RAY
(1936–91)

Welsh actor, much seen on TV from the 1960s. Coming from mining stock himself, it seemed appropriate that he appeared in the drama serial, SAM (as collier George Barrowclough), and played punch-drunk boxer Dai Bando in the BBC's 1976 adaptation of *How Green Was My Valley*. As DI Firbank, Smith was partner to Frank Marker in PUBLIC EYE, and he was also seen as Albert Mundy in WE'LL MEET AGAIN and Sir Bert in the sitcom, *Struggle*, although it is as the bawling boss of DEMPSEY AND MAKEPEACE, Chief Supt. Gordon Spikings, that he will be best remembered. His last screen appearance came in BBC 2's version of *The Old Devils*. Smith's career also took in series like Z CARS, A FAMILY AT WAR, CALLAN, GIDEON'S WAY, *Flying Lady* and such dramas as *Rogue Male*, *The Sailor's Return* and *Masada*.

SNOW, JON
(Jonathan Snow; 1947–)

Award-winning, Sussex-born newscaster, a former IRN/LBC radio news reporter who joined ITN in 1976. He became its Washington correspondent in 1983 and was later its diplomatic correspondent, before taking over as anchor for *Channel 4 News* on the departure of Peter Sissons in 1989. He is the cousin of fellow journalist Peter Snow.

SNOW, PETER
(1938–)

Dublin-born journalist and presenter, working for many years on NEWSNIGHT and the BBC's election coverages (complete with 'swingometer') and then moving on to TOMORROW'S WORLD in 1997. While preparing a report for the science show, he was almost killed in a light aircraft crash in the USA. Snow was formerly a reporter and newscaster for ITN, which he joined in 1962. He is the cousin of newscaster Jon Snow.

SO HAUNT ME
UK (Cinema Verity) Situation Comedy. BBC 1 1992–4

Yetta Feldman	**Miriam Karlin**
Sally Rokeby	**Tessa Peake-Jones**
Pete Rokeby	**George Costigan**
Tammy Rokeby	**Laura Simmons**
	Laura Howard
David Rokeby	**Jeremy Green**
Mr Bloom	**David Graham**
Carole Dawlish	**Julia Deakin**

Creator/Writer: **Paul A. Mendelson**
Producers: **Caroline Gold, Sharon Bloom**

A family discover their new home is haunted by a Jewish ghost.

When Pete Rokeby threw in his job as an advertising executive to concentrate on full-time writing, he and his family aimed to keep their overheads low by moving house, from an upmarket neighbourhood to a dowdy street. Their new home, they quickly discovered, was prone to icy blasts, bumps in the night and, strangely, a lingering smell of chicken soup – all down to the ghost of one-time resident Yetta Feldman. Following her death (choking on a chicken bone), Yetta's spirit had driven away everyone who had taken over her home, but the Rokebys proved to be different. Gradually making herself visible to them one by one, Yetta became a nagging grandmother to kids Tammy and David, and an annoying cuckoo to Pete and his beleaguered wife, Sally. All the same, the family sort of adopted the old lady and helped find her long-lost daughter ('Carole, with an E'). Yetta's Jewish mothering instincts were brought to the fore again later, when Sally gave birth to a new baby. Also seen was Mr Bloom, the Rokebys' melancholy neighbour.

Creator Paul A. Mendelson drew partly on autobiographical experiences when working on this comedy. He, too, was once in advertising and left to pursue a writing career. With hits like MAY TO DECEMBER and *So Haunt Me*, he was clearly more successful than Pete Rokeby.

SOAP

US (Witt-Thomas-Harris) Situation Comedy. ITV 1978–82

Jessica Tate	**Katherine Helmond**
Chester Tate	**Robert Mandan**
Corrine Tate	**Diana Canova**
Eunice Tate	**Jennifer Salt**
Billy Tate	**Jimmy Baio**
Benson Dubois	**Robert Guillaume**
Grandpa Tate ('The Major')	**Arthur Peterson**
Mary Dallas Campbell	**Cathryn Damon**
Burt Campbell	**Richard Mulligan**
Jodie Dallas	**Billy Crystal**
Danny Dallas	**Ted Wass**
The Godfather	**Richard Libertini**
Claire	**Kathryn Reynolds**
Peter Campbell	**Robert Urich**
Chuck Campbell	**Jay Johnson**
Dennis Phillips	**Bob Seagren**
Father Timothy Flotsky	**Sal Viscuso**
Carol David	**Rebecca Balding**
Elaine Lefkowitz	**Dinah Manoff**
Dutch	**Donnelly Rhodes**
Sally	**Caroline McWilliams**
Det. Donahue	**John Byner**
Polly Dawson	**Lynne Moody**
Saunders	**Roscoe Lee Browne**
Carlos 'El Puerco' Valdez	**Gregory Sierra**
Announcer	**Rod Roddy**

Creator/Writer/Producer: **Susan Harris**
Executive Producers: **Tony Thomas, Paul Junger Witt**

Parody of US daytime soap opera, featuring two related families.

The Campbells and the Tates lived in the town of Dunn's River, Connecticut. Jessica Tate and Mary Campbell were sisters but, otherwise, the families had little in common, for the Tates were wealthy and lived in a mansion and the Campbells were working class and lived on the other side of town. Their day-to-day lives were depicted in serial form, just like an American soap opera, but the events were always hugely exaggerated.

These families certainly had their problems. Each member had a hang-up of some kind. Jessica was married to Chester Tate, a wealthy but untrustworthy stockbroker, and they had three troublesome children. Corrine was their flirtatious daughter, Eunice was involved with a married senator, and then there was their 14-year-old adolescent brat, Billy. The household was completed by Jessica's father, the Major, whose mind was still in World War II. They were all looked after by an obnoxious black manservant, Benson, who refused to cook anything he disliked himself. When he left to star in his own spin-off series, *Benson*, he was replaced by a new butler, Saunders.

Mary lived with her impotent second husband, Burt, a nervous wreck who struggled to control his wayward stepsons, Jodie, a transvestite, and delinquent Danny, who found himself involved with the Mob. Burt also had two sons from his previous marriage: Chuck, who thought his ventriloquist dummy, Bob, was real, and Peter, an amorous tennis coach who was murdered in the shower.

Even before it reached the screens, *Soap* invited a torrent of criticism by pre-publicizing its open treatment of taboo issues, especially extra-marital sex, homosexuality, racism, religion and terminal illness. But, when the producers promised to tone things down a little, and the first episodes were actually seen in all their overplayed glory, criticism subsided. All the same, *Soap*'s storylines still meandered between such risqué topics as divorce, voyeurism, irresponsible affairs, illegitimate children and cold-blooded murders. It also touched on cloning, abduction by aliens, and even the seduction of a priest and the exorcism of a baby.

SOAP OPERA

The tag given to open-ended, long-running, mainly domestic dramas involving a stable cast of characters, usually of middle- or working-class background. Each episode generally involves a number of continuous storylines at various stages of development.

The term derives from 1930s American radio, when soap and detergent companies used to sponsor the 15-minute radio series which ran daily to fill the daytime schedules. In these dramas, everyday problems assumed crisis proportions and dialogue easily outstripped action. With the arrival of television as a mass medium in the 1950s, the format transferred to the screen, although programmes now ran for 30 minutes. The soap manufacturers remained heavily involved. One company, Procter & Gamble, even set up a TV studio to produce their own.

Britain's first attempt at TV soap opera was THE GROVE FAMILY, on BBC in 1954. Of course, the detergent makers had no involvement and, unlike many of their successors, the Groves didn't last long – a mere three years. With the birth of commercial television in 1955, Britain was treated to its first daily soap, *Sixpenny Corner*, the everyday story of a garage, run by Bill and Sally Norton (Howard Pays and Patricia Dainton) in a new town called Springwood. EMERGENCY – WARD 10 added a medical dimension in 1957, but it wasn't until 1960 that the soap concept really took off in the UK, with the arrival of CORONATION STREET. Even then, the *Street* – like *The Grove Family* and *Ward 10* screened only twice a week – was not a soap in the truest sense. Nearer was CROSS-ROADS, transmitted five days a week from 1964, until the IBA eventually cut it back to three.

The mundane nature of the soap opera has been pushed aside since the late 1970s. The arrival of DALLAS, DYNASTY and other glitzy offerings, shot like small feature films, gave rise to the 'supersoap', where the action took place on quite another plane from the down-to-earth world of the original soaps. British versions have also changed their spots. BROOKSIDE and EASTENDERS have introduced a new and vigorous reality, and issues like abortion, rape, drug abuse and gruesome murder now pervade many such series. Exceptions are the tame melodramas from Australia (such as NEIGHBOURS and HOME AND AWAY), that have filled UK screens in the afternoons.

SOFTLY, SOFTLY/SOFTLY, SOFTLY – TASK FORCE

UK (BBC) Police Drama. BBC 1 1966–76

Det. Chief Supt. Charlie Barlow	Stratford Johns
DCI/Det. Supt./Det. Chief Supt. John Watt	Frank Windsor
DS/DI/DCI 'Harry' Hawkins	Norman Bowler
PC Henry Snow	Terence Rigby
DC 'Reg' Dwyer	Gilbert Wynne
ACC Bill Calderwood	John Welsh
PC Greenly	Cavan Kendall
PC Tanner	David Quilter
DC/Insp. Gwyn Lewis	Garfield Morgan
Mr Blackitt	Robert Keegan
DC Matthew Stone	Alexis Kanner
DC Box	Dan Meaden
Sgt/DS Evans	David Lloyd Meredith
DC Digby	Gavin Campbell
Chief Constable Cullen	Walter Gotell
ACC Austin Gilbert	John Barron
DC Morgan	Howell Evans
Policewoman/DS Allin	Peggy Sinclair
Chief Constable Calderwood	John Welsh
DI Jim Cook	Philip Brack
Policewoman/DC Donald	Susan Tebbs
Sgt Jackson	David Allister
PC Ted Drake	Brian Hall
Policewoman/DC Forest	Julie Hallam
Policewoman/DS Green	Heather Stoney

PC Knowles	Martin C. Thurley
Det. Supt. Adler	John Franklyn-Robbins
PC Nesbitt	Grahame Mallard
DS Stirling	Warren Clarke
PC Dodds	Nigel Humphreys
PC Perry	Malcolm Rennie
PC Lincoln	Peter Clough
DS Grant	Peter Childs
PC Pearson	John Flanagan

Creator: **Elwyn Jones**
Producers: **David E. Rose, Leonard Lewis, Geraint Morris**

The further cases of detectives Barlow and Watt.

One of the most successful spin-offs ever, *Softly, Softly* ran for ten years in parallel with Z CARS, its mother series. It took up the story of the 'nasty and nice' double act of Barlow and Watt, after they left Newtown and headed south to the fictional region of Wyvern (somewhere near Bristol). Promoted to the ranks of detective chief superintendent and detective chief inspector respectively, one of the first people they encountered was their retired former desk sergeant, Blackitt (now a newsagent), and his dog, Pandy. Among their new colleagues were the jovial Welshman, Sgt Evans, miserable dog-handler PC Henry Snow (and his most famous charge, Inky) and a local detective inspector, Harry Hawkins. The show's title was derived from the adage 'Softly, softly, catchee monkey'.

In 1969 *Softly, Softly* became the more cumbersome *Softly, Softly – Task Force* and saw Barlow and Watt working for Thamesford Constabulary's CID Task Force. In 1969 Barlow went his own way, branching out into BARLOW AT LARGE and *Barlow*. He was reunited with Watt, however, for a novel re-investigation of the Jack the Ripper case in 1973 and a subsequent series, SECOND VERDICT, in 1976, which looked at other such mysteries.

SOLDIER, SOLDIER

UK (Central) Drama. ITV 1991–7

Major Tom Cadman	David Haig
Laura Cadman	Cathryn Harrison
L/Cpl./Cpl./Sgt Paddy Garvey	Jerome Flynn
Cpl./Sgt Nancy Thorpe/Garvey RMP	Holly Aird
CSM Chick Henwood	Sean Baker
Colour Sgt Ian Anderson	Robert Glenister
Cpl./Sgt Tony Wilton	Gary Love
Lt. Nick Pasco	Peter Wingfield
Fusilier/Lance Cpl. Dave Tucker	Robson Green
Lt. Col. Dan Fortune	Miles Anderson
Carol Anderson	Melanie Kilburn
Juliet Grant	Susan Franklyn
Joy Wilton	Annabelle Apsion
Donna Tucker	Rosie Rowell
2nd Lt./Lt./Capt. Kate Butler	Lesley Vickerage
Sgt Sally Hawkins	Debra Beaumont
Sheena Bowles	Lena Headey
Sgt Dennis Ryan	Colin Salmon
Major Bob Cochrane	Simon Donald
Fusilier 'Midnight' Rawlins	Mo Sesay

Fusilier Jimmy Monroe .... **Ian Dunn**
Rachel Elliot/Fortune .... **Lesley Manville**
Padre Simon Armstrong .... **Richard Hampton**
2nd Lt. Alex Pereira .... **Angus MacFadyen**
Lt. Col. Mark Osbourne .... **Patrick Drury**
Capt./Major Kieran Voce .... **Dorian Healy**
CSM/Lt. Michael Stubbs .... **Rob Spendlove**
Marsha Stubbs .... **Denise Welch**
Fusilier Luke Roberts .... **Akim Mogaji**
Bernie Roberts .... **Rakie Ayola**
Lt. Col. Nicolas Hammond .... **Robert Gwilym**
Major Tim Radley .... **Adrian Rawlins**
Sandra Radley .... **Suzanne Burden**
Lt. Col. Ian Jennings .... **John Bowe**
Isabelle Jennings .... **Gabrielle Reidy**
Fusilier Eddie Nelson .... **Paterson Joseph**
Tracy Whitwell .... **Kelly Deeley**
Major James McCudden .... **John McGlynn**
Lt./Capt. Jeremy Forsythe .... **Ben Nealon**
Lilian Malanjie/Forsythe .... **Nthati Moshesh**
Fusilier/Sgt Joe Farrell .... **David Groves**
Colette Daly .... **Angela Clarke**
Cpl. William Markham .... **Razaaq Adoti**
Fusilier Andy Butcher .... **Danny Cunningham**
L/Cpl. Steve Evans .... **Shaun Dingwall**
Capt. Sadie Williams .... **Sophie Dix**
Sgt Brad Connor .... **Richard Dillane**
Major Rory Taylor .... **Dougray Scott**
Lt. Col. Paul Phillips .... **Duncan Bell**
Fusilier Mel Briggs .... **Simon Sherlock**
Deborah Osbourne/Briggs .... **Laura Howard**
Cpl. Mark Hobbs .... **Ian Curtis**
Cate Hobbs .... **Kate Ashfield**
Pte. Stacey Grey/Butcher .... **Kate O'Malley**
Sgt Chris McCleod .... **Jonathan Guy Lewis**
Sgt Angela McCleod .... **Fiona Bell**
Major Tim Forrester .... **James Callis**
2nd Lt. Samantha Sheridan .... **Biddy Hodson**
Lt. Col. Mike Eastwood .... **Philip Bowen**
Dr Sarah Eastwood .... **Alison Skilbeck**
Fusilier Jacko Barton .... **Thomas Craig**
Fusilier Tony Rossi .... **Chris Gascoyne**
Lt. Col. Philip Drysdale .... **James Cosmo**
Major Jessica Bailey .... **Lucy Cohu**
CSM Alan Fitzpatrick .... **Conor Mullen**
Karen Fitzpatrick .... **Joanna Phillips-Lane**
Julie Oldroyd .... **Michelle Butterly**

Creator: **Lucy Gannon**
Producers: **Chris Kelly, Christopher Neame, Ann Tricklebank**

The rigours of an army career and its effect on personal lives.

Soldier, Soldier focused on the men and women of the King's Own Fusiliers Infantry Regiment as they toured the world on active and inactive duty. The first episode saw them return to their Midlands base from a six-month tour of duty in Northern Ireland. Later series followed them to Hong Kong, New Zealand, Germany, Bosnia, Cyprus, Australia and Africa, as well as guard duty at the royal palaces in the UK. In addition to the tough routine of army life, the series examined the cama-

raderie of the force and witnessed the stresses and strains such an existence placed on the personal lives of soldiers and their families. New additions to the battalion arrived every series as some members left or were tragically killed. Among the most memorable characters were Paddy Garvey, his military policewoman girlfriend, Nancy Thorpe, his hapless mate, Dave Tucker and his unfaithful wife, Donna, plus the ill-fated Tony Wilton.

SOLO
UK (BBC) Situation Comedy. BBC 1 1981–2

Gemma Palmer .... **Felicity Kendal**
Danny .... **Stephen Moore**
Mrs Palmer .... **Elspet Gray**
Gloria .... **Susan Bishop**
Sebastian .... **Michael Howe**

Creator/Writer: **Carla Lane**
Producer: **Gareth Gwenlan**

A 30-year-old woman kicks out her boyfriend, chucks in her job and goes it alone.

Discovering that her live-in boyfriend, Danny, had been having an affair with her best friend, Gloria, Gemma Palmer decided to reassert her independence. She turfed Danny out of her flat and her life, broke off relations with Gloria and, for good measure, resigned from her job. Going solo was not without its problems, however, but thankfully Gemma's supportive mum was usually at hand in times of crisis. In the second series, Danny had left the scene for good and Gemma had gained a new platonic friend, Sebastian.

SOME MOTHERS DO 'AVE 'EM
UK (BBC) Situation Comedy. BBC 1 1973–5; 1978

Frank Spencer .... **Michael Crawford**
Betty Spencer .... **Michele Dotrice**
Mr Lewis .... **Glynn Edwards**

Writer: **Raymond Allen**
Producer: **Michael Mills, Sydney Lotterby**

A kind-hearted but naïve simpleton courts disaster at every turn.

Frank Spencer was an accident waiting to happen. Sporting a knitted tank-top, unfashionable long mac and a beret, wherever he went he brought chaos and confusion. DIY jobs resulted in the systematic destruction of his house while, at work (whenever he found any), machinery exploded and his bosses despaired. And yet poor Frank, with his infantile voice, unfortunate turn of phrase, expressive shoulder-twitches and hurt looks, always tried hard and meant well. He was gravely offended by criticism and deeply shocked at everything untoward. At his side through thick and thin were his over-loyal wife, Betty, and baby daughter, Jessica. Mr Lewis, the irascible neighbour seen in the last series, was just one of Frank's many adversaries.

Some Mothers Do 'Ave 'Em made a star out of Michael

Crawford, but the actor worked hard for his success. His characterization was so precise that it kept impressionists in gags for years after. He also chipped in with occasional ad-libs, plotted the stories for some episodes and even performed many of his own stunts that included driving a car halfway over a cliff, and narrowly escaping a collapsing chimney stack. Series creator Raymond Allen was working as a cinema cleaner on the Isle of Wight when he began writing the scripts.

SOMERVILLE, GERALDINE

Red-haired, Irish-born actress best recalled as 'Panhandle' in CRACKER. Her other credits have included the roles of Bridget Millican in CATHERINE COOKSON's *The Black Velvet Gown*, Deborah Bennett in *Heaven on Earth*, Lady Emily in ARISTOCRATS and Val McArdale in *Daylight Robbery*, as well as parts in CASUALTY, AGATHA CHRISTIE'S POIROT, *Romeo and Juliet* and *Performance*'s *The Deep Blue Sea* (Ann Welch) and *After Miss Julie* (title role).

SOMERVILLE, JULIA
(1947–)

British journalist and news presenter, who joined the BBC as a sub-editor in 1973 after working on magazines, and who went on to become labour affairs correspondent and then, from 1984, to anchor *The Nine O'Clock News*. She was poached by ITN in 1987, for whom she was one of the mainstays of *News at Ten*. She still presents other bulletins and has also hosted the current affairs series, *3D*.

SONGS OF PRAISE
UK (BBC) Religion. BBC 1 1961–

Television's longest-running religious programme.

A well-rehearsed combination of hymns, prayers, blessings and inspirational interviews, *Songs of Praise* has been an integral part of Sunday evenings for some 40 years. A different venue has hosted proceedings each week and efforts have been made to reflect all denominations and all parts of the UK (and sometimes overseas). The first transmission came from Tabernacle Baptist Chapel in Cardiff.

The programme's presenters have been many and diverse. In recent years they have included Cliff Michelmore, Pam Rhodes, Debbie Thrower, Roger Royle, Sally Magnusson, Gloria Hunniford, Alan Titchmarsh, Hugh Scully, Steve Chalke, Harry Secombe, Deborah McAndrew, Diane Louise Jordan and Stephanie Hughes, with Cliff Richard, Russell Harty, Jimmy Savile and even Eddie Waring listed among one-time hosts.

SOOTY
See CORBETT, HARRY.

SORRY!
UK (BBC) Situation Comedy. BBC 1 1981–2; 1985–8

Timothy Lumsden	**Ronnie Corbett**
Mrs Phyllis Lumsden	**Barbara Lott**
Mr Sidney Lumsden	**William Moore**
Muriel	**Marguerite Hardiman**
Kevin	**Derek Fuke**
Frank	**Roy Holder**
Freddie	**Sheila Fearn**
Chris	**Chris Breeze**
Jennifer	**Wendy Allnutt**
Pippa	**Bridget Brice**

Writers: **Ian Davidson, Peter Vincent**
Producer: **David Askey**

A 40-year-old librarian can't break free from his overpowering mother.

Short, bespectacled, moped-riding bachelor Timothy Lumsden lived at home in Oxfordshire with his domineering, blue-rinsed mother and his hen-pecked, timid father (if his father hadn't been banished to the shed). Although his sister, Muriel, had married and moved away, Timothy had never had the courage to do so, largely because his mother refused to let him, not believing he had grown up. She still cajoled him with kiddy talk and threatened him with all manner of kiddy treats and punishments. As a result, Timothy was bashful, rather apologetic (hence the programme title) and always a little uncertain in the company of females. He enjoyed a few pints down at the pub with his friend, Frank, and was well placed in the library where he worked, but, whenever the prospect of his leaving the nest materialized, his mother always put her foot down and ensured he remained firmly tied to her apronstrings.

Timothy certainly did not live at home for the comforts: Mrs Lumsden's cooking was something to avoid, with everything from starters to desserts likely to be curried. Nor was privacy a possibility. Yet it was soon clear that Timothy was as wary of leaving home as his mother was determined to keep him there. And it was this stop-go dash for independence which ran at the heart of the series. *Sorry!* was not entirely dissimilar to an earlier Ronnie Corbett vehicle, NOW LOOK HERE . . .

SOUL, DAVID
(David Solberg; 1943–)

Blond American actor/singer, once billed as the Mystery Singer on *The Merv Griffin Show* in the USA, for which he donned a hood. Moving into acting, Soul secured guest parts in various series (including STAR TREK) and minor roles in US shows like *Here Come the Brides* and *Owen Marshall, Counselor At Law*, before getting his big break with the all-action police series, STARSKY AND HUTCH, in 1975. As Detective Ken 'Hutch' Hutchinson, Soul became an international star, and this led to another foray into the music world, resulting in two number one hits in the UK ('Don't Give Up On Us' and 'Silver Lady'). He co-hosted the magazine show, *Six Fifty-Five Special* (with Sally James), in 1982 and played Rick Blaine in a TV remake of *Casablanca* a year later. He has since taken roles in the series, *The Yellow Rose* and *Unsub*, and has been seen in many TV movies.

SOUTH BANK SHOW, THE
UK (LWT) Arts. ITV 1978–

Presenter/Editor: **Melvyn Bragg**

Acclaimed Sunday-night arts programme.

The successor to AQUARIUS, *The South Bank Show* picked up where the former left off, thoughtfully and unhurriedly covering all corners of the arts world, from the classical elements through to pop culture. Conducted throughout by Melvyn Bragg, the programme has combined in-depth interviews with studio performances and film profiles, to great effect. The 2000 series, for instance, included features on subjects as varied as Shakespeare, Sam Mendes, Michael Douglas and the Millennium Dome. The theme music has been Julian Lloyd-Webber's *Variations*.

SOUTH PARK
US (Comedy Central) Animation. Channel 4 1998–

Voices:

Stan Marsh	**Trey Parker**
Kyle Broslofski	**Matt Stone**
Eric Cartman	**Trey Parker**
Kenny McCormick	**Matt Stone**
Chef	**Isaac Hayes**
Mr Hanky	**Trey Parker**
Mr Garrison	**Trey Parker**

Creators: **Trey Parker, Matt Stone**
Executive Producers: **Trey Parker, Matt Stone, Anne Garefino, Deborah Liebling**

Crude (in more than one sense) animation, featuring the pupils of a Colorado school.

A new era in adult animation arrived with *South Park*. It took the provocative nature of THE SIMPSONS and advanced it a mile or two with its depiction of a bunch of vulgar kids (round-headed, quirky figures) who attended school in a snow-bound, little American town called South Park. The main protagonists were level-headed Stan, Jewish Kyle, fat bully Cartman and Kenny – a shy, parka-wearing character that was fated to die in every episode (to the catchphrase cry: 'Oh my God, they killed Kenny!'), usually by the most grotesque methods. Also seen were Mr Hanky (a turd), teacher Mr Garrison (who toyed with a hand puppet), and the school's Chef (bass-voiced by soulster Isaac Hayes). Most of the dialogue and humour was focused on bodily functions and sex, and bad language was the norm. Guest stars queued up to provide their voices, including Elton John, Meatloaf,

Jennifer Aniston and George Clooney, who barked for a gay dog.

In the UK, the series debuted on Sky One before being picked up for terrestrial airing by Channel 4. A feature film, *South Park: Bigger, Longer, Uncut*, was released in 1999.

SOUTH RIDING
UK (Yorkshire) Drama. ITV 1974

Sarah Burton	**Dorothy Tutin**
Robert Carne	**Nigel Davenport**
Mrs Beddows	**Hermione Baddeley**

Writer: **Stan Barstow**
Producer: **James Ormerod**

A schoolteacher finds the going tough in the poverty-stricken 1930s.

This 13-part adaptation of Winifred Holtby's novel was set in 1932, in the fictitious South Riding of Yorkshire. It told of a progressive schoolmistress, Sarah Burton (head of Kipling Girls High School), who found her plans for her pupils hindered by injustices in society. Also prominent were Alderman Mrs Beddows and Councillor Robert Carne. The series was repeated on Channel 4 in 1987.

SOUTHERN TELEVISION

Southern was the ITV contractor for the South of England from 30 August 1958 until 31 December 1981, when its franchise was taken over by TVS. There was, however, considerable surprise, if not shock and fury, at the decision of the IBA to terminate Southern's licence, as the company had a good record in local programming and was also a more than useful contributor to the ITV network. Its national offerings included drama series like WINSTON CHURCHILL – THE WILDERNESS YEARS and the quiz show, WHEEL OF FORTUNE, but it was through children's programmes that Southern gained particular respect. *Freewheelers*, *Bright's Boffins*, *The Saturday Banana*, *Runaround*, HOW!, *Little Big Time* and WORZEL GUMMIDGE were just some of the company's many contributions to children's viewing. In addition to its programming record, Southern had never been formally criticized by the IBA, except for some concern over the make-up of the company (62.5 per cent was owned jointly by Associated Newspapers Group and D. C. Thomson), and its perceived weak coverage in certain parts of Kent. Southern believed the latter wasn't entirely their problem since the IBA had ordered key transmitters to broadcast signals from London instead of Southern's. It was interesting to note that when the new franchise was awarded to TVS, the official name of the transmission area was changed from South of England to South and South-East of England (thereby, perhaps, upholding Southern's argument).

SPACE

US (Dick Berg/Stonehenge/Paramount) Science Fiction.
ITV 1987

Norman Grant	James Garner
Elinor Grant	Susan Anspach
John Pope	Harry Hamlin
Penny Hardesty/Pope	Blair Brown
Stanley Mott	Bruce Dern
Rachel Mott	Melinda Dillon
Martin Scorcella/Leopold Strabismus	David Dukes
Dieter Kolff	Michael York
Liesl Kolff	Barbara Sukowa
Randy Claggett	Beau Bridges
Debbie Dee Claggett	Stephanie Faracy
Senator Glancey	Martin Balsam
Finnerty	James Sutorius
Tucker Thomas	G. D. Spradlin
Cindy Rhee	Maggie Han
Funkhauser	Wolf Kahler
Marcia Grant	Jennifer Runyon
Skip Morgan	David Spielberg
Paul Stidham	Ralph Bellamy

Writers: **Dick Berg, Stirling Silliphant**
Executive Producer: **Dick Berg**
Producer: **Martin Manulis**

Dramatization of the race into space.

This 13-hour mini-series told the story of America's space programme, using the lives of fictional characters to reveal the real stresses and strains brought about by the space effort. Picking up from the end of World War II, it focused on the battle between the Americans and the Russians for Nazi Germany's top rocket specialists. It continued through US political wrangles in the 1950s to the foundation of NASA and its subsequent space race successes, including the spectacular trips to the moon. Its lead characters were naval hero-turned-senator Norman Grant, his alcoholic wife, Elinor, her devious lover Leopold Strabismus (a TV evangelist whose real name was Martin Scorcella), and Penny Pope, Norman's mistress who was an ambitious lawyer with the Senate Space Committee. Also prominent were muck-raking reporter Cindy Rhee, German rocket scientist Dieter Kolff and dedicated astrophysicist Stanley Mott, with former Korean War pilots John Pope (Penny's husband) and Randy Claggett taking the honours as the astronauts on the lunar project. The series was based on James A. Michener's novel of the same title and cost a staggering £35 million to make. Sadly, its audience figures never justified this expense.

SPACE: 1999

UK (ITC/RAI/Gerry Anderson/Group Three) Science
Fiction. ITV 1975–7

Commander John Koenig	Martin Landau
Dr Helena Russell	Barbara Bain
Prof. Victor Bergman	Barry Morse
Capt. Alan Carter	Nick Tate
First Officer Tony Verdeschi	Tony Anholt
Maya	Catherine Schell
Sandra Benes	Zienia Merton
Yasko	Yasuko Nagazumi
Paul Morrow	Prentis Hancock
David Kano	Clifton Jones
Dr Bob Mathias	Anton Phillips
Moonbase computer	Barbara Kelly (*voice only*)

Creators: **Gerry Anderson, Sylvia Anderson**
Executive Producer: **Gerry Anderson**
Producers: **Sylvia Anderson, Fred Freiberger**

A nuclear waste dump on the moon explodes and the inhabitants of a moonbase are hurled out into space.

Space: 1999 was conceived as a kind of British STAR TREK by puppet experts Gerry and Sylvia Anderson. It focused on the adventures of the crew of Moonbase Alpha (or Alphans, as they became known) who found themselves stranded in space. On 13 September 1999, a nuclear waste depository on the dark side of the moon exploded and jettisoned the moon, its space research station and all 311 inhabitants out, through a black hole, into deepest space. As they whizzed through the galaxies, desperately trying to find a new home before their supplies ran out, the reluctant travellers encountered all manner of *Star Trek*-like aliens. One such alien, Maya, who possessed the ability to turn herself into plants or animals and who was the last survivor of the planet Psychon, joined the crew and became the girlfriend of Tony Verdeschi, the first officer.

Stars of the show were ex-MISSION: IMPOSSIBLE heroes, husband and wife Martin Landau and Barbara Bain. Here, Landau played the grim moonbase commander who had just taken up his post when the explosion occurred. Bain was the chief physician. Other prominent characters were the chief pilot, Alan Carter, and Professor Victor Bergman, the brains behind the moonbase (written out after the first series).

Space: 1999 was made in association with Italy's RAI organization and was widely acclaimed for its advanced special effects, masterminded by expert Brian Johnson. Years of detailed model-making had taught the Andersons how to stage quite spectacular space scenes, but other aspects of the production were roundly criticized, from the wooden acting to the somewhat far-fetched concept. Not even the arrival of former *Star Trek* producer Fred Freiberger managed to save the day, and the series ended without a proper conclusion.

SPACE PATROL

UK (National Interest/Wonderama) Children's Science
Fiction. ITV 1963–4

Voices:

Capt. Larry Dart	Dick Vosburgh
Husky	Ronnie Stevens
Slim	Ronnie Stevens
Col. Raeburn	Murray Kash

Prof. Haggerty	**Ronnie Stevens**
Marla	**Libby Morris**
Cassiopea	**Libby Morris**
Gabblerdictum	**Libby Morris**

Creator/Writer: **Roberta Leigh**
Producers: **Roberta Leigh, Arthur Provis**

A tri-planetary space force protects the solar system.

In the year 2100, Space Patrol was the active unit of the United Galactic Organization, a peace-keeping body formed by the natives of Earth, Mars and Venus. This series featured the exploits of its lead ship, *Galasphere 347*, and its crew of Earthman Captain Larry Dart, the Martian Husky and the Venusian Slim. Back at base, Colonel Raeburn gave the orders, assisted by his Venusian secretary, Marla. Professor Haggerty was the unit's somewhat erratic scientific genius, and Cassiopea his daughter. Also seen was the Gabblerdictum, a kind of Martian parrot.

Space Patrol reached the screen just as Gerry Anderson's futuristic adventures were beginning to take off, with SUPERCAR and FIREBALL XL5 already on the air. It was scripted by Anderson's former colleague, Roberta Leigh.

SPALL, TIMOTHY
OBE (1957–)

London-born actor who is still remembered as boring Barry in AUF WIEDERSEHEN, PET, even though he has taken countless other roles since. In 1993 he donned the mantle of would-be wide-boy Frank Stubbs in FRANK STUBBS PROMOTES and, the next year, was both slovenly Kevin Costello in OUTSIDE EDGE and anarchic Phil Bachelor in *Nice Day at the Office*. Spall's other credits have included works as diverse as *The Cherry Orchard*, *Great Writers*, BOON, *Tracey Ullman: A Class Act*, the *Performance* presentations *Nona* (Chico) and *Roots* (Jimmy Beales), *Our Mutual Friend* (Mr Venus), the single comedy, *Neville's Island* (Gordon), *Shooting the Past* (Oswald Bates), MURDER MOST HORRID, *The Thing about Vince . . .* (Vince Skinner), and the travelogue, *African Footsteps*.

SPECIAL

An individual, usually celebratory (for holidays, etc.), episode of a long-running series, or a one-off variety show.

SPECIAL BRANCH
UK (Thames/Euston Films) Police Drama. ITV 1969–70; 1973–4

DI Jordan	**Derren Nesbitt**
Supt. Eden	**Wensley Pithey**
Det. Supt. Inman	**Fulton Mackay**
DCI Alan Craven	**George Sewell**
DCI Tom Haggerty	**Patrick Mower**

DS North	**Roger Rowland**
Commander Nicols	**Richard Butler**
Commander Fletcher	**Frederick Jaeger**
Strand	**Paul Eddington**

Executive Producers: **Lloyd Shirley, George Taylor**
Producers: **Reginald Collins, Robert Love, Geoffrey Gilbert, Ted Childs**

The investigations of an élite division of Scotland Yard.

Although this series is best remembered for the exploits of snappily dressed detectives Craven and Haggerty, they were latecomers to *Special Branch*. For the first two seasons, the featured officers were Inspector Jordan and his superior, Supt. Eden (later substituted by Supt. Inman). Alongside Craven and Haggerty, DS North and Commander Nicols were also added, though they were soon replaced by Commander Fletcher and a snooty civil servant named Strand.

The thrust of *Special Branch* investigations was international crime and espionage. The team were assigned to high-pressure, undercover operations which involved plugging gaps in security, preventing murders and foiling attempts at sabotage. It was the first series to show a British copper in trendy clothing (Jordan) and is also notable for being the first programme made by Thames TV's offshoot, Euston Films, which took over production after the first two seasons had gone out on videotape.

SPEED, DORIS
MBE (1899–1994)

As snooty Annie Walker, landlady of the Rovers Return, Doris Speed elevated herself above other residents of CORONATION STREET for 23 years. Born into a showbiz family, Speed had worked part-time on stage, radio and early television (series like SHADOW SQUAD and *Skyport*), before she became Annie at the age of 61. It was a role that *Street* creator Tony Warren had written specifically for her; but she had to be persuaded to accept it and, in doing so, she took retirement from an office job with Guinness, having been with the brewery for over 40 years. Speed left the series in 1983, shortly after the tabloid press had revealed her true age to be 84, much to the surprise even of her bosses at Granada, who believed it to be 69.

SPEIGHT, JOHNNY
(1921–98)

Controversial London-born comedy writer, the creator of TILL DEATH US DO PART's Alf Garnett in 1965. By putting bigoted statements and bad language into the mouth of his number one character, Speight attracted the full wrath of Establishment figures. Others, however, recognized that such frankness exposed prejudices in society and applauded the writer. But worse was to come for Speight when he penned the sitcom, CURRY AND CHIPS in 1969. Starring Eric Sykes and a blacked-up Spike

Milligan, it was seen as a racist joke too far and did not survive longer than one season. Speight, a former milkman, also wrote for Frankie Howerd, Max Wall, Norman Evans, Cyril Fletcher, Dickie Valentine, Bernard Braden, Marty Feldman, Graham Stark and Mike Reid. Among his other major credits were *The Arthur Haynes Show*, SYKES, the early sketch show, *Two's Company*, *Them* (a comedy about tramps), its female counterpart, *The Lady is a Tramp*, SPOONER'S PATCH (with Ray Galton) and *The Nineteenth Hole*.

SPELLING, AARON
(1923–)

American TV executive, specializing in glossy, glitzy dramas. A former actor and writer (on series like WAGON TRAIN), Spelling's early successes as a producer included BURKE'S LAW. He then joined with fellow executive Leonard Goldberg to produce series like STARSKY AND HUTCH, THE LOVE BOAT, CHARLIE'S ANGELS, FANTASY ISLAND and HART TO HART. His next partner was Douglas S. Cramer, with whom he collaborated on popular series such as DYNASTY (and its less successful spin-off, THE COLBYS), *Vega$*, HOTEL and BEVERLY HILLS 90210. With Cramer he established Aaron Spelling Productions, later renamed Spelling Entertainment Inc. He is the father of actress Tori Spelling.

SPENDER
UK (BBC/Initial/Big Boy) Police Drama. BBC 1 1991–3

Spender	**Jimmy Nail**
Stick	**Sammy Johnson**
Supt. Yelland	**Paul Greenwood**
DS Dan Boyd	**Berwick Kaler**
Frances	**Denise Welch**
Keith Moreland	**Tony McAnaney**
Laura	**Dawn Winlow**
Kate	**Lynn Harrison**
Det. Chief Supt. Gillespie	**Peter Guinness**

Creators: **Jimmy Nail, Ian La Frenais**
Producers: **Martin McKeand, Paul Raphael**

A maverick Geordie cop is seconded back to his home city to work undercover.

Detective Sgt Spender, a plain-clothes cop with unorthodox methods, worked for the Metropolitan Police. However, his superiors were increasingly frustrated by his approach to the job and, when a partner was badly injured, they transferred Spender back to his home patch of Newcastle-upon-Tyne, after 15 years away. Although it was intended as a one-off assignment, Spender soon found himself permanently back on the Tyne, snooping around where the local cops – being too well known – could not tread. He was perfect for the job: his dishevelled looks and rough-diamond appearance, with tousled hair, pierced ear and chiselled face, hardly marked him out as a policeman, and his thick Geordie accent firmly established him as a local.

Despite his years away, Spender could still count on a few useful contacts, most notably Stick, a convicted building society robber, whom he dragged into investigations and tapped for the word on the streets. DS Dan Boyd, a ring-rusty desk clerk, was assigned as Spender's police liaison, and they occasionally met up at the music shop owned by crippled rock guitarist Keith Moreland. Not being the shy type, Spender always found his way into the thick of the action, usually ending up on the wrong end of a bust-up. But his individual approach generally brought results (after a set-back or two along the way), satisfying his no-nonsense boss, Supt. Yelland (Det. Chief Supt. Gillespie from the second series).

There were other sides to Spender's personality, too. Beneath his gritty, determined façade he possessed a heart of gold. He remained on good terms with his ex-wife, Frances, who still lived in the city; and his two young daughters, Laura and Kate, brought out an even softer part of his nature. But Spender was committed to his job and, even when Frances was killed in the third series and Spender was given permanent custody of his children, he found it hard to balance his responsibilities.

Spender was a series with character. Newcastle's distinctive accents and familiar streets and bridges offered an intriguing backdrop, and a driving rock soundtrack helped keep up momentum. Jimmy Nail not only starred in the programme, he also co-created it with Ian La Frenais and provided scripts for a number of episodes.

SPENSER: FOR HIRE
US (John Wilder/Warner Brothers) Detective Drama.
BBC 1 1989–93

Spenser	**Robert Urich**
Hawk	**Avery Brooks**
Susan Silverman	**Barbara Stock**
Assistant DA Rita Fiori	**Carolyn McCormick**
Lt. Martin Quirk	**Richard Jaeckel**
Sgt Frank Belson	**Ron McLarty**

Executive Producer: **John Wilder**
Producers: **Dick Gallegly, Robert Hamilton**

A cultured private eye stalks the streets of Boston.

Spenser (first name not given) was a rarity among private detectives. This ex-cop was a man of principle who knew and enjoyed literature, his trademark being quotes from Wordsworth and other classic writers. He was also a former boxer, and a *cordon bleu* cook to boot. He cruised the streets of Boston in a vintage Mustang car, assisted in his work by Hawk, a bald, Magnum-toting, black street-informer who was later given his own spin-off series (*A Man Called Hawk*). Guidance counsellor Susan Silverman was Spenser's girlfriend in early and later episodes, with Assistant DA Rita Fiori keeping our hero on his toes in the interim. Lt. Quirk was the local police contact and Belson was his colleague from the homicide department. The series was based on the books by Robert B. Parker.

SPITTING IMAGE
UK (Central) Comedy. ITV 1984–96

Voices: **Chris Barrie, Enn Reitel, Steve Nallon, Jan Ravens, Harry Enfield, Jon Glover, Jessica Martin, Rory Bremner, Hugh Dennis, Kate Robbins, Steve Coogan, Alistair McGowan, John Sessions**

Creators: **Martin Lambie-Nairn, Peter Fluck, Roger Law**
Producers: **Jon Blair, John Lloyd, Tony Hendra, Geoffrey Perkins, David Tyler, Bill Dare, Giles Pilbrow**

Cruel satire from latex puppets.

With respect for no one, be they the royal family, Mother Teresa or especially Margaret Thatcher, the *Spitting Image* team pulled the rug from under prominent personalities for 12 years. Using rubber puppets skilfully crafted by Peter Fluck and Roger Law, and some of the country's leading impressionists and comedians for voices, the series slaughtered holy cows while poking fun at politicians, entertainers, sportsmen and other world figures. The wit was topical and direct, if at times patchy, initially drawing controversy but later earning a degree of respect or at least resignation. Some celebrities even declared themselves honoured to have had their caricature captured in latex. Among the most memorable depictions were Kenneth Baker as a slug, Norman Tebbit as a skinhead, the Pope as a swinging dude and Gerald Kaufman as Hannibal Lecter.

Developed by Fluck and Law from an idea by LWT graphics artist Martin Lambie-Nairn, the series' early writers included the likes of Ian Hislop, Rob Grant and Doug Naylor. But, as well as humour, there was pathos, particularly in some of the musical numbers. At the other end of the scale, though, was 'The Chicken Song', a chart-topping 1986 spin-off that ridiculed the Benidorm brigade and their summer disco songs.

SPONSORSHIP

Although common in the USA in the 1950s, sponsorship is relatively new to British television. In America, sponsors virtually owned the programmes, paying for production and the cost of the airtime, gaining editorial control and reaping the benefits of the exposure their products gained. The system went out of favour in the 1960s when production expenses increased and sponsors were forced to share costs with other advertisers. A form of sponsorship has arrived in the UK since 1991 (having been banned previously), with newspapers, chocolate companies, banks and biscuit manufacturers attaching their names to game shows, sports coverage or travel programmes. Unlike in the USA, the sponsor is allowed no editorial influence, nor can its products be prominently displayed in the programme. Indeed, so-called 'product placement' is prohibited in any programme, sponsored or not. News and current affairs programmes are debarred from taking sponsorship.

SPOONER, DENNIS
(1932–86)

British writer who scripted parts of Tony Hancock's unsuccessful ITV series, *Hancock*, and other comedies before finding his niche in the world of science fiction and adventure dramas. Spooner contributed episodes to DOCTOR WHO, NO HIDING PLACE, FIREBALL XL5, STINGRAY, THUNDERBIRDS, THE AVENGERS, THE BARON, THE PROTECTORS, UFO, DOOMWATCH, HAMMER HOUSE OF HORROR, BERGERAC and THE PROFESSIONALS. However, he particularly endeared himself to cult TV fans by creating or co-creating MAN IN A SUITCASE, THE CHAMPIONS, DEPARTMENT S and RANDALL AND HOPKIRK (DECEASED).

SPOONER'S PATCH
UK (ATV) Situation Comedy. ITV 1979–82

Insp. Spooner	**Ronald Fraser**
	Donald Churchill
DC Bulsover	**Peter Cleall**
PC Killick	**John Lyons**
PC Goatman	**Norman Rossington**
Kelly	**Dermot Kelly**
Mrs Cantaford	**Patricia Hayes**
Jimmy the Con	**Harry Fowler**

Creators/Writers: **Johnny Speight, Ray Galton**
Producer: **William G. Stewart**

The day-to-day events in a hopelessly inept police station.

Inspector Spooner, head of the small, suburban Woodley police station, craved a quiet, comfortable life. Sadly, rather than heading out on to the golf course each day, he found himself called down from his upstairs flat to clear up the mess his corrupt and incompetent juniors had created. DC Bulsover, for instance, was one officer to keep in check, a CID man who thought he was Starsky or Hutch and who drove around in a flashy red and-white-motor. There were also the bigoted PC Goatman and the sarcastic PC Killick to watch over, although some of Spooner's biggest problems came from the quick-tempered traffic warden, Mrs Cantaford. To add to the confusion, Kelly, an Irish grass, plagued the station with his presence, before he was replaced by another informer, Jimmy the Con.

No fewer than three actors played the title role in this relatively short-lived series. Ian Bannen starred in the pilot episode, followed in the series proper by Ronald Fraser and then by Donald Churchill. Although it combined the writing talents of Johnny Speight (TILL DEATH US DO PART) and Ray Galton (HANCOCK'S HALF HOUR and STEPTOE AND SON), the series proved a disappointment to most viewers.

SPORTS REVIEW OF THE YEAR
UK (BBC) Sport. BBC 1 1954–

Annual sports showcase with awards for the best achievers.

Sports Review of the Year was launched way back in 1954 and has become one of the BBC's major annual events. Transmitted live, early in December, with a tense, nervous atmosphere, it has focused on the sporting year just passed, replaying the key action and interviewing the winners and losers. In a light-hearted diversion, good 'sports' like Frank Bruno have tried their hands at silly stunts, such as fairground shooting stalls, taking hockey penalties, performing snooker tricks, changing the tyres on a Formula One racing car and pitting their wits against electronic games. The 'Sports Personality of the Year' award has provided the climax to the evening (a full list of winners is given below), with other presentations made to 'Overseas Personality of the Year' and the best team. In 1999, new awards were introduced: 'Coach of the Year' and the 'Helen Rollason Award' for inspiration (in tribute to the late BBC sports presenter). The 1999 programme was actually titled *Sports Personality of the Century* and saw Muhammad Ali collect the eponymous award. Cool-headed hosts Steve Rider and Sue Barker have held the show together in recent years, succeeding the likes of Peter Dimmock, David Coleman, Harry Carpenter, Frank Bough and Desmond Lynam.

'SPORTS PERSONALITY OF THE YEAR' WINNERS:

1954	Chris Chataway
1955	Gordon Pirie
1956	Jim Laker
1957	Dai Rees
1958	Ian Black
1959	John Surtees
1960	David Broome
1961	Stirling Moss
1962	Anita Lonsbrough
1963	Dorothy Hyman
1964	Mary Rand
1965	Tommy Simpson
1966	Bobby Moore
1967	Henry Cooper
1968	David Hemery
1969	Ann Jones
1970	Henry Cooper
1971	HRH The Princess Anne
1972	Mary Peters
1973	Jackie Stewart
1974	Brendan Foster
1975	David Steele
1976	John Curry
1977	Virginia Wade
1978	Steve Ovett
1979	Sebastian Coe
1980	Robin Cousins
1981	Ian Botham
1982	Daley Thompson
1983	Steve Cram
1984	Torvill and Dean
1985	Barry McGuigan
1986	Nigel Mansell
1987	Fatima Whitbread
1988	Steve Davis
1989	Nick Faldo
1990	Paul Gascoigne
1991	Liz McColgan
1992	Nigel Mansell
1993	Linford Christie
1994	Damon Hill
1995	Jonathan Edwards
1996	Damon Hill
1997	Greg Rusedski
1998	Michael Owen
1999	Lennox Lewis
2000	Steve Redgrave

SPORTSVIEW
UK (BBC) Sport. BBC 1954–68

Presenters: **Peter Dimmock, Brian Johnston, Frank Bough**

Editors: **Paul Fox, Ronnie Noble, Cliff Morgan, Alan Hart**

Early midweek sports round-up.

Replaced after 14 years on air by *Sportsnight* (later *Sportsnight with Coleman*) in 1968, *Sportsview* was the BBC's first major sports showcase, predating GRANDSTAND by four years. Peter Dimmock was the programme's first host, introducing such sporting milestones as Roger Bannister's four-minute mile on 6 May 1954. *Sportsview* was also adventurous technically. It was the first BBC programme to use a teleprompter and among its other innovations was the placing of cameras inside racing cars. A younger viewers' version, *Junior Sportsview*, with hosts including Peter Dimmock, Billy Wright and Kenneth Wolstenholme, ran between 1956 and 1962, and the annual SPORTS REVIEW OF THE YEAR was another by-product.

SPOT THE TUNE
UK (Granada) Quiz. ITV 1956–62

Presenters: **Ken Platt, Ted Ray, Jackie Rae, Pete Murray**

Producers: **Wilfred Fielding, Johnny Hamp**

Musical quiz game.

In this self-explanatory quiz, contestants were asked to spot the tune, given only a few bars to work on. There was a jackpot (increasing by £100 a week), to be won by those with an ear for music. Singer Marion Ryan (mother of 1960s pop stars Paul and Barry Ryan) helped pose the questions, accompanied by the Peter Knight Orchestra.

The format was revived in the 1970s as *Name That Tune*, a segment of the variety show, *Wednesday at Eight*, and subsequently a programme in its own right. Tom O'Connor and, later, Lionel Blair hosted proceedings, Maggie Moone was the resident songstress and the Alan Braden band struck up the tunes.

SPRING AND AUTUMN
UK (Thames) Situation Comedy. ITV 1973–6

Tommy Butler .... **Jimmy Jewel**
Charlie Harris .... **Charlie Hawkins**
Vera Reid .... **June Barry**
Brian Reid .... **Larry Martyn**
Betty Harris .... **Jo Warne**

Creators/Writers: **Vince Powell, Harry Driver**
Producers: **Ronnie Baxter, Mike Vardy, Anthony Parker**

*A lonely old man finds company with a
12-year-old lad.*

It seemed life was over for 70-year-old former railway worker Tommy Butler when his home was demolished and he was forced to live with his daughter and son-in-law, Vera and Brian Reid, in a high-rise flat. It was clear that he wasn't really wanted in their home and, to be fair, the cantankerous old moaner made little effort to fit in. His only friend was Nelson, a stuffed green parrot. However, Tommy found a new soul-mate in the form of Charlie Harris, a cheeky, somewhat wayward young Cockney lad who was neglected by his hard-up, divorced mother, Betty. Tommy and Charlie became firm friends and shared many an outing. Their mutual interest in football and railways bound them together, and Charlie loved Tommy's far-fetched tales of the past.

This gentle comedy, with moments of sentimentality, followed on from a one-off 1972 play in which Tommy's daughter and son-in-law were Betty and Joe Dickinson (played by Gaye Brown and Larry Martyn).

SPRINGER, JERRY
(1944–)

London-born host of sensational US daytime talk shows, a career he has pursued after success in American politics – he was an aide to Robert Kennedy and was elected Mayor of Cincinnati. In 1999 he recrossed the Atlantic to record a pilot celebrity chat show for ITV, which was followed by a short series the following year. In 2000 he hosted MISS WORLD.

SPYDER'S WEB
UK (ATV) Spy Drama. ITV 1972

Charlotte 'Lottie' Dean .... **Patricia Cutts**
Clive Hawksworth .... **Anthony Ainley**
Wallis Ackroyd .... **Veronica Carlson**
Albert Mason .... **Roger Lloyd Pack**

Creator: **Richard Harris**
Producer: **Dennis Vance**

*International intrigue with three agents of a secret
governmental unit.*

The 'Web' of this programme's title was a top-secret, undercover, anti-espionage organization, and 'Spyder' referred to any of its agents. There were three prominent activists: Lottie Dean, Clive Hawksworth and Wallis Ackroyd. Individually or collectively, they investigated bizarre and complicated cases of infiltration and international deception. Albert Mason, Lottie's butler, was also seen. This light-hearted thriller was created by Richard Harris and penned mainly by comedy writer Roy Clarke (later responsible for LAST OF THE SUMMER WINE, OPEN ALL HOURS, etc.).

SQUIRRELS, THE
UK (ATV) Situation Comedy. ITV 1975–7

Mr Fletcher .... **Bernard Hepton**
Rex .... **Ken Jones**
Susan .... **Patsy Rowlands**
Harry .... **Alan David**
Burke .... **Ellis Jones**
Carol .... **Karin MacCarthy**

Creator: **Eric Chappell**
Producer: **Shaun O'Riordan**

*Petty squabbles with the staff of a TV rental
company.*

Beginning as a one-off play in 1974, this comedy focused on life in the offices of International Rentals, a television hire firm. Head of the accounts staff was Mr Fletcher, and bickering beneath him were his hapless minions, Rex, Susan, Harry, Burke and Carol (played by Susan Tracy in the pilot). Joining creator Eric Chappell in scripting the series were writers like Kenneth Cope (of RANDALL AND HOPKIRK fame) and BROOKSIDE's Phil Redmond. Chappell revamped the idea for the sitcom, *Fiddlers Three* (ITV 1991), which starred Peter Davison and Paula Wilcox.

STAFF, KATHY
(Minnie Higginbottom; 1928–)

Northern actress, most familiar as the redoubtable Nora Batty in LAST OF THE SUMMER WINE. However, Staff has also been seen in both CORONATION STREET (corner shopkeeper Vera Hopkins) and CROSSROADS (Doris Luke), as well as a third soap, EMMERDALE FARM (Winnie Purvis). She was Mrs Blewitt, one of Arkwright's customers, in OPEN ALL HOURS and later played interfering grandmother Molly Bickerstaff in the comedy, *No Frills*. Her other credits have included *Castle Haven*, HADLEIGH, *Sez Les, Dawson and Friends* and *The Benny Hill Show*.

STANWYCK, BARBARA
(Ruby Stevens; 1907–90)

After a long and successful career in Hollywood, spanning nearly 40 years, Barbara Stanwyck at last ensured herself television posterity in 1965 when she was cast as Victoria Barkley, the matriarch of the Barkley family, in the Western, THE BIG VALLEY. Her earlier excursions into TV had comprised guest spots in series like THE

UNTOUCHABLES, RAWHIDE and WAGON TRAIN, in addition to her own short-lived anthology series, *The Barbara Stanwyck Show*. *The Big Valley* ran in the USA until 1969 and, after making a few TV movies, Stanwyck officially retired from the business in 1973. She was tempted back to the small screen on two occasions, however. In 1983 she played Mary Carson in THE THORN BIRDS and in 1985 was Constance Colby in THE COLBYS. Her second husband was actor Robert Taylor.

STAR MAIDENS
UK/W. Germany (Scottish/Portman) Science Fiction.
ITV 1976

Fulvia	**Judy Geeson**
The President	**Dawn Addams**
Adam	**Pierre Brice**
Shem	**Gareth Thomas**
Octavia	**Christine Kruger**
Rudi	**Christian Quadflieg**
Liz	**Lisa Harrow**
Prof. Evans	**Derek Farr**

Creators: **Graf Von Hardenberg, Graefin Von Hardenberg**
Producer: **James Gatward**

Two male refugees from a female-dominated planet escape to Earth.

Adam and Shem were male slaves on Mendusa, a planet ruled exclusively by women. There, men were no more than the subservient race, confined to a life of drudgery while their womenfolk lived in luxury. Making a break for it, the two men stole a spaceship and fled to Earth, pursued by Adam's mistress, Supreme Councillor Fulvia, and her assistant, Octavia. Their arrival was monitored by Earth scientist Professor Evans, whose young colleagues, Rudi and Liz, were then taken hostage and whisked off into space when Fulvia failed to corner her escapees. With two Mendusans on Earth and two humans on Mendusa, the series followed the battle against the 'Star Maidens' on both worlds.

Thirteen episodes of *Star Maidens* were produced as a joint venture between British and West German companies, although the series (played mainly for laughs) was never successful in the UK, enjoying only sporadic screenings around the ITV network. A planned second series was quickly shelved.

STAR TREK
US (Norway/Paramount/Desilu) Science Fiction. BBC 1
1969–71

Capt. James T. Kirk	**William Shatner**
Mr Spock	**Leonard Nimoy**
Dr Leonard McCoy	**DeForest Kelley**
Mr Sulu	**George Takei**
Lt. Uhura	**Nichelle Nichols**
Engineer Montgomery Scott	**James Doohan**
Nurse Christine Chapel	**Majel Barrett**
Ensign Pavel Chekov	**Walter Koenig**
Yeoman Janice Rand	**Grace Lee Whitney**

Creator/Executive Producer: **Gene Roddenberry**
Producers: **Gene L. Coon, John Meredyth Lucas, Fred Freiberger**

The voyages of the starship Enterprise.

In the 23rd century, Earth had become a member of the United Federation of Planets, a galactic union that ran a joint defence organization, Starfleet. Its starships plied the cosmos, hoping to bring peace to other civilizations, or at least to discover more about alien life-forms. The USS *Enterprise* was one of those ships, and *Star Trek* followed its adventures on a five-year mission to 'boldly go when no man has gone before'.

The *Enterprise* was a massive exploration-cum-messenger craft which cruised at 'warp' speeds, all of which were faster than light. Protected by high-tech deflector shields and phasers, it whisked its crew of 428 from galaxy to galaxy and from one life-threatening adventure to another. The spaceship never landed: the crew were simply 'beamed down' on to the surface of a planet, to tackle new adversaries (with the minimum of special effects).

Commander of the ship was 34-year-old Captain James Tiberius Kirk, an American from Iowa. His Chief Navigator was the Japanese Mr Sulu, assisted by the Russian, Chekov (added in the second season to provide international balance). Lt. Uhura, the communications officer, was a sultry African, and Chief Engineer was Montgomery 'Scotty' Scott. However, the key members of Kirk's team were always his First Officer, Mr Spock, and the ship's doctor, 'Bones' McCoy. McCoy, an expert in space psychology from Georgia, USA, always considered himself to be a simple 'country' doctor. He was an emotional chap, quite unlike his perennial sparring partner, Spock, who, being half Vulcan, was devoid of human instincts. Green-blooded and pointy-eared, Spock was interested only in what was logical, his mind working through the facts like a computer. Kirk proved to be a mixture of the two, an often impetuous man with strong powers of leadership, a (sometimes) athletic frame and a firm belief in humanity as a force for overcoming evil. Consequently, *Star Trek* stories (beginning and ending with Kirk's vocal entry into the Captain's Log) usually had a moral theme, with the crew facing up to alien civilizations which echoed the cruellest regimes our own world has seen, such as the ancient Romans and the Nazis. Social issues of the day, such as civil rights and the Vietnamese war, were also reflected. The *Enterprise* had two main enemies, the militaristic Romulans and the greasy, barbarous Klingons, although all kinds of weird and wonderful foes were likely to turn up.

Star Trek was devised by Gene Roddenberry, previously scriptwriter on HAVE GUN WILL TRAVEL, and he perceived the programme as a sort of WAGON TRAIN in space. It was not an instant hit; in fact it flopped in the USA. In the UK it was eventually picked up by the BBC and screened only after the entire run had ended in America. However, re-runs have ensured that the programme has gained a cult following, manifested in a legion of international fans known as 'Trekkies' for whom part of the attraction are the show's many clichés and sayings. A UK chart-topper from 1987, 'Star Trekkin'' by a group called The Firm, parodied its classic lines like 'Klingons on the starboard bow', 'It's life, Jim, but not as we know it' and 'It's worse than that, he's dead, Jim'. In January 2000, Sky One even produced a four-part *Star Trek* quiz, *Trekmasters*.

Star Trek's pilot episode, *The Cage*, starred Jeffrey Hunter as Christopher Pike, the first captain of the *Enterprise*, but it has been rarely seen, with some of its footage reworked into a later episode called *The Menagerie*. Only Leonard Nimoy and Majel Barrett from the main cast appeared in the pilot. A series of nine feature-length movies was made years after filming of the TV show finished in 1969, and a cartoon version was also issued. STAR TREK: THE NEXT GENERATION (see below) picked up the story again in 1989, and two further spin-offs, STAR TREK: DEEP SPACE NINE and STAR TREK: VOYAGER, have also now been produced.

STAR TREK: DEEP SPACE NINE
US (Paramount) Science Fiction. BBC 2 1995–

Commander Benjamin Sisko	**Avery Brooks**
Odo	**Rene Auberjonois**
Dr Julian Bashir	**Siddig El Fadil/Alexander Siddig**
Lt. Jadzia Dax	**Terry Farrell**
Jake Sisko	**Cirroc Lofton**
Chief Miles O'Brien	**Colm Meaney**
Quark	**Armin Shimerman**
Major Kira Nerys	**Nana Visitor**
Lt. Commander Worf	**Michael Dorn**
Ezri Dax	**Nicole de Boer**

Creators: **Rick Berman, Michael Piller**
Executive Producers: **Rick Berman, Michael Piller, Ira Steven Behr**

Trouble and strife on an extreme outpost in the backyard of space.

Set, like STAR TREK: THE NEXT GENERATION, in the 24th century, this series, for once, did not feature a wandering USS spacecraft. Instead, the static setting was the eponymous *Deep Space Nine*, a run-down space station orbiting the wasted (by rival race the Cardassians) planet Bajor, way, way out in space. Its position close to a newly discovered 'wormhole' – a crack in space – meant that it soon gained strategic importance and was a popular stopover for trans-galactic travellers using the wormhole to catapult across light years. This made *DS9* akin to a Wild West frontier town, with visitors of all persuasions dropping by to wreak havoc with the station staff. The crew included the understandably disgruntled widower, Commander Benjamin Sisko; his brattish teenage son, Jake; First Officer Major Kira Nerys, a patriotic Bajoran; Chief Miles O'Brien, the pessimistic operations director (ex of the USS *Enterprise*); newly graduated medical man Dr Julian Bashir, who held a torch for science officer Lt. Jadzia Dax, a Trill whose beautiful outer form concealed a 300-year-old slug-like symbiotic core; the seedy Quark, a typically greedy Ferengi who specialized in dirty money (bars and holographic brothels); and Odo, a

shape-shifting, naturally liquid creature who kept his human form while on duty as a security officer. Odo's own race, the Founders of the Dominion, become one of Starfleet's new enemies, and to head them off *DS9* employed a prototype fighter spacecraft called the *Defiant*. Joining the crew later was Lt. Commander Worf, another *Next Generation* cross-over, who became Strategic Operations Officer.

Considerably darker than STAR TREK's two previous incarnations, *Deep Space Nine* was also grittier and far less optimistic, featuring characters who exhibited traits like distrust, spite and anger.

STAR TREK: THE NEXT GENERATION
US (Paramount) Science Fiction. BBC 2 1990–6

Capt. Jean-Luc Picard	**Patrick Stewart**
Commander William T. Riker	**Jonathan Frakes**
Lt. Commander Geordi La Forge	**LeVar Burton**
Lt. Worf	**Michael Dorn**
Lt. Tasha Yar	**Denise Crosby**
Dr Beverly Crusher	**Gates McFadden**
Counsellor Deanna Troi	**Marina Sirtis**
Lt. Commander Data	**Brent Spiner**
Wesley Crusher	**Wil Wheaton**
Dr Katherine Pulaski	**Diana Muldaur**
Guinan	**Whoopi Goldberg**
Ensign Ro Laren	**Michelle Forbes**
Transporter Chief Miles O'Brien	**Colm Meaney**
Q	**John de Lancie**

Executive Producer: **Gene Roddenberry**

The voyages of the starship Enterprise, *resurrected.*

In this STAR TREK sequel, time had moved on to the 24th century, about 80 years after the exploits of Kirk and Co. The new *Enterprise* was much flashier – a Galaxy-class starship eight times as spacious as the original, with over 1,000 crew members (including families), and greatly advanced technology.

The ship's commander was stubborn Jean-Luc Picard, not as emotional or impetuous as his predecessor, Kirk, and less inclined to soil his hands. He delegated off-ship missions to his hard-working 'Number 1', the bearded Riker. Also on the bridge was Lt. Geordi La Forge, a blind black helmsman who could see by wearing a VISOR (Visual Instrument and Sight Organ Replacement) band. He later became Chief Engineer. Deanna Troi, Riker's ex, was a half-Betazoid who worked as an adviser, warning of impending danger by reading people's emotions (her mother, Lwaxana, was seen occasionally, played by *Star Trek* original Majel Barrett). Data, a pale-faced, encyclopaedic android, and Lt. Tasha Yar, the security chief who was killed by the alien Armus, also appeared. Often violent Lt. Worf was a Klingon, from the race that was once Starfleet's enemy, and the ship's medical officer was widow Dr Beverly Crusher, later temporarily replaced by Dr Kate Pulaski. Crusher's kid-genius son, Wesley, was also on board, and comedienne Whoopi Goldberg dropped in from time to time, playing the part of Guinan, bartender in the ship's Ten Forward lounge. Guest stars included Leonard Nimoy as Spock, James Doohan as Scotty and Stephen Hawking as himself.

Storylines, as in the original series, generally offered a moral, and the show was warmly received by 'Trekkies'. But *Star Trek: The Next Generation* was slow to come to the UK. It turned up first in video shops, before being bought by Sky. BBC 2 secured the rights for terrestrial transmission, but episodes were screened some time after premiering on satellite.

STAR TREK: VOYAGER
US (Paramount) Science Fiction. BBC 2 1996–

Capt. Kathryn Janeway .... **Kate Mulgrew**
Chakotay .... **Robert Beltran**
B'Elanna Torres .... **Roxann Biggs-Dawson**
Kes .... **Jennifer Lien**
Lt. Tom Paris .... **Robert Duncan McNeill**
Neelix .... **Ethan Phillips**
Doctor .... **Robert Picardo**
Tuvok .... **Tim Russ**
Ensign Harry Kim .... **Garrett Wang**
Seven of Nine .... **Jeri Ryan**

Creators: **Rick Berman, Michael Piller, Jeri Taylor**
Executive Producers: **Rick Berman, Michael Piller, Jeri Taylor, Brannon Braga**

A Starfleet ship is lost in the outer reaches of the universe.

Some time in the 24th century, the USS *Voyager* (one of Starfleet's smaller ships) was hit by a wave of energy and sent hurtling 70,000 light years across the galaxies to the Gamma Quadrant. The efforts of its captain, Kathryn Janeway, and her team to return to parts of space that were more familiar formed the basis of this LOST IN SPACE-like series.

Her crew consisted of a uneasy mix of Starfleet officers and Maquis terrorists who found themselves similarly marooned and reluctantly reliant on the *Voyager* for the hope of a journey home. Asian rookie communications officer Harry Kim; Vulcan security officer Tuvok; impetuous ex-pilot Lt. Tom Paris; and Native American Chakotay (former Maquis leader) were key members of the team, along with half-Klingon B'Elanna Torres; an impatient holographic medical man known only as the Doctor; a treacherous Kazon named Seska; Neelix, a Talaxian cook-cum-handyman; and Neelix's Ocampan lover, Kes – the last three just some of the new species *Voyager* encountered in these uncharted regions of space. One notable later addition to the cast was the stunning half-Borg, Seven of Nine.

STARR, FREDDIE
(Freddie Fowell; 1943–)

Unpredictable British comedian and impressionist with a cheeky grin, coming to the fore on OPPORTUNITY KNOCKS and establishing himself on WHO DO YOU DO?. Starr's career has experienced several ups and downs, the ups including several series of his own, such as The *Freddie Starr Show* and *The Freddie Starr Showcase* (a talent show). In 1980 he shared the limelight with Russ Abbot in *Freddie Starr's Variety Madhouse* which, when Starr left, was renamed *Russ Abbot's Madhouse*. Starr has also been a popular variety show and panel game guest, and took to straight drama as Lance Izzard in *Supply and Demand*. In 1999 he fronted the Sky game show, *Beat the Crusher*.

STARS AND GARTERS
UK (Associated-Rediffusion) Variety. ITV 1963–6

Hosts: **Ray Martine, Jill Browne, Willie Rushton**

Producers: **Daphne Shadwell, John P. Hamilton, Rollo Gamble, Elkan Allan**

Traditional pub entertainment presented from a fake hostelry.

A cross between the earlier CAFÉ CONTINENTAL and the later WHEELTAPPERS' AND SHUNTERS' SOCIAL CLUB, *Stars and Garters* was a variety show dressed up as pub entertainment. Host Ray Martine and his pet mynah bird invited viewers to share in the pubby atmosphere and watch top acts, supported by resident performers like Kathy Kirby, Tommy Bruce, Clinton Ford, Kim Cordell, Vince Hill, Debbie Lee, Al Saxon, Queenie Watts and Julie Rayne. The Alan Braden and Peter Knight orchestras provided musical accompaniment. Martine was later replaced as host by EMERGENCY – WARD 10 star Jill Browne, who compered events with Willie Rushton. The title became *The New Stars and Garters* at the same time.

STARS IN THEIR EYES
UK (Granada) Entertainment. ITV 1990–

Presenters: **Leslie Crowther, Matthew Kelly**

Executive Producer: **Dianne Nelmes**
Producer: **Jane Macnaught, Kieron Collins, Matthew Littleford, Nigel Hall**

Viewers impersonate their favourite singing stars.

A cross between a talent show and a vehicle for impressionists, *Stars in Their Eyes* has offered members of the public the chance to emulate their favourite musical performers. Togged up in appropriate gear by the wardrobe department and given the looks of their idols by make-up, the contestants have then performed with the Ray Monk Orchestra to prove that they can sound like the real thing, too. A grand final (live) has been held at the end of each series and in 1999 a *Champion of Champions* show pitched the first ten series' winners against each other, the winner (the 1999 series champion) impersonating Chris de Burgh. Also in 1999, editions of *Celebrity Stars in Their Eyes* were introduced, with showbiz names paying tribute to their heroes. Leslie Crowther was the series' original host, replaced after his tragic car accident by Matthew Kelly.

STARS ON SUNDAY

UK (Yorkshire) Religion. ITV 1969–79

Presenter/Executive Producer: **Jess Yates**

Cosy, Sunday-evening celebrity showcase with a religious slant.

Stars on Sunday, ITV's answer to SONGS OF PRAISE, specialized in attracting top showbusiness names into the studio to sing hymns or give Biblical readings. Masterminded and presented by Jess 'The Bishop' Yates (assumed father of Paula), its mixture of big stars and spiritual comforts made it extremely popular, and viewers' requests flooded in. Among the international celebrities to contribute were Bing Crosby, Princess Grace of Monaco, Johnny Mathis, Raymond Burr and Howard Keel, while heading the home-grown talent were the Beverley Sisters, James Mason, Harry Secombe, Gracie Fields, John Gielgud, John Mills and Anna Neagle. The Archbishops of Canterbury and York also made appearances, as did Prime Minister Edward Heath. The resident singing troupe were The Poole Family, fronted by little Glyn Poole, and, as well as traditional hymns, moral modern pieces were also featured.

In 1974 the programme was rocked by the 'actress and the bishop' scandal, when Yates's relationship with Anita Kay, a showgirl more than 30 years his junior, was splashed over the tabloids. Yates was forced to leave the series and his career never recovered. His immediate short-term replacement as host was Anthony Valentine, but numerous personalities picked up the reins for the show's last five years on air. These included Moira Anderson, Wilfred Pickles, Robert Dougall, Cliff Michelmore and Gordon Jackson.

STARSKY AND HUTCH

US (Spelling-Goldberg) Police Drama. BBC 1 1976–81

Det. Dave Starsky	**Paul Michael Glaser**
Det. Ken ('Hutch') Hutchinson	**David Soul**
Capt. Harold Dobey	**Bernie Hamilton**
Huggy Bear	**Antonio Fargas**

Creator: **William Blinn**
Executive Producers: **Aaron Spelling, Leonard Goldberg**
Producer: **Joseph T. Naar**

Two buddy-buddy undercover cops patrol the seedier areas of LA.

Dave Starsky and Ken 'Hutch' Hutchinson were cops. More than that, they were pals and it showed in their work. Hutch was blond, Starsky was dark-haired, and their lifestyles contrasted just as sharply. Starsky enjoyed junk food and streetlife, Hutch preferred health foods and the quiet life. But the main thing was that they knew they could depend on each other, and this ran right to the heart of their working relationship.

Stationed in one of LA's seamiest districts, the casually dressed duo concentrated on only the most serious crimes, hustling drug-pushers, pimps and other society dregs, and apprehending muggers, rapists and racketeers. Screaming around the streets in Starsky's souped-up, red Ford Torino with a loud white strip along its side, they were hardly inconspicuous for undercover policemen. What's more, if they could enter a car through a window rather than the door, then they would, probably leaping on to the bonnet first. Yet they still got results, usually bending the rules along the way, but ultimately keeping their fiery boss, Captain Dobey (played by Richard Ward in the pilot), happy. Huggy Bear was their hip street-contact.

The show became less aggressive over the years in response to anti-violence campaigns in the States, but the programme always enjoyed greater success in Britain, where the two principals were big stars. Paul Michael Glaser's chunky cardigans became fashion items and David Soul was able to reprise his recording career, notching up a string of middle-of-the-road hits, including a couple of number ones, 'Don't Give Up On Us' and 'Silver Lady'.

STAY LUCKY

UK (Yorkshire) Drama. ITV 1989–93

Thomas Gynn	**Dennis Waterman**
Sally Hardcastle	**Jan Francis**
Kevin	**Chris Jury**
Lively	**Niall Toibin**
Pippa	**Emma Wray**
Samantha Mansfield	**Susan George**
Franklyn Bysouth	**Ian McNeice**
Isabel	**Rula Lenska**
Jo	**Leslie Ash**

Creator: **Geoff McQueen**
Executive Producer: **Vernon Lawrence**
Producers: **David Reynolds, Andrew Benson, Matthew Bird**

A Cockney wide-boy meanders between jobs, follows his heart and finds unlikely girlfriends.

On the run from the London underworld, Thomas Gynn met up with recently widowed, northern businesswoman Sally Hardcastle at an A1 service station and, more by chance than design, the two reluctantly ended up sharing a houseboat. At one point, Thomas – ducking and diving – drove minicabs in Newcastle, while the headstrong Sally ran her narrowboat charter company in Yorkshire. By the third season, Thomas had spent time behind bars and Sally had long since left the scene. Thomas then saved the life of Samantha Mansfield, administrator of the Yorkshire Industrial Museum, who gave him a job and more besides, before he enjoyed a fling in Eastern Europe with Isabel, a British trade official in Hungary. Finally, Jo, a dancer, became the new girl in his life. Pippa and Lively, two old friends, were usually on the scene and Franklyn Bysouth was Thomas's one-time cellmate. Now a dodgy businessman, he took Thomas under his wing and offered him work.

STEADMAN, ALISON
OBE (1946–)

Liverpool-born actress, for many years the wife of playwright Mike Leigh, in some of whose works (*Nuts In May* and ABIGAIL'S PARTY) she has also been seen. Steadman's TV career opened in the early 1970s. She was WPC Bayliss in Z CARS, appeared in *Frost's Weekly* and took the part of Bernadette Clarkson in *The Wackers*. In the 1980s she played Mrs Marlow and Lili in THE SINGING DETECTIVE, and in the 1990s she was Edda Goering in *Selling Hitler*; Lauren Patterson in *Gone to the Dogs* and Hilda Plant in its 'sequel', *Gone to Seed*; Elinor Farr in *The Wimbledon Poisoner*; Mrs Bennet in PRIDE AND PREJUDICE; Evelyn Hamilton in *No Bananas*; Mrs Haynes in KARAOKE; Christine Peacock in *The Missing Postman*; and Madame de Plonge in *Let Them Eat Cake*. In 2000 she was Betty Simpson in *Fat Friends* and followed this with the role of Pauline Mole in *Adrian Mole: The Cappuccino Years* in 2001. She also appeared in *Coogan's Run*, narrated the documentary, *Love Town*, and provided voices for the animations, *Crapston Villas* and *Stressed Eric*. Her TV series have been underpinned by roles in single dramas like *Through the Night*, *P'tang Yang Kipperbang*, *The Muscle Market* and *The Caucasian Chalk Circle*.

STEPHENSON, PAMELA
(1951–)

Actress and comedienne born in New Zealand, a member of the NOT THE NINE O'CLOCK NEWS team from 1979. Her other credits have included appearances in WITHIN THESE WALLS, SPACE: 1999, TARGET, THE NEW AVENGERS, THE PROFESSIONALS, HAZELL (alongside her first husband, Nicholas Ball), *Funny Man*, *Lost Empires*, *Move Over Darling* and the American series, *Saturday Night Live*. Her second husband is Billy Connolly.

STEPTOE AND SON
UK (BBC) Situation Comedy. BBC 1 1962–5; 1970–4

Albert Steptoe	**Wilfrid Brambell**
Harold Steptoe	**Harry H. Corbett**

Creators/Writers: **Ray Galton, Alan Simpson**
Producers: **Duncan Wood, John Howard Davies, Graeme Muir, Douglas Argent**

A pretentious bachelor can't escape his grubby old father and the rag-and-bone business they share.

There are few shows in the history of television which have reaped such wide appreciation as *Steptoe and Son*, Ray Galton and Alan Simpson's saga of a socially-aspirant son and the dirty old dad who kept him anchored to the mire of a scrapyard. Harold Steptoe, in his late 30s, dreamed of a life away from the squalid, junk-filled house he shared with his father at 24 Old Drum Lane, Shepherd's Bush. He longed to progress his cultural interests and to embark on some romantic journey but was always hauled back to sub-working-class grime by his disgusting, emaciated old man. His plans for soirées in gentrified circles usually collapsed into nights at The Skinner's Arms or argumentative evenings in front of the box, thanks to the efforts of his seedy father. Albert Steptoe was vulgarity personified, a man who washed his socks only when taking a bath. He cooked and generally ran the house, while Harold did the rounds with Hercules (later Delilah) the carthorse, but Albert's idea of culinary finesse was edging a pie with his false teeth. Albert's greatest skill lay in scuppering his son's dreams of a better life. Whenever Harold made a dash for freedom, the clinging, devious old man always stood in the way, using emotional blackmail to deny his son independence.

The gloriously coarse series – which was as much a tragedy as it was a comedy – ran in two bites, in the early 1960s (it first aired in 1962 as a COMEDY PLAYHOUSE episode called *The Offer*) and then in the early 1970s. A radio series was also produced, and the show spawned a US cover version, *Sanford and Son*, as well as two far less successful feature films, *Steptoe and Son* and *Steptoe and Son Ride Again*.

STEVENS, CRAIG
(Gail Shekles; 1918–)

American actor popular at the turn of the 1960s, thanks to his portrayal of suave detective *Peter Gunn* and his role as photo journalist Mike Strait in MAN OF THE WORLD. A third series, *Mr Broadway*, proved less successful. In later years, he played David McCallum's boss, Walter Carlson, in THE INVISIBLE MAN, Asher Berg in RICH MAN, POOR MAN and, for a while, Craig Stewart in DALLAS.

STEWART, ALASTAIR
(1952–)

British journalist, presenter and newscaster. Stewart's initial TV work was for Southern Television in the late 1970s, before he joined ITN as its industrial correspondent in 1980. He was later Washington correspondent and anchor on various news bulletins, including *News at Ten*, *News at 5.40* and *Channel 4 News*. He also worked on ITN specials, like election coverages, but left to launch *London Tonight*, Carlton TV's regional news programme in 1993. Since 1994 he has presented *The Sunday Programme* for GMTV and he has also hosted *Police, Camera, Action* and *Missing*.

STEWART, WILLIAM G.
(1935–)

British comedy producer/director and latterly quiz show host. Stewart made his name in the late 1960s and early 1970s through programmes like MRS THURSDAY, FATHER, DEAR FATHER, BLESS THIS HOUSE, LOVE THY NEIGHBOUR, MY GOOD WOMAN, AND MOTHER MAKES FIVE, *Doctor Down Under*, *Down the Gate*, *The Many Wives of Patrick*, *Paradise Island*, *My Name is Harry Worth*, SPOONER'S

PATCH and THE RAG TRADE. In the 1980s he worked on the short-lived Alf Garnett revival, *Till Death . . .* and also the Channel 4 comedies, *The Lady Is a Tramp*, *The Nineteenth Hole* and *The Bright Side*. Other credits include shows for comics like Frankie Howerd, Max Bygraves, Al Read, Larry Grayson, Tom O'Connor and Tommy Cooper, as well as the ITV game show, THE PRICE IS RIGHT. Since 1987 he has both produced and presented (very drily) the daily quiz show, FIFTEEN TO ONE, for Channel 4.

STILGOE, RICHARD
(1943–)

Surrey-born humorist, musician and presenter. Cambridge Footlights graduate Stilgoe was a familiar face in the 1970s, writing topical ditties for THAT'S LIFE and NATIONWIDE. Later he was the front man on the sketch series, A KICK UP THE EIGHTIES, and also appeared in *And Now The Good News*, the sketch shows, *Psst!* and *Don't Ask Us*, and the sitcom, *A Class by Himself*, which he also wrote. Stilgoe has also been involved in the theatre. Among his successes have been the musicals, *Starlight Express* and *Phantom of the Opera*, for which he penned lyrics.

STINGRAY
UK (AP Films/ATV/ITC) Children's Science Fiction. ITV
1964–5

Voices:

Capt. Troy Tempest	**Don Mason**
George 'Phones' Sheridan	**Robert Easton**
Atlanta Shore	**Lois Maxwell**
Commander Sam Shore	**Ray Barrett**
Titan	**Ray Barrett**
Sub Lt. Fisher	**Ray Barrett**
X20	**Robert Easton**

Creators: **Gerry Anderson, Sylvia Anderson**
Producer: **Gerry Anderson**

The crew of a supersub save the world.

Stingray was the number-one craft of WASP, the World Aquanaut Security Patrol, which operated out of the city of Marineville, in the year 2000. With peace now established on land, the Earth's population had begun to harvest the minerals and other riches of the sea, which is where they encountered new enemies. WASP was the Earth's response to the dangers of the ocean.

Head of WASP was Commander Shore, a man crippled in a sea battle and now confined to a hoverchair. His assistant was Sub Lt. Fisher, and Shore's daughter, Atlanta, also lived and worked in Marineville. Most of the action centred on the daring crew of Stingray itself, and in particular its fearless commander, Captain Troy Tempest. Voted 'Aquanaut of the Year', Tempest was the hero of the series, although he did have a juvenile tendency to sulk. His patrol partners were the amiable Phones (real name George Sheridan), who operated the craft's hydrophone sonar system, and Marina, a beautiful mute girl from the shell-like undersea world of Pacifica, where she grew up as the daughter of Emperor Aphony. Tempest had saved her life and now she was in love with him. Back at Marineville, Marina owned a pet seal, Oink, and vied with Atlanta for Troy's attentions.

The arch-enemy of WASP was Titan, ruler of Titanica, who was assisted by his inept land-based agent, X20. Titan was also the power behind the evil Aquaphibians, who menaced the ocean in mechanical Terror Fish, firing missiles from the large, fishy mouths. Stingray, a high-tech, blue-and-yellow supersub (with a number 3 on its tailfins), fired back Sting Missiles. Atomic-powered, the supersub could also leap from the waves like a salmon and dive deeper and travel faster than any other submarine.

Stingray was Gerry Anderson's third venture into Supermarionation. It was also the first British TV programme to be filmed in colour, even though it could only be shown in black and white on its initial run in the UK. Tension, for viewers, began to mount from Commander Shore's opening words at the start of each episode: 'Stand by for action. Anything can happen in the next half-hour!', but the closing theme song, 'Aquamarina', sung by Garry Miller, provided a soothing finish.

STOCK, NIGEL
(1919–86)

Malta-born, one-time child performer who grew into one of Britain's most prolific actors. His film career began in the 1930s, and he was also an early arrival on television. In 1947 he appeared in the Borstal play, *Boys in Brown*, and the farce, *The Happiest Days of Your Life*, and he continued to pop up in dramas for the next 30-odd years. In the 1960s he guested in THE TROUBLESHOOTERS and THE PRISONER and in 1965 took on the mantle of Dr Watson for the BBC's SHERLOCK HOLMES, a role he reprised three years later. Soon after, he joined THE DOCTORS and then graduated to the title role of Dr Thomas Owen in *Owen, MD*. In the 1970s he was Hoof Commissaris Samson in VAN DER VALK and appeared in series like COLDITZ and TINKER, TAILOR, SOLDIER, SPY. In 1981 he was cast as Wally James in TRIANGLE. Other appearances included parts in *And No Birds Sing*, *Churchill's People*, *A Tale of Two Cities*, *A Man Called Intrepid*, YES, MINISTER and *The Pickwick Papers*.

STOPPARD, Dr MIRIAM
(1937–)

British TV pop doctor who came to the fore in the 1970s as host and expert on YTV's science series, DON'T ASK ME, *Don't Just Sit There* and WHERE THERE'S LIFE. Other credits have included *The Health Show* and *People Today*. She was formerly married to playwright Tom Stoppard.

STOPPARD, Sir TOM
CBE (Thomas Strausler; 1937–)

Czech-born British playwright, a former freelance journalist who has contributed mainly to stage, radio and films, specializing in complex and intellectual productions. His *Professional Foul* (a 1977 *Play of the Week*) was an award winner. Among his other television offerings have been *Every Good Boy Deserves Favour* (1979), an adaptation of *Three Men in a Boat* (1975) and the TV film, *Squaring the Circle* (1984).

STORYBOARD
UK (Thames) Drama Anthology. ITV 1983–6; 1989

Intermittent series of drama pilots.

Much in the style of COMEDY PLAYHOUSE, *Storyboard* was Thames TV's experimental drama anthology, giving airtime to assorted pilot episodes in the hope that some would turn into fully fledged series. Some, indeed, did. These were THE BILL (derived from the 1983 *Storyboard* episode entitled *Woodentop*), LYTTON'S DIARY, MR PALFREY OF WESTMINSTER (from a pilot called *The Traitor*), *King and Castle* and *Ladies in Charge*.

STORYTELLER, THE
UK (TVS/Jim Henson) Children's Entertainment. Channel 4 1988

The Storyteller .... **John Hurt**

Classic European folktales brought to life with imaginative and colourful special effects.

Using all the invention of Jim Henson's Creature Shop, *The Storyteller* was TVS's award-winning rendition of the great European fairytales. The Hobbit-like Storyteller related each tale in dramatic fashion at the side of his hearth, with his easily startled dog at his feet. Skilful animation by the Muppet team and complex special effects ensured that the series captured the imagination.

A follow-up series, *Jim Henson's Greek Myths* (1991), hosted by Michael Gambon, recalled the fabulous stories of ancient Greece concerning Theseus, Perseus, Orpheus and Eurydice, and Icarus and Daedalus.

STOTT, KEN
(1955–)

Scottish actor whose best-known TV work has been as hospital radio DJ Eddie McKenna in *Takin' over the Asylum*, Joe Hickey in *Bad Company*, fish farm manager McCaffrey in *A Mug's Game*, Barney Barnato in *Rhodes*, Redfern in *Screen Two*'s *Stone, Scissors, Paper*, Inspector Pat Chappel in *The Vice*, striker Tommy Walton in *Dockers* and criminal Martin Cahill in *Vicious Circle*. An early credit came in THE SINGING DETECTIVE.

STOURTON, EDWARD
(1957–)

Nigeria-born BBC newsreader, featuring in all the main bulletins and in current affairs programmes like PANORAMA, *Correspondent* and the religious series, *Absolute Truth*, having previously worked for ITN and *Channel 4 News*.

STRACHAN, MICHAELA
(1966–)

Popular British children's presenter, seen first on TV-am hosting *Wide Awake Club* and *Wacaday*. Her other kids' series have included *Hey Hey It's Saturday*, *Michaela*, *Owl TV*, *But Can You Do It On TV?*, *Go-Getters* and *The Really Wild Show*, and she was also seen with Pete Waterman in the late-night music show, *The Hit Man and Her*.

STRANGE REPORT
UK (Arena/ITC) Detective Drama. ITV 1968–9

Adam Strange .... **Anthony Quayle**
Hamlyn Gynt .... **Kaz Garas**
Evelyn McLean .... **Anneke Wills**
Chief Supt. Cavanagh .... **Gerald Sim**
Prof. Marks .... **Charles Lloyd Pack**

Creator/Executive Producer: **Norman Felton**
Producer: **Robert Buzz Berger**

The adventures of a retired criminologist and his young assistants.

Adam Strange was a renowned expert on the criminal mind, a former Home Office criminologist. Although retired, he was called back into action whenever the authorities were baffled by a case or needed help in sensitive areas. The investigations were complex and the crimes intricate, but Strange always had the answers, combining his vast experience with the latest techniques in a forensic laboratory at his Paddington flat. Assisted by a young American museum researcher, Ham Gynt, and a model and artist neighbour, Evelyn McLean, Strange, rather unusually, raced to the scenes of crime in an unlicensed black taxicab. Each episode was given a 'report' number: 'Report 4407 HEART – No Choice for the Donor', for instance, concerned an investigation into plans to use a live donor for a heart transplant, and 'Report 3906 COVER GIRLS – Last Year's Model' revolved around a mystery in the fashion world.

STRANGE WORLD OF GURNEY SLADE, THE
UK (ATV) Situation Comedy. ITV 1960

Gurney Slade .... **Anthony Newley**

Creator: **Anthony Newley**
Writers: **Sid Green, Dick Hills**

Producer: **Alan Tarrant**

A young man wanders through life in a state of fantasy.

In this bizarre, whimsical but short-lived series (only six episodes were made), the title character of Gurney Slade lived in a world of his own imagination. Talking to trees and animals, fantasizing about women, conjuring up unusual characters and bringing static beings to life, this young Londoner meandered his way through a number of weird situations.

Anthony Newley, the programme's creator and star, allegedly plucked the character's name from that of a Somerset village and, in devising this series, he developed a concept which was simply too far ahead of its time. Audiences in 1960 were used to comfortable domestic comedies and that's what *The Strange World of Gurney Slade* appeared to be, when it began by focusing on a family squabbling at home. But when Gurney suddenly stood up and walked off the set and into his own surreal world, he failed to take the bemused audience with him, and the programme quickly came to an end.

STRANGERS

UK (Granada) Police Drama. ITV 1978–82

DS/DCI George Bulman .... **Don Henderson**
DC/DS Derek Willis .... **Dennis Blanch**
DS David Singer .... **John Ronane**
WDC Linda Doran .... **Frances Tomelty**
WDC Vanessa Bennett .... **Fiona Mollison**
DCI Rainbow .... **David Hargreaves**
Det. Chief Supt. Jack Lambie .... **Mark McManus**
Insp. Pushkin .... **George Pravda**
William Dugdale .... **Thorley Walters**

Producer: **Richard Everitt**

Scotland Yard detectives infiltrate crime rings in the North-West.

Notable for the return of the glove-wearing, inhaler-sniffing, Shakespeare-quoting Sgt Bulman, first seen in THE XYY MAN, *Strangers* once again teamed the quirky detective with DC Derek Willis. This time they found themselves based in Manchester, joined by WDC Linda Doran, an expert in self-defence who was later replaced by WDC Vanessa Bennett, a car fiend. They operated as Unit C23, literally 'strangers' in a neighbourhood where local police officers would have been too well known. Assisted by DS Singer, who provided local knowledge, they took their assignments from the somewhat ineffective DCI Rainbow.

After two seasons, the format was changed. The team moved back to London but could be given missions anywhere in the country. They became the 'Inner City Squad', under the command of Det. Chief Supt. Lambie, a tough, no-nonsense officer played by Mark McManus in a rehearsal for TAGGART. Bulman was also introduced to William Dugdale, a university lecturer who had secret service connections and who was to assist him even more in the follow-up series, BULMAN. Willis was pro-moted to detective sergeant, and Bulman himself became a detective chief inspector in the penultimate season. The series ended with Bulman planning to marry Lambie's ex-wife. However, by the time *Bulman* reached the screen, the engagement had clearly fallen through.

STRAUSS FAMILY, THE

UK (ATV) Historical Drama. ITV 1972

Johann Strauss .... **Eric Woofe**
Johann Strauss, Jr .... **Stuart Wilson**
Anna Strauss .... **Anne Stallybrass**
Adele Strauss .... **Lynn Farleigh**
Emilie Trampusch .... **Barbara Ferris**
Josef Lanner .... **Derek Jacobi**
Eduard 'Edi' Strauss .... **Gary Miller**
                                                                          Tony Anholt

Writers: **David Butler, Anthony Skene, David Reid**
Executive Producer: **Cecil Clarke**
Producer: **David Reid**

The life and times of Austria's famous musical family.

Spanning most of the 19th century and tracing 75 years of musical creativity from father and son Johann Strauss, Sr and Jr, this biopic wafted along to the strains of authentic Viennese waltzes, sweepingly performed by the London Symphony Orchestra. But, beyond the music, the duo's lives and loves were also depicted. The series was made as part of ATV's historical drama spree in the mid-1970s.

STRAUSS, PETER

(1942–)

Largely seen in TV movies and blockbuster mini-series, American actor Peter Strauss made his TV name in the two RICH MAN, POOR MAN serials, playing Rudy Jordache. He was also Eleazar ben Yair in *Masada*, Dick Diver in *Tender Is the Night* and Abel Rosnovski in *Kane and Abel*, as well as starring as Peter Gunn in a 1989 TV movie revival of the 1950s detective.

STREET-PORTER, JANET

(1946–)

British presenter and TV executive. A former fashion journalist, Street-Porter came to the fore as a presenter for LWT, hosting, among other programmes, *Saturday Night People* with Clive James and Russell Harty. At the turn of the 1980s, she switched to behind-the-scenes work and then joined Channel 4, where she developed teenage output through *Network 7*. In 1988 she moved to the BBC to become Head of Youth Programming, which resulted in the DEF II programme strand and the commissioning of series like *Rough Guide to . . .* and *Rapido*. She was later the BBC's Head of Independent Entertainment Productions, bringing in series like *Paramount City*, *Ps and Qs* and *How Do They Do That?*. In 1994 she joined

Ffyona Campbell on the last leg of her global charity trek in *The Longest Walk*, and the same year left the BBC to be managing director of cable station, Live TV, a post she quit after a year. Back in front of the camera, she has presented *Street-Porter's Men*, followed the work of art historian Nikolaus Pevsner in one of the *Travels with Pevsner* series, continued her walks in *As the Crow Flies*, and made a series of *Cathedral Calls*.

STREETS OF SAN FRANCISCO, THE
US (Quinn Martin) Police Drama. ITV 1973–80

Det. Lt. Mike Stone	**Karl Malden**
Insp. Steve Keller	**Michael Douglas**
Insp. Dan Robbins	**Richard Hatch**
Lt. Lessing	**Lee Harris**
Sgt Sekulovich	**Art Passarella**
Officer Haseejian	**Vic Tayback**

Executive Producer: **Quinn Martin**
Producers: **William R. Yates, John Wilder, Cliff Gould**

A veteran police officer and his young assistant tackle crime in the Bay Area of San Francisco.

Detective Lt. Mike Stone was a widower with 23 years' experience in the force. He now worked for the Bureau of Inspectors Division of the San Francisco Police Department, where he was paired with 28-year-old Insp. Steve Keller, a college graduate. Stone's tried-and-tested techniques were occasionally questioned by Keller, whose ideas were more modern, but they struck up an effective, wise-old-head/eager-young-enthusiast partnership. When Keller left to take up teaching, he was replaced by another young cop, Dan Robbins, for the programme's last season (1976–7 in the USA).

For realism, some of the filming actually took place in the offices of the San Francisco Police Department, and the city's hilly streets were put to good use for the many car chases. The inspiration and the characters were drawn from Carolyn Weston's novel, *Poor, Poor Ophelia*.

STRIDE, JOHN
(1936–)

British actor, star of THE MAIN CHANCE (solicitor David Main) and WILDE ALLIANCE (fiction writer/detective Rupert Wilde). He also played Lloyd George in *Number Ten* and was seen in *Diamonds* (Frank Coleman), the BBC Television Shakespeare production of *Henry VIII* and the dramatization of *The Trial of Klaus Barbie*. Other credits have included LOVE STORY, LYTTON'S DIARY, *The Old Devils*, AGATHA CHRISTIE'S POIROT and THE INSPECTOR ALLEYN MYSTERIES.

STRIKE IT LUCKY / STRIKE IT RICH
UK (Thames/Central) Quiz. ITV 1986–94/1996–

Presenter: **Michael Barrymore**

Producer: **Maurice Leonard**

Easy-going game show involving quiz questions and a bank of illuminated TV screens.

A game of general knowledge and chance, *Strike It Lucky* was a very effective vehicle for the talents of Michael Barrymore. His ease with the general public was highlighted in his dealings with (and gentle mockery of) the three pairs of contestants, and his manic, physical style of comedy was accommodated by a large, sprawling set.

The six contestants were divided up into question answerers and 'screen strikers'. By choosing to give two, three or four correct answers to questions in a given category (with a list of possible responses shown on a screen to help them), a contestant allowed his or her partner to advance the equivalent number of steps along a wide, raised stage. Each step housed a TV screen which, when 'struck' revealed a prize or a 'hot spot'. Contestants were able to stick with the prize or advance further along the stage. A hot spot cancelled all the prizes won in that turn, and attention then switched to the next pair of contestants.

The first contestants to cross the stage were offered a jackpot question which, if answered correctly, took them to the grand finale. For this finale the two contestants progressed along the stage together, striking screens, occasionally answering questions and hoping to avoid a set number of hot spots which would end their bid for the top cash prize. These prizes were significantly increased when the show was renamed *Strike It Rich* in 1996.

STRIPPING

A scheduling term meaning the transmission of the same programme on the same channel at the same time, five or more consecutive nights a week (as NEIGHBOURS has been in the UK, for instance).

STRITCH, ELAINE
(1926–)

American actress with a number of comedies and quizzes behind her in her native USA, as well as stage and film credits, but primarily known to UK viewers as writer Dorothy McNab, alongside Donald Sinden, in the culture-clash sitcom, TWO'S COMPANY. She has also been seen in the UK in the comedies, *My Sister Eileen* (Ruth Sherwood) in 1964 and *Nobody's Perfect* (Bill Hooper) in 1980, plus series as diverse as TALES OF THE UNEXPECTED and THE COSBY SHOW.

STRONG, GWYNETH
(1959–)

London-born actress most familiar as Cassandra in ONLY FOOLS AND HORSES but seen in many other programmes, too. These have included *Bloody Kids*, THE KRYPTON FACTOR, *Nice Town* (Linda Thompson), *99–1* (Charlotte), *The Missing Postman* (WPC McMahon), REAL WOMEN

(Janet), A TOUCH OF FROST, *Forgotten* (Denise Longden) and *Lucy Sullivan is Getting Married* (Hetty).

STUBBS, UNA
(1937–)

British dancer and actress, first appearing in series like COOL FOR CATS, SUNDAY NIGHT AT THE LONDON PALLADIUM (in the chorus), *Moody in . . .* and NOT ONLY . . . BUT ALSO . . . . In 1966 she began a nine-year (on and off) run as Alf Garnett's daughter, Rita, in TILL DEATH US DO PART, reprising the role occasionally in the follow-up series, *In Sickness and in Health*, in the 1980s. Stubbs was one of the team captains in the charades game, GIVE US A CLUE, and played Aunt Sally in WORZEL GUMMIDGE. She appeared in the kids' comedies, *Morris Minor's Marvellous Motors* and *Tricky Business*, and was also seen in FAWLTY TOWERS and *Happy Families*. Her two husbands were both actors: Peter Gilmore and Nicky Henson.

SUBTITLE

Text superimposed on the screen (usually at the bottom) to provide a translation of foreign dialogue or to allow viewers with hearing difficulties to follow the action.

STV
See SCOTTISH TELEVISION.

SUCHET, DAVID
(1946–)

British actor, the brother of ITN newscaster John Suchet, undoubtedly best known for his work as AGATHA CHRISTIE'S POIROT, although he has enjoyed many other prominent roles. He played Blott in BLOTT ON THE LANDSCAPE, Edward Teller in *Oppenheimer*, Inspector Tsientsin in REILLY – ACE OF SPIES, Sigmund Freud in *Freud*, Shakespeare's *Timon of Athens*, Adolf Verloc in *The Secret Agent* and Morris Price in *Seesaw*. Among his other credits have been parts in dramas like *Oxbridge Blues*, *Ulysses*, *King and Castle*, *Nobody Here But Us Chickens* and *Time to Die*.

SUCHET, JOHN
(1944–)

British journalist and newscaster, once with Reuters and the BBC but since 1972 on ITN's staff. As well as working as ITN's Washington correspondent in the early 1980s, Suchet has fronted most of the main news bulletins, including *News at Ten*, *News at 5.40* and the lunchtime programmes. His brother is actor David Suchet and he is the father of actor Damian Suchet.

SUGDEN, MOLLIE
(1922–)

Yorkshire-born actress, the first choice of many producers when casting interfering, over-the-top mother figures. She played Mrs Clitheroe (Jimmy's mum) in JUST JIMMY, Mrs Hutchinson (Sandra's mum) in THE LIVER BIRDS, Mrs Waring (Duncan's mum) in DOCTOR IN CHARGE, Mrs Bassett (George's mum) in MY WIFE NEXT DOOR, Terry Scott's mum in *Son of the Bride* and Ida Willis (Robert Price's natural mum) in the adoption comedy, THAT'S MY BOY. She was also Mrs Crispin in HUGH AND I, Flavia in UP POMPEII!, Mrs Noah in COME BACK MRS NOAH, Nora Powers in *My Husband and I* (opposite her late real-life husband, William Moore) and Nellie Harvey, landlady of The Laughing Donkey, in CORONATION STREET. Undoubtedly, her most popular character, however, has been Mrs Slocombe in ARE YOU BEING SERVED? and *Grace and Favour*. She has also been seen in other comedies like PLEASE SIR!, FOR THE LOVE OF ADA and *Just William*, dramas like *Oliver's Travels* (Mrs Robson), the consumer show, THAT'S LIFE, and panel games like WHODUNNIT? and CLUEDO.

SULLAVAN BROTHERS, THE
UK (ATV) Drama. ITV 1964–5

Paul Sullavan	Anthony Bate
John Sullavan	Tenniel Evans
Beth Sullavan	Mary Kenton
Robert Sullavan QC	Hugh Manning
Patrick Sullavan	David Sumner

Creator: **Ted Willis**
Producer: **Jack Williams**

Legal eagling with a family law team.

The Sullavan Brothers were three solicitors and a barrister who worked in tandem for the benefit of their distressed clients. The barrister was Robert, a big, bulldozing type who took on the most serious cases. The team administrator was Paul, a logical, level-headed thinker; John was the blind, cultured idealist; and youngest brother Patrick was a handsome, vintage car aficionado who did most of the leg work. Also involved was John's wife, Beth.

SULLIVAN, ED
(1901–74)

The most famous of all variety show hosts, Ed Sullivan's background was in newspaper journalism. It was as a Broadway columnist that he was introduced to the major showbusiness names of the 1930s, leading to his own immersion in radio and film work as an impresario and compere. When TV began to take off, Sullivan was quickly in the action, pioneering the variety show format with *The Toast of the Town* (soon renamed *The Ed Sullivan Show*) from 1948. In this legendary Sunday-night

American programme, Sullivan introduced to viewers many budding or emerging stars, and gave countless others their TV debut. They ranged from Dean Martin and Jerry Lewis (in the very first show) to Elvis Presley and The Beatles. The series ran until 1971. Never known for his ease in front of the camera, Sullivan, nicknamed 'The Great Stone Face', was nevertheless one of TV's early giants.

SULLIVAN, JOHN
(1946–)

London-born comedy writer, a former scene-shifter at the BBC who knew he could write better scripts than the ones he was servicing. He talked producer Dennis Main Wilson into looking at his idea for a comedy based around a South London Marxist revolutionary, and CITIZEN SMITH was born, initially as an episode of *Comedy Special*. Sullivan's next creation has been widely acclaimed as his greatest, namely ONLY FOOLS AND HORSES, although he has also entertained viewers with JUST GOOD FRIENDS, DEAR JOHN, SITTING PRETTY, ROGER ROGER, *Heartburn Hotel* (with Steve Glover) and the two-part wartime comedy-drama, *Over Here*. His London roots tend to show through in most of his work.

SULLIVANS, THE
Australia (Crawford) Drama. ITV 1977–82

David Sullivan	**Paul Cronin**
Grace Sullivan	**Lorraine Bayly**
John Sullivan	**Andrew McFarlane**
Tom Sullivan	**Steven Tandy**
Terry Sullivan	**Richard Morgan**
Kitty Sullivan	**Susan Hannaford**
Harry Sullivan	**Michael Caton**
Geoff Sullivan	**Jamie Higgins**
Jim Sullivan	**Andy Anderson**
Maggie Hayward/Baker	**Vikki Hammond**
Anna Kaufman/Sullivan	**Ingrid Mason**
Lotte Kaufman	**Marcella Burgoyne**
Hans Kaufman	**Leon Lissek**
Jack Fletcher	**Reg Gorman**
Magpie Haddern	**Gary Sweet**
Rose Sullivan	**Maggie Dence**
Mrs Jessup	**Vivean Gray**
Major Barrington	**Roger Oakley**
Melina	**Chantal Contouri**
Bert Duggan	**Peter Hehir**
Caroline O'Brien	**Toni Vernon**
Michael Watkins	**John Walton**
Alice Morgan	**Megan Williams**
Norm Baker	**Norman Yemm**

Executive Producers: **Hector Crawford, Jock Blair**

An Australian family struggles to come to terms with World War II.

Beginning in 1939, *The Sullivans* told the continuing story of the Melbourne-based Sullivan family, headed by engineering foreman dad Dave and devout Catholic mum Grace. They had four children: John was a medical student but also a pacifist, and he joined the army very reluctantly; his brother, Tom, was also recruited, while third son Terry was still only a freckle-faced youth when hostilities began. The family's daughter was 13-year-old Kitty (played by 24-year-old actress Susan Hannaford). Anna Kaufman was John's girlfriend, a beautiful girl who suffered cruel abuse as anti-semitism spread around the world.

Inspired by Granada's A FAMILY AT WAR, *The Sullivans* followed the family through thick and thin as the war took a grip on the Antipodes. Scenes of desert and jungle conflicts were combined with everyday domestic ups and downs, but many of the most poignant moments came after the war had ended. Terry's demise into petty crime was disturbing enough, but more shocking still was Kitty's suicide following a visit to the devastation of Hiroshima with her photographer husband.

The Sullivans was a popular lunchtime offering in the UK, beginning just a year after its Australian première and conceived by ITV as a ready replacement for EMMERDALE FARM, which had been promoted to peak hours. In its native country, the series paved the way for later international hits like PRISONER: CELL BLOCK H, NEIGHBOURS and HOME AND AWAY, with many of *The Sullivans'* performers popping up in new guises in Wentworth, Erinsborough and Summer Bay.

SUNDAY NIGHT AT THE LONDON PALLADIUM
UK (ATV) Variety. ITV 1955–67; 1973–4

Comperes: **Tommy Trinder, Hughie Green, Alfred Marks, Robert Morley, Arthur Haynes, Dickie Henderson, Bruce Forsyth, Don Arrol, Dave Allen, Norman Vaughan, Jimmy Tarbuck, Des O'Connor, Roger Moore; Jim Dale**

Creator: **Val Parnell**
Producers: **Albert Locke, Francis Essex, Jon Scoffield, Colin Clews**

Weekly showcase of international stars, at the world's number-one variety theatre.

Sunday Night at the London Palladium was a British institution in the 1950s and 1960s. It was the show that everyone talked about the next day at work and it brought the world's most celebrated stars, plus the best of home-grown talent, into the living room of the ordinary citizen. The first ever show featured Gracie Fields and Guy Mitchell, and other stars appearing during its initial 12-year run included Judy Garland, Bob Hope, Johnny Ray, Liberace, Petula Clark, The Beatles and The Rolling Stones. The cheeky Italian mouse puppet, Topo Gigio, was a regular visitor. The programme's first host was music-hall comedian Tommy Trinder, who set the tone with his sharp ad-libs and fast talk. Others are listed above with, apart from Trinder, the main presenters being Norman Vaughan, Jimmy Tarbuck and Bruce Forsyth. Forsyth, like Trinder before him, was the perfect compere for the show's games interlude, *Beat the Clock*, which was based on the American quiz show of the same name and involved couples performing silly tricks or stunts within a set time-period. Bruce kept order by yelling 'I'm in charge', and prizes were awarded to successful participants. THE GENERATION GAME was a logical progression.

The format of *Sunday Night at the London Palladium* seldom varied. Lasting an hour, it began with the high-kicking Tiller Girls and then a welcome from the compere. He introduced a couple of lesser acts, before launching into *Beat the Clock*. The second half of the show was devoted to the big name of the week, and the programme was rounded off with the entire cast waving goodbye from the famous revolving stage. Although cancelled in 1967, *Sunday Night at the London Palladium* was revived briefly in 1973, with Jim Dale as host, but its heyday had long gone and it survived only one year. However, that didn't stop another revival in 2000, with Bruce Forsyth in charge of *Tonight at the London Palladium*.

SUPERCAR
UK (AP Films/ATV/ITC) Children's Science Fiction.
ITV 1961–2

Voices:

Mike Mercury	**Graydon Gould**
Prof. Popkiss	**George Murcell**
	Cyril Shaps
Jimmy Gibson	**Sylvia Anderson**
Dr Beaker	**David Graham**
Mitch	**David Graham**
Masterspy	**George Murcell**
	Cyril Shaps
Zarin	**David Graham**

Creators: **Gerry Anderson, Reg Hill**
Writers: **Martin Woodhouse, Hugh Woodhouse, Gerry Anderson, Sylvia Anderson**
Producer: **Gerry Anderson**

Adventures with the crew of an amazing land, sea and air vehicle.

Gerry Anderson's first science fiction series was based around a unique vehicle: a car, a plane and a submarine all rolled into one. Test pilot of Supercar was racing-driver-cum-airman-cum-deep-sea-diver Mike Mercury, who was joined on his missions by Professor Popkiss and the stammering Dr Beaker, co-inventors of the car. Also aboard were freckly ten-year-old Jimmy Gibson (one of two brothers whom Mike and Supercar had rescued at sea) and Mitch, Jimmy's talking monkey. The Supercar team were based at a secret laboratory in an American desert, but their travels saw them helping people and averting disasters all over the world. Their day-to-day enemies were the Sidney Greenstreet/Peter Lorre-type partnership of Masterspy and his sidekick, Zarin, who aimed to steal Supercar and use it for their evil ends. Of course they never succeeded.

Somewhat primitive by the standards of his later efforts, *Supercar* nevertheless was a breakthrough for Gerry Anderson, taking his puppet expertise to new levels and cementing his new partnership with Lew

Grade's ITC production and distribution company. It was also the series that coined the phrase, 'Super-marionation', to express the elaborate style of puppetry involved.

SUPERGRAN
UK (Tyne-Tees) Children's Comedy. ITV 1985–7

Granny Smith ('Supergran')	**Gudrun Ure**
The Scunner Campbell	**Iain Cuthbertson**
Inventor Black	**Bill Shine**
Insp. Muggins	**Robert Austin**
Muscles	**Alan Snell**
Dustin	**Brian Lewis**
Edison	**Holly English**
PC Leekie	**Terry Joyce**
Tub	**Lee Marshall**
Willard	**Ian Towell**

Writer: **Jenny McDade**
Producers: **Keith Richardson, Graham C. Williams**

An old lady becomes a superheroine and uses her powers to help others.

Struck by a beam from a magic ray machine, gentle old Granny Smith found herself accidentally endowed with superhuman powers. Adopting the guise of Supergran, she set out on her amazing 'flycycle' to defend the good folk of Chisleton against baddies like The Scunner Campbell. Also in the action was Inventor Black, the man whose magic ray had transformed the old lady. Supergran was based on the books by Forrest Wilson. Billy Connolly co-wrote the programme's theme music.

SUPERMAN
US (Lippert/National Periodical Publications) Science Fiction. ITV 1956–7

Superman/Clark Kent	**George Reeves**
Lois Lane	**Phyllis Coates**
	Noel Neill
Jimmy Olsen	**Jack Larson**
Perry White	**John Hamilton**
Insp. William Henderson	**Robert Shayne**

Producers: **Robert Maxwell, Bernard Luber, Whitney Ellsworth**

TV's first rendition of the comic-strip saga.

Created by Jerome Siegel and Joe Shuster in 1938, Superman was a refugee from the planet Krypton who lived on Earth and was endowed with superhuman powers. Under his *alter ego* of Clark Kent, he lived in Metropolis and worked as a reporter for *The Daily Planet*, an ideal position for hearing about crime as it happened. Stripping off his spectacles and donning his tights and cape, Superman raced to the rescue of helpless civilians, who often turned out to be his friends and colleagues. Demonstrating his superhuman strength by smashing down walls and bending iron bars, he was hailed as 'faster than a speeding bullet', once spectators had worked out that it was not a bird or a plane that had just flown past, but Superman himself. Those friends and colleagues included top reporter Lois Lane (in love with Superman, but disparaging of Clark Kent) and hapless trainee newshound Jimmy Olsen. His boss was pipe-smoking editor Perry White, who was often heard to exclaim, 'Great Caesar's ghost,' whenever anything startling happened, which was pretty often.

George Reeves, who had played Brent Tarleton in *Gone with the Wind*, suffered chronically from typecasting after this role, to the point where he was unable to work and eventually took his own life. Co-star Noel Neill reappeared briefly in the 1970s film version, this time as Superman's mother. Superman returned to the TV screens in 1994, in *The New Adventures of Superman*, with Dean Cain as the 'Man of Steel' and Teri Hatcher as Lois Lane.

SUPERSONIC
UK (LWT) Pop Music 1975–7

Creator/Producer: **Mike Mansfield**

State-of-the-art 1970s pop showcase.

One of ITV's many attempts to match the success of TOP OF THE POPS, *Supersonic* suffered from the usual problem – networking (or lack of it), being shown at various times around the ITV regions (mostly Saturday mornings). The man behind the show was producer/director Mike Mansfield, who conceived the idea of a music show without a regular host. Instead, a camera was installed in the director's gallery and the acts were introduced simply by being cued in – along with the cameras, sound, etc. – by Mansfield himself ('Good luck, everybody, and roll *Supersonic*'). On the studio floor, the latest techniques were employed – roving cameras, stars perched on crane lifts over the audience, bubble machines, fireworks and the usual sea of dry ice and smoke. In his control box, Mansfield called up special effects like crazy wipes and multiple images. Four or five bands/artists appeared in each show, some performing more than once, and not just their current releases.

SUPERSTARS, THE
UK (BBC) Sport. BBC 1 1975–82; 1985

Presenters: **David Vine, Ron Pickering**

Producers: **Ian Smith, Peter Hylton Cleaver**

International sportsmen tackle representatives from other sports in a contest of fitness and skill.

Beginning as a domestic event (initially entitled *Sporting Superstars*) but later going international, *The Superstars* was an innovative test of power, fitness, skill and adaptability. It aimed to discover which sports provided the best all-round athletes and competitors by pitting top names against each other in a series of contests. These ranged from gym tests (push-ups, squat thrusts, etc.), to disciplines like football control, rifle shooting, distance

running, sprinting, cycling, basketball, archery, weightlifting, swimming and rowing. Competitors were not allowed to compete in their own sports or in sports akin to their own. The series made household names of lesser-known sportsmen like judo star Brian Jacks and rugby league's Keith Fielding. A spin-off series, *The Superteams*, matched team competitors from various sports.

SURGICAL SPIRIT
UK (Humphrey Barclay/Granada) Situation Comedy.
ITV 1989–95

Dr Sheila Sabatini	**Nichola McAuliffe**
Dr Jonathan Haslam	**Duncan Preston**
Joyce Watson	**Marji Campi**
George Hope-Wynne	**David Conville**
Neil Copeland	**Emlyn Price**
Simon Field	**Lyndam Gregory**
Giles Peake	**Simon Harrison**
Sister Cheryl Patching	**Suzette Llewellyn**
Dr Michael Sampson	**Beresford Le Roy**
Daniel Sabatini	**Andrew Groves**

Creator: **Peter Learmouth**
Producer: **Humphrey Barclay**

A senior surgeon's tongue is as sharp as her scalpel.

Sheila Sabatini was a hard-working surgeon at the Gillies Hospital. She was also hot-tempered, opinionated and sharp-tongued, but this didn't prevent her anaesthetist colleague, Jonathan Haslam, from beginning a relationship with her (once her divorce had come through). Their on-off affair ran for six years amid weekly hospital crises and against a backdrop of open conflict in the operating theatre. Involved in matchmaking was the hospital's gossipy administrator, Joyce Watson, and her efforts paid off when the two were wed in 1994. Also seen were fellow surgeon Neil Copeland, houseman Giles Peake, sister Cheryl Patching, her live-in boyfriend, Dr Michael Sampson, George Hope-Wynne, a consultant surgeon with more interest in private medicine, and Sheila's teenage (later medical student) son, Daniel.

SURPRISE, SURPRISE
UK (LWT) Entertainment. ITV 1984–97

Presenters: **Cilla Black, Christopher Biggins, Bob Carolgees, Gordon Burns**

Producers: **Bob Merrilees, Brian Wesley, Linda Beadle, Colman Hutchinson, Nina Donaldson**

Magic-wand show in which members of the public are given heart-warming surprises.

Surprise, Surprise was created as a showcase for Cilla Black and was her first TV series for over eight years. It paired her initially with Christopher Biggins, but he was dropped after the first series, to be replaced later by Bob Carolgees. The aim of the show was to make dreams come true in JIM'LL FIX IT fashion for members of the general public, acting on advice from relatives and friends. One segment, entitled *Searchline*, hosted for five years by Gordon Burns, hoped to re-establish contact between broken families and long-lost friends. Another feature was celebrities making unexpected visits to fans' homes. In true Cilla tradition there were a 'lorra lorra laffs', but plenty of tears, too. A one-off *Cilla's Surprise, Surprise Mother's Day Special* was screened in 1999.

SURVIVAL

UK (Anglia) Natural History. ITV 1961–

Creator: **Aubrey Buxton**

Long-running, award-winning wildlife series.

Undoubtedly Anglia Television's greatest product, *Survival* has been seen in more countries (112) around the world than any other British programme (in some cases under the title of *The World of Survival*). Beginning in 1961 with a short series of films about London wildlife (with production assistance from Associated-Rediffusion), *Survival* has since expanded to cover nature stories all over the globe. Creator Aubrey Buxton was associated with the programme for many years and introduced some of the early episodes. His daughter, Cindy Buxton, has carried on the tradition, once famously being trapped on South Georgia during the 1982 Falklands conflict while filming for the series. Colin Willock has also been a major influence. The painstakingly made half-hour films (occasionally an hour in length, when they have been billed as *Survival Special*) have been narrated by the likes of David Niven, Peter Scott, Kenneth More, John Hedges, Brian Blessed, Duncan Carse, Ian Holm, Dennis Quilley, Andrew Sachs, T. P. McKenna and Robert Hardy. Programmes have focused on the threat to wildlife, the environment and native peoples. Some of the best remembered have been *Tarantula!*, *The Painter and The Fighter* (African tribespeople) and *Polar Bear – Hunters on Ice*. John Forsythe has introduced the series for American viewers. Around 800 programmes have now been produced and *Survival* has picked up some 130 international awards.

SURVIVORS

UK (BBC) Science Fiction. BBC 1 1975–7

Abby Grant	**Carolyn Seymour**
Greg Preston	**Ian McCulloch**
Jenny Richards	**Lucy Fleming**
Charles Vaughan	**Denis Lill**
Dave Long	**Brian Peck**
Tom Price	**Talfryn Thomas**
John	**Stephen Dudley**
Lizzie	**Tanya Ronder**
	Angie Stevens
Vic Thatcher	**Terry Scully**
Paul Pitman	**Christopher Tranchell**
Mrs Emma Cohen	**Hana-Maria Pravda**
Charmian Wentworth	**Eileen Helsby**
Agnes	**Sally Osborn**
	Anna Pitt

Arthur Russell	**Michael Gover**
Alan	**Stephen Tate**
Seth	**Dan Meaden**
Pet Simpson	**Lorna Lewis**
Ruth Anderson	**Celia Gregory**
Hubert	**John Abineri**
Jack	**Gordon Salkilld**
Melanie	**Heather Wright**
Daniella	**Gigi Gatti**
Dave	**Peter Duncan**
Alec	**William Dysart**

Creator: **Terry Nation**
Producer: **Terence Dudley**

The survivors of a killer plague struggle to rebuild civilization and establish a future for the world.

Imagine a world that suddenly grinds to a halt. A world where 95 per cent of the population is wiped out in just a few weeks by a rogue virus and where the remaining 5 per cent has to battle to stay alive. Imagine a world where, for all the modern technology around him, man is forced to fall back on primitive skills to feed himself and to establish a pattern of law and order. This was the imagination of Terry Nation, the creator of the Daleks and the inspiration behind *Survivors*.

As graphically depicted in the programme's opening titles, the world had been gripped by a deadly virus, accidentally released when a scientist in the Far East smashed a test-tube. Inadvertently spread by jet-setting businessmen, the virus had quickly reached Britain, where *Survivors* took up the story. It centred on a motley band of individuals, people who had either been immune to the plague or who had somehow recovered from it. At the forefront was suburban housewife Abby Grant, who watched her husband die in the first episode but who still hoped to find her lost son, Peter. Twenty-six-year-old secretary Jenny Richards, 38-year-old architect Charles Vaughan and the group's leader-elect, 35-year-old civil engineer Greg Preston, were also prominent. The first episodes revealed how they found each other as they wandered around derelict towns and villages, seeking food, shelter and, above all, other people. After that, attention turned to their efforts to re-establish civilization and to harness whatever specialist talents remained in the survivors around them – the likes of doctors, electricians and teachers. Along the way, they encountered unpleasant characters, such as weaselly Welsh labourer Tom Price, and other communities which expressed their own perverse forms of law, order and justice.

Getting all the survivors to work in harmony proved impossible. Suspicion was rife and greed and power were two elements they found hard to subdue. Effectively, the Dark Ages had returned. The desperate need to reclaim society and to re-invent the skills needed to replenish supplies of food, medicine, transport, power and other essentials formed the backbone of the series which, after three seasons, ended on a more optimistic note than it had begun. Common sense and human spirit were beginning to shine through and, although the going remained tough, at least some kind of future was beckoning.

SUTHERLAND'S LAW
UK (BBC) Legal Drama. BBC 1 1973–6

John Sutherland	**Iain Cuthbertson**
Alec Duthie	**Gareth Thomas**
Christine Russell	**Maev Alexander**
Sgt McKechnie	**Don McKillop**
Dr Judith Roberts/Sutherland	**Edith MacArthur**
Gail Munro	**Harriet Buchan**
Insp./Chief Insp. Menzies	**Victor Carin**
David Drummond	**Martin Cochrane**
Sheriff Derwent	**Moultrie Kelsall**
Helen Matheson	**Virginia Stark**
Kate Cameron	**Sarah Collier**

Creator: **Lindsay Galloway**
Producers: **Neil McCallum, Frank Cox**

The cases of a procurator fiscal in a Scottish fishing town.

In the small town of Glendoran, John Sutherland held the post of procurator fiscal, a legal position somewhere between an investigative prosecuting lawyer, an American district attorney and a coroner. Under Scottish law, the police do not prosecute criminals themselves, they have to go to the procurator fiscal for action. So it was that Iain Cuthbertson, fresh from playing the rogue Charlie Endell in BUDGIE, became a reformed character and, as Sutherland, began to act on behalf of the people against the criminal fraternity, solving baffling mysteries along the way. He was supported at various times by Alec Duthie, Christine Russell, Gail Munro, David Drummond and Helen Matheson. The beautiful West Coast views were a bonus. The series stemmed from a 1972 *Drama Playhouse* presentation.

SUTTON, SHAUN
OBE (1919–)

British writer, producer and director, working mostly on children's comedies and dramas (such as BILLY BUNTER OF GREYFRIARS SCHOOL, BONEHEAD, *The Great Detective* and *The Silver Sword*) before becoming the BBC's Head of Drama, 1969–81. Among his other work was direction on THE TROUBLESHOOTERS, Z CARS, *Kipling* and DETECTIVE. He later produced some of the *BBC Television Shakespeare* presentations.

SWEENEY, THE
UK (Euston Films/Thames) Police Drama. ITV 1975–8

DI Jack Regan	**John Thaw**
DS George Carter	**Dennis Waterman**
Chief Insp. Frank Haskins	**Garfield Morgan**

Creator: **Ian Kennedy Martin**
Executive Producers: **Lloyd Shirley, George Taylor, Ted Childs**

Rough, tough and violent crime-busting with a no-nonsense pair of Flying Squad detectives.

Taking its name from the Cockney rhyming slang for Flying Squad ('Sweeney Todd'), this was one of television's most physical cop shows. It featured the investigations of door-smashing, crook-thumping, heavy-drinking DI Jack Regan and his junior partner, DS George Carter, who screamed around London in a gold-coloured Ford Granada. Hard, and sometimes unquestioning, Regan had little time for rules and regulations. In his leather jacket and '70s-style kipper ties, he was also a bit of a lad, found off-duty in the boozer, chatting to the local villains, or in bed with yet another woman (he was, not surprisingly, estranged from his wife). Carter was his loyal number two, learning the trade from his mentor and picking up the bad habits along with the good. Like his boss, he too was pretty useful with his fists. Supervising the operations, often in desperation at the tactics involved, was Chief Insp. Haskins.

The series began seven months after a pilot episode, *Regan*, part of the *Armchair Cinema* anthology, was screened in 1974, and it ended in 1978, when Regan was banged up for allegedly taking bribes. No charges were brought, but Regan had had enough and decided to call it a day. Through *The Sweeney*, the public was introduced to a new kind of policeman, one the authorities tried to deny existed but one which certain real-life lawmen privately acknowledged to be alive and kicking, especially kicking. Indeed, Jack Quarrie, a former Flying Squad officer, was the programme's technical adviser. But, for all its bad language and excessive violence, the series also had its humorous side, highlighted in the Regan–Carter Cockney repartee and an episode which featured Morecambe and Wise as guest stars. Two feature films were also made.

SWIFT, CLIVE
(1936–)

British actor seen in numerous supporting roles, most prominently as the hen-pecked Richard Bucket in KEEPING UP APPEARANCES. He was DI Waugh in *Waugh on Crime* (six *Thirty-Minute Theatre* productions in 1970), and was Mr Nesbitt in the sitcom, *The Nesbitts are Coming*. Among his many other credits have been parts in COMPACT, *Dig This Rhubarb*, *Clayhanger*, THE BROTHERS, LOVE STORY, THE LIVER BIRDS, SOUTH RIDING, *The Barchester Chronicles*, TALES OF THE UNEXPECTED, WINSTON CHURCHILL – THE WILDERNESS YEARS, *Beasts*, THE GENTLE TOUCH, SHELLEY, DOCTOR WHO, MINDER, A VERY PECULIAR PRACTICE, INSPECTOR MORSE, various adaptations of the classics, and more. He is the brother of actor David Swift.

SWIT, LORETTA
(1937–)

Blonde American actress of Polish descent, M*A*S*H's Margaret 'Hotlips' Hoolihan, but also Christine Cagney in the pilot movie for CAGNEY AND LACEY (although not the series). She has since been seen in many other TV movies, with her earliest appearances coming in series like GUNSMOKE, HAWAII FIVE-O and MANNIX.

SWORD OF FREEDOM
UK (Sapphire/ITC) Adventure. ITV 1958–61

Marco del Monte .... **Edmund Purdom**
Angelica .... **Adrienne Corri**
Sandro .... **Rowland Bartrop**
Duke de Medici .... **Martin Benson**
Francesca .... **Monica Stevenson**
Machiavelli .... **Kenneth Hyde**

Executive Producer: **Hannah Weinstein**
Producer: **Sidney Cole**

Robin Hood in an Italian Renaissance setting.

Marco del Monte was a 15th-century Florentine painter, much sickened by the excesses of the city-state's ruling family, the Medicis. Supported by Angelica, his former pickpocket model, and his broad-shouldered friend, Sandro, he constantly took on the might of the authorities, displaying a flair for swordsmanship as well as art as he rode to the rescue of many an oppressed compatriot. In his sights were the Duke de Medici and his cruel sister, Francesca.

SYKES
UK (BBC) Situation Comedy. BBC 1 1960–5; 1972–9

Eric .... **Eric Sykes**
Hattie .... **Hattie Jacques**
Mr Charles Brown .... **Richard Wattis**
Corky .... **Deryck Guyler**

Writers: **Johnny Speight, Eric Sykes**
Producers: **Dennis Main Wilson, Sydney Lotterby,
Philip Barker, Roger Race**

*A hapless brother and sister share a suburban
home.*

Life at 24 Sebastopol Terrace, Acton, was seldom simple. Home to bachelor brother Eric and spinster sister Hattie, it played host to assorted domestic crises. With Eric constantly trying to better himself, misunderstandings were rife and often involved Eric and Hattie's snooty, interfering neighbour, Mr Brown, or Corky, the pompous neighbourhood bobby.

Initially, this long-running series went out under the title of *Sykes and . . .*, with the object, implement or creature that was about to cause chaos inserted into the title. Examples included *Sykes and a Telephone* and *Sykes and a Plank*. Some early episodes were scripted by Johnny Speight, but the lion's share of programmes were penned by Eric Sykes himself. The title became simply *Sykes* when the series was revived in the 1970s.

SYKES, ERIC
OBE (1923–)

British comedian and writer, who broke into radio after the war, penning scripts for *Educating Archie* and other series. He also wrote for television: *The Howerd Crowd* for Frankie Howerd in 1952, gags for Max Bygraves, Harry Secombe and Jimmy Logan, and Tony Hancock's first TV sketches, screened as *The Tony Hancock Show* by ITV in 1956. The Goonish *Idiot Weekly, Price 2d* was another of his early outlets, and he was also involved in the film world by the time his long-running sitcom, SYKES, began in 1960. Apart from a seven-year hiatus in the middle, the series ran until 1979. Originally, the *Sykes* scripts were written by Johnny Speight, but Eric soon took control himself, although his relationship with Speight was to resume in 1969, when Sykes played the liberal factory foreman in the controversial CURRY AND CHIPS. He and Speight teamed up again in 1989 for another sitcom, *The Nineteenth Hole*. Sykes has also been known for his visual humour, exemplified in the silent films, *The Plank, It's Your Move* and *Mr H Is Late*. He also directed the TV film, *If You Go Down to the Woods Today*, in 1981 and other credits in his long career have included *Sykes Versus ITV* (a mock court case), *Sykes and a Big Big Show* and guest spots in NOT ONLY . . . BUT ALSO . . . More recently, he provided the voice of the lion in TELETUBBIES, guested in DINNERLADIES and appeared as Mollocks in *Gormenghast*.

SYLVANIA WATERS
Australia (BBC/Australian Broadcasting Company)
Documentary. BBC 1 1993

Producer: **Paul Watson**

*Warts-and-all, 12-part documentary about the
daily life of a typical Australian family.*

In the fly-on-the-wall tradition of his earlier programme, THE FAMILY, producer Paul Watson captured the domestic ups and downs of the Baker–Donaher family in one of Sydney's well-off suburbs. Heads of the family were rich divorcees Noeline Baker and Laurie Donaher, proud of the hard-working way in which they had built up their wealth and determined to enjoy it to the full. Intra-family squabbles added spice to the story, with running arguments between Noeline and her elder son, Paul, the unfolding drama of his wife Dione's pregnancy and the teenage trials of younger son, Michael, who narrated the programme.

These real-life NEIGHBOURS caused a storm in their native Australia when they were criticized for their brash, bigoted behaviour and their heavy drinking/ smoking lifestyle.

SYNDICATION

An American term for the sale of programmes to independent stations (rather than the national networks) for screening locally. Old, repeat episodes of prime-time series are syndicated, as are new series which the major networks decline to take up. Some programmes are made specifically for syndication (low-budget features, game shows, etc.) and occasionally a major series begins or only airs in syndication (STAR TREK: THE NEXT GENERATION is one example). Many British series have been seen in the USA only in syndication.

T. J. HOOKER

US (Spelling-Goldberg/Columbia) Police Drama. ITV
1983–5

Sgt T. J. Hooker	**William Shatner**
Officer Vince Romano	**Adrian Zmed**
Capt. Dennis Sheridan	**Richard Herd**
Fran Hooker	**Lee Bryant**
Vicki Taylor	**April Clough**
Officer Stacy Sheridan	**Heather Locklear**
Officer Jim Corrigan	**James Darren**

Creator: **Rick Husky**
Executive Producers: **Aaron Spelling, Leonard
Goldberg**
Producer: **Jeffrey Hayes**

*An experienced police officer teaches rookies rights
and wrongs.*

Honest and decent, plain-clothes detective T. J. Hooker
had grown tired of investigations and longed to return
to the beat. Reverting to his former role of sergeant, he
was assigned to the Academy Precinct of the LCPD
where his keen young partner was Vince Romano. While
performing his duties in an exemplary fashion, Hooker
became a role-model for trainee officers, educating them
in the moral dimensions of policing, as well as the strategic and physical aspects. He had seen one of his partners killed in action and over the years had had plenty
of time to contemplate the good and bad sides of law
enforcement.

Hooker was divorced but was still friendly with his
ex-wife, Fran, a nurse. His police family included rookies
Vicki Taylor and Stacy Sheridan, the latter the daughter
of his hard-nosed boss, Captain Dennis Sheridan. She
was later promoted to patrol officer and teamed up with
experienced Jim Corrigan. Cameo appearances from
stars like the Beach Boys and Leonard Nimoy were
common. The 'LC' of LCPD was never explained, nor
were Hooker's initials, T. J.

TAGGART

UK (Scottish) Police Drama. ITV 1983–

DCI Jim Taggart	**Mark McManus**
DS Peter Livingstone	**Neil Duncan**
Supt. Jack McVitie	**Iain Anders**
Supt. Murray	**Tony Watson**
DC/DS/DI/DCI Mike Jardine	**James Macpherson**
Jean Taggart	**Harriet Buchan**
Alison Taggart	**Geraldine Alexander**
Dr Stephen Andrews	**Robert Robertson**
WDC/WDS Jackie Reid	**Blythe Duff**
DC Stuart Fraser	**Colin McCredie**
DI Robbie Ross	**John Michie**

Creator: **Glenn Chandler**
Producers: **Robert Love, Murray Ferguson, Paddy
Higson, Bernard Krichefski, John G. Temple, Frank Cox,
Richard Handford, Mike Dormer, Emma Hayter**

Gruesome murder investigations with a gritty Glaswegian detective.

Jim Taggart worked for the Glasgow CID. Covering the Northern Division, he was hard-nosed, firm and dedicated, yet was saddened by his job to the point of cynicism. His wife, Jean, had been wheelchair-bound for over 20 years (since the birth of their daughter, Alison) and she was largely resigned to her husband's devotion to work, not that he had a lot to say when he did eventually return home. Working with the down-to-earth Taggart was the university-educated DS Peter Livingstone, a man with quite different social roots. Livingstone was later replaced by Mike Jardine, a keen, young teetotaller (much to the disgust of Taggart, a malt whisky connoisseur) who worked his way up from detective constable under his mentor's tutelage. Their assignments involved the grisliest, most distressing and baffling murders, all set against the distinctive backdrop of Glasgow city, with a touch of wry Scottish humour to sugar the pill.

Combining one-off stories with short serials, in a somewhat intermittent fashion, *Taggart* began with a thriller entitled *Killer* in 1983 and seemed likely to end with the premature death of its star, Mark McManus, in 1994. However, Taggart continued, with Jardine and DS Jackie Reid moving on to centre stage.

TAKE A LETTER
UK (Granada) Game Show. ITV 1962–4

Presenter: **Bob Holness**

Producers: **John Hamp, Max Morgan-Witts**

Crossword-based family puzzle game.

By solving clues and choosing letters to complete mystery words, the contestants in this popular programme attempted to win small cash prizes. The amount won depended on the number of letters selected before the correct answer was given. Future BLOCKBUSTERS host Bob Holness took charge of proceedings.

TAKE HART
See VISION ON.

TAKE THE HIGH ROAD / HIGH ROAD
UK (Scottish) Drama. ITV 1980–

Elizabeth Cunningham	**Edith Macarthur**
Fiona Cunningham/Ryder	**Caroline Ashley**
Isabel Blair/Morgan	**Eileen McCallum**
Brian Blair	**Kenneth Watson**
Jimmy Blair	**Jimmy Chisholm**
Alice McEwan/Taylor	**Muriel Romanes**
Dougal Lachlan	**Alec Monteath**
Gladys Aitken/Lachlan	**Ginni Barlow**
Grace Lachlan	**Marjorie Thomson**
Donald Lachlan	**Steven Brown**
Alan McIntyre	**Martin Cochrane**

Davie Sneddon	**Derek Lord**
Mrs Mary Mack	**Gwyneth Guthrie**
Lorna Seton	**Joan Alcorn**
Mr Obadiah Arthur Murdoch	**Robert Trotter**
Alex Geddes	**James Cosmo**
Tom Kerr ('Inverdarroch')	**John Stahl**
Bob Taylor	**Iain Agnew**
Fergus Jamieson	**Frank Wylie**
Ken Calder	**Bill Henderson**
Dr Sandy Wallace	**Michael Elder**
Archie Menzies	**Paul Kermack**
Max Langemann	**Frederick Jaeger**
Jane Steedman	**Ingrid Hafner**
Sheila Lamont/Ramsay	**Lesley Fitz-Simons**
Sir John Ross-Gifford	**Michael Browning**
Lady Margaret Ross-Gifford	**Jan Waters**
Eric Ross-Gifford	**Richard Greenwood**
Joanna Simpson/Ross-Gifford	**Tamara Kennedy**
Emma Aitken	**Amanda Whitehead**
Greg Ryder	**Alan Hunter**
Sam Hagen	**Briony McRoberts**
Jockie McDonald	**Jackie Farrell**
Sadie McDonald	**Doreen Cameron**
Trish McDonald	**Natalie Robb**
Gary McDonald	**Joseph McFadden**
Carol McKay/Wilson	**Teri Lally**
Lynne McNeil	**Gillian McNeill**
Mr Ian McPherson	**John Young**
Effie MacInnes/McDonald	**Mary Riggans**
Jennifer Goudie	**Victoria Burton**
Paul Martin	**Peter Bruce**
Alun Morgan	**Mike Hayward**
Menna Morgan	**Manon Jones**
Nick Stapleton	**Stephen Hogan**
Sgt Murray	**James McDonald**
Revd Michael Ross	**Gordon MacArthur**
Morag Stewart	**Jeannie Fisher**
Tee Jay Wilson	**Andrew Gillan**
Miss Symonds	**Harriet Buchan**
Eddie Ramsay	**Robin Cameron**
George Carradine	**Leon Sinden**
Sarah Gilchrist/McDonald	**Shonagh Pryce**
Callum Gilchrist	**Jim Webster**
Judith Crombie	**Anne Marie Timoney**
PC Douglas Kirk	**Graeme Robertson**
Phineas ('Fin') North	**William Tapley**
Tiffany Bowles	**Rachel Ogilvy**
Chic Cherry	**Andy Cameron**
Susan Duncan/Ross	**Jacqueline Gilbride**
Dominic Ramsay	**Gary Hollywood**
Paul Lafferty	**Simon Weir**
Lachie McIvor	**Alec Heggie**
Ewan Logan	**Gordon Brown**
PC Tony Piacentini	**Alan McHugh**
Victor Kemp	**Iain Andrew**
Sally McGann	**Catriona Evans**

Creator: **Don Houghton**
Producers: **Clarke Tait, Frank Cox, John G. Temple, Mark Grindle**

Life in a rural Scottish community.

A sort of EMMERDALE FARM north of the border, *Take the*

High Road is the long-running saga of the good folk of Glendarroch and the next-door parish of Auchtarne. The main characters have included local gossip Mrs Mack, shopkeepers Isabel and Brian Blair, their heart-throb son, Jimmy, and roguish Irish land-manager Davie Sneddon. Others to feature have been the hypocritical Mr Murdoch, postman Fergus Jamieson, farmer Inverdarroch, old-fashioned Dr Wallace, minister Mr McPherson, *Auchtarne Herald* reporter Sheila Ramsay and Ardvain crofter Dougal Lachlan; but the series has also focused on the Lairds of Glendarroch House, to whose estate the village has belonged. When the first Lady Laird, Elizabeth Cunningham, was dramatically killed in a car accident in 1987, and her daughter, Fiona, also left the house (she later married ruthless businessman Greg Ryder), Glendarroch gained new Lairds in the shape of Sir John and Lady Margaret Ross-Gifford. Being English, they were looked upon with distrust. Action has taken place in such settings as Blair's Store and the Ardnacraig Hotel, the latter run by the Ross-Giffords' son, Eric, and his wife, Joanna. The real-life village used for filming has been Luss on Loch Lomond.

Despite enjoying large audiences in its native Scotland, *Take the High Road* has only gained an afternoon time-slot elsewhere in the UK. The title was shortened to *High Road* in 1994, but ITV regions have gradually lost interest and begun dropping the series. Outside Scotland, only the Border, Central, Ulster and Westcountry regions were still carrying the series in 2000.

TAKE THREE GIRLS
UK (BBC) Comedy Drama. BBC 1 1969–71

Kate	**Susan Jameson**
Avril	**Angela Down**
Victoria Edgecombe	**Liza Goddard**
Mr Edgecombe	**David Langton**
Jenny	**Carolyn Seymour**
Lulie	**Barra Grant**

Creator: **Gerald Savory**
Producer: **Michael Hayes**

Ups and downs in the lives of three girl flatsharers.

The three girls in question were the cello-playing deb, Victoria (one of life's losers), failed actress Kate (a struggling single parent) and Cockney art student Avril. Together they shared a flat in London SW3 and with it their experiences of life as single women in the capital. Four of the 50-minute episodes were devoted to each girl's story. Also seen was Victoria's mean dad, Mr Edgecombe. When the second series began, only Victoria remained of the original trio, Kate having been married off and Avril leaving to work in Paris. Victoria was joined by new flatmates, 23-year-old Jenny, a journalist, and Lulie, an American psychology graduate. A four-part reunion special, entitled *Take Three Women* and featuring Victoria, Kate and Avril, was screened in 1982. Thirteen years on from the earliest episodes, it saw Victoria widowed and raising her young daughter alone, Kate living with the teacher of her 13-year-old son and Avril proprietress of an art gallery. Music for early and later episodes was performed by folk, jazz and blues band Pentangle.

TAKE YOUR PICK
UK (Associated-Rediffusion/Arlington/Thames) Quiz. ITV
1955–68; 1992–8

Hosts: **Michael Miles, Des O'Connor.**
Announcer: **Bob Danvers-Walker**

Producer: **Brian Klein**

Popular quiz game played for laughs.

Hosted by New Zealander Michael Miles, billed as 'your quiz inquisitor', *Take Your Pick* took its place in the very first ITV schedules and stayed there (alongside its great rival, DOUBLE YOUR MONEY) for 13 years. Like *Double Your Money*, it graduated to television from Radio Luxembourg, where it had been a hit for three years. *Take Your Pick* involved contestants answering three general knowledge questions successfully so as to pick up a key to a numbered box. Each box contained details of a prize, although three of the prizes were worthless – a prune or a clothes peg, for example. Before the box was opened, Miles attempted to buy the key from the contestant, offering him or her ever-increasing sums of money. 'Take the money or open the box?' he asked, at the same time encouraging the audience to yell their advice. While some heads were turned by the prospect of cash in hand, others risked all on the turn of the key. To add to the excitement, there was also the mysterious Box 13, the contents of which were unknown even to Miles, and the additional prospect of winning the Treasure Chest of Money or Tonight's Star Prize. The booming voice of Bob Danvers-Walker announced the prizes and Harold Smart gave a quick burst on the organ to add to the thrill.

To reach the questions stage, contestants – plucked from the studio audience just minutes before the show began – had to survive a gruelling ordeal in which Miles asked them questions about their life, work, hobbies, family, etc. Without hesitation, and without nodding or shaking their head, participants had to respond avoiding the use of the words 'yes' and 'no'. Those who lasted longest progressed to the general knowledge phase. The 'Yes/No Interlude', as it became known, was patrolled by Alec Dane, who banged a gong whenever the forbidden words were uttered.

A year after *Take Your Pick* ended, Michael Miles resurfaced with a similar concept entitled *Wheel of Fortune* (1969–71). Not to be confused with the later American import (hosted in the UK by Nicky Campbell and others; see separate entry), this *Wheel of Fortune* offered star and booby prizes just like *Take Your Pick*, only this time they were determined by the spin of a large wheel. Danvers-Walker and Smart were again in support. *Take Your Pick* itself was revived with some success in 1992. Des O'Connor took over from the late Miles and Jodie Wilson acted as his assistant and gong-mistress, before she gave way in 1994 to the Australian twins Gayle and Gillian Blakeney, once of NEIGHBOURS fame, then to Sarah Matravers and Sasha Lawrence.

TALES FROM EUROPE

Europe (various, including BBC) Children's Drama Anthology. BBC 1 1964–9

Producer (UK): **Peggy Miller**

Anthology of Euro-fairytales with an English commentary.

Effectively a pooling of material, *Tales from Europe* was the umbrella title given to a collection of children's drama serials (mostly fairy stories like *Rumpelstiltskin*) produced by television companies all across the Continent. Each was shown in its native language, with an English narrative dubbed on top. Probably the best-remembered offering was a 1958 East German film called *The Singing Ringing Tree*, starring Christel Bodelstein as a beautiful but bad-tempered princess who wanted a magic tree for a wedding gift. Charles-Hans Vogt played the prince who tried to find her one and Antony Bilbow gave the English narrative.

TALES OF MYSTERY

UK (Associated-Rediffusion) Suspense Anthology. ITV 1961–3

Algernon Blackwood .... **John Laurie**

Executive Producer: **John Frankau**
Producer: **Peter Graham Scott**

Suspense anthology centring on the supernatural.

John Laurie, the rolling-eyed, spooky undertaker from DAD'S ARMY, was the host of this series of half-hour thrillers. He took on the guise of writer Algernon Blackwood, the author of many of the bizarre tales that were adapted for the programme. Laurie generally introduced ghost stories, but the base was extended in the second and third seasons to include other supernatural yarns with a twist in the tail. Plenty of established British actors filled the lead roles, including Harry H. Corbett, Patrick Cargill, Peter Barkworth, Francesca Annis and Dinsdale Landen.

TALES OF PARA HANDY, THE

See PARA HANDY – MASTER MARINER.

TALES OF THE RIVERBANK

Canada (Dave Ellison/Ray Billings) Children's Entertainment. BBC 1960–4

Narrator (UK): **Johnny Morris**

Creators/Writers/Producers: **Dave Ellison, Paul Sutherland**
Producer (UK): **Peggy Miller**

Messing about on the water with a cute little hamster and his big friend, a white rat.

Tales of the Riverbank – screened by the BBC as part of the WATCH WITH MOTHER lunch-time strand from 1963, but before that at around 5 p.m. – concerned the everyday affairs of busy Hammy Hamster, his friend Roderick the Rat and their wildlife associates, like GP the guinea-pig. The animals were real, with words put into their mouths by the whimsical Johnny Morris. Their homes were furnished as human homes and they enjoyed all human comforts, including musical instruments, cars, aeroplanes and even a little boat in which to travel up and down the river. Produced in Canada, the series was filmed at high speed, so that the rodents' movements appeared slower and more deliberate in playback. And, because hamsters lose their looks after about nine months, dozens of look-alikes were called up to play Hammy over the years. The series was repeated on BBC 1 until 1971 and also aired under the title of *Hammy Hamster's Adventures on the Riverbank* on ITV (1974–6). A sequel, entitled *Further Tales of the Riverbank*, was also seen on Channel 4 in the 1990s.

TALES OF THE UNEXPECTED

UK (Anglia) Suspense Anthology. ITV 1979–88

Executive Producer: **John Woolf**
Producer: **John Rosenberg**

A collection of tales with a twist.

Originally introduced by Roald Dahl, whose short stories formed the core of this anthology, *Tales of the Unexpected* (*Roald Dahl's Tales of the Unexpected* for the first series) offered a weekly carousel ride of suspense and black humour, always with a neat, unsuspected, quirky ending. Sinister fairground music played over the opening titles, which featured the slinky silhouette of a siren female dancer.

Some of Dahl's stories had already been treated to TV interpretation by ALFRED HITCHCOCK PRESENTS, but these mystery tales forwent Hitchcock's sardonic, odd-ball introductions, concentrating instead on a simple moral warning from the author. Even these were phased out when other writers were brought in. With a different cast for every episode, guest stars abounded, ranging from John Gielgud, Telly Savalas and Joan Collins to Joseph Cotton, Brian Blessed and Wendy Hiller. The series was a great export success for Anglia.

TALES OF WELLS FARGO

See WELLS FARGO.

TALK SHOW

Although the term talk show can apply to all kinds of interview programmes, it is more precisely connected with American audience-participation shows like *Jerry Springer* and *The Oprah Winfrey Show* (and UK equivalents like *Kilroy* and *Vanessa*), where selected members of the studio audience reveal their emotional hang-ups and particular points of pique. Because of their low production costs, talk shows are popular choices for daytime programming. The term can also apply to celebrity interviews in the *Parkinson* and *Wogan* vein, although these are generally known as chat shows in the UK.

TALKING HEADS/TALKING HEADS 2
UK (BBC) Drama. BBC 1 1988/BBC 2 1998

Writer: **Alan Bennett**
Producers: **Innes Lloyd, Mark Shivas**

Two series of acclaimed monologues.

Alan Bennett's 1988 series of six monologues – inspired by his success in scripting *A Woman of No Importance* for Patricia Routledge – was so well received (even finding its way on to A-level syllabuses) that it is something of a surprise that it was ten years before he served up another helping (he claimed he found it difficult to write such pieces). Written in his typically gossipy style, focusing (on the face of it) on parochial matters, each script, however, had great depth, spotlighting some truly sad, often pathetic, characters. Their depressing tales – emotional reflections on wasted lives with hints of dark secrets and obscure obsessions, all mixed up with tittle-tattle and talk of voluntary workers and the social services – were lightened by a generous sprinkling of Bennett's noted flair for social observation and moments of wry humour.

The first series consisted of the following monologues: *A Chip in the Sugar* (Alan Bennett himself in a tale of the relationship between a mother and her middle-aged son); *A Lady of Letters* (Patricia Routledge as a woman whose sole pleasure in life is correspondence); *Bed Among the Lentils* (Maggie Smith as a vicar's wife with little time for God); *Soldiering On* (Stephanie Cole as a stockbroker's widow now bereft of her assets, including her memories) *Her Big Chance* (Julie Walters as an aspiring actress who lands a role in a porn film but makes out it's serious drama); and *A Cream Cracker under the Settee* (Thora Hird as the pensioner who suffers a fall and spots the eponymous item). The 1998 series was made up of: *Miss Fozzard Finds Her Feet* (Patricia Routledge as a spinster shop assistant whose home life is dominated by her stroke-victim brother and whose only pleasure is in a visit to the chiropodist); *The Hand of God* (Eileen Atkins as an antiques dealer who develops an unhealthy interest in the possessions of a sick acquaintance); *Playing Sandwiches* (David Haig as an efficient park-keeper with a mysterious past and a black secret to hide); *The Outside Dog* (Julie Walters as a hygiene-mad wife who despises her husband's dog); *Nights in the Gardens of Spain* (Penelope Wilton as a gardening-obsessed woman who befriends her murdering neighbour); and *Waiting for the Telegram* (Thora Hird as a pensioner awaiting 100th birthday congratulations from the Queen and recalling a telegram of a more tragic nature that arrived during World War I).

In addition to Bennett's dialogue, the performances of the actors were highly acclaimed. Singled out particularly were Julie Walters and the BAFTA award-winning Thora Hird.

TARBUCK, JIMMY
OBE (1940–)

Liverpudlian comic turned TV quizmaster. A former Butlins redcoat, Tarbuck arrived on our screens in 1963 in programmes like *Comedy Bandbox* and, more notably, SUNDAY NIGHT AT THE LONDON PALLADIUM, on which he proved to be an overnight success. He was so popular, in fact, that he made a number of quick return visits and, just two years later, took over as the show's compere. In tandem with the Merseybeat boom, he swiftly grew into one of the biggest names of the 1960s and 1970s, a familiar face on various star-studded shows and launching numerous series of his own. These included *It's Tarbuck*, *Tarbuck at The Prince of Wales*, *Tarbuck's Back*, *The Jimmy Tarbuck Show*, *Tarbuck's Luck* and *Tell Tarby*. He later tried his hand at quizzes and chat shows. He hosted the gambling quiz, WINNER TAKES ALL, for many years and later presented *Tarby's Frame Game* and the golf game, *Full Swing*. He was in the chair for *Tarby and Friends* and another talk show, *Tarbuck Late*, and appeared as Mr Belafonte in the single comedy, *Brazen Hussies*, although he has not forgotten his variety roots, emceeing events *Live from Her Majesty's* and *Live from the Palladium* in the 1980s. Actress/presenter Liza Tarbuck is his daughter.

TARGET
UK (BBC) Police Drama. BBC 1 1977–8

Det. Supt. Steve Hackett	**Patrick Mower**
DS Louise Colbert	**Vivien Heilbron**
Det. Chief Supt. Tate	**Philip Madoc**
DS Frank Bonney	**Brendan Price**
DC Dukes	**Carl Rigg**

Producer: **Philip Hinchcliffe**

The rough, tough tactics of a regional police force.

In *Target*, viewers were, for once, treated to a police series based outside the big cities. But this was no village bobby fantasy. Instead, it surveyed the hard-hitting tactics of a Hampshire regional crime squad, working in and around an unidentified major port. Seventies trendy Patrick Mower was the actor charged with bringing the series some sex appeal as it was pitched into rivalry with ITV's THE SWEENEY to see which cops could punch the hardest. *Target* probably won fists up, but was criticized for its excessive violence and for its lack of humour, which, for many, was *The Sweeney*'s saving grace. A second series followed, but with the action toned down somewhat, though its main man, 39-year-old divorced Liverpudlian Steve Hackett, was just as unscrupulous as ever. 'Target' was the name police gave to a person active in the commission of a serious crime.

TARGET LUNA
See PATHFINDERS.

TARMEY, WILLIAM
(William Piddington; 1941–)

Mancunian actor, a former builder and shopkeeper who entered showbusiness as a part-time singer, gradually picking up 'extra' work on a number of TV series. He appeared in dramas like CROWN COURT, STRANGERS and *The Ghosts of Motley Hall* before, in 1979, he was given the chance to appear as Jack Duckworth in CORONATION STREET and, since becoming a regular cast member, has never looked back.

TARRANT, CHRIS
(1946–)

British presenter, a former teacher who broke into television as a reporter with ATV in Birmingham. As host and producer of the anarchic TISWAS, he brought a new strain of children's television to the UK, making the show a cult favourite with adults, too. His attempt at a proper grown-up, late-night version, *OTT*, failed miserably, however, and was replaced by another Tarrant offering, *Saturday Stayback*, after one series. Tarrant then headed into radio, taking over as breakfast presenter on London's Capital Radio, while making a name for himself in the advert voice-over world and contributing to LWT's *The Six O'Clock Show*. He succeeded Clive James and Keith Floyd in the chair of what became *Tarrant on TV*, presented the 'help' show, *Hotline*, and has since hosted numerous game shows, including *Everybody's Equal, Lose a Million, The Main Event, Pop Quiz, The Opposite Sex, Prove It, Man O Man* and the phenomenally successful WHO WANTS TO BE A MILLIONAIRE?.

TARZAN
US (Banner) Adventure. ITV 1967–70

Tarzan	**Ron Ely**
Jai	**Manuel Padilla, Jr**
Jason Flood	**Alan Caillou**
Rao	**Rockne Tarkington**
Tall Boy	**Stewart Raffill**

More adventures with the apeman created by Edgar Rice Burroughs.

In this television version, Tarzan (the Earl of Greystoke) returned from civilization to live once again among his animal friends. This time there was no Jane and no pidgin-English, but at least the Tarzan yodel was authentic – they used the Johnny Weissmuller original. Now Tarzan was accompanied by a chimpanzee called Cheetah and Jai, a young native orphan he had befriended. Tracking down illegal hunters and other *persona non grata*, the Lord of the Jungle became a kind of gamekeeper and animal doctor. Also seen were Jai's tutor, Jason Flood, Rao, the local vet, and Rao's assistant, Tall Boy. The show was shot in Mexico and Brazil.

TAXI
UK (BBC) Comedy Drama. BBC 1963–4

Sid Stone	**Sid James**
Fred Cuddell	**Bill Owen**
Terry Mills	**Ray Brooks**
Madeleine	**Vanda Godsell**
Sandra	**Diane Aubrey**
Bert Stoker	**Toke Townley**
Dolly Stoker	**Clare Kelly**
Jean Stoker	**Janet Kelly**

Creator: **Ted Willis**
Writers: **Ted Willis, Harry Driver, Jack Rosenthal**
Producers: **Michael Mills, Harry Carlisle, Douglas Moodie**

A London taxi-driver involves himself with other people's problems.

Driver Sid Stone owned his own cab and plied his trade on the streets of London. Unfortunately, Sid also had a flair for interfering in other people's business, be they his fare-paying customers, his partner, Fred Cuddell, or his young colleague, Terry Mills. The three drivers shared rooms in a converted house and, in the second season, the upstairs neighbours, Bert and Dolly Stoker (with daughter Jean), were introduced. By that time, however, Fred had left the scene. Sid's girlfriends were Madeleine (in the first series) and Sandra (thereafter).

TAXI
US (Paramount/John Charles Walters) Situation Comedy. BBC 1 1980–5

Alex Reiger	**Judd Hirsch**
Bobby Wheeler	**Jeff Conaway**
Louie De Palma	**Danny De Vito**
Elaine Nardo	**Marilu Henner**
Tony Banta	**Tony Danza**
Latka Gravas	**Andy Kaufman**
John Burns	**Randall Carver**
'Revd' Jim 'Iggie' Ignatowski	**Christopher Lloyd**
Simka Dahblitz Gravas	**Carol Kane**
Jeff Bennett	**J. Alan Thomas**
Zena Sherman	**Rhea Perlman**

Creators/Writers/Executive Producers: **James L. Brooks, Stan Daniels, Ed Weinberger, David Davis**
Producers: **Glen Charles, Les Charles**

The sad, frustrated lives of a team of New York cabbies.

If you can't do the job you want, you can always drive a taxi until a suitable position becomes available. It'll only be for a while. Well, that was what the drivers at the Sunshine Cab Company believed. Here was a bunch of rainbow-chasers, dreamers hoping that the right door would open so they could leave the grubby garage and move on to their chosen career. Sadly, you knew that they were likely to be driving taxis for the rest of their lives.

Among the crew was Tony Banta, a boxer who lost every fight, Bobby Wheeler, a failed actor, and Elaine Nardo, a single mother who longed to run an art gallery. More intriguing were Latka Gravas, the immigrant garage mechanic who could hardly speak English, and the wacky Reverend Jim, a burned-out hippie who lived in a condemned flat and was oblivious to the world around him. While they planned their perfect futures they were hustled and hassled by the firm's lecherous dispatcher, the vicious, pint-sized Louie De Palma who barked out instructions from his 'cage'. He charged the cabbies for phone messages, spied on Elaine as she changed clothes and generally became their common enemy. Only one cabbie was happy with his lot. That was kind, thoughtful Alex Reiger, a man with limited horizons. He was number one driver, a father figure and the best friend of all his colleagues.

Other characters who appeared were naïve, romantic student John Burns (a driver for one season), and Simka, a scatter-brained compatriot of Latka's who went on to become his wife. Also seen was Rhea Perlman as Louie's girlfriend, Zena, a vending-machine stocker. She and Danny De Vito were actually married during a *Taxi* lunchbreak and when the show's producers moved on to create CHEERS they took Perlman with them. De Vito and Christopher Lloyd soon became major Hollywood names, starring in films like *Romancing the Stone* and *Back to the Future* respectively, but Andy Kaufman, who played the zany Latka, tragically died of cancer in 1984.

TAYLFORTH, GILLIAN
(1955–)

London-born actress becoming famous as Kathy Beale/Mitchell in EASTENDERS, having previously been seen in the PLAY FOR TODAY, *Eleanor*, and series like *Zigger Zagger*, THE RAG TRADE (Lyn), *Watch This Space*, *Sink or Swim* and MINDER. Since leaving Albert Square, Taylforth has starred in the drama, *Big Cat* (Polly), and guested in *Operation Good Guys*. She is a sister of actress Kim Taylforth.

TAYLOR, GWEN
(Gwen Allsop; 1939–)

British actress seen mostly in comedy or light drama roles on television. Most prominent have been the parts of Amy Pearce in DUTY FREE, Rita Simcock in A BIT OF A DO, Liz in *Sob Sisters*, Celia Forrest in *The Sharp End*, Annie in *Screaming*, Gen Masefield in *Conjugal Rites*, Tilly in *Pilgrim's Rest*, Barbara in *Barbara*, and Laura, the deputy mayor, in *A Perfect State*. Earlier credits included RUTLAND WEEKEND TELEVISION, *Took and Co.*, *Sounding Brass* and numerous single dramas, including Alan Plater's PLAY FOR TODAY, *The Land of Green Ginger*.

TAYLOR, KEN
(1922–)

British writer responsible for dramas like *China Doll* (1960), *Into the Dark* (1963), *The Devil and John Brown* (1964) and a trilogy, *The Seekers* (also 1964). He adapted H. G. Wells's *Days to Come* in 1966 and was later co-writer of THE BORGIAS. Somewhat more successfully, Taylor wrote the screenplay for THE JEWEL IN THE CROWN and adapted Mary Wesley's *The Camomile Lawn*. He has also contributed to popular series like MISS MARPLE.

TAYLOR, SHAW
(1924–)

British presenter, most familiar urging viewers to 'keep 'em peeled' as host of POLICE FIVE (from 1962). Previously, Shaw had been quizmaster on the show, DOTTO, and was later seen in ITV's motoring magazine, *Drive-In*.

TCM
(Turner Classic Movies)

Digital film channel making the most of the MGM, Warner Brothers and RKO movie libraries owned by its parent company, AOL-Time Warner. As its name suggests, Hollywood favourites abound.

TELECINE

A machine which allows films and film inserts to be shown on television by converting them into electronic signals. In news programmes, filmed reports converted by telecine have now been replaced by videotape and VCRs.

TELEGOONS, THE
UK (BBC/Grosvenor Films) Comedy. BBC 1963–4

Writers: **Spike Milligan, Eric Sykes, Larry Stephens**
Producer: **Tony Young**

Animated, visual version of classic radio scripts from The Goon Show.

Although some new material was specially recorded, this puppet series essentially made use of archive radio programmes for its soundtrack. As in the radio days, *The Telegoons* were voiced by Peter Sellers, Harry Secombe and Spike Milligan, taking the parts of the characters Neddy Seagoon, Major Denis Bloodnok, Bluebottle, Eccles, Henry Crun, Moriarty, Minnie Bannister, Brigadier Grytpype-Thynne and others.

TELEPLAY

An old-fashioned word (used in the 1950s and 1960s) for the script of a fictional drama programme, equivalent to screenplay in the cinema.

TELERECORDING

A primitive means of recording TV pictures on to film, used in the days before videotape as a way of preserving live broadcasts. Effectively, the TV screen was filmed and a telecine machine was used for playback. The system was known as kinescope in the USA.

TELETEXT

A TV screen-based data system that conveys information about news, sports, weather, recipes, travel, etc. It also offers subtitles for hearing-impaired viewers on certain programmes. The viewer with a Teletext TV set can call up the information at the press of a button. For the technically minded, the information is carried in the blanking interval of the TV waveform (i.e. it uses the spare lines which make up the screen image). The BBC's text service is known as CEEFAX and was first made available in 1974. ITV's service, starting a year earlier, was initially known as ORACLE (Optional Reception of Announcements by Coded Line Electronics) and run by a company jointly owned by the ITV companies. However, since 1993 the licence has been operated by Teletext Ltd and the service known simply as Teletext. Teletext Ltd also provides the service for Channel 4 and S4C, while Channel 5's service (5 Text) is supplied by Sky Five Text Ltd.

TELETHON

The name given to a television broadcast marathon (lasting an entire evening or longer), specifically designed to draw attention to one or more causes and usually tied in with a charity appeal. The name was appropriated by ITV for their regular appeals in the late 1980s, although the best-known annual telethon is the BBC's CHILDREN IN NEED. Others have included COMIC RELIEF.

TELETUBBIES
UK (Ragdoll) Children. BBC 2 1997–

Tinky Winky .... **Dave Thompson**
Dipsy .... **John Simmit**
Laa-Laa .... **Nikky Smedley**
Po .... **Pui Fan Lee**

Creators: **Anne Wood, Andrew Davenport**
Writer: **Andrew Davenport**

Hugely successful pre-school series featuring four colourful gibberish-speakers.

The Teletubbies lived in Teletubbyland (actually a grassy hill in Warwickshire) which they shared with some nibbling rabbits, talking flowers, a magic windmill and periscope-like voice-trumpets which surfaced to make announcements. Their home was the Tubbytronic Superdome, which they shared with their vacuum-cleaner named the Noo-noo. Played by actors in costumes, the radiant, dancing, prancing stars – akin to giant alien babies – in descending order of size were Tinky Winky (a purple creature with a triangular aerial on his head; prone to falling over and carrying a handbag – a gay icon), Dipsy (green, with a spike aerial; sang 'Bptum, bptum, bptum, bptum'), Laa-Laa (yellow, with a curled aerial; the happiest of the bunch) and Po (red, with a loop aerial; easily worked up and sang in Cantonese). All had grey squares in the centre of the tummy on which at times were projected films of real-life activities. Their diet consisted of Tubby Custard and Tubby Toast. Also seen were a toy lion and bear (voiced by Eric Sykes and Penelope Keith, respectively), and all was watched over by a giggling baby framed in the corona of the sun. Toyah Willcox provided the opening narration.

These bizarre creations caused quite a furore when they first appeared. Parents were up in arms over the way they shunned proper English for 'goo-goo' talk ('Eh-oh' for 'Hello', for example). The creators hit back, explaining that their mission was to encourage under-fives to learn through play, inspiring them to inter-react with the characters. Contact with the adult world was kept to a minimum or approached only through the eyes of a real toddler (in the deliberately repetitive filmed sequences). Toddlers immediately loved the Teletubbies, and not just in the UK. The series became one of the BBC's biggest exports and the source for some extremely lucrative merchandising, including the 1997 chart-topper, 'Teletubbies Say Eh-Oh!'. 'Time for Tubby Bye Bye!'

TELEVISION
UK (Granada) Documentary. ITV 1984

Narrator: **Ian Holm**

Producers: **Leslie Woodhead, Norman Swallow**

The history of television, by television.

Tracing the development of the 20th century's major communications medium, right from the pioneering days of Logie Baird and others (although not in strict chronological order), this 13-part documentary squared up to the difficult task of evaluating the impact and style of television. Old footage, interviews, discussions, reconstructions and plenty of illustrative clips and flashbacks helped the producers to reflect on television's treatment of news, politics, drama, comedy, commercials, etc. Filming took place right across the globe, showing East Berliners watching West German TV, extracts from a Samurai drama in Japan, an outside broadcast in Indonesia and the transmission of Soviet news simultaneously in places as far apart as Tashkent and Siberia. An edited version was prepared for transmission in the

USA, taking out certain British examples and adding American substitutes.

TELEVISION DANCING CLUB
UK (BBC) Entertainment. BBC 1948–64

Producer: **Richard Afton**

Long-running dance showcase.

Predating its sister programme, COME DANCING, by two years, *Television Dancing Club* was largely devoted to the dance music of Victor Sylvester and his Ballroom Orchestra. Sylvester also offered dance instruction and was assisted by hostesses Patti Morgan and Sylvia Peters. For the last season, 1963–4, the title was shortened to *Dancing Club*.

TELEVISION SOUTH
See TVS.

TELEVISION SOUTH WEST
See TSW.

TELEVISION TOP OF THE FORM
UK (BBC) Quiz. BBC 1 1962–75

Presenters: **Geoffrey Wheeler, David Dimbleby, Paddy Feeny, John Edmunds, John Dunn**

Producers: **Innes Lloyd, Bill Wright, Mary Evans**

General knowledge tournament for grammar school kids.

Launched on radio in 1948 and emulated on television from 1962, *Top of the Form* was a contest for well-behaved high school children. Schools were invited to put forward a team of four pupils, of varying ages, to compete in a national tournament to find who really was 'Top of the Form'. In the early days, two questionmasters were employed, one in the assembly hall of one school and the other similarly housed at another. Geoffrey Wheeler and David Dimbleby were the first to fill these roles and Boswell Taylor was the programme's chief questionsetter. In 1967 a special *Transworld Top of the Form* was seen. Linking teams in the UK and Australia, it was chaired by Aussie anchorman Bill Salmon.

TELEVISION WALES AND WEST
See TWW.

TELFORD'S CHANGE
UK (BBC) Drama. BBC 1 1979

Mark Telford	**Peter Barkworth**
Sylvia Telford	**Hannah Gordon**
Keith Everley	**Albert Welling**
Peter Telford	**Michael Maloney**
Tim Hart	**Keith Barron**
Maddox	**Colin Douglas**
Helen Santon	**Zena Walker**

Creator: **Peter Barkworth**
Writer: **Brian Clark**
Producer: **Mark Shivas**

A successful banker opts for the quiet life and, in so doing, puts his marriage on the line.

High-flying, middle-aged international bank official Mark Telford had reached a crossroads in life. Should he continue in the fast lane or was it time to take things a little more easily? He opted for the latter, accepting an appointment as the manager of a branch in Dover. His wife, Sylvia, however, refused to be dragged away from London, where she was carving out a career in the theatre world. The result was a ten-episode soapy drama that focused on the intriguing clients of the provincial bank and the various twists and turns of the Telfords' marriage, which was threatened by the intrusion of Sylvia's friend, Tim Hart. The series was based on an idea that star Peter Barkworth first conceived in 1968.

TELL IT TO THE MARINES
UK (Associated-Rediffusion/Jack Hylton) Situation Comedy. ITV 1959–60

Leading Seaman White	**Alan White**
Cpl. Surtees	**Ronald Hines**
Lt. Raleigh	**Henry McGee**
Petty Officer Woodward	**John Baskcomb**
Whittle	**Ian Whittaker**
Kilmartin Dalrymple	**Ian MacNaughton**
Commander Walters	**Ian Colin**
Major Howard	**Jack Allen**

Creator: **Ted Willis**
Producer: **Jack Hylton**

The Navy and the Marines share a traditional rivalry.

Exploiting the long-standing tensions between the men of the Royal Navy and those of the Royal Marines, *Tell It to the Marines* featured petty squabbles, minor battles and endless joking between the two forces. Principal among the protagonists were Leading Seaman White and Marine Cpl. Surtees, with superior officers like Lt. Raleigh and Major Howard also in the fray. The premiss was that the tensions between the forces had come to a head after a squabble over girls in a pub, leading to the top brass deciding to stamp out the animosity by arranging a series of 'friendly' sports events – an exercise that was doomed to failure.

TELLY ADDICTS

UK (BBC) Quiz. BBC 1 1985–98

Presenter: **Noel Edmonds**

Producers: **Juliet May, John King, Richard L. Lewis, Helen Lott**

Teams of contestants test their knowledge of television.

In this light-hearted quiz, two teams of four competed to show off their knowledge of television history. For the first nine years, the teams were made up of family members only, but in 1994 the rules were relaxed to allow friends, workmates, etc., to make up the numbers. (Also in 1994, *The Archers* actor Charles Collingwood was recruited to fool around while reading out the scores.) A knockout tournament unearthed each year's *Telly Addicts* champions. The first winning team was the Payne family from Swindon, but in that inaugural series the rules were different. Instead of progressing through a knockout, the winning family stayed on to meet new challengers week after week. In 1995, the series celebrated its tenth anniversary with *Champion Telly Addicts*, an additional tournament designed to find the best of the best. For the final season, in 1998, the couch potatoes were dragged from their armchairs as *Telly Addicts* was revamped into a quiz for three teams of two, played on a stage that required much moving around.

The origins of *Telly Addicts* lay in a series entitled *Telly Quiz*, presented by Jerry Stevens, which was seen on BBC 1 between Christmas Eve 1984 and 2 January 1985. In *Telly Quiz*, celebrities took on viewers, as they did in an early rival to *Telly Addicts*, ITV's *We Love TV*, which was hosted by Gloria Hunniford.

TEMPO

UK (ABC) Arts. ITV 1961–7

Presenters: **Lord Harewood, Leonard Maguire**

Creator: **Kenneth Tynan**

Editors: **Kenneth Tynan, Peter Luke, Clive Goodwin**

Fortnightly arts magazine.

Conceived as a response to the BBC's successful MONITOR programme, *Tempo* was a 50-minute (later 25-minute) arts indulgence hosted first by Lord Harewood, then by Leonard Maguire and others. As well as the classic arts of painting, sculpture, ballet and music, *Tempo* also reviewed film, literature and drama, with the aim of allowing a mass audience to appreciate the artistic world without the intrusion of academic opinion.

TENKO

UK (BBC) Drama. BBC 1 1981–4

Rose Millar	**Stephanie Beacham**
Marion Jefferson	**Ann Bell**
Sylvia Ashburton	**Renee Asherson**
Major Yamauchi	**Bert Kwouk**
Dr Beatrice Mason	**Stephanie Cole**
Kate Norris	**Claire Oberman**
Minah	**Pauline Peters**
Vicky Armstrong	**Wendy Williams**
Sally Markham	**Joanna Hole**
Nellie Keene	**Jeananne Crowley**
Gerda	**Maya Woolfe**
Mrs Domenica Van Meyer	**Elizabeth Chambers**
Christina Campbell	**Emily Bolton**
Blanche Simmons	**Louise Jameson**
Dorothy Bennett	**Veronica Roberts**
Joss Holbrook	**Jean Anderson**
Debbie Bowen	**Karin Foley**
Verna Johnson	**Rosemary Martin**
Maggie Thorpe	**Elizabeth Mickery**
Alice Courtenay	**Cindy Shelley**
Edna	**Edna Doré**
Col. Clifford Jefferson	**Jonathan Newth**
Bernard Webster	**Edmund Pegge**
Cpl. Jackson	**Colin Dunn**
Major Sims	**David Gooderson**
Sister Ulrica	**Patricia Lawrence**
Miss Hassan	**Josephine Welcome**
Johnny Saunders	**Gregory de Polnay**
Harry Milne	**Andrew Sharp**
Father Lim	**Ric Young**
Tom Redburn	**Daniel Hill**
Jack Armstrong	**Ivor Danvers**
Simon Treves	**Jeffrey Hardy**
Dolah	**Ronald Eng**
Shinya	**Takashi Kawahara**
Kasaki	**Takahiro Oba**
Yukio	**Peter Silverleaf**
Sato	**Eiji Kusuhara**
Joan	**Dawn Keeler**
Timmy	**Nigel Harman**

Creator: **Lavinia Warner**

Writers: **Jill Hyem, Anne Valery, Paul Wheeler**

Producers: **Ken Riddington, Vere Lorrimer**

The hardships of female prisoner-of-war camps in 1940s Malaya.

Following the invasion of Singapore by Japan in 1942, the expatriate women of Britain and Holland were torn from their menfolk and imprisoned in makeshift holding camps. *Tenko* – meaning 'roll call' in Japanese – told the story of one such group of women, trapped in filthy conditions, abused, beaten and degraded, thousands of miles from home and out of reach of assistance. Their appalling living conditions, their relationships with their captors, and the relationships among the women themselves (where race and class became prominent issues) were documented in this hugely popular programme which ran for three seasons.

Appointed head of the women was Marion Jefferson, the wife of a colonel and the obvious choice as leader. Around her were gathered the likes of rape victim Rose Millar, Beatrice Mason, a formidable doctor, nurses Kate Norris and Nellie Keene, ageing academic Joss Holbrook, Dorothy Bennett who, having lost both her husband

and her child, turned to prostitution with the guards, tarty Cockney Blanche Simmons and the ladylike Verna Johnson. The formidable Sister Ulrica was head of the Dutch section, which also featured the nauseatingly selfish Mrs Van Meyer. The cruelty of their captors was too underplayed, according to some viewers, but nevertheless the prisoners were subjected to enormous humiliation, torturous working conditions, malnutrition, disease, long marches to new camps and insufferable indignity beneath a baking Asian sun.

The first series depicted how the women struggled to adjust to captivity and how the hope of release lingered long in their minds. By the second season, that hope had largely disappeared, replaced by a determination to survive, as their personal values changed dramatically. The last series concerned the end of the war and the efforts of the survivors to come to terms with life back in society, coping with estranged husbands and shattered lifestyles. A one-off reunion episode, played as a murder mystery and set in 1950, was produced in 1985.

The series was created by Lavinia Warner, who had researched the history of Japanese POW camps for a THIS IS YOUR LIFE programme on Margo Turner, a nursing corps officer who had once been held captive. Warner developed the idea into an OMNIBUS documentary before dramatizing the harrowing events in *Tenko*.

TERRAHAWKS
UK (Anderson Burr/LWT) Children's Science Fiction. ITV
1983–6

Voices:

Zelda	**Denise Bryer**
Sgt Major Zero	**Windsor Davies**
Capt. Mary Falconer	**Denise Bryer**
Dr Tiger Ninestein	**Jeremy Hitcher**
Lt. Hiro	**Jeremy Hitcher**
Lt. Hawkeye	**Jeremy Hitcher**
Capt. Kate Kestrel	**Anne Ridler**
Yung-Star	**Ben Stevens**
Cy-Star	**Anne Ridler**
Hudson	**Ben Stevens**
Space Sgt 101	**Ben Stevens**

Creator: **Gerry Anderson**
Writer: **Tony Barwick**
Producers: **Gerry Anderson, Christopher Burr**

*A defence force protects the Earth from an ugly
alien witch queen.*

In Gerry Anderson's major contribution to 1980s television, his 'Supermarionation' progressed into 'Supermacromation', an advanced form of glove puppetry. However, following the tried and tested Anderson formula, the heroes were unsurprisingly familiar. They were the Terrahawks, an élite squad of dare-devils who risked life and limb to save the Earth from alien invasion in the year 2020.

Headed by Dr Tiger Ninestein, the ninth clone of Austrian-American scientist Gerhard Stein, the Terra-

hawks consisted of ace pilot Mary Falconer; Hawkeye, an American with computer-aided vision; Lt. Hiro, the team's computer boffin; and pop singer-turned-pilot, Kate Kestrel. From Hawknest, a secret South American base, they faced the cunning might of the cackling, prune-faced android, Zelda, and her equally hideous allies from the planet Guk. These included her useless son, Yung-Star, and her spiteful twin sister, Cy-Star. With the use of cube-shaped robots, and other agents like Yuri, the space bear, and MOID (Master of Infinite Disguise), Zelda aimed to take over the planet. The Terrahawks, in their spaceship known as *Hawkwing*, covered her every move, assisted by round robots called Zeroids. These were controlled when on Earth by Sgt Major Zero and when in space by Space Sgt 101, pilot of the Zeroid spacecraft, *Spacehawk*. Also on display was Hudson, a Rolls-Royce with a mind of its own.

TERRY AND JUNE
UK (BBC) Situation Comedy. BBC 1 1979–87

Terry Medford	**Terry Scott**
June Medford	**June Whitfield**
Sir Dennis Hodge	**Reginald Marsh**
Beattie	**Rosemary Frankau**
Malcolm	**Terence Alexander**
	Tim Barrett
	John Quayle

Creator: **John Kane**
Producers: **Peter Whitmore, Robin Nash, John B. Hobbs**

*Mishaps and misunderstandings in the life of a
typical suburban couple.*

Terry and June Medford were an ordinary middle-class couple whiling away their middle age in suburban Purley – except that Terry was bumptious, ham-fisted, over-ambitious and helplessly accident-prone, and June was the archetypal long-suffering wife who had to pick up the pieces. Terry commuted into the city, where he worked for Sir Dennis Hodge, a man likely to call at the Medfords' home just at the wrong moment, usually with farcical consequences.

Safe, silly and unspectacular, *Terry and June* was effectively a reworking of an early Scott/Whitfield sitcom, HAPPY EVER AFTER, but without the old lady, the mynah bird or occasional visits from grown-up children seen in the earlier outing.

TERRY-THOMAS
(Thomas Terry Hoar Stevens; 1911–90)

Although largely known for his film work, gap-toothed, plummy comedian Terry-Thomas was one of TV's earliest stars, appearing on the BBC from the 1940s in programmes like *To Town With Terry*, *How Do You View?* and *Strictly T-T*. He later headed for the USA, where his 'frightfully-Englishness' led to more TV success (including guest appearances in series like BURKE'S LAW), but he found his better days behind him when he returned to the BBC in 1968 for a short-lived comedy entitled *The*

Old Campaigner, in which he played travelling salesman James Franklin-Jones.

TEST CARD

A card marked with colours, shades, patterns and lines of various sizes and thicknesses, used by engineers to calibrate cameras and monitors for best performance. The test card was a familiar sight until daytime television arrived in the 1980s, with TV installers using it to set up and adjust receivers. The BBC colour test card featured a schoolgirl, a blackboard and some toys. The girl's name was Carol Hersey and she consequently holds the record for being the most-seen person on British television.

TFI FRIDAY

UK (Ginger). Channel 4 1996–2000

Presenter: **Chris Evans**

Producers: **Suzie Aplin, David Granger, Will Macdonald, Stephen Joel**
Executive Producers: **Chris Evans, John Revell**

Lively, Friday tea-time mix of entertainment and chat.

Chris Evans bounced back on to the small screen, fresh from Radio 1 breakfast show success, with this youth-orientated show which majored on pop bands, showbiz gossip and daft stunts and games. The letters in the title standing for *Thank Four It's Friday*, the show was broadcast from the Riverside Studios in Hammersmith, with a set that conveyed the impression of a nightclub below and a manager's office (from where Evans anchored the show) above. Producer Will Macdonald joined Evans to present a series of intriguing 'pub tricks', involving matches, glasses, etc. Star guests dropped by for a chat, ugly people paraded their best features, and there were plenty of other similarly wacky competitions. The programme was repeated at around 11 p.m. the same evening. By the time of the final series, in autumn 2000, Chris Evans had left the show and the programme was fronted by different celebrity guests each week, winding up with Sir Elton John.

THAMES TELEVISION

Formed by the merger of two ITV contractors (ABC and Associated-Rediffusion) at the instigation of the ITA, Thames took over the London weekday franchise on 29 July 1968. Its franchise was retained during the 1980 reviews but was surprisingly taken away from the company in the 1991 auctions, when Thames was outbid by Carlton Communications. This decision, among others, seriously brought into question the logic of the new auction system, whereby the franchise was awarded to the highest bidder, providing the ITC was satisfied that business plans were viable and commitments to programme quality would be met. It effectively ignored Thames's remarkable programming record, which had brought many notable contributions to the ITV network. Among the company's biggest hits were THE SWEENEY, MINDER, MAN ABOUT THE HOUSE, THE WORLD AT WAR, ROCK FOLLIES, BLESS THIS HOUSE, THIS WEEK and THE WIND IN THE WILLOWS.

Thames subsequently concentrated on programme production and also helped establish the satellite channel, UK Gold. A consortium headed by Thames was the sole bidder for the proposed Channel 5 project when it was first touted but, with doubts about the viability of the new network and the company's business plan, the licence was not awarded by the ITC. In 1993 Thames was bought by Pearson plc, becoming part of Pearson Television, where it has been joined by companies like Alomo, Witzend and Grundy. The company continues to make programmes for BBC and commercial networks, including the long-running THIS IS YOUR LIFE, THE BILL, WISH YOU WERE HERE . . . ? and *Des O'Connor Tonight*, plus *Heroes of Comedy* and *Family Affairs* (the last with Grundy).

THANK YOUR LUCKY STARS

UK (ABC) Pop Music. ITV 1961–6

Presenters: **Keith Fordyce, Brian Matthew, Jim Dale**

Producers: **Philip Jones, Helen Standage, Keith Beckett, Milo Lewis**

Successful Saturday-evening pop show.

Planned as ITV's answer to JUKE BOX JURY, *Thank Your Lucky Stars* presented the pop sensations of the day miming to their latest tracks. Keith Fordyce and, later, Brian Matthew were the main frontmen, although in earlier programmes hosts included the likes of Jimmy Savile, Pete Murray, Alan Dell, Sam Costa, Barry Alldis, Kent Walton, Jimmy Young and Don Moss. The segment known as Spin A Disc (a shamelessly direct copy of *Juke Box Jury*) called on a panel of celebrities and local teenagers to give their views on record releases, and it was in this part of the programme that 16-year-old office clerk Janice Nicholls was discovered in 1962. Her broad Black Country accent, displayed when she declared 'Oi'll give it foive', made her an instant favourite and ensured she became a programme regular. *Thank Your Lucky Stars* also gave The Beatles their first national television exposure, in February 1963. Jim Dale took over as presenter in 1965, but the programme was cancelled a year later, just as the British beat boom was coming to a close. The summer programmes in 1963–5 went out under the title, *Lucky Stars Summer Spin*.

THAT WAS THE WEEK THAT WAS

UK (BBC) Comedy. BBC 1962–3

David Frost, Millicent Martin, Lance Percival, Bernard Levin, William Rushton, Roy Kinnear, Timothy Birdsall, Kenneth Cope, David Kernan, Al Mancini, Robert Lang, Irwin Watson

Producer: **Ned Sherrin**

Hard-hitting, revolutionary satire, week by week.

That Was The Week That Was broke new ground for television. Airing on a Saturday night, it was a product of the BBC's current affairs department rather than its light entertainment crew, a fact reflected in its commitment to topicality and its biting tone. The programme looked at the major events of the previous week, ridiculed them, drew comment and exposed ironies. At the helm was a young David Frost who became host after Brian Redhead had declined the position. Frost's team included the likes of Willie Rushton, Roy Kinnear, Lance Percival, Bernard Levin and Millicent Martin, whose opening song recalled the week's news in its lyrics. The remainder of the programme was given over to sketches, interviews and guest spots, with scripts written by the likes of Kenneth Tynan, Dennis Potter and Keith Waterhouse. For the first time, sacred cows like racism, royalty, politics and religion were slaughtered in a humorous fashion, prompting much criticism from the Establishment. Individuals, such as then Home Secretary Henry Brooke, were also singled out for treatment. Bernard Levin upset many viewers with his forthright opinions (to the point where one night a member of the studio audience knocked him off his stool). In addition, the programme adopted a technically *laissez faire* approach which allowed cameras to wander into shot and the studio audience to be seen, something which had seldom been experienced before on prim-and-proper British television.

The format and title also transferred to the USA, again with Frost in the chair. His Stateside collaborators included Alan Alda and Tom Bosley, but the show didn't really click. Back in the UK, *TW3* (as it became known) was taken off before the election year of 1964 (in case it influenced voters) and was succeeded by two short-lived sequels, NOT SO MUCH A PROGRAMME, MORE A WAY OF LIFE and BBC-3.

THAT'S LIFE
UK (BBC) Consumer Affairs. BBC 1 1973–94

Presenters: **Esther Rantzen, George Layton, Bob Wellings, Kieran Prendiville, Glyn Worsnip, Cyril Fletcher, Paul Heiney, Chris Serle, Bill Buckley, Doc Cox, Gavin Campbell, Michael Groth, Joanna Munro, John Gould, Maev Alexander, Adrian Mills, Grant Baynham, Mollie Sugden, Howard Leader, Simon Fanshawe, Scott Sherrin, Kevin Devine**

Creator: **John Lloyd**
Producers/Editors: **Esther Rantzen, Henry Murray, Peter Chafer, Michael Bunce, Ron Neil, Gordon Watts, John Morrell, Bryher Scudamore, Shaun Woodward, John Getgood**

Consumer/light entertainment magazine filled with silly stunts, painful puns and invaluable investigations.

Originally planned for just a six-week run, *That's Life* continued instead for 21 years. The series was conceived as a follow-up to the Saturday night offering, BRADEN'S WEEK, in which Bernard Braden and a team of reporters made people laugh and fought consumers' battles. One of those reporters was Esther Rantzen and, installed in the new *That's Life* format, she quickly made the series her own.

Rantzen was assisted by an ever-changing team of mostly male reporters, with George Layton and Bob Wellings her first co-stars. Cyril Fletcher joined in 1974 to recite his odd odes and to pick out funny misprints from newspapers (a job later done by Mollie Sugden and Doc Cox among others), and Richard Stilgoe, the Fivepenny Piece and Victoria Wood were recruited to provide witty songs. A weekly *vox pop* saw Esther out on the streets of London, challenging punters to sample strange items of food or drink. Invariably, she bumped into Annie, an elderly lady who became a stalwart of the programme.

That's Life also offered plenty of daft stories about talented pets and quirky pastimes, but its real merit was as a consumers' champion. It presented a 'Heap of the Week' award for shoddily made goods, dished out 'Jobsworth' and plain English accolades for excessive bureaucracy and tackled con-men on their doorsteps. More importantly still, the programme also campaigned heavily for the protection of children, a crusade which resulted in the establishment of the Childline charity.

In 1984 a story which moved every viewer concerned two-year-old Ben Hardwicke, a toddler suffering from an incurable liver disease. Ben sadly died, but not before the case for child organ transplants had been thoroughly aired. As part of the campaign, Marti Webb released a version of Michael Jackson's 'Ben', which reached the Top Five in 1985.

That's Life, with its careful balance of the silly and the serious, its brassy theme music and topical closing cartoons (drawn by Rod Jordan), became an intrinsic part of the weekend for many viewers. In 1979 there was also a version for younger fans, *Junior That's Life*, from the same team.

THAT'S MY BOY
UK (Yorkshire) Situation Comedy. ITV 1981–6

Ida Willis	**Mollie Sugden**
Dr Robert Price	**Christopher Blake**
Angie Price	**Jennifer Lonsdale**
Mrs Price	**Clare Richards**
Wilfred Willis	**Harold Goodwin**
Miss Parfitt	**Deddie Davies**

Writers: **Pam Valentine, Michael Ashton**
Producer: **Graeme Muir**

A housekeeper discovers her employer is really her son.

After endlessly pestering a domestic employment agency, fearsome Ida Willis was finally installed in the position of housekeeper to young Dr Robert Price and his model wife, Angie. Gradually realizing that Robert was the son she gave away for adoption at birth, Ida became increasingly possessive of him, much to the despair of his adoptive mother. The young doctor was left to dither between the two. The family (and house-keeper) later moved out of London to Yorkshire, where Ida gained a friend, Miss Parfitt, and also had her brother, Wilfred, to keep her occupied.

THAW, JOHN
CBE (1942–)

Characters as well defined as INSPECTOR MORSE, THE SWEENEY's Jack Regan, KAVANAGH QC and HOME TO ROOST's Henry Willows testify to the versatility of award-winning British actor John Thaw. Thaw's TV debut came in an anthology series called *The Younger Generation* in 1961 and his first starring role was in REDCAP in 1964, playing military policeman John Mann. Apart from the series listed above, he has also been seen as Stan in the comedy, THICK AS THIEVES; Francis Drake in a 1980 TV movie, *Drake's Venture*; crime reporter *Mitch*; wartime RAF supremo, *Bomber Harris*; Stanley Duke in *Stanley and the Women*; Peter Mayle in A YEAR IN PROVENCE; Labour Party leader George Jones in *Screen Two's The Absence of War*; Harry Barnett in the murder mystery, *Into the Blue*; Tom Oakley in the award-winning *Goodnight Mr Tom*; plastic surgeon Joe MacConnell in *Plastic Man*; legal clerk Joshua Mantle in the spy drama, *The Waiting Time*; and the title character in *Monsignor Renard*. Guest appearances in programmes like Z CARS, THE AVENGERS, THE MORECAMBE AND WISE SHOW and THE ONEDIN LINE, and narration work on series such as *The Second World War in Colour*, have added to his credits. Thaw is married to actress Sheila Hancock. He is the father of actress Abigail Thaw and step-father of actress Melanie Thaw.

THEAKSTON, JAMIE
(1970–)

Tall, youth TV presenter, the host of series like *The O Zone*, *Live and Kicking*, TOP OF THE POPS, *The Priory* and *A Question of Pop*.

THEY THINK IT'S ALL OVER
UK (Talkback/BBC) Quiz. BBC 1 1995–

Presenter: **Nick Hancock**

Producers: **Harry Thompson, Jim Pullin**
Executive Producer: **Peter Fincham**

Irreverent sports quiz.

More akin to HAVE I GOT NEWS FOR YOU than its BBC 1 stablemate, A QUESTION OF SPORT, this comedy quiz show has featured the talents of chairman Nick Hancock and resident comedians Rory McGrath and Jonathan Ross (initially Lee Hurst). Adding sporting authenticity to the mirth have been team captains David Gower and Gary Lineker, both – inevitably – the butt of much of the humour, as well as varied sporting guests. Rounds have included explaining bizarre goal celebrations, unravelling a photofit image of three personalities, 'Feel

the Sportsman' (blindfolded reveal-the-identity) and guessing as many names of sports stars as possible from clues given by team colleagues within a time limit. The programme title (and part of its opening sequence) was taken from Kenneth Wolstenholme's famous closing commentary on the 1966 World Cup Final.

THICK AS THIEVES
UK (LWT) Situation Comedy. ITV 1974

George Dobbs	**Bob Hoskins**
Stan	**John Thaw**
Annie Dobbs	**Pat Ashton**
Tommy Hollister	**Trevor Peacock**
Daphne	**Nell Curran**

Creators/Writers: **Dick Clement, Ian La Frenais**
Producer: **Derrick Goodwin**

Two crooks share one house and one woman.

When petty criminal George 'Dobbsie' Dobbs was released from prison after three years, he returned home to Fulham to discover his best pal, Stan, shacked up with his missus, Annie. Rather than punching each other's lights out, they reluctantly agreed to share the house, with predictable consequences, especially when on-the-run jailbird Tommy Hollister also moved in. Daphne was Annie's friend and much-needed confidante.

Only eight episodes were produced, although creators Dick Clement and Ian La Frenais had made plans to develop the series, sending its two main protagonists back inside. Instead, largely because actor John Thaw had been signed up for THE SWEENEY, they returned to the BBC, for whom they developed their Ronnie Barker pilot, *Prisoner and Escort*, into another old lag comedy – PORRIDGE.

THIN BLUE LINE, THE
UK (Tiger Aspect) Comedy. BBC 1 1995–6

Insp. Raymond Fowler	**Rowan Atkinson**
Sgt Patricia Dawkins	**Serena Evans**
PC Maggie Habib	**Mina Anwar**
PC Kevin Goody	**James Dreyfus**
PC Frank Gladstone	**Rudolph Walker**
DI Derek Grim	**David Haig**
DC Kray	**Kevin Allen**
DC Gary Boyle	**Mark Addy**

Writer: **Ben Elton**
Producers: **Ben Elton, Geoffrey Perkins**

The misadventures of an incompetent police inspector and his equally inept team.

Ben Elton has often declared his admiration for the sitcom genius of DAD'S ARMY, and in *The Thin Blue Line* there was more than an echo of Captain Mainwaring and his bumbling platoon, albeit in a cruder, 1990s style. The setting was Gasforth police station, ruled over with a rod of plastic by stick-in-the-mud traditionalist Inspector Raymond Fowler. Joining him in the force was his eminently more sensible live-in girlfriend of ten years, Sgt Dawkins, and other members of the team were Constable Habib (an Asian from Accrington and another voice of womanly reason), languid West Indian Constable Gladstone (filled with irrelevant recollections of the old days) and the jumpy, vain and decidedly effeminate (despite his lust for Habib) Constable Goody. Friction at the station came from the CID division, headed by the angry, unscrupulous DI Grim (prone to mixed metaphors) and his right-hand men, initially the smirky Kray then the bluff Boyle.

Collectively, the Gasforth crew faced difficult situations such as dealing with young offenders, martialling football hooligans, policing anti-road protesters, flushing out drug-dealers and making themselves attractive for a TV documentary. Two series were made.

THIN MAN, THE

US (MGM) Detective Drama. BBC 1957–8

Nick Charles	**Peter Lawford**
Nora Charles	**Phyllis Kirk**
Lt. Ralph Raines	**Stafford Repp**
Lt. Steve King	**Tol Avery**

A husband, a wife and their dog are a team of amateur detectives.

The first thing to forget about this series is the Thin Man. There wasn't one. That character had appeared in the film from which the series was derived and in which our heroes, Nick and Nora Charles, made their debut. Played by William Powell and Myrna Loy, this pair of amateur sleuths appeared in five more cinema features before arriving on TV in the persons of Peter Lawford and Phyllis Kirk.

Nick had been a private eye with the Trans-American Detective Agency, but now, fabulously rich, he and his new wife, Nora, had retired to a swanky apartment on New York's Park Avenue and settled into a world of good living. However, Nick found old habits die hard, and he soon returned to the detective game, this time with his devoted wife at his side. The couple's wire-haired fox-terrier, Asta, also played a part, sniffing out clues like a bloodhound. What the plots lacked in depth was compensated for by the sparkling husband-and-wife repartee.

These characters, created by novelist Dashiell Hammett, have proved highly influential. If you ever wondered where the likes of HART TO HART, McMILLAN AND WIFE and WILDE ALLIANCE found their inspiration, look no further.

THIRD MAN, THE

UK/US (BBC/National Telefilm/British Lion) Drama. BBC 1959–65

Harry Lime	**Michael Rennie**
Bradford Webster	**Jonathan Harris**
Arthur Shillings	**Rupert Davies**

Executive Producer: **Vernon Burns**

Producer: **Felix Jackson**

The further adventures of Graham Greene's treacherous Viennese double-dealer.

In a move away from the famous cinema version starring Orson Welles, the TV *Third Man* cast Michael Rennie as Harry Lime, a charming amateur sleuth – quite unlike the film character – officially running an import-export agency but travelling the world to pin down crooks and help people in trouble at the same time. Specializing in works of art, the suave, sophisticated Lime's companies included Harry Lime Ltd, in London, and its equivalent, Harry Lime Inc., in New York. In his work he was assisted by his treasurer-cum-manservant, Bradford Webster (played by a pre-LOST IN SPACE Jonathan Harris), and on his investigations he enjoyed a close liaison with Scotland Yard's Arthur Shillings (Rupert Davies in training for his future role as MAIGRET). A joint UK/US production, filming took place in both Shepperton Studios and Hollywood.

THIRTYSOMETHING

US (MGM/United Artists) Drama. Channel 4 1989–92

Michael Steadman	**Ken Olin**
Hope Steadman	**Mel Harris**
Elliot Weston	**Timothy Busfield**
Nancy Weston	**Patricia Wettig**
Melissa Steadman	**Melanie Mayron**
Ellyn Warren/Sidel	**Polly Draper**
Prof. Gary Shepherd	**Peter Horton**
Janey Steadman	**Brittany and Lacey Craven**
Ethan Weston	**Luke Rossi**
Brittany Weston	**Jordana 'Bink' Shapiro**
Miles Drentell	**David Clennon**
Susannah Hart/Shepherd	**Patricia Kalember**
Steve Woodman	**Terry Kinney**
Jeffrey Milgrom	**Richard Gilliland**
Lee Owens	**Corey Parker**
Billy Sidel	**Erich Anderson**

Creators: **Ed Zwick, Marshall Herskovitz**
Producers: **Ed Zwick, Marshall Herskovitz, Paul Haggis**

Light-hearted drama series centring on a group of upwardly mobile friends in Philadelphia.

Against a background of disappearing youth and unfulfilled careers, *thirtysomething* introduced viewers to seven professional people in their thirties, children of the baby-boomer generation, now adults in a yuppie world. There were two couples and three singles, and the programme traced their lives, their loves, their fears and their ambitions.

Michael and Elliot were colleagues at an advertising agency who branched out into their own business. Hope and Nancy were their respective wives. Hope was a Princeton graduate and writer who put her own career on hold in order to raise little Janey (and, later, Leo); Nancy was a 1960s flower child with artistic pretensions who looked after her and Elliot's school-age children, Ethan and Brittany. The three other protagonists were

Gary Shepherd, a college classics lecturer, Melissa Stead-man, Michael's photographer cousin, and Ellyn Warren (Hope's best friend), an administrator at the City Hall. Both Melissa and Ellyn drifted in and out of affairs, before Ellyn eventually married an old flame, Billy Sidel.

The series focused on each of the characters as they reached the crossroads and crises that affect everyone's lives, like the death of a parent (Michael's father), marital problems (Nancy and Elliot went through a messy separation) and personal illness (Nancy was diagnosed as having ovarian cancer). Career matters were always under discussion, particularly when Michael and Elliot's business collapsed and they were forced to work for the devious Miles Drentell. Romance was never far away, as when Gary married Susannah Hart and they had baby Emma. Nor was death. Gary was then killed in a car accident.

It was not surprising to discover that most of the programme's audience were in their 30s themselves. Viewers clearly identified with the series, sharing the characters' childhood memories and facing up to the same challenges of maturity.

THIS IS YOUR LIFE
UK (BBC/Thames) Entertainment. BBC 1955–64; ITV 1969–94; BBC 1 1994–

Presenters: **Eamonn Andrews, Michael Aspel**

Creator: **Ralph Edwards**
Producers: **T. Leslie Jackson, Vere Lorrimer, Robert Tyrrel, Malcolm Morris, Jack Crawshaw, John Graham, Sue Green**

The life story of an unsuspecting celebrity retold with the help of surprise guests.

Taking people unawares, surrounding them with friends and family, and reliving the major moments in their life is what this programme has been all about. *This Is Your Life* began on American TV in 1952, with Ralph Edwards, its creator, also acting as host. In the UK it has meandered between channels, beginning first on the BBC in 1955 and running for nine years. After a five-year hiatus, Thames picked up the format for ITV, and the company continued to produce the show when it returned to the BBC in 1994. Over the years, it has consistently topped the ratings.

The same formula has been followed from the start. The unsuspecting victim has been cornered by the presenter (usually in disguise) at a public event or at a contrived meeting, informed 'This is your life' and then whisked away to a nearby TV studio, where close family and friends have welcomed the fêted one. Other guests have been introduced as the host has worked his way chronologically through the person's life, reading from a large red book. Mystery voices hidden behind closed doors have given way to forgotten faces and warm embraces. Amusing anecdotes have been told and glowing tributes have been paid. The final guest has usually been someone special: a child from the other side of the world, an inspirational teacher from the distant past, a

person who has saved the celebrity's life, or vice versa. Buckets of tears have been shed.

The very first victim was Eamonn Andrews, who was already signed up to be the programme's regular host. Ralph Edwards had flown over from the USA to conduct the inaugural programme but, after the *Daily Sketch* had spoiled the launch by revealing that the subject was going to be Stanley Matthews, a new victim had to be found. Andrews expected boxer Freddie Mills to be the target. Instead, it was Andrews himself. When Thames revived the series, its first victim was Des O'Connor. Some celebrities refused outright to appear. Soccer star Danny Blanchflower was one; novelist Richard Gordon (of *Doctor in the House* fame) was another. To avoid such embarrassments, the programme is now pre-recorded.

Not all those featured have been famous. One or two guests per series have come from the ranks of anonymous worthies – brave airmen, industrious charity workers, selfless foster-parents, etc. Probably the highest-profile victim was Lord Mountbatten, the subject of a *This Is Your Life* special in the Jubilee Year of 1977.

When Eamonn Andrews died in 1987, Michael Aspel picked up the big red book. The one used on screen contains just the programme script, but a real biographical scrapbook is later presented as a memento to the featured guest. Regular consultants to the series have been Roy Bottomley and Tom Brennand.

THIS LIFE
UK (World/BBC) Drama. BBC 2 1996–7

Miles	Jack Davenport
Milly	Amita Dhiri
Warren Jones	Jason Hughes
Egg	Andrew Lincoln
Anna	Daniela Nardini
Hooperman	Geoffrey Bateman
O'Donnell	David Mallinson
Graham	Cyril Nri
Jo	Steve John Shepherd
Delilah	Charlotte Bicknell
Kira	Luisa Bradshaw-White
Kelly	Sacha Craise
Dale	Mark Lewis Jones
Jerry	Paul Copley
Therapist	Gillian McCutcheon
Rachel	Natasha Little
Ferdy	Ramon Tikaram
Nicki	Juliet Cowan
Montgomery	Michael Elwyn
Paul	Paul J. Medford
Sarah	Clare Clifford
Mrs Cochrane	Steph Bramwell
George	Gregg Prentice
Lenny	Tony Curran
Francesca	Rachel Fielding

Creators: **Amy Jenkins, Tony Garnett**
Producer: **Jane Fallon**
Executive Producer: **Tony Garnett**

The lifestyle of professional young Londoners, through the eyes of five housesharers.

Quickly gathering cult status, *This Life* was the brainchild of BBC 2 controller Michael Jackson and was developed by award-winning producer Tony Garnett and writer Amy Jenkins. It featured five young lawyers (Jenkins was herself a legal clerk) who were disillusioned with the restrictions of office work and led turbulent social lives – casual sex, drugs and heavy language were par for the course.

Three of the five – Miles (slightly arrogant), Milly (hard-working perfectionist-achiever) and her boyfriend, Egg (sensitive, nice guy) – had been good friends at university and now shared a house in Benjamin Street, Southwark. However, they needed a couple more people to help with the rent and so brought in Anna (brash, witty and impetuous), who had once slept with Miles – a perennial source of tension – and another work colleague, the (on the face of it) hyper-confident Welshman, Warren, who was gay. Hand-held cameras followed them to work, to the wine bar, to the bathroom and to bed. The introduction of additional characters like the bulimic Delilah, a girlfriend of Miles, Warren's cousin Kira (who discovered his homosexuality, a secret back in Wales) and barrister's clerk Jo (one of Anna's one-night stands), plus Egg's uncertainty over his chosen career path (he'd rather have been a novelist, a football writer or a cook), allowed a wide range of twentysomething troubles to come to the fore.

Two series were made, the second a mighty 21 episodes long.

THIS WEEK
UK (Associated-Rediffusion/Thames) Current Affairs. ITV
1956–78; 1986–92

Presenters: **René Cutforth, Leslie Mitchell, Michael Westmore, Ludovic Kennedy, Daniel Farson, Brian Connell, Alastair Burnet, Jonathan Dimbleby**

Editors/Producers: **Caryl Doncaster, Peter Hunt, Cyril Bennett, Peter Morley, Jeremy Isaacs, Cliff Morgan, Phillip Whitehead, David Elstein**

Award-winning weekly current affairs reports.

ITV's answer to PANORAMA, *This Week* began life as a simple topical news magazine with the slogan 'A window on the world behind the headlines'. In the mid-1960s *This Week* changed to adopt the single-investigation format it employed until its demise in 1992. Among its celebrated crew were reporters like Desmond Wilcox, James Cameron, Robert Kee, Llew Gardner and, later, Jonathan Dimbleby. For some reason, the programme was renamed *TV Eye* in 1978 (when one of its reporters was the temporarily unseated Labour MP, Bryan Gould), but the original title was restored in 1986. *This Week*'s stirring theme music was an excerpt from Sibelius's 'Karelia Suite'.

THOMAS, ANTONY
(1940–)

British documentary film-maker, known for his passionate involvement in his work. His prize-winning trilogy, *The South African Experience*, aired in 1977, although infinitely more controversial was his DEATH OF A PRINCESS in 1980, a dramatized account of the execution of an Islamic princess who had adopted some western ideas and so questioned the values of Islam. It led to an international row and the disruption of diplomatic relations between Britain and Saudi Arabia. Other contributions have included *Where Harry Stood*, *The Japanese Experience* (both 1974), *The Arab Experience* (1975), *The Good, The Bad and The Indifferent* (1976) and *The Most Dangerous Man in the World* (1982).

THOMAS, GARETH

Welsh Shakespearean actor who has enjoyed a number of popular roles on television. Probably his most prominent was as the rebel leader Roj Blake in BLAKE'S 7, even though he was a member of the cast for only the first two seasons. He was also DC Ron Radley in *Parkin's Patch*, Dr Philip Denny in *The Citadel*, Reverend Mr Gruffydd in *How Green Was My Valley*, Major General Horton in BY THE SWORD DIVIDED, scientist Adam Brake in *Children of the Stones*, Owen in *The Knights of God*, refugee Shem in STAR MAIDENS and Morgan in *Morgan's Boy*. Thomas has also appeared in *Shades of Darkness*, HAMMER HOUSE OF HORROR, MEDICS, *Crown Prosecutor*, LONDON'S BURNING and numerous single dramas.

THOMAS THE TANK ENGINE AND FRIENDS
UK (Clearwater/Britt Allcroft/Central) Animation. ITV
1984–6; 1992

Narrators: **Ringo Starr, Michael Angelis**

Writers: **Britt Allcroft, David Mitton**
Executive Producer: **Britt Allcroft**
Producers: **Britt Allcroft, David Mitton, Robert Cardona**

The adventures of a steam railway engine and his fellow vehicles.

Narrated initially by Beatle Ringo Starr and then in the same dry, Liverpudlian manner by Michael Angelis, *Thomas the Tank Engine and Friends* was the television incarnation of Reverend Wilbert Awdry's children's stories from the 1940s. Star of the show was Thomas, the blue tank engine bearing the number 1. Unlike most children's characters, Thomas was not always a goodie and was prone to bouts of moodiness, depicted in his expressionful face and rolling eyes (painted on the front). All the same, he became a hero for toddlers, and a massive merchandising business took off as a result.

Joining Thomas in his scrapes on the island of Sodor were old Edward, the blue number 2 engine, Henry (green, number 3), Gordon (blue, number 4), James, the mixed traffic engine (red, number 5), Percy, the saddle tank (green, number 6), Toby, the tram engine (brown, number 7), Montague, a Great Western engine familiarly known as 'Duck' because he waddled (green, number 8), the twin black engines, Donald (number 9) and Douglas (number 10), and Oliver (green, number 11). Thomas's carriages were Annie and Clarabel, and also seen were Daisy, the diesel rail car, Diesel, a diesel engine, and Henrietta, another carriage. Several new engines and vehicles were added in later series. All operated under instructions from the Fat Controller (Sir Topham Hat), who, like the drivers, firemen and other human characters, was simply seen as a static figurine. Thomas's other acquaintances were Terence the tractor, Harold the helicopter and Bertie the bus.

Thomas the Tank Engine and Friends, made using models, was one of the few British animations to be sold to the USA.

THOMPSON, EMMA
(1959–)

Versatile British actress and all-purpose entertainer, the daughter of Eric 'MAGIC ROUNDABOUT' Thompson and former PLAY SCHOOL presenter Phyllida Law. Now an international film name, Emma, a Cambridge Footlights graduate, has also been acclaimed for her television work, which began with the comedy series, ALFRESCO. She played Suzi Kettles in the musical drama, TUTTI FRUTTI, and in FORTUNES OF WAR she starred as Harriet Pringle opposite her future husband, Kenneth Branagh. Unfortunately, her adventurous sketch series, *Thompson*, a showcase for her multi-talents in 1988, was not so well received. She has also guested in THE YOUNG ONES and CHEERS, and appeared with Jasper Carrott in *Carrott's Lib*. She is the sister of actress Sophie Thompson.

THOMSON, JOHN

English comedian and actor, coming to the fore as Fat Bob in Steve Coogan's Paul Calf programmes and as dim publican Ken in MEN BEHAVING BADLY. He has since supported Coogan in *Coogan's Run*, been a member of THE FAST SHOW team and starred in ROGER ROGER (Barry), COLD FEET (Pete Gifford) and PLAYING THE FIELD (Eddie), also appearing in series like MURDER MOST HORRID, *Is It Legal?*, SOLDIER, SOLDIER, *The World of Lee Evans* and the nativity short, *It's a Girl*. In 2001, he provided the voice for Bill in the revival of FLOWER POT MEN.

THORN BIRDS, THE
US (ABC) Drama. BBC 1 1984

Father Ralph de Bricassart	**Richard Chamberlain**
Meggie Cleary	**Sydney Penny**
	Rachel Ward
Mary Carson	**Barbara Stanwyck**
Fiona 'Fee' Cleary	**Jean Simmons**
Archbishop Contini-Verchese	**Christopher Plummer**
Luke O'Neill	**Bryan Brown**
Paddy Cleary	**Richard Kiley**
Rainer Hartheim	**Ken Howard**
Justine	**Mare Winningham**
Luddie Mueller	**Earl Holliman**
Anne Mueller	**Piper Laurie**
Dane	**Philip Anglim**

Writer: **Carmen Culver**
Producers: **David L. Wolper, Stan Margulies**

Forbidden love in the Australian outback.

The Thorn Birds was the story of ambitious and handsome Catholic priest Ralph de Bricassart who found himself dragged off the straight and narrow by Meggie Cleary, the beautiful daughter of an Australian sheepfarmer, a girl he had known from an early age (Sydney Penny played Meggie as a child). Set between the years 1920 and 1962, the five-part serial chronicled the consequences of their illicit love affair, for the priest's conscience and his clerical career, and for Meggie, who gave birth to a son, Dane, who followed his father into the church. Hovering in the background was Meggie's matriarchal grandmother, Mary Carson, who herself had designs on the heart-throb churchman. *The Thorn Birds* was adapted by Carmen Culver from Colleen McCullough's steamy novel. Richard Chamberlain resumed the role of Ralph for a two-part sequel, *The Thorn Birds: the Missing Years*, in the 1990s.

THORNE, ANGELA
(1939–)

British actress, typically seen in upper-class parts, as characterized by her roles in TO THE MANOR BORN (Marjory Frobisher), THREE UP, TWO DOWN (Daphne Trenchard) and *Farrington of the F.O.* (Harriet Emily Farrington). She also appeared in ELIZABETH R (Lettice Knollys), *Cold Comfort Farm* (Mrs Hawk-Monitor), the sketch show, *World in Ferment*, and the kids' comedy, *The Bagthorpe Saga* (Laura Bagthorpe), and other credits have included *The Canterville Ghost*, *Haunted* and THE GOOD GUYS.

THORNTON, FRANK
(Frank Thornton Ball; 1921–)

Staunch British comedy support, coming into his own in the guise of Captain Peacock in ARE YOU BEING SERVED? and *Grace and Favour*. Previously, Thornton had been seen largely as a straight man to many comics, including Tony Hancock (HANCOCK'S HALF HOUR), Michael Bentine (IT'S A SQUARE WORLD), Spike Milligan (*The World of Beachcomber*) and Harry Worth. Thornton was also Commander Fairweather of HMS *Paradise* in the 1964 sitcom of the same name, and has appeared in STEPTOE AND SON, JANE and THE UPPER HAND, among many other programmes. More recently, he played legal clerk Geoffrey Parker-Knoll in *All Rise for Julian Clary* and starred as Truly in LAST OF THE SUMMER WINE.

THORP, RICHARD
(1932–)

EMMERDALE's Alan Turner has, in fact, enjoyed a long career on TV. Surrey-born actor Richard Thorp first appeared on our screens back in the 1950s, when he played heart-throb Dr John Rennie in EMERGENCY – WARD 10, also starring in its spin-off, *Call Oxbridge 2000*. He was later seen in series like HONEY LANE, A FAMILY AT WAR, PUBLIC EYE, *The Cedar Tree*, STRANGERS and TO THE MANOR BORN before he joined *Emmerdale Farm* as 'Fatty' Turner, then boss of NY Estates, in 1982.

THREE OF A KIND
UK (BBC) Comedy. BBC 1 1981–3

Tracey Ullman, Lenny Henry, David Copperfield

Producer: **Paul Jackson**

Comedy sketch show featuring three promising performers.

As a showcase for emerging talent, *Three of a Kind* certainly delivered the goods. Lenny Henry had already been seen on NEW FACES, THE FOSTERS and TISWAS, and Tracey Ullman had appeared in West End musicals. They were drawn into a team with fellow comic David Copperfield (not to be confused with the American illusionist) by producer Paul Jackson and presented two series of sketches and monologues which were well received. Everyone knows what happened to Henry and Ullman, but the fate of David Copperfield remains a mystery to many viewers (he retired to the world of cabaret).

Three of a Kind was also the title of another vehicle for up-and-coming talents, which was screened in 1967. The three in question then were Lulu (not that she was *that* new), Mike Yarwood and Ray Fell (the David Copperfield of the trio, who went on to appear on the Las Vegas cabaret circuit).

3–2–1
UK (Yorkshire) Game Show. ITV 1978–87

Presenter: **Ted Rogers**

Executive Producer: **Alan Tarrant**
Producers: **Derek Burrell-Davis, Mike Goddard, Ian Bolt, Terry Henebery, Graham Wetherell**

Game show in which contestants decipher clues to win prizes.

3–2–1 was based on the Spanish quiz, *Uno, Dos, Tres*, and focused on three married couples as they battled for the right to win valuable prizes. The first segment of the game was a quiz (often 'list' questions), after which the leading couple went away to return in the next programme. In early editions, a second round consisted of physical games and observation questions about a performed sketch, but the format employed for the rest of the show, devoted to a series of playlets, songs and sketches featuring surprise celebrity guests, was soon used from the end of round one onwards. Resident comics Chris Emmet, Dougie Brown and Debbie Arnold were known as 'The Disrepertory Company', and the Brian Rogers' Connection was the supporting dance troupe. The sketches all followed a theme: Arabian Nights, the circus, Merrie England, etc., and, following each skit, one of the performers read out a related riddle which referred to a prize. When the two remaining couples had been whittled down to one by an elimination question, the final couple then had to decide which of the cryptic clues to discard in the search for the best prize (usually a car). One prize they all wanted to avoid was the new metal rubbish-bin, representing the show's robotic mascot, Dusty Bin. Compere Ted Rogers fast-talked his way through each show, twirling his fingers in a 3–2–1 salute. He was supported by a team of hostesses known as The Gentle Secs.

THREE UP, TWO DOWN
UK (BBC) Situation Comedy. BBC 1 1985–9

Sam Tyler	**Michael Elphick**
Daphne Trenchard	**Angela Thorne**
Nick Tyler	**Ray Burdis**
Angie Tyler	**Lysette Anthony**
Major Giles Bradshaw	**Neil Stacy**
Wilf	**John Grillo**
Rhonda	**Vicki Woolf**

Creator/Writer: **Richard Ommanney**
Producers: **David Askey, John B. Hobbs**

A stuck-up widow and a down-to-earth widower share a flat and a grandchild, but have little else in common.

With a new son (Joe) to look after and finances stretched, photographer Nick Tyler and his model wife, Angie, decided to install one of the child's grandparents in their basement flat, as a live-in baby-sitter. This meant that either Nick's working-class dad, Sam, or Angie's well-bred mum, Daphne, would take up residence, but, because of a mix-up, both were invited and both accepted. Reluctantly agreeing to share the flat, in order to be near their grandchild, Cockney Sam and Cheltenham-raised Daphne became the worst of enemies, despite Sam's obviously warm feelings towards his cold, snooty flatmate. His easy-going, earthy manner frustrated her and his taxidermy hobby only made matters worse, filling the flat with stuffed penguins and other dead creatures. However, after a disastrous fling with con-man Giles Bradshaw, Daphne finally realized that the kind-hearted Sam was really the man for her, despite their many differences, and the two embarked on a rather more harmonious co-existence. Wilf was the theatrically-minded zoo-keeper who provided animals for Sam to stuff, and also seen in later episodes was flirty neighbour Rhonda.

THRELFALL, DAVID
(1953–)

Northern Shakespearean actor who took the part of Leslie Titmuss MP in John Mortimer's *Paradise Postponed* and *Titmuss Regained*. He was also seen in the RSC's *The Life and Adventures of Nicholas Nickleby* (Smike), played Prince Charles in BSkyB's *Diana: Her True Story* and turned to comedy for the sitcoms, *Nightingales* (security guard Bell) and *Men of the World* (travel agent Lenny Smart). In addition, Threlfall appeared with Sheila Hancock in *Jumping the Queue*, and other credits have included *Scum*, *The Gathering Seed*, *A Murder of Quality*, *Clothes in the Wardrobe* and *Sex, Chips and Rock 'n' Roll* (Norman Kershaw).

THRILLER
UK (ATV) Suspense Anthology. ITV 1973–6

Creator: **Brian Clemens**

Series of feature-length film thrillers.

Created and largely written by Brian Clemens, *Thriller* offered a collection of twist-in-the-tail stories designed to keep the audience on the edge of their seats. The best-remembered contributions included *A Coffin for the Bride* (starring Helen Mirren), *Only a Scream Away* (Hayley Mills), *Nurse Will Make It Better* (Diana Dors) and *The Crazy Kill* (Denholm Elliott).

THROUGH THE KEYHOLE
UK (Yorkshire/David Parradine) Game Show. ITV 1987–94; BBC 1 1997–

Presenters: **David Frost, Loyd Grossman**

Executive Producer: **Kevin Sim**
Producers: **Ian Bolt, Chantal Rutherford Browne**

Who-lives-where game show featuring celebrity panellists.

In this easy-going, family panel game, Loyd Grossman has led a camera team through the various rooms of a celebrity's house, pointing out features of décor, their style of living and evidence of hobbies and professions. Three famous guests have then had to guess to whom the house belongs, taking note of extra clues from host David Frost. The householder has subsequently strolled on to confront the panellists.

After being axed by ITV, *Through the Keyhole*, produced by David Frost's own production company, was picked up by BBC 1 for its daytime schedules.

THROWER, DEBBIE
(1957–)

British presenter and newsreader, born in Kenya. After working in newspapers and radio, Thrower joined BBC South as a reporter on the news magazine, *South Today*, before going national and reading the main BBC news bulletins. At this time, she was also seen in programmes like *Out of Court*, *Lifeline*, action reports like *Hospital Watch* and as host of SONGS OF PRAISE. Returning to regional broadcasting, she took over as presenter of TVS's *Coast to Coast*, which evolved into *Meridian Tonight*. She has also presented other local programmes and Channel 4's *Collectors' Lot*.

THROWER, PERCY
MBE (1913–88)

Percy Thrower, as host of GARDENING CLUB for 12 years from 1955 and its successor, GARDENERS' WORLD (filmed at his own home), from 1968, was the king of TV gardeners. But, as well as having green fingers, he proved to be a popular TV personality, popping up in numerous other programmes, including BLUE PETER (1974–88), for which he designed a famous Italian sunken garden in 1978.

THUNDERBIRDS
UK (AP Films/ATV/ITC) Children's Science Fiction. ITV 1965–6

Voices:

Jeff Tracy	**Peter Dyneley**
Scott Tracy	**Shane Rimmer**
Virgil Tracy	**David Holliday**
	Jeremy Wilkin
Alan Tracy	**Matt Zimmerman**
Gordon Tracy	**David Graham**
John Tracy	**Ray Barrett**
Lady Penelope Creighton-Ward	**Sylvia Anderson**
Brains	**David Graham**
Parker	**David Graham**
The Hood	**Ray Barrett**
Tin-Tin Kyrano	**Christine Finn**
Kyrano	**David Graham**
Grandma	**Christine Finn**

Creators: **Gerry Anderson, Sylvia Anderson**
Producers: **Gerry Anderson, Reg Hill**

A 21st-century family runs a global rescue service, using advanced aircraft and technology.

In the year 2063 International Rescue (IR) had been established by retired astronaut Jeff Tracy in a mountain refuge on his isolated Pacific island. Utilizing futuristic aircraft devised by Brains, a stammering, bespectacled genius, he sent into action a squad of brave, humanitarian rescuers – all his own sons, named after the first five Americans in space and dedicated to averting disasters.

The stars of the show were the Thunderbirds themselves, wonderfully high-tech vehicles capable of incredible speeds and amazing manoeuvres. Thunderbird 1 (with Scott, Jeff's eldest son and second-in-command, at the helm) was a combination of reconnaissance jet and rocket. Thunderbird 2 (piloted by the softly spoken, piano-playing Virgil) was the fleet's freighter, carrying machinery like the burrowing tool, The Mole, and the team's submarine, Thunderbird 4, in a series of six pods which could be inserted into its belly. Thunderbird 4, when called into use, was controlled by aquanaut Gordon Tracy, an enthusiastic practical-joker who was always keen for action. Their blond-haired, impetuous brother, Alan, piloted the rocket, Thunderbird 3, taking it into orbit to join the team's space-station, Thunderbird 5, manned by the fifth son, John, the loner of the family. John and Alan sometimes switched jobs.

The Thunderbirds (which Anderson named after Thunderbird airfield in Arizona) could be called out at any time. Usually the siren was sounded by Thunderbird 5, picking up distress messages from all around the globe. Thunderbird 1 was the first on the scene, making full use of its 7000 m.p.h. velocity, allowing Scott to liaise with base and advise the slower Thunderbird 2, following in its wake. The elaborate take-off procedures from Tracy Island were a highlight of the show. Swivelling walls and sinking sofas conveyed the pilots out of the luxurious Tracy home to the hangars beneath, with chutes and slides positioning them perfectly in their craft, before swimming pools retracted and palm trees fell back to reveal hidden launch-pads. Once in action, the boys reported back via a video intercom which superimposed their faces on to wall portraits. All messages were punctuated with the acknowledgement 'F.A.B.'

However, the whole International Rescue set-up was a mystery to the rest of the world, and the identity of the Thunderbird pilots shrouded in secrecy. The only parties in the know were the Tracys themselves, their island staff and a special London agent and her butler. The staff were Kyrano, Jeff's oriental manservant, and his daughter, Tin-Tin (an electronics expert and Alan's romantic interest). The London agent was Lady Penelope Creighton-Ward, a true aristocrat with a cool, calm approach to dealing with thugs. She travelled in a souped-up, well-armed, pink Rolls-Royce (registration FAB 1; FAB 2 was her luxury yacht), which was driven by her shifty-looking, safe-cracking butler, Parker, a Cockney best remembered for his loyal 'Yes M'Lady'. Hounding the rescuers was the evil, bald-headed Hood. He was Kyrano's half-brother and lived in a temple in a Thai jungle, but he was also a master of disguise and travelled the world trying to ensnare the Tracy brothers and their fabulous machines. He also had power over Kyrano, his eyes lighting up whenever he cast his 'hoodoo' spell.

The series has been widely acknowledged as Gerry Anderson's masterpiece. Filmed in 50-minute episodes to corner the prime-time market, the format provided plenty of scope for character development and tension-building. By this stage, the Supermarionation production technique had almost reached perfection. The puppets' eye- and lip-movements were synchronized with the dialogue and their control wires were so thin (one 5,000th of an inch) that they were barely noticeable. With its stirring theme music by Barry Gray, sophisticated special effects and multitude of explosions, *Thunderbirds* captured an adult, as well as a children's, audience. A bandwagon rolled out in *Thunderbird* merchandise, and two feature films were also produced, *Thunderbirds Are Go* and *Thunderbird Six*. A digitally remastered version of the series was screened on BBC 2 in 2000.

TILBURY, PETER
(1945–)

British writer and actor, the creator of SHELLEY and CHEF!. His other writing credits have included episodes of BIRDS OF A FEATHER and the sitcoms, *Sorry, I'm a Stranger Here Myself* (with David Firth) and *It Takes a Worried Man* (in which he also starred as Philip Roath). In addition, his acting career has taken in series like DIXON OF DOCK GREEN, THE EXPERT, C.A.T.S. EYES, FORTUNES OF WAR, FIRST BORN, CASUALTY and THE BILL.

TILL DEATH US DO PART
UK (BBC) Situation Comedy. BBC 1 1966–8; 1972–5

Alf Garnett	**Warren Mitchell**
Else Garnett	**Dandy Nichols**
Rita	**Una Stubbs**
Mike	**Anthony Booth**
Bert Reed	**Alfie Bass**
Min Reed	**Patricia Hayes**

Creator/Writer: **Johnny Speight**
Producers: **Dennis Main Wilson, Brian Winston, David Croft**

A bigoted East End docker shares his home with his dim wife, his liberal daughter and her left-wing husband.

Alf Garnett remains one of TV's most memorable creations. He has been loved and he has been hated, but he is unlikely to be forgotten. The man who brought racist views and foul language into British living rooms is a hard act to follow. Although the 1980s' 'alternative' comedians aimed to shock, their impact was negligible in comparison with TV's first controversial loudmouth.

The Garnetts lived in London's decaying East End, long before the Isle of Dogs was transformed into a yuppie paradise. Their little docker's terraced house was home to four adults: Alf, his wife, Else, daughter, Rita, and son-in-law, Mike. Such close habitation induced claustrophobia and an endless amount of personal friction. On one side, there was Alf, a bald, bespectacled bigot, patriotically standing up for the Queen and cheerfully pushing the blame for the country's ills on to 'Darling Harold' Wilson and immigrants. Mind you, if he had succeeded in shipping out the immigrants and dislodging the Labour Party from government, he still wouldn't have been happy with Edward Heath in charge – he was a grammar school boy, not a traditional Tory like Winston Churchill. On the other side was Mike, a long-haired, unemployed, Liverpudlian socialist, 'Shirley Temple' or 'randy Scouse git', as he became known. In between were the phlegmatic, rather dopey Else and the giggly Rita.

Alf's rantings were heavily criticized by the church, Mary Whitehouse and politicians, but his character had other sides to it, too. He was incredibly selfish, and extremely mean to his long-suffering wife. Yet Else took it all in her rather sluggish stride, shrugging off insults like 'silly old moo' and conjuring up sharp retorts to put Alf firmly in his place. Whenever that happened, he donned his West Ham scarf and skulked off to the pub. When Dandy Nichols briefly left the series in the 1970s (Else went to visit her sister in Australia), Alf's invective was directed against his neighbours, Bert and Min.

Till Death Us Do Part began as an episode of COMEDY PLAYHOUSE in 1965. In this pilot, Warren Mitchell played Alf Ramsey (as in the football manager), with Gretchen Franklin (Ethel in EASTENDERS) as his maligned wife. The series proper ran from 1966 to 1968 and was exhumed for a new run in 1972. A short-lived 1981 version, *Till Death . . .* (produced by ATV), was followed by a new BBC revival in 1985. This time the title had been changed to *In Sickness and in Health*, ironically appropriate considering the obvious illness of Dandy Nichols. The Garnetts had been rehoused in a new development, without Rita or Mike, and the antagonizer's role was filled by a gay, black home-help, provocatively named Winston. This series continued even after Nichols's death in 1986 (Alf's neighbour, Mrs Hollingbery, played by Carmel McSharry, became his new sparring partner) but by this time the political climate had changed. Even though Alf could slate the incumbent Tory government for being a bunch of spivs ruled over by a grocer's daughter, the bite had disappeared and the series was far less successful. Johnny Speight's monstrous creation had had his day. An American version of *Till Death Us Do Part*, ALL IN THE FAMILY, was just as big and controversial.

TILT

The pivoting of a camera vertically up and down, as opposed to a pan, which involves horizontal movement from left to right or vice versa.

TIME TUNNEL, THE
US (Twentieth Century-Fox/Irwin Allen) Science Fiction.
BBC 1 1968

Dr Tony Newman	**James Darren**
Dr Doug Phillips	**Robert Colbert**
Dr Ann MacGregor	**Lee Meriwether**
Lt. Gen. Heywood Kirk	**Whit Bissel**
Dr Raymond Swain	**John Zaremba**

Creator/Executive Producer: **Irwin Allen**

Two scientists are trapped in a man-made 'time tunnel' and are thrown into assorted historical adventures.

Tony Newman and Doug Phillips were working on a top-secret project to build a machine which could transport people backwards or forwards in time. When a penny-pinching goverment official arrived at their research centre, hidden beneath the Arizona desert, to demand evidence of progress, Tony was forced to enter the 'time tunnel' to prove it worked. However, as he

knew, the machine was not yet perfected and his risk backfired, leaving him swirling in the mists of time. He eventually materialized on the deck of the *Titanic* on the day before it sank. Seeing him trapped, Doug volunteered to rescue him. Despite their best efforts to convince the ship's captain of the impending doom, he, of course, took no notice and the pair had to be whisked away from the disaster just as it happened.

This set the pattern for other adventures. The team back at base (Drs Swain and MacGregor), while not able to retrieve the scientists, could, however, move them in and out of situations and occasionally caught glimpses of their lost colleagues. Tumbling through time, the travellers fell into adventure after adventure, always arriving at a key point in history – the Alamo before its capitulation, Krakatoa on the point of eruption, Pearl Harbor in advance of the Japanese attack. They also witnessed the French Revolution, the siege of Troy and the Battle of Gettysburg. Ample use was made of old cinema footage to keep expenditure within the show's very limited budget.

TIMESLIP
UK (ATV) Children's Science Fiction. ITV 1970–1

Liz Skinner	**Cheryl Burfield**
Simon Randall	**Spencer Banks**
Frank Skinner	**Derek Benfield**
Jean Skinner	**Iris Russell**
Commander Traynor	**Denis Quilley**
Frank	**John Alkin**
Devereaux	**John Barron**
Beth Skinner	**Mary Preston**
2957	**David Graham**

Creators: **Ruth Boswell, James Boswell**
Writers: **Bruce Stewart, Victor Pemberton**
Producer: **John Cooper**

Two teenagers move backwards and forwards in time through an invisible time-barrier.

On holiday in the Midlands village of St Oswald with her parents, Liz Skinner and her friend Simon Randall were intrigued by the disappearance of a young girl at the site of an old wartime weapons base. Also interested was the mysterious Commander Traynor, Liz's dad's CO when the base had been active. The teenagers discovered an invisible fence and felt their way along it until they came to a hole. Squeezing through, they found themselves back in 1940 and embarked upon an adventure in which they helped a young Mr Skinner to dismantle a secret laser before it was stolen by the Germans. The job done, Liz and Simon returned through the time-barrier to find themselves not in their original 1970 but in 1990, at an Antarctic research station called the Ice Box. Experiments were being performed there on human beings, using a longevity drug known as HA 57. They met up with Beth, an unpleasant older version of Liz, and also discovered her parents, with her father entombed in ice, the victim of a botched experiment. Leading the project was base director Morgan C. Devereaux, who, it transpired, was actually a clone. The kids escaped back to their own time, only to be persuaded to return to the future once more by an anxious Commander Traynor.

On this occasion, they arrived again in 1990, but in a tropical, baking-hot Britain, the result of a failed experiment in climate control. They encountered a friendly Beth and also an older Simon, known simply by the number 2957, who was in charge of a team of clones. But that was not the last of their adventures, and they discovered that Commander Traynor was not all he seemed when they took another trip through the barrier and surfaced in 1965.

The first episode of this imaginative science-fiction series was introduced by ITN's science correspondent, Peter Fairley, who was called up to explain to the young audience the general concept of time travel. The fact that such a prologue was necessary indicated how complex the subsequent episodes were, as they followed the two friends backwards and forwards through time, discovering the unavoidable interdependence of the past and the future, and of actions and consequences.

Timeslip's four adventures (*The Wrong End of Time*, *The Time of the Ice Box*, *The Year of the Burn-up* and *The Day of the Clone*) ran back to back, as one 26-week series. It is fondly remembered by science-fiction fans and was co-created by ITV sci-fi specialist, Ruth Boswell, later producer of THE TOMORROW PEOPLE.

TIMOTHY, CHRISTOPHER
(1940–)

Welsh-born actor whose role as vet James Herriot in ALL CREATURES GREAT AND SMALL has dominated his TV career. However, Timothy has also been seen in series like SOME MOTHERS DO 'AVE 'EM, KATE and *Jackanory Playhouse*, plus single dramas and Shakespearean classics. More recently, he played Dr Brendan McGuire in the daytime series, *Doctors*.

TINTIN
See HERGÉ'S ADVENTURES OF TINTIN.

TINKER, TAILOR, SOLDIER, SPY
UK (BBC) Spy Drama. BBC 2 1979

George Smiley	**Alec Guinness**
Toby Esterhase	**Bernard Hepton**
Roy Bland	**Terence Rigby**
Percy Alleline	**Michael Aldridge**
Bill Haydon	**Ian Richardson**
Peter Guillam	**Michael Jayston**
Sir Oliver Lacon	**Anthony Bate**
Ricki Tarr	**Hywel Bennett**
Control	**Alexander Knox**
Insp. Mendel	**George Sewell**
Jim Prideaux	**Ian Bannen**
Connie Sachs	**Beryl Reid**
Karla	**Patrick Stewart**
Spikely	**Daniel Beecher**
Ann Smiley	**Siân Phillips**

Writer: **Arthur Hopcraft**
Producer: **Jonathan Powell**

A British spy-catcher is brought out of retirement to lead the hunt for a mole.

World-weary British intelligence agent George Smiley suddenly found himself dragged back into the field of international espionage when his help was needed in tracking down a mysterious double-agent. Back at the 'Circus' – as the intelligence agency in London's Cambridge Circus was known – Smiley discovered that some of the top men (Esterhase, Bland, Alleline and Haydon) were under suspicion, each being targeted for investigation under codenames like 'Tinker', 'Tailor', 'Soldier' and 'Poor Man'. Despite struggling with the humiliation of his wife's adultery, Smiley diligently set about his task and painstakingly uncovered vital clues which put him on the road to unmasking the mole.

Based on John Le Carré's novel of the same name, *Tinker, Tailor, Soldier, Spy* was dramatized by Arthur Hopcraft in seven episodes and won enormous acclaim. It wasn't the end of Smiley's intelligence career, however. Three years later he resurfaced (again played by Alec Guinness) in another of Le Carré's offerings, *Smiley's People*. The character reappeared once more in a 1991 two-hour Thames production called *A Murder of Quality*, in which he was played by Denholm Elliott.

TISWAS
UK (ATV/Central) Children's Entertainment. ITV 1974–82

Presenters: **Chris Tarrant, John Asher, Trevor East, Sally James, Lenny Henry, John Gorman, Sylvester McCoy, Frank Carson, Bob Carolgees, Gordon Astley, Fogwell Flax, Den Hegarty, David Rappaport**

Producers: **Peter Harris, Glyn Edwards, Chris Tarrant**

Anarchic Saturday morning live entertainment.

Tiswas was the series which tore up the rulebooks of kids' TV. In contrast with MULTI-COLOURED SWAP SHOP, its BBC Saturday morning rival, *Tiswas* ditched goody-goody, wholesome fare in favour of raucous, get-stuck-in slapstick. Custard pies and buckets of water reigned supreme. Silly sketches featured the likes of Lenny Henry and Frank Carson, plus Bob Carolgees and his punk dog, Spit. Former Scaffold member John Gorman played the appropriately named Smello, but who was the Phantom Flan Flinger who terrorized the studio audience with his foaming pies? Anchors Trevor East, John Asher and particularly Chris Tarrant and Sally James made no attempt to restrain the erupting chaos as they struggled to introduce cartoons, interview pop stars and take competition calls on the Wellyphone (made of old gum boots).

Tiswas began as a regional show in the Midlands in 1974 and took several years to gain full network coverage. ITV companies then opted out of various segments of the show in order to drop in their own cartoons and adventure series. Apart from its sheer anarchy, what made *Tiswas* such a cult series was the fact that adults loved it, too, and there were plenty of dubious, 'grown-up' gags thrown in for them to enjoy. There was even a waiting list of 'mature' viewers demanding to be trapped in 'The Cage' and subjected to regular dousings. This adult following eventually led to a late-night spin-off entitled *OTT* (*Over the Top*) in 1982, hosted by most of the *Tiswas* crew, with the addition of Helen Atkinson-Wood and Alexei Sayle. Sadly, crudeness took over and the series was quickly cancelled. *Tiswas*, too, suffered, largely from the loss of Chris Tarrant, and it soon followed *OTT* into the TV archives.

Tiswas (the name was said to be an acronym for Today Is Saturday, Watch And Smile) also generated a hit single when Tarrant, James, Carolgees and Gorman joined forces as The Four Bucketeers to enter the 1980 Top 30 with 'The Bucket of Water Song'.

TITCHMARSH, ALAN
(1949–)

Yorkshire-born, Kew-trained gardening expert turned television presenter. In addition to green-fingered programming (fronting GARDENERS' WORLD and GROUND FORCE in particular), Titchmarsh has become associated with SONGS OF PRAISE, PEBBLE MILL and other daytime programmes. Other credits have included NATIONWIDE, BREAKFAST TIME, POINTS OF VIEW and *Titchmarsh's Travels*. He is also a published novelist.

TITLES
See CLOSING TITLES and OPENING TITLES.

TNT
(Turner Network Television)

Entertainment channel launched on cable in the USA by Turner Broadcasting (now AOL-Time Warner) in 1988, majoring on old movies and sports. It transferred to Europe in 1993, broadcasting from the Astra satellite system, but omitting the sports element. TNT screens classic American movies from the former MGM and Warner Brothers libraries, with soundtracks available in several languages. In the digital age it has been joined (and looks set to be superseded) by a similar channel, TCM (Turner Classic Movies).

TO PLAY THE KING
See HOUSE OF CARDS.

TO THE MANOR BORN
UK (BBC) Situation Comedy. BBC 1 1979–81

Audrey fforbes-Hamilton	**Penelope Keith**
Richard DeVere	**Peter Bowles**
Marjory Frobisher	**Angela Thorne**
Brabinger	**John Rudling**
Mrs Polouvicka	**Daphne Heard**
Rector	**Gerald Sim**
Brigadier Lemington	**Anthony Sharp**
Ned	**Michael Bilton**
Mrs Patterson	**Daphne Oxenford**

Creator: **Peter Spence**
Producer: **Gareth Gwenlan**

A widow is forced to sell her stately home and move into more limited surroundings.

When Audrey fforbes-Hamilton's husband, Martin, died, he left her his stately pile, Grantleigh Manor, but also a mound of death-duties to pay. Not being able to keep up the estate, Audrey was forced to sell the property (it fetched £876,000 at auction) to Richard DeVere, a former costermonger and now the tycoon head of supermarket and catering chain Cavendish Foods. She being strictly old money and he being *nouveau riche*, she was desperate to keep an eye on his activities, to make sure he did not destroy the character of the estate. By moving into one of the manor's lodges with her ageing butler, Brabinger, and with the use of a pair of binoculars, at least she was able to monitor proceedings. But not even that was enough. Distrusting the new Lord of the Manor, resenting his position and also fancying him quite a bit, Audrey was always meddling in DeVere's affairs. She guided him in the etiquette of lordship and ensured – as far as she could – that Grantleigh was still run on traditional lines. Audrey's old school chum, Marjory Frobisher, dropped in regularly to keep her friend in her place, while Richard's Czech mother, Mrs Polouvicka, acted as a matchmaker for her son and Audrey, whom she considered perfect for each other. Her efforts bore fruit at the end of the series when the two were married – and Audrey was at last back in charge at the manor.

The series was filmed at Cricket St Thomas in Somerset. The series was originally devised for radio, and a pilot show was recorded, featuring Penelope Keith and Bernard Braden (as an American). However, it was never broadcast, although a radio version was produced in 1997, with Keith Barron slipping into the role of DeVere, alongside Penelope Keith.

TODD, BOB
(1921–92)

One of the UK's leading comic supports, Bob Todd played straight man to numerous comedians, including Dick Emery, Michael Bentine, Jimmy Tarbuck, Des O'Connor, Jim Davidson and, particularly, Benny Hill. Todd arrived in showbusiness late, having served in the RAF and worked as a cattle farmer. In addition to a marathon stint in *The Benny Hill Show*, he worked on series like *The Marty Feldman Comedy Machine*, *The Best Things in Life* (Mr Pollard), DOCTOR AT SEA (Entertainments Officer), *What's on Next?*, JANE, *Funny Man*, *The Steam Video Company*, *Q8* and *Q9*, *Cribbins* and his own comedy, *In for a Penny* (in which he starred as Dan, a lavatory supervisor). He was similarly well known for commercials, once advertising stock cubes with a cry of 'It's beef!'

TODDLERS' TRUCE

The historic one-hour gap in transmission, between 6 and 7 p.m., designed to allow mums to put children to bed (after children's programmes had finished) and to allow older children to get on with their homework. The Truce was respected by both BBC and ITV until February 1957. Commercial considerations then gained the upper hand. ITV filled the gap with action series like THE ADVENTURES OF ROBIN HOOD, while the BBC went for the news/current affairs audience with TONIGHT on weeknights and the youth market on Saturday with SIX-FIVE SPECIAL.

TODMAN, BILL
(1918–79)
See GOODSON, MARK.

TOM AND JERRY
US (MGM) Animation. BBC 1 1967

Creators: **William Hanna, Joseph Barbera**
Producer: **Fred Quimby**

A cat and a mouse are the worst of enemies, with violent consequences.

Tom and Jerry have been playing cat and mouse since 1940, when these short theatrical cartoons were first screened. On television, they have become two of the most popular and enduring characters, with the BBC happily dropping in the five-minute episodes whenever programmes have run short or technical problems have delayed regular transmissions.

Each cartoon has adopted the same format, effectively an extremely violent, breathtaking chase around a house, a garden, a ship, etc., with the cat (Tom) desperately trying to get even with the wily mouse (Jerry). Much flattening of faces, crumbling of teeth and crushing of tails has been witnessed, but viewers have also noticed various differences in animation styles from film to film. The first (and generally regarded as the best) selection came from the years up to 1958, when the characters' creators, Bill Hanna and Joe Barbera, were still employed on the project at MGM. The studio then decided to drop out of animation and Hanna and Barbera went their own successful way, developing the likes of HUCKLEBERRY HOUND, THE FLINTSTONES and SCOOBY DOO. MGM commissioned 13 more *Tom and Jerry*s from Czechoslovakia in 1961, and then more films were made by cult animator Chuck Jones with Les Goldman in the mid-1960s. Further episodes were made as part of a longer children's cartoon compilation in 1975, but received little acclaim.

TOMLINSON, RICKY
(1939–)

Liverpudlian actor, a former construction worker, who has received greatest acclaim as Jim Royle in THE ROYLE FAMILY but was previously seen in BOYS FROM THE BLACKSTUFF and as Bobby Grant in BROOKSIDE, DCI Wise in CRACKER and Cinders the cook in *Roughnecks*. Always in demand, Tomlinson has also starred in *The Fix* (Gordon), PLAYING THE FIELD (Jim Pratt), *Hillsborough* (John Glover), *Dockers* (Macca Macaulay), *The Greatest Store in the World* (Santa) and *Safe as Houses* (Lawrence Davidson).

TOMORROW PEOPLE, THE
UK (Thames/Tetra) Children's Science Fiction. ITV 1973–9; 1992–5

John	Nicholas Young
Stephen Jameson	Peter Vaughan-Clarke
Carol	Sammie Winmill
Kenny	Steve Salmon
Tim	Philip Gilbert (*voice only*)
Jedekiah	Frances de Wolff
	Roger Bizley
Prof. Cawston	Brian Stanion
Elizabeth	Elizabeth Adare
Tyso Boswell	Dean Lawrence
Mike Bell	Mike Holloway
Hsui Tai	Misako Koba
Andrew Forbes	Nigel Rhodes
Ginge	Michael Standing
Lefty	Derek Crewe
Adam	Kristian Schmid (*1992–5*)
Megabyte	Christian Tessier (*1992–5*)
Lisa	Kristen Ariza (*1992–5*)
Kevin	Adam Pearce (*1992–5*)
Ami	Naomie Harris (*1992–5*)

Creator: **Roger Price**
Producers: **Ruth Boswell, Roger Price, Vic Hughes**

A team of telepathic teenagers use their powers to save the Earth.

The Tomorrow People were homosuperions: the first exponents of the next stage in man's development after Homo sapiens (or 'saps', as they became known). They were teenagers endowed with powers of telepathy, telekinesis and ESP, and became Earth's first 'ambassadors' to the Galactic Empire. By employing their advanced minds, they were able to thwart malevolent aliens and protect the Earth from invasion and interference.

The first Tomorrow Person to become aware of his special powers and to come to terms with them was 17-year-old John, a lean, dark-haired, level-headed lad who was able to counsel and help other youngsters enduring this painful transition, known as 'breaking out'. The next two were Carol and Kenny, who left after the first series to work on the Galactic Trig (a Galactic Empire space-complex), but new Tomorrow People broke out on a regular basis and took their places in the cast. They were Stephen (in the programme's first episode), Elizabeth, Tyso, Mike (played by Mike Holloway, the drummer in the teenage band, Flintlock), Hsui Tai and Andrew. They travelled by 'jaunting', a process of teleportation in which mind power alone took them from place to place, and they even went back in time and into space to confront villains like the bearded Jedekiah, an evil alien robot. In and out of their secret hideout ('The Lab'), constructed in a disused London Underground station, using funds generated by John's inventions, they were assisted and guided by a deep-voiced, paternal, biological computer called Tim.

The Tomorrow People was touted as an ITV rival to DOCTOR WHO, filling the kids' fantasy slot vacated by ACE OF WANDS. At first it was intriguing and adventurous, but after a few seasons the plots thinned and the special effects became very weak. Its creator, Roger Price, pursued the idea yet again in a new version (1992–5), which cast NEIGHBOURS star Kristian Schmid as a Tomorrow Person.

TOMORROW'S WORLD
UK (BBC) Science. BBC 1 1965–

Presenters: **Raymond Baxter, James Burke, William Woollard, Michael Rodd, Judith Hann, Anna Ford, Kieran Prenderville, Maggie Philbin, Su Ingle, Peter Macann, Howard Stableford, Kate Bellingham, Carmen Pryce, John Diamond, Carol Vorderman, Shahnaz Pakravan, Vivienne Parry, Rebecca Stephens, Richard Mabey, Monty Don, Philippa Forrester, Jez Nelson, Craig Doyle, Peter Snow, Anya Sitaram, Lindsey Fallow, Nick Baker**

Producers/Editors: **Glyn Jones, Max Morgan-Witts, Michael Latham, Peter Bruce, Lawrence Wade, Dick Gilling, Michael Blakstad, David Filkin, Richard Reisz, Dana Purvis, Edward Briffa, Saul Nassé**

A weekly look at new inventions and discoveries.

Initially titled *Tomorrow's World . . . in the Making Today*, this long-running, popular science programme has looked at the very latest innovations and discoveries over four decades, explaining how they work and describing how the new technology could be of use to mankind in major or minor ways. Among the many items introduced by the series have been hole-in-the-wall cash machines, TV tennis (the earliest video game) and the compact disc. Studio experiments and dry runs have illustrated proceedings.

For years, *Tomorrow's World*'s chief presenter was Raymond Baxter, supported by the likes of James Burke, William Woollard and Michael Rodd, although the number of participants has increased significantly in the last 15 years. An occasional inventors' insert has been compiled by Bob Symes. Transmitted live for most of its existence (with hazardous consequences when experiments backfired), it has been pre-taped in recent years, allowing its reporters to travel the world in search of innovations.

Annual fixtures have included a visit from the Prince of Wales to present his *Award for Innovation*, and *Megalab*, a programme of live experiments in which viewers can participate.

In 1997 and 1998, a sister programme for summer, *TW Time Machine*, reported on inventions showcased in previous years and their relative success or failure.

TONIGHT
UK (BBC) Current Affairs. BBC 1957–65

Presenter: **Cliff Michelmore**

Producers/Editors: **Donald Baverstock, Alasdair Milne, Antony Jay, Peter Batty, Gordon Watkins, Derrick Amoore**

Easy-going but influential nightly news magazine.

Conceived as a means of filling the TODDLERS' TRUCE on weeknights, *Tonight* offered a review of the major events of the day, mixed with songs, unusual items and bits of humour. Presented by the unflappable Cliff Michelmore (whose closing remarks were 'The next *Tonight* will be tomorrow night'), *Tonight* numbered among its reporters Alan Whicker, Derek Hart, Fyfe Robertson, Geoffrey Johnson Smith, Trevor Philpott, Polly Elwes, Julian Pettifer, Macdonald Hastings, Kenneth Allsop, Brian Redhead and Magnus Magnusson. Robin Hall and Jimmie Macgregor were the resident folk singers who rounded off each show.

When *Tonight* ended in 1965, many of its crew were shunted off into its late-night replacement, 24 HOURS. Of its producers, Alasdair Milne went on to become BBC Director-General and Antony Jay later co-wrote the hugely successful comedy, YES, MINISTER. *Tonight*, as a title, was revived in 1975, with presenters Sue Lawley, Donald MacCormick, Denis Tuohy and John Timpson hosting a show (again late in the evening) which was altogether less frivolous than the original early-evening show. It ran for four years on BBC 1.

TOOK, BARRY
(1928–)

London-born comedy writer and performer, discovered on a Carroll Levis talent show in 1952. As well as performing stand-up routines, Took then went on to write for radio and television, scripting series like *Colonel Trumper's Private War* and various other comedies in collaboration with Marty Feldman (see Feldman's entry for joint credits). Took also produced Kenneth Horne's *Horne a Plenty*, wrote for the BOOTSIE AND SNUDGE follow-up, *Foreign Affairs*, created and produced the stand-up show, *Grubstreet*, adapted *The World of Beachcomber* and *One-Upmanship*, devised and starred in the sketch show, *N.U.T.S.*, and introduced comedy guests in *Took and Co.* His other work has included the sitcom, *A Roof Over My Head*, the drama, *Scoop* (adapted from the Evelyn Waugh novel), and the illiteracy campaign series, ON THE MOVE. As a consultant to the BBC comedy department in the late 1960s, he was instrumental in seeing that MONTY PYTHON'S FLYING CIRCUS reached the screen and helped THE GOODIES get off the ground. Took also brought his wry humour to bear from the chair of POINTS OF VIEW for many years, and among his other credits have been the television magazine, *TV Weekly*, and UK Gold's chat show, *Funny You Ask*.

TOP CAT
See BOSS CAT.

TOP GEAR
UK (BBC) Motoring Magazine. BBC 2 1978–

Presenters: **Angela Rippon, Barrie Gill, Noel Edmonds, William Woollard, Sue Baker, Jeremy Clarkson, Quentin Willson, Tiff Needell, Chris Goffey, Tony Mason, Janet Trewin, Michele Newman, Steve Berry, Andy Wilman, James May, Kate Humble**

Executive Producer: **Dennis Adams**
Producers/Editors: **Derek Smith, Tom Ross, Jon Bentley, Ken Pollock, John Wilcox, Chris Richards, Julie Clive**

Long-running motoring magazine.

Road-testing new models, highlighting innovations and generally keeping the motorist well informed, *Top Gear* was given a test drive in the BBC Midlands area in 1977 before being given the green light nationwide a year later. Its first hosts were Angela Rippon and Barrie Gill. Noel Edmonds was behind the wheel for a while, but Jeremy Clarkson held pole position for many years. Quentin Willson, Tiff Needell and Kate Humble have set the pace most recently. Sister programmes, *Top Gear GTi, Top Gear Motorsport* and *Top Gear Waterworld*, were also screened in the late 1990s.

TOP OF THE FORM
See TELEVISION TOP OF THE FORM.

TOP OF THE POPS
UK (BBC) Pop Music. BBC 1 1964–

Producers: **Johnnie Stewart, Colin Charmey, Stanley Dorfman, Mel Cornish, Robin Nash, Brian Whitehouse, David G. Hillier, Stanley Appel, Michael Hurll, Paul Ciani, Ric Blaxill, Mark Wells, Chris Cowey, Lee Lodge**

The UK's premier chart-music show.

With the immortal words, 'It's Number One, it's Top of the Pops,' Britain's top pop programme made its bow on New Year's Day 1964 and quickly became the most influential music programme on air. From the start, record companies clamoured for their artists to appear, recognizing the boost the programme gave to new releases and to fledgling or fading careers. It remains just as important to the trade today.

The programme has unashamedly been based around the Top 30/Top 40 singles chart, and albums have never had much of a look-in. To emphasize this, each programme has given a rundown of the latest chart positions and ended with the number one song. Other contributions have come from chart (or soon to be chart) artists, most appearing in the studio. For many years, when important artists were not available, the resident *Top of the Pops* dancers performed to the records. Pan's People (Babs, Ruth, Dee Dee, Louise, Andrea, plus choreographer Flick Colby and, later, Cherry and Sue) enjoyed this privilege for nine years up to 1976. Ruby Flipper, Legs and Co. and finally Zoo replaced them, but dance troupes were abandoned in 1983, in favour of pop videos.

The very first presenter was Jimmy Savile, who hosted the show from its original home in a converted Manchester church. On that landmark programme were stars like The Rolling Stones, The Dave Clark Five, The Swinging Blue Jeans, Dusty Springfield and The Hollies. Savile and three other DJ colleagues, Pete Murray, David Jacobs and Alan Freeman, took turns to host the show during its formative years. Other radio personalities (mostly drawn from Radio 1) dominated the programme in later years. These included Tony Blackburn, Noel Edmonds, Dave Lee Travis, Ed Stewart, David 'Kid' Jensen, John Peel, David Hamilton, Peter Powell, Simon Bates, Tommy Vance, Mike Read, Andy Peebles, Gary Davies, Richard Skinner, Mike Smith, Steve Wright, Janice Long, Bruno Brookes, Simon Mayo, Mark Goodier, Nicky Campbell and Jakki Brambles. In October 1991 the 'personality DJ' was abandoned in favour of lesser-known, younger hosts like Tony Dortie and Mark Franklin. At the same time *Top of the Pops* inherited a new home at BBC Elstree and began to focus more on live bands, for the first time wavering from its chart-only format. Later, celebrities, including pop stars like the Spice Girls and comedians like Jack Dee, shared the compering, before the Radio 1 DJ was re-installed, in the form of presenters such as Mark Radcliffe and Marc Riley, Zoë Ball and Jo Whiley, along with the likes of Jayne Middlemiss, Jamie Theakston, Kate Thornton and Gail Porter. A sister radio programme was added in 1997, featuring interviews with, and other music from, artists appearing in each week's show. In summer 1999, *Top of the Pops* left its Elstree home and headed out on a short tour of provincial cities.

Before miming to records was officially outlawed by the Musicians' Union in 1966, records were visibly placed on a turntable and guests simply mouthed the words. Denise Sampey spun the discs in the earliest programmes, but model Samantha Juste took over and is the girl older viewers remember at Jimmy Savile's side, even though she hardly ever spoke. When the mime ban came into force, artists had to pre-record their contributions or perform live. Accompaniment usually came from Johnny Pearson and his *Top of the Pops* Orchestra, with the Ladybirds providing backing vocals.

During the 1970s, CCS's version of Led Zeppelin's 'Whole Lotta Love' was used as the *Top of the Pops* theme music, and this was revamped and reintroduced in 1998. In 1981, 'Yellow Pearl' by Phil Lynott launched the show, followed by other theme tracks in the 1980s and 1990s.

In 1994, BBC 2 introduced a spin-off programme, *TOTP 2*, featuring highlights from the previous week's *Top of the Pops*, plus selections from the archives. Steve Wright has been the main (unseen) presenter.

TOP SECRET
UK (Associated-Rediffusion) Spy Drama. ITV 1961–2

Peter Dallas .... **William Franklyn**

Miguel Garetta .... **Patrick Cargill**
Mike .... **Alan Rothwell**

Producer: **Jordan Lawrence**

*The all-action adventures of a pair of secret agents
in South America.*

Peter Dallas was a tough but likeable British intelligence
agent based in Argentina. Given a year's secondment,
he found himself working for local businessman Miguel
Garetta (who also had secret service connections) in a
fight against crime and subversion. Delving into matters
which the everyday law-enforcers could not touch,
Dallas worked undercover to undermine crooks and
spies throughout South America and was joined on his
assignments by Mike, Garetta's young nephew.

The show made a star out of William Franklyn (later
the Schweppes 'Shh! You know who!' man), while Patrick Cargill moved on from this serious role to specialize
in farces and sitcoms like FATHER, DEAR FATHER. Alan
Rothwell is better remembered as David Barlow in CORO-
NATION STREET. The show's theme tune, 'Sucu Sucu' by
Laurie Johnson, was a hit in 1961 for several artists.

TOP SECRET LIFE OF EDGAR BRIGGS, THE

UK (LWT) Situation Comedy. ITV 1974

Edgar Briggs .... **David Jason**
The Commander .... **Noel Coleman**
Buxton .... **Michael Stainton**
Jennifer Briggs .... **Barbara Angell**
Spencer .... **Mark Eden**
Cathy .... **Elizabeth Counsell**

Creators: **Bernard McKenna, Richard Laing**
Producer: **Humphrey Barclay**

*Counter-espionage capers with a bumbling British
secret agent.*

Edgar Briggs worked for SIS, the Secret Intelligence Service, and was strangely successful at his job, considering
that he was probably the most incapable agent British
security ever employed. A paperwork error had resulted
in his transfer to the position of personal assistant to the
Commander of SIS and meant that the hapless Briggs
was involved in the most hush-hush undercover operations. Inevitably, he fouled up the best-laid plans – by
shredding vital documents, inadvertently announcing
secret tactics over a tannoy system or handing over his
holiday snaps instead of an important film. But, amazingly, Briggs had the knack of bringing matters to a
satisfactory conclusion. This early starring role for David
Jason lasted only 13 episodes.

TORCHY, THE BATTERY BOY

UK (Pelham Films/AP Films/ABC) Children's
Entertainment. ITV 1960

Voices: **Olwyn Griffiths, Kenneth Connor, Jill Raymond,
Patricia Somerset**

Creator/Writer/Producer: **Roberta Leigh**

*A battery-powered doll has fun at a toys' refuge
in space.*

Torchy, the battery boy, lived in Topsy Turvy Land, a
haven in space where abused and neglected toys savoured their freedom, and walked and talked like
humans. The land (where the only rain was orange juice)
was ruled by King Dithers from his Orange Peel Palace
and had its mixture of good and bad toys. These ranged
from the pirate doll, Pongo, to Pom Pom the poodle,
Sparky the baby dragon, Squish the space boy, Pilliwig
the clown and Flopsy the rag doll, most living in the
settlement of Fruitown (all the houses being made of
fruit, with Torchy's a pineapple). Torchy, boarding his
giant rocket, was also able to travel back to Earth, where
he assisted his friend, dear old Mr Bumbledrop, and ran
into old adversaries like Bossy Boots, a domineering little
girl, and Bogey, a particularly naughty boy. Only Torchy
and Pom Pom were able to visit Earth, because they were
moving toys; the others would have reverted to their
static former selves. But even Torchy had his problems.
Occasionally, he hit trouble when his battery failed and
the magic beam from the lamp on his hat grew dim.
Future puppetmaster Gerry Anderson directed some of
the episodes.

TORS, IVAN

(1916–83)

Hungarian writer who moved to the USA and became a
successful producer of wildlife adventures series, most
notably SEA HUNT, FLIPPER, DAKTARI and *Gentle Ben*,
through his own Ivan Tors Productions. Among his
other credits were action series like RIPCORD.

TOTP 2

See **TOP OF THE POPS**.

TOUCH OF FROST, A

UK (Yorkshire/Excelsior) Drama. ITV 1992–

DI William Edward 'Jack' Frost .... **David Jason**
Supt. Mullett .... **Bruce Alexander**
DCI Allen .... **Neil Phillips**
DC Clive Barnard .... **Matt Bardock**
Shirley Fisher .... **Lindy Whiteford**
DS Toolan .... **John Lyons**
Rosalie Martin .... **Isla Blair**
DS Liz Maud .... **Susannah Doyle**
Kitty Rayford .... **Gwyneth Powell**
Sgt Brady .... **James McKenna**
PC Ernie Trigg .... **Arthur White**

Executive Producers: **Vernon Lawrence, Richard Bates,
Philip Burley, David Jason**
Producers: **Don Leaver, Simon Lewis, Martyn Auty, Lars
Macfarlane**

The investigations of a lonely and rather disorganized detective.

Representing a change of career direction for comic star David Jason, the 'serious' role of DI Jack Frost of the Denton police revealed new talents in Britain's top sitcom actor (Jason's brother, Arthur White, also appeared).

Frost, a moustached, greying little copper, was a terrier-like investigator. Despite being almost shambolically disorganized and having a grudge against both technology and authority (represented by the disapproving Supt. Mullett – 'Hornrimmed Harry'), he proved himself to be perceptive and thorough, if old-fashioned in approach. The fact that his wife was terminally ill (she died in the first episode) was not allowed to interfere with his work, but his irritability when trying to give up smoking did, however, shine through. Viewers instantly took to the sandwich-munching, George Cross-winning policeman who had once been shot on duty. Frost was the creation of novelist R. D. Wingfield.

TOUCHING EVIL
UK (Anglia/Coastal) Police Drama 1997–

DI Dave Creegan	**Robson Green**
DI Susan Taylor	**Nicola Walker**
DC Mark Rivers	**Shaun Dingwall**
DS Jonathan Kreitman	**Adam Kotz**
Commander Enright	**Michael Feast**

Creator: **Paul Abbott**
Executive Producers: **Simon Lewis, Michele Buck, Damien Timmer, Sandra Jobling**
Producers: **Jane Featherstone, Philip Leach**

A maverick cop joins an élite squad of detectives in tracking down serial criminals.

DI Dave Creegan was a member of the Organized and Serial Crime Unit (OSC), a rapid-response force of specially trained officers covering the whole of the UK (though based in London) and charged with tracking down serial killers, child abductors and the like. The unit had been pulled together by Commander Enright as a British equivalent of the FBI, in response to the increase in serial crime. Although his language was often rich and his temper quick, Creegan – a divorced father of two – was also a thoughtful copper, an intelligent detective quickly climbing the police ladder. Imbued with a deep sense of justice, Creegan had already fought his way back from mental illness, having been shot in the head on duty. Working closely with Creegan was 28-year-old Susan Taylor, another high-flyer who initially doubted his unorthodox methods but who soon gave him full support. They were backed up by the youngest member of the squad, the seemingly confident DC Mark Rivers, and also by DS Jonathan Kreitman, a usually dependable family man who tended to be overtaken by events. For once, the action was well and truly focused on the cases in hand, with little attention paid to the characters' personal lives.

TRAINER
UK (BBC) Drama. BBC 1 1991–2

Mike Hardy	**Mark Greenstreet**
Rachel Ware	**Susannah York**
John Grey	**David McCallum**
James Brant	**Nigel Davenport**
Hugo Latimer	**Patrick Ryecart**
Joe Hogan	**Des McAleer**
David Ware	**Marcus D'Amico**
Kath Brant	**Sarah Atkinson**
Frances Ross	**Nicola King**
Jack Ross	**Ken Farrington**
Nick Peters	**Floyd Bevan**
Mo Ratcliffe	**Audrey Jenkinson**
Alex Farrell	**Claire Oberman**
Robert Firman	**John Bowe**
Sue Lawrence	**Melanie Thaw**

Creator/Producer: **Gerald Glaister**

A young trainer tries to succeed in the competitive world of horse racing.

Mike Hardy was the lead character in this horse saga, set among the padded anoraks and green wellies of the Sport of Kings. Given the chance to set up as a trainer in his own right, Hardy secured the backing of grouchy businessman James Brant, who sent his best horses to Hardy's Arkenfield Stables. Also on Hardy's side was wealthy widow and stud owner Rachel Ware, local gambler John Grey and head lad Joe Hogan. However, Hardy also had his enemies, including his former boss, rival trainer Hugo Latimer, and he also battled with a drink problem. After an only moderately successful first season, *Trainer* rode on to a second year, which saw James Brant disappear and Hardy fall in love with Alex Farrell, the girl sent to administer Brant's estate.

Trainer was filmed on the Berkshire downs and on racecourses up and down the country. The village pub, The Dog & Gun, was actually The Crown & Horns at East Ilsley, just north of Newbury. The theme song, co-written by disc jockey Mike Read, was performed by Cliff Richard.

TRAINING DOGS THE WOODHOUSE WAY
UK (BBC) Information. BBC 2 1980

Host: **Barbara Woodhouse**

Producer: **Peter Riding**

Education for dog-owners.

What was intended as a straightforward course for would-be dog-handlers turned into a cult TV hit, thanks to the eccentricities of its bossy, senior-citizen host. Barbara Woodhouse, aged 70, and a former horse trainer, had developed her own forceful techniques for teaching dogs obedience. Her snapped commands and shrill requests soon made her a household name, with her personality and character enhanced by a staid, woolly-kilt-and-sensible-shoes appearance. Her techniques received much criticism at the time and have continued to do so since her death in 1988, although it was always the nervous owners who looked terrified, not the hounds.

TRANSPONDER

The satellite component that collects signals beamed up from the ground, amplifies them and sends them back to dish receivers.

TRAVANTI, DANIEL J.
(1940–)

American actor who, after some 20 years of playing bit parts in series like *Route 66*, THE MAN FROM UNCLE, PERRY MASON, THE DEFENDERS, LOST IN SPACE, GUNSMOKE, KOJAK and HART TO HART, suddenly found fame as Captain Frank Furillo in HILL STREET BLUES in 1981. He has since been seen in the 1989 BBC political drama, *Fellow Traveller*, and in the US cop series, *Missing Persons*, as well as in numerous TV movies.

TRAVELLING MAN
UK (Granada) Drama. ITV 1984–5

Lomax .... **Leigh Lawson**
Robinson .... **Terry Taplin**

Creator: **Roger Marshall**
Executive Producer: **Richard Everitt**
Producer: **Brian Armstrong**

A former drug squad officer, freed from prison, sets out to find his son and to track down the man who framed him.

The life of Detective Inspector Lomax of the Metropolitan Police Drugs Squad had suddenly fallen apart. Framed for the theft of £100,000 after a drugs seizure went awry, he spent two years behind bars for a crime he did not commit. On his release, he found that his wife, Jan, had left him for Canada, and Steve, his dropout son, was hiding away on Britain's canal network. To add to his worries, the police had placed him under surveillance (in case the money turned up), and the underworld were also on his tail. Almost as threatening was Robinson, an investigative reporter in pursuit of a story.

Stepping aboard his own narrowboat, named *Harmony*, Lomax made off along the waterways and mixed with canal folk, hunting for the man who set him up and hoping to trace his missing son. The result was a sort of THE FUGITIVE for the 1980s.

TREACHER, BILL
(1937–)

British actor best known as Arthur Fowler in EAST-ENDERS. Earlier credits included Z CARS, *Bold as Brass*, BLESS THIS HOUSE, GRANGE HILL, ANGELS, THE PROFESSIONALS, THE AGATHA CHRISTIE HOUR, *Maggie and Her*, *Sweet Sixteen* and *The Bright Side* (prisoner Chadwick). Radio fans will remember his voice as that of Sidney, the milkman, in *The Dales*.

TREASURE HUNT
UK (Chatsworth) Game Show. Channel 4 1982–9

Presenters: **Kenneth Kendall, Anneka Rice, Wincey Willis, Annabel Croft**

Creator: **Ann Meo**
Producers: **Malcolm Heyworth, Peter Holmans**

Helicopter-orientated adventure game.

In this all-action game show, two studio-bound contestants yelled directions to a 'runner' who darted around the countryside in a helicopter, looking for clues. Each treasure hunt took place within a 50-mile radius of its starting point and, by using maps and solving five riddles discovered on the way, the contestants aimed to claim the treasure (£1,000) within the 45-minute time-limit. Kenneth Kendall tried to keep calm in the studio along with Wincey Willis, while Anneka Rice (and, in 1989, ex-tennis star Annabel Croft) acted as runner, supported by an athletic roving camera team. Croft also appeared in the similarly styled *Interceptor* (1989–90), in which contestants attempted to avoid enemy agents.

TRETHOWAN, Sir IAN
(1922–90)

British political journalist (*Daily Sketch*) who joined ITN in 1958, working as newscaster, diplomatic editor and political editor. He switched to the BBC in 1963, to contribute to PANORAMA and *Gallery*, then, between 1970 and 1975, was Managing Director of BBC Radio, on one occasion famously sacking Kenny Everett for making a joke about the wife of a politician. He became Managing Editor of BBC Television in 1976 and the BBC's Director-General in 1977, holding the position for five years. He was later Chairman of Thames Television. Trethowan was knighted in 1980.

TREVOR, WILLIAM
CBE (William Trevor Cox; 1928–)

Irish novelist and dramatist, known for his sensitive treatment of old folk and women. Among his offerings have been *The Baby Sitter* (1965), *The Mark-Two Wife* (1969), *O Fat White Woman* (1971), *The General's Day* (1972), *Eleanor* and *Love Affair* (1974), *Mrs Acland's Ghost*

(1975), *Secret Orchards* (1980), *Matilda's England* (a trilogy, 1981), *Autumn Sunshine* and *The Ballroom of Romance* (both 1982).

TRIALS OF LIFE, THE
UK (BBC) Natural History. BBC 1 1990

Presenter/Writer: **David Attenborough**

Executive Producer: **Peter Jones**
Producer: **Keenan Smart**

The survival of the fittest in the animal world.

Produced by the BBC's Natural History Unit, *The Trials of Life* formed the third part of David Attenborough's epic wildlife documentary series, which had begun with LIFE ON EARTH and continued with THE LIVING PLANET. In this 12-part voyeuristic examination of animal behaviour, Attenborough turned his attention to the struggle for survival of the planet's many species, from birth to death, via feeding, reproduction, etc. The colourful and detailed footage was painstakingly shot over a three-year period, by over 30 cameramen, sometimes in truly life-threatening situations. Attenborough's next project was *The Private Life of Plants*, shown in 1995.

TRIANGLE
UK (BBC) Drama. BBC 1 1981–3

Katherine Laker	**Kate O'Mara**
John Anderson	**Michael Craig**
Matt Taylor	**Larry Lamb**
Tom Kelly	**Scott Fredericks**
Wally James	**Nigel Stock**
Nick Stevens	**Tony Anholt**
Marion Terson	**Diana Coupland**
George Larsen	**Dennis Burgess**
Christine Harris	**Sandra Payne**
Dougie Evans	**Christopher Saul**
Charles Woodhouse	**Paul Jerricho**
Jo Bailey	**Elizabeth Larner**
Peter Nuttall	**Jonathan Owen**
Tony Grant	**Philip Hatton**
Judith Harper	**Joan Greenwood**
Mrs Landers	**Dawn Addams**
Sarah Hallam	**Penelope Horner**
Penny Warrender	**Sandra Dickinson**
Kevin Warrender	**Peter Arne**
David West	**George Baker**
Arthur Parker	**Douglas Sheldon**
Sandy McCormick	**Helena Breck**
Joe Francis	**David Arlen**

Creator/Producer: **Bill Sellars**

Drama with the passengers and crew of a North Sea ferry.

Triangle is one of those programmes its producers and participants probably want to forget, given the amount of flak fired in its direction. Indeed, the twice-weekly series lasted only three seasons, the last without its star (Kate O'Mara), who had already quit. The premiss was fairly simple. Action took place aboard a ferry making the triangular journey of Felixstowe–Gothenburg–Rotterdam–Felixstowe. Initial intrigue followed the appointment of a new chief purser, Katherine Laker, who turned out to be the daughter of a Triangle Lines bigwig. Subsequently, there was much vying for position and numerous skulking visits to strange cabins in the dead of night.

Bravely experimenting with new lightweight equipment and actually filming aboard a moving ship (the *Tor Scandinavia*), the team, unfortunately, encountered all manner of unforeseen problems. Most daytime cabin shots had to be taken with the curtains drawn to avoid glare, and the movement of the North Sea upset the crew and performers alike. Worse still, there was little viewer interest. The bleak and icy waters of northern Europe just didn't have the appeal of the warm, azure Caribbean lagoons that made THE LOVE BOAT such a success.

TRINDER, TOMMY
CBE (1909–89)

Chirpy Cockney comedian who arrived on television after years of musical-hall and film work. In 1955 he was the first compere of SUNDAY NIGHT AT THE LONDON PALLADIUM, which benefited from his quick thinking and skill with the ad lib. His own series, *Trinder Box*, followed. 'You lucky people' became his catchphrase.

TRINITY TALES
UK (BBC) Drama. BBC 2 1975

Eric, the Prologue	**Francis Matthews**
Stan, the Fryer	**Bill Maynard**
Dave, the Joiner	**Paul Copley**
Judy, the Judy	**Susan Littler**
Nick, the Driver	**Colin Farrell**
Smith, the Man of Law	**John Stratton**
Alice, the Wife of Batley	**Gaye Brown**

Creator/Writer: **Alan Plater**
Producer: **David Rose**

A group of rugby fans tell tall stories on the way to a cup final.

Writer Alan Plater took Chaucer's *Canterbury Tales* and placed them in a contemporary setting for this innovative six-part series. It concerned a minibus of Wakefield Trinity fans making their way down to Wembley for the Rugby League Challenge Cup Final. To while away the miles, they each told a story (all of which were somewhat far-fetched, with slapstick elements). The six episodes were subtitled *The Driver's Tale*, *The Fryer's Tale*, *The Judy's Tale*, *The Joiner's Tale*, *The Wife of Batley's Tale* and *The Man of Law's Tale*.

TRIPODS, THE
UK (BBC) Children's Science Fiction. BBC 1 1984–5

Will Parker	John Shackley
Henry Parker	Jim Baker
Beanpole (Jean-Paul)	Ceri Seel
Duc de Sarlat	Robin Langford
Count	Jeremy Young
Countess	Pamela Salem
Eloise	Charlotte Long
Ozymandias	Roderick Horn
Vichot	Stephen Marlowe
Mme Vichot	Anni Lee Taylor
Fritz	Robin Hayter
Krull	Jeffrey Perry
Ulf	Richard Beale
Master 468	John Woodvine
Boll	Edward Highmore
Borman	James Coyle
Coggy	Christopher Guard
Ali Pasha	Bruce Purchase
Speyer	Alfred Hoffman
Jeanne	Elizabeth McKechnie

Writers: **Alick Rowe, Christopher Penford**
Producer: **Richard Bates**

Three youths flee tyrannical alien machines in a medieval world of the future.

The Tripods was an adventurous exercise in science fiction by the BBC. Sadly, the ratings and expenses did not balance out and the series was cancelled two-thirds of the way through, leaving viewers stranded in mid-story.

The tale concerned a trio of youths living in the year 2089 at a time when the Earth had been ruled by ruthless, three-legged alien machines known as the Tripods for over 100 years. A medieval society had been restored to the planet, with all children 'capped' at the age of 16 to ensure complete subservience. Two English teenagers about to be processed (which involved attaching a metal plate to the head) decided to make a break for it in an attempt to reach the White Mountains of Switzerland, where the Free Men allegedly lived. The two were cousins Will and Henry Parker. Making it as far as France, they were joined by a local youth, Beanpole, and together they lurched from danger to danger, progressing south to the safe lands.

Series two picked up in the year 2090 as the three boys and their Free Men hosts plotted to overthrow the Tripods and free the human race. A newcomer, Fritz, replaced Henry, and the trio headed for the Tripod Annual Games in the guise of competitors, in an attempt to infiltrate the Tripods' City of Gold. They encountered the Masters, the monsters from the planet Trion which had devised the machines, and learned of their sinister plans for the Earth. And that was where the BBC left it – with the Tripods still in control and the boys back on the run.

Twenty-five episodes were made in total, although sci-fi fans were left crying out for a few more to set the story straight. Those keen enough will have turned to the original novels by John Christopher: *The White Mountains, The City of Gold and Lead,* and *The Pool of Fire.*

TRIPPER'S DAY/SLINGER'S DAY
UK (Thames) Situation Comedy. ITV 1984/1986–7

Norman Tripper	Leonard Rossiter
Hilda Rimmer	Pat Ashton
Alf Battle	Gordon Gostelow
Mr Christian	Paul Clarkson
Hardie	Philip Bird
Laurel	David John
Higgins	Andrew Paul
Sylvia	Liz Crowther
Marlene	Charon Bourke
Dottie	Vicky Licorish
Cecil Slinger	Bruce Forsyth (Slinger's Day)
Fred	David Kelly (Slinger's Day)
Colin	Charlie Hawkins (Slinger's Day)
Shirley	Jacqueline De Peza (Slinger's Day)
Miss Foster	Suzanne Church (Slinger's Day)

Creator: **Brian Cooke**
Producers: **Michael Mills, Anthony Parker**
(*Tripper's Day*), **Mark Stuart** (*Slinger's Day*)

Days in the life of a harassed supermarket manager.

This comedy series pitched Leonard Rossiter into the role of Norman Tripper, manager of the Supafare supermarket. Tripper marshalled his staff like a US police chief, reflecting his fascination with American cop series, and flirted with canteen manageress Hilda Rimmer. Also seen were secretary Sylvia, elderly security guard Alf Battle, shop steward Hardie, management trainee Mr Christian and oafish staffer Higgins. It proved to be Rossiter's last TV offering and, following his untimely death, the programme was retitled and recast. It became *Slinger's Day*, with Bruce Forsyth enrolled as Supafare's new manager, Cecil Slinger, but with only two members of Tripper's supporting staff maintained, namely Mr Christian and Hardie.

Don Adams, star of the 1960s comedy, *Get Smart*, was enrolled for a Canadian version, entitled *Check it Out!,* in the mid-1980s.

TRODD, KENITH

Acclaimed British producer, closely associated with playwright Dennis Potter, working on *Double Dare, Brimstone and Treacle* (both 1976), PENNIES FROM HEAVEN (1978), *Blue Remembered Hills* (1979), *Blade on the Feather, Rain in the Roof, Cream in my Coffee* (all 1980), THE SINGING DETECTIVE (1986), *Christabel* (1988) and Potter's final works, KARAOKE and *Cold Lazarus* (1996). Trodd, a campaigner for filmed, rather than videotaped, drama, has also been responsible for *Dinner at the Sporting Club* (1978), *A United Kingdom* (1981), *Screen Two's Femme Fatale* (1993) and *The Fix* (1997), among other dramas.

TROUBLESHOOTERS, THE
See MOGUL.

TROUGHTON, PATRICK
(1920–87)

British Shakespearean actor who first worked on television as early as 1948. He appeared in *Toad of Toad Hall* in 1950, starred in a 1953 BBC version of *Robin Hood*, played Sir Andrew Ffoulkes in THE SCARLET PIMPERNEL in 1955 and was Captain Luke Settle in the 1960 Civil War drama, *The Splendid Spur*. Troughton also took the small roles of George Barton in CORONATION STREET and Eddie Goldsmith in COMPACT, but it was as the second DOCTOR WHO (1966–9) that he became a household name. Later, he played the Duke of Norfolk in THE SIX WIVES OF HENRY VIII, Nasca in *The Feathered Serpent*, journalist J. P. Schofield in the comedy, FOXY LADY, Sextus in THE CLEOPATRAS and Perce (Nicholas Lyndhurst's grandad) in THE TWO OF US. Seldom away from the small screen, Troughton was also seen in many other productions, including THE INVISIBLE MAN, MAN OF THE WORLD, A FAMILY AT WAR, SPECIAL BRANCH, THE PROTECTORS, THE SWEENEY, THE SAINT, THE GOODIES, DOOMWATCH, DR FINLAY'S CASEBOOK, COLDITZ, *Churchill's People*, MINDER, Z CARS, SURVIVORS, *Sally Ann*, *The Box of Delights*, INSPECTOR MORSE, ALL CREATURES GREAT AND SMALL and assorted single dramas. One of his last roles was as the rebel, Arthur, in *Knights of God* in 1987. He was the father of actors David and Michael Troughton.

TRUMPTON
See CAMBERWICK GREEN.

TSW
(Television South West)

The ITV contractor for South-west England from 12 August 1981 to 31 December 1992, TSW succeeded Westward Television on to the air. This was one of the more predictable changes of the 1980 franchise round, as Westward had suffered badly from boardroom turmoil in the run-up to the reallocations. TSW broadcast from a Plymouth base, but made little contribution to the ITV network during its 11-year franchise tenure, the most prominent being editions of HIGHWAY and *About Britain*, plus the canine quiz, *That's My Dog*. In applying for the continuation of its licence in the 1991 franchise auctions, the company was deemed to have 'overbid' by the ITC, which then appointed Westcountry Television as the new contractor for the South-west region.

TTT
See TYNE TEES TELEVISION.

TUBE, THE
UK (Tyne Tees) Rock Magazine. Channel 4 1982–7

Presenters: **Jools Holland, Paula Yates, Leslie Ash, Muriel Gray, Gary James**

Producers: **Malcolm Gerrie, Paul Corley**

Influential 1980s rock magazine.

The READY, STEADY, GO! of the 1980s, *The Tube* was presented live on a Friday teatime from the studios of Tyne Tees in Newcastle. Live bands, star interviews, reviews and reports were combined to produce an up-to-the-minute look at the rock music scene, and the programme became a launching pad for many of the decade's most prominent names, including Frankie Goes To Hollywood, Paul Young, U2 and The Eurythmics. Established stars like Elton John, David Bowie and Tina Turner also made appearances. Model and pop columnist Paula Yates was accompanied as host by former Squeeze keyboards man, Jools Holland, and their flippant and controversial presentational style (Holland was once suspended for using a four-letter word in a programme trailer), combined with numerous technical fluffs, contrasted sharply with the slick patter of the fab DJs and the glossier presentation of TOP OF THE POPS. Muriel Gray, Gary James and, briefly, Leslie Ash also hosted proceedings.

In November 1999, Sky One recreated the series as a one-off show, *Apocalypse Tube*, broadcast from the same Newcastle studio, with hosts Chris Moyles and Donna Air.

TUCKER'S LUCK
See GRANGE HILL.

TUGBOAT ANNIE
See ADVENTURES OF TUGBOAT ANNIE, THE.

TULLY, SUSAN
(1967–)

London-born actress-director, on TV since her teens hosting Saturday morning series like *Our Show* and *The Saturday Banana*. She took the role of Suzanne Ross in GRANGE HILL and then joined EASTENDERS at its inception in 1985, playing Michelle Fowler until 1995. She has since returned to Albert Square as programme director. Other credits have included the documentary series, *Genderquake* (presenter), *Holiday Reps* (narrator) and *Black Cab* (director).

TURN OUT THE LIGHTS
See PARDON THE EXPRESSION.

TURNER BROADCASTING SYSTEM
See AOL-TIME WARNER.

TURNER CLASSIC MOVIES
See TCM.

TURNER NETWORK TELEVISION
See TNT.

TURNER, ANTHEA
(1960–)

Staffordshire-born presenter, moving from radio to BLUE PETER and then on to GMTV, THE NATIONAL LOTTERY LIVE, *Pet Power*, *All You Need Is Love*, *Change Your Life Forever*, TOP OF THE POPS, WISH YOU WERE HERE . . . ? and *Turner Round the World*. She was once married to her manager, former DJ Peter Powell, and is the sister of presenter Wendy Turner Webster, with whom she hosted the game show, *Your Kids Are in Charge*.

TURNER, TED
(1938–)

Flamboyant and ambitious American TV executive, head of Turner Broadcasting System (TBS) and one of the most influential TV magnates of the 1980s. Turner sold off his family's advertising business in the early 1970s, purchasing instead a small Atlanta television station, which he renamed WTBS. In 1976, by beaming its signal off a satellite to cable systems in other parts of the USA, Turner created one of the first 'superstations'. In 1980 he defied the advice of experts and set up a 24-hour cable news station. That was CNN, now globally relayed by satellite and one of the world's most watched channels, its reputation enhanced by coverage of the Gulf War (1991). TBS also launched the TNT channel (Turner Network Television) to screen old movies from the MGM/United Artists archives (also in Turner's ownership) and Cartoon Network. In 1996 TBS was sold to Time-Warner, with Turner joining the board as head of its cable TV divisions. He is married to (but separated from) actress Jane Fonda.

TURTLE'S PROGRESS
UK (ATV) Drama. ITV 1979–80

Turtle	John Landry
Razor Eddie	Michael Attwell
Supt. Rafferty	James Grout
	David Swift
Ethel Wagstaff	Ruby Head
WPC Andrews	Jo Ross

Creator: Edmund Ward
Producers: Joan Brown, Nicholas Palmer
Executive Producer: David Reid

A petty crook and his accomplice have trouble from both the police and other felons.

Six months before viewers were treated to the dodgy dealings of Arthur Daley and his muscle-bound sidekick, Terry, in MINDER, ITV launched this not too dissimilar light drama. The focus was on Turtle – a character first seen in the 1975 thriller serial, *The Hanged Man* – a lovable, unrepentant, small-time crook who lived with his Aunt Ethel and was joined in his petty larceny by the big-eating Razor Eddie (a giant former hooligan, now 'bettering himself'). Indicative of this duo's criminal ambitions was the fact that they nicked a van for the modest fee of £35. What they didn't realize was that the van contained a hoard of stolen safety-deposit boxes, which their rightful and wrongful owners soon demanded back. Keeping out of the reach of both police and fellow law-breakers, Turtle and Eddie discovered that the boxes contained a fortune. They hid half in a safe in a scrapyard and the other half in a neighbour's loft, and set up a company, 'Guaranteed Security Inc.' (which specialized in murky underworld operations), with some of the lolly, taking a five-year lease on a high-rise office in Victoria. Unfortunately, each security box (one opened per episode) also contained a headache for the lads – top-secret documents, important chemical formulae – that they needed to shake off.

The setting was Fulham, and Turtle's local was The Robin Hood, where the redoubtable Aunt Ethel worked as a barmaid, calling time while her husband was inside doing it. The part of Turtle's nemesis, Supt. Rafferty, was taken over by David Swift after original incumbent James Grout broke a leg. Alan Price wrote and sang the theme song.

TUTTI FRUTTI
UK (BBC) Comedy Drama. BBC 1 1987

Danny McGlone	Robbie Coltrane
Suzi Kettles	Emma Thompson
Eddie Clockerty	Richard Wilson
Vincent Diver	Maurice Roeves
Bomba MacAteer	Stuart McGugan
Fud O'Donnell	Jake D'Arcy
Dennis Sproul	Ron Donachie
Janice Toner	Katy Murphy

Creator/Writer: John Byrne
Producer: Andy Park

On the road with a Scottish rock'n'roll band.

Returning home from New York for the funeral of his brother, Big Jazza ('The Beast of Rock'), who had been killed in a car crash, failed artist Danny McGlone stumbled into singer Suzi Kettles, an old flame. Donning drainpipes and crêpe soles, he found himself enrolled alongside her into his late brother's rock'n'roll band, The Majestics, billed as 'Scotland's Kings of Rock'. The Majestics comprised guitarist Vincent Diver, bass-player Fud O'Donnell and drummer Bomba MacAteer and were shakily managed by the staid Eddie Clockerty. As they set out on tour to celebrate 25 years in the business, their roadie was Dennis Sproul. The six-episode series followed the band as they travelled from gig to gig, and watched the developing relationship between the slobbish Danny and the hard-nosed Suzi.

TV-AM

TV-am won the franchise for the ITV breakfast slot in 1980 and went on air with its *Good Morning Britain* programme on 1 February 1983. This followed early difficulties that delayed the launch and allowed the BBC to get ahead of the game by presenting its own BREAKFAST TIME on 17 January the same year. TV-am's teething troubles were not over, however, as advertising problems and other matters continued to dog the early days.

The company ambitiously took to the air with a self-declared 'mission to explain'. Its 'Famous Five' presenters were all big names: Robert Kee (who hosted the earliest segment of the day, known as *Daybreak*), Angela Rippon, David Frost, Michael Parkinson and Anna Ford. Peter Jay was the company's chief executive. However, its formal, somewhat highbrow approach soon lost favour with viewers, who preferred the BBC's warmer, more casual style. As audiences shrank, changes needed to be made. Jay left after only six weeks. Rippon and Ford quickly followed, sacked by station boss Timothy Aitken, to make room for fresher presenters like Anne Diamond and Nick Owen. Greg Dyke was brought in from LWT as Editor-in-Chief to mastermind a revival, and he instigated a more lightweight style of programming. The station's fortunes were improved yet further in 1983 when a glove puppet named Roland Rat was introduced during school holidays. The streetwise rodent quickly built up a cult following and eventually transferred to his own series on BBC 1. A weekend segment for kids, *Wide Awake Club*, hosted by Timmy Mallett, was also added. When Greg Dyke left to become programme controller at TVS, he was succeeded by Bruce Gyngell, who was introduced by fellow Australian Kerry Packer, who had bought into TV-am. Gyngell, who had been the first person seen on Australian TV, ran the station for the rest of its time on air, shrugging off a walk-out of technical staff by handing out dismissal notices in 1987. On the studio couch new hosts Lorraine Kelly and Mike Morris took over from Diamond and Owen. By the time of the 1991 franchise renewals, TV-am was in good shape financially and enjoyed a sizeable audience. David Frost's and, later, Maya Even's Sunday programme was an important part of the political week. This was not enough, however; when the company was outbid by Sunrise Television (later renamed GMTV), the ITC awarded the franchise to their rivals, to the fury of all at TV-am. Even former premier Margaret Thatcher, whose Government had introduced the auction system, was contrite. She wrote to Gyngell apologizing for TV-am's downfall. TV-am's last day on air was 31 December 1992.

TV EYE

See THIS WEEK.

TVS
(Television South)

TVS was the company that controversially 'stole' the South and South-east of England ITV franchise from the well-established Southern Television during the 1980 licensing round. Making an application for the contract under the consortium name of South and South-East Communications, the company's strongest cards were its original personnel, which included notable broadcasting executives like Michael Blakstad (formerly of the BBC and Yorkshire Television) and Anna Home (from BBC children's programmes). Awarded the licence, it adopted the broadcasting name of TVS, bought the old Southern studios in Southampton and went on air on 1 January 1982. The company proceeded to open up new studios in Maidstone and split its regional news coverage into southern and south-eastern sectors. It made programmes like C.A.T.S. EYES, *Davro's Sketch Pad*, *Fraggle Rock*, THE STORYTELLER and CATCHPHRASE for the ITV network and expanded internationally, ambitiously taking over the MTM Entertainment company (producers of HILL STREET BLUES and LOU GRANT among other shows) in 1988, a move which unfortunately caused TVS some financial distress. When reapplying for its licence in 1991, TVS was deemed to have 'overbid' by the ITC and lost its franchise to Meridian Television, broadcasting finally on 31 December 1992. The TVS company and its Maidstone studios were subsequently bought by The Family Channel (now Challenge TV, part of Flextech).

TW3

See THAT WAS THE WEEK THAT WAS.

24 HOURS
UK (BBC) Current Affairs. BBC 1 1965–72

Presenters: **Cliff Michelmore, Kenneth Allsop, Ian Trethowan, Michael Barrett, Robert McKenzie, David Dimbleby, Ludovic Kennedy**

Producers/Editors: **Derrick Amoore, Anthony Whitby, Anthony Smith, Peter Pagnamenta, Tony Summers, John Dekker, Gordon Watts, David Harrison, Michael Bukht, Michael Townson**

Late-night current affairs series.

The replacement for TONIGHT, *24 Hours* reviewed the day's news events from a late-night (10.30 p.m.) standpoint, rather than a teatime position. It inherited many members of the *Tonight* crew, including anchorman Cliff Michelmore, and ran for seven years, before giving way to *Midweek* in 1972. Among the reporting team were the likes of Michael Parkinson, Robin Day, David Lomax, Julian Pettifer, Fyfe Robertson, Leonard Parkin and Philip Tibenham.

Its most controversial moment came in 1971 with a film entitled *Yesterday's Men*. Referring to a slogan used by the Labour Party about the Conservatives in the previous year's general election, it featured an interview with ex-Prime Minister Harold Wilson in which reporter David Dimbleby quizzed him about the profits he received from his published memoirs. This angered Wilson and a cut was made, but the whole style of the film, with its satirical Gerald Scarfe cartoons and songs by The Scaffold, still caused a furore when broadcast. Matters were complicated by the following evening's *24 Hours* film about the Conservatives, a much kinder documentary entitled *Mr Heath's Quiet Revolution*. The BBC Programmes Complaints Commission was established as a consequence of this particular dispute.

TWILIGHT ZONE, THE
US (Cayuga) Science Fiction. ITV 1963–6

Host/Narrator: **Rod Serling**

Creator/Writer/Executive Producer: **Rod Serling**
Producers: **Buck Houghton, Herbert Hirschman, Bert Granet, William Froug**

Cult anthology of science-fiction thrillers.

The Twilight Zone was a labour of love for one man, Rod Serling. An Emmy-winning TV playwright, Serling not only created and produced the series, he also wrote most of the episodes and appeared on screen as host and narrator. He developed a simple format of half-hour playlets (some one-hour episodes were also produced), which succinctly told a story with a curious, often shocking, twist in the tail. The storylines effectively merged illusion and reality, introduced intriguing concepts and ideas, and conveyed a moral message. Some episodes were subtle human parables, others were downright spooky. The black-and-white footage added a sinister tone, but special effects were virtually non-existent.

One classic episode concerned a bank clerk who loved to read. Sneaking away into a vault one lunchtime to delve into his book, he emerged to find that a nuclear disaster had destroyed all life on Earth. He was the only survivor. At last he could read to his heart's content. Then he dropped and broke his glasses. Another episode told of an alien which arrived on Earth to offer help. It accidentally left behind a book called *To Serve Man*. By following the alien's advice, Earth was rid of hunger and war, and humans began to pay visits to the alien's home planet. Then a translator finished decoding the book, to find it was actually a cookery manual. And then there was the episode starring Agnes Moorehead as a woman whose home was invaded by miniature alien spacemen. Once she had fought them off, it was revealed that the spacemen were actually NASA astronauts who had landed on a planet of giants. It was she who had been the alien.

The series played host to a horde of guest stars, ranging from William Shatner, Charles Bronson and Burt Reynolds, to Mickey Rooney, Roddy McDowall and Robert Redford. Airing between 1959 and 1965 in its native USA, *The Twilight Zone* received only sporadic screenings in the UK. ITV first transmitted some episodes, but further runs (including previously unseen episodes) came on BBC 2 and Channel 4 in the 1980s.

The concept was picked up again for a 1983 cinema film, *Twilight Zone the Movie*, in which four directors (Steven Spielberg, John Landis, Joe Dante and George Miller) reworked three original TV scripts, plus one unused story by Serling. A second television version came along in 1985. Filmed in colour, in an hour-long format, featuring two or three stories per episode, it met with little success. There was no Rod Serling this time.

TWIN PEAKS
US (Lynch/Frost/Spelling Entertainment/ABC) Drama.
BBC 2 1990–1

Agent Dale Cooper	**Kyle MacLachlan**
Sheriff Harry S. Truman	**Michael Ontkean**
Leland Palmer	**Ray Wise**
Sarah Palmer	**Grace Zabriskie**
Laura Palmer/Madeleine Ferguson	**Sheryl Lee**
Jocelyn 'Josie' Packard	**Joan Chen**
Catherine Martell	**Piper Laurie**
Pete Martell	**Jack Nance**
Major Garland Briggs	**Don Davis**
Bobby Briggs	**Dana Ashbrook**
Benjamin Horne	**Richard Beymer**
Audrey Horne	**Sherilyn Fenn**
Jerry Horne	**David Patrick Kelly**
Shelly Johnson	**Mädchen Amick**
Leo Johnson	**Eric Da Re**
Dr William Hayward	**Warren Frost**
Donna Hayward	**Lara Flynn Boyle**
Eileen Hayward	**Mary Jo Deschanel**
Big Ed Hurley	**Everett McGill**
Nadine Hurley	**Wendy Robie**
James Hurley	**James Marshall**
Hank Jennings	**Chris Mulkey**
Norma Jennings	**Peggy Lipton**
Lucy Moran	**Kimmy Robertson**
Dr Lawrence Jacoby	**Russ Tamblyn**
Deputy Andy Brennan	**Harry Goaz**
Deputy Tommy 'The Hawk' Hill	**Michael Horse**
Mike Nelson	**Gary Hershberger**
Richard Tremayne	**Ian Buchanan**
Margaret, the log lady	**Catherine E. Coulson**
Windom Earle	**Kenneth Welsh**
Annie Blackburne	**Heather Graham**

Creators/Executive Producers: **David Lynch, Mark Frost**

Surreal mystery-cum-soap-opera set in the Pacific North-west of America.

Twin Peaks exemplified the power of hype. This bizarre series arrived with such a fanfare that the TV public around the world simply couldn't ignore it. Early episodes in the USA topped 35 million viewers and, despite its relegation to BBC 2, it attracted an extremely healthy audience in the UK. However, for all the promotion and the merchandising which followed, the series failed to hang on to its viewers and it ended with a whimper rather than a bang.

At least partly responsible for its decline was its incredibly weird plot, which meandered in and out of minor tales without getting to the bottom of the main question: 'Who killed Laura Palmer?' That was the mystery that FBI agent Dale Cooper was hoping to resolve when he arrived in the sleepy lumber town of Twin Peaks, in pine-covered Washington State. Laura, a 17-year-old homecoming queen, had been fished out of the lake, her body naked and draped in a plastic sheet. Through his investigations, Cooper was to uncover more and more about Laura's shady lifestyle, and about the dark secrets, skulduggery and sexual intrigue that went to make the town of Twin Peaks the Peyton Place of the 1990s.

Cooper's detection methods were strange, to say the least. For a start, most of his leads came from ESP or from dreams involving midgets. His findings were then dictated to his never-seen assistant, Diane, via a microcassette recorder, between mouthfuls of his favourite cherry pie and 'damn fine coffee'. Of little help were the local sheriff, Harry S. Truman, a man of few words, and his tearful deputy, Andy Brennan. But, little by little, Cooper uncovered the truth about this spooky, misty backwater. Illicit love triangles were unearthed, nasty plots to take over the town's Packard Sawmill were exposed, and some of the strangest people kept cropping up – like a dwarf who talked backwards, like the Log Lady, who nursed a piece of timber in her arms, and like Audrey Horne, the teenage seductress who tied knots in cherry stalks with her tongue. Yet, although the finger of suspicion pointed at most of the eccentric townsfolk, the identity of Laura's killer remained obscure. Eventually, to most viewers' relief, it was revealed to be Laura's own father, Leland, but only because he had become possessed by the so-called Killer BOB. Even then Cooper did not take the hint. He stayed in Twin Peaks, investigating other murders, and the arty quirkiness of the series continued into a second season.

Criticized as being the proverbial triumph of style over substance, *Twin Peaks* was, at least initially, powerful viewing. A creation of cult film director David Lynch (of *Eraserhead*, *The Elephant Man* and *Blue Velvet* fame), and HILL STREET BLUES writer Mark Frost, its haunting, sinister atmosphere was skilfully manufactured. The dreamy, oddball feel and cinematic look were later echoed in the more successful NORTHERN EXPOSURE and the weird *Eerie, Indiana*. The haunting theme music was by Angelo Badalamenti and location shooting took place in the once-peaceful, one-horse town of Snoqualmie Falls, Washington, a community now besieged by devoted fans.

TWIZZLE

See ADVENTURES OF TWIZZLE, THE.

TWO IN CLOVER

UK (Thames) Situation Comedy. ITV 1969–70

Sid Turner	Sid James
Vic Evans	Victor Spinetti

Creators/Writers: **Vince Powell, Harry Driver**

Producer: **Alan Tarrant**

Two City clerks move to the country and find it less appealing than they imagined.

Londoner Sid Turner and Welshman Vic Evans were clerks in a City insurance office and thoroughly fed up with their lot. Throwing in their jobs, they purchased Clover Farm, a smallholding in the country. However, with problematic livestock to look after, and the insular locals difficult to agree with, they soon realized that country life was not as calm and trouble-free as they had first thought. Their rustic dream became more of a nightmare.

TWO OF US, THE

UK (LWT) Situation Comedy. ITV 1986–90

Ashley Phillips	Nicholas Lyndhurst
Elaine	Janet Dibley
Perce	Patrick Troughton
	Tenniel Evans
Colin Phillips	Paul McDowell
Lillian Phillips	Jennifer Piercey

Creator/Writer: **Alex Shearer**
Producers: **Marcus Plantin, Robin Carr**

Two young people live together despite having different outlooks on life.

Computer programmer Ashley and his girlfriend, Elaine, didn't always see eye to eye. In fact, they usually talked at cross purposes. Nevertheless, they were happy to share a flat and a relationship of sorts. Ashley was keen on marriage, Elaine was not; but they did eventually tie the knot and settled down to a life of marital ups and downs. Ashley's parents and his widowed grandad, Perce, were also seen.

2 POINT 4 CHILDREN

UK (BBC) Situation Comedy. BBC 1 1991–9

Bill Porter	Belinda Lang
Ben Porter	Gary Olsen
Rona Harris	Julia Hills
Jenny Porter	Clare Woodgate
	Clare Buckfield
David Porter	John Pickard
Gerry	Leonard O'Malley
Angelo Shepherd	Ray Polhill
Christine	Kim Benson
Bette/Aunt Belle	Liz Smith
Pearl	Barbara Lott
Tina	Patricia Brake
	Sandra Dickinson
Tony	Tom Roberts
Declan	Alex Kew

Creator: **Andrew Marshall**
Producers: **Richard Boden, Andrew Marshall, Marcus Mortimer, Rosemary McGowan**

A working mum struggles to balance professional and domestic responsibilities.

Centring around the Porter family of 142 Chepstow Road, Chiswick, *2 Point 4 Children* viewed (sometimes surreally) the life of a working mum, her easy-going, child-like husband and their two troublesome teenagers as they sought to make ends meet. Head of the household was Bill Porter, first seen working in Hanson's bakery with her man-hungry friend and neighbour, Rona. They later moved to an airline meals factory, before setting up their own catering company, working from home. Bill's husband, Ben, was a central heating engineer who employed a Scot named Gerry, then the rebellious Christine, as his assistant. The Porters' two children were stroppy, boy-crazed Jenny and adolescent David, who was usually to be found dabbling in murky pursuits. Occasional visitors, much to everyone's dread, were Bill's mum, Bette (pally with Rona's Auntie Pearl), Bette's sister, Belle, and Ben's snooty sister, Tina. During early episodes, a mysterious biker named Angelo Shepherd haunted Bill's every move until his sudden death on the M25. A late addition to the family was Declan, a young boy the Porters fostered when Jenny left for college.

Beginning very much like a UK version of ROSEANNE, *2 Point 4 Children* quickly found its own direction. With fantasy sequences becoming more and more the norm, it also gained in popularity and secured itself a run of Christmas spectaculars (including music and dance), in addition to regular series.

TWO RONNIES, THE
UK (BBC) Comedy. BBC 1/BBC 2 1971–87

Ronnie Barker, Ronnie Corbett

Executive Producers: **James Gilbert, Michael Hurll**
Producers: **Terry Hughes, Peter Whitmore, Brian Penders, Paul Jackson, Marcus Plantin, Michael Hurll**

Gags and sketches from a long-standing comedy partnership.

Messers Barker and Corbett, the big and the small of TV comedy, had first worked together in the mid-1960s when contributing to various David Frost programmes. Although they each enjoyed individual opportunities to shine (such as SORRY! for Corbett and PORRIDGE for Barker), their joint efforts are equally well remembered.

The Two Ronnies ran for 16 years from 1971 and was hugely successful. Most programmes were shown on BBC 1, but some aired under the *Show of the Week* banner on BBC 2. Calling upon a host of talented scriptwriters (including the likes of David Nobbs, David Renwick and assorted *Pythons* – as well as Gerald Wiley, a pseudonym used by Barker himself), each show followed a simple format, opening and closing with mock news items. In between, 'in a packed programme', viewers were treated to cocktail party sketches, a boisterous costume musical, a meandering Corbett monologue delivered from a big chair, and doses of Barker's astounding pronunciation power, with a decent helping of gentle smut thrown in

for good measure. There were also spoof serials like *The Phantom Raspberry Blower of Old London Town* (written by Spike Milligan), *The Worm That Turned* and the cases of private investigators, Charley Farley and Piggy Malone. Regular musical guests broke up the humour. These included middle-of-the-road performers such as Barbara Dickson, Elaine Paige and the Nolan sisters. Finally, it was 'Goodnight from me, and goodnight from him'.

TWO'S COMPANY
UK (LWT) Situation Comedy. ITV 1975–9

Dorothy McNab .... **Elaine Stritch**
Robert Hiller .... **Donald Sinden**

Creator: **Bill MacIlwraith**
Producers: **Stuart Allen, Humphrey Barclay**

Friction between a brash American author and her staid British butler.

American thriller-writer Dorothy McNab had taken up residence in London, employing traditional butler Robert Hiller to manage her household. As depicted by the bald eagle and proud lion in the programme's titles, this was no happy arrangement. For a start, Dorothy was one of the worst type of Americans, loud and rather uncouth, a cheroot-smoker with a pushy attitude to life. Hiller was very much of the old school, a champion of etiquette and decorum with impeccable manners. Their love-hate relationship provided the humour. An American version, *The Two of Us*, starring Peter Cook and Mimi Kennedy, followed in 1981 (UK, ITV 1983).

TWW
(Television Wales and West)

TWW was the original ITV contractor for South Wales and the West of England, taking to the air on 14 January 1958 from studios in Cardiff and Bristol. Coverage of the northern and western parts of the Principality did not fall into its initial remit but was instead looked after by Wales West and North (WWN), which began broadcasting in 1962. However, when WWN folded a year later, TWW was allowed to absorb its territory. TWW's contributions to the national ITV network were few (most notable, probably, was *Land of Song*), but it did have the added obligation of producing a number of programmes in the Welsh language. TWW lost its franchise to Harlech Television in the 1967 reshuffle, eventually leaving the airwaves on 3 March 1968.

TYNAN, KENNETH
(1927–80)

British theatre/film critic, infamous for being the first person to use the 'F' word on British television. The controversial utterance came not as a piece of thoughtless abuse but as part of a debate about theatre censorship taking place on the satirical programme, BBC-3, in 1965. Robert Robinson was the interviewer at the time. This has tended to overshadow Tynan's other television achievements, which included editing TEMPO – ITV's answer to MONITOR – and taking part in the 1950s quiz, THE 64,000 QUESTION, in which he answered questions on jazz. He also made some programmes about method acting and contributed to the documentary series, *One Pair of Eyes*.

TYNE TEES TELEVISION
(TTT)

Tyne Tees Television took to the air on 15 January 1959, to serve the far North-east of England from its Newcastle-upon-Tyne studios. Its successful consortium included film producer Sidney Box and *News Chronicle* impresarios George and Alfred Black.

Having one of the smallest ITV regions, the company's ambitions were always modest in the early days. However, horizons were raised in 1974 when its programmes were broadcast for the first time to most of North Yorkshire, following a transmitter swap with Yorkshire Television, which was instigated by the IBA. At the same time, in order to stabilize finances and maximize advertising potential, Tyne Tees and Yorkshire set up a joint holding company known as Trident

Television. (The third 'prong' of Trident was intended to be Anglia Television, which had also exchanged transmitters with Yorkshire, but the IBA ruled out Anglia's involvement.) Trident was eventually disbanded on the instructions of the IBA when it reappointed both Tyne Tees and Yorkshire to their franchises in 1980. However, following successful bids by the two companies in the 1991 auctions, they again merged under the Trident name, before both being swallowed up by Granada.

Among Tyne Tees' best-remembered programmes have been daytime variety and game shows like *Those Wonderful TV Times*, the current affairs series, *Face the Press*, the children's drama, SUPERGRAN, the drama-documentary, *Operation Julie*, and the pop shows, *The Geordie Scene*, *Razzamatazz* and, for Channel 4, THE TUBE.

TYZACK, MARGARET
(1931–)

British actress, seen in a number of prominent roles in classic serials. She was Winifred Forsyte in THE FORSYTE SAGA, Bette Fischer in *Cousin Bette*, Princess Anne in THE FIRST CHURCHILLS, Antonia in I, CLAUDIUS and also appeared in the 1979 revival of QUATERMASS. More recent credits have included *The Young Indiana Jones Chronicles* (teacher Helen Seymour) and *Family Money* (Delia).

UFO

UK (ATV/Century 21/ITC) Science Fiction. ITV 1970–3

Commander Edward Straker	Ed Bishop
Col. Alec Freeman	George Sewell
Capt. Peter Carlin	Peter Gordeno
Lt. Gay Ellis	Gabrielle Drake
Col. Paul Foster	Michael Billington
Gen. Henderson	Grant Taylor
Col. Virginia Lake	Wanda Ventham
Dr Jackson	Vladek Sheybal
Joan Harrington	Antonia Ellis
Nina Barry	Dolores Mantez
Lt. Mark Bradley	Harry Baird
Capt. Lew Waterman	Gary Myers
Lt. Ford	Keith Alexander
Skydiver navigator	Jeremy Wilkin

Creators: **Gerry Anderson, Sylvia Anderson**
Executive Producer: **Gerry Anderson**
Producer: **Reg Hill**

A secret defence agency protects Earth from space invaders.

UFO was puppet-specialists Gerry and Sylvia Anderson's first full attempt at real-life action, and in this series Earth was pitted against a mysterious alien force, some time in the 1980s. Arriving in weird, pyramid-shaped spacecraft, the intruders were seldom seen. Viewers did learn, however, that they had green skin and breathed not air but liquid, and that they were a sterile race, having lost the power of reproduction. The only way for them to survive was by kidnapping humans and stealing their organs for transplantation.

The general public was not alerted to the threat, for fear of causing widespread panic. Instead, a secret global defence unit was formed to anticipate UFO attacks and thwart any landings. SHADO (Supreme Headquarters, Alien Defence Organization), whose command centre, Control, housed deep beneath the Harlington-Straker film studios on the outskirts of London, was spearheaded by abrasive USAF officer Ed Straker, working under the cover of a film producer. Straker was assisted by the amiable Colonel Freeman, the moody Captain Carlin (who had lost his sister to the intruders), dare-devil test pilot Colonel Paul Foster and Lt. Gay Ellis, the shapely commander of the organization's futuristic Moonbase, the first line of defence (where, for some reason, all operatives wore white catsuits, string vests and purple wigs).

SHADO was well prepared for a UFO attack. Its Interceptor spacecraft, crewed by females and launched from the moon, were first into action, when alerted by the SID (Space Intruder Detector), a reconnaissance satellite. If this line was breached, Skydivers were called into play. These nuclear submarines were capable of underwater and aerial combat. If all else failed, and land defence was required, SHADO air-dropped its SHADO-mobile supertanks into the fray.

UFO was clearly more adult-orientated than the Andersons' Supermarionation series. The characters had fuller profiles, the plots had darker tones and the uniforms (being filled with real people, not woodentops) were certainly more provocative. One or two episodes touched on murky subjects such as hallucination, drugs and sex, and contrived to give the series a falsely risqué reputation. As a result, it was denied a network screening on ITV and floated between Saturday mornings and late nights around the country. It seems schedulers could not make up their minds whether this was kids' or adults' fare.

UK DRAMA

UK Drama replaced UK Arena within the UKTV portfolio of satellite/cable/digital channels, removing the arty features and concentrating on quality drama re-runs, both old and recent.

UK GOLD

Satellite/cable/digital channel established in 1992 by the BBC and Thames Television to transmit their archive material, plus some programmes from overseas. It is now part of the UKTV group of channels but still specializes in re-runs of popular British programmes, some from many years back.

UK HORIZONS

Satellite/cable/digital channel that majors on documentary and docu-soap re-runs. Part of the UKTV group of channels.

UK LIVING
See LIVING.

UK STYLE

Satellite/cable/digital channel devoted to lifestyle programming, reshowing series like CHANGING ROOMS, GARDENERS' WORLD and *Ready, Steady, Cook*. Another of UKTV's group of specialist channels.

UKTV

Umbrella company, jointly owned by BBC Worldwide and Flextech, which operates five satellite/cable/digital channels, specializing in re-runs of mostly British programmes. The five channels are UK Gold, UK Style, Play UK, UK Drama and UK Horizons.

ULLMAN, TRACEY
(1959–)

British actress, comic and singer, a hit on both sides of the Atlantic. Ullman first came to light in 1981 on THREE OF A KIND, in which she shared the honours with Lenny Henry and David Copperfield. She also appeared in A KICK UP THE EIGHTIES and then became one of the GIRLS ON TOP (Candice) in 1985. After heading off to Hollywood, Ullman was given her own sketch programme, *The Tracey Ullman Show*, in 1987, which ran for three years, was a ratings success and won her an Emmy. It also helped launch the cartoon series, THE SIMPSONS, but did not take off when screened in the UK, being deemed 'too American'. Back home, Ullman appeared in *A Class Act*, a satire in three parts, in 1993 for the new ITV company, Meridian, of which her producer husband, Allan McKeown, was a director. This led to the one-off, three-part satire, *Tracey Ullman Takes on New York*, which gave rise to a whole series of *Tracey Ullman Takes on . . .* in the USA. More recently, she has been seen as psychiatrist Dr Tracey Clark in ALLY McBEAL.

ULSTER TELEVISION
(UTV)

Ulster Television, or UTV as it is now known, has provided the Independent Television service for Northern Ireland since 31 October 1959. Always having to tread a fine line politically, because of the region's sensitivities, Ulster has had one of the more difficult tasks in the ITV network. Nevertheless, it has survived every franchise shake-up. Notable contributions to ITV's national output have been few, however.

UNITED!
UK (BBC) Drama. BBC 1 1965–7

Gerry Barford	David Lodge
Jack Birkett	Bryan Marshall
Jimmy Stokes	George Layton
Kenny Craig	Stephen Yardley
Horace Martin	Harold Goodwin
Ted Dawson	Robin Wentworth
Frank Sibley	Arnold Peters
Mary Barford	Ursula O'Leary
Kevin Barford	Peter Craze
Dan Davis	Arthur Pentelow
Mick Dougall	Robert Cross
Curly Parker	Ben Howard
Jean Jones	Mitzi Rogers
Danny South	Mark Kingston
Dave Rockway	Christopher Coll
Bryn Morrison	Derek Sherwin
Mark Wilson	Ronald Allen
Dick Mitchell	Tony Caunter
Chris Wood	Mike Redfern

Creator: **Brian Hayles**
Producers: **Bernard Hepton, Anthony Cornish, David Conroy, John McRae**

Life in and around a struggling soccer club.

As one strand of the BBC's autumn 1965 soap offensive (the other strand was THE NEWCOMERS), *United!* was another attempt by the Corporation to break the popular drama stranglehold held by CORONATION STREET. Airing on Monday and Wednesday evenings, it focused on the struggling Second Division team of Brentwich United just as the new manager, Londoner Gerry Barford, was drafted in to keep the club afloat. Sadly, his best efforts failed to boost the team's affairs and, by 1966, another new boss, Mark Wilson, had succeeded him.

Most prominent among the team members were goalkeeper Kenny Craig and strikers Jimmy Stokes and Jack Birkett (the team captain). Club trainer was Horace Martin, Ted Dawson was the chairman and the secretary was Frank Sibley. Dan Davis was chairman of the supporters' club. Boardroom battles, personal problems and domestic friction combined with the soccer stories throughout, and also seen were Barford's wife, Mary, and their soccer-mad, 18-year-old son, Kevin. Jimmy Hill acted as technical adviser and match action was filmed at Stoke City's Victoria Ground. These efforts were all in vain, however, and *United!* left the screen in 1967.

UNIVERSITY CHALLENGE
UK (Granada) Quiz. ITV 1962–87; BBC 2 1994–

Presenters: **Bamber Gascoigne, Jeremy Paxman**

Creator: **Don Reid**
Producers: **Barrie Heads, Patricia Owtram, Douglas Terry, Peter Mullings, Kieran Roberts, Peter Gwyn**

Long-running intellectual quiz for teams of university students.

A decade before MASTERMIND made its debut, Granada's *University Challenge* had already cornered the market in high-brow trivia, becoming, like *Mastermind*, an unexpected success. No one could have anticipated that a programme which posed questions about nuclear physics or Renaissance artists would run for 25 years.

Scholarly questionmaster Bamber Gascoigne took delight in taxing Britain's brightest young brains and added a touch of personality to what was otherwise a drably presented programme. Two four-person teams from competing universities or colleges did battle for a half-hour in a bland set, with a split screen employed to impose one team above the other. A round of questions opened with a 'starter for ten' (which became a catchphrase), and continued with three bonus questions. There were no holds barred and topics ranged from the sublime to the ridiculous, from Rachmaninov's piano concertos to First Division goalkeepers. The winning team stayed on to face a new challenge the following week, hoping to achieve three consecutive wins and earn a place in the end-of-the-series knock-out. The first contest took place between the universities of Reading and Leeds. In 1994 the programme was exhumed by Granada, who sold it to the BBC. Jeremy Paxman was installed as host and a somewhat jazzier set was employed. A straight knock-out tournament replaced the original 'challenge' format.

University Challenge was closely modelled on the US series, *College Bowl*, and champion teams from both sides of the Atlantic occasionally faced off in a special match. A number of notable personalities appeared as contestants in their youthful days, including writer Clive James, comedian Stephen Fry, TV journalist John Simpson and Conservative politicians Malcolm Rifkind and David Mellor.

UNSUITABLE JOB FOR A WOMAN, AN
UK (Ecosse/HTV/WGBH Boston). Detective Drama 1997–

Cordelia Gray	**Helen Baxendale**
Edith Sparshott	**Annette Crosbie**
Det. Chief Supt. Fergusson	**Struan Rodger**

Executive Producers: **Douglas Rae, Rebecca Eaton**
Producers: **Colin Ludlow, Debbie Shewell**

A rookie detective inherits her boss's investigation agency.

Cordelia Gray, in her late twenties, worked for private eye Bernie Pryde but his sudden suicide changed her life. His bequest to her of the ropey detective agency in London's Brick Lane meant she was no longer an apprentice private eye but the head of the firm, and she found herself thrown right in at the deep end when hired by a scientist to look into the suspicious death of his son, a Cambridge student. After this first three-part investigation, Gray never looked back, renaming the company Gray's Detective Agency. Intelligent and bookish, she hid her inexperience behind a dogged determination and a deep sense of natural justice. Adding not always welcome advice and lending a hand with the cases was matronly office manager Edith Sparshott. To coincide with star Helen Baxendale's own pregnancy, Gray was also shown expecting in later episodes.

The series was based on a character created by P. D. James.

UNTOUCHABLES, THE
US (Desilu/Langford) Police Drama. ITV 1966–9

Eliot Ness	**Robert Stack**
Agent Martin Flaherty	**Jerry Paris**
Agent William Youngfellow	**Abel Fernandez**
Agent Enrico Rossi	**Nick Georgiade**
Agent Cam Allison	**Anthony George**
Agent Lee Hobson	**Paul Picerni**
Agent Jack Rossman	**Steve London**
Frank ('The Enforcer') Nitti	**Bruce Gordon**
Al Capone	**Neville Brand**
'Mad Dog' Coll	**Clu Gallagher**
Narrator	**Walter Winchell**

Executive Producers: **Jerry Thorpe, Leonard Freeman, Quinn Martin**
Producers: **Howard Hoffman, Alan A. Armer, Alvin Cooperman, Lloyd Richards, Charles Russell, Fred Freiberger**

A US Treasury official and his incorruptible men home in on gangsters in Prohibition Chicago.

Based on the life of the real Eliot Ness, who brought Al Capone to book in 1931 (for non-payment of taxes), *The*

Untouchables told the story of an honest, upright and dedicated Treasury man as he sought to rid Chicago of organized crime. The dour, tight-lipped Ness and his whiter-than-white colleagues earned themselves the nickname 'The Untouchables' from the fact that they couldn't be bribed or influenced in any way.

The capture of Capone had been portrayed in a two-part TV special starring Robert Stack as Eliot Ness, which was screened in the USA as part of the *Desilu Playhouse* anthology. It proved so successful that this series ensued, although fact quickly gave way to fiction as it took hold. Although it showed the agents rounding up the likes of Frank Nitti (Capone's right-hand man), Ma Barker, Bugs Moran, Dutch Schultz, Walter Legenza and 'Mad Dog' Coll, the real Ness had had nothing to do with these events. Criticism also came from Italianate Americans, who complained how their names were being dragged through the mud in every episode. In response, the producers added a disclaimer to the end of the show, admitting that much of the action was fictional, and also cut down the number of Italian criminals.

The Untouchables was a notably violent programme, filmed in stark, realistic black and white, with plenty of gunfire to keep its large audience enthralled. It aired in its native USA from 1959 to 1963. ITV companies in the UK were slower to bite. Kevin Costner took over the Ness role for a 1987 cinema version, directed by Brian De Palma.

UP POMPEII!
UK (BBC) Situation Comedy. BBC 1 1970

Lurcio .... **Frankie Howerd**
Ludicrus Sextus .... **Max Adrian**
                                                          Wallas Eaton
                                                          Mark Dignam
Ammonia .... **Elizabeth Larner**
Erotica .... **Georgina Moon**
                                                      Jennifer Lonsdale
Nausius .... **Kerry Gardner**
Senna .... **Jeanne Mockford**
Plautus .... **William Rushton**

Creator: **Talbot Rothwell**
Writers: **Talbot Rothwell, Sid Collin**
Producers: **David Croft, Sydney Lotterby**

Innuendo and double entendre *in old Pompeii.*

The centre of attention in this Roman farce was Lurcio, the weather-beaten slave of randy senator Ludicrus Sextus. Constantly diverted from his attempts to deliver '*The Prologue*' to the viewing audience, Lurcio was obliged to act as a go-between for Ludicrus and the rest of his household and their friends as they all sought to bed one another. Lurcio kept viewers informed about the goings-on through asides to the camera. Ammonia was Ludicrus's wanton wife, Erotica the appropriately named daughter and Nausius the wimpy son. Other characters (and numerous guest stars) floated in and out of the action, not least batty old Senna, the soothsayer who foolishly predicted the destruction of the town.

Based on Frankie Howerd's stage success in the musi-

cal, *A Funny Thing Happened on the Way to the Forum*, *Up Pompeii!* began life as a *Comedy Playhouse* pilot in 1969. It went on to spawn a feature film, leading to various other '*Up*' movies for Howerd, and also gained a TV sequel in 1973, *Whoops Baghdad!*, with the action transferred to the Middle East and Howerd adopting the guise of servant Ali Oopla. In addition, two revival specials have been seen, both called *Further Up Pompeii!*, one in 1975 and the other (for ITV) in 1991. The programme's heavy innuendo was notably daring for the time.

UPPER HAND, THE
UK (Central) Situation Comedy. ITV 1990–6

Charlie Burrows .... **Joe McGann**
Caroline Wheatley .... **Diana Weston**
Laura West .... **Honor Blackman**
Joanna Burrows .... **Kellie Bright**
Tom Wheatley .... **William Puttock**
Michael Wheatley .... **Nicky Henson**

Executive Producer: **Paul Spencer**
Producer: **Christopher Walker**

A former footballer becomes housekeeper to a female advertising executive.

Injured soccer star Charlie Burrows needed a new vocation. A widower, he also needed a good environment in which to bring up his 11-year-old daughter, Joanna. So he applied for and was taken on as live-in housekeeper to Henley-based business executive Caroline Wheatley, mother of seven-year-old Tom and separated wife of Michael, a wildlife film-maker. Caroline's man-hungry mother, Laura West, her assistant at the Blake and Hunter advertising agency, was also on the scene.

Problems with the kids, as well as more mundane domestic matters, drew Charlie and Caroline into conflict but, at the same time, helped foster their growing romance. After four seasons of amiable squabbling, love finally won through and Charlie and Caroline were engaged to be married. A one-off, hour-long special in 1995 saw the dithering duo finally make it to the altar and, in the last series, they struggled to come to terms with their new status as man and wife.

The Upper Hand was based on the US sitcom, *Who's the Boss* (and largely followed the same scripts), but shared the same theme music as another American series, KNOTS LANDING.

UPSTAIRS, DOWNSTAIRS
UK (LWT/Sagitta) Drama. ITV 1971–5

Mr Angus Hudson .... **Gordon Jackson**
Mrs Kate Bridges/Hudson .... **Angela Baddeley**
Rose Buck .... **Jean Marsh**
Lord Richard Bellamy .... **David Langton**
Lady Marjorie Bellamy .... **Rachel Gurney**
Capt. James Bellamy .... **Simon Williams**
Elizabeth Bellamy/Kirbridge .... **Nicola Pagett**
Georgina Worsley .... **Lesley-Anne Down**

Daisy .... **Jacqueline Tong**
Edward .... **Christopher Beeny**
Sarah .... **Pauline Collins**
Emily .... **Evin Crowley**
Alfred .... **George Innes**
Roberts .... **Patsy Smart**
Pearce .... **Brian Osborne**
Lawrence Kirbridge .... **Ian Ogilvy**
Hazel Forrest/Bellamy .... **Meg Wynn Owen**
Ruby .... **Jenny Tomasin**
Thomas Watkins .... **John Alderton**
Virginia Hamilton/Bellamy .... **Hannah Gordon**
Frederick .... **Gareth Hunt**
Alice .... **Anne Yarker**
William .... **Jonathan Seely**
Lily .... **Karen Dotrice**
Sir Geoffrey Dillon .... **Raymond Huntley**
Lady Prudence Fairfax .... **Joan Benham**
Marquis of Stockbridge .... **Anthony Andrews**
Violet .... **Angela Walker**

Creators: **Jean Marsh, Eileen Atkins**
Executive Producer: **Rex Firkin**
Producer: **John Hawkesworth**

Events in the lives of a turn-of-the-century London family and their loyal servants.

Much praised, fondly remembered and hugely successful, *Upstairs, Downstairs* focused on life at 165 Eaton Place, the Belgravia home of Tory MP Richard Bellamy, his lady wife, Marjorie, and their two children, James and Elizabeth. The family was rich, but not extravagantly so, with most of their wealth inherited on Lady Bellamy's side (she was the daughter of a prime minister). So Richard's career was vital to the upkeep of the family's home and its standing in society, something which the indiscretions of his wayward children continually placed in jeopardy.

But, as the title suggested, the 'Upstairs' goings-on were only half the story, with the 'Downstairs' world of the Bellamys' domestic staff equally prominent. Head of the servants was Mr Hudson, the highly responsible, softly spoken but firm Scottish butler, a man who knew his place and made sure other staff members knew theirs. A father figure to the servants, he masterminded the team effort which kept the house afloat, ably assisted by Mrs Bridges, the gruff, plump cook, and Rose, the level-headed chief housemaid. Beneath them worked the younger staff – feisty, daydreaming under-parlourmaid Sarah, maturing footman Edward, loyal housemaid Daisy (later Edward's wife), pathetic maid Ruby, and, in later episodes, new footmen Thomas and Frederick.

The series began in November 1903, shortly after the death of Queen Victoria, and ran through until 1930. Along the way, in cosy, soap-opera fashion, it depicted the household's struggles to win through in times of adversity, whether social (such as a visit by the King for dinner) or real (when Rose's fiancé was tragically killed in the Great War). It reflected all the early fads and fashions of the 20th century, from the Suffragette movement to the jazz age, writing historical events into the plot. The General Strike was one example and the loss of Lady Marjorie on the *Titanic* another. Lord Bellamy remarried (to Scottish widow Virginia Hamilton), his ward Georgina moved in to replace the petulant Elizabeth, and other characters came and went, both above and below stairs, before disaster struck at the end of the series. The family's wealth was lost in the 1929 Wall Street Crash, James committed suicide and the house had to be sold. The final episode saw Hudson marry Mrs Bridges and, together with Ruby, set off to run their own guest house. Edward and Daisy became butler and maid to Georgina and her new husband, the Marquis of Stockbridge, and Rose was the last to leave, wandering through the rooms and closing up the house, with voices from the past reminding her of events, happy and sad, that had dominated her life in Eaton Place.

Upstairs, Downstairs – widely acclaimed for its historical accuracy and shrewd social comment – was the brainchild of Jean Marsh and fellow actress Eileen Atkins (who had created the role of Sarah for herself but found herself committed to stage work when the programme began). They repeated the exercise in devising THE HOUSE OF ELIOTT in the 1990s. *Upstairs, Downstairs* enjoyed sales all across the world and led to a spin-off series, *Thomas and Sarah*, which followed the two young servants as they took up a new appointment in the country. An American version, *Beacon Hill*, set in 1920s Boston, was also attempted but didn't succeed.

UTV
See **ULSTER TELEVISION**.

V

US (Daniel H. Blatt and Robert Singer/Warner Brothers)
Science Fiction. ITV 1984–5

Mike Donovan	**Marc Singer**
Dr Julie Parrish	**Faye Grant**
Diana	**Jane Badler**
Nathan Bates	**Lane Smith**
Robin Maxwell	**Blair Tefkin**
Elizabeth	**Jenny Beck**
	Jennifer Cooke
Ham Tyler	**Michael Ironside**
Willie	**Robert Englund**
Elias	**Michael Wright**
Kyle Bates	**Jeff Yagher**
Lydia	**June Chadwick**
Sean Donovan	**Nicky Katt**
Mr Chiang	**Aki Aleong**
Charles	**Duncan Regehr**
Martin/Philip	**Frank Ashmore**
Lt. James	**Judson Scott**
Howard K. Smith	**Himself**

Creator: **Kenneth Johnson**
Executive Producers: **Daniel H. Blatt, Robert Singer**

Earth is taken over by Nazi lizards from outer space.

V began as two successful mini-series (*V* and *V: The Final Battle*) and then expanded into a weekly run, which was never as popular. The 'V' in the title actually stood for 'Visitors' and 'Victory', with the storyline revolving around an alien invasion of Earth and the underground resistance to it. The Visitors came from somewhere near the star, Sirius, arriving in Los Angeles in the late 20th century in massive spacecraft, ranging in size from three to five miles wide. They ostensibly came in peace, offering advice and technical help to the Earth's population in return for some vital minerals. However, once the human race had been wooed, the Visitors began to take over the planet, using subtle coercion and clever propaganda.

If this sounds familiar, it was because *V* was modelled on the rise of fascism in Germany before World War II. But in case the metaphor passed some viewers by, there were some even more obvious references. The aliens dressed in uniforms with swastika-type motifs. They formed an élite squad of stormtroopers, like the SS, and rounded up all opposition, confining subversives in concentration camps. But, like the Nazis, they also met resistance.

Working against them was TV journalist Mike Donovan, who had penetrated an alien spaceship and discovered their true intentions. He learned that the Visitors were not humanoids at all but forked-tongued, giant, rodent-eating reptiles whose scaly skin was revealed whenever their flesh was torn. They had come to steal Earth's water and, more menacingly, to take back frozen humans as food. Pursued by the aliens, Mike teamed up with scientist Julie Parrish (a concentration camp escapee), mercenary Ham Tyler, a friendly alien named Willie (played by the film world's future Freddie Kruger, Robert Englund) and young Robin Maxwell, who had been seduced by a Visitor and given birth to a hybrid child, Elizabeth. They hid out in the Club Creole and adopted the 'V for Victory' sign as their emblem. Thankfully, by the end of the mini-series, they had seen off the oppressors with the aid of a specially produced bacterial red dust.

When the weekly series began, the Visitors soon regained the upper hand. Diana, their evil, duplicitous leader, was back in control, thanks to chemical magnate Nathan Bates (whose Scientific Frontiers Corporation had manufactured the lethal red dust), who sprang her from a Nuremburg-style trial. The underground still battled valiantly and the half-alien Elizabeth rapidly developed into a teenager with special mental powers. When the climax came, Diana and her cronies were thwarted by a mutual desire for peace between the two races.

V is well remembered for one classic scene in which Jane Badler, as Diana, swallowed a mouse. It was actually done using chocolate mice, a mechanical jaw for close-ups and a false expandable throat, which showed the mouse slipping down, but it looked very realistic and upset the squeamish.

VALENTINE, ANTHONY
(1939–)

British actor, often cast in sinister, sneery roles. Among these have been the parts of Toby Meres in CALLAN and Major Mohn in COLDITZ. As a teenager in the 1950s Valentine was one of the actors to play Harry Wharton in BILLY BUNTER OF GREYFRIARS SCHOOL. He also appeared in *Whirligig* and the 1955 adaptation of *Children of the New Forest* and went on, in the 1960s, to pop up in DR FINLAY'S CASEBOOK, playing Bruce Cameron. Valentine was TV's RAFFLES in the 1970s and had prominent roles in JUSTICE and the thriller series, *Codename*. As Maurice, he was an occasional visitor to MINDER and, as Simon De Belleme, he was a mystic sorcerer in ROBIN OF SHERWOOD. He has been seen in numerous single dramas and his guest parts have included series like DEPARTMENT S, THE AVENGERS, SPACE: 1999, HAMMER HOUSE OF HORROR, TALES OF THE UNEXPECTED, BERGERAC, THE CASEBOOK OF SHERLOCK HOLMES, LOVE-JOY, THE HOUSE OF ELIOTT (Victor Stride), *Body and Soul*, and *Jilly Cooper's Riders* (Col Carter). In complete contrast, he also once hosted STARS ON SUNDAY.

VAN DER VALK
UK (Thames/Euston Films/Elmgate) Police Drama.
ITV 1972–3; 1977; 1991–2

Piet Van der Valk	**Barry Foster**
Arlette Van der Valk	**Susan Travers**
	Joanna Dunham
	Meg Davies
Kroon	**Michael Latimer**
Samson	**Nigel Stock**
	Ronald Hines
Wim Van der Valk	**Richard Huw**

Creator: **Nicholas Freeling**
Executive Producers: **Lloyd Shirley, George Taylor, Brian Walcroft**
Producers: **Michael Chapman, Robert Love, Geoffrey Gilbert, Chris Burt**

The investigations of a Dutch detective.

Set against the cosmopolitan backdrop of Amsterdam, with its reputation for drugs and prostitution, this series explored the world of local CID officer, Van der Valk. The blond, curly-haired, impulsive detective scoured the canals and polders of the Dutch city in his search for common criminals and those involved in more subversive activity.

After an initial two-year run, the series was brought back in 1977 by Euston Films, with Joanna Dunham now in the part of Arlette, Van der Valk's wife. It was revived yet again in 1991, cashing in on the Morse, Dalgliesh, Wexford and Taggart success stories. This time yet another actress, Meg Davies, came in to play Arlette and Van der Valk now also had a policeman son, Wim. The role of his boss, Samson, was taken by Ronald Hines on this occasion. In this two-hour series, Van der Valk, greying and still rather uncharismatic, had been promoted to Commissaris.

The character of Van der Valk was created by author Nicholas Freeling in 1962. The programme's catchy theme music, 'Eye Level' by the Simon Park Orchestra, surprisingly topped the British singles chart in 1973.

VAN DYKE, DICK
(1925–)

American entertainer whose showbusiness ambitions seemed limited when he worked as an announcer for southern TV stations, having already failed to make the grade in a mime act. But, moving to New York, he gained a foothold on Broadway, guested in THE PHIL SILVERS SHOW and then launched his own sitcom, THE DICK VAN DYKE SHOW, in 1961. The series, in which he played writer Rob Petrie, brought him international fame and a host of Emmy awards. It ran for five years. Van Dyke then looked for greater achievements in the movies, but his material, by common consent, was not the best and he returned to television. His later series (such as *The New Dick Van Dyke Show*, with Dick as talk-show host Dick Preston) did not prove particularly successful, however, and he was largely seen in specials and TV movies until fighting back as doctor-detective Mark Sloan in the series, *Diagnosis Murder*, in 1993.

VAN OUTEN, DENISE
(1974–)

Basildon-born actress/presenter of Dutch descent, a former member of the Those 2 Girls pop group, who made her name as host of THE BIG BREAKFAST, having previously been seen in the programme's weather helicopter. Earlier, she had fronted the kids' series, *Massive* and *Scratchy & Co.*, and she has since starred in the sitcom, *Babes in the Wood* (Leigh), and the TV pantomime, *Jack and the Beanstalk* (Jill), and presented the late-night shows, *Something for the Weekend* and *Prickly Heat*. Van Outen has also guested in THE BILL.

VARNEY, REG
(1922–)

London-born comic actor, initially working as a teenage singer and ragtime pianist in workingmen's clubs. He moved on to the music halls and, after the war, teamed up with Benny Hill, who acted as Reg's stooge. It wasn't until the turn of the 1960s that Varney began to make television inroads. He was cast as Reg, the foreman, in the very popular sitcom, THE RAG TRADE, and followed it up with a children's series, *The Valiant Varneys*. He also starred in BEGGAR MY NEIGHBOUR in 1967, playing Harry Butt, before, in 1969, ON THE BUSES arrived. Hugely successful, it ran for four years and even had three film spin-offs. It was very much Varney's series, and his clippie-chasing Stan Butler character was always at the centre of the action. When *On the Buses* ended, Varney was given his own showcase programmes on ITV and starred in yet another sitcom, but *Down the Gate*, featuring Reg as fishmarket porter Reg Furnell, proved to be short-lived. As a result of his working on stage elsewhere in the world, and convalescing after heart problems, UK viewers have seen little of Reg Varney in recent years.

VAUGHAN, JOHNNY
(1966–)

London-born comedian and presenter of light entertainment programmes, particularly *The Fall Guy*, *Here's Johnny*, *Moviewatch*, *The Johnny Vaughan Film Show* and THE BIG BREAKFAST (forming a successful on-screen partnership with Denise Van Outen in the last). Vaughan has also hosted *The Brit Awards* and fronted a number of celebrity interview specials, most notably with the stars of FRIENDS in *The One Where Johnny Makes Friends*.

VAUGHAN, NORMAN
(1927–)

Liverpudlian entertainer who made his name as compere of SUNDAY NIGHT AT THE LONDON PALLADIUM in 1962. Vaughan, then a comparative unknown, had previously worked as a compere in stage shows and had first been seen on TV in 1954, later appearing in *The Harry Secombe Show* and with Terry Scott in *Scott Free*. However, by the time his three-year spell at the Palladium ended, he was one of Britain's brightest stars. Along the way, he conjured up the thumbs-up, thumbs-down catchphrases of 'Swinging' and 'Dodgy'. Another catchphrase was 'Roses grow on you', taken from his commercials for chocolates. He was given his own series by both ITV (*A Touch of the Norman Vaughans*) and the BBC (*The Norman Vaughan Show*). In 1972, he took over from Bob Monkhouse as host of the popular game show, THE

GOLDEN SHOT, but stayed with the programme for only one year. He hadn't finished with game shows, though, as he went on to co-devise BULLSEYE for Central Television. Working more on stage as an actor, Vaughan's TV appearances have been mostly in panel games and variety shows in the last few decades, although he did compere *Pebble Mill Showcase* in 1978.

VAUGHAN, PETER
(Peter Ohm; 1924–)

Silver-haired, Shropshire-born actor, one of whose best-remembered creations was that of pampered prison baron, 'Genial' Harry Grout, in PORRIDGE. He followed this with another sitcom success as Charlie Johnson, Wolfie's prospective father-in-law and class enemy in CITIZEN SMITH. However, Vaughan's TV career stretches back to the 1950s. One of his first starring roles was in the 1960 newspaper drama, DEADLINE MIDNIGHT, and he went on to play Bill Sikes in a 1962 adaptation of *Oliver Twist* and Long John Silver in a 1968 version of *Treasure Island*. He was seen in the sitcom, *Our Man from St Mark's*, took the lead in 1969's THE GOLD ROBBERS (Det. Chief Supt. Cradock) and starred as Billy Fox in the 1980 series, FOX. He was David Kimber-Hutchinson in *Game, Set and Match* in 1988. In 1995 he played Frank Ashworth in *The Choir* and was Delaney in *Oliver's Travels*, and a year later appeared as Gabriel Betteredge in *The Moonstone* and Alzheimer's victim Felix Hutchinson in OUR FRIENDS IN THE NORTH. In 2000 he was Ray Skinner in *The Thing about Vince . . .* and Sonny in *Face*. Vaughan has also been seen in many other productions, including mini-series and more adaptations of the classics, including Mr Boffin in *Our Mutual Friend* and Sir Ensor Doone in *Lorna Doone*. Both his wives have been actresses: Billie Whitelaw and Lillias Walker.

VAUGHN, ROBERT
(1932–)

One of TV's international stars of the 1960s, Robert Vaughn was Napoleon Solo, THE MAN FROM UNCLE. He remained a man undercover in the 1970s, when he returned to our screens as Harry Rule in THE PROTECTORS. Vaughn's first appearances came in the 1950s, when he took minor roles in series like DRAGNET, and his first prime-time lead arrived in 1963 in a US drama called *The Lieutenant*. For most of the 1970s, Vaughn was cast in TV movies and glossy mini-series, and he continued to be active in the cinema (he had been one of *The Magnificent Seven* back in 1960). He played Chief of Staff Frank Flaherty in WASHINGTON: BEHIND CLOSED DOORS in 1978 and resurfaced in 1986 to take the role of General Hunt Stockwell in THE A-TEAM. In the 1990s, he hosted the spoof adventure series, *Danger Theatre*.

VCR
See VIDEOTAPE.

VERNON, RICHARD
(1925–97)

Reading-born actor, often cast in upright, slightly aristocratic roles. One of his best remembered was as Oldenshaw in THE MAN IN ROOM 17 and THE FELLOWS, in the mid-1960s. Vernon also starred in THE DUCHESS OF DUKE STREET (Major Smith-Barton), EDWARD THE SEVENTH (Lord Salisbury), THE SANDBAGGERS ('C'), *A Gentlemen's Club* (George), *L for Lester* (bank manager Mr Davies), *Leaving* (Mr Chessington), ROLL OVER BEETHOVEN (crusty dad Oliver Purcell), THE HITCHHIKER'S GUIDE TO THE GALAXY (Slartibartfast) and *Class Act* (Sir Horace Mainwaring). Other credits included Dick Emery's *Legacy of Murder, Something in Disguise, Return of the Antelope, Paradise Postponed* and numerous single dramas, including *Suez 1956*.

VERY PECULIAR PRACTICE, A
UK (BBC) Comedy Drama. BBC 2 1986–8

Dr Stephen Daker	Peter Davison
Dr Bob Buzzard	David Troughton
Dr Jock McCannon	Graham Crowden
Dr Rose Marie	Barbara Flynn
Lyn Turtle	Amanda Hillwood
Chen Sung Yau	Takashi Kawahara
Maureen Cahagan	Lindy Whiteford
Mrs Carmen Kramer	Gillian Rainer
Ernest Hemmingway	John Bird
Dorothy Hampton	Frances White
Dr Grete Grotowska	Joanna Kanska
Jack B. Daniels	Michael J. Shannon
Julie Daniels	Toria Fuller
Sammy Limb	Dominic Arnold
Prof. George Bunn	James Grout
Nuns	Sonia Hart
	Elaine Turrell

Creator/Writer: **Andrew Davies**
Producer: **Ken Riddington**

Surreal tales of life at an ailing university medical practice.

Keen, idealistic, rather neurotic young doctor Stephen Daker had a rude awakening on his arrival at Lowlands University. Accepting a position in the medical centre, in the hope of starting a new life after a messy marital break-up in Walsall, he discovered anarchy and moral decline all around him and chiefly among his professional colleagues. His genial but boozy boss, Jock McCannon, had hopelessly lost control of the practice and spent most of his time dictating his forthcoming book, *The Sick University*. This left room for the cynical and amoral Bob Buzzard to introduce dubious money-making schemes and for the devious arch-feminist Dr Rose Marie (who believed that illness was something men inflicted on women) to scheme against the male species. Daker at least found humanity in the form of

chirpy police student Lyn Turtle, and his Burmese mathematician flatmate, Chen Sung Yau.

In the second series, when Lyn had departed, the prickly Pole Grete Grotowska, an art historian, became Daker's new girlfriend. At this time, sinister forces were on the move at Lowlands. An unscrupulous new American vice-chancellor (Jack B. Daniels) had been appointed and right-wing market forces were taking over. Throughout both series, two mysterious, silent nuns flitted around the campus, rummaging in waste-bins, doing quirky things and generally becoming the programme's trademark. Elkie Brooks sang the theme song, which was written by Dave Greenslade.

In 1992 Andrew Davies followed up *A Very Peculiar Practice* with a *Screen One* presentation entitled *A Very Polish Practice*. Set in Warsaw amid decaying Communism and advancing capitalism, it featured Stephen, Grete (now his wife) and Bob Buzzard, who was in town on a business trip and hoping, as ever, to make a fast buck.

VH-1
See MTV.

VHS

Video cassette format established by JVC in Japan in 1976 and now the standard for domestic users. It was initially challenged in the marketplace by Sony's Betamax system, launched a year earlier, which some claimed provided a better image. However, although both systems use $1/2$-inch-wide tape inside the cassette, the VHS tape recorded and played back longer and gradually saw off its rival. VHS stands for Video Home System.

VIACOM

Major international media group whose television interests now include America's MTV channels (including VH-1 and Nickelodeon), Paramount Television, the UPN network, the Showtime networks, Spelling Television and Comedy Central. The company was formed in 1971 as an off-shoot of CBS, dealing in programme syndication.

VICAR OF DIBLEY, THE
UK (Tiger Aspect) Situation Comedy. BBC 1 1994–

Geraldine Granger	Dawn French
David Horton	Gary Waldhorn
Hugo Horton	James Fleet
Alice Tinker/Horton	Emma Chambers
Letitia Cropley	Liz Smith
Frank Pickle	John Bluthal
Jim Trott	Trevor Peacock
Owen Newitt	Roger Lloyd Pack
Simon Horton	Clive Mantle

Writers: **Richard Curtis, Paul Mayhew-Archer**
Producers: **Jon Plowman, Sue Vertue, Margot Gavan Duffy**

A new female vicar adds zest to life in a sleepy village.

When Pottle, the ancient vicar of St Barnabas in the rural village of Dibley, finally passed on, there was much speculation about his successor. What the villagers didn't expect was a woman. The arrival of Geraldine Granger certainly raised a few eyebrows, especially those of the local squire, David Horton, who set his face against her from the start. It wasn't just that she was female, she had these crazy liberal values, too, not to mention a radical, almost flippant, approach to Christianity. A more favourable response came from David's dozy son, Hugo, and the girl (later wife) he had his eye on, drippy, naïve, ultra-dim verger Alice Tinker – clearly a product of local inbreeding. The other villagers were also positive about the change: boring Frank Pickle, who went on to stun the community by revealing his homosexuality; lavatorial farmer Owen Newitt; sexually liberated, stuttering pensioner Jim Trott ('No, no, no, no, no . . . yes'); and organist/flower arranger Letitia Cropley, who 'treated' the parish council meetings to her finest culinary creations, such as a cake iced with Marmite, before dying one Easter.

Geraldine herself was what she might call a small-time sinner – sex and chocolate her major vices – but by the time she was actually contemplating a move to a new parish (to chase after David's hunky brother, Simon), she had even won over Horton, thanks to her boundless energy and novel ideas which not only encouraged larger congregations but fostered a new spirit in the village.

A trademark of each episode was a post-credits ending in which Geraldine tried to explain a smutty joke to Alice, always without success.

VICTORY AT SEA

US (NBC/Project 20) Documentary. BBC 1952–3

Narrator: **Leonard Graves**

Producer: **Henry Saloman**

American history of World War II sea battles.

Introduced for British audiences by Michael Lewis, Professor of History at the Royal Naval College in Greenwich, this ground-breaking documentary examined the maritime context of the war effort. Using combat footage (from both sides of the conflict) in 26 parts, it discussed key events like the bombing of Pearl Harbor. The production team worked closely with the US Navy, and Richard Rodgers provided a rousing musical score. The series' award-winning status ensured plenty of re-runs in the early 1950s.

VIDEO WALL

A bank of television monitors, each showing different images or each contributing one part to a larger image.

VIDEOTAPE

Video Tape Recording or VTR – a means of translating television signals on to magnetic tape, for future playback – was first pioneered in the early 1950s, but the technology was primitive and the resolution poor. It wasn't until the Ampex Corporation launched a completely new system in 1956 that the industry began to take it seriously. Colour versions arrived two years later and the Ampex system remained in international use until the late 1970s, by which time simpler, cheaper and better-quality reel-to-reel systems had been introduced. Professionally, 2-inch and 1-inch Quad tape systems have been in use, though $^{3}/_{4}$-inch U-matic, $^{1}/_{2}$-inch VHS and Betamax, and $^{1}/_{4}$-inch Quatercam have also been employed (the smaller tapes mostly by amateurs). Cassette-based systems (Video Cassette Recorders, or VCRs) are now commonplace and have provided more flexibility in news gathering. They have also enabled domestic viewers to enjoy record and playback facilities, of course. Sony's Video 8 (8-mm. tape) and its high-resolution sister, Hi-8, are popular with camcorder users.

VINE, DAVID
(1936–)

British sports frontman, a newspaper journalist who entered television with Westward TV but joined the BBC in 1966. He has focused largely on skiing (as host of *Ski Sunday*), show-jumping and snooker, but has been involved with most sports and most BBC sports programmes. He was the first questionmaster of A QUESTION OF SPORT (following on from hosting QUIZ BALL), and has introduced THE SUPERSTARS, IT'S A KNOCKOUT, MISS WORLD and the EUROVISION SONG CONTEST.

VIRGIN OF THE SECRET SERVICE
UK (ATV) Spy Drama. ITV 1968

Capt. Robert Virgin .... **Clinton Greyn**
Mrs Virginia Cortez .... **Veronica Strong**
Doublett .... **John Cater**
Karl Von Brauner .... **Alexander Doré**
Klaus Striebeck .... **Peter Swannick**
Col. Shaw-Camberley .... **Noel Coleman**

Creator: **Ted Willis**
Producer: **Josephine Douglas**

The dangerous assignments of a patriotic British agent in the early 1900s.

Intrepid Captain Robert Virgin more than worked for the British secret service: he lived and breathed to defend

British honour at a time when the Empire was beginning to crumble. From the North-west Frontier of India to all parts of the Middle and Far East, and even South America, Virgin fought for his country, obeying the orders of his superior, Colonel Shaw-Camberley, protecting his lady assistant, Mrs Cortez, and physically fending off his ruthless opponents, Karl Von Brauner and Klaus Striebeck. Doublett was his loyal batman.

VIRGINIAN, THE/
THE MEN FROM SHILOH

US (Universal) Western. BBC 1 1964–73

The Virginian	**James Drury**
Judge Henry Garth	**Lee J. Cobb**
Trampas	**Doug McClure**
Steve Hill	**Gary Clarke**
Molly Wood	**Pippa Scott**
Betsy Garth	**Roberta Shore**
Randy Garth	**Randy Boone**
Sheriff Brannon	**Harlan Wade**
Deputy Emmett Ryker	**Clu Gulager**
Belden	**L. Q. Jones**
Jennifer	**Diane Roter**
Starr	**John Dehner**
John Grainger	**Charles Bickford**
Stacy Grainger	**Don Quine**
Elizabeth Grainger	**Sara Lane**
Sheriff Abbott	**Ross Elliott**
Clay Grainger	**John McIntire**
Holly Grainger	**Jeanette Nolan**
David Sutton	**David Hartman**
Jim Horn	**Tim Matheson**
Col. Alan MacKenzie	**Stewart Granger** (*Shiloh*)
Roy Tate	**Lee Majors** (*Shiloh*)
Parker	**John McLiam** (*Shiloh*)

Executive Producer: **Norman MacDonnell**
Producers: **Howard Christie, Paul Freeman, Jim McAdams**

An eastern ranch foreman brings new methods to a western cattle farm.

This cowboy series was set on the Shiloh Ranch in Medicine Bow, Wyoming Territory. At the thick of the action was the ranch foreman, known only as 'The Virginian'. Little else was ever revealed about this mystery man of few words but, stern, level-headed and imbued with a strong sense of justice, he was a respected figurehead for the local community. His presence at Shiloh reflected how eastern influence and modern thinking spread across America in the 1880s, eroding primitive western ways.

The ranch was owned initially by Judge Garth, then by brothers John and Clay Grainger, and finally by Englishman Colonel McKenzie (by which time the era had moved on to the 1890s and the programme retitled *The Men From Shiloh*). On the range Trampas was The Virginian's impulsive young friend, one of a supporting cast of family members, ranch-hands and assorted lawmen. Many top stars were introduced in one-off supporting roles – Bette Davis, Ryan O'Neal, George C. Scott, Charles Bronson, Telly Savalas and Lee Marvin, to name but a handful – and, as in WAGON TRAIN, stories tended to focus on these visitors, rather than on the rather aloof members of the regular cast.

The Virginian was TV's first feature-length Western series, presenting virtually a movie a week. It was loosely based on the turn-of-the-century book of the same name by Owen Wister, which had also been covered three times for the cinema, most notably starring Gary Cooper in 1929.

VISION MIXER

The name given to the equipment that enables its operator (also known as a vision mixer) to select, mix, cut and fade different camera shots (or introduce visual effects) during recording or transmission on the instructions of the director.

VISION ON

UK (BBC) Children's Entertainment. BBC 1964–76

Presenters: **Pat Keysell, Tony Hart, Larry Parker, Ben Benison, Wilf Lunn, Sylvester McCoy, David Cleveland**

Producers: **Ursula Eason, Leonard Chase, Patrick Dowling**

Juvenile entertainment accessible to youngsters with hearing impediments.

Vision On was the more politically correct follow-up to a programme baldly entitled *For Deaf Children*, which had begun in 1952. Aiming to cater for children with hearing difficulties as well as those with adequate hearing, *Vision On* was, as its name suggested, a visual extravaganza. Arty features by Tony Hart, a former graphic artist, dominated the show and one regular feature was 'The Gallery', displaying drawings sent in by young viewers. There were also crazy inventions to look at, lots of sight gags and sketches, plus the misadventures of pipe-cleaner men Phil O'Pat and Pat O'Phil. Co-host Pat Keysell signed for those who could not hear and, in the first series, there was also an emphasis on lip-reading. From the second series, however, words became increasingly irrelevant, and the programme had little verbal content beyond a courteous hello and goodbye each week. However, lively music and weird and wonderful sounds remained important to the make-up as the producers recognized that deaf people could pick up vibrations and appreciate the feel of the programme in this way.

When *Vision On* ended in 1976, it was succeeded by a more obvious art programme, again hosted by Tony Hart and entitled *Take Hart* (1977–83), which itself was superseded by *Hartbeat* (1984–93). It was in *Take Hart* that the popular plasticine creature named Morph (created by future *Wallace and Gromit* Oscar-winner Nick Park) made his debut.

VITAL SPARK, THE
See PARA HANDY – MASTER MARINER.

VOLUME

The intensity of sound reproduction and the control on the receiver to adjust this.

VORDERMAN, CAROL
MBE (1960–)

Brainy British presenter, coming to the fore as a number-crunching hostess on COUNTDOWN in 1982 but since seen on a variety of science-based or educational programmes, including HOW 2, *Notes and Queries with Clive Anderson* and TOMORROW'S WORLD. Her many other credits include *The Wide Awake Club*, *Entertainment Today*, *Out of This World*, *Put It to the Test*, *The Antiques Inspectors*, *Mysteries with Carol Vorderman*, THE NATIONAL LOTTERY LIVE, *Computers Don't Bite*, *Testing . . . Testing*, *Hot Gadgets*, POINTS OF VIEW, *What Will They Think of Next?*, *Carol Vorderman's Better Homes*, *Dream House*, *Find a Fortune* and *Tested to Destruction*, plus coverage of the World Chess Championship.

VOX POP

The views of people in the street when stopped by a reporter, which are then edited into a sequence for use in current affairs or magazine programmes.

VOYAGE TO THE BOTTOM OF THE SEA
US (Twentieth Century-Fox/Irwin Allen) Science Fiction.
ITV 1964–6

Admiral Harriman Nelson	**Richard Basehart**
Commander/Capt. Lee Crane	**David Hedison**
Lt. Commander Chip Morton	**Robert Dowdell**
CPO Curley Jones	**Henry Kulky**
CPO Francis Sharkey	**Terry Becker**
Stu Riley	**Allan Hunt**
Kowalsky	**Del Monroe**
Crewman Sparks	**Arch Whiting**
Crewman Patterson	**Paul Trinka**
Doctor	**Richard Bull**

Creator/Executive Producer: **Irwin Allen**

The crew of a super-submarine take on threats to the world.

The *Seaview* was the world's most advanced nuclear submarine, created by its commander, Retired Admiral Harriman Nelson, and housed in a pen 200 feet down at his Nelson Institute of Marine Research, at Santa Barbara, California. Six hundred feet long, the supersub could dive deeper (4450 feet) and travel faster (70 knots) than any of its rivals, and was equipped with all the latest devices, including atomic torpedoes. It carried a separate mini-sub, a diving bell, a snowcat and an innovative 'flying fish', a small vessel capable of both water and air travel.

The action was set 13 years in the future and, although their role was meant to be research, Nelson and his crew were constantly called upon to maintain peace below the waves, by thwarting aggressors, whether human, fish or alien. After a reasonably serious beginning, the storylines soon plummeted to ridiculous depths. One of the most memorable villains was Professor Multiple, played by Vincent Price, who tried to take over the *Seaview* using life-like puppets. In addition, the ship confronted all manner of outrageous monsters from the deep. There were werewolves, enemy orchids, giant jellyfish, supersquids, even Nazis. One adventure took place inside a whale.

Valiantly assisting Nelson in his protection of our planet were the youngest submarine captain ever, Captain Lee Crane, and fellow officers Chip Morton, Francis Sharkey and Curley Jones. The show was created by low-budget sci-fi specialist Irwin Allen (LOST IN SPACE, LAND OF THE GIANTS, etc.), and was spun off his 1961 cinema version starring Walter Pidgeon. Much of the film footage was re-used in the TV series, and the sub itself was also a relic of the movie.

VTR
See VIDEOTAPE.

WACKY RACES

US (Hanna-Barbera/Heatter-Quigley) Cartoon. BBC 1
1969–70

Voices:

Dick Dastardly	**Paul Winchell**
Muttley	**Don Messick**
Peter Perfect	**Daws Butler**
Penelope Pitstop	**Janet Waldo**
Luke and Blubber Bear	**John Stephenson**
Rufus Ruffcut	**Daws Butler**
Rock and Gravel Slag	**Daws Butler**
Prof. Pat Pending	**Don Messick**
The General	**John Stephenson**
Clyde	**Paul Winchell**
Sergeant	**Daws Butler**
Pte. Pinkley	**Paul Winchell**
Red Max	**Daws Butler**
The Ant Hill Mob	**Mel Blanc**
Big Gruesome	**Daws Butler**
Little Gruesome	**Don Messick**
Sawtooth	**Don Messick**
Ring-a-Ding Convert-a-Car	**Don Messick**
Narrator	**Dave Willock**

Creators/Executive Producers: **William Hanna, Joseph
Barbera**

*Animated series of hair-raising contests between
eccentric drivers and their weird vehicles.*

Based loosely on the film, *The Great Race*, *Wacky Races*
drew together America's finest drivers, each behind the
wheel of the strangest speed machines. In each episode,
the 11 daredevil teams lined up for a cross-country race,
eager to claim the title of 'The World's Wackiest Racer'.
In car No. 1, the Boulder Mobile, were the cavemen Slag
brothers, Rock and Gravel, and they were joined on the
starting grid by the Gruesome Twosome in the Creepy
Coupé (No. 2), inventor Professor Pat Pending in his
Ring-a-Ding Convert-a-Car (3), the Red Max in the Crim-
son Haybailer (4), girl racer Penelope Pitstop in the Com-
pact Pussycat (5), the General, Sgt and Private Pinkley in
the Army Surplus Special (6), gangster Clyde and The
Ant Hill Mob in the Bulletproof Bomb (7), Luke and
Blubber Bear in the Arkansas Chugabug (8), the all-
American Peter Perfect in his Turbo Terrific (9), and
Rufus Ruffcut and Sawtooth in the Buzz Wagon (10).
Villain of the piece was the appropriately named Dick
Dastardly in the Mean Machine (00), whose sole aim
was to win at all costs, especially if it meant cheating.
Thankfully, usually through the ineptitude of his snig-
gering dog sidekick, Muttley, Dastardly's attempts to
impede his rivals always backfired.

The series, one of the most popular cartoons to come
out of the prolific Hanna-Barbera studio, gave birth to
two spin-offs, *The Perils of Penelope Pitstop* and *Dastardly
and Muttley in their Flying Machines*, a clone of *Those
Magnificent Men in their Flying Machines*, in which they
tried to 'Stop the pigeon', but never did. 'Drat and triple
drat,' Dastardly exclaimed.

WAGNER, LINDSAY
(1949–)

TV's BIONIC WOMAN (Jaime Sommers), Lindsay Wagner's road to fame began with modelling and rock singing in the 1960s. Turning to acting, she appeared in shows like THE ROCKFORD FILES and MARCUS WELBY, MD, but her break came with an episode of THE SIX MILLION DOLLAR MAN, in which she played his girlfriend. Despite the fact that she died in the episode, the producers liked her so much they spun her off into her own bionic series. Her later work has involved a US prime-time police drama, *Jessie*, plus plenty of TV movies and mini-series.

WAGNER, ROBERT
(1930–)

American actor who first came to light in the cinema in the 1950s. A decade later, movie work not proving so fruitful, Wagner moved into television, starring in the adventure series, IT TAKES A THIEF, playing Alexander Mundy. He crossed the Atlantic to take the part of Flt Lt. Phil Carrington in COLDITZ but then returned to Hollywood to star in *Switch*. In 1979 he began possibly his most successful role, that of millionaire adventurer Jonathan Hart in HART TO HART. His most notable series since has been the drama series, *Lime Street* (1985), which ran to only five episodes as a result of the death of one of his co-stars, Samantha Smith (the schoolgirl who had gained global fame by writing to Soviet leader Yuri Andropov to ask for peace). In recent times, Wagner has largely been seen in TV movies and glossy dramas. His wife – on two occasions – was the late Natalie Wood.

WAGON TRAIN
US (Revue/Universal) Western. ITV 1958–62/ BBC 1962–3

Major Seth Adams	**Ward Bond**
Flint McCullough	**Robert Horton**
Charlie Wooster	**Frank McGrath**
Bill Hawks	**Terry Wilson**
Christopher Hale	**John McIntire**
Duke Shannon	**Scott Miller**
Cooper Smith	**Robert Fuller**
Barnaby West	**Michael Burns**

Producer: **Howard Christie**

The adventures of a wagon train as it crosses the West in the 1880s.

This wagon train, although studio-bound in reality, supposedly ran from St Joseph ('St Joe') in Missouri to California, echoing the hazardous journey across the plains and the Rocky Mountains endured by many 19th-century settlers. The train's leader was middle-aged father figure, Major Seth Adams, replaced by Chris Hale when actor Ward Bond died in 1960. Ensuring that Indians did not impede progress was frontier scout Flint McCullough, later replaced by Duke Shannon and Cooper Smith. Other regulars were lead wagon driver Bill Hawks and cook Charlie Wooster. A 13-year-old orphan, Barnaby West, found wandering the trail alone, also joined the train.

In many ways, the regular cast merely provided the backdrop. For while they sometimes had their own tale to tell, most of the action was introduced by travellers who came and went, briefly joining the train and then heading off again.They brought with them hopes, experiences, but usually trouble, ensuring a different story every week. Many episodes were simply known as *The . . . Story*, with the name of the guest character filling the gap. John Wayne, James Coburn, Ernest Borgnine, Shelley Winters, Jane Wyman, Lee Van Cleef, Lou Costello, Bette Davis, Mickey Rooney and Ronald Reagan were all among the big names taking on these roles. *Wagon Train* also tried its hand at the classics, with a couple of episodes devoted to what were effectively revamps of *Great Expectations* and *Pride and Prejudice*. The series was based on the 1950 John Ford movie, *Wagonmaster*, in which Ward Bond had appeared, although not in the same role.

Wagon Train was one of those oddity programmes which switched channels in the UK (from ITV to BBC) during its first showing. Most episodes were an hour long, but some feature-length films were also made. Actor Robert Horton left the show in 1962, allegedly fed up with Westerns. However, his next starring role came in another oater, A MAN CALLED SHENANDOAH, and co-star John McIntire also held on to his spurs, moving on next to THE VIRGINIAN.

WAITING FOR GOD
UK (BBC) Situation Comedy. BBC 1 1990–4

Diana Trent	**Stephanie Cole**
Tom Ballard	**Graham Crowden**
Harvey Bains	**Daniel Hill**
Jane Edwards	**Janine Duvitski**
Geoffrey Ballard	**Andrew Tourell**
Marion Ballard	**Sandy Payne**
Jenny	**Dawn Hope**
Basil Makepeace	**Michael Bilton**
Davey	**Ross Thompson**
Jamie Edwards	**Paddy Ward**
Revd Dennis Sparrow	**Tim Preece**

Creator/Writer: **Michael Aitkens**
Producer: **Gareth Gwenlan**

Two stroppy inmates keep the staff of an old folks' home on their toes.

Tom Ballard and Diana Trent were neighbours at the Bayview Retirement Home in Bournemouth. Tom, a former accountant, had been dumped in the home by his thoughtless son, Geoffrey, and grasping daughter-in-law, Marion, in the series' first episode, but remained philosophical about it all. His natural cheer, his eccentric sense of humour and his flair for adventure remained undiminished. He paired up, to form a formidable, subversive geriatric duo, with the next-door resident, retired photo-journalist Diana Trent, for whom 'trout' would have been a more appropriate surname. Domineering and dismissive, the acid-tongued Diana had largely given up on enjoyment before Tom arrived, but now they led the home's cynical manager, Harvey Bains, and his fawning, drippy assistant, Jane Edwards, a merry dance. They scuppered all Harvey's cost-cutting measures with threats of bad publicity and goaded their fellow residents into demanding more from life. When finances became tight, Diana was forced to move in with Tom, but she fought tooth and nail against marriage. Also seen were Jenny, the good-natured waitress, OAP colleagues like Basil, Davey and Jamie, and, later, spaced-out vicar Dennis Sparrow.

WALDEN, BRIAN
(1932–)

Brian Walden took over as host of the political programme, WEEKEND WORLD, in 1977 and gained a reputation as a relentless interviewer. He eventually relinquished the hot seat to Matthew Parris nine years later but, when the programme ended in 1988, he returned to interrogate parliamentarians in *The Walden Interview* (later retitled simply *Walden*). In the 1990s, he presented two series of unscripted, one-take lectures, *Walden on Heroes* and *Walden on Villains*. Prior to TV, he had been Labour MP for Birmingham All Saints and Birmingham Ladywood (1964–77). He is the father of actor Ben Walden.

WALES WEST AND NORTH
(WWN)

The short-lived ITV contractor for West and North Wales (TWW held South Wales) which came on air on 14 September 1962 but went out of business, because of low advertising revenue, on 26 January 1964. To date, WWN has been the only ITV franchise-holder to go broke. Appreciating that the transmission area was too small to support an independent station, the ITA amalgamated it into the South Wales and West of England ITV region, allowing TWW to expand its coverage across the whole of the Principality.

WALKER, CLINT
(Norman Eugene Walker; 1927–)

Massive American actor who became an overnight success in 1955 when cast as the mysterious wanderer, CHEYENNE. Contractual wrangles led to his walking out for a while (Ty Hardin was introduced as Bronco Layne to fill the gap in production), but Walker eventually returned to the series. When his contract ended in 1962, he spent most of his time away from showbusiness, making just a handful of cameo appearances. He made a comeback in the 1970s, but without much success. His TV movies were not particularly well received and a new prime-time drama, *Kodiak*, didn't make the grade.

WALKER, MURRAY
OBE (1923–)

Veteran motor-racing commentator, for both BBC and ITV. The son of racer/commentator Graham Walker, he followed his father into broadcasting in 1949 and they worked together for 13 years. Like David Coleman, Walker is famous for his much-loved, over-excited commentaries and clangers such as 'Do my eyes deceive me or is Senna's Lotus sounding a bit rough', 'The boot is on the other Schumacher' and 'You can cut the tension with a cricket stump'.

WALKER, ROY
(1940–)

Northern Irish entertainer, first seen on NEW FACES in 1977 and then as one of THE COMEDIANS, before hosting the guessing game, CATCHPHRASE. He has also had his own series, *Licensed for Singing and Dancing*, and compered *Summertime Special*. His son Mark is also a TV presenter.

WALL, MAX
(Maxwell Lorimer; 1908–90)

British comedian, famed for his silly walks, pained expressions and ridiculous black tights and big boots. After years on the stage and in radio, Wall was given his own television show in the 1950s and continued to make guest appearances on variety shows in the following decades. He played Tommy Tonsley in the 1978 sitcom, *Born and Bred*, and also made cameo appearances in CORONATION STREET (Harry Payne, a friend of Elsie Tanner), EMMERDALE FARM (Arthur Braithwaite), CROSSROADS (Walter Soper, a cousin of Arthur Brownlow), MINDER (Ernie Dodds, a jailbird) and the kids' series, *Danger – Marmalade at Work* (a judge).

WALTER, HARRIET
CBE (1950–)

British Shakespearean actress seen in such series as *A Dorothy L. Sayers Mystery* (Harriet Vane) and the Channel 4 kidnap thriller, *The Price*, plus the play, *Amy*, in which she starred as aviator Amy Johnson. More prominently, Walter played Charity Walton in the steamy academic serial, THE MEN'S ROOM, Amy in the sitcom, *Unfinished Business*, Mildred in the drama, *A Dance to the Music of Time*, and Felicity Normal in the spoof, *Norman Ormal: a Very Political Turtle*, among many other parts.

WALTERS, JULIE
OBE (1950–)

Acclaimed British actress, known for her versatility. She appeared with Victoria Wood in the Granada series, *Wood and Walters*, and the two have worked together many times, in plays like *Talent*, the series, *Victoria Wood – As Seen on TV* (charlady Mrs Overall in the CROSSROADS spoof, *Acorn Antiques*) and *Victoria Wood*, and TV films like *Pat and Margaret*. Walters appeared in BOYS FROM THE BLACKSTUFF, played Pauline Mole (Adrian's young mum) in THE SECRET DIARY OF ADRIAN MOLE and Mrs Murray (Robert Lindsay's pensioner mum) in GBH. She also delivered some of Alan Bennett's TALKING HEADS monologues, starred in her own special, *Julie Walters and Friends*, and took the parts of Diana Longden and Alice in *Screen One*'s *Wide-Eyed and Legless* and *Bambino Mio*, respectively; publican Maureen Hardcastle in the feature-length comedy, *Brazen Hussies*; Julie Diadoni in *Jake's Progress*; Paula in *Melissa*; Petula, Bren's mother, in DINNERLADIES; Mrs Mann in *Oliver Twist*; and both the girl and her grandmother in *Roald Dahl's Little Red Riding Hood*.

WALTON, KENT
(1925–)

Canadian sports commentator, for years ITV's voice of wrestling on Saturday afternoons. In the late 1950s, however, Walton worked in a quite different field, that of pop music, as host of the teenage music show, COOL FOR CATS, and DJ with Radio Luxembourg.

WALTONS, THE
US (Lorimar) Drama. BBC 2 1974–82

John Walton	**Ralph Waite**
Olivia Walton	**Michael Learned**
Zeb (Grandpa) Walton	**Will Geer**
Esther (Grandma) Walton	**Ellen Corby**
John Boy Walton	**Richard Thomas**
	Robert Wightman
Mary Ellen Walton/Willard	**Judy Norton-Taylor**
Jason Walton	**Jon Walmsley**
Erin Walton	**Mary Elizabeth McDonough**
James Robert 'Jim-Bob' Walton	**David W. Harper**
Ben Walton	**Eric Scott**
Elizabeth Walton	**Kami Cotler**
Ike Godsey	**Joe Conley**
Corabeth Godsey	**Ronnie Claire Edwards**
Aimee Godsey	**Rachel Longaker**
Sheriff Ep Bridges	**John Crawford**
Mamie Baldwin	**Helen Kleeb**
Emily Baldwin	**Mary Jackson**
Verdie Foster	**Lynn Hamilton**
Revd Matthew Fordwick	**John Ritter**
Emily Hunter/Fordwick	**Mariclare Costello**
Yancy Tucker	**Robert Donner**
Flossie Brimmer	**Nora Marlowe**
Maude Gormsley	**Merie Earle**
Dr Curtis Willard	**Tom Bower**
Revd Hank Buchanan	**Peter Fox**
J. D. Pickett	**Lewis Arquette**
John Curtis Willard	**Marshall and Michael Reed**
Rose Burton	**Peggy Rea**
Serena Burton	**Martha Nix**
Jeffrey Burton	**Keith Mitchell**
Cindy Brunson/Walton	**Leslie Winston**
Toni Hazleton	**Lisa Harrison**
Arlington Wescott Jones ('Jonesy')	**Richard Gilliland**
Narrator	**Earl Hamner Jr**

Executive Producers: **Lee Rich, Earl Hamner Jr**

Sentimental tales of a Virginian family during the Depression and World War II.

The Walton family lived in the town of Walton's Mountain, in the Blue Ridge Mountains of Jefferson County, Virginia. Mom and Dad were Olivia and John, she a caring, devoted mother, he a solid father figure and part-owner of the family's sawmill, with Grandpa Walton.

The Waltons had seven children, plus a dog named Reckless. The eldest was John Boy, a fresh-faced youth with writing ambitions. He majored in English at Boatwright University, started a local newspaper, *The Blue Ridge Chronicle*, had a novel published which took him to New York, then worked as a war correspondent during the hostilities. The next in line was Mary Ellen, who became a nurse, married Dr Curtis Willard, gave birth to little John Curtis and then saw her husband die at Pearl Harbor (or so it was thought). When he resurfaced in Florida, he decided not to return to Virginia, leaving Mary Ellen with the new man in her life, fellow pre-med student Jonesy. The Waltons' other sons were Jim-Bob, Jason and Ben, and the two youngest daughters were Elizabeth and Erin. They didn't play such prominent roles but were always on hand to help out during family crises, of which there were plenty.

Grandma was taken ill, then Grandpa died (actor Will Geer passed away between seasons). Olivia suffered an attack of tuberculosis and was sent away to recuperate in a sanitarium, with her place as housekeeper given to her cousin, Rose. Then the war arrived and saw the boys taken off with the armed forces, leaving the sawmill short-staffed and forced into temporary closure. Meanwhile the other townsfolk also had their ups and downs. Most prominent were storekeeper Ike Godsey and his prim wife, Corabeth, the vicar, Reverend Fordwick, who married schoolteacher Emily Hunter, and two fading spinster sisters, Mamie and Emily Baldwin.

The Waltons shunned sex and violence for human tragedy and family drama. It showed the children growing up and getting married, followed domestic upheaval after domestic upheaval and portrayed a good-natured family struggling to survive in one of America's poorest areas at a time of great deprivation. All stories were told through the moist eyes of John Boy.

The series was created by Earl Hamner Jr, who also acted as narrator. The stories were based on his own life, which had first been dramatized in a 1963 Henry Fonda film, *Spencer's Mountain*. *The Waltons* (which began as a

TV movie called *The Homecoming*) was so squeaky-clean and wholesome that it attracted much parody, particularly for its closing sequence when the family, tucked up in bed, all called 'Goodnight' to each other as the household lights were dimmed one by one. After the series ended, three TV movie specials were produced to update events in Walton's Mountain.

WANAMAKER, ZOE
CBE (1949–)

American-born actress, the daughter of US actor/director Sam Wanamaker. She has been seen in EDGE OF DARKNESS (Clemmy), INSPECTOR MORSE, *Paradise Postponed*, PRIME SUSPECT, *Screen Two*'s *Memento Mori* (Olive Mannering), *The Blackheath Poisonings* (Charlotte Collard), the *Performance* presentation of *The Widowing of Mrs Holroyd* (title character), *The English Wife* (Madame Griveau), *A Dance to the Music of Time* (Audrey Maclintick), *David Copperfield* (Miss Murdstone), *Gormenghast* (Clarice) and other dramas, plus the sitcom, *My Family* (Susan). However, it was as Tessa Piggott alongside Adam Faith in LOVE HURTS that she became widely known. She is married to actor Gawn Grainger.

WAR GAME, THE
UK (BBC) Drama. BBC 1 1985

Writer/Producer: **Peter Watkins**

Graphic portrayal of nuclear destruction.

One of the BBC's most controversial projects, *The War Game* depicted in harrowing images the aftermath of an imaginary nuclear attack on the UK. Initially showing civilians preparing for the onslaught, the 50-minute film then revealed in stark black-and-white footage the horrors of the resulting chaos.

The War Game was made in drama-documentary style as a film for MONITOR in 1965 and producer Peter Watkins employed mostly non-professional actors to add to the realism. However, the overall effect was so startling and distressing that Director-General Sir Hugh Greene banned its transmission, fearing it would alarm or confuse the old and fretful in society. Although it was released for cinema showings, it was not televised until 20 years later, when it was screened as part of the BBC's 40th-anniversary commemoration of the bombing of Hiroshima.

WAR IN THE AIR
UK (BBC) Documentary. BBC 1954–5

Narrator: **Robert Harris**

Writer/Producer: **John Elliot**

Analysis of the role of aircraft in combat.

With Sir Philip Joubert as series adviser, *War in the Air* was a 15-part retrospective on the role played by air power before, during and immediately after World War

II. The half-hour programmes were made in collaboration with the Air Ministry. Sir Arthur Bliss composed the theme music, which was performed by the London Symphony Orchestra under Muir Mathieson.

WARING, EDDIE
MBE (1910–86)

For many years Eddie Waring was the voice of rugby league on the BBC, and his excitable commentaries were as much a part of the entertainment as the match itself. His northern accent, novel approach and well-oiled catchphrases like 'early bath' and 'up and under' readily exposed him to the impressionists of the day. Waring gave his first TV commentary in 1946, having previously managed both Dewsbury and Leeds rugby league clubs. Additionally, he was one of the presenters of IT'S A KNOCKOUT and *Jeux Sans Frontières* (usually taking charge of the Mini-Marathon). Always game for a laugh, Eddie was also seen as a guest in THE GOODIES and *The Morecambe and Wise Show*. At one time, in complete contrast, he hosted SONGS OF PRAISE. He retired in 1981.

WARING, RICHARD
(1925–94)

British comedy writer majoring on domestic sitcoms. Among his contributions were LIFE WITH THE LYONS, *On the Bright Side*, *The Eggheads*, MARRIAGE LINES, *The World of Wooster*, NOT IN FRONT OF THE CHILDREN, *Ukridge*, BACHELOR FATHER, AND MOTHER MAKES THREE/FIVE, MY WIFE NEXT DOOR, *Second Time Around*, *The Many Wives of Patrick*, *My Honourable Mrs*, MISS JONES AND SON, RINGS ON THEIR FINGERS, *Partners* and *Tears Before Bedtime*. Waring provided some early scripts for Richard Hearne, Charlie Drake and Tommy Cooper, wrote episodes of DIXON OF DOCK GREEN and was also seen as an actor. He played Henry Blagrove alongside Richard Briers in the 1962 comedy, BROTHERS IN LAW (some episodes as writer as well), and was seen in SIX FACES OF JIM. He was the brother of actor Derek Waring.

WARK, KIRSTY
(1955–)

Kilmarnock-born journalist and current affairs presenter, a regular anchor of NEWSNIGHT and also host of *The Late Show*, *One Foot in the Past* and *Rough Justice*, as well as a political show for Scotland. She runs her own production company, Wark Clements, with her husband, Alan Clements.

WARNER, JACK
OBE (Horace John Waters; 1895–1981)

As the totally reliable copper, George Dixon, in DIXON OF DOCK GREEN, Jack Warner became a national institution. Born in London's East End, Warner, the brother of radio and stage entertainers Elsie and Doris Waters (otherwise known as Gert and Daisy), followed his sisters into showbusiness. He won fame on radio, 'Mind my bike' becoming his catchphrase in *Garrison Theatre* during the war, and he also played Joe Huggett, head of the Huggett family, in a series of films and radio programmes. In 1949 Warner played PC Dixon in the film, *The Blue Lamp*, and was shockingly shot dead. However, the character struck a chord with cinema audiences, and prolific writer Ted Willis was encouraged by the BBC to furnish Dixon with his own TV series. *Dixon of Dock Green* started in 1955 and ran for 21 years. Apart from occasional variety appearances, and the linkman's job on the BBC's *Christmas Night with the Stars* package, it was Warner's only major TV role. He was 80 when it ended.

WARSHIP
UK (BBC) Drama. BBC 1 1973–7

Commander Nialls .... **Donald Burton**
Lt. Commander Beaumont .... **David Savile**
Lt. Commander Kiley .... **John Lee**
Lt. Last .... **Norman Eshley**
Lt. Parry .... **Richard Warwick**
MAA Heron .... **Don Henderson**
Leading Regulator Fuller .... **James Cosmo**
Commander 'Murky' Murton .... **Malcolm Terris**
Lt. Boswall .... **Christopher Coll**
Lt. Commander Junnion .... **Rex Robinson**
Lt. Wakelin .... **Graeme Eton**
Lt. Palfrey .... **Michael Cochrane**
LMA Milner .... **Colin Rix**
Lt. Peek .... **Andrew Burt**
Commander Glenn .... **Bryan Marshall**
Lt. Tagg .... **James Leith**
MAA Burnett .... **Frank Jarvis**
Capt. Edward Holt .... **Derek Godfrey**
Lt. Commander James Napier .... **Robert Morris**
L/Seaman Anderson .... **Nigel Humphries**
Zoe Carter .... **Prunella Ransome**

Creators: **Ian MacKintosh, Anthony Coburn**
Producers: **Anthony Coburn, Joe Waters**

Drama on the high seas with a Royal Navy frigate.

Routine and not-so-routine manoeuvres gave rise to the action in this durable military soap opera. Amid much naval banter and a plethora of stiff upper lips, the crew of HMS *Hero*, a Royal Navy frigate (number F42), stuck loyally to its chores in places as far apart as the Mediterranean and the Far East, which involved anything from NATO exercises to Cold War face-offs, policing fishing wars or picking up defecting spies. Most of the attention focused on the commissioned ranks. In the last series, journalist Zoe Carter was also featured. The BBC worked closely with the Navy on the series and the military collaboration even extended to the supply of a real warship for filming.

WASHINGTON: BEHIND CLOSED DOORS
US (Paramount) Drama. BBC 1 1977–8

President Richard Monckton .... **Jason Robards**
William Martin .... **Cliff Robertson**
Linda Martin .... **Lois Nettleton**
Sally Whalen .... **Stefanie Powers**
Frank Flaherty .... **Robert Vaughn**
Esker Anderson .... **Andy Griffith**
Bob Bailey .... **Barry Nelson**
Myron Dunn .... **John Houseman**
Carl Tessler .... **Harold Gould**
Adam Gardiner .... **Tony Bill**
Hank Ferris .... **Nicholas Pryor**
Lars Haglund .... **Skip Homeier**

Creator: **David W. Rintels**
Executive Producer: **Stan Kallis**
Producer: **Norman Powell**

Fictional tale of intrigue in 1970s American politics.

Based on the novel, *The Company*, by John Ehrlichman, a former aide to President Nixon, this six-part mini-series was essentially Watergate with the names changed. It didn't take viewers long to realize that President Richard Monckton was meant to be Nixon, or that his predecessor, Esker Anderson, was Lyndon Johnson. Robert Vaughn played Monckton's devious right-hand man, Frank Flaherty, as the White House manoeuvred to avoid being implicated in a political scandal.

WATCH WITH MOTHER
UK (BBC) Children's Entertainment. BBC 1953–80

Programmes for pre-school-age children.

Watch with Mother was an umbrella title for various offerings from the BBC's children's department. In the immediate post-war years, its predecessor had been FOR THE CHILDREN (with MUFFIN THE MULE, *et al.*), but in 1953 the title was changed to complement the radio series, *Listen with Mother*, and new component programmes were introduced. Originally, *Watch with Mother* aired at around 3.45 in the afternoon, Tuesday–Thursday, as part of the *Children's Television* sequence, but more familiar is the 1.30 p.m. slot it occupied for most of its 27 years on air.

Running from Monday to Friday, the classic *Watch with Mother* line-up consisted of PICTURE BOOK on Mondays, ANDY PANDY on Tuesdays, FLOWER POT MEN on Wednesdays, RAG TAG AND BOBTAIL on Thursdays and THE WOODENTOPS on Fridays. Later additions in the 1960s were TALES OF THE RIVERBANK, CAMBERWICK GREEN, POGLES' WOOD, *Joe* (1966–7; 1971), TRUMPTON, THE HERBS, *Bizzy Lizzy* (1967; first seen in PICTURE BOOK), CHIGLEY and *Mary, Mungo and Midge* (1969). Other favourites in the 1970s were MR BENN, BAGPUSS, *Fingerbobs* (1972), *Barnaby* (1973) and *The Mister Men* (1974–6). In 1980, the formula was maintained but, with occupational and viewing habits changing, the name *Watch with Mother* was discarded in favour of the less politically troublesome *See-Saw*.

WATCHDOG
UK (BBC) Consumer Affairs. BBC 1 1985–

Presenters: **Nick Ross, Lynn Faulds Wood, John Stapleton, Anne Robinson, Alice Beer, Charlotte Hudson**
Editors: **Lino Ferrari, Nick Hayes, Sarah Caplin, Steve Anderson, Helen O'Rahilly, Mark Killick**

Effective consumer-affairs programme.

Launched as a programme in its own right, having been a segment of the defunct NATIONWIDE and its equally defunct successor, *Sixty Minutes*, *Watchdog* was initially presented by Nick Ross with Lynn Faulds Wood. Faulds Wood was later joined as co-host by her husband, John Stapleton. Anne Robinson took over in 1993, assisted by Alice Beer, with, among other reporters in subsequent years, Chris Choi, Simon Walton, Johnathan Maitland, Denise Mahoney, Andy Webb, Liz Kershaw, John Nicolson, Beaky Evetts, Matt Allwright, Adrian Goldberg and David Bull. Nicky Campbell was inked in to replace Robinson in 2001. The aim of the series has been to expose con-men, lift the lid on shoddy workmanship and give the real facts about consumer goods. Viewers have been invited to write and ring in with their personal experiences.

In 1995, Judith Hann and Alice Beer presented *Watchdog Healthcheck*, which focused on medical matters, and other spin-offs have been *Watchdog: Face Value* (cosmetics consumerism), *Watchdog: Value for Money* (high street rip-offs), *Watchdog: the Big Dinner* (food and catering investigations), *Watchdog on the House* (DIY cons) and *Weekend Watchdog* (leisure industry concerns).

WATCHING
UK (Granada) Situation Comedy. ITV 1987–93

Malcolm Stoneway	**Paul Bown**
Brenda Wilson	**Emma Wray**
Mrs Marjorie Stoneway	**Patsy Byrne**
Mrs Joyce Wilson	**Noreen Kershaw**
Pamela Wilson/Lynch	**Liza Tarbuck**
Terry Milton	**Perry Fenwick**
David Lynch	**John Bowler**
Lucinda Stoneway	**Elizabeth Morton**
Harold	**Al T. Kossy**
Cedric	**Bill Moores**
Gerald Wilson	**Andrew Hilton**
Jonathan Macmillan	**Richard Good**

Creator/Writer: **Jim Hitchmough**
Executive Producer: **David Liddiment**
Producers: **David Liddiment, Les Chatfield**

A couple struggle to keep their relationship on the rails.

Set in Merseyside, *Watching* took its name from the bird-watching hobby enjoyed by its dithering lead couple, men's outfitter Malcolm Stoneway and his sarcastic girlfriend, Brenda Wilson. Brenda lived in Liverpool with her sister, Pamela, and frequented the local boozer, The Grapes, where they 'watched' the male talent and pondered their single lifestyle. Malcolm – proud owner of a 1939 Norton 500 motorcycle and 1936 sidecar – lived across the Mersey, in the affluent district of Meols on the Wirral, with his mother.

As the series progressed, Malcolm opened his own motorcycle repair shop, Brenda went to work as a barmaid at The Grapes for dopey landlord Harold, and Pamela married social climber David Lynch and gave birth to two daughters (Sarah and Zelda). Also introduced was Brenda's potty mum and her naval-minded, child-genius brother, who lived, regrettably for Malcolm's snooty mum, in deprived Toxteth. Unfortunately, Malcolm and Brenda's relationship was seldom stable and there was much to-ing and fro-ing across the Mersey to their respective mothers' homes as one tiff led to another. When this happened, they spent more time watching each other than watching birds.

During one period of 'divorce', Malcolm married Lucinda, a nurse from the Royal Hospital, but the marriage broke down (she became pregnant by doctor Jonathan Macmillan) and he and Brenda were soon watching each other again. The Mersey-crossed lovers eventually married in the final episode. The programme's theme song, 'What Does He See in Me?', by Charles Hart, was sung by star Emma Wray.

WATER MARGIN, THE
Japan (NTV) Drama. BBC 2 1976–8

Lin Chung	**Atsuo Nakamura**
Kao Chia	**Kei Sato**
Wu Sung	**Hajine Hana**
Hu San-niang	**Sanae Tschida**
Hsiao Lan	**Yoshiyo Matuso**

Writer: **David Weir**

Flailing swords and mystic magic in medieval China.

Adapted by David Weir from translations of the original Japanese script, *The Water Margin* told of 108 chivalrous knights aroused from their graves to combat tyranny and corruption in the Orient, from their base in the water margins of Lian Shan Po. The hero was Lin Chung, with Hsiao his wife. This Japanese treatment of the 14th-century Chinese classic by Lo Kuan-Chung proved surprisingly popular. Among those voicing the English version were Bert Kwouk and Miriam Margolyes. In 1979 Weir adapted another Japanese/Chinese serial, Wu Ch'eng-en's *Monkey*, which starred Masaaki Sakai as a Buddhist pilgrim.

WATERHOUSE, KEITH
CBE (1929–)

British newspaper journalist, novelist and TV script-writer. His series have generally involved humour or light drama and most have been in conjunction with Willis Hall (see Hall's entry for their joint credits). Alone, Waterhouse has also written *West End Tales*, *Andy Capp*, *The Happy Apple*, CHARTERS AND CALDICOTT, *The Upchat Line*, *The Upchat Connection* and the TV film, *Charlie Muffin*.

WATERMAN, DENNIS
(1948–)

British leading man, a one-time schoolboy actor, on TV since the late 1950s. In the 1970s he became familiar as tough nut George Carter in THE SWEENEY, but he has also taken on lighter roles, such as MINDER's Terry McCann, millionaire East Ender Tony Carpenter in the sitcom, ON THE UP, and wide-boy Thomas Gynn in STAY LUCKY. Waterman's TV career began with plays like *Member of the Wedding* (1959) and *All Summer Long* (1960), and the title role in *William* (an early JUST WILLIAM) in 1962. He appeared as Judy Carne's brother, Neville Finch, in the transatlantic sitcom, *Fair Exchange*, the same year and subsequently guested in series like JOURNEY TO THE UNKNOWN and MAN ABOUT THE HOUSE. He played King Harold in *Churchill's People* and was seen in Alan Plater's *Première* film, *Give Us a Kiss, Christabel*. Waterman was instrumental in bringing the story of the victory of a Durham miners' football team in the first ever 'World Cup' to our screens in the drama *The World Cup – A Captain's Tale* (as co-producer and star) in 1982 (his love of football was manifested again later when he presented the series, *Match of the Seventies*). He was seen as Bobbo in THE LIFE AND LOVES OF A SHE DEVIL, SAS man John Neil in *Circles of Deceit* and villain John Danson in *The Knock*. His third wife was actress Rula Lenska and he is the father of actress Hannah Waterman.

WATKINS, PETER
(1936–)

Pioneering British film-maker who employed documentary newsreel techniques and non-professional actors in his dramatic reconstructions. His *Culloden* in 1964 surprised viewers with its graphic depiction of the last battle to be fought on British soil, but more controversy followed THE WAR GAME, a year later. This account of the aftermath of a nuclear attack was, in fact, banned from transmission by the then BBC Director-General, Sir Hugh Greene. It was eventually shown in 1985 as part of a season of programmes marking the 40th anniversary of the dropping of the atomic bomb on Hiroshima. Watkins later worked in Scandinavia, his Edvard Munch biopic being screened in the UK in 1976.

WATLING, JACK
(1923–)

British actor familiar in the 1960s as Don Henderson in THE PLANE MAKERS and THE POWER GAME. He also guested in DOCTOR WHO, NO HIDING PLACE, DIXON OF DOCK GREEN, HANCOCK'S HALF HOUR, BOYD QC and other series, and was a late arrival in THE NEWCOMERS (Hugh Robertson). Watling, the father of actress Deborah Watling, and the step-father of actress Dilys Watling, continued to work in television throughout the 1970s and 1980s. In 1972 he played Doc Saxon in the wartime RAF series, *The Pathfinders*. In 1977 he appeared in *Lord Tramp* and in 1981 starred as Dr Carmichael in the sitcom, *Doctor's Daughters*. Later, he was occasionally seen in HOT METAL and as Frank Blakemore in BERGERAC.

WAX, RUBY
(Ruby Wachs; 1953–)

Chicago-born comedienne, actress and interviewer, the loud, intrusive host of *Don't Miss Wax*, *Wax on Wheels*, *Hit and Run*, *The Full Wax*, *Ruby's Health Quest*, *Ruby Does the Season*, *Ruby Wax Meets . . .*, *Ruby* and *Ruby's American Pie*. Among her earliest work in the UK were sketches for NOT THE NINE O'CLOCK NEWS and the satire, *For 4 Tonight*. In 1985 she co-wrote and co-starred in GIRLS ON TOP (Shelley) and went on to be script editor for ABSOLUTELY FABULOUS and write the Joan Collins one-off comedy, *Mama's Back*. Wax has also guested in THE COMIC STRIP PRESENTS. She is married to producer/director Ed Bye.

WE ARE THE CHAMPIONS
UK (BBC) Children's Game Show. BBC 1 1973–87

Presenter: **Ron Pickering**

Producer: **Peter Charlton**

Long-running, inter-school sports contest.

The BBC's Mr Athletics, Ron Pickering, hosted this durable series which pitched school versus school (by region) in a sequence of physical contests and races. Competition was played down in favour of taking part and kids didn't need to be superb athletes to be involved. Games, held both on the field and in the pool, were often based around mini-assault courses. Star guests like Gary Sobers, Sebastian Coe, David Wilkie, Sharron Davies and Ian Rush egged on the youngsters. A special edition for children with disabilities was aired in 1987. The series ended the same year, but a number of one-off 'specials' were shown in the 1990s.

WE'LL MEET AGAIN
UK (LWT) Drama. ITV 1982

Dr Helen Dereham .... **Susannah York**

Major Ronald Dereham .... **Ronald Hines**
Patricia Dereham .... **Lise-Ann McLaughlin**
Major Jim Kiley .... **Michael J. Shannon**
Albert Mundy .... **Ray Smith**
Vera Mundy .... **June Barry**
Letty Mundy .... **Natalie Ogle**
Peter Mundy .... **Patrick Pearson**
Jack Blair .... **Patrick O'Connell**
Rosie Blair .... **Lynne Pearson**
Violet Blair .... **Kathryn Pogson**
Col. Rufus Krasnowici .... **Ed Devereaux**
M/Sgt Joe 'Mac' McGraw .... **Christopher Malcolm**
M/Sgt Chuck Ericson .... **Joris Stuyck**

Creator: **David Butler**
Writers: **David Butler, David Crane, John Gorrie**
Producer: **Tony Wharmby**

An Englishwoman falls for an American major during the wartime 'invasion' of Britain by the USA.

'Overpaid, oversexed and over here' was the familiar description applied to US military personnel stationed in the UK during World War II, and this 13-part drama set out to prove its validity. Based around the sleepy Suffolk market town of Market Wetherby, *We'll Meet Again* focused on the impact made on its residents by the arrival of 2,000 men from the US Eighth Air Force 525th Bomb Group in 1943. At the forefront of the action was hospital doctor Helen Dereham, wife of army man Ronald Dereham, who found herself drawn to the charms of suave Yank Jim Kiley, second-in-command at the US airbase. The Derehams' daughter, Patricia, was also present, having refused to return to her academic studies in Cambridge. Local resentment to the 'intruders' was fuelled by grouchy grocer and ARP warden, Albert Mundy, but there was more of a welcome at the pub, The Plough, run by Jack Blair and his two daughters, the flighty Rosie and the more sensible Violet. Chuck Ericson was the US NCO who saved Violet's life.

To keep within the show's modest budget, only one B-17 bomber was seen, with the rest of the action involving models or stock footage.

WEAKEST LINK, THE
UK (BBC) Quiz. BBC 2/BBC 1 2000–

Presenter: **Anne Robinson**

Producers: **Ruth Davis, Phil Parsons**

Winner-takes-all quiz in which the contestants themselves nominate the losers.

Designed as a late-afternoon offering on BBC 2, *The Weakest Link* quickly gained a cult following. Despite premiering only in August 2000, by October it had graduated to BBC 1 and a peak-hour evening slot. Anne Robinson hosted proceedings like a strict schoolmistress, chastising contestants for performing poorly and brutally sending a loser down the so-called 'Walk of Shame' at the end of each round ('You are The Weakest Link: Goodbye!').

Nine contestants began each programme, answering general knowledge questions in sequence over eight timed rounds, each question adding more money to the jackpot to be claimed by the eventual winner. Prize money jumped substantially for each consecutive correct answer, with a total of £1,000 available for stringing together nine correct answers in each round. Although contestants could 'bank' the money gained at any point, a wrong answer took the total for the run of questions back to zero. Money gained in the eighth round was trebled, making a potential daily jackpot of £10,000. When each round was completed, the contestants each nominated the person they felt to be 'The Weakest Link' and the person with the most votes (whether or not he or she was actually statistically the weakest in terms of correct answers or banked money) was evicted from the game. Their comments on being voted off were then recorded and edited in to the finished programme. In the final, the remaining two contestants were each asked five questions, with the higher scorer taking all the accumulated money. If scores were level after the five questions, 'sudden death' was employed, with the first wrong answer deciding the winner and loser.

The evening version, initially entitled *The Weakest Link: Champions' League*, introduced a studio audience, doubled the potential prize money to £20,000 and pitted previous winners against one another. Another evening show focused on 'Bad Losers', bringing back contestants who felt they were unjustly voted off during their previous afternoon performance. A celebrity edition was shown at Christmas 2000.

WEATHER

The world's first television weather forecast was broadcast by the BBC on 20 November 1936 at 4.01 p.m. and lasted six minutes. An anonymous hand sketched in the isobars on a weather chart, while an off-screen voice provided the forecast over a bed of light music – all somewhat different from today's world of computer graphics and personality weather-presenters. The first on-screen meteorology men appeared in Canada and the USA, quickly bringing a showbiz element to proceedings in an attempt to keep viewers switched on. In the UK no weather man was seen until 1954, when George Cowling gave the first in-view summary for the BBC on 11 January. Cowling, like his successors, was a Meteorological Office employee, not a BBC man. The first weather woman was Barbara Edwards, who made her bow in 1974. Among other notable weather folk (on the BBC) have been Bert Foord, Graham Parker, Jack Scott, Keith Best, Michael Fish, Ian McCaskill, Jim Bacon, John Kettley, Bernard Davey, Suzanne Charlton, Peter Cockroft, Rob McElwee, Penny Tranter, Richard Edgar, Helen Young, David Lee, Isobel Lang, David Braine, Philip Avery, Peter Gibbs, Sarah Wilmshurst, Darren Bett and Francis Wilson (who worked on BREAKFAST TIME forecasts). Bill Giles took over as head of the BBC's team in 1983, a move that coincided with the introduction of flashy computer imagery and a new emphasis on the personalities of the presenters. ITV began its own national weather forecasts in 1989, with Alex Hill, Siân

Lloyd, Trish Williamson, Martyn Davies, Laura Greene, Fiona Farrell, John Hammond and Clare Nasir the most prominent forecasters. BBC has also screened *The Weather Show* (1996–9), a lunchtime series of short programmes fronted by weather presenters, revealing how the weather affects people's lives. In the USA, The Weather Channel is a 24-hour cable service which reports on national and local conditions. In the 1990s, a sister channel for the UK proved very short-lived.

WEAVER, DENNIS
(1924–)

American actor who made his TV debut in the 1950s, in series like DRAGNET. Weaver went on to take the role of Matt Dillon's deputy, Chester Goode, in GUNSMOKE and stayed with the series for nine years. He left to star in his own vehicle, *Kentucky Jones*, but it failed to take and, instead, Weaver headed into children's adventures as family man Tom Wedloe in *Gentle Ben*. He then found himself another durable role when he was cast as McCLOUD, the backwaters sheriff who brought his southern ways to New York City. When it ended in 1977, Weaver was still in demand and he has since taken parts in a host of prime-time US series and dramas such as *Buck James*, which have not, however, transferred to the UK. He has also been seen in numerous TV movies.

WEBB, JACK
(1920–82)

One of American TV's golden greats, former radio announcer Jack Webb made his mark as the glamourless, 'just the facts' policeman Joe Friday in the long-running crime series, DRAGNET. It was, in effect, Jack Webb's show. It was he who created it for US radio in 1949, bringing a new realism into police series and using genuine police files as sources for his stories. Webb had previously played other cops on radio, but none with the down-to-earth character of Friday, and none with the same success. When it transferred to TV in 1952, Webb was also its producer. The series ran for seven years and was revived for another three years in 1967. He did very little acting otherwise, but his Mark VII production company did turn out a number of US series, including *The DA*, *Pete Kelly's Blues*, *Adam 12* and *Hec Ramsey*. He also produced the final season of 77 SUNSET STRIP and was in charge of Warner TV for a while. Webb was once married to actress-singer Julie London.

WEDNESDAY PLAY, THE
UK (BBC) Drama Anthology. BBC 1 1964–70

Adventurous and influential vehicle for 1960s dramatic talent.

Quickly gaining a reputation for breaking new ground in television drama, *The Wednesday Play* was a showcase for emerging playwrights. Taking its cue from ABC's ARMCHAIR THEATRE and the angry young men of the late 1950s, its gritty social commentaries also furnished it with a left-of-centre image. The first *Wednesday Play* was Nikolai Leskov's *A Crack in the Ice*, dramatized by Ronald Eyre, and among other notable offerings were Sartre's *In Camera*, adapted by Phillip Saville (1964), David Mercer's *And Did Those Feet?*, Dennis Potter's *Vote, Vote, Vote for Nigel Barton* and *Stand Up, Nigel Barton*, Nell Dunn's *Up the Junction* (all 1965) and Jim Allen's *The Lump* (1967). Probably the most controversial and important play was Jeremy Sandford's study of a homeless family in CATHY COME HOME (1966).

In addition to the writers listed, others like Peter Nichols, James Hanley, James O'Connor, Nigel Kneale and Michael Frayn also contributed memorable material, and production and direction was skilfully handled by the likes of Rudolph Cartier, Don Taylor, Tony Garnett, Ken Loach, Gilchrist Calder, Kenith Trodd, James MacTaggart, Waris Hussein, Jack Gold, Alan Bridges, Roger Smith, Irene Shubik and Charles Jarrott.

With a change of transmission day and the start of a new decade, *The Wednesday Play* eventually gave way to PLAY FOR TODAY.

WEEKEND WORLD
UK (LWT) Current Affairs. ITV 1972–88

Presenters: **Peter Jay, John Torode, Mary Holland, Brian Walden, Matthew Parris**

Producers: **John Birt, Barry Cox**

Influential Sunday lunchtime political programme.

Weekend World was the programme that introduced politics to Sunday lunchtimes. Launched as a means of filling the gap between news bulletins and current affairs series like THIS WEEK and WORLD IN ACTION, the series brought leading politicians and industrialists into the studio and quizzed them over the state of the nation, economic plans, foreign policies, etc. Major events in the week ahead were flagged up. John Torode and Mary Holland shared the presentation with Peter Jay in the early days, although Jay soon became sole frontman. When he left to take up an appointment as British Ambassador to the USA in 1977, he was replaced by former Labour MP, Brian Walden. Ex-Tory MP Matthew Parris was in charge for the final two years from 1986. The programme's powerful theme music was 'Nantucket Sleighride' by American rock band Mountain.

WEEKS, ALAN
(1923–96)

BBC sports commentator (from 1951), specializing in ice events in his latter years, but also heard over football matches, swimming, gymnastics and on other major occasions. He also fronted POT BLACK and GRANDSTAND. Prior to working in television (and sometimes during), Weeks publicized ice shows and the Brighton Tigers Ice Hockey Club.

WEINSTEIN, HANNAH
(Hannah Dorner; 1911–84)

American independent film-maker of the 1950s, formerly a *New York Herald Tribune* journalist and a publicist. Her interest in film began in the early 1950s and led to her joining forces with ATV to produce action series like THE ADVENTURES OF ROBIN HOOD, SWORD OF FREEDOM and THE BUCCANEERS. She also produced COLONEL MARCH OF SCOTLAND YARD and THE FOUR JUST MEN. Weinstein then returned to the USA, where she spoke out against racial discrimination in the film industry.

WELDON, FAY
CBE (1931–)

British novelist and playwright noted for her feminist stance and her portrayal of women who dare to break free from men's shadows. Among her TV offerings have been the plays, *The Fat Woman's Tale*, *A Catching Complaint* (both 1966), *Poor Cherry* (1967), *Splinter of Ice* (1972) and *Life for Christine* (1980). She also contributed episodes to THE DOCTORS, UPSTAIRS, DOWNSTAIRS (including the pilot) and the anthology series, *Menace*, and, in 1980, she adapted Jane Austen's *Pride and Prejudice*. Her novel, THE LIFE AND LOVES OF A SHE DEVIL, was dramatized to great acclaim by the BBC in 1986, and a year later *Heart of the Country* was also well received. In 1991 ITV produced her *The Cloning of Joanna May*, followed in 1992 by *Growing Rich* and in 1998 her series, *Big Women*, was shown on Channel 4. In an earlier job in advertising, she was credited with developing the slogan 'Go to work on an egg'.

WELLAND, COLIN
(Colin Williams; 1934–)

Liverpool-born actor and writer. In front of the camera his most familiar performances have been in Z CARS (PC David Graham), *Cowboys* (Geyser), Dennis Potter's *Blue Remembered Hills*, Screen Two's *Femme Fatale* (Harty), *The Fix* (Harry Catterick) and *Trial and Retribution* (Mallory). As a writer, he has contributed plays like *Bangelstein's Boys* (1969), *Slattery's Mounted Foot*, *Say Goodnight to Your Grandma*, *Roll On Four O'Clock* (all three 1970), *Kisses at Fifty*, *Jack Point* (both 1973), *Leeds – United!* (1974) and *Your Man from the Six Counties* (1976), plus the series *The Wild West Show* (1975). After winning an Oscar for *Chariots of Fire*, he eventually returned to television writing with the *Screen One* film, *Bambino Mio* (1994).

WELLS FARGO
US (Overland/Juggernaut/Universal) Western.
BBC 1957– 64

Jim Hardie	**Dale Robertson**
Beau McCloud	**Jack Ging**
Jeb Gaine	**William Demarest**
Ovie	**Virginia Christine**
Mary Gee	**Mary Jane Saunders**
Tina	**Lory Patrick**

Producers: **Earle Lyon, Nat Holt**

The adventures of a stagecoach company troubleshooter in the Gold Rush days.

In the 1860s Jim Hardie was a roaming agent for the passenger and shipping company of Wells Fargo, Incorporated, based in the Californian town of Gloribee. His duties extended from ironing out problems with employees to preventing the hijacking of coaches and the theft of the gold bullion they carried. The series, initially a half-hour in length, was expanded to full-hour episodes in 1961, when it switched production companies from Overland to Juggernaut. At the same time, Hardie settled down a little, bought the Haymaker Farm ranch on the outskirts of San Francisco and was given a cast of co-stars. These were his ranch supervisor, Jeb Gaine, his young assistant, Beau McCloud, and a widowed neighbour, Ovie (who fancied Jeb), plus her two daughters, Mary Gee and Tina. Despite these distractions, Hardie still fulfilled his duties for the company in exemplary fashion.

Properly titled *Tales of Wells Fargo*, the series was known only as *Wells Fargo* in the UK.

WEST, TIMOTHY
CBE (1934–)

British actor, often seen in distinguished, hard-nosed or blustery roles, with probably his best-remembered portrayal that of EDWARD THE SEVENTH. That apart, West has taken major parts in very many series and plays. They include BIG BREADWINNER HOG (Lennox), *Churchill and the Generals* (Winston Churchill), THE EDWARDIANS (Horatio Bottomley), THE MONOCLED MUTINEER (Brigadier General Thomson), A VERY PECULIAR PRACTICE (the aptly named Dr Furie), *Crime and Punishment* (Inspector Porfiry), BRASS (Bradley Hardacre), *The Good Dr Bodkin Adams* (Adams), *Masada* (Vespasian), *Framed* (DCI McKinnes), *Over Here* (Squadron Leader Archie Bunting) and *Cuts* (TV magnate Lord Mellow). Among other important credits have been HINE, *Cottage to Let*, *Hard Times*, THE BBC TELEVISION SHAKESPEARE's *Henry VIII* (and other TV classics), *Harry's Kingdom*, *Shadow on the Sun* and Screen One's *Blore MP*. He is married to actress Prunella Scales, with whom he once guested in AFTER HENRY, and is the father of actor Sam West.

WESTCOUNTRY

The ITV franchise-holder for the South-west of England, Westcountry first went on air on 1 January 1993, having outbid the existing service provider, TSW. A judicial review followed the ITC's move to award the contract to Westcountry, but the decision was upheld. From the start, Westcountry went for an entirely new approach to regional programming, bringing in the latest technology and a host of new faces. This initially alienated some viewers, but gradually audiences settled down. The company has since been taken over by Carlton Communications and the station has been renamed Carlton Westcountry. Its main studios are in Plymouth, but there are smaller studios across the region. There has been little contribution to the national network to date.

WESTWARD

Serving South-west England, Westward took to the air on 29 April 1961 and remained the ITV contractor for the region until 11 August 1981. The company became indelibly linked to its outspoken executive chairman, Peter Cadbury, who campaigned vehemently for the South-west ITV region to be enlarged up as far as Bristol (the part of the West Country controlled by TWW and, later, HTV West). Cadbury also found himself involved in internal disputes, and a major boardroom tussle in 1980 helped seal Westward's fate as the franchise re-appraisals loomed large. Even though programme standards were deemed to be good and there was local satisfaction with the service provided, the licence was awarded instead to TSW, which then purchased Westward's Plymouth studios. For many years, Westward was administratively joined to Channel Television, in an effort to maximize advertising potential for the two stations and keep down office costs. Westward produced few national programmes of note.

WHACK-O!
UK (BBC) Situation Comedy. BBC 1956–60; 1971–2

Prof. James Edwards	**Jimmy Edwards**
Mr Oliver Pettigrew	**Arthur Howard**
	Julian Orchard (1971–2)
Mr F. D. Price Whittaker	**Kenneth Cope**
Mr S. A. Smallpiece	**Norman Bird**
Mr Lumley	**John Stirling**
Mr R. P. Trench	**Peter Glaze**
Mr Halliforth	**Edwin Apps**
	Peter Greene (1971–2)
Parker	**David Langford**
Mr Forbes	**Keith Smith**
Mr Proctor	**Brian Rawlinson**
Mr Dinwiddie	**Gordon Phillott**
	Harold Bennett (1971–2)
Mr Cope-Willoughby	**Frank Raymond**
Matron	**Barbara Archer**
	Elizabeth Fraser
	Charlotte Mitchell
Taplow	**Gary Warren** (1971–2)
Potter	**Greg Smith** (1971–2)

Creators/Writers: **Denis Norden, Frank Muir**
Producers: **Douglas Moodie, Eric Fawcett, Douglas Argent**

A public school is tyrannized by its bumptious, cane-swishing headmaster.

Professor James Edwards, MA, was the principal of Chis-elbury School, an educational establishment that he ruled with an iron cane. While the schoolboys were always easy targets for the bullying, manipulative head-master, so, too, were his staff and in particular his weedy right-hand man, Mr Pettigrew (played by Leslie Howard's brother, Arthur). Other members of staff came and went during the programme's four-year run.

A spin-off film, *Bottoms Up*, was released in 1959, and *Whack-O!* was briefly revived on TV in 1971, with Julian Orchard in the role of Pettigrew and the indomitable Jimmy Edwards again donning the boozy principal's cap and gown.

WHAT THE PAPERS SAY
UK (Granada) Current Affairs. ITV 1956–82; Channel 4 1982–9; BBC 2 1990–

Presenters: **Kingsley Martin, Brian Inglis, Stuart Hall**

Weekly review of newspaper headlines.

What the Papers Say is one of those programmes that have done the rounds of the channels, and yet it has been produced by the same company, Granada, since its inception in 1956. The first hosts were *New Statesman* editor, Kingsley Martin, and *The Spectator's* assistant editor, Brian Inglis, who alternated appearances. Inglis eventually became sole host. Under the temporary title of *The Papers*, in 1969 Stuart Hall inherited the presenter's chair, and various other personalities and Fleet Street scribes have filled that seat since. The role of them all has been to consider the week's newspaper coverage, to discuss the headlines, to analyse the treatment of big issues and to follow lines of opinion and bias, often with a light and very humorous touch. Each edition has lasted 15 minutes.

WHAT'S MY LINE?
UK (BBC/Thames) Panel Game. BBC 1 1951–63; BBC 2 1973–4; ITV 1984–90

Hosts: **Eamonn Andrews, David Jacobs, Penelope Keith, Angela Rippon**

Creators: **Mark Goodson, Bill Todman**
Producers: **T. Leslie Jackson, Dicky Leeman, Harry Carlisle, John Warrington, Richard Evans, Ernest Maxin, Maurice Leonard**

A celebrity panel tries to guess contestants' occupations.

What's My Line? was one of the biggest successes in television history. Not only did it enjoy three runs on British television but it was also a hit in its native USA, where it eventually ran for 25 years. And yet the formula was remarkably simple. Contestants 'signed in', gave a brief mime to illustrate the work they did (or part of it), and four celebrity panellists then tried to guess the profession, by asking the contestant questions which elicited no more than a yes or no answer. If the occupation was not discovered by the time ten 'nos' had been received, the contestant was declared the winner and took away a certificate to prove it. The host acted as adjudicator to ensure that fair questions were asked and that contestants always told the truth.

The first UK host was Eamonn Andrews and he chaired the quiz until its cancellation in 1963 (except for a short period when Australian Ron Randall took over in 1954 and a few other occasions when Gilbert Harding, Jerry Desmonde and Elizabeth Allen took charge of events). David Jacobs was frontman for the short-lived 1970s version and Andrews returned for an ITV revival in 1984. On Andrews's death in 1987, Penelope Keith and then, more permanently, Angela Rippon were drafted into the presenter's chair. Panellists varied, but the classic 1950s line-up was Barbara Kelly, David Nixon, Lady Isobel Barnett and the notoriously grouchy Gilbert Harding. Under the guidance of David Jacobs, the panel consisted of Lady Barnett, Kenneth Williams, William Franklyn and one other. Barbara Kelly returned in 1984, accompanied most often by Jilly Cooper and George Gale.

What's My Line? was revived yet again, this time as a regional programme (not fully networked) by Meridian Television (1994–6). Emma Forbes was installed as presenter and Roy Hudd, Kate Robbins, June Whitfield, Peter Smith and Denise Black were among the regular panellists.

WHATELY, KEVIN
(1951–)

North-eastern actor who came to the fore as Neville in AUF WIEDERSEHEN, PET in 1983, but won even more acclaim for his subsequent performance as INSPECTOR MORSE's genial sidekick, Detective Sgt Lewis. Whately has also starred in the medical drama series, PEAK PRAC-TICE (Dr Jack Kerruish), *Screen Two's Skallagrigg* (Hopkins), *Screen One's Trip Trap* (abusive husband Ian Armstrong) and *Gobble* (MAFF official Colin Worsfold), and *The Broker's Man* (insurance investigator Jimmy Griffin). One of his earliest TV appearances was as a miner in WHEN THE BOAT COMES IN. He is married to actress Madelaine Newton.

WHATEVER HAPPENED TO THE LIKELY LADS?
See LIKELY LADS, THE.

WHEEL OF FORTUNE
UK (Scottish) Quiz. ITV 1988–
Presenters: **Nicky Campbell, Bradley Walsh, John Leslie**

Executive Producer: **Sandy Ross**
Producers: **Stephen Leahy, Anne Mason**

Colourful game show broadly based on Hangman.

Derived from the phenomenally popular American show of the same name, *Wheel of Fortune* gave Scottish Television its first big success in the world of networked game shows. Hosted by Radio 1 disc jockey Nicky Campbell, the programme invited three contestants to answer general knowledge questions, spin a large wheel marked with variously numbered segments and guess the missing letters of a mystery phrase. Whichever number was indicated by the pointer when the wheel stopped was translated into points in the player's bank. Contestants correctly identifying the phrase picked up an extra prize, and the highest overall scorer attempted one more phrase in the grand finale, in the hope of collecting even bigger rewards – a car or a large cash sum. Angela Ekaette was the hostess/letter-turner in the early programmes, with Carol Smillie and then Jenny Powell taking over later. When Nicky Campbell left the show to concentrate on more cerebral TV and radio, he was succeeded by Bradley Walsh, who in turn soon gave way to John Leslie. In 1999 *Wheel of Fortune* was switched out of prime time and into the afternoon schedules.

Wheel of Fortune was also the name of a successor programme to TAKE YOUR PICK, offering star and booby prizes on the turn of a wheel, hosted by Michael Miles.

WHEELER, Sir MORTIMER
(1890–1976)

Distinguished British archaeologist, discoverer and recoverer of many important sites, who became an unlikely television personality in the 1950s, thanks to his appearances on the erudite panel game, ANIMAL, VEGETABLE, MINERAL?.

WHEELTAPPERS' AND SHUNTERS' SOCIAL CLUB
UK (Granada) Variety. ITV 1974–7

Presenters: **Bernard Manning, Colin Crompton**

Creator/Producer: **John Hamp**

Variety show with a northern clubland atmosphere.

Presented from the fictitious Wheeltappers' and Shunters' Social Club, this series offered a collection of decent acts from the northern clubs scene plus some international names, all performing in the smoky, noisy atmosphere of a mock-up club concert hall. Earthy comedian Bernard Manning was compere, competing for attention with bell-ringing 'concert chairman' Colin Crompton, who was for ever interrupting to announce that the meat pies had arrived or that the bingo would start in half an hour.

WHELDON, Sir HUW
OBE (1916–86)

Once described as 'the best Director-General the BBC never had', Welshman Huw Wheldon joined the Corporation in 1952 as a publicity officer. He then became a senior producer, working on programmes such as *Press Conference* and *Men in Battle*. Wheldon also appeared in front of the camera, conducting interviews for PANORAMA and hosting kids' shows such as ALL YOUR OWN.

More famously, he became editor and presenter of the arts magazine, MONITOR. Wheldon was subsequently promoted to the positions of Head of Documentary and Music Programmes (1963–5) and Controller of Programmes (1965–8). In 1968 he took over as Managing Director of Television, becoming Deputy Director-General in 1976. On leaving the boardroom, Wheldon returned to presenting, with the series, *Royal Heritage* (timed to coincide with the Queen's Jubilee in 1977). From 1979 until shortly before his death in 1986, Sir Huw was President of the Royal Television Society.

WHEN THE BOAT COMES IN
UK (BBC) Drama. BBC 1 1976–7; 1981

Jack Ford	**James Bolam**
Jessie Seaton/Ashton	**Susan Jameson**
Bella Seaton	**Jean Heywood**
Bill Seaton	**James Garbutt**
Tom Seaton	**John Nightingale**
Billy Seaton	**Edward Wilson**
Dolly Headley/Ford	**Madelaine Newton**
Matt Headley	**Malcolm Terris**
Arthur Ashton	**Geoffrey Rose**
Sir Horatio Manners	**Basil Henson**
Mary	**Michelle Newell**
Lady Caroline	**Isla Blair**
	Lois Baxter
Duke of Bedlington	**William Fox**
'Geordie' Watson	**Ian Cullen**
Miss Laidlaw	**Catherine Terris**
Len Laidlaw	**Peter McGowan**
Roddy	**Martin Duncan**
Channing	**Christopher Benjamin**
Mary Routledge/Seaton	**Michelle Newell**
Sarah Headley	**Rosalind Bailey**
Doughty	**Bryan Pringle**
John Hartley	**William Squire**
Tania Corley	**Judy Loe**
Nigel Scott-Palliser	**Clive Merrison**

Creator: **James Mitchell**
Producers: **Leonard Lewis, Andrew Osborn, David Maloney**

Lives and loves in the depressed North-east.

Centring on one Jack Ford, a shipyard fitter who dabbled in unionism and politics before working his way up the capitalist ladder, *When the Boat Comes in* depicted the hard days of the 1920s in the cobbled streets of Gallowshield (based on South Shields, where author James Mitchell's dad had once been mayor). Ford was a Jack the Lad-type figure, a rough diamond with a good heart who was closely allied to the Seaton family, especially attractive daughter Jessie, a schoolteacher. Her brother, Tom, was Jack's miner friend and her younger brother, Billy, became a doctor and brought free medicine to the local people. Dolly was the girl who became Ford's wife and Ashton was the po-faced teacher Jessie married.

Using Ford, man of the people, as guide, and beginning in 1919 with his return from the Great War to a land rife with injustice, Mitchell effectively portrayed the deep, grim poverty of this proud industrial region and the earthy but noble character of its people. After three series, the programme ended with Jack heading for a new life in the USA, only to return six years later in dubious circumstances, having made a fortune from bootlegging during Prohibition and then losing it all in the Wall Street Crash. This last season, set in the 1930s, saw our hero involved in the Jarrow marches and also taking part in the Spanish conflict.

Familiar through its jaunty 'Dance Ti Thi Daddy' theme song (written by David Fanshawe and sung by Alex Glasgow), *When the Boat Comes in* introduced viewers to the peculiarities of the lilting Geordie dialect and has since been fondly remembered as a poignant piece of social history.

WHERE THE HEART IS
UK (United/Anglia) Drama 1997–

Margaret 'Peggy' Snow	**Pam Ferris**
Ruth Goddard	**Sarah Lancashire**
Vic Snow	**Tony Haygarth**
Simon Goddard	**Thomas Craig**
Stephen Snow	**William Ash**
	Jason Done
Lucy Snow	**Jessica Baglow**
Wendy Atkins	**Susannah Wise**
Patricia Illingworth	**Maggie Wells**
Deborah Allis	**Laura Crossley**
Dick Lampard	**William Travis**
Henry	**Andrew Knott**
Terry	**Simon Ashley**
Jacqui Richards	**Marsha Thomason**
	Paulette Williams
Cheryl Lampard	**Kathryn Hunt**
Sandra Harrison	**Melanie Kilburn**
Keith Harrison	**Neil McCaul**
Craig Harrison	**Alex Carter**
Alison Storey	**Katrina Levon**
Anna Kirkwall	**Lesley Dunlop**
Luke Kirkwall	**Christian Cooke**
Chris Eckersley	**Vincenzo Pellegrino**
Karen Buckley	**Leslie Ash**
David Buckley	**Philip Middlemiss**
Jess Buckley	**Kelly Wenham**

Creators: **Ashley Pharoah, Vicky Featherstone**
Executive Producers: **Simon Lewis, Michele Buck, Damien Timmer**
Producers: **Kate Anthony, Simon Lewis, Avon Harpley, Richard Broke**

Heartwarming tales concerning nurses at a Yorkshire health centre.

'A series about everyday things like living and dying', according to its star, Pam Ferris, *Where the Heart Is* was the story of two sisters-in-law working as district nurses in the Yorkshire town of Skelthwaite. While committed to their work, they also recognized the responsibilities they faced with their own families.

Kind-hearted, 48-year-old Peggy was the wife of Vic and mother of teenage son Stephen and young daughter

Lucy. Ruth, wife of Peggy's astute businessman brother, Simon, was about to give birth to their first child, Alfie, as the series opened. Simon owned the toilet paper factory where Vic worked. Action focused more on wholesome, human stories rather than medical crises, with plenty of humour, a few pints of Chapstons down The Skelthwaite Arms, and a little sporting spice, through Vic's involvement as the ageing player-coach of the Skelthwaite Skorpions rugby league team, all thrown in for good measure. Featuring later were new nurse Jacqui Richards, an 'outsider' with new ideas who started a relationship with Stephen and lodged with widow Maggie Wells, a member of the Skelthwaite Medical Centre team; Vic's sister, Sandra, and her new-in-town family; recently widowed mum, nursing sister Anna Kirkwall (who replaced Ruth – who had walked out on Simon and gone to Australia); and Chris Eckersley, the town's first male nurse. When tragedy struck and Peggy was killed in a car accident involving a runaway horse, her place was taken by new nurse Karen Buckley, an old friend of Anna's who arrived with husband David and 17-year-old daughter Jess in tow.

Paddy McAloon of the band Prefab Sprout wrote and performed the theme song.

WHERE THERE'S LIFE
UK (Yorkshire) Medical. ITV 1981–9

Presenters: **Miriam Stoppard, Rob Buckman**

Executive Producer: **Duncan Dallas**
Producers: **John Fanshawe, David Taylor, Ian McFarlane, Derek Goodall, Irene Garrow, Anne Pivcevic, David Poyser, Paul Bader**

Discussion programme about medical matters.

Hosted by doctors Miriam Stoppard and Rob Buckman, the long-running *Where There's Life* talked to ordinary people about the medical traumas in their life and instigated debate about healthy lifestyles. It also considered new ideas and developments in the world of medicine.

WHICKER, ALAN
(1925–)

Britain's most-travelled TV reporter, Alan Whicker, was born in Egypt. After entering journalism, he became a war correspondent and then joined the influential current affairs series, TONIGHT, when it began in 1957. His dry, distinctive delivery and his ability to play the ordinary Brit abroad led to his own series for the BBC, *Whicker's World*, in 1959. Initially, a compilation of his *Tonight* reports, it soon broadened into new assignments, many under individual series titles, like *Whicker Down Under* in 1961. In 1968 he defected to the newly formed Yorkshire Television, where he continued to notch up air mile after air mile in the pursuit of oddities overseas and insights into other people's lifestyles. He later returned to the BBC and, in the 1980s, presented *Living with Uncle Sam* and *Living with Waltzing Matilda*, series about British expatriates in the USA and Australia.

He then turned down the chance to emulate Phileas Fogg and go AROUND THE WORLD IN 80 DAYS (Michael Palin stepped in and reaped the rewards), preferring instead to take things rather more easily in *Around Whicker's World: The Ultimate Package*, in which he shadowed a wealthy tour party as they made their champagne circumnavigation. Among his other offerings have been *Whicker on Top of the World* (1962), *Whicker Down Mexico Way* (1963), *Whicker's New World, Whicker in Europe* (both 1969), *Whicker's Walkabout* (1970), *The World of Whicker* (1971), *Whicker's Orient, Whicker Within a Woman's World* (both 1972), *Whicker's South Seas, Whicker Way Out West* (both 1973), *Around Whicker's World in 25 Years* (1982) and *Whicker's World: A Taste of Spain* (1992). He also gained unexpected access to Haiti dictator Papa Doc Duvalier for a famous 1969 documentary, *Papa Doc – The Black Sheep.*

WHIPLASH
UK (ATV) Western. ITV 1960–1

Christopher Cobb	**Peter Graves**
Dan	**Anthony Wickert**

A Western set not on the plains of America but in the Australian bush.

Chris Cobb was an American who had arrived in Australia in the 1850s to establish Cobb & Co., the country's first stagecoach line. Even though he was based Down Under, and not in the Wild West, he faced the usual collection of cowboy outlaws. Thirty-four episodes were made, but star Peter Graves made more of an impression when he later appeared as Jim Phelps in MISSION: IMPOSSIBLE.

WHIRLYBIRDS
US (CBS/Desilu) Adventure. BBC 1958–62

Chuck Martin	**Ken Tobey**
Pete 'PT' Moore	**Craig Hill**
Janet Culver	**Sandra Spence**
Helen Carter	**Nancy Hale**

Producer: **N. Gayle Gitterman**

Two helicopter pilots find adventure.

Chuck Martin and PT Moore were two young pilots who founded their own helicopter charter company, Whirlybird Service, based in Longwood Field, California. Every day proved to be an adventure, as the young daredevils flew their aircraft into tense and dangerous situations, hunting for missing folk or apprehending villains. With stunts aplenty, this was an all-action series that appealed to younger viewers. It was produced by Lucille Ball and Desi Arnaz's Desilu company.

WHISTLE TEST
See OLD GREY WHISTLE TEST.

WHITE, BETTY
(1924–)

American comic actress, a US hit as early as 1953 with her first sitcom, *Life with Elizabeth*, and successful throughout that decade in quizzes, variety shows and the comedy, *Date with the Angels*. However, it wasn't until the 1970s that she began to attract the attention of viewers elsewhere in the world, having fallen out of the mainstream in the 1960s. As man-hungry Sue Ann Nivens in THE MARY TYLER MOORE SHOW her prime-time career took off again, and she followed it with game show appearances and her own comedy, *The Betty White Show*, in which she played Joyce Whitman. For most people, however, White is the naïve, dim-witted but caring Rose Nylund from THE GOLDEN GIRLS and *The Golden Palace*, a role she picked up in 1985 when in her sixties. Since these ended she has appeared in Bob Newhart's sitcom, *Bob*, and alongside Marie Osmond in the comedy, *Maybe This Time*.

WHITE, CAROL
(Carole White; 1942–91)

British actress, a child film star in the 1950s, on TV in the mid-1960s and then quickly moving on to Hollywood. White's forte was the ingenue, the girl who was easily led, attracted by bright lights and ending up in trouble, as she exemplified in the powerful dramas, *Up the Junction* and CATHY COME HOME.

WHITE, FRANCES
(1938–)

Yorkshire-born actress, seen in many roles on TV since the 1970s. She was Andrea Warner in *A Raging Calm*, Julia in I, CLAUDIUS, Linda Clark in *A Little Bit of Wisdom*, Sister May in *I Woke Up One Morning*, Molly Cramer in DANGERFIELD, and secretaries Dorothy Hampton in A VERY PECULIAR PRACTICE and Kate Hamilton in CROSSROADS. However, White is probably best known as Miss Flood in MAY TO DECEMBER.

WHITE HEATHER CLUB, THE
UK (BBC) Variety. BBC 1 1958–68

Presenters: **Robert Wilson, Andy Stewart, Robin Hall, Jimmie Macgregor**

Producer: **Iain MacFadyan**

Singing and dancing, Scottish style.

An extension of the traditional Hogmanay parties, *The White Heather Club* was an excuse for Scottish performers to don their best kilts and jig around to the best folksongs and ballads north of the border. Featuring stars like Moira Anderson, Duncan Macrae, Roddy McMillan, The Joe Gordon Folk Four, James Urquhart, Jimmy Logan, dancers Isobel James and Dixie Ingram and bandleaders Jimmy Shand and Ian Powrie, the series, produced by the BBC at its Springfield Road studio in Glasgow, ran and ran – for 285 editions. Tenor Robert Wilson was the first host, giving way after six programmes to Andy Stewart and the TONIGHT pairing of Robin Hall and Jimmie Macgregor.

WHITE HORSES, THE
Germany/Yugoslavia (Jugoslavija Film) Children's Drama.
BBC 1 1968

Julia	**Helga Anders**
Uncle Dimitri	**Helmuth Schnider**
Hugo	**Franz Muxeneder**

A teenage girl enjoys horsey adventures during her holidays.

Fifteen-year-old Julia lived in Belgrade but was given the chance to spend her holiday at the stud farm run by her Uncle Dimitri and his head groom, Hugo. Julia instantly fell in love with the farm's white Lippizaner horses, particularly one named Boris who led the girl into a series of adventures.

Made on the Continent and dubbed into English, the series proved to be enchanting children's hour escapism. Its evocative theme song, also called 'White Horses', was a hit in 1968 for Jacky (later, as Jackie Lee, to record another theme song hit with 'Rupert').

WHITE HUNTER
UK (ITP) Adventure. ITV 1958–60

John Hunter	**Rhodes Reason**

Producer: **Norman Williams**

Adventures in the African jungle with the appropriately named John Hunter, guide and game-handler.

This series was based on the true-life tales of John A. Hunter, author of the books, *African Safari* and *Hunter's Tracks*. *White Hunter* was filmed in East Africa and made full use of the abundant wildlife. Thirty-nine episodes were made.

WHITEHOUSE, MARY
CBE (1910–)

Former schoolteacher who turned moral crusader when establishing her Clean-Up TV campaign in 1964 and formalizing it as The National Viewers' and Listeners' Association a year later. TILL DEATH US DO PART (not surprisingly) was one programme to raise her blood pressure, and she was particularly critical of the works of Dennis Potter. The regime of Sir Hugh Greene, the BBC's Director-General in the permissive 1960s, was blamed for contributing to moral decay. She formally retired from the campaign in 1994 and had nothing to do with the comedy sketch show, *The Mary Whitehouse Experience*!

WHITELAW, BILLIE
CBE (1932–)

Warwickshire-born actress who arrived on TV in the 1950s, appearing in series like THE ADVENTURES OF ROBIN HOOD and playing Mary, the daughter of DIXON OF DOCK GREEN, soon to be married to his young colleague, Andy Crawford. She left *Dixon* after just one year but went on to support Bob Monkhouse in *My Pal Bob*, was Josephine in Thames TV's 1974 series, *Napoleon and Love*, and, in 1981, she turned to comedy again, taking the role of Bertha Freyer in PRIVATE SCHULZ. Among her many notable performances have been parts in the ARMCHAIR THEATRE offerings, *No Trams to Lime Street* and *Lena, O My Lena*, the *Supernatural* presentations, *Countess Ilona* and *The Werewolf Reunion*, plus *Jamaica Inn*, *The Dressmaker*, *A Murder of Quality*, *The Cloning of Joanna May* (Mavis), *Firm Friends* (Rose Gutteridge), *Performance*'s presentation of *The Entertainer* (Phoebe Rice), *Screen Two*'s *Skallagrigg*, *Merlin* (Ambrosia) and CATHERINE COOKSON's *A Dinner of Herbs* (Kate Makepeace).

WHITELEY, RICHARD
(1943–)

Yorkshire-born presenter, the first face seen on both Channel 4 (as the punning host of the long-running COUNTDOWN) and Yorkshire Television (spending no less than 30 years at the helm of the regional news magazine, *Calendar*, after an ITN traineeship). Whiteley has also hosted *Richard Whiteley Unbriefed*, in which he has bravely interviewed famous guests without being told who they are or given any research notes.

WHITFIELD, JUNE
CBE (1925–)

RADA-trained, London-born comedy actress, the archetypal suburban sitcom wife, thanks to her long partnership with the late Terry Scott in HAPPY EVER AFTER (June Fletcher) and TERRY AND JUNE (June Medford). Whitfield had previously appeared with Scott in *Scott On . . .* After success on radio in *Take It from Here* (Eth in The Glums) and other series, Whitfield's first TV appearances came in the 1950s, in shows like *Idiot Weekly, Price 2d*, *The Benny Hill Show* and then HANCOCK (she was the nurse in *The Blood Donor*). She appeared again with Hancock in 1967, playing Esmeralda Stavely-Smythe, a waitress in *Hancock*'s, his last TV series. Whitfield was seen in *The Arthur Askey Show* (and his earlier *Before Your Very Eyes*), supported Jimmy Edwards in THE SEVEN FACES OF JIM and Stanley Baxter in *Baxter On . . .*, was Rose Garvey in BEGGAR MY NEIGHBOUR and starred as Mabel Pollard, Harry H. Corbett's fiancée, in the *The Best Things in Life*. She has also gamely turned her hand to 'newer' comedy, guesting with Julian Clary in *Terry and Julian* and *All Rise for Julian Clary*, and playing the part of Jennifer

Saunders's mum in ABSOLUTELY FABULOUS. More recently, Whitfield, who has also featured in various sketch shows and panel games, was seen in *Time Keepers of the Millennium*, as Mrs Birkstead in CATHERINE COOKSON's *The Secret* and as Annie in *Last of the Blonde Bombshells*. She is the mother of actress Suzy Aitchison.

WHITNEY, JOHN
(1930–)

British TV executive, a former writer and producer who scripted for 1950s and 1960s series like *The Verdict Is Yours*, HARPERS WEST ONE, *The Hidden Truth* and THE INFORMER, in collaboration with Geoffrey Bellman (the last three also as creators), and the sitcom, *In for a Penny*, with John Hawkesworth. He was script editor on THE PLANE MAKERS and later became Head of LWT, before advancing to the position of Director-General of the IBA (1982–9).

WHO DARES, WINS . . .
UK (Holmes) Comedy. Channel 4 1984–8

Rory McGrath, Philip Pope, Jimmy Mulville, Julia Hills, Tony Robinson

Producers: **Denise O'Donoghue, Andy Hamilton**

Comedy sketch show featuring an up-and-coming team of writers/comedians.

In the view of most critics, the often satirical but not necessarily topical *Who Dares, Wins . . .* succeeded where similar 'alternative' sketch shows failed, because it was innovative. Among the best-remembered items was a series on pandas plotting to escape from a zoo. Julia Hills played a tense, accident-prone TV interviewer and Tony Robinson spent two programmes totally naked. The series followed a one-off 'special' in 1983 and early episodes carried a sub-title, such as 'A Camping Holiday in Beirut' or 'A Ticket for the Cup Final'.

WHO DO YOU DO?
UK (LWT) Comedy. ITV 1972–6

Freddie Starr, Peter Goodwright, Faith Brown, Janet Brown, Margo Henderson, Roger Kitter, Barry Cryer, Johnny More, Jerry Stevens, Len Lowe, Dailey and Wayne, Paul Melba, Little and Large, Aiden J. Harvey

Creator/Producer: **Jon Scoffield**

Comedy sketches featuring top impressionists.

Although leaning heavily on the talents of Freddie Starr and Peter Goodwright, *Who Do You Do?* also featured most of the other leading impressionists of the day in a series of gags and skits. Tightly editing together its various components, the programme offered a gag a second in the style of THE COMEDIANS. The series was renamed *New Who Do You Do?* in 1975 and *Now Who Do You*

Do? in 1976 (when the cast incorporated new faces like Michael Barrymore, Les Dennis and Dustin Gee).

WHO WANTS TO BE A MILLIONAIRE?
UK (Celador) Quiz. ITV 1998–

Presenter: **Chris Tarrant**

Creators: **David Briggs, Mike Whitehill, Steve Knight**
Producers: **Guy Freeman, Colman Hutchinson, David Briggs**

DOUBLE YOUR MONEY *for the turn of the millennium.*

It's often the simplest programming that is the most successful, and *Who Wants to Be a Millionaire?* has certainly been successful, the format being sold all round the world. It has also seemed simple on the face of it: a contestant pitched into the hot seat, working his way up a ladder of cash prizes, having to decide whether to quit while ahead or gamble big money in the hope of an even bigger cash prize. However, this synopsis tends to ignore the planning that has gone into staging the contest, so that the game is easy to follow and viewers are enthralled by the unfolding drama. A carefully lit set, the constant throbbing of background music and an edgy studio atmosphere have all been key elements in lifting this quiz above the ordinary. Questionmaster Chris Tarrant's encouragement – repeating the options available, making sure they have understood their situation ('Is that your final answer?') – has also added to the tension. However, it has been the sheer magnitude of the prize money that has proved the biggest draw.

Contestants have progressed from a £100 base to the possible jackpot of £1 million via a series of 15 questions. For each question, four possible answers have been shown and the contestant has even had the options of asking the audience for help, eliminating two of the answers by going '50/50', or phoning a friend for assistance. But questions have become increasingly difficult and the pressure of gambling away many thousands of pounds has deterred all but the bravest from aiming for the top – even though the producers have built in guaranteed prizes of £1,000 and £32,000 for contestants who reach those levels. To take part in the show, viewers have been invited to phone in and answer eliminator questions, the cost of the calls covering the show's prize money. Ten viewers have then been selected for the programme and a place in the hot seat has been won by answering a 'fastest finger first' question, involving placing four answers in the correct order in the quickest time.

The first person to go all the way to the jackpot came in the American version. John Carpenter scooped the $1 million prize in November 1999. A year later, Judith Keppel became the first £1 million winner in the UK.

WHO-DUN-IT
UK (ATV) Mystery Anthology. ITV 1969

Insp. Jeremy Moon .... **Gary Raymond**

Creator: **Lewis Greifer**
Producer: **Jack Williams**

Series of single plays with a murder theme, offering viewers the chance to spot the culprit.

Hosted by and starring fictional detective Inspector Jeremy Moon, this 13-episode series of Agatha Christie-type murder mysteries was set in the 1930s. Each week, after the discovery of a body – on one occasion that of a Hollywood film star on a transatlantic liner – the Inspector would begin his investigations, pausing at the end of the second act to invite the viewing public to hazard a guess as to *Who-Dun-It*, before finally revealing all.

WHODUNNIT?
UK (Thames) Panel Game. ITV 1972–8

Hosts: **Edward Woodward, Jon Pertwee**

Creators/Writers: **Jeremy Lloyd, Lance Percival**
Producers: **Malcolm Morris, Robert Reed, Dennis Kirkland, Anthony Parker, Leon Thau**

Celebrity panellists attempt to spot the culprit in a series of half-hour mysteries.

Hosted initially by Edward Woodward and then by Jon Pertwee, this light-hearted panel game offered celebrity guests the chance to find the killer in a mystery playlet. After seeing the action on tape, each celebrity was allowed to request a short action replay of a telling moment and then to question all the characters involved. Finally, they were called upon to name the guilty party, who would, in a great show of bravado, stand up to take the rap. The performers changed from week to week, but a handful of panellists became regulars, most notably Patrick Mower and Anouska Hempel. Created by comedians Jeremy Lloyd and Lance Percival, the formula was rehashed for CLUEDO in the 1990s.

WHOOPS APOCALYPSE
UK (LWT) Comedy. ITV 1982

Johnny Cyclops .... **Barry Morse**
Premier Dubienkin .... **Richard Griffiths**
The Deacon .... **John Barron**
Commissar Solzhenitsyn .... **Alexei Sayle**
Kevin Pork .... **Peter Jones**
Foreign Secretary .... **Geoffrey Palmer**
Chancellor of the Exchequer .... **Richard Davies**
Shah Mashiq Rassim .... **Bruce Montague**
Lacrobat .... **John Cleese**
Jay Garrick .... **Ed Bishop**
Abdab .... **David Kelly**

Creators/Writers: **Andrew Marshall, David Renwick**
Producer: **Humphrey Barclay**

A world dominated by crackpot politicians rushes towards World War III.

In this irreverent comedy, attempts to restore Shah

Mashiq Rassim to the throne of Iran by the use of the nuclear Quark bomb proved disastrous when events went haywire and Israel was blown up. This action sent the world spinning towards Armageddon, with the balance of power fought over by US President Johnny Cyclops (a lobotomized former actor from Omaha) and Soviet Premier Dubienkin. In the middle was idiotic British Prime Minister Kevin Pork. The Deacon was the USA's crazed security adviser, and also in the fray was international terrorist Lacrobat. A feature-film version, starring Peter Cook and Loretta Swit, was released in 1986.

WHOOPS BAGHDAD!

See UP POMPEII!.

WHOSE LINE IS IT ANYWAY?

UK (Hat Trick) Comedy. Channel 4 1988–

Presenter: **Clive Anderson**

Creators: **Dan Patterson, Mark Leveson**
Producer: **Dan Patterson**

Celebrity improvisation game show.

Transferring to television from Radio 4, *Whose Line Is It Anyway?* has brought the drama school discipline of improv – improvisation – into the world of mainstream comedy. Each programme has featured four ad-libbing comedians working singly, in pairs or all together, to execute a series of parlour games. Host Clive Anderson has asked the studio audience for suggestions for some games, others have been predetermined, but all have demanded instant response and imagination from the assembled performers. Favourite guests have included Tony Slattery, John Sessions, Josie Lawrence, Greg Proops, Paul Merton, Sandi Toksvig, Mike McShane, Ryan Stiles, Stephen Fry, Caroline Quentin and Colin Mochrie. Music has been supplied by Richard Vranch at the piano. Editions have also been made in the USA for airing on both sides of the Atlantic.

A similar concept, entitled *Impromptu*, was shown on BBC 2 in 1964. Produced by David Croft, it called on a resident team of performers (Victor Spinetti, Lance Percival, Anne Cunningham, Peter Reeves and Betty Impey) to act out a whole programme, working from basic instructions given to them on cards by Jeremy Hawk.

WHYTON, WALLY

(1929–97)

Former skiffle musician Wally Whyton was one of ITV's favourite children's entertainers from the 1950s to the 1970s. He began his showbiz career with The Vipers group (who notched up three hits in 1957) and found his way into television by sitting in for Rolf Harris on one show. Whyton was soon in demand for series like *Small Time*, *Musical Box*, *The Three Scampis* and FIVE O'CLOCK CLUB, where he worked with puppets like Pussy Cat

Willum, Ollie Beak, Fred Barker, Joe Crow and Spike McPike. He was later seen in PLAY SCHOOL and as co-host of the pop show, LIFT OFF.

WIDESCREEN

Widescreen (pioneered in the UK by Channel 4 and S4C and now commonly available, thanks to digital broadcasting) is a means of displaying the TV picture so that it more natually fits the human eye. Widescreen imagery has a ratio of 16:9 (16 units high and nine units wide), as opposed to the picture on conventional TV screens which has a 4:3 ratio (or, to compare like with like, 12:9). The added width allows the new technology to assimilate more closely the human field of vision and is, therefore, reputedly more comfortable to watch. Viewers with old-style sets can use their digital control box to switch to widescreen format, which displays the whole widescreen picture but with black horizontal bars at the top and bottom. When programmes made in the old 4:3 ratio are viewed on a dedicated widescreen television, there are three options available to the viewer. The first involves allowing the picture to sit in the middle of the screen, with black bars vertically down each side. The second is for the set to crop the picture at the top and bottom, and then stretch the edges of the image to fill out the screen (stretching the whole image results in distorted figures). The third option zooms in on the image to fill out the screen, but the top and bottom of the image are then lost.

WIDOWS/WIDOWS II/SHE'S OUT

UK (Thames/Euston Films) Crime Drama. ITV 1983/1985/ 1995

Dolly Rawlins	**Ann Mitchell**
Linda Perelli	**Maureen O'Farrell**
Shirley Miller	**Fiona Hendley**
Bella O'Reilly	**Eva Mottley**
	Debby Bishop (*II*)
DI Resnick	**David Calder**
DS Fuller	**Paul Jesson**
Harry Rawlins	**Maurice O'Connell**
Audrey Withey	**Kate Williams**
DC Andrews	**Peter Machin**
Boxer Davis	**Dudley Sutton**
Kathleen Resnick	**Thelma Whiteley**
Trudie	**Catherine Neilson**
Arnie Fisher	**Jeffrey Chiswick**
Tony Fisher	**Chris Ellison**
Vic Morgan	**Stephen Yardley** (*II*)
Micky Tesco	**Andrew Kazamia** (*II*)
Ester Freeman	**Linda Marlowe** (*She's Out*)
Gloria Radford	**Maureen Sweeney** (*She's Out*)
Julia Lawson	**Anna Patrick** (*She's Out*)
Connie Stephens	**Zoe Heyes** (*She's Out*)
Angela Dunn	**Indra Ove** (*She's Out*)
Kathleen O'Reilly	**Maggie McCarthy** (*She's Out*)
DS Mike Withy	**Adrian Rawlins** (*She's Out*)
DCI Ron Craigh	**Hugh Quarshie** (*She's Out*)
DS John Palmer	**Douglas McFerran** (*She's Out*)

Creator/Writer: **Lynda La Plante**
Executive Producers: **Verity Lambert, Linda Agran,
Johnny Goodman**
Producers: **Linda Agran, Irving Teitelbaum,Verity
Lambert**

*Four inexperienced female crooks pull off a daring
armed robbery.*

When arch-villain Harry Rawlins was killed in an
attempted hold-up, his wife, Dolly, inherited his well-
laid plans for future robberies. One involved attacking a
security van in a subway, and Dolly fancied her chances
of pulling it off. She assembled around her three other
widows: attractive, blonde Shirley Miller and dark-
haired Linda Perelli (whose husbands were killed along
with Harry), plus black stripper Bella O'Reilly, whose
husband had died of a drugs overdose. Together they
planned the raid meticulously, but with the Fisher
brothers (Harry's old adversaries) lurking around, and
Detective Inspector Resnick deeply suspicious, keeping
their secret was not easy. Yet all went swimmingly and
the four girls flew off to Rio with suitcases full of cash.

It was in the sequel, two years later, that their troubles
began. Their tongues became loose and their behaviour
invited comment. Most alarming was the fact that Harry
was not dead but had faked his death to live with another
woman and was now out to regain the money that was
rightly his. In this second series, Bella was played by
Debby Bishop, following the death of Eva Mottley.

The story was picked up yet again in 1995 in a second
sequel entitled *She's Out*. This saw Dolly Rawlins released
from an eight-year jail-term and hoping to set up a
children's home, yet surrounded by a new troupe of
female felons, as well as numerous other unsavoury
characters, all after her stashed-away loot.

WILCOX, DESMOND
(1931–2000)

Award-winning British documentary-maker and current
affairs reporter, married to Esther Rantzen, with whom
he worked when co-editor of the long-running MAN
ALIVE series and editor of BRADEN'S WEEK. In the early
1960s Wilcox was a reporter with THIS WEEK and he
was later Head of General Features at the BBC, but he
returned in front of the cameras in 1983 as anchor of
Sixty Minutes, the short-lived successor to NATIONWIDE.
That same year he began writing, presenting and producing *The Visit*, a series which accompanied people undertaking dramatic, life-changing journeys. The highlight
was the story of *The Boy David*, a young Peruvian Indian
receiving facial plastic surgery in the UK. Wilcox
employed the same documentary techniques when
following the wedding plans of a young couple from
Cardiff in another 1980s series, *The Marriage*. Later contributions included *The Lost Children* (1991, about Colom-
bian street-kids) and its follow-up, *Children of the Sewers*
(1999).

WILCOX, PAULA
(1949–)

Manchester-born actress, starring as Beryl in THE
LOVERS, after appearances in series like THE DUST-
BINMEN and CORONATION STREET (Ray Langton's sister,
Janice). Around the same time, she popped up in another
comedy, *On the House*, but enjoyed far more success as
Chrissy in MAN ABOUT THE HOUSE. When this series
ended, Wilcox was cast in her own sitcom, the daring
(for the time) single-parent comedy, MISS JONES AND
SON (Elizabeth Jones). After a few quiet years, Wilcox
resurfaced in the 1985 Channel 4 comedy, *The Bright Side*,
playing prison widow Cynthia Bright. In the 1990s she
took the role of Ros in the sitcom, *Fiddlers Three*, and
then appeared as Ivy in Frank Skinner's comedy, *Blue
Heaven*, Sylv in *Life After Birth*, Mrs Parker in the children's series, *The Queen's Nose*, and Mrs Walwyn in *The
Stalker's Apprentice*. Other credits over the years have
included guest spots in THE ONEDIN LINE, THE LIVER
BIRDS, HADLEIGH, KATE, BOON and BROOKSIDE.

WILDE ALLIANCE
UK (Yorkshire) Detective Drama. ITV 1978

Rupert Wilde	**John Stride**
Amy Wilde	**Julia Foster**
Christopher Bridgewater	**John Lee**
Bailey	**Patrick Newell**

Executive Producer: **David Cunliffe**
Producer: **Ian MacKintosh**

*A thriller-writer and his wife become involved in
real-life intrigue.*

Rupert Wilde was a successful author of detective novels
and lived with his attractive wife, Amy, in a luxurious
country mansion in Yorkshire. However, for the Wildes,
life imitated art, and the lively couple themselves
became sleuths as they stumbled into a series of investigations, any of which could have come from Rupert's
books. Rupert's agent, Christopher Bridgewater, was also
dragged into the action. This was a short-lived British
attempt at a McMILLAN AND WIFE/HART TO HART/THE
THIN MAN-type series. Just 13 episodes were made.

WILDE, BRIAN
(1924–)

British actor, best known for his roles as starchy Foggy
Dewhurst in LAST OF THE SUMMER WINE and prison
warder Mr Barrowclough in PORRIDGE. Earlier, Wilde
had appeared in the drama, *The Men from Room 13*, and
the sitcoms, *The Love of Mike* and *Room at the Bottom*,
and also played Bloody Delilah in THE DUSTBINMEN.
Other credits have included the parts of radio station
boss Roland Simpson in *The Kit Curran Radio Show* and
Major Wyatt in *Wyatt's Watchdogs*.

WILL SHAKESPEARE
UK (ATV) Drama. ITV 1978

Will Shakespeare	**Tim Curry**
Christopher Marlowe	**Ian McShane**
Edward Alleyn	**André Morell**
Earl of Southampton	**Nicholas Clay**
Hamnet Sadler	**John McEnery**
Sir Thomas Walsingham	**Simon MacCorkindale**
Anne Hathaway	**Meg Wyn Owen**
Ingram Frizer	**Simon Rouse**

Writer: **John Mortimer**
Producer: **Peter Wood**

The life of the Bard of Avon.

With historical facts rather thin on the ground, writer John Mortimer added more than a touch of fiction to his dramatization of the life and times of William Shakespeare. This bustling six-part series followed young Will as he broke through into theatrical circles and gradually established himself as the finest playwright of his generation. Viewers were treated to a new 'human' angle on the bard, with Tim Curry portraying him as a bawdy and romantic type, hovering around the Globe Theatre and mingling in the court of Queen Elizabeth.

WILLIAM
See JUST WILLIAM.

WILLIAM TELL
See ADVENTURES OF WILLIAM TELL, THE.

WILLIAMS, ANDY
(1930–)

Easy-going American singer, once a member of the Williams Brothers singing group, who hosted his own variety series in the USA through most of the 1960s and 1970s. The show was carried by the BBC in the UK and, among other things, introduced viewers to the Osmond Brothers.

WILLIAMS, DORIAN
OBE (1914–85)

BBC equestrian events commentator from 1951, retiring in the early 1980s. Williams, an acknowledged horse expert, also wrote numerous books on equine matters.

WILLIAMS, KENNETH
(1926–88)

British comedian and comedy actor, well known from *Carry On* films and various radio series but also familiar on television, his catalogue of funny voices and shocked faces and his skill as a raconteur making him popular on chat shows and panel games. He supported Tony Hancock in the early days of HANCOCK'S HALF HOUR, hosted *International Cabaret* for several years and was given his own sketch show by the BBC. His last contributions included the kids' series, *Whizzkid's Guide* and *Galloping Galaxies* (the voice of the computer, SID), and he also provided the voices for the *Willo The Wisp* cartoon series and many commercials.

WILLIAMS, MICHAEL
(1935–2001)

Versatile British actor, at home with both dramatic and comedy roles. In the former vein, he played The Duke of Alençon in ELIZABETH R, Philip Hart in *A Raging Calm*, Alan Crowe in *The Hanged Man*, William Essex in *My Son, My Son*, Uncle Davey in *Love in a Cold Climate*, Billy Balsam in SEPTEMBER SONG and Ted Jeavons in *A Dance to the Music of Time*. Comedy-wise, Williams was Mike Selway in A FINE ROMANCE (with his real-life wife, Judi Dench), N. V. Standish in *Double First* and Barry Masefield in *Conjugal Rites*. He enjoyed many other credits, too, including *TV Shakespeare*, A FAMILY AT WAR and *Tracey Ullman Takes On New York*.

WILLIAMS, ROBIN
(1952–)

Energetic, quickfire, quirky American comedian who shot to fame in the 1970s when he was spotted playing LA nightclubs. A master of improvisation and ad-lib, he was given a role in the short-lived revival of LAUGH-IN and contributed to *The Richard Pryor Show*, but a bigger break came with a guest appearance in the sitcom, HAPPY DAYS. Cast as zany alien Mork from Ork, he proved such a hit that his own series, MORK AND MINDY, was soon on the screens. That took Williams into the cinema and he has since become one of Hollywood's biggest names.

WILLIAMS, SIMON
(1946–)

British actor winning fans with his portrayal of Captain James Bellamy in UPSTAIRS, DOWNSTAIRS and later seen in the comedies, AGONY (Laurence Lucas), KINVIG (Buddo) and DON'T WAIT UP (Dr Charles Cartwright). He also played Simon Company in the musical drama, *Company and Co.*, was cast as Ken Hawkes in *Demob* and barrister Gerald Triggs in the sitcom, *Law and Disorder*, and took the lead in the pilot for THE INSPECTOR ALLEYN MYSTERIES. He has also featured in series like THE REGIMENT, WODEHOUSE PLAYHOUSE, STRANGERS and BERGERAC. Williams is married to actress Lucy Fleming and his children, Tam and Amy, are both actors.

WILLIS, BRUCE
(1959–)

American actor born in Germany who shot to fame as the jive-talking, ultra-casual detective, David Addison, in MOONLIGHTING in 1985, having previously acted on stage and made a few TV appearances in shows like HART TO HART and MIAMI VICE. He quickly turned his attention to the movie world and also notched up a few hit singles. He married actress Demi Moore.

WILLIS, Lord TED
(1918–92)

One of TV's most prolific writers and programme creators, Ted Willis pioneered working-class, 'kitchen sink' dramas and social realism with his scriptwriting in the 1950s. Among his brainchildren – revealing a flair for both comedy and straight pieces – were DIXON OF DOCK GREEN, TELL IT TO THE MARINES, SERGEANT CORK, TAXI, THE SULLAVAN BROTHERS, MRS THURSDAY, VIRGIN OF THE SECRET SERVICE, *Coppers End* and HUNTER'S WALK. In all, he created 41 television series. In addition, his plays included *Woman in a Dressing Gown*, the ARMCHAIR THEATRE presentation, *Hot Summer Night*, and an adaptation of Richard Gordon's *Doctor in the House*. He was made a peer in 1963.

WILSON, DENNIS MAIN
(1924–97)

Long-serving British light entertainment producer and occasional director, initially working in radio but associated with numerous TV sitcoms, such as *The Two Charleys*, SYKES, THE RAG TRADE, TILL DEATH US DO PART, *Scott On . . .*, *Them*, *Well Anyway*, CITIZEN SMITH, *Mr Big*, *Time of My Life*, *L for Lester*, *Roger Doesn't Live Here Anymore* and *The Lady Is a Tramp*. Other comedies included *Lance at Large*, *A Series of Bird's*, *The Dick Emery Show*, *Marty* and countless programme pilots and single pieces.

WILSON, DONALD
(1910–)

British screenwriter, script editor and producer, largely on BBC historical dramas (he was one of the Corporation's early contract-writers). Among his writing credits have been *The Six Proud Walkers* (1954 and again in 1962), *The Royalty* (1957, with Michael Voysey), *No Wreath for the General* (1960), *The Flying Swan* (1965), THE FIRST CHURCHILLS (1969, as writer, director and producer), *Anna Karenina* (1977, as writer and producer) and, most celebrated of all, THE FORSYTE SAGA (1967, as producer and co-writer).

WILSON, FRANCIS
(1949–)

Scottish weather-presenter, known for his relaxed, easygoing style which initially won him fans while working on *Thames News* (1978–82). Wilson then moved to the BBC's BREAKFAST TIME and *Breakfast News* before defecting to Sky News in 1992.

WILSON, RICHARD
OBE (Iain Wilson; 1936–)

Award-winning Scottish actor and director, a former scientist who, after years of supporting others, playing vicars, doctors and barristers, found his niche as the grumpy Victor Meldrew in ONE FOOT IN THE GRAVE. Otherwise, Wilson has played Revd Martin Hooper in MY GOOD WOMAN, Jeremy Parsons QC in CROWN COURT, Dr Gordon Thorpe in ONLY WHEN I LAUGH, the TV chaplain in *Room at the Bottom*, newspaper managing editor Richard Lipton in HOT METAL, Eddie Clockerty, the manager of the Majestics, in TUTTI FRUTTI, bank manager Richard Talbot in *High and Dry*, Hector Duff in *Unnatural Pursuits*, Mr Lichfield in *The Life and Times of Henry Pratt*, Revd Green in CLUEDO, Prime Minister James Forth in *Screenplay's The Vision Thing*, Ben Glazier in *Under the Hammer* (also as director), Bill Webster in *Screen One's The Lord of Misrule*, the Professor of Language in *Gulliver's Travels*, Lord Tone in *In the Red*, river policeman Prof in *Duck Patrol* and John Doone in *Life Support*. In addition, he has narrated the docu-soap, *The Zoo Keepers*, and been seen in *A Sharp Intake of Breath*, DR FINLAY'S CASEBOOK, INSPECTOR MORSE, WHOOPS APOCALYPSE and many other series and single dramas.

WILTON, PENELOPE
(1946–)

Yorkshire-born actress, probably best recalled as Ann, the long-suffering wife of the pedantic Martin Bryce, in EVER DECREASING CIRCLES. However, Wilton was also a member of the cast of *The Norman Conquests* and played Beatrice in Carla Lane's *Screaming* and Homily in *The Borrowers*. She also appeared in THE MONOCLED MUTINEER (Lady Angela Forbes) and has taken roles in dramas like *King Lear*, *The Widowing of Mrs Holroyd*, *The Sullen Sisters*, the *Performance* production of *The Deep Blue Sea* (Hester Collyer) and *Talking Heads 2* (Rosemary). Her two husbands have both been actors: the late Daniel Massey and Ian Holm.

WIND IN THE WILLOWS, THE
UK (Thames) Animation. ITV 1984–8

Voices:

Mole	Richard Pearson
Rat	Peter Sallis
Toad	David Jason

Badger .... **Michael Hordern**

Producers: **Mark Hall, Brian Cosgrove**

Rural roving in Edwardian England with a motley band of creatures.

Following the success the previous year of a 90-minute, animated musical adaptation of Kenneth Grahame's 1908 classic novel, Thames launched this series of additional rodent tales in 1984. Peter Sallis took over the role of Rat from Ian Carmichael, but otherwise the principal voicers remained in place. The success of the series lay chiefly in the quality of the animation, with each model reputedly costing around £5,000 to build.

WINDS OF WAR, THE
US (ABC) Drama. ITV 1983

Commander Victor 'Pug' Henry	**Robert Mitchum**
Natalie Jastrow	**Ali MacGraw**
Byron Henry	**Jan-Michael Vincent**
Warren Henry	**Ben Murphy**
Madeline Henry	**Lisa Eilbacher**
Rhoda Henry	**Polly Bergen**
Berel Jastrow	**Topol**
Aaron Jastrow	**John Houseman**
Palmer 'Fred' Kirby	**Peter Graves**
Pamela Tudsbury	**Victoria Tennant**
Alistair Tudsbury	**Michael Logan**
Leslie Slote	**David Dukes**
President Franklin D. Roosevelt	**Ralph Bellamy**
Winston Churchill	**Howard Lang**
Adolf Hitler	**Gunter Meisner**
Brigadier Gen. Armin Von Roon	**Jeremy Kemp**
Narrator	**William Woodson**

Writer: **Herman Wouk**
Producer: **Dan Curtis**

The globe-trotting escapades of an American military attaché in the early years of World War II.

Beginning with the German advance into Poland in 1939 and continuing through to the Japanese attack on Pearl Harbor in 1941, this mammoth drama was the story of one man's war. It focused on 'Pug' Henry, an American naval officer who was sent around the world, meeting the likes of Churchill and Hitler, but who found personal problems along the way. These came from his unfaithful wife, Rhoda, pilot son Warren, artistic son Byron and student daughter Madeline, as well as an English rose named Pam, with whom he embarked on an affair, and an eccentric Jewish girl, Natalie, who found herself in Poland as the Germans invaded and who became Byron's lover.

The Winds of War, adapted in eight parts from his own novel by Herman Wouk, cost £26 million to make and was heralded with a loud fanfare of publicity. However, viewers and critics were less than impressed on the whole. A sequel, *War and Remembrance*, which dramatized the remainder of Wouk's book and covered the final years of the war, was screened in 1989.

WINDSOR, BARBARA
MBE (Barbara-Ann Deeks; 1937–)

Diminutive blonde actress, for many years a stalwart of the *Carry On* movies but reviving her career on television as Peggy Mitchell in EASTENDERS. Earlier she had appeared as Judy in THE RAG TRADE, Millie in *Wild, Wild Women*, Saucy Nancy in WORZEL GUMMIDGE and Myrtle in YOU RANG, M'LORD?. She also provided voices for the cartoon, *The Great Bong*.

WINDSOR, FRANK
(1927–)

Frank Windsor, for most viewers, is John Watt, star of Z CARS and SOFTLY, SOFTLY. However, before arriving in Newtown, the Midlands-born actor had been seen in the Shakespearean anthology, AN AGE OF KINGS, and as scientist Dennis Bridger in A FOR ANDROMEDA. Among his later credits have been the title roles in *The Real Eddy English* and *Headmaster* (Tom Fisher), and the parts of Harry Bradley in the Rolls-Royce drama, *Flying Lady*, Cyril Wendage in SEPTEMBER SONG, Simon Armstrong in *Screen One*'s *Trip Trap* and William in *Anchor Me*. Other performances have come in CROWN COURT, WHODUNNIT?, *Kidnapped*, *Into the Labyrinth* and BOON, as well as a 1973 attempt to discover the truth behind *Jack the Ripper* (again in the guise of John Watt) and a follow-up series looking at other unsolved crimes, SECOND VERDICT.

WINFREY, OPRAH
(1954–)

American Oprah Winfrey was the first black woman to host a major US daytime talk show (*The Oprah Winfrey Show*, 1986) and proved so successful that she quickly became the richest woman on TV. Her career began as a teenager in Nashville, where she worked as a newsreader. Moving to Baltimore and then Chicago, she transferred into talk shows, rapidly outgunning her daytime rivals and soon being syndicated nationwide. Her shows (screened initially on Channel 4 in the UK) are highly charged emotionally and sometimes have a strong personal involvement from Oprah, such as her admission of childhood abuse and her well-publicized weight-watching regime. She now owns her own production company, Harpo Productions, and has several acting credits to her name, including in the series, *Brewster Place*.

WINGS
UK (BBC) Drama. BBC 1 1977–8

Sgt/2nd Lt. Alan Farmer	**Tim Woodward**
Capt. Owen Triggers	**Nicholas Jones**
Lt./2nd Lt. Charles Gaylion	**Michael Cochrane**
Lt. Richard Bravington	**David Troughton**
Lt. Michael Starling	**Michael Jayes**

Sgt Mills	**Roger Elliott**
Harry Farmer	**John Hallam**
Molly Farmer	**Anne Kristen**
Lorna Collins	**Sarah Porter**
2nd Lt. Favell	**Simon Turner**
Tom	**Reg Lye**
Kate Gaylion	**Celia Bannerman**

Creator: **Barry Thomas**
Producer: **Peter Cregeen**

Stirring action in the skies during World War I.

Over two series, and beginning in February 1915, *Wings* focused on the daring pilots of the Royal Flying Corps, the pioneers of air combat during the Great War. Tackling the Hun in their sheepskin jackets, leather hats and goggles were French-based aviators Farmer, Triggers, Gaylion, Bravington and others. Farmer was initially the odd man out, being a poorly educated blacksmith's son who taught himself to fly and subsequently gained promotion from the NCO ranks to join the snooty commissioned men. The series took as its inspiration events in the lives of real RFC airmen and made good use of numerous re-created old flying machines. Alexander Faris composed the sweeping period theme music.

WINKLER, HENRY
(1945–)

American actor, producer and director, whose creation of Fonzie, the superhuman biker with the heart of gold, turned the sitcom, HAPPY DAYS, from a ratings also-ran into America's number-one show. Winkler was with the series for its entire run (1974–84), becoming a US institution in the process. When it ended, he moved behind the scenes, creating (with John Rich) *MacGyver* and producing other projects. He has also been seen in a few TV movies.

WINNER TAKES ALL
UK (Yorkshire) Quiz. ITV 1975–87

Presenters: **Jimmy Tarbuck, Geoffrey Wheeler**

Creator: **Geoffrey Wheeler**
Producers: **Guy Caplan, Lawrie Higgins, Ian Bolt, Don Clayton, Terry Henebery, Graham Wetherell**

Long-running quiz in which contestants gambled on the answers to questions.

Jimmy Tarbuck welcomed the guests and the unseen Geoffrey Wheeler asked the questions in this popular general knowledge quiz show. The four contestants competed in a little knock-out tournament to find one winner who would 'take all', namely a big cash prize, at the end of each programme. The winner then stayed on the following week, risking a proportion of his winnings in the pursuit of more money.

Five questions were offered, one at a time, together with six possible answers. Each answer was accompanied by appropriate odds, ranging from even money, through 2–1, 3–1, 4–1 and 5–1 to the rank outsider at 10–1. The contestants had to select an answer and back it with a proportion of their points bank, losing the gambled points if the answer was wrong, but reaping the rewards if they gambled correctly. The contestant with the most points was the winner. In the final round, pounds replaced points, but only the winner could take away his final total. When Jimmy Tarbuck left the series in 1987 to present a new game show, *Tarby's Frame Game*, Geoffrey Wheeler (who was also the deviser of the series) was brought into vision as joint host and question master.

WINSTON CHURCHILL – THE WILDERNESS YEARS
UK (Southern) Historical Drama. ITV 1981

Winston Churchill	**Robert Hardy**
Clementine	**Siân Phillips**
Stanley Baldwin	**Peter Barkworth**
Neville Chamberlain	**Eric Porter**
Samuel Hoare	**Edward Woodward**
Bernard Baruch	**Sam Wanamaker**
Brenden Bracken	**Tim Pigott-Smith**

Creators: **Martin Gilbert, Richard Broke**
Executive Producer: **Mark Shivas**
Producer: **Richard Broke**

Dramatization of Churchill's period of political 'exile'.

After a meteoric rise to prominence in the early decades of the 20th century, Churchill's political career ground dramatically to a halt during the 1930s. A change in leadership in the Conservative Party and momentous movements on the world stage left the always outspoken Churchill sitting in the shadows, his voice singing out of tune with many of his own political colour. This drama looked back at those 'wilderness years', viewing how the great man bided his time, speaking out in vain on issues such as the rise of fascism and self-government for India, offering support for Edward VIII in the Abdication Crisis and waiting for that moment when the country would again call upon his services. The eight-part series was one of Southern Television's last productions.

WINSTONE, RAY
(1957–)

East London-born actor starring in programmes like *Get Back* (Martin Sweet), *The Ghostbusters of East Finchley* (Thane), *Our Boy* (Woody) and *Births, Marriages and Deaths* (Alan). He also appeared in series such as FOX (Kenny Fox), ROBIN OF SHERWOOD (Will Scarlet), FAIRLY SECRET ARMY (Stubby Collins), *Father Matthew's Daughter* (Father Charlie), MURDER MOST HORRID, *Tough Love* (DC Lenny Milton) and *Face* (Dave), and featured in the single drama, *Scum*.

WINTERS, MIKE

(Michael Weinstein; 1930–) and **BERNIE** (Bernie Weinstein; 1932–91)

British comedy double-act of the 1950s–1970s, real-life brothers who originally worked together as part of a music and impressions band. After gaining radio experience, they were given regular exposure on SIX-FIVE SPECIAL in 1957 and, after a few ups and downs, were hosts of *Big Night Out* and *Blackpool Night Out* in the 1960s. They also starred in *Mike and Bernie's Show*, *Mike and Bernie's Scene* and the sitcom, *Mike and Bernie*. Their act was essentially traditional music-hall crosstalk, with Mike the straight man and Bernie the idiot who referred to his brother as 'Choochy Face'. However, differences came to the fore and the brothers split up in 1978. Mike became a businessman in Florida, while Bernie teamed up with Schnorbitz, his St Bernard dog, and starred in his own series, *Bernie*, and hosted the game show, *Whose Baby?*. He also perfected an impersonation of Bud Flanagan and performed it on stage and TV, with Leslie Crowther as his partner, Chesney Allen.

WINTON, DALE

(1955–)

Light entertainment presenter, coming to the fore as host of the cult day-time game show, *Supermarket Sweep*. He has since moved into prime time with *Pets Win Prizes*, THE NATIONAL LOTTERY LIVE and *The Other Half*, as well as hosting GMTV. The son of 1960s TV starlet Sheree Winton (who allegedly named him after actor Dale Robertson), Winton began his career in radio, with the United Biscuits Network and then Radio Trent in Nottingham. He moved into TV as presenter of *Pet Watch* in 1986, and worked on *Network 7*, *Home Today* and *Public Enemy Number One*, as well as satellite television, before *Supermarket Sweep* made him a star.

WIPE

A visual effect in which one camera shot displaces another on the screen, 'wiping' across from side to side, top to bottom or even breaking through in contrived patterns. The facility was much employed in 1970s pop-music programmes.

WISDOM, Sir NORMAN

OBE (1915–)

Acknowledged as one of Britain's great screen clowns, diminutive Norman Wisdom has made his mark in the story of television, too, even though his TV work generally fitted in and around his film career. London-born Wisdom was given his first TV series, *Wit and Wisdom*, in 1948, followed in 1953 by *It's Wisdom* and, in 1956, by *The Norman Wisdom Show*. On one famous TV occasion, he was the lone star of SUNDAY NIGHT AT THE LONDON

PALLADIUM, taking over the whole show, papering the set and eventually being chased off by compere Bruce Forsyth. With his best cinema days behind him, he turned to sitcom in 1970 with *Norman*, a series about a taxman-turned-musician, and followed it with *Nobody Is Norman Wisdom*, as Nobody, a daydreamer. His next series, *A Little Bit of Wisdom*, ran for three years, with various situations and characters. In contrast, his performance as a man dying of cancer in the 1981 drama, *Going Gently*, won much acclaim and, enjoying his switch to straight acting, he was later seen as a guest in BERGERAC, LAST OF THE SUMMER WINE and CASUALTY.

WISE, ERNIE

OBE (Ernest Wiseman; 1925–99) See MORECAMBE, ERIC.

WISE, HERBERT

(1924–)

British director responsible for I, CLAUDIUS and *The Norman Conquests*, plus episodes of such series as *The Victorians*, Z CARS, *Six Shades of Black*, UPSTAIRS, DOWN-STAIRS, THE SIX WIVES OF HENRY VIII, ELIZABETH R, THE BBC TELEVISION SHAKESPEARE, RUMPOLE OF THE BAILEY, INSPECTOR MORSE, THE RUTH RENDELL MYSTERIES and the P. D. JAMES Adam Dalgliesh story, *Death of an Expert Witness*. Single dramas include *The Cruel Day*, *The Big Donkey*, *Walk with Destiny* and *The Woman in Black*.

WISH ME LUCK

UK (LWT) Drama. ITV 1988–90

Liz Grainger	**Kate Buffery**
Mathilde 'Matty' Firman	**Suzanna Hamilton**
Col. James 'Cad' Cadogan	**Julian Glover**
Kit Vanston	**Michael J. Jackson**
Faith Ashley	**Jane Asher**
Colin Beale	**Jeremy Northam**
Claudine de Valois	**Shelagh McLeod**
Lois Mountjoy	**Abigail McKern**
Col. Werner Krieger	**Warren Clarke**
Laurence Grainger	**Nigel Le Vaillant**
Vivien Ashton	**Lynn Farleigh**
Emily Whitbread	**Jane Snowden**
Gordon Stewart	**Stuart McGugan**
Lewis	**Jeremy Nicholas**
Virginia	**Catherine Schell**
Renard	**Trevor Peacock**
Nicole	**Felicity Montagu**
Gen. Stuckler	**Terrence Hardiman**
Col. Max Dubois	**Damien Thomas**

Creators: **Jill Hyem, Lavinia Warner**
Executive Producer: **Nick Elliott**
Producers: **Colin Shindler, Lavinia Warner, Michael Chaplin**

Brave men and women infiltrate German-occupied France.

Like the similarly styled MANHUNT and SECRET ARMY,

Wish Me Luck was set in World War II and focused on the daring young people who risked life and limb to spy on the enemy and sabotage the Nazi advance. Two women in particular were highlighted, both fluent in French, with a local's knowledge of Normandy. One was well-bred blonde Liz Grainger from Devon, a twenty-something mother of a five-year-old daughter, who answered an appeal for pictures of Normandy and was duly recruited. Her brother had been killed in action and her husband, Laurence, was away with the forces. The other was earthy 22-year-old Cockney, Matty Firman, whose mother was French and whose father was a London Jew. She was recruited as a wireless operator. Both worked as agents of the Special Operations Executive (casually known as 'The Outfit'), run by Colonel James 'Cad' Cadogan, assisted by Oxford graduate Faith Ashley (dubbed 'The Snow Queen') and wireless receiver Lois Mountjoy (the teenage daughter of a vicar).

The unlikely duo worked together behind enemy lines, along with baronet's son and Oxford blue, Kit Vanston (the chief intelligence officer in the area), fellow agent Colin Beale (naval experience) and Claudine (a wealthy former Sorbonne buddy of Liz's, now forced to work for a living and who took an instant dislike to the 'common' Matty). Claudine developed a risky 'friendship' with the increasingly cruel local Nazi boss, Colonel Krieger, later replaced by General Stuckler. New agents were also introduced in later series, primarily Vivien (a recently widowed former dancer) and Emily (a Catholic doctor's daughter).

WISH YOU WERE HERE . . . ?
See HOLIDAY.

WITCHELL, NICHOLAS
(1953–)

Red-haired BBC journalist, a former Northern Ireland reporter and foreign correspondent (Beirut and the Falklands) who joined the Corporation as a trainee in 1976. He has fronted all the main bulletins (especially *Breakfast News*), and contributed to PANORAMA. He was made diplomatic correspondent in 1995 and royal correspondent in 1998.

WITHIN THESE WALLS
UK (LWT) Drama. ITV 1974–8

Faye Boswell .... **Googie Withers**
Charles Radley .... **Jerome Willis**
Chief Officer Mrs Armitage .... **Mona Bruce**
Dr Mayes .... **Denys Hawthorne**
Miss Clarke .... **Beth Harris**
Helen Forrester .... **Katharine Blake**
Susan Marshall .... **Sarah Lawson**

Executive Producer: **Rex Firkin**
Producer: **Jack Williamson**

Drama centring on the governor of a women's prison.

Set in HMP Stone Park, *Within These Walls* focused on its newly installed governor, Faye Boswell, as she set out to liberalize the firmly run institution. She quickly realized that all would not be plain sailing and she met resentment not only from the inmates but from the staff, too. The impact on her personal life was also scrutinized. Boswell lasted three years before making way for a new governor, Helen Forrester, who was in turn succeeded by Susan Marshall in 1978. The series was the inspiration for the Australian soap, PRISONER: CELL BLOCK H, which proved much more durable.

WITT, PAUL JUNGER
(1943–)

American producer, working on series like THE PARTRIDGE FAMILY in the early 1970s, before producing the comedies, SOAP and *Benson* (both written by his wife, Susan Harris), in partnership with Tony Thomas. Joining forces in Witt-Thomas-Harris Productions, they have since handled all Harris's other hits, including THE GOLDEN GIRLS, *The Golden Palace, Empty Nest* and *Nurses*. Witt and Thomas have also produced BEAUTY AND THE BEAST, *Blossom, Herman's Head* and *Pearl*.

WKRP IN CINCINNATI
US (MTM) Situation Comedy. ITV 1981–2/Channel 4
1983–4

Andy Travis .... **Gary Sandy**
Arthur Carlson ('Big Guy') .... **Gordon Jump**
Jennifer Marlowe .... **Loni Anderson**
Les Nessman .... **Richard Sanders**
Herb Tarlek .... **Frank Bonner**
Gordon Sims (Venus Flytrap) .... **Tim Reid**
Bailey Quarters .... **Jan Smithers**
Johnny Caravella (Dr Johnny Fever) ....
.... **Howard Hesseman**
Lillian 'Mama' Carlson .... **Carol Bruce**

Creator: **Hugh Wilson**

A dying radio station is kicked into life when a new programme director takes over.

WKRP, one of Cincinnati's 18 radio stations, was losing money hand over fist. Its drab playlist attracted only a drab, ageing audience and drab advertising sponsors. But all that changed when new programme controller Andy Travis arrived. He encouraged the station's elderly owner, Mama Carlson, and her son, Arthur, the incompetent station manager (commonly known as 'Big Guy'), to take a chance, make the switch to rock music and put some life back in the programming. Mrs Carlson bought the idea and the ratings began to take off. All the same, it was obvious that this radio station would never be a huge success.

The WKRP team consisted of Les Nessman, a bumptious news, weather and farming reporter, Bailey

Quarters, Andy's young assistant, who became a journalist, and the station's top two DJs, Dr Johnny Fever (real name Johnny Caravella), the laid-back, jive-talking morning presenter, and Venus Flytrap (Gordon Sims), a cool, black night-time jock. Holding the station together was busty, blonde secretary, Jennifer Marlowe, constantly pursued by obnoxious ad salesman Herb Tarlek.

Nine years after the series ended, a new version was produced for syndication in the USA. Only three members of the original cast were recalled: Arthur Carlson, Herb Tarlek and Les Nessman.

WODEHOUSE PLAYHOUSE
UK (BBC) Comedy. BBC 1 1975–8

John Alderton, Pauline Collins

Writer: **David Climie**
Producers: **David Askey, Michael Mills, Gareth Gwenlan**

Anthology of P. G. Wodehouse comedies.

Adapted by David Climie from the short stories of P. G. Wodehouse, this collection of 1920s high society farces starred the husband-and-wife pairing of John Alderton and Pauline Collins in a variety of different roles. Wodehouse himself introduced the earliest episodes. Three series were made.

WOGAN, TERRY
OBE (Hon.) (1938–)

Irish presenter and chat show host. A one-time bank clerk, then a presenter with RTE in Dublin, Wogan joined the BBC in the 1960s and was one of Radio 1's original team of presenters in 1967. His Radio 2 breakfast show in the 1970s and early 1980s gained a cult following and established his distinctively witty, self-effacing presentational style. Items like 'Fighting the Flab' and 'Wogan's Winner' characterized the show, and his constant digs at DALLAS ensured that the soap became a hit in the UK. Although he had already hosted a chat show, *Lunchtime with Wogan*, for ATV in 1972, and the pop quiz, *Disco*, in 1975, it wasn't until 1979, when he began five years at the helm of the panel game, BLANKETY BLANK, that his TV career began to take off. In 1980 he turned his hand to chat shows with *What's On Wogan*, a live Saturday tea-time programme. Two years later, it metamorphosed into *Wogan* and was transmitted late on a Saturday night, before being promoted in 1985 to an early-evening, thrice-weekly live event. Terry quickly became *the* TV personality of the 1980s and was seldom off British screens. When *Wogan* ended to make way for ELDORADO in 1992, he returned to his old Radio 2 morning slot, saving room all the same for another music-and-chat show, *Wogan's Friday Night*, and the Ireland travelogue, *Wogan's Island*. He has been co-host of the annual charity telethon, CHILDREN IN NEED, since 1980, and can be heard every year disparaging the entries on the EUROVISION SONG CONTEST. Among his other TV credits have been COME DANCING, MISS WORLD, *You Must Be Joking!*, *Do the Right Thing* and the bloopers programme, *Auntie's Bloomers*, and its spin-offs. He is the father of actress Katherine Wogan and TV chef Mark Wogan.

WOLFE, RONALD
See CHESNEY, RONALD.

WOLSTENHOLME, KENNETH
DFC (1920–)

British soccer commentator, a contributor to *Sports Special* in the 1950s and the voice of football with the BBC in the 1960s, thanks to his work on MATCH OF THE DAY. It was Wolstenholme who uttered the famous words, 'They think it's all over. It is now' at the end of the 1966 World Cup Final. He left the BBC in 1971 to make way for a new generation of commentators after 23 years with the Corporation, but continued to cover soccer for Tyne Tees before retiring. He has since made numerous guest appearances and has become something of a cult figure. Prior to entering broadcasting, Wolstenholme had been a bomber pilot in the war and was awarded the DFC.

WOMAN OF SUBSTANCE, A
UK (Portman Artemis) Drama. Channel 4 1985

Emma Harte	Jenny Seagrove
	Deborah Kerr
Henry Rossiter	John Mills
Laura Spencer	Diane Baker
Bruce McGill	George Baker
Olivia	Gayle Hunnicutt
Adele Fairley	Nicola Pagett
Paula	Miranda Richardson
Paul McGill	Barry Bostwick
Shane O'Neill	Liam Neeson
Murgatroyd	Barry Morse

Writer: **Lee Langley**
Producer: **Diane Baker**

An ambitious servant girl drives her way to the top.

Told in flashback and beginning in 1905, *A Woman of Substance* was the rags-to-riches story of Emma Harte, a Yorkshire lass from the serving classes who made her way up through society. Her ambitions took her out of the scullery and into the world of business. She moved to the USA and became one of the world's wealthiest women, owning a major chain of department stores. Jenny Seagrove played Emma up to the age of 49, with Deborah Kerr taking over for the heroine's later years. Adapted by Lee Langley from Barbara Taylor Bradford's romantic novel, this mini-series was shown on three consecutive nights on Channel 4 in 1985. A year later, a sequel made in America and entitled *Hold That Dream* once again saw Seagrove and Kerr in the role of Harte.

WOMBLES, THE

UK (Filmfair/Cinar Films) Children's Entertainment. BBC 1 1973–5/1990–1; 1998–

Narrator: **Bernard Cribbins**

Creator/Writer: **Elisabeth Beresford**

A small colony of cuddly conservationists keeps Wimbledon Common free of litter.

'Underground, overground, wombling free', the long-nosed, furry Wombles of Wimbledon Common were Britain's foremost ecologists in the 1970s. 'Making good use of the things that they find, things that the everyday folk leave behind', the incredibly devious Wombles turned trash into useful items – useful to a Womble at least. Their burrow was wallpapered in discarded newsprint and there was always some new contraption being conjured up. Headed by Great Uncle Bulgaria, the Wombles were Tomsk, Orinoco, Tobermory, Wellington, Bungo and their French housemaid, Mme Cholet.

Based on the stories by Elisabeth Beresford (once married to broadcaster Max Robertson), the five-minute Wombles tales, animated by Ivor Wood, were whimsically narrated by Bernard Cribbins. Mike Batt performed the theme music, which became a hit in 1974 and led to a spate of other Wombling pop pieces. A feature film, *Wombling Free*, was released in 1977, and the busy little creatures were resurrected by ITV in 1990–1 for two one-off stories. In 1998 the Wombles were back, with four new members in the clan: Stepney (a Cockney), Obidos (a pan piper from Brazil), Shanshi (from China) and the skateboarding Alderney, who lived in a tree-house. Contemporary technology like womfaxes and the Internet made life easier for the fluffy ecologists.

WONDER WOMAN

US (Warner Brothers) Science Fiction. BBC 1 1978–80

Diana Prince/Wonder Woman	**Lynda Carter**
Steve Trevor	**Lyle Waggoner**
Joe Atkinson	**Normann Burton**
IRA	**Tom Kratochzil** (*voice only*)

Executive Producer: **Douglas S. Cramer**
Producer: **Bruce Lansbury**

A superwoman uses her powers to fight subversion.

Wonder Woman, a creation of cartoonist Charles Moulton, actually appeared in two different settings on TV in the 1970s. Firstly, in a series entitled *The New, Original Wonder Woman*, she lived in the 1940s. She was discovered among a race of Amazon women on Paradise Island, an uncharted piece of land somewhere in the Caribbean, by a crash-landed US major, Steve Trevor. The women, refugees from ancient Greece and Rome, had lived on the island since about 200 BC, having stumbled across a magical material called Feminum which, when moulded into bracelets or belts, gave them superhuman powers.

The future Wonder Woman was Princess Diana, daughter of Hippolyte, the Queen of the Amazons. Nursing the wounded soldier back to health, she fell in love and returned with him to civilization. There, she assumed the identity of Diana Prince and became his secretary in the War Department. However, whenever trouble beckoned, she took on the mantle of Wonder Woman, performing a quick change of clothes by spinning herself around and donning a patriotic red, white and blue costume, complete with Feminum belt to give her strength and Feminum bracelets to deflect bullets. The magical lasso she carried forced her enemies (usually Nazis) to tell the truth.

This series was not shown in the UK. We did catch up with her, however, in the second series, *The New Adventures of Wonder Woman*, in which the setting was 1970s America. Diana had once again returned from Paradise Island, showing no sign of ageing, to take up a post as an agent for the Inter-Agency Defense Command (IADC). Her boss was Joe Atkinson and her close colleague was the son of her former friend, Steve Trevor, conveniently the double of his father (and also called Steve). For the IADC, Diana fought against crazed scientists, saboteurs, terrorists and aliens, and, like all the agents, was assisted by a talking Internal Retrieval Associative computer (IRA). Only IRA knew Diana's *alter ego*.

The statuesque Lynda Carter was perfectly built to fill this Amazonian role – she had been Miss America in 1973. All the same, a 1974 pilot film cast Cathy Lee Crosby in the title role.

WONDER YEARS, THE

US (Black/Marlens) Situation Comedy. Channel 4 1989–93

Kevin Arnold	**Fred Savage**
Kevin Arnold (adult)	**Daniel Stern** (*voice only*)
Jack Arnold	**Dan Lauria**
Norma Arnold	**Alley Mills**
Wayne Arnold	**Jason Hervey**
Karen Arnold	**Olivia d'Abo**
Paul Pfeiffer	**Josh Saviano**
Gwendolyn 'Winnie' Cooper	**Danica McKellar**
Coach Ed Cutlip	**Robert Picardo**

Creators: **Neal Marlens, Carol Black**
Executive Producers: **Neal Marlens, Carol Black, Bob Brush**

Light-hearted, nostalgic tales of growing up in suburban America in the late 1960s.

The Wonder Years focused on young Kevin Arnold, a 12-year-old (at the programme's beginning), just starting out at the Robert F. Kennedy Junior High School in 1968 and desperate to make the right impression with his peers, especially the girls. The adult Kevin (never seen) acted as narrator, telling viewers just what his younger self had been thinking at that time. The result was a whimsical, poignant observation of adolescent woes in an era of social change.

Kevin was the youngest child of a typical suburban family. His mom and dad were 1940s teenagers turned parents and householders, overtaken somewhat by time and finding it difficult to relate to their children (especially after a hard day's work). Wayne, Kevin's obnoxious brother, teased him mercilessly, while his sister, Karen, was into every peace and protest movement of the day. Kevin's best friend was Paul, a gangly, nerdy type with glasses and a brace, and Winnie Cooper was the girl next door whom Kevin had his eye on.

Old newsreel clips added period atmosphere, as did music of the time (the show's theme was Joe Cocker's 'With a Little Help from My Friends'), but this was a programme whose success came from the strength of its characterization and its scripts, not cheap, nostalgic in-fills.

WOOD, DUNCAN

(1925–97)

BBC comedy producer of the 1950s–1970s, working with Benny Hill, Frankie Howerd and Ken Dodd, and also responsible for such classic sitcoms as HANCOCK'S HALF HOUR and STEPTOE AND SON. *Strictly T-T, Great Scott – It's Maynard!*, CITIZEN JAMES, THE BED-SIT GIRL, HUGH AND I, *Harry Worth*, OH BROTHER!, THE FURTHER ADVENTURES OF LUCKY JIM, *The World of Beachcomber* and *Now Take My Wife* were other notable production credits. He moved to Yorkshire Television in the 1970s as Head of Light Entertainment, where he commissioned series like RISING DAMP, *Hello Cheeky*, OH NO! IT'S SELWYN FROGGITT and 3–2–1.

WOOD, VICTORIA

OBE (1953–)

Lancashire-born comedienne, musician and writer, coming to light in the NEW FACES talent show in 1975 and its spin-off, *The Summer Show*. A year later, she secured herself fortnightly work writing topical songs for THAT'S LIFE and by the end of the decade was moving into her own comic plays like *Talent, Nearly a Happy Ending* and *Happy Since I Met You*, usually with her regular partner, Julie Walters. Together they hosted a show for Granada entitled *Wood and Walters*, before Victoria switched to the BBC and began a run of successful comedies, among them *Victoria Wood – As Seen on TV* (a sketch and monologue show with a repertory cast of Walters, Celia Imrie, Duncan Preston and Susie Blake, and featuring the CROSSROADS spoof, *Acorn Antiques*), and the playlet series, *Victoria Wood*. In 1994 she starred again with Julie Walters in the *Screen One* comedy, *Pat and Margaret*, in 1996 took one of the *Great Railway Journeys*, and in 1998 launched her own sitcom, DINNERLADIES, appearing herself as Bren. In 2000 she hosted *Don't Panic! The Dad's Army Story*. Wood is married to entertainer Geoffrey Durham (aka The Great Soprendo).

WOODENTOPS, THE

UK (BBC) Children's Entertainment. BBC 1955–8

Voices: **Peter Hawkins, Eileen Brown, Josephina Ray**

Creators: **Freda Lingstrom, Maria Bird**
Producer: **Freda Lingstrom**
Writer: **Maria Bird**

Idyllic life down on the farm with an industrious puppet family.

Friday's WATCH WITH MOTHER offering was brought to the screen by the same team responsible for Tuesday's (ANDY PANDY) and Wednesday's (FLOWER POT MEN). The Woodentops were Daddy Woodentop (seldom seen with a shirt on his back), Mummy Woodentop (so busy in the kitchen that she needed daily help from Mrs Scrubbitt), high-pitched twins Jenny and Willy Woodentop and, completing the family, Baby Woodentop, still in his mother's arms. Also seen was Sam, the man who helped Daddy Woodentop in the garden, as well as Buttercup the cow and a rascally hound by the appropriate name of Spotty Dog, in fact 'the biggest spotty dog you ever did see'. With action thin on the ground, the best that toddlers could hope for was Jenny or Willy getting into a scrape and being late for dinner, or Spotty taking the odd liberty with his caring owners. All ended well, however, and the whole cast waved goodbye over the closing credits. Once again Audrey Atterbury and Molly Gibson pulled the strings.

WOODHOUSE, BARBARA

(1910–88)

Irish-born doctor's wife and farmer who became an unlikely TV celebrity as an animal trainer. After years of supplying star animals for the media, Barbara Woodhouse's heyday arrived in 1980 when she hosted an educational series entitled TRAINING DOGS THE WOODHOUSE WAY, which was considered to be light entertainment of the first order by many viewers. The bossy granny in a Scottish kilt and sensible shoes pioneered 'quick training' methods for dogs, barking shrill orders and yanking them into submission with her much-criticized choke-chains. But she was equally tough on inept owners who failed to bring their pets into line. She later took her message around the country in *The Woodhouse Roadshow* and also hosted other canine and equine programmes.

WOODWARD, EDWARD

OBE (1931–)

British actor fond of tough, determined roles like that of secret agent CALLAN and avenging angel Robert McCall in THE EQUALIZER. Among his other credits have been DETECTIVE (Edgar Allan Poe's Auguste Dupin), 1990 (journalist Jim Kyle), WINSTON CHURCHILL – THE WILDERNESS YEARS (Sir Samuel Hoare), *Nice Work* (labour official Edwin Thornfield), COMMON AS MUCK (Nev), the American crime series, *Over My Dead Body* (detective-novelist Maxwell Becket), and *Gulliver's Travels* (Drunlo). He also appeared in the 1977 drama, *The Bass Player and the Blonde*, hosted the anthology series, *In Suspicious Circumstances*, and has plenty of single plays in his portfolio. His earliest guest appearances came in 1960s series like MOGUL, THE SAINT and MYSTERY AND IMAGINATION. The father of actors Tim, Peter and Sarah Woodward, and husband of actress Michele Dotrice, he also hosted the 1970s panel game, WHODUNNIT?, and was occasionally heard singing in 1970s variety shows such as his own *The Edward Woodward Hour*.

WORD, THE

UK (24 Hour/Planet 24). Channel 4 1990–5

Presenters: **Terry Christian, Amanda de Cadanet, Kate Puckrik, Mark Lamarr, Dani Behr, Huffty, Jasmine Dottiwala, Andrew Connor**

Editors: **Charlie Parsons, Sebastian Scott, Paul Ross, Duncan Grey**
Producers: **Dele Oniya, Richard Godfrey, Tamsin Summers, Asif Zubairy**
Executive Producer: **Charlie Parsons**

Controversial, late-night music and chat show.

For middle-aged critics *The Word* was everything that was bad about early 1990s television. A new generation of youth culture had finally arrived and, pre-empting even less disciplined programmes like *The Girlie Show*, this magazine led the way with its laddish approach, gossipy interviews and sometimes ignorant interviewees. One notorious slot was called The Hopefuls and featured members of the general public who would do, it seemed, absolutely anything to get on television, from outrageous stunts to revolting things with their bodies. The series started out in a 6 p.m. transmission slot but was soon moved to around 11 p.m. – indicative of its appeal to the post-pub crowd. But *The Word* was at least live and lively, with a buzzing audience milling around the guests, and among its achievements was providing Oasis with their first ever TV exposure. Paul Ross (brother of Jonathan) was editor for a time.

WORKER, THE

UK (ATV) Situation Comedy. ITV 1965; 1969–70

Charlie .... **Charlie Drake**
Mr Whittaker .... **Percy Herbert**
Mr Pugh .... **Henry McGee**
Writers: **Charlie Drake, Lew Schwarz**
Producers: **Alan Tarrant, Shaun O'Riordan**

An unemployable nuisance is the scourge of the local labour exchange.

Although he was known as the Worker, Charlie didn't – work, that is, at least not for more than one day at a time, such was his inability to hold down a job. Apparently he had fouled up nearly 1,000 jobs in 20 years. As a result, the irrepressible, ginger-haired imp banged on the counter of the Weybridge labour exchange every other morning, much to the frustration of the clerks, first Mr Whittaker then, more famously, Mr Pugh (or Mr Peooow, as our hero dubbed him). Such antagonism unfailingly ended with Pugh grabbing Charlie by the throat and winching him off the ground. After a gap of four years, the series was brought back in 1969, and it was briefly revived once more in 1978 as part of *Bruce Forsyth's Big Night*, with Drake and McGee again doing battle in the job centre.

WORKING TITLE

The provisional title of a programme, used during preparations and planning but which may be changed before the programme reaches the air.

WORLD ABOUT US, THE

UK (BBC) Natural History. BBC 2 1967–86

Long-running series featuring the wonders of nature and assorted global explorations.

Initially making use of amateur footage, but soon becoming fully professional in its contributions, *The World About Us* ran for nearly 20 years. It was commissioned by David Attenborough (then head of BBC 2) to illustrate the scope of colour television (which had just been introduced), the glorious hues of the natural world providing the perfect subject-matter. Major geographical expeditions were also featured (one went up the Orinoco and Amazon by hovercraft), and Jacques Cousteau's undersea explorations also formed part of the package.

WORLD AT WAR, THE

UK (Thames) Historical Documentary. ITV 1973–4

Narrator: **Laurence Olivier**

Producer: **Jeremy Isaacs**

Eye-opening account of World War II.

Thoroughly researched (with historical accuracy monitored by Noble Frankland), *The World at War* looked at the 1939–45 conflict in 26 episodes. From the rise to power of Hitler to the bombing of Hiroshima, all the dramas and horrors of the war were documented using old film footage (some newly unearthed) and harrowing eye-witness accounts. The accompanying book sold half a million copies and the series won awards all round the world. It was repeated on BBC 2 in 1994 and 2001.

WORLD IN ACTION

UK (Granada) Current Affairs. ITV 1963–98

Creator: **Tim Hewat**
Producers: **Tim Hewat, David Plowright, Leslie**

Woodhead, Jeremy Wallington, Gus McDonald, Denis Mitchell, Michael Apted, Mike Wooller, John Birt, Ray Fitzwalter, Alex Valentine, Brian Lapping, Nick Hayes, Charles Tremayne, Steve Boulton

Long-running, award-winning current affairs series.

Launched with the intention of providing 'not simply the news but the full background story', *World in Action* became one of the world's most acclaimed public affairs series. From the first edition, when it focused on the nuclear arms race, the series was never afraid to confront authority. Its hard-hitting, in-depth investigations caused embarrassment to many politicians and industrialists, exposing scandals and unearthing hidden facts. Programmes were generally half an hour in length and aired on Monday evenings.

WORLD OF SPORT
UK (Various) Sport. ITV 1965–85

Presenters: **Eamonn Andrews, Richard Davies**

Four-and-a-half-hour Saturday sports marathon.

ITV's answer to GRANDSTAND, *World of Sport* tried somewhat unsuccessfully to compete with its BBC rival for 20 years, before finally throwing in the towel. Although, as an overall package, it was never on terms with *Grandstand* (largely because the BBC controlled all the major events), *World of Sport* did enjoy a sizeable following for its minority sports, particularly horse racing and wrestling.

World of Sport was a team effort involving most ITV companies, with studio facilities and programme production provided by LWT in later years. Its first host was Eamonn Andrews, supported by a team of Fleet Street sub-editors who clattered around in the background, thrusting latest scores and other news items into his hand as he talked to camera. Richard 'Dickie' Davies took over in 1968 and remained in charge until the programme was cancelled in 1985. Fred Dinenage was Davies's relief presenter.

For many years the running order featured football to start, followed by horse racing and the likes of snooker, darts and motor sports, with wrestling taking over the second half of the programme and leading into the results service at about 4.45 p.m. Some events were screened under the umbrella subtitle of *International Sports Special*, which embraced anything from show-jumping and water skiing to Australian rules football and arm wrestling. In the early days, Fred Trueman and Ian Wooldridge were specialist contributors to the programme and Peter Lorenzo previewed the day's soccer. When the football slot was retitled *On the Ball*, Brian Moore and Jimmy Hill were drafted in as hosts. Ian St John and Jimmy Greaves were the last football pundits, and when *World of Sport* was cancelled their slot survived as a separate programme, entitled *Saint and Greavsie*. (*On the Ball* was revived as a programme in its own right in 1998, with presenters Gabby Yorath and Barry Venison.) *World of Sport* was the pioneer of multi-course racing

coverage, as an all-action alternative to one-card racing. Its *ITV Seven* (an accumulator based on the winners of all seven featured races) became a popular bet. Trilby-hatted John Rickman took charge of racing affairs for many years, and also seen were John Oaksey, Ken Butler, Brough Scott and Derek Thompson, with commentaries by Tony Cooke, John Penney, Raleigh Gilbert and Graham Goode and results from John Tyrrel. Wrestling was in the capable hands of former disc-jockey Kent Walton, and other commentators included Tony Green for darts, John Pulman for snooker, Adrian Metcalfe for athletics and Reg Gutteridge for boxing.

WORTH, HARRY
(Harry Illingsworth; 1917–89)

Yorkshire-born comedian and comic actor, generally seen as a genial, bungling interferer who ended up confusing all and sundry. Breaking into showbiz as a ventriloquist, Worth, a former miner, abandoned his dummies on the advice of Stan Laurel and became a stand-up comic. In 1959 he began his first TV series, the sitcom, *The Trouble With Harry*, and less than a year later starred in HERE'S HARRY, in which he introduced his trademark shop-window routine, using his reflection to make it look as if he was waving all four limbs at once. *Here's Harry* ran for five years and was followed during the 1960s and 1970s by *Harry Worth, Thirty Minutes' Worth, My Name Is Harry Worth* (titled after his catchphrase), *How's Your Father* (as Harry Matthews, an out-of-touch widowed father of two teenagers) and *Oh Happy Band!* (playing himself as a brass band conductor). He was also seen as William Boot in the BBC's 1972 serialization of Evelyn Waugh's newspaper spoof, *Scoop*.

WORZEL GUMMIDGE
UK (Southern) Children's Adventure. ITV 1979–81

Worzel Gummidge	**Jon Pertwee**
Aunt Sally	**Una Stubbs**
The Crowman	**Geoffrey Bayldon**
John Peters	**Jeremy Austin**
Sue Peters	**Charlotte Coleman**
Mr Peters	**Mike Berry**
Mrs Braithwaite	**Megs Jenkins**
Mr Braithwaite	**Norman Bird**
Saucy Nancy	**Barbara Windsor**
Dolly Clothes-Peg	**Lorraine Chase**
Mrs Bloomsbury-Barton	**Joan Sims**
Mr Shepherd	**Michael Ripper**

Writers: **Keith Waterhouse, Willis Hall**
Executive Producer: **Lewis Rudd**
Producer: **James Hill**

The adventures of a living scarecrow.

Worzel Gummidge, a warty scarecrow with a turnip head, straggly straw hair and a unique line in yokelese, was the friend of young John and Sue Peters. They had just moved to the country, with their dad, having lost their mum, when they stumbled across this mischievous character in Ten Acre field of Scatterbrook Farm, and he transformed their life with his clumsy antics and good-natured humour. Wherever Worzel went, disaster followed. His girlfriend was Aunt Sally, a skittle doll, although he also fell for Saucy Nancy, a ship's figurehead, and flirted with a tailor's dummy called Dolly Clothes-Peg. The Crowman was Worzel's creator and could fashion new heads for him to change his character, if required.

The series, written by Keith Waterhouse and Willis Hall, was based on the books of Barbara Euphan Todd and was largely the idea of star Jon Pertwee. In marked contrast to his role as DOCTOR WHO, this part gave him the chance to show off his comedy skills, which had been honed on BBC Radio for many years. When Southern Television lost its ITV franchise, production was halted, until the idea was picked up by a New Zealand company in 1987, with Worzel taking up residence in the Antipodes in a series called *Worzel Gummidge Down Under* (UK, Channel 4 1987–9). Jon Pertwee also had a minor chart hit with 'Worzel's Song' in 1980.

TV's first Worzel Gummidge was Frank Atkinson, who played the part in the 1953 series, *Worzel Gummidge Turns Detective*.

WRATHER, JACK
(1918–84)

Texan oil and TV executive who purchased the rights to LASSIE and THE LONE RANGER and reaped the benefits of his foresight when both proved to be perennial and global hits. His company, Wrather TV Productions, produced both series, plus other juvenile action series like *Sergeant Preston of the Yukon*. He was also prominent in television sales and syndication, with Lew Grade forming the American wing of ITC, ITC Inc., to distribute Wrather and ITC programmes in the USA, although he was later bought out by Grade. He was married to actress Bonita Granville.

WWN
See WALES WEST AND NORTH.

WYATT EARP
See LIFE AND LEGEND OF WYATT EARP, THE.

WYCLIFFE
UK (HTV) Police Drama. ITV 1993–8

Det. Supt. Charles Wycliffe	**Jack Shepherd**
DI Lucy Lane	**Helen Masters**
Helen Wycliffe	**Lynn Farleigh**
DI Doug Kersey	**Jimmy Yuill**
DS Andy Dixon	**Aaron Harris**
DC Ian Potter	**Adam Barker**
Franks	**Tim Wylton**
David Wycliffe	**Greg Chisholm**
Ruth Wycliffe	**Charlie Hayes**
DCC Stevens	**Michael Attwell**
Supt. Le Page	**Sharon Duce**

Producers: **Pennant Roberts, Geraint Morris, Michael Bartley**
Executive Producers: **Jenny Reeks, Steve Matthews**

The cases of a glum-looking Cornish detective.

Based on the novels of W. J. Burley, this series followed the investigations of Det. Superintendent Charles Wycliffe – named by Burley after John Wycliffe, who translated the Bible back in the 1500s. This Wycliffe was a man who knew his own mind, was thoughtful and fairly tolerant but who didn't suffer fools gladly. He was not a Cornishman himself and viewed local folk with a certain objectivity. He was assisted in his work (in and around Penzance, with excursions to picturesque coves, deserted tin mines and Bodmin Moor) by DIs Doug Kersey and Lucy Lane (the latter played by Carla Mendonca in the 1993 pilot episode, which was subtitled '. . . and the Cycle of Death').

Wycliffe's family was kept largely in the background for the first two series, then he was given a domestic dimension with more appearances from his wife, Helen (Lucy Fleming in the pilot), and the introduction of his teenage kids, David and Ruth. In a later series, Wycliffe was shot and badly injured, taking several episodes to make a full recovery. Star Jack Shepherd also directed some stories.

WYMAN, JANE
(Sarah Jane Faulks; 1914–)

Oscar-winning American actress who has enjoyed two bites of the TV cherry. In the 1950s, on the back of her Hollywood success, Wyman was called up by US TV to host two series of drama anthologies. In the 1960s and 1970s, her small-screen appearances were relatively few, but she bounced back in 1981 when cast as Angela Channing, matriarch of the vineyards in FALCON CREST. She played the part for nine years and has also been seen in numerous TV movies. Wyman was married to Ronald Reagan from 1940 to 1948.

WYMARK, PATRICK
(Patrick Cheeseman; 1926–70)

Popular British actor of the 1960s. Formerly a Shakespearean stage performer, Wymark shot to fame as John Wilder, the ruthless managing director in THE PLANE MAKERS and its sequel, THE POWER GAME. Sadly, he had little time to capitalize on his success, dying suddenly at the age of 44, not long after the last series of *The Power Game* ended.

WYNDHAM-GOLDIE, GRACE
OBE (1900–86)

Influential BBC current affairs producer of the 1950s. Moving into television from radio, she became Assistant

Head of Talks in 1954 and, from this position, was responsible for shaking up and revamping PANORAMA in 1955 and launching TONIGHT two years later. In 1962 Wyndham-Goldie was promoted to Head of Talks and Current Affairs. She retired in 1965.

WYNGARDE, PETER
(Cyril Louis Goldbert; 1928–)

French-born actor whose earliest television appearances came in 1950s plays like *Rope* and *A Tale of Two Cities*. In subsequent years he starred in episodes of the anthology series, *On Trial* and OUT OF THIS WORLD, before becoming a familiar guest face in ITC action series like THE BARON, THE AVENGERS, THE PRISONER and THE CHAMPIONS. In 1969 he was cast in his most famous role, that of flamboyant novelist/secret agent Jason King in DEPARTMENT S, and, although only one of a trio of agents, he proved so popular that he was brought back in his own spin-off, entitled simply JASON KING, in 1971. His TV work has been thin since, but he has been spotted in DOCTOR WHO, BULMAN, THE TWO RONNIES and THE COMIC STRIP PRESENTS.

X-FILES, THE
US (Ten-Thirteen/Twentieth Century-Fox) Science Fiction.
BBC 2/BBC 1 1994–

Agent Fox Mulder	**David Duchovny**
Agent Dana Scully	**Gillian Anderson**
Deep Throat	**Jerry Hardin**
Cigarette-Smoking Man	**William B. Davis**
X	**Steven Williams**
Assistant Director Walter Skinner	**Mitch Pileggi**
Alex Krycek	**Nicholas Lea**
Frohike	**Tom Braidwood**
Byers	**Bruce Harwood**
Langly	**Dean Haglund**
Well-Manicured Man	**John Neville**
Agent Jeffrey Spender	**Chris Owens**
Agent Diana Fowley	**Mimi Rogers**
Michael Kritschgau	**John Finn**

Creator: **Chris Carter**
Executive Producers: **Chris Carter, Frank Spotnitz**

*Two FBI agents investigate cases involving the
paranormal.*

American Fox Mulder was an Oxford graduate in psychology who believed his eight-year-old sister had been abducted by aliens when he was 12. He joined the FBI, where he put his preoccupation with the paranormal to good use by delving into the 'X-Files', classified documents detailing unsolved investigations which seemed to involve alien encounters or other weird occurrences. He was assisted in his work by red-haired Dana Scully, a doctor who had given up medicine for the challenges the FBI offered. After two years' experience with the agency, she had been given the job of Mulder's partner, largely to keep an eye on his activities and, using her scientific knowledge, to throw cold water on his extravagant theories. Shady figures like Deep Throat and the Cigarette-Smoking Man provided leads and advice in 'Watergate' fashion, while Mulder's chief, Skinner, was among those who contrived to cover up his discoveries. Gradually, however, as the parade of UFO sightings, out-of-body experiences, spontaneous combustions, etc., kept rolling by – not to mention her own abduction by aliens – it crossed Scully's sceptical mind, too, that 'the truth' really was 'out there'.

A delight for conspiracy theorists, *The X-Files* was the creation of Chris Carter, at the time a writer for a surfing magazine. Filmed in Vancouver, it was undoubtedly the number one sci-fi show of the 1990s and enjoyed cult status across the globe. In the UK, Sky One was first off the mark, screening episodes well ahead of the BBC. An *X-Files* feature film was theatrically released in 1998.

XENA: WARRIOR PRINCESS
US (Renaissance) Drama. Channel 5 1997–

Xena	**Lucy Lawless**
Gabrielle	**Renee O'Connor**

Joxer	**Ted Raimi**
Autolycus	**Bruce Campbell**
Ares	**Kevin Smith**
Callisto	**Hudson Leick**
Salmoneus	**Robert Trebor**

Executive Producers: **Sam Raimi, Robert Tapert, R. J. Stewart**

In ancient times, a battle-hardened maiden rescues folks in distress.

Xena: Warrior Princess was a spin-off from another adventure series set in the ancient world of myths and magic entitled *Hercules: The Legendary Journeys* (Channel 5 1997–). In this, Xena was portrayed as an evil warrior, but in her own series she turned to the side of good, roaming around the world on her horse, Argo, rescuing the underdog. At her side was blonde runaway village girl Gabrielle, who considered herself something of a bard, and occasionally the cack-handed but well-meaning Joxer. Ares, a war god, showed up from time to time, as did the thieving Autolycus and Xena's nemesis, Callisto. But the star of the show was the Amazonian Xena, her skimpy bodice and martial arts skills turning her into a lesbian icon among viewers as she kicked, fenced and threw her enemies into their places. The series was shot in New Zealand, star Lucy Lawless's home country, and in the UK was aired on Sky prior to screening on the fledgling Channel 5.

XYY MAN, THE
UK (Granada) Spy Drama. ITV 1976–7

William 'Spider' Scott	**Stephen Yardley**
Maggie Parsons	**Vivienne McKee**
DS George Bulman	**Don Henderson**
DC Derek Willis	**Dennis Blanch**
Fairfax	**Mark Dignam**
Laidlaw	**William Squire**

Producer: **Richard Everitt**

A genetically odd cat-burglar is recruited by British intelligence.

Spider Scott was different. In his cell structure he had a spare chromosome, an extra 'Y' chromosome which made him noticeably tall and instilled in him the urge to steal. He had become a practised cat-burglar, one of the best, but had retired – until the mysterious Fairfax of the British secret service enticed him to commit a break-in at a foreign embassy. After the embassy affair and its drawn-out consequences, Spider found it difficult to go straight again, especially when Fairfax reappeared, asking him to spring a criminal from jail. On his trail at all times were Det. Sgt Bulman and DC Willis of Scotland Yard (and later of STRANGERS). This early incarnation of Bulman was quite unlike the quirky later model. Here he was far from sympathetic, and was rough and unstinting in his pursuit of the elusive Spider.

The series was based on the book by Scottish author Kenneth Royce and began with a three-part mini-drama in 1976.

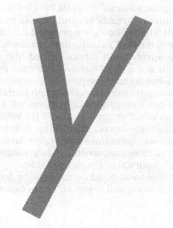

YARDLEY, STEPHEN
(1942–)

Tall British actor, now popular for the 'man you love to hate' type of role, thanks to his portrayal of slimy Ken Masters in HOWARDS' WAY. Previously, Yardley's most prominent credit had been as Spider Scott, the burglar with the genetic defect, in THE XYY MAN, although his TV appearances began in the 1960s in series like DR FINLAY'S CASEBOOK, UNITED! (goalkeeper Kenny Craig) and Z CARS (PC Alec May). Yardley was also in the cast of the BBC's 1981 version of *The Day of the Triffids* and has been seen in series like *Morgan's Boy*, SECRET ARMY (Max Brocard), WIDOWS, REMINGTON STEELE, *Virtual Murder* (Inspector Cadogan) and CORONATION STREET.

YARWOOD, MIKE
OBE (1941–)

Britain's number one impressionist of the late 1960s–1970s, Mike Yarwood's career really took off in a 1964 edition of SUNDAY NIGHT AT THE LONDON PALLADIUM, when his impersonation of premier Harold Wilson, among others, put him on the map. Yarwood soon grew into one of TV's top attractions, hosting his own series and Christmas Day extravaganzas. Wilson remained probably his greatest success, although he also won applause for his general attention to detail (particularly for his victims' mannerisms) and for his mimicry of the likes of Brian Clough, Eddie Waring, Alf Garnett, Robin Day and Ted Heath. With such a political bias to his act, the arrival of the inimitable Mrs Thatcher at Number 10 contributed to his demise and his career sadly veered off course in the 1980s. At a time when comedy was demanding a harder edge, Yarwood quickly lost ground to Rory Bremner and a new breed of satirists. His cause was not helped by a run of personal problems and a few mini-comebacks since have failed to bring him back into the limelight. Yarwood's major series over the years have been THREE OF A KIND (with Lulu and Ray Fell), *Will the Real Mike Yarwood Stand Up?*, *Look – Mike Yarwood!* and *Mike Yarwood in Persons*.

YATES, JESS
(Jesse Yates; 1918–93)

British TV presenter and producer, generally associated with the long-running STARS ON SUNDAY showcase, through which he earned the nickname 'The Bishop'. However, Yates, a former cinema organist, worked in television from the early 1950s, climbing his way up from designer to writer, producer and director. Series like THE GOOD OLD DAYS, *Top Town* and COME DANCING gave him a grounding in light entertainment that he was to exploit when, after some years away from the business, he returned to TV with the fledgling Yorkshire Television in 1968. Under his auspices as Head of Children's Programmes, such series as *Junior Showtime*, *The Flaxton Boys*, *The Boy Dominic*, *Origami* and the educational *How*

We Used to Live reached the screen, before Yates turned his attention to religious programming with *Choirs on Sunday* and eventually *Stars on Sunday*. He was unceremoniously dropped from the show in the mid-1970s after disclosures about his private life and he never returned to television in a big way afterwards. Scandal continued to mark him even after his death, when it was revealed that he was not the father of model/presenter Paula Yates as was generally believed, the news breaking after the funeral of her real father, Hughie Green.

YATES, PAULA
(1960–2000)

British model turned TV presenter whose troubled life seldom failed to make the headlines. Yates was the daughter of actress/writer Heller Toren and her father was thought to have been Toren's husband, STARS ON SUNDAY host Jess Yates. However, it was later announced that her father was actually OPPORTUNITY KNOCKS frontman, Hughie Green. Yates herself married Boomtown Rats singer Bob Geldof, but left him for Michael Hutchence of the band, INXS, who was found dead in his hotel room in 1997. Yates herself was found dead in 2000. Her TV career highlights included fronting THE TUBE with Jools Holland and being part of the founding team of THE BIG BREAKFAST, for which she interviewed celebrities on a lavish double bed.

YEAR IN PROVENCE, A
UK (BBC) Comedy Drama. BBC 1 1993

Peter Mayle	John Thaw
Annie Mayle	Lindsay Duncan
Colombani	Jean-Pierre Delage
Amedée Clément	Jo Doumerg
Antoine Rivière	Marcel Champel
Marcel	Bernard Spiegel
Madame Hermonville	Annie Sinigalia
Huguette Clément	Francine Olivier

Writer: **Michael Sadler**
Producer: **Ken Riddington**

Twelve-part dramatization of Peter Mayle's best-seller about life in the South of France.

Peter and Annie Mayle, an advertising executive and an accountant, bravely abandoned their rat-race jobs to move to their farmhouse home in the Luberon where, they hoped, a relaxing new world awaited them. However, things did not quite work out as planned. While the views were beautiful and the food glorious, the local French neighbours and workers proved totally unpredictable; petty disasters, plus the constant threat of British visitors, lurked around every corner. Mayle's attempts to settle into writing a novel proved fruitless and a far better book eventually emerged from the frustrating and complicated situations which unfolded as they tried to set up their new home.

Although much promoted by the BBC and supported by a serialized feature on *Peter Mayle's Provence* in *Radio Times*, *A Year in Provence* was considered by most critics to be one of the flops of 1993.

YENTOB, ALAN
(1947–)

London-born producer (a BBC trainee from 1968) who became Controller of BBC 2 in 1988 and of BBC 1 in 1993, moving on to be the Corporation's Director of Programmes and Director of Television. As a producer, he worked on series like OMNIBUS and ARENA (creator), which led to his appointment as Head of Music and Arts in 1985.

YES – HONESTLY
See NO – HONESTLY.

YES, MINISTER/YES, PRIME MINISTER
UK (BBC) Situation Comedy. BBC 2 1980–2/1986–8

Right Hon. James Hacker MP	**Paul Eddington**
Sir Humphrey Appleby	**Nigel Hawthorne**
Bernard Woolley	**Derek Fowlds**
Annie Hacker	**Diana Hoddinott**
Sir Arnold Robinson	**John Nettleton**

Creators/Writers: **Antony Jay, Jonathan Lynn**
Producers: **Stuart Allen, Sydney Lotterby, Peter Whitmore**

An ambitious government minister is put firmly in his place by his chief civil servant.

Yes, Minister followed the political career of one Jim Hacker, initially an MP for an unnamed party, but later divulged to be a Tory. It opened with Hacker taking up his first ministerial position (Administrative Affairs) and teaming up with Permanent Under-Secretary Sir Humphrey Appleby. Filled with bright ideas for cleaning up his department, Hacker began to set the wheels in motion, only to find himself stymied by the career civil servant, who was intent on keeping the power out of politicians' hands and firmly in the control of the permanent staff. And it was these concepts of idealism against political reality, and perceived power against real power, which underpinned the entire series, with Hacker flying ambitious kites and Sir Humphrey cheerfully shooting them down.

While the persuasive Sir Humphrey bamboozled Hacker with his tongue-twisting, jargon-loaded, overstretched explanations, Hacker's genial Private Secretary, Bernard Woolley, hovered nervously in the middle, gently offering opinions on the implications and complications of this or that decision (especially if they affected Hacker's political future). But Hacker must have heeded their advice pretty well in the first three series, for a major career move quickly followed. When the incumbent prime minister resigned, three candidates stood for the top job – two extremists and the rather mundane Hacker. By stealing the middle ground, Hacker (somewhat by default) found himself installed in Downing Street for the final two seasons, which went out under the title of *Yes, Prime Minister*.

The series was much acclaimed by real politicians, who enjoyed the show's cynical dismissal of Whitehall intrigue and its insight into the machinations of government. Even Margaret Thatcher dubbed it her favourite (before dubbing writer Antony Jay a knight in the Honours' List).

YESTERDAY'S MEN
See 24 HOURS.

YOGI BEAR
US (Hanna-Barbera) Cartoon. ITV 1960–4

Voices:

Yogi Bear .... Daws Butler
Boo Boo .... Don Messick
Ranger John Smith .... Don Messick
Cindy Bear .... Julie Bennett
Snagglepuss .... Daws Butler
Yakky Doodle .... Jimmy Weldon
Chopper .... Vance Colvig

Creators/Executive Producers: **William Hanna, Joseph Barbera**

A hungry bear preys on picnickers in a national park.

Holidaying families were never safe when Yogi was around, for the crafty bear with the healthy appetite was always likely to talk them out of their lunch. Dressed in a tie and a pork-pie hat, Yogi, with his bear-cub sidekick, Boo Boo, prowled the expanses of Jellystone National Park, skilfully avoiding the attentions of Ranger John Smith. After all, as Yogi himself declared, he was 'smarter than the average bear'. Also seen at times was Yogi's southern sweetheart, Cindy Bear, prone to cries of 'Ah do declare'.

Yogi Bear (named after New York Yankees pitcher, Yogi Berra) first appeared in THE HUCKLEBERRY HOUND SHOW, although he quickly outgrew his second-fiddle status. Awarded his own series, Yogi was himself then supported by other cartoons. These featured the theatrical lion, Snagglepuss (fond of thespian exclamations like 'Heavens to Murgatroyd'), and a garrulous duck, Yakky Doodle, who was closely guarded by his pal, Chopper the Bulldog. In the 1970s, in later series, Yogi moved out of Jellystone and into more adventurous situations, taking on environmental crusades and even risking space travel.

YORKIN, BUD
(Alan Yorkin; 1926–)

American TV executive in partnership with Norman Lear when creating such 1970s series as ALL IN THE FAMILY, its spin-offs, *Maude* and *The Jeffersons*, and *Sanford and Son*. Together they founded Tandem Pro-

ductions. Earlier, Yorkin had produced variety shows, before working with Lear in the cinema in the 1960s.

YORKSHIRE TELEVISION
(YTV)

Yorkshire Television has been the ITV contractor for the region east of the Pennines since 1968, when previous incumbent Granada was obliged by the ITA to refocus its coverage on the North-west. A consortium known as Telefusion Yorkshire Ltd won the franchise in 1967 and, on 29 July a year later, Yorkshire Television (its chosen broadcasting name) went on air, hastily constructing purpose-designed studios in Leeds. Former BBC producer Donald Baverstock was its first programme controller and he was succeeded in 1973 by another BBC executive, Paul Fox. Alan Whicker was another board member and major shareholder.

Yorkshire's initial 'trading' area was not just the county of Yorkshire, but also parts of Derbyshire and Nottinghamshire. However, changes were made in the early 1970s, when the company lost most of North Yorkshire to Tyne Tees (thanks to an IBA transmitter swap) and then gained Lincolnshire and Humberside from Anglia (another transmitter reallocation). To stabilize the three companies (Yorkshire, Tyne Tees and Anglia) and to maximize advertising revenue, a new holding company, known as Trident Television, was proposed. However, the IBA declined to allow Anglia to join, and Trident was formed out of Yorkshire and Tyne Tees only. When, in 1980, both companies' franchises were renewed, the IBA insisted on them leaving Trident and becoming independent once more. The Trident partnership was resumed after the 1991 franchise auctions, which were again successful for both companies. However, both Tyne Tees and Yorkshire now belong to Granada.

From the start, Yorkshire was charged with the role of a network provider, that is being one of the big five companies which supply the bulk of ITV's national programmes. Its successes have been many, including *Whicker's World*, THE SKY'S THE LIMIT, EMMERDALE FARM, WHERE THERE'S LIFE, WINNER TAKES ALL, HADLEIGH, THE MAIN CHANCE, RISING DAMP, THE BEIDERBECKE AFFAIR, DUTY FREE, 3-2-1, FOLLYFOOT, A BIT OF A DO and THE DARLING BUDS OF MAY.

YOU BET!
UK (LWT) Game Show. ITV 1988–96

Presenters: **Bruce Forsyth, Matthew Kelly, Darren Day, Diane Youdale**

Executive Producer: **Marcus Plantin**
Producers: **Richard Hearsey, Alasdair Macmillan, Linda Beadle, Mark Linsey**

Light-hearted panel game in which celebrities and the studio audience bet on the skills of a guest enthusiast.

Hosted originally by Bruce Forsyth, then by Matthew

Kelly from 1991, with Darren Day and Diane Youdale taking over for the final season, *You Bet!* was a showcase for the skills and talents of its many guests, who attempted to perform odd feats related to their hobbies or professions within a given time. Could three divers put up a tent underwater, for example? How much would politician Roy Hattersley know about his favourite programme, CORONATION STREET? Each guest was sponsored by one of the celebrity panellists and, if the guest failed in his task, the celebrity was forced to accept a forfeit. The studio audience, meanwhile, gambled on whether the guest would make the grade, and all profits were directed to charity. The series was originally based on a Dutch format.

YOU RANG, M'LORD?
UK (BBC) Situation Comedy. BBC 1 1990–3

Alf Stokes	**Paul Shane**
Ivy Teasdale	**Su Pollard**
James Twelvetrees	**Jeffrey Holland**
Mrs Lipton	**Brenda Cowling**
Lord George Meldrum	**Donald Hewlett**
Hon. Teddy Meldrum	**Michael Knowles**
Poppy Meldrum	**Susie Brann**
Cissy Meldrum	**Catherine Rabett**
Lady Lavender Meldrum	**Mavis Pugh**
Henry	**Perry Benson**
Mabel	**Barbara New**
PC Wilson	**Bill Pertwee**
Sir Ralph Shawcross	**John Horsley**
Lady Agatha Shawcross	**Angela Scoular**
Myrtle	**Barbara Windsor**

Creators/Writers: **Jimmy Perry, David Croft**
Producer: **David Croft**

Life up- and downstairs in an eccentric 1920s household.

An hour-long pilot, screened in 1988, set the scene for this UPSTAIRS, DOWNSTAIRS send-up which had more than an echo of other Perry/Croft sitcoms, especially HI-DE-HI!. It began in 1918, in the trenches of World War I and with the discovery of the body of an army officer by two foot-soldiers. One of the soldiers, Alf Stokes, looted the officer's possessions, as the other, James Twelvetrees, vainly argued against the theft. However, discovering that the officer was not in fact dead, the two men carried him to safety. He turned out to be Captain Edward Meldrum, known to others as 'the Honourable Teddy', and in return for their life-saving efforts he promised the men a favour.

Back in civvy street, nine years later, Twelvetrees had cashed in his favour and had been taken on as head of the household at the Meldrum residence, which was presided over by the well-meaning Lord Meldrum. When their butler died, the bad penny Stokes arrived and, much to Twelvetrees's disgust, talked his way into the job. He brought with him as parlourmaid his daughter, Ivy, but kept their relationship secret (she used her mother's maiden name). Like all the parlourmaids employed before her, Ivy, despite her plain looks, was relentlessly pursued by the randy Teddy, a true upper-class twit, while his flighty sister, Poppy, took a similar shine to Twelvetrees. The other Meldrum family members included the lesbian Cissy, who dressed like a man, and the bedridden, food-throwing Lady Lavender, the lord's batty mother. Family friends were Sir Ralph and Lady Agatha Shawcross, Lady Agatha also being Lord Meldrum's secret lover.

The serving staff comprised cook Mrs Lipton, boot-boy Henry (regular recipient of clipped ears) and, lowest of the low, scullery maid Mabel. A regular visitor to the kitchen was the scrounging local bobby, PC Wilson, a devotee of Mrs Lipton's culinary skills. While the upright Twelvetrees conducted his affairs in the most honest and decent fashion, the sly Stokes worked on plans to swindle his betters and line his own pockets. And so the series continued for three years, finally ending when the Meldrum family fell on desperate times and were forced to give up their home and staff.

The programme's theme song was sung by Bob Monkhouse and Paul Shane.

YOUENS, BERNARD
(Bernard Popley; 1914–84)

Remembered as one of TV's most lovable characters, the boozy, work-shy Stan Ogden in CORONATION STREET, Sussex-born Bernard Youens was, in real life, a totally different person from the slob he played on screen. Far from only being able to garble, 'A pint and a pie, missus,' Youens was an eloquent, well-spoken performer. Indeed, one of his first jobs in television was as a continuity announcer at Granada. His first TV acting parts were also with Granada, in series like SHADOW SQUAD and KNIGHT ERRANT. He joined *Coronation Street* in 1964 and stayed with the series (through considerable restricting illness in later years) until his death in 1984.

YOU'LL NEVER GET RICH
See PHIL SILVERS SHOW, THE.

YOUNG, ALAN
(Angus Young; 1919–)

British-born actor/comedian, raised in Canada, who became a reasonable success in the USA. By far his most memorable role was as Wilbur Post, straight man to MISTER ED, the talking horse, in the early 1960s, although, by that time, Young had already picked up an Emmy and headlined in his own variety series, *The Alan Young Show*, and the USA's *Saturday Night Revue*. In the late 1950s and early 1960s he starred in his own ITV showcases, including *Personal Appearance*. In the 1980s he was cast in the retirement sitcom, *Coming of Age*.

YOUNG, KIRSTY
(1968–)

Scottish presenter and newscaster, entering broadcasting with BBC Radio Scotland and then Scottish Television, on which she had her own chat show. After featuring in programmes like HOLIDAY, FILM 96 and *The Street*, Young was snapped up to front the new *Channel 5 News*, from which she was poached in 1999 to anchor ITN news bulletins. In 2000, she hosted the quiz *The People Versus*.

YOUNG, MURIEL
(1928–2001)

British presenter, one of Associated-Rediffusion's earliest continuity announcers. However, it was as a star of kids' TV in the late 1950s and early 1960s, in series like *Small Time, Tuesday Rendezvous* and FIVE O'CLOCK CLUB, that she became known to viewers nationwide, working with puppets Ollie Beak, Fred Barker, Pussy Cat Willum and others. In the late 1960s she moved north to Granada to become Head of Children's Programmes. There, as producer, she established such favourites as CLAP-PERBOARD, LIFT OFF WITH AYSHEA, *Get It Together* and other pop shows for stars such as the Bay City Rollers (*Shang-a-Lang*), Marc Bolan (*Marc*) and *The Arrows*. She retired from television in 1986.

YOUNG ONES, THE
UK (BBC) Situation Comedy. BBC 2 1982–4

Rick .... **Rik Mayall**
Neil .... **Nigel Planer**
Vyvyan .... **Adrian Edmondson**
Mike .... **Christopher Ryan**
Jerzy Balowski (and his family) .... **Alexei Sayle**

Writers: **Ben Elton, Rik Mayall, Lise Mayer**
Producer: **Paul Jackson**

Four anarchic students share a decrepit house.

The Young Ones were Rick, Neil, Vyvyan and Mike. Sneering Rick was the Cliff Richard fan who owned a pet hamster known as SPG (Special Patrol Group), long-haired Neil was the melancholic, vegetarian hippie and the stud-headed Vyvyan was gormlessly aggressive. Diminutive Mike was the most 'normal' of the bunch, although his wide-boy tendencies and moments of paranoia marked him out, too, from the rest of the public. In an atmosphere of absolute squalor (even the stale food began to move), the four led a life of mindless violence and brainless conversation, rebelling against the world outside. The storylines were vague and the comedy was heavily slapstick, usually involving the destruction of the house or of each other, but there were bizarre moments of surreal humour, too. The boys' Russian landlord, Jerzy Balowski (or other members of his family, all played by Alexei Sayle), was given his own slot in the programme and, unusually for a comedy, contemporary pop groups also performed their stuff.

Viewers tuned in to *The Young Ones* to be shocked. The younger generations loved it and felt the series was right on their wavelength. More 'mature' critics were appalled at the wanton violence, infantile jokes and total disrespect for society; but many of these, too, were won over as the series progressed. It was a series that certainly shook up television comedy and heralded the age of the 'alternative' comedian. Indeed, *The Young Ones* has continued well beyond its 12 episodes, with Mayall and Edmondson's later offerings, FILTHY RICH AND CATFLAP and BOTTOM, essentially extensions of the series. Nigel Planer, in the guise of Neil, also had a spin-off hit single in 1984, with a cover of Traffic's 'Hole In My Shoe', and the foul foursome joined Cliff Richard on a chart-topping remake of 'Living Doll' for charity in 1986.

YOUNG, ROBERT
(1907–98)

American movie actor of the 1930s who never really found his niche until television arrived. There his homely, kindly features were put to good use in an award-winning domestic sitcom, *Father Knows Best* (dad Jim Anderson), that ran for six years (having already been a hit on radio). Unusually, it also enjoyed prime-time repeat showings until 1963, although the 1960s were generally leaner years for Young, and another comedy, *Window on Main Street*, didn't take. However, in 1968, his first TV movie, MARCUS WELBY, MD, sparked another long-running series, in which Young played a gentle, understanding family practitioner. It ended in 1976 and Young did little television afterwards, save the odd commercial, occasional TV movie, a couple of *Father Knows Best* reunions and some impressions in *Kopykats*.

YOUR LIFE IN THEIR HANDS
UK (BBC) Documentary. BBC 1958–64; BBC 2 1980–6;
1991

Producers: **Bill Duncalf, Peter Bruce, Humphrey Fisher, John Mansfield, Fiona Holmes, Stephen Rose**

The wonders of surgery explored in close detail.

This innovative series was conceived with a tripartite purpose in mind: to investigate new medical techniques, to applaud the medical profession, and to provide 'reassurance' for citizens at home. However, with its blood-and-guts visuals, *Your Life in Their Hands* excited some viewers and alarmed others.

The pre-recorded programmes interviewed sick patients, watched their admission to hospital, heard the prognosis of the experts and learned of the action intended by the surgeon. Overhead mirrors, microscopes and numerous cameras were then used to capture events in the operating theatre, before the patient's recovery was monitored in the weeks and months that followed. Never before had gallstones been removed on British television. Open-heart surgery was even more dramatic and, caesarean birth was demonstrated just as graphically. Predictably, there was an outcry from the Establishment. The British Medical Association criticized it for frightening, rather than reassuring, viewers and there were reports of sick people preferring suicide to treatment, having seen the programme. Other doctors warmly applauded the programme's frankness and its educational value.

When the series was revived in 1980, operations were shown for the first time in full, gory colour and were definitely not for the squeamish. For this series, surgeon Robert Winston acted as the informative narrator. Five more editions were screened in 1991.

YOU'VE BEEN FRAMED
UK (Granada) Comedy. ITV 1990–

Presenters: **Jeremy Beadle, Lisa Riley**

Producers: **Jane Macnaught, Kieran Roberts, Mark Gorton, Mark Wells, Nigel Hall, Kieron Collins**

Selections of home video howlers.

You've Been Framed has ridden the wave of interest in home video bloopers that has swept around the world since the introduction of the camcorder. Emulating similar programmes in the USA, Japan and elsewhere, it has gathered together some of the most amusing clips of video footage, most of which have shown people falling over, children unwittingly misbehaving or pets displaying unusual talents. A contest for the best British clip was incorporated into early programmes but was later abandoned. EMMERDALE star Lisa Riley took over as presenter in 1998 and some episodes have been aired under the title, *New You've Been Framed*. The BBC attempted to cash in with its own version, *Caught in the Act* (BBC 1, 1992), hosted by Shane Richie, but it failed to take off.

YTV
See **YORKSHIRE TELEVISION**.

YUS MY DEAR
See **ROMANY JONES**.

Z

Z CARS
UK (BBC) Police Drama. BBC 1 1962–78

DCI Charlie Barlow .... **Stratford Johns**
DS/Det. Chief Supt. John Watt .... **Frank Windsor**
PC William 'Fancy' Smith .... **Brian Blessed**
PC John 'Jock' Weir .... **Joseph Brady**
PC/DC/Sgt/Insp. Herbert 'Bert' Lynch .... **James Ellis**
DI/Supt. Dunn .... **Dudley Foster**
PC Bob Steele .... **Jeremy Kemp**
PC Ian Sweet .... **Terence Edmond**
Sgt Twentyman .... **Leonard Williams**
Mary Watt .... **Gwen Cherrell**
Sgt Blackitt .... **Robert Keegan**
PC David Graham .... **Colin Welland**
Det. Supt. Miller .... **Leslie Sands**
DI Sam Hudson .... **John Barrie**
Chief Supt. Robbins .... **John Phillips**
PC Ken Baker .... **Geoffrey Whitehead**
PC Raymond Walker .... **Donald Gee**
DS Tom Stone .... **John Slater**
PC Owen Culshaw .... **David Daker**
PC Alec May .... **Stephen Yardley**
WPC Jane Shepherd .... **Luanshya Greer**
PC Steve Tate .... **Sebastian Breaks**
PC Finch .... **Christopher Denham**
DC Kane .... **Christopher Coll**
PC Jackson .... **John Wreford**
WPC Parkin .... **Pauline Taylor**
PC Bannerman .... **Paul Angelis**
PC Roach .... **Ron Davies**
PC Horrocks .... **Barry Lowe**
DS Cecil Haggar .... **John Collin**
DC Scatliff .... **Geoffrey Hayes**
PC Render .... **Allan O'Keefe**
PC Covill .... **Jack Carr**
PC/Sgt Bowman .... **John Swindells**
DS Miller .... **Geoffrey Whitehead**
PC Yates .... **Nicholas Smith**
Insp. Ralph Pratt .... **Graham Armitage**
DC Braithwaite .... **David Jackson**
WPC Bayliss .... **Alison Steadman**
DS/DI Terry Moffat .... **Ray Lonnen**
DI Connor .... **Gary Watson**
Sgt Culshaw .... **John Challis**
WP Sgt Cameron .... **June Watson**
Sgt Chubb .... **Paul Stewart**
DC Bowker .... **Brian Grellis**
PC Bill Newcombe .... **Bernard Holley**
DI Brogan .... **George Sewell**
DI Todd .... **Joss Ackland**
DI Alan Witty .... **John Woodvine**
PC/Sgt Quilley .... **Douglas Fielding**
DI Neil Goss .... **Derek Waring**
PC/DC Joe Skinner .... **Ian Cullen**
WPC Jill Howarth .... **Stephanie Turner**
Sgt Chubb .... **Paul Stewart**
DI Maddan .... **Tommy Boyle**
DC Braithwaite .... **David Jackson**
DS Bowker .... **Brian Grellis**
WPC Jane Beck .... **Victoria Plucknett**

PC Roger Stevens .... **Ralph Watson**
BD girls .... **Anjula Harman**
Jennie Goossens

Creator: **Troy Kennedy Martin**
Producers: **David E. Rose, Colin Morris, Ronald Travers, Richard Beynon, Ron Craddock, Roderick Graham**

Long-running and influential police drama series, highlighting the work of patrol car policemen.

In 1962 the DIXON OF DOCK GREEN type of police series was already looking dated. The cosy life of a community copper had been lost for ever, certainly in the big cities at least, and it was time for television to reflect this change. However, it wasn't until writer Troy Kennedy Martin was ill in bed with mumps and, to while away the time, tuned into the police wavelengths that such a change became a possibility. Martin instantly recognized that what he was hearing was a world away from George Dixon's weekly homilies and decided to work his findings into an idea for a new programme. The result was *Z Cars*, a police series that aimed to portray the *real* relationship between the police and the community.

Filled with northern grit and heavily influenced by contemporary 'kitchen sink' dramas, *Z Cars* was set on Merseyside, at a time when the Liverpool docklands were undergoing radical social change. Traditional streets, now designated slums, were making way for high-rise blocks of concrete flats, functional but soulless living spaces that rapidly turned into fertile breeding-grounds for unrest. The pace of life was quickening and crime was responding in its own unpleasant fashion. To combat this crime wave, police were taken off the beat and placed in patrol cars, with the aim of providing a swifter response. *Z Cars* depicted the efforts of one such patrol team as it roamed the streets of both the old district of Seaport and the modern development of Newtown.

The very first episode revealed how the death of a police officer had led to the formation of the team. Det. Insp. Barlow and DS Watt were invited to select their new élite squad, and it introduced viewers to the four patrolmen who were chosen. In the first patrol car, Z Victor 1, were burly northerner 'Fancy' Smith and rugby-playing Scot, Jock Weir. In Z Victor 2 were Irishman Herbert Lynch and red-headed Bob Steele. Both cars were Ford Zephyrs, initially Mark 4s, later Mark 6s. Supervising events back at the station was old-fashioned copper Sgt Twentyman, replaced after a year by Sgt Blackitt when actor Leonard Williams suddenly died.

However, *Z Cars* didn't just focus on the new type of crime in the early 1960s, or the police response to it, but, for the first time on British television, it actually dared to suggest that policemen were not as wholesome as they ought to be. Troy Kennedy Martin had wanted the crooks to win through now and again, to show that police were not infallible, but this was too much to ask of a staid BBC. However, he did get away with showing policemen as real human beings, with complicated home lives and vices of their own. Martin and his colleagues painted them as gamblers, drinkers and, most controversially of all, even wife-beaters. Real-life police withdrew their co-operation in response to such excesses.

Another innovation was the portrayal by Stratford Johns of Charlie Barlow as a nasty superior officer, not averse to dishing out aggression. Johns was tired of seeing bumbling, ineffective TV detectives. What he wanted was a police officer who actually made the running, was hard on his subordinates and was not afraid to pound suspects into submission. Together with the gentler John Watt, he offered the classic combination of the nice and the nasty; and such was their success, they headed off to the Regional Crime Squad after three years and a series of their own, SOFTLY, SOFTLY.

Watt and Barlow's departure in 1965 was intended to be the finale for *Z Cars*, but it returned to the screens in 1967, installing John Barrie and John Slater as DI Hudson and DS Stone, their replacements. New Panda cars roared into action and some fresh constables were added to the team, although continuity was maintained through Weir and Lynch (a man who was to rise steadily through the ranks). The format switched from 50-minute episodes to two 25-minute programmes a week, and continued in this vein until 1971, when the longer forms were re-introduced.

Other notable characters to come and go over the years were young PC Ian Sweet, who was tragically drowned in a heroic rescue attempt; Leigh-born PC David Graham, Lynch's second partner (an early break for actor/writer Colin Welland); the sarcastic Insp. Dunn; and Geordie heart-throb PC Joe Skinner and his partner, PC Quilley. Indeed, future stars fared rather well, either as guests or as regulars. They included John Thaw, Judi Dench, Kenneth Cope, Alison Steadman, David Daker, Stephen Yardley, George Sewell, Joss Ackland, Patrick Troughton and Ralph Bates, whose character pulled a gun on Joe Skinner and shot him dead.

Like *Dixon of Dock Green* before it, *Z Cars* found itself left behind by other cop shows in the 1970s. Not only were the likes of KOJAK and STARSKY AND HUTCH screaming on to British TV screens, but there was also our own THE SWEENEY to contend with. Still *Z Cars* rolled on, probably showing a more realistic image of 1970s policing than its contemporaries, until the end finally arrived in 1978.

Originally transmitted live, making use of crude techniques like back-projection for car scenes, *Z Cars* looks very dated today. However, the quality of writing, from the likes of Martin, Alan Plater, Elwyn Jones and John Hopkins, is still apparent in the few surviving episodes from those early days. The last episode, penned by Martin, brought the newly promoted Det. Chief Superintendent Watt back to Newtown and featured cameo appearances from Joseph Brady, Brian Blessed, Jeremy Kemp and Colin Welland. Over the previous 16 years, the programme's unforgettable theme tune (based on the folk song, 'Johnny Todd', with an ominous drumbeat intro) had become synonymous with TV policing.

ZERO ONE

UK (BBC/MGM) Adventure. BBC 1 1962–5

Alan Garnett .... **Nigel Patrick**

Maya	**Katya Douglas**
Jim Delaney	**Bill Smith**

Producer: **Lawrence P. Bachmann**

The cases of an airline detective.

Zero One was the call-sign of International Air Security, an organization dedicated to the safety of air travel all around the world. Its London agent was Alan Garnett and he was called up to combat hijackers, prevent disasters and generally preserve peace in the air and at airports. Jim Delaney was his assistant and Maya his secretary.

ZIMBALIST, EFREM, JR

(1918–)

American actor, the son of classical music entertainers Efrem Zimbalist and Alma Gluck. Zimbalist Jr enjoyed two major starring roles between the late 1950s and mid-1970s. He was Ivy League-educated detective Stu Bailey in 77 SUNSET STRIP for six years from 1958 and then quickly donned the mantle of Inspector Lew Erskine of THE FBI, to ensure he remained on US TV screens until 1974. He has since appeared in HOTEL (Charles Cabot), TV movies and mini-series, as well as a revival of ZORRO (Don Alejandro). Among his numerous guest appearances over the years have been spots in THE PHIL SILVERS SHOW, MAVERICK (Dandy Jim Buckley) and REMINGTON STEELE (alongside his daughter, Stephanie Zimbalist).

ZOO GANG, THE

UK (ATV/ITC) Adventure. ITV 1974

Tommy Devon	**John Mills**
Stephen Halliday	**Brian Keith**
Alec Marlowe	**Barry Morse**
Manouche Roget	**Lilli Palmer**
Lt. Georges Roget	**Michael Petrovitch**
Jill Burton	**Seretta Wilson**

Creator: **Paul Gallico**
Producer: **Herbert Hirschman**

Four French Resistance fighters reunite to maintain law and order on the Riviera.

Nearly 30 years after disbanding at the end of the war, the so-called Zoo Gang found themselves back in business. Each member of this crack Resistance unit possessed individual skills and operated under animal codenames. Team organizer was Tommy Devon, or Elephant, as he was known. When an old Nazi adversary walked into his jewellery shop on the French Riviera, he called up surviving members of the squad to bring the war criminal to book. His colleagues were Stephen Halliday (a New York businessman and electronics expert, codenamed Fox), Canadian Alec Marlowe (Tiger, a mechanical genius) and Madame Manouche Roget (Leopard, the widow of another team member, Claude Roget – or Wolf – who had been killed by the Gestapo). Manouche ran a bar in Nice and was skilled in explosives. Her son,

Georges, a French policeman, was also seen. Having nailed the Nazi, the four stayed together to bring justice to the Côte d'Azur in Robin Hood fashion for five more episodes. The theme music was provided by Paul and Linda McCartney.

ZOO QUEST

UK (BBC) Natural History. BBC 1954–61

Producers: **David Attenborough, Paul Johnstone**

Global expeditions in search of rare wildlife.

Zoo Quest, a collaboration between the BBC Talks Department and London Zoo, recorded zoological searches for rare animals in the far corners of the world, such as the hunt for paradise birds in Madagascar. The aim was to bring examples back for exhibition and protection at the zoo. Individual series' titles reflected the nature of the expedition. They included *Zoo Quest to Guiana*, *Zoo Quest for a Dragon* (the komodo dragon) and *Zoo Quest in Paraguay*.

ZOO TIME

UK (Granada) Natural History. ITV 1956–68

Presenters: **Desmond Morris, Harry Watt, Chris Kelly**

Producers: **Milton Shulman, Derek Twist, David Warwick, Peter Mullings**

Studies of animal behaviour at London Zoo.

Initially introduced by animal watcher Desmond Morris, and aimed at the younger viewer, *Zoo Time* focused on the inmates of London Zoo and examined their innate behaviourial instincts. Harry Watt became host in 1960 and Chris Kelly took over in 1967, by which time the action had switched to Chester Zoo. Spin-off programmes like *A to Zoo*, *Breakthrough* and *Animal Story* were produced contemporaneously.

ZORRO

US (Walt Disney) Western. ITV 1958–

Don Diego de la Vega ('Zorro')	**Guy Williams**
Don Alejandro de la Vega	**George J. Lewis**
Bernardo	**Gene Sheldon**
Capt. Monastario	**Britt Lomond**
Sgt Garcia	**Henry Calvin**
Cpl. Reyes	**Don Diamond**
Nacho Torres	**Jan Arvan**
Elena Torres	**Eugenia Paul**
Magistrate Galindo	**Vinton Hayworth**
Anna Maria Verdugo	**Jolene Brand**
Senor Gregorio Verdugo	**Eduard Franz**

Executive Producer: **Walt Disney**
Producer: **William H. Anderson**

A mysterious masked cavalier continually thwarts the local tyrant.

In 1820 Don Diego de la Vega had been summoned home from Spain to southern California by his father, Don Alejandro, to assist in the overthrow of the new local tyrant. Merciless Captain Monastario had taken control of the local Fortress de Los Angeles, and all the nobles of the area felt under threat. Much was expected of the well-educated Don Diego. Sadly, it seemed that their hopes were to be dashed, as the young nobleman turned out to be something of a fop. But, under the secret disguise of Zorro, a swashbuckling masked swordsman, he made sure that the cruel Captain and his cronies – the stupid, slobbish Sgt Garcia and Corporal Reyes – were put firmly in their place.

Everyone knew when Zorro had visited – he carved a distinctive 'Z' with the point of his sword – but only one man knew his true identity, his dumb servant, Bernardo, who also pretended to be deaf in order to spy for his master. Don Diego's two trusty steeds were the black Tornado (for use as himself) and the white Phantom (ridden by Zorro). Anna Maria Verdugo was Don Diego's romantic interest.

Zorro, meaning 'fox' in Spanish, was created by author Johnston McCulley in 1919. The character had already been played in the cinema by the likes of Douglas Fairbanks and Tyrone Power before Guy Williams took on the role. Williams himself is possibly better remembered as Professor John Robinson in LOST IN SPACE.

ZWORYKIN, VLADIMIR K.
(1889–1982)

Russian-born American engineer, one of the pioneers of television. In the 1920s he produced an all-electronic television system that quickly found favour over Baird's electromechanical units. It was based on his development of the iconoscope (the cathode ray tube used in cameras) and the kinescope (the tube in the receiver).

BIBLIOGRAPHY

The information in this book has been obtained from many, many sources and primarily from the programmes themselves, from press releases and from the invaluable weekly listings magazines, *Radio Times* and *TV Times*. Other facts and figures have been unearthed from official websites, and from programme producers and actors' agents, who have kindly helped with inquiries. Scores of books have also been consulted and the most helpful general publications have been listed below.

MAGAZINES AND ANNUALS:

Radio Times
TV Times
Look-In
Television & Radio, IBA, various editions
Encyclopaedia Britannica, 1999

BOOKS:

Bolton, Jane (ed.): *British Hit Singles*, Guinness Publishing, 1999

Brooks, Tim, and Earle Marsh: *The Complete Directory to Prime Time Network and Cable TV Shows*, Ballantine Books, 1999

Brooks, Tim: *The Complete Directory to Prime Time TV Stars*, Ballantine Books, 1987

Brown, Les: *Les Brown's Encyclopedia of Television*, Visible Ink, 1992

Cain, John: *The BBC: 70 Years of Broadcasting*, BBC 1992

Castleman, Harry, and Walter J. Podrazik: *Harry and Wally's Favorite TV Shows*, Prentice Hall Press, 1989

Cornell, Paul, Martin Day and Keith Topping: *The Guinness Book of Classic British TV*, Guinness Publishing, 1996

Crowther, Bruce, and Mike Pinfold: *Bring Me Laughter*, Columbus Books, 1987

Crystal, David (ed.): *The Cambridge Biographical Encyclopedia*, Cambridge University Press, 1998

Davis, Anthony: *TV's Greatest Hits*, Boxtree, 1988

Donovan, Paul: *The Radio Companion*, Grafton, 1992

Down, Richard, and Christopher Perry: *The British Television Drama Research Guide*, Kaleidoscope Publishing, 1997

Down, Richard, and Christopher Perry: *The British Television Music & Variety Research Guide*, Kaleidoscope Publishing, 1997

Down, Richard, Richard Marson and Christopher Perry: *The British Television Children's Research Guide*, Kaleidoscope Publishing, 1999

Fischer, Stuart: *Kids' TV The First 25 Years*, Facts on File, 1983

Fulton, Roger: *The Encyclopedia of TV Science Fiction*, Boxtree, 1995

Gambaccini, Paul and Rod Taylor: *Television's Greatest Hits*, Network Books, 1993

Grade, Lew: *Still Dancing*, Fontana, 1987

Greenfield, Jeff: *Television, The First Fifty Years*, Crescent Books, 1981

Halliwell, Leslie, and Philip Purser: *Halliwell's Television Companion*, Granada, 1986

Harbord, Jane, and Jeff Wright: *40 Years of British Television*, Boxtree, 1992

Hayward, Anthony and Deborah: *TV Unforgettables*, Guinness Publishing, 1993

Hayward, Anthony, *et al.*: *Who's Who on Television*, various editions

Hayward, Anthony: *The Guinness Who's Who of Soap Operas*, Guinness Publishing, 1995

Hill, Tom (ed.): *Nick at Nite's Classic TV Companion*, Simon & Schuster, 1996

Home, Anna: *Into the Box of Delights*, BBC Books, 1993

Housham, David, and John Frank-Keyes: *Funny Business*, Boxtree, 1992

Hunter, Allan (ed.): *Chambers Film & TV Handbook*, Chambers, 1991

Jarvis, Peter: *Teletalk*, BBC Television Training, 1991

Javna, John: *Cult TV*, St Martin's Press, 1985

Javna, John: *The Best of Science Fiction TV*, Harmony Books, 1987

Javna, John: *The Best of TV Sitcoms*, Harmony Books, 1988

Kingsley, Hilary, and Geoff Tibballs: *Box of Delights*, Macmillan, 1989

Kingsley, Hilary: *Soap Box*, Macmillan, 1988

Lewisohn, Mark: *Radio Times Guide to TV Comedy*, BBC Worldwide, 1998

Marschall, Rick: *The Golden Age of Television*, Bison Books, 1987

McLeish, Kenneth: *Good Reading Guide*, Bloomsbury, 1991

McNeil, Alex: *Total Television*, Penguin, 1996

Miall, Leonard: *Inside the BBC*, Weidenfeld & Nicolson, 1994

Monaco, James: *The Virgin International Encyclopedia of Film*, Virgin Books, 1991

Morton, Alan: *The Complete Directory to Science Fiction, Fantasy and Horror Television Series*, Other Worlds Books, 1997

Penney, Edmund F.: *The Facts on File Dictionary of Film and Broadcast Terms*, Facts on File, 1991

Rogers, Dave: *The ITV Encyclopedia of Adventure*, Boxtree, 1988

Sachs, John, and Piers Morgan: *Secret Lives*, Blake Publishing, 1991

Schwartz, David, Steve Ryan and Fred Wostbrock: *The Encyclopedia of TV Game Shows*, Facts on File, 1995

Taylor, Rod: *The Guinness Book of Sitcoms*, Guinness Publishing, 1994

Terrace, Vincent: *The Ultimate TV Trivia Book*, Faber and Faber, 1991

Tibballs, Geoff: *The Boxtree Encyclopedia of TV Detectives*, Boxtree, 1992

Tibballs, Geoff: *The Golden Age of Children's Television*, Titan Books, 1991

Vahimagi, Tise: *British Television*, Oxford University Press, 1994

Walker, John (ed.): *Halliwell's Film & Video Guide*, HarperCollins, 1999

Walker, John (ed.): *Halliwell's Who's Who in the Movies*, HarperCollins, 1999

Woolery, George W.: *Children's Television: The First Thirty-Five Years* (2 volumes), Scarecrow Press, 1983 and 1985

APPENDIXES

Anglia Television
Anglia House
Norwich NR1 3JG
Tel.: 01603 615151
www.anglia.tv.co.uk

BBC TV
Television Centre
Wood Lane
London W12 7RJ
Tel.: 020 8743 8000
www.bbc.co.uk

Border Television
The Broadcasting Centre
Durranhill
Carlisle CA1 3NT
Tel.: 01228 525101
www.border-tv.com

British Sky Broadcasting Ltd
Grant Way
Isleworth
Middlesex TW7 5QD
Tel.: 020 7705 3000
www.sky.com

CNN International
CNN House
19–22 Rathbone Place
London W1P 1DF
Tel.: 020 7637 6800
www.cnn.com

Carlton Television
101 St Martin's Lane
London WC2N 4AZ
Tel.: 020 7240 4000
www.carlton.com

Carlton Central
Gas Street
Birmingham B1 2JT
Tel.: 0121 643 9898
www.carlton.com

Carlton Westcountry
Langage Science Park
Western Wood Way
Plymouth PL7 5BG
Tel.: 01752 333333
www.carlton.com

Channel 4
124 Horseferry Road
London SW1P 2TX
Tel.: 020 7396 4444
www.channel4.com

Channel 5
22 Long Acre
London WC2E 9LY
Tel.: 020 7550 5555
www.channel5.co.uk

Channel Television
The Television Centre
St Helier
Jersey JE1 3ZD
Tel.: 01534 816816
www.channeltv.co.uk

Discovery Channel
160 Great Portland Place
London W1N 5TB
Tel.: 020 7462 3600
www.discovery.com

GMTV Ltd
The London Television Centre
Upper Ground
London SE1 9TT
Tel.: 020 7827 7000
www.gmtv.co.uk

Grampian Television
Queen's Cross
Aberdeen AB15 4XJ
Tel.: 01224 846846
www.grampiantv.co.uk

Granada Television
Quay Street
Manchester M60 9EA
Tel.: 0161 832 7211
www.granadatv.co.uk

HTV Wales
The Television Centre
Culverhouse Cross
Cardiff CF5 6XJ
Tel.: 029 2059 0590
www.htv.co.uk

HTV West
The Television Centre
Bath Road
Bristol BS4 3HG
Tel.: 0117 972 2722
www.htv.co.uk

ITN (Independent Television News)
200 Gray's Inn Road
London WC1X 8XZ
Tel.: 020 7833 3000
www.itn.co.uk

LWT
The London Television Centre
Upper Ground
London SE1 9LT
Tel.: 020 7620 1620
www.g-whizz.net/lwt

MTV Networks Europe
Hawley Crescent
London NW1 8TT
Tel.: 020 7284 7777
www.mtv.com

Meridian Broadcasting
Television Centre
Southampton SO14 0PZ
Tel.: 023 8022 2555
www.meridian.tv.co.uk

Pearson Television
1 Stephen Street
London W1P 1PJ
Tel: 020 7691 6000
www.pearsontv.com

S4C
Parc Tŷ Glas
Llanishen
Cardiff CF4 5DU
Tel.: 029 2074 7444
www.s4c.co.uk

Scottish Television
Cowcaddens
Glasgow G2 3PR
Tel.: 0141 300 3000
www.stv.co.uk

Tyne Tees Television
The Television Centre
City Road
Newcastle-upon-Tyne NE1 2AL
Tel.: 0191 261 0181
www.g-whizz.net/tttv

Ulster Television (UTV)
Havelock House
Ormeau Road
Belfast BT7 1EB
Tel.: 028 9032 8122
www.utv.co.uk

Yorkshire Television Ltd
The Television Centre
Leeds LS3 1JS
Tel.: 0113 243 8283
www.g-whizz.net/ytv

Appendix B:
THE ITV COMPANIES

Area	Programme company	On air	Off air
London (weekdays)	Associated-Rediffusion	22.9.55	29.7.68
	Thames Television	30.7.68	31.12.92
	Carlton Television	1.1.93	
London (weekends)	ATV	24.9.55	28.7.68
	London Weekend Television (LWT)	2.8.68	
Midlands (weekdays – and later all week)	ATV	17.2.56	31.12.81
	Central Independent Television	1.1.82	
Midlands (weekends)	ABC	18.2.56	28.7.68
North of England (weekdays)	Granada Television	3.5.56	26.7.68
North of England (weekends)	ABC	5.5.56	28.7.68
Central Scotland	Scottish Television	31.8.57	
Wales and the West of England	TWW	14.1.58	3.3.68
	HTV	4.3.68	
South of England (later South and South-east England)	Southern Television	30.8.58	31.12.81
	TVS	1.1.82	31.12.92
	Meridian Broadcasting	1.1.93	
North-east England	Tyne Tees Television	15.1.59	
East of England	Anglia Television	27.10.59	
Northern Ireland	Ulster Television	31.10.59	
South-west England	Westward Television	29.4.61	11.8.81
	TSW	12.8.81	31.12.92
	Westcountry Television	1.1.93	
The Borders	Border Television	1.9.61	
North of Scotland	Grampian Television	30.9.61	
Channel Islands	Channel Television	1.9.62	
West and North Wales (later absorbed into Wales and the West of England)	Wales West and North	14.9.62	26.1.64
North-west England	Granada Television	29.7.68	
Yorkshire	Yorkshire Television	29.7.68	
National Breakfast Service	TV-am	1.2.83	31.12.92
	GMTV	1.1.93	

N.B.: The Midlands weekends franchise was amalgamated into the weekdays franchise in 1968. At the same time the North of England weekdays and weekends franchises were restructured into two new, all-week franchise areas, North-west England and Yorkshire.

Appendix C:
RIGHTS TO BROADCAST

The rights to broadcast programmes are generally still held by the production companies. However, in some cases, the production companies no longer exist. The following is a list of known rights-holders for material produced by such companies.

ABC:
Canal Plus Image UK Ltd
Pinewood Studios
Iver
Buckinghamshire SL0 0NH
Tel.: 01753 631111

Associated-Rediffusion:
Archbuild Ltd
Greenland Place
115–123 Bayham Street
London NW1 0AG
Tel.: 020 7424 0450

ATV:
Carlton International Media Ltd
35–38 Portman Square
London W1H 0NU
Tel: 020 7224 3339

ITC:
Carlton International Media Ltd
35–38 Portman Square
London W1H 0NU
Tel.: 020 7224 3339

Southern Television
(general programmes):
Saban Entertainment
338 Euston Road
London NW1 3AZ
Tel.: 020 7554 9000

(news footage):
Meridian Broadcasting
Television Centre
Southampton SO14 0PZ
Tel: 023 8022 2555

Thames Television:
Pearson Television
1 Stephen Street
London W1P 1PJ
Tel: 020 7691 6000

TVS (general programmes):
Saban Entertainment
338 Euston Road
London NW1 3AZ
Tel.: 020 7554 9000

(news footage):
Meridian Broadcasting
Television Centre
Southampton SO14 0PZ
Tel.: 023 8022 2555

TSW:
TSW Film & Television Archive
New Cooperage
Royal William Yard
Stonehouse
Plymouth PL1 3RP
Tel.: 01752 202650

TV-am
Moving Image Communications
61 Great Titchfield Street
London W1P 7FL
Tel.: 020 7580 3300

TWW:
HTV Ltd
The Television Centre
Culverhouse Cross
Cardiff CF5 6XJ
Tel.: 029 2059 0590

Westward:
TSW Film & Television Archive
New Cooperage
Royal William Yard
Stonehouse
Plymouth PL1 3RP
Tel: 01752 202650

Appendix D:
NOTABLE DATES IN BRITISH TELEVISION HISTORY

1922 18 Oct. British Broadcasting Company Ltd is established.

1923 8 Sept. First edition of *Radio Times*.

1925 30 Oct. First transmission of a human face (that of teenager William Taynton) by television, during an experiment by John Logie Baird in London.

1927 1 Jan. British Broadcasting Corporation is established.

1929 20 Aug. First BBC television trials, using Baird's 30-line equipment.

1932 22 Aug. The BBC's experimental television service begins from Broadcasting House.

1936 2 Nov. The world's first regular high-definition television service is launched by the BBC at Alexandra Palace. Baird's technology is eventually abandoned in favour of Marconi-EMI's 405-line system.

1939 1 Sept. The BBC television service is closed down with the advent of war.

1946 7 June The television service is resumed.

1953 2 June The Coronation of Queen Elizabeth II – an occasion covered live by the BBC, which inspires thousands of citizens to purchase their first TV sets.

1954 30 July The Independent Television Authority (ITA) is inaugurated to oversee and regulate commercial television in the UK.

1955 20 Sept. *TV Times* is first published (London area).
22 Sept. ITV begins with broadcasts to the London area by Associated-Rediffusion.
10 Oct. Test transmissions for colour television begin.

1957 16 Feb. Toddlers' Truce is abandoned.
24 Sept. BBC schools service is inaugurated.

1960 29 June BBC Television Centre at Shepherd's Bush is opened.

1962 11 July First live transatlantic broadcast, courtesy of the Telstar communications satellite.

1964 20 April BBC 2 begins transmissions on 625 lines, though much of the first night's output is blacked out by a power failure.

1967 25 June *Our World* – the first worldwide live satellite link-up – is broadcast.

1 July The UK's first regular colour transmissions begin on BBC 2.

1969 21 July Man first walks on the moon, watched by millions, thanks to television.
15 Nov. Colour transmissions are extended to BBC 1 and ITV.

1971 3 Jan. Open University broadcasts begin on the BBC.

1972 12 June The ITA takes control of independent radio as well as television and is renamed the Independent Broadcasting Authority (IBA).

1974 23 Sept. CEEFAX, the BBC's teletext service, begins transmissions. ITV's answer, ORACLE, begins in July 1975.

1982 1 Nov. S4C, the Welsh fourth channel, begins transmissions.
2 Nov. Channel 4 takes to the air.

1983 17 Jan. The BBC's breakfast television service (*Breakfast Time*) begins.
1 Feb. ITV's breakfast television service (through TV-am) begins.

1984 16 Jan. Sky television starts broadcasting via satellite and cable systems to selected conurbations in the UK.

1986 27 Oct. The BBC begins daytime (all day) broadcasts.

1989 5 Feb. Sky's direct-to-home satellite service begins, broadcasting from the Astra satellite, over a year before 'official' rival British Satellite Broadcasting (BSB) commences transmissions from the Marco Polo satellite.

1990 2 Nov. Sky and BSB merge to form BSkyB.

1991 1 Jan. The Independent Television Commission (ITC) replaces the IBA as regulator of ITV companies and their output.
15 Apr. BBC World Service Television is inaugurated.

1997 30 Mar. Channel 5 takes to the air.
9 Nov. BBC News 24 begins broadcasting.

1998 23 Sept. BBC launches BBC Choice, soon followed by other new digital channels.
1 Oct. BSkyB is the first to offer digital television, by satellite.
15 Nov. ONdigital starts terrestrial digital transmissions.

2000 1 Aug. ITN launches its digital, 24-hour ITN News Channel.

Appendix E:
LONGEST-RUNNING PROGRAMMES STILL ON UK TELEVISION

Programme	First Broadcast	Programme	First Broadcast
1. Panorama	11 November 1953	6. Coronation Street	9 December 1960
2. What the Papers Say	5 November 1956	7. Survival	1 February 1961
3. The Sky at Night	24 April 1957	8. Songs of Praise	1 October 1961
4. Grandstand	11 October 1958	9. Top of the Pops	1 January 1964
5. Blue Peter	16 October 1958	10. Horizon	2 May 1964

These are programmes which have run more or less continuously from their first transmission dates, although some, like *Panorama* and *Survival*, are not shown every week of the year. News programmes have not been included. *This Is Your Life* first aired on 29 July 1955 and is still being screened today, but it was off-air for five years between 1964 and 1969. The same applies to *Points of View*, transmitted from 1961 to 1971, and from 1979 to today.

PENGUIN ONLINE

READ MORE IN PENGUIN

In every corner of the world, on every subject under the sun, Penguin represents quality and variety – the very best in publishing today.

For complete information about books available from Penguin – including Puffins, Penguin Classics and Arkana – and how to order them, write to us at the appropriate address below. Please note that for copyright reasons the selection of books varies from country to country.

In the United Kingdom: Please write to *Dept. EP, Penguin Books Ltd, Bath Road, Harmondsworth, West Drayton, Middlesex UB7 0DA*

In the United States: Please write to *Consumer Services, Penguin Putnam Inc., 405 Murray Hill Parkway, East Rutherford, New Jersey 07073-2136*. VISA and MasterCard holders call 1-800-631-8571 to order Penguin titles

In Canada: Please write to *Penguin Books Canada Ltd, 10 Alcorn Avenue, Suite 300, Toronto, Ontario M4V 3B2*

In Australia: Please write to *Penguin Books Australia Ltd, 487 Maroondah Highway, Ringwood, Victoria 3134*

In New Zealand: Please write to *Penguin Books (NZ) Ltd, Private Bag 102902, North Shore Mail Centre, Auckland 10*

In India: Please write to *Penguin Books India Pvt Ltd, 11 Community Centre, Panchsheel Park, New Delhi 110017*

In the Netherlands: Please write to *Penguin Books Netherlands bv, Postbus 3507, NL-1001 AH Amsterdam*

In Germany: Please write to *Penguin Books Deutschland GmbH, Metzlerstrasse 26, 60594 Frankfurt am Main*

In Spain: Please write to *Penguin Books S. A., Bravo Murillo 19, 1°B, 28015 Madrid*

In Italy: Please write to *Penguin Italia s.r.l., Via Vittorio Emanuele 45la, 20094 Corsico, Milano*

In France: Please write to *Penguin France, 12, Rue Prosper Ferradou, 31700 Blagnac*

In Japan: Please write to *Penguin Books Japan Ltd, Iidabashi KM-Bldg, 2-23-9 Koraku, Bunkyo-Ku, Tokyo 112-0004*

In South Africa: Please write to *Penguin Books South Africa (Pty) Ltd, P.O. Box 751093, Gardenview, 2047 Johannesburg*

READ MORE IN PENGUIN

POPULAR SCIENCE

In Search of Nature Edward O. Wilson

A collection of essays of 'elegance, lucidity and breadth' *Independent*.
'A graceful, eloquent, playful and wise introduction to many of the
subjects he has studied during his long and distinguished career in
science' *The New York Times*

Clone Gina Kolata

'A thoughtful, engaging, interpretive and intelligent account ... I
highly recommend it to all those with an interest in ... the new
developments in cloning' *New Scientist*. 'Superb but unsettling' J. G.
Ballard, *Sunday Times*

The Feminization of Nature Deborah Cadbury

Scientists around the world are uncovering alarming facts. There is
strong evidence that sperm counts have fallen dramatically. Testicular
and prostate cancer are on the increase. Different species are showing
signs of 'feminization' or even 'changing sex'. 'Grips you from page
one ... it reads like a Michael Crichton thriller' John Gribbin

Richard Feynman: A Life in Science John Gribbin and Mary Gribbin

'Richard Feynman (1918–88) was to the second half of the century
what Einstein was to the first: the perfect example of scientific genius'
Independent. 'One of the most influential and best-loved physicists of
his generation ... This biography is both compelling and highly
readable' *Mail on Sunday*

T. rex and the Crater of Doom Walter Alvarez

Walter Alvarez unfolds the quest for the answer to one of science's
greatest mysteries – the cataclysmic impact on Earth which brought
about the extinction of the dinosaurs. 'A scientific detective story par
excellence, told with charm and candour' Niles Eldredge

READ MORE IN PENGUIN

POPULAR SCIENCE

How the Mind Works Steven Pinker

'Presented with extraordinary lucidity, cogency and panache . . .
Powerful and gripping . . . To have read [the book] is to have consulted
a first draft of the structural plan of the human psyche . . . a glittering
tour de force' *Spectator*. 'Witty, lucid and ultimately enthralling'
Observer

At Home in the Universe Stuart Kauffman

Stuart Kauffman brilliantly weaves together the excitement of
intellectual discovery and a fertile mix of insights to give the general
reader a fascinating look at this new science – the science of complexity
– and at the forces for order that lie at the edge of chaos. 'Kauffman
shares his discovery with us, with lucidity, wit and cogent argument,
and we see his vision . . . He is a pioneer' Roger Lewin

Stephen Hawking: A Life in Science
Michael White and John Gribbin

'A gripping account of a physicist whose speculations could prove as
revolutionary as those of Albert Einstein . . . Its combination of
erudition, warmth, robustness and wit is entirely appropriate to their
subject' *New Statesman & Society*. 'Well-nigh unputdownable' *The
Times Educational Supplement*

Voyage of the *Beagle* Charles Darwin

The five-year voyage of the *Beagle* set in motion the intellectual
currents that culminated in the publication of *The Origin of Species*.
His journal, reprinted here in a shortened version, is vivid and
immediate, showing us a naturalist making patient observations,
above all in geology. The editors have provided an excellent
introduction and notes for this edition, which also contains maps and
appendices.

READ MORE IN PENGUIN

LANGUAGE/LINGUISTICS

Language Play David Crystal

We all use language to communicate information, but it is language play which is truly central to our lives. Full of puns, groan-worthy gags and witty repartee, this book restores the fun to the study of language. It also demonstrates why all these things are essential elements of what makes us human.

Swearing Geoffrey Hughes

'A deliciously filthy trawl among taboo words across the ages and the globe' *Observer*. 'Erudite and entertaining' Penelope Lively, *Daily Telegraph*

The Language Instinct Stephen Pinker

'Dazzling . . . Pinker's big idea is that language is an instinct, as innate to us as flying is to geese . . . Words can hardly do justice to the superlative range and liveliness of Pinker's investigations' *Independent*. 'He does for language what David Attenborough does for animals, explaining difficult scientific concepts so easily that they are indeed absorbed as a transparent stream of words' John Gribbin

Mother Tongue Bill Bryson

'A delightful, amusing and provoking survey, a joyful celebration of our wonderful language, which is packed with curiosities and enlightenment on every page' *Sunday Express*. 'A gold mine of language-anecdote. A surprise on every page . . . enthralling' *Observer*

Longman Guide to English Usage
Sidney Greenbaum and Janet Whitcut

Containing 5000 entries compiled by leading authorities on modern English, this invaluable reference work clarifies every kind of usage problem, giving expert advice on points of grammar, meaning, style, spelling, pronunciation and punctuation.

READ MORE IN PENGUIN

ART AND ARCHITECTURE

Ways of Seeing John Berger

Seeing comes before words. The child looks before it can speak. Yet there is another sense in which seeing comes before words ... These seven provocative essays – some written, some visual – offer a key to exploring the multiplicity of ways of seeing.

The Penguin Dictionary of Architecture
John Fleming, Hugh Honour and Nikolaus Pevsner

This wide-ranging dictionary includes entries on architectural terms, ornamentation, building materials, styles and movements, with over a hundred clear and detailed drawings. 'Immensely useful, succinct and judicious ... this is a book rich in accurate fact and accumulated wisdom' *The Times Literary Supplement*

Style and Civilization

These eight beautifully illustrated volumes interpret the major styles in European art – from the Byzantine era and the Renaissance to Romanticism and Realism – in the broadest context of the civilization and thought of their times. 'One of the most admirable ventures in British scholarly publishing' *The Times*

Michelangelo: A Biography George Bull

'The final picture of Michelangelo the man is suitably three-dimensional and constructed entirely of evidence as strong as Tuscan marble' *Sunday Telegraph*. 'An impressive number of the observations we are treated to, both in matters of fact and in interpretation, are taking their first bows beyond the confines of the world of the learned journal' *The Times*

Values of Art Malcolm Budd

'Budd is a first-rate thinker ... He brings to aesthetics formidable gifts of precision, far-sightedness and argument, together with a wide philosophical knowledge and a sincere belief in the importance of art' *The Times*

READ MORE IN PENGUIN

DICTIONARIES

Abbreviations
Ancient History
Archaeology
Architecture
Art and Artists
Astronomy
Biographical Dictionary of
  Women
Biology
Botany
Building
Business
Challenging Words
Chemistry
Civil Engineering
Classical Mythology
Computers
Contemporary American History
Curious and Interesting Geometry
Curious and Interesting Numbers
Curious and Interesting Words
Design and Designers
Economics
Eighteenth-Century History
Electronics
English and European History
English Idioms
Foreign Terms and Phrases
French
Geography
Geology
German
Historical Slang
Human Geography
Information Technology

International Finance
International Relations
Literary Terms and Literary
  Theory
Mathematics
Modern History 1789–1945
Modern Quotations
Music
Musical Performers
Nineteenth-Century World
  History
Philosophy
Physical Geography
Physics
Politics
Proverbs
Psychology
Quotations
Quotations from Shakespeare
Religions
Rhyming Dictionary
Russian
Saints
Science
Sociology
Spanish
Surnames
Symbols
Synonyms and Antonyms
Telecommunications
Theatre
The Third Reich
Third World Terms
Troublesome Words
Twentieth-Century History
Twentieth-Century Quotations